Also by Gerald Gunther

Constitutional Law

Individual Rights in Constitutional Law

John Marshall's Defense of *McCulloch* v. *Maryland*

Learned Hand

Learned Hand

The Man and the Judge

GERALD GUNTHER

with a Foreword by
Justice Lewis F. Powell, Jr.

Alfred A. Knopf New York 1994

THIS IS A BORZOI BOOK
PUBLISHED BY ALFRED A. KNOPF, INC.

Copyright © 1994 by Usingen Corporation
Foreword copyright © 1994 by Lewis F. Powell, Jr.

Library of Congress Cataloging-in-Publication Data
Gunther, Gerald.
Learned Hand: the man and the judge / by Gerald Gunther;
with a foreword by Lewis F. Powell, Jr.—1st ed.
p.   cm.
Includes bibliographical references and index.
ISBN 0-394-58807-X
1. Hand, Learned, 1872–1961. 2. Judges—United States—Biography.
3. United States. Circuit Court (2nd Circuit)—Biography.
I. Title.
KF373.H29G76   1994
347.73'22'34—dc20
[B]
[347.307234]
[B]
93-22868
CIP

Manufactured in the United States of America

First Edition

For Barbara
for her indispensable love and support
and her (nearly) inexhaustible patience

Contents

Photographs follow pages 232 and 424

all to Elisabeth Sifton, one of today's truly great book editors, whose deeply engaged and skillful efforts improved this biography immeasurably. I will always be in her debt. My thanks, too, to the sensitive and thoughtful copyediting of Benjamin Dreyer, and to the work of Barbara Bristol and Paul Schnee at Knopf in helping this book to publication. Finally, I am very grateful for the extraordinary devotion of the secretaries who have worked with me over the years. My special thanks to Bess Hitchcock, Beth Sherman, Frances Martin, and Mary Ann Rundell, and especially to my two most recent secretaries, Jody Conrad and Pat Moates, for unsurpassably calm, splendid effectiveness.

Learned Hand

I

The Early Years

ON JANUARY 27, 1872, a cold winter day, a second and last
child was born to Lydia and Samuel Hand of 224 State Street in Albany,
New York. The Hands named their only son Billings Learned Hand.
Late in life, Hand would recall Albany as "a hick town up the river,"[1]
but the Albany boosters of his youth would have challenged that description. After all, Albany, less than 150 miles from New York City,
was the state's capital; after all, its population of about seventy thousand
in 1870 made it the fourth largest city in the state, the twentieth largest
in the nation; after all, there was reason to hope that the post–Civil
War industrial boom would spur growth in Albany as it was doing
elsewhere. At first, the local hopes seemed vindicated: as its population
rose to ninety thousand by 1880, Albany's rate of growth kept pace
with New York City's, Buffalo's, and Boston's. Yet soon growth ground
to a halt; during the 1890s, sleepy Albany's population actually shrank;
by 1900, it dropped from being America's twentieth largest city to only
the fortieth.[2]

Learned Hand had his own spacious room in his parents' comfortable
redbrick home on Albany's principal residential street. Through his
windows, he saw the lush green trees during the summer, the dirt-gray
snow cover during the winter. Horse-drawn trolleys ran on State Street;
a few blocks closer to the Hudson River, farmers parked their wagons
at the curb to sell their produce. Learned's father, a successful appellate
lawyer, earned enough to make the Hands comfortably well off. Unlike
the wealthiest families—those of fledgling industrialists and bankers—
they did not have their own horse and carriage, but they were at least
at the fringe of the town's upper class. There was a nursemaid during

Learned's early years, and a housemaid throughout his childhood. Learned was hardly aware of the poor, of the Irish and German immigrants, or of the workers receiving wages averaging less than $400 a year.

On the surface, Learned's family environment seemed secure and stable. Four protective women hovered over him, the only young male in the household: the maid; his sister, Lydia (Lily), eight years older; his doting mother; and his equally doting aunt—his mother's unmarried sister Harriet Learned, who lived with the Hands and treated the youngster as if he were her own cherished baby.[3] On weekends and in the evenings, Learned's busy father joined the family. Hand would recall: "He adored me, they said. I don't remember, but they said he did what he could to spoil me."[4]

There were darker undercurrents beneath the surface serenity. "I used to have night terrors," Hand later recalled as one of his earliest memories. "I would wake up screaming."[5] As a child, Learned was often fearful; and over the years, even as honors proliferated, he was beset with extraordinary self-doubts and anxieties. Throughout his life, the introspective Hand searched for explanations for his unconfident makeup and his low self-esteem. Was his deep-rooted apprehensiveness an inherited trait? Was it a product of his environment? He guessed that it was some of both. "I was, of course, like my father and the whole damn crew, a neurasthenic, a neurotic," he once said.[6] And in another reflection, when in his eighties, he acknowledged: "I was very undecided, always have been—a very insecure person, very fearful; morbidly fearful."[7] The best he could do toward self-understanding was to speculate that he had "a naturally overresponsive sensorium, in an environment which helped."[8]

A closer look at his early years indeed discloses suggestive data pointing to both heredity and environment as contributing causes to Hand's insecurity. Even his distinctive name contains clues. He was christened Billings Learned Hand, a "formidable" name that made him uncomfortable.[9] The explanation for it is simple enough: Hand's mother, Lydia Coit Learned Hand, came from a family that had long used family surnames as given names: her father and her brother were both named Billings Peck Learned. Hand's parents showed some mercy in naming their only son: they thought, Hand later recalled, that "it was going pretty strong to call a little boy Billings Peck Learned Hand, so they left out the Peck."[10] But to the youngster, the two weighty first names were burdensome enough.

Fortunately, Learned did not have to cope with being called "Billings Learned" in his day-to-day relations. Apparently, no one thought of simply calling him "Bill." The women in his family usually addressed him as "Bunny" or "Bun," a nickname that evolved into a simple "B," by which he was known to close friends throughout his life. However, even in childhood, his father and often his mother as well called him "Learned"; and the family always referred to him as "Learned" in their letters.

For years, Hand searched self-consciously for a more congenial substitute for his oppressive given names. He was concerned about his image and his identity: What impression would his name make upon others? Were "Billings" and "Learned" adequately "masculine," as he recurrently wondered, or did they suggest a "sissy," as he sometimes feared? Yet he did not feel free to rid himself of the unwelcome name for many years. He signed all of his childhood letters with the full "Billings Learned Hand." Only when he left Albany for Harvard did he begin an open retreat from it. At college and at law school, he signed himself "B. Learned Hand." (Some of his classmates translated the initial into "Buck," a welcome relief: Hand thought "Buck" was "all right because it was a masculine name.")[11] But not until 1899, when he was in his twenties, did he muster the courage to drop the "Billings" entirely and identify himself simply as "Learned Hand." His long-delayed decision brought him great relief: "I was sorry, I couldn't carry all that."[12] Even "Learned" was formidable enough, but family usage had accustomed him to it. And the shortened name did not shield him from questions and occasional sarcasm. (Near the end of his life, for example, he recalled an "officious" British journalist, interviewing him on a trip to England, whose curiosity focused on his unusual name. It was clear, Hand imagined, that the reporter thought, "Now, look, isn't that like an American? That man's a judge, so it's a good thing if he has the name 'Learned,' just as if a fellow is a colonel and he is called 'Colonel Courageous Stanton.' " Hand patiently explained how he had gotten his name and denied (not entirely truthfully) that it had given him embarrassment; the journalist replied superciliously, "I fancy it may here.")[13]

The three family surnames also symbolized deeper sources of lifelong pressures. His name was a constant reminder of ancestry, traditions, and family anticipations, and it impressed upon him that much was expected of him because of his lineage.

Samuel Hand, Learned's father, was no doubt the most important family member casting a shadow over Learned's youth and, indeed, his entire life, though he died in 1886, at the age of fifty-three, when Learned was only fourteen. Samuel Hand's influence on his son rested less on Learned's actual experience of his father than on the idealized image impressed upon the young man after his father's early death, for Learned had never felt intimate or even at ease with his father when he was alive.[14] But Samuel Hand's death deprived Learned of the opportunity to assess his father as a fellow adult and instead left him with an image that, encouraged if not forced upon him by his mother, he tended to embellish and exaggerate.

For Learned, the postmortem portrait of his father was a picture not of a flesh-and-blood human being, with limitations as well as strengths, but rather of a larger-than-life model of excellence that he might strive to emulate but, he felt, could never match. Even in his last years, Hand would say that his father was not only an outstanding lawyer but also "a scholar" who would have reached "wonderful" heights had he lived; he would also say, with a deep belief in the accuracy of this evaluation, that Samuel Hand "had more brains than I did."[15] This judgment helped to foster Learned's self-doubts, curbed his sense of self-worth, yet also spurred his efforts.

Even after the world had come to appreciate Learned Hand's extraordinary intellect and to applaud his achievements, he continued to speak of—and believe in—his father's unmatchable qualities. During Samuel Hand's lifetime, however, he most often felt distant from his father. "I can remember," he once said, "when his key rattled in the door, it always gave me a little sense of fear. . . . I had always been a little afraid of him."[16] He received periodic lectures from his father, delivered in "a rather traditional way," and occasionally, Samuel Hand would show a "quick temper": "[He] would fly out at me and that would scare me too."[17] True, in rare moments when Samuel Hand was not immersed in his professional career or his beloved library, he sought out his son's company and took him for walks. But Learned found these outings "rather trying": his father "didn't seem to have the gift [of] forgetting the distance between us in years." In sum, his relations with his father "were not really intimate."[18]

Yet from the time Learned's father died, Lydia Hand incessantly drilled the image of paternal perfection into her son. She had found in Samuel the "man with brains" she had always wanted to marry, and she eagerly conveyed her awe of her husband to her son.[19] By the time Learned began law practice in 1896, he had thoroughly adopted her portrait of Samuel as an intellectual giant. Repeatedly, to please her, he spent hours making copies of his father's occasional writings and of laudatory obituaries of him.[20] And for the rest of his life, he would labor over idealized biographical sketches of his father whenever publishers sought them.

The breadth of Samuel Hand's career interests was indeed notable for late-nineteenth-century Albany; however, his achievements were considerably more modest than the family maintained. After reading law under his father's supervision in the small Adirondack town of Elizabethtown, New York, Samuel Hand had sought legal work in Albany at the age of twenty-six, in 1859. He joined one of a small number of law firms specializing in cases before the highest state court, the Court of Appeals; by the time he was thirty-two—a remarkably short time since he had joined the firm—he had become its leading lawyer. (In one of the biographical sketches of his father that he revised, Learned emphasized the "unprecedentedly early age" at which his father had begun his career in the Court of Appeals;[21] he wrote this when he himself was nearly the same age; at this time he viewed himself as an unsuccessful lawyer, with little confidence in his skills as an advocate and with virtually no experience in appeals.) Samuel Hand remained a leader of the appellate bar for the remaining two decades of his life, and enjoyed statewide prominence. Even though most major law offices were in New York's large cities, the Court of Appeals sat in Albany, and in that epoch big-city lawyers typically referred their appeals to specialists in Albany rather than arguing the cases in person. As a result, Samuel Hand argued appeals before the highest state court "in greater number and importance than those argued by any other lawyer in New York during this same period."[22]

Samuel Hand's activities ranged well beyond the courtroom. He became a confidential adviser to a number of Democratic governors. True to family tradition, he was a lifelong Jeffersonian Democrat with reformist inclinations. In New York State, this meant opposition to New York City's political machine, Tammany Hall. Samuel Tilden, an anti-Tammany governor and an unsuccessful candidate for the presidency in 1876, chose Hand as one of his most trusted political advisers, a position achieved not because of any strong personal warmth or charm but because of Samuel Hand's intellectual gifts and his personal equanimity amid bitter partisan battles. The emotional self-control that served Hand well in appellate advocacy helped to assure success in politics. Samuel Hand's political involvement produced recurrent offers of public positions, a few of which he accepted in his early years at the bar. For three years, for example, he spent some of his time producing six volumes of the *Reports* of the Court of Appeals. His greatest opportunities came during the 1870s. In 1875, when he was only forty-two, Governor Tilden offered to name him to the New York Supreme Court, the state's trial court, but he declined. A year later, he was pressed to accept the Democratic nomination for governor, as Tilden's successor. After losing much sleep for more than a week, he again refused: earning money to support his growing family had "not yet" ceased to be "a necessity" for him.[23] (Learned Hand, only four at the time, was not aware of his father's agonies over this offer. But he recounted later—from family stories that, for a change, were not wholly uncritical of Samuel—that more than financial pressures explained the rejection of the offer: "My mother, who knew him, persuaded him not to [run for governor]. He was a very, very nervous, apprehensive kind of man, always imagining that he was sick or something—one of his apprehensions was that he was going blind. She was right [about his anxieties]."")[24]

Briefly, Samuel Hand did achieve high office. In 1878, one of Tilden's successors named him to fill a vacancy on the Court of Appeals. Samuel Hand was forty-five then, and only one man had ever been appointed to that court at a younger age. But his judicial career was short-lived. In a matter of months, his seat came up for election, and though by then Hand was ready to accept the nomination, he did not get it, for the state Democratic party had temporarily fallen into Tammany hands.[25] This lost opportunity for a longer judicial tenure loomed even larger in his survivors' eyes after Samuel Hand died eight years later. In his last years, he had become an intimate adviser of still another governor, Grover Cleveland, who, unlike Tilden, became president, in 1893. Cleveland's final appointment to the United States Supreme Court was Judge Rufus W. Peckham of New York, five years younger than Samuel Hand and among Hand's friends and admirers; Peckham had reached the Court of Appeals in 1886, the year Samuel Hand died. Learned Hand believed that had his father lived, he would have been selected for that seat—and that Samuel Hand, not Rufus Peckham, would have moved to the Supreme Court in 1895.*

Samuel Hand's capacity to combine professional success with public affairs, remarkable as it seemed to his son, was not unusual among nineteenth-century lawyers. What made Samuel Hand truly atypical

---

* Hand said: "I rather think that if he had lived when Cleveland came to make [the appointment of] Rufus Peckham, he would have appointed my father" (Family Interview II, 13).

   This must have been an especially agonizing reflection, because Learned Hand for years yearned for appointment to the Supreme Court and never achieved it. The story has an additional ironic aspect: Learned Hand, for most of his life, was a vehement opponent of Supreme Court obstructions to legislative policy-making through the vehicle of an expansive reading of the due-process clauses of the Constitution. The source and symbol of that much criticized substantive-due-process approach was a 1905 decision, *Lochner v. New York*, in which Justice Peckham wrote the majority opinion. Hand's most important writing before he became a judge in 1909 was an attack on *Lochner* in the *Harvard Law Review* in 1908, and contempt for *Lochner* persisted throughout his life. Learned Hand's respect for and awe of his father must have tempted him to guess that, had Samuel lived, there would have been no majority opinion as objectionable as Peckham's in *Lochner*.

were his interests and talents beyond those spheres. Learned viewed his father as a true "egghead"[26]—inquisitive about ideas, a bibliophile, a voracious reader of classical and contemporary literature, and an occasional essayist to boot. In a biographical sketch, Learned Hand referred to his father's lifelong "wide and careful reading . . . coupled with a natural bent to reflection and speculation," a bent that "had given his mind a breadth and a humane sympathy which made him preeminent not only as a distinguished advocate, but as a cultivated gentleman," which was, Hand added, "unusual among men."

Samuel Hand had begun collecting books even while striving to support his family in his law practice. His library, which grew to three thousand volumes, became one of the finest private collections in Albany, "the most complete and valuable" in French literature.[27] He was "a great collector of books; that was his great extravagance,"[28] an enthusiasm he demonstrated soon after he moved to Albany, when in 1861 he published the first American edition of a fourteenth-century English volume, Richard de Bury's *Philobiblon*, a work in praise of books. In 1869, he delivered an elaborate lecture in Poughkeepsie on "Cervantes and His Times." (Within weeks of Learned's return to Albany from law school in 1896, he prepared, at his mother's behest, a forty-two-page typewritten transcript of this lecture; he preserved it in his own papers for the rest of his life. Interestingly, Samuel emphasized the "melancholy" aspect of Cervantes.)[29]

Learned Hand's awe of his father as a lawyer was probably justified: as a practitioner, Samuel Hand was far more successful, in achievements and material success, than Learned ever became. But the son's views of the father's nonlegal achievements were vastly exaggerated. Learned, too, was a voracious, broad-ranging reader all his life, and his father's occasional extraprofessional writings do not come close to matching his own in style or substance.

From personal experience, Learned Hand could sympathize with the descriptions of his father as "sensitive" and "by nature of melancholic disposition." Yet for most of his life, blinded by his deeply ingrained family perception of Samuel as an intellectual giant of unmatchable talents, he could not acknowledge his father's flaws, and only in old age could he concede that some of these flaws imposed substantial costs on his family. Belatedly, these perceptions brought him closer to his father than he had ever been during the fearful associations of his youth or the many years of distant awe. Finally he was able to say that his father had been "too dependent on what people thought"; unlike himself, he "did not have many friends," for he "didn't give out enough." And he recalled the dark side of his father's bookishness: "In the evening, he was just buried in books. . . . He was a selfish man, I think, in a way, and of course he was encouraged to be so by his adoring wife, who venerated him." Hand acknowledged as well that his father "didn't have much gift with people" and that his hard-won self-control precluded warmth and engagement. Recalling his mother's saying that her husband had believed "that if he could always feel [as] he did when he had two or three drinks under his belt, his whole life would have been different," Hand added, "I understand that, because I often feel that way."[30]

Tales told by family members, not firsthand experience, created the awe Learned felt about his father. By contrast, decades of personal association fashioned his perceptions of his mother, Lydia Coit Learned Hand. Even while her husband was still alive, Lydia was the pervasive, dominant presence in the home, and after Samuel's death, she became the sole source of parental nurture. She had many years to lavish her love on her son: she lived until 1921, when she was in her eighties and her son in his fiftieth year.

Toward Learned, in his middle age as well as youth, Lydia poured out an inexhaustible flow of warm, protective concern. When he was a little boy, she would worry about the risks she feared he was taking in his rare ventures into the cold, wet snow of Albany winters; after he married and moved to New York in 1902, she continued to lecture him about getting enough sleep, taking care of his health, having his hair cut regularly. After he became a judge in 1909, she expected— and *received*—daily letters from him; even after she had ostensibly reconciled herself to his moving from Albany, she was nevertheless thrown into depressions when she contemplated the miles that separated them.[31] Hand never voiced resentment of his mother's hovering, sometimes smothering, attention—instead, as both a child and an adult, he was ever ready to obey and eager to please her. His mother's solicitude was clearly one of the causes of his lifelong anxiety, for he never thought he was doing enough for her. Despite his continuing flow of letters and frequent visits, he would apologize when he had to skip writing for a day or send only an abbreviated note.

Learned was well aware that his mother had been raised in an atmosphere conducive to anxieties. Lydia's father, struggling to make his way in banking after giving up the law, had been relieved to "palm off" his two older daughters into the care of his childless sister, Betsy.[32] She was a religious fanatic, an obsessed devotee of a Puritan, Calvinist heritage. Lydia's upbringing in the home of Aunt Betsy and her husband, "a Congregationalist clergyman of the strictest faith," as Learned recalled, instilled in the child a fear of God and of Hell that Lydia passed on to her own children in transmuted form as an anxious sense of duty.

In his own old age, Learned Hand still retained a graphic sense of how "my mother got this terrific brand of Calvinism."[33] Nightly, Aunt Betsy would tell her nieces that "they had to go over everything they had done and try to find the selfish motive back of it, which, but for the sacrificial death of Jesus Christ upon the Cross, would justify their eternal torment." This "eternal torment" was described to the girls in such vivid detail that Lydia, throughout her long life, found it ever threatening.[34]

The mature Hand, unlike his mother or great-aunt, was not devout and did not attend church, yet he was quite aware that he had not shed the Puritan traits they shared. For example, Aunt Betsy had instilled in his mother "this awful sense of expiation," as he put it—the drive to extinguish the burdens of guilt and to seek atonement for offenses, unwitting as well as conscious; even in old age, he insisted that he still had some of that in his own makeup: "I don't know just what form it takes, but I know it is there." One form it took was his feelings toward his mother—feelings not only of love but also of duty and guilt. In his eighties, Hand also brooded about why he could not claim a "happy, contented disposition" even though he had enjoyed a "most protected" life. Searching for explanations, he pointed to his mother and her background: "My mother was a very fearful woman. That was the bad thing about the whole Puritan tradition. It was apt to leave a constant anxiety complex," from which, he acknowledged, he too suffered.

Forebears beyond his parents also left imprints on Learned Hand. The ancestry symbolized by his names could be traced back several centuries to the *Mayflower* generation. Although Hand had no enthusiasm for genealogy, he grew up with a strong sense of family and repeatedly speculated about the effect of ancestors. In his view, the earlier Hands were far more important than the Learneds in shaping his own personality.

Hand recalled most of the members of his mother's family as undistinguished—"obstinate, stupid, lethargic and uninteresting," in his own words, though he thought that their "qualities of self-respect and integrity" lifted them "far above many more shining people."[35] This limited regard for the Learneds arose from his own experience of them: his maternal grandfather, Billings Peck Learned, had studied law, lived in Albany, and, until his death when Learned Hand was twelve, had frequently visited his daughter's home; but he "wasn't very good" at lawyering and turned to banking instead; Hand remembered

him only as a reasonably well-to-do but quite conventional person.[36]
Yet the American roots of the Learneds were as deep as the Hands',
and some Learneds were successful lawyers long before any Hand had
even a significant formal education.

The Learneds, like the Hands, descended from early-seventeenth-
century immigrants from England to Massachusetts. Each of the families quickly moved south, with the Learneds settling in Connecticut
and the Hands crossing the Sound to the eastern tip of Long Island.
But for young Hand, the Learned lawyer tradition was remote and
insignificant. The Hand family left a far deeper imprint. Family legends
conveyed to young Learned a picture of seventeenth- and eighteenth-
century Hands as God-fearing, hardworking folk.[37] The first American
Hand was one of the original settlers of East Hampton on Long Island
(one of the town's streets still bears the name "Hand's Lane"); the next
four generations scratched a living from the land and the surrounding
sea, and farming, fishing, and whaling, Learned knew, afforded "a
very, very narrow living" indeed. Learned himself was most struck by
what he called their "New England qualities": the respect for books
even among those who were not well read; the Puritan piety, which
considered hard work on earth a duty to a wrathful deity.

For Learned, the story of the "modern" Hands did not fully begin
until his great-great-grandfather Nathan decided to leave Long Island
and head north. Tantalized by tales of rich wheat-bearing farmland
along the Vermont–New York border, Nathan, then forty-five years
old and the father of nine children, borrowed funds to buy two hundred
acres of land on Lake Champlain, just outside the village of Shoreham,
Vermont, not far from Middlebury. There, at a "very beautiful" site
across the lake from Fort Ticonderoga, Nathan established the home-
stead Learned would visit as a boy. Nathan Hand's house, built of solid
blocks of wood and made notable by a large chimney that heated the
four large rooms downstairs and the four smaller ones above, still stands,
overlooking what is called to this day "Hand's Cove."[38]

The crops on Nathan's lands proved as rich as the rumors had forecast.
In 1796, after only four years in Vermont, Nathan's wife, Anna, urged
her oldest son, Samuel, to help his father on the farm. "[Y]our Dada
is old & a cripple & has a good farm & over run [*sic*] with business,"
she wrote Samuel. "I must think it would be best for you to come
home soon as possible. [He] is willing you should possess one-half of
the estate and stock."[39] This Samuel Hand, Learned's great-grandfather,
dutifully heeded this call. He left his job as master on a freight-carrying
sloop on the Hudson River and soon became an even more successful
farmer than Nathan. During the War of 1812, he led a local militia

battalion and carried the title of "Captain" for the rest of his life. (Learned was always skeptical of the tales of heroism that many of his relatives relished, for he knew that Captain Samuel had never seen battle.)[40]

Learned, raised to admire the achievements of this first truly successful Hand, thought of his great-grandfather as a greatly respected farmer who "managed to squeeze enough out of the land" to give his children a good education and to build an "extremely good-looking" brick residence on the hill above the old wooden house. He was impressed by his great-grandfather's reputation as an "active, driving fellow" with considerable self-confidence.[41]

In Learned's eyes, some of the moodiness that made his own personality so complex was traceable to Samuel's wife, his great-grandmother Elizabeth Sill Hand. Once, speculating about "how I turned out to be such a nut," he ventured, "I think it came from my great-grandmother Sill. I think it was the Sill blood."[42] She was indeed reputed to be "sensitive," a rare adjective in descriptions of Learned's ancestors.[43] And she certainly left her mark on his appearance: he inherited her pronounced eyebrows, penetrating eyes, large mouth, and strong chin.[44]

The family pattern with which Learned was most familiar, a pattern of formal education and entry into the professions, did not emerge until the early nineteenth century, with the children of Samuel and Elizabeth Sill Hand. All six of them, four daughters and two sons, received training beyond the local schools. Hand remembered frequent visits to his great-aunts on the Shoreham farm; above all, he remembered a house full of "books—mostly devotional books."[45] Samuel and Elizabeth persuaded their older son, Richard, to enter the ministry; he was the first Hand to go to college. The Reverend Richard Hand proved a decent enough man, but, as Hand recalled, not "very brilliant."[46] The younger son, Augustus, was expected to take over the family farm, but he defied his parents' wishes and enrolled in a law course; this Augustus, Learned's grandfather, was the first Hand to become a lawyer and judge, the preeminent model of professional success for his male descendants.

Although Augustus died when his grandson was only six years old, Learned retained a vivid memory of a formidable figure with a stocky body, a large head with ample hair, prominent eyebrows, piercing eyes, and a wide mouth. But it was less his childhood memories than his lifelong awareness of Augustus's achievements that accounts for his grandfather's significance to him: next only to his father, Augustus Hand was Learned's most awe-inspiring but also most anxiety-inducing model.

Early in life, Augustus concluded that Shoreham was unbearably oppressive, doomed forever to "monotony," "insipidity," and "selfishness."[47] In 1827, when he was twenty-four, he escaped the small village: relying on his limited savings, small loans from his father, and above all his own energy and determination, he enrolled at America's earliest law school, Litchfield Law School in Connecticut. Classes, which a Judge Tapping Reeve had begun in the 1780s, were being taught by Reeve's successor, James Gould, by the time Augustus arrived. Augustus endured the rote lectures and filled thousands of pages with notes, viewing the law as "the study & business of man's life, not the mere smattering to be 'admitted,' "[48] and he used his legal education to build a successful law practice and a considerable public life.

After being admitted to the bar in 1828, Augustus opened his law office in a small New York town across Lake Champlain from Shoreham and, after waiting for his childhood sweetheart to complete her education, married. To a degree unusual for his time, he sought intellectual as well as personal companionship in marriage. "Truly, education makes the woman," he wrote his future wife. "The graceful step [and] vivid glance may make our hearts flutter, but the brightness of the polished mind visits the whole soul."[49]

Soon after, Augustus moved once again, to become Essex County surrogate, a part-time office that left time for private law practice. The county seat was Elizabethtown, a small town in an Adirondack valley twenty-five miles northwest of Shoreham. With Augustus's move there in 1831, Elizabethtown replaced Shoreham as the Hand family base. From a stock of farmers and seafarers, Augustus fashioned a new family pattern of lawyers. The solid brick law office that Augustus built adjacent to his new home still stands; Elizabethtown, not Albany, was young Learned's favorite place, the eagerly anticipated site for winter visits and summer excursions.

Early in his career, Augustus took a middle name, Cincinnatus, but even the self-confident Augustus was reluctant to use this imposing chosen name in his informal correspondence. ("I think he was rather ashamed of it," Learned once mused; his grandfather had used only the modest abbreviation "C.") But Augustus did not need a pompous signature to succeed: his book-filled, file-choked office showed the signs of rapid success, and from his small-town base he reached out to wider forums, handling cases in other parts of New York and even in international law. And law offered an outlet for his political interests as well. All his life, Augustus was "a passionate Democrat" of the traditional, Jacksonian variety, deeply suspicious of expanding national power. Essex County was Whig and, later, Republican territory, yet in 1839 Augustus managed to get elected as a Democrat for a term in the U.S. House of Representatives. Other offices soon followed: he served successively as a state senator, a delegate to the state constitutional convention, a justice of the New York Supreme Court, and, briefly, a judge on the New York Court of Appeals.

Learned was brought up on tales of the career of the first judge in the Hand family, the rebellious farm boy who "somehow, by hook or crook, God knows how, managed to get down to Judge Gould's law school in Litchfield" and who, because he was "very industrious" and had "great competence," achieved much. Learned was impressed, too, by Augustus's love of books: it showed he was a "bookworm." (Augustus did indeed assemble a remarkably wide-ranging law library for a country lawyer of his day, and Learned liked knowing that his grandfather truly "knew [and] studied" all his books.)[50]

Augustus C. Hand had three sons: Clifford, the eldest; Samuel, Learned's father; and Richard. The children were less free to develop in their own ways than their father, a self-made man breaking away from his father's farm, had been. From their earliest years through college, Augustus preached to his sons about the virtues of education, hard work, and ambition, about the endless opportunities in a growing nation, about the desirability of entering a profession. His instructions were unchanging: "[Y]ou can be nothing, without application long [and] severe"; it was essential to avoid unproductive "hobbies" and "trifling"; a college education was a necessary but not sufficient condition for success. "Knowledge now in America is a tremendous lever of power," he said. "But the knowledge I speak of costs labour & cannot be obtained as the honey is sipped by insects buzzing here & there. [I] do admire the strong minded man of real knowledge." He told his sons that they could either "take it comfortably" and accept what came or "put on the armour & with inflexible purpose & unremitting energy command your position." Only the latter, he made clear, was conducive to "power, wealth (oftentimes) & respectability."[51] They could choose which professional career to pursue, so long as they demonstrated "industry, honesty, and independent thinking";[52] but his own preference was always clear: "The highest post a man can hold in the U.S. is that of a distinguished member of the bar."[53]

Augustus's stern advice bore at least some fruit in each of his sons. All three went to college, all three became lawyers. But Clifford, Samuel, and Richard had varying levels of self-worth and anxiety. Their father considered Clifford the "prodigy" in the family—he tackled every academic and professional challenge with total confidence—while he described Samuel as a "sulky ill-natured clever fellow,"[54] the most gifted of the brothers in the long run, but torn by doubts. Both Clifford and Samuel, after studying law in their father's office, left Elizabethtown for larger cities. Richard, initially as anxious as Samuel, remained in Elizabethtown all his life. He became a successful country lawyer, with some statewide recognition, though not approaching his father's. Only Clifford absorbed his father's preachings without the by-products of recurrent anxieties; he moved to Brooklyn to become a successful practitioner and a pious, tradition-revering and tradition-bound, rather smug and dull man.

The middle son, Samuel, struggled for years to come to terms with Augustus's powerful personality. Always uncertain of his father's approval, he worked harder for fewer emotional satisfactions, and adopted early a firm belief in the power of self-control as an answer to self-doubt. As he wrote in 1847, when he was only fourteen, it "is the duty of every young man to learn to face the world. . . . [I]t is foolish and cowardly in me to shrink."[55] He steeled himself to accept and absorb his father's didactic letters. At eighteen, he graduated from Union College as the youngest member of his class—a fact that Learned took care to emphasize in one of his biographical sketches of his father.[56]

When Samuel left Elizabethtown for Albany in early 1859, he felt he was escaping a confining hometown environment: much as his father had spoken of Shoreham (and as his son would speak of Albany), Samuel thought the "diminutive city" of Elizabethtown, "our little burgh," a place of "intolerable dullness."[57] His sense of having inadequately satisfied his father's expectations also provided some of the impetus for leaving. But Samuel succeeded in his struggle for self-control. By late 1859, when his brother Richard confessed his fears to Samuel—his lack of "self-possession," his need to convince his father that "I am neither brainless, unambitious, or unenergetic"[58]—Samuel was ready with an older brother's calm-sounding advice: he himself had "failed" and "was at fault" in going to Albany, and warned Richard that he too would fail "unless you cultivate *force of will* which we both lack."[59] Samuel assiduously exercised that "force of will" in gaining a foothold at the Albany bar. Yet his developing self-discipline could not wholly disguise the persisting emotional tensions. Advising Richard that his worries about pleasing their father demonstrated "morbidity," Samuel, nearly thirty years old, offered his own prescription to combat the anxious undercurrents: "Put it in plain words. You are afraid, when you hear a footstep, for fear they will ask you [for] advice. So are you afraid in the dark sometimes, at least I am. Does it hurt me? *Shall I yield to it?* On the contrary, every man nerves himself against it and his mind compels him to a *contempt* of the feeling and in a word he *conquers* it."[60]

Young Learned knew little of his father's inner tensions and flaws. When, in his twenties, he prepared a typescript of the eulogies and obituaries occasioned by his father's death, he followed his mother's wishes and sanitized Samuel's portraits. An obituary in the *Brooklyn Eagle*, for example, had stated: "[Samuel Hand's] mien was austere and his manners were formal and unsympathetic. [That], however, was only the shell of a kind disposition." As expurgated in Learned's transcript, the passage read simply: "He had a kind disposition."[61] Only much later, as an old man, did Hand, reflecting on the family moodiness, suggest that though "Clifford didn't have [it], my father had it, and Richard had it," that his father was "by nature of melancholic disposition. He was too sensitive."[62]

Even when Learned Hand came to appreciate that his father's remoteness constituted acquired behavior, he continued to view his grandfather Augustus as the personification of equanimity, and he showed only the most sporadic recognition that there might have been unstable elements in Augustus as well. Neither Samuel nor Learned Hand fully recognized that their own searches for personal equilibrium followed in Augustus's well-concealed footsteps. In a letter to his wife, Augustus once stopped himself from excessive brooding about life and death and religion with the comment *"I fear I am getting too sensitive for manhood on this subject."*[63] But he revealed these anxieties only rarely.[64] Similarly, Samuel's more deliberate efforts to control his own much deeper sensitivities produced for young Learned a sense of a distant, cold individual who revealed little of his inner self. For Learned, the Hand legacy, especially of his grandfather and father, was a source of pride and a model for emulation, but it was also a heavy burden.

FROM THE FIRST, young Learned was the center of attention and he grew up as "the precious male," as he put it, "spoiled" by the entire family.[65] When he was a baby of six months and his paternal grandmother took care of him for a few days, she promptly wrote to his maternal grandmother, in a passage that speaks volumes about family goals, "You would think he was going to make a speech so earnestly does he look into your face—we call him Judge Hand. We are all devoted to his honor."[66]

In Hand's early recollections of his parents, they too were "devoted," but their strictness, discipline, and frugality were unforgettable: as a very young boy, he was "taught always when I went by to turn out the gas light." When friends spoke about his "miserliness," Learned could only agree: "I was brought up a tightwad."[67] Even more insistently, his mother "tried to keep the faith in me," he recalled. She persistently urged him to read the Bible: "I mean, that was the thing to do. If you really were going to be good, you had to know the Bible." And she made him go to church every Sunday, even though he was "terribly bored with it," and she barred any activity that interfered with her fervent belief in the Puritan Sabbath. "Sunday was a gloomy atmosphere, do-nothing. I was allowed to draw, but not to paint. The rule was that on Sunday you shouldn't write anything."[68] It is no surprise to discover that Learned turned agnostic in adolescence yet carried remnants of his mother's training throughout his life: when he sang at his desk, for example, Calvinist hymns would alternate with Gilbert and Sullivan; when he wrote opinions and letters, biblical allusions in the literary style of the King James Version readily surfaced.

The emotional restraint Samuel had painfully cultivated to curb his own moodiness was early transmitted to his son. For example, when Learned was not yet nine, his father proudly reported to his own mother that he had managed to improve Learned's school behavior, even though the boy was already unusually well behaved: "[He] seems capable of being shamed out of his freaks & able to exhibit self-control." When Learned received a bad grade in "deportment" for whispering in class, Samuel reported: "I talked with him about it, showed the absurdity of it & he has never had a demerit mark since—that strikes me as showing a fair amount of self-control for a little boy of eight."[69]

Not surprisingly, young Learned's favorite hours were those he could spend in his own room on the top floor of the Hands' solid brick house on State Street. Even there, he could not escape symbols of confinement. At his mother's insistence, the windows were "kept tight shut—I can remember in the morning the condensed breath would be all over, frozen on the windowpanes."[70] Still, in this welcome retreat, he could play with his toys, indulge in his hobbies, and, in later years, curl up with his books. As a little boy, he loved working with his scroll saw, and he spent hours enthralled by the pictures of distant places projected by his magic lantern, his most cherished possession.[71] In his earliest preserved letter, the nine-year-old Learned eagerly told his cousin Gus about his growing stamp collection and reported even more enthusiastically about his "three section maps, [of] New York state, [of] the United States, and [of] the world."[72]

Young Learned spent far more of his free time in his own room than with playmates. Occasionally, he would visit other children's homes for an afternoon snack or as part of his dancing lessons, but there is no record of children ever joining him at his own home. He played outdoors infrequently: one winter, he complained that he had been able to ride his bicycle only once; as he reported, "I fell in a snowbank and wet my clothes."[73] A sense of physical awkwardness, which he had from his earliest days, persisted throughout his life. Repeatedly he forced himself to try sports, but thought himself poorly coordinated, and his usual attitude when other youngsters played outdoor games was that of a sideline observer. "I was never any good as an athlete, oh, no! I was big enough—but I wasn't any good. I couldn't use my body, and I didn't like [athletics] enough."[74] He tried boxing lessons and was a second-stringer on a school football team, yet he always fell short of his own aspirations; and these failures reinforced his doubts about his aggressiveness and masculinity. The good behavior drilled into him at home reinforced his reluctance to romp on playing fields. The Hands' maid described him as a "little gentleman," and he himself thought he had been "a very good boy indeed" if something of a "sissy."[75]

No wonder, then, that the hours in his own room provided his happiest moments. The joys of this retreat increased dramatically after he learned to read. Hand would later recall that as a child he had not been "much of a reader," only average, "betwixt and between" at best; certainly not "avid."[76] But in fact, he read a great deal; he was average only by comparison with Samuel Hand—and of course Learned always made this comparison. As Learned turned eight, his father reported in letters, he was reading books about knighthood and Hawthorne's *Tanglewood Tales*, and had already delved into the "old classic stories"—"the Argonauts & their adventures; Theseus & the Minotaur; Perseus & the Gorgons; Ceres & Europa & so on"—and was able to retell the myths "in his own way."[77] Most of Learned's own childhood letters are also filled with reports on reading: children's books of stories from Livy and Herodotus were among his favorites. And he had access to his father's Dumas volumes. *The Count of Monte Cristo* evoked special enthusiasm: Learned thought it "bully," even though "Mama won't let me read on Sunday." His mother's ban on all nonreligious reading on the Sabbath ("a great privation," as young Learned wrote to his cousin Gus[78]) and on "trash" at any time chafed even in the Judge's old age: "I wasn't allowed to read dime novels," he recalled, or any Dickens.

The education Learned received in Albany fit his father's prescription. Samuel Hand believed that education was "something like calisthenics": training in the basics—in mathematics, classical languages, other traditional subjects—was "like going on chest weights." By studying the fundamentals, Samuel told Learned, "you got muscles in your brain";

the basics were just right for stretching the mind, for training in discipline and thoroughness.[79] Myths and adventure stories and modern literature, like history, were subjects to be indulged in during spare time, not at school.

Learned's two years in the small primary school near his home were devoted to the study of reading, writing, and arithmetic. In 1879, when he was seven, he went to a far more imposing building farther down State Street, Albany Academy, where he spent the next ten years—five in the lower school downstairs, five more in the upper grades on the second floor.

The city's best families had long considered the academy, founded in 1813, the outstanding local school for their sons. Its massive building, with its somber, dark red stone and grand, Romanesque design, presented a forbidding façade. Yet Learned recalled it as "very beautiful," with its "great large rooms, two wings, [and] a cupola."[80] (The building survives, in its original park setting, on Albany's most prominent hill, between the state capitol and the Court of Appeals.)

The magnificence of the building and its site far exceeded the intellectual stimulation of what went on inside. Hand's memories of his lower-school years were predominantly unpleasant—a sense of "being scared," perhaps an understandable reaction from a sheltered youngster finding himself amid two hundred or so other boys for the first time. He rarely enjoyed even the recesses from classes: in the big yard, he felt himself an outsider, "not knowing exactly what to play, what it was all about." All his teachers in the lower school were women; all stressed discipline, Bible reading, and the three R's; the one who made the most lasting impression did so, Hand recalled, because he was "rather afraid of her."[81] The academy only further developed Learned's drive to work hard and do well even at unpleasant tasks. In his last year there, he reported punctiliously to Cousin Gus: "I stood 2 in my class in the semi-annual work, the boy who stood ahead being 97 240-480, and I stood 97 227-480, he being 13-480 ahead of me."[82] Clearly an excellent student despite the lack of intellectual excitement, Learned encountered as stimuli only the competition for grades and the satisfaction of completing assigned tasks.

EVEN AS A CHILD, Learned thought Albany a dreary and joyless town. The strictness of the academy routine and his home environment bred a restlessness that could not be wholly suppressed. Throughout the school year, he looked forward to the escapes from Albany during vacations, when the vitality buried in the somber boy burst forth. During most winter vacations, and always in the summer, Learned and his family would go to Elizabethtown, his favorite destination: "I can remember going down just to look at the tracks that led up to [Elizabethtown], anticipating the wonderful revelations that were going to be there, of interest, and beauty too."[83]

The winter visits to the Adirondacks nourished Learned's vision of endless stretches of pure white snow, contrasting sharply with the gray slush left by Albany storms. "I remember the enchantment of seeing the rabbit tracks in the snow," Hand said in his eighties. "A rabbit has four legs but he makes only three tracks. . . . I shall never forget that."[84] He wished that he could live in Elizabethtown "the year round," he told his father when he was eight, especially when there would be "such glorious clean snowdrifts" to gaze upon, walk through, and coast down with Cousin Gus.[85]

His friendship with Augustus Noble Hand, Uncle Richard's son, was formed and cemented during those visits. Augustus—Cousin Gus— was two and a half years older than Learned, which seemed in the childhood years a more "enormous difference" than decades later, when they viewed each other as contemporaries on the federal court bench in New York City. From the beginning, Gus and Learned had "the most fabulous times" together. The visits each August were especially memorable. For example, in the summer of 1882, when Learned was ten, he and Gus went on daylong walks over the hills, taking in their magnificent vistas: "You could hear the echo of every word we said."[86] No wonder that Learned wrote to Gus from Albany during the winter: "You don't know how much I would like to be with you in the country, and how often I think of the good times [we] have together in Elizabethtown."[87]

In Elizabethtown, the "little gentleman" of Albany turned into one of the "wild boys," especially when he and Gus took their overnight camping trip, the highlight of each summer visit. They called their camp "Cudgo's Cave"; it was sited only a mile from the house by boat, but to the boys it was the middle of the wilderness. Preparing the evergreen hut at the campsite was a joy that never paled: "You cut the two forked sticks which were the entrance, then you add some longer sticks, [and you place them] on a little slope—the front was the down end." The frame consisted of "some latticework of sticks." Nails were prohibited: "If a nail was used it showed that we were not real woodsmen." And then came Learned's major task, to thatch the hut with evergreens: "I was supposed to be an expert thatcher and the question was whether I thatched so that the rain wouldn't come through." One of Uncle Richard's handymen helped the boys take the supplies to the campsite and left them there alone. The boys would say good-bye to him with "beating hearts. . . . And then the night would finally come" and the boys would ensconce themselves beside a big fire. When the eight-year-old Learned faced the first of these evenings, "I was terribly scared and I got my foot in the water getting out of the boat and began to cry and wanted to come home but they didn't let me. I was glad they didn't. I don't know how much sleep we had but I remember waking up in the middle of the night wondering whether the sun would ever come up."[88]

Almost daily there were hours in the woods and on the trails overlooking Lake Champlain. "Oh, it was a lovely place," the Judge recalled. "I can remember with Gus going up there and lying on our bellies looking off and imagining how Burgoyne's army [came] down the lake. In my mind's eye [I could] see the glitter of the red uniforms, and the Indian scouts." Historical legends about the area abounded; for example, Rogers's Rangers had allegedly fought there in Colonial days. ("My father as a young man wrote a poem about this fight," Hand would recollect, and all his life he remembered a line: "On the shore those dead men stilly lie." Perhaps the poem was "not so much," he conceded; but "I couldn't have done it. I don't think any member of the family but he could have done it."[89]) Still, the summers in Elizabethtown were all too short, barely long enough to sustain Learned's spirits throughout the constrained Albany winters.

IN MAY 1886, when Learned was fourteen, his father died of cancer. Samuel Hand's fatal illness had been diagnosed months earlier, but the news had been kept from Learned until a few days before the end. When Samuel stopped going to his office, Learned could no longer be sheltered, and he was at his father's bedside during the final agonies. Two days after Samuel's death, Learned, writing on black-bordered mourner's stationery, shared his grief with his cousin Gus.

Learned's long letter[90] contains expectable reflections on the shock of "the sad news of Papa's death": it "seemed hardly as if it could happen"; it was "a terrible loss." Far more startling to anyone who knew of Learned Hand's agnosticism during the subsequent seven decades was the extraordinary depth of the religiosity he voiced; given that he was writing to his closest friend, we must presume that, for the moment at least, the faith was genuine. "If you could imagine one half the comfort my religion has given to me in this terrible loss, you would see that Christ never forsakes those who cling to him," he wrote. "I cling to Jesus Christ always as my counsellor, guide, comforter and father throughout the short school of life to be worthy of that crown of life my earthly father obtained."

The immediate and more lasting effect of the death was the inevitable heightening of Learned's sense of responsibility as the family's sole surviving male. He had absorbed his father's advocacy of self-control —he told Gus that he had "tried" to hold back tears; he had "not cried much"—and then he dwelt on his new burdens: "I am now I suppose at the head of our little branch of the family and I try to feel my responsibility, indeed I think I do, and with God's help I shall I hope be able to do so. I want you to pray [to] the Almighty to sustain me in this new and important care which it is best for me to bear while I am young. . . . What I must try to do is to be worthy of the name of Hand which I bear." He thanked God for assuring that his father had left to him "to carry on as spotless and pure a reputation as any body on the wide world ever had or will have."

Learned's anxious, somber letter worried Gus, who urged him not to feel too oppressed by his new obligations. Learned's emphasis on duty, Gus suggested, reeked of a mechanical response to society's expectations, a response individuals were expected to demonstrate as if they were "trained animals." Learned quickly protested that "what I said to you I meant exactly." His sense of responsibility, he insisted, was his own choice and came from his heart: "[T]o begin with, trained animals have no sense of duty for what they do is either through force of habit or through love of their master and not as if they considered what they did a good act but merely to obtain their master's praise." Learned insisted that he was different: "[N]ow duty is in my estimation a sense of something which drives you on because you feel that it is a right thing and has to be done to fulfill this sense and another thing, I think that duty is one of the highest of motives which can influence anyone to anything."[91]

In the summer of 1886, he was promptly called on to demonstrate this heightened sense of obligation, especially toward his mother. He had planned to spend some of his vacation visiting Gus, but as summer approached, Learned found that he was no longer free to make such plans. "Mama" was more worried than ever about the problems her cherished son might encounter with train connections and other travel hazards, and while privately Learned was convinced that he could manage the trip perfectly well, he canceled his plans. As he told Gus, "It would only cause [Mama] some uneasiness of which she has had enough already."[92]

Another immediate consequence of his father's death was an intensification of the internal pressure to do well at school. Within two weeks, for example, Learned spent a near sleepless night "to study quite hard" for an impending Latin examination. He had moved upstairs at Albany Academy less than two years earlier, and he completed the six-year college preparatory course in the upper school in five. He was a driven youngster, and he achieved high grades, but his performance was a triumph of determination over lack of inspiration. The curriculum was traditional and narrow, limited to no-frill basics. Pursuing it at least assured him that he was following his father's wishes. "The thing, my boy, you must do is what develops your mind," Samuel had repeatedly told Learned.[93] Albany Academy offered "not a bit" of English; as Hand would later recall, there was "no Shakespeare, no literature of any sort." The history courses, mainly in ancient history, were "just enough" to meet the college prerequisites. The elementary physics course was "interesting," and Learned would have liked to take more, but nothing further was offered. He was exposed to a little German and French, also just enough to satisfy college prerequisites, but most of the work in languages was in the classics, in Greek and Latin.[94]

Military drills were the major out-of-class preoccupation. The students were organized into a battalion structure, issued uniforms, and given mock muskets. All this reflected the prevalent "hangover of military notions," Hand thought later, the "military atmosphere in the air" in the aftermath of the Civil War. (His classmate Freddie Townsend's father, for example, enjoyed special respect because he had been a brigadier general in the war, even though Learned thought of him as "a pompous ass who never did anything after he married a rich wife.") Learned unenthusiastically turned out for the mandatory daily drills.[95] When later he became a trustee of the Academy, more to further his career as a young lawyer than because of any innate affection for the school, he performed his duties conscientiously, except for one rejection of an institutional summons: when he was asked to attend a drill exercise, he replied that he was "not very keen about such matters," and if the drills should "suffer from the august absence of Trustees, I think the school will not be the worse."[96]

It is no wonder that an educational atmosphere so lacking in joy or excitement left few traces in Hand's memories. He had a vivid recollection of only one of his teachers, mainly because this one taught mathematics, Hand's favorite subject among those designed to develop "muscles in the brain." "I remember what we used to call the originals in algebra and geometry. I can to this day [remember] the pleasure that came when I felt, 'God, I've got the forms; I've devised the form that fits this thing!' "

Devising "the form that fits" proved a lifelong source of satisfaction to Hand, and consolation as well whenever his disbelief in absolutes brought gloom. In law, too, there could at least be the rock-bottom gratification of creating an intelligible "form that fits" the disorderly array of legal precedents and human behavior. He could not bring himself to believe that "the sequence, the flux" of the universe revealed any God-imposed order; but, he added:

> I think the real salvation of mankind rests in what I like to call the craftsman spirit. Homo sapiens [does] take a strange [and] lively satisfaction in imposing a notion, an idea, a picture, what you will, on the medium outside. Whether it's painting a picture, whether it's writing a poem, singing a song, or pleasing a lady [or] a man. Doing something well, something that's in himself, that he's succeeded, by God, in putting there.[97]

Satisfaction in craftsmanship, the aesthetic satisfaction of imposing a form on milling fragments, was to Hand a significant bulwark against uncertainty spilling over into paralyzing despair.

At college and law school, Hand would encounter inspiring teachers whom he admired throughout his life, but not at Albany Academy. He recalled only one person with real warmth—Henry P. Warren, the headmaster for most of Learned's years at the school. On the surface, Warren was a traditional preacher of "the good-sounding clichés," but he was decent and warm, and his emphasis on public service had special appeal for Learned: "I don't mean political service but [that] everyone should be brought up with the idea that he must justify his existence in the terms of the society in which he lives; he must not be an idler, he must be a contributor, he must stand for the better life."[98]

The impression Warren left was all the more vivid because Learned's contacts with him were not limited to the academy. Warren joined Learned (by now sixteen), Lydia Coit Learned, and several others on a European trip during the summer of 1888. For Learned, it came at the traditional time for the grand tour, but his reason for going was that his mother, who complained of illnesses all her life, had decided to take the waters at Karlsbad. Judging by Learned's reports to Gus, he was not very impressed by the traditional tourist sights as the party moved from Great Britain through France and Switzerland to the Hapsburg Empire. The high spot came while his mother waited for the baths to take effect: during those few weeks Learned was able to travel with Henry Warren, mainly to Switzerland. For Learned, it was like the glorious outdoor days in the Adirondacks writ large: he and the headmaster walked more than one hundred miles in the glorious Alpine scenery. When he returned to his mother's side for the final weeks, he wished that "the Karlsbad business" were finished; he was worried about what he might miss in the early weeks of his senior year at Albany Academy; and he was especially apprehensive about the results of the Harvard entrance examination he had taken at the end of the spring.[99]

As would so often be true, his anxieties proved groundless. He was graduated near the top of his class and was admitted to Harvard. Choosing Harvard was somewhat unusual for an Albany Academy graduate: most went to Williams, some to Yale; only "the swells" opted for Harvard, which was regarded "as a stuck up, snobbish school."[100] Learned was not one of the "swells"; in his case, intellect, not wealth and status, explained his decision. Albany Academy, like its city, was a gray and confining environment. The atmosphere that would make intellectual verve and challenging inquiry second nature to Hand lay 150 miles to the east, in Cambridge.

AS HAND LATER REMEMBERED IT, he arrived in the "strange and new surroundings" of Harvard College in 1889 as a "frank barbarian from a small New York town," an "untamed native," "a rather unsophisticated boy from a small city," "a guileless youngster."[101] As a graduate of a good private school and a member of a respectable family, he was hardly a barbarian; yet his recollections coincide with his contemporaneous impressions of the rigidly stratified social atmosphere at Harvard. One of his first letters from Cambridge reported that the students were "in a great measure a pretty snobbish lot."[102] The Harvard preoccupation with social standing cast a cloud over most of his college years, deepened his self-doubts, intensified the fragility of his self-esteem, and left scars that would never heal.

Relations among Harvard students during Learned's college days were marked by a deep chasm. Those most readily accepted into the ranks of the socially prominent "swells" were typically the sons of the best families of New England and New York, graduates of the best private preparatory schools, students with the best contacts in Boston society. Clearly relegated to the other side of the chasm were the public school graduates, young men who had not grown up on the East Coast, merely middle-class boys, and sons of ghetto Jews or Irish Catholics. A student's placement in the social ranks dominated much of his extracurricular life, from dinner and dance invitations to positions in student organizations and even his residence in Cambridge. And the most visible symbol of social position turned on a student's place, if any, in Harvard's cluster of social clubs.

Hand usually described his Harvard position as that of an "outsider."[103] Harvard's leading historian insists that the exclusiveness of the social clubs inflicted no " 'inferiority complex' on outsiders": allegedly, those who could not hope to be chosen by the clubs did not feel hurt because, "strange as it may seem, nobody seems to care."[104] Arguably, that is an accurate assessment for those who could have no hope at all. And if Hand had indeed been clearly beyond the pale, the scars left by his social experience would not have been so deep. But Hand was not a graduate of a midwestern high school or the son of recent immigrants. He was at least marginally qualified for acceptance into the inner circle, he did care, he was considered but rejected by the desirable clubs, and he never forgot it. Having been at the margin— "on the fringe," as he once put it[105]—he was legitimately in the competition, and rejection hurt all the more because of that.

Like his father, Hand cared about what others thought of him, perhaps too much. And he was very much aware of the social hierarchy symbolized by the clubs. For example, in the summer of 1888, when Gus was already at college but Learned still a year away, Learned had said to his cousin, "Gus, Fred Townsend says the important thing in Harvard College is to join the Porcellian Club," the most exclusive of all. Gus replied, "I never heard of it. I think it must be abandoned now because there isn't any such thing."[106] This is a revealing anecdote, both about Learned's early sensitivity to the club system and about Gus's equanimity: Gus was never given to moody introspection; for Learned, far more preoccupied with appearances and about belonging, failure to make the Porcellian rankled to the end of his life.

During their freshman year, socially ambitious students were encouraged to "say, do, wear, the 'right thing,' avoid the company of all ineligibles, and, above all, eschew originality." The formal club-selection process began in the sophomore year, with elections to "the Institute of 1770," from which the elite clubs selected their members. Only about one fourth of the class would be chosen for the institute, in groups of ten; and the names of the chosen were printed in the local press, Hand recalled, "in the exact order of the election, which wholly served as an index of social rating." Most of those elected to the institute were then selected for the next rung in clubdom's social ladder, the DKE—"the Dickey," whose members were known as "Deeks."[107] From the ranks of the Dickey, in turn, the smaller, even more exclusive clubs, with eating, drinking, and sleeping facilities, with bars and billiard tables and card rooms, chose their members. At the top of the small-club pyramid was the most exclusive of all, the Porcellian. To be a Porcellian was to be of the crème de la crème, the epitome of the "swell" and the "grandee."

Learned was elected to the institute, but nowhere near the top ten. He did not make it even close to the Porcellian; indeed, he was not even selected for the Dickey. In the spring of 1891, more than eighty members of the class of about three hundred were elected to the institute; about seventy of these made it into the Dickey. As Learned recalled, he was one of the "few leftovers or also-rans," one of the "thirteen second graders" who went into the institute but not the Dickey; and that result, he felt, made one "distinctly déclassé." Fred Townsend, who had the same Albany Academy background (although his family was wealthier and socially more prominent than the Hands), got beyond the institute rung of the social ladder. "Freddie got in," Hand recalled when in his eighties. "He got in with the swells more than I."[108]

Freshman students ambitious for social acceptance knew that they had to watch their step very carefully. Intellect was not a barrier so long as it was tactfully concealed; association with the right people was more important. Despite his eagerness to belong, Learned did not follow these prescriptions. He worked as hard, and did as well, in his first year at Harvard as he had at Albany Academy, and he was perceived to be a top student: as one classmate recalled, Hand seemed "the intellectual leader, far and away, of our college class" from the outset.[109] But his opposition to exclusiveness and to stereotyped generalizations was apparent from the beginning, even though it was at war with his desire for acceptance:

> There is a very prevalent idea that one should take great pains not to meet men who will injure [one's] position in the college [he wrote to Richard Hand, Gus's father]. . . . [I]t strikes me that to choose your companions with a view to the social position which you have from them is the very essence of 'snobbery.' [It] seems as though I had heard nothing since I came here except 'be careful what crowds you get in with' or something like it. . . . [I]t is very sad to see fellows who are snobbish or exclusive.[110]

Learned's feelings were even more intense a decade later. He had advised a Harvard freshman from Elizabethtown to join the debating society; the freshman's older brother opposed that advice because it would throw the freshman in "with men that are not desirable." That was "hardly a worthy point of view," Learned said. "I do not mean by this that I do not understand the advantages of knowing what we commonly call 'the right sort of men,' but I do mean that a man who consciously shapes his college career with that in view has lost something which is of greater value than anything else he can take from it—his self-respect."[111] The older brother persisted in arguing that "it is best to begin with the fellows whom he would be more apt to ask to pass Sundays with his family,"[112] but Learned rejected that view even more firmly: "[O]ne's acquaintances or friends should not be governed by the antecedents or parentage of the man whom one meets." And he added: "[W]e should certainly not attempt to select our friends from 'our own set.' I am quite aware that in this, I am at variance with most people, [but] I own that it strikes me as rather the manliest attitude to accept men and have them as friends simply for the personal qualities which you may find in them and regardless of what may be the connections or associations they come from."[113] Sentiments such as these could not have endeared Learned to the gatekeepers of the Dickey and the Porcellian.

Exclusion from the best clubs left Hand feeling "booted about" socially.[114] The clubs' decision affected other areas of extracurricular life: it meant he would not live in the elegant "private dormitories" off campus where "the swells [had] their private clubs";[115] nor did he live in the more primitive but centrally located quarters within Harvard Yard. Instead, he and Fred Townsend moved into the newly built Hastings Hall (still in use today as a law school dormitory). Learned found Room 4 at Hastings—actually, a wood-paneled suite of two bedrooms and a study—"most comfortable." Indeed, his suite was probably just as comfortable as the private dormitories "where the grandees lived," albeit physically and socially at the fringe.[116]

As his early years at Harvard passed, Learned's circle of acquaintances among his classmates grew. Virtually all of them belonged to clubs, though, and when they left for their "sacred precincts," Hand's sense of social alienation was reinforced. He recalled that he was one of "the very obedient, docile little boys. We went to our classes. We didn't drink. We didn't consort with the hetaerae. We worked every night. And we were nice boys."[117] This circumscribed life was a consequence not only of the club rejections, but also of his mother's Puritan standards: his college classmates did "a great deal of drinking," but, as he remembered, "I didn't drink or smoke at all in college. Mother didn't want me to. I was kind of a sissy, I guess."[118]

Learned tried out for the glee club, but his voice was not good enough and, as he put it, "they canned me, threw me out." He sought acceptance by athletic teams, again unsuccessfully. He "wasn't good enough" to make the football team. He made an even more determined effort to join the crew—partly because he enjoyed rowing, partly because membership on the crew carried some social cachet. But he "wasn't good enough" to make the crew either, other than as a substitute. Still, even rowing with the substitutes proved "a pleasant experience," not only for its own sake but also to help overcome his sense of being a "sissy." He was accepted by the other boys there, who called him "Buck." He began to sprout a mustache and beard, and his appearance earned him some comradely nicknames—"Mad Russian" and "Mongolian." At crew practice, he recalled, "they used to call me the 'Mongolian Grind' "—"Mongolian" for his appearance, "Grind" for his reputation for studiousness.

Learned's devotion to studies put a stop even to the rowing: "I gave it up after a year because I thought it interfered with my work. I was a serious boy, oh boy, wasn't I a serious boy!" Thereafter, his physical activities were limited to solitary physical exercises in the gymnasium: "I did chest weights and things like that, just to keep up my body, so that my mind would be all right, you know. This was Hand stuff, inherited Hand stuff, these ideas. This mental stuff came from my father, his admonitions when I was young."[119]

When Learned would leave campus to mingle with Boston society, the excursions brought only limited satisfaction. Some Albany friends, he recalled, "got me into the Saturday Evening Dancing Class [in Boston], and that was where the swells were. But I didn't know any girls, and I didn't know [the swells], and they were in the clubs, and I wasn't in the clubs." Typically, Learned would simply watch "those great swell boys," "in full dress, tailcoats [and] white waistcoats," go off to their dances. Very occasionally, he himself would go to one of the cotillions, or "germans," as they were also called, that were outgrowths of the dancing class. But once again, he was doomed to be "on the fringe." Typically, he was introduced to girls only when a more elegant acquaintance needed a partner for "some unattractive cousin or sister."[120] When after his sophomore year he at last encountered a young woman he was attracted to, a visitor from Chicago, it was not at college but during his summer vacation. For the first time, Hand thought he was in love: "I was deeply in love, I couldn't have been more in love. . . . Oh, awfully noble love!" Months later, when he chaperoned his older sister on a visit to Chicago, he saw his summer love again, and it became clear that she did not reciprocate his "overwhelming passion."[121] Learned returned to his usual nonrelationship to women, speculating about "girls in general" in his correspondence, pronouncing such notions as "I neither like a fast foolish thing nor a silly prude."[122] But he never came close to moving beyond theory during his time at Harvard.

In his last two years at college, Learned began to have some success in finding a place in extracurricular activities. He was "getting in more or less with quality . . . not like being in one of the clubs, but at least not being booted about. . . . I began [to] get a little more acquaintance with the class; I wasn't quite the hermit I had been." In his junior year, he automatically became a member of the Hasty Pudding Club as a result of his earlier election to the Institute of 1770. As a lowly member of the cast of the Pudding's student musical for 1892, he played a chorus girl in the club's performance in New York City. Painted with big black eyebrows, bedecked in a blond wig, Learned danced and sang; he could remember some of the lyrics decades later. It was not the top of the social pyramid, but it signified a limited entry into the mainstream of student life; and the New York City appearance in particular was "pretty hot stuff."[123]

In the spring of his junior year, Hand was elected president of the *Harvard Advocate*, a student literary magazine.[124] Yet even this position did not add much to his self-esteem. The *Advocate* was not at the top of the heap of student publications: as a humor magazine, it had been replaced by *The Harvard Lampoon*; as literary publications were concerned, the best people and the best work were with the newer *Harvard Monthly*. And Learned was convinced that "the scarcity of editors accounted for the fact that when [the prior] board went out they put me in as President."[125] Others wrote short stories and poetry; Hand limited himself to brief editorials. He took little retrospective pride in them, recalling them as "priggish," "conceited and opinionated," and "shallow." That was unduly harsh, but his contributions do indicate that he did not tackle his job with his maximum energy and talents. Early in his senior year he resigned, to "the great contempt of the others," because he thought the *Advocate* was interfering with his work: "everything was interfering with my work," he recalled later. By the time he left himself open to attack as a "quitter," his immersion in his studies was providing whatever boosts to his self-confidence he could garner.[126] The effects of social rejection would never leave him, but he now enjoyed the satisfaction of outstanding grades in challenging courses.

THROUGHOUT HIS LIFE, Learned Hand reiterated his gratitude for what Harvard College "had done" for him.[127] What he had in mind was certainly not the blows to his self-esteem but what he had gained from certain faculty members and classes. The educational experience at Harvard opened vast intellectual vistas and prompted fond recollections:

> Harvard was to me the awakening of all those things that since then have been dearest.[128]

I have often thought what a blessed advantage it was, how few
people had a chance to be thrown—a raw little boy from a hick
town up the river—to be thrown [with] men like those men at
the College, James, Santayana, Royce, Palmer, Norton, Taussig.
[What] an unequalled opportunity![129]

Hand was graduated from the college summa cum laude, having
taken the maximum possible number of courses and done so well in
them that he was awarded a master's as well as a bachelor's degree for
his four years there; his classmates elected him to deliver the Class Day
oration at the June 1893 commencement. The honors might suggest
only the ceaseless efforts of a self-described "greasy grind," an inveterate
"marks hound," which Hand in fact had been during his first years at
Harvard. But during the second half of his sophomore year, he had
begun to break away.

Neither Fred Townsend nor Cousin Gus ever deviated from the
traditional approach: they concentrated on classical studies throughout
their college years. Learned, by contrast, took no course in either Latin
or Greek after his freshman year. Only a mathematics course brought
real satisfaction; for the rest, in classical and modern languages as well
as in the required writing classes (in which he received his lowest
grades), he was stimulated neither by the instructors nor by their materials. He took lots of courses because he "was supposed to be an eager
student,"[130] but he did not recall them as "very important." His father's
admonitions were still with him: Samuel Hand had "always said that
he thought the important thing in college was to take classics and
mathematics. . . . [W]hat he left in my mind was [that they] trained
your mind a little as gymnastics trained your muscles."[131] And so
Learned endured the drudgery of Latin and Greek in order to add "power
to the brain," even though he "didn't care much" about them, since
the teachers did not "regard the substance of what was said. What you
read in Greek and Latin as literature was treated with scorn."

But then Learned broke with his father's confining views of college
education. "I think wisely," he recalled, "I made up my mind that
there was really not any warrant for keeping on; that this development
of the cerebrum was a mistake on my father's part." This breakthrough
toward a questioning of received traditions was spurred by "something
new that happened" at the end of his sophomore year. The "important
thing, what really counted," was "those courses in philosophy and
economics."[132] Intellectual excitement, spurred by great minds engaged
in great teaching, inspired Learned and left a permanent imprint; at
last, he was exposed to the aspects of the college closest to Harvard

president Charles W. Eliot's heart, and the student was never the same thereafter.

Eliot was at the halfway point of his forty-year incumbency in 1889, when Learned Hand entered Harvard. Eliot was an educational visionary with the talents of a practical reformer, and his leadership transformed Harvard from a hidebound school struggling to hold on to a slipping regional reputation into the nation's pace-setting university. His most daring innovation was to cut back sharply on required courses and substitute a wide-ranging elective system. By the last decade of the nineteenth century, Harvard neared the zenith of its Olympian age. In his inaugural address, Eliot had described the aim of the college he envisioned as the production of graduates with "an open mind, trained to careful thinking, instructed in the methods of philosophic investigation, acquainted [with] the accumulated thought of past generations, and penetrated with humility."[133] Few of the students of Eliot's years could have personified the realization of those ideals as well as Hand.

Hand's concentration on courses in philosophy and economics in his junior and senior years did not make him a philosopher or economist. Far more important than the specific knowledge he gained was the cast of mind he developed in response to his inspiring teachers and as he underwent a difficult maturing process toward greater independence.

Philosophy, Hand would recall, was his "first love": that "attracted me more than anything else."[134] After a basic philosophy course and related lectures in his sophomore year, he took most of his classes in that field and was awarded double honors for his work. The major reason for this sudden love affair with philosophy was Learned's encounter with three memorable teachers: George Santayana, William James, and Josiah Royce. These men were "the most shining stars" in the Harvard firmament at that time,[135] and these giants of Harvard's golden age of philosophy provided the first genuine intellectual stimulation for Learned in Cambridge. "We got the great star figures at once," he remembered, "and I swallowed it, hook, bait, and sinker."[136]

The actual contents of the courses were not the main reason for the importance of philosophy to Learned. True, it was useful to obtain a fuller, more systematic acquaintance with the ideas of great thinkers, and this was congenial to Learned's emerging tendency toward speculativeness. And the extensive reading in the courses spurred a lifelong interest in reading philosophy. (In later years he would come to know personally as well as to read John Dewey, Morris Raphael Cohen, Bertrand Russell, and Alfred North Whitehead.) All his letters and speeches disclose a ready familiarity with ideas absorbed at Harvard, the ideas of Hume, Kant, and Descartes as well as those of his teachers.

But most important was the effect of the Harvard philosophers on Learned's personal and intellectual makeup. In his early years at college, he was a young man very much at sea: he was uncomfortable about the growing number of questions that he could raise and the dwindling number of answers he found adequate. He was skeptical of his father's notions of education, and he had deeper doubts than ever about his mother's religious beliefs. About that time, he made his "abjuration" of religious faith: "I could see no bearing in anything I could understand in it."[137] What philosophy signified for Learned, then, can best be understood in the context of his near vacuum of convictions and beliefs. Alone and adrift, he was initially attracted to it as a beckoning refuge and rock. "I wanted a home to go to," as he once put it. Perhaps the emotional pains of personal and intellectual doubts could be calmed through the process of "absolute rigorous deduction": "I wanted something that I couldn't escape because, if I couldn't escape it, I could live with it, and that's what I wanted."[138]

Hand "didn't get much" by way of answers to replace his lost certainties, but he absorbed a sense that his own uncertain, uncomfortable search was a legitimate stance. Instructors who offered confident answers struck him as "flabby" and vacuous; those he respected were the great questioners—untiring and unbiased in their inquiries and unafraid to challenge traditions, confident about the need to ask questions rather than to supply answers. Learned found that being a seeker rather than the supplier of answers was not necessarily discreditable. He later recalled that one of his teachers made students "rather proud of being skeptics: the old notions were all trash." In short, Harvard's philosophers channeled and legitimated Learned's doubts, and reinforced his emerging skepticism.[139]

During his introductory philosophy course, Hand turned from a merely hardworking student into a genuinely engaged one. The readings often seemed impenetrable: "I think a great many of the words had no meaning. I sort of had the notion that if I read it over enough, the fog might clear a little."[140] But the teachers were always absorbing. To Learned, George Santayana, the youngest and least prominent, was the most attractive. He was only about eight years older than Hand and seemed even younger than that. An engaging, iconoclastic, vivacious young intellectual, he lived in bachelor quarters far from the social elite on Shady Hill and Irving Street. Unlike most faculty members, he did not keep his distance from students. Instead, he relished long evening talks over wine in his apartment with a select number of undergraduates, and Learned became an occasional member of that group.

Even in his eighties, Hand's face would glow as he recalled the young Santayana:

> We thought him really the most wonderful thing that ever was made. He had a very detached impersonal way, but everything was welcome. He seemed to be entirely without bias. He started every question as though it was a question of what's that on the street, is it a grain of sand, or is it a pocketbook, or what you will.[141]

Santayana was not prepossessing: Hand recalled him as "a slight man" with "a very light mustache and a curious birdlike quality in speaking and moving his body." When students asked him an unexpected question, he would, disconcertingly, stop, glance about the room, and often make the questioner seem ridiculous. Yet, Hand said, "we all admired the clarity of his mind so much, and how he stripped off conventions of any sort. You felt as though you were getting from this man what was fresh and original in that sense—it was *him* you were getting."[142]

The great attraction of Santayana for Hand lay not only in the philosopher's intellectual stance but also in the much needed social support he gave Learned. In later years, when Hand read Santayana's books as they appeared, he often reacted with puzzlement or dissatisfaction, and when he had sporadic meetings with Santayana, Hand found his pessimistic, somewhat supercilious attitude uncongenial; but he would always cherish the memory of the young instructor's magnetic personality and fair-minded spirit as he had come to know it at college.

William James was near fifty when Hand first encountered him, and the two never had much personal contact. Yet James's liveliness of mind and philosophical inclinations were especially congenial. James was already a renowned and respected figure: after twenty years on the Harvard faculty, he had just published his two-volume *Principles of Psychology*, an influential work that grew out of his research in his psychology laboratory.[143] James was at a turning point of his own, increasingly moving from psychology toward the philosophical analyses that became his major work. And some of the themes of his later writings, especially in his *Pragmatism*,[144] were foreshadowed in his classroom lectures and in the psychology treatise Learned used as a text.

What struck the most responsive chord in Learned was James's distrust of absolutes, his doubts about metaphysics, and his emphasis on the empirical; and that intellectual rapport made Learned Hand an engaged albeit critical reader of James for the rest of his life. The older James's personality was far more shielded from his students than Santayana's was: had Hand known James better, he would have recognized kindred traits of melancholy, anxiety, and self-doubt; but the face James presented in class concealed the darker shadows.

Hand studied psychology under James and later claimed, "All the psychology I ever knew I think I got from that."[145] He vividly remembered having to dissect sheep's and calves' brains. "I'd eaten calves' brains and I think I got just as much from eating them as I did from dissecting them"; nevertheless, "it was interesting." Hand found James "a most stimulating kind of teacher. We felt as though the angels had come and kissed him in his cradle and had poured gifts out to him. He had the strangest, most vagrant imagination you could think of; he would go into all kinds of things that were new and enlightening." At first, "I despised him a little because he wasn't given to absolute rigorous deduction which was what I was looking for." But at least "he didn't go in for metaphysics"; and James's lack of "absolute rigorous deduction" itself taught Hand an important lesson—that there were no logically unchallengeable truths to be found, that imaginative, hardheaded, often agonizing questioning was all there would be. James's *Principles of Psychology* "was a negative kind of book; he very readily disposed of any such thing as the soul as an entity." But there could be virtue in destroying unsustainable beliefs, and Learned accepted the skepticism proudly.

In his classes, James occasionally tried to emphasize as his "main thesis" "the parallelism in the mental and the nervous life." References to this "parallelism" occasionally surfaced in Hand's later writings, but he conceded that the students "didn't really get very far in that" under James. "But, after all, we got James. And James [was] a living angel. He was descended from whatever powers there are that make this planet a decent place." Hand summarized his debt to James by describing him as representing the epitome of "hard thinking"; and Hand would invoke no labels more frequently than James's later distinction between the "tough-minded" and the "tender-minded."[146]

Josiah Royce was thirteen years younger than James and had been brought to Harvard by him; he had, however, committed himself to philosophy several years before James did. Hand recalled him warmly for his human traits: Royce was "a noble kind of creature. [You] loved him because he had such a pure heart." His appearance was memorable: he had "a tousled red curly head" and "a pudgy face which looked as if, if you stuck your finger into it, it would be like putty"; "he looked a little like those things you see on Greek vases, or, I tell you, he looked a little like fifteenth-century Italian commedia dell'arte."

But Hand viewed Royce's ideas with some reserve. Royce was a system builder, and more rigorously analytical than James, yet his conclusions were often vague and metaphysical—"I think they called it subjective idealism," Hand accurately recalled.[147] Hand realized that James and Royce represented contrasting approaches. Where James put his faith in human experience and observation, Royce was committed to the dialectic method. Where James reinforced Hand's doubting nature, Royce pursued an analytical route toward stabilizing universalities. Where James moved toward pragmatism, Royce became the foremost exponent of a post-Kantian idealism. Where James's pragmatism tended to reinforce questioning, Royce searched for the absolute and encouraged loyal devotion to the ideal of community.

For Learned, these contrasting positions mirrored elements of his own mind. Royce's commitment to reason was more congenial than James's imperfect analytical rigor; yet the products of Royce's thinking were often ethereal concepts cast in absolute terms, as uncongenial to the doubting student as, in later years, to the mature judge. Royce's striving to bring intellectual order out of observed chaos appealed to Learned's yearning for a solid replacement for his lost religious faith; yet James's relativism was more attuned to Learned's growing conviction that only by self-delusion, only because of fear of confronting the unanswerable, could one perceive a purposive order in the chaotic universe. Royce's appeals to loyalty, character, and community struck a responsive chord, though Learned could not accept Royce's cosmology; while James's approach was more palatable to Hand, Royce's emphasis on idealism, social duties, and community did not fall on entirely fallow ground.*

Frank W. Taussig,[148] of the economics department (the field was called "political economy" at the time), taught a stimulating introductory course that prompted Learned to take several more economics courses. The great attraction of Taussig's economics courses lay far more in the teacher than in the subject matter: Learned thought Taussig "a highly interesting creature, oh very!" and "really a great teacher."

Taussig's approach in his economic-theory classes was becoming outdated by the 1890s. He used John Stuart Mill's *Principles of Political Economy* as his textbook—"antiquated very largely," Hand would recall. Yet the teacher and the book assured "a grand discipline for a young

---

* Hand's philosophy for most of his life was far closer to James's than Royce's, especially in its skepticism and suspicion of absolutes. Yet Royce's call for "invincible loyalty to a constructive social ideal," in an article published in 1908, fell on receptive ears among Hand's acquaintances, especially Herbert Croly (whose writings Hand enthusiastically embraced and publicized), and informed the resultant Progressive campaign in the years before World War I. (See Arthur Schlesinger, Jr.'s, introduction to the John Harvard Library edition of Herbert Croly, *The Promise of American Life* [Cambridge: Harvard University Press, 1965].)

fellow, discipline in analysis. [It] really was cerebral chest weights."
Hand's appreciation was especially strong because Taussig, unlike his
other college teachers, had gone to the Harvard Law School and used
its Socratic method in his teaching: "You didn't tell the student what
you believed. You wormed it out of him by cross-questions. You asked
him what he thought about things and then showed him how little he
had thought. [It] was rather formidable for the student, but it was
awfully good for him." As with the philosophers, it was above all
Taussig's disciplined spirit of inquiry that attracted Hand.* And Taussig
may have had added appeal because he was also an outsider at Harvard,
being from St. Louis, the son of a Jewish immigrant. He was considered
a "rude [and] uncultivated fellow," and was not accepted by the inner
social circle of the Harvard faculty. As Hand would vividly remember,
"Taussig lived under the shadow of Shady Hill, and it was some shadow,
because this gross St. Louis Jew who talked economics was not regarded
benignly from above by Shady Hill."[149]

By contrast, Charles Eliot Norton, who also had a significant effect
on Learned, occupied one of the loftiest positions in Harvard society.
Learned took a fine-arts class with Norton in his junior year—Art 4,
"Roman and Medieval Art," with an emphasis on the "Development
of Gothic Architecture."[150] Learned, typically, was attracted by the
reputation of the teacher. Norton was already legendary as Harvard's
"principal means of inculcating in our 'young barbarians at play' an
urbane and civilized point of view."[151] His warnings about the degrading
impacts of mass opinion, and his references to the wide circle of famous
people he had known, from Emerson and Longfellow in New England
to Ruskin and Carlyle in England, attracted some of his pupils;[152] but
an equally strong reason for his "huge course, given in a large classroom,
was that he had a reputation for being an easy grader. Students would
appear while attendance was taken and then vanish via the fire escape."
But not Learned: "I didn't know the score," he recalled; "[I] sat up in
front, eagerly and raptly drinking in every word and getting culture."
Hand, who for decades delighted in mimicking Norton, gathered from
his lectures "the general impression [of] great mournfulness and de-
jection that the American people were so benighted and so unliterary
and so unaesthetical and anything you like"; Norton "seemed to sigh

---

* Hand's affection for Taussig contrasted sharply with his contempt for the sociologist Edward
Cummings. Cummings's course on "the social and economic condition of workingmen" was
hardly antiquated; indeed, the subject was becoming of vital interest to Hand. Yet Cummings's
impact was negligible: he seemed to Hand a "softy," giving a "very poor" course "full of the
vaguest kind of uplift. . . . There was really no severe thinking or attempt at severe thinking.
You just went on" (Family Interview II, 43).

a great deal, as though he spoke from a deep burden of resignation and discouragement [about] the task before him."[153]

Norton provided a welcome awakening to art, but ultimately his influence on Learned Hand was negative: he instilled an awe of rigid artistic criteria that became a barrier to Hand's enjoyment of art for decades, and his lectures reinforced the young man's sense that he lacked polish. As Hand later recalled:

> There wasn't a bigger gosling that ever sat under Charles Eliot Norton, and I owe him an enormous amount. After all, I didn't know anything. The arts in Albany, well, they didn't exist. It wouldn't have been so if my father had lived, but the Learneds didn't [care]—they largely were readers. . . . And the rest of us were just untamed barbarians. . . . So I owe whatever I have had of my interest in the arts to [Norton].[154]

Yet for years Norton's "purist" standards intimidated Learned, and alienated him from art: just before his senior year, while on his second trip to Europe, Learned told Gus that he was not quite trained enough to enjoy all "the wonderful artistic things," which "you might get if you were good enough."[155] It took many more visits to Europe before Hand felt free to respond to art more emotionally and intuitively.

Hand's long acquaintance with the connoisseur Bernard Berenson later helped to free him from the rigid constraints of Norton's standards. "[Y]ou give one the right to trust to his untutored feelings," he wrote to Berenson in 1949. The more spontaneous response to art for which Hand credited him was "a boon":

> When I came to Harvard College almost sixty years ago, there never entered a greener fledgling, with a pathetic pathological suggestibility, which incidentally he was never to shake off. Those Puritans ruthlessly seized hold of my flaccid self, and, chiefly through C. E. Norton, made me think that the enjoyment of art was possible only by a discipline which made a Yogi seem like a voluptuary. 'Art' was something to approach with awe and humility; it must never be a mere spontaneous outgoing. [I] suppose it came from the confusing of Art with Morals, for Norton, as you know, took his inspiration from Ruskin.
>
> Well, B.B., the damage they did me has never been undone and can't be; I shall never break the evil domination of connoisseurship; but you have at least shown me that beyond the bars of my mor-

alistic cell is a land of sunshine and spontaneous joy—'life enrichment' as you like to call it—which, if the repressions of my
background have prevented me from sharing, has at least in passing
moments been mine own. Thanks for it.[156]

What Learned absorbed from Norton with the least damage was the
teacher's critical stance toward American civilization and public affairs:
although his outlook was never so gloomy as Norton's, Hand, too,
would in later years voice concern about the capacity of civilized standards to survive mass democracy.

DURING HIS LAST YEAR IN COLLEGE, Learned Hand ago-
nized over his choice of a career. This decision was the most difficult
he had ever faced: he had come to Harvard imbued with the family's
expectation that he would become a lawyer; yet now philosophy had
become his great love. At Christmas 1892, when he returned home
for the holidays, he had just completed his second course with Royce,
he was absorbed in his senior-year studies with Santayana, and the
memory of his full year under James was still vivid. Increasingly, he
perceived his "bent toward philosophy" and thought about graduate
study in that field. His mother, he knew, would not be happy with
this, and the family's surviving lawyer-spokesmen, his uncles Richard
Hand and Clifford Hand, would surely try to dissuade him. Yet he
mustered the courage to raise the issue with them.

Richard Hand's response was predictably cool. A few days later,
Richard introduced Learned to a judge of the highest state court, who
asked the young man whether he planned to study law. Before Learned
could answer, Richard interjected that at Learned's age (he was a few
weeks short of his twenty-first birthday) "one thought that philosophy
was more attractive." Richard's tenor was a mixture of amusement,
condescension, and concern, and his attitude, Learned confessed, "took
the feet from under some of my ideas for the minute."[157]

Yet Learned pressed on. As soon as he returned to his room in
Hastings Hall, he wrote a twelve-page letter to Richard to review his
arguments.[158] He tried to calm his uncle's concern by assuring him that
he had not yet reached a firm decision, though he made the case for
philosophy and summoned the strength to insist that he might yet go
in that direction. "When the thoughts of possibly following another
profession than the almost hereditary one of the law came into my
mind," he had "dreaded broaching" the possibility, and he did not want

his uncles to think that his doubts about becoming a lawyer were intended to denigrate the profession, but he felt a special congruence between his own personal traits and the philosopher's life:

> The men of action, those who take genuine hold of things and carry them through, are undoubtedly indispensable and more important than the others, but the others have great uses and those uses are in this country, which is so eminently practical, liable to be forgotten. I think that if I were fitted for [a life of observation], it would be a very important and valuable one for me to devote myself to.

Learned's final paragraph summarized his own ambivalence; yet it contained a rare note of affirmation as well. He had always imagined he would be a lawyer, he wrote, and worried about what he might miss in the "life of action." Yet, he warned, "I have always felt myself to be unfitted for practical affairs; I have no readiness of decision and a general inaptitude for handling a number of details with any skill. [The] life of a man of contemplation and of study does not call for so much decision." But more important was "the natural desire which has grown in me for philosophy and which at times seems strong enough to last. . . ."

Learned admitted that he had begun the study of philosophy "with a view to finding in it a religion and guide of life," and he confessed that "so far I have not succeeded in working out my own salvation." But, he added, even if "salvation proved out of reach," such a result "seems to me worthwhile to attain." He would "often become disgusted" with his musings about philosophy, but the alternative was to "plunge into the world of action and experience and live *unthinkingly* in that." His tentative conclusion: "[Philosophy] seems in a measure to suit my temperament, to be attractive to my mind, to offer me the hope of some sense with regard to my position in the universe and my fate in it, and to be a worthy occupation at this practical time and [in this practical] country. . . ."

For young Learned, this unprecedented insistence on independence and autonomy could not obscure his continuing insecurities. He was strong enough to resist recurrent family pressures in the ensuing weeks, but he lacked the confidence to make a firm decision. He was clear about his inclination, but not about his talents, and to do graduate work, he felt, required a shoring up from one of Harvard's "masters."

There was indeed encouragement from Frank Taussig. In response to a paper the young man submitted on rent and interest, Hand later recalled, Taussig "called me and offered me a place as a Fellow." He added: "I think if I had stayed on I could have been taken on as an economist, and maybe it would have been better if I had."[159] But much as Learned admired Taussig, further work in economics did not attract him.

For the unconfident student, pursuit of philosophy required reinforcement from one of the great men in that department. Santayana was too young; James was not one of Learned's teachers in his senior year. That left only Royce, and Learned accordingly turned to him: "I talked to Royce about it and he was very friendly and said, 'Well, if you want to go on, you have to go to Germany, and spend a year there.' But he didn't show any enthusiasm. I don't think I had impressed him that I was any good, beyond the fact that, like so many others, I had got A's."[160]

"But he didn't show any enthusiasm"—this was a blow Learned's shaky ego could not withstand. His doubts about his talents for philosophy were fatally reinforced. If his teachers had encouraged him, "I'm quite sure I'd have taught philosophy," he later recalled, "but I didn't inspire anyone."[161] Almost lethargically, he gave up his dream and glided into law school. In the end, it was his "weakness," his "great and almost, as it seems, unconquerable nervousness and lack of confidence," that moved him toward law as if by default.[162]

When he reflected on his choice decades later, Hand claimed he felt a deficiency in the very subject of philosophy: "[T]he feeling came to me that [philosophy] was rather like shoveling smoke anyway. . . . It was a sort of wilderness of words, and I felt the unreality of it enough so that I decided that that was not my field." He acknowledged, too, that he abandoned philosophy "particularly as I had obviously not impressed anybody that I was good at it."[163] But this evaluation smacks of rationalization. He took the path of least resistance:

> You see, the family had all been lawyers. . . . And there it was. Law has always been a kind of slop box for boys who don't know what else they want to do anyway. It's decent and it may lead to something or it may not. So I found myself in the law school. And there were a lot of men I knew who had gone in for the same reason—they didn't know what else to do.[164]

In 1893, Learned thought that he had turned his back forever on the searching intellectual quests he had admired in the great philosophers. He did not yet know that he would overcome and transcend the distinction between the lawyer's life of "action" and the philosopher's life of "contemplation."

RESIGNED AND PESSIMISTIC, Hand "drifted" into Harvard Law School in the fall of 1893.[165] He assumed it would offer little intellectual stimulation and expected that he would spend the long class hours as a bored, passive recorder of black-letter rules of law. In fact, the law school years proved to be Learned's happiest ones yet. His social and intellectual self-esteem strengthened; while he continued to doubt that he was cut out to be a practical, decisive "man of action," those qualms could be shelved temporarily amid a new circle of warm friends and admirable teachers.

In the 1890s, texts and lectures still predominated in most law schools; instruction was much as it had been when his grandfather Augustus had laboriously filled his notebooks at Litchfield. But Harvard Law School no longer operated that way. In the 1870s, President Eliot had brought a bookish, nearsighted, reclusive New York lawyer named Christopher Columbus Langdell to the deanship to shake up the lethargic faculty. By the time Learned entered, Langdell's revolution had triumphed, and the law school's golden age was under way. The atmosphere was vibrant and triumphant, full of confidence that Langdell's method was the unchallengeable wave of the future.

Austin Hall, the Harvard Law School's sole building in 1893, seemed warm and welcoming. The ten-year-old Romanesque building of dark red stone, designed by Henry Hobson Richardson, was the most elegant Harvard structure of its day, with its triple arches over stately front steps and redbrick interiors offset by dark wood paneling. But what went on in Austin Hall's classrooms was at first bewildering, even off-putting, to Learned and most of his classmates. The most distinctive ingredient of Langdell's new approach was the case method of instruction. Most of the readings were volumes of selected court rulings. In their purest form, these enormous casebooks contained no explanatory materials, no historical or theoretical background at all. Instead, the students were expected to deduce the organizing principles from the morass of decisions.[166] President Eliot himself had once been a scientist, and he was attracted by Langdell's view that "law is a science": students and teachers were to examine the results of the cases, with little regard for the judges' reasons, much as a botanist would scrutinize plants in order to classify them.[167] Learned thought it all "rather a silly way" to proceed. He remembered, for example, "reading a fifteenth-century [case] on property. I hadn't any idea what the words meant. You read it over and over and over, until sort of by osmosis, it would come in."[168] Yet he was too disciplined a student to be paralyzed by the chaos: he worked hard, he mastered the materials, and he soon found rewards in the law school's new approach.

In college, Learned had found that social isolation awaited a student perceived as a "grind." But his fear that this might occur at law school did not materialize. Law school was more meritocratic; one's reputation as an intellectual was not a hindrance to social acceptance and could indeed help. Learned discovered that he could take pride in his grades and yet develop a larger circle of friends than he had at college. And, by notable contrast, the warmest social circles grew informally. The two top extracurricular organizations were the Pow-Wow Club and the *Harvard Law Review*, but their social and intellectual aspects were not sharply divided, and members of the Pow-Wow and the *Review* found outlets in each for gregarious as well as academic inclinations.

The Pow-Wow was the oldest and most prominent of a number of clubs in which students might practice appellate arguments by arguing moot court cases before upperclassmen. The invitation to join it was a source of special satisfaction to Learned, as was becoming an editor of the *Harvard Law Review* in 1894. The *Review*, founded in 1887, was a young institution, but already launched on a trailblazing route. Law reviews are unique academic institutions: only in law are the major professional journals student-run, with contributions from novices as well as established figures. Even in 1894, academic promise was an important basis for selecting students for the *Review*; Learned was one of only three invited to join the *Review* in the spring of 1894, before the first examinations. The April 1894 issue was the first to list his name—as "Billings L. Hand"—among the fifteen editors.[169] Learned's selection was a tribute to the intellectual reputation he already carried: from the first, fellow students identified him as part of "the heavy artillery of our class."[170]

Election to the Pow-Wow and to the *Law Review* were significant achievements: Learned was on the inside at last. Yet he never became very active in the Pow-Wow, and he resigned from the *Review* later in 1894, after working on only four issues. His social needs, he came to feel, were met outside these formal structures, and his intellectual energies could be directed to better purposes. He resigned from the *Review*, he said later, because "I thought it took too much time away" and "I didn't think I got anything out of it." He decided that he was at the school "to get a legal education, not to edit or write parts of a magazine, a law magazine." (Reminiscing sixty years later, he remarked, "Think of saying that now! That's worse than heresy; it's blasphemy!'")[171]

When Learned received his first-year grades, the "heavy artillery" evaluations proved justified. Under Harvard's grading system, then as now, a grade of 75 was an A; 80 and over constituted a high A (a grade not so rare in those days). Learned's average at the end of his first year was an 83; and though his grades fell slightly in his final two years, he graduated with an 80 average, placing him sixth in his class.[172] This was clearly gratifying (though when he was in his seventies, he told a Harvard faculty member that his standing did not "make flattering reading"[173]); at the same time he gained far greater social acceptance. "I got to know people more. [I] began to see some girls [while] in the law school. . . . I was asked out some. It wasn't as severe a grind; but you were kept pretty busy." He shaved off the dark Vandyke beard and trim mustache he had grown at college. He began attending Boston Symphony concerts, and found that music "meant a great deal" to him.[174]

During his first year in law school, Learned continued to live in the Hastings Hall quarters he had shared with Fred Townsend, even though Fred had decided to delay entry into law school by a year. But Learned came to spend more and more time with the students who lived in a boardinghouse at 52 Brattle Street, where Santayana had once lived. Most of them were seniors, in Gus's class, and two acquaintances from Learned's college class were also there, Charles Lowell Barlow from New York and Robert Pendleton Bowler from Maine.[175] When the seniors moved out in 1894, Learned hastened to take over one of the vacancies. Townsend soon joined the group, as did a proper Bostonian, Harold J. Coolidge.

Barlow, Bowler, Townsend, Coolidge, and Hand became close friends during their two years at 52 Brattle. They were all Harvard graduates; they all loved good talk; they all had broad intellectual interests. And though they were excellent students, they dared to deviate from the developing norm that "the best men" should be on the *Review*, having either resigned from it after a brief period or not participated at all; they took law seriously, but they liked informal discussions. This intellectually lively group realized that there were other dimensions to life than legal studies, and they regaled one another with philosophical and literary banter, and with bawdy tales. Other classmates soon joined the circle, including a debonair, lively New Yorker, Gordon Knox Bell. Bell, a favorite at Santayana's get-togethers, at last afforded Learned a friendship with a reasonable facsimile of a "swell."

Learned's resignation from his editorship on the *Review* soon after he moved to 52 Brattle was in part an act of conformity to the pattern of his circle of friends. He had never been part of such a circle before (and its members stayed in touch for many years after graduation, visiting one another's homes and taking vacations together). At last, Hand had found the rewards of acceptance and friendship.

EARLY ON, Learned perceived that the Langdellian case method had immense value even if one rejected its originator's conviction that students learned best when plunged into the raw materials of cases without further help. The pure model of that system, Learned realized, left a good deal to be desired. And the obsession with organizing the results into overarching systems was a flaw of Langdell's excessive belief that law was analogous to the physical sciences; his search for "underlying syntheses" gave his enterprise an unrealistic, "esoteric flavor."[176] As Hand would frequently say, the Langdellian purist viewed the judge "like Balaam's Ass"——only the results counted, without presupposing any "conscious intelligence in the being from whom they proceeded": "[Langdell] paid no attention to [the judges'] reasons, but only to the results. He would take the facts and then use them as if [this] had been an experiment, and by induction he would attempt to learn what the underlying rule must have been, regardless of what rule the utterers said they were following." Langdell's neat, logical structures lacked adequate reality; although Langdell in one sense was "a great scholar," Hand admitted, his learning was limited and ultimately "nothing but chopped straw."[177]

Preoccupation with logic-chopping classifications and distinctions was never enough to satisfy Learned Hand. But he saw that Langdell "builded better than he knew."[178] During his brief association with the *Law Review*, in a book note signed "B.L.H.," Hand identified the strongest element of the case system: it was "a method which offers to the student a chance to do his own thinking, in preference to [teachers] working out his own conclusions for him,"[179] and he was immensely attracted by the intellectual engagement it could produce. What was going on in Austin Hall, he discovered, was remarkably similar to the stimulating spirit of inquiry he had absorbed from his masters in college. And Learned relished this experience. As he put it later, the driving insight that underlay the case method was "that one cannot teach law [by] merely lecturing to one's pupils; they must dig out the truth for themselves."[180] At its best, Langdell's method converted students from passive listeners to active participants in their own education.

Langdell's innovations were widely criticized at the time—for emphasizing theory over practice, for building a faculty of full-time scholars rather than part-time practitioners, for making legal education too inaccessible (by moving toward making a bachelor's degree a prerequisite for law school, and requiring a three-year residency). The Langdellians responded that their approach was practical, that it trained students "how to think like lawyers" rather than merely drilling rote legal rules into them.[181] Ultimately, Harvard's success was assured, for society was at the same time—with increased industrialization, urbanization, and commercial complexity—demanding well-trained professionals, and Harvard's elitist professional training satisfied the striving for self-esteem and social visibility of many offspring of America's middle class.

HAND ONCE CONFESSED that "maybe I have stayed more adolescent than most" in his responses to the men who taught him at law school,[182] and it is true that his portraits of the Harvard law faculty often feature idealized supermen. But in fact, Hand was quite discriminating: he perceived the weaknesses and limitations as well as the strengths of his teachers, yet drew inspiration from the strongest qualities of each. By Learned's student days, the faculty had grown to eight men; Learned studied under seven of them.[183] When he evaluated them individually rather than as segments of a whole, he made it clear that he was least attracted to the dogmatic logicians and to those who merely focused on the practical, and that his greatest admiration went to those who tempered theory with wisdom, judgment, and warm human qualities.

Fortunately for the students, the teachers Langdell recruited did not rigidly adhere to his purist notions of case study. Instead, the best were more at ease with inconsistencies and conflicts than the dean could be, and they were flexible enough to leave room for practicalities and common sense. Learned relished their theoretical speculations, and their good sense combined with his own reflectiveness to protect him against the rigid neatness of the pure Langdellians' logic.

Langdell himself and his most recent recruits, Samuel Williston and Joseph Beale, were at the most logic-obsessed end of the spectrum; Jeremiah Smith was at the most practical end. But Hand's favorites were those in the middle—James Barr Ames, John Chipman Gray, and, above all, James Bradley Thayer, the most unassuming of all. Yet even the flawed ones among the "greats" had value to give:[184] the theoretical would remind Hand of the ideal; the practical would provide needed ties to reality.

Dean Langdell, the leader of Harvard's "crusaders and pioneers" and by Learned's day near the end of his career, left the least inspiring impression of all. "He was like a little mole, running in and out," Hand later recalled. "He was a strange, half-blind creature, with a big long beard and green goggles." Oddly enough, Langdell was the only one who did not teach via the case method by then: his eyes were too weak to read and discuss with his students "in the Socratic way," and he lectured instead. He was best when he engaged in "eviscerating the decisions" and sought to "disembowel a case";[185] but these were cold and confining, albeit essential, skills, lacking the breadth and the contact with reality necessary for greatness.

Jeremiah Smith, who had joined the faculty just a few years before Learned started law school, was already over fifty after a long career at the bar and on the New Hampshire Supreme Court. He was not "much given to speculation";[186] instead, he tried to convey "the sense of what it really was all about."[187] But his matter-of-fact realities, Learned realized, were as limited as Langdell's excessive theorizing.

Young Joseph Beale, just past thirty, looked timid, but the "little fellow" with the "pop eyes" was a terror in class.[188] Learned had some admiration for this "brilliant dialectical fencer," as one writer put it,[189] but the foil and saber left needless scars: Beale's impetuousness and "the inexorability of his dialectic" could "take your hide off"; though he could be a "dear fellow, lovely fellow" in private, Learned did not take to his cast of mind.[190] In his passion for system building, Beale was a caricature of a pure Langdellian. "I have always thought of him as a kind of spiritual descendant of St. Thomas Aquinas," Hand once wrote.[191] The deeply religious Beale believed that "were we only true to ourselves, law would emerge as the will of God." Adequate diligence, he insisted, would reveal eternal "principles of justice" from which specific rules could be readily deduced.[192]

Samuel Williston was also very young, a recent addition to the law faculty. He, too, was extraordinarily skillful in the classroom. His field, like Langdell's, was contract law, and in the 1890s he claimed to be breaking away from the Langdellian mold but was not yet overpoweringly confident; he still engaged with his students in the search for understanding. Williston (who would outlive Hand) had many dealings with his onetime student in later years, and Hand had repeated occasion to write public assessments of his former teacher (including the foreword to Williston's autobiography), in which he portrayed Williston as an example of his own preferred model of tempering the search for logical constructs with breadth, sensitivity to reality, and humanity.[193] Yet Hand's more intimate reflections suggest that Williston's cast of mind was also too Langdellian, too rigid and theoretical, to be wholly palatable: "[He] was so secure in his thinking, so prepared to encounter dissidence and gently dispose of it, that one wondered what was the perfect mechanism that his skull enclosed. He seemed to be indifferent as to the effect of law, measured in human values, so long as it was consistent and clear."[194] And he added: "[H]is serene intelligence [was] unshaken by dissent. In [the] classroom it were best not to cross swords with him, unless you were a master yourself, which no one was in my time."[195]

With James Barr Ames, who succeeded Langdell as dean while Learned was a student, virtues clearly outweighed flaws. The classroom skill and personal grace of this slight, unprepossessing, soft-spoken man elicited special affection from Learned. Like Langdell, Ames emphasized theory rather than the articulated reasons of judges, but he did not pursue symmetry for its own sake, and he was ready to infuse notions of fairness and justice into the fabric of the law. Above all, Hand would remember Ames as a superb teacher. He was near fifty, at the peak of his powers after more than two decades on the faculty. Learned found him "so charming and so alluring that to sit under him was to love him."[196] And Ames's commitment to teaching carried beyond the classroom: "No one felt more than he the sacredness of his calling; no one was more available to all who chose to seek his counsel or his advice"; he was, all in all, "a delightful, charming creature."[197] Yet, as Hand once put it, "I always felt peeping out from under his professorial robe the face of some herald of good tidings"; he was "at heart a reformer." The students got little appreciation of what the law of trusts or of partnerships was really like; "but one did get a deep conviction of what they ought to be, and what we should try to make them."[198]

John Chipman Gray, Hand remembered, was "a great gentleman, lettered, urbane, charming, witty, affable, though never familiar, without condescension and always open to approach." Though his poise made for distance from his less secure students,[199] he seemed the "best of them all" precisely for combining social ease with legal talent: "He was a great master [in the law]. He was a very fine gentleman. He was a swell in the sense that none of the others [on the Harvard faculty] were swells. He lived on Beacon Street. He was one of the leaders of the Boston bar."[200] Happily, consistency and logical neatness were not the highest virtues for the robust, tall, and imposing Gray, as they were for Langdell and Beale: Gray recognized that generalities were often inadequate; as Hand once put it, he was "content to accept the variants with the theorem."[201] And, deviating from Langdell's ideal of full-time teacher-scholars, Gray managed to conduct a major law practice in Boston throughout his forty years on Harvard's faculty. His special field was real property—legal rights in land—although he had once taught constitutional law (which he abandoned because he was convinced that "there was no such thing," that constitutional law was merely politics). Hand could never quite understand how Gray could have chosen "so jejune a subject" as real property, for Gray "had wide horizons, and a most genial and capacious overview of the law as a whole."[202] As the years passed, Gray seemed ever more enviable, and Hand wished he could be like him. To a remarkable degree he was, but he could never quite believe it.

James Bradley Thayer was the one teacher Hand admired in every respect: "on the whole the best of the lot," "the most original of them all," and without doubt "the teacher who counted most with me."[203] In many ways Thayer was also the most unconventional of the lot: he had joined the Harvard faculty twenty years earlier, after two decades in law practice[204] in which he had never been wholly absorbed; unlike most of his colleagues, he was a person of very broad interests, like Learned Hand's own father. He was truly engaged in the humanities: he had written literary criticism and had composed translations of the classics.[205]

Moreover, Thayer long resisted the Langdellian crusade for casebooks and Socratic teaching. Not until Learned's student days did Thayer publish casebooks; and Thayer's, unlike Langdell's, were far more than collections of raw material. For example, in his 2,500 pages on constitutional law published in 1895, he interspersed highly readable excerpts from political histories and elegant comments of his own among the decisions. Nor was Thayer a natural teacher. He lacked a talent for fluent extemporaneous commentary, and he was not given to pyrotechnical displays of Socratic techniques. Yet Learned, like many of the best students of his day, looked back to Thayer's courses as "the fitting crown of the whole three years" of law school. The modesty and thoughtfulness of this droopy-eyed, gray-bearded man in his sixties captivated his admirers. Thayer was undogmatic and refused to pursue logically airtight unifying systems. Not mental gymnastics but more sustaining qualities of mind and character were his strengths. As Hand recalled, "[O]ne did not get—or at least I did not—many working propositions out of [Thayer's courses]. . . . [H]e was always tentative and moderate, as though dealing in an unpredictable medium on which no one could count."[206] This "tentative and moderate" approach—this rejection of extremes and unwillingness to advance confident conclusions—was marvelously encouraging to the tentative and moderate young student from Albany.[207]

Learned first encountered Thayer in a second-year course on evidence, a subject that can be dry and confusing. But Thayer's path through the tangle was the un-Langdellian one of eschewing the search for orderly systems and emphasizing instead the historical and human dimensions too often ignored by his colleagues. He defended the rules that excluded certain kinds of evidence from trials for practical, historical, and policy reasons. Thayer's sensitivity to human fallibility and to history stirred Hand's interest in the field. (One of Hand's earliest scholarly publications, about evidence, was written with Thayer's active encouragement.)[208]

But Thayer's greatest impact on Learned came in a third-year course in constitutional law. An article Thayer had published in the *Harvard Law Review* during Learned's first year at law school—Felix Frankfurter called it the most important article on constitutional law ever published[209]—conveyed his views, but his message was more subtly reiterated in his casebook and in his course. The result of Thayer's approach to constitutional law, as Hand once put it, "was to imbue us with a scepticism about the wisdom of setting up courts as the final arbiters of social conflicts, [a skepticism] which many of [us] always retained." What the students learned "step by step," Hand remembered, was "that most of constitutional law had been constructed out of circular propositions, which justified the predetermined attitudes of the judges."[210] And what he found "most original" was that Thayer saw "pretty plainly what would result if the courts [made] themselves into what is really a legislative body with a veto. He foresaw that and said that the only way for them to behave was to hold back and have a certain moderation."[211]

Thayer's position on judicial review proved to be extraordinarily prescient: he had put his finger on what would become a pervasive, divisive problem in the twentieth century, and one of central concern to Hand throughout his career. This most influential advocacy of judicial restraint was fashioned by Thayer and absorbed by Hand several years *before* the Supreme Court began to strike down a wide range of laws as unduly interfering with "liberty" and "property" under the due-process clauses of the Constitution; "activist" federal judges were not even on the horizon. Within a decade, however, federal courts did begin to intervene in legislative compromises, initially on behalf of economic rights, later on behalf of personal liberties. And Thayer's advocacy of restraint proved, as Hand once put it, to be "an even more 'subversive' influence" than Langdell's: it came "to be feared and deeply deprecated by those who set their hopes [upon] that repository of eternal principles: a judicature, invulnerable to popular assaults."[212]

Over the years, Hand frequently viewed himself as articulating variations on Thayer's theme. In 1958, three years before he died, Hand's Holmes Lectures at Harvard were his most extreme restatement; when he sent a copy of these lectures to his friend Bernard Berenson, he described them as "an old grievance I have nurtured for over sixty years, derived from one of the great masters I had the good luck to be under at the Law School."[213] Hand often wondered whether he had carried Thayer's teachings too far; and it is true that he sometimes converted "skepticism about the wisdom of setting up courts as the arbiters of social conflicts," a central Thayerian belief, into open hostility. In 1959, he wrote to an acquaintance: "I have often asked myself how far [Thayer] would recognize as legitimate descendants my own views about constitutional law; [but] there is no doubt that—bastards or not—they are his get."[214]

In 1902, when Thayer died, Learned was "really much grieved." It was "quite clear," he wrote a Boston friend, that "no one of the rest of the Law School was quite such a scholar as he": Thayer had "more sympathetically reflected the character of our law" in his specialties than "any of the others did in theirs." He added, "Besides, I had a real personal regard, perhaps almost an affection for him, on account of his character, which it seems to me represented the very best you people in Eastern New England can produce, albeit perhaps a little unworldly for the great mass of mankind."[215]

From his law school experience Hand drew important "legal lessons," guidelines that would serve him well as lawyer and judge: a mix of conservatism and innovativeness, a loyal regard for legal traditions combined with an awareness that the legacy must be used "flexibly," a recognition that the function of judges is confined but not uncreative, and a perception that "orderly change" is essential if civilization is not to perish "either by atrophy, or by convulsion." But Hand's sense of the virtues of the Harvard Law School faculty also provided personal solace and inspiration. As he would describe one consequence of this "experience in a young man's life": "If the example of these men— devoted, without stint and without deviation, to the pursuit of truth— was not a perpetual reminder to him of what life might be, he was past hope. On them he could draw when the world about him seemed sordid and base and meaningless; they made a picture, which, though he could not reproduce it, he could try to copy."[216]

Hand's final, and most memorable, reflection on his law school experience came when he returned to Austin Hall in 1958. In a moving coda to his Holmes Lectures, he tried to sum up what he had found there in the 1890s. He had ascertained, he said, not the various legal rules alone:

> I did get those so far as I was able to absorb them, but I got much more. I carried away the impress of a band of devoted scholars; patient, considerate, courteous and kindly, whom nothing could daunt and nothing could bribe. The memory of those men has been with me ever since. Again and again they have helped me when the labor seemed heavy, the task seemed trivial, and the confusion seemed indecipherable.[217]

The ultimate help came from an attitude, an intellectual stance, that Hand had first perceived in Harvard's great philosophers and had relished in his happiest days in the law school, and that he developed ever after: "From them I learned that it is as craftsmen that we get our satisfactions and our pay. In the universe of truth they lived by the sword; they asked no quarter of absolutes and they gave none."[218] His mentors were fortunate enough to have an unusually perceptive student with the capacity to absorb from each the qualities most valuable in them, and most congenial to him.

IN 1896, Learned Hand, now twenty-four, prepared to enter law practice. Law school had proved far more satisfying than he had anticipated, but his success there, amid a warm circle of friends and under "a band of devoted scholars," had not wholly stilled his doubts about his suitability for lawyers' work. What had been so unexpectedly attractive was that the study of law had been far more broad-gauged than the narrow technical training he had anticipated. But what good would that do in practice? While legal education had been transformed during Langdell's deanship, law practice had remained essentially unchanged. What use would exciting models of probing inquiry be in the day-to-day routine? Would the exhilarating law school experience truly enrich law practice? Or would it merely make the practitioner's life seem dispiritingly drab by contrast?

Early in June, Learned wrote to his cousin Gus to explain why he had decided to return home to Albany. Gus, who had completed law school two years earlier, was already well established as an associate in an excellent New York City firm. Learned told Gus that he felt a "need of justifying myself for selecting a smaller town than you have selected," and he accurately specified the two central reasons that made his choice easy: his lack of self-confidence; and the ever-present expectations of his family. "For myself," Learned wrote, "I am quite sure New York would not do, because I have not the nerve to live in its distraction much less to take an active share in its activity." Gus had "stouter timber" in him, he thought, and could therefore "thrive under what I should wilt beneath." In any event, Learned, as he reminded Gus, had "justification enough" for his decision "in the peculiar construction" of his family—in his role as the sole surviving male who was expected to follow in his father's footsteps.[219]

Learned moved back into his childhood home on State Street, affectionately welcomed by his mother and his aunt Harriet Learned, (Sister Lily had married an Albany doctor, but lived only a few steps away and had not left the family circle.) He was now an adult, yet the adoring but demanding love of the women of his family quickly suffused him. "The chief danger is that I make myself a petty tyrant," as he told Gus. "I get everything so much my own way."[220] He spent many of his early weeks back home responding to his mother's entreaties to prepare typescripts of the writings of and eulogies about his father.

Returning to Albany did at least smooth Learned's first step into law practice. As a classmate reminded him, "[Y]ou come of a well-known legal family";[221] and family contacts got him his first job. He was hired by his uncle Matthew Hale, once a law partner of Samuel Hand and long a leader at the bar. Hale's background was in Elizabethtown, and his late first wife was one of Samuel's sisters. The heavyset, muttonchopped, bald, genial Hale looked benignly on the prospect of training young Learned toward partnership, especially since his own sons were still years away from law school. But only a few months later, in March 1897, Hale died; and without the family tie, there was no permanent place for Learned in Hale's firm.

During the few months with Hale, Learned's anxieties about succeeding in law practice subsided. At law school, his classmates had come to know of Learned's contempt for those who went into law simply for its material rewards: that objective, according to Learned, branded an aspiring lawyer as "wholly lost" to the proper pursuit of a profession already too filled with a "sordid wealth-loving, money-seeking spirit." He would "point [his] finger of scorn" at those who went into practice because they "wanted to make money."[222]

In Hale's firm, Learned sensed some prospect that he might not have to make the choice between the practical and the reflective life after all. Hale had a high-quality appellate practice, much like Samuel Hand's, and Learned even found time to write his first scholarly article. (This appeared in the *Harvard Law Review* in the spring of 1897. It dealt with a legalistic debate about "unjust enrichment," a debate then raging in the pages of the *Review*. Hand's contribution was the earnest commentary of a good recent graduate.)[223] But Hale's death demanded reabsorption in the search for a job.

Less than three weeks later, Learned was able to report to James Bradley Thayer that he would soon go into the office of "Mr. Marcus T. Hun of reportorial fame" (Hun was the longtime reporter of the decisions of the New York State Court of Appeals, a job once held by Samuel Hand). "I think myself very fortunate in the change now that Mr. Hale is gone," Learned assured Professor Thayer, "because I believe I shall have as good an opportunity as I could have anywhere in the city."[224] This was probably true, though it was not so promising a position as the aborted one in Hale's firm. Hun was a competent, modest lawyer with a decent law practice, but not one of the elite Albany practitioners. Nor was there a great promise of room at the top: Hun himself was only fifty-two, and his one partner only thirty-three.

Hand made moderate progress in his five and a half years with Hun's firm. At the beginning of 1899, after less than two years, he was designated a "partner," and in a letter to his uncle Richard Hand he tried to put this promotion in the best possible light: the partnership meant "a substantial position in the Bar here," he wrote, "and incidentally gives me the satisfactory income of $1,500 a year, as I am not to share in the profits."[225] But this "incidental" feature rankled. To Gus, Learned complained of his "small" financial rewards and his disappointment that the firm's name was not changed to include his. (The firm became "Hun, Johnston & Hand" a year later, in 1900, when Hand began to draw a small, very junior percentage of the partnership income; it never exceeded 15 percent. The firm income being small, his earnings remained meager.)

Learned's association with Hun was rewarding personally, however. Hun was not only a patient tutor in practical know-how; he was also a model of professional integrity and a respected leader in Albany's municipal-reform movement. Moreover, he was a man of great personal warmth, with a near paternal interest in Learned. Their affectionate mutual regard radiates from the many letters between "My dear Learned" and "My dear Mr. Hun." And, perhaps most important to Learned's development, Hun thought highly of his young associate and provided much-needed support for his shaky ego. "I can only say that I have at least one merit," Hun told Hand, the merit "of being able to appreciate an intelligence greater than my own, and in your case, I think I have made no mistake."[226]

But Learned, despite his best efforts, was never satisfied with his professional performance in Hun's firm. Given his idealized image of his father, Learned probably would not have been satisfied even if he had made faster progress; while his uncles sought to calm his doubts about himself, their reassurances were typically interlaced with references to the giant Samuel Hand had been. Clifford Hand would send admonitions to "have the faith in yourself that I have in you," and at the same time reiterate, as if the reminder were needed, "Were my dearly beloved brother your father living, there would today be no limit to his practice"; no one else had attained similar prominence, for reasons "in no small degree personal. Who survived him that could reasonably claim to assume the accession?"[227]

Yet the nature of the law practice Learned handled gave real grounds for dissatisfaction. During his first two years with Hun, Learned devoted himself single-mindedly to succeeding at the bar, abandoning virtually all other interests, including scholarly writing. He found some opportunities to prepare appellate briefs, but almost none to argue appeals; Hun's firm handled few, and Hun argued those himself; Learned was relegated to doing the detailed, often dull research, and to reducing the arguments to writing. Other lawyers at times retained him, for small fees, to write briefs for them. Hun repeatedly urged Learned to concentrate on research and brief writing, the kind of work, as he put it, "for which I think you are best fitted."[228]

Appellate work was indeed the most congenial to Learned, for it did not require a lawyer to make quick decisions on his feet and placed a premium instead on research, reflection, and writing. But he feared becoming merely a back-room, bookish writer of arguments for others, and he was convinced that contacts with clients and trial experience were essential to success at the bar. He briefly thought that his "partnership" in Hun's firm would afford this kind of experience. "My work is to be concerned almost altogether with litigation," he told his uncle Richard, "that being the branch of the law in which I intend to practice in so far as I shall have any opportunity to choose."[229] But this hope proved illusory. Hun continued to handle most of the few courtroom appearances that came the firm's way. Learned spent some of his hours on chores for out-of-town lawyers—collecting debts, filing papers with the state government, keeping an eye on Albany issues in which these lawyers were interested. For this tedious work, Learned, timid about asking for fees when his intellectual resources were untapped, sought and received even less than the very small amounts—two to five dollars a job—that were appropriate. (Gus was among several of Learned's friends who pressed him to ask for some pay: "There is no sense in your bothering to do things [for] nothing. [These chores] are a nuisance and should be charged for at reasonable rates. [I] advise you therefore to make charges for these things in all cases.")[230] Learned found little more stimulation in drafting wills for small estates and contracts for small businesses. Many beginning lawyers have to endure this kind of routine work, but it was still commonplace for Learned after three or four years in practice. Increasingly, he pressed for client contacts and trial practice.

In his dutiful correspondence with his uncles, Learned continued to express doubts about his capacity to do the work he was determined to pursue. As he wrote to his uncle Richard when he still had hopes of engaging mainly in litigation:

> I am of course not by any means thoroughly equipped for my work. [I] find what I understand to be the prevailing weakness of our [family] obtains very strongly with me, a great and almost, as it seems, unconquerable nervousness and lack of confidence whenever I must go into a matter—as a trial—the issue of which depends upon how one can meet and cope with unexpected matters which admit of no preparation. An argument I do not fear, but anything where I must depend upon the moment and upon that alone I find very difficult to meet. As this is no doubt a constitutional failing I must meet it only by much experience and self-control.[231]

The need to be quick-witted and composed in the service of a client clashed with Learned's inclination to be reflective and high-minded. His worst fears were confirmed in one of his earliest opportunities to confront human beings rather than law books. In 1898, a Fitchburg, Massachusetts, lawyer, Charles Ware, enlisted Learned's assistance in representing a woman named Alice Houghton, who claimed that her illegitimate child had been fathered by one Seymour Pierce, a poor, married barber. Pierce and his parents had recently moved to the Albany area. Before their move, the parents had paid Houghton a little money for her medical bills, and Houghton had executed a release. Ware claimed that her release was invalid because she was still a minor, and he asked Learned to track down the Pierces in their new residence and to press Houghton's claim for more money.

Learned, eager for any law-related work, promptly expressed his "hearty sympathy" for Houghton, readily agreed to take on her claim, and assured Ware that he would help "for nothing."[232] But the only results of his good intentions were hours of work, no pay, and considerable embarrassment to boot. He tracked down the Pierces and, on a cold January day, nervously called on them. He encountered not only

Seymour Pierce's mother (who, though "much excited," seemed prepared to think about paying a few more dollars to protect her son) but
also Seymour's angry wife, who told him in no uncertain terms that
"she would not do a thing" and "would not let anyone else do anything
for Alice."[233] Learned, beset with self-condemnation about his poor
performance as well as anxiety about Houghton's fate, promptly sent a
fifty-dollar check of his own to Ware, for her. He was moved to do
so, he told Ware, by "the possibility of the delays resulting in acute
suffering to the woman."[234]

Ware, a more tough-minded practitioner, immediately wrote to Seymour Pierce's parents offering to drop all further claims if they would
pay Houghton $350. The Pierces in turn retained an Albany-area
lawyer, T. A. Griffin, who quickly confronted the already shaky
Learned Hand in a tenor that greatly troubled the young lawyer: Griffin
claimed there was no practical way for Houghton to pursue her paternity
charges in a New York court; what she was really threatening, he
insisted, was the instigation of an adultery prosecution against Seymour
Pierce unless she was paid some money, and this would amount to
blackmail.

Learned thought Griffin's suspicion "most embarrassing" and assured
him that he would have nothing to do with any adultery claim. As it
happened, Ware himself had become leery of the case, and Houghton
now assured him that she did not want to press charges; it was her
parents behind the demand. The case was dropped, but Learned's embarrassment was not yet at an end: Ware returned to him his check,
expressing long-standing doubts that "it was wise" to give it to Houghton,[235] and Learned had to concede that his attempted gift was "unjustified and hysterical upon the facts," reproaching himself for not
behaving with the cool hardheadedness he thought appropriate to a
competent practitioner.[236]

Learned got no greater satisfaction from his rare courtroom appearances. His experience in a suit to collect a debt in a small upstate town
was typical. He knew that his best hope for inner calm lay in thorough
preparation, but he was not ready for the courtroom atmosphere created
by a tired, bad-tempered trial judge. The case was the last one to be
heard for the day, and the judge was "exceedingly impatient" with
Learned's careful presentation of his evidence. Learned quickly became
flustered: "the judge would not let me get my evidence in without
hassling and rushing me," he reported to his uncle Clifford, "so that
I got quite excited."[237] Matters worsened when the testimony ended.
The judge dismissed Learned's claim, which Learned was prepared for:
he pulled from his briefcase a recently decided case (so recent that it

was "not even yet in the advance sheets") to persuade the judge to change his mind. But the judge "glanced at the opinion perhaps half a minute," Learned reported, and adhered to his own ruling. Learned was dejected: as he later told Gus, the judge "gave me rather a short and swift rope [and] beat me at once."[238]

Gus told Learned to stop worrying: from his own greater experience, he assured his cousin, he knew how often careful preparation had no effect on "the idiots who are on the bench."[239] But Learned's anxieties would not be stilled: he told his uncle Clifford that the judge's quick ruling "very possibly" was traceable to "a certain ineptitude of the presentation of it on my own part."[240] Nevertheless, he persisted in seeking trial experience—he volunteered to defend poor criminal defendants, tried to set up an Albany version of a legal-aid society, and undertook charity cases. But these, too, offered few opportunities and fewer satisfactions.

AFTER MORE THAN TWO YEARS of focusing exclusively on law practice, by the beginning of 1900 Learned had very little to show for his efforts. His search for practical experience had yielded embarrassing episodes at worst, trivial cases at best. Increasingly, he was engulfed by gloom. His cases seemed "very dull"; he saw himself as running very hard, yet standing still: "I am really getting to feel that something must be done or all my years will be gone with nothing to show for it."[241] Comforting words from those close to him rang hollow in his ears. Gus argued that Learned was doing well "for a beginner in Albany" and well enough "for the time you have been at it."[242] But Gus's New York City practice was enviable by comparison: he was immersed in major antitrust, international, and constitutional-law issues. As Learned wrote to a law school friend, the "pleasing aphorism [that] 'there is always room at the top,' while morally inspiring, has as yet not appealed to me as of great practical value."[243]

Increasingly, Learned found that Albany struck "a kind of deadness into my soul."[244] He was not yet ready to give up, but he feared that his depression would mount if he persisted in thinking only of professional success. He was "afraid to do anything which would upset Albany's strangely rigid routine," and worried about becoming "a miserable misanthrope,"[245] but he also concluded that he had suppressed his intellectual interests for too long. He knew that reimmersion in books would do little for his career: law firms, he recognized, were "anxious to eschew geniuses in so far as [they] can discover them beforehand."[246] Yet his affinity for ideas burst forth once more, partly to assuage his frustrations, partly because it was irrepressible. Hungrily, he devoured books of history, economics, biography, and philosophy, exploring old areas of interest and reaching out for new ones.

In the spring of 1900, Learned's reabsorption in ideas was enhanced when Gus told him that a number of his young acquaintances—mostly New York City and Boston lawyers—were organizing a discussion group. Gus offered to nominate Learned; by the fall, Learned eagerly accepted, saying, "I mean to go to as many [meetings] as possible." The "no name" club met at monthly dinners to hear and discuss talks prepared by its members; Learned regularly took the train down the Hudson to New York City for the sessions. The topics were usually related to law, but not to the day-to-day concerns of practitioners: discussions ranged from "the Negro question" to "modern reform movements" and "the right to personal liberty."[247] Gus explained that the group was "something like" the law school clubs, "only more serious and not legal except in membership, and not for promiscuous drooling speeches."[248] For Learned, the sessions were oases of stimulation reminiscent of the happy evenings of talk in Cambridge, and they permitted him to get to know some stimulating young lawyers. But inevitably, Learned's eager participation in the "no name" club only reinforced his sense of the intellectual aridity of Albany: Albany had a similar discussion group, the Fortnightly Club, but its sessions were so dull that Learned had no desire to attend regularly. He reengaged in scholarly writing, and that year published an article on the uses and abuses of expert testimony in an obscure medical journal, *Albany Medical Annals*. The piece's reception, for style as well as content, was sufficiently enthusiastic that Learned arranged for two hundred reprints and distributed them to acquaintances. Soon after, he submitted the same essay to the *Harvard Law Review*, which reprinted it in 1901.[249]

The tone of the article, no longer that of a recent graduate, shows the distinctive voice of the mature Hand for the first time. Writing with power, grace, and wit, he intertwined historical, logical, and practical arguments to attack the "absurd" practice under which litigants paraded before a lay jury their hired experts on complex scientific questions. Hand advocated reform, urging that judges and juries be aided in resolving the contending submissions of the parties' expert witnesses by an advisory tribunal of independent, court-appointed experts.

Gus was not impressed by some of Learned's stylistic flourishes. After the Albany publication, Gus took his cousin to task for "utterly uncalled for," "cheap and indefensible" asides on common-law traditions. A reference, for example, to the common law as "the foster mother of absurdities" was the sort of comment that should not be uttered casually, "with a sneer." This "reckless habit" to express *"one's mood,"* Gus insisted, had no place in a formal article.[250] The cousins' exchanges reflected their unusual intimacy: neither could have spoken so candidly to anyone else, yet their disagreements did not damage their relationship. (Learned did take Gus's criticism enough to heart to make one small change in phrasing before the article was republished; but in every other respect he stood his ground.)[251]

In June 1901, Harvard's philosophy department asked its alumni for contributions to fund a new philosophy building. Hand's response was remarkable: he pledged a thousand dollars, and this at a time when he was concerned about his limited income and his usual charitable contributions ran from five to twenty-five dollars. The chairman of the department, stunned by the unanticipated contribution, told Hand that his gift "stands for all times as the *first* official pledge toward our Emerson Hall . . . the first definite promise."[252] Hand's contribution was nearly half the total pledged over the first two years of the fund-raising effort, and he had no regrets: the "project [is] very important to me," he wrote, "and would mean much [to] Harvard and to the whole community which Harvard influences."[253]

Hand's gift to Harvard was a private matter, and could not impair his efforts to cultivate the image of a practical lawyer. But a simultaneous decision, to become a part-time law teacher, risked just that. During the 1901–02 academic year, he taught a course at Albany Law School, and he considered doubling his teaching load for the following year. His lawyer uncles tried to discourage this academic interest, but he needed these intellectual outlets, and his reengagement with ideas served to revive for him the kind of intellectual life he had enjoyed at Harvard.

IN ONE RESPECT, Hand's years in Albany opened new areas of interest. For the first time, he became truly aware of politics.

At Harvard during America's Gilded Age, distant, aloof contempt for politics was the fashionable attitude in Hand's circle. Politicians were a distant world of crude climbers, often of immigrant stock, scrambling for petty spoils; principles seemed remote from party divisions, where the issues apparently did not go much beyond battles between the ins and the outs. Learned was of course aware of a greater engagement in politics in his own family: his grandfather and father had been loyal Democrats; over the years he had heard his uncle Clifford's numerous avowals of loyalty to the Hands' Democratic traditions; and Gus, he knew, unquestioningly followed that path. But party disputes were of no concern to Learned at college and law school.

Hand's alienation from politics began to fade when the Spanish-American War broke out in 1898. In the spring, after the sinking of the battleship *Maine* in Havana Harbor, President William McKinley, a Republican, bowed to the agitation against Spanish "atrocities" in William Randolph Hearst's newspapers, and Congress authorized American intervention. Soon, the Philippines were drawn into the battle, and Commodore George Dewey occupied Manila. Cuba fell quickly, after the storming of San Juan Hill by Teddy Roosevelt and his Rough Riders at the beginning of July. In August, the four-month war ended; in December, the peace treaty ceded the Philippines (also Puerto Rico and Guam) to the United States. Suddenly, America had become a world power. Learned's uncle Clifford and cousin Gus, as Jeffersonian Democrats unceasingly suspicious of national power, despised this new American imperialism as a betrayal of traditional ideals and a threat to traditional morals. Learned could not avoid listening to Clifford's long lectures or reading Gus's long letters. At first, he echoed their antiwar sentiments, enough to evoke from his acquaintances semi-serious charges that he was "unpatriotic." But as Clifford's outbursts grew ever more shrill, Learned was pressed to think more carefully about the family's traditional allegiances, and that process brought greater maturity and autonomy.

Learned's letters to Gus in 1898 were his declaration of awakening political consciousness and independence.[254] To him, Uncle Clifford's defense of Jeffersonian Democratic ideals was attractive only in that it was "clearly defined" and "confidently accepted," in contrast to his own uncertainties. Yet he found it "doctrinaire" and therefore not wholly acceptable. Clifford's arguments against imperialism and colonialism, Hand saw, were extrapolations from a "good Jeffersonian, French Revolution and J.J. Rousseau individualism," but he asked whether the Jeffersonian notions were suitable to the modern age. He confessed that "the amorphous mixture of socialism and laisser faire [*sic*]" reflected in contemporaneous government practices made more sense to him. "[Y]ou and I cannot be quite so naively confident in the policy of letting everyone alone and must sacrifice robustness and lucidity of ideas to what I in the end believe to be a wider scope and a better if a less consistent social philosophy." He argued that a "hands-off" role for government was not "an inevitable principle"; instead, "in a vast multitude of cases the State must and should regulate the conduct of individuals for their own welfare and modify the contractual relations which they assume toward one another." And, he added, "In particular I at least believe that in the matter of regulating the safety and healthfulness of factories and the maximum hours of work for women and children this obtains." Professor Thayer's teachings about the breadth of the state's police power—the state's power to further the health, welfare, and morals of its population—lurked behind these words, but they were also the words of a young man struggling for the first time with those academic ideas in a concrete political setting, and rejecting substantial parts of his political legacy in the process.

Local concerns also prompted Learned's search for his own political voice. The New York gubernatorial election was at hand. Teddy Roosevelt had put aside his cavalry commission to become the Republican candidate against an undistinguished, Tammany-supported Democrat. To traditional Democrats such as Clifford and Gus, the choice was easy: a vote against Roosevelt was essential to repudiate this symbol of America's misguided, immoral foreign policy. But Learned would not yield: despite repeated efforts, his uncle and his cousin could not persuade him to follow their lead; instead, he cast his vote for the Republican Roosevelt. Like the rest of the family, Learned abhorred Roosevelt's "militant imperialism," but in TR's campaign speeches he saw some of the "amorphous mixture of socialism and laissez faire," as he expressed it to Gus, that he himself advocated. Moreover, Roosevelt, a well-born Harvard graduate, was an intellectual who was genuinely engaged in politics, a new breed very different from both the Harvard students he had known and the politicians they held in contempt.

Equally important was Learned's belief that votes on state and local elections should not turn on one's view of national politics. He told Gus that he had reservations about Teddy Roosevelt's style—the " 'big army, big navy, bow-wow' kind"—and added that if this were the true issue of the campaign, he would "of course not vote for him"; but after all, Learned pointed out, Roosevelt was running for a statewide office, not a national one. A "great gain would be made," he insisted, if every voter "could be made to feel that he voted only upon those questions which were within the jurisdiction of the man for whom he voted and if he therefore [had] to make up his mind [as] to what he wanted in casting that particular ballot." For governor, surely the Tammany nonentity did not warrant support: "Certainly if character and [TR's] past record of honesty and integrity are anything, the assurances of his conducting himself admirably are great. Unwise he sometimes is and in bad taste he has been most of the time since he was nominated, but still perfectly independent." By contrast, Tammany Hall's followers "always remain what they are, the refuge and the strength of the criminal and those who are only unconvicted."

Yet this plea for separating state elections from national issues was not Learned's most basic reason for supporting TR. What counted most was that he was unpersuaded by Clifford's and Gus's fears that American colonialism had to be combated at any cost. He refused to believe that American control of the Philippines *"necessarily* implies the destruction of the Republic.*"* He thought that there was clear national power to acquire new territories and that maintaining colonial possessions could be consistent with American traditions. These ideas were heretical enough in a Democratic family, but he was not yet through. He argued that those obsessed with fear of American colonialism would be well advised to pay less attention to overseas developments and more to unsolved problems at home, and he presciently advocated the view that the national government should address domestic problems such as those of the environment and the condition of minorities. He urged attention to "the plight of the poor Indian"; he argued that "when one considers the Negro, I can't see how he can have any very sanguine confidence in the beneficent effect of that glorious American liberty of which we talk so much"; and he insisted that the major risk to democratic government lay not in acquiring overseas territories but in neglecting domestic problems such as making "our cities safe—e.g., from the contamination of their water supply."

Another two years passed before Learned was ready to make public statements of his political independence. In 1900, Governor Roosevelt was the Republicans' vice presidential candidate on the McKinley ticket. Learned had gotten to know TR somewhat since 1898, both in sporadic professional dealings and through occasional social contacts. He liked what he saw in the man; and he found most of the Republican planks, especially the party's commitment to the use of the power of the national government, more palatable than the hands-off attitude of Jeffersonian Democrats. Once again, Uncle Clifford advocated loyalty to Democratic traditions. This time, Learned mustered the courage to tell Clifford that he disagreed, and then went beyond: he registered as a Republican. This was quite a risky step, professionally as well as in terms of family relations. As he wrote Gus: "I am afraid that you will think this is unwise and I am certain that, from a personal point of view, it may well cause damage to me in Albany, where I have perhaps some affiliations with the Democratic Party, which might be useful to me, and none with the Republicans." Yet the Republicans had more often been "on the right side [of] most public questions than the Democrats," and he preferred the Republicans' policies in the coming election.[255]

Registering as a Republican, Learned told Gus, did not seem "in any sense binding upon me in the future";[256] but for now, it was the candid thing to do. Moreover, he now felt strong enough to tell Uncle Clifford that family traditions would not keep him within the Democratic fold. Yet Hand had not embraced a dogmatic ideology of his own. His registration and vote in 1900 were a choice for that election only. In 1904 he voted for the Democratic presidential candidate against Teddy Roosevelt; for the rest of his life, his presidential votes went to Democrats as often as they did to Republicans—and, once, to a third-party candidate.

Other, more continuous involvements in public affairs occurred during Hand's Albany years as outgrowths of his professional work. The most demanding was a by-product of his work for Marcus Hun's firm. Ever since the 1880s, Hun had been the head of the Albany Citizens' Association, a reform group battling graft and corruption in city government. Its main focus had turned to needless spending of public funds, and its work was carried on through a "Committee of Thirteen." Soon after Hand joined Hun's firm, Hun named him counsel to the committee; Hand had to appear on behalf of the committee in administrative hearings (at least when Hun chose not to be the spokesman). The halls of the state capitol were a livelier environment than the law office, but most of Hand's time went to tedious scrutiny of the details of state vouchers. Questioning the use of public funds for the support of deaf-mutes and accompanying public officials to inspect pavements to assure that contractors had done their work properly were hardly exhilarating tasks. But occasionally there were chances for oral arguments, an experience Hand craved. Yet even some of these opportunities were disappointingly like his frustrating exposures to trial courts. When Learned appeared before the state comptroller to urge that payments for certain state printing expenses be disallowed, he did not prevail; more embarrassingly, a local newspaper commented critically on his excessively complicated arguments: "HAND EXPOUNDS—A BUSHEL OF FIGURES" read the headline; the story noted, "Mr. Hand's argument was bristling with technical verbiage of the printer's art, and was exceedingly difficult for the layman to follow."[257]

Only once did Hand's work for the Committee of Thirteen attract sustained newspaper attention. For two weeks in May 1901, Hand was enmeshed in a controversy that filled the front pages of the Albany newspapers day after day with unaccustomed banner headlines. The occasion was a violent labor strike by workers on the new electric trolley cars. The spreading national phenomenon of stormy labor-management relations had come to Albany at last. Around the country, skilled laborers sought not only pay raises but greater protection of the right to form unions. When workers went on strike, employers often resorted to strikebreakers. Picket-line brawls were common; sometimes, they erupted into serious violence.

The most divisive issue in Albany was the central question of union strength: nine of the several hundred employees of the United Traction Company were not union men, and the strikers insisted on a union shop. A week after the strike began, the company brought in its first strikebreakers. By 10:00 a.m. on May 14, trolleys rolled out of the Quail Street carbarn at great speed. The first one made it through; the second was blocked by more than a thousand strikers and their sympathizers. The motorman of the second car was hit by one of the many stones and bricks being thrown. Emotional newspaper descriptions reported he was near death, and some reports added that the police had simply stood by, in evident sympathy with the strikers.

This report roused the Committee of Thirteen to action. The committee, suspecting that the police had violated the law, assigned Hand to conduct an investigation. While he interviewed a large number of witnesses, the emotional atmosphere became ever more heated. Crowds gathered in the streets as more and more strikebreakers arrived; soon, National Guardsmen were brought in to keep order. A few days later, some militiamen fired their rifles and killed two innocent bystanders.

Hand remained remarkably calm during his two-week investigation. Early on, he remedied an injustice prompted by the committee's successful demand that the policemen on the injured motorman's trolley car be suspended for "conniving with the riotous mob":[258] finding that one of the suspensions had been based on mistaken identity, he had it revoked. And in his final report, he stood firm against the prevailing hysteria. He insisted that it was impossible to identify individual culprits, unfair to blame members of the police rank and file, and important to distinguish fact from conjecture. For once in his early career, Hand survived a tense situation without succumbing to anxieties.

Yet his judicious, thorough report was also a very narrow one, focusing exclusively on the allegations of police misconduct, and was wholly silent about the underlying causes of the labor dispute. Hand's inattention to the social and economic context is understandable, given his narrow charge from the committee, but there is no indication that at any time he thought at all about the low pay of workers or the obstacles to effective union organizing that underlay these abrasive strikes in Albany and elsewhere. Intellectually, he recognized even then that public action on behalf of workers was constitutionally justified: as he had told Gus in the course of their discussion of Jeffersonian laissez-faire philosophy, "the State must and should regulate the conduct of individuals,"[259] especially with respect to working conditions. But there is no indication that genuine empathy with workers' problems had yet become part of Learned's makeup.

A year later, Hand showed greater emotional involvement while studying another public-affairs issue, the conditions in a state mental hospital. Through Gus he had met James B. Ludlow, a New York lawyer and bon vivant who impressed Hand as having an unusually broad intellectual range. One of Ludlow's interests was the State Charities Aid Association, an organization led by members of the social elite who were not content with patrician, remote gestures toward the poor, and instead engaged in active lobbying. After Hand met some of them at the association's annual meeting in Albany in 1900, he helped their work by checking on the progress of proposed legislation, a minimal involvement motivated largely by a young lawyer's search for contacts. But one assignment evoked from Hand a depth of human empathy quite uncharacteristic of his distant attitude toward social problems at this time. In 1902, he was named a "visitor" to inspect and report on the conditions in the Hudson River State Hospital in Poughkeepsie. (Years earlier, the association had successfully lobbied for laws removing some of the mentally ill from local almshouses and asylums to state hospitals; these laws also authorized the association to name "visitors" to check on the hospitals' effective operation.) Hand undertook his work with his typical attention to detail, visiting the hospital twice and preparing an eleven-page report. (On reading it, the association's staff director commented that it was "really very remarkable" that Hand should have "gained so extensive a knowledge of the subject" in so short a time.)[260] Learned's voice, no longer merely that of a technically competent lawyer, conveyed empathy with human suffering and a commitment to reform. Hand was especially effective in criticizing the hospital's policy of devoting identical care to incurables and curables. The incurables, he acknowledged, required "reasonable comfort," if only because of the demands of "a decent humanity"; but the curable inmates, he insisted, deserved even greater attention.[261] The overcrowded conditions were especially reprehensible for those who could benefit from treatment, and merely custodial care failed to realize the possibilities of cure. In Learned's own eyes, his work had clearly evolved from the chore of a struggling young lawyer to the advocacy of an emotionally engaged citizen.

BUT ENGAGEMENTS with intellectual issues and public affairs were the exception in Albany. Most of Hand's days were devoted to menial legal tasks, and hard as he tried, he could find little satisfaction in them. He joined some local organizations, but meetings of groups such as the chamber of commerce or the board of a local bank were of little help to his professional career and even more unsatisfying socially and intellectually. The most rewarding breaks in the legal routine, he recognized, did not draw upon Albany at all: the young lawyers' "no name" club met in New York City; the assignment to inspect the mental hospital had come through New York City contacts. It was harder and harder to suppress the thought that he might be happier in a larger city. He was haunted by the thought that perhaps he should escape the confining, sterile atmosphere of Albany, for the sake not only of his career but also of his life as a thinking human being. For years, he agonized over the question. But his hometown exerted a strong pull. How could he expect to succeed as an unknown elsewhere if he had not demonstrated his capacity to build a practice in familiar surroundings? How could he reject his "duty" by abandoning his family?

As early as 1897, a lawyer who had moved from Albany to New York City had warned him that "Albany is a delightful place to revisit, but not so good to make one's living in";[262] by 1898, Hand was prepared to concede that professional prospects were better in the big cities. In 1899, James Ludlow told him bluntly, "The only thing for you to do is to come to [New York City] for good. You will come to it, sooner or later."[263] Indeed, the more Hand persisted in pouring his energies into his Albany efforts and in repressing thoughts of escape, the more depressed he became. To a law school contemporary who also felt "blue" about law practice, Hand confessed that he was beset by "troubles of [his] own making, imaginings light as air." The even more melancholy friend tried to console him: "Don't let your spirits sag, and if you do have that tendency, don't let their very lowness make you feel that there must be some great cause of it. With you, and lots of us, it is just some little playfulness of the nerves. . . . Forget the law for a minute or two."[264] Hand followed the advice only to the extent of curbing his obsession with "the importance of the work—only work"[265] enough to indulge in a few intellectual diversions.

In 1901, after more than four years of struggle at the Albany bar, Hand mustered the courage to look seriously for job opportunities elsewhere. He asked acquaintances in New York City and Boston and even Buffalo whether a young lawyer without local connections had any hope of succeeding in those places. As he acknowledged in his letters to friends,[266] the situation in Albany looked "so very questionable that I am strongly inclined to take the first good chance I can get to clear out and go somewhere where there is more doing." Soon he concluded that Boston and Buffalo were a "closed way" and turned to New York City, where he believed the "great prizes" were to be had. His search continued for more than a year, and he uncovered a few opportunities. But there was a long distance between his having an intellectual conviction that he had to escape Albany and his finding the emotional strength actually to make the move. Tortured by ambivalence, he took one step back for every two forward. Even his law school classmate Charlie Barlow impatiently complained about Hand's recurrent "shrieks and gyrations."[267]

In 1901, Learned's uncle Clifford died and Gus left his position as a junior partner in a Wall Street firm to join Clifford's smaller but well-established one. Learned carefully drafted a letter to his cousin suggesting that he, too, join the firm for a six-month trial period. While Learned awaited an answer, Gus's father, Learned's uncle Richard, visited Albany. Ever protective of his son, Richard Hand made it clear that he was not happy about the proposition: as Learned wrote to his cousin, Richard felt that "if the business was not such at the end of the time set [as] to justify [Gus] and the others in taking me in, it would be a rather disagreeable situation." That was enough to make Learned shrink back: the proposed move, he told Gus, "would be disagreeable for me, though I take my chances in any move, and disagreeable for you too, in a way perhaps somewhat more delicate than I had before appreciated."[268] He quickly let the matter drop.

James Ludlow suggested to Learned the possibility of the young lawyer's "joining forces with me," assuring Learned that "I can at least give you enough to do to keep you busy."[269] But this vague offer came to nothing, mainly because the family pressures to remain in Albany resurfaced. Ludlow reassured Learned that "you are coming here, sometime, notwithstanding all the futile considerations of reasons to the contrary, & (unless domestic considerations make it seem impossible) you might as well come now."[270] Sporadically, Learned checked out other opportunities. The best available one in the fall of 1901 proved to be a position that would be "largely devoted to brief making."[271] But "brief making" still lacked appeal: Hand told the potential employer that his Albany experience had been "rather more than I should wish in the preparation of briefs and less the business side of the law—which as far as I can see, seems to offer the best chances." He continued convinced that "the active side of the profession, in contact with clients," offered the best prospects.[272] By the end of the year, as Albany law business temporarily picked up and the prospects in New York seemed dim, Hand set aside his search. "For the time being,—no opening being apparent—," he wrote a New York acquaintance, "I have given up getting in at New York." Still, he added, "I am on the lookout for any place there that seems to have any promise in it and believe in the end I shall get it."[273]

An opportunity with "any promise in it" soon developed. On an elevated train during a visit to New York, Hand encountered J. Archibald Murray, a socially prominent partner in the small Wall Street firm of Zabriskie, Burrill & Murray. The Zabriskie firm, it turned out, did need a young man, and Murray invited Hand to his office for interviews. An offer materialized—and brought several weeks of renewed agony for Hand, for reports were mixed about the firm. The opening was for a salaried associate, not a partner; the firm was not of the top rank; the well-to-do partners were not very energetic, which might dim the firm's prospects (although "an infusion of brain power would fill a long felt want," a friend reported).[274]

In February 1902, Learned turned down the offer. Family pressures were once again decisive. Hand wrote the firm that he would have gone "if I'd been willing to go at all," but his "peculiar family situation" still took its toll: "While I think that it will probably be somewhat less advantageous for me to stay here, the personal reasons [have] finally seemed to me to be properly of greater weight than the relative business advantages, and I have determined to stay where I am. [While] things are as they are I do not mean to leave Albany."[275]

In the fall of 1902, Hand resumed the search. This time, he saw it through to the end with unprecedented speed. Fortunately, the Zabriskie firm still needed a young man. During a brief meeting with Archibald Murray on October 2, Hand accepted on the spot the offer he had spurned in February. He would only be the "managing clerk," not a partner, and his salary would be only $1,500 a year, the salary he had reached at Marcus Hun's firm years earlier.

Hand's mounting impatience with Albany partly explains his turnabout. But two additional developments were even more important: By the fall of 1902, he had learned that he would receive a legacy under his uncle Clifford's will; this would assure some financial independence. More significantly, he had decided to marry. Learned Hand and Frances Fincke had met in the summer of 1901, and Learned proposed to her then; in the summer of 1902, she accepted; in mid-November, three weeks before their wedding, Learned moved to New York City to join the Zabriskie firm.

One of Hand's few certainties was that he was lucky to have escaped from Albany. Repeatedly, for the rest of his life, he would reflect on "what [his] life would have been" had he stayed there: "I get a sense of such a terrible escape that it positively seems to me as though the peril were still actual and I was living [there], long since melancholic, a failure."[276] Repeatedly, he would think of the years he had spent in Albany "with a kind of mournful dreariness which has never existed in the Great Metropolis."[277]

II

Learned Hand and Frances Fincke

LEARNED HAND met Frances Fincke, his future wife, in July 1901, while both were vacationing in Murray Bay, a summer resort for the well-to-do on the St. Lawrence River in Quebec. Learned, then nearing thirty, thought himself destined for permanent bachelorhood, for he had never developed a serious interest in any young woman. Meeting Frances, a charming, beautiful twenty-five-year-old Bryn Mawr graduate from Utica, New York, dramatically changed that. Almost overnight, Learned, though typically indecisive on most questions, resolved that he wanted to marry Frances. A year after they met, they became engaged; six months later, in December 1902, they married. And the marriage gave Learned the strength to escape from Albany at last.

Years later, recalling their engagement, Learned Hand told his wife: "I like to think that we had some reason for acting as we did, for each could discern, and did, in the other things that he or she wanted. Still, it was a risk. . . ."[1] The marriage was indeed "a risk": it inflicted sharp pains yet also brought deep rewards for both Learned and Frances. What were the qualities that "each could discern [in] the other"— qualities that account for the durability of (as well as the tensions in) the marriage that lasted until his death nearly sixty years later?

GROWING UP IN LATE-VICTORIAN AMERICA, Learned Hand knew the era's attitudes toward women. In his family and social circle, women were admired for their grace and beauty; marriage, domesticity, and child rearing were their unquestioned realms. By adolescence, Learned began to appreciate feminine beauty,[2] and the appeal of attractive women did not diminish during his college years, though it was something to be relished only from a distance. The Harvard clubmen whom Learned envied courted the attractive debutantes of Boston society and boasted of indulging in pleasures of the flesh among the demimonde; Learned only watched from afar and brooded. He did not think himself handsome or debonair, and he was not socially at ease. With women, he regarded himself as an outsider.

Learned was well aware that his major source of information about women was his acquaintances' romantic entanglements. Thus, when his cousin Gus told him about his ambivalent reactions to an Elizabethtown "masher," a woman who was an ostentatious flirt, Learned composed and then tore up four pages of advice to Gus that had consisted only of vague philosophical speculations—worthless, he concluded, for he did not "know about what I [was] talking." He could only counsel Gus, quite magisterially, "neither like a fast foolish thing, 'a deep dyed scheming masher'; [nor] a silly prude." For himself, he ventured, he liked girls with "a deal [of] wit and life," for "after all these are very attractive. . . ."[3]

Six years later, during his final days at Harvard Law School, Hand's general thoughts about women—still those of a distant observer—had evolved to include dissatisfaction with the prevalent model of female domesticity. Replying to a note from Gus about a mutual acquaintance who had just become engaged, Learned commented, with evident distaste:

> Most of the women I have met are better fitted for matrimony than anything else, but there are some that God made with matrimony so much in his mind that they are married in soul as soon as they have any characters at all, and long before they know any one man better than Tom, Dick, or Harry. They are so well fitted for matrimony that their fitness for other things seems merely ineptitude in comparison. Lela is one of that sort of woman. She was completely domestic and really what else she could have done besides get married [one] trembles to think of.[4]

Women primarily "fitted for matrimony" were not for Learned, even in the days when he could only speculate abstractly about such matters. When he returned to Albany to practice law, he had repeated occasions to meet such women—women who were often graceful, sometimes flirtatious, but always, in Learned's eyes, mainly interested in settling into a life limited to domesticity. He had no interest in any of them.

Learned's entry into law practice provided the first occasions for him to engage actively in social relations with young women, as he tried to mold himself into a "normal" young attorney advancing his prospects as a "practical" trial lawyer. Involvement in civic affairs was part of that effort, and so was his brief immersion in the social life of country clubs, dances, and dinner parties. He quickly came to be seen in Albany as a handsome, gracious guest, a prime eligible bachelor, attracting the interest of young women and fueling the hopes of their parents. His efforts to suppress his intellectualism did not dampen his gift for words: his letters and conversations were fluent and witty, and they even showed some talent for flirtatious banter. These social skills, along with his family's respectability and his reputed professional promise, helped open the doors to the dining rooms and country retreats of Albany's best families.

But after only two years of these social rounds, Hand found the conversations vacuous, the young women uninteresting. By late 1900, he reembraced the intellectual life and withdrew from most of the increasingly monotonous social pursuits.

Three wealthy, prominent Albany families—the Bowditches, the Tremains, and the Olivers—were the main focuses of Learned's short-lived efforts to join the social whirl. Each family, not coincidentally, included marriageable young women, so that invitations for dinners and entertainment came regularly to Learned. The Bowditches, old family friends of the Hands, had an unmarried female relative in Boston, and Learned took her to dances often enough to rouse the hopes of her elders, hopes finally dashed by his engagement to Frances.[5]

Far greater expectations were generated in the Tremain family, with two unmarried daughters, Emily and Mabel.[6] That "nice young man" Learned Hand quite regularly accepted their parents' invitations to the family's summer retreat near Syracuse, joining in the weekend meals, walks, and lawn games. Although he found Emily dreary, Mabel was at first somewhat more intriguing: at least she would engage in an occasional political discussion, such as chatter about Learned's hostility to the Spanish-American War.[7] But her liveliness, while a refreshing change from her blander contemporaries, was not enough to sustain Learned's interest.[8] When a college friend of Learned urged him to join in a trip that would bring them near the Tremains' summer home in 1900, Learned took great pains to avoid meeting the daughters once more.[9]

Learned's withdrawal from the dreary social scene especially risked embarrassment in the case of the Olivers. Brigadier General Robert Shaw Oliver and his wife, even more prosperous and socially eminent than the Tremains and Bowditches, also had two unmarried daughters. One of the daughters, Cora, known as "Coco," soon became engaged to Learned's closest friend, Fred Townsend; the other, Elizabeth, nick-named "Bessie," had an obvious interest in Learned. Learned became increasingly uncomfortable about the Olivers' invitations to their summer "cottage" in Murray Bay, Quebec, telling a friend that he was "uneasy [about the Oliver girls] and would be till [he] saw them married."[10]

In 1898, Learned summarily declined an invitation to Murray Bay, and when the invitation was renewed for the next summer, he had added reason to avoid the place, for Bessie Oliver had sent him an effusive letter on his professional progress that carried expectant undercurrents: "My boyfriends are doing so much in the way of partnership, matrimonial and otherwise, that I suppose they must be quite grown up and I along with them."[11] Fred Townsend, who was spending his summer at Murray Bay in the company of his fiancée, warned Learned not to offend the Olivers. If Learned were to stay away, Fred suggested, Bessie might well feel insulted. Indeed, she had told Fred that "if [Learned] came when she had gone she would feel sure that [he] had arranged the date with the purpose of avoiding her." Moreover, the Olivers, Fred thought, had begun to suspect that Learned's interest in Bessie was not nearly as strong as that of the Olivers in Learned, and "as long as the truth has occurred to them as a possibility, you had better not give them the opportunity to believe it a fact."[12] Learned knew that the Olivers were fond of him, but he found their expectations oppressive, and so he declined their invitation once more.

By 1900, however, when Learned received yet another invitation to visit "Château Oliver" in Murray Bay, he felt impelled to maintain social relations with the influential family, and accepted. On leaving Canada after that vacation, he politely sent violets to the daughters, a courtesy that spurred another round of mildly flirtatious letters from Bessie.[13] Learned's efforts at civility were so successful that the Olivers were among the last to suspect the seriousness of his interest in Frances Fincke. When Learned returned to Murray Bay in the summer of 1901—and met and fell in love with Frances—he stayed with the Bowditches, not the Olivers. And a year later, shortly before setting off on another trip to Murray Bay in July, the visit that culminated in Learned's engagement to Frances, Bessie still expected "dear B" (Billings Learned, that is) to spend much of his time with her and looked forward to long carriage drives.[14]

By the end of the summer of 1902, the disappointment of the Olivers' hopes could no longer be avoided: Frances and Learned publicly announced their engagement. Though everyone maintained a surface decorum, the Olivers' pain was not wholly concealed. Charlie Barlow, one of Learned's law school friends, himself a frequent visitor to Murray Bay, reported a few months after Learned's engagement that his, Charlie's, sister, while returning from Europe, had overheard a man's voice transmitted to her cabin by the ship's ventilating system. The stranger had said:

> I happened to be in Murray Bay last summer, & there was a young lawyer named Hand, a nice fellow & very comfortably off, who was just engaged to a girl from Utica—Mrs. Oliver gave them a breakfast, which I went to, & it was quite pathetic to see her expression—"Another good chance lost."[15]

But the "chance" had never been "good," no more so for Bessie Oliver than for any of the other young Albany women. None of them sustained Learned's interest; all seemed shallow and unabsorbing to him.

As one after another of Learned's Harvard friends got married, he seemed one of those "cut [out] for permanent bachelors." But he was not content with that status. Replying to a marriage announcement from a Harvard College classmate, he acknowledged: "It has its depressing side [to] see the men of his own age stepping away from the state of singleness till one feels that he, the last, goes forth companionless." To another, he wrote: "I wish I might be able to tell that I saw an end to these bachelor days, but alas, I seem to have lost that faculty." His closest friends recognized that he did not cherish the prospect of spending his life alone. As one put it to him, his "remarks on the subject of matrimony suggested [that] something was stirring within you." And that friend, George Rublee, also perceived that Learned had a special need for the reassurance and stability a wife might provide: "Few men seem to me more capable of being happy in marriage than you and few seem to need such happiness more."[16]

As Learned neared thirty in 1901, he had never met a young woman he thought he could love. Indeed, there is no indication that he had ever even kissed one. His Harvard friends in New York City would brag about the abundance of beautiful society women there; and they would hint that their "weak flesh" sometimes succumbed to the well-beaten paths to houses of prostitution.[17] But Learned had not yet met a "respectable" woman whom he could imagine spending his life with, and he avoided prostitutes. As Charlie Barlow wrote after an evening spent taunting Learned about his abstinence from worldly temptations: "Chastity, sir, is certainly the greatest aim of mankind on earth, & I trust that you will cling to yours."[18] Many years later, Hand reminisced with his wife about the timid, sheltered life he had been leading when he met her: "I was such a gosling, so naive and simple about what people really were. I wonder if most men of thirty are such simps. . . ."[19]

IN 1901, when Learned decided to spend the last few weeks of the summer in Murray Bay and accepted an invitation from the Bowditches, Charlie Barlow, a regular guest at the estate of another family, the Minturns, there, had assured him of a sociable "gang of playmates."[20] Learned's brief taste of Murray Bay the year before had convinced him that it was indeed a congenial place to visit. A major summer resort for socialites from the New York City area, it ranked with Newport, Rhode Island, and Bar Harbor, Maine, and easily rivaled them in natural attractions.

Murray Bay, 90 miles downriver from the city of Quebec, 250 miles from Montreal, is situated on the northwest bank of the St. Lawrence River as it widens and winds its way northeast toward Newfoundland and the Atlantic Ocean. At Murray Bay, the tidal river is fifteen miles wide, with attractive sheltered settings on its shores.[21] For turn-of-the-century New York City residents, Murray Bay was somewhat more inaccessible than Newport or Bar Harbor: a long train ride to Montreal followed by a voyage on a river steamer down the St. Lawrence was the most common route. But, once there, the vacationers could walk on gentle hills, delight in a fresh river, and enjoy the beach.[22] Salmon and trout fishing, golfing and tennis, writing, walking, boating, and bathing were the prime diversions; but even more important were the lively card games, charades, teas, and dinners. Above all, there was good talk.[23]

After Learned arrived in Murray Bay for a month's stay in early August 1901, he spent far less time with his hosts, the Bowditches, than with the Minturns, a wealthy New York City family, heirs to one of the largest shipping fortunes of the mid-nineteenth century. Susanna Shaw Minturn, widow of the son of the fortune's founder, owned and presided at the Minturn "cottage"—a large, spacious house with nearly a dozen bedrooms and large verandas overlooking the river, and the frequent site for social gatherings and musicales. One of Mrs. Minturn's daughters, Mildred, three years out of Bryn Mawr, was spending the summer there, and she had invited along her closest friend and college housemate, the twenty-five-year-old Frances Fincke of Utica.

Initially, Learned's attraction to the Minturn cottage was the presence there of Charlie Barlow. But very quickly the major magnet became Frances Fincke: Learned showed far greater interest in becoming better acquainted with her than in exchanging his usual banter with Charlie. By the time he prepared to return to Albany in early September, he felt certain that he had met the woman he wanted to marry. Indeed, he proposed to Frances during his final days at Murray Bay, but she postponed an answer. The few friends of Learned who knew of the proposal were startled by this deviation from his typical indecisiveness. Charlie was among them: he told Learned that he hoped "that after a couple of weeks' absence and reflection you do not find that your action—so contrary to your general character—was hasty." Many in the Murray Bay crowd were aware that Learned was paying unusual attention to Frances; but most, including the Bowditches and the Olivers, failed to perceive the depth of his feelings. As Charlie Barlow reported, "No one I am certain suspects that you have done, or intend, anything serious." But he understood: "The more I see of the lady the less I wonder that you went off as you did."[24]

For the next few months, even as Learned renewed his effort to find a position with a New York City law firm, his courtship of Frances preoccupied him. In October, he wrote to his cousin Gus that much of his attention was "to a large degree shared by something else than this matter" of job hunting;[25] he had already given Gus a hint during an earlier conversation. Soon, rumors that Learned was "pretty busy in [the] western part of [the] state" spread to a wider circle of acquaintances.[26]

Learned's determination in proposing to Frances was not matched by self-confidence in the aftermath. He was beset by fears that she would reject him, and the family watched his anxieties with mixed emotions. Learned's mother, torn between fear of losing her son and concern about his brooding, assured him that she "suffered" with him during "this trying year."[27] Gus was as usual eager to jolt Learned out of his recurrent bouts of self-deprecation. He sympathized with Learned's impatience for an answer from Frances ("It has doubtless seemed long"), yet had no patience with Learned's concern that he was not worthy of Frances:

> You, of course, "know" you don't deserve her, and you don't in one sense, simply because you are coming face-to-face with your ideal woman about whose perfection poets have sung and mystics dreamed. Everybody must feel not only worthless but at times very miserable for such a contrast as there is between that far removed but "not *impossible* she" and himself.[28]

A full year went by, and Frances still did not make up her mind. Learned sent letters and occasionally visited Utica, but she gave him no indication of her decision. In the summer of 1902, Learned accordingly once more accepted invitations to visit Murray Bay—very eagerly this time, because he knew Frances would again be summering with the Minturns. On August 1, he went by train from Albany to Montreal; the next morning, he took the half-day trip down the St. Lawrence to Murray Bay on the steamship *Quebec*. For the first two weeks, he was once again the guest of the Bowditches; for the final days, he moved to the more spacious, more lively cottage of the Olivers.[29]

For months, he had prepared carefully for this summer visit; during the spring, for example, he had taken riding lessons in Albany and ordered riding breeches from Montreal in order to join less self-consciously in one of Murray Bay's favorite pastimes.[30] But whether riding or playing charades or joining in tea and dinner conversations, Learned's mind was always fixed on Frances.

The summer went quickly. Near the end of August, Learned still had no answer from Frances. On one of his last evenings in Murray Bay, he called on Frances once more and pressed his proposal. At last, Frances said yes. And for the first time in the year they had known each other, Learned and Frances kissed. Learned returned to his room at the Olivers, elated and relieved.

Now it was Frances's turn to have an agonizing night. Though she had acquiesced, she was still not sure. She knew that Learned would return to the Minturn cottage the next morning to call on her. She slept fitfully, tossing and turning for hours. When she awoke the next morning, she thought she had resolved her doubts. She said to herself, "I can't go through with it," and she decided to tell Learned that she had to take back the word she had uttered only hours earlier. But as she was dressing, she heard him coming up the footpath singing and whistling, obviously overjoyed by the success of his long courtship. Frances changed her mind again, because, she concluded, "I can't disappoint him now." She slowly descended the staircase and greeted her fiancé in the Minturns' "suitors' room."[31]

Hand never forgot that night and morning in Murray Bay. Nearly five decades later, he wrote to his wife:

[W]hat strange importance it had in our lives when you kissed me for the first time that night at the Minturns! What a tremendous fearful critter was I! And you repentant the next day. In a sense both of us were right for it was momentous to us [as] nothing else was and has been, and who can tell what such commitments will carry in their train? You and I knew this, and that is what made it seem like taking a long chance. . . .[32]

When Hand hurried back to Albany from Murray Bay in early September, exhilaration about Frances's answer, not trepidations about the future, filled his mind. Winning his "ideal woman" had temporarily dispelled his moodiness. He plunged into extraordinarily busy work, and promptly renewed negotiations with Zabriskie, Burrill & Murray, whose offer he had spurned earlier. In the spring, the pull of his mother and the rest of the Albany family circle had prevailed; but now he quickly accepted Archibald Murray's offer, and told him that he would begin by November. By then, he hoped, he and Frances would be married. He worked feverishly to clear up his business in Albany and devoted much of his time to the details of the wedding arrangements.

COUSIN GUS, recently married himself, advised an early and simple wedding. He repeatedly urged that the engagement not last longer than a few months. He thought three months "useful so that you may really know each other better than you doubtless suppose you do already," but "[d]elay beyond that is only tantalizing, so you must be married in October. . . ." Then he pressed, "Why can't you be married in October[?]" and closed with the postscript "whatever you do, don't have too theoretical a courtship."[33]

Learned, left to his own choice, would have preferred to get married simply and soon. But simplicity and speed were not within easy reach. Throughout the fall of 1902, wedding arrangements dominated the engaged couple's conversations and correspondence. Learned complained about "going over [guest] lists till I am tired. I fear I shall have nearly a thousand names."[34] At times, he feared that the immersion in details would corrode his relationship with Frances. He yearned to talk to her about "things that are neither here nor now, and don't concern anything concrete or in particular at all. Do you ever feel as if you must get away from what concerns the very present or you should go off the hooks and blow up? That's the way I am getting to feel. . . ."[35] Although Frances's letters revealed no such weariness, Learned, fearful that her patience might also be wearing thin, urged her to maintain cheer: "Courage, mon amie, in 6 wks. we shall be wed."[36]

Graver concerns than the details of the wedding ceremony preoccupied Learned that fall. Foremost was his felt need to reconcile his mother to his decision to marry and move to New York City. Although her tendency to cling to him was no longer enough to dissuade him, everyone who knew her well recognized that his departure would be traumatic for her. Even Gus, ever ready to condemn Learned's excessive anxieties, had to concede that there was good cause in this instance: "It is really a great waste of nervous energy on your part to worry about [your decision to marry], except in a single aspect, the loss your mother will feel by your going away. That is absolutely the only thing to cause any worry in reason."[37]

Frances tried to help by visiting Albany a few times during the engagement period, to become better acquainted with Learned's family.[38] On the surface, all went with proper decorum, but the strain could not be wholly disguised. His mother assured Learned that she was "prepared to love 'The Angel' " and "to think of her with *respect*." She hoped that Frances would like her "as not a mother-in-law but as a mother who would be only too happy to sacrifice herself to a dear daughter." But her characteristic martyr's stance also impelled her to assure her "good boy" that, after all, "I have had you thirty years."[39]

The perceived delicacy of reconciling Learned's mother to her impending loss was best revealed in a letter to her, soon after the engagement, from Fred Townsend, who was in an unusually good position to observe her capacity to stir her son's sometimes suffocating sense of filial duty. Though obviously hesitant to interfere in family tensions, Fred ultimately pushed himself to write. In a letter marked "Destroy When Read," he disavowed any intention to intrude upon the relations "between you & your boy," but hoped that "it might make you feel a little more assured for his future happiness if one who knows her a little & him so well should tell you how wonderfully fortunate I really believe he is." Apologizing for any possible "indiscreet" remarks, he added, in an obvious effort to persuade her to accept the marriage graciously, "[I]f it is almost too hard for you to face the prospect of giving him up to anyone, there is one other who finds it only [slightly] less hard & yet also can wish him Godspeed now with a clear conscience, if not with a light heart, & that is your affectionate Frederick Townsend."[40]

Neither concern about his mother's feelings nor annoyance with wedding details deflected Learned from his determination to marry at the earliest possible date. For a while, Learned feared that the organizational difficulties might push the wedding into 1903.[41] But, ultimately, Saturday, December 6, 1902, was chosen—less than three weeks after Learned was to begin work at the Zabriskie firm.

The wedding took place at two in the afternoon in Utica on that Saturday.[42] Fred Townsend served as best man, Mildred Minturn as maid of honor. Gus joined Learned's Harvard friends to fill the ranks of ushers.[43] About seventy invited guests attended, crowding the Fincke home for the post-wedding reception.[44] And by late afternoon, relieved to have the formalities behind them, Frances and Learned Hand boarded a train for New York City.

YOU AND I were really very different critters to hitch up together; we had little knowledge of each other, and it [is] somewhat to our credit that we should have come to see in each other so much that we could admire and love."[45] So, thirty years after their wedding, Learned reflected. In his letters to Frances, he often speculated about what attracted them to each other, and he usually concluded that "each could discern, and did, in the other, things that he or she wanted."[46]

Learned's attraction to Frances is easily understandable. She was a beautiful young woman: her face, with its high brow, wide mouth, and strong cheekbones, readily elicited attention. She carried herself with poise and pride. She exuded extraordinary charm and vitality, and she moved with easy grace among the socially secure with whom Learned had always felt something of an awkward outsider. But the major reasons for Learned's attraction lay deeper, in her qualities of mind and personality. Unlike every other woman Learned had ever known, Frances seemed an intellectual, genuinely interested in ideas. None of the Albany women in his circle had more than a traditional finishing-school education designed to equip them for marriage and domesticity. Frances, by contrast, was a graduate of Bryn Mawr College, which prided itself in developing its students' minds rather than womanly graces. It strove to shape independent young women with a sense of their own autonomy and with a determination to pursue a career built on their scholarly inclinations. Frances was a member of the first generation of American women with a serious college education, a graduate of a college that helped to fashion the "New Woman" by insisting that women were as intellectually gifted as men. Bryn Mawr imposed entry qualifications as rigorous as those of any men's college and offered a program as demanding as the best Ivy League schools. Thus, Frances, like Learned, had to demonstrate proficiency in Greek, Latin, and mathematics to qualify for college, and Learned could freely express his facility with Latin and Greek and include phrases in classical languages in his long letters to her.[47] Indeed, Frances was more at ease with modern languages, particularly French, than was Learned.[48]

Learned liked Frances for the way she flaunted her general interest in books and ideas, but her curiosity was not as thoughtful and deep as Learned's, for she tended to be more of a dilettante, though Learned could not have suspected that during their courtship. What counted most to him was that she appeared to be an eager listener, and he could talk to her for hours about philosophy, history, and current events. Occasionally he worried whether she was truly absorbed in what he was saying, but most often he gloried in his luck.

Learned wooed Frances with words, in long letters and even longer conversations. Once, during their engagement, he exclaimed, "I should like to sit on a sunny bank and talk about God after the manner of [my doubting journalist friend] Norman Hapgood, and if it was not you who wanted to talk, I should want to have you there, but most of all to have you do the talking yourself."[49] After knowing her for a year, though, he was more doubtful about how much she really wanted to talk rather than just listen. He had received a "little note" from her and confessed that it was "somewhat of a surprise [that it was] so short."[50] Throughout their correspondence, covering more than sixty years, her letters are remarkably brief and usually limited to day-to-day matters; his are usually long and rich in both emotions and ideas.

In the midst of discussing wedding arrangements, for example, he broke off from "this welter of stuff which I confess offends my taste and my ideals" to say that he wished they could be doing "something together really interesting." And he promptly poured forth paragraph upon paragraph of the kind of talk he truly relished: on negotiations between the coal-mine operators and the mine workers' union; on a book of philosophy he had just read, demonstrating the "absurdity of the old theory of natural rights"; and on an explanation why, to positivists such as he, the "sovereign [is] necessarily . . . omnipotent, irresponsible and untrammeled." He went on and on like that, with a concluding "There, my dear, now I feel better" and a note of concern about her response: "I know it is not the conventional way to address one's sweetheart and perhaps I am wrong, but after all I wooed you with this kind of thing and I really only feel at peace and happy when we get for a good deal of time on this basis. How is it with you? . . . Good-night, my dearest, it has been a great pleasure so to talk to you. Your lover."[51]

Shortly after his engagement, Learned had described the "rational" wedding ceremony he dreamed would soon take place. It was to be performed, he told Charlie Barlow, "by the Chief of the Brotherhood of Locomotive Engineers, Elizabeth Cady Stanton & George Santayana."[52] That trinity symbolized the exhilaration Learned found in his extensive albeit often rather one-sided conversations with Frances: the union leader, because of their discussion of current events, including labor-organizing efforts; Stanton, the pioneering upstate New York feminist, convener of the Seneca Falls Women's Rights Convention in

1848, who was still carrying on her crusade for women's suffrage in the 1890s, to symbolize Frances's determination to adhere to the ideals of autonomy and intellectual development she had absorbed at Bryn Mawr; Santayana, his teacher and the author of books Frances had been reading, to bless their penchant for philosophical speculation.

Learned was especially drawn to Frances because her personality was in many ways the opposite of his own. She was not a brooder but, rather, stable, strong, confident, independent, and cheerful; she lived for the present. Her optimism, even-temperedness, and serenity were traits that Learned most lacked, and they were qualities that he most wanted and needed in her; yet they were also the traits that would cause most of the strains in their marriage.

Learned's friends expressed predictable compliments on first meeting Frances. To Gordon Bell, for example, she seemed "very beautiful"; to Charlie Barlow, she was "one of the most unusually attractive people I ever saw."[53] But his most sensitive friends also perceived a good deal more in her. Gus Hand was especially aware of Learned's needs and Frances's strengths. In one of his periodic admonitions that Learned overcome his brooding, Gus wrote, soon after the engagement, "I do not expect one thing from you and that is any more 'nerves' and threnodies from you. They mar the usefulness of an able man and I hope your lady will buy some hob-nailed golf 'specials' and kick them out of you without a grain of mercy or hesitation, for they are nonsense and at times fit you for [a] neurotic symphony."[54] Others were convinced that Frances could do just that, even without golf shoes. Fred Townsend put it well while urging Learned's mother to reconcile herself to the loss of her son: "Marriage is the only thing in the world that can steady and quiet him, and she is exactly the woman to be his perfect complement. She has the head to appreciate him and the heart to love him."[55]

Learned was captivated by Frances's strength, practicality, and good cheer from the start, and throughout their life together, he often dwelt gratefully on those characteristics. Even before their marriage, he thanked her for "the pellucid serenity of your temper."[56] She could not eradicate the moodiness central to his personality, but, as he frequently reiterated, she made it easier for him to bear. "Most women," he believed, "would have been unable to adjust themselves to the vagaries of such a neurotic" as he; Frances did, and Learned considered this his "inestimable fortune." Without her, he was convinced, he would have been perennially "melancholic, a failure [because] I should have thought myself so, and probably single and hopelessly hypochondriac."[57] As he once wrote, thanking her for her advice on a career decision, "I cannot tell you how much your response has meant to me; it is exactly the kind of answer which heartens a man, especially a man of my makeup, the unquestioning conviction which admits of no variation. . . ."[58] Frances's "unquestioning conviction which admits of no variation," her assurance and serenity, probably reflected to some extent her occasional insensitivity and shallowness, but Learned found in her a welcome, necessary antidote to his uncertainty and periodic gloom. Her good cheer and practicality never ceased to amaze him: "[Y]ou do pretty well in the schedule of finders of the 'Good Life.' I suspect it is a good deal because you live here & now, take your pay while it is current, and have not the very bad habit of being sorry for yourself."[59]

Over the years of their marriage—especially after Learned's periodic visits to his mother in Albany—he repeatedly thanked Frances for "rescuing" him. "[I]f I had not married you," he once wrote, "it seems to me likely that I should have stuck on here, just as I was doing, and become a miserable misanthrope. . . . afraid to do anything which would [have] upset this strangely rigid routine."[60] He relished her "joy of living" and drew sustenance from it, and often he would apologize for his inability to change his personality, "so full of fears and so vacillating."[61] Again and again he attributed his survival despite his moodiness to her "marvelous powers of happiness." Contemplating those around him who were "washed up," he said, "I see myself but for your steadying hand."[62] Recurrently, too, Learned was beset by waves of guilt, because of his belief that he tended to curb Frances's autonomy, so that self-criticism, recriminations, and apologies flowed from him over the later years.

Frances was unconventional in her attitudes, an early feminist even though she moved comfortably in the most traditional social circles. True to her Bryn Mawr ideals, she vehemently rejected the late-Victorian model of the demure young woman and subservient wife, and Learned fell in love with her because of that. During her visits to Albany when they were engaged, she and Learned were both nervously aware of the contrast between her and the typical young Albany woman. Frances knew that she would be scrutinized to determine whether she measured up to the conventional criteria; Learned, proud of her independence and intellectually committed to a marriage that would accommodate her needs, was nevertheless also concerned. These were tense visits, but Frances readily passed muster. The head of the Bowditch family, for example, pronounced her "a sweet girl."[63] This was the general reaction: Frances raised no hackles; only Learned's announcements about the type of marriage he contemplated risked Albany resistance. As Learned reported to Frances after one of her visits:

It seems [that] I have already been putting my foot in it in my talk. [Mother thinks] it would jeopardize my reputation as a really loving lover, if I should let out my ideas on the subject of the equality of burden taking and absence of the shield-protection-and-cherish standard, which we both believe in and which I, again evidencing the less stable, living faith, am perhaps rather prone to promulgate with emphasis and some heightening of intonations.[64]

His letter is especially revealing about his sense of her most important traits, the distinctive qualities that cast her (as he put it three years later) in a "rich crimson" glow far more absorbing than the "thin pink" he associated with "other women":

When all is said and done—and as you know, my love, with me that means a good deal said, however little done—I must confess [that] all their chatter about "lovely" and "sweet" has very little attraction for me and serves to arouse a decidedly perceptible underglow of irritation. How is it with you? Indeed, dear heart, I know well enough without asking; that in fact being many times more non-conventional, if not unconventional, than I, it raises very little feeling or interest of any kind, because you are quite serenely indifferent to them and their general opinion, which, dearest, is one of the things from the outset I liked most about you.[65]

Over the many years of their marriage, Frances had repeated occasion to demonstrate that she was indeed "unconventional" and "serenely indifferent" to the opinions of others. Learned, in turn, frequently condemned himself for not sharing that trait: although he was intellectually unconventional, he repeatedly berated himself for being too concerned with what others thought. He envied her unconventionality; he was also to suffer from it.

FRANCES FINCKE OWED HER POISE in large part to her family background and to her Bryn Mawr education. Her hesitancy about marriage reflected the difficult choice with which women of her generation often struggled. *After College, What? For Girls* was both the title of a widely read pamphlet published near the turn of the century[66] and the pervasive question for Frances and her classmates. When Learned proposed to Frances, she was less than four years out of college and was grappling with the question of her future; her failure to resolve it may account for her indecision.

Yet indecision was out of character for Frances Fincke. The dominant person in the Fincke family in Utica was her father, Frederick G. Fincke, a hardheaded, tough-minded, successful business lawyer. Frances's mother was a demure, quiet, rather weak woman—the family structure was clearly patriarchal—who died in the fall of 1901, soon after Frances met Learned. By all accounts, Frances took her mother's death in stride. As Learned wrote Gus, although Frances was "the only daughter, [it] was she who gave support instead of receiving it,"[67] and so she was not likely to be shaken by the loss of her mother (as Learned certainly would have been by the death of his clinging mother). An old Fincke family friend in Utica confirmed that Frances had always been self-reliant, and domineering toward her mother: "Kitty was mother to her mother & to all the neighboring children. She took this dignified position about when she [was old enough for] her dolls." And he recalled that Frances had led her mother "first by the hand, then by the nose."[68]

Frances's closest family bonds were clearly with her father, and many of her strongest traits mirrored his. A Harvard College graduate,[69] he had achieved a reputation for being very bright but also for not being overly preoccupied with ideas. Unlike Learned, he "could go to Boston [for] an evening and not once talk of college."[70] His social poise and self-confidence gained him admission to the Porcellian, a distinction that Learned always envied.

Frederick Fincke was a practical man of the world, given to few but forceful words. He was never speculative or anxiety-ridden, and Learned as well as Frances was frequently showered with his advice, typically delivered in staccato, blunt sentences that sounded like telegrams. As Fincke once wrote to Hand, in his usual style:

> Not having an introspective, analytical or philosophical turn of mind, I cannot answer [you] in kind. Am not much interested in the ultimate causes of things. Haven't time. Proximate cause & its effect on the matter in hand is about my limit. . . . You & I don't look at the details of life alike & it is no wonder. You are different to start with & had an entirely different bringing up and environment.[71]

Fincke was immensely proud of his two children (Frances had a younger brother, Reginald, called Rex, who also went to Harvard and was also elected to the Porcellian),[72] and their notable self-esteem was a product of the loving reassurances he heaped upon them. Unlike his

father, Rex was not a brilliant student, but he had the Fincke assurance
and joy of life; he became a stockbroker. His postgraduate achievements
were never extraordinary, but to his father, any compliments about Rex
simply confirmed the obvious: "The boy must be unusual [to] excite
such affection. And by God! he is."[73] Learned grew very fond of Rex
soon after the Hands moved to New York: he saw in Rex the very
model of the assured bon vivant, the "Porc" he could never be.

But it was Frances who was the special apple of Frederick Fincke's
eye. He called her "Kitten" or "Kitty," and these sobriquets symbolized
his love and pride in his only daughter.[74] Frances, like her father, was
tough-minded and practical—indeed, Fincke thought she was even
more practical than he about the "little things of life, as if she had been
brought up in a mechanic's home who worked for wages in a factory."[75]
To Frederick Fincke, the ideal young woman was "not introspective
or self-analyzing" but instead "strong, well, blooming." He himself
did not "care a damn for philosophizing"; and his daughter met his
aspirations and emulated him.[76]

When Frances decided that she wanted to attend Bryn Mawr, her
father suppressed his concerns that the school might turn her into a
philosophizing intellectual, and wholeheartedly supported her.[77] She
readily met the difficult entrance requirements and began her studies
there in 1893.

TO GO TO BRYN MAWR in 1893 was to enter a select, elitist,
self-consciously intellectual college determined to mold its graduates
into strong, independent, career-oriented women. Less than 3 percent
of American women between the ages of eighteen and twenty-one attended college in 1890,[78] and most of the colleges that admitted
women—typically, coed ones in the Midwest and a handful of newly
established women's schools in the East—trained their students for the
traditional role of domesticity, without serious scholarly pretensions
and offering such fields of study as "domestic science." Bryn Mawr
was different, and it was different because of its determined leader,
Martha Carey Thomas.

Thomas had written as a young girl: "I ain't going to get married
and I don't want to teach school. I can't imagine anything worse than
living a regular ladies' life."[79] She had been graduated from Cornell
University in 1877, "spurning Vassar as an advanced female seminary,"
had tried unsuccessfully to pursue graduate work at Johns Hopkins in
the face of the sex barrier, and then pursued studies at German uni-

versities, especially Leipzig. But no German university was yet willing to grant a doctorate to a woman, and so she obtained hers at Zurich— the first woman to do so—and with honors. Yet she found the burdens of scholarship boring and sought an alternative way to promote women's intellectual development. Thus, before she returned to the United States, she applied for the presidency of the newly established Bryn Mawr College, relying on the presence of her father and an uncle on its board of trustees. The board was unwilling to give her the presidency but made her the college's first dean when it opened in 1884. For the next decade, she was often the de facto president, serving as chief assistant to an aging male president. In 1895, she became Bryn Mawr's president in title as well as in fact, and held that position for nearly thirty years. Frances's years at Bryn Mawr, then, coincided with Thomas's earliest, most influential years at its helm.

No student attending Bryn Mawr in the mid-1890s could escape Thomas's dominant personality. To her, "the intellectual life was an exalted end to be pursued with all the strength that the spirit possessed."[80] From the time the students passed the rigorous entrance exams, Thomas's intense, indefatigable sense of mission was ever present. Students were never left in doubt that they belonged to a special group possessing superior intellectual ability. They not only listened to Thomas's regular addresses in the chapel, but also had to review academic programs with her. Grades were posted after examinations, producing a tense, competitive atmosphere unlike that at other women's colleges.[81] Thus, to pass her final language examination, each student had to present herself in full academic dress to President Thomas and translate from sight, quickly and accurately, passages in French and German. Many students dreaded that experience, but Thomas thought it furthered her objective of instilling discipline. To enhance this uncompromising atmosphere, Bryn Mawr announced, "No part whatever need be taken by the student in the care of her own room."[82] Other women's colleges had their students take care of their own quarters to help train them in household management so that they might in the future better serve as wives and mothers; but Bryn Mawr had nothing but contempt for that concession to domesticity. Similarly, Thomas shunned "frivolous" subjects: "[d]rawing, painting, instrumental music, domestic science, . . . typewriting, [and] manual training have no place whatever in a college course [because] they do not give the kind of mental work that should be given by college studies," she insisted. With single-minded fervor and near religious zeal, she announced, "A woman's college is a place where we take those wonderful, tender and innocent freshmen with their inherited prejudices and ancestral emotions and mold them by four years of strenuous intellectual discipline into glorious thinking, reasoning women fit to govern themselves and others."[83]

In part, Thomas's zeal was a defensive response to the prolific literature of the day that preached that women's intellectual activity violated feminine nature and caused poor health among educated women. Excessive studying, critics warned, would degenerate women's reproductive organs and lead to hysteria and insanity. Even Charles Eliot, Harvard's president during Learned Hand's years there, joined this chorus of criticism.[84] Thomas neglected no opportunity to attack such critics head-on. She accused Eliot of having "sun spots" on his brain and claimed that a well-known book on adolescence reflected the views of men who were themselves "pathological, blinded by neurotic myths of sex, unable to see" that women were human beings.[85]

Frances Fincke and her friends thrived at Bryn Mawr, and after graduation they returned to the college as often as they could; Frances herself took a lifelong interest in its affairs through its alumnae association and as an alumna member of its board of trustees; she and many of her classmates nostalgically looked back to their college days as the most memorable in their lives. As Mildred Minturn expressed it in her diary, the graduates never forgot

> the good old companionship of college—perfect freedom, endless talk, absolute liberty, some people would call it license, of speech, affection, discussion &, I'm not ashamed to say, sentiment in talking over the good old days. We agree that they were absolutely the *best* years of our life—that Bryn Mawr and what it stood for [will] mean more to us than any other one thing in our experience. . . . I am unalterably thankful for those years for my friends and intercourse with them, a rare and perfect gift, the best possession I have, I do think.[86]

The statistics of the postgraduate life of students at Bryn Mawr during Frances's years are a remarkable tribute to the effectiveness of Thomas's efforts to inculcate upon her students a sense of mission about the capacity of women for independence and intellectual pursuits. Thus, 61 percent of Bryn Mawr graduates between 1889 and 1908 went on to graduate study, and nearly 90 percent pursued an occupation. Moreover, only 47 percent married (a particularly low percentage in light of the 88 percent marriage rate reported for women in the 1910 census);[87] of those attending during Frances's college years, 1892–97, 64 percent never married.[88] Bryn Mawr graduates differed sharply not only from the national norm for women, but also from that of women graduates of most other colleges.[89] No wonder they were viewed by outsiders as "eccentric, elitist, unusually intelligent, but markedly undomesticated."[90]

To Carey Thomas, marriage was incompatible with women's careers and intellectual development. As she once reportedly put it, "Our failures only marry";[91] Bryn Mawr graduates took with them a commitment to a life "where domestic values would not encroach on life styles or careers."[92] At the least, they left imbued with a strong skepticism about marriage, a fear that it would bar their realization of Bryn Mawr ideals.[93] As Thomas's influence at Bryn Mawr waned, she began to acknowledge that marriage was not necessarily incompatible with careers.[94] But women of Frances's college generation never forgot the undiluted message.

Nor was President Thomas the only influence steering Bryn Mawr graduates toward careers and autonomy. She regularly invited distinguished intellectuals to visit the campus. In the fall of 1896, during Frances's senior year, a twenty-four-year-old Englishman, "a rising man . . . said to be quite remarkable," of whom much was expected in academic circles,[95] turned up with his wife. The British visitor was Bertrand Russell, recently named a fellow at Trinity College of Cambridge University and at the beginning of his career. Russell had married into the Thomas family: the handsome, abrasive young man had wed Carey Thomas's cousin Alys Pearson Smith two years earlier.[96] The Russells lectured at Bryn Mawr for only a week or two, but with great effect. Russell was supposed to lecture on non-Euclidian geometry, but expanded his subject to advocate socialism as well, propagandizing because "everyone is so anti-socialistic here."[97] Alys Russell talked too, supposedly on the history of the women's movement, but it sounded to some in her audience as if she were endorsing free love. The lectures created quite a stir: the Russells' unconventional statements and radical theories forced President Thomas to do a lot of explaining and justifying.[98] But the Russells had even more impact through their social relations with students. Mildred Minturn especially caught their eye: the Russells found her "extremely clever" and "spent a long time trying to persuade her to revolt utterly against her mother and study economics at the London School," taking her out for long walks, "though Carey [Thomas did] not know it," and preaching "the Revolt of the Daughters to her. . . . [She] spread it among her friends like a new Gospel."[99]

The Russells' sojourn clearly reinforced the ideals Bryn Mawr students were supposed to take with them upon graduation; in the case of

Frances Fincke and Mildred Minturn, the visit was long remembered. In later years, Mildred claimed that the Russells radically changed her aspirations in life,[100] and Frances wrote Mildred, more than two years after they left Bryn Mawr, "What long years ago it seems since the Russells worried our little excitable brains. I wonder if we are much wiser now than we were then."[101]

THE MOST MEMORABLE ASPECTS of life at Bryn Mawr for Frances and her closest friends were the supportive emotional relationships with fellow students. Bryn Mawr, like all such colleges, was an enclave relatively free of the immediate influences of family members and of social relationships with young men. The social mores of the day barred much dealing with the male students at nearby Haverford College or elsewhere, so the women were left to their own social resources, with ample opportunities to express their affection for one another and their commitment to the college's ideals. As Frances Fincke wrote to Mildred Minturn within a year of graduating:

> Dear old B.M.C.—Do you remember our first year, dearie, & the little red room & the evening brews & talks & speculations! And how we used to wander down to Radnor in the moonlight after teas & be glad we were there together. . . . We've had a chance to live & learn much there. . . . [W]e can't forget it ever, love, I'm sure.[102]

As both Frances and Mildred quickly discovered after graduation, Bryn Mawr little prepared them for the difficult choices confronting them in the real world. Career opportunities for educated women were sharply limited, and these two women's differing responses are instructive.

For Mildred, family interests soon began to exert their pull. Her rich and domineering mother, the widowed Susanna Shaw Minturn,[103] had reluctantly permitted her to attend Bryn Mawr, but now tried to compel her to forget about a career. When Mildred was offered a teaching position at Brearley, a private girls' school in New York City,[104] her mother objected:

> The more I think of it the more sure I am that I want you to stay at home, so you must just give up this cherished plan and make it easy for yourself to bear this disappointment by remem-

bering how much more you have had than most girls so far . . .
I am sorry to disappoint you but this is my final conclusion and
we must rest on this.[105]

Mildred accepted this ruling, took a long trip to Japan instead, and fell
seriously ill for months on her return, as she would repeatedly for years.

Mildred's stress in battling with and then succumbing to her mother's
demands, and in the frustration of abandoning a promising career,
produced what was called "neurasthenia," a catchall diagnosis of the
day for nervous stress and exhaustion, and the very "disease" that
"experts" had warned would befall women who pursued excessive intellectual ambitions.[106] As Mildred wrote in her diary: "It was a
wretched summer. Mamma got another Homeopathic doctor who said
just what the Mental Healer I had treat me in town did—i.e. that it
was a case of absolute nerve exhaustion, to be cured by complete rest
—'Live the life of a clam.' "[107]

As would become usual after a bout of nerves, Mildred returned to
Bryn Mawr for an "almost happy 3 weeks," where she could "almost
live again after that black year." A few months later, one of her sisters
married, and Mildred again fell ill after she "settled down to playing
only daughter a little too fiercely. . . . [T]he rush of N.Y. life was
too much for me." Once again, she returned to Bryn Mawr, in early
1901, where Frances Fincke—"my Kleine [my little one]—came,"
and "we moved into rooms of our own. It was a joyous time, reading
& talking hours in the delicious old way, perfectly intimate & perfectly
happy at being together." She particularly recalled an evening discussing
"the problems suggested by Charlotte Perkins Stetson's book, gathered
about a soft . . . wood fire, the air heavy with cigarette smoke. Good
days, good nights, friendships & freedom & always some new idea to
be discussed together."[108]

Frances Fincke, unlike Mildred Minturn, had no such family pressures to overcome. Her subservient mother deferred to her father, who
strongly supported his daughter's independence, and no one stood in
the way of her efforts to live in accordance with her Bryn Mawr ideals.
She was not buffeted by competing pressures and did not suffer recurrent
nervous breakdowns. True, she took a leave of absence because of ill
health during her last semester at Bryn Mawr, and this may have been
a stress-related illness prompted by the competitive college atmosphere
and the pending final oral examinations,[109] but for the rest of her life,
she seemed able to maintain her calmness and equilibrium. Yet Frances
found it difficult to discipline herself after college. Although her letters

to Mildred frequently mentioned ambitious reading plans, she rarely achieved these objectives.

> [A]ll the ambitions & views of worldly people seem so trivial—ours is as you say, dear, "the cleaner, greener land." Nothing can take it away from us. It is going to be hard, very hard for us to settle down & try to hold . . . to our ideals. Not so hard for you as for me & others who *are* lazier & who lapse. I keep thinking of our Sunday evening meetings & remember how comparitively [*sic*] easy it seemed to think of holding firm & living with courage & a purpose but, love, it is a different thing to practice it. . . .[110]

Living at home in Utica, Frances made efforts at self-improvement through reading, and traveled often, on occasional journeys to Europe or to visit Mildred in New York City. But she was notably lacking in the drive toward intellectual achievement that Mildred, with far greater obstacles, pursued. Frances would tell Mildred of her "vain attempt" to finish "that old essay—such rot."[111] Once, while in Europe, she wrote, "I need to continually shake myself up or I find myself living absolutely superficially—not a 'strenuous life' as [William] James says."[112] And as she put it in one characteristic letter:

> I am still leading a vegetable-like existence. Have been reading Froude's Life & Letters of Carlyle—a most pathetic picture, & poor Mrs. Carlyle's fate would have made a stone weep. I don't think that I should *ever* be willing to be the door-mat of a man of genius—(for all my life).[113]

Repeatedly, Frances envied Mildred's cosmopolitan life. "[Y]ou are a lucky woman to reside in the metropolis," she wrote in 1898. "[D]on't forget it."[114] Her deeply implanted Bryn Mawr elitism manifested itself in various forms of snobbery: speaking of a young man with whom she had gone for a drive, she reported tartly that "he is *not* intellectually stimulating";[115] about a train trip to Nice in the company of Europeans, she opined, "Surely the Greeks and Romans didn't have such unattractive people in their civilizations." Anti-Semitic comments recur in her letters, as when she applauded Mildred's decision to abandon Dr. Gorodizche for Dr. Janet as her physician in 1904: "I'm glad you've left him and 'tis well he was revealed in his true light. You know, Babe, the—(I was going to say something foolish & anti-Semitic but will resist)."[116] Her sporadic, discursive reading and occasional stabs at writing were dilettantish and superficial; though she felt a tension between living up to Bryn Mawr standards and succumbing to her own "laziness," she settled for a fairly unchallenging existence. When she

first met Learned in 1901, Frances was as bored by Utica as he was by
Albany.

FRANCES FINCKE delayed her response to Learned Hand's proposal
of marriage for more than a year. She knew that marriage would entail
compromises, and she had few real models to follow. In theory at least,
work and a career seemed a far nobler aspiration than marriage, but on
the other hand, the career opportunities available to her were minimal.
(In 1900, only 5.6 percent of all American wives held jobs, and most
of these women were immigrants or blacks. Professional schools were
largely hostile to women, so that the principal opportunities were teaching or social work.)[117] But her lack of self-discipline and her apparent
failure to look for a regular job in the more than four years between
her graduation and her marriage cast doubt on the seriousness of her
career ambitions.

A central reason for Frances's hesitation in accepting Learned's proposal was no doubt her repeatedly discussed plan of not marrying at all
and living instead with Mildred in a lifelong replication of their happy
days at Bryn Mawr. Even though Frances's life was marked by languor
and drifting, by mere toying with books and ideas, the abstract appeal
of an independent, fulfilling intellectual life haunted her, and her friendship with Mildred offered a way to realize it.

The intimacy of this close friendship persisted for a decade after their
graduation. In their letters, they addressed each other as "O.S."—often
"Dearest O.S.," "My dear love," "My dearest dear," "My dearest
O.S.," or "My Darling little friend."[118] "O.S." most probably meant
"Own Sister," a term not uncommon between close female friends in
the Victorian era.[119] When visiting each other, they spent much of their
time alone together, reading poetry, walking hand in hand, and sharing
their most intimate thoughts. For both, their friendship meant more
than any other relationship and helped to make their Bryn Mawr days
"the *best* years of our life."[120]

Such relationships between unmarried, independent young women
were quite common in the late nineteenth century. Though Frances's
and Mildred's effusive expressions of love to each other might arouse
suspicions of lesbianism today, their mutual endearments were acceptable and conventional at the time, and there is no indication that their
relationship was ever marked by overt sexual behavior. Rather, their
devotion may show the limits on social relations between college women
and men in those days. Mildred's mother was fully aware of the friendship and never raised an eyebrow, nor did anyone else. Indeed, their

closeness thrived on gossipy accounts of flirtations with eligible young men; for them, thoughts of marriage comfortably coexisted with serious contemplation of never marrying at all.[121] For two women, especially professional New Women, living together was not uncommon at the turn of the century. Frances and Mildred knew such couples: Carey Thomas of Bryn Mawr and her companion, for example.[122] To women who sought more than domesticity, a living arrangement with another woman who shared similar aspirations was thought to be more supportive and rewarding than a traditional marriage, especially when one had not yet met a man who could be a "husband-friend" as well as a "husband-lover" and who would respect one's autonomy.[123] These long-term relationships between two unmarried women became known as "Boston marriages."[124]

By 1900, a "Boston marriage" between Mildred and Frances was clearly in their plans. Mildred had already spent some time in a small cottage rented from her friends Louisa and Pierre Jay in Mount Kisco, in northern Westchester County, and was "busily planning my own little house here at Mt. Kisco on the rocky corner of land I had bought fr. Loulie & Pierre, & there we were to have had our retreat together, there at last we were to have known perfect independence & our own tiny home that we had talked of for years."[125] This prospect of independence with Mildred—a life of reading to each other and good talk, perhaps even emulating Mildred's disciplined study and research[126]— was probably the primary reason for Frances's uncharacteristic hesitancy in the face of Learned Hand's marriage proposal.

For the next year, as Frances and Mildred saw each other with unusual frequency, it became clear to the chagrined Mildred that Learned was making progress: her closest friend was developing a real interest in the young suitor from Albany. "I never shall forget how physically sick the thought of losing her made me feel," she wrote in her diary.[127] For example, Frances told Mildred of a trip to Albany spent mainly in the company of Learned:

> It seemed O.S. *very* nice to see him again. I have seen him every day now for a week and feel as if I knew him very well and I like him *exceedingly*. . . . We walked & drove and went to a trial. A pleasant & amusing game, the law. . . . Nearly every night L.H. and F. Townsend came in and we chatted or played ping-pong.[128]

Soon after, when Frances came to New York City for "her usual long visit," Mildred recorded that she "began . . . to suspect that Frances was going to take Learned Hand, who had been in love w. her nearly a year."[129] Finally, in August, at Murray Bay, Frances told Mildred that she had accepted Learned's marriage proposal.[130]

Just two weeks before Frances and Learned's wedding date, Mildred was still mourning the loss of her closest friend and distressed that Frances was so busy planning her wedding:

I did, of course, plan to *have* Kleine here [in Mount Kisco] most of the winter & she agreed to come even aft. she was engaged, but she hasn't even spent a single night here, but has gone instead to Albany six Sundays running, tired out as she has been with shopping & useless house hunting. Well, I've lost her & I must just change all my plans & learn to live unto myself & hope perhaps to find a man that I can love as she loves B. & who will be as sympathetic to me as he is to her.

[A]ll the dear old days of perfect hour by hour intimacy & sympathy would come sweeping over me & I would feel a great rush of loneliness & longing for the old uninterrupted relationship, the perfect joy in each other's society, the happy building of castles in the air & voyages in Spain.

But Fate, in that curiously neat way she has, broke up our life together at the very minute it was to have reached its culmination. I cld. have borne to give her up better if we had ever had the trip in Italy that we had always planned, if she had ever lived here with me, even for one year—Well, it's over, & it's just *Life*.[131]

Within a few weeks, Mildred was ruminating about her own "feminine yearnings for . . . a sweet, blessed, friendly marriage," doubting all the while that it was truly possible without compromising her independence.[132] By the summer of 1903, the emotional strains of the year produced another "relapse" in her health, and she took up residence in France, in part for medical care—by Dr. Gorodizche and, later, Dr. Janet—all the while remembering that "[no] one could take Kleine's place in my heart, ever. . . ."[133]

In many respects, Frances shared Mildred's ideals, but ultimately, it must have come to seem to her that marriage to Learned offered a near perfect compromise. After three years of marriage, she wrote to Mildred: "B. was speaking the other day of the dread he had of being merely one of the countless mediocre—do you feel that? I don't. Life to me is so interesting and fruitful a thing by and in itself that I don't mind now the idea of having no effect."[134] Being "one of the countless mediocre" would no doubt have appalled M. Carey Thomas, and it would not have satisfied Mildred; but for Frances, the ability simply to enjoy life—be it reading a novel, working in the garden, or walking in the woods—was satisfaction enough.

In Learned, Frances found a "husband-friend" and "husband-lover" who appreciated her unconventionality, intellect, and independence, a man who was himself an intellectual with a promising future. Moreover, he claimed to view marriage as a partnership of two equals and professed to have strong convictions on "the subject of the equality of burden taking and absence of the shield-protection-and-cherish standard."[135] A relationship based on freedom of thought and emotion, intellectual growth, and mutual support was what Frances had envisioned with Mildred. The prospect of such a relationship with a husband seemed an attractive opportunity; and she had good reason to believe that marriage to Learned did not even require her to end her intimacy with Mildred: after all, Mount Kisco was near New York City.

THE POSITION OF WANDERERS in this city is not wholly agreeable," Learned Hand reported to a friend in the spring of 1903, when he had been in New York City for six months.[136] He had in mind the discomforts of living in temporary quarters while searching for a permanent home, but his description proved apt for a longer time and for a broader range of concerns. A permanent residence for Hand and his new wife turned out to be elusive for years, and a satisfying position at a law firm was beyond his grasp.

As a bachelor in Albany, Hand had always lived with his mother on State Street, and he was neither calm nor practical enough to take in stride the ordeals of house hunting. Learned had to begin at the Zabriskie firm three weeks before his wedding; even before he moved to New York, he had corresponded with his few acquaintances there about a place to live, but nothing had turned up by the time the newly married couple were ready to settle down, and they had to make do with rented hotel rooms for their first few weeks together.[137]

In February 1903, the Hands located temporary quarters somewhat more satisfactory than cramped hotel accommodations. For six months, they sublet the furnished Park Avenue house of a physician while intensifying their hunt for a place of their own.[138] But nothing acceptable turned up: available houses were either too far uptown for their needs, in the East Seventies and Eighties, or too far downtown, in the East

Twenties and Thirties; in any event, the prices—in the high $30,000 range—seemed too high.[139]

By late summer of 1903, Learned heard about a house on East Fifty-fifth Street available on a long-term lease. He was so "discouraged," so uncomfortable with not knowing "where we shall go next fall," and so exhausted by the "annoyance and trouble of moving," that he signed a three-year lease even though the owners refused to give him an option to buy.[140] "The moving and the continued work which she has had to do has had a bad effect upon Frances, who is now pretty well tired out," he reported to Fred Townsend. But Hand himself seemed in even worse shape: "You have no idea until you try it how harassing and exhausting it is to move into a new house and get everything arranged."[141] Slowly, as furniture filled the empty rooms and books crowded the shelves, the leased house turned into a more comfortable environment for Learned's reading and cigar smoking and whiskey drinking. Yet only the books were truly his old friends. Virtually everything else was far more familiar to Frances than to Learned: the linens, the dishes, the utensils, and even the furniture were all shipped from Utica by Mrs. Hand's doting father.

The need to find a permanent home pressed upon the Hands throughout their stay on East Fifty-fifth Street. Yet when their lease drew to a close, they resigned themselves to returning to apartment living, an unwelcome prospect averted only at the last minute: when a house became available in a desirable location, the Hands bought it in the spring of 1906 and moved in even while alterations were still under way. Located on the south side of a tree-lined block between Third and Lexington avenues, 142 East Sixty-fifth Street was a narrow, four-story brownstone on one of the most attractive blocks in Manhattan, then and now. It was to be the Hands' home for more than fifty years. Even though real estate prices had dropped somewhat during the three years, the new house cost nearly $30,000.[142]

That they could purchase a house at that price suggests a substantial improvement in the Hands' financial position, but Learned's professional income remained low; his inheritance from his uncle Clifford was the source of his security. Money worries persisted, though Learned's real estate investments indicate that in reality his economic situation was quite comfortable, for in early 1906, at about the time they moved to East Sixty-fifth Street, he and Frances also spent about $20,000 on a country home. Among young professionals in the Hands' circle, a summer place was the norm. Spending the warm and humid summer in the city seemed unthinkable; summering in cooler seashore or mountain environments was de rigueur. During the first two summers of their marriage, the Hands had made do with visits to friends' country homes and short-term vacation rentals; then, in 1905, they rented a cottage in Mount Kisco, and before they returned to New York City, they resolved to build a permanent summer home there.

III

From Wall Street Lawyer to Federal District Judge

IN MID-NOVEMBER 1902, Learned Hand had begun his New York law practice at the Wall Street firm of Zabriskie, Burrill & Murray. He had known that the position was chancy professionally, and he feared from the outset that a young lawyer who had failed to make his mark in Albany would be even more submerged in the "maelstrom" of New York City. Fred Townsend tried to allay these misgivings:

> I think you are doing the right thing and I know you will make a go of it. You are not the kind of man who is swallowed up and never heard from more in New York. Don't let that sort of pitfall worry you. Look at old Gus for instance: he has abilities along the same lines as yours, only they don't go so far. I haven't the least doubt of your wisdom in making the move, or the conspicuous success that will demonstrate it.[1]

But Learned was never confident about "conspicuous success." After all, Gus was already well established in a flourishing New York firm. The outlook for the Zabriskie office was far more questionable.

Hand's doubts about his new firm soon proved to be justified. His agreement to join the Zabriskie office as managing clerk, falling short as it did of the partnership he had wanted for so long, could have been adequate if the firm's business were flourishing. He had accepted the position at a salary of $1,500, but the firm had promised an increase after a few months and consideration for a partnership after a year's trial. Hand's modest expectations were quickly cast in doubt. During his first few weeks, he discovered that an important old client had left, that new ones were not coming in, and that his tasks were as routine and unchallenging as they had been in Albany.

The firm had only two truly hardworking lawyers—the senior partner, George Zabriskie, and Hand himself.[2] Hand's role was to assist Zabriskie and to handle whatever work might arise from the very few cases under Archibald Murray's supervision. The cases Hand worked on—administration of some old estates, insolvency claims, dull commercial matters—did not much differ in nature or difficulty from his routine business at Marcus Hun's firm, although the amounts in dispute were somewhat larger than the Albany norm.

Hand's relations with the seniors were good enough: Zabriskie, though cold and distant, appreciated his skills in legal research and writing; Murray, much warmer personally, was often away from the office. But as the firm's workload shrank, the partners were not "enterprising in hunting up business,"[3] and by the spring of 1903, Learned began to fear that his daring move had only entrapped him, perhaps doomed him to oblivion in a stagnant firm. Perhaps, he speculated, he himself bore some of the blame; perhaps his own talents were not up to Wall Street standards. Frances repeatedly tried to cheer him up: "I think you ought to have a little more confidence in your own ability (this is just a gentle reproach, Dear)."[4] But her reassurances could not lift his gloom.

In April 1903, after less than five months with the firm, Hand was approached by a seemingly more energetic law office, Gould & Wilkie, with a tempting offer, but for months he was reluctant to consider it seriously. He feared being viewed as ungentlemanly: he had agreed to go with Zabriskie for a year and thought it unseemly to negotiate with others during that period. Only strong pressure from his tough-minded, practical father-in-law, Frederick Fincke, got Learned to think seriously about the Gould offer.

Throughout the many months of 1903 during which Hand tried to choose between the Zabriskie and Gould firms, Frederick Fincke bombarded Hand with a flow of reminders about his lack of practical business sense. For example:

> At the start you want to throw aside all regard for the interests of Z.B.&M. and G.&W. The action of both is governed by purely selfish business considerations, the only consideration which should enter into a purely business proposition. There is just one person you should think about and whose interests you should seek most intelligently and persistently to promote, and that person is one L. Hand.

But Fincke was not confident that his son-in-law, whom he regarded as sentimental and weak, would see it that way: "Have not the slightest doubt this will be so as far as they are concerned. Am not so sure of you. . . . Too great modesty is a crime in business when one has reached a certain point and you have reached and passed that point."[5]

This was Fincke's characteristic tone in his long efforts to put some steel into his son-in-law. Most of the time, Hand recognized that he needed practical counsel and heeded Fincke's advice, yet these admonitions also reinforced his doubts about himself, even while he was pressed ever more into the dealings of the practical world that he found unsavory and uncongenial. Later, Fincke reminded Hand that pursuit of professional success was not an occasion "for gentlemanly self effacement and an invocation [of] those unwritten rules of conduct which characterized the knights of old."[6] This was an especially pointed reference to the essential difference between the Fincke and Hand families—between practical, nonintrospective people and uncertain, anxious, brooding ones, between a clan of ambitious modern entrepreneurs and a family uncomfortable with the ways of the market.

At times Learned resented Fincke's intrusiveness, once finding the courage to suggest that his father-in-law "advised his children too much."[7] But he appreciated his father-in-law's experience, accepted much of the advice that came via Frances, and, in any event, Fincke's comments were more helpful than those Learned received from his mother, who did little more than reinforce his own nervousness about major decisions: "[I]t makes me cold through and through to decide or rather have you decide such an important question."[8]

Within a few months, Learned was ready to follow Fincke's advice that he should unearth "the volume of business and character of business done by G&W—examine their books, find out their clients, their gross earnings for say five years back and the net," and, armed with that information and the firm's best offer in hand, go to Zabriskie for better terms, including a partnership commitment: "You can then take the offer which is better for B. Hand. [U]nless you look out for B. Hand's side of the proposition, no one else will."[9]

Hand's inquiries quickly produced more information about the Gould firm than he had about Zabriskie's. Charles W. Gould offered Learned a partnership, with a guaranteed $3,000 a year. And when Hand, following Fincke's strategy, told George Zabriskie about the Gould offer, Zabriskie responded by offering Learned an assured income of $4,000.[10] A chorus of advisers—his mother and several of his New York acquaintances—urged Hand to stay with the "older firm," and Fincke too thought that Hand would more quickly become a major figure with Zabriskie (who would probably step aside for Hand more readily than John L. Wilkie, the key partner at the Gould firm). But Hand was not so sure, and his vacillation evoked Fincke's impatient admonition: "Think only of B. Hand. He has been wagged long enough and now that the tail seems to be wagging the dog, . . . see to it that it wags easily and well for the tail and give no thought to the dog."[11] Hand agreed that Fincke had properly stated the ultimate choice—"On the one side, an old, respected and influential firm doing a business considerably larger than the other and earning their income from fewer transactions because of the amounts involved and the character of clients; on the other, a less known and influential firm doing a business of somewhat recent creation with evidences of growth and development" —but he disagreed with Fincke's conclusion that the balance was "manifestly in favor of the older firm."[12] In the end, he chose Gould & Wilkie: the Gould firm had made him feel more valuable and important; the Zabriskie offer, by contrast, was merely a response to competition. Moreover, he thought the Gould prospects were better, and against that promising future, $1,000 in additional yearly income from Zabriskie seemed insignificant.

Hand's decision to go his own way by moving to Gould & Wilkie expressed a growing maturity, independence, and assertiveness. As he perceived it, nothing in his law practice in Albany or at Zabriskie had given him grounds for optimism about professional success, and he was no longer content to wait patiently for better things to happen. Restless and frustrated, he seized another, perhaps final chance to succeed in law practice, and he dared to do so against strong contrary advice.

At the beginning of January 1904, Hand moved down to 2 Wall Street to his new office at Gould & Wilkie. But within a very few days his uncharacteristic optimism was clouded with feelings of anxiety and disappointment with which he was all too familiar. By January 7, the image of the law partnership of Gould & Wilkie had become badly tarnished: Hand, who had expected to be a junior, profit-sharing partner, found instead that he was to be on probation for the first six months; only if these went well would he be entitled to a percentage of the profits. Disheartened, he promptly complained to Fincke that Gould had misled him. Fincke assured him that the probationary clause was reasonable and that his prospects were attractive, but he could not help adding the first of many "I told you so" reminders: "The wisdom of the decision by which you dumped ZB&M is something different, but that is done for, well or not."[13]

Hand's disappointment was not easily allayed, and he seriously considered leaving his new firm after only a week in order to go into practice on his own. Fincke virtually shouted at Hand about this:

> The suggestion merely of your quitting and trying it alone is concentrated foolishness, irrespective of your income. You have what you consider not and what I consider a good chance—just as good practically as the chance you thought you were getting. . . . Jump in and do your damndest and at the end of six months, faith will have given place to right and then you can make larger demands [about] future relations. . . . When the time comes remember it is a business proposition solely all around.

Reverting to the telegraphic style into which he lapsed at his most emotional, he added, "Think you are a bit too introspective and analytical."[14] Hand came to see that he really had no choice, and so he gritted his teeth and stayed put.

Hand's day-to-day practice at his new firm was no more challenging than it had been with the other ones: his assignments, he told his father-in-law, included "no piece of business so important and complicated that it needed and received my study and ability."[15] When he did achieve partnership status, his seniors apportioned him a percentage share that Learned found disappointingly below 10 percent. There was a good reason for this: the practice had lessened that year, and Gould was not about to take a reduced share; as Fincke tried to explain, it was "simply a case of too small a business and too many divisions already." Yet the prospect of joining an expanding enterprise had prompted Hand's move, and no matter how rational Gould's behavior, the firm's decline intensified Hand's gloom. When he mustered the courage to tell Gould that he was "not entirely satisfied with the present arrangement,"[16] the senior partner would not budge. Hand took little comfort from his father-in-law's reassurance that his confrontation with Gould would at least "set [him to] thinking" and put him into a better position to act "if any better chance should unfold itself."[17] There was no "better chance"; no other firm made overtures to Hand.

The early months of 1905 were the nadir of Hand's years in Wall Street practice. His worries as a nervous father-to-be and an unsuccessful practitioner soon took their toll. Yet when he fell ill with pneumonia, the firm was unexpectedly humane, continuing his salary while he recuperated.[18] Still, the professional situation did not improve after he returned to his desk in the fall. He attracted only two clients of his own during his five years at Gould & Wilkie, both stemming from old Albany contacts, and only one case, a controversy over mining claims to Pennsylvania lands, which Hand shepherded to a successful settlement, brought in a substantial fee.[19]

At the end of 1905, Hand considered joining the prosecutorial staff of the flamboyant, reformist New York district attorney William Travers Jerome, a possibility that probably arose through Hand's ongoing friendship with his college classmate Howard S. Gans, who was Jerome's chief appellate lawyer. The prospect reawakened his Albany dreams of successful trial work, but he gave up these dreams when Fred Townsend reminded him of his earlier failures: "Unless you made a considerable reputation as a court lawyer, you might find yourself stranded after a few years: & in all frankness—I doubt if your gifts lie specially that way."[20]

By 1907, Hand's guarantee at the Gould firm had risen to only $5,000, and thereafter his situation deteriorated further. He was convinced he had made a mistake and felt trapped. Many of his friends in law were doing far better, and the professional success of his closest friend of all, his cousin Gus Hand, constantly reinforced his own sense of failure: Hand could not have been cheered, for example, when he heard that Gus had been retained to represent the Venezuelan government in a major case.[21]

Hand's sense of defeat in law practice helped to prompt his first effort to obtain a federal judgeship, in 1907. When that failed, he had no choice but to continue with the law firm; still, Gould & Wilkie seemed less attractive than ever. True, the firm profits in 1906 and 1907 were high enough to boost his annual income to $6,000,[22] but by the spring of 1908, the senior partners no longer got along and John Wilkie decided to leave. Hand was caught in the middle: both Wilkie and Charles Gould wanted to have him as a partner. Fincke, as usual, was ready with practical advice: Play both ends against the middle; work out the best deal you can; and for heaven's sake don't be your usual modest self; blow your own horn, for talent will not be rewarded unless the possessor touts it.

Hand decided to stay with Gould: although Gould was even less congenial than Wilkie,[23] he could hope for major business with him once Wilkie was gone. Fincke urged him to insist on a 15 percent share of the profits as his price for staying, but once again, Hand was frustrated. Gould refused to raise Hand's share beyond 10 percent, and, making that news even more unpalatable, the offer of an increased share was coupled with a reduction from $5,000 to $3,000 in his guaranteed income. Frances shared Learned's disappointment. As usual, she recommended that he seek "dad's advice" and urged him not to give Wilkie the impression that he was "perfectly ready to go on indefinitely the way you are."[24] But what was there to do? Fincke reluctantly agreed that the Gould firm was indeed a dead end; Learned once again threatened to leave in disgust; his father-in-law once more urged him to stick with it, on the simple ground that it would be easier to "keep your job, but keep your eyes and ears open for a better one."[25] Learned's doting mother shared his resentment and, characteristically, only deepened his gloom: "[I]t has distressed me to have you there. I always felt you were put upon."[26]

In 1909, then, after more than seven years of law practice in New York City, Hand had little to show for his efforts. In later years, Hand repeatedly told often incredulous listeners about what he considered an utter failure: "I was never any good as a lawyer," he said once in a public confession, "I didn't have any success, any at all."[27] The bench seemed more appealing than ever, and in the spring of 1909, Hand, with the aid of friends, mounted a second campaign for a federal judicial appointment. This time, he succeeded.

AT SOCIAL GATHERINGS, and especially in the reform activities of New York's intellectually oriented lawyers, Hand gained the renown that was escaping him at the bar. From his earliest days in New York, his friends recognized his acuity and breadth and admired the independence of his mind. These impressions led Hand's circle to support him as an ideal candidate for the federal bench, at a rare time when the national administration genuinely wished to nominate an independent intellectual.

In New York as in Albany, friendships, talk about ideas, and occasional ventures into reformist politics gave Hand vital breaths of air, essential to surviving an arid and disappointing practice. He had been attracted to New York by the hope that it would offer him escape from the dreary, parochial confinements, and his high expectations were, after all, based on some experience. The young New York lawyers who predominated in Hand's circle during his early years in the city, even while they strove for professional success, maintained some interest in the life of the mind and the political health of the city. Learned's new circle in New York City included some old Harvard classmates, including Gordon Bell and Charles Barlow, but not all his acquaintances were lawyers. For example, Norman Hapgood, a Harvard Law School contemporary of Gus, had begun a distinguished career in writing and investigative journalism, becoming the editor of *Collier's* magazine, a leading reform-oriented periodical, in 1903.

Hand came to know a few older men as well. Charles C. Burlingham, fourteen years Hand's senior, was one of his favorites and ultimately proved most important to his career. Throughout his very long life, "C.C.B." loved younger, lively minds, and he took to Learned quickly. On the surface, C.C.B. was merely another downtown lawyer, a partner in a leading maritime-law firm who was no intellectual and never held an important public office. Yet Burlingham's informal influence over more than fifty years of New York public life was phenomenal. The genial, straight-talking C.C.B. had a great passion: he loved pulling strings.[28] To him, involvement in what others might view as tireless meddling was simply a means to pursue a lifelong devotion to good government. Over the years he was an effective foe of the party machines that staffed public offices with people chosen on the basis of their clubhouse connections. He fought for a merit system of civil service appointments and, above all, for better quality on the local, state, and federal benches. In form he was an independent Democrat, but in fact his contacts included the powerful of both parties at all levels of government. He launched a number of distinguished judicial careers— including Learned Hand's in 1909 and, four years later, Benjamin Cardozo's.

Soon after the Hands moved to New York, Learned met C.C.B. through Gus; before long, the Hands and the Burlinghams exchanged dinner invitations. In the time Learned could spare from his routine legal tasks, he occasionally wrote memoranda for C.C.B.'s briefs on admiralty issues, a field to which C.C.B. had introduced him (he had never encountered it in law school or Albany law practice) and one in which he became the nation's most eminent judge. C.C.B.'s extracurricular enthusiasms proved contagious as well: by the end of Learned's first year in New York, he was engaged in a mayoralty campaign in which C.C.B. was among the leaders favoring municipal reform.

Hand's acquaintance with Burlingham quickly flowered into a warm friendship. At first, C.C.B. addressed Learned as "Dear Hand," but this became "Dear Learned" by 1906 and "Dear B" by early 1907; and in that year, Hand began addressing Burlingham as "Dear C.C.B." Indeed, C.C.B.'s affection for Learned was already evident in 1905, when Hand survived his life-threatening bout with pneumonia. "It is a thing to be directly thankful for," C.C.B. wrote Hand, "that God has kept you here a bit longer. . . . I'd like to lay my eyes on you and hope I may anon. *This to the fire,* with this *sentimental rubbish*—true though. Love to your lady wife."[29] (Hand's reprieve proved to be quite "a bit longer": Hand lived to be eighty-nine; C.C.B., one hundred.)

Hand's "lady wife," who had come to her marriage with far greater social graces than her husband, was one reason his social life expanded so rapidly. Frances hosted dinner parties with ease, and Learned relished the good conversations they spurred. At first, Frances aspired to high society, and Learned dutifully subscribed to *The Social Register*, asking that he and Frances be listed in it. But by 1907, they were dropped from the *Register*, after Learned angrily complained about being charged for publications he had not ordered. The Social Register Association notified him: "As Mr. Hand reserves the liberty of interpreting his own contract in his own way, . . . the Association begs to suggest that an entire cancellation of the subscription would be a graceful solution to the difficulty."[30] Hand had no regrets: informal, stimulating contacts were more important to him than high-society listings. Increasingly, this stimulation came in the settings of the University and Harvard clubs, the Century Association, and the City Bar Association, and especially in informal social gatherings and growing engagements in political reform.

Involvement in municipal reform politics was a natural activity for bright young New York lawyers with any interests beyond narrow career ones. For many of them, state and national politics evoked ennui and hopelessness, if not contempt. But at the local level, they thought, something might be accomplished. While the politics of the city had been dominated since the 1850s by Tammany Hall, the Democratic organization, backlashes against its machine patronage, graft, and corruption were common, and anti-Tammany movements periodically arose. And once in a while, a reform administration would be elected. Hand moved to New York in 1902 during one of these rare periods: the reformer Seth Low was occupying the mayor's office. When Low ran for reelection in 1903, Tammany was determined to defeat him; Hand and some of his acquaintances joined in the effort to keep the reformers in their unaccustomed position of power, but Low was defeated.

Low's defeat was the typical fate of New York reformers. C. C. Burlingham led most of the few anti-Tammany efforts that succeeded over the decades—he was at Low's side at the beginning of the century; a few years later, he organized the city's first anti-Tammany "Fusion" movement, which built a coalition of Democrats and Republicans that elected John Purroy Mitchel as mayor in 1913; and he crowned his achievements by founding a new Fusion party in the early 1930s, assuring the election of Fiorello H. La Guardia as mayor for twelve years. But most of the time, Tammany's chieftains were not truly worried by the reform forces. They knew they had staying power and viewed the reformers—the "goo-goos," the "good government" crusaders—with unconcealed contempt. The colorful observations of long-time Tammany district leader George Washington Plunkitt typified Tammany's attitude.[31] Academics and philosophers, Plunkitt once noted, always debated the subject "Why Reform Administrations Never Succeed Themselves." The reason was clear: the reformers lacked political endurance because they were amateurs, without the career investment and patience of the professionals. As Plunkitt put it: "They were mornin' glories—looked lovely in the mornin' and withered up in a short time, while the regular machines went on flourishin' forever, like fine old oaks."[32]

To Hand and his fellow reformers, Tammany was an unmitigated evil. They thought government should be in the hands of a meritocracy devoted to efficiency and enlightened stands on public issues. Tammany, by contrast, seemed to seek power for its own sake: to get out the vote, win elections (often by unsavory means), and divide the spoils. Tammany, they insisted, cared nothing about issues such as the tariff or American colonialism or curbing the evils of concentrated economic power.

All this was true, but it does not explain Tammany's successes. Clearly, Tammany was superbly well organized: it served as the major social welfare agency of its day, helping out needy supporters, facilitating the voters' relations with government, and, in an age of mass immigration, familiarizing hordes of new citizens with their rulers. The reformers, by contrast, could not reach the masses, not only because they were not full-time political professionals but also because most of them were not at ease with the new immigrants and their children who, increasingly, populated the city. To some reformers—although not to Hand or most in his immediate circle—restoring the masses' deference to patricians was indeed one of the attractions of the reform cause.

Hand rejected such narrow class politics: the substantive issues, not just engagement with the concerns of his friends, were the reasons why he participated in reform politics. While quite well off himself, he detested abuses of wealth such as the excessive concentration of economic power in the hands of larger companies and "robber barons" and the overwhelming role of money in political campaigns. Moreover, he despised the scrambling for material rewards reflected in the patronage and graft of the machine politics of the day. Concerns such as these induced him to participate not only in Low's mayoralty campaign but also, for even longer periods, in the work of the Civil Service Reform League, the Citizens Union, and similar "goo-goo" groups. There was substantial overlap among the leadership of the few reform organizations to which he belonged and the larger number to which he contributed. Usually, Hand's closest friends participated, too, and C. C. Burlingham was often among the leaders.

In state and national politics, Gus Hand had remained loyal to the Democratic family tradition; Learned declared his independence by 1900, but the cousins comfortably joined in the effort to reelect Low; indeed, the combination of civic-minded Republicans and independent, non-Tammany Democrats had made possible Seth Low's election in 1901. Low, then president of Columbia University, had emphasized the need for complete separation of municipal and national politics, a theme congenial to these reformist lawyer-intellectuals. And once in the mayor's office, Low concentrated on civic reform, particularly through restraints on patronage; this endeared him all the more to the patrician reformers. During the 1903 reelection campaign, then, the reform crowd campaigned for him with unprecedented zeal.

Hand felt a growing commitment to the reform cause. Among his friends, C.C.B. was continuously involved in planning sessions, and Cousin Gus as well was "up to his eyes in the attempt to save the City."[33] A few weeks before election day, Hand joined in. As he reported in late October: "I am much interested in the campaign and am to make my maiden speech tonight at the Citizens Union mass meeting on the Bowery. We have good hopes of success; in particular the registration has been very large in our district, and not so large in the Tammany district. . . . What we have most to fear is apathy not hostility."[34]

Tammany worked ceaselessly for victory, but the incumbent Fusion movement fought back with unusual skill, and Hand felt "great admiration" for its organizers. Yet he was not cheered by his own efforts. Speaking in the strange and noisy venue of the Bowery was an unaccustomed activity: nothing in Albany had prepared him to sway the masses. And Hand did not think he covered himself with glory. As he told his Albany mentor, Marcus Hun, "I began my career as a cart-tail speaker last night to a phlegmatic crowd of east-siders on Second Avenue. I did not seem to stir their souls to rapture, either of rage or delight."[35]

A few days later, he felt no more confident about his talents:

> I still continue to address the electorate from the end of a truck. I wish I could feel more encouragement as to the usefulness of my efforts. I cannot find that the average denizen of the Bowery seems to be greatly impressed by any oratorical or recommendative

efforts which may proceed from me. Perhaps it may be the incessant roll of the elevated and the rattle of the surface cars that
may interrupt my efforts. Certainly the combination is not hopeful.
The only real satisfactory element in the matter is that my voice
seems to hold out extraordinarily well, and I at least have the
satisfaction of feeling that I am on the right side.[36]

Hand's ineffectiveness is not surprising; what is remarkable is that, for
the first time, he was moved enough to engage in public politicking at
all. As Fred Townsend wrote him from Albany, "I admire your [cour-
age] in doing it. It would be beyond my pluck however good the
cause. I never should be able to talk to the public except in the way of
law."[37]

Learned told his uncle Richard Hand, Gus's father, right after Tammany's victory: "I cannot say that I bore in any sense the honorable
and efficient part that Gus did in the vain effort which was made to
keep this City from plunging once more in[to] the debauchery of [a
Tammany] administration. I did do a very little, and I felt a good deal
more than I did. Of course it is all lost now."[38] Yet the "very little"
he did gave him some visibility among the reformers, and the "good
deal more" he "felt" had a lasting effect. Although he never again took
so active a part in a mayoral campaign, he stayed involved in municipal
good-government groups for years to come, and his experience laid the
emotional groundwork for his far deeper involvement in Teddy Roosevelt's Progressive movement a decade later. For the first time, he
overcame his characteristic, skeptical distance; for the first time, albeit
only briefly, he participated actively.

Hand's continued detachment from state and national issues, meanwhile, mirrored the attitude of most of his acquaintances. "Everything
is rotten and I have no convictions except negative ones," Gus once
put it.[39] Norman Hapgood captured the prevailing disenchantment when
he wrote to Hand, "Principles seem to have little to do with party
divisions at present. It is the ins versus the outs and I cannot see that
the outs promise to do better than the ins."[40]

Though Hand shared much of this "a plague on both your houses"
attitude, on occasion he did support one candidate over another. We
have seen that in his Albany days, he broke with his family's allegiance
to the Democrats in order to vote for McKinley and the Republicans
in 1900. While he continued to criticize the Republicans' imperialist
ventures in the Philippines and their protective tariff, he considered
them generally more attuned to the economic realities of the new century

than the Democrats, who still pursued Jeffersonian ideals of smallness and agrarianism, which Hand thought anachronistic: to him, curbing big business, not breaking it up, seemed the preferable solution. Indeed, his chief political concern was how government could curb the abuses of concentrated wealth without lapsing into Jeffersonian nostalgia. Like his cousin Gus, for example, he was offended by Herbert Parsons's candidacy for Congress in New York's Silk-Stocking District, long an oasis of Republican strength encompassing the relatively well-to-do residential areas of Manhattan's Upper East Side. Parsons might be a good man (indeed, he was a young intellectual lawyer himself), but that he was backed by substantial amounts of family money was profoundly troubling. As Gus wrote Learned, "A sufficient expenditure of money from the bucket-shop of his father-in-law will elect [him]"; "money is the whole business and the old question comes whether the necessity justifies a temporary corruption of voters. If it does, there is mighty little difference in the mode of getting elected in the best and the worst politicians."[41] Learned's reply uncharacteristically revealed even firmer convictions than Gus had expressed: "[I]f your anticipations are correct, it can make no difference how admirable the record he makes, the whole outcome will be disastrous. I think that is one thing which we must all set our faces against absolutely uncompromisingly, that the necessity never justifies those particular means."[42]

Hand's developing concern about abuses of economic power explains his somewhat unusual position in the presidential election of 1904, when he voted for Judge Alton B. Parker, the Democratic candidate, instead of supporting Teddy Roosevelt, who had succeeded to the presidency after McKinley's assassination.

A number of Hand's acquaintances misunderstood his position. An upstate family friend was delighted that "the sons of honored Democrats are drawn back to the fold,"[43] but Hand had no such permanent return in mind. Instead, he simply considered the candidates' stands on central issues more important than traditional party allegiances, and in 1904 he concluded that Parker's Democrats offered the better prospect for curbing wealth. Some of Hand's friends were not persuaded. The Boston lawyer Arthur Dehon Hill, for example, insisted that Learned was misguided: party positions on curbing big business were not grounds for choosing between the candidates, for the money problem underlay "the whole political system" and would not be "remedied by electing Parker." With the usual alienation from national politics that prevailed among young intellectual lawyers, Hill argued, "As for the principles of the Democratic party and the Republican party too, I am sick of the whole business. Neither party platform has any more sincerity than a breakfast food ad. Teddy is a man, and when I see a man I will vote for him and to Hell with formulas."[44] But Learned would not budge. To him, the need to curb economic power *was* central. As he explained to Marcus Hun, he feared that trusts would develop more readily under the Republicans.

In the 1904 campaign, Hand did little more than discuss politics with friends and then vote; he played no public part at all; the one Democratic meeting he attended proved uninspiring and he never returned. He scorned the charge common among Parker supporters that Teddy Roosevelt was too strong an individual, too dangerous an expression of "the admiration always felt by the crowd for 'the man on horseback,' "[45] and, even while supporting the Democratic ticket, defended Roosevelt against charges of demagoguery.

On September 16, *The New York Times* published a report, sponsored by the Parker Constitutional Club and signed by a number of Democratic lawyers, that accused Roosevelt of abusing presidential power and that criticized Roosevelt's executive order loosening the eligibility rules for Civil War veterans seeking pensions. The club claimed that Roosevelt, in "a bid for the pension vote," had engaged in "lawless" and "most reprehensible" behavior. Hand wrote a three-page rebuttal on the same day. He argued that the club's charges were "strikingly incorrect and unjust" and proceeded to defend at length the clear constitutional power of the president to issue the order:

> All the talk about the President's lawlessness has, no doubt, a very deep basis, whether just or unjust, in the popular suspicion based upon his ardent manner, his consuming activity and his unrestrained expression. There [is] some ground in his acts for that opinion. But a party only serves to weaken its cause when it pushes to the fore so weak a case as [this], and any good Democrat could do no better service to his party than to try to lay at rest this phantom bugabear [*sic*] conjured originally from the ingenious and fertile brain of that delightful tergiversator, [Tammany congressman] Bourke Coc[k]ran. If the Parker Constitution[al] Club seeks lawless deeds done in high places, they can surely find better pabulum than this.[46]

The letter was too long and technical for the *Times*'s pages and was not published, but Roosevelt hardly needed Hand's help during the 1904 election: the charismatic president soundly defeated the colorless Parker by a margin of 20 percent in the popular vote and 200 votes in the Electoral College.

IN ALBANY, Hand had been quite indifferent to social problems not touching his own class. His report on the treatment of the mentally ill had been motivated mainly by the boredom of law practice and his hunger for a reputation; his work during the city's transit strike revealed no awareness that the workers had been frustrated in their drive for unionization. After he moved to New York City, Hand's advocacy of causes such as restrictions on child labor and improved safety inspections of factories showed no greater emotional engagement. Typically these involvements were mere by-products of Hand's friendships with reformist lawyers, among whom support for social causes ranked second to campaigns for good government.

There was one significant exception to Hand's usual detachment: his energetic hostility to the prevailing anti-Semitism of his class. Hand had little occasion to meet Jews in the patrician circles he moved in during his youth, though in his easy dealings with Jews over the years he emulated one of his father's traits: during the 1870s, a Jew named Nathan Swartz was a partner in the Albany law firm that Samuel Hand had founded. Swartz died at a young age, but his widow recalled, decades later, the Hands' warmth toward the Swartzes and remembered Learned as " 'the little fellow' I often saw" in visits to the Hand home.[47] There were few Jews at Harvard, and they were invisible on the rolls of the clubs. The references to Jews that Hand heard as a young lawyer were usually contemptuous; stereotypical remarks about their pushiness were commonplace. But it was at Harvard that Hand had met Howard Gans, apparently the only Jew in the college from New York's immigrant Lower East Side,[48] and this acquaintance reflected his unusual empathy with the feelings of a social outsider—Hand, of course, thought himself an outsider as well—and his lifelong pattern of treating people on their own terms.

After college, Gans obtained his legal education in New York City and, the doors of Wall Street firms being closed to Jews, went to work in the Manhattan district attorney's office. When William Travers Jerome ran for district attorney in 1901, in the anti-Tammany election campaign that made Seth Low mayor, Gans enthusiastically supported him, and soon after Jerome's victory was put in charge of the office's appeals before the state court in Albany. His frequent trips to the capital while Learned Hand was in practice there led them to renew their college friendship; Hand invited Gans to his wedding in November

1902.[49] Gans did not come, perhaps because he feared that, as a solitary Jew among the guests, he would be uncomfortable.

The Gans affair stemmed from what Fred Townsend called "the Jew exclusion feeling"[50] at Albany's preeminent club, the Fort Orange Club, whose members included lawyers and judges, doctors, and the top echelons of the business community; Hand had been an active member for years, resigning only when he moved to New York City. Gans, now a frequent visitor to Albany, thought it would be convenient to have access to the club's eating and sleeping facilities; he had good professional relations with the members of the state's highest court, and one of the court's most respected judges, John Clinton Gray, offered to nominate him for membership.[51] Gans mentioned this to Hand, who warned him about the club's anti-Semitic policy.[52]

Nonresident members were elected by the club's board of trustees rather than by the full membership, and the procedure included literal blackballing: each board member was given a white ball and a black ball—an affirmative vote was cast with the white ball, a negative vote with the black, and a single black ball constituted an absolute veto on admission.[53] Townsend confirmed that Gans would indeed face serious obstacles: it was "the unwritten law of the FOC to exclude all Jews."[54]

Gans promptly asked Judge Gray not to propose him. But Gray urged Gans to press ahead, assuring him that the club's "race prejudice" was not "anything like as strong" as Hand feared and that there was only a handful of rigidly anti-Semitic members. Reassured, Gans permitted Gray to move ahead with the nomination in November 1903, but he told Hand, "I am eager that you should not suppose me [as] one of those who would willingly force himself into a social circle where for any reason, good, bad, or indifferent, he was not welcome."[55]

Hand thought that there was more reason to worry than Gans or his sponsor suspected, and was moved to consider stronger measures than any other social issue had evoked from him—to write a forceful letter to every member of the board, for example. But he made the mistake of mentioning his plan in the presence of his father-in-law, who was in New York on one of his regular visits from Utica. Frederick Fincke promptly sought to dampen what he considered to be Learned's misguided zeal. As Learned told Fred Townsend, Fincke was "very strongly of the opinion that it would be an impropriety—and in his mind a very great impropriety—to write such a letter . . . a very gauche and stupid thing to do."[56]

Learned was not yet ready to take a strong stand in the face of his father-in-law's "great force,"[57] but neither was he ready to abandon Gans's cause. Instead, he devised an alternative: "to write to six of [the trustees] whom I know and ask them to state [to their colleagues] that they had received a letter from me" in support of Gans.[58] The board members he knew covered a wide range: an officer of a leading Albany bank, the head of a manufacturing company, a member of one of Albany's oldest families, and a publisher.[59] All the responses were favorable, but all rested on special reasons: every trustee made clear that he acted solely as a favor to Hand and because of the strong feelings of Judge Gray; none suggested that he had any personal eagerness to see Gans in the club or felt any opposition to club policy.

Luther H. Tucker, Jr., the publisher of an Albany agricultural newspaper, was especially outspoken. He was confident that Gans would be admitted at the board's December 1903 meeting, but he left no doubt about his own misgivings: "Indeed, I am rather sorry that the candidate has thought fit to make such a dead set for admission—it has a little too much the Hebraic flavor to my thinking, but I daresay he is a proper man enough, and of course he feels that he has a prejudice to overcome."[60] Even Fred Townsend showed no enthusiasm. In most of his letters to Learned, Fred referred to Gans as "*your* dear young friend Mr. Gans"; after all, he explained, "I have met him [only] once since college and I did not know him [there] at all."[61] Though Fred would not blackball Gans if he had a vote, neither was he willing to raise a finger on Gans's behalf. Of all the past and present members of the club whose views are preserved, only Hand and John Gray criticized the anti-Semitic exclusion rule and enthusiastically favored Gans's admission.

In the end, Gans was not blackballed. He had assured Learned that if the club admitted him only reluctantly, "as the result of much pressure and influence, I shall want to resign after a short period of membership."[62] But Gray's support and Hand's letters made for smooth sailing. Gans thanked Hand for his "effective contribution" and became a nonresident member.[63]

Hand's battle on behalf of Howard Gans clearly heightened his sensitivity to the treatment of excluded social groups, and it foreshadowed further public expressions of that sensitivity in later years, as when his beloved Harvard considered imposing a quota on Jewish undergraduates—a proposal Hand's forceful intervention helped to kill.

Hand's friendship with Gans also afforded him a view of New York City's immigrant quarter. East European Jewish immigrants at the turn of the century typically settled on New York's Lower East Side, separated by only a few miles but by an enormous social gap from the Hands' Upper East Side residence. Gans invited the newly married Hands to dine at his "East Side lodging house" and visit a Yiddish theater with him once they moved to New York City. As he put it, it might "amuse you and Mrs. Hand to see how the submerged $^{99}/_{100}$ live."[64] Learned promptly accepted the invitation but did not follow up on it until a year later, in November 1903. Gans was delighted with the prospect but somewhat nervous as well: "By the way—if the suggestion is not an impertinence—would you tell Mrs. Hand that Rutgers Street would drop dead if she came in evening clothes."[65] Presumably, she did not.[66]

LEARNED HAND'S MOST SIGNIFICANT WORK during his early New York City years was the writing of a fifteen-page essay entitled "Due Process of Law and the Eight-Hour Day." Published in the May 1908 issue of the *Harvard Law Review*,[67] the article was a response to a landmark decision by the Supreme Court in 1905, *Lochner v. New York*,[68] a ruling that initiated three decades during which the Court intensively scrutinized and frequently struck down state and federal economic legislation. The name of the case still provides the colloquial label for those decades: the power wielded by the justices during "the *Lochner* era," when the Court engaged in "Lochnerizing" and frequently invalidated popularly supported laws, ultimately provoked public wrath. Hand's strong criticism of the ruling and the kind of judicial behavior it represented was one of the first published attacks on the decision, and one of the most trenchant. His analysis devastated the economic and jurisprudential underpinnings of the ruling and the reign of judicial supremacy—in his view, the abuse of judicial power—that *Lochner* initiated.

Hand's attack on *Lochner*, published in the nation's most widely read professional journal not long after his first, unsuccessful try for a judgeship, made him more visible, in New York and beyond. But ambition was not his prime motive. Rather, he was eager to elaborate a position on the proper role of the Supreme Court that he had first absorbed in James Bradley Thayer's classes at Harvard Law School, one that he believed in very deeply for the rest of his life. Hand's essay was not only a cutting critique of the legal justifications for the Court's behavior but also a sharp economic and political commentary, unusually blunt for the stately pages of the *Harvard Law Review*.

Lochner v. New York was a 5–4 decision holding unconstitutional a New York law that prohibited the employment of bakery workers for more than ten hours a day or sixty hours a week. The constitutional obstacle to the law, according to the *Lochner* majority, was the due-process provision of the Fourteenth Amendment, which bars any state from depriving "any person of life, liberty, or property without due process of law."[69] The fate of the New York law struck down in *Lochner* was far less important than the approach that the Court's ruling signified: *Lochner* indicated that the justices would review very carefully, and would not hesitate to invalidate, many economic regulations, including the new worker-protective provisions that legislatures were beginning to adopt (decades after they had become commonplace in Europe). Hand's attack on *Lochner* presciently identified the harms that would flow from this judicial attitude, both in the obstruction of the popular will and in the abuse of judicial power.

Lochner was the first Supreme Court decision invalidating a law aiding workers on the ground that it violated due process, but the battle over the proper judicial role in applying due-process standards had raged since the ratification of the Fourteenth Amendment in 1868. "Due process" in its traditional meaning imposed very little restraint on legislatures; historically, it required only that laws be applied through fair procedures. In 1873, soon after the Fourteenth Amendment was adopted, a narrowly divided Court adhered to that narrow interpretation: it set its face strongly against using the due-process clause to establish the Court as "a perpetual censor upon all legislation . . . with authority to nullify such as it did not approve."[70] But by the end of the century, this judicial self-restraint began to break down. Instead, the Court began to hint that in due-process cases it would be prepared to consider arguments not only on the fairness of the procedures invoked but also on the substantive merits of the law itself, on the question of whether it was "reasonable" or whether it interfered excessively with basic rights.

When Hand was a law student in the mid-1890s, the Court had not yet struck down a single law on such "substantive due-process" grounds. But Professor Thayer spent much of Hand's constitutional-law course warning about the threatening cloud on the horizon—the risk that the justices would abuse their power and read their political and economic biases into the Constitution.[71] In 1897, some of Thayer's forebodings came true. The Court, in its first major effort to delineate the "liberty" protected by the due-process clause, interpreted it very broadly. Most important, the justices held that "liberty" included a wide range of economic rights, including the right of the individual "to pursue any livelihood or avocation, and for that purpose to enter into all contracts which may be proper, necessary and essential to his carrying out [his] purposes."[72] This identification of the "liberty of contract" as a fundamental right protected by due process planted the seed for the Court's anti-government-regulation, pro-laissez-faire approach of the *Lochner* era. But not until 1905, in *Lochner* itself, did the Court use its newfound power to strike down an economic-reform law.

The *Lochner* majority sounded modest enough, purporting to inquire only into the rationality of New York's law protecting bakery workers. But in fact the *Lochner* decision went much further, demanding a far stronger justification than mere "reasonableness" before it would permit government to interfere with the free economic market. The majority's new "censorship" of regulatory laws rested on its ill-concealed hostility toward the trend to regulate employer-employee relations for the latter's protection. As the *Lochner* majority opinion put it, the Court would not stand idly by while the individual rights of autonomous employees and employers to contract with one another on whatever terms they pleased were placed "at the mercy of legislative majorities." If laws such as New York's were upheld, it insisted, then "[n]ot only the hours of employés, but the hours of employers, could be regulated and doctors, lawyers, scientists, all professional men, as well as athletes and artisans, could be forbidden to fatigue their brains and bodies by prolonged hours of exercise. . . . [T]here would seem to be no length to which legislation of this nature might not go." And, the majority opinion added, "We do not believe in the soundness of the views which uphold this law." To the *Lochner* Court, simply, laws restricting the hours "in which grown and intelligent men may labor" were "mere meddlesome interferences with the rights of the individual."[73]

Many of Hand's objections were initially voiced in the two dissenting opinions in *Lochner*, by Justice Oliver Wendell Holmes, Jr., and the first Justice John Marshall Harlan, but Hand articulated them more fully and broadly. One argument in defense of New York's law was that it would promote the health of bakery employees: this was the focus of Justice Harlan's dissent, which argued that reasonable people had long advocated restrictions on working hours and that legislatures around the world had in fact enacted such laws; he insisted that the existence of such a body of opinion and legislation precluded the Court from branding the law as "irrational." A different argument addressed the economic welfare of the bakery workers, claiming that the law was justifiable as an effort to redress the inequalities in bargaining power between employers and employees. This argument, the core of Justice Holmes's famous dissent, challenged the claim that any attempt by the state to redress economic inequalities was illegitimate. Holmes argued that the *Lochner* majority was engaged in a raw exercise of judicial power. "This case is decided upon an economic theory which a large part of the country does not entertain," he contended. Whether the Court agreed or not with the increasingly popular views supporting economic regulation had "nothing to do with the right of the majority to embody their opinions in law." In an especially well known passage, Holmes added:

> The Fourteenth Amendment does not enact Mr. Herbert Spencer's Social Statics. . . . [A] constitution is not intended to embody a particular economic theory, whether of paternalism and the organic relation of a citizen to the State or of *laissez faire*. It is made for people of fundamentally differing views, and the accident of our finding certain opinions natural and familiar or novel and even shocking ought not to conclude our judgment upon the question whether statutes embodying them conflict with the Constitution. . . . I think that the word liberty in the Fourteenth Amendment is perverted when it is held to prevent the natural outcome of a dominant opinion, unless it can be said that a rational and fair man necessarily would admit that the statute proposed would infringe fundamental principles as they have been understood by the traditions of our people and our law. It does not need research to show that no such sweeping condemnation can be passed upon the statute before us.[74]

By 1908, when Hand wrote his article, the Court had reinforced its *Lochner* ruling with two similar decisions whose implications he also condemned.[75] He emphatically agreed with Holmes's contention that the majority had "perverted" due process in *Lochner* and its progeny; indeed, he went beyond Holmes in narrowing the function of courts in cases claiming due-process violations. And his forceful conclusion made clear his disagreement with the *Lochner* majority:

> The question for the courts is not whether the problems have been wisely answered, but whether they can be answered at all, or whether they are taboo. So far as concerns laws limiting the hours of work, the present position seems quite untenable.

The decisive factor, he insisted, was that reasonable persons differed about the economic merits of such laws, and this threw "the whole matter open for exclusive consideration, and for exclusive determination, by the legislature, unless the Court is to step out of the role of interpreter of the Constitution and to decide the question itself as another legislature."[76] Not only was free-market economic theory[77] too amorphous and controversial to be an adequate guide; more important, the very attempt to evaluate the wisdom of protective laws was simply beyond the competence of the judges:

In short, the whole matter is yet to such an extent experimental that no one can with justice apply to the concrete problems the yardstick of abstract economic theory. We do not know, and we cannot for a long time learn, what are the total results of such "meddlesome interference with the rights of the individual." . . . The only way in which the right, or the wrong, of the matter may be shown, is by experiment; and the legislature, with its paraphernalia of committee and commission, is the only public representative really fitted to experiment. That the legislature may be moved by faction, and without justice, is very true, but so may even the court. There is an inevitable bias upon such vital questions in all men, and the courts are certainly recruited from a class which has its proper bias, like the rest.[78]

Hand's clear implication that the justices in the *Lochner* majority were reading their economic biases into the Constitution went further than most commentators were willing to go. But Hand had the youthful courage to speak out. A fervent plea for judicial restraint, a strong endorsement of legislative power to engage in experimentation, a sharp attack on exercises of judicial authority in the *Lochner* mode—these were Hand's central themes.

Hand set forth his supporting arguments succinctly and lucidly. In a passage revealing his deep convictions about the dangers of permitting judges to consider the wisdom or expediency of challenged laws, he stated:

Whether it be wise or not that there should be a third camera with a final veto upon legislation with whose economic or political expediency it totally disagrees, is a political question of the highest importance. In particular it is questionable whether such a power can endure in a democratic state, while the court retains the irresponsibility of a life tenure, and while its decisions can be reversed only by the cumbersome process of a change of the federal Constitution. . . . [I]f the court is to retain the absolute right to pass . . . on the expediency of statutes passed by the legislature, the difficulty is inherent and in the end it may demand some change, either in the court or in the Constitution.[79]

The risk, in short, was that the *Lochner* philosophy allowed unelected, politically unaccountable judges to decide whether a particular legislative purpose was or was not legitimate. Courts, Hand argued, were not super-legislatures: they exceeded their legitimate powers unless they deferred to elected legislatures on debatable issues.

Hand's second line of attack drew on his readings in economic theory. He argued that it was justifiable to restrict hours of labor, for this promoted the economic welfare of workers. Could it really be claimed that the protective laws made no contribution to that welfare, either under classic free-market theories or under more modern, paternalistic ones? In this part of his essay, Hand invoked recent "trades-unionist theory" and cited a book he had recently read, *Industrial Democracy*, by the British Fabian socialists Sidney and Beatrice Webb. So long as the economic arguments for a law existed, he insisted, that was "as far as the court can inquire." Nor were restraints on contract merely a fiction of socialist theory. Following Holmes, Hand cited the unquestioned validity of usury laws and argued further: "For the state to intervene to make more just and equal the relative strategic advantages of the two parties to the contract, of whom one is under the pressure of absolute want, while the other is not, is as proper a legislative function as that it should neutralize the relative advantages arising from fraudulent cunning or from superior physical force."[80] Hand had evidently broadened his intellectual horizons; his article showed a heightened empathy for the economic and social arguments supporting a more interventionist role for the state.

Hand's essay elicited considerable attention and helped to make him attractive to those eager to place more articulate and independent individuals on the bench. A few years later, C. C. Burlingham would put it well in writing to President William Howard Taft's attorney general, George W. Wickersham, on behalf of another promising young New York intellectual, Van Vechten Veeder.[81] C.C.B. told Wickersham that Veeder, although not well known at the bar, had a reputation as a fine writer: "I admit that in a way creates a prejudice against him because ordinary New York lawyers, worshipping at the shrine of Efficiency and Dispatch, are rather shy of learning."[82] But, he insisted, an eloquent writing style, combined with a good mind, should be considered an attractive trait in a judicial nominee. A man who could write well *and* think well, turn out the work, and had a modicum of good sense to boot—such phrases described Hand even better than they did Veeder. And when C.C.B. made a similar appeal to Wickersham in Hand's case, it succeeded equally well, in part because of the trenchancy and eloquence Hand had demonstrated in criticizing the *Lochner* approach.

HAND'S QUEST FOR A FEDERAL JUDGESHIP began in 1907, when at the age of thirty-five he became convinced that success on Wall

Street was forever out of reach. As it happened, a misunderstood remark by the person who most strongly opposed Hand's quest first sparked Learned's interest: during a brief visit to New York City in March 1907, Frederick Fincke mentioned that a federal judge he knew was planning to retire, and added cryptically that it might be nice if someone in the family filled the vacancy; Hand thought he was the family member Fincke had in mind and, shortly after Fincke returned to Utica, wrote that he was eager to try for the federal bench.[83]

Fincke replied the next day with a hasty but vehement six-page letter. His "casual remark," he wrote, concerned "a U.S. *Circuit*, not *District*, Court judgeship," and more important, he explained, "I had myself in mind, not you, when I spoke of [the] vacant place." Besides, he assured Learned, he had spoken "all in jest": "as you know I would not take the place if offered to me on a gold platter."

Fincke's arguments against Hand's consideration of a judgeship were, typically, mainly financial: it was simply "absurd & indeed impossible" for a man of "first class ability" to settle for a $6,000 judicial salary unless he was independently wealthy. And despite his inheritance from his uncle Clifford Hand, Learned was not independently wealthy; all that he could count on beyond his salary was about $9,000 a year. Once again, Fincke urged that "patience & time" on Wall Street would ultimately bring riches. And the rewards of a law partnership, Fincke argued, were "far worthier" than a mere judgeship: "The invisible, intangible & largely theoretical honor of the place has no audience with me," he exclaimed. "It does not buy houses, maintain them, educate children, or afford them a fair start in life." To give up on law practice for a mere $6,000 salary, he bluntly told Learned, was "suicidal."[84]

Fincke's accusation that Hand was contemplating a cowardly flight from the pursuit of material success touched some of Learned's deepest self-doubts. More than ever, Hand felt that in his father-in-law's eyes he was only a pale shadow of the model set by the more ambitious Fincke children. (As Fincke would pointedly note in a letter to Frances the next day, his son, Rex, had curbed his impatience at the outset of his career, had absorbed his father's advocacy of the "doctrine" of patience, and had become a successful stockbroker—"he believed me, kept the faith & look at him now.")

These aspects of Fincke's angry sermons were familiar: they resembled the recurrent messages Learned received from Utica whenever he expressed dissatisfaction with law practice. But Fincke's admonitions this time contained a novel ingredient that Learned found especially difficult to accept. Fincke saw no countervailing value in the alternative Hand was considering: he could not perceive anything truly worthwhile in a judgeship. For Hand, a judgeship had very powerful, affirmative attractions, but Fincke apparently did not understand this part of his son-in-law's makeup at all.

These criticisms were only the opening salvo. After mailing his letter on Saturday, March 9, Fincke tossed and turned all night, worrying that only stronger words could convey the depth of his antipathy toward a judgeship. He had enough self-possession to realize that another letter to Learned would be too heavy-handed. Still, he decided, he could write to his daughter, and he did so the next morning.[85] Frances, after all, was always more receptive to her father's materialistic appeals and, pregnant with her second child, would surely be susceptible to arguments relating to the financial needs of a growing family. And Fincke knew that anything he wrote to Frances would reach Learned. Indeed, by the time he got to the end of his seven-page letter, he had apparently forgotten he was not addressing Learned directly. By then, the "you" was clearly Hand himself:

> I feel so deeply about it that I must butt in as I have in this letter—& put myself on record. . . . My advice is to stay where you are, give up any idea of change, be patient & wait & look out every minute for your own advantage & press it when it comes, but always in the place you are in . . . & never tolerate the suggestion of a change unless it implies *large & certain* betterment. If you do this, the result in a few years will make you wonder that you ever considered seriously a place at $6,000 per year.

To his daughter, Fincke explained that he had written Learned the day before "in hot haste," but not "nearly strongly enough." To give up practice after only a few years, "to lie down supinely and give up the fight," was "the height of folly." Nothing about a judgeship warranted such a decision:

> It looks like quitting to me to take the same [salary] plus some alleged honor, rather than to fight it out & reach infinitely larger rewards. . . . [At best, he will gain] only $1,000 per year & the ermine, which is largely cotton batten, with burnt cork marks on it for tails—& that's the end—at 35.

For his pregnant daughter, the shrewd Fincke added an especially effective argument: to seek a judgeship might "perhaps" be defensible if the aspirant were thinking simply about "himself & wife"—"but for their children, no." Fifteen thousand dollars a year—Learned's salary plus the inheritance—was simply not enough "to educate two or three children at good preparatory schools & college & professional schools."

And a federal trial judge "cannot do for his boys, if he has boys, as a lawyer in full practice & with clients in all the walks of life. He is practically like a college professor, so far as the world & men are concerned. Now what would you gain by the change . . . ?"

Learned Hand winced in the face of his father-in-law's outbursts, but held his ground. Patiently he stated and restated his views, and perhaps sensing that his own efforts might not persuade his father-in-law, he enlisted his cousin Gus to write Fincke and plead the case.[86] Even though Fincke considered Gus not much less woolly-headed than Learned,[87] Gus's letter was both blunt and shrewd: "I think you are wrong and do not realize the position that a federal judgeship gives a young man here in New York," he argued. "I think [Learned] would make an ideal judge and is better fitted to do judicial work than to be a business lawyer." He only nodded at the honor of a judicial post, though, and spent most of his letter arguing that Learned could cash in on it. Although he knew perfectly well that Learned had no such aspiration, Gus assured Fincke that Learned could ultimately return to a far more lucrative practice than he'd leave. Thus, from a career standpoint, a judgeship could be a useful stepping-stone that "would hasten [Learned's] success more than anything he can do."[88]

Fincke was not persuaded, by Gus or by Learned. But he was a devoted family man, unswervingly loyal to his children and their families. Thus, even as he urged Learned to abandon his quest, he promised him all possible assistance should Learned insist on pursuing the appointment.

Fincke was at his best as a skillful adviser. He admired those who "not only know, but also know how," and recurrently urged Learned to emulate the practical men of affairs while seeking a judgeship: "[G]et to work, stop all philosophizing, argument, weighing of the pros & cons, & don't approach the problem as a judge, for you are not a judge, but as a politician, starting the right measures through the right men & the right way to succeed, whether or not they are the ideal steps to be taken to produce such a result or not."[89] Federal judges, he recognized, were selected by political officials, typically on the basis of connections. Learned's intellectual friends were interested in politics, but as civic reformers they were despised by the political machines that could make or break an appointment. Despite his claim that as "an upstate farmer" he was not very familiar with city politics, Fincke proved to be the best source of advice on whom to contact.

The most important local politician to enlist, Fincke thought, was Congressman Herbert Parsons: "My notion would be to have your cause taken up by Parsons, through [Charles] Burlingham or some like person who can reach Parsons."[90] Parsons was indeed the most influential Republican in the city, and he carried special weight in Washington as President Roosevelt's trusted guide through the morass of New York City politics. But Hand was uncomfortable about soliciting Parsons: he had opposed Parsons's use of family wealth in his congressional campaigns. Not surprisingly, Parsons was no direct help to Hand at all.

Fincke also recommended that Hand enlist "friends" to support his cause, so long as they were "practical" friends "like [George] Wickersham, Henry Taft, [New York lawyer James] Byrne, et omne genus & not such chaps as Charlie Barlow & Gus Hand." He advised that once Parsons (or "the next most influential politician") was lined up, "the candidacy & the recommendation should be pressed upon the President by the Secy. of War [William Howard Taft], through his brother Henry & every one else who has weight with the Secy. & also by anyone & everyone who has personal influence with the President."[91] Learned must have felt quite helpless in the face of these recommendations. He barely knew President Roosevelt. Secretary of War Taft, whom Learned had met briefly in visits to Murray Bay, probably remembered little about him. Taft's brother Henry was a New York lawyer whom friends such as Burlingham might reach, but Hand did not know him well either. Moreover, Learned would have difficulty coming up with anyone else with "weight with the Secy." other than an old Albany acquaintance, Brigadier General Robert Shaw Oliver, who had become assistant secretary of war under Taft. His father-in-law's counsel could not but remind Learned how much of an uphill struggle he faced.

Fincke offered to use his own influence as soon as the groundwork was laid by others. He promised that he would "not hesitate to take" Learned's candidacy to the president, with "my personal request that not only for you & for the good of the courts, but also as something very near & dear to my own heart, he should make the appointment."[92] But Fincke's clout was weaker than he thought: Taft felt bound by the political structure, and apparently the failure of Congressman Parsons to endorse Hand was a critical omission. Fincke's interpretation of this setback was perhaps self-serving: he pointedly noted, when he told Learned of the president's discouraging response at the beginning of May, "As I told you at the very start, Parsons is the influence to get —Chas Burlingham, Henry Taft, et al, are all well enough—but as I said & supposed, Parsons is the real toad in the puddle."[93]

Yet Learned Hand's aspiration in 1907 was not an impossible dream. His competition did not seem insurmountable. While ordinarily the strongest claimants would be those well connected to the Republican organization, most of the gossip focused on reform lawyers. Lorenzo Semple, long a leader of the Citizens Union, looked like the strongest rival, for he had recently left that organization to become "an active adherent of Herbert Parsons," and he had a reputation for ability and integrity. The other aspirant, Samuel H. Ordway, was even more prominent in good-government circles, although he lacked Semple's political connections. Gus described him as "a lawyer of some ability, about 48 years old, a great civil service reformer and general kicker." Ordway mustered some support from "certain friends of the President," but he did not impress Gus as the "type of man that the President will care for in the least, as he is too much of a 'goo-goo.' "[94]

Against this competition, Hand had a genuine chance. Despite his youth (at thirty-five, he was younger than his rivals), the other contenders were not men of great political influence. The practical Gus thought Learned's chances fairly good from the outset:

> I do not think Semple has any strong following, though I believe both he and Ordway are good lawyers and would be good judges. It would seem to me under the conditions, that if no other candidates appear having strong political claims, Learned ought to have a chance, and I am entirely convinced that he will make a much stronger judge than either of the men under consideration.[95]

But in 1907, Hand and his competitors were chasing after a mirage: there was in fact no vacancy in the Southern District of New York; New York City lawyers had assumed Congress would establish a new judgeship, but no such bill was introduced. Yet Hand's efforts were by no means futile. When, in February 1909, Congress authorized a new judgeship at last in the Southern District, his experience stood Hand in good stead.

At the turn of the century, there had been only a single federal trial judge in Manhattan. For a decade, Congress heard pleas and conducted studies regarding the court's workload and the need for added personnel; in 1903, a second judgeship was created, and in 1906 a third. Although extensive statistics gathered by a House committee in 1906 led observers to expect a fourth in 1907, the new judgeship that finally materialized in 1909 came after another, even more extensive committee report.

Ironically, it was Congressman Parsons who took the lead on the floor in urging his colleagues to act, arguing that the need in the Southern District of New York was greater than in either Pennsylvania or Washington, where new judgeships had just been approved.[96] As one of his colleagues put it, the Southern District was "the federal district having the largest population and doing the most business in the United States," and a new judge was "absolutely necessary."[97] The House overwhelmingly approved the Parsons bill on February 16, 1909; less than a week later, the Senate agreed;[98] on March 2, President Roosevelt signed the bill just two days before leaving office.[99] The new president, William Howard Taft, had the opportunity to fill the new vacancy.

Hand reentered the competition without hesitation. His irritations with Gould & Wilkie had increased in the intervening two years. Within weeks of his 1907 hopes being dashed, moreover, he had taken steps to improve his chances: mindful of his weak political connections, he joined his neighborhood Republican Club in late May 1907,[100] and during the 1908 election campaign, he volunteered as a speaker for the Republican County Committee's Speakers Bureau. (Early in October, he received his first and apparently last assignment: he was asked to join William M. Chadbourne, another Wall Street lawyer, at the Metropolitan Temple on Fourteenth Street and Seventh Avenue in supporting the proposition "That the Expenditures of the National Government During the Last Administration Have Been Justified by the Results Achieved.")[101] But such gestures hardly qualified Hand as an active party man. His candidacy would turn, as it had before, on his reputation as an independent intellectual, and he would succeed only if he were recommended by bar leaders, above all if the new administration stood ready to withstand political attacks on a merit appointment.

Fortunately for Hand, quality appointments were a high priority for the new administration. This nonpartisan zeal is surprising in light of Taft's later reputation. By 1912, when Theodore Roosevelt bolted the Republicans to form his Progressive party, Taft was cast as a conservative party loyalist warding off the assaults of a reform-minded insurgent, but at the outset of his term, he was eager to establish his independence and was, indeed, more ready to defy the party organization than Roosevelt had been.

One of President Taft's first acts was to select George Wickersham as attorney general. Wickersham, a law partner of Henry Taft, the president's brother and political confidant, was a distinguished Wall Street lawyer at the height of his career; he had built his reputation by defending corporate interests, especially railroads and banks. But as the president no doubt knew from his brother, Wickersham was no lackey: he was outspoken and energetic, and though he had long been valued as a Republican adviser, his counsel was high-minded and reform-oriented rather than narrowly political. Taft chose him in part because

Wickersham, with his intimate knowledge of corporate practices, might be an especially effective enforcer of antitrust laws. Taft's hopes were fulfilled: despite Roosevelt's trust-busting reputation, the Taft administration brought more actions against leading corporations than the Roosevelt regime had in nearly twice the time.[102]

The accession of a reformist president and an independent attorney general encouraged Hand's aspirations. He knew Wickersham (although he was hardly a close friend); more important, Henry Taft was a supporter. And crucially, Burlingham knew both Wickersham and Henry Taft well and was eager to support Hand enthusiastically. As soon as Wickersham made clear that he was looking for quality candidates, Hand supporters—especially the bar leaders whom Wickersham respected—conveyed their recommendations.

Hand's second campaign for a judgeship proved mercifully shorter than the first and far less abrasive within the family. Frederick Fincke no more shared his son-in-law's dreams than he had before, but in 1909 there was little opportunity to hammer Learned about the glories of the New York bar. Fincke was still not ready to abandon his opposition, however:

> You can't get too much honor & distinction for me, provided only you don't get the judgeship. . . . [A]spire & aspire & don't stop at District Judge. . . . State Judge. Judge of [New York] Ct. of Appeals. U.S. Circuit Judge. Judge of the U.S. Supreme Court; only don't by any slip-up *land*. Keep them all fastened to yr. head & put ahead of yr nose & yr time will come as sure as trees make shingles, when you can have what you want & can afford to take it, which in my judgment, you cannot now.[103]

But these acidulous remarks did not deter his now confident and resolute son-in-law. On April 1, Hand wrote that the attorney general was urging the president to submit his name to the Senate.[104]

Charles C. Burlingham deserved, claimed, and received much of the credit for Hand's nomination: after all, he was Hand's closest friend among senior New York lawyers, and he had Wickersham's ear.[105] But Wickersham was the critical element in fulfilling Hand's dream. Felix Frankfurter, then a promising young assistant United States attorney in the Southern District, portrayed the situation thus when he recalled it many years later:

> In sponsoring Learned Hand's appointment . . . , Attorney General Wickersham showed a keen scent for intellectual powers and a realization of their need particularly on the federal bench. Learned

Hand would hardly have appeared as an inevitable choice had there been deference to the usual considerations guiding the selection of federal judges. While the discerning were at once excited by Mr. Wickersham's bold recommendation of Hand to President Taft, it took the pedestrian members of the profession some time to make their adjustment to this new planet in the judicial sky.[106]

Hand's nomination provoked a flood of congratulatory letters. Some of these must surely have stirred Learned's old anxieties about his self-worth, for among their words of satisfaction they reminded him that he had a weighty legal and judicial tradition to emulate.[107] Still, most of the correspondence was genuinely warm and some of it was especially perceptive. For example, Fred Townsend wrote as soon as he learned the "glorious news" from Hand's mother: "Of course, I am delighted because you wanted it & because it is a good thing in itself for you any way you look at it. You will be a good judge for one thing & I fancy you will find the point of view more congenial than that of the advocate."[108]

Even Fincke responded with real generosity and warmth: "I congratulate you unconditionally, unreservedly & sincerely. . . . I am proud of you to my fingertips. You will realize for me my ideal of what a judge should be, an ideal almost obliterated by my frequent contact with the courts—To be sure you have sacrificed a great lawyer but only to make a greater judge." Fincke abandoned almost overnight his long-held reservations about Learned's ability to support a family on a judge's salary:

> It's all right from my point of view. You can afford it, which some of them can't. While the salary is wickedly small, it is substantial and with what you inherited from your lawyer father & lawyer uncle, guarantees a comfortable and even liberal upkeep for the kids. It's up to me to add ultimately to the family store when my life's action has been dismissed with costs. . . . Surely I am a most fortunate man & envy no one—with such sons and daughters what could I have more? The family circle is small, B, but thank God it is intimate, loving & loyal—not a peasant in the lot.[109]

Hand joined in the celebratory spirit, despite his reservations. Thanking James Byrne for his important support, for example, Hand acknowledged:

> I believe that this opportunity is a very fine one, if I am man enough to discharge the duties. If not, the sooner that is understood

the better, but I have hopes that it will go after some time of trial. Of course, it means to abandon the chance for much temporal return. That is a kind of sacrifice I have imposed [upon my family]. It has many times occurred to me to wonder whether some day they may ask what was the quid pro quo to them, but at least I may say to you what I can't say to others who know less about me, that if perhaps they will lose more than seems [now] in prospect, it is still very prospective and there was no present cash value to surrender. . . . As for me personally, this is what I want; now I only want to justify the authorities who appointed me and to satisfy my friends that there has not been a blunder.[110]

But Hand soon succumbed to anxiety. The president's submission of the nomination to the Senate produced nothing but silence from Capitol Hill as April passed, and this mysterious delay intensely worried Hand. Fred Townsend expected that Hand would lapse into brooding. "[Y]ou are such a nervous case," he had written Learned before,[111] and now he assumed that "with your 'neurotic' pessimism, you worried some over the delay in your confirmation." He had heard that Hand's "mother had [worried]," and commented, "[I]f she did you must have."[112]

In fact, Hand had little to worry about. The explanation for the Senate's inaction lay in Attorney General Wickersham's Washington inexperience, his independence of political channels, and his occasional "tactlessness."[113] Preoccupied with seeking merit appointments, Wickersham had ignored the long-standing courtesy of consulting the New York senators before submitting the nomination.[114] This breach of political etiquette stung the pride of the senior senator from New York, Chauncey M. Depew. Depew was a Republican stalwart, a candidate for the presidential nomination in 1888 who had achieved great success as a corporate lawyer and entrepreneur. He was especially not a person to slight, because he sat on the Senate Judiciary Committee, which processed judicial nominations.[115]

Depew learned of Hand's nomination not from the attorney general but from the newspapers. He had assumed that the new president would "follow the custom observed by all Presidents prior to Mr. Roosevelt in making appointments: namely, to consult in advance the senators from the state where the vacancies existed." Yet the Taft administration, to the growing annoyance of organization Republicans, was flouting tradition.[116] Accordingly, Depew would not lift a finger to move Hand's nomination along. Jealous of their prerogatives, the committee members decided that "[u]nless a Senator [could] vouch for the standing, ability and general worthiness of an appointee," the committee would not act.

As a result, they set aside any further consideration of the nomination. Meanwhile, the hostility of congressional Republican stalwarts hardened, as it became clearer that the Taft administration was even less inclined than Roosevelt's had been to handle nominations through traditional political channels.

But Attorney General Wickersham's feistiness was not so readily suppressed. A few weeks later—Hand's New York friends had expressed their concern about the Senate's inaction—Wickersham telephoned Senator Depew "and in an agitated voice inquired why Hand's nomination had not been confirmed." Depew coldly replied, "Chiefly because the New York senators know nothing about Mr. Hand." Wickersham would not be silenced: with barely curbed impatience, he "explained at great length that he knew all about Judge Hand; that he had been acquainted with him for years, and had watched his rise with pride and satisfaction; in short, that he had selected Mr. Hand for this place himself because of his special fitness for it." Senator Depew decided that the better part of valor lay in retreat. Wickersham's intensity, and his recital of the support Hand had attracted from Depew's own colleagues on Wall Street, no doubt persuaded him that Hand's nomination was not the occasion for obstructionism. He thanked Wickersham and allowed that the information he had conveyed was, at last, "satisfactory." Depew's consent provoked a prompt favorable vote in the Judiciary Committee; soon after, the Senate confirmed Learned Hand's nomination as United States district judge for the Southern District of New York, and on April 30, 1909, Hand took his judicial oath and donned his robe at last.[117]

GRATIFIED AS HE WAS by the support of his friends and the realization of his dream, Hand could not shake one nagging doubt: Could he satisfy his supporters' expectations, let alone the impossible ones he set for himself?

This doubt never wholly left Hand during his fifty-two years on the federal bench, and his anxiety was especially strong at the beginning. One source of his worries was the memory of his long-dead father, a memory that was more of a myth than of a reality. Samuel Hand had served as a judge for a few months, and his few judicial opinions were no more than workmanlike. Still, many of the congratulatory notes on Learned's appointment recalled Samuel Hand's reputation and made Learned feel that his obligation as Samuel's only son was to emulate his father's (exaggerated) achievements. His mother was the chief offender here. In her uncharacteristically happy letter about her son's appointment, she could not help exclaiming, "Oh! the memories of past days have been very hard to bear—your father's delight to see his son, his darling, distinguished would have filled his heart with pride & joy."[118]

One expression of Hand's response to his arrival on the bench, in May and June 1909, can be found in a series of letters he dutifully sent to his mother in Albany. Ever the obedient, devoted, solicitous son, he wrote her almost daily; when work pressures caused him to miss a day, he apologized, guiltily and profusely. Even at the age of thirty-seven, seven years after his marriage and move to New York, he was still very much in her grip. Her mixture of physical and psychological complaints, her suspicion of anyone who threatened to wrong him, and even her attempts at encouragement spun the silken threads that tied Learned to her.

Lydia Coit Hand's letters to Learned were filled with worries about his health, her own aches, and every cold that beset a family member. "I wonder what next," she once exclaimed after reciting her latest litany. "I am feeling rather shaky—you know what a weak woman I am and always inclined to look on the dark side."[119] She suffered from the usual physical pains of advancing age, but the far more wearisome source of her complaints was "nerves." As she would repeatedly tell Learned, "I have had a very hard time with my nerves & sleeplessness."[120] "Nervousness" and "sleeplessness" were traits she passed on to her son, and her own maladies helped to increase his. When anyone in the family fell ill, she would write, "You can imagine my frantic state."[121] Even in a rare moment when she acknowledged happiness, as when she learned of Wickersham's support of Hand's nomination, she could not resist opening her letter with a recurrent refrain: "[T]wo Seconal tablets did not give me the sleep I should have had."[122]

Their correspondence well reflects the difficulties Learned had in his relationship with his mother.[123] When he mentioned fatigue, she admonished him to get more sleep; when he noted the wearying repetition of some kinds of cases, she suspected that his seniors were assigning especially boring ones to him; even after he had been on the bench for nearly two years, his relief on finishing a task led her to wonder, "Does [judging] weigh on you more than office work & do you fear it [may be] too much for you?"[124] Hand knew she was inclined to "see the dark side" in his reports, and he made some effort to avoid stirring her worries, but he never quite succeeded: it was nearly impossible to relate his work day by day without arousing her concern; perhaps, too, after years of maternal coddling he needed to elicit her sympathetic reactions.

The greatest importance to us of Hand's reports to his mother lies in their clear expression of his anxiety about his new tasks. During the second week of his judgeship, for example, he briefly filled in for the federal judge in Rutland, Vermont. He found that this produced "plenty of work for all my waking moments," and worried whether he would have time to get it all done. During an account of one of his earliest trials, a case that proceeded "very peaceably," as he told her, he echoed her nervousness: the absence of courtroom confrontations, he admitted, gave "a great rest to my nerves, for I find that when the lawyers fight it sets me all on edge and is very wearing."[125]

From Vermont, he headed back to New York City, to settle down to his court work there and to attend a celebration of his appointment at a dinner given "by twelve lawyers who used to meet together long ago" as members of the old "no name" club whose sessions had opened up the vistas of New York intellectual life for him years earlier.[126] But continuous exposure to trial court work in New York City made him very dissatisfied with himself: "I find that I am kept very busy with the work and I do not really satisfy myself with the way I discharge it," he told his mother.

> Perhaps I do it as well as I can be expected to, but it seems to me as though most everything that comes up I really do not know, and I have a sort of feeling that I talk too much. I hope, as time goes on, I shall feel a little better contented with the way I am doing, and no doubt I shall find myself in time, though it will probably take a good while.

He found it especially uncomfortable to decide so many issues that one could only "guess at": "[I]t is unpleasant when you do not have time really to familiarize yourself with the work."[127]

Two quite distinct problems underlay these concerns. One is common to most new judges, particularly those who, like Hand, had limited courtroom experience. The United States, unlike most countries, has never had a professional judiciary; practitioners come to the bench without training in judging. Only experience can teach the new American judge how to steer through the complexities of trial procedures and preside calmly over a lawsuit. The difficulty is aggravated for new federal judges, who are often unfamiliar with the specialties of federal judicial business. Although the range of problems before federal courts in 1909 was narrower than it is today, judges then did deal with many issues: problems of torts, contracts, and other fields of common law— with which most new appointees were likely to be acquainted from their law practice—but also more esoteric federal fields such as bankruptcy, patent, copyright, and admiralty. Hand had no familiarity with any of these.

The second problem was still more difficult. While experience had taught Hand how a courtroom is run and had acquainted him with federal law, the need "to decide so many things" that he could only "guess at," without adequate opportunity for study and reflection, would always trouble him. When presiding over a trial, the judge must often shoot from the hip, issuing immediate rulings from the bench that grant or deny motions, determine admissibility of evidence, and in general keep the proceeding going without long pauses for studying and writing an opinion on a controverted issue. This aspect of the work was especially uncongenial to a person as thorough, and sometimes indecisive, as Learned Hand—the man whom Felix Frankfurter occasionally called "the modern Hamlet."[128]

After his first few weeks on the bench, Hand had reason to regret the candor of his reports to his mother. She pounced on every sign of fatigue or anxiety as an indication that a terrible fate had befallen him. Even when Learned assured her that he was "getting the hang of it a little better" and that once he got used to his work, "I believe I shall like it extremely, much better than anything else I have done,"[129] she seized upon his confessions that judging required enormous energy. Occasionally he became testy: "You rather misinterpreted what I said about my work," he once told her with some impatience. True, his new job placed "a good deal of strain" upon him and left him "tired," but he expected the burdens to ease as he became more accustomed to them.[130]

In his early weeks, the pressure to issue on-the-spot rulings troubled Hand; and always, the dilatory tactics of lawyers annoyed him: "A good deal of my time is wasted, in view of the fact that the attorneys take so long to try their cases. The whole matter could often times be disposed of in about half the time they take, but I can't do more than sit still and listen."[131] Formulating his charges to juries added to the pressures. He sought to follow the law and produce lucid instructions, yet also hoped to steer the jury panel toward just decisions—not always successfully. As he reported to his mother in late May:

> I have produced about the results that I had thought just and wanted to produce until today, when I could not get the jury to bring in a verdict for the defendant, who had killed a man with his automobile. Of course, they are perfectly free to do as they think best and I have no right in any way to control their judgment

on the facts, but I was rather in hopes that as I had charged them they would take my view of the matter, which was, that the defendant was entirely blameless. However, as they disagreed, that perhaps is not a very bad result, the only difference being that nothing has been accomplished and precious time has been wasted. . . . My mind seems to be full of law and nothing but law all the while, even at night.[132]

Early in June, he was assigned to handle bankruptcy cases for the first time—cases that produced more than half of his written opinions during his first year on the bench. After a day of it, he reported to his mother, "I seem to be all tired out, but I have recovered now, and I think that after a little I shall get along well."[133] Promptly, his mother asked who was responsible for heaping such difficult work upon him. "It is not that the bankruptcy cases are more difficult to decide than others," he replied patiently, "only there are so many of them, and I get mixed up; and besides that, I am constantly interrupted by people who come in asking usually for what they ought not to have." All he had tried to say, he explained, was that "the strain of four hours' attention to one thing after another and being talked at continually was very wearing, but I think that was only because it was the first, and I am enjoying it a great deal."[134]

In his passing remark about interruptions by those "asking usually for what they ought not to have," Hand tried to make light of a problem that in fact he took very seriously. When creditors of insolvent businesses asked a court to appoint a receiver to manage and wind up the insolvent's estate, federal judges traditionally appointed private lawyers.[135] Appointment as a receiver was considered a plum by attorneys eager to supplement their incomes, and political pressures on judges to appoint loyal clubhouse workers were a routine aspect of the patronage system. Hand was the rare judge who had not been appointed because of his political connections, but he was not exempt from these pressures. As he wrote to C. C. Burlingham, more frankly than he had to his mother:

I wish some benevolent person would abolish the power to appoint receivers and substitute standing receivers [permanent functionaries], like the referees. I find that I have about half my time taken up by obsequious gentlemen who come in with letters either from Herbert Parsons, who did the best he could to keep me out, or the politicians to whom my appointment must be equally grateful.[136]

For years, Hand struggled with these annoying requests for political favors. He tried his best to appoint receivers only on the basis of merit, and he repeatedly pressed for reform of the system, without success.

The flood of cases involving business failures, bankruptcies as well as receiverships, was ever more time-consuming and irksome. Soon he told his mother, "I am afraid that I am slowly dropping behind in the work, which is piling on at great length. I have simply got to do it in the best way I can without elaborating too much, or I shall be over-whelmed." But he quickly caught himself: he did not want to stir a new round of worries, and so he reassured her, "I enjoy it more than I can tell you." Yet he conceded that "I am getting pretty tired. . . . It would be all right if I could only sleep without dreaming about the pesky stuff, but after a day like yesterday my sleep consists mainly of hearing arguments on various things that have come up before me, and that is not very restful."[137] (He wrote the letter from which this passage comes after a four-day gap in his correspondence, for which he profusely apologized.)

By his second month on the bench, Hand began to feel more comfortable. When he took on his "first patent case," he was able to acknowledge without any great agony that "naturally, I knew absolutely nothing about the whole subject."[138] Patent cases, common grist for the federal judicial mill of the day, required extensive study of complex mechanical and chemical descriptions. While Hand had never shown much technological or scientific aptitude, nor had he ever handled any patent case in his law practice, he soon produced some of the most meticulous and probing patent opinions extant, and before long achieved a reputation as one of the nation's great patent judges.

By late June, Hand reported, "I am working quite constantly now, but it does not seem anything like as hard as it used to." True, there was a "cloud on the horizon: As it gets less hard it seems a little less interesting [and] the last few days have been rather uninteresting, as the subject was itself quite dull."[139] But this was an unusual commentary; not until later years did the boring aspects of his work produce a recurrent feeling that he was engaging in mere "crossword puzzles."

This letter was the last of the sequence of reports Hand sent to his mother during his early weeks as a judge. Soon after, she went to Europe for a year, and he wrote less frequently. But his devotion to and attendance upon her did not diminish. Frances pretty well ignored her, although Lydia was free with advice about how Frances should raise her children, what she should do about nurses and maids, et cetera. Almost all of Learned's visits to his mother's in Albany were made by him alone, without Frances or the children—but they were regular visits until Lydia's death in the early 1920s.

IN ONE OF HAND'S recurrent efforts to allay his mother's concerns, he told her that he had moved into newly painted permanent chambers that assured a "very fresh and clean," "much more comfortable" working environment. There was little sunlight, but that was "a commodity very scarce in the downtown district of New York." In any event, his new working space meant "I shall have as much [room] as I had at any time in Gould & Wilkie's and I think, indeed, a little more."[140] In fact, however, his quarters were not so cheerful. Throughout his fifteen years on the district court, he labored in surroundings that symbolized the low, unappreciated position of the federal trial judge of his day. The environment was shabby, the salary low, and he was compelled to plead repeatedly for books, furniture, and even typewriter ribbons.[141]

When Hand took his seat, the federal trial court was housed in the dingy old Post Office–Court Building at the south end of City Hall Park in lower Manhattan. The building had been unattractive even when it opened in 1875; by 1909, it had become a "dilapidated" place "disfiguring" the adjacent park.[142] Throughout his years on the court, Hand complained about the gloomy, "antiquated and inadequate building."[143] The limited space on the fourth floor of the Post Office–Court Building was insufficient as the court's caseload mounted and the number of judges grew. Bar association reports urged that plans be made to replace the court accommodations "universally recognized as disgraceful,"[144] but all the government would do for the judges was to rent additional space, on the twelfth floor of the nearby Woolworth Building. In 1914, Hand moved his chambers just across Broadway to this recently completed, handsome skyscraper, then the world's tallest.[145] Eventually, all the district judges joined him there, but the courtrooms remained divided between the two buildings.[146]

The low priority the government gave to the needs of federal judges was reflected even more clearly in its provisions for their salaries and staff assistance. Hand's salary was $6,000 when he took his seat. With his inheritances added on, he could get by on that well enough, but the amount was insufficient for judges whose sole income it was, and several federal judges resigned to seek better income in private practice.[147] When World War I prompted a sharp rise in the cost of living, Hand had to plead with the Justice Department to authorize a salary increase for his stenographer, so that her income might remain reasonably competitive.[148] But for himself, the lack of a pay raise mainly constituted a symbol of the government's disregard for judges' needs.[149] He was not prepared to accept a small increase as a sop: when Congress considered a judicial pay raise from $6,000 to $7,500, Hand opposed it, arguing that the bill would postpone for years consideration of a just raise.

To Hand, the government's failure to provide sufficient staff assistance was at least as annoying. He was entitled only to his stenographer, at a salary of $1,000 a year. There was as yet no system of hiring recent law school graduates to serve as personal assistants, do legal research, and help on opinions. The lack of professional assistance was especially significant to as scholarly a judge as Hand, and he quickly sought to remedy the problem with an innovative solution. Hand was decades ahead of his time when, in 1909, the day after he was nominated to the judgeship and weeks before he was confirmed, he turned to the law schools for a recent graduate who could help out with correspondence and other office tasks.[150] He asked his onetime property teacher at Harvard Law School, John Chipman Gray: Was there a graduating senior with some office skills to serve as his legal assistant?[151] Hand suspected, and Gray confirmed, that the pickings would be slim: all Hand could offer was the $1,000-a-year position as "stenographer." But Hand was ready to take his chances in this "experiment," in the interest of finding legal help from someone who might also, on the side, do the little clerical work he required. Gray recommended, and Hand promptly hired, a young Mainer, Ralph L. Collett (the only one of Hand's early legal assistants who was in fact "a first-rate stenographer," though he was hardly "a brilliant man").[152] The experiment worked well enough so that, in April 1910, Hand wrote Gray that he was "anxious to continue" the practice.[153] Gray urged Hand to consider Richard M. Hallet, concededly a "B man," not "remarkable," not trained in stenography, but at least an "honest, straightforward fellow." Though Gray was apologetic about recommending Hallet,[154] he turned out to be the most successful of Hand's early law clerks. Hallet was the last law clerk Gray managed to produce: by 1911, he could find no one willing to forgo law practice for such a strange position with a little-known judge. The Harvard Law School dean found Hand another young man from Maine, Arthur L. Robinson,[155] but Hand's bold experiment ended in 1912.

The fourth Harvard graduate Hand employed, Lewis P. Meade, was neither very healthy nor very competent. Hand temporarily hired a young secretary, Mrs. Helen Bergman, and called on her periodically while Meade took recurrent sick leaves. As much as Hand preferred the professional assistance of law graduates, good ones were hard to find, and not until the late 1920s, after his promotion to the Court of Appeals, did he resume the practice of having legal assistants—at first, by paying for them out of his own pocket; after 1930, with government funds.[156]

Hand's relations with his early legal assistants were cordial enough, but seldom as intimate and affectionate as would be his rapport with his later law clerks—the assistants whom he called "puny judges."[157] The only exception was Hand's affinity with his second assistant, Richard Hallet, whom he came to know unusually well and with whom he corresponded thereafter. Indeed, decades later, they renewed their acquaintance: in 1957, when Hand was eighty-five, he and Frances drove their 1939 Plymouth to visit the Hallets in Boothbay Harbor, Maine.

Dick Hallet evoked in Hand the characteristic admiration and envy the judge often felt for people who engaged in adventures and risks, men with a panache his own timid self could not attain. He told Hallet, late in life, "There was in your blood a craving for more scope to the unknown and unexplored, and this has as good a claim upon one as anything else. After all, [in] the end we must give rein to what pushes us about."[158] Hand perceived what pushed Hallet about early on, especially during their long walks in 1910 and 1911 from Hand's chambers to his home on East Sixty-fifth Street. Dick Hallet had a craving to go to sea and explore the world, and at the end of his clerkship he talked his way into a job on a British sailing ship, "a bald-headed barque" heading for Australia. He looked forward to "the time of my life," he told Hand, and he readily found it. During his 112-day journey from New York City to Sydney, he encountered "the wildest kind of incident, storms, fist-fights, & food famines." His shipmates were a rowdy lot who had come aboard "of their own accord, or drunk, or in slings—the toughest, but the gamest men in the world." When they arrived in Australia, they were so eager for their "beer and folly" that they abandoned the ship, penniless. Hallet himself promptly set off on his own, equipped with only "an army roll, a frying pan, a tent, a camera, a violin, & a hopeful air." On his way to the western Australian bush, he worked as a stone breaker, sheep shearer, and boundary rider; thereafter, he headed for Singapore, "and from there as the mood takes us." As he exulted to Hand, "It is the best fun ever."[159] The Hands devoured Hallet's letters. Frances as well as her husband was "greatly inspired by his extraordinary adventures": "He seemed to have done the most thrilling things and we greatly admire his courage and his love of life." As Hand told Hallet's father: "I cannot tell you how much I envy him [such] adventures."[160]

Young Hallet eventually made his way to Europe as a furnace stoker on a British mail packet. His father grew increasingly concerned about his future, fearing that it would be "hard for him to settle down on his return," but Hand urged him to let Dick continue his travels: "He has such a fine spirit [that] I rather dislike the idea of his going back into routine work" prematurely.[161] And to Dick Hallet himself, Hand confessed regret to learn that the young man planned to settle down to law practice: "It seems to me, as I sit in not too vigorous health and grind out this stuff here, that it might be well to keep to the road forever." Hand urged him to stay away as long as possible: "after the life you have been leading, you would probably go crazy if you came to New York and did nothing but read [law]. Routine is a kind of narcotic, it keeps one's mind so occupied that one thinks very little of what really matters,—losing the forest for the trees. Still after all it is not unpleasant."[162]

Hallet did find a way to escape a lawyer's routine. He was a gifted, vigorous writer, and he had sold a few pieces of fiction to small magazines even before he sailed for Australia. After he returned to America in 1912, he sold his account of his adventures in a steamer's furnace room to the *Saturday Evening Post*.[163] By then, Hand had persuaded C. C. Burlingham to hire Dick for his firm's admiralty practice. But the sale to the *Post* "tilted the beam" for Dick and prompted him to quit the law.[164] To Hand's great delight, Dick found a way to continue his adventures and make a living at them: he became a professional writer and editor and produced short essays and stories as well as six travel books, even while taking on such jobs as boiler-room crewman on Great Lakes steamers, copper miner in Arizona, and timber cruiser in Canada.[165]

At the time of his reunion with Hand in the 1950s, Hallet claimed to "see now how pivotal to my life was my association with you" but conceded that his services as law clerk "were of the sketchiest." Hand would probably have agreed about the quality of his legal assistance; but the spirit Hallet brought to their relationship meant a great deal to the judge. Near the end of Hand's life, Hallet wrote him, "Like yourself, I have sometimes wondered 'what the whole show is about,' but I have enjoyed it all."[166] Hand did wonder throughout his life what the show was about, but he could not have said that he had enjoyed it all. Still, his associations with ebullient men such as Hallet sometimes gave him a joyousness he could seldom attain on his own. Once, when he heard from Hallet after years of silence, Hand wrote that his oldest surviving law clerk's letter was "like a breeze from the sea or the woods": "I think you did right to follow your bent."[167] Hand had also followed his own bent, with greater worldly renown but less joy. Throughout his life, Hand found relief from melancholy in companionship. Hallet, with his diverting tales of adventures, was an especially welcome addition to Hand's circle.

THE LIFE OF A DISTRICT JUDGE when Hand went on the bench was lonesome, considerable in power but cut off from most human contact in the conducting of official business. Beyond his one assistant in his chambers, the only staff personnel Hand communicated with regularly were the court clerk (about administrative matters), the United States attorney (about criminal cases), and employees of the Justice Department (in pleas for trifles from the limited federal judicial budget). The only officeholders Hand saw regularly beyond these were his fellow district judges, a small group of mixed ability.

When Hand took his oath of office in 1909, the three other judges in the district were George B. Adams, named in 1901, who had become ill from overwork after a year and a half and never fully recovered (when he did sit, it was mainly in admiralty cases, his specialty); George C. Holt, appointed in 1903, a workmanlike judge but mediocre at best; and Charles Merrill Hough, on the bench since 1906, a gruff, conservative, yet witty and warm man who was Hand's only early colleague in his own intellectual league, and the only one who became a close friend.[168]

Immediately above Hand and his fellow trial judges, to review their decisions and correct their errors, were the three members of the appellate court for the Second Circuit.[169] Hand not only was subordinate to the circuit court but participated in its work from time to time. The Second Circuit would frequently designate a district judge to sit with it when it needed help to catch up with its backlog. Hand was selected to sit with the circuit judges as early as his first month on the bench, in May 1909. Thereafter, he frequently served as a temporary appellate judge, mainly because of his evident ability. Adams was clearly unavailable because of his narrow competence, and his illness; Holt was undistinguished; only Hough and Hand seemed to the Second Circuit worthy of selection for appellate work. Hand enjoyed his opportunities to participate in appeals. Appellate work was always especially attractive to him, for it allowed him to write opinions regularly rather than sporadically, and to deliberate before issuing a ruling. The opinions he produced as a member of a three-judge appellate panel greatly enhanced his rapidly growing reputation.

The Second Circuit in 1909 was able but not outstanding. Its judges were Alfred C. Coxe (who resigned in 1917), Henry G. Ward (who retired in 1921), and Walter C. Noyes (a distant relative of Hand, who resigned in 1913 to make more money in private practice). Later, the appellate court became somewhat stronger: Charles Hough was promoted to the Second Circuit in 1916, and he was a judge Hand could genuinely admire. Far less impressive was Martin T. Manton, a Democratic clubhouse politician whose promotion to the Second Circuit in 1918 Hand unsuccessfully opposed. At the outset, Hand was nearly as doubtful about Julius M. Mayer, a politically well connected Republican who, like Manton, came to the federal bench after Hand but was promoted ahead of him. But Mayer slowly rose in Hand's estimation; unlike Manton, he took his job seriously and could produce better-than-adequate opinions.[170] But the glory years of the Second Circuit, during which it became known as the nation's outstanding appellate court, lay far in the future.[171]

In 1909, when the fourth judgeship on the Southern District was established, its congressional proponents portrayed the district as the nation's busiest federal trial court, whose business would continue to grow. Court demands kept a young, energetic judge such as Hand busy enough, but his official duties did not prove unduly burdensome. Indeed, for several years after his appointment, Hand objected to proposals to increase the size of the court. He knew that a visiting judge from another district could always be brought in when the caseload became heavy, and he saw no need to add additional permanent seats before World War I. In 1910, for example, only about 3,000 cases were filed, nearly half of which involved bankruptcy matters. The rest were divided among the general law and equity calendar (which included patent, copyright, and antitrust cases as well as ordinary civil suits), admiralty cases, and the criminal docket.[172] World War I and its aftermath changed all that: by 1920, although bankruptcy cases remained stable, the rest of the docket jumped from about 1,800 to more than 7,600 cases. During 1910–20, the rise in admiralty and criminal cases was especially dramatic.[173] So eventually Hand was ready to join in pleas to Congress to allow for more judges. Congress responded in late 1922, when it created the first new seats in the Southern District since Hand's in 1909.

Even though Hand occasionally produced sparkling and important opinions on the district court, his workload left him often fatigued and sometimes bored with the seemingly interminable flow of routine cases.

He enjoyed mastering new fields such as patent and admiralty law, but the bankruptcy cases that took much time were an oppressive burden. Yet every case, the many small ones as well as the few big ones, received Hand's careful attention. He wrote page after page, laying out the facts of a complex patent claim or a ship collision, an especially difficult task when, as was often the case, witnesses for both sides were—at least—embroidering the truth. As one of Hand's great modern successors on the Second Circuit, Judge Henry J. Friendly, aptly put it, "[Hand's] stature as a judge stemmed not so much from the few great cases that inevitably came to him over the years . . . as from the great way in which he dealt with a multitude of little cases, covering almost every subject in the legal lexicon."[174]

One of Hand's greatest challenges as a district judge was his routine duty of supervising ordinary lawsuits. Conducting trials that were often frustrated by lawyers' obfuscations and delays occupied an enormous part of his time and energy. In the courtroom and in his correspondence, Hand frequently voiced irritation about the tactics of attorneys who imposed needless obstacles.

Only once did Hand present his trial experiences systematically. In November 1921, after twelve years on the bench, he addressed a gathering of lawyers at the City Bar Association on the subject "The Deficiencies of Trials to Reach the Heart of the Matter."[175] In the decade or so that the bar association had been having "Lectures on Legal Topics," few were so apparently mundane or technical as those Hand addressed: pleadings and evidence in trials. Yet Hand's lecture stands out as a gem: it was an eloquent example of his vigorous style, drawing richly not only on his judicial experience but also on his readings in history and literature. Some of the judges and lawyers who gave lectures offered extemporaneous and rambling performances;[176] others spoke with dull detachment, draining all vitality from history or indulging in so many platitudes that the audience could not have paid much attention.[177] Hand's presentation stood in sharp contrast: his was a carefully prepared, engaging, and polished presentation.

Hand converted his narrow assignment into a search for the causes of inefficient trials—the mechanical application of irrational rules, the heavy-handed judicial review by appellate courts, and the combativeness of lawyers. Ruefully, he acknowledged that one could not "expect lawyers who are half litigants to forego the advantages which come from obscuring the case and supporting contentions which they know to be false."[178] The price paid for such tactics was clear: "the atmosphere of contention over trifles, the unwillingness to concede what ought to be conceded."[179] What he had seen in his years conducting trials did not cheer him: "After now some dozen years of experience I must say that as a litigant I should dread a lawsuit beyond almost anything else short of sickness and death."[180]

Hand began his lecture modestly enough, by addressing the rules of pleading: the statements in the complaint and the response, which in theory sharpen the central disputed issues to be resolved at trial. The theory was simple enough; the trouble was "nobody will follow it." Instead, Hand said, lawyers filled their pleadings with unwarranted arguments about legal theory and melodramatic recitals of the facts. Drawing on one of his favorite writers, he warned that if this pattern continued, "we shall be philogrobolized [*sic*] like the Pundits in Rabelais and six hundred bags of papers and testimony will accumulate with no results but to parboil our brains and throw us into such interminable a welter of confusions, doubts and suspicions as never in the course of thirty years we can unravel." If lawyers could be deterred from mustering "all the rhetoric of passion and the efflorescence of literary imagination," they would "make the issues clearer," so that "the case may be laid bare to its bones in advance." But instead of simplifying the trial, the pleadings usually created new issues to resolve: "I dare say that an ingenious actuary might find upon irrefragable computation that in general loss of time, misprision of judges, consequent appeals, discouragement of suitors and the like, the annual loss to our country through bad pleadings equalled the cost of four new battleships, or complete refashioning of primary education."[181]

Hand recalled that in his earliest days on the bench he had tried to penalize attorneys for bad pleadings: "I must own that in my salad days, when the lust of combat still raged within me, I rather welcomed the opportunity afforded by the meandering trickle of a sloppy pleading. Here was indeed an occasion to teach practitioners that unless they had learned their craft they should have a short shrift and a long rope." But now he doubted that lawyers could be effectively disciplined, and, he confessed, "I make no effort to disentangle from the junk pile presented to me those structural pieces, which, had they been properly chosen and erected, would have made a fair building." But he continued to insist that good pleadings did in fact pay.

In protesting the artificial and irrational technicalities that governed the admissibility of particular types of evidence in trials, Hand argued that the rules failed to pick out the types of information that ordinary people would consider in making important decisions. The average client watching a trial could only view with "a baffled sense that there is going on some kind of game which, while its outcome may be tragic to him, in its development is incomprehensible." In Hand's view, such evidence was relevant that "human beings would think to prove the issue, if they had never heard of a court," and the accuracy of a judge's evidentiary rulings should be assessed by the standards not of "a learned lawyer, but [of] a sensible man." He added, "Much of the delay and bickering which does more than deface a court room would be avoided by a recognition that the rules of evidence are practical and discretionary."

Yet the discretion of the practical judge was constantly questioned by the lawyers and often curbed by the appellate courts. Would deference to the typical trial judge's good sense truly place near dictatorial powers in his hands? Hand did not think so. Voicing a theme for the first time that he would later apply to problems of constitutional law, Hand argued that a system of rules without discretion was impracticable: "[A] government of laws without men is as visionary as a government of men without laws; the solution will always be a compromise based on experience." Accordingly, leaving most evidentiary issues to the sound judgment of the trial judge was the only sensible strategy. But in America, by contrast to Great Britain, a trial judge tended to be "straitjacketed and gagged and told to walk this slack rope to-day and climb that pinnacle to-morrow": "Go into a court room and see him baited and excepted to, till you wonder who is on trial." The trial judge was by no means perfect, Hand conceded, but leaving most evidentiary rulings to him was "the best way to settle disputes":

> With all his sins upon him, his self-importance, his ignorance, his bad manners, his impatience, he is all you have got, and I believe he will produce better results if you give him a little more room to roam about. At least let me say . . . that for myself, taking us even as we are, I believe we should get through the day's work with better satisfaction to you all, if in the conduct of these incidentals we were left to muddle it out alone, and you were to forego that supernal clarifier, the appellate court.[182]

Hand closed with an eloquent appeal for self-restraint by lawyers. A "change of heart in ourselves," not "formal changes," offered the only cure for the sorry condition of trial procedures. "Without a bar which is willing to co-operate, a bench more virtuous and wise than any we are ever to get would do very little. . . . You get out of a community what there is in it, out of a bar . . . what the character and capacity that bar contains, and neither laws nor principalities nor powers will in the end help you jot or tittle."

Hand's argument proceeded more from his fundamental philosophical convictions than from any hope for successful legal reform. Whether or not such reform would be realized, he argued, "we must in one way or another live by faith, and perhaps the highest test of it is when it is stricken by a doubt that after all it may be mistaken." Reaching the height of his eloquence, he confessed:

> [S]till at times I can have the hope that in America time may at length mitigate our fierce individualism, may teach us the knowledge we so sorely lack that each of us must learn to realize himself more in our communal life whose formal expression is and as I believe will continue to be the law. If through some such conversion we can be taught to abate the intensity of our own wills, to subject our desires to what has been laid down for us, even when we dislike and distrust it, then in this which seems so trivial and minor a detail, the management of our private disputes, we may succeed. But not, I fear, short of something like that; we are made all of a piece, and the cloven hoof will show however well the bestial heart be covered.[183]

Lawyers regularly attending the bar association's lectures could not have heard a more powerful address on such a technical subject. Hand's capacity to turn remarks upon mundane subjects into sparkling jewels was unique. But of course when he went back to his bench, he found the day-to-day conduct of trials little changed. He was as frustrated as ever by legal delays and chicanery, his own struggles with the artificial rules, and the possibly ineradicable obstacles to efficient trials. Hand's hopes for efficiency, rationality, and focus in the resolution of factual disputes still await realization.

MOST OF HAND'S OPINIONS on the district court, even those that illuminated old problems with sharper and deeper insights, dealt with technical subjects. Occasionally, however, a case came before him that allowed him to rethink and articulate concerns central to the faith of the skeptical liberal. *United States v. Kennerley,* a 1913 ruling on the contentious subject of obscenity, was one such case.[184] In *Kennerley,* in an opinion occupying only about a page of the court reports, Hand articulated his deepest feelings about the protection a free society should afford even allegedly obscene materials. His opinion, the first on a problem to which he returned in later decades, constitutes "some of the most powerful prose ever written on this delicate subject."[185]

Kennerley illustrates aspects of Hand's characteristic manner of judging. While he privately preferred to dismiss the indictment, he felt constrained by an unbroken line of precedent to rule against the publisher's motion for dismissal. In following precedent rather than his private preference, Hand reflected, as he would again and again, his understanding of his limited role. As he would say in a later case, it is not "desirable for a lower court to embrace the exhilarating opportunity of anticipating a doctrine which may be in the womb of time, but whose birth is distant."[186] In his view, the lower courts in the federal judicial hierarchy had to obey clear commands of their superiors; this limitation, he thought, was essential to a democratic government under law. Yet bowing to precedent did not prevent him from expressing sharp and thoughtful criticism of the prevailing law, or from suggesting a better approach. And his *Kennerley* remarks were influential: the case has frequently been cited by later courts, including the Supreme Court; most of his suggestions have become the modern law of the land; and in some respects, his formulations are more appealing than modern obscenity law.

The book that led to the *Kennerley* prosecution was *Hagar Revelly*, a novel about the life of a young working woman in New York City.[187] Hand called it a "novel of manners"; to modern eyes, it is an earnest effort at social realism. As Hand described it, the novel portrayed the central character as "impulsive, sensuous, fond of pleasure, and restive under the monotony and squalor of her surroundings." Her "virtue" was successfully assailed by a man she loved; after her seduction, in Hand's words, "she has several amorous misadventures and ends with a loveless marriage and the prospect of a dreary future. In order to give complete portrayal to the girl's emotional character, some of the scenes are depicted with a frankness and detail which have given rise to this prosecution."

These few brief scenes, taken in isolation and without regard to their context, were enough to allow a jury to decide whether the book was obscene as the law stood in 1913. The rule governing all federal courts at the time originated in a mid-Victorian English decision, *Regina v. Hicklin*.[188] Adopting the *Hicklin* rule, federal law allowed juries to determine that a book was obscene by examining isolated passages rather than the work as a whole. Moreover, the *Hicklin* standard measured a book's obscenity by its most susceptible audience, not by its acceptability to the community at large. Hand followed this test because, as he said, it had been "accepted by lower federal courts until it would be no longer proper for me to disregard it." He accordingly found that there were passages in the novel that "certainly might tend to corrupt the morals of those into whose hands it might come and whose minds were open to such immoral influences. Indeed, it would be just those who would be most likely to concern themselves with those parts alone, forgetting their setting and their relevancy to the book as a whole."

This finding ended the formal part of Hand's task: as a lower court judge, he was compelled to rule that the prosecution could not be dismissed and that the obscenity issue had to be left to the jury.[189] Yet his belief in freedom of expression was too strong to let it go at that.

> I hope it is not improper for me to say that the rule as laid down, however consonant it may be with mid-Victorian morals, does not seem to me to answer to the understanding and morality of the present time. . . . I question whether in the end men will regard that as obscene which is honestly relevant to the adequate expression of innocent ideas, and whether they will not believe that truth and beauty are too precious to society at large to be mutilated in the interests of those most likely to pervert them to base uses. Indeed, it seems hardly likely that we are even to-day so lukewarm in our interest in letters or serious discussion as to be content to reduce our treatment of sex to the standard of a child's library in the supposed interest of a salacious few, or that shame will for long prevent us from adequate portrayal of some of the most serious and beautiful sides of human nature.

There should at least be no prosecutions for the sole purpose of protecting a susceptible, immature group in the potential audience, he argued. The standards of the community should govern, standards a jury could properly ascertain. "I scarcely think that [society] would forbid all which might corrupt the most corruptible, or that society is prepared to accept for its own limitations those which may perhaps be necessary to the weakest of its members." At least, "obscene" should be interpreted as indicating merely "the present critical point in the compromise between candor and shame at which the community may have arrived here and now"; and only a jury could determine that. "To put thought in leash to the average conscience of the time is perhaps tolerable," he concluded, "but to fetter it by the necessities of the lowest and least capable seems a fatal policy"—fatal because it would drastically reduce the scope of literary expression in an open society.[190]

Several decades passed before federal obscenity law caught up with Hand's position. The part of the *Hicklin* rule that permitted conviction on the basis of isolated passages rather than the work as a whole went down to defeat at the hands of the Second Circuit itself, after Hand became a member of its appellate court.[191] More important, not until the 1950s, more than four decades after *Kennerley*, did the Supreme

Court at last agree with Hand that a book should not be banned simply because it might reach the eyes of an especially susceptible reader,[192] and that the standards of the community as a whole were central in determining obscenity.[193]

In one significant respect, modern obscenity law is still less protective of free expression than Hand's approach in *Kennerley*. Hand suggested that all writing "which is honestly relevant to the adequate expression of innocent ideas" should be immune from obscenity convictions.[194] This hope has not yet been realized; instead, the Supreme Court continues to emphasize community standards, and has wrangled for decades about what the level of "redeeming social value" should be.[195] Hand's analysis in *Kennerley* is more focused, clearer, and more consistent with First Amendment doctrine as it has evolved in other areas. The obscenity morass today supports Hand's criticisms in 1913. He would probably be disturbed by the continuing strength of speech-restrictive forces in society, but he would not be surprised. He once commented, in a 1937 ruling, that "[n]o civilized community not fanatically puritanical would tolerate such an imposition."[196] Yet, as he well knew in his own life, society's repressive, puritanical forces are strong and resilient.

THE *KENNERLEY* CASE presented one of the most difficult issues of Hand's district court years. But one other case, *Masses Publishing Co. v. Patten*, in 1917,[197] raised questions even more central to the protection of freedom of expression under the First Amendment: When, if at all, may the state penalize political dissenters—those who criticize government leaders and their policies? *Masses* compelled Hand to draw on his deepest personal resources of courage and independence and evoked the most important, pathbreaking opinion of his trial court tenure—an analysis that, decades later, became the law of the land.

The government's lawsuit in *Masses* arose because, two months after the United States entered World War I, Congress enacted the Espionage Act of 1917.[198] For the first time in nearly 120 years, criticism of governmental policies became a federal crime. One portion of the new law declared that publications containing statements made illegal by the act could be banned from the mails. The first magazine to feel the bite of the law was *The Masses*, "a monthly revolutionary journal." Two weeks after the enactment of the law in June 1917, Thomas G. Patten, the postmaster of New York City (acting on orders of Postmaster General Albert S. Burleson), prohibited *The Masses* from mailing its forthcoming issue. The magazine promptly went to federal court to block the threatened ban. The case came before district judge Learned

Hand, and it fell to him to be the first judge to interpret the new law. On July 24, Hand issued an eloquent opinion and enjoined the postmaster from banning the magazine.

In its immediate result, the ruling proved only a fleeting triumph, both for Hand and for *The Masses*: the Circuit Court of Appeals quickly overturned Hand's decision.[199] The circulation of *The Masses* dropped precipitously because it was unable to reach most of its audience. Some of its editors were soon indicted for conspiracy to violate the Espionage Act. Although two successive trials ended in hung juries, the defendants gave up their efforts to publish their journal in the face of a hostile government: by the end of the year, *The Masses* had gone out of business.

In its brief life span, *The Masses* had reached a circulation of nearly thirty thousand. To its readers, its demise meant the loss of a spirited, iconoclastic magazine whose pages had attracted some of the leading artists and writers of the day. For Hand, the case spurred an act of courage that, although costly in its immediate consequences, produced his major contribution to the intellectual and legal history of free speech.

The immediate costs to Hand were real. After only eight years on the district court, the bar had come to admire his analytical skills and lucid style, but the speedy and unanimous overturning of his well-publicized ruling tarnished his otherwise shining reputation. And the reversal came while Hand was under consideration for promotion to the Circuit Court of Appeals. He was passed over, in part because of his unpopular decision.

But these immediate setbacks could not permanently obscure the importance of what Hand had wrought. His *Masses* opinion was an original, penetrating analysis, an expression of an outsider's deepest belief about the importance of dissent in a democratic society. Hand was free to place this philosophical statement in the judicial reports because he was in effect writing on a blank slate: no other court had yet interpreted the 1917 act, and the Supreme Court's few prior decisions on the First Amendment gave no relevant guidance. Hand's opinion was extraordinarily speech-protective, far more so even than Justice Oliver Wendell Holmes's well-known standard announced less than two years later. Hand strongly believed in his approach to free speech, and he tried to persuade Holmes and others to adopt it in the ensuing years. He failed at the time, and he died more than four decades later believing that his venture had been doomed. But he was wrong. By the late 1960s, the Supreme Court announced its most speech-protective standard ever. And that standard is essentially an embracing of Hand's *Masses* approach.[200]

Hand knew from the moment the case reached his desk that it would not be an easy one. He was acquainted with *The Masses* and with the central figure on its staff, Max Eastman, as well. His first impression was that *The Masses* had a strong case; he also knew that, were he to rule against the government and for a radical, antiwar, unpopular journal, he would be strongly criticized and would seriously impair his chances for promotion.

The brief, chaotic life of *The Masses* had effectively begun in 1912, when Max Eastman became its chief editor and tried to give some leadership to the anarchic editorial board.[201] The magazine's platform asserted little beyond a commitment to freedom—freedom for the editors to do essentially as they pleased; they promised a "revolutionary and not a reform magazine; [a] free magazine, frank, arrogant, impertinent, searching for true causes; a magazine directed against rigidity and dogma wherever it is found; [a] magazine whose final policy is to do as it pleases and conciliate nobody, not even its readers."[202]

The Masses attracted a remarkable group of contributors. Max Eastman was just finishing a dissertation in philosophy under the pragmatist John Dewey at Columbia University and was already building a reputation as a poet, public speaker, and political organizer. He had been brought aboard by the artist Art Young, a cartoonist who became an editor and regular contributor. Like most of the twelve art editors, Young had been associated with the painter Robert Henri, an early American realist and occasional contributor to *The Masses*; unlike most of the artists, Young was an avowed partisan, a devoted socialist. Many of the artists with *The Masses*—John Sloan, George Bellows, and Stuart Davis among them—helped to found the "Ashcan School." They, like its writers, varied in their political beliefs and had little in common beyond a penchant for iconoclasm and confrontation. Not only Max Eastman and John Reed but also Louis Untermeyer, Bill Haywood, Carl Sandburg, and Floyd Dell contributed prose and poetry. *The Masses* was unusually handsome, with bright-colored covers and oversize pages filled with bold drawings and lively social satire, political criticism, and intellectual commentary.

The magazine quickly found an audience, albeit not among the masses it hoped to reach—it was essentially a magazine for intellectuals—but it did not achieve an ideological identity until after the outbreak of World War I. Eastman, Reed, and Young opposed the war from the beginning, viewing it as the machination of business interests, and editorials against militarism, the war, and the draft soon proliferated.

Hand was no radical. He was an internationalist, he supported the Allies, and he applauded America's entry into the war. But he had a lively mind, and he occasionally read *The Masses*. Moreover, he too was an outsider, though not in the same sense as Eastman and what the press came to call "the *Masses* crowd." In the language of *The Masses'* manifesto, he was committed to political "reform," and he was no "revolutionary." Nor was he an avant-garde bohemian, and he had nothing to do with the artistic and literary groups centered in Greenwich Village that presided over the birth of American modernism. But New York intellectuals were not so numerous and isolated from one another that there was no overlap between Hand's circle and that of "the *Masses* crowd." Eastman had been an organizer for a women's suffrage group just before he became *The Masses'* editor, and Frances Hand was devoted to achieving the vote for women during that time. Eastman also recalled later—after his politics had moved from support of the Russian Revolution to praise of Trotsky, staunch opposition to Stalinism, and ultimately an editorial post with *Reader's Digest*—that he had once lectured on "radicalism" at the Colony Club, one of New York's exclusive women's clubs, and that Learned Hand (perhaps at the urging of Mrs. Hand, a member) had introduced him.[203]

Eastman's slight acquaintance with Hand prompted him to seek the judge's help in a difficulty *The Masses* encountered the year before the United States entered the war. *The Masses'* problem in 1916 stemmed not from its controversial political stands but from the offense to religious sensibilities aroused by one of its freewheeling contributors, who had written an allegedly blasphemous poem that likened the Virgin Mary to an unwed mother. The magazine's foe was the Ward & Gow Company, the distributor of periodicals to newsstands in New York's rapid transit system; the "blasphemy" prompted Ward & Gow to order its dealers to stop carrying *The Masses*. Eastman pleaded that if Hand would compose a statement "that you believe *The Masses* ought to be on those stands, it will be the favor of a lifetime."[204] The letter was to be presented to a state legislative committee holding hearings on the Ward & Gow ban. Hand immediately supplied an eloquent response defending the right of *The Masses* to be circulated. He told Eastman, "I do not feel sympathy with your approach to the question of social and economic reorganization, or the means by which you seek to bring it about," but, he quickly added, "[t]hat I prefer another way, does not blind me to the wisdom of giving you the chance to persuade men of yours."

> Yours is a way, whether it is a good way or a bad way, of getting men to think and feel about those things in which it is most important that they should think and feel. I can conceive of no

possible defence for excluding you except either that such matters must not be discussed, or that they must be discussed only in a way which accords with the common standards of taste. One alternative is tyrannous absolutism, the other, tyrannous priggism.[205]

Hand's defense fell on deaf ears; the Ward & Gow ban stood, and the magazine's circulation fell, although its publication continued.

Hand's immediate reaction to *The Masses'* plea a year later for an injunction to stop the postal authorities' threatened action graphically emerges from a letter he wrote to Frances on the very day he received the legal papers in the case. On first reading, he sensed that the editors "had not done anything which could possibly be illegal, though, of course, their bias is clear enough. I should think that in fairness I should be obliged to protect them." If the case were not settled quickly, he added, "my decision would go against [the government], and then whoop-la your little man is in the mud, assuming he is not there anyway." Yet he then immediately asserted, in a stirring statement of the obligations that most judges profess but few manage consistently to heed:

I must do the right as I see it and the thing I am most anxious about is that I shall succeed in giving a decision absolutely devoid of any such considerations [as the prospect of promotion]. There are times when the old bunk about an independent and fearless judiciary means a good deal. This is one of them; and if I have limitations of judgment, I may have to suffer for it, but I want to be sure that these are the only limitations and that I have none of character.[206]

In claiming that the challenged issue of *The Masses* violated the Espionage Act, the government pointed to several pieces. The prosecution's selection must have pleased those contributors who thought of the magazine mainly as a vehicle for art: the charge specified four cartoons, three articles, and a poem. The most objectionable cartoons were one by Henry Glintenkamp and another by Art Young. Glintenkamp's "Conscription" showed a cannon with nude men labeled "Youth" and "Labor" chained to it, and a nude woman labeled "Democracy" crucified on its carriage. Young's "Congress and Big Business" depicted Congress as a disconsolate bystander ignored by a group of businessmen inspecting a document labeled "War Plans." Congress was depicted as asking: "Excuse me, gentlemen, where do I come in?" Big Business replies: "Run along now! We got through with you when you declared war for us."

As for the articles, they expressed admiration for the self-reliance and sacrifice of draft resisters. The first conceded the state's right to imprison these "heroic young men" and argued merely that, instead of jailing them as "slackers" and thereby encouraging contempt from the press, the government should at least proceed with "a certain sorrowful dignity." The others expressed similar admiration for conscientious objectors: one reported on the prosecution of Alexander Berkman and Emma Goldman, in one of the first cases under the Espionage Act, for having urged conscientious objectors to refuse to register. *The Masses* added that it was prepared to receive contributions to help Berkman and Goldman air their "working class protest against the plans of American militarism."[207]

Though *The Masses* indeed opposed the war and admired those who resisted service in it, it fell short of telling readers that they *must* violate the law. What prompted Postmaster General Burleson and his attorneys from the Justice Department to argue that such comments constituted criminal behavior was Section 3 of the newly enacted Espionage Act: it specified three offenses, each punishable by a maximum of twenty years in prison and a $10,000 fine—first, making "false statements with intent to interfere with the operation or success of the military or naval forces . . . when the United States is at war"; second, causing or attempting to cause "insubordination . . . or . . . refusal of duty" in the military forces; and third, obstructing "the recruiting or enlistment service of the United States."[208]

Had *The Masses* crossed the line into illegality? And if the Espionage Act were interpreted to reach this type of criticism, could it be squared with the First Amendment? To most judges of the time, the answers were clear. The kind of antiwar talk published by "the *Masses* crowd," the typical response went, surely bred dissatisfaction with the government and the war; to the extent the articles had an audience, they could interfere with the "success" of the armed forces and the government's recruitment and conscription efforts. The embryonic state of First Amendment law left ample room for this restricted view of permissible criticism of government. Nothing like the 1917 act had ever been on the federal statute books. (The closest predecessor was the Federalists' Sedition Act of 1798, which punished false, scandalous, and malicious criticism intended to bring the federal government into contempt or disrepute.[209] The victory of the Jeffersonians in the election of 1800 had meant the end of that law, although it took nearly two centuries, until 1964, for the Supreme Court to acknowledge a "broad consensus" on the view that the 1798 law could not be squared with the First Amendment.)[210]

The prospect that *The Masses* could legally be banned from the mails was especially strong when the case came before Hand. The political and legal climate of the day was strikingly inhospitable to dissent. Radicals preaching pacifism, conscientious objection, or worse were anathema to most Americans, and the government's arguments in the *Masses* case reflected the prevailing legal analyses. According to most judges, speech was punishable if violation of the law was the probable effect of the words—the focus was on guesses about the consequences of speech.[211] And the few judges who appreciated the value of freedom of expression—including Justice Holmes—did not quarrel with this focus on the consequences of words; their response was to require a closer causal relationship between the offensive words and the later illegal acts. (This insistence on closer ties between expression and action was soon expressed in such formulations as that only words presenting a "clear and present danger" of bad consequences were punishable.)

The originality and daring of Hand's decision in *Masses* emerge sharply against this background. Unlike other judges, Hand was not satisfied with efforts merely to shrink the chain of causation between words and deeds, and indeed he stepped wholly outside this framework of argument. Conceding that a causal relationship between dissident words and illegal action often *did* exist—and acknowledging that speech could indeed cause effects harmful to the war effort—he argued that tightening the required chain of causation was not an apt or effective method of protecting the range of speech essential in a democratic society.

To second-guess legislators and administrators about the probable consequences of dissident speech was to Hand a highly questionable function for courts: judges had no special competence to foresee the future; moreover, most judges—and even more, most juries—were not likely to be immune to the "herd instinct" of wartime hysteria. A legal standard inviting speculation about the consequences of words—whether immediate or remote—would allow judges and juries to succumb to majoritarian, speech-repressive sentiments.

Hand's solution focused on the speaker's *words*, not on their probable consequences. Instead of asking in each case whether the words had a tendency to produce unlawful conduct, he tried to fashion a more "absolute and objective test" focusing on the language that was at issue.[212] What he urged was "a test based upon the nature of the utterance itself," an "incitement" test: if the words constituted solely a counsel to violate the law, solely an instruction that it was the listener's duty or interest to violate the law, they could be forbidden; in a democratic society, all other utterances had to be protected. As he wrote: "[T]o assimilate agitation, legitimate as such, with direct incitement to violent resistance, is to disregard the tolerance of all methods of political agitation which in normal times is a safeguard of free government." Emphasizing the importance of the line he was establishing, he added: "The distinction is not a scholastic subterfuge, but a hard-bought acquisition in the fight for freedom."[213]

In this extraordinarily speech-protective interpretation of the 1917 law, Hand raised no doubts about its constitutionality; he purported to be dealing simply with congressional purpose. But he interpreted legislative purpose in the context of constitutional values—and he expressed these values in a manner as noble as any on the books. In his opinion, Hand invoked these values only to justify the narrow interpretation of the law, but he intended that the "incitement" test be understood as essential to the protection of dissent in a free society, and a constitutional standard as well.

Hand's statement of democratic norms is notable for several reasons: the *Masses* opinion contrasts sharply with Holmes's early confrontations with the same issues in *Schenck* and its companion cases in the spring of 1919, its eloquence ranking with Holmes's much quoted phrases when at last he began to exhibit greater awareness of free-speech values in his *Abrams* dissent in the fall of 1919; most important, the values Hand emphasized in *Masses* inspired his partially successful appeals to Holmes in subsequent years.

Hand's ingenious technique is especially well illustrated by his handling of the Espionage Act's ban on willfully causing insubordination in the armed forces. Instead of second-guessing the government's causation argument, he accepted it and then insisted that it was inconsistent with adequate protection of free speech. For Hand, predictions about the possible effect of speech, empirically plausible as they might be, would not do as a legal standard consistent with the safeguarding of free speech:

> [T]o interpret the word "cause" so broadly would . . . involve necessarily as a consequence the suppression of all hostile criticism, and of all opinion except what encouraged and supported the existing policies, or which fell within the range of temperate argument. It would contradict the normal assumption of democratic government that the suppression of hostile criticism does not turn upon the justice of its substance or the decency and propriety of its temper. Assuming that the power to repress such opinion may rest in Congress in the throes of a struggle for the very existence

of the state, its exercise is so contrary to the use and wont of our people that only the clearest expression of such a power justifies the conclusion that it was intended.[214]

The "normal assumption of democratic government," the "use and wont of our people," or, as Hand put it elsewhere in the opinion, the "right to criticise either by temperate reasoning, or by immoderate and indecent invective, which is normally the privilege of the individual in countries dependent upon the free expression of opinion as the ultimate source of authority"[215]—these were the primary sources Hand's values articulated in *Masses*. They were derived from history and, especially, philosophy: the voice was that of Billings Learned Hand, the thoughtful Harvard undergraduate specializing in philosophy, and Learned Hand, the lawyer and judge of an inescapably philosophical bent.

How were those values to be translated into effective law? If an adequate legal standard "could become sacred by the incrustations of time and precedent," Hand wrote in one of his letters, "it might be made to serve just a little to withhold the torrents of passion to which I suspect democracies will be found more subject than for example the whig autocracy of the 18th century."[216] For him, the best hope for avoiding the "suppression of the free utterance of abuse and criticism of the existing law" lay in his "objective" standard of "incitement": "Words are not only the keys of persuasion, but the triggers of action, and those which have no purport but to counsel the violation of law cannot by any latitude of interpretation be a part of that public opinion which is the final source of government in a democratic state." This perception was the touchstone:

> To counsel or advise a man to an act is to urge upon him either that it is his interest or his duty to do it. While, of course, this may be accomplished as well by indirection as expressly, . . . the definition is exhaustive, I think, and I shall use it. . . . [T]o assimilate agitation, legitimate as such, with direct incitement to violent resistance, is to disregard the tolerance of all methods of political agitation which in normal times is a safeguard of free government.[217]

"Direct incitement" to illegal action was a standard focused on the content rather than the effect of speech. This standard would have protected much of the unpopular speech that was condemned by prevailing doctrines in 1917—and condemned, too, by Holmes's "clear and present danger" test of the postwar era. For Hand, the question was not whether "the indirect result of the language might be to arouse a seditious disposition, for that would not be enough," but whether "the language directly advocated resistance to the draft."[218]

The civil libertarian nature of this standard is illustrated by Hand's application of it to passages in *The Masses* praising conscientious objectors, Emma Goldman, and Alexander Berkman. To most judges of the day, written admiration for such "martyrs" encouraged readers to emulate them, and this contributed at least indirectly to violation of law; that was enough to justify punishment. Not so for Hand. *The Masses* indeed held up "martyrs" to "admiration, and hence their conduct to possible emulation." But that was not enough:

> One may admire and approve the course of a hero without feeling any duty to follow him. There is not the least implied intimation in these words that others are under a duty to follow. The most that can be said is that, if others do follow, they will get the same admiration and the same approval. Now, there is surely an appreciable distance between esteem and emulation; and unless there is here some advocacy of such emulation, I cannot see how the passages can be said to fall within the law.[219]*

The immediate response to Hand's *Masses* decision was as negative as he had feared from the outset of the case. As he recalled, "[I]t seemed to meet with practically no professional approval whatever."[220] The most formal indication of this disapproval appeared in the official reports of court decisions within two weeks, when Judge Hough took the unusual step of blocking, pending appeal, the enforcement of Hand's injunction against the postmaster's ban. Hough, the widely admired, forceful son of a brigadier general, was "never tortured by doubt."[221] He was readily attracted to the postmaster's position and openly skeptical of Hand's contrary approach:

> [I]t is at least arguable whether there can be any more direct incitement to action than to hold up to admiration those who do act. Oratio obliqua has always been preferred by rhetoricians to oratio recta; the Beatitudes have for some centuries been considered highly hortatory, though they do not contain the injunction "Go thou and do likewise."[222]

---

* This strict, perhaps even strained, rule in the interest of speech protection had its problems. As some contemporaries recognized, it could not easily deal, for example, with the indirect but purposeful incitement of Mark Antony's oration over the body of Caesar. Nor did it cope with the problem of the "harmless inciter," a speaker explicitly urging violation of the law but with little realistic hope of success.

When the case came before the full Circuit Court of Appeals in November 1917, Judge Henry Wade Rogers's unanimous opinion reversed Hand's order outright. Rogers did not have a mind as able as Hough's, but his capacities were adequate to reflect the mainstream of contemporary legal thinking. Noting Hand's incitement test, he replied: "This court does not agree that such is the law. If the natural and reasonable effect of what is said is to encourage resistance to a law, and the words are used in an endeavor to persuade to resistance, it is immaterial that the duty to resist is not mentioned, or the interest of the persons addressed in resistance is not suggested."[223]

The repudiation of Hand's position was not limited to official statements from the bench. As Hand wrote to C. C. Burlingham, "I think all this building [the federal courthouse] is against me. . . . Gus thinks of it as nothing more than another instance of my natural perversity."[224] Soon after the decision, Hand told Walter Lippmann, "I am getting convinced that I must be out of [the competition for the Second Circuit vacancy]; perhaps the *Masses* was enough."[225] And he would recall three years later: "The case cost me something, at least at the time. . . ." The Second Circuit appointment went to a more political, less distinguished district judge (Martin T. Manton).

Despite his frustration over the reversal of his ruling, Hand remained committed to his position. As he wrote to Burlingham:

> [T]he perversity is there all right and God knows how much my subconscious self, which is no doubt a cross-grained critter, may have been fooling with my cerebral centres, but I never was better satisfied with any piece of work I did in my life. I do not mean that I was pleased with it as a judicial performance, but with the result. There is a bit of it that is arguable, no doubt; in the main outline I have been very happy to do what I believe was some service to temperateness and sanity.[226]

His self-deprecation about pride in "result" rather than "judicial performance" was characteristic; in fact, he took pride in both. He engaged in years of effort to spread the message of his *Masses* argument, to heighten sensitivity to the importance of protecting free speech, and to urge his view on how legally to implement sensitivity. His "judicial performance" is surely the source of the eventual lasting strength of his approach.

THE FIRST SALVO of Hand's campaign was fired in the summer of 1918, and the target was Justice Holmes. Hand's aim was not yet to urge the *Masses* doctrine in detail—no Espionage Act case had yet come to the Supreme Court—but to persuade Holmes of the importance of special sensitivity to free-speech values. The first confrontation was a brief but revealing chance one, when Hand and Holmes shared a train ride from New York City most of the way to Boston, on Wednesday, June 19, 1918. Holmes, at the end of the Supreme Court's term, was on his way to his Beverly Farms residence near Boston; Hand was traveling to his summer home in Cornish, New Hampshire. They talked about the majority's right to suppress dissent. Holmes insisted that the majority had a legal right to prevail in this area as in all others; Hand objected that the courts must curb the majority when the minority's free-speech interests were at stake, difficult as that might be when, for example, majoritarian wartime hysteria was squelching antiwar dissidents. Echoes of their conversation are preserved because Hand, brooding about it in New Hampshire, decided he had given up "rather more easily"[227] than he should have and decided to restate his position for Holmes; and Holmes promptly replied.

Holmes and Hand were indeed very far apart, a gap in values all the more remarkable because Hand and Holmes shared a common philosophical outlook in most respects. Neither believed in absolutes or eternal truths; both were skeptics; and both doubted the effectiveness and even the legitimacy of judicial restraints on legislative enactments. Yet from these premises Hand was able to derive arguments for the judicial protection of minority views, more than a year before Holmes finally arrived at a similar (albeit weaker) conclusion.

The dispute was remarkable at a more personal level as well. That Hand would disagree with Holmes on anything, and would do so strongly and persistently, was extraordinary. Although Hand rarely suffered from hero worship, his admiration, even idolatry, of Holmes was extreme, expressed in both public and private, a veneration that exceeded even the esteem he felt for his Harvard professors. Holmes was "the epitome of what a judge should be," a continuous object of "affection," "a dear friend, a wise guide and the example of all that I most cherish."[228] What spurred the forty-six-year-old Hand, only nine years a federal trial judge, to do battle with the most revered judge and legal philosopher in the land, a justice more than three decades older than he with almost three decades more experience on the bench, were deeply held beliefs. Only a matter of utmost significance could move Hand to challenge a man he regarded with a reverence second only to what he felt for his father.

What Hand's letter to Holmes set forth was the credo that had spurred his *Masses* opinion—a credo Holmes was unable to accept until the following year, and never able to effectively implement. "Opinions are at best provisional hypotheses, incompletely tested," Hand argued, so "we must be tolerant of opposite opinions or varying opinions by the very fact of our incredulity of our own." Deference to majoritarianism was ordinarily central to Hand's beliefs, but here he could not follow Holmes's guide. Yes, he agreed, silencing "the other fellow when he disagrees" was indeed "a natural right," but not one that a democratic society and its law could afford to endorse.[229]

Hand's insistence on the need to protect dissenters because of the fallibility of widely held opinions was not yet acceptable to Holmes. But it was strikingly similar to the famous defense of free speech that Holmes ultimately presented in his *Abrams* dissent more than a year later, where he advocated a "free trade in ideas" and insisted that "the best test of truth is the power of the thought to get itself accepted in the competition of the market." He added, "That at any rate is the theory of our Constitution,"[230] but this "theory of our Constitution" had not yet revealed itself to Holmes in 1918.

Characteristically, Holmes tried to meet Hand's 1918 argument with the assertion "I agree with it throughout," but he admitted to one, all-important, disagreement: Free speech, Holmes insisted, "stands no differently than freedom from vaccination," a "freedom" that could be readily overridden by a majority, as a Supreme Court decision Holmes had joined thirteen years earlier made clear. As Holmes told Hand, occasions "when you cared enough" to squelch the dissident might indeed be rare, "but if for any reason you did care enough you wouldn't care a damn for the suggestion that you were acting on a provisional hypothesis and might be wrong. That is the condition of every act."[231]

Within months, this philosophical debate between Holmes and Hand could be seen in concrete legal differences. In March 1919, it fell to Holmes to write for the Supreme Court in its first encounters with the very provisions of the Espionage Act of 1917 that Hand had construed narrowly in *Masses*. This produced Holmes's first statement of the widely acclaimed "clear and present danger" test. It was not a useful civil libertarian doctrine but, rather, little more than a legal manifestation of the philosophy he had expressed in his June 1918 letter to Hand—a view that recognized no justification for limiting the right of the majority to "kill" the dissident minority.[232] Holmes consequently —and to Hand's regret if not surprise—found no compelling reason to elaborate adequate legal safeguards for free speech.

The Supreme Court decided *Schenck v. United States* on March 3, 1919.[233] One week later, it ruled in *Frohwerk v. United States* and *Debs v. United States*.[234] In each case, the Court was unanimous: speaking through Justice Holmes, it affirmed the convictions of antiwar speakers under the 1917 Espionage Act. *Schenck* enunciated the "clear and present danger" test; *Frohwerk* and *Debs* applied it. As that test has come down through the years of praise from civil libertarian commentators, it stands for the view that speech cannot be punished unless it creates an *immediate* risk of harm. But the correspondence between Hand and Holmes confirms what commentators have come to appreciate only in recent years: the "clear and present danger" test showed neither special sensitivity to free-speech values nor special concern for interpreting constitutional law to implement those values (by, for example, insisting that the risk of harm must be *immediate* before speech can be punished). Holmes had actually not moved at all from his 1918 position of blindness to any effective legal limit on curtailing majority suppression of dissent; he was still immune to any persuasion that special doctrinal safeguards, such as those Hand had enunciated in *Masses*, were needed to protect free speech.

While the cases were pending, Hand tried to induce Holmes to think about his *Masses* formulation. Holmes told him that he did not have "the details in my mind" of the *Masses* case, and Hand got only a perfunctory acknowledgment: Holmes assumed he would "come to a different result" but praised Hand's forcefulness and "admirable form."[235] Then, after *Debs*, Hand wrote again to Holmes, but his arguments appeared again to make no impact. Quite simply, Holmes missed the central issue. "I don't quite get your point," Holmes wrote Hand in April 1919.[236] To Holmes, the cases were essentially routine criminal appeals; by the end of the spring, Hand had written to a rare academic critic of *Debs*, "I own I was chagrined that Justice Holmes did not line up on our side; indeed, I have so far been unable to make him see that he and we have any real differences."[237]

The Supreme Court's upholding of the conviction of the Socialist party leader and presidential candidate, Eugene V. Debs, aroused strong contemporary protests. As Holmes described the speech Debs had given that led to his indictment, its main theme "was socialism, its growth, and a prophecy of its ultimate success." But Holmes had been willing to speculate about damaging innuendos, and from these fragments, he concluded, a jury could find "that one purpose of the speech, whether incidental or not does not matter, was to oppose not only war in general but this war, and that the opposition was so expressed that its natural and intended effect would be to obstruct recruiting."[238] "Natural tendency and reasonably probable effect" were enough to send Debs to jail. As a modern commentator has remarked, it was "somewhat as though

George McGovern had been sent to prison for his criticism of the [Vietnam] war."[239]

Professor Zechariah Chafee, Jr., the creator and chief promulgator of the idea that Holmes was, from the outset, committed to maximum First Amendment protections, claimed that Holmes was merely "biding his time until the Court should have before it a conviction so clearly wrong as to let him speak out his deepest thoughts about the First Amendment."[240] But this assertion is wrong, as the exchange of letters between Hand and Holmes shows. Hand was so distressed by *Debs* that he was moved to renew his campaign for greater protection of speech, though he had little hope of success; his views, he told Holmes, were "already fast receding in the seas of forgotten errors. . . . I bid a long farewell to my little toy ship which set out quite bravely on the shortest voyage ever made."

The thrust of Hand's March 1919 letter to Holmes, just days after *Debs*, contrasts sharply with Holmes's approach. Hand once again acknowledged that words might have practical consequences, but denied that mere risk of consequences was enough to incur legal culpability:

> In nature the causal sequence is perfect, but responsibility does not go pari passu. I do not understand that the rule of responsibility for speech has ever been that the result is known as likely to follow. It is not—I agree it might have been—a question of responsibility dependent upon reasonable forecast. . . . The responsibility only began when the words were directly an incitement.

There was far more than speculative philosophy behind Hand's approach; it was prompted, too, by his practical awareness of the risks if juries were permitted to punish on the basis of guesses about the speaker's intent or the "reasonable consequences" of his words.

> All I say is, that since the cases actually occur when men are excited and since juries are especially clannish groups, . . . it is very questionable whether the test of motive is not a dangerous test. Juries won't much regard the difference between the probable result of the words and the purposes of the utterer. In any case, unless one is rather set in conformity, it will serve to intimidate —throw a scare into—many a man who might moderate the storms of popular feeling. I know it did in 1918.[241]

This practical concern about the administration of law at the hands of impassioned juries, and the reference in the same letter to the postmaster general's "legal irresponsibility" in terrorizing some of the press by declaring antiwar publications "nonmailable," reveal important differences between Hand and Holmes. Holmes was the Olympian observer, a relatively unconcerned Stoic watching the combatants from afar as they fought their battles. There were ample detachment and skepticism in Hand's ironic philosophy, but there was also greater human sympathy, a greater concern with what we now call the "chilling effects" of prosecuting dissidents, with the real-life impact of legal doctrine. Neither supported the prosecutions as a matter of policy; but while Holmes viewed them simply as illustrations of mankind's folly, to Hand they were genuine tragedies.

Holmes's quite different perspective on the appropriate legal standards was clear in his response to Hand. He quoted the full "clear and present danger" test from *Schenck* and added this remarkable comment: "I don't see how you differ from the test as stated by me." After all, Hand had stated in *Masses* that words may constitute a violation of the statute, without proof of an actual obstruction. "So I don't know what the matter is, or how we differ so far as your letter goes."[242]

But very much was the matter. Of course Hand recognized that words could sometimes be punishable. Virtually everyone agreed on that point. But the real challenge was to articulate a legal standard that would protect most criticism of government while punishing unacceptable expressions. Eight months later, Justice Holmes at last began to get some of the point: in the fall of 1919, in a dissent to the majority opinion in *Abrams v. United States*, his best-known view of the First Amendment,[243] it was as if the message of critics such as Hand were having a delayed, if only partial, effect. Holmes's dissent in *Abrams* is classic primarily because of its eloquent concluding passages, with their emphasis on the "free trade in ideas" as "the theory of our Constitution." Those passages indeed respond to Hand's sense of the values of free speech. But on the second part of Hand's argument, on the need for adequate legal implementation of free-speech values, Holmes's dissent was less satisfying. And Hand was not satisfied.

The majority opinion affirming the convictions of the *Abrams* defendants dismissed their constitutional objections as untenable under *Schenck*. It is in fact hard to see significant differences between this opinion and the opinions Holmes himself had written the previous spring. Indeed, the words the *Abrams* defendants had used were a good deal more threatening than those of the earlier defendants; the *Abrams* defendants were Russian-born aliens, self-confessed "revolutionists" and "anarchists" who in August 1918 in New York City had thrown thousands of leaflets into the street—some in English, some in Yiddish—that opposed American intervention in the Russian Revolution and appealed to workers in ammunition factories to stop producing weapons used "to murder their dearest," the Soviet revolutionaries.[244]

Yet Holmes, joined by Justice Louis Brandeis, now dissented. In part, Holmes relied on a constitutional argument—a newly invigorated "clear and present danger" test, infused at last with an immediacy element. And he now saw the force of the historical argument to which he had been oblivious earlier: the First Amendment did not leave "the common law as to seditious libel [which permitted criminal prosecutions for mere criticisms of government] in force. History seems to me against the notion. I had conceived that the United States through many years had shown its repentance for the Sedition Act of 1798."[245] Holmes's dissent left many questions unanswered; but it did provide a real basis for regarding "clear and present danger" as speech-protective at last.

Hand's reaction to Holmes's dissent was intriguing. He welcomed it for its values, but he did *not* endorse its legal standards. To have Holmes finally recognize free speech as worthy of special protection was gratifying, and writing to Holmes in late November, he mainly expressed his appreciation of finding added judicial support for his own special concern for speech. But, more important to Hand, "clear and present danger," even in its revised form, was still less attractive than his own incitement test.

Hand must have found it especially hard to repress his reservations about Holmes's standard, because the underlying practical risks to dissidents were greater than ever. As he told Holmes, "the merry sport of Red-baiting goes on, and the pack gives tongue more and more shrilly." He ended his letter with an especially powerful line: "For men who are not cock-sure about everything and especially for those who are not damned cock-sure about anything, the skies have a rather sinister appearance."[246] With Holmes's short reply,[247] the Hand-Holmes correspondence about the First Amendment ended: Hand thought it pointless to pursue his advocacy of the "incitement" test with Holmes, but he advocated his position for a while longer, this time addressing his appeals to Zechariah Chafee.

By the end of 1919, Chafee had begun to build a reputation as a scholar of civil liberties. Free speech was a very recent interest with him, but at a time when few academics were concerned with the First Amendment, even two years' exposure to the field was enough for incipient prominence. (Chafee's research had produced little of use until he came across *Masses*. As he told Hand, "It was really your opinion in the *Masses* case that started me on my work.)"[248] Then, in 1920, Chafee published *Freedom of Speech*, which was to be for the next three decades a leading study of the First Amendment, and which immensely enhanced the importance of Holmes's "clear and present danger" test.

The occasion for many of the Hand-Chafee letters was Chafee's ironic decision to dedicate his Holmes-praising *Freedom of Speech* not to Holmes himself but to Hand. The truth is that Chafee had a secret preference for Hand's approach in *Masses*.[249]* Perhaps the ultimate irony is that Hand wrought better than he knew: though he had lost hope that his test would ever be accepted, he persisted for several years in elaborating its advantages to Chafee; and these private messages reiterated the lessons that the Supreme Court ultimately learned decades later. The legend on the dedication page of Chafee's book reads, "To Learned Hand who during the turmoil of war courageously maintained the tradition of English-speaking freedom and gave it new clearness and strength for the wiser years to come."[250]

What, then, made Chafee a propagandist for Holmes's test? Perhaps Chafee became an unwitting captive of the Holmes mythology he had created. Also, there are pragmatic explanations: Holmes's position was on the Supreme Court books; *Masses* was not; one might as well make the most of the second best. Hand himself understood Chafee's emphasis on Holmes in that light. As he wrote to Chafee at the beginning of 1921, "You have, I dare say, done well to take what has fallen from Heaven and insist that it is manna rather than to set up any independent solution. 'Immediate and direct' is all we have; for God's sake let us not look it in the mouth."[251]

Yet Hand himself did not view the differences between him and Holmes as "minor." He wrote to Chafee:

> I do not altogether like the way Justice Holmes put the limitation. I myself think it is a little more manageable and quite adequate a distinction to say that there is an absolute and objective test to language. I daresay that it is obstinacy, but I still prefer that which I attempted to state in my first "Masses" opinion, rather than to say that the connection between the words used and the evil aimed at should be "immediate and direct."[252]

This was no offhand remark. When Chafee suggested some other variations in free-speech doctrine, Hand carefully reformulated his view:

> I prefer a test based upon the nature of the utterance itself. . . . There could be no objection to the rule of the Supreme Court,

* Only once did Chafee acknowledge this publicly: in a 1952 pamphlet, he confessed, "I still like better Judge Learned Hand's phrase in [*Masses*], 'direct incitement to violent resistance.' " But, characteristically, he added, even then, "Yet these are only minor variations" (Zechariah Chafee, Jr., *Thirty-five Years with Freedom of Speech* [New York: Roger M. Baldwin Civil Liberties Foundation, 1952], 9).

tendency plus a purpose to produce the evil, . . . if one were sure
of the result in practical administration. . . . My own objection
to the [Holmes approach] rests in the fact that it exposes all who
discuss heated questions to an inquiry before a jury as to their
purposes. . . . My own belief is that a jury is an insufficient
protection. I think it is precisely at those times when alone the
freedom of speech becomes important as an institution, that the
protection of a jury on such an issue is illusory. The event seems
to me to have proved this. . . . In taking sides I suppose one will
range oneself according to one's degree of natural scepticism about
opinions in general. For myself I think our chief enemies are
Credulity, and his brother Intolerance.[253]

A few months later, Chafee asked Hand for permission to dedicate
Freedom of Speech to him; Hand was delighted. But the difficulty still
remained. In what may be the most impressive of his letters to Chafee,
Hand reiterated:

I am not wholly in love with Holmesy's test and the reason is
this. Once you admit that the matter is one of degree, while you
may put it where it genuinely belongs, you so obviously make it
a matter of administration, i.e. you give to Tomdickandharry,
D.J., so much latitude [here Hand wrote and struck out "as his
own fears may require" and continued] that the jig is at once up.
Besides even their Ineffabilities, the Nine Elder Statesmen, have
not shown themselves wholly immune from the "herd instinct"
and what seems "immediate and direct" to-day may seem very
remote next year even though the circumstances surrounding the
utterance be unchanged. I own I should prefer a qualitative formula, hard, conventional, difficult to evade.

It was a splendid letter to crown a sparkling sequence. Throughout,
Hand combined the qualities of a judicial craftsman with the concerns
of a committed civil libertarian, and there were also glimpses of the
warm, modest, and charming human being, expressing a final joy about
Chafee's dedication of the book:

[Y]ou have made *me* feel very happy, and you have pleased three
little girls too, who I am glad to say have never regarded their
father hitherto as much more than an elderly man with a not
wholly reliable amiability, though buttressed with a taste for
buffoonery.[254]

As Hand wrote to Chafee, in a noteworthy last paragraph of his final letter in their exchange:

> I can't help wondering whether a good many years from now when you are old and I am dead, you may not pick up the book and reading the first page, smile with some amusement and some regret. . . . [I]f I were there then—and perhaps I shall come back to plague you for your thoughts, because ghosts have no respect for freedom of opinion—I should feel a little as though I have passed off on you some false coin.[255]

Hand's characteristically self-deprecating words had a serious undercurrent. As he wrote to the civil liberties lawyer Walter Nelles two years later, "I have not much hope that my own views as stated in the Masses case would ever be recognized as law."[256] And from the reaction to *Masses* in the next decades, it seemed indeed destined to be viewed as "false coin." Chafee himself did not adhere to his dedication: when he published a revised edition in 1941, the dedication went instead to former Harvard president A. Lawrence Lowell.[257] By then, *Masses* seemed forgotten, the revised "clear and present danger" test had made its way from Supreme Court dissents into majority opinions, and the Holmesian phrase had become the major rallying point for civil libertarians.

But "clear and present danger" was always a standard more popular than sturdy. During the 1940s, "clear and present danger" came under increasing attack. It flourished largely in contexts far from its origin in the problems of allegedly seditious speech. And when the Supreme Court returned to the subversion context with the prosecution of Communist party leaders under the Smith Act, in *Dennis v. United States* in 1951,[258] "clear and present danger" proved of little help in the protection of free speech.*

By the end of the Earl Warren era, the incitement criterion, so long urged by Hand, finally became part of the law of the land. Hand's analysis was precious metal, never "false coin"; the problem always lay in the eyes of the appraisers. Hand's courageous teaching made sense in 1917 and 1918, in 1920 and 1921; nearly five decades later, the American legal system came to appreciate it.

* See pp. 598–605.

IV

The Marriage and Its Tensions

MOUNT KISCO, where the Hands decided to build a summer house, was an accessible summer retreat for New York financiers and businessmen, a social circle not likely to entice Learned Hand. Yet the couple had friends there, Learned could readily travel to and fro for weekends, and Mount Kisco's trees and flowers and lawns satisfied some of his wife's cravings for gardening, the outdoors, and escapes into nature's solitude. For Frances, the special attraction of Mount Kisco was the prospect of being with Mildred Minturn; for Learned, it was the companionship of their friends Pierre and Louisa (Loulie) Jay, who had first enticed him and Frances to Mount Kisco in 1905, when the Jays rented the Hands a cottage on their property, with the Hands keeping a horse for their carriage at the Jays' stable, taking vegetables from their garden, and sharing a caretaker with them.

The search for land to build a house turned out to be easy. After a few months of negotiations with a Wall Street banker who offered to sell some nearby land, during which Learned tried to be as businesslike as possible even while dealing with a social acquaintance, he bought a property for about $6,000[1] and immediately plunged into planning a house and stable even while he was completing the purchase of the New York house on East Sixty-fifth Street. His meticulous attention to detail resurfaced in his dealings with William A. Delano, the architect, and the contractor on the summer house. (Delano was also Hand's architect in remodeling the East Side house; Hand thought Delano was an even better designer than the well-known architect Charles Platt, later his neighbor and friend in Cornish, New Hampshire.) During the summer of 1906, while construction was under way, the Hands once again rented the Jays' cottage. Learned hovered about with suggestions (and complaints) throughout the building process, and, to Frances's annoyance, construction workers were still underfoot when they moved in during the summer of 1907. The total cost of the Mount Kisco home was $20,000.

Between 1905 and 1909, the Hands' three daughters were born—Mary Deshon in 1905, Frances in 1907, and Constance in 1909. The private family life was not tranquil—and this was not just because of the turbulence of child rearing. By 1908, when the Hands had their first opportunity to enjoy the house in Mount Kisco in peace, with the workmen gone at last, they had become disenchanted. Learned had hoped that the businessmen and financiers who were their neighbors would have broad interests, but Pierre Jay was an exception: most of the others seemed narrow and politically conservative; their uncritical echoings of received wisdoms set his teeth on edge. So the highlight of the Hands' summer was the time they spent elsewhere—in a rented house in Cornish, New Hampshire, on the Connecticut River a few miles south of Hanover. By the end of some weeks there, they decided to move to Cornish for their summers; beginning in 1910, they rented summer homes there virtually every year; in 1912, they sold the Mount Kisco house to Joseph P. Cotton, one of Hand's good friends among Wall Street reformist lawyers; and in 1919, they bought a house in Cornish and used it as their country home for the rest of their lives.

Cornish, already well established as a writers' and artists' colony, was an ideal setting for unwinding from city tensions, an unusually lovely, wooded place with rambling roads and paths beckoning to long walks. Ideas and good talk filled the air, and Learned, disenchanted with Wall Street's pursuit of greed and hungry for intellectual stimulation, quickly grew fond of it. And it appealed even more to Frances, no doubt the initiating force behind the move north. For her, Mount Kisco's attractiveness had dropped precipitously in 1908, when Mildred Minturn married and moved to Europe permanently. Moreover, Frances had been enchanted by Cornish well before Learned ever saw it. On visits to her Bryn Mawr classmate Frances Arnold there,[2] she had been introduced to the community's intellectual ferment (Cornish was known to some New Yorkers as "the Athens of America").[3] And she loved the more spacious countryside of New Hampshire, knowing that it would inspire richer engagement with nature and wider opportunities for long walks and gardening.

Cornish residents were more diverse than those of Mount Kisco, far more catholic in their interests, and more liberal and progressive in their politics (although hardly as radical in arts and politics as the

Greenwich Village bohemians of the day). Yet for the risk-averse, anxiety-ridden Learned, the thought of going so far north—so far from New York City and so soon after investing so much energy and money in Mount Kisco—could not but add to his unsettled feelings. Mount Kisco was readily reachable for weekends; to get to Cornish required a nine-hour train ride from New York City, and the place was therefore usable by him only for extended summer stays. But Frances's obvious attraction to New Hampshire and Learned's own interest in its informal, stimulating atmosphere ultimately prevailed.

Even more unsettling to Learned were his recurrent anxieties about health—his own and that of his family. Not only did he have to battle a serious illness, but the joys of having three children in the span of five years were diminished by his irrepressible capacity to fret—about his wife's stamina, about family planning and birth-control methods, and about his daughters' nutrition and health. For the rest of his life, he remembered February 26, 1905, as the "ominous day" when he "fell ill" with pneumonia and "nearly went out."[4] Pneumonia was a serious disease in the days before antibiotics, and whether or not Learned would survive remained in doubt throughout March and well into April. His friends in Albany and Boston as well as New York gave what encouragement they could.[5] The crisis passed at last by May, when Learned's friends could express relief that he had returned "from the borderland country into which you journeyed, and toward which we followed you with anxious hearts."[6] The complete recovery lasted months longer: Learned was unable to return to a full work schedule until the early fall. Throughout these difficult months, Frances supplied calm and loving reassurance, and he was forever grateful for her ministrations, even while she gave birth to and cared for their first child, Mary Deshon, born in March. As he wrote Frances thirty-nine years later, "I think of how faithful and loyal you were to me in those terrible days. . . . [It] is wonderful to have spent one's life with a person who [has] that absolutely unconquerable courage and loyalty."[7]

When Learned's victory over pneumonia allayed his fears for his own health, he returned to his more typical apprehensions about the health of those close to him. During these outbreaks of concern, he frequently turned for advice and reassurance to his sister's husband, Dr. Henry Hun of Albany. Ordinarily, "Harry" Hun's conservative politics and trite philosophizing held little attraction for Learned, but Harry was a competent physician and Learned a nervous layman who was uninformed about family-planning matters beyond the elementary facts of life. Learned's mother surely would have considered talk about conception and pregnancy sinful: as Harry once commented to Learned, the "older theology of your mother's day [made] sin absolute." And Learned felt more comfortable supplementing his knowledge by turning to his brother-in-law rather than to forbidding New York City doctors.

Learned's inquiries to Harry Hun began as early as 1904. When difficulty in conceiving their first child led to some impatience in Frances and considerable brooding by Learned, Harry Hun quickly provided reassurance, some basic physiological information, and pointed warnings lest Frances resort to needless surgery or Learned doubt his own virility: "If at first you don't succeed try try again. Tell your fair bride that 'all things come to her who knows how to wait.' Rome was not built in a day nor can the heir of the Hand family be perfected 'ab ovo' on any ordinary chance occasion."[8] Dr. Hun might be prone to clichés, but reassuring homilies were just what Learned needed, and Hun provided them throughout the Hands' early married years.

Then, by the summer of 1905, concerns about baby Mary's health and proper feeding preoccupied Learned. Frances was breast-feeding successfully, yet Learned worried. On a visit to Boston, he engaged in a "vigorous, raucous" dispute with an old Harvard friend "over the advisability of bottle as against breast feeding." The Boston friend strongly recommended "bottling a baby at once,"[9] but Frances continued right on with breast-feeding until the baby was eight months old. When Mary briefly became cranky while being weaned, her father had another serious attack of "nerves." Hun once more provided reassurance: "There is apt to be some little difficulty in separating a child from its first fountain of youth but at the age of eight months there is no danger. She will take to her new liquor in time. Frances is getting experience in life and thereby a knowledge which she could never acquire in Bryn Mawr."[10]

Only rarely did Hun reveal impatience with Learned's need for reassuring consultations. After dealing with Learned's mother and her gastric worries, he burst out, "It is a joy not without alloy to live in a family where apprehension daily reaches the intensity of insanity,"[11] but a few days later he was once again ready with soothing words about baby Mary's minor glandular infection: "Babies are troubles and cares, and children do not fail to cause anxieties also."[12]

The Hands' second child, Frances, was born in the spring of 1907.[13] The presence of two young children in the house only doubled the occasions for Learned's concern, and when a polio epidemic broke out in New York City in the fall, Learned feared for his children with good reason. But his anxiety attack in late 1907—the first of many—was triggered by something quite different, a worry that despite their care about birth control, he and Frances would confront an unplanned pregnancy. "Fear not," Hun reassured him: unplanned pregnancies were most unlikely when prophylactics were used. "Even in this rapidly changing and capricious world a few scientific rocks still stand firm."[14] Learned's "cautious and wavering nature" was averse to any "positive statement," Hun knew, but he was so confident that Learned's fears were unjustified that he bet on it, and a few weeks later Learned sent Hun a check to pay off the wager.[15]

In 1909, when Learned became a judge, a third and last child, Constance, was born. By now, Learned's experiences as a father precluded needless worries about childhood illnesses, but his anxieties about unplanned pregnancies continued. Dr. Hun was exasperated: "You and your fair bride are cowards. You are dreading a danger which is only possible and not probable. . . . I think that you may reasonably expect an escape."[16]

Despite these worries, Learned considered his early years in New York City to be among the happiest of his married life. His recovery from near fatal pneumonia unleashed an unaccustomed burst of cheeriness, and the endearments in his letters reached new heights of affection. He addressed Frances as "Kitten" or "Kitty," occasionally as "Dearest Puss," "Dearest Heart of Life," and "My Dearest of Women."[17] Most often, he ended his letters with a deft little drawing of a feline mate, a "Cat" for his "Kitten";[18] affectionate signatures included "Your Woodcockie" and "Your Own Pucky Catnip Boy."[19] And even though he may have regretted that none of his children was a boy (or so Dr. Hun assumed),[20] he took genuine delight in the babies. When Mary was about a year old, Hand wrote his wife:

> The baby was too sweet for words this morning, and between ourselves I think she is utterly fascinating. . . . [H]er merry little chuckles were most engaging. I think that the queer little slits she makes of her eyes were most bewitching. They look like this [here Hand sketched a small, happy face]; do you recognize your little offspring?[21]

And a month later:

> I think of that dear little pink back roaring out her infant energy and it fills me with deep satisfaction. I certainly never expected to be so happy as I have [been] for some time. . . . I feel . . . this is something which nothing can now take from me. . . .[22]

Yet strains were developing in the Hands' marriage, although Learned did not yet perceive them. Working hard, he lacked the time and energy to respond to Frances's needs. She, burdened by the demands of household and motherhood and the recurrent need to calm her often anxious husband, grew increasingly restless. In later years, in long, self-flagellating birthday letters to his wife, Hand often brooded about his early insensitivity to her and blamed his own driven nature. As he once acknowledged, "I blame myself [for] so much in our early years. [If] I had been less ambitious for things that in the end don't come to much I should have neglected less what would have satisfied you."[23]

Signs of Frances's restlessness and withdrawal appeared from the start. At first, she spent her time much as she had before she and Learned married: her days were filled with visits to and from friends, her evenings with dinner parties. Her letters to Mildred Minturn featured reports of get-togethers with old friends, gatherings dominated by news of engagements and marriages, and other gossip.[24] She would complain: "You, having lived so long in interesting circles, O.S., probably have forgotten how unusual it is here to get people who can talk. I should just love to hear good talk." Yet in the next sentence she would report on her latest rounds of visitors and their "very satisfactory" chitchat "about life, women, the West, etc." Visits from Bryn Mawr friends stimulated her most: with these, she could have "a pleasant collegy time."[25] To Frances, "good talk" certainly did not include the details of domestic life. As she reported to Mildred on returning from a vacation with Learned in upstate New York, most of "the women folk" there seemed "terrible": "An awful feeling of deadly boredom came over me one day when I walked up w. two of them . . . to the golf club, and literally the conversation never for a moment swerved from servants, children and domestic details. It is an evil indulgence to allow myself to get bored but I lay prone then. There were no books to speak of and no view."[26]

Yet Frances demonstrated no greater determination to commit herself to systematic studies or a career than she had before her marriage. During their engagement, Learned had suggested to her, "[W]hy not inquire of Giddings [a sociologist who had moved from Bryn Mawr to Columbia] or Columbia generally about the course of instruction for [a] Ph.D.?" But there is no indication that Frances ever pursued that suggestion. By late 1904, in any event, Frances had become pregnant with Mary Deshon; the birth of three children in five years, and Frances's decision to nurse them, kept her very busy. Yet even during the free hours that her ample household help permitted her, she could not bring herself to adhere even to a regime of reading. As before, she reported to Mildred, "As to reading, I find it so difficult to do decently."[27] Once again, she promised, but did not implement, a more disciplined literary diet: "My leisure for reading is getting less and less so that I am thinking of doing what [William] James suggests for character exercise viz. 2 hrs. per diem."[28]

Nor did Frances pursue social or political causes in any persistent way. During the 1904 presidential election campaign, she told Mildred, "How I wish we could vote and be in it for the sake of the experiment."[29] But for another decade she showed no greater interest than that in the women's suffrage movement. Only one social project captured her attention: she became active in a trade school for underprivileged children. "The work of the boys has really been very good," she reported, "& the thing is a living & a fine & stimulating work. The girls (27) are doing pretty good work in millinery. The drawing is rather a waste of time I think." The school principal lacked interest in the girls' development, and Frances advocated merging the two single-sex schools; but this, she reported, was a "very delicate" matter, though "*most* necessary."[30] The trade school managed to elicit her interest for several years, and she helped bring about the unification of the girls' and boys' departments.[31] Moreover, she took some interest in her college's alumnae affairs. Reporting to Mildred about a Bryn Mawr dinner in New York City, she sketched a diagram showing where everyone sat, but criticized Carey Thomas's speech as "the dullest I've ever heard her make": "[S]he seemed to me to have degenerated because she made several remarks such as 'B.M. is the only college of standing which has a woman at the head and men serving in subordinate capacity under her,' etc. Not meant perhaps egotistically, but considering the fact that there seems to be an increasing dislike among some men to come to B.M. just because they have to be under Miss T., it was unfortunate to mention it."[32] In June 1918, Frances was elected an alumnae trustee.[33]

The summer days spent in Mount Kisco from 1905 to 1908 were at first satisfying for Frances. Loulie Barlow Jay was an engaging acquaintance, and, more important, Mildred Minturn's nearby little cottage offered the prospect of renewed good talks and reading to each other in the old Bryn Mawr way. But, to Frances's great disappointment, Mildred's presence in Mount Kisco proved more hope than reality. In the fall of 1903, Mildred, at her mother's behest, had gone to France in the wake of "another relapse"—a renewed bout of the neurasthenia she had suffered after the Hands' marriage—where she recovered enough to immerse herself in studies of French socialism, cooperatives, and workers' conditions.[34] Frances and Mildred wrote to each other frequently during these two years that Mildred spent in France, Frances typically the less faithful correspondent, frequently apologizing for the delays in her responses. Clearly she missed Mildred and yearned for

her company. "I long to see you again. When are you coming back?";
"I long for the flowers and grass. I wish you were in yr. little Mount
Kisco house"; glimpsing Mildred's "little house" on a visit to Mount
Kisco "made me so homesick, just the sight of the smoke curling out
of the chimney, that I didn't go down to it" immediately; "I wonder
when we shall live near each other again"; "When are you coming
back to USA?"; "I wish you could be here to lie w. me and read poetry.
Do you remember? We shall have good times yet, O.S."; "I feel as if
I couldn't bear to have you abroad another winter, almost as if you
were drifting away from me. . . . I hope our paths won't be so long
separate again. I long to see you."[35]

These entreaties prompted Mildred to plan a lengthy visit to Mount
Kisco for the early fall of 1905. Frances's spirits lifted dramatically:
"It will be perfect when we are both, at no distant date now, ensconced
in our 2 separate & cunning little houses at Mount K. I could only
wish dear O.S. that we were under one roof for [the] times to do real
talking come then." Although Frances, like Learned, found her firstborn
daughter enchanting, the chores of nursing and the dullness of her social
routines cast shadows. "I have such an attack of 'wanderlust,' " she
reported to Mildred, "that I feel as if a little encouragement would start
me going." And even the demands of the baby did not stop her from
leaving to see friends with surprising regularity. Frances and Loulie
Jay found time for a five-day visit to Boston for a "change of scenes."
Learned, busy in his law office, would try to cheer her up. When he
thought she "might feel 'down,' " he would bring her "a lot of lovely
roses. . . . Wasn't it sweet of him?" Frances told Mildred.[36]

Frances expected perhaps too much from Mildred's return to America,
especially as an antidote to her mounting restlessness. When the time
for Mildred's arrival drew near, Frances wrote, "I may say w. all honesty
O.S. dear that I am yearning to see you and feel a strange sense of
excitement and exhilaration to think of our meeting again." She had
been observing "2 O.S. friends here," two young women obviously
attached to each other, "and they make me homesick. There is a satisfied
look in the eyes of each and they go off hand in hand w. a tea basket
& book for the afternoon." She added, "Our time is coming and we
shall make the different pasts of the last 2 years one."[37]

Mildred's visit went well: as she herself reported, she had "a happy
autumn with Kleine & B. & little Mary, & Loulie & her 3 babies, in
my own little home."[38] But by mid-November 1905, she decided she
had to return to France for a while longer. Frances impatiently awaited
what she expected would be Mildred's imminent return. Even as she

reported that life was "full of interest" at last, and that she and Learned would soon move into the house they had bought on East Sixty-fifth Street, she hinted that Mildred's permanent return to Mount Kisco was necessary to make her life complete.[39] When Mildred delayed month after month, Frances repeatedly reminded her: "It will be good to have you back again."[40]

By the summer of 1906, the letters from Mildred carried hints that threatened to dash Frances's hopes. In the spring, Mildred had met a young Englishman at the home of new friends. Arthur H. Scott seemed "intelligent, high-minded, nice-looking & attractive"; from the outset, Mildred thought he might "turn out to be Alexander Augustus" (a mythical husband-friend and husband-lover she had concocted). For several months, Mildred vacillated about considering marriage, sometimes berating herself for entertaining such romantic dreams about someone who, though her contemporary, seemed years younger than she,[41] and who had his hands full trying to direct an English-style boys' boarding school in the French provinces. Repeatedly, she sought to banish such thoughts by plunging herself into work, especially her efforts to write a book. Yet at other times, she feared that if she did not marry, she would give up her last chance for passion and happiness.[42]

Frances watched Mildred's emotional struggle with trepidation. Once, when she opened a letter from Mildred "w. a quaking qualm," she feared "that you were going to tell me that you had cast your line w. [Scott]." When a letter indicated that Mildred was leaning against marriage, Frances voiced her "great relief": "I felt almost as if you had come back to me." In early September, an uncharacteristic silence from Mildred filled Frances with renewed fear: "Every now & again there drifts through my mind a kind of foreboding that the silence means a struggle going on w. [Scott] or some unknown!" Now, when she referred to the anticipated permanent reunion in Mount Kisco, her uncertainty was palpable: "Shall we ever see each other again & live cheek by jowl? I'm counting on Mount Kisco for that."[43]

Frances's concern was well based. A letter was on its way to her from Mildred, then staying with her mother at a cottage near the home of the Bertrand Russells in England, assuring Frances that Mildred was "not feeling a bit as if I could ever leave you for anyone." Yet, she acknowledged, another "impulse" came in "waves"—her attraction to Arthur Scott: "[S]ometimes I wonder whether it wldn't be wisest to cut & run *now* when there is no real danger & I could do it easily!" Her mother had asked her to invite Scott for a September weekend, and Mildred thought it might be "foolhardy to risk such important things on the chance of emotion coming in & playing an unforeseen part." There might be no risk, but "I have a suspicion that there is one." Though she was tempted to "escape at the end of the month with Mamma," she ultimately decided to risk another meeting: if she did run away, she speculated, "& then never had a drawing to anyone again, & lived a sterile old maid all my days, I suppose I should regret it. It's probably sensible to give the other side a chance. And yet—Oh, Dear, O.S. I wish you were here."[44]

In early September 1906, Mildred told Frances how the weekend visit by Scott had gone. During her stay in Mount Kisco the previous fall, she had promised Frances not to marry without first coming home; now, though still undecided, she explained the new situation: "[Arthur Scott and I] walked & drove together & talked endlessly all day long, & darling . . . I want you to release me from a promise I made at Mount Kisco. . . . I have not decided, dearest little friend, but I must be free to do so if I want. He is very dear O.S. & very fine & I think charming." Still, the "balance *may* tip the home way. I can't tell yet." Mildred claimed to be "dreadfully torn," but her leanings were frighteningly obvious to Frances: "He is so cosmopolitan he doesn't quite understand how I feel about the idea of leaving America. Nobody over here will. You are such a large part of America to me, friend of my heart, that it is hard for any third person, no matter how sympathetic, to see. Well, O.S., I may come back, a cheery old maid, to you & Mary & our little houses & our jogging drives through the country & morning readings."[45]

Frances, pregnant with her second daughter,[46] received Mildred's letter two weeks later and promptly replied:

[I]t has left me with a heavy heart and a sense of loss, all this selfishly speaking of course. As for you, dear, I can only feel gladness if you have decided that you are in love and have found fairy prince. Being married is so blessed a state that one wants it very much for one's near & dear. I could think of nothing else all yesterday and when I passed the little cottage I felt a lump in my throat. How little we can foretell the future. I shall wait so *palpitatingly* for your next letter O.S.—don't be long awriting.

And she added a postscript to this letter, addressed to "Dearest" and signed "Yr. very loving O.S.": "I love you very much and last night under the 'starry canopy of heaven' I felt that I cldn't lose you out of my life."[47]

But lose Mildred she did. Mildred, uncertain until the end about marrying Scott, couldn't "face the idea of going back to America alone & never seeing him again." Bertrand Russell, who didn't "know any of the complications," urged her "to do it." And Arthur Scott proposed marriage. On September 25, they "finally took the plunge of telling people," and Mildred sent a cablegram conveying the news to Frances. She and Scott decided to get married three weeks hence, in October, and Mildred at last could write in her diary, "I am very content."[48]

That evening, Frances, sitting by the fire in her little Mount Kisco green room "with the dark outside and that crispness in the air which used to make us feel the joy of the fire," wrote Mildred of her sadness:

> You can't know O.S. how life has changed for me since your cable. Every drive I take and every hour of the day brings to me the memory of our planned years together here. . . . I thought of the years without you. I know how you felt when I married but if your life were only to be here I should so rejoice. I shall anyway O.S. for these are all selfish mournings, for the joy of marriage gives one such a hold on the springs of life that I want it for you. It is only that the kind of friendship we have had is so rare a thing that the separation is so hard a thing to bear. I care more my dear since I've been married & had the baby than I could have before. I'll read a little poem tonight pour le bon souvenir but somehow my eyes get very wet.[49]

With Mildred's commitment to remain in Europe, most of the attraction of Mount Kisco waned for Frances, and for the remainder of her years there she mourned Mildred's absence. "Oh O.S. dear I wish you were here by my side," she wrote nearly two years later. "It is now night and I am alone. This combination always make me think to you-ward & wish you were near & we could read & talk until we went to sleep."[50] By then, Mildred was expecting a child of her own.

Frances was also prompted to move to New Hampshire by more inchoate feelings of restlessness and ennui. The "deluge of the prosperous newly married," the "dull young married people,"[51] who were flooding Mount Kisco reinforced her desire to escape the "struggling temper of the men" in the competitive life of New York City. All the jockeying for worldly achievements, she thought, "was apt to make life, this straining for success, so arid in other directions that it seemed wrong." She clearly preferred a simpler life: she loved the peacefulness of nature and even flirted with the "ancient idealism of poverty": "the liberation from material attachments, the unbribed soul, the manlier indifference, the paying our way not by what we have but what we are, the right to fling away our life at any moment irresponsibly—the more athletic trim, in short, the moral fighting shape, etc."[52]

This could not have been taken literally. After all, she enjoyed her comfortable residences, her household staff, and her freedom from financial pressures. But her dissatisfaction was real: she yearned for simplicity. Her husband loved her, did not overvalue material acquisitions, took delight in their children, exercised his talents for mimicry and elaborate games as he rolled on the floor with the youngsters. Yet in Mount Kisco as well as Manhattan, she was ever more surrounded by "struggling" men. And Learned, too, was preoccupied with a quest for worldly achievements, with "straining for success." He came to Mount Kisco as often as he could in the summer, and spent most evenings with her and the children when the family was in New York. But he was driven and insecure, and he worked immensely hard. That left little time for long walks and reading aloud to each other poetry and prose, and Frances was discontented.

A desire for greater spiritual fulfillment added to her discontent. When she had first suspected that she was pregnant with little Frances, she had told Mildred, "[I]t's rather a solemn business though, this calling of children into the world. I feel more & more that [we] have so few convictions [and] faiths to hand on to our children." No more religiously observant than Learned, she nonetheless began attending church for a while, "to hear . . . one whose profession it was to think about spiritual matters speak." And she acknowledged to Mildred: "I have come to feel that we, of the free mind, have a great lack in having *no* rituals which we can take part in, in order to refresh us spiritually."[53]

All these emotions prompted Frances to gain Learned's agreement to make Cornish rather than Mount Kisco their summer retreat. Learned was not nearly so enthusiastic, and urged her to go slowly before reaching a decision: "I want you to please yourself and if you feel strongly you must do it, but I must confess . . . that it was a hard blow to me to look forward to [Cornish] every summer till I was through. I really don't think I have got to you how I do feel about it."[54] The long travel time to New Hampshire explains a good part of his reluctance, but more important, he sensed that he was losing her companionship.

For Frances, the attractions of Cornish were always clear. There was a lively social scene with her and Learned's friends the Rublees, the Churchills, the Platts, and the Littells, as well as her classmate Frances Arnold; there was also the even more powerful magnet of Cornish's extraordinary physical beauty. But most important of all, not long after the Hands moved to Cornish, Frances found there a close and intimate friend to take Mildred Minturn's place in her life.

THE NEW FRIEND was Louis Dow, professor of French at nearby Dartmouth College in Hanover. Dow, a year older than Learned, was tall and handsome, with a quick wit, a gentle temperament, and a scholar's intellect.[55] He was already a part of the Cornish social circle when the Hands began to spend their summers there. Dow and the Hands quickly became good friends. Even by the end of the Hands' first summer in Cornish, Dow and Learned corresponded on an intimate first-name basis, with letters between "Dear 'B' " and "My dear Louis."[56] At the outset, Dow lived with his wife, Rebecca; in 1912 and 1913, she developed a mental illness, and she spent the rest of her life in mental hospitals.[57]

By 1913, when Dow had commenced his bachelor-like existence, repeatedly complaining of loneliness, he spent an increasing amount of time with the Hands. In October 1913, for example, Frances and her three young daughters visited Dow in Hanover, and Dow told Learned about the "good time we had"—"[i]t was a hive of merry voices from morning until night. I don't know when I have enjoyed anything as much."[58] By 1914, the relationship between Dow and the Hands had grown so close that Constance, the Hands' youngest daughter, then five years old, spent several weeks with him in Hanover.[59] By then, Dow retained "very little hope that [his wife] will get well"[60] and began spending considerable time in Frances's company. From 1917 to 1919, he was a regular houseguest at Low Court in Cornish when Frances was in residence there; the Hand children, and sometimes Frances as well, called him "Uncle Louis."

As Frances extended the duration of her visits to Cornish over the years—stretching the length of her summer vacations, frequently visiting in the fall, and sometimes adding trips during winter as well—strains in her marriage with Learned deepened. Her many letters to him contained, typically, hasty narratives of daily doings rather than the extensive outpourings of ideas and emotions characteristic of his. (Hardly any of her notes to Learned over sixty years match her letters to Mildred Minturn in length or depth.) The expressions of love that Learned so clearly craved[61] and with which she sprinkled earlier letters were now infrequent and usually combined with details about daily routines, as when she wrote, "Tell me . . . that you still hold me in affectionate remembrance and by the way what arrangement is made by the Mt. Kisco Telephone Co. about our telephones in winter. Do they allow a reduction & how much?"[62]

In 1911, Frances went to Europe with the children, and Learned told her that though he was happy she was making the journey he loved her "so dearly" that he was discontented that she was away, and that he did not have her with him, even as he had "an amorous pleasure" in writing to her. His letters were written "from no sense of duty," he said, in implied criticism of the quality of hers, "but from a craving, as if in this way I got near to you as I cannot in any other." And he once more voiced the yearning that had been so central during their engagement a decade earlier: "I should like to be able [to] have some good book to read aloud to you lying somewhere out in the grass and in the open country."[63]

Yet after Louis Dow became a regular houseguest in Cornish, Learned's dreams of being with Frances in the countryside were most often realized by Dow. Frances mentioned Dow in virtually every letter to her husband—the long walks with him, the picnics and riding, the motor trips, and especially studying and reading French together. Unself-consciously, she would report on Louis staying overnight at Low Court or having his meals there.[64]

The relationship between Louis Dow and Frances Hand was bound to raise eyebrows, and it must surely have prompted feelings of jealousy and inadequacy in Learned. The most serious tensions seem to have arisen in 1917–19, as Frances came close to purchasing a home in Cornish, despite Learned's reluctance. In 1918, for example, while Learned was spending most of the summer alone in New York City, driven as always to complete his work on the district court, he wrote to her that he loved to get her letters "more than you can imagine," yet was not really "content," for "I miss you increasingly." He regretted as well that his letters seemed "to have nothing to say to you of any intimate kind, just the usual exchange of daily news which surely means nothing or almost nothing"[65]—a description that in fact applies to her letters far more than to his.

> I wish there were some way we could see more of each other. It is all so unsatisfactory, these hurried trips and the general rush of town. I feel as if the years were passing and we had so little to show. I guess it is mostly my fault, preoccupied and rushed, where it would be possible to be serene and possessed.

He wanted to "correct" their long separations, but doubted they could: "Can we? I wonder. Shall we? I think not."[66] Although terms of endearment would occasionally recur in Frances's letters, they were composed in ever more impersonal and detached tones.

Louis Dow certainly did not overtly contribute to any alienation between Frances and Learned. Indeed, he seemed more sensitive than she to Learned's need for reassurance about his continued centrality in Frances's life. His own letters to Hand are filled with copious accounts of the doings of the children, and they have the tenor of a loving uncle, or attentive governess. Dow would listen to the children's problems, offer them advice, shower them with presents, and always defer to Learned's role in the family.[67] And whenever Frances and Louis traveled abroad without Learned (as they did several times, as in 1930 and 1939), it was he rather than she who showed the greater sensitivity in assuring Learned that his place in their lives was not forgotten.[68] In addition, Louis repeatedly thanked Learned for his emotional support during his several illnesses and for allowing Frances to travel to Cornish during these periods.[69]

It was far more than Louis Dow's companionship, however, that prompted Frances to go to Cornish so often and for so long. She had a genuine craving for the countryside and truly came to life there: the solitude of the environment and the pleasure of outdoor work gave not only physical but spiritual satisfaction. "It is *so* lovely here and the simple life in the frame of the great serene nature [is] good for the spirit!"; "I do *love* this simple life. I like doing the work"[70]—remarks like these recurred through her letters over the years. The country life allowed her to work with her hands, in tending to her garden or cleaning her house, and gave her a chance for reading and quiet reflection. The countryside brought her senses fully into play and delighted her with its beauty; "so beautiful it was, the apple blossoms just open, the grass a brilliant green, the air full of delicious smells, lilacs & violets, and then the blue Italian landscape in the distance."[71] Once, she told Learned, she walked through the meadows and

> I got boiling & then in the isolation of the place I slipped off garment after garment till I finally got to my hat & my stockings & walked with *immense* enjoyment. Don't tell anyone for it wld. sound foolish . . . but it was delicious & I can understand clearly the joys of the vie de la nature.[72]

Occasionally, she would continue to voice her yearning for spiritual satisfactions of a more traditional sort. "It is the isolated facing of the universe which is difficult," she noted; for a while she decided to read two chapters of the Bible regularly at breakfast.[73] But her reading more often consisted of French novels, read aloud with Louis Dow, from the

works of Anatole France to Romain Rolland's *Jean Christophe.*[74] But
above all, it was gardening, riding horses, swimming in the brook,
and other physical activities that nourished her spirit. As she exclaimed
in 1920, when she was forty-four years old, "Isn't it absurd to take
such pleasure in physical things at my age?"[75]

Learned Hand, alone and usually uncomplaining in New York City,
had difficulty understanding her infatuation with country life. He would
tease her with "I think of you up there on the mountain heights
consulting w. your soul and it gives me an affectionate feeling."[76] At
other times, he voiced concern that her absorption in nature indicated
an excessive withdrawal from human contacts: "At times . . . I fear
that there is a danger you will become quietistic,—willing to withdraw
from people, all but a few. It is of course well, if you find that this is
what truly suits you, and yet I sometimes think that one accepts such
things without quite calculating the changes that a withdrawn life brings
about, almost unconsciously."[77] Yet Frances would assure him that she
was happy—she had had "a fine hard morning of house work and
garden. I love it," and "I *positively* enjoy the simple things more and
more."[78] In 1919, she extended her summer in Cornish into October,
with undiminished exuberance. She and the sculptor Frances Grimes
together with Louis Dow went off on a picnic lunch and read aloud to
one another until a rain began, she reported, and she had "one perfect
& glorious time"; she was "happy as a cat."[79] Living her life as she
"wanted to" was her central drive.

The long separations from Frances troubled Learned. He wrote her
lengthy letters of love, admiration, and, only rarely, veiled criticism.
Once she replied, "I think I am influenced by your goodness—even if
I have never done much in my life that I haven't wanted to do."[80] Her
search for personal satisfaction and serenity sometimes bruised him, as
she, rather insensitively, would fill her letters with recitals of her
satisfying times alone in nature or reading, picnicking, riding, and
motoring with her friends, especially Louis.[81] Learned's often fragile
self-respect could not but be impaired by the prominence of Louis Dow
in Frances's life.

Dow's regular attendance upon Frances concerned her Cornish friends
as well. Frances Arnold, who never married (and may have been in-
fatuated with Dow), once told her that it seemed improper, in appearance
as well as in fact, to have Dow rather than the Hands' oldest daughter
sit at the head of the table during the many meals he enjoyed at Low
Court. Frances Hand's response, according to Frances Arnold, was that
she was entitled to live her life in her own way in accordance with her

credo: "I have never done much in my life that I haven't wanted to do." She would have her guest at whatever seat at the table she chose, and if others wanted to raise eyebrows about the presence of an unattached male in her home, she would not stoop to satisfy them by barring him. She had nothing to feel immoral or guilty about, and she would not change her life-style because of unjustified gossip; the community would just have to take her as she chose to be and was.[82]

There is no proof that Frances Hand and Louis Dow ever had a physical affair, though some speculated that they were lovers.[83] Learned himself never suggested anything on this score, and all that can be said is that given his great dependence on her, he stayed married. Still, his concern over appearances as well as his dissatisfaction with their frequently interrupted conjugal life eventually prompted him to confront Frances about her long absences. The tone of their correspondence strongly suggests that the pleas he made for more time with her fell on deaf ears. In all likelihood, Frances replied to Learned essentially as she had to Frances Arnold: her conscience was clear, she found immense satisfaction and joy in her life in Cornish, and she was not prepared to change it. Learned—who never failed to reiterate his great need for his wife, and who frequently told her and others that without her he would be a neurotic, depressed failure—accepted her decision and acquiesced in her desires. Afraid of losing her and being cast adrift, he apparently agreed not to stand in the way of Frances's enjoyment of her Cornish life-style, even when he was unable to join her. He accepted Louis Dow's prominence in her life, even as he vowed to find more time to spend with her.

For the rest of Louis Dow's life, until his death in 1944, Learned continued his friendship and correspondence with him. With his wife, Learned's letters became apologetic, and he berated himself for failing to understand her better in earlier years and for seeking to impose too many restraints on her. Brought up in a home where guilt was a central theme, he now found new ways to apologize for what he construed as his, not her, inadequacies in the marriage. Thus, even in the midst of the crisis, he wrote to Frances, "Do you know you have a way in your letters of so satisfying me that I am very important and dear to you, I should be willing to stand nearly anything from you, if need were. I would believe you against anything."[84] Even as he hoped that "there was some way we could see more of each other," he would add, "I guess it is mostly my fault."[85] Occasionally, he expressed confusion about her: "Sometimes I think it is hard to live up to you; sometimes I feel I understand you and then again I wonder."[86] But above all, the recurrent refrain in his letters (especially in his long birthday greetings to her) was his determination to make the necessary accommodations and to accept blame for his own shortcomings.

Learned's letters make clear that he simply adapted to a situation in which much of his wife's time was spent with another man. He had evidently accepted that the cost of having Frances spend as much time as she wished in Cornish, whatever people might think, was well worth the benefit of having her at his side at least some of the time; he could not have faced the prospect of losing her entirely. Yet occasionally he would confide to close friends that the situation was difficult. "I don't know if I can take this," he once told an old acquaintance, who took the remark as referring to the situation with Frances. But he went on ascribing much of the blame to himself. In 1919, while she was spending the fall in Cornish, he wrote:

> [A]s I think over our years together they seem to be so little full of those hours of delight that we might have had. I blame myself . . . w. so much in our early years, the blindness and insensibility to what you wanted and to your right to your own ways when they differed from mine. If I had been less ambitious for things that in the end don't come to much I should have neglected less what would have satisfied you.
>
> You realized what you wanted and w. another mate you could have had experiences to live upon till you died. But you got precious little out of me, but worries and anxieties about how I was to get along in the world, and a sort of pseudo-obligation to make my mark. Whatever it was, I won't defame it, but it never occurred to me, I believe, that the aim for the "good life," "the noble employment of leisure," was to be pitted against it. . . . I do believe I have come to see the right you have to follow your way, and I think I have learned not to trammel you as I did in the early years.[87]

On her forty-seventh birthday, in 1923, he wrote in the same mode:

> I was thinking over our start the other day, and believing I could now have made it much better than I did. Really, I gave too little thought in the early years to you and what you wanted. Most women . . . would have been unable to adjust themselves to the

vagaries of such a neurotic. I often wonder how much of what seemed to me as necessary, morally or dutifully or however one likes to put it, was a disguised egoism. As I think of it, it seems all to have been some curious feeling that there was an inevitable compulsion which I had to yield to.[88]

V

The Peak of Political Enthusiasm:
Herbert Croly, Theodore Roosevelt, and
the Progressive Years

AS HAND GAINED GREATER CONFIDENCE as a district judge, he reported to Herbert Croly that his judicial work was an "intoxicant."[1] The word has a double meaning, suggesting the dually captivating and numbing effect that mastering arcane federal court specialties had upon him. And the intellectual stimulation of his job only whetted his appetite for intellectual and personal challenges less circumscribed than those of the law.

Hand found these challenges in a new devotion to social, economic, and political activities. The casual interest with which he had previously viewed national affairs became a passionate commitment—to the cause of decent conditions for workers, to the curbing of abuses of concentrated economic power, and above all, to combating judicial obstruction of legislative reform. He also became a major progressive figure, helping to plan *The New Republic* magazine and contributing commentary (often anonymously) to its pages. For once in his life, he was a true believer, in the "New Nationalism" and the progressive cause.

What was the nature and extent of Hand's involvement in political issues during these years? What motivated him? How did he reconcile his own political engagements with principles of appropriate judicial behavior?

Hand's interest in American politics was closely related to his friendships, and the friendship most important to him during his first years on the bench was with Herbert Croly, the political commentator who later founded *The New Republic*. Hand established an immediate and warm rapport with Croly in Cornish during the summer of 1908: while many found Croly reclusive, shy, and painfully difficult to talk with, Hand discovered him to be engaging; they walked in the woods together, played tennis and golf, and spent many hours in easy conversation. As Felix Frankfurter recalled, "while [Croly] was inhibited in company, he was a free talker à deux."[2]

They were kindred souls in many respects. Like Hand, Croly came from a comfortable upper-middle-class background, although his fore-bears had not been rooted in American soil nearly as long as Hand's. Croly's father, David Goodman Croly, was an Irish immigrant who achieved a significant career in journalism; his mother, Jane Cunningham Croly, daughter of an English clergyman, was a person of even more remarkable drive who became America's first full-time newspaperwoman. David and Jane Croly were leading American advocates of positivism, Auguste Comte's allegedly scientific "religion of humanity." Yet Herbert Croly, like Learned Hand, grew up with considerable insecurities. His mother's career left her little time for her children. His father, by contrast, spent many years inculcating his son with his unusual views of life, religion, and the power of reason, views that echoed through many of Herbert Croly's writings (he dedicated his most famous book, *The Promise of American Life*, to his father), much as the image and renown of the far more remote Samuel Hand served both as a model and a source of anxiety for his son. Croly, like Hand, attended Harvard College, starting three years before Hand, in 1886. For Croly, too, the Harvard philosophers James, Royce, and Santayana were stimulating undergraduate influences, opening up new intellectual vistas. And as with Hand, the move to Harvard allowed Croly to break free from family influence: as one of Croly's friends reported, Harvard induced in him a "profound spiritual crisis . . . [a] revolt against Auguste Comte."[3] But whereas Hand finished his undergraduate work at Harvard in the normal four years, Croly's Harvard College career was frequently interrupted by self-doubts and personal crises: his sporadic attendance was spread over twelve years, from 1886 to 1897.

What Hand found most attractive in his friend was that Croly, unlike any of his other contemporaries, was leading the life that Hand had found so enticing at Harvard, the life of a philosopher. By the time Hand met him in 1908, Croly had married a wealthy woman, settled in Cornish, given up the one steady job he had held as editor of *Architectural Record*, and was able to devote full attention to writing *The Promise of American Life*.

The book was partly an account of American history, partly philosophy, and partly a systematic plan for political reform. Above all, it was a speculative, brooding book about important issues, and Croly, the speculative, brooding political philosopher, could not have been more aptly tailored to Hand's inclinations. As Hand would write Croly:

> It is a great pleasure to find a person, and you I think are nearly the only one whom I have found, who has in fact led successfully the kind of life that I once mapped out for myself and abandoned perhaps through weakness of will, though I have never been certain that it was not wise for me personally to abandon it.

Hand quickly recognized that Croly's stimulating talk and writing might help prevent the atrophy of his own intellectual interests—the atrophy threatened by Hand's work first at the bar and then on the bench. As he told Croly in early November 1909, only days after Croly's book had come off the press and only seven months after he himself had become a judge, "While this is a pleasant life to me it is really, in a sense, a kind of intoxicant. I look forward to your book as a sort of bromo-seltzer, to help clear the head."[4] And, a year later: "I am reading nothing and thinking nothing but how to construe statutes and work out laborious facts. I hope it keeps my wits sharp; it certainly keeps them narrow, and I suppose that sharpness is nothing but the ultimate expression of narrowness. Please never desert me, and leave me to be nothing but a word exchanger."[5]

Almost from the outset, Hand and Croly were on a first-name basis. After their first encounter in the summer of 1908, the Hands spent part of the year-end holiday season visiting the Crolys. Beginning in 1909, Herbert Croly and Learned Hand corresponded and saw each other often, not only in Cornish but also in New York during Croly's periodic visits there. Typically, Croly stayed at the Players' clubhouse on Gramercy Park, but sometimes he roomed with friends. Soon, Hand was inviting Croly to sleep at his and Frances's house and would meet him for dinner downtown whenever possible.

In early November 1909, Croly sent Hand one of the first copies of his newly published *The Promise of American Life*. Hand was immediately enthusiastic. Invitations to dine at the Hands', usually issued discriminatingly, soon proliferated in Croly's case. Early in December, for example, Hand suggested three alternate dinner dates for one week but quickly added, as he almost never did with any other guest, "If you can, come all three nights."[6] By New Year's, Hand took the unusual step of reviving an old and not very intimate acquaintance with Theodore Roosevelt to commend Croly's book to TR's attention. Hand was the first person to do so; and Roosevelt soon credited Croly with many of the ideas he aired in his political writings at the time and, soon after, in his 1912 Bull Moose campaign to return to the White House.

The ideas articulated in Croly's book struck an especially responsive chord in Hand. Croly's volume of more than 450 pages was at times long-winded and turgid; his vision of reform was short on details, and he lapsed occasionally into mystical realms of humane religiosity (traces of David Goodman Croly's influence that could only have made Hand impatient). Yet the book was a remarkable, hardheaded attempt to view the problems of twentieth-century America in the context of the nation's historical development. Croly astutely recognized the changes that industrialization and concentration of economic power had wrought and, like Hand, distrusted old formulas and shibboleths. His notable achievement was to locate his historical analysis within a pragmatic philosophical approach; in this way he was able to develop a sharply focused commentary on contemporary social, economic, and political problems, and to sketch a program for solving them. While most of Croly's ideas were indeed in the air, no one before him had put anything like them together in such a systematic and comprehensive way.

The central conclusion of Croly's overview of American history echoed Hand's strongest political convictions: the old Jeffersonian political vision of small farmers and businessmen in an agrarian nation was inadequate for an increasingly national economy dominated by large corporate enterprises. Croly's analysis rested on a central debate in American political theory: the conflict between Hamiltonians, who advocated a vigorous exercise of national powers, and Jeffersonians, who distrusted all government, and centralized government in particular. While Croly's views were on the whole Hamiltonian in that he advocated stronger national power, he praised Jefferson for his strong commitment to democracy and criticized Hamilton for viewing stronger national powers merely as devices to aid the wealthy. Federal power, he argued, should be used for more democratic and egalitarian ends; in short, he advocated the use of Hamiltonian means to achieve Jeffersonian ends. Among his proposals were public control of corporations and public support of the trade-union movement, as well as protective legislation for factory workers, women, and children.

The Promise of American Life also preached that bigness in economic organization was an inevitable consequence of industrial development. Croly, like Hand, had little patience with those who urged that large corporations produced what Louis Brandeis called the "curse of bigness" and must therefore be broken up. Bigness often meant efficiency, Croly insisted. A political and economic policy that sought to turn back the clock to a Jeffersonian era of small entrepreneurs seemed to him misguided in twentieth-century America. This naïve Jeffersonianism had prompted the Sherman Anti-Trust Act of 1890, whose "trust-busting" goal was mistaken, Croly thought, as was its invitation to lengthy and complicated court proceedings. Instead, Croly advocated national regulation and control of large corporations. He was vague about the specifics of implementation, although he hinted that a commission of experts that could regulate whole industries would be more effective than a system of ad hoc adjudication before unsophisticated judges and juries.

While Croly's thinking on social issues was generally more developed than Hand's, Hand was able to instruct his friend on the threat that a recalcitrant judiciary (especially the conservative justices of the Supreme Court) posed to the progressive movement. Croly viewed constitutional debates as arcana for lawyers, and he was reluctant to discuss issues about which he felt so ill informed; his remarks on the legal profession in *The Promise of American Life* were brief. He conceded that the "reform movement" had "brought into prominence many public-spirited lawyers," and certainly the lawyers among his acquaintances—including George Rublee and Learned Hand—fit that description. But he lamented that "the majority of prominent American lawyers are not reformists. The tendency of the legally trained mind is inevitably extremely conservative." Croly noted, moreover, that the "ablest American lawyers have been retained by the special interests" and that the "retainer which the American legal profession has accepted from the corporations inevitably increases its natural tendency to a blind conservatism." In Croly's view, "thoroughgoing reorganization" of the American political system could only "be brought about in spite of the opposition of the legal profession."[7]

Croly's remarks on Lochnerism were still briefer. He never mentioned the *Lochner* jurisprudence that, as Hand well knew, threatened the wide-ranging reforms he proposed, but limited himself to asserting that "the lawyer, when consecrated as Justice of the Supreme Court, has become the High Priest of our political faith." For that reason, it was "of the utmost importance that American lawyers should really represent the current of national public opinion"; if future judges were drawn from the increasingly specialized, conservative corporate bar, the cause of reform would no doubt suffer. These were sentiments that Hand could readily agree with, but Hand's deeper awareness of the problems of constitutional law and judicial review allowed him to speak with far greater confidence and specificity about these issues.[8]

Croly's book sold only about 7500 copies during his lifetime, but its audience included many of the leaders in the growing national progressive movement. Less than three years after the book's publication, many Eastern professionals and intellectuals enlisted in Teddy Roosevelt's Bull Moose third-party campaign for the presidency, Learned Hand and Herbert Croly among them, and, at various times, many of their friends—George Rublee, Joseph Cotton, Philip Littell, Winston Churchill (the American novelist), and Norman Hapgood. While Croly's book was hardly the sole cause of pre–World War I progressivism, his efforts did give the movement an intellectual cohesiveness.

Few could have anticipated the publication of Croly's book more eagerly than Hand. He had had previews of its ambitious scope and proposals in his frequent conversations with Croly for more than a year. At the beginning of November 1909, when he thanked Croly for sending one of the first copies off the press, he expressed his "confidence that I shall enjoy it very much," and added: "I feel that you think out my thoughts for me, or at least help to, and in this book I hope to find them thoroughly worked out."[9]

This indeed was what the book did for Hand. When Croly visited New York three weeks later, Hand had read through a good part of it, remarking that he was "lost in a maze of admiration at your excellent work." He added, using superlatives with rare freedom: "I mean you to believe quite literally what I say when I tell you that I consider it a most remarkable book of reasoning and certainly it is the result of the best reflection which any man of my acquaintance and anywhere near my age has given forth, with perhaps the exception of Santayana."[10]

Croly was ecstatic about Hand's enthusiasm:

> Your reference to the book overwhelmed me. Is it really as good as that? Others have been generous in their appreciation of it, but none so generous as you. Naturally I hope that it is really good not merely because I have my own share of vanity, but because it needs to win friends. It is essentially a reconnoitering expedition into territory hitherto not very well occupied in this country; and I cannot expect to hold my ground unless I [can] obtain support. I have always hoped that it would win some converts. . . .[11]

During the year after the book's publication, Hand repeatedly bought copies to send to acquaintances. This was unusual behavior: ordinarily he watched his expenditures very carefully, buying books to satisfy his own appetite for voracious reading, but rarely as gifts for others. Soon, he wrote to Croly, in the course of a twelve-page letter:

My dear friend, you are becoming an authority. I have no doubt that in a few years, myths will be established about you. Perhaps you will take on the form of the Sun God. That is the common retroactive metamorphosis of heroes. . . . I find that by actual mention of my intimacy with you, I acquire a distinct political significance, the only one I have ever reached, or expect to.[12]

Hand now went to work to persuade the authorities at Harvard to confirm the formal recognition that Croly clearly craved. In March 1910, he wrote a florid plea—humorous in style but serious in purpose—to the dean of Harvard College. "My friend, Herbert Croly," he explained, had spent parts of twelve years at Harvard and had taken "a great many courses"—enough, Hand thought, to justify B.A. and M.A. degrees, except for his "omission to qualify in Preliminary Entrance Greek": "The time goes on and with the mellowing of the years, he feels a craving for the rights and privileges of a scholar, but Preliminary Entrance Greek stands in his path,—a huge elephant, a bestial Behemoth; turn wheresoe'er he may by night or day, he is confronted with Preliminary Entrance Greek." Could not Harvard waive that requirement? Must Croly forever "encounter the fearful Monster," or could not the faculty "with gently anaesthetic hand" tame it so that "it lie quiescent while he nimbly leaps over to his goal"? Noting that Croly's book had received "much eulogistic comment," Hand went on: "May not this perhaps stand in place of Preliminary Entrance Greek? Could it not serve as a cloak or mask? . . . Surely the academic authorities cannot be less resourceful, or full of benign shifts, than we hacks of judges, and had it come before me, I should have no difficulty in presuming that I could not possibly distinguish the two, if justice so required."[13] Hand's pleas were largely successful: the Harvard authorities could "see no possible objection" to a retroactive B.A.[14]

Croly's reputation grew with the many thoughtful and favorable reviews of *The Promise of American Life*.[15] The book's renown stemmed largely from the future prominence of some of its readers. Felix Frankfurter, for example, insisted that "Croly's *'Promise'* [belongs on] any list of half a dozen books on American politics since 1900. . . . It may fairly be called seminal for American political thinking."[16] And Walter Lippmann, who was also to become an intimate of Croly and Hand, would say that the book was "the political classic which announced the end of the Age of Innocence with its romantic faith in American destiny and inaugurated the process of self-examination."[17] But Croly's book became especially famous because of its perceived impact on a single reader: Theodore Roosevelt.

When *The Promise of American Life* was published, Roosevelt was overseas on an extended trip, having turned over the White House to his protégé William Howard Taft. When the ebullient Roosevelt came home in the late spring of 1910 and read the book, he paid repeated homage to it as he reentered the political forum, in a series of speeches and articles that culminated in his third-party candidacy in 1912.

Croly's chief hope for his book had been that one day his proposals might become political policy, and Roosevelt was the political leader on whom he clearly banked his hopes. TR's name surfaced repeatedly in the book, and one of its central chapters—on "Reform and the Reformers"—concluded with two sections devoted to him.[18] Croly's claim that TR was the one reformer "whose work has tended to give reform the dignity of a constructive mission" had some basis in fact. Roosevelt had long been associated with reform efforts, as New York State legislator, federal civil service commissioner, New York City police commissioner, New York governor, and, ultimately, president. While Roosevelt's vision seemed to have been as limited as that of the other reformers whom Croly chastised, Croly had reason to single out TR as particularly promising: he had actually attained major public office and a national reputation; he was young enough to have a further political career ahead of him; and, above all, he was a charismatic, vigorous leader with wide popular appeal.

Croly's book conceded some of Roosevelt's shortcomings. He acknowledged that the rhetoric of then President Roosevelt's "Square Deal" had often exceeded its achievements. Moreover, President Roosevelt had too often engaged in the kind of purposeless moralizing that Croly had criticized in other reformers, tending to be "an example more of moral than intellectual independence." And to Croly, TR had lacked the highest virtues of "consistent thinking and plain speaking."[19] Yet considering all that, Croly, with an admixture of wishful thinking and detached observation, insisted, "In truth, Mr. Roosevelt has been building either better than he knows or better than he cares to admit." TR's career "stood for an idea from which the idea of reform cannot be separated—namely, the national idea." In rather inflated terms, he insisted that Roosevelt was "the founder of a new national democracy" and that "his influence and his work have tended to emancipate American democracy from its Jeffersonian bondage." More concretely, he noted that Roosevelt seemed committed to one of Croly's favorite notions, reliance on experts.

In the course of this discussion, Croly became an overt party advocate. Throughout his review of American history, he had condemned the Democratic party's bondage to Jeffersonian conceptions of individualism and limited government. Now, he praised Roosevelt for having rallied the Republican party to his brand of national democracy. Croly recognized the danger that the Republican party's "alliance with the 'vested interests' would make it unfaithful to its past as the party of responsible national action." However, "due chiefly to the personal influence of Theodore Roosevelt," the party seemed to have escaped that risk. Although the Republicans were divided and although some of their support for TR seemed shallow, Croly argued, "A Republican party which was untrue to the principle of national responsibility would have no reason for existence; and the Democratic party . . . cannot become the party of national responsibility without being faithless to its own creed."[20]

Perhaps betraying lingering uncertainty about Roosevelt's commitment to reform, Croly concluded, "Mr. Roosevelt and his hammer must be accepted gratefully, as the best available type of national reformer; but the day may and should come when a national reformer will appeal and be figured more in the guise of St. Michael, armed with a flaming sword and winged for flight."[21] And similarly, Croly in the very last sentence of his book exhorted:

> The common citizen can become something of a saint and something of a hero, not by growing to heroic proportions in his own person, but by the sincere and enthusiastic imitation of heroes and saints, and whether or not he will ever come to such imitation will depend upon the ability of his exceptional fellow-countrymen to offer him acceptable examples of heroism and saintliness.[22]

But none of these dreams could be realized unless Roosevelt could be gotten to read *The Promise of American Life*. Croly had never met Roosevelt and therefore felt helpless in bringing that about. But Hand had a limited acquaintance with TR, stemming from their Albany years. Soon after returning from Christmas with the Crolys in Cornish in 1909, Hand inquired of William H. Wheelock, a vice president of a New York real estate firm headed by one T. Douglas Robinson, who happened to be Roosevelt's brother-in-law, whether Wheelock could get Roosevelt's present address.[23] All that Hand knew was that Roosevelt was somewhere in Africa: TR had set off ten months before to go on safari, hunting lions. Wheelock replied immediately: Roosevelt's address was probably "Nairobi, British East Africa."[24]

Hand did nothing with the Nairobi address, but three months later, early in April, Roosevelt was more accessible: he was on a whirlwind tour of European capitals before heading home. On April 8, Hand wrote to Roosevelt: "I am recalling to you an acquaintance, long since past, to send you the book of my friend Herbert Croly, 'The Promise of American Life,' which goes under a separate cover." He closed with an expression of his "most agreeable memories of the time when I used to occasionally see you in Albany," but he devoted most of his letter to enthusiastic praise of the book:

> I hope that you will find in it as comprehensive and progressive a statement of American political ideas and ideals as I have found. I think that Croly has succeeded in stating more adequately than anyone else,—certainly of those writers whom I know,—the bases and prospective growth of the set of political ideas which can fairly be described as Neo-Hamiltonian, and whose promise is due more to you, I believe, than to anyone else. I do not suppose that you will agree with it all, but I should be much disappointed if you failed to be interested in much the greater part of it, if you could find a chance to read it.[25]

Less than two weeks later, Roosevelt, writing from the American embassy in Paris, assured Hand that he looked forward to reading the book; a week after, there was another letter acknowledging receipt and stating that he would read it "with real pleasure."[26]

Croly was overjoyed. "You certainly hit the game," he told Hand. "Now let's see whether he drops." Croly was particularly hopeful that Roosevelt might use his ideas in *The Outlook*, a somewhat religious, mildly reformist magazine that TR was about to join as a contributing editor: "I have great confidence in the fact that he has got to supply copy for The Outlook; and the book would be one of those subjects, prized by every editorial writer, [that is] up-to-date without being contentious."[27] For nearly three months, Croly fretted lest his target escape his sights after all. But at the end of July, he was able to write Hand, "What you say about T.R. & The Promise of American Life is confirmed by the following letter received yesterday which I transcribe." The letter was the first Croly had ever received from Roosevelt, and he was overjoyed. Roosevelt had written:

> I do not know when I have read a book which I felt profited me as much as your book on American life. There are a few points on which I do not entirely agree with you, yet even as to these my disagreement is on minor matters; indeed chiefly on questions of emphasis. All I wish is that I were better able to give my advice to my fellow countrymen in practical shape according to the principles you set forth.

I shall use your ideas freely in speeches I intend to make. I know
you won't object to my doing so, because, my dear sir, I can see
that your purpose is to do your share in any way for the betterment
of the national life; that what you care for is to see this betterment
secured. Can't you come in to see me at the Outlook office. I
want very much to have a chance to talk to you.[28]

Roosevelt's letter, Croly's biographer has said, was "the most important
letter he was ever to receive."[29] It was as if Croly's dream had come
true: the intellectual working in his lone study in New Hampshire had
apparent proof that ideas could matter in the real world. "I am deeply
grateful to you, my dear Learned," Croly wrote, "for being the instrument that forged the bond."[30]

Roosevelt's subsequent political career proved that the bond was much
less firm than Croly had hoped. Croly was also mistaken in thinking
that Hand deserved sole credit for calling *The Promise* to Roosevelt's
attention. For, as neither he nor Hand knew, the conservative Republican senator from Massachusetts, Henry Cabot Lodge, had also recommended it. A later visitor to Sagamore Hill, Roosevelt's estate in
Oyster Bay on the North Shore of Long Island, reported that TR's copy
of the book was heavily underlined and annotated;[31] TR must have
pounced on a book that could appeal so strongly to people on such
different parts of the political spectrum.

The recommendations from Hand and Lodge, and Roosevelt's assertion that he would use Croly's "ideas freely in speeches," were
documented only in private correspondence, though. What catapulted
Croly into national prominence was a speech Roosevelt delivered at the
end of August 1910, soon after his return from Europe, at the site of
John Brown's bloody abolitionist uprising in Osawatomie, Kansas.[32]
"The New Nationalism" has been described as "probably . . . the most
radical speech ever given by an ex-President."[33] It was certainly not
intended to be radical, yet contrary to TR's intention, it led inexorably
toward a split in the Republican party and the formation of the Progressive–Bull Moose movement. The title of the speech prompted the
widespread impression that Roosevelt's Bull Moose platform had Croly's
book as its foundation, but the case rests on a slender reed. Croly used
the phrase only once in his 454 pages, and only in passing (distinguishing Roosevelt's nationalism from that of the property- and business-
oriented Hamilton: "The new Federalism or rather new Nationalism
is not in any way inimical to democracy").[34]

Still, in the Osawatomie speech, Roosevelt advocated a new strategy
that revealed Croly's influence. Although he had made his reputation

as a trustbuster, he now insisted, with Croly, that "combinations in industry" were the inevitable consequence of economic forces and that the "way out lies, not in attempting to prevent such combinations, but in completely controlling them in the interest of the public welfare." He urged that federal administrative agencies should be strengthened to assure that control, and should be staffed by experts. Proclaiming that "every man holds his property subject to the general right of the community to regulate its use to whatever degree the public welfare may require," Roosevelt called for a strong conservation policy, minimum-wage and maximum-hours legislation, and comprehensive workmen's compensation programs. Moreover, he demanded not only strengthened congressional action but also an enhanced executive power that would be "the steward of the public welfare," as well as a judiciary that "shall be interested primarily in human welfare rather than in property. . . . [O]ur public men must be genuinely progressive."[35]

The "New Nationalism" speech was only one of many Roosevelt delivered on a tour that took him to sixteen states of the Trans-Mississippi West, but none received more applause or created more furor. While "Roosevelt for 1912" cries arose among his western supporters, the eastern conservatives, including some of his oldest allies, were outraged. Henry Cabot Lodge told Roosevelt that his advocacy of limits on property had "startled" people everywhere and that his critics were describing him as "little short of a revolutionist."[36] And the conservative sector of the eastern press—led by *The New York Times* and *The New York Sun*—warned of a new Napoléon on the horizon.

Roosevelt himself claimed repeatedly that he had not intended to make an open break with President Taft or to begin a third-party movement, but wanted instead to be a peacemaker among the increasingly clashing wings of the Republican party; he claimed that his speeches were intended to pacify the rapidly developing "insurgent," anti-Taft movement among Republicans in the West. Still, he moderated his initial radical tenor, though he never took back his words in the "New Nationalism" speech, and indeed eventually moved to the forefront of the anti-Taft forces.

Meanwhile, Croly became ever more prominently associated with the Roosevelt name. By the time the 1912 election drew near, with Roosevelt the candidate of the Bull Moose Progressives, *American Magazine* declared what was by then widely assumed, printing a full-page picture of Croly with the caption "The Man from Whom Col. Roosevelt Got His 'New Nationalism.' "[37] TR repeatedly paid tribute to Croly in an article in *The Outlook*, calling *The Promise* "the most profound and illuminating study of our national conditions which has appeared for many years" and elaborating one of Croly's central themes, that the purpose of government must be "a genuine effort to achieve true democracy—both political and industrial."[38]

Historians have had great difficulty in assessing Croly's impact on Roosevelt. The popular view of TR's contemporaries, that Croly directly exerted a decisive influence, converting Roosevelt from a fairly conservative ex-president into a progressive leader, persisted into the 1940s.[39] In the 1960s, many historians argued instead that it was Roosevelt who influenced Croly. But more recent and moderate reevaluations seem sounder: as Croly's biographer has put it, Croly had an "unspectacular, quiet, confirming influence" on Roosevelt; he did not produce any "startling conversion."[40] This subtle influence was not unlike the effect that *The Promise of American Life* had on Hand. For both Roosevelt and Hand, Croly helped crystallize their thought, deepen it, and stimulate new interests and positions. In these senses, Croly's *The Promise* clearly did exert influence.

ALTHOUGH LEARNED HAND was an early and wholehearted convert to Croly's New Nationalism, he was not nearly so quick to hail Theodore Roosevelt as the leader who would transmute progressive ideals into practice: he was far more ambivalent about Roosevelt than about the merits of the reform program. A letter to Croly demonstrates this clearly:

> Every month reassures me of the Colonel's position. No one, I think, in the country has anything like the real breadth of vision that he has; no one the foresight; granting his violence, and his lying, his personal untrustworthiness, he is today the best patriot we have. It seems to me incredible that in the situation which the next ten years will bring us, he should not again come to the front. I believe he will, provided he lives and does not go crazy.[41]

By 1912, however, Hand was led from skepticism to enthusiasm by Roosevelt's stand on three critical issues—Roosevelt's opposition to the *Lochner* Court's abuse of judicial power, his plan to control corporate power through regulation rather than trust-busting, and his advocacy of new laws to address the needs of the weak and underprivileged. In each of these areas, Hand made important contributions to the progressive cause.

Despite his promising beginning at Osawatomie in the summer of 1910, Roosevelt's return to national politics faltered. Far from uniting the progressive Republicans with the anti-government, business-oriented wing that supported President Taft, Roosevelt's peacemaking efforts managed to alienate both factions.

The outcome of state elections in which Roosevelt intervened, and the New York gubernatorial campaign of 1910 in particular, illustrate the problems.[42] His home state had seemed an ideal setting for his activity as peacemaker: moderate Republicans were more numerous in New York, and even the Taft administration supported the more liberal elements, such as outgoing governor Charles Evans Hughes, against New York's Old Guard. Here, Roosevelt saw an opportunity to attack conservatives without battling the administration, and to advocate a strategy of reconciliation.

Nevertheless, Roosevelt's image emerged badly tarnished. His support for Hughes's election-reform efforts failed against Old Guard resistance in the state legislature, and his attempt, at Hughes's behest, to carry this reform battle to the state Republican convention backfired when Hughes left state politics for a position on the Supreme Court and President Taft became increasingly uncooperative. Only after considerable infighting with Taft and his supporters did Roosevelt win election as temporary chairman of the convention, and the maneuverings led both Taft and Roosevelt to conclude privately that their relations were irreparably breached. Even the progressives, who were prepared to cheer TR's support for the liberal lawyer Henry L. Stimson as the gubernatorial candidate, were alienated by Roosevelt's keynote address, which praised Taft's achievements in the White House and even endorsed the protectionist Payne-Aldrich Tariff Act. And although Roosevelt stumped so hard for Stimson that he injured his voice, Stimson was badly defeated by a mediocre Democrat, John A. Dix. Roosevelt stumbled on his tightrope all across the East, as most of the candidates he supported on his extensive tour went down to defeat.

Both Hand and Croly, especially Hand, followed the New York political scene closely. And for both, Roosevelt's 1910 performance in New York caused them to question their support for the once promising leader. Perhaps the only ray of hope Hand saw was Roosevelt's support for Stimson. Hand knew about Stimson's stellar work at the district court, where he had been U.S. attorney before Hand went on the bench, and they were approaching something of a formal friendship. Stimson was a most reserved person, though, both with Hand and on the hustings. Hand remarked to Croly, "Sometimes I wonder whether he has a heart."[43] But Felix Frankfurter, an assistant to Stimson at the U.S. attorney's office, gave Hand admiring reports, and by the time Stimson left the prosecutor's office in 1909, he had in any case built a remarkably apolitical, high-quality operation. Hand never doubted that Stimson was a true progressive, and Stimson saw Hand as a political comrade. As he confirmed to Hand soon after his nomination in the fall of 1910, "I cling fast to you as a fellow progressive of the truest blue and only hope that during the campaign I shall not inadvertently say anything which offends you or Herbert Croly or any other of the dear disciples of Alexander Hamilton."[44]

Yet Hand was not sanguine about Stimson's political prospects. "[I] can't see anything but defeat," he wrote to Croly—even though Croly kept insisting to the end that he could not "believe" Stimson would lose.[45] As for Roosevelt's behavior and the future of the progressive cause, Hand found no reason to cheer. "[I] am at times thoroughly disgusted with the Colonel's conduct of the campaign. At times he has been guilty of the worst sort of unfair play, which I do not think even he can be blind to."[46] Ten days before the election, Hand learned from Lloyd Griscom, the county Republican leader, that he thought Roosevelt had reentered local politics simply to aid Griscom and Congressman Herbert Parsons, the two most powerful Republicans in New York City, since otherwise they "would have been put out of business here in New York." Hand was disturbed: "[I] must say that the thought of T.R. undertaking the whole business merely to save Herbert Parsons and Lloyd Griscom has a certain element of the comic in it," he told Croly.[47] If only he had waged "a fine fight" on the issues, as Princeton University's president, Woodrow Wilson, had been making in the New Jersey gubernatorial race. (This is almost the only kind word about Wilson in Hand's entire correspondence.) Instead, Roosevelt was engaged in renewed exchanges of "miserable, childish vituperation":

> It seems a long way off to any of the things you and I want; I begin to wonder whether we are a lot of academic doctrinaires. At least there seem to be so few people who look at these matters as we do, that we don't seem likely to count for very much, whether we are right or wrong. . . . Of course I mean to be loyal, but to you I feel privileged to a good curse.[48]

Hand's political alienation was prompted not only by ideological disgust but by fatigue from his judicial work and his perennial battles with physical ailments. For months, he had been complaining about digestive problems and other aches and pains; Herbert Croly as well as Frances Hand and Loulie Jay recommended that he consult an osteopath. Hand considered that kind of medicine heresy—"to take any real faith in these people is to me a sign of the sort of intellectual vulgarity that is distressing."[49] Some of his physician's traditional medications soon began to alleviate his symptoms, but his distress about the 1910 campaign lasted for months. In February 1911, in a twelve-page letter to Croly written while Hand was confined to bed (this time with tonsillitis), he lamented that the Old Guard was back "in control of New York. A pretty pickle we are in." The Democrat, John Dix, was proving to be as mediocre a governor as Hand had expected, and as even his erstwhile supporters now recognized.[50] And while Lloyd Griscom had not yet been booted out as Republican county chairman, his hold on the office only indicated that "the Colonel is not so dead a lion yet that one can kick him wantonly in the stomach. . . ."[51]

Yet Hand's disenchantment did not cause him to withdraw from politics. There was in fact reason to be hopeful even then about the future of progressivism. Despite certain disasters in the East, progressives had done remarkably well in a number of western campaigns. Yet the largely agrarian progressives of the West were too populist and demagogic for eastern elitist reformers—even Robert La Follette, the recently victorious senator from Wisconsin, a man far more able than Hand and Croly thought. To Hand, the western "insurgents" had little real understanding of the New Nationalism. As he wrote Croly:

> They have about as much sense of what you are after and the few individuals here in the East who sympathize with you, as they have [of] Neo-Cart[es]ianism. Their damned nostrums [of] popular government are all well enough, in their way, but I doubt whether they have even understanding of those, and I can't see that their plans go any further or contemplate any administrative program. Some of them must be disgusting whelps.[52]

Hand's journalist friend Mark Sullivan had told him that a leading Oregon progressive had said that "the collective judgment of a hundred people was always better than that of any single one." To Hand, that was "such loathsome talk that it is difficult to reconcile it with sincerity." When a congressional proposal to increase federal judicial salaries from $6,000 to $7,500 per year (which would raise the pay of federal judges to that of senators) was beaten in part because of a western progressive onslaught, Hand charged the distinguished progressive senator George Norris with "disgusting cant" for claiming that the pay increase would put judges out of touch with the common people.[53]

Hand's and Croly's deepest fears about East-West splits in the progressive ranks were soon confirmed in the debate over a proposed reciprocity treaty to lower tariffs on Canadian trade. Taft's support for the treaty allied him with eastern progressives against those of the West, led by Senator La Follette, who opposed the lower tariffs and condemned the treaty as a sacrifice of the farmer to urban interests. In an unusual alliance, Old Guard Republicans, traditionally high-tariff, joined these western progressives. Nevertheless, after Taft called a special session of Congress, the treaty was approved in the late summer (only to be defeated in the Canadian parliament).

For the easterners, the 1911 tariff debate cast further doubt on progressive chances. Taft looked more attractive than he had for a long time, and the western progressives seemed more questionable allies than ever. To Croly, the western progressives' position showed that they were factionalists who "still conceiv[ed] tariff-making as a distribution of plums among various interests."[54]

Other developments, too, endangered the New Nationalism. A few progressives saw attractions in the Democratic party for the first time in a decade. The perennially losing presidential candidate of the Democrats, the Jeffersonian populist William Jennings Bryan, had at last been replaced by new faces. In scoring election successes in 1910, a host of promising progressive Democratic leaders—especially New Jersey's new governor, Woodrow Wilson—had emerged. Roosevelt went into unaccustomed seclusion at Sagamore Hill, his prestige tarnished and his normal ebullience suppressed by melancholy. When La Follette's forces formed a National Progressive Republican League in early 1911, neither TR nor most of his eastern supporters joined it.[55]

Matters began to turn around before the end of 1911. During that year, Hand visited Roosevelt a number of times in Oyster Bay and carried on a substantial correspondence with him. At the same time, Roosevelt stopped believing that his political career was over, and he began to emerge as a candidate for the Republican nomination for the presidency in 1912. By the end of February 1912, when Roosevelt publicly threw his hat into the ring, Hand had gotten to know him more intimately and, despite some continuing misgivings, had moved clearly to his side.

One of Hand's earliest encounters with Roosevelt as TR reentered national politics in late 1911 related to the problem of trusts. Converts to the New Nationalism considered antitrust enforcement through Sherman Act lawsuits misguided and ineffectual: national regulation, not destruction of the trusts, was their preferred solution. The issue produced strange alliances: western progressives and Democrats were confirmed trustbusters; eastern progressives joined the plutocratic, standpat Republicans in opposition. The issue heated up when President Taft launched a surprisingly aggressive antitrust enforcement policy, warning the business community in October 1911 that he had ordered Attorney General George Wickersham to enforce the Sherman Act vigorously.

During the last two years of Taft's administration, antitrust enforcement became a priority.

Politically, Taft's antitrust policy was probably the most foolish among his many questionable moves. By the fall of 1911, he had already lost the support of most progressives, and the wiser path would have been to placate his natural allies, the business interests. But near the end of October, the administration brought its most publicized case of all, charging that the United States Steel Corporation had violated the Sherman Act. The occasion for the suit was U.S. Steel's allegedly monopolistic acquisition of the Tennessee Coal and Iron Company a few years earlier, during Roosevelt's presidency. The subject was a sensitive one for Roosevelt, since as president he had personally assured U.S. Steel that his administration would not raise antitrust objections, apparently believing the company's assurance that the transaction would help restore stability to Wall Street during the stock market panic of 1907. Roosevelt had been attacked ever since for allowing himself to be duped, or worse, and while he ultimately conceded that the motives of U.S. Steel's officials were not wholly pure and benign, he bristled at suggestions that he had been fooled.

Against this background, the U.S. Steel suit may well have been, as a historian has said, "the most costly political mistake of [Taft's] entire career."[56] Taft's institution of the suit outraged Roosevelt, who saw it not only as an attack on his competence but also as personally reprehensible behavior, since Taft had never raised a voice against the transaction while a member of Roosevelt's cabinet. Indeed, Roosevelt recalled, Taft had emphatically endorsed the acquisition at the time.

In an eight-page signed editorial, "The Trusts, the People, and the Square Deal," Roosevelt's familiar justification for his handling of the U.S. Steel case was rehearsed again. But he took the occasion to go further, and to outline a more general strategy for controlling large-scale business organizations, a more detailed and more ambitious position than he had ever proposed before. His arguments now paralleled those of Croly's *The Promise of American Life* even more closely. The only solution, Roosevelt thought, was to "abandon definitely the *laissez-faire* theory of political economy, and fearlessly champion a system of increased Governmental control, paying no heed to the cries of the worthy people who denounce this as Socialistic." He insisted that "the only way to meet a billion-dollar corporation is by invoking the protection of a hundred-billion-dollar government." This strategy required "a course of supervision, control, and regulation of [the] great corporations—a regulation which we should not fear, if necessary, to bring to the point of control of monopoly prices."[57]

All this was a clear expression of Croly's message and Hand's beliefs. Hand agreed with Roosevelt's argument that Congress's failure to specify detailed antitrust policy, leaving to courts the case-by-case determination of what was monopolistic and unfairly competitive, had required judges to "legislate"—ad hoc in particular cases, and without the necessary expertise. But another aspect of Roosevelt's article troubled Hand. He voiced his criticism to TR in a personal encounter, and Roosevelt suggested that he put his views into writing. Roosevelt published Hand's remarks in the next issue of *The Outlook*—as a letter printed anonymously, at Hand's request.[58] Hand also suggested to TR that "it might be better to indicate your correspondent as a vaguely wise and competent person, than as a lawyer," advice Roosevelt took.[59]

Hand's letter sought to correct a misimpression Roosevelt had created in his remarks on the Tobacco Trust litigation. Just days before Roosevelt's article appeared, the Second Circuit Court of Appeals had implemented a recent Supreme Court decision approving dissolution of the trust. Roosevelt had noted that the final decree "practically leaves all of the companies [in the Tobacco Trust] still substantially under the control of the twenty-nine original defendants. Such a result is lamentable from the standpoint of justice. The decision of the Circuit Court, if allowed to stand, means that the Tobacco Trust has really been obliged to change its clothes, that none of the real offenders [has] received any real punishment. . . . Surely, miscarriage of justice is not too strong a term to apply to such a result."[60]

To Hand it was clear that Roosevelt had not understood the case. The circuit court's failure "to break up the community of ownership feature in the new tobacco companies," he wrote, "needs a little supplementing." In several earlier antitrust rulings, the Supreme Court had approved decrees "which necessarily resulted in a community of ownership." And in the tobacco case, the attorney general had stated that "in view of these decisions, he felt that he could make no objection to the plan." Under these circumstances, the circuit court, bound as it was by Supreme Court precedent, had no choice but to approve the proposed decree, and its decision—contrary to Roosevelt's assertion— therefore would not be read as approving in principle a final remedy in antitrust cases that left the ownership of the dissolved companies in the same hands. While Hand was no lover of the trusts, he believed that the Second Circuit judges and the defendants deserved to have the case stated accurately.

Replying to Hand's letter, Roosevelt implicitly accepted the correction, but immediately went on to say that Hand's suggestion did not alter the "vital" issues—that current antitrust law did not provide an adequate answer to the trust problem, and that to try to handle the problem "merely by lawsuits" was "to insure failure." To these sentiments, Hand of course had no inclination to object.[61]

The episode was a preview of the pattern Roosevelt repeatedly followed in response to Hand's suggestions in the ensuing months: Roosevelt would assure Hand that his suggestions were helpful and would incorporate his ideas into articles or speeches, but at the same time he would insist that he had not been moved to change his basic position.

Roosevelt's writing on trusts produced an "extraordinary degree" of interest in "both the public and the newspapers," *The Outlook* claimed. In *The Outlook*'s view, the popular reaction suggested that "the country is ripe for an effective policy, carried on under strong and wise leadership, of 'trust regulation' instead of 'trust busting.' " Yet *The Outlook* denied any presidential ambitions on TR's part: "Those who really know Mr. Roosevelt's mind know that he is not a presidential candidate, that he does not desire to be such a candidate, and that the thought of such a candidacy never occurs to him in his discussions of questions of public and National interest."[62] Of course, just the contrary was true: those who "really" knew Roosevelt, and TR himself, recognized that he was at last ready to battle Taft openly in the 1912 campaign.

By the time Hand approached Roosevelt about the antitrust article, the two had already discussed another issue dear to progressivism, the troubled relation between judicial and legislative power. Judicial obstructions of legislative reform, especially by politically motivated interpretations of the due-process clauses, was something Hand criticized throughout his life and had opposed ever since his studies under James Bradley Thayer at Harvard Law School. As Hand became more committed to the reform program of the New Nationalism, he recognized that many of its regulatory proposals would be scuttled by the Court's rigid protection of "liberty of contract" and property rights, exemplified in the Supreme Court's 1905 *Lochner v. New York* decision.

Croly had not tackled the issue of judicial power in *The Promise of American Life*, but Roosevelt had no inhibitions about doing so and had attacked judicial obstructionism as early as his Osawatomie speech in 1910. Judicial power, like antitrustism, was an issue on which Hand and Roosevelt agreed as to goals. And Hand applauded Roosevelt's attempt to develop public awareness of the problem; he himself had tried to do the same thing in his *Harvard Law Review* article in 1908. But they disagreed on appropriate remedies. Roosevelt was far readier than Hand to propose drastic measures, such as "judicial recall" (the people's power to remove judges) or "recall of judicial decisions" (the people's power to overturn obstructive judicial decisions). By 1912,

Roosevelt's advocacy of recall of judicial decisions became the most controversial aspect of his program. Hand, who feared the populist, sometimes demagogic qualities of Roosevelt's progressivism, thought that TR's cure was worse than the disease, and frequently told him so, both in face-to-face encounters and in correspondence.

Hand's exchanges with Roosevelt on this issue began in May 1911. A mutual friend told Hand that Roosevelt was preparing an article for *The Outlook* on a recent decision involving employees' interests, and that TR would be "glad of a call from anyone who was interested in the subject." Hand certainly was interested. During a weekend visit to friends on the North Shore of Long Island, he walked several miles to Roosevelt's Oyster Bay residence, only to find that the ex-president was at church. Hand promptly sent Roosevelt his *Harvard Law Review* article on *Lochner*, "which says some of the things I had in mind and which perhaps says all I could say myself."[63] And in his cover letter Hand proceeded to summarize his views on judicial power—the first of many such letters to Roosevelt in the next two years.

The decision that had prompted Roosevelt to think of writing an article was not made by the Supreme Court, but rather by New York's highest court, the Court of Appeals. In a unanimous, highly publicized and much criticized decision handed down on March 24, 1911, that court held, in a case called *Ives v. South Buffalo Ry. Co.*,[64] that New York's recently enacted workmen's compensation law was unconstitutional. Judge William E. Werner's long opinion embodied the *Lochner* philosophy; indeed, the ruling was a blow to progressives such as TR and Hand not just because it struck down an important piece of pro-worker reform legislation, but because it illustrated with a vengeance the evils of Lochnerism.

The 1910 New York law had counterparts in many other industrialized nations, although few in the United States. The prevailing American rule governing compensation for work-related injuries was notoriously unsatisfactory: the injured employee could recover only if he showed the employer to have been at fault ("negligent"). And even if the employer had been negligent, the employee would recover nothing if he had been guilty of any "contributory negligence," or if any of the other rules favorable to employers came into play (such as the notion that an employee "assumed the risk" of being hurt by "voluntarily" going to work in a dangerous business). In practice, injured employees could rarely clear these hurdles.

The New York statute had been drafted by the Wainwright Commission, which the legislature had established to study the problem of industrial accidents. The commission prepared what even the New York judges called an "excellent," "comprehensive" report, the premise of which was that injuries to workers in especially dangerous occupations were a "necessary, substantially unavoidable" part of doing business. However, the report said, the common-law system of compensating employees was "economically unwise and unfair" and imposed the financial burdens of unavoidable industrial accidents on the group least able to bear them. In the view of the study commission and the legislature, imposing liability on employers made sense because they could spread the costs of accidents by passing them along to their consumers.[65] Yet this reasoning did not persuade the court: the judges insisted that they "must regard all economic, philosophical, and moral theories, attractive and desirable though they may be, as subordinate to" the constitutional barriers; the very purpose of a constitution was to protect the people "against the frequent and violent fluctuations of . . . 'public opinion.' "[66] In short, the protections of property and liberty in the due-process clauses could not yield simply because the majority and good sense supported the legislation.

For Hand, the *Ives* decision dampened hopes that a line of recent Supreme Court decisions had kindled. Two months earlier, the unanimous Supreme Court, in the so-called Oklahoma Bank case, *Noble State Bank v. Haskell*, had taken a very broad view of the state's police power and a narrow view of due-process restraints. The opinion, by Justice Holmes (who had dissented in the *Lochner* case), warned against "pressing the broad words of the Fourteenth Amendment to a drily logical extreme" and stated that "the police power extends to all the great public needs." Holmes added that this power may be used "in aid of what is sanctioned by usage, or held by the prevailing morality or strong and preponderant opinion to be greatly and immediately necessary to the public welfare."[67] This approach was precisely what Hand had advocated in his *Harvard Law Review* article three years earlier. Croly, to whom the jubilant Hand had sent a newspaper clipping about the *Noble State Bank* ruling, commented, "You must have some personal satisfaction in watching this truly therapeutic process of bleeding the 14th amendment to death, for most assuredly your article must have made [its] contribution to this astonishing reversal of recent precedents."[68] In the context of this cheery omen from Washington, the New York *Ives* decision seemed all the more a rude awakening. What Hand "especially deplore[d]" was the "kind of interpretation of such vague clauses as 'due process of law' [that] takes away from the legislature the power to do those things which are recognized as within the legislative power in every civilized country of the world." The idea that due process "embalms individualistic doctrines of a hundred years ago

I believe myself to be heretical historically and very serious practically."[69] Moreover, however permanent the Supreme Court's apparent change of course, Hand realized, the *Ives* case showed that state courts could block state legislative reform on their own: the obstructionist New York court in *Ives* was not even subject to review by the Supreme Court, since it had rested its decision not only on the federal Constitution, but also on the counterpart due-process clause in the New York Constitution.

When Hand heard in May 1911 that TR planned to write an article for *The Outlook* on the *Ives* case, he sent the ex-president a copy of his *Lochner* article, noting (with some wishful thinking) that the *Lochner* philosophy was "now happily rather superseded by the later decisions of the Supreme Court." Hand's letter was his first effort to educate Roosevelt about the general question of judicial power. Hand agreed with Roosevelt's 1910 condemnation of obstructionist courts, but showed little patience with TR's increasingly frequent calls for direct democracy, advocating instead the policy of instilling in the courts a more welcoming attitude toward legislative reform. This, he told Roosevelt, was necessary "if the system of constitutional control by courts is to survive at all." Unless the courts adopted a more receptive attitude toward legislation, Hand argued, "I am quite certain that . . . either the courts must give up their constitutional prerogative, a by no means unthinkable alternative," or most reform laws would have to be validated through constitutional amendments, with the result that constitutions would look like codes of legislation—surely, "a cumbersome form of making law."[70]

Hand later regretted that his early advice to Roosevelt did not differentiate more clearly between the responses to judicial obstructionism that he approved of and those that troubled him. Hand was delighted to see TR advance arguments that would help persuade judges to adopt the Holmes-Hand due-process position, but he had serious reservations about TR's advocacy of direct popular restraints on judges. Roosevelt, whose capacity for sustained rational thought Hand and Croly repeatedly had reason to doubt, either did not understand this distinction or was not persuaded by it. Roosevelt's first *Outlook* comment on the judicial power question, in the May 13, 1911, issue,[71] in addition to noting quite appropriately that it was "out of the question that the courts should be permitted permanently to shackle our hands as they would shackle them with such decisions as . . . the decisions in the Bake Shop cases [*Lochner*] shackled them," insisted that "the people" must have the ultimate power:

I wish to see the judge given all power and treated with all respect; but I also wish to see him held accountable by the people. [T]hey must have the power to act. And not only should they exercise this power in the case of any judge who shows moral delinquency on the bench, but they should also exercise it whenever they have been forced to come to the conclusion that any judge, no matter how upright and well-intentioned, is fundamentally out of sympathy with the righteous popular movement, so that his presence on the bench has become a bar to orderly progress for the right.[72]

This idea of popular restraints on individual judges was a measure that a few western progressive states had already adopted, and it soon divided progressive and conservative Republicans when, a few weeks later, the proposed constitution for the new state of Arizona was drafted to allow the electorate to recall state judges. President Taft lambasted the scheme as one that would convert justice into "legalized terrorism," asserting that "the people at the polls no more than kings upon the throne are fit to pass upon questions involving the judicial interpretation of the law."[73] By contrast, Roosevelt suggested that judicial recall was necessary, that it was in fact only a moderate reform, and that decisions such as *Ives* "would, in the end, render it absolutely necessary for the American people, at whatever cost, to insist upon having a more direct control over the courts."[74]

Until early 1911, Roosevelt had resisted endorsing measures like judicial recall, so his attack on *Ives* was the first sign that he might flirt with western populist notions of direct democracy. These notions only alarmed eastern progressives like Hand and Croly, for whom true progressivism required national policy-making based on expertise.

Two major causes account for Roosevelt's change in attitude. The first was his outrage at the *Ives* case itself. But as he moved ever closer to candidacy in late 1911, he also found the pressures from western progressives difficult to resist. And when he became a public candidate for the Republican nomination early in 1912, the furor over these direct-democracy proposals diverted attention from his New Nationalist platform and doomed his campaign. Roosevelt then abandoned his flirtation with the idea of recall of judges, but he did not retreat all the way to Hand's position. Instead, beginning in the fall of 1911, TR began to advocate the recall of judicial *decisions*. Rather than endorsing the removal of individual judges by popular vote, he now urged that the people be given the power to overturn state court decisions that interpreted due-process clauses in state constitutions as prohibiting state reform laws—a proposal that would meet the *Ives* decision itself but not the underlying problem of restrictive interpretations of due process generally, of Lochnerism.

This idea had blossomed in Roosevelt's mind during the summer of 1911, while the Hands were in England; as it happened, its stimulus may well have come from English developments. While the Hands were there, England was much in the news, in part because of Americans' fascination with the ceremonial trappings of the coronation of King George V, in more significant part because the long campaign to curb the veto power of the House of Lords had finally succeeded. In his correspondence with English friends, Roosevelt wrote about the need to overturn the similar blocking power of the American courts: "[I]t is all right for them to have power to stop hasty, ill-considered action and make the people think, but . . . once the people have thought the subject out, the people must have the power to carry their determination into effect."[75]

Roosevelt announced his revised plan to curb the judiciary in a New York City speech to an overflow crowd at Carnegie Hall on Friday evening, October 20, 1911. Roosevelt's address was quaintly entitled "The Conservation of Womanhood and Childhood," and much of the speech was indeed devoted to a plea for laws to prohibit child labor and limit working hours of women as well as men. But these proposals went virtually unnoticed in the next morning's newspapers. What was new in Roosevelt's speech was his call for popular power over the decisions of the courts. He criticized judges "who have proved their devotion, not to the Constitution, as they thought, but to a system of social and economic philosophy which in my judgment is not only outworn, but to the last degree mischievous." Abuses of the courts' power to adjudicate constitutionality had to be curbed, and his preferred method of controlling the courts, he insisted, was not radical but the only alternative to radicalism: "The people should be enabled with reasonable speed and in effective fashion themselves to determine by popular vote whether or not they will permit the judges' interpretation of the Constitution to stand."[76]

Despite Roosevelt's protests that his plan was moderate, his proposal, reiterated and elaborated for months to come, proved to be an egregious political mistake. The vehement reaction it provoked was even more costly than the one that a Roosevelt of a later generation encountered, when Franklin D. Roosevelt's Court-packing plan of 1937 alienated many liberal friends and proved a bonanza for anti–New Deal conservatives. Astonishingly, Teddy Roosevelt took this important political step without consulting anyone. Apparently it was not until TR read the attacks on his Carnegie Hall speech, and realized that his general proposal raised knotty problems of detail as well as principle, that it occurred to him to seek advice. Some of his supporters pressed him to seek legal counsel. Brooks Adams, the pessimistic historian of the Adams clan, observed mordantly that it was highly desirable that "some thoroughly competent constitutional and economic lawyer—if you know such a one—advise you always before you speak."[77] To consult someone before every speech was clearly not in Roosevelt's character, but he did know of a "thoroughly competent" lawyer, and he did seek his advice. The person he turned to was Judge Learned Hand.

Roosevelt sent Hand proofs of "The Conservation of Womanhood and Childhood," asking for comments. On November 20, 1911, Hand replied. Thinking that the speech was to be published within the week, Hand had little hope of changing the nature of the text, but he expected that this would not be the last word from TR on the issue, and he hoped to influence Roosevelt's future course. With respect to TR's general attack on abuses of judicial power, Hand made it clear, "I have said very often almost the same thing and there is really none of it that I can disagree with." But agreement as to the evil did not mean agreement with TR's remedies: "[T]o appeal to the people not to endorse such opinions as [*Ives*] is to ask a remedy which is either impracticable, or, as I think, very dangerous." The danger was that recall of decisions threatened judicial independence, and indeed the very office of a judge:

> [I] cannot quite swallow the necessity of having public pressure put on a judge for any purpose, for it so utterly perverts the assumption which is fundamental in his function. He should properly have no duty, but to interpret words which have been used by the sovereign itself, and in doing that I think it is fatal in the end to his integrity to try to find the sovereign's meaning except in its formal declarations.

In short, so long as judges possessed the power of judicial review, a conscientious judge must try to interpret the words of the Constitution and not bow to the most recent referendum on the popular will. The problem, of course, was that general clauses such as "due process" were difficult to interpret in particular cases. But if it came to a choice between judicial independence and the general clauses, Hand made clear that he would opt for the former, not the latter:

> Really, we [judges] have got ourselves into the mess we are now in here in America, by failing to remember how strictly our duties should be interpretive. . . . In construing the vague clauses of the

Bill of Rights we have done the most damage, and something must be done to change it, but I really think that I had rather take them out of the constitutions altogether than make the judges respond to any popular pressure. . . .

Assuming, however, that the "vague clauses" were retained, judges had to make sure that they interpreted the text faithfully and did not merely give voice to personal or even popular opinion:

The popular will, when clearly ascertained, cannot wisely be withstood in a democracy, but there are a good many occasions when before it has been authoritatively expressed [in the text of a constitution or statute], a judge is tempted to interpret what he finds about him in popular form. Except in so far as that helps him to an honest interpretation of what has reached authoritative expression, I have not the least doubt that he should, and indeed he must, wholly disregard them. If he does not, he is just as much a usurper of authority if they be popular . . . as though he followed his personal, but unpopular, predilections.

Hand was a great deal blunter now than he had been in May. He tried to persuade Roosevelt that curbing judicial abuse through popular pressure on the courts was worse than the disease of a handful of regrettable due-process decisions. And so he hammered at Roosevelt:

Now, to be perfectly frank with you, I think that the end of your paper will almost inevitably result in making people suppose that by some sort of popular pressure ad hoc, judges should be influenced in their decisions. [T]here are only two ways of meeting the difficulty, one, by changing the formal expression of the fundamental law . . . and the other by securing such men as understand it in a different sense. The first is a so much better way of meeting the evil than the second, which lends itself to exploitation by men of facile convictions, that we ought to prefer it. Indeed, so inherent are the defects of the system which has grown up under the general clauses of the Bill of Rights, that I am feeling with increasing force that the evils which would result from their abolition might be less than those under which we now labor. . . . If Justice Holmes's opinion,—I hope you will not get to hate that man's name in my mouth,—in the Oklahoma Bank cases could become well riveted into all the law, that would solve the difficulty.[78]

Roosevelt's first response to Hand's November 20 letter was typical: TR voiced general agreement without changing the substance of his position. "Evidently I must try to make my expression more clear," Roosevelt told Hand:

> I absolutely agree with you as to bringing pressure to bear on the judges, but in constitutional cases the alternative must be to secure the right of appeal from the judges. Take the New York cases to which I refer. My idea would be to have the [New York] Constitutional Convention provide that the people shall have the right to vote as to whether or not the judges' interpretation of the law in such a case is correct, and that their vote shall be decisive. Evidently I have got to get you to come out again and talk this matter over with me.[79]

The "but" in TR's first sentence was of course crucial: "the right of appeal" to the people, in Hand's view, was itself a form of "pressure" on the judges, not an alternative to pressure. Thus the "agreement" with Hand that Roosevelt professed was quite illusory. As Hand remarked to Croly, in sending him a copy of his exchange with TR, "Even allowing for the noble phrasing of the gallant Colonel, his remedy is wholly imaginary. Without changing the Fourteenth Amendment all he could do would be to eliminate the present Court of Appeals of the State of New York." In any event, nothing in TR's proposals struck at the ultimate source of the evil, Lochnerism. Hand's hopes for slaying that dragon, he told Croly, lay elsewhere: if the Supreme Court adhered to its most recent decisions, due-process restraints on legislatures would be "practically valueless."[80]

Roosevelt, perhaps forgetting that he had already acknowledged Hand's November 20 letter, once again thanked the judge a few days later, this time with a clearer indication that he had gotten Hand's point:

> I would much prefer that the judges should themselves change their attitude, and adopt the attitude that Holmes took in the Oklahoma Bank cases. I hope that criticism such as mine will tend to bring about this result. If it does not, then there will have to be a change in the fundamental form of the law of the land.[81]

Hand quickly wrote again, enclosing a recent Supreme Court decision along the lines of Holmes's permissive opinion in the Oklahoma Bank case. The new opinion, upholding a Massachusetts law protecting employees,[82] was in Hand's view "not particularly good," but it did contain some useful language about the breadth of the police power and the need for judicial deference to legislatures. According to Hand's optimistic reading, the decision was "important as one more stone in the cairn which marks the real decease of that once menacing ghost," the *Lochner* philosophy. He quoted some of the opinion, underlined additional helpful passages, and concluded, "If you should read the opinions which now regularly follow one another without dissent, you would feel that that court anyway is safe for a long time from any danger of narrow usurpation." This evidence, Hand urged TR, should "moderate your scorn" about the prospect of Supreme Court restraint, as well as his growing enthusiasm "in favor of a 'pure Democracy.' " And then he lightened his message with some humorous references to the accusations of totalitarianism that TR's Carnegie Hall speech had provoked: "Of course, to one meditating a permanent dictatorship this may seem only an indication of flabby imbecility, but pray recall that boards of usurpers have always proved ineffective; and, besides, how much they might have interfered with your ruthless, vaulting ambition!"[83]

Roosevelt was properly amused:

> My dear judge, I chuckled heartily over your allusion to the probable thoughts of the would-be dictator. Seriously, these decisions please me immensely, . . . because they represent the kind of attitude which if regularly taken means that any effort to assault the Federal judiciary will be abandoned; and therefore we shall preserve what is of inestimable value, the power of the Court *on great occasions* to steady our governmental structure by declaring what the Legislature or Executive can do and what it or he cannot do. [Your letter comes] in the nick of time for me to insert it in an article I have been writing about New York State Courts.[84]

But when Hand saw the article that TR had been writing, his hopes were once more dashed. The January 6, 1912, issue of *The Outlook* featured "Judges and Progress," Roosevelt's longest and most careful statement yet on the issue of judicial power. The conclusion was as provocative as ever: Roosevelt still advocated recall of judicial decisions.[85] By now, Roosevelt had all but announced as a presidential candidate; the article was probably his misguided effort to attract support from the broadest possible coalition. Yet he was persisting in a stand that alienated many potential supporters. TR had reason to worry that westerners would prefer the more populist progressive, La Follette. Yet by continuing to advocate recall of decisions (though not recall of judges), and indeed making this position clearer than ever, he quickly lost the support of conservative Republicans, and moderate progressives such as Hand would view Roosevelt with mounting distrust.

Yet Hand could take some limited personal satisfaction from TR's essay, since it incorporated several of his own suggestions. But once again, the old pattern recurred: Hand's formulations served as theses for populist antitheses with which he did not agree. Roosevelt was trying to square the circle: to avow loyalty to the courts' independence from popular pressure, yet insist on the people's legitimate right to overturn judicial decisions. He closed his essay with the final words of his Carnegie Hall address: "What I have advocated is not revolution. It is not wild radicalism. It is the highest and wisest kind of conservatism."[86] Hand feared that the ex-president was advancing a position that was no more politically wise than it was intellectually coherent.

In January 1912, the very month of TR's *Outlook* article, rumors circulated that Roosevelt was maneuvering behind the scenes to position himself closer to a presidential candidacy, rumors that reached Hand's ears quickly and that Croly promptly confirmed. By late January, Hand was fully convinced that Roosevelt would run. "It looks to me as though the Colonel certainly was the Man of Destiny," Hand wrote, but he was not genuinely enthusiastic and felt some sympathy for Taft: "I really think he has not had a square deal. The good things that he has done have been interred long before his bones, and the evil seems to bedevil and cling on to him more than he deserves. I am sorry."[87]

A few weeks later—just days before TR's formal announcement— Hand voiced more fully his reservations about a Roosevelt candidacy in a letter to a Roosevelt publicist named Whitridge. Hand conceded that Roosevelt's instincts, if not his reasoning, were remarkable. The "marvellous child," Hand wrote, "is almost always right; I think he does not have to prick out the path of reason, but is drawn on by the goal." But Hand complained that TR's instincts had led him astray on the judicial power issue: "I wish you or someone else could have sidetracked the appeal by referendum, which is really a stupid make-shift." The best that could be said for these proposals was that they were perhaps the inevitable retribution for conservative judges' thickheadedness:

> Little as the worthy judicial Cobdenites, e.g., [Justices] Brewer and Peckham, expected, when by their decisions they thought to have embalmed friend Bentham in the Constitution, they were, I believe, more directly making for initiatives, referendums, etc., etc. than for anything else.

Like Henry Stimson, Learned Hand began to think TR had better wait until 1916. As Hand told Whitridge:

> As for his running now, I am sorry that you are for it. Why not have a Democrat? In that party I have absolute confidence that it carries in itself absolute chaos and imbecility. Still, we have to

work off old Jeffersonian poisons once in a while; . . . we need now a purge which nothing but four years of the good old Democratic irresponsibility will give us. Then for the Colonel and an open field. . . . Why not let a Democrat quite mess up the business, till the country demands [Roosevelt]? He is young enough for that and I had rather have him in with so broad a warrant, that he could make his plans systematic and thorough-going.[88]

On February 21, 1912, three days before Roosevelt announced, "I will accept a nomination for President if it is tendered to me,"[89] he delivered a major speech before the Ohio Constitutional Convention at Columbus in which he once again urged recall of judicial decisions and asserted he would support even the recall of judges as a remedy of last resort.[90] This speech alienated many of Roosevelt's supporters and gave Taft and his cohorts their chief weapon for attacking TR in the ensuing primary campaign. Many of Roosevelt's allies abandoned him, even his old friend Henry Cabot Lodge, who promised not to support "anyone else" but soon was building a national organization to fight the recall of judicial decisions.[91] Hand, too, was distressed; he did not yet give up all hope of persuading Roosevelt to change his tune. Instead, for most of the spring, he sought to encourage TR to adopt still another moderate remedy, one that his longtime New York and Cornish acquaintance George Rublee had suggested. Hand had recently introduced Rublee to Roosevelt (and Rublee would soon join the inner circle of TR advisers). Rublee in turn brought his partner, Joseph Cotton, into Roosevelt's circle.[92]

Rublee's idea, Hand wrote to TR, seemed to go "to the very heart of the difficulty" in a "more thorough-going fashion" than anything he had earlier suggested. The restrictive reading of due process that *Lochner* and *Ives* exemplified could be overcome, Rublee and Hand thought, by a constitutional amendment that would define "due process of law" as the recent, more liberal Supreme Court decisions had defined it. Now that the Court had endorsed "the most amazingly latitudinarian canon," Hand argued, what could be better than to suggest that this latest interpretation "be written into the Bill of Rights as a definition"? Roosevelt need not commit himself "to any given phrase": "It is enough that the interpretation should be finally fixed in the B. of R. itself substantially embodying the best present doctrine of the Supreme Court."

For once, Hand did not limit himself to claiming that his remedy made more sense in principle. Fully aware of the popular outcry against Roosevelt's recent statements, he ventured into political punditry as well: "The genius of the idea is that it absolutely quiets the hardest-shelled Bourbon. They have always banked on the Sup. Ct. and haven't yet waked up to the fact that that august body has been sadly treacherous of late, consistently, deliberately treacherous." In a long postscript, Hand drafted four "tentative definitions of 'due process of law' or, what is the same thing, the 'Police Power' " as possible constitutional amendments Roosevelt might support. Of these he preferred the second and fourth—one paraphrasing Holmes's opinion in the Oklahoma Bank case of 1911, the other stating, "An act of the legislature shall be deemed due process of law whenever it does not clearly prescribe what is beyond the scope of any reasonable view of the welfare or convenience of the people."[93]

Throughout March, Learned Hand and his closest friends bombarded Roosevelt with pleas that he embrace the Rublee-Hand constitutional-amendment route. Rublee, Cotton, and even Croly, usually the least critical of TR in Hand's circle, joined this campaign,[94] as did a new, soon to be intimate, friend of Hand.

This new face in the progressive movement was an effervescent, engaging young intellectual, Felix Frankfurter. Frankfurter was ten years younger than Hand, much younger than the other reformist lawyers in his circle, but this difference in age was no obstacle to a fast-developing friendship that deepened for the rest of Hand's life. They had met soon after Hand went on the bench in 1909: the twenty-seven-year-old Jewish immigrant from Vienna, recently out of Harvard Law School and hired for the staff of U.S. Attorney Henry Stimson, soon called on the new thirty-seven-year-old judge in his chambers. Their rapport was immediate. They saw each other frequently while Frankfurter remained an assistant U.S. attorney. When Taft persuaded Stimson to join his cabinet as secretary of war in 1911, Stimson brought Frankfurter along to Washington. Officially, Frankfurter was assigned to the War Department's Bureau of Insular Affairs; in fact, he was Stimson's chief assistant and confidant. Hand and Frankfurter each relished letter writing, and a proliferating correspondence soon flowed between them. In the early years, both were progressives who were especially interested in the question of judicial power. They had their differences at times, then and later, but their relationship was sufficiently close to be unusually candid.

By 1911, when Frankfurter went to Washington, he was already a convert to the New Nationalism and an admirer of Croly and his book. Frankfurter's progressive, pro-Roosevelt sympathies of course put him into a difficult posture in the Taft administration; his position made it impossible for him to support TR publicly. Frankfurter agonized about whether to stay in the administration, ultimately remaining in part because he thought he could assure a progressive voice there, and perhaps also because he was concerned about his career and his income: unlike many progressive lawyers, he had no private wealth to draw on. But his public affiliation did not keep him from expressing his sympathies in private.

To Frankfurter, Hand communicated his thoughts on the courts at greatest length and with greatest candor. Frankfurter, knowing of the judge's preoccupation, regularly fed Hand the latest developments on their favorite topic. Early in 1911, for example, he sent Hand a recent conservative diatribe by James M. Beck, among the most reactionary of Wall Street lawyers and constitutional commentators, who had written confidently that the Fourteenth Amendment protected the nation against "Socialism."[95] It was just the kind of remark to anger Hand: "So far as I know we could have 'Socialism' to-morrow if we wanted it," so long as the state's legitimate regulatory powers were properly recognized. Ultimately, Hand argued, "stand-patters" like Beck had "no courage in their convictions." They were true believers in private property, "but they have no confidence that they can justify it before the people at large," and that is why "they want to put the whole weight of government on nine elderly gentlemen at Washington." "You and I," Hand told Frankfurter, do not admire private property "as unreservedly as they," and "we are willing to let it be mauled about a bit. . . . For myself I have no delusions of the vox populi vox dei character, but . . . if we can't make the 'people' realize that the institution is worth keeping, it is in the end better to let it go by the board." Hand had no patience with conservatives who talked "a lot of platitudes about 'Socialism,' whatever that may mean, all designed to show that the Beatitudes were delivered in Manchester and not on the Mount."[96] True to Holmes's dissent in *Lochner*, neither Hand nor Frankfurter could rest easily with the notion that the views of Adam Smith or of Herbert Spencer had been constitutionalized by the framers of the Fourteenth Amendment.

Frankfurter was enthusiastic about Hand's slashing attack: "It's refreshing, at least for an iconoclast like me, to read a consideration of the Constitution that doesn't consist of merely phrases uttered with dogmatic finality." But for Frankfurter as for Hand, the tenor of the Supreme Court's recent rulings spurred hope that "for the next ten years there'll be little cause for complaint." And Frankfurter, as if anticipating his campaigns decades later to advance Hand's name for appointment to the Supreme Court, concluded his letter, "I shall jealously conceal your views with the hope that someday we may get you inside the house, past the unsuspecting Trojans."[97]

With their shared beliefs about due process and the courts, Hand and Frankfurter were understandably in frequent contact as Roosevelt's primary campaign developed. Knowing that Frankfurter was "with us in spirit," Hand felt free in early March to unburden himself to his young friend about issues of central concern:

> I regret very much the [judicial power] issue as the Colonel has framed it. The institutional changes for the most part I am opposed to and the only good one—recall of judicial decisions—is good only for its purpose and thoroughly unworkable and pernicious in its plan. Indeed I think it could only serve to reinforce the very evil against which it is directed. That evil is the power of the courts to take the responsibility from the legislature, the only efficient organ of democracy in my judgment. As you know I am opposed to that function [of the courts] and I am becoming all the time more and more prepared for extreme and radical action [to take away the courts' judicial review authority]; and the reason for that position in most part arises from the fact that the alternative is direct popular action in which I have almost no belief. That is the alternative which the Colonel proposes.[98]

In the same letter, Hand reported to Frankfurter that he had seen Roosevelt "twice last week and labored as well as I could along those lines." But he had mounting, well-justified fears that it was getting to be too late: "[I]f we could have got at him earlier something might have been done, but it is of course very difficult now."[99] Frankfurter agreed only in part. "I wish you had gotten hold of the Colonel earlier," he acknowledged. He was a good deal more sympathetic to TR's populist proposals than Hand could ever be: "While I do not expect much from [institutional changes], I'm for them as weapons in the arsenal—I mean the initiative, referendum and recall. . . . I don't share your fear that they will lead to direct action." But he agreed with Hand's assessment of Roosevelt's character: "The essence of his leadership for me, too, lies in his purposes and his capacity for noble expediency, stimulated by the right faith and sympathies, rather than in any formulated program."[100]

On March 15, 1912, Hand made his last, most elaborate effort to persuade Roosevelt on the judicial reform issue. Knowing that TR planned additional speeches on the court question, Hand undertook a ghostwriting effort to suggest an approach that seemed to him "to present a somewhat different aspect from what we have talked of." The evil, he argued repeatedly in the speech he drafted for TR, was the power of American courts to interpret the hopelessly vague due-process clauses.

Because "due process" lacked any clear content, judicial interpretations were inevitably merely policy judgments. Due-process rulings had only the appearance of legal decisions; they were legal only in form. What the courts did in fact, Hand argued, was to second-guess the legislature on the merits of a given statute. "If the court believes that there is beyond question no good public policy served, it calls the act not due process of law," Hand urged TR to say.

> Such a power I am unalterably against; it exists in no other country; it did not exist in this for many years after our governments began; it is today opposed by a majority of political students in this country, not generally a revolutionary class.

By this time, Hand had surmised that the ex-president was not enthusiastic about a constitutional amendment, so his central aim was to persuade TR to leave the question of remedies open. According to Hand's draft, Roosevelt would say:

> As I have repeatedly said, I am not in the least concerned with means, and if any community thinks it better to define "due process of law" in such clear terms that no court can have excuse for substituting its own view of public policy for the legislatures, I should be wholly satisfied.

But the amorphous due-process clauses themselves, Hand insisted, not a crusade for any particular remedy, should be Roosevelt's central target.[101]

Roosevelt promptly thanked Hand for his suggestions: "I think I can use them" in forthcoming speeches.[102] But soon, TR made it even clearer that he would not budge. On March 20, two days after he received Hand's final suggestion, he gave the talk in which he had promised to use the judge's thoughts—a widely publicized speech before three thousand people who packed New York's Carnegie Hall, with an overflow in an adjacent auditorium eager to hear him. Once again, some of Hand's suggestions made it into the speech. But the overwhelming message of TR's second Carnegie Hall speech, "The Right of the People to Rule," adhered more strongly than ever to the proposal Roosevelt had first put forth in his November 1911 speech, clarified in his January 1912 article, and reiterated in Columbus in late February.

What was especially depressing to New Nationalists was that the speech contained barely a nod to substantive reform proposals. The entire address was devoted to institutional mechanisms. Roosevelt made it clear that his preferred immediate remedy continued to be the recall of judicial decisions, and he specifically rejected the idea of a constitutional amendment as "wholly inadequate."[103]

Whether Roosevelt would have gained the Republican nomination in 1912 if he had followed the advice of Hand and his circle is impossible to say. Clearly, though, he would have had a better chance, for nothing cost Roosevelt more support than his stubborn insistence on his pet remedy. The uproar over Roosevelt's views on judicial power increasingly filled the air during the early months of the campaign, and diverted attention from the New Nationalism proposals that had attracted eastern progressives in the first place.

For weeks after the second Carnegie Hall speech, Roosevelt's campaign grabbed the newspaper headlines. Most of the press coverage, however, focused on the latest invectives the candidates had hurled at each other. Taft, with uncharacteristic forcefulness, resorted to name-calling; Roosevelt replied in kind. To Hand, this deterioration was distressing. Matters turned worse when Roosevelt launched unfounded charges that the Taft Republicans were engaging in fraud and theft in the selection of delegates to the Republican National Convention. "I should not want to announce this publicly," Hand told Frankfurter, "but I am quite willing to tell you that I am really deeply disappointed in the Colonel and his candidacy. [N]early everything he is saying now fills me with regret and indeed with dismay. I wish he could be chloroformed for eight months and then elected. There is no doubt about it that as a campaigner he makes the judicious grieve." Hand no longer felt like a crusader:

> Nearly everyone wants to be known vaguely as a Progressive, and almost all really want to be Progressive. We are being bedeviled beyond any measure by sympathies and sentiments, and so far the result is only to tinker over the old machine. . . . I am sick of clamor, of mutual suspicion, and of abuse: what we need is, Licht, mehr Licht!, like Goethe. I am weary to death of the Rule of the People and a millennium created by constant elections and never-ending suspicion of authority. [I] say I am sick of the whole lot, either they are full of sound and fury and signify nothing, or they twist around a whirligig with prayers written on it, like the Grand Lhama [*sic*] of Tibet, and think that they can exorcise all the devils within the four seas.[104]

Soon after, Hand told Frankfurter that George Rublee had lectured him on his "lack of faith" for speaking in that vein. Rublee complained that Hand was "standing outside and merely barking," and that since he "really was in sympathy with the movement as a whole," he "ought to give that sympathy more expression." "Well, I suppose he is right," Hand told Frankfurter. "I suppose I am in sympathy with the movement though I am pretty doubtful just what that movement is." And he could not suppress his dismay: "It looks to me rather a recrudescence of bourgeois Jacksonianism than the kind of thing that I really want, but it is beyond human nature, or at least beyond my human nature, to become very kindly, when nearly all the declarations of the leaders fill me with a sadness and even with contempt."[105]

Yet Hand still did not abandon the campaign. Instead, he overcame his disappointments and tried to salvage what he could in the Roosevelt candidacy. His persistence reveals much about the depth of Hand's commitment to the New Nationalism. Following Frankfurter's advice, he put aside his difference with TR and focused once more on the social reforms that had originally attracted him. He began work on the planks for Roosevelt's political platform, fervently hoping that TR would return to the fundamental issues that had been obscured in the fog of the primary campaign.

When Frankfurter recommended in mid-March that Hand begin drafting Roosevelt's platform, TR's prospects for nomination looked dim. Frankfurter, like many eastern progressives, did not "believe the Colonel has a decent chance."[106] Even La Follette seemed to be doing better in the battle for the Republican nomination. By the middle of April, however, the odds began to change. With the clamor over the judicial issue fading somewhat, and the campaign shifting to states that used direct primaries rather than conventions, Roosevelt's prospects improved dramatically. Every week seemed to bring news of new TR victories, from Illinois and Pennsylvania to California, Minnesota, and Nebraska. Roosevelt's surge crested in the Ohio primary in May, when a bitter three-way battle among Taft, La Follette, and Roosevelt produced a smashing victory for TR, and in Taft's home state.[107]

HAND'S INVOLVEMENT in the drafting of Roosevelt's platform began with a long letter of May 23 to Norman Hapgood at the editorial office of *Collier's Weekly* magazine. With the Republican National Convention only a month away and Roosevelt's campaign on the rise, Hand wrote, "Now that it seems likely that the Colonel will be nominated, I wish very much that you and George [Rublee], if either or both of you can have any influence on him, would bestir yourselves towards getting him interested in the Platform on which he will run." Could not Roosevelt be persuaded to interest himself "in the things which I at least believe to have more pressing importance"—the substantive ideas of the New Nationalism? Hand enclosed "a few suggestions" he had drafted. He sought no more than brief and general statements; the point was simply "to commit the party to a certain attitude on the subjects they touch."[108]

Hand's enclosures are not preserved, but his cover letter shows his focus on what he would call the "social and industrial" planks. What he had in mind was primarily the assurance of improved conditions for workers and the control of the economic power of corporations. Maximum hours, minimum wages, prevention of child labor: issues such as these were now in the forefront of Hand's attention. Hand assumed that unless he and his eastern friends acted quickly, "the Platform will be practically dominated by the western Progressives." On the same day that Hand sent his platform proposals to Hapgood, he forwarded copies to Croly and Rublee. Croly, isolated in Cornish, had fallen out of touch with Roosevelt—perhaps jealous of the attention that Hand, Rublee, and Cotton received; Rublee was becoming ever more involved, and Hand emphasized that his drafts were designed to "stir" both Rublee and his law partner, Joseph Cotton, to work on the basic issues.[109]

Time was indeed short, since the Republican convention was scheduled to convene in Chicago on June 18. But as that date approached, Hand had growing reasons for confidence. When Massachusetts went to TR, for example, Rublee told Roosevelt that "Cotton, Hand and I have been rejoicing all morning."[110] And the prospect of convincing Roosevelt to return to the New Nationalist fold seemed brighter as Rublee managed to install himself in the inner group when the TR forces gathered in Chicago a few days before the convention.[111] Hand continued to work on the social and industrial plank, sending new revisions to Rublee that emphasized more strongly than ever the need for the exertion of national legislative power. Hand was politically astute enough, however, to realize that these controversial proposals would need some camouflage: "I think it is a good thing to try to make acceptable to the States Rights people a plank which is very radical and in the end giving Congress an enormous extension of power." However controversial the party's statement about social and industrial justice might be, Hand insisted, it was "a most important plank, at least in principle, [and] I am sure it is right."[112]

But when the Republican convention met in Chicago, all the platform efforts seemed to have gone for naught. While TR clearly had the overwhelming support of Republican voters, as the direct primaries and newspaper polls made clear, neither primaries nor polls seated delegates, and the Taft forces controlled the machinery that did. Taft was put in nomination by a flamboyantly oratorical Ohio newspaper editor, Warren

G. Harding, and the convention was his. Roosevelt was furious. TR himself was convinced that the nomination had been stolen from him, as were his delegates, many of whom abstained in protest.

Roosevelt had hinted for weeks that he would not accept defeat at the hands of the Republican bosses. Before the convention ended, he followed through on his threat: most Republican progressives bolted the party, and a new third party, the Progressive party, was formed. This split in the Republican party created a three-way race for the presidency among Taft, TR, and whoever the Democratic nominee might be. It also helped guarantee that progressivism "as a potent force within the Republican Party was dead for at least thirty years."[113] Hand was among the progressives who had urged Roosevelt to bolt in the weeks preceding the nomination. In a visit to Oyster Bay early in June, Hand told Croly, he had emphasized this possibility: "I particularly ran home the idea [that] there was a principle at stake now which would justify a bolt regardless of stealing the contests or not, that being a futile issue practically." Hand mistakenly thought that his advice had not had "the least effect."[114] He underestimated how many others would urge the same course on TR, and above all how averse TR was to accepting defeat.

Nor was Hand's work on the Republican platform as futile as he feared when he heard the Chicago results. Norman Hapgood wrote him two days after the convention adjourned that he would "have plenty of time" to present the issues that concerned him "to the Progressive party for its platform," since the new party's convention was not scheduled until the first week of August, also in Chicago.[115] For the remainder of the campaign, Hand remained intensely involved. And the new party heeded his call for more specific platform planks.

The very long document that emerged as the Progressive National Platform included a major section on "Social and Industrial Justice." The ideas of the New Nationalism were amply expressed in specific promises, on the child-labor problem, minimum-wage standards for working women, and the eight-hour day.[116] Another plank contained a commitment to something like the "radical" strengthening of congressional power that Hand had urged: "bringing under effective national jurisdiction those problems which have expanded beyond reach of the individual States," including elimination of "unequal" state laws on such matters of "common concern" as child labor, women's health, and protection of workers. Joined with this was an attack on the Democratic party's "extreme insistence on States' rights," which demonstrated "anew its inability to understand the world into which it has survived."[117] Hand promptly joined the Progressive party. "I don't think you have made any mistake," wrote Croly. "It seems to me a clear case."[118]

Roosevelt had reasonable hopes of winning the presidency, especially if the Democrats were to nominate an anti-nationalist who would drive progressive Democrats into TR's movement. But the Progressive party's prospects for the upcoming election soon dimmed. The Democrats nominated Governor Woodrow Wilson of New Jersey, and many Roosevelt Progressives were drawn to him (as happened with Hapgood and Rublee in later months). Croly, slowly being drawn back into TR's campaign (he prided himself on having received a luncheon invitation from TR at last), was not about to give up his old loyalty: "[A] third party even under the existing somewhat dubious conditions certainly contains more promise for future good government than any recent movement in American politics. You will find it driven," he assured Hand, "by the logic of its own work and situation towards nationalization." To Croly, the Progressive party included "the most vital ingredients in American political opinion, . . . the men who want to do something and who are willing to use the agency of the government for the realization of their program."[119]

Hand shared these beliefs about the party; more than Croly, he detested Wilson and thought him a hypocritical Jeffersonian orator. Unlike Croly, though, he had no illusions that success beckoned in 1912. Instead, he viewed the campaign mainly as the first step in a lasting movement of national reform. Soon he agreed with Frankfurter that the campaign "should be fought on the assumption of not being successful this year."[120] Of course, hopes of building a lasting movement also turned on assuring that the new party would not simply become a vehicle for TR. As Hand remarked to his Cornish friend Philip Littell, "I don't know whether the present third party will survive; it certainly has no right to be born, much less survive, as a Roosevelt party— [although] he happens to be the most effective expression of the demands that make the movement."[121]

As the Progressive convention neared, Hand found new energy for the cause. "There was a time, for about two weeks after the Democratic Convention," he wrote to Frankfurter in late July, "when I was rather unhappy, because I didn't know exactly what to do, because Wilson's nomination removed the last chance of victory for the new Party, and because it first seemed to me as though it would greatly serve to confuse the issues." But soon he became certain of "the proper course to follow," and, once he concluded that the Progressives still warranted his support, he was "practically without any misgivings." Hand was distressed by Progressive backsliding on national issues for the sake of local success, but his faith overcame his doubts. He sensed new growth at the grass roots:

> There is immense enthusiasm throughout the country, a real sense, I believe, of political liberation. While the party remains unsuccessful there ought to be much to inspire devotion. If it ever should become successful it will falter, I suppose, and trim like all other organizations, political, ecclesiastical and social. That's the condition of cooperation. . . . [But] I think there is good ground for enthusiasm. . . . There is lots of backing [all] over the country. This may be the beginning of a real national democracy; no one can tell. I am sorry there is so much T.R. in it, but that you can't help—without him, we must concede, it would cut a small figure.[122]

Hand's perception of "backing [all] over the country" is suspect. He and his friends were upper-middle-class eastern intellectuals; indeed, he was better acquainted with Europe than with the country west of the Hudson. From his parochial vantage point, he had no perspective on the strength of TR's support among the masses. While Hand was probably right when he assured Roosevelt two weeks later that the "greater part of the conscience and brains—under forty—of the country that I see are fine Bull Moose,"[123] this small group of displaced intellectuals, critical of the insensitivities and abuses of wealth around them, hardly constituted a nationwide wave.[124]

The Progressive convention in early August had more the air of a religious crusade than a political gathering, and it featured a triumphant performance by Roosevelt. Throughout his long acceptance speech the crowd cheered ecstatically and waved red bandannas, the new symbol of the Bull Moose Progressives. Even Hand was enthusiastic about TR's "Confession of Faith"; it was indeed as clear a statement of the New Nationalism's principles as Hand and Croly could have desired. Although Roosevelt did not abandon his direct democracy proposals, he did, with greater vigor than ever, urge all of Hand's favored reforms, from a national industrial commission that would regulate industry to a long list of measures to aid the underprivileged. And the platform that emerged was a detailed, nationalistic statement.

The incipient strains within the Progressive party, however, could not wholly be mended. The antitrust issue was particularly contentious. Although the platform still called for national agencies that would regulate corporations, the financier George Perkins, after some intense parliamentary maneuverings, managed to eliminate a provision that would have advocated strengthening the Sherman Act. Hand was not disturbed, for he agreed with Perkins on the issue, but the western Progressives and TR's radical supporters around the nation were offended.

The Bull Moose commitment to administrative regulation rather than Sherman Act enforcement also made Roosevelt vulnerable to attack from the progressive elements in the Democrats' campaign. Wilson increasingly attacked Roosevelt as "pro-business" on the antitrust issue, relying on Louis D. Brandeis for ammunition. Hand complained that "Brandeis's effort to throw us into the camp of the monopolists" was "falsifying the actual issue." But the debate, he thought, was healthy: "Indeed, it is only one of the numerous instances of how the new party has already begun to clarify the issues; it proves abundantly what we all believed, that the stimulus to thought would come when the lines were once drawn."[125]

During the final weeks of the campaign, Hand joined the local Progressive Club as well as the national party, and he contributed money generously.[126] But he had growing misgivings about how active his participation should be, given his position as a judge. In his correspondence with Henry Stimson earlier in the year, Hand had revealed that he was aware of some rumblings around the courthouse about his political activism. By September, he expressed his mounting misgivings in correspondence with a Progressive party official who solicited him, a young economist and journalist named Walter E. Weyl. Weyl asked Hand to aid the party's campaign in a number of ways: drafting short editorials on Progressive platform planks, writing signed letters to local newspapers, speaking to voters, and giving informal talks to students in the college wing of the party.[127] After several days of reflection, Hand, expressing a "good deal of regret," declined to participate:

> [I]t seems to me that any active participation in campaign work is to be deprecated on the part of any judge. . . . I should like to be able to do some work, but I think that you will agree that a judge should keep himself free from any active partisanship. Cases arise not infrequently where it is important that his mind should be quite free from party bias, and he certainly loses the confidence of the community insofar as he allows himself with much ardor upon the one side or the other in advance.[128]

Hand was obviously treading a thin and occasionally imperceptible line: behind the scenes he had already done a great deal for the party; and in the next year, his compunctions did not keep him from being a candidate for New York's Court of Appeals to aid the Progressive ticket.

But for the remainder of the 1912 campaign, he avoided public activities.

However, Hand did attend the climax of Roosevelt's campaign, a mass meeting in New York's Madison Square Garden at the end of October. Roosevelt probably gave his best speech, before an audience of sixteen thousand who cheered their candidate for forty-five minutes even in the face of TR's uncharacteristic efforts to quiet them.[129] Hand was deeply moved and inspired, for Roosevelt's advocacy of the New Nationalism was crisper and more forceful than ever. This time, even Roosevelt's support for the recall of judicial decisions did not restrain Hand's enthusiasm. Two days later, he wrote an emotional note to Mrs. Corinne Roosevelt Robinson, TR's sister:

> Your brother certainly never appeared more gallant. The occasion absolutely suited his genius, and he showed himself most truly a great leader of men. I shall never forget the lofty and inspiring phrases in which he put our aims, nor his solemn fervor as he assured us now with the added emphasis of the last two weeks of his consecration to a great cause.

Perhaps sensing Roosevelt's impending defeat, he closed the letter with something of a eulogy:

> I hope, and I believe, that when history comes to be written, the greatest service he would have done his country—and his worst enemy admits that there are many—will be said to be when he became the inspiration and the leader, as he had been the real creator, of the Progressive Party.[130]

A few days later, the election took place, and Roosevelt was indeed defeated. However, he ran a strong second, and he soundly thrashed Taft, receiving over 4 million votes to Taft's fewer than 3.5 million. Roosevelt carried six states and won eighty-eight electoral votes, to Taft's two states and eight electoral votes. Wilson, with only a plurality of the total vote, won easily over the divided Republicans. For Hand, the unprecedented strength of Roosevelt's third-party campaign nourished hopes for the future of the Progressive cause.

LIKE MOST PROGRESSIVES, Learned Hand saw the 1912 election as only the beginning of the New Nationalist crusade. Greater challenges lay ahead. Could a permanent Progressive movement emerge from a campaign so intimately associated with Roosevelt himself? TR expressed no doubts: the Progressive party's achievements in just a few

Ancestors

Augustus C. Hand (1803–1878), Learned Hand's grandfather, founded the Hand family's legal tradition. Learned held his grandfather in awe, convinced that he could never match his talents or drive. *(Bruce L. Crary Foundation)*

Samuel Hand, Learned Hand's father (1833–1886), was a successful Albany lawyer. His death when Learned was only fourteen left his son with a larger-than-life ideal that his son was pressed to emulate. *(Bruce L. Crary Foundation)*

Youth

Billings Learned Hand in 1875, age three, with his mother's sister, Harriet W. Learned, one of the three female members of the household in which Learned was usually the only male. *(Family Collection)*

Billings Learned Hand, posing with his father, Samuel—in matching coats and hats—in 1876. Learned was then four years old, already earnest and obedient, with few opportunities, then or later, to form close bonds with his bookish and distant father. *(Family Collection)*

Learned Hand's mother, Lydia Coit Learned Hand. Until her death in the 1920s, she exerted the most important family influence on her son. *(Family Collection)*

Billings Learned Hand, age fourteen, in 1886, the year his father died of cancer. His father's death stirred deep feelings of responsibility in Learned, the sole surviving male in the family. *(Family Collection)*

Learned Hand (standing, fourth from the left) as a member of Albany Academy's first football team in 1887, when he was fifteen. Hand always felt awkward about participating in organized sports. *(Albany Academy Archives)*

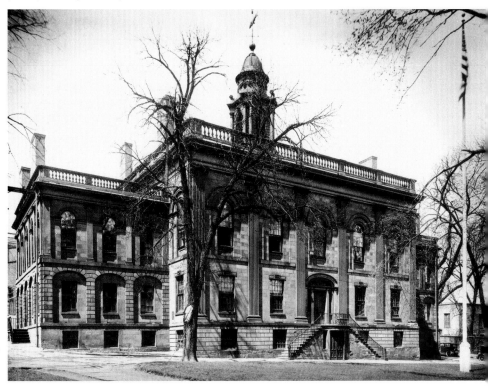

Albany Academy, which Learned Hand attended from 1879 to 1889. The building, dating from 1813, still stands, in a park between the state capitol and the state Court of Appeals. *(Albany Academy Archives)*

Learned Hand in 1893, the
year of his graduation from
Harvard College. Because of his
beard, college classmates often
called him "the Mad Russian"
and the "Mongolian Grind."
Though he was inclined to pursue graduate study in philosophy, family pressures persuaded
him to go to law school instead.
(Harvard University Archives)

Austin Hall, the Harvard Law School building during Learned Hand's student days (1893–1896) and
the site of his *Bill of Rights* lectures in 1958. *(Harvard Law Art Collection)*

Marriage and the Young Family

Frances Fincke, a strong-minded young girl, in Utica in the 1880s. *(Family Collection)*

Frances Fincke at twenty, at Bryn Mawr Colleg *(Courtesy of Constance Jordan)*

The "Minturn Cottage" at Murray Bay, Quebec, on the St. Lawrence River. Here, in 1901, Learned Hand met Francis Fincke, a young Byrn Mawr graduate, and proposed to her before the end of the summer. *(Courtesy of Leslie Minturn Allison)*

Frances A. Hand in 1903, soon after her marriage to Learned Hand.
(Courtesy of Constance Jordan)

ildred Minturn, Frances Fincke's housemate and
sest friend at Bryn Mawr, on graduating in 1897.
ourtesy of Leslie Minturn Allison)

The young couple summering in Mount Kisc in July 1905, with their firstborn, Mary Desh Hand. *(Family Collection)*

Frances Hand with her daughters Mary a Frances, ca. 1908, perhaps during their firs visit to Cornish, New Hampshire. *(Family Collection)*

The family complete, ca. 1912: Learned and Frances Hand with daughters Mary, Frances and Constance in Cornish. *(Family Collection)*

months, he proclaimed right after the 1912 election, were "unparalleled in the history of free government." The party, he insisted, had "come to stay," and "the battle has just begun."[131] But to rally the masses to the high-minded reforms conceived by such intellectuals as Croly and Hand would be no easy task.

In the weeks after the election, Progressives gathered in state and national conferences to plan for the future. They sought not only to superimpose an elaborate party structure upon the existing grass roots organizations, but to develop a parallel educational structure, the "Progressive Service" organization, designed to bring the reform message to legislators and the masses. The Progressive Service—proposed by the well-known social worker Jane Addams—sought to coordinate within the party the scattered reform groups from whose ranks so many Progressives came—groups devoted to eliminating child labor, achieving women's suffrage, improving factory conditions. Thus, the "social workers," who Hand had once predicted would be an important source of party strength, now had their day. Through education and persuasion, the party hoped, Progressive reform would flourish.

Hand participated eagerly in these organizational efforts. He was among the first to pledge annual contributions to assure permanent financing for the national party organization.[132] The New York party organization asked Hand to serve on two subcommittees of its legislative committee, groups seeking Progressive enactments concerning the courts' relation to legislation and the removal of public officials. Hand was not enthusiastic about his subcommittee assignments. In mid-December 1912, he wrote William L. Ransom, the chair of the legislative committee, that he preferred to serve on a group "dealing more directly with labor legislation."[133] Soon after, Hand began to have more serious second thoughts: "I have thought considerably about what I ought to do in relation to this and I have a feeling that it is not quite proper for a judge to be connected with a political party in this way."[134] After meeting with Ransom, Hand concluded that he had better not participate at all—that "it was advisable for me not to have any formal or active connection with any such committees."[135]

By the fall of 1913, Hand's decision to avoid public involvements with Progressive party activities was put to a severe test. On September 24, while vacationing in Cornish, he received a startling letter from T. Douglas Robinson, TR's brother-in-law and the chairman of the state committee of the Progressive party, inquiring on behalf of Colonel Roosevelt whether Hand "would accept the Progressive nomination for Judge of the Court of Appeals if such nomination were made." As Robinson explained, the New York Progressives were "in a peculiar position in regard to these nominations." The party could not endorse incumbent associate judge William E. Werner, a candidate for the chief judgeship, because he had written the opinion in *Ives*. If the Progressives were to run a separate ticket for the two vacancies, one candidate was already available: Samuel Seabury, a respected independent who had won a New York City judgeship in Seth Low's 1901 Fusion sweep and, since 1906, had held a seat on the New York Supreme Court, the state trial court. Seabury's availability still left the Progressives one candidate short, which led the party to Hand:

> The Colonel and other leaders of the Party hope that you will consent to accept the nomination in case the state committee of the Progressive Party is forced to select men not already selected by the Republicans, and in all probability not to be selected by the Democrats. Will you wire me "Yes" or "No" . . . ?[136]

Hand knew that the New York Progressives had decided to run a separate ticket for a significant number of state offices. He also knew that the party could not endorse any judge who had participated in the infamous *Ives* decision. The nomination thus appeared to be Hand's for the taking, but seemed inconsistent with his withdrawal from public participation in politics. Robinson's request thus put Hand in a quandary. After considering Robinson's urgent appeal for five hours, Hand wired, "Cannot reply unconditionally. Am writing." All that evening and much of the next day he fretted as he drafted and redrafted his letter. Finally, he told Robinson:

> Naturally I regard it as a great honor to be selected for so important a place, and if it is necessary and best for the party I will run, though I must confess that I am very loath to do so in view of the great probability that we should make an extremely poor showing this year. I hope very much that matters will so fall out that we need not be counted at all, as I have said from the first.[137]

Hand's groping response was prompted partly by his ignorance of recent political developments. Because he had just returned to Cornish from a three-week vacation trip to the Far West, he did not know that in early September both he and Seabury had appeared on a State Bar Association Committee list of sixteen judges from which the parties should pick their nominees.[138] Nor did he know that the Republicans had already selected their candidates: Werner for chief judge and Frank H. Hiscock, another incumbent, for associate judge. Hand's response was that he would accept the Progressive nomination if the Democratic nominees proved unsuitable. But the Progressives were slated to name their candidates within a very few days, while the Democrats would not meet until early October.

Hand realized that his condition put the party in a difficult position. He wrote Robinson that he hoped the Progressives could delay their judicial nominations, and then firmly added one more condition: "Finally, I assume, of course, that no candidate, who is already a judge, will be expected to take any part in the campaign. Last year there was some talk of Progressive candidates for judicial positions campaigning like others. That I could not do."[139]

On September 27, two days after Hand's letter to Robinson, the Bull Moose convention selected Learned Hand as its candidate for chief judge of the New York Court of Appeals and Samuel Seabury as its candidate for associate judge. Hand was praised as "a man relatively young, strong in physical characteristics, a man already on the bench, descended from a distinguished legal family, and, above all, a Progressive to the core —a man who looks at social questions with such an insight as Progressives feel that they do."[140] Robinson promptly telegraphed Hand in Cornish to notify him of the decision, and Hand bowed to the Progressives' nomination without awaiting the Democrats' choice. "[I] accept subject to the conditions mentioned in my letter of Sept. 25, which I assume are agreeable to the State Committee," he telegraphed Robinson.[141] Robinson promptly acknowledged that the Progressive state committee had indeed "agreed" to Hand's conditions and added that his entire committee appreciated "to the full your acceptance of this nomination and so does Colonel Roosevelt."[142]

The Democrats' choice for chief judge was Willard Bartlett, a conservative Court of Appeals judge who, like Hand's Republican opponent, Werner, had participated in *Ives*. Understandably, the Court of Appeals race promptly became a focus of political controversy, as the Progressives used the opportunity to continue their attack on the *Ives* judges, and Hand's resolve to avoid public statements during the campaign was repeatedly put to the test. He turned down all invitations to attend political dinners or participate in other party functions; privately, he thanked local party functionaries for their efforts on behalf of the Progressive ticket,[143] but that is as far as he would go. The greatest pressure came from party pleas that he at least make the judicial nominee's traditional public acceptance statement. Even the incumbent Court of Appeals judges in the race did not hesitate to do this, and Seabury was especially eager to have Hand lend his voice to the anti-*Ives* campaign. Hand, true to the condition he had imposed on his acceptance of the nomination, refused to do so. "I was already on the bench and the thought of haranguing the electorate was more than I could bear," Hand

recalled long after.[144] Seabury was irritated, insisting that judicial nominees, like other candidates, had a duty to define the issues for the
electorate. But given his vow of silence, Hand could not even counter
newspaper editorials that overwhelmingly favored the other candidates
and that linked the Progressive candidates to TR's 1912 advocacy of
the recall of judicial decisions.[145] A *New York Sun* editorial that Hand
clipped and saved in his files made this point clearly:

> Considering the general tendencies of the Progressive party with
> respect to the judiciary, as illustrated by the attitude of Colonel
> Roosevelt and other leaders with radical views on the subject of
> popular reversal of decisions from the bench, to the eyes of con-
> servative citizens the Progressive nominee, Judge HAND [will]
> not seem to be a desirable alternative to either Judge BARTLETT
> or Judge WERNER in the present state of public opinion.[146]

Privately, Hand expressed his strong hope for a respectable Progressive showing in the state election: he knew that 1913 was a critical
test of whether the party had a future without TR on the ticket. And
while national results were mixed, New York, together with Massachusetts, proved a bastion of relative strength. The "shining"[147] New
York results included a sweep for the New York City Fusion ticket
that the Progressives had joined and, even more important, the election
of twenty-three Progressives to the New York State Assembly.[148] But
in the contests for the Court of Appeals, the outcome was what Hand
had expected all along: he and Seabury, running without major party
support, were defeated. In the chief-judgeship race, Bartlett, the Democrat, beat Werner by only 3,000 votes out of more than 1.5 million.
Hand's statewide vote was slightly over 195,000—about 13 percent of
the total, and nearly 2,000 more than Seabury garnered.

Hand acknowledged to Frankfurter that there was "no denying that
it was a satisfactory result": "I was myself a good deal gratified at the
size of the vote, which was the very top figure that I had hoped."[149]
Frankfurter had all along considered Hand's nomination "a deeply satisfying symbol" of "what ought to be," for it demonstrated his "availability" for a higher position, perhaps even the Supreme Court. Even
if the New York race proved unsuccessful, the youthful Frankfurter
reminded Hand, "the world is still wondrously young for you. . . ."[150]

In Hand's own assessment, it was unwise to read too much into the
gratifying results. As he wrote the civil liberties lawyer Gilbert E. Roe:

> In some ways I am sorry about all this trouble over judges. As a
> judge myself I am very conscious of the fact that it is hard to be

indifferent to the popular feeling as it exists now, in those cases in which one ought to be indifferent to it. All of us must recognize, of course, that a judge is not the authoritative source of public opinion and that his first duty is honestly to try to get at the legislative meaning when it is written.

The hostilities provoked by judges exceeding their powers might, Hand thought, in the long run threaten judicial independence: "I agree with you that the time may come when we will have to fight hard to preserve what is right in our law. It will be harder for people like you and me because we will be charged with having caused exactly the excitement which at that time we shall be trying to stem."[151]

DEFEAT AT THE POLLS, but a satisfying contribution to the Progressive cause, were the immediate results of Hand's reluctant participation in the 1913 campaign. There were potential harms as well. Would regular Republicans remember his maverick behavior when Hand was considered for higher judicial offices in later years? Hand apparently gave no thought to his career prospects when he accepted the 1913 nomination, but he did pay recurrent attention to a related issue: Was his candidacy consistent with the standards of propriety appropriate for a federal judge? He found himself increasingly concerned with this issue, and in his eighties, while reflecting on his politically active years, he commented, "I ought to have lain off, as I now view it; I was a judge, and a judge has no business to mess into such things even though he doesn't appear. Mea culpa, mea culpa!"[152]

Hand apparently perceived a fairly clear line separating proper from improper judicial involvement in political affairs. At that time, he thought it appropriate for a federal judge to offer private advice, as he so frequently did with Theodore Roosevelt, so long as there was no prominent public identification with the cause. This view of acceptable judicial conduct, while not unusual at the time,[153] was less restrictive than today's official view[154] or Hand's later view. By the time he was on the appellate court, Hand consistently avoided political involvements and public identification with causes that could be seen as "agitation." In November 1922, for example, he firmly insisted, "If a judge is to become actively interested in politics, I think he should resign."[155] Bowing by early 1923 to Holmes's advice "to avoid all 'heated subjects,' "[156] he abstained from all public partisan activity, although he remained an engaged observer of the political scene throughout his life and shared his views in his private correspondence with his friends.

Hand's far greater involvement during the Progressive years stands in sharp contrast to his later self-imposed restraint. Limits on acceptable judicial behavior were less certain then, but the key explanation surely lay in his profound commitment to the cause of the New Nationalism. Even as an old man, he had no regrets: "I was indeed an ardent 'Rooseveltian.' . . . I have never repented and should do it again."[157] Hand's commitment to Progressivism and, some of the time, to TR as its leader overcame most of his nagging doubts about the propriety of his activities.

Soon after Hand accepted the Progressive nomination, Croly, knowing that the question of propriety was on Hand's mind, wrote, "Dear B:—What's the news? What think your learned and cherished confreres of your candidacy?"[158] Hand replied that he had spoken to only two of his judicial colleagues and that "they took it better than I supposed." He was far less certain about the reaction among lawyers: "I should not be surprised . . . if I had incurred a good deal of odium from a number of the older members of the bar, who must look upon the Progressive Party in general as anathema and think any judge who will lend himself to it is already condemned."[159]

But there had been a great deal of objection from another source, a source that troubled Hand considerably. As Hand wrote Croly, "I was a little surprised to learn that Brandeis had told both George [Rublee] and Norman [Hapgood] that he thought that I ought not to have done it. His theory was that a judge ought never to run for any elective office." By 1913, Brandeis, fifteen years older than Hand, was already an imposing national figure. During the years in which Hand's awareness of national issues developed, Brandeis contributed in many ways to progressive causes. From his base in Boston corporate practice, he had gained a controversial reputation not only as one of the first public-interest lawyers but also as a reformer on many fronts. By 1913, he was coming to be known as an austere, moralizing, distant figure; many years later, during the New Deal, Hand, like others, referred to Brandeis as "Isaiah." No wonder that Hand was irritated when he found himself a target of the prophet's denunciations. In any case, Hand somewhat defensively rejected Brandeis's contention:

> [T]his is perfectly absurd if it is to be extended to State judges for largely it necessarily involves not running to succeed yourself for the same office. The theory that your impartiality is affected has undoubtedly something in it, in fact, is a good argument against electing judges anyway, but it seems to me preposterous when you have the institution, to lay down any such rule as that.

Yet what of the propriety of nonelected, life-tenured federal judges running in state judicial elections?

> I believe he confined [his argument] to Federal judges, but it seems to me just as absurd to apply it to Federal as to State judges, and certainly the strictest tradition up to the present time has not discountenanced it in the least. . . . I think [Brandeis] is going to stick his standard of disinterestedness so high that few of us can possibly hold office or even important positions. Things will have to be run by people who are willing to sacrifice a great deal more than anybody that I know,—unless it be Brandeis himself.[160]

This response is not wholly persuasive. Even Hand recognized that standing for election could affect judicial impartiality, or at least the appearance of judicial impartiality. While elected state judges could not avoid this risk, federal judges, appointed for life, certainly could. (Three years later, when President Wilson named Brandeis to the Supreme Court, he was confirmed only after a rancorous battle in the Senate. Hand wrote a letter in support of his confirmation. Ironically, Brandeis as a Supreme Court justice repeatedly engaged in behind-the-scenes political advising, from the Wilson era to that of the New Deal—often with the collaboration of Felix Frankfurter.)

Some of Hand's friends worried, with good reason, about possible damage to his career. Frankfurter reported that a former federal judge "seemed really pleased that you ran. He thought that the talk of 'harm' was nonsense."[161] Yet William Howard Taft, Chief Justice of the United States from 1921 to 1930, never forgot or forgave Hand's association with the Bull Moose movement and repeatedly managed to block consideration of Hand for promotion to the Supreme Court during the Republican administrations of the 1920s.

Hand's 1913 candidacy was his last major service to the Progressive party. His withdrawal stemmed less from second thoughts about the propriety of his candidacy than from his growing realization that the Bull Moose crusade had no future. Woodrow Wilson's New Freedom had stolen its thunder: forward-thinking Democrats controlled the Democratic party, and their program echoed the Progressives' aims in many respects. The involvement of his friends Rublee and Hapgood in the Wilson administration symbolized the flight of some old Progressives to the Democratic camp. But the main reason Hand lost faith in the Progressive party's future lay in the fact that so many Progressives continued to assign a central role to Roosevelt. Hand expressed his opposition to that strategy in the spring of 1914, when a Progressive acquaintance sought to persuade him to support the idea of Roosevelt's running in the New York gubernatorial race, in part as a stepping-stone toward a renewed run for the presidency in 1916. Hand sharply disagreed, stating that he did "not want him to run for governor":

> [I] am sick of having the party represent Roosevelt and nothing but Roosevelt, and think that if it continues to do so, it is and ought to be doomed. I am not interested in a party which cannot support itself by the ideas which it can make clear to the people. If the Progressive Party has not the virtue or the intelligence to declare its position so that it will become popular, I do not believe that Roosevelt can or will save it.[162]

Hand urged Rublee to write TR "as strong a letter as you can" to keep him from running,[163] and, drawing on his growing acquaintance with TR,[164] gave the same advice to TR directly: "I hope you will not let them push you into running for governor." Any arguments for running, Hand argued, were reasons "of desperation. Every sound consideration of reason makes against it, and it will finally demonstrate that the Progressive Party has only one card to play, yourself. . . . You will understand that I am not belittling the effect of your presence in the campaign; rather it is because it will overshadow everything else that I speak. Those who wish you see no further than an immediate victory."[165] To Hand's great relief, Roosevelt replied, "I absolutely agree with you and absolutely agree with your reasoning. I will not run for governor."[166]

As the 1916 election drew near, the remaining leaders of the Progressive party once again pressed TR to become a presidential candidate. But by then, Hand had even more firmly concluded that the party had no future. He carefully drafted his final substantive letter to Roosevelt, once more urging TR not to accept any Progressive nomination. When Hand wrote, on June 13, 1916, the Republicans had just named Charles Evans Hughes to run against Wilson, and Hughes had resigned his Supreme Court position to accept the nomination. Hand thought Hughes a potentially acceptable, reasonably liberal Republican, and certainly a far cry from the conservative Taft. Hughes might well prove acceptable to Progressives, Hand insisted to TR, and "[i]f he will show a genuine sympathy for our general point of view, . . . we shall not betray anything in going with him." Roosevelt would be "wise and patriotic" to give Hughes the chance to demonstrate his liberal sympathies. As for Hand himself, he told TR, he could not personally remain loyal to the Progressives: "I shall join the Amalekites [exiles]; I can see no room . . . for a third party."[167] If pressed, he preferred to go into political exile. Roosevelt promptly assured Hand that "I agree exactly with what you say."[168] TR kept his word. A few days later, the Progressive National Convention nominated Roosevelt for the presidency; TR declined immediately.

Roosevelt's refusal to run killed the Progressive party. The Progressives nominated no substitute candidate, and the party quickly disintegrated. Hand, like Roosevelt, voted for Hughes in 1916; Hughes's defeat threw the Republican party back into the hands of its most conservative elements. Learned Hand went into effective political exile: through most of the 1920s, he felt that both major parties had abandoned the positions he held dear. As a Progressive, he had written Walter Lippmann in 1914: "My Progressive flag is nailed to the mast and I propose to play the Star Spangled Banner while the ship sinks. My position in the band is to beat the bass drum softly."[169] But Hand's interest in beating the drum waned. He had continued to make financial contributions to the party through 1915, and was a founding supporter of a new Progressive party journal in Massachusetts.[170] But eventually he lost all patience with the party. "I would like to find a new home," he wrote poignantly to Felix Frankfurter. "If you know any congenial political boardinghouse where we could live for a while, I wish you would advise me."[171] The home Hand found was not in partisan activities but in what he called "the House of Advanced Thought," the headquarters of Herbert Croly's new magazine, *The New Republic*.

CROLY BEGAN SERIOUSLY PLANNING for a new magazine in the fall of 1913. The first issue of *The New Republic* was published on November 7, 1914, right after the congressional elections, and quickly found a substantial audience: in its first year circulation reached fifteen thousand, twice the audience of *The Promise of American Life*, and its circulation kept growing for several years, attaining a peak of forty-three thousand in 1920. Hand was deeply involved in the organizing discussions, and once the magazine was launched, he remained involved, often attending staff sessions and contributing commentary as well.

The magazine was conceived as a platform for the democratic nationalism so dear to Croly's heart. But much as Croly might have wanted to reach a wider audience than he had with his book, he could not even consider the project without financial support. While Hand relieved some of Croly's financial woes in the summer of 1913, loaning him some $2,000 and settling Croly's overdue account at the Harvard Club in New York City,[172] Croly lacked the capital to start a national magazine.

Croly soon found his patron. One evening in the fall of 1913, at a dinner at the Long Island mansion of Willard and Dorothy Straight, Croly's angry denunciation of Norman Hapgood's increasingly anti-Progressive, pro-Wilson editorials in *Harper's* led his hostess first to suggest that Croly publish a weekly, and then to offer to finance it. Mrs. Straight was not dissuaded by Croly's warning that it would take a great deal of money and a good many years to make the magazine self-supporting. "[L]et's go ahead," she insisted.[173]

Dorothy Straight, the daughter of William C. Whitney, a Wall Street financier, was only twenty-six at the time of her conversation with Croly; her husband, Willard, was seven years older. She had inherited a large fortune at seventeen and was imbued with a social worker's concern for the underprivileged. The Straights had spent some time in China, where Willard sought to secure greater investments by American bankers and where he and his wife read *The Promise of American Life*. Their admiration for the book prompted them to seek out Croly on their return and ultimately to offer to finance the magazine. Although some *New Republic* staffers and more outside critics thought that the financial arrangements were bound to subvert the magazine's independence, the Straights in fact gave Croly and his staff full editorial independence and, essentially, a blank check. During its first ten years, *The New Republic* received more than $800,000 from the Straights, and Dorothy Whitney Straight continued her support into the 1950s, long after Croly's death in 1930.[174]

With financial support assured, Croly energetically set off on his meticulous planning, and no person was closer to him during this planning than Hand. The Straights purchased two adjacent town houses in New York City to serve as editorial and business offices for *The New Republic*. Croly threw himself into arranging the offices, drawing on the tastes he had cultivated in his days as editor of the *Architectural Record*. The four-story, yellow brick house on West Twenty-first Street soon came "to resemble a gentlemen's club as much as an editorial plant." Croly hired a French couple as cook and caretaker, and they prepared and served the elegant meals served at staff gatherings. Frequently consulting with Hand, Croly began rounding up the most important ingredient of his new venture, the editorial staff.[175]

As Felix Frankfurter recalled, the "editors were brought together the way a producer . . . looks around and asks for suggestions in filling the roles of a new play."[176] Croly's first two recruits were Walter Weyl and Walter Lippmann.

Weyl's professional background was in muckraking journalism, and with a Ph.D. in economics, he was also the only member of the founding group not afraid of statistics. He had written a book entitled

The New Democracy that was published in 1912; in it he had discussed American progressivism much as Croly had in *The Promise of American Life*. Like Lippmann but unlike Croly, Weyl was a fluent, graceful writer, which Croly appreciated. He was a year younger than Hand, four years younger than Croly. These men, all in their early forties, were the oldest in *The New Republic*'s founding circle.

Walter Lippmann was far younger. Theodore Roosevelt said in 1915 that Lippmann was "on the whole the most brilliant young man of his age in all the United States."[177] Only twenty-five then, Lippmann was already known as remarkably prolific. He had arrived at Harvard College in 1906, completed its requirements in three years, and stayed on as George Santayana's assistant. He so impressed the Fabian socialist Graham Wallas, then a visiting lecturer at Harvard, that Wallas dedicated his next book to him. Two years after Lippmann left college, he published his first book, *A Preface to Politics*, which dazzlingly combined political analysis with a theory of human nature, drawing heavily on Freud, Nietzsche, Bergson, and other modern European thinkers. Lippmann argued that reform movements had to take into account the darker, irrational elements of human personality, a theme that the sometimes gloomy, often skeptical Hand appreciated. A year later, in 1914, Lippmann had a second book published, *Drift and Mastery*, in which he abandoned his emphasis on the irrational and instead preached that the scientific method should be the basic tool of reformers.

Weyl and Lippmann agreed with Croly and Hand on most important issues—particularly on the promise of democratic nationalism and on the trust question. All four were critics of Woodrow Wilson; all were followers of Teddy Roosevelt, at least at the outset. Croly signed up Lippmann for the magazine after Hand had described him as "an interesting mixture of maturity and innocence." Hand exulted: "I consider him as a gift from Heaven for the enrichment of the *Republic*. I don't know where I could find a substitute with so much innocence or conviction, united with so much critical versatility. . . . He'll throw a few fire crackers under the skirts of the old women on the bench & other high places."[178] Even though Lippmann managed to charm Croly, his self-confidence and detachment could also alienate associates: he appeared unusually arrogant, indeed Olympian. John Reed, his Harvard classmate and collaborator in founding a Socialist Club there, perceived this quality early on. Reed—a romantic radical throughout his short life—wrote in a poem that Lippmann "wants to make the human race, and me, march to a geometric Q.E.D."[179] Hand, too, noted Lippmann's excess of detached intellectualism[180] and the alarming self-righteousness with which he successively defended conflicting views. Later, he criticized Lippmann's habit of using others' ideas and suggested that he "was a man of temporary enthusiasms who tended to ricochet off on whatever idea had last been presented to him,"[181] but his reservations did not prevent the two from developing an extraordinarily intimate friendship.

Croly rounded out his founding staff of five coeditors with Philip Littell and Francis Hackett. Littell was the only editor Croly had known before 1913: he was a well liked and admired member of the Cornish circle. Croly recruited him to help edit the magazine's cultural features, and to write a weekly column, "Books and Things." Littell proved a useful peacemaker in the occasional disputes among the editors. Hackett, an Irish-born essayist, had been "editing the best book review page of any paper in the land [at] the *Chicago Daily News*,"[182] and he was put in charge of the cultural back pages. Justice Holmes, never much interested in politics, thought him "the only genius in the lot."[183] A year after publication began, Alvin Johnson, an economics professor at Cornell, joined the board.

Hand found all of them congenial, lively, and stimulating, and the editorial group quickly welcomed Hand into their "Inner Circle."[184] The editors met regularly on Mondays or Tuesdays at *The New Republic*'s offices to plan the next issue, and Croly held biweekly dinners there for the editors and a selected few friends. Hand had a standing invitation to attend, and he frequently did, as did Felix Frankfurter, who came down from his new faculty post at Harvard Law School whenever he could. Had Croly had his way, Frankfurter and Hand would have been formally named to the board of editors, for "Croly was closer to these two men than to any others."[185]

Croly several times tried to persuade Hand to leave the bench and join *The New Republic*, as either an editor or regular columnist.[186] Early in the summer of 1914, for example, he wrote, "I sincerely wish that you had the time actually to serve on the editorial staff, and from my own point of view, I should be particularly happy, in case you discarded the dignity of being a judge and threw your fortunes in with those of the *Republic*." Hand was not prepared to leave the bench, but he responded readily to Croly's assurance that "I want just as much of your time and counsel as you are inclined to give."[187] Throughout the organizing year, he was regularly at Croly's side on a wide range of concerns—not only in selecting editors, but also as chief consultant in preparing a circular to solicit potential subscribers, and even in hiring the circulation manager.[188] Three weeks before the first issue appeared in November, Hand attended his final pre-publication dinner at *The New Republic*'s offices and left with high hopes. "I felt happy and confident when the evening was over," he told Croly shortly after the dinner. "You have put together a real unity and it is bringing out the best in you and them. I am full of *bienaise* [*sic*]."[189]

Progressive domestic reform was the all-consuming passion of the eager young planners of *The New Republic*. But three thousand miles away, the great European powers prepared for war. On the day the staff moved into the magazine's quarters, World War I broke out; by the time the first issue appeared on November 7, the battlefields of Europe were already bloody. For the optimistic Croly, the war seemed less a threat than an opportunity for the magazine. The war, he thought, would inevitably result "in making over the European international system." And that could only help:

> The war will . . . prove in the end an actual help to *The New Republic*. It will tend to dislocate conventional ways of looking at things and to stimulate public opinion to think about the greater international problems which are now pressing for solution. It will create, that is, a state of mind in which a journal [of] political and social agitation will find its words more influential and more effective in modifying public opinion.[190]

To Hand, the outbreak of war was a far less happy omen. "Today, my 'psychology' is genuinely overshadowed by the terrible prospects of the general war," he wrote Frankfurter on July 31, a month after the assassination of Archduke Francis Ferdinand at Sarajevo, three days after Austria declared war on Serbia, a few days before Germany declared war on Russia and France: "It obsesses my mind to think that where ten days ago there were millions of men engaged in peaceful and profitable pursuits, now apparently they are all to begin killing each other as rapidly as possible, so far as I can see only because some Austrian nobles have decided that it ought to go on." The major European powers were bound to declare a war on one another soon:

> It seems a vicious circle, but I suppose perhaps it is all inevitable, men being men and land being limited. I have not a vast deal of confidence that the fundamental causes of war are going to be removed by Hague tribunals and not much of anything else. I doubt whether there is any other way finally of testing out which people is entitled to hold a country except those who are the strongest. That may seem a very brutal test, but I seem rather despondent; that I should live, perhaps, to see it, I regret.[191]

The New Republic's position of cautious sympathy for the Allies led to conflict with some of the magazine's erstwhile friends—most notably

Theodore Roosevelt, who took an ever more belligerent stance and attacked Wilson for his weakness. In the summer, TR had referred to the inner circle of the magazine as those "young idealists,"[192] but a sharp attack on Wilson's policy toward Mexico in December led *The New Republic* to criticize Roosevelt's outburst as "an example of the kind of fighting which has turned so many of his natural admirers into bitter enemies. . . . [H]e struck blindly and unfairly."[193] Roosevelt would not accept this kind of criticism from even his staunchest supporters. He told Francis Hackett that he thought Croly and his associates had been "disloyal." Croly promptly wrote Roosevelt: "In writing and publishing that critical paragraph, we all of us considered it merely as the same kind of criticism which candid friends continually pass upon one another, and we had no idea that any question of loyalty or disloyalty would be raised by it. . . . I do not see that at the present time we were under any obligation not to express our opinions such as they were upon any public utterance by you."[194] Roosevelt's reply was chilling: he objected to having "an unworthy motive" attributed to him and insisted that the magazine's comment "merely shows that we can't work together, which would be important if we were active party associates, but is not important as between an independent editor and an independent politician."[195] This exchange effectively ended the relationship between the magazine and TR, just two months after its initial publication. Privately, TR turned ever more bitter toward *The New Republic* crowd: the magazine was being run by "three anemic Gentiles and three international Jews"; the editors were "well-meaning geese," "nice old ladies" who were "sinning against the light."[196]

Hand wrote several brief essays for *The New Republic*—all but one published anonymously, and most during the magazine's first year. Usually, he wrote about judicial power and social reform, issues central to his involvement with the Progressive party. But once he ventured beyond, in his first contribution to the magazine, an unattributed editorial entitled "An Unseen Reversal," in the January 9, 1915, issue.[197] This crisp and forceful essay was Hand's most important extrajudicial statement of his views on public control of corporate economic power. He greeted the newly enacted Federal Trade Commission Act enthusiastically and emphasized its "unseen reversal" of antitrust policy. Whereas antitrust enforcement had traditionally relied upon private lawsuits in which lay juries and generalist judges made decisions, the FTC Act established an administrative agency of experts to evolve standards of antitrust policy. To Hand, this was a "clear recognition" of "the proper mental attitude toward the trust question." It reflected "a spirit strangely contradictory to the campaign theories of [President

Wilson]," who, following Brandeis, had been virulently hostile to "bigness" in corporations. The new law, by contrast,

> contained the possibility of a radical reversal of many American notions about trusts, legislative power, and legal procedure. It may amount to historic political and constitutional reform. It seems to contradict every principle of the party which enacted it. It seems to strike at the root of ancient American prejudice. But the opposition [to the act] has been negligible, so negligible that it stirs a little wonder as to whether Congress and the press realize that the quiet phrasing and ingenuity of this bill were another Trojan Horse.*

The new commission, Hand wrote, "will focus attention not on possibilities, but on performance, not on monopoly, but upon unfair trade methods."[198] Moreover, it might at last relieve the courts of the antitrust tasks they were so unfit to handle; at least the time-consuming fact-finding tasks would be left to experts. Hand's hopes proved too optimistic. The commission never realized the promise of intelligent expertise Hand had envisioned, and the courts remained very much in the business of developing antitrust generalizations—a task they continued to bungle for decades.

Hand's other essays for *The New Republic* dealt with the issues of judicial power and social reform. By 1914, Hand had abandoned his hope that the Supreme Court would become less hostile to reform legislation. The Court had returned to its pattern of transforming personal biases into constitutional doctrine. As the Court reconvened in the fall of 1914, a month before *The New Republic* began publication, Hand, in a letter to Frankfurter, denounced "the fatuous floundering of the Supreme Court which goes by the name of Constitutional Law. Am I perverted that I alone of those who touch it have acquired such a contempt for that subject? I can scarcely think of a matter to which the human mind has been applied with less credit to itself than that." He was especially outraged by the justices' lack of self-awareness and by their hypocrisy:

---

* An exchange of letters with George Rublee had helped to crystallize Hand's thoughts on this subject. Rublee, in Washington advising Brandeis and Wilson on antitrust policy, turned to Hand for assistance. Hand's review of the Supreme Court's decisions confirmed his view that courts were incompetent to develop coherent antitrust policies. The decisions lacked "any clear reasoning," he told Rublee: "I can find absolutely no general rule which applies. It seems to me you can only try to steer about in the cases in the most haphazard and unscientific way" (Hand to Rublee, 9 June 1914). He welcomed Rublee's support for "the Bull Moose idea" of a Federal Trade Commission empowered to prevent unfair competition (Rublee to Hand, 31 May 1914; Hand to Rublee, 1 June 1914; all in 107–2).

They suppose they are compelled by a rigid dialectic, that they are
engaged in a deductive analysis (those of them who would know
what the words meant), and their work is pitiable from that aspect;
most of it would disgrace any capable boy of 20 who had been
trained by you and your colleagues in [Harvard Law School]. I
should honestly have much more respect for a trained pupil of St.
Thomas, than for most of those worthy mastiffs. . . . I cannot
take seriously that solemn farce; it is the rarest thing in the world
to find any honest avowal of the real reasons which dictate their
decisions. . . . Even Holmes, shrewd analyst that he is, has to
conceal in part the main-springs. Out upon the accumulated mass
of rubbish! Let all [the] ponderous asses . . . be condemned to the
pleasant Hell for them of smearing and gumming up the glutinous
heterogeneous mass with their secretions in saecula saeculorum. [199]

Soon after, the Court announced one of its most criticized, most
reactionary decisions of the *Lochner* era, in a case called *Coppage v.
Kansas.* [200] *Coppage* struck down a Kansas law that prohibited the "yellow
dog" contract, under which nonmembership in a labor union was made
a condition of employment. To the Court's majority, this law unconstitutionally interfered with the "freedom of contract." The majority
opinion went even beyond *Lochner*, declaring that it was simply beyond
a state's power to redress perceived economic inequalities by protecting
labor-union membership. It insisted that "it is from the nature of things
impossible to uphold freedom of contract and the right of private property
without at the same time recognizing as legitimate those [normal]
inequalities of fortune that are the necessary result of the exercise of
those rights." [201]

Hand was outraged. He promptly submitted an essay, printed in the
February 6, 1915, issue of *The New Republic* under the title "Normal
Inequalities of Fortune." The state's regulatory power, he insisted, was
broad enough to cover anything "which serves the public interest"; the
proper standard judges should apply was simply "whether a fair man
could believe that the law as enacted really served any genuine public
interest. Between all reasonable differences of opinion, the legislature
has the right to choose."

Hand thought it "inconceivable" that a law redressing the "normal
inequalities of fortune" could seriously be considered beyond the police
power. No plausible constitutional doctrine, he argued, could support
such a frustrating principle. Angrily, he attacked the justices' narrowness
and bias:

Are we not finally driven to the conclusion that such decisions come from the prejudices of that economic class to which all the justices belong, and that they are merely unable to shake off the traditions of their education? How else shall we interpret an imagination which has failed to comprehend the hopes and aspirations of hundreds of thousands of living men? How else is it possible to understand such blindness to the beliefs of certainly half the economists of the present time?

The result was hideous, the reasoning unpersuasive, and worst of all was "the political system which permits either." Once again, the due-process clauses had been invoked as constitutional barriers to popular legislation. These clauses, Hand argues, "can never be other than a means by which courts exercise a legislative function. . . . No amount of judicial protestation to the contrary can disguise the facts."

During the 1912 campaign, Hand had suggested amending the due-process clauses to make clear that popular opinion should ordinarily prevail. Now, he went significantly beyond this to recommend total repeal of the due-process provisions. Without such constitutional change, he maintained, constitutional government would face the people's "impotent rage":

> The possible uses [of due process] at best are trifling compared with the evils which come from decisions like these; it will be a great gain to take out of all constitutions such provisions as the Fifth and Fourteenth Amendments. No state can safely risk the creation of that impotent rage which will come to great numbers of men from a declaration that the law will not permit any legislation which affects the inequalities of economic power.

At the root of the evil, Hand insisted, was "the fatuity of the system which grants such powers to men it insists shall be independent of popular control!" If the courts were to retain their legislative power under the guise of interpreting the due-process clauses, they must either "abdicate their exercise except on rare visitations," or "submit to a popular control which they rightly enough resent." Judicial self-restraint and popular control of the judiciary were the only two possibilities consistent with democracy: "One or the other is a condition of democracy; it is a condition of anything but ceremonial dancing before the ark of the covenant."[202]

These twin themes—the abuses of judicial power and the desirability of social reform to aid the underprivileged—reverberated in three additional articles Hand contributed to *The New Republic* in 1915. In "The Bill of Rights Again," a response to conservative New York lawyer Elihu Root's keynote speech to the New York Constitutional Convention, Hand attacked the natural-rights philosophy that was accepted unquestioningly by the conservative Wall Street bar as well as a majority of the Supreme Court. He argued that the notion of natural rights had become a mere apologia "in behalf of the institution of property in the extreme individualistic sense of the term"; the doctrine had "become the mainstay of conservatism." Hand's major objection was that the philosophy of natural rights was "wholly unworkable in practice." In trying to distinguish between choices properly left to the individual and those where social action was appropriate, the Court insisted upon "invoking abstract principles, instead of trying to determine for concrete cases whether social control should supersede individual initiative." Conservative natural-rights talk produced predictable results: it served "to preserve the institution of property" and squelched the people's role in democratic self-government. Due process, Hand argued, was insufficient justification for the Court's political decisions:

> It is a faith, not an idea, and, as with all faiths piously held, its content is chiefly feeling. Vague, conflicting, turgid, abstract, as anyone may see who interprets the decisions of the courts, it offers no comfort to the mind, but is a balm to the timid heart of reaction.[203]

Two weeks later, *The New Republic* printed "The Hope of the Minimum Wage."[204] This article, Hand's only signed contribution to *The New Republic*, was also the only one Croly had specifically commissioned (probably at Frankfurter's suggestion), and it was signed at Hand's specific request.[205] He may have overcome his concern about judicial propriety in this case because the main focus of the article was on Australian, rather than American, developments. But the topic had an obvious relation to reform efforts that regularly came before domestic courts, and the essay clearly reflected Hand's commitment to reform on behalf of the underprivileged. The Hand who wrote this essay was not a detached judge uninterested in policy and results, or merely a commentator, but a committed reformer.

"The Hope of the Minimum Wage" took as its point of departure a recent *Harvard Law Review* article that described Australia's national intervention to ensure "fair and reasonable" wages for employees—in effect, a "living wage" for each employee. Hand noted ruefully that the clear pro-labor slant of the Australian law "contrasts strangely with the doctrine of our own Supreme Court" in *Coppage*, a decision that cast added doubt on the constitutionality of minimum-wage laws. He offered a thoughtful, fair-minded analysis of the economic and philosophical arguments for and against minimum-wage laws, recognizing the possibility that a minimum wage might have the effect of forcing some marginal employees into unemployment. But he left no doubt that he favored allowing states to experiment with such laws, not only because of his philosophical belief in judicial deference to the legislature but also on humanitarian and efficiency grounds:

> Some relief from the oppression of physical privations, some security for a future, some provision against disease and unemployment, may so change the workman's approach to his daily routine as to make the increased wage a cheap industrial expedient, even when viewed in the most mechanical way. The result stands in trial, not in dialectic; but we must insist upon the reasonable expectation of those who view it hopefully, and we must seek to advance it, at least until it has been demonstrated to be false.[206]

For several years, Hand continued to attend gatherings at the magazine and to remain on intimate terms with its editors, especially Croly, Lippmann, and Littell,[207] but his judicial workload had increased, and when the war ended, he, like others, had profound disagreements with Croly over American participation in the League of Nations. In 1923, in part as a gesture toward reviving his friendship with Croly, he contributed a final anonymous editorial comment, "The Legal Right to Starve,"[208] remarks prompted by a Supreme Court decision, *Adkins v. Children's Hospital*,[209] that was the high-water mark of the *Lochner* era. *Adkins* held that the District of Columbia's minimum-wage law for women violated due process; this startlingly reactionary decision showed that the Court had become more conservative than ever. Regulation of wages, like regulation of prices, was, for these justices, simply outside the bounds of legislative experimentation. The members of the Court, Hand argued, seemed unable to free themselves from their own class prejudices:

> A man does not get to be a justice of the Supreme Court chiefly because he can detach himself from the convictions and prejudices of his class or his time. He emerges in large part because he has established his position in his community, by force of character and by reputation for integrity and strength of will. These are high qualities, but they do not necessarily go along with a tolerant acceptance of other men's opinions. Such men are . . . not ac-

customed patiently to accept opinions which seem to them mischievous and deadly.[210]

Hand now modified a proposal by Senator William Borah, the maverick Idaho progressive: the Supreme Court, Hand suggested, should
be able to declare a law unconstitutional on due-process grounds only
if two thirds of the Court voted that way.[211] This, Hand thought, would
"avoid those strains upon the authority of, and confidence in, the Court
which have been more serious than it ought be called on to bear." Too
often, Hand argued, the justices had confused the question of the wisdom
of a law, an issue not properly before them, with the only question
they could legitimately consider, "whether any one can think [the law]
wise."[212] Even if the justices could not be compelled to ask only the
latter question, a super-majority requirement would at least have produced a desirable result in most of the objectionable decisions of the
Lochner era. But neither Hand's nor Borah's proposal had any success.
Only the passage of time and a change in the composition of the Court
finally removed the due-process obstacles to economic and social reforms
that Hand so bitterly opposed.

IN 1 9 1 5 , while most Americans remained preoccupied with domestic
problems, Hand became an anxious observer of what was happening at
the front. He quickly perceived that the United States had a stake in
the battle between the European democracies, especially England, and
their authoritarian opponents.

Members of the American political elite differed sharply in their
responses to the war. Woodrow Wilson, echoing the nation's traditional
isolationism, promptly proclaimed American "neutrality." Some of
Hand's acquaintances, by contrast, urged immediate intervention on
the side of the Allies. Hand's friends at *The New Republic* advocated a
third, intermediate position. By 1915, Croly, Lippmann, and company
were urging a "benevolent," "differential" neutrality with a distinct tilt
in the Allies' direction. Hand, more skeptical and realistic, never shared
the editors' illusions that war would help realize progressive ideals, nor
was he ever convinced that war would make the world safe for democracy; but clearly he wanted the Allies to prevail.

By 1916, Germany's unrestricted U-boat warfare edged the administration closer to intervention. *The New Republic* took the lead in urging
the use of American moral and economic power against the aggressors.
In the 1916 election, the magazine, speaking mainly through the

confident voice of Walter Lippmann, backed Wilson. Most of the old Bull Moose sympathizers, including Rublee, Frankfurter, and Hapgood, also endorsed Wilson, and this support helped him gain his narrow electoral victory. Hand, who still considered Wilson an ineffectual leader given to vague moralizing, was one of the few in the old circle who preferred Charles Evans Hughes.

Hand's independent path was an early sign of his growing differences with *The New Republic*. He agreed with his old friends about ultimate aims: supporting the Allies, achieving a just and nonpunitive peace, and committing the United States to a greater international role; he was not ready to move from disdainful reserve to strong enthusiasm for Wilson. What began in 1916 as a disagreement about the presidential candidates would culminate three years later in sharply conflicting positions on the acceptability of the Treaty of Versailles.

By 1917, *The New Republic* enjoyed the reputation for having Wilson's ear and reflecting Wilsonian policy,[213] and indeed, Lippmann and Croly met weekly with Colonel Edward M. House, Wilson's closest adviser, getting information and offering advice. Along with *The New Republic*'s new ties to the administration came a rapid increase in its circulation: over thirty thousand copies were sold each week, and sometimes the figure reached forty-five thousand. Not surprisingly, the magazine began to respond to the nationalistic sentiments of its broader readership. Throughout early 1917, *The New Republic* took the lead in pressing for war against Germany. Slowly, Wilson followed that path. On April 2, 1917, the president asked Congress for a declaration of war; four days later, Congress complied. The once-critical *New Republic* intellectuals had become enthusiasts, convinced that they could ride the tiger of nationalistic ambitions.

Meanwhile, Hand had begun to feel increasingly restless and isolated as a judge. The routine of a docket comprised heavily of bankruptcy and maritime cases seemed very remote from the ongoing battles. And as he watched many of his friends go off to serve the country, his sense of remoteness grew more acute. Felix Frankfurter took a leave from Harvard to serve as special assistant to Secretary of War Newton D. Baker; Walter Lippmann left *The New Republic* to join Frankfurter on Baker's staff; George Rublee joined the War Shipping Board, charged with strengthening America's merchant marine. Hand's doubts about the draft[214] evaporated once war was declared, as all around him men were being drafted or were volunteering for service. At Harvard in June, where he was class marshal at commencement, Hand watched a parade of young men in uniform and subsequently reported to his wife:

> We were all much moved when the regiment passed; we old fellows [Hand was then forty-five] were, many of us, close to the point of tears and were ready at a word to make fools of ourselves. There was no exhilaration, no gloire de guerre about any of it, but we thought what another twelve months might bring to these serious faced little chaps and how we by the merest chance were out of it.[215]

Everywhere he turned, his friends were thinking about what they could do for the war effort: "Oh such a restlessness all around; everyone wanting to do something and not knowing what or how to do it."[216] Hand himself mused about what he would do if he were to enter military service. He decided he would choose the artillery rather than the infantry: "[Y]ou have a great deal more work in learning how, trajectory, ordnance and the whole business of fire and camouflage. That would certainly be my affair. Besides, if I was to 'get mine' I should much prefer to have it by a bomb or a shell than by some friendly Fritz sticking me in the belly with a bayonet. Holmes says that no man dies a hero's death who gets wounded below the diaphragm, and I believe him."[217] He also repeatedly considered the possibility of serving in some civilian role, even if it meant giving up his judgeship. Frances agreed that if called upon, he must serve: "exactly the kind of answer which heartens a man," Learned told her, "especially a man of my make-up."[218]

The first opportunity arose at the Harvard commencement, where he spoke with a bright, engaging engineer who had been catapulted into national fame by chairing the Commission for Relief in Belgium. Herbert Hoover, two years younger than Hand, was getting an honorary LL.D. from Harvard; he took the opportunity to seek Hand's advice on a legal staff for his new, war-related job in Washington as U.S. food administrator. During the course of the conversation, Hand realized, as he reported to Frances, that it might bring him "so near what may be an important, even a momentous moment in what I might be pleased to call my career." Hand told Hoover that his friend Joseph Cotton "would serve in any way he wanted." But Hoover had more on his mind.

> Whereat he, "Why shouldn't B Hand serve in some way?" Thus came the sudden critical moment, hits you right in the face as you turn the corner. . . . I told him that I was at his service absolutely, if he wanted me, that all I asked was that I might be allowed a vacation before I began, which I needed, and that I would throw up my job and he could do with me what he wanted.[219]

This response was extraordinarily uncharacteristic for such a deliberate and self-doubting individual, but Hand was genuinely caught up in the excitement of war. "Never," he acknowledged to Frances, "have I done anything which may make a deep difference to us with so little friction and hesitation." "We all felt so moved at seeing the boys [in uniform marching at commencement] . . . that it had something to do with my accepting H.'s offer so promptly. So be it; we must live in part by our feelings."[220]

Hand eagerly awaited a firm offer from Hoover. "It will be really fun if he wants me to do a big part of the job and I shall especially like it, a change and the sense of larger affairs," he told Frances. But by the end of the week, there was still no word. On second thought, the prospect of resigning from the bench seemed less feasible than it had in the first rush of emotion, and Hand decided to inquire "whether I cannot get a floating judge on the job while I am gone."[221] Frances was relieved: careful checking before rushing into the job with Hoover was what she had been "trying to make clear"; it would be "foolish" to rush to Washington without "something very definite & specific to do."[222] With continued silence from Hoover, Hand told his wife, "I begin to think it is all off, and, really, I hope so."[223] Frances assured Learned that she could understand that he was "restless," but "it wouldn't do for you to throw up yr. job in the elan everybody gets in without something very definite."[224]

Work under Hoover was only the first of several war-related positions Hand considered. In October 1917, Walter Lippmann returned to New York from his War Department post to work on a secret project, on assignment from Colonel House. The task of a small group of men (ultimately dubbed "the Inquiry") was to draft proposals for postwar peace negotiations—essentially, to sketch the American vision of the postwar world. According to Lippmann, Hand quickly offered to leave the bench in order to work on the peace project.[225] But "the Inquiry" sought experts, not generalists like Hand, and nothing came of this proposal.

In the late spring of 1918, Hand once more thought about resigning from the bench, this time in order to join Bernard Baruch's staff in Washington. Baruch, the New York financier, had held various government positions since 1916, all directed toward mobilizing American industry for war production. In 1918, he attained his most important World War I post, as chair of the War Industries Board. He needed a confidential adviser and turned to Hand as a possibility. While Philip Littell did not think the position worthwhile, Joseph Cotton was much more enthusiastic. Hand leaned in Cotton's direction. As Learned explained to Frances, Baruch "needs a guide, philosopher and friend content to stay in the background, not expected to see many people, but able to give more guidance to [his] thought than he can himself. . . . [T]he whole thing is personal and the job will be to do his thinking for him."[226] Within a few days, Baruch selected someone else. Frances was irritated about the stirring of false hopes,[227] and Hand continued to be a restless nonparticipant in the war effort.

Not until the closing weeks of the war did Hand at last have a chance to serve his country in a role other than judge, a chance that arose because of his rapidly developing reputation in deciding patent, trademark, and copyright cases. In August 1918, the State Department asked him to chair a committee to study wartime disruptions in the law of intellectual property and suggest revisions in treaties regarding international arrangements for the protection of literary property.[228] By October 1918 Hand had put together a group that undertook the State Department study,[229] and throughout October and early November, the committee worked feverishly to prepare its report. The issues studied by Hand's committee ranged from adjustment and restoration of rights compromised by the war to amendments of existing treaties and proposals for desirable new international arrangements.[230] The work included suggested provisions for the peace treaty for the American negotiators at the Paris Peace Conference.[231] And while Hand's committee was at work, David Hunter Miller, the State Department official with whom Hand dealt most often, invited him to accept the position of "Delegate for Patents and Trademarks" to the Paris conference. Hand's responsibility was apparently limited to technical legal matters that might not even be reached at the conference, but he had little hesitation about accepting the assignment. He received permission from his senior judge to take a leave of absence and promptly told the State Department that he would be "glad to undertake that work if the Department thinks fit."[232] Once again, Hand's hopes were crushed. Miller reported to him from Paris late in December that Washington had severely trimmed the size of the delegation and that for this reason he was not invited.

In fact, the reasons for Hand's exclusion were more complex. The delegation that went to Paris—which was hardly small, consisting of thirteen hundred Americans—had undergone a change of leadership. At first, Colonel House had expected to head the American group; and he drafted Walter Lippmann to join the delegation. But Wilson had invested too much of his own ego in his dreams for a permanent democratic peace to permit House, a man he had come to distrust, to take all the glory. In the ensuing maneuvers, Wilson went to Paris himself, named his secretary of state as his chief deputy, and shunted

House and his aides aside. Hand's displacement from the delegation was related to these changes.

Hand had been eager to join the delegation because he would have been at the center of the action, and reunited with his friends Lippmann, Rublee, and Frankfurter. But when the offer was canceled, he claimed at first to be relieved. "I had [begun] to have great misgivings about going over," he told David Miller, "for I felt sure that I should have absolutely nothing to do when I got there. . . . It is a pleasure to me to know that you wanted me to go over and we should have had a very interesting time, but in the back of my head I should have always had the sense that I ought not to be there."[233] Relief changed to regret when he learned that the intellectual-property assignment was only a cover, and that, had Washington politics not barred the way, he might have participated in drafting the central provisions of the peace treaty.[234]

EVEN WHILE HAND FLIRTED with opportunities to leave the bench for the war effort, he was also exploring the possibility of a judicial promotion. Most of his work as district judge had turned routine and dull. Moving to the Court of Appeals seemed ever more enticing: there, he thought, he could devote himself more fully to questions of law rather than fact, to problems of greater interest and consequence. Hand knew he had formidable rivals; and the administration, busy with wartime problems, was in no hurry to fill the vacancy in the Second Circuit that occurred in mid-1917. Yet for more than eight months, into early 1918, Hand persisted in his pursuit. As he confessed to Lippmann, "I loathe this damnable job-hunting inexpressibly, but I want the job."[235]

Hand's New York and Cornish friends—George Rublee, Felix Frankfurter, Walter Lippman, Herbert Croly, and C. C. Burlingham—worked diligently on his behalf. And Hand himself went to unusual lengths to land the appointment. Rublee opened up the possibility of promotion by urging Hand's name on Attorney General Thomas W. Gregory early in May.[236] A month later, the prospect of success seemed strong enough to prompt Hand to visit Washington himself, seeking to advance his chances. As he reported to his wife, he "[w]ent right to the House of Truth" in order to consult with Frankfurter and Lippmann. There he met William Hitz, one of the most knowledgeable people in Washington about the convoluted workings of the Wilson administration. After leaving his private law practice to become a Justice Department official in 1914, Hitz had become a justice of the Supreme Court of the District of Columbia in 1916, but retained his interest in politics. Hand and Hitz liked each other immediately and were "as thick as thieves in an hour."

Hand wrote Frances a detailed report about his visit. "[I]t was getting time for the great event," he told her: "I was to meet the High Dispenser of the Yob," Attorney General Gregory, an old-time Texas Democrat. Frankfurter and Hand went to Justice Brandeis's home to meet Gregory—"serenissimus superbus, with a good square downright head and a good open face in front of it," "familiar, real and obvious," an "upstanding sort of fellow, true to all the small prejudices of his place and time, and not by any means confined to them either." Hand was reasonably optimistic about the evening: "I *think* we made a hit, he and I, but quien sabe? I was at my prettiest. The insinuating-gracious was my cue. . . ." The trip "was a success and may do the trick, though I confess it seemed not at all certain." (He feared that Abram Elkus, an unsuccessful candidate for the New York Court of Appeals in the 1913 race, might get the post, in view of his much better standing in the Democratic party.)[237] A day later, Hand was a bit more encouraged: "I can't possibly judge whether my chances are good or not, but I know that I bettered them and bettered them considerably."[238]

A week later, Hand's spirits fell. Rublee told him the most recent rumor: Gregory had decided to recommend New York patent lawyer Thomas Ewing. "I will do anything I can," Rublee assured Hand, even though the attorney general was now "so crowded by people who are after him that he doesn't seem to like suggestions and receives them rather irascibly."[239] The disappointing news about Ewing's rising prospects caused Hand to lose hope momentarily: "I regard the Circuit Judge business now as nearly as good as over and it is surprising how little I care," he told Frances. Yet he did care: by the end of June, he told Frances that he wished he "knew definitely about this blessed Circuit Judge job. I would be more comfortable to have it certainly out of the way than to feel it hanging around as a vague possibility."[240] A few days later, he learned of another apparently disappointed rival for the job: district judge Martin T. Manton, a clubhouse Democrat named to Hand's court only a year earlier, had hoped that Wilson would promote him; but Manton, too, had heard about Ewing's ascendancy and was "a good deal chagrined." Hand now thought that there was "little doubt" that Ewing would get the position.[241]

Rublee had more encouraging news at the beginning of July. An especially important ally had come forward in support of Hand's promotion: Colonel House, Wilson's chief confidant, had promised to work for Hand behind the scenes. House attributed the rumors about Ewing to Gregory's preference for "a lawyer familiar with the patent laws" for the Court of Appeals. House had a ready answer: "[N]o man can be on that bench for any number of years without becoming thoroughly grounded in patent law. . . . In my opinion, [Gregory] could make no better appointment than Learned Hand." House promised to approach Wilson directly. While this development seemed to enhance Hand's prospects, Rublee had a word of caution: "I hope you will not become optimistic. The chances are against you, and I don't want you to be disappointed. But there is no harm in knowing that your friends are still active."[242]

In mid-July, Learned reported to Frances that C. C. Burlingham was "as busy as a bee intriguing," though he thought it was all for naught: "It rather amused me, but I think there is nothing in it."[243] In any event, on the day Hand learned of Burlingham's maneuverings, a case came before him that he recognized might well cast a fatal cloud over his chances. It was the suit by *The Masses* to challenge the postmaster's effort to ban the radical magazine from the mails, and it would produce Hand's most courageous and important First Amendment decision.[244]

Though the *Masses* ruling did impair Hand's chances for the circuit judgeship,[245] the administration still had not made a decision on the Second Circuit vacancy, and Hand's friends continued to press for his promotion. Croly and Lippmann, now holding regular meetings with Colonel House, argued the case for Hand, and Croly informed Frances that he would also "see Felix [Frankfurter] and try to get him on the job again."[246] Frankfurter, who had been one of the first to press Hand's name on the administration in the spring of 1917, did indeed get reinvolved. (Frankfurter had disclosed some of his lifelong tendency to embellish the truth in the course of promoting good causes by asserting that "no one was more passionately eager for Wilson's reelection than Hand." Hand, Frankfurter had also insisted, was "without doubt . . . one of the half dozen outstanding intellects in the American Judiciary.")[247]

By mid-October, Rublee reported that while the front-runner had changed, Hand's chances remained doubtful. Thomas Ewing was "no longer in the running"; Martin Manton would be appointed, the latest rumors indicated: "[T]oday Manton is the leading man."[248] According to William Hitz's informed assessment, Hand's candidacy had waned because of Frankfurter's intervention: "Felix injured you. A feeling of prejudice and hostility against Felix . . . is growing up here, and Felix's advocacy is likely to set back any man. . . ."[249] The volatile, ebullient Frankfurter was apparently too much for Gregory, who conceivably also had his share of anti-Semitism, but Gregory was not the only person put off by Frankfurter's often overbearing pleas on behalf of appointments for his friends.

The Manton candidacy disturbed Hand for reasons beyond the obstacle it presented to his own ambitions. Manton seemed the least competent of his fellow district judges, in part because he apparently spent more time with his political cronies and on self-promotion than in preparing adequate opinions. According to Rublee, Hitz had advised that a "vigorous protest against Manton from the right sources in New York might have an effect. . . . Could not C.C. [Burlingham] arrange that?" And, Hitz had suggested, perhaps others should be enlisted as well to protest the promotion of Manton.[250] Hand did not need this advice, for he had already begun to move in that direction. Frances Hand briefly thought in early January 1918 that Learned's campaign to block Manton's promotion had succeeded,[251] but she was wrong. Hand had learned from his Washington sources that the attorney general had firmly decided not to nominate him and that Manton's candidacy was still alive. On January 9, he wrote to Frankfurter to confirm his "elimination," to thank him for his efforts, and to urge him not to press Attorney General Gregory for reconsideration: "It is better not to touch it, for though I understand I have been out of it for long, G. seems to have some unreasonable shimmer against you, dating . . . way back in the summer. . . . He ought to have decided six months ago; it would have given him less trouble. At least I hope he will select a better man than Manton."[252]

But Gregory and President Wilson chose Manton after all. On March 18, 1918, Manton, the junior district judge, took his seat on the Second Circuit. Apparently, loyalty to a devoted Democratic party worker had proved decisive. Frances guessed that "undoubtedly it was the *Masses* decision which had hurt you but dear, I feel just as you do about it. You couldn't have done differently and it was a fine thing to do and if it cost in the end you will be glad to have done it. The inside satisfactions are in the end the things that count."[253]

But Hand thought his rejection also rested on reasons beyond *Masses*, on a political independence that made him unacceptable to the Wilson administration. As he wrote to Frankfurter, "I don't believe that anybody could have pushed me over the line. I am an outsider . . . and who can expect such a one to stand for preferment?" He was lucky to have a judgeship at all, he reflected:

I ought rather to be thankful that G.W.W. [George W. Wickersham, who had been Taft's attorney general in 1909] ever thought of pulling me out of my obscurity to land me even here. The world doesn't like non-joiners, and sometimes I wonder whether the world is not half right. Most of the oxen that won't pull in harness well are at bottom egoists, and that's the reason they don't pull.[254]

It was not in Hand to be anything but a political maverick. Except for his Bull Moose enthusiasm, he was never a party loyalist, and he paid the penalty: as future Second Circuit vacancies developed, he was passed over repeatedly.

IN 1918, with the war drawing to a close and his chances for a Second Circuit appointment waning, Hand focused increasingly on the prospects of postwar international relations. To him and his ex-Progressive friends, future bloodshed could be averted only if a just peace were assured. In their view, the peace would be just if it minimized nationalistic rivalries and imperialistic ambitions, and if it did not oppress the vanquished with impossible demands for reparations that would plant seeds of revenge. Peace could only be lasting, they believed, if the United States assumed international responsibilities. Above all, a just peace required that an organization be established to settle international disputes peacefully—in short, a League of Nations.

Within days of the Armistice in November 1918, a group of nearly one hundred intellectuals published a statement of principles for a new organization—the League of Free Nations Association.[255] Learned Hand was among the signers of this organizing statement, the only federal judge on the list. The roster of signers was liberally sprinkled with Hand's old Progressive associates—the novelist Winston Churchill, Herbert Croly, Felix Frankfurter, Francis Hackett, Norman Hapgood, and Alvin Johnson. The purpose of the association was to engage in "propaganda in favor of American participation in an international society."[256] Over the next two years, Hand was both observer and participant in the effort to achieve a just peace and American participation in the League.

During the last months of the war, before the association was founded, Hand had become increasingly supportive of Wilson's foreign policy. The president had anticipated the goals of the association in a speech to a joint session of Congress in early 1918, when he announced the Fourteen Points outlining his dreams for a postwar world.[257] The next day, Hand told Frankfurter, with rare enthusiasm about Wilson, "Most of W.W.'s last I liked exceedingly. Of course a good deal of it is vague, but it must be. This is a nearer approach to definition than we have had before and all in the right way."

Eight of Wilson's Fourteen Points pertained to postwar borders (for France, Italy, Poland, Turkey, Belgium, and the former constituents of the Austro-Hungarian Empire). Wilson added to those details the broader goals especially close to his heart, including "open covenants . . . openly arrived at," reduction of economic barriers to international trade, disarmament, and, in the Fourteenth Point, a "general association of nations" to afford "mutual guarantees of political independence and territorial integrity to great and small states alike."

Hand's enthusiasm for the Fourteen Points was not unqualified. For example, he told Frankfurter that he was "not too much in love with the smaller nations, but I shall grow more so if they do not insist upon being too damned national." Yet his doubts did not overcome his belief that, all in all, he liked Wilson's proposals "exceedingly"—we "must try to put into practice the beginnings of such a thing." By the time Hand voiced these modest hopes, The New Republic was more strongly in Wilson's corner than ever. In an early signal of differences with Croly, Hand reported that he was beginning to find it difficult to discuss his less ambitious hopes with his old friend, "for he always gets impatient and peremptory when I do."[258]

Wilson's Fourteen Points were merely a unilateral American pronouncement, not a declaration of Allied policy; Wilson had not informed the Allied governments of his proposals before he addressed Congress, partly because he feared that they would reject them. And the secret treaties that carved up conquered territory were not wiped out by Wilson's speech. What Wilson was trying to do was to go over the heads of the Allied governments to gain the support of the people directly.

Hand and his fellow internationalists anxiously followed the rumors about the progress of peace negotiations and sought to shape American public opinion in favor of the League. Organizations like the League of Free Nations Association were vitally important in this respect, for Wilson himself was far too busy in France to pay much attention to domestic developments.[259] By late January 1919, Hand began to fear that "things were shaping up for a general game of grab" in the Paris negotiations, and that this endangered a just peace: "If everybody is allowed to put his hand in the bag as deep as he likes, any League of Nations would only be a means of preserving a bad status quo." He was equally worried about "recent sinister developments" in American public opinion: "The matter is here fast becoming a party one, Republicans opposed to any but a denatured League of Nations, the Democrats, as usual, having no ideas and no policies at all, and the liberals relying on the President for anything good which may come up, and that, too, without any sanguine expectations."[260]

Yet anxiety did not mean despair. Instead, Hand busied himself ever more in work for the League. Despite his reservations about participating in public political activities, he agreed to speak to citizens' groups in New York City's suburbs, where he found the audience responses encouraging. Public opinion had "certainly changed," he told Rublee: "[I] find nearly everybody here receptive and enthusiastic [about the League]. The real difficulty is that they don't know what it is all about. They are yearning for the right but don't know what the right is."[261] At the beginning of March, with proceedings in Paris still secret, Hand thought that "[o]ver here the trend just at present is distinctly in favor of a League of Nations."[262]

In early May 1919, when the Paris negotiations ended, the terms of the peace treaty leaked into the American press, and many internationalists were outraged. Walter Lippmann, who had rejoined the *New Republic* staff, published as his first contribution an extensive, hard-hitting analysis of the peace terms and the League, filled with pleas for just terms and for revisions in the proposed covenant for the League of Nations. At the end, he sounded an ominous warning to Europe: "[I]f you make . . . a peace that can be maintained only by the bayonet, we shall leave you to the consequence and find our own security in this hemisphere."[263]

Hand was impressed by both the style and much of the substance of Lippmann's article. "If you can sustain such power and scope you will make yourself a noticeable force in American political ideas," he predicted. "The war was a bad enough thing, but it certainly has been a blessing for you."[264] But he qualified his praise with criticism of particulars: he questioned, for example, Lippmann's attack on Article X of the proposed covenant, which bound the signatories to guarantee one another's territorial integrity. Lippmann worried both that the United States would be bound to go to war whenever any state's borders were threatened, and that there would be no opportunity for later changes in boundaries. Hand did not think it necessary to interpret Article X so rigidly: he argued that the covenant left room for later treaty modifications.

Lippmann warned that America would return to isolationism if a just peace were not concluded. This possibility soon seemed more ominous. When the full peace terms were published in April, the Allies' power grab was plain for all to see. The proposed boundaries flagrantly disregarded Wilson's plea for self-determination; the new contours of

Italy, Poland, and other nations meant that Europe would be Balkanized. Above all, the treaty threatened Germany's ability to take its place among the peaceful nations: it imposed not only a ruinous $15 million indemnity obligation but additional and undetermined future reparations.

These unsatisfactory terms put the "war liberals" in Hand's circle to a critical test. Should they endorse the imperfect treaty, hoping that, if the treaty were ratified and the League of Nations established, at least that council might one day modify the terms of peace? Or should they turn their back on the League as well as the peace treaty and oppose Wilson's efforts to obtain American ratification? *The New Republic* quickly and angrily took the latter path. Hand, by contrast, continued to support the League, and the imperfect peace, to the end. This division about the most important issue of American postwar foreign policy quickly led to an estrangement between Hand and the *New Republic* editors, especially Croly, and left Hand in political exile. Hand told Frankfurter, "I can flock with no tories and my old crowd I am on the outs with."[265]

Early in May, the editors of *The New Republic* decided unanimously to oppose the treaty and the League. They unleashed their attack with the words "IS IT PEACE?" emblazoned on the cover of the May 17 issue. In the next issue, *The New Republic* answered its own question: the cover read, "THIS IS NOT PEACE."[266] Lippmann, in the May 17 editorial, insisted that the treaty was simply "the prelude to quarrels in a deeply divided and hideously embittered Europe."[267] Alvin Johnson continued in the May 24 editorial, in a manner indistinguishable from that of rock-ribbed isolationists: "Looked at from the American point of view, it would be the height of folly to commit a great people as the guarantor of a condition which is morally sick with conflict and trouble."[268] Article X of the covenant, pertaining to mutual defense, became a major target of *The New Republic* and for anti-League forces generally. For nearly a year, while the treaty and the covenant were pending in the Senate, *The New Republic* carried on a vituperative attack, not only on the treaty but also on Wilson personally.

The New Republic's position reflected a state of mind Learned Hand found repugnant. He accurately described himself as unlike those "men of action" who were unable to "distinguish bet[ween] persuading people and breaking their faces." With only a trace of humor, he claimed he was one of the few "democrats": to him, being a democrat was identified with the virtues of patience, receptivity to the other side's argument, tolerance of differing opinions, and calm reasoning. Rublee, by contrast, "would never be a democrat any more than H.C. [Croly] could be; or perhaps anyone else who ever leads or wants to lead":

> I am nearly the only democrat in the world, except Phil Littell and Holmes. It is fortunate, probably, that there are so few democrats or there might be nothing to eat or to wear. Real democrats get food and clothes only because there are so few that they get ignored in the general hand-out. If there were many enough to be noticed, they would be put in the cellar and would there be tolerant to each other till they starved to death.[269]

Frankfurter had a sharp, interesting response: "Is Hamlet the only democrat? There is at least one man of decision on mundane matters that I know who I think is also a real democrat—Brandeis."[270] Yet Hand, however tolerant and open-minded, was capable of reaching firm conclusions. He listened carefully to the criticisms of the peace treaty, and while he found many of them justified, he emphasized attainable consequences—especially the acceptance of international responsibility that would be symbolized by American participation in the League. As he told Frankfurter in early December 1919, "I seldom have been surer that I was right about a public matter than about the ratification. At first I was very wobbly, but time has taken it from me."[271]

The New Republic's shrill hostility to Wilson, the treaty, and the League led Hand to part ways with his old friends. Both Lippmann and Croly became part of the strange alliance of disappointed liberals and conservative isolationists that opposed Wilson and American ratification. Hand managed to maintain civil relations with Lippmann most of the time, but relations with Croly became increasingly strained. No doubt angry and frustrated by the consequences of his new involvement in party politics, Croly turned on the Paris terms and on Wilson with the greatest vituperativeness. Hand found his old friend increasingly difficult to bear. In June 1919, for example, he told Frances:

> I own that I am out of temper with the whole outfit; I had best not discuss [*The New Republic* group] at present, for their arrogance and assumption really have made me sick. . . . [F]or the time being I had better not see them, at least H.C. . . . I do hope I may be able to avoid H.C. without offense until the fit wears off. I don't want to hurt him, but God! Just for a while I don't want to see him.[272]

The correspondence between Hand and Croly, which for a decade had consisted of lively, intimate exchanges, deteriorated into occasional, brief, social notes. As Croly later wrote Hand, "I have had rather a forlorn feeling of recent years that the N.R. was making a difference between me & the friendship of some of the people I most loved. . . ."[273]

By early December, Hand's support of ratification had become unshakable. The Senate had rejected the treaty not because of its unjust terms, he told Frankfurter, but only "to establish the precedent that we are opposed to any international order." American participation, he argued, was essential to the postwar order. However imperfect, the treaty contained "a chance of its holding long enough to be modified by 'collective bargaining,' " and America had to be party to that bargaining. "Without us the prospect is perilous. I know that the answer is, [the treaty] had better go, the sooner the better and by an upheaval. I think it very doubtful that the upheaval will result [in] a more liberal attitude and what it may bring no one can tell. At present we need cement, not explosives."[274]

Hand's stance distinguished him from both *The New Republic*'s liberals and right-wing isolationists. Public opinion moved to the extremes; support for moderate views like Hand's shrank rapidly. Hoover was one of the few who remained on Hand's side, pleading, in a letter to Wilson, that he compromise in order to get the League in some form, virtually any form.[275] Any prospect of compromise was crushed between the confident assertions of the left and the right. As Hand complained to Frankfurter soon after the first negative vote from the Senate:

> As a result of it all, we have lost our chance to modify and ameliorate the conditions imposed on Germany which are, as you & I both agree, most pressing. I really can see in the attitude of the N.R. nothing but the intransigent position of those who would have no bread, if they must put up with half a loaf. Their continued hostility to Wilson, full of personal feeling, has spread in me feelings I don't like to have toward my intimate friends.[276]

In March 1920, the Senate rejected the treaty a second and final time and necessarily with it the League of Nations. Wilson had remained adamant, opposing even minor amendments that would have gained the support of Republican moderates. When the senators refused to give the treaty the necessary two-thirds approval, the possibility of American participation in the League ended. In a long postmortem to F. D. MacKinnon, a Scottish acquaintance, Hand reflected pessimistically on what had happened and what lay ahead. The peace treaty was vulnerable to justified criticism: "It was conceived in a spirit of oppression and without any view to possibilities. I was glad enough to take all the

German cash and property which we could lay our hands on, . . . but as for the indemnities, they seem to me merely preposterous."[277] Still, the realist Hand recognized that the treaty's harsh terms were not a shocking surprise: "I have never felt, in spite of the disgust of my liberal friends, that it was possible during the period when the Treaty was made to make either England or France agree to any of the terms. Some treaty had to be made and the real hope lay in its execution." And there lay the rub: the internationalists' only hope was that the League could ameliorate the treaty's harsh terms, yet American rejection of the treaty thwarted that hope entirely.

Hand laid much of the blame at the president's feet, despite his admiration for Wilson's well-intentioned efforts. If only Wilson had been willing to compromise, he could have assured ratification and support for the forces in Europe working for a more just postwar world. The consequence of Wilson's rigidity was the final Senate rejection:

> I am entirely satisfied that the Senate has acted throughout in a spirit of pure faction. They were greatly outraged by Wilson's ignoring them, in which he made a quite inexcusable mistake, and being a jealous, bureaucratic body, they were determined to assert their power at any cost. It would all have been very easy if Wilson had been less of an egoist and more accustomed to accommodation and compromise, as everyone who aspires to statecraft must be, in my opinion.

But Wilson had to be Wilson. He had been incapable of overcoming his own rigid, moralistic makeup, traits that Hand had long criticized:

> And so the fat is all in the fire and we are an unhappy example of the dangers of wealth and security. Even at the last minute Wilson could have accomplished the essence of what he wanted had he been willing to show any reasonable spirit of compromise. But he has always been a dour (shall I be offensive if I say, Scotch) Presbyterian who would have his way and all his way.

The bitter battles of 1919 and early 1920 had costs beyond foreign policy. While Wilson concentrated on Europe, he had largely ignored domestic developments, and reactionary forces were flourishing. Even during the war, Postmaster General Albert S. Burleson and propaganda chief George Creel had systematically repressed dissent, particularly that of pacifists and socialists. Hand's courageous stand in *Masses* was exceptional: the federal appellate courts uniformly endorsed interpretations of the Espionage Act of 1917 that were hostile to free expression. After the war, the opportunities for robust debate shrank still further. The

new attorney general, A. Mitchell Palmer, launched a virulent Red-
baiting campaign, arresting and deporting thousands. The New York
Assembly expelled five members because they were Socialists, and as
the 1920 election approached, the Democratic party was in disarray.
When Wilson refused to recognize the new Soviet government—a
course Hand thought would merely strengthen the worst elements in
the U.S.S.R.—Red-baiting became American foreign policy as well.
Hand was dismayed:

> If the Russians are content with the kind of militant oligarchy
> they have got now, or if not being content they have not the public
> spirit to overthrow it, we do our best by our present attitude to
> consolidate its power and to give it the enormous support of all
> national Russian sentiment. . . . [I]t is an intolerable government
> we are all doing our best to maintain and consolidate . . . and
> this last announcement of Wilson is only another prop.

The New Republic, desperately searching for an acceptable Democratic
candidate in 1920, launched a trial balloon for Herbert Hoover, but
Hoover announced that he was a Republican. When the Democratic
convention gathered, the strongest candidates were the Red-baiting
Mitchell Palmer and William G. McAdoo, Wilson's son-in-law and
former secretary of the treasury. Most members of *The New Republic*'s
circle preferred McAdoo, but neither Palmer nor McAdoo was able to
muster the votes necessary for nomination. The delegates turned instead
to a compromise candidate, Ohio governor James M. Cox, an inoffensive man with little chance to win. (Cox's running mate was the
popular assistant secretary of the navy, Franklin Delano Roosevelt of
New York.) Hand did not expect much from Cox, whom he thought
"not inspiring," but the Republican choice was worse. The liberal
Republicans were as disorganized as the liberal Democrats, leaving the
Old Guard in charge of the convention; Warren G. Harding emerged
from the smoke-filled rooms as the candidate. Against Harding's competition, Hand said, Cox "certainly will have my vote," but it would
be in vain. A Harding victory, Hand gloomily but accurately predicted,
meant

> we are in for four years of stout Bourbonism,—years which prom-
> ise to present to us the most formidable questions of internal policy
> which we have experienced since 1865, years which ought to be
> met by the best thinking and the most courageous statesmanship
> that we can muster. We promise to meet it by a refusal either to
> think of or take any position. I suppose we shall get through, for

we are so grossly rich that apparently we can with safety neglect all the common precautions in our public affairs of intelligence and character.

Harding announced that his motto was "Return to Normalcy." In fact, Americans, surrendering to the fatigue produced by the war and the long debate about the peace treaty and the League of Nations, embraced apathy, disillusionment, and cynicism about politics. For Hand and his old Progressive colleagues, it was a bleak ending to a decade that had begun with high hopes for American reform and regeneration.

VI

Promotion to the Second Circuit

BY THE SPRING OF 1917, after only eight years on the bench, Hand was the most senior judge of his district. He had grown more confident about his talents, and the increasing attention to his rulings by lawyers, fellow judges, and professional publications reinforced his self-esteem. He enjoyed the opportunities to reflect upon the law and the facts in those cases that lent themselves to written rulings. Yet many of his daily chores as a district judge seemed ever more routine and dull. The workload of hearing motions and presiding over trials both short and long filled with conflicting testimony made for wearying steady pressure yet rarely provided outlets for his analytical skills. Increasingly, the Second Circuit summoned him to hear appeals, and he found that the appellate work gave him some of his most enjoyable and rewarding days. A permanent seat on the Circuit Court of Appeals, he knew, would assure him of regular work on legal problems of interest and significance.

Hand's dream of promotion to the Second Circuit moved closer to realization when word spread in March 1917 that a vacancy was about to arise: Alfred C. Coxe, who had been a federal judge since 1882 and a member of the appellate court since 1902, was thinking of retirement. Although self-advancement was ordinarily uncongenial to Hand, he now pursued promotion with unaccustomed determination. Throughout his nine-month campaign, Hand realized that he had formidable rivals and that his involvement with the Progressives would not endear him to the Wilson administration, yet his friends urged him on. But he did not succeed: the unpopularity of his decision in the *Masses* case, and above all his lack of party loyalty, prompted the administration to name

Martin T. Manton, the junior district judge, to fill the vacancy in January 1918.[1]

After this frustrating failure, Hand's routine chores on the district court grew ever more irksome. With the adoption of nationwide Prohibition (through the 1919 Volstead Act), the court docket was more bloated than ever, and Hand, who had no sympathy with this national moral crusade but was duty-bound to enforce the law, found the endless stream of liquor cases the most irritating part of his duties. The Volstead Act, he complained, had turned the criminal side of the district court "into so much of a police court as to be thoroughly disgusting."[2]

No further vacancy on the four-seat Second Circuit arose until 1921. By then the Republican party had swung sharply to the right: while Hand had hoped that the relatively liberal Herbert Hoover would be the Republican nominee in 1920, Warren G. Harding had been chosen in the "smoke-filled room," representing all the conservative, business-oriented forces that TR had sought to overcome eight years earlier. Unenthusiastically, Hand had cast his vote for the colorless Democratic candidate, James M. Cox. President Harding, who named a surprisingly strong cabinet, unfortunately selected Harry M. Daugherty, a longtime Ohio political ally with a shady past, as attorney general. With these Old Guard Republicans in power, Hand knew he had no chance for promotion and decided to back his junior colleague Julius M. Mayer instead. President Taft had put Mayer, a well-connected New York City Republican, on the district court in 1912, and despite his considerable ego, Mayer was a conscientious, competent judge, especially strong in patent and receivership cases.[3] Hand's relations with Mayer, distant at first, had grown warmer, and Hand knew that Mayer would be a far stronger circuit judge than Manton; he pitched in to help defeat the only significant opposition to Mayer's promotion, from a Vermont competitor. As Hand told Mayer, "[B]eing out of it myself I would much rather have you have it than the outsider."[4] Moreover, Hand thought it "preposterous" to have an appellate court half of whose members were not from New York, and he gathered statistics for Mayer to show that 94 percent of cases came to the Second Circuit from federal courts in New York rather than those in Connecticut or Vermont.[5] When Mayer was nominated in September, he was understandably grateful, telling Hand "how very, very deeply I appreciate your generous attitude."[6]

BY MID-1924, when Judge Mayer decided to resign in order to return to private law practice, Hand thought the political situation had changed sufficiently to warrant another try for promotion. Harding was dead, and Calvin Coolidge had succeeded him. Even more important, Harry Daugherty had just resigned: his Justice Department had been marked by inefficiency and beset by charges of fraud and corruption. Coolidge, perceiving the need for housecleaning, brought in as his new attorney general Harlan Fiske Stone, former dean of the Columbia Law School (later, he would be made Chief Justice of the United States). Moreover, Hand's national reputation was growing. With mounting frequency, he had sat on the Second Circuit by designation, and among New York lawyers, he was widely recognized as the strongest district judge. Professional journals paid increasing attention to his opinions, and academics thought his promotion long overdue, as a "tardy recognition" of his excellence.[7]

Justice Louis D. Brandeis, for example, told Frankfurter, "Learned Hand's opinions are the best Federal Court opinions that come before us for review,"[8] and talk even spread that Hand's rightful place was on the Supreme Court, especially when the conversation concerned the Court's increasingly conservative direction. The notion of Hand's moving to the Supreme Court was wishful thinking on the part of those sympathetic to the justices in the beleaguered liberal minority. Felix Frankfurter, for example, told Hand, "Ever since I was entitled to have an opinion about . . . the Supreme Court I have entertained an eager conviction that you are among the very few on the bench who ought to be one of the Nine."[9] Hand himself knew better than that: "The chances are so remote . . . as to be merely in the realms of mathematical possibilities."[10]

Harding had been able to reinforce the conservative majority by filling four vacancies that arose during his little more than three years in the White House. (Wilson had been able to name only three justices in his eight years in office; Harding's successors, Coolidge and Hoover, between them named only four in more than two terms.) The four justices chosen by Harding not only assured conservative dominance for the decade but provided the backbone of the solidly anti–New Deal majority into the mid-1930s. Harding's first nominee to the Court, William Howard Taft, heavily influenced all the president's subsequent appointments. In 1921, when Chief Justice Edward D. White died, Harding named Taft, once a circuit judge and law professor (as well as a president), to succeed him. Taft typically voted on the conservative side, though he could not stomach his colleague James C. McReynolds, the most abrasive and extreme of the conservatives.[11] And Taft's influence ranged well beyond the votes he cast, for he took an extraordinary interest in judicial administration and an even more extraordinary one in judicial appointments. He frequently volunteered his advice to the president and the attorney general, and Harding and Daugherty eagerly accepted and often relied on it.

During the 1920 election campaign, Taft had written an article criticizing Wilson's appointments of Louis D. Brandeis and John H. Clarke in 1916; he argued that the most important election issue was "the maintenance of the Supreme Court as the bulwark to enforce the guaranty that no man shall be deprived of his property without due process of law."[12] The Court's use of the due-process clauses to block economic and social-reform laws had been a central target for Theodore Roosevelt a decade earlier; Taft as Chief Justice and counsel to the administration assured that this judicial hostility to reform would continue and intensify.

In the fall of 1923, for example, when Justice Oliver Wendell Holmes and his young British intellectual friend and Labour politician Harold J. Laski entertained themselves by putting together their ideal Supreme Court, Hand easily made it onto their list. (Holmes suggested adding Benjamin Cardozo as well, and Laski went along, though he thought Cardozo did not have "the brilliance of Hand.")[13] In 1922, the resignation of Justice Clarke, whose voting record had been even more liberal than Brandeis's, had prompted Laski to tell Holmes, "If God is good, you will have Learned Hand" as a colleague; but he realistically recognized that the place would probably go to Utah senator George Sutherland, and Sutherland indeed went on the Court, as the ablest member of the conservative bloc.[14]

Then, late in 1922, Justice William R. Day retired. It was clear that the administration would seek a Roman Catholic to replace him, for Chief Justice White's death had left the Court without an occupant of "the Catholic seat." The chief rivals for the vacancy proved to be Pierce Butler, a Minnesota railroad lawyer, and New York federal judge Martin Manton. Chief Justice Taft shared the views of the New York legal establishment that Manton did not deserve to be on the Court, despite Manton's strong support from his archbishop and the Democratic machine, so Taft took the lead in orchestrating Butler's campaign. Harding nominated Taft's candidate after a close race.[15] Hand had watched the battle with great concern and was relieved by Manton's defeat. "Whatever [Butler] may turn out to be," he wrote Frankfurter, "he certainly saved us from Manton, and he will be welcome for that." Manton had come frighteningly close. "I know whereof I speak," Hand reported. "The hierarchy was solid behind him; the White House was flooded with telegrams. [How] he got such backing, I don't know. One must credit him with the most amazing astuteness. Now I think his day is done. . . ."[16]

But Harding's opportunities to strengthen the Court's conservative majority were not yet at an end. A third 1922 vacancy arose when Mahlon Pitney of New Jersey retired. The New York bar assumed that the replacement would come from that state, though various New York lawyers and judges competed for the seat. Frankfurter, knowing that Hand had no chance, wrote to him cheerfully, "I wish to God that you were 100% Republican, one of the best minds and special friend of that great jurisconsult Harry M. Daugherty. For then we'd have you with the Nine Popes."[17] Yet Chief Justice Taft was sufficiently nervous about Hand's growing reputation that he strongly urged President Harding not to nominate him. Conceding that Hand was of "proper age," "an able judge and a hard worker," and reminding Harding that he had placed Hand on the district court in 1909, "on Wickersham's recommendation," Taft offered a decisive political argument: Hand had "turned out to be a wild Roosevelt man and a Progressive, and though on the Bench, he went into the [Bull Moose] campaign," he told Harding. Clearly, so unreliable a maverick could not be trusted on the Supreme Court: "If promoted to our Bench, he would most certainly herd with Brandeis and be a dissenter. I think it would be risking too much to appoint him."[18]

Hand did not know about this letter, but it would not have surprised him. Hand had defended Taft in 1921 as a writer of "professionally tip top" opinions in the face of Frankfurter's insistence that Taft was a narrow-minded mediocrity and a "lazy bones,"[19] but Hand realized that Taft had never forgiven him for his Bull Moose criticisms of the Supreme Court's abuses of due process. Hand saw Taft regularly, not only at meetings on judicial administrative matters but during vacations as well, for Taft often spent parts of his summers at Murray Bay in Quebec, and the Hands occasionally returned there. During one visit, in the summer of 1921, Hand wrote to Frankfurter, "I can't understand why he should treasure aught against poor little me, but apparently he does. Strange, and yet not strange! I suppose it was the sin against the Holy Ghost to touch the Ark of the Covenant. . . . However that all may be, I am in Dutch, I fear, with his nibs."[20] In the summer of 1922, again at Murray Bay, Hand had "several delightful talks with the Chief Justice," he wrote to Taft's brother Henry; indeed, they played golf together, with Hand gracefully recording that the Chief Justice was "as far above me in golf as he is in judicial hierarchy."[21] Yet neither personal association nor professional respect could deflect

Taft from keeping a Bull Moose advocate of restrained judicial review off the Supreme Court. And the seat went to a candidate from Tennessee, Edward Terry Sanford, as Harding's final appointment.

THE POLITICAL and ideological storms over judicial appointments that marked the Harding years sharply abated by the summer of 1924. And selecting a new circuit judge was a more placid, less controversial task than selecting a Supreme Court justice: ideological concerns about protecting property rights were far less central in the makeup of the lower federal courts than when the Supreme Court's composition was at issue, for circuit courts of appeals rarely decided due-process questions (most such challenges came to the Supreme Court from the state courts).

Hand entered the race for promotion in July 1924, and within a month, he learned that the nomination was his. Even Chief Justice Taft thought his promotion to the Second Circuit "well-deserved," and in urging Hand's name on the administration, he told Hand, "it needed no urging."[22]

Calvin Coolidge was receptive to merit considerations, for he was eager to put the sordid politics of the Harding era behind him. And Attorney General Harlan Fiske Stone claimed to be on Hand's side. He recommended the appointment, he told Hand, for reasons beyond his "duty": "It was a mighty great satisfaction to me also to have it . . . my pleasure."[23] Hand was not surprised: he had respected Stone before he became attorney general, and his respect continued throughout Stone's subsequent career (despite Frankfurter's persistent claim that Hand's admiration was excessive). But in fact, Stone was not nearly so enthusiastic as he asserted: in a letter to Taft, he expressed worries that Hand was too "radical and erratic in his political thinking"—while the far more conservative Taft paradoxically backed Hand on the ground that he was "the best man" for the position.[24]

Hand's easy road to the Second Circuit was assured by the support he received from the judge whom he succeeded there, Julius Mayer.[25] Mayer had not forgotten Hand's support of his own promotion three years earlier and told Hand that he had written Stone on Hand's behalf and that the attorney general's answer "indicates chances all in your favor."[26] Mayer was too experienced in politics, however, to leave the outcome to chance. He resorted to his wide range of contacts, from New York Republican senator James Wadsworth to "the local political people," to ensure Hand's promotion.[27] (Among the "local political people" was an especially influential one, Charles D. Hilles—once personal secretary to President Taft and now chair of the Republican party's finance committee.) Hand's supporters arranged for the usual outpouring of letters on his behalf, including strong ones from two major rivals of 1917, New York Democrat Abram Elkus and the patent lawyer Thomas Ewing.[28]

By late August, Hand learned that the attorney general had formally recommended him to the president. When Coolidge postponed sending the nomination to the Senate, Hand did not fret about the delay: Mayer had told him early on that the timing was governed by the impending presidential election, since the administration preferred delaying all nominations until after the vote.[29] On December 2, having handily defeated Democrat John W. Davis, Coolidge sent Hand's nomination to the Senate at last. There was a brief delay because a senator had mislaid the papers, but the Senate confirmed Hand, unanimously and without hesitation, on December 20.[30] A few days later, Hand received his commission as circuit judge, and on December 29 he was sworn in by senior judge Charles M. Hough.[31]

Hand's promotion had come virtually by acclamation. Superlatives filled the congratulatory letters that soon descended upon him. Those writers who knew Hand especially well perceived accurately that he would find the appellate work far more congenial than that of a district judge. And several viewed the promotion as simply a step toward the Supreme Court: as one supporter put it, Hand was the only American judge who deserved to be "bracketed with [Holmes] and Brandeis."[32] The most widely noted praise came from Walter Lippmann. In an editorial in the *New York World*, he congratulated the administration for its "admirable choice" of a judge who was "one of the great figures of the American courts, recognized wherever law is expounded in this country as a mind of extraordinary richness and distinction." Hand's appointment, Lippmann insisted, was "the real answer to criticism and distrust of the courts," for the true remedy for "sterile legalism" lay not in rhetoric but only in naming judges "who know the law and know life and know human motives."[33]

Hand himself took special delight in the fact that, despite his reputation as an erratic independent, a conservative administration had promoted him. With unusual daring, he agreed to speak with a reporter from the *World* on the day the nomination was announced. Hand bluntly insisted that he did not regard himself a Republican, and even though the Republican Senate had not yet confirmed his designation, he told the journalist that, ever since the Bull Moose debacle, he had been left "without a party," left "alone on a life raft" so far as politics were concerned.[34] (This interview prompted civil liberties lawyer Walter Nelles to congratulate him on this "brave statement of political disaffiliation": "It is testimony to the vitality of certain qualities of mind and heart that the fluctuations of the political morass occasionally put them where they can count.")[35]

Hand knew that many in the administration considered him a dangerous radical, a charge he thought bizarre: "Radical—God save the mark! Think of anybody thinking me radical—a man who always finds the new experiments too hazardous to be tried just now."[36] Nevertheless, he had achieved his long-sought promotion at last; and amid his glee, he was especially delighted when a well-wisher wrote:

> Even your best friends must admit that there is something essentially remarkable about your character & attainments which compels conservatives of the style of Taft & Coolidge to hand out promotions to one of the . . . well-known liberal, semi-radical . . . members of our judiciary.[37]

VII

The Second Circuit Court of Appeals
in the 1920s and 1930s:
Hand as First Among Equals

WHEN HAND TOOK HIS SEAT on the Second Circuit, he knew that he could now devote himself exclusively to appellate decisions, which would give him frequent opportunities to address questions of law, and that he would have no further obligation to tackle the burdensome routines of a trial judge. A distinctive feature of the work on a federal appellate court is that the judge is not solely responsible for a case. Appellate courts are staffed by more than one judge, and federal appeals courts dispose of most of their work in panels of three. (In the Second Circuit, the four judges rotated in three-man panels, usually sitting two weeks out of four each month.) This feature puts a premium on collegiality. In every case, Hand knew, he would have to work closely with two other judges, reaching decisions through exchanges of written memoranda and drafts and in informal talks and conferences. Hand was of course familiar with this aspect of the work, and he knew the men he would be dealing with.

The Second Circuit in 1924 was manned by four judges: in addition to Hand, there were senior judge Henry Wade Rogers, Charles Merrill Hough, and Martin Manton. Hand had special difficulty mustering the respect desirable for harmoniousness with regard to Manton, who was a loner, preoccupied with his political cronies and incapable of turning out memoranda and opinions that could earn him respect from the bar or bench. And as far as Hand was concerned, Rogers was intellectually not much better; he was not a political judge, but he was periodically ill and, even when able to work, contributed little of quality. (Though Rogers had come to the court from the deanship of Yale Law School, Hand's typical hero worship of law professors was not so blind as to blur his perceptions of quality—and the Yale Law School during Rogers's decade-long tenure was far from the leading institution it would become. Rogers was an adequate administrator and the school improved under his aegis, to be sure—it had been third-rate and he had brought it to the second rank. Yale continued to hold out against the case method that Langdell had instituted at Harvard and that had spread to other leading schools, and remained committed to outmoded rote lectures from law texts. Rogers made progress in moving from part-time teachers to a full-time faculty, but his recruits included only two distinguished scholars, the analytic philosopher Wesley N. Hohfeld and the brilliant young contracts expert Arthur L. Corbin. Yet Hohfeld and Corbin were happy to see Rogers depart—indeed, they led the forces that compelled him to resign when he, true to the part-time tradition of the school, tried to remain dean after being named a circuit judge.)[1]

So among Hand's new colleagues on the Second Circuit, only Charles M. Hough, a judge of distinguished ability, could elicit Hand's real affection and respect. On the surface, they could not have been more different. Hough's great regret was that he was too frail to have qualified for the armed services. His father had entered the army at the beginning of the Civil War as a private, decided to make army life his career, and rose through the ranks to become a brigadier general; Hough had dreamed of following in his father's footsteps, but that road was blocked and he resigned himself to attending Dartmouth rather than West Point. Nevertheless, he carried the demeanor of a military man throughout his life: he tended to be gruff and brusque, and he intimidated lawyers and judges alike. Moreover, he was a lifelong conservative Republican, contemptuous of sentimental reformers. Yet Hand, who was usually able to gaze beyond the surface of people (he had an "all seeing eye," Anne Morrow Lindbergh once told him), perceived the warmth beneath Hough's crusty surface. He liked Hough's directness and his willingness to engage in argument. And he appreciated Hough's scholarly bent (Hough wrote a history of the federal trial court in New York City). Most important, Hand thought him a first-rate judge, with impressive capacities for thoroughness and analysis, and an even more admirable ability to curb his traditional, conservative biases in the interest of fair-minded adjudication.

Hough was fourteen years older than Hand and had preceded him by three years to the district court (President Wilson had promoted him to the Second Circuit in 1916, a rare merit appointment of so conservative a Republican by a Democratic president), so at first Hand looked up to him as a father figure, but they soon formed a warm friendship, though not until he was near death in 1927 was Hough prepared to reveal the "unusual gentleness" and "tenderness" that Hand knew was obscured by his "commanding and brusque manner." In a moving deathbed note to Hand, he wrote, "For more years now than it is necessary to count, I have found more pleasure (saving only the companionship of two or three men whom I knew as boys of seventeen) in considering affairs of the world with you. With you I could loaf and invite my soul—the pleasure and the rest that one doesn't always find even with those you esteem and are fond of. . . . I want you to know how many years of my life have been made more pleasurable by knowing you."[2] And Hand in turn never forgot Hough's "kindness and forebearance of what must at times have been trying for him to get along with,"[3] as he wrote to Hough's widow, who in turn told Hand that her husband especially appreciated his "newer outlook": "He often said that you made him *think* as almost no one else did."[4] And it was true that Hand had the capacity to engage and admire colleagues of sharply differing philosophies, be they to the right or the left of him, so long as they engaged in discussions candidly and held positions resting on solid intellectual foundations.

An exchange between Hough and Hand in 1926 illustrates the candor of their engagements. The Supreme Court had just handed down an important early decision on free speech, *Gitlow v. New York*, in which the majority upheld the constitutionality of New York's anti-subversion criminal-anarchy law and affirmed the conviction of a leading left-wing member of the Socialist party. Holmes, joined by Brandeis, had issued a brief but powerful dissent, applying his "clear and present danger" standard to defend Benjamin Gitlow's First Amendment rights. "If in the long run the beliefs expressed in proletarian dictatorship are destined to be accepted by the dominant forces of the community," Holmes had said, "the only meaning of free speech is that they should be given their chance and have their way."[5]

Hough was puzzled, even outraged, by Holmes's performance in the *Gitlow* dissent. At about the same time, Holmes had written for the Supreme Court in a decision that went against a suing worker in an injury case. "Holmes does cheer my soul every now and then," Hough wrote to Hand, by insisting on holding "that darling infant of most judges," "the injured laborer," to rigid standards of proof. Decisions like these heartened him: he thought Holmes's tough-mindedness indicated there was "some remnant of the soldier" in Holmes after all. But, he went on, "I cannot reconcile [Holmes's] conduct in negligence cases with his (to me) conscienceless & easy going sufferance of 'imperial jaw' from every kind of social vermin. His dissent in [*Gitlow*]—

standing alone—could lead one to think him either daft or an enemy of his race & country."

Hand could not bear this attack in silence. Ever since the *Masses* decision, he had frequently expressed his criticisms of Holmes's "clear and present danger" formula, for his commitment to free speech was even deeper than Holmes's, a commitment springing from the depths of his skepticism about dominant truths and his fierce allegiance to keeping open the channels of debate. And so, passionately and eloquently, he now took issue with Hough. Without something like the *Gitlow* dissent, Hand insisted, "the whole doctrine of free speech goes by the board." He added, "I had rather lose any right but that of the right to talk," "the most important," as well as "probably the most dangerous, of all rights." Hand was in no doubt about the proper outcome of *Gitlow*: "I should join in [Holmes's] dissent." He was not as confident as Holmes that a stronger protection of speech would ever become law, but he was "all for keeping the flag flying, whether you would describe it as 'red' " or, as Hand would view it, "as 'stars and stripes.' " And with special heat, he challenged Hough's derogatory adjectives: Holmes's views were not "conscienceless" or "easy going" but rested on "a conviction about the relations of men to one another, which . . . go as deep as any can into the core of the very meaning of morality." Holmes's position was truly important, Hand insisted, "only at a time when most men are greatly excited and intolerant, when they are quite as likely to turn upon those who wish to be tolerant as upon those who actively oppose them, perhaps more so." Hand spoke from years of experience as a defender of those whose positions were far more radical than his, and his relations with Hough were such that he felt wholly free in stating his case openly and powerfully.[6]

Hough was especially appealing to Hand because he was the only other powerful intellect on the Second Circuit when Hand started there. And from virtually the first moment, Hand yearned for other able and congenial companions. He was eager to prevent additional second-rate political appointments and to ensure high professional quality. He frequently avowed his inexperience in political maneuverings, but he was unusually active in pressing for strong candidates, and he knew whom he would like most to see on his bench: first of all there was his cousin Gus Hand, who had become a district judge in 1914, and also the present Yale Law School dean, Thomas W. Swan. He worked energetically toward these ends, and he succeeded: Swan was named to the circuit court in 1926, Gus a year later. These designations put in place the core of what for decades would be recognized as the strongest appellate court in the United States.

Identifying desirable future colleagues was far easier than awaiting vacancies and ensuring that Gus Hand and Thomas Swan would be appointed to them. One alternative was to persuade Congress to enlarge the size of the court. And it was true that the Second Circuit's work load was growing steadily: at the time, its docket was substantially heavier than that of any of the ten other federal circuit courts, even though some of these also had four judges, and one (the Eighth, covering an area ranging from Minnesota to Arkansas) had six. Hand repeatedly pleaded with members of the House and Senate Judiciary committees as well as with Chief Justice Taft to sponsor legislation providing a fifth judge for the Second Circuit, and as early as 1926, he thought that the law would soon be enacted (and dreamed of having Gus promoted to the new seat). But the bills were blocked repeatedly, usually by New York members of the House majority, who held out for assurances that new district judges would be created simultaneously, which would provide valuable patronage for loyal members of the Democratic machine.

Critical aid came not from Congress but from fate. Judge Henry Wade Rogers, never intellectually powerful or energetic, became even less effective by late 1925 because of periodic bouts of illness. The added burden his absences placed on the other judges was sufficiently serious so that Hough was moved to seek help from Chief Justice Taft and Attorney General John Sargent to hasten Rogers's retirement.[7] But no formal action proved necessary. In August 1926, Rogers died and Hough became the senior judge. Gus Hand had no chance for the new vacancy: one of the Second Circuit's positions had traditionally been held by a non–New Yorker, Rogers had been the Connecticut incumbent, and the replacement would probably have to come from that state.

For Hand, Thomas Swan was the obvious choice, though he did not know him very well and had learned from Rogers's performance that a Yale deanship did not guarantee outstanding quality. But Hand realized that the Yale Law School had risen steadily in reputation under Swan's leadership. Moreover, Ned Burling, Hand's friend who had practiced law with Swan in Chicago before World War I, assured Hand that Tom Swan was a first-rate professional. Hand also knew that Swan had graduated with distinction from Harvard Law School (four years after Hand himself had). Indeed, Swan had been brought to the Yale deanship in part to pilot Yale's conversion to Harvard's approach to legal education, which had by then become the hallmark of all leading law schools and was heading into an even more progressive direction at Harvard itself.[8] Although Swan was personally conservative, under his leadership Yale made great progress toward its modern reputation as a first-rank law school.

Hand was the leading promoter of Swan's appointment to the Second Circuit, playing the unaccustomed role of chief persuader and lobbyist. It took many letters to persuade Swan to announce a willingness to be considered, for Swan did not want to impair his relationship with Yale's law faculty or president, and he did not want to appear as an office seeker engaging directly with Connecticut senator Hiram Bingham, whose support was essential. (His reluctance did not stem from financial concerns, for he had married Mabel Dick, the daughter of the office-machine magnate A. B. Dick.) Hand also took the lead in overcoming Bingham's doubts that Swan would be willing to leave Yale, helped rally the bar in Swan's support, and was in frequent contact with Chief Justice Taft to press Swan's candidacy.

Taft proved extraordinarily helpful. With his preoccupation with effective judicial administration—a task he performed far more assid-uously than he did the normal duties of a judge—he vehemently disliked judicial appointments being treated as mere political patronage, and he consistently crusaded for lower court nominees of high quality, as free with advice during the Coolidge years as he had been in the Harding era. Hand and Taft were allies on a range of issues—nominations to the Second Circuit, selections of district judges, and proposals to add new judgeships in New York. No one was more expert than Taft in the inner workings of judicial politics, and he constantly advised Hand on how to promote a favorite candidate, prodding him to be even more energetic in rounding up local support. Repeatedly, Hand would protest that his political contacts were limited; repeatedly, Taft would insist that good judicial nominations did not happen without a lot of political work. So Hand wrote letters to Washington as best he could, and Taft worked with his powerful Washington acquaintances, especially Pres-ident Coolidge and the attorney general.

Taft was an enthusiastic supporter of Coolidge's administration. But, as he told Hand, "Cal's" incapacity to identify strong appointees, in-cluding judicial ones, was a pervasive weakness: he was all too likely to be buffeted about by shifting political winds. Coolidge's selection of an attorney general after Harlan Fiske Stone went to the Supreme Court in 1925 was, for example, symptomatic of Coolidge's flaws, as well as being a problem in its own right. John Sargent, whom Coolidge plucked from his native Vermont, was a timid, uninformed soul. Thus Taft went to work ever more energetically to strengthen the backbones of the Vermonters on judicial appointments. Of course, Hand feared that

Coolidge and Sargent would try to place a Vermont candidate on the Second Circuit, and there was good reason for anxiety on that score, since Vermont lacked outstanding lawyers and judges. (The only Vermont district judge, Harland B. Howe, was one of the least competent and most disagreeable individuals sitting on a federal court anywhere in the nation.) But Tom Swan was finally nominated in late 1926, and easily confirmed.

Hand's satisfaction at having Swan as a colleague was offset by his disappointment that there was still no place for his cousin Gus. The bills to add a new circuit judge continued to be stalled in Congress (as they would be until 1929). But in the spring of 1927, Hough's death provided an opportunity. Hand was grief-stricken by the loss of his one congenial colleague. And he plainly thought it unseemly to take the leading part on behalf of a cousin who was also his closest friend since childhood.[9] Once again, Chief Justice Taft lent important assistance, especially by eliminating the Hands' fears that Gus, a lifelong Democrat, would run into difficulty with the Republican administration. Indeed, Gus's party affiliation was an attraction for Taft: in the Chief Justice's eyes, occasional selections of Democrats could only help the Republican administration, especially at a time when the opposition controlled the House of Representatives. And Taft, like Hand, was a strong proponent of promoting district court judges to the appellate court, all other things being equal. Not only did the district court experience provide a better record of a candidate's mettle, but merit promotions also provided incentives and rewards for those lawyers who had chosen to leave law practice for the bench. With judicial salaries far less than private-income opportunities even then, some of the best lawyers, especially in high-income cities such as New York, refused to become judicial candidates; and some sitting judges—Julius Mayer was a recent example—chose to resign in order to relieve financial pressures.

Gus Hand's nomination came quickly, but confirmation was annoyingly delayed for several months. With this promotion assured, the Learned Hand–Augustus Hand–Tom Swan triumvirate was in place at last. (Learned's good friend the witty, engaging Washington lawyer Ned Burling once cheerfully embraced his secretary's transcribing error and told Hand that the real Second Circuit consisted of "Ellhand, Gushound, and Tomswine.")[10] For the next quarter century, this court symbolized the highest judicial quality for the nation. The three men quickly formed a tightly knit nucleus, based on mutual professional admiration and personal congeniality. Manton went his own way, not only socially and politically but also in his high-handed manner of exercising the limited administrative functions of the senior judge.

Far closer to the triumvirate was Judge Julian W. Mack, who during the 1920s served in effect as a half-time member of the Second Circuit. Mack, an outstanding Harvard Law School student in the class of 1887, a founder of the *Harvard Law Review* who became a respected Chicago lawyer and law professor, had been named to the Commerce Court in 1911—a new court created to review railroad regulation cases whose three judges were given the rank of circuit judges. This early experiment in specialized courts was short-lived: the Commerce Court was caught in a political cross fire, targeted by the industry as well as those advocating more stringent regulation; and when one of its judges, Robert W. Archbald, was impeached by the House and convicted by the Senate in 1913 for taking gifts and loans from litigants, Congress abolished the court. The remaining two judges were left as "floating" judges without a specific assignment, available for duty on any federal court in the nation. Mack sat from time to time on the courts in Chicago but increasingly spent most of the year as a district or circuit judge in New York City. He contributed few written opinions: although he was one of the nation's most distinguished trial judges, he suffered from "pen paralysis," as Felix Frankfurter once put it. But behind the scenes, in contributions to the court's conferences and, to some extent, in his memoranda—Mack found them easier to produce because he was not writing for publication—he was a very able member of the Second Circuit.[11]

It did not take long for Hand to develop a liking and respect for Mack, whose background was precisely the kind likely to impress Hand. With the Second Circuit burdened by a mounting workload, the availability of another able jurist dividing his time between the trial and appellate courts assured some lightening of the task. Moreover, Mack was a congenial companion—a large, jovial man who talked well and loved fine food (despite suffering from diabetes). Only Mack's uninhibited involvement in extrajudicial matters prompted Hand to be at all critical. While Hand increasingly withdrew from public participation in controversial causes, Mack zestfully threw himself into his favorite contentious issues. With Louis Brandeis, for example, he was at the core of the American Zionist movement, and he had attended the Versailles Peace Conference as a Zionist observer. For Hand, it was not Mack's ethnicity that gave pause as such, but his well-publicized, energy-consuming preoccupation with nonjudicial affairs. (By contrast, Mack's Jewishness was strongly disliked by Frances Hand: she would not have him as a dinner guest, even though Mack was among the most assimilated of Jews, more readily accepted in usually exclusive circles—from his longtime service as a member of the Board of Overseers of Harvard University to his presidency of the Harvard Club of New York—than most Jews of his day.)

One additional judge joined the Second Circuit before the decade was out. In 1929, the proposed legislation to add a fifth regular judge to the Second Circuit was at last adopted by Congress. Hand and his New York City friends pressed to have district judge Thomas D. Thacher, appointed by President Coolidge in 1925, named to the newly created position, for they considered him among the strongest of trial judges. But the competition for the new position was, as usual, fierce. After extensive maneuvering, the lame-duck Coolidge ("I do not choose to run for President in 1928," he had announced) nominated a Vermonter. Harrie Brigham Chase, a young man on the state's Supreme Court, was wholly unknown to Hand and his friends. As Hand told Taft, "[M]y heart sinks a little at a man who carries the name 'Harrie.' " Yet Hand was prepared to "wait & see": after all, "there were all sorts of possibilities; perhaps we got off better than we might."[12]

When Hand sent a cordial welcoming letter to Chase, the new appointee replied with a note of thanks: "While I do not dare hope that you will find me all that you have the right to expect, I do believe that you will find me always willing to work hard and eager to learn."[13] This modest self-evaluation proved to be an accurate one; Chase never claimed to be an intellectual or a penetrating student of the law, but he did possess integrity and competence—unlike Manton, he was not a political judge preoccupied with cronyism; still, he preferred his outings on the golf course to his struggles with arguments and judicial opinions. The taciturn Chase never became a member of the central core of the Second Circuit, but neither was he ever at the remote distance of Manton. He spent most of his time in Brattleboro, and commuted to New York only when necessary for court work; his geographical preference for his hometown meant that he never enjoyed the social intimacy with the Second Circuit triumvirate any more than he was part of its intellectual intimacy.

With Chase's appointment in January 1929, the Second Circuit's makeup was in place for the next decade, and calm descended. Not until 1938, when Congress created a sixth circuit judgeship, was there any change in personnel.

THE UNMATCHED QUALITY of the Second Circuit in Learned Hand's years showed what could happen on a court with a majority of unusually able judges devoting themselves month after month, year after year, to fair-minded, top-caliber decision making, using superior craftsmanship in taking the contested issues seriously and working through them with the utmost intellectual discipline. The significance of their processes for tackling the workload paled in comparison; Hand himself believed that procedural rules were far less important than the quality of the men who worked with them. Still, one aspect of the Second Circuit's methods, he recognized, was of central importance in assuring focused individual attention by the three judges on each case. This feature was the pre-conference memorandum, a practice already in use when Hand joined the Second Circuit in 1924 that achieved its greatest flowering during Hand's years of service over the next three and a half decades.

The use of pre-conference memos makes the Second Circuit unique among American appellate courts. The usual practice in both federal and state appellate courts is for the judges to meet soon after the oral arguments have been made in order to reach a tentative decision, but this means that unless all the judges have studied the lawyers' briefs beforehand or have gotten a grasp of the issues during the oral argument, the shaping of the court's ruling may fall to just one of them, whoever is sufficiently familiar with the field to take the lead. The Second Circuit, by contrast, devised the pre-conference memo procedure in order to promote individual consideration of each case prior to giving collegial attention to it. During Hand's years, members of the judicial panel hearing a case typically did not discuss its issues until more than a week after the end of the week in which they had heard arguments. Meanwhile, each judge individually worked through the case and reached tentative conclusions before ever consulting with his colleagues. In each judge's chambers, the secretary would type an informal memorandum on long legal pages, with carbon copies on onionskin sheets to be distributed to the other judges. Most of the time, a judge's memos made no reference at all to his colleagues' memos; ordinarily, a judge had not read them until after he had completed his own. Then, when the judges met face-to-face a week or two later, they had a far greater familiarity with the facts and legal issues than was possible otherwise.

The pre-conference memo (which continues in modified form on the Second Circuit today, where it is now called a "voting memo") assured an unequaled degree of intellectual engagement. Forcing each judge to think through a case to a tentative conclusion risks a premature rigidity of viewpoint and a divided court, but in fact no such rigidity showed in Hand's years. Each judge recognized that his memo stated only tentative conclusions, and was designed to promote more focused, better-informed discussion; this was indeed the usual consequence. And no judge could easily be inattentive: having to write the memos—they typically ran two to four pages (in Hand's case, sometimes as long as ten)—obliged the judges to articulate their reasoning, and as a result, the time needed to confer was often shorter than it would have been otherwise, for the discussion could concentrate on areas of disagreement, and the hours were not wasted on floundering efforts to identify the central issues.

Learned Hand saved virtually all the pre-conference memoranda he and his colleagues wrote during his more than thirty-five years on the Second Circuit.[14] These files offer rare glimpses not only of his central role on the court but also of the quality of the collegial exchanges. Repeatedly, the ultimate decision in a given case and, especially, the court's written opinion bear the imprint of the pre-conference memos: some tentative positions, of course, changed in the face of colleagues' memoranda; the ensuing discussion was more focused; and the shape and quality of the final opinion were enhanced.[15] Thus, the pre-conference memo system was a significant mechanism to ensure that the actual process on appeals approximated its ideal, for it promoted group deliberation based on independent preparation rather than a final decision reached, in effect, by one judge.

ONE OTHER INSTITUTIONAL ARRANGEMENT, the use of law clerks by the judges, also contributed importantly to the special personal and intellectual atmosphere of the Second Circuit. Law clerks are no longer unique to the Second Circuit, but the Second Circuit, and Hand especially, were pioneers in using them; Hand's manner was, moreover, significantly different from that of any federal judge in our history.

When Hand became a district judge in 1909, the judges lacked funding for law clerks, and Hand imaginatively used his small financial allotment for a stenographer to hire a law-trained assistant instead. He asked acquaintances at Harvard to tell him about recent law graduates whom he could use, and in his first three years he hired young men to help out with secretarial chores and to assist him in legal research.[16] But the very low salary made it impossible to attract top Harvard graduates. Hand formed close social relations with some of his law secretaries, but he could not get from them the close intellectual engagement he cherished; he abandoned the practice before World War I.

After his promotion to the Second Circuit in 1924, faced with the greater obligations for legal analysis and writing that the appellate judge-ship entailed, Hand was more eager than ever to have a young law-trained companion at his side, but Congress still made no funding available for such a position. After Thomas Swan joined the court, Hand found a temporary solution: for three years beginning in 1927, he and Swan shared a law clerk whose salary—$2,000 a year—they paid out of their own pockets. In 1930, the law at last caught up with the institutional support with which Hand had long experimented: Congress began to provide a law clerk for each appellate judge. The initial salary was $3,000 a year, sufficient at last to attract the best law school graduates. As the Depression deepened, Congress reduced the salary, but outstanding young graduates continued to serve as clerks even during these low-paying years. (As late as 1953, the law clerk's salary was still only $3,600 a year; by contrast, modern appellate judges may have as many as three law clerks, and a clerk's salary nowadays is well over $30,000.)

During the brief period of joint Hand-Swan law clerks, the clerks came from Yale, for Swan had recent contacts with New Haven. But once Hand was assured of his own clerk, in 1930, he turned regularly to his alma mater. Felix Frankfurter was the central source of supply: he was already choosing clerks for Justices Holmes and Brandeis, and he happily added Hand to his list. (After Frankfurter moved to the Supreme Court in 1939, Harvard's dean's office took over the selecting of clerks for Hand.) Unlike most judges today, who entertain applications from many candidates and select their clerks after interviews, Hand relied entirely on Frankfurter, who would choose a single person whom Hand usually accepted sight unseen. Typically, his clerks— Hand called them his "puny judges"—had been presidents or senior officers of the *Harvard Law Review*, and they went on to distinguished careers in government, academia, or private practice.

The most distinctive aspect of clerking with Hand was the extraordinary intellectual intimacy of the relationship, stemming entirely from face-to-face contacts rather than written work. Virtually every other judge, then and since, relied on law clerks to produce a vast amount of written work, from research memoranda on cases about to be or just argued, to investigations and reports on knotty issues, to draft opinions to be revised by the judge and issued under the judge's name. Not so with Hand: every opinion that bears Hand's name was produced, word by word, by the judge himself and no one else. The task of a Hand law clerk was to familiarize himself with the cases before the court as best he could, reading the briefs and supplemental legal materials, so as to be ready to discuss them with the judge. In every case Hand considered at all unclear—and he was uncertain about the proper result in most cases, even after decades of judicial experience—he would spend many hours with his clerk at every stage of the decisional process, before and while writing his pre-conference memoranda, before and while writing his formal opinions, repeatedly asking for the clerk's criticisms and responses.

In writing his memos and opinions, Hand worked with a legal-size pad of yellow paper, which he propped on a board resting on his knees or set on his desk. Before getting down a word, he would tell the clerk what he planned to write in, say, the first two paragraphs, and then invite—indeed, press—him to offer criticisms; Hand took these very seriously. The clerk would then return to his own desk while Hand wrote out the first paragraphs in longhand. Soon, Hand would give the yellow sheets to the clerk for renewed criticism; if the clerk had objections and Hand saw merit in them, he would try again. He repeated that procedure for page after long yellow page of his drafts, continuing to press for comment; in the most difficult cases, he would go through as many as thirteen draft opinions with many crossings-out and much rewriting before he permitted his secretary to prepare a typewritten version and distribute it to his fellow judges. And often he was still not wholly satisfied.

Most of Hand's clerks, fresh out of law school, were startled to find this experienced jurist, a near mythic figure, a household word to every law school graduate, the master judge of his generation, asking for help and insisting on candid criticism and continuous oral participation in the decision process. Was it really conceivable, they would wonder, that Hand was seriously interested in their views when they were just months away from the classroom? Or was Hand's quest for critical reactions merely a courteous gesture designed to make them feel important? As the clerks got to know Hand better, most realized that he was entirely serious about his constant prodding to elicit critical analysis, and that this unique way of working with his clerks was part and parcel of his distinctiveness as a judge. Obviously, Hand had far more experience with the legal issues that came before him than the clerk possibly could, but less obviously, he had a deep-rooted open-mindedness and skepticism about his work, a capacity to doubt his own tentative conclusions and to insist on putting them to the test of the most rigorous analysis. He was not cocksure; he had a genuine capacity for listening and, indeed, a hunger for points of view different from his own; he was not satisfied until he had explored all sides of an issue; and these traits made him view his intimate contact with a succession of bright young lawyers as essential to his performance of his function, as vital to an inquiring mind that never grew complacent, was never closed.

One of Hand's former clerks once spent a long afternoon with him while Hand went over a list of all his previous law clerks and reminisced about the characteristics of each. The judge did not hold them all in equally high regard, but his evaluations were usually positive, and significantly, there was a common quality in the very few less than satisfactory clerks: he would say of them that they held back too much and were too unwilling to engage with him. He had no desire for brash, abrasive, or callow clerks, but he very much wanted involved, critical ones. And difficult as it was for law school graduates in their early twenties to challenge—indeed, try to tear apart—the reasoning of a judge of Hand's ability and experience, Hand's best clerks did just that.

It is not surprising that for most of Hand's clerks, their year's service with him was one of the most rewarding of their careers. For some, everything that followed was anticlimactic; for all of them, the clerkship was unforgettable, a demanding, intense, intellectually engaged experience with a rare judge and human being. And for Hand himself, the clerks assured him not only close encounters with different viewpoints and modern ideas in the law schools but, above all, a zestful, ceaseless searching for answers, answers that Hand was sure could never be unchallengeable, permanent ones.[17]

THE DISTINCTIVE ROLE Hand played on the Second Circuit during his first decades there emerges clearly in the many hundreds of pre-conference memoranda he preserved. Their most notable characteristic is the sheer joyful thoroughness with which he tackled each case. The court confronted a very wide range of subjects in a seemingly endless flow of cases, many of them of little apparent interest to anyone other than the litigants' lawyers. Yet whatever the subject—patents and copyrights, maritime law, bankruptcy, corporate and commercial law, citizenship and aliens' deportation, criminal law, problems of evidence and jurisdiction—Hand unflaggingly sought to get to the bottom of the facts and the law. Repeatedly, a colleague's memo would suggest that the case was easy and presented nothing of substance, but Hand typically found issues worth discussing. Frequently, he began his memoranda (as his colleagues rarely did) with the remark "This is an interesting case."[18] He would skillfully dissect and explain the technical data about a complex mechanical or chemical patent, for example, or, as if he were an experienced seafarer, the hows and whys of a ship collision. And after a masterful summary of the data that had left his colleagues bewildered, he would probe and articulate the applicable legal principles and bring them trenchantly to bear on the disputed evidence. As the workload mounted, Hand memos as long as ten pages were rarer, but his frequent three- and four-page statements still exceeded those of his colleagues. His persistence in unraveling each of the myriad cases that came before him is the clearest demonstration of the assertion, as Judge Henry Friendly put it, that Hand's major achievement stemmed from "the great way in which he dealt with the multitude of little cases."[19]

Hand's extraordinary thoroughness might suggest a judge in the painful grip of a compulsion to dot every *i*, cross every *t*, but this impression is wrong: what emerges most clearly from Hand's memos is his enjoyment of the process of preliminary analysis. His memos are full of humor and wordplay. He was gifted with a great command of the language, and he relished playing with it. Literary allusions flowed naturally from his pen, from Shakespeare and the Bible to Greek classics and Rabelais. His sense of humor and his sarcasm were unmatched on the court. Charles Hough and Gus Hand and, less often, Harrie Chase would sometimes join in the humorous banter, but only in Hand's memos was this a major, recurrent characteristic.

Hand's sense of humor made it possible to convert a memo on even a routine case into wit. In one small case, for example, a tie manufacturer claimed that a competitor had copied his novel design for a tie; the plaintiff had gotten a design patent for a style featuring a "merrowed edge" at the tie end. (Hand commented, "I cannot find 'merrowed' in the dictionary.") Manton's and Mack's memoranda disposed of the case in a very few lines; by contrast, Hand's memorandum was a funny little essay on the treatment of design patents that argued for a relatively lenient, protective approach. He had not the "slightest idea" what an earlier court might have said, he wrote—he himself had "always been far more friendly" than most judges to design patents—and here, the novel shape and unusual edge seemed "mildly pleasant," and that was enough: "What will please folks nobody can say. . . . God forbid we shall make the test whether it attracts us." That the defendant had copied the plaintiff's design showed that he at least thought it was aesthetically pleasing, and if he "says it is not beautiful, let him avoid it. . . . Apparently nobody has thought of finishing a necktie like this before. To me that is enough; there being no approach shots anywhere near the green." Hand went on to reject a contrary decision from another circuit court that had claimed that "only what shows above the waistcoat can be a design for a tie." Hand answered:

> People buy their ties for all sorts of reasons. I do not see why the wearer should not look with pleasure on his clothes before he puts them on. I wish I could. Most design patents are footling affairs and this is one. It is indeed easy to adopt a high and mighty attitude

towards them, vaguely suggestive that [these matters] are beneath such important personages as ourselves, but it is childish to do so.[20]

Hand had fun with the facts in a case even when the legal issues were far from earthshaking. A 1934 case is illustrative. His colleagues Gus Hand and Harrie Chase wrote only a dry paragraph each in finding that a claimed business-expense deduction by a taxpayer was not allowable because it was not "ordinary and necessary." He agreed with this conclusion, but let his wry imagination run freely in reaching it. The case involved Inecto, a manufacturer of hair dyes, which had engaged a well-known cosmetician, a Mrs. Maurer, to help promote its dyes. Inecto had given her some stock in another company in addition to her salary and had guaranteed her a minimum income from it. When the dividend income proved less than expected, she received cash payments instead under the guarantee, and the company claimed that these payments to her were "ordinary" business expenses.

As Hand described the facts, this "Mother of the Beauty Shop" was expected merely to "shed the effulgence of her restrained poisonality" over Inecto's product. If all worked well, she would be a "propagandist" among beauticians who had an "almost pathological affection for Mother." (Hand referred to Inecto as "that dispenser of the disguise of the ravages of years, hair dye that takes away the dignity and beauty of a face in which the lines should show the gentleness that time can bring, and put the spotlight on all that's hard and unredeemed.") And he added, "Oh, 'tis a goodly calling, to be a Beautician, a Cosmetician, a Disguitician! . . . It may be assumed that if Mother even in her sleep thought Inecto, all the sheep would baa 'Inecto.' " To Hand, the guarantee on dividend returns to "Mother" was certainly no "ordinary" expense, just an unusual payment to keep her loyal: "She was a wild, untamed thing out of a Wisconsin newspaper office, full of the wisdom of the badger and the winged freedoms of Lake Michigan fish hawk."[21]

Sometimes, the mere name of a ship in an otherwise ordinary case was enough to set him off. *United States v. S.S. Manuel Arnus* involved a law permitting suits against ships that brought aliens to the United States without making sure that they had gone through the proper immigration channels. Tom Swan and Gus Hand wrote brief, technical memos, but Hand devoted an entire page to playful embroidery on the name of the ship:

Arnus, Arnus? Who is Manuel Arnus? His name has unpleasant connotations, but he must have been some punkins. Was he arnus mirabilis; or arnus Dei irae? Well, never mind; I can't see how the case can very well turn on that. It might; it might of course. But then, pshaw! Why follow out these pedantic sophistries? Are we not practical men? The first thing I know you'll be thinking is that my mind is ranging into irrelevancies, like old Henry Wade Codgers [former senior judge Rogers], whom Tomasso [Tom Swan] succeeded. . . .

I am a gentleman, even if I didn't make the Porcellian Club. And I am going to show you both, demonstrate it, *that* I am a gentleman, a *perfect* gentleman. Well, well! After all there must be an end. Some exordium is all right of course, but for God's sake let's have an end on't. Tristram Shandy is not the proper standard for a busy man, a *very* busy man. My lads, let us stow all this guff and man the yards. Start your chanty, Bosun. Here she blows.[22]

And with that, he proceeded to a straightforward dissection of the statute and the governing cases.

Occasionally, Hand framed his legal memo with a few lines of poetry composed for the occasion.[23] At other times, he would couch a technical legal issue in more lucid and far funnier prose than any lawyer's brief or, indeed, any printed opinion could. One case, for example, involved a claim by a landlord who had leased space to Montgomery Ward for what he thought would be a chain-store branch; Montgomery Ward, however, decided to use the space for other purposes. The landlord was disappointed: the branch store, he had hoped, would raise the value of his adjoining properties, and he claimed that Montgomery Ward had breached the lease and owed him money for the expected profits that never materialized. The case merely presented the issues of whether there had in fact been a breach of the lease and whether loss of expected profits was recoverable. All the judges—Swan and the two Hands— agreed that there had been no breach, because the lease had not required Montgomery Ward to use its rented space for a branch store. But Learned Hand went on to discuss the more difficult issue of whether, had there been a breach, the landlord could sue for profits he might have made. Hand thought he could, and explained:

If there was really a contract here, I think that the defendant was a scurvy wight [a]nd ought to be hooked. Suppose I want to get up a Methodist consortium and buy a plot of land, put up bungalows and prepare an auditorium. Suppose I say to the Rt. Rev. Cannon: "Doc, if you will agree to spend a month every year for ten years at this God-hopping paradise, you shall have it rent free. Your presence will attract all the godly, grim, ascetic, bare, stark, joyless, unlovely, tyrannous, compulsive, envious, loveless Methodists of high repute in this Land of Freedom. There they can plot to make the lives of others as dreary, sunless, miserable, hard, starved soulless and narrow as their own. I shall reap largely by this holy company, and you can get your vacation,—if you can be said to know what a vacation really is,—for nix." If the Rt. Rev. Son-of-a-sea cook . . . agreed to occupy for ten years [and does not do so], I don't quite see why he should not be stuck with my loss, measured by the difference that his sacred presence would have made in the value of my aforesaid paradise.

After spinning out this example, Hand proceeded to two additional pages of lengthy, straight-faced analysis of the legal issues, only occasionally broken by mocking asides (such as "To be sure, [allowing such damages] opens up a horrid possibility . . . of having twelve Red Men, Kiwanis and Odd Fellows get even with chain store operators, and T.W.S. [Swan] will rear on his hind legs and snort like Behemoth at the risk. But a contract's a contract and if the damages were really kept to honest increases in value, what injustice is there in it?")[24]

Hand's humor and literary gifts were not deployed only on occasions when he wanted to enliven routine cases. Even in areas where he cared deeply, as in alien deportation and naturalization, he could speak colorfully about the human situation involved and explode forcefully at the injustice of the law, even though he was duty-bound to apply its clear mandates. The *Neuberger* case, for example, involved a German immigrant who had grown up in the United States but returned to Germany before World War I, was compelled to join the German army, and sought citizenship after he returned to the United States. The gruff, militaristic Charles Hough had no sympathy at all for the applicant: he insisted that Neuberger had not shown the necessary devotion "to the principles of the Constitution," for he had been in the United States ever since he was a youngster without applying for citizenship and then became an officer in the German army; that made him "not a proper person to be made an American citizen." Hand rejected that stance: although he agreed with the denial of citizenship because Neuberger's absence had been too long to satisfy the law's residence requirement, he insisted that an alien's motives were irrelevant; the residence requirement existed "to get him broken in to the traditions of this great and glorious land of $15 wages"; but he surely could not be treated as undevoted to "the principles of the Constitution":

So far as we know he has behaved about like any other fish in similar circumstances. I have no idea that he is a John Hampden [the outspoken parliamentary opponent of King Charles I] or an Abraham Lincoln; but I dare be sworn that he is not a [traitor] or even a Babe Ruth. I should think he was of the ordinary dough, and doughy.[25]

Another early case involved an attempt to deport an alien found to lack the required good moral character because he had immigrated with his mistress and had continued their adulterous relationship in this country. Hand thought the law unjust, because the Congress unfairly expected aliens to meet standards not imposed on Americans: "I hate the Puritanical pharisaism which enacted the blessed law and set a standard for aliens that the incolae [natives] make only a poor pretense to follow." Still, Congress had the constitutional power to impose such offensive restrictions, and the rejection of the alien had to be sustained. But Hand could not restrain himself in describing the facts. The alien's name was Vincenzo Della Femina: "This alien is well named, for he is an adept in the ways to the heart of woman." Here, there could be no doubt "that this subtle son of the sunny south and his Lombardian beauty immigrated under the influence of the Cyprian and pursued their dalliances after arriving." In the case "of this most noble Vincenzo," Hand could feel no compunctions.[26]

Hand also held strong feelings about overzealous prosecutors and vindictive trial judges. As an appellate judge, he had no authority to modify the trial judges' sentences, but he never tired of chastising judges and prosecutors for their harsh indulgence in technicalities. In one case, for example, he stated that he had examined the briefs "with the most hostile eye that I could, for I wanted to reverse in view of the outrage committed on the defendants. [But I] really do not see how I can honestly avoid voting to affirm." Still, he was "not content to let this case go without some comment upon what [the trial judge] did." "[He] had seen fit to throw [the circuit court's views] to the winds and act like a God on a mountain." And, Hand added, "I will not be canned, though in conscience I cannot vote to reverse":

In the words of the lamented William Lloyd Garrison, than whom there has never been a than whomer, "I *will* be heard," if only to write myself down an ass more indelibly than as is. The spectacle of these little solemn donkeys [the trial judges] visiting the pangs of Atlanta upon crooks, be they never so villainous, by such verbal tricks, is more than I can bear.

To Hand, the lower courts' behavior was "dirty evasion," and he insisted that he would not be silent; his anger was all the more powerful for the graceful wit in which he couched it.[27]

Hand's humor was especially evident in the most technical, least emotionally engaging cases. For example, he would interrupt a carefully honed discussion of corporate taxation with a contemptuous sideswipe at fashionable jargon: " 'Group as a whole' is a '$50' phrase; it would please Jerome Frank [a leading legal realist of the day and later a colleague on the Second Circuit] and the Yale and Columbia Law Schools. Hail to the filii aurorae!!!"[28] ("Children of light" was a common Hand term for sentimental reformers.) Or, in a government suit that relied on alleged administrative discretion: "These bureaucrats will go just as far as they are allowed. I would not allow their ipse dixits (which I have looked up in a lexicon and which means, 'For he himself has said it and it's greatly to his credit that he *is* an Amurri*can*') to be the substitute for what the statute provides. . . . If we don't do anything now, we never shall,—we are really telling these highbinders that they can do what they damn well please."[29] And another case allowed Hand to fashion an excursus on the technical steps necessary to allow a foreign government to invoke sovereign immunity in a federal court. A seaman had sued a ship for wages, and the defendant claimed the ship was owned by the Portuguese government and therefore could not be sued. Hand argued that Portugal did not invoke the immunity properly, and then dissected the technicalities, leading to this passage:

> [M]ere proof of the fact that the particular cow you've got by the tail is a sovereign's cow is of no moment at all. You could have it proved by 16 bishops and it would not help a particle. The sovereign has got to come in, set himself up as a sovereign and claim his rights. He has to say: "I'm here, because I'm here, because I'm here, because I'm here. You can tell I am a sovereign by examining the marks on my linen. Being here I claim the cow; she is my cow. Come across with the bovine." Proof is nothing but claim is everything.[30]

Hand's memoranda quickly established him as the leader of the Second Circuit. Indeed, deference to his views was notable from his first year. Charles Hough repeatedly noted that a Hand memo had convinced him,[31] even when he could not restrain himself from commenting on their obvious differences. "The real difference between Hand and me," he once wrote, "is that his complex (which he has to call his conscience because there is no other word for it) balks at convicting anybody of anything [on] contradictory and slender evidence."[32] Julian Mack was even more deferential: his brief memoranda again and again echoed with the refrain "I entirely agree with LH's memo."[33]

Respect for Hand's view did not mean that the judges always agreed with him. In the more than one thousand cases for which pre-conference memos are preserved in Hand's files from his first decade on the Second Circuit, the judges agreed about the results at the pre-conference stage slightly less than 60 percent of the time, though their reasoning often differed. Hand was the sole dissenter in about 12 percent of the cases; in about 25 percent, he was with the majority on a divided court. In the published opinions, the court was more unified than that, unanimity frequently replacing initial difference at the judges' conferences. Hand was ready to speak out separately where an important issue of law was involved; but most often, he worked hard for collegiality and institutional harmony and served as a peacemaker on a bench where irritations, especially with Martin Manton, periodically erupted.

For example, Hand guided Mack in the mores of the court and curbed Mack's tendency to be excessively picayune in criticizing others' draft opinions. In 1924, he commented on a seven-page memorandum Mack wanted to send on a proposed Hough opinion: "The practice here has never been to go over the opinions with as much care as you have and I am rather afraid that it will annoy Hough a little," he told Mack. He himself always accepted colleagues' opinions "as they came unless there was some clear statement of law such as I could not join in. [I] seldom find another opinion which says the thing as I should have." Personally, he would have preferred to have each judge express his opinion separately in every case, "but the American practice" was "all the other way."[34] Thereafter, Mack typically sent his minor differences with others' opinions to Hand, so that the more politic Hand could communicate the criticisms to the author if he chose.[35] In late 1926, for example, Hand was instrumental in quelling an incipient battle between Mack and Manton.[36]

At times, Hand's trait of avoiding open disagreements with his colleagues unless the issue was important caused him considerable discomfort. Hand was a strong believer in precedent: as a judge of a lower court, he felt more duty-bound than most judges to follow Supreme Court holdings even when he disagreed with them; he felt almost as deeply that he should follow prior decisions of the Second Circuit in the interest of continuity and predictability. He often complained in his memos that he wished he had not joined in an earlier opinion yet now felt obliged to adhere to it. As he once put it, "I wholly dissent" from an earlier ruling, but "there [it] stands. . . . I have so often fallen in with a ground I did not approve of that it seems [now] rather hypocritical to accept this as the decision when it directly contradicts what I believe. Still, . . . I think we must say that it was the meaning of all the judges." And so he "regretfully" applied the prior decision in the case.[37] Or, as he said in another case, an earlier opinion by Gus Hand had "nailed down the rotten rule so we can't budge. I participated and I am gagged. . . . Holding my nose, I . . . affirm."[38] To Learned Hand, it was "only in a rare case that we ought to back out of our decisions, deliberately made."[39]

While the decisions of his own court carried a strong presumption that they were binding, clear Supreme Court holdings were even more authoritative. True, Hand would distinguish an unappealing precedent whenever possible. His own inclination, for example, was to recognize patent claims generously (although he saw signs of growing hostility to patents on the Supreme Court), and so long as there was no clear Supreme Court barrier to applying his own views, he would go his own way. But even when he felt strongly about the correctness of his own position, he applied clear Supreme Court precedent, although at times he urged that the Second Circuit opinion express its disagreement with "the Nine" in Washington. As he once said, "I cannot see any escape without overruling not only ourselves but the Supreme Court. [But] I suggest it might be worth while telling the hardship as we see it."[40] The Supreme Court precedents Hand found binding included those in which his own rulings were overturned. As he commented in one such instance, "I wrap my head in my toga, like your friend, G. J. Caesar, and fall before the daggers of ruthless men who do not understand the force of reason."[41]

Hand's strong sense of obedience to higher authority in the judicial hierarchy prevailed even when the issue was as central to his beliefs as the freedom of speech. Such a case came before the Second Circuit in April 1931, in *Gitlow v. Kiely*, challenging a postmaster's ban of an allegedly revolutionary magazine. Fourteen years earlier, in 1917, Hand had forcefully objected to such a prohibition, in one of the most speech-protective statements in American legal history, but in the intervening years, the Supreme Court majority had failed to follow Hand's *Masses* approach, and in 1926, the Supreme Court had affirmed Benjamin Gitlow's criminal conviction; as we have seen, Hand had strongly supported Holmes's dissent. Hand had not changed his mind about the protected nature of Gitlow's "subversive speech," yet now, as a circuit judge bound by Supreme Court precedents, he refused to intervene in what he considered a violation of Gitlow's First Amendment rights.

Among the publications with which Gitlow's criminal conviction had been concerned was one that was "substantially the same kind of document" as the postmaster now banned. To Hand, the Supreme Court ruling in *Gitlow* had answered "the only possible question here; we have no right to question that decision, whether we like it or not," and he urged a simple affirmance on the authority of the Supreme Court's *Gitlow* ruling. He probably would have preferred having the Second Circuit express disagreement with the Supreme Court's approach before applying its holding, but he knew that that was a futile hope. The memos of his colleagues in the case, Manton and Chase, showed no doubt at all about the justification for handing Gitlow another defeat. "If we get into a discussion of the theoretical limits of free speech," Hand well knew, "we are sure to get mixed up and probably shall not agree."[42]

As a peacekeeping member of the court, Hand avoided directing any of his well-known sarcasm at his sitting colleagues. True, he did not mind needling those he liked and respected. For example, he would joke about Swan's preoccupation with procedural and jurisdictional niceties. "I am treading as nicely as I can for I fear to arouse that Hircanian Tiger, T.W.S., on this procedure stuff," he once wrote; or, as he threatened in another case, "if TWS gets jurisdictional scruples I shall take to the woods."[43] Hand did not know what lay ahead: Swan's preoccupation was as nothing compared with that of Charles E. Clark, who became a colleague in 1938. Hand would typically refer to Clark, even in memos directed at colleagues when Clark was not sitting, as "the GLAPP"—"the Greatest Living Authority on Practice and Procedure." But Hand had no inhibitions about filling his memoranda with sarcastic remarks about incompetents who were not his colleagues, whether they were dead circuit judges, live trial judges, or lawyers.

For example, Hand assumed that all his colleagues shared his low regard for senior judge Henry Wade Rogers when he invoked his memory in a case that came before him, Swan, and Chase six years after Rogers's death. The case involved a weak claim by a defendant convicted of car theft. Hand wrote that he was tempted to limit his memo to saying simply that the case "is all bunk," as Rogers had once done:

> Once I had the honor to sit in a court with the Hon. Henery Wormwood Rogers, a knight errant of the law, well known for voluminous comment on the principles of jurisprudence, for penetration and scope, and chiefly perhaps because he never took his

eye off the ball, for he never saw it. He followed all the play but not the important player, him with the pigskin. If he got the ball himself and had an open field, he could have run as much as ten yards when he tripped over his own feet and fell; and when the play was resumed it was always found that he had made for his own goal. Now this jurisconsult reported on cases just as we do and his reports were models of condensity, for he never did any work on them. Once he said, "I think this case is all bunk," than which no memorandum could have been more complete, terse and adequate. I have always envied him this gift, which you will both agree the gods have not given me, as these remarks themselves prove, if indeed proof be necessary.[44]

Hand's sarcasm was far more biting when turned against poor lawyers and incompetent district judges, and he would occasionally berate himself for impatient outbursts in the courtroom, outbursts that caused some lawyers to blanch and shake. (Once, his critical questioning at a student moot-court argument caused a fledgling advocate to faint.) Hand was a gentle person, but he hated lawyers who wasted his time with unprepared or irrelevant arguments, and attorneys who did not respond to his sharp questions. Sometimes, he would simply turn his seat 180 degrees to express his contempt for a poor argument; at other times, he would urge a lawyer to get to the point or, if he did not have a more genuine contribution to make, simply to sit down. He did not limit his wrath to the inexperienced and the unknown: he was, if anything, harsher to renowned, highly paid senior members of the bar.

In the privacy of his pre-conference memos, Hand heaped contempt on the incompetent without fear of hurting feelings. Any lawyer ought to be disbarred for making so ridiculous a claim, he once wrote; the only proper criticism of the trial judge's challenged remarks was that they were "altogether improper in their mildness": "The only way to treat that miserable little wretch is to beat him on the head continually. I would have pardoned and commended the judge who did not let him open his mouth."[45] He called one "nagging" attorney "the most annoying trial lawyer I know";[46] he characterized another's brief as "rotten";[47] and he erupted in still another case with "This is the most miserable of cases, but we must dispose of it as though it had been presented by actual lawyers."[48] These periodic comments went on year after year: "The idiotic trouble with [this] brainless boob of a lawyer is,—how nice it would be if we could write opinions this way!— . . .";[49] "Oh, how my bowels yearn in pitch and pity for these ineffable lobsters. Lawyers! I could make better lawyers out of a garbage heap."[50]

The mockery aside, Hand was reconciled to the unevenness of counsel before him, and he got some comfort from the truly outstanding practitioners. But he was far less forgiving of below-par trial judges: there, Hand's ideals were at their highest, and failure to meet adequate standards was particularly painful. Appellate judges regularly reviewing lots of cases from a few district judges inevitably form opinions about the competence of the latter; Hand's memos were replete with sarcastic remarks about the worst offenders. The Eastern District of New York, covering Staten Island, Brooklyn, and Long Island, had an unusual percentage of marginal judges during Hand's years. His treatment of district judge Robert A. Inch in the confidential context of his memos is a graphic illustration of his critical judgment.

Inch served as a district judge in Brooklyn from 1923 to 1961, the year Hand died. From the beginning, Hand found little to praise and much to condemn in Inch's rulings. Latterly, he referred to him as "Judge Millimeter"; earlier, there were plentiful references to "Inch, J.—how well named he is"; "that ineffable Inchworm"; the purpose was so plain "that no one but Judge Millimeter could doubt it"; "What Millimeter, J., was thinking about when he struck out the other defences would amaze me but for other instances of that jurist's perspicacity and divine insight."[51] Once, Hand mockingly invoked the name of a series of great British judges in the course of castigating Inch, calling him "this modern Justinian" who

> managed as usual to do all he could to muss up the result when he refused to give [the] fourth request to charge. . . . We have got to find that somewhere in his charge Lord Mansfield gave the jury to understand that [the defendant] was not liable in such an event. Amid a lot of flapdoodle intended to be [cozy], Lord Ellenborough emitted the following. . . . That is the customary blameless inanity quite appropriate in the mouth of this great man. Fortunately after rambling along aimlessly for a long while, Lord Cockburn finally permitted himself the following. . . .[52]

Hand was sarcastic about Inch even when he agreed with him: "In spite of the fact that Inch, J., decided the case and seems not to have understood it, as usual, I vote to affirm."[53] Or, "By God, Millimeter, J., got it right. Let me note it on my tablets that a man may talk and talk and be a jurist still. At least 'tis so in Brooklyn."[54] Only very rarely did he find occasion to give Inch the kind of praise he readily bestowed on more competent district judges: "Inch, J., wrote a good opinion and . . . considered every point. . . . I vote to affirm on Inch's opinion."[55]

HAND NEVER PERMITTED sarcastic contempt to get in the way of full and fair examination of the cases. Similarly, his strong sense of the authoritative voice of precedent, and his deference to the legislature's choice of public policy, misguided as it might be in his own eyes, did not mean detachment and aloofness from the tribulations of mankind. Hand's memoranda resonated with awareness that the cases involved human beings, and he typically demonstrated more sympathy than his other colleagues. A strong commitment to fairness radiates through the memos: in his view, the people were entitled not only to be protected against oppression by government officials, but to have the courts attending fairly to the arguments; indeed, this conviction helps explain the thoroughness of his memos. As he once wrote, "I hope that in justice to the plaintiff Judge Hough will not dismiss this claim without some discussion. It has troubled me more than I suppose it ought."[56] Repeatedly he would say, "[T]his case has troubled me more than it has you two."[57]

Hand's engaged, humane view of the disputes before him is especially well illustrated by two groups of cases: aliens challenging deportation orders and criminal defendants attacking convictions. In both areas, his hands were tied. Congressional power over immigration and aliens is very broad, he recognized, and as a judge he could not legitimately argue with the underlying policy of alien legislation, no matter how cruel and perverse it might be. So with the substance of criminal law: Congress has broad authority to enunciate policies, misguided as they may be. Yet Hand could and did sympathize with the victims of these questionable policies, and he used every opportunity within the sharply confined limits of his discretion to come to their aid. As a judge, he properly insisted on procedural fairness in applying statutes; and with regard to especially heinous policies affecting aliens, he protested against injustices and pressed for changes in the law even when he was forced to apply it.

Hand again and again aired his pain about having to apply unjust provisions, even while most of his colleagues displayed no similar agonies—and sometimes, as in Hough's case, even took pride in safeguarding America for Americans and against "foreign scum." "I feel very earnestly about this case," Hand once said, "because the result seems to me cruel and inhuman. I must say I am shocked and disgusted down to my boots."[58] Soon after, he complained of "a particularly mean and heartless case": "These aliens are to be sent back to Greece because of a lot of damned red tape. . . . Doesn't it make you both ashamed?"[59] True, Hand was not averse to using the racial epithets commonplace in the 1920s: like his colleagues', his memos refered to "Chinks" and "Wops." But these terms did not bar sympathetic engagement. As he once put it, "I am a little sensitive in these Chinese cases: the jury goes into the box committed against them and the lawyers take their money and 'submit on our briefs.' "[60]

One feature of immigration law that particularly outraged Hand was a provision that allowed deportation of aliens for immoral behavior even if they had come to the United States as children and had grown up here. To Hand, it was disgustingly uncivilized to throw out such a person, a human being for whose behavior American society itself surely bore great responsibility. His memos repeatedly decried this policy as shameful. As he commented in one case, "She must go to a country as alien to her as it would be to us. Even if we ignore the conditions in which she was brought up, American conditions which we create, and if we treat her as individually and personally responsible—and so I suppose we must—the penalty seems to me monstrous for the offense."[61] He reiterated, a few years later, "It is a cruel law to exile a person who has been here since infancy."[62] Nor was Hand satisfied to limit his criticisms of the law to his memos and opinions. He engaged in lengthy, eloquent correspondence with the commissioner of immigration and with members of Congress whom he pressed for legislation to ameliorate these injustices, and indeed suggested draft language toward these ends.

Hand's humanity, concern with fair procedures, and awareness of his limited role as a judge enforcing the legislature's purposes similarly predominate in the criminal cases. Hand was not softhearted or sentimental: he did not assume that every criminal defendant's protestation of innocence was well based, and he rigorously deferred to the trial judge's assessments of credibility and resolutions of conflicting statements when there was substantial evidence on each side of a case. Moreover, in this as in other areas, he could spot lying witnesses when the testimony was clearly inconsistent or obviously implausible. Yet he steadfastly insisted that even the clearly guilty were entitled to fair procedures, he was outraged by overzealous law-enforcement officials who did not heed the commands of procedural guarantees in the law, and he never forgot that defendants were human beings.

Repeatedly, Hand regretted the injustice of certain laws even while he felt bound to apply them. "This is a hard provision, but I can see no escape from it as the statute reads, and as the Supreme Court has ruled" was a characteristic refrain.[63] To him, issues of fair procedure, especially procedures established by the Constitution, offered far greater justification for judicial intervention, and he did not hesitate to use his legitimate power. His numerous protests against the "disgusting practice" of imposing cumulative sentences when in essence only one rather than several crimes had been committed were not the only instances of his approach.[64] Like Benjamin Cardozo, Hand did not think that the constitutional guarantee against self-incrimination was always central to civilized justice, but he enforced it in appropriate cases. Hand felt most strongly that confessions must not be coerced[65] and that searches and seizures had to be curbed in accordance with strict readings of the Fourth Amendment.

The Fourth Amendment, which bans general warrants, insists that search warrants specifically describe the property to be seized and demonstrate probable cause that a crime has been committed, and in effect prohibits free-roaming intrusions into the privacy of a suspect's home or office, is one of the major restraints on the behavior of law-enforcement officers. From the beginning of the twentieth century, federal courts were required to exclude evidence obtained through illegal searches, even if the cost was to let the accused go free and even though the evidence seized was entirely reliable. As a result, the Fourth Amendment is a major battleground between the forces of law and order and those concerned with protecting individual rights. In this controversy, Hand throughout his career was on the side of the individual's constitutional guarantees and a vehement foe of overreaching law enforcers. His opinions on the Fourth Amendment—from rulings handed down while he was a district judge to those on the circuit court decades later—were widely quoted and influential; Supreme Court justices repeatedly cited them (usually emphasizing that they were relying on a Learned Hand opinion).[66] Not surprisingly, perceived violations of the guarantee evoked some of the most vitriolic outbursts in Hand's pre-conference memoranda. As he put it once, for example, it was "a high-handed outrage" that a federal law-enforcement officer had made "a blanket seizure of everything in seven storehouses" instead of a genuine, limited search: "Afterwards he began to sift out what he wanted. . . . This appears to me to have all the vices of a general warrant with none of its protection. To say that an officer making an arrest may clamp upon everything in seven buildings and take possession of it, is to countenance the worst kind of evils."[67]

No criminal law that Hand had to enforce in his years on the Second Circuit offended him more than the Volstead Act of 1919, adopted by Congress to enforce the liquor-prohibition amendment, the Eighteenth

Amendment to the Constitution. His hostility to Prohibition rested on reasons far deeper than his personal inconvenience: he liked a social drink, but throughout the Prohibition era, he dutifully avoided alcohol unless it was clear that it came from private stock bought prior to the act. A deeper objection came from the effect of Prohibition on a federal judge's workload. Hand's last years on the district court were darkened by an endless run of Volstead Act prosecutions, which he complained turned the federal courts into little more than police courts. But Hand's most basic opposition to Prohibition stemmed from his hostility to enacting a particular species of morality into national law, one visible consequence being that of turning millions of law-abiding Americans into violators and breeding a general disrespect for law. He had to decide numerous Volstead Act cases on the Second Circuit; he had no right to deny enforcement, for he realized that Congress had explicit authority to enact the law, but his private correspondence and memoranda are filled with sarcastic references to the absurdity of Prohibition.

Not until December 1933—when the Twenty-first Amendment, repealing the Eighteenth, was ratified—did this misguided era come to an end. Two months later, a case came before Hand's court in which a tax provision of the now moribund Volstead Act was involved. Hand could not resist writing a delicious, Rabelaisian tangent hailing the repeal: "God! How good it is to speak freely about it! Free, free, free!!!!" His eulogy over the grave of Prohibition characterized the Volstead Act as follows:

> Curst be its name, its memory, its parent, its fosterers, its de-
> signers, its sycophants, its proposers, its backers, its executors;
> curst be all who ever had part or parcel in that Sycorax, that
> Hecate, that blotch, that abortion, that stain, that blazon, that
> stench, that enormity, that changeling, that hybrid, that monster,
> that nightmare, that vile stew, that serpent, that horror, that nas-
> tiness, that misery, that Harpy, that miscarriage, that Hypocrisy,
> that snare, that delusion, that illusion, that ignis fatuus, that fraud,
> that venom, that damnation, that hallucination![68]

HAND'S THOROUGHNESS and attention to detail, the tightly reasoned persuasiveness of his memoranda, could be seen in many typical concerns of lawyers and judges—contract disputes, issues of statutory interpretation and corporate law, and torts cases of injuries to persons and property. But the fruits of Hand's special skills were especially notable in the fields of maritime law and patent law.

To most lawyers and judges, admiralty and patent cases are particularly arcane. Most maritime and patent litigation is handled by a specialized bar, with its own bar associations whose members seem to occupy a legal world apart. Yet Hand recurrently had to resolve disputes in these fields, and when Congress periodically considered establishing specialized courts to decide patent cases, he steadfastly opposed those proposals: he believed that it was healthy, for the judges and for the law, that generalists decide disputes even in specialized areas; he feared that specialized tribunals would produce unduly narrow judges.[69] And maritime and patent lawyers would have had little reason for worry about generalist judges if all incumbents had matched Learned Hand. From his earliest days on the bench, Hand evoked admiration for his mastery of these esoteric fields.

New York City, as a major port, had a century-long tradition of expert federal admiralty judges, but Charles Hough was the only one among Hand's contemporaries to achieve a renown equal to his; and no other judge achieved a reputation on a par with Hand's in the patent field. Hand's achievements were especially remarkable because he came to the bench without any background in either maritime or patent law. He had had no training nor shown any natural inclination for the complexities that are characteristic in disputes over mechanical, electrical, or chemical patents, and nothing in his legal background had acquainted him with the doctrinal paraphernalia that determined whether an alleged inventor had shown enough originality to claim a valid patent. Nor, except for occasional childhood ventures on a small sailboat near an uncle's hotel in New London, Connecticut, did he have any exposure to seafaring skills to help him adjudicate controversies over accidents on navigable waters or resolve disputes over cumbersome marine insurance policies.

Yet Hand quickly mastered the intricacies. The best illustrations of his skills are found in his decisions in numerous ship-collision cases. Hand recognized the notorious tendency of witnesses to distort the facts and was skeptical about the testimony he read as he waded through the voluminous records. Yet taking the statements at face value, he proceeded to test them for internal inconsistencies and against those aspects of the accidents on which both sides agreed. Then he reconstructed as best he could what actually happened. He would take pens and pencils and inkstands on his desk to represent the ships or piers and move them around to establish the courses described in the testimony. He would consult tide tables and weather reports and draw diagrams, and, from early on, he seemed comfortably familiar with seamen's jargon. This was not happenstance: among the first books he ordered when he became a judge was Knight's *Seamanship,* a standard manual that became his maritime bible.

A simple-looking case early in Hand's appellate career illustrates his skillful attention to detail. A steam tug pulling a heavy load of barges on the East River collided with the abutment of a bridge maintained by the New York Central Railroad. The tug owner conceded that his ship was partly at fault, but claimed that the railroad company should pay part of the damages because of the admiralty rule dividing the loss among all those at fault: New York Central had improperly maintained some wooden "fenders" that were designed to afford protection in collisions with the bridge pier, he argued. A lower court decision had agreed, and Hough and Manton both urged that the decision be affirmed without opinion; to them, the case was easy. (Hough, for example, did not even "know nor care" just what part of the bridge abutment the tug had struck.)

Hand was not so readily satisfied. His memo noted that "this pesky little case" had troubled him a great deal, because he had not been able to figure out just how the tug had incurred its damage only eighteen inches below its waterline. He consulted the tide tables and extrapolated from them that at the time of the collision (8:00 a.m. on July 15, 1924) the incoming tide was about two hours away from high water. Ascertaining the mean range of the tide at the bridge, he found that the tide must have been three and a half feet above mean low water; this meant that the part of the abutment protected by the wooded fender was under more than eight feet of water. Carefully analyzing the run of the water at the bridge, he concluded that the tug had in fact ripped away the loose fenders but could not have run into the bridge at the point where they protected it. And so he urged his colleagues to reexamine the case in light of his data, for these made clear that this was "not a question of weight of probability" at all, but that the trial judge, in finding that the tug had collided with that part of the bridge that should have been protected by the wooden fenders, had "found an impossibility to be a fact."[70] The case is characteristic of Hand's attention to detail, but highly atypical in terms of his effect: he failed to shake his colleagues' convictions; two weeks after his memo, the court affirmed the trial judge without an opinion.[71]

In a second collision case heard by the same panel of judges later that year, Hand was, characteristically, more influential. Like the tugboat case, this accident took place in New York waters near Manhattan; but this collision involved two ocean liners, one French and one German, that had collided near the middle of the Hudson River while leaving to head for Europe. The French ship, after leaving its Manhattan pier, was straightening out its course when the German vessel backed out into the river from a New Jersey dock on the west bank of the Hudson. Each ship mistakenly thought it had the right-of-way; in fact, in this situation each vessel was obligated to heed the other in order to avoid collision, and neither did. The trial judge, relying on mistaken views about the respective rights-of-way, found both ships at fault.

Hough and Manton once again limited themselves to pre-conference memoranda of less than a page each. Hough did not think it was his "duty to read all of this record"; Manton similarly found it unnecessary to determine how the collision might have occurred. Only Hand analyzed the facts at length, critically examined the testimony about each ship's maneuvers, reached an informed judgment about the specific place of the collision, and determined its cause by inferences from photographs of the damage to the French ship. To make his point clear, he drew a simple diagram showing how the stern of the German ship made contact with the side of the French liner and explaining why it was clear "that the Germans are right as to the angle of collision and the French are wrong." Further, he explained why an alleged precedent Manton had relied on was not relevant, but that the finding of joint fault was nevertheless correct because the German ship "kept on backing too long" and the French ship did not adequately act to avoid the collision: "Each acted on the assumption that the other would do more than she did. The safe rule requires each to do enough to escape collision if the other fails to do her part." Hand's analysis was not wasted even though his colleagues' more superficial scrutiny led to the same result; and the published opinion repeatedly echoes his thoroughness.[72] Similarly, in a fairly simple case of a collision in New York City's Gowanus Bay between a motor vessel and a barge being towed by a tug, Hand's memo delineated the facts with special clarity. Although the dispute merely involved the straightforward application of the Inland Rules of Navigation, determining what actually happened was not easy. But Hand's investigation lifted the fog:

> A line drawn along the pier-ends on the Brooklyn shore of Gowanus Bay is exactly,—so far as I can plot it,—at a six point angle to the long side of the pier. This means that a vessel running in the bar parallel to the pier-ends cannot be two points abaft the beam of one emerging parallel to the long side until the emerging boat crosses her course.[73]

Often, the cases were more complex than that, on the facts and in the law. Yet Hand, with unmatched familiarity with right-of-way rules and seafaring practices, dogged persistence in using all the ascertainable facts available to determine the causes of the accident, and a perceived duty to make the best sense he could of the controversies before him, produced a cohesive whole out of a myriad of small cases. He was modest about his abilities, yet he was not afraid to make the judgment calls that some of the disputes inevitably involved. As he once put it, "[I]t is always a little impertinent for us landlubbers to substitute our judgment for that of the man on the spot; we ought to give him the benefit of any doubt"; but he nevertheless went on to fault a tug master who had persisted in pulling his five loaded sand scows from Long Island toward New York City in the face of a storm rather than doing his best to reach a safe harbor on Long Island's North Shore.[74] Where necessary, moreover, he was ready to impose clear rules on the prevailing morass:

> I hope that we may agree upon a strong declaration that any such custom [of going on the wrong side of the channel when the tug deemed it unsafe to go where the rule required] is wholly unlawful, that we altogether repudiate the supposed excuse and that a tug which chooses so to obstruct travel will be held grossly at fault. . . . I confess to some feeling on the subject. . . . If these tows will choose to cross the bows of such ships, requiring of them quick movements in confined waters, it seems to me that they richly deserve what they get.[75]

Soon after, he was equally firm in urging clear guidelines for ships at sea:

> The law being in an entirely unsettled condition, I think that we ought to fix the rule we mean to follow, else the cases will continue to be at odds indefinitely. On the whole the best rule is that an overtaking vessel assumes the risk of changes in the course of the overtaken vessel until there has been an exchange of signals.[76]

Untangling conflicting stories about accidents by no means exhausted the duties of an admiralty judge. Frequently, the central issue was the computation of damages. In such cases, Hand's early skill in mathematics was put to good use, and he worked out the proper allowances and allocations with meticulous care. In one case, for example, the issue involved the allowance to a salvor who had saved more than twenty-seven thousand bags of coffee worth more than $300,000 from a shipwrecked vessel in a Mexican harbor. Augustus Hand announced that he did not "favor a minute analysis of the expenses of the salvors"; Harrie Chase eschewed all mathematical analysis; only Learned Hand went into the issues at length, with analytical rigor and his characteristic humor. (One problem in the case was the damage caused by the delay of the cargo in a Vera Cruz warehouse, where the salvor had stored it. Commented Hand, "I have been at Vera Cruz; the True Cross is said to have been a poor place to occupy, but it has nothing on Vera Cruz. However, it may not have been so bad for coffee.")[77] The computational skills these maritime cases demanded were ultimately no different from those Hand displayed in handling contracts, torts, patents, and bankruptcy cases. Yet Hand knew that a good mathematical mind was a necessary but not a sufficient talent for judging: each type of case also required a subtle awareness of the factual context; and Hand's abilities were equal to that challenge as well.

Patent cases similarly required judges to apply vague legal standards to complex issues of fact. The facts presented in patent disputes were even more remote for Hand than those in maritime cases, and the legal principles even murkier, but here, too, his intense absorption in the factual tangles and his untiring effort to make sense out of the legal rules quickly became legendary. As early as 1912, the Second Circuit, in affirming one of Hand's trial court opinions, had gone out of its way to praise the opinion as "most exhaustive," and as dealing with "the difficult chemical questions presented" with "the greatest clearness."[78]

The patent cases brought before Hand a breathtaking range of alleged inventions, from the most important to the seemingly trivial, from the Wright brothers' airplane and the electronics work of Lee De Forest, Reginald Fessenden, and Edwin H. Armstrong to methods of repairing runs in stockings and improving underarm dress shields. Year after year, his pre-conference memos reveal a remarkable understanding of the contraptions before him, a mastery gained through careful study, hard work, and lucid, forceful explanations of his modifications of received legal wisdoms.

As he did in the maritime area, Hand occasionally drew careful diagrams to make clear how an alleged patent was supposed to work, as when he scrutinized a complex machine to improve the making of handbags[79] or, with the aid of three sketches, delineated the difference between a patentee's method of making ladies' undergarments and that of the alleged infringer.[80] Hand was the only judge who regularly probed the facts sufficiently to explain them; and amid the technicalities, he revealed his humanity as well. In examining a complex new way of building a spring trap to catch animals by their legs, for example, he found the patent "plainly valid and a contribution to this bloody and atrocious art, which I wish might be held immoral."[81]

In many of Hand's cases, the facts were far more complicated than those involving women's undergarments and dress shields. Only a few months after he was promoted to the Second Circuit, for example, he, Hough, and Manton were confronted by a claimed infringement of a patent for electrically welding thin-walled tubing, the kind of tubing that might be used in bicycle wheels. The defendant had developed a faster method of welding; the central issue was whether he had infringed the plaintiff's invention. Analyzing this question required scrutiny of mountains of complex electrical, metallurgical, and mechanical evidence. Hand drew on his own resources when he could, as when he relied on his early geometry training:

> Since in the defendant's practise the pressure is radial to the tube, the greatest pressure will be at the centre of the line of contact. . . . Geometrically he is right, since the pressure must vary with the cosine of the angle which the direction of the pressure makes with the tangent of the point of contact.

Yet to probe the mysteries of the welding case fully, Hand was forced, reluctantly, to fall back on the conflicting testimony by the expert witnesses on each side. In the most lucid memo written in the case, he ultimately concluded that the defendant had not infringed the patent; still, Manton and Hough were not persuaded, and Hand registered a brief, modest dissent. The patent, he thought, produced its weld through a "single condensed shot" of current; the defendant had instead achieved his "culmination of heat" from "several diffused shots"; hence, there was no infringement. But, he added, "I have not [been] able to persuade my brothers to my view, and that inability has, very naturally, I think, added to the doubts which are inevitable under the circumstances." He did not see any point in spelling out the details of his doubts in "this complicated case"; the main reason for his dissent was to vent once more his hostility to the prevailing system of using partisan experts rather than court-appointed ones. Hand had argued for impartial experts ever since his first published article in his Albany days, and he continued to press for them, both in his opinions and in testimony before Congress. And so in the welding case he noted, "The system which submits such questions to the decision of laymen upon the evidence of partisan experts apparently satisfies the profession"; but in his view it was a very poor system.[82] He was more comfortable when he could rely on data other than the experts' testimony, as when he drew on uncontested evidence about the chemistry of inks to decide a dispute about a patent for making soluble inks for use on fabrics.[83]

When a new industry repeatedly raised its claims before his court, Hand had a chance to develop more confident expertise. This was the situation with respect to the developing technology of radio receivers. The battles among Edwin H. Armstrong, Lee De Forest, and others over rights to some of the most basic inventions that made possible modern wireless communication repeatedly reached the Second Circuit.[84] Many of these cases involved multiple patents and required long memos about such issues as the circuitry of audio amplifiers; Hand's memos ran as long as twelve pages.[85]

Underlying Hand's probing of the factual underpinnings of patent disputes was his concern with clarifying the legal framework. During most of his years on the bench, Hand confronted a body of law that ranged from useless generalizations to annoying technicalities. Much of his reputation was gained by his skill in laying bare in intelligible language what was truly at stake, and in castigating obscuring platitudes. His discourse on the recurrent issue of *when* a new device is entitled to patent protection shows this. What constitutes a "patentable invention"? Hand's response began with an insistence that the courts' frequent talk of "objective rules" by which to recognize an invention offered no real help. It was impossible to say that something was a breakthrough, a true invention, without considering what had gone before and what the alleged inventor's contribution was; not abstract rules but the context of a particular field was decisive. As one of his opinions put it, the "putatively objective principles by which it is so often supposed that invention can be detected are illusion, and the product of unconscious equivocation; the inexorable syllogism which appears to compel the conclusion is a sham."[86] And how much of an advance in the art did the invention have to represent? In Hand's view, the monopoly that Congress granted was available not only to geniuses, though an invention required more than routine craftsmanship produced. Somewhere in between lay the answer, and concrete contexts, not broad rules, had to be the guide, which made it all the more important that a judge pay careful attention to the factual context of the case.

> It would indeed be absurd to rank [as] invention [only those] great pioneers such as come only at rare intervals and are the work of genius. Indeed, it is precisely those which probably need no patents to call them forth; the stimulus of profit has little or no part in their production. The patent law is aimed at animating a lower order of imagination and skill than that; more, it is true, than the ordinary rub of competition automatically brings out from competent workmen in the art, but not the superlative skills. . . . When all is said, there will remain cases where we can only fall

back upon such good sense as we may have. [There] comes a point when the question must be resolved by a subjective opinion as to what seems an easy step and what does not.[87]

Yet to Hand this did not mean wholly arbitrary decision making; for him, this was merely to reject arguments that there were automatic tests to divine patentability:

[I]nventions depend upon whether more was required to fill the need than the routine ingenuity of the ordinary craftsman. Such a standard is no more of a will-o'-the-wisp than others which the law adopts, reasonable care, reasonable notice and the like; the effort is to fix that standard by recourse to average propensities, dispositions and capacities. Any attempt to define it in general terms has always proved illusory; it is best to abandon it.[88]

These statements from his opinions show the characteristically lucid, elegant language he produced when he wrote for the printed reports. In pre-conference memoranda, the basic ideas reverberate with even greater frequency, and in more pungent prose. For example, in a memo on a case involving a new kind of zipper, he commented that the jargon used in court was merely "an easy way of disguising the question, which really is, whether the collocation of the old slider with the old lock required more than the ingenuity of an ordinary boob, of a judge for instance."[89] And in the dress-shield case, he exploded at a lawyer's resort to a technicality: "While I agree that you can find plenty of saws about it in the books, I deny that it is a rule as to invention, just as I deny any such rules, except that an invention is a new article which the ordinary plantigrade bozo has not the wit to think of."[90]

The dress-shield case afforded Hand an opportunity to criticize judges who tried to dismiss patent claims by a shortcut, claiming to be able to determine, from the mere description of the alleged invention, that it was not enough of an advance to be patentable. A woman had devised a disposable paper dress shield to replace the traditional rubber one then used by customers trying on dresses in stores. The trial judge had summarily dismissed her claim without examining the factual context. Hand objected forcefully:

I can't say that no possible setting in the art might show this to be an invention; the test is of that setting and we can't know anything about it from the face of the patent. . . . Suppose that customers object to swapping armpits with earlier Janes who have sweated their fill upon the old ones. . . . I don't see why a girl who thinks that it is neater and tidier . . . to use [a shield] once and throw [it] away, may not have invented something. . . . [Yet our] friends, the district judges, like to get rid of such cases, because it saves them trouble. I'm absolutely set against it, and I want them to understand so. There is no issue, I maintain, more proper for . . . surrounding evidence than invention.

Hand's colleagues disagreed. Mack needed few words to conclude derisively, "Her invention, if it can be called that, consists merely in substituting the cheap paper in this temporary dress shield for the more expensive material in the more permanent dress shield; in that there is no invention."[91] Hand lost this battle, but he won the war: his insistence on full consideration of context, and his opposition to avoiding the context by using broad but wooden rules, became the Second Circuit approach; his patent-law opinions were the most cited by other courts and the most quoted by commentators.[92]

No area displays Hand's superlative traits as a judge more richly than his work in copyright law. His opinions over more than five decades as a federal judge continue to be cited and quoted, and when Congress revised the copyright statute in 1976, the legislators relied heavily on his insights and incorporated many of them. The important Hand opinions and pre-conference memos show how Hand creatively shaped the law, though he was unusually loyal to the authoritative commands from the Supreme Court and Congress. His copyright opinions are especially attractive because they arise in fascinating contexts, involve a limited number of pervasive issues, and illustrate his distinctive style and breadth at their best.

The federal copyright law that produced a steady flow of cases was the product of Congress's exercise of its constitutional power to "promote the Progress of Science and useful Arts, by securing for limited Times to Authors and Inventors the exclusive Right to their respective Writings and Discoveries."[93] Most of the cases arose under the Copyright Act of 1909, in force for more than six decades thereafter. The 1909 law, like those before and since, is filled with details about such matters as the formalities of obtaining a copyright in a work, but it left the most basic questions open to the ultimate decisions of judges interpreting the law; they, in turn, had little guidance other than American and English precedents and, above all, their own good sense and appreciation of the law's purposes. Neither the constitutional grant of power nor the statute explains, for example, who is an "Author" or what is a copyrightable "Writing." Moreover, though the statute speaks of infringement of copyrights, it does not explain when a copyright holder's rights are "infringed" by someone producing a similar work. Hand's copyright rulings, then, illustrate how even a seemingly specific law can leave very broad choices to a judge. During Hand's years, most of the answers came from the judicial gloss on the constitutional and statutory language; and many of the most influential answers came from Hand's own pen.

The basic purpose of the constitutionally protected copyright is to provide economic incentive to the production of original expression. The copyright power encourages Congress to promote artistic innovation by creating limited monopolies in the marketplace of ideas, and the notion that the monopolies are indeed "limited" is an important one: monopolies that are too broad restrict public access to information and prevent later creators from building on the work of their predecessors; yet monopolies that are too narrow offer the creative individual too small an economic return on his activities to ensure that he will engage in them. Ultimately, then, intelligent interpretation of the copyright scheme must balance against each other the interest in free public access and the interest in artistic incentive.[94]

An unsophisticated judge is likely to take sides between the competing images of the artist-as-creator and the copier-as-pirate.[95] One of Hand's great achievements was his constant refusal to divide the world into such angels and devils and instead to strike a sensible balance between the competing aims. In a wide range of contexts, from motion pictures to codebooks, popular music, and comic books, he never lost sight of the basic principles, and he never failed to focus on and articulate them.

Hand's copyright opinions and memoranda convey the sense that he enjoyed deciding them; they certainly are a joy to read. Often, the cases involved famous personalities and intriguing facts, though most often Hand made it clear that he did not think much of the artistic creations before him. His attraction to the issues stemmed in part from a humanistic judge's appreciation of true creative artists and in part from the intellectual challenges presented. The two pervasive issues of copyright law that recurrently came before him were, first, what constitutes sufficiently original "Writing" to be entitled to copyright protection and, second, when does an alleged plagiarist "infringe" on an author's copyright?

On the first issue, Hand took a very lenient attitude. The notion of "originality" had been read into the copyright law well before Hand became a judge, but its contours were still to be clarified. "Originality" might have been viewed as a requirement that the author had made significant advances over prior "Writings," and the judge had to evaluate the artistic merit of the author's creativity. Hand firmly rejected these notions.

In the very first significant copyright case to come before him (only months after he was named a district judge), *Hein v. Harris*, decided in January 1910,[96] Silvio Hein had copyrighted a song called "The Arab Love Song"; he sued to restrain the defendant from publishing a song entitled "I Think I Hear a Woodpecker Knocking at My Family Tree," claiming that it infringed his copyright. One of the defendant's arguments was that "The Arab Love Song" had little merit; indeed, both songs were of "the lowest grades of the musical art," examples of the then popular ragtime, and, as Hand put it, "all [had] the same general character," with "a monotonous similarity." At the time, Hand had no more background in copyright than in maritime or patent law, and he wrote his opinion without any citation of authority and without any apparent awareness of prior decisions. (He seemingly did not know of Holmes's landmark 1903 opinion that established the principle that the artistic merit of a particular work was not a factor in determining copyrightability.)[97] He insisted that the plaintiff's copyright was valid even though the song was "strongly suggestive" of earlier ones in the same genre and lacked creativity: the lack of

> originality and musical merit . . . is . . . of no consequence in law. While the public taste continues to give pecuniary value to a composition of no artistic excellence, the court must continue to recognize the value so created. Certainly the qualifications of judges would have to be very different from what they are if they were to be constituted censors of the arts.

At the outset, then, Hand recognized that "originality" in the sense of copyrightability meant no more than that the "Writing" was a product of the author's own mind; it merely meant that the author had not copied someone else's work.[98] More basically, as Hand perceived, a minimal requirement of originality ensured that the marketplace itself judged the value of the author's work. This followed from the constitutional scheme of relying on the market as a major means of encouraging science and the arts: though a judge might not think much of the quality of the art, the public's judgment was entitled to prevail and might indeed be no worse than that of judges.

Silvio Hein, the plaintiff in *Hein v. Harris*, was the first of many litigants to discover that Hand could be a damning critic even though he did not regard himself a "censor of the arts" in his official capacity. Fifteen years later, Hein's lawyer wrote to Hand: "Poor Silvio Hein never quite recovered from your characterization of his song as being 'in the lowest stage of the musical art' and as adding 'to the general degradation of the style of music which they represent.' I had great difficulty at the time in restraining him from approaching you with the view of convincing you of the artistic merit of his production." Hand replied apologetically, much as he often did after his outbursts of temper against incompetent lawyers in the courtroom: "I am sorry that Hein felt badly about my comment," but "that [was] nearly fifteen years ago and I hope I should not use such language any longer."[99]

Hand was not wholly averse to popular culture: he occasionally went to vaudeville performances and musical comedies, although his tastes in music usually reached no lower than Gilbert and Sullivan, which he adored; he liked the theater, but he rarely attended movies; he enjoyed creative literature, but he preferred Rabelais, Montaigne, and Shakespeare to modern novels and potboilers. In case after case, he aired his contempt for the works before him. In a 1916 case, he found that a song that was found to infringe "I Didn't Raise My Boy to Be a Soldier" was "of a most ephemeral and trivial character."[100] A year later, when he found that the motion picture *The Strength of Donald MacKenzie* had infringed the copyright of the plaintiff's play *The Woodsman*, it was obvious that he thought little of the latter: he characterized its plot as "trite and conventional in the extreme," involving "a simple-hearted and poetic hero, a north woods guide, who wins the heart of a person described as a society girl, whatever that may be."[101] Two decades later, in holding that particular defendants had not copied a popular song, he described one of the alleged infringers as "a one-finger composer who had no reputation" and whose "gifts were very limited," and another as a composer who "could apparently write the kind of treacle which passes in a popular love song, but such mawkish verses are reeled off by hundreds of poetasters all over the country."[102]

Ordinarily, Hand's sarcasms were merely asides. In holding that the 1939 motion picture *The Mortal Storm*, adapted from a 1938 novel, did not infringe the copyright of the plaintiff's movie script *The Mad Dog of Europe*, he described one difference between the movie and the script as merely an effort to make the piece "more sentimentally appealing to . . . immature tastes." And, in dismissing the plagiarism charge, he remarked that courts had become accustomed to copyright plaintiffs who, relying on "the finest gossamers of similarity," brought actions "without shadow of merit." Similarly, he criticized one litigant as responsible for a "cheap and vulgar plagiarism" and another as a "paranoiac" with "a persecution complex."[103]

Some of America's best popular composers were involved in cases before Hand; but Jerome Kern, Sigmund Romberg, Irving Berlin, and Cole Porter all lost. The most frequent litigants, and typical winners, were Tin Pan Alley publishers and run-of-the-mill composers, scriptwriters, and novelists. Usually, Hand immersed himself in complex legal doctrine, drew on his considerable knowledge of the best in art and music, and used his finest prose for the sake of resolving clashes between two pieces of pop art that he found essentially worthless. In this kind of litigation, the social goal involved—the promotion of "the Progress of Science and useful Arts"—was unusually clear, yet far removed from the reality of the cases. Nevertheless, Hand would labor arduously, even to the point of bringing pianos into the courtroom and scheduling special performances of plays that he would watch alone.[104] The frequently poor quality of the works before him never interfered with his analysis of the law: his low opinion of the works did not affect his conviction that a judge was never to be a censor, or his insistence that the market's evaluation was determinative, or, above all, his belief that originality was to be very broadly construed and that a copyright was to be recognized as sufficiently "original" so long as the author had not copied from someone else. Indeed, in more than fifty years of copyright decisions, Hand *never* found that a plaintiff's work was insufficiently original to qualify for copyright protection.[105] For Hand, then, copyright law did not often concern itself with vindicating the rights of truly creative geniuses, but, rather, protected rights through a complicated statutory scheme that advanced the "Progress of Science" circuitously and indirectly.

Hand was equally generous in interpreting the *range* of "Writings" for which copyright protection was available. Were "Writings" limited to words with meaning, or did nonsense words also qualify? This novel issue came before Hand three years before his promotion to the Second Circuit, in *Reiss v. National Quotation Bureau*,[106] a case that gave him the challenge of filling a blank slate, much as *Masses* had four years earlier: it was a rare instance of a trial judge being presented with a question on which there was no guidance in prior federal decisions and for which to find the answer he had to look directly to the Constitution. In an opinion of only six sparkling paragraphs that have been described as "brilliantly imaginative and convincing,"[107] Hand persuasively resolved the problem. As one commentator has remarked, *Reiss* "best represents Hand's judicial skills in copyright. The case requires neither difficult nor profound aesthetic judgments about truth and beauty and art, but rather clear-headed analysis of the interests involved."[108]

Edward D. Reiss had printed a book consisting of nothing but 6,325 coined words of five letters each constructed so as not to be readily confused with one another, listed alphabetically. The words, which had no meaning but were all pronounceable, were designed to serve as a cable code, and the book was sold to those who might use them as a private code by assigning meanings to the made-up words. The book attained considerable commercial value. The defendant copied parts of it for a standard commercial code; his defense to the copyright infringement charge was that there could be no valid copyright in a book composed only of nonsense words.

Hand's opinion argued compellingly that there was no justification for limiting "Writings" to creations that "already have a meaning." He relied directly on the scope of the copyright clause in the Constitution: since the 1909 law had purported to cover "all the writings of an author," he interpreted it "to cover all those compositions which, under the Constitution, can be copyrighted at all."[109] With that background, Hand moved immediately to useful analogies: "Suppose some one devised a set of words or symbols to form a new abstract speech, . . . a kind of blank Esperanto. [Or suppose] a mathematician were to devise a new set of compressed and more abstract symbols, and left them for some quite conventional meaning to be filled in." There was no reason to deny such creations copyright protection, he suggested.

> Not all words communicate ideas; some are mere spontaneous ejaculations. Some are used for their sound alone, like nursery jingles, or the rhymes of children in their play. Might not some one, with a gift for catching syllables, devise others? There has of late been prose written, avowedly senseless, but designed by its sound alone to produce an emotion. Conceivably there may arise a poet who strings together words without rational sequence— perhaps even coins syllables—through whose beauty, cadence, meter, and rhyme he may seek to make poetry. Music is not normally a representative art, yet it is a "writing."

> Works of plastic art need not be pictorial. They may be merely patterns, or designs, and yet they [are copyrightable]. . . . If [such] paintings are "writing," I can see no reason why words should not be such because they communicate nothing. They may have their uses for all that, aesthetic or practical, and they may be the production of high ingenuity, or even genius. Therefore, on principle, there appears to be no reason to limit the Constitution in any such way as the defendants require.

These simple but wide-ranging paragraphs were the essence of Hand's reasoning in this case. Beyond these, he said only that he could find no "remotely relevant" American case, though two nineteenth-century English cases supported him; he defended using these, even though they had come after the adoption of the American Constitution, on the basis of a remarkably broad view of constitutional interpretation.[110]

A final question—When is a creation sufficiently original to warrant copyright protection?—was decided in a pathbreaking Hand opinion of 1924, just a few months before he was promoted to the Second Circuit. The case was a copyright infringement suit against the composer Jerome Kern.[111] The plaintiff had copyrighted a song called "Dardanella," which Hand described as "being of ephemeral quality," and soon after the popularity of "Dardanella" had waned, Kern wrote a song entitled "Ka-lu-a" for his musical comedy *Good Morning, Dearie*. "Ka-lu-a," like "Dardanella," became extremely popular. The claimed infringement lay in the accompaniment to the refrain in "Ka-lu-a," allegedly plagiarized from the accompaniment to "Dardanella," a sequence of only eight notes, repeated again and again. This ostinato produced the effect of a rolling underphrase for the melody—"something like the beat of a drum or tom-tom," as Hand put it—and was designed "to indicate the booming of the surf upon the beach." The similarity was so striking that Hand had little difficulty finding that Kern had copied from the plaintiff's song. Kern swore that "he was quite unconscious of any plagiarism," and Hand gave him the benefit of the doubt, but that left the possibility that Kern had unintentionally, "unconsciously," copied the accompaniment. Could "unconscious" copying be an infringement? Hand readily decided against Kern on this new issue: "Dardanella" had been so popular that Kern must have heard it; in writing "Ka-lu-a," he must have "unconsciously" copied "what he had certainly often heard only a short time before." Hand added, "I cannot really see how else to account for a similarity, which amounts to identity." Since an author's "copyright is an absolute right to prevent others from copying his original collocation of words or notes, and does not depend upon the infringer's good faith" or intent, that Kern's memory might have "played him a trick" was "no excuse."

Kern had another defense that raised an equally novel and far more complex issue. Kern claimed that the plaintiff's copyright was invalid because substantially the same ostinato had been used by earlier composers and was in the public domain. That, Hand noted, was "the most important point of law in the case": Was it fatal to a copyright that the precise work had independently appeared before?[112]

In deciding that this prior use of the musical figure did not invalidate the plaintiff's copyright, Hand focused with unprecedented clarity on the differences between patents and copyrights, making it sharply clear that a copyright, unlike a patent, does not enable the property holder to halt *independent* efforts that produce identical results. All that was needed to establish a valid copyright was that an independent intellectual creation by the author had produced the work for purposes of copyright;

it did not matter at all that others had "anticipated" the creation so long as he had not copied their work. In short, the "originality" requirement in copyrights was once again interpreted in the most generous terms.

Hand expressed this characteristic of copyright law in one of his most quoted passages in a movie infringement case a dozen years later:

> [A]nticipation as such cannot invalidate a copyright. Borrowed the work must indeed not be, for a plagiarist is not himself pro tanto an "author"; but if by some magic a man who had never known it were to compose anew Keats's "Ode on a Grecian Urn," he would be an "author" and, if he copyrighted it, others may not copy that poem, though they might of course copy Keats's.[113]

The systems of patent and copyright that Hand clarified reflect two very different kinds of protection of intellectual property. Patents, extending over a shorter time period than copyrights, give the property holder rights against the world in his work, but bar him from obtaining a patent if his work repeats that of someone else, even though he did not copy it. Copyright, by contrast, gives the property holder only the right to prevent piracy, but ensures the freedom to create without fear of interfering with the rights of others, so long as he does not copy from someone else.

From these considerations, Hand drew his major insight: the two basic tenets of copyright law—that authors are protected in whatever they write if they do not copy from others, but that this protection only gives the author the right to prevent others from copying his work— necessarily follow from each other. As Hand put it in Kern's case, "[T]he rule of the patent law governing validity" is not to be "carried over into copyrights": "It appears to be very obvious that the rule as to infringement has, and indeed must have, as its correlative, the rule that originality is alone the test of validity."[114]

Hand also had frequent occasion to address—and gain even greater renown from—the second major recurrent issue in copyright cases: whether an alleged copyright infringer had in fact plagiarized an author's work. Copying is a critical ingredient of liability for infringement; the defendant must have had access to the plaintiff's work, and it is not illegal to come up with an identical work so long as it is arrived at independently. But this perception merely introduces one of the most difficult issues in identifying plagiarism: *How much* may the second author take before he passes the forbidden line?

Hand cast clarifying light on the basic principle that an *idea* is not protected by copyright and that the copyright covers only the *form* of expression. A copyright holder's basic ideas are part of the public domain and can be used by anyone, so long as not too much of the work is taken by the alleged infringer. As Hand put it in an unreported district court opinion in 1919, a copyright holder's right is limited to his actual sequence of words and to "any equivalent expression which gives substantially the same impression to the mind as the author's words." How much is too much was the recurrent issue. As in the patents area, Hand was skeptical of drawing the line via deceptive generalities; case-by-case adjudication would have to do. His contribution lay not only in writing his opinions with extraordinary grace, but also in developing a lucid technique for drawing that line. Limiting the author's rights to the expression rather than the underlying idea, he recognized, "is of the utmost consequence to freedom of thought."[115]

Two famous Hand opinions illustrate his style and skill. Each case involved a claim by a playwright that a motion-picture company had infringed the copyright for a play. The first, *Nichols v. Universal Pictures Corp.*, was a claim by Anne Nichols, the playwright of the enormously successful farce *Abie's Irish Rose*, that Universal was guilty of plagiarism in making a silent movie, *The Cohens and the Kellys*.[116] (*Abie's Irish Rose*, first produced in 1922 and involving Jewish and Irish families who feuded because of the marriage of their offspring, became the longest-running play in Broadway history to that time.)[117] In the second case, *Sheldon v. Metro-Goldwyn Pictures Corp.*,[118] Hand's most widely quoted copyright opinion, the plaintiffs charged that Metro-Goldwyn's 1932 movie *Letty Lynton* had plagiarized their copyrighted play, *Dishonored Lady*. (The movie was among Joan Crawford's first big commercial successes.)

Nichols, the *Abie's Irish Rose* case, illustrates Hand's characteristic approach. First, he described both the protected work and the putatively infringing one in a felicitous, entertaining style. Next, he found that the second work had indeed copied from the first and proceeded to examine whether it had taken too much. To do so, he identified a highly detailed common "pattern." Finally, he considered whether this pattern was an unprotected "idea" or whether, because of the similarity in characters and the parallelism in incident, it was "the very web of the authors' dramatic expression."

There was clearly some similarity between the play and the silent movie. Both were about a love affair and marriage between the children of feuding Jewish and Irish families. But in the play, the Jewish and Irish fathers were religious zealots, and religion was the major reason for their quarrel; in the movie, the major dispute was over an inheritance. As Hand put it, "The only matter common to the two is a quarrel between a Jewish and an Irish father, the marriage of their children, the birth of grandchildren and a reconciliation."

The pre-conference memos indicate that the judges had no difficulty finding that the movie had not copied enough to infringe Anne Nichols's copyright. Yet all three judges were convinced that the scriptwriters had deliberately copied parts of Nichols's play. As Learned Hand suggested, "It appears to me too probable to doubt that [they] knew of the plaintiff's play [and] that they copied some parts of it"; moreover, they had probably done so because *Abie's Irish Rose* had "proved so successful. [The] purpose seems to me plain to trade on her [Nichols's] success."

Only Learned Hand's memo went beyond the facts to consider the appropriate legal analysis. A "plagiarist must come closer to the original before the law takes hold," he noted. "How close nobody can say. . . . [I]t only confuses counsel to attempt definition." He concluded, with his usual aversion to simplistic absolutes:

> No standard probably exists; it is like invention; we must make the standard in each instance as it arises, with no better guide than general admonition on the one hand that there are variances which will not exonerate the plagiarist and on the other that it is only the concrete expression which the law protects.[119]

When Hand wrote his formal opinion—produced in less than two weeks, amid other pending cases—he included a brilliant discussion of the central considerations pertaining to alleged plagiarism. There is, he said,

> a point in this series of abstractions [about the general similarities in the plot and the characters of the play] where they are no longer protected, since otherwise the playwright could prevent the use of his "ideas," to which, apart from their expression, his property has never extended. Nobody has ever been able to fix that boundary, and nobody ever can. . . . In these cases we are concerned with the line between expression and what is expressed. As respects plays, the controversy chiefly centers upon the characters and sequence of incident, these being the substance.

To breathe life into his answer, Hand alluded to examples that would be familiar to literate readers:

> If Twelfth Night were copyrighted, it is quite possible that a second comer might so closely imitate Sir Toby Belch or Malvolio as to infringe, but it would not be enough that for one of his characters

he cast a riotous knight who kept wassail to the discomfort of the household, or a vain and foppish steward who became amorous of his mistress. These would be no more than Shakespeare's "ideas" in the play, as little capable of monopoly as Einstein's Doctrine of Relativity, or Darwin's theory of the Origin of Species. It follows that the less developed the characters, the less they can be copyrighted; that is the penalty an author must bear for marking them too indistinctly.

Hand's last sentence was not intended as a backhanded way of rewarding authors whose characters have depth and subtlety; rather, he wanted to emphasize that copyright protection at too general a level would limit the freedom of later writers to improve upon the efforts of earlier ones. Granting a monopoly simply to a basic "idea" would unduly restrict "the Progress of Science and the useful Arts."

And in *Nichols*, neither characters nor plots were sufficiently alike to warrant a finding of copyright infringement. His concluding passages echoed comments in his pre-conference memo about the difficulties of drawing the line; still, case-by-case analysis could guide one on the relevant considerations:

> Whatever may be the difficulties a priori, we have no question on which side of the line this case falls. A comedy based upon conflicts between Irish and Jews, into which the marriage of their children enters, is no more susceptible of copyright than the outline of Romeo and Juliet. [120]

The facts in the *Sheldon* case were more complex. Like *Nichols*, it involved a movie and a play, but there were two other narratives to be considered as well. The underlying story in both play and movie was based on an actual event, the trial of one Madeleine Smith in Glasgow in 1857 for poisoning her lover, Emile L'Angelier, a young Jerseyman of French descent, to whom she had written "letters of the utmost ardor and indiscretion" before she decided to marry someone else. And the authors of the play and the movie script were not the only writers to be inspired by the Smith affair: an English novelist had copyrighted a book, *Letty Lynton*, based on the same episode.

Metro-Goldwyn officials saw the plaintiffs' play, *Dishonored Lady*, and seriously considered making a movie based on it. While negotiating with the playwrights in the spring of 1930, the studio learned that Will Hays—the first head of the industry self-censorship system—thought the play obscene. Metro-Goldwyn therefore returned the play to the authors, but continued to hope that the Hays Office would relent. A few months later, in 1931, Irving Thalberg, the preeminent genius among Metro-Goldwyn executives, read the novel *Letty Lynton* and bought the rights to it. So now, in the suit, Metro-Goldwyn defended itself by claiming that its movie was based solely on the Scottish trial of 1857, which was in the public domain, and on the novel, and not at all on *Dishonored Lady*. However, the playwrights-plaintiffs asserted that there was "substantial identity between passages in the picture and those parts of the play which are original with them."

In the trial, district judge John M. Woolsey took Hand's opinion in *Nichols* as his guide—and concluded that Metro-Goldwyn, like Universal, was not guilty of infringement.[121] Yet Hand, in an opinion that a distinguished Philadelphia lawyer said "exhibits craftsmanship at its best and is entitled to be ranked as a model of judicial style,"[122] reversed Woolsey's ruling, finding that Metro-Goldwyn had in fact plagiarized the play. Even a critic who has argued that Hand's distinctions are too vague and subjective concedes that the opinion is "a virtuoso piece of writing."[123] Accolades such as these are largely directed at Hand's incomparably felicitous style in telling the story four successive times, as he had to: he was required not only to describe the historical incident about Madeleine Smith in Scotland, but also the play, the novel, and finally the movie. As another commentator has justifiably said, "Each telling is more delightful than the last, and, instead of boredom, a certain suspense is built up."[124] Yet Hand's opinion is even more impressive for the sheer persuasive power of its legal analysis.

The essence of Hand's skill in his tellings of the four versions of the story was not only to entrance the reader but also to point out the essential similarities and differences among the versions. To start with, the historical Smith fell in love with the Jerseyman, Hand noted, even though her respectable parents had sent her to boarding school: "They supposed her protected not only from any waywardness of her own, but from the wiles of seducers. In both they were mistaken."[125] She then decided to marry an older man, but her lover threatened to expose her by revealing her letters to him. She poisoned the ex-lover by putting arsenic in his cup of chocolate, but the Scottish jury returned a "not proven" verdict after hearing alibi testimony from her younger sister.

The plaintiffs' play elaborated considerably on the skeleton of the plot, which Hand described as "the acquittal of a wanton young woman, who to extricate herself from an amour that stood in the way of a respectable marriage, poisoned her lover." The leading character was now Madeleine Carey, a well-to-do New York woman, "intelligent, voluptuous, ardent and corrupt." Her lover and victim was an Argentinian, a nightclub dancer who regularly wooed her by "singing a

Gaucho song." Subsequently, she fell in love with a young British Labour peer. Her final visit to the Argentinian's apartment was designed to get him to accept that their affair was over. Instead, he lured her to bed once more and, as Hand said, "[t]he play must therefore wait for an hour or more until, relieved of her passion, she appears from his bedroom and while breakfasting puts the strychnine in his coffee." This Madeleine also gets off via an alibi, provided by an old family friend who claims (as falsely as the original Madeleine's sister had) that he had spent the critical night with the accused.

The novel *Letty Lynton* portrayed a young Englishwoman who, after an affair with a half-English Swede, meets an older, unmarried nobleman and decides to marry him—more, Hand commented, "because it is a good match than for any other reason." The Swedish lover threatens to expose her letters to him. "His motive," Hand wrote, "is ambition rather than love, though conquest is a flattery and Letty a charming morsel." Letty plans to commit suicide by swallowing arsenic, but changes her mind and poisons her lover instead. At a coroner's inquest, she is acquitted through an alibi she arranged by asking for help from a passing cyclist.

When Hand finally turned to the movie script, he told the same basic story a fourth time, and with great artistry. The notable similarities between the movie and the play—and the differences between it and the novel—emerged clearly. Thus, the movie, like the play, was set in New York's wealthy circles (relating the central character's decision to poison her lover, for example, Hand wrote, "Desperate, she chances on a bottle of strychnine, which we are to suppose is an accoutrement of every affluent household, and seizes it"), and each had a South American villain. Other characters were very similar; the incidents were often alike, including the actions of the jilted lover in "using among other aphrodisiacs the Gaucho song."

Woolsey had also tracked the plot and character in detail; he had concluded that the similarities were trivial in comparison with the large part of the movie taken from the public-domain material of the Scottish trial and from the novel. But the differences between the Woolsey and Hand analyses were far more basic than mere variations in counting the number of similar episodes. Woolsey dissected the play carefully and methodically counted the number of similarities and differences. Hand's ultimate point was very different from Woolsey's: he was trying to show not copying of details as such—to him, using the same city, a similar villain, and a similar alibi was simply a repetition of "ideas," insufficient to show copyright infringement—but how the details flowed together as a product of a writer's storytelling craft. He stressed that copyright protection extends to the way in which an author sorts through and presents the ingredients in his story. Woolsey took apart the works in question piece by piece; Hand, by contrast, watched the stories unfold. Where Woolsey sought discrete details, Hand perceived the larger patterns.

Sheldon was a close case, and Hand's opinion has been criticized for making too much of a few similar details, but that criticism misses the point: what Hand made clear was that protectable "expression" lay precisely in telling the story in a distinctive way. As one careful observer has said:

> The flaw in Woolsey's analysis [in] Hand's eyes seems to have been its unwillingness to find "dramatic expression" in the *sequence* of character and incidents. Detail by detail, matters such as the nationality of the villain, the sex alibi or the New York locale are not "dramatic expressions" that give the author of them the monopoly right to prevent others from using them. But when many such details are strung together, they become [quoting Hand's opinion] "the very web of the authors' dramatic expression, [the] essence of the authors' expression, the very voice with which they speak."[126]

After emphasizing his underlying theme that "others may 'copy' [the] 'ideas' [of] a work, though not its 'expression,' " Hand focused on the similarities in character and on "the parallelism of incident." He pointed out that a play may be pirated without using the dialogue; but Metro-Goldwyn *had* lifted "substantial parts" of the play, he concluded.[127] In short, the similarities in characters and sequence were the critical elements central to a plagiarism finding: Metro-Goldwyn's telling of the story had taken too much of the playwrights' work.

HAND OBVIOUSLY FOUND the copyright cases absorbing, in part because they provided an outlet for his interest in literature, and in part, too, because they were occasions to air his commitment to freedom of expression. These values were far more in evidence in another kind of case that regularly came before Hand, involving challenges to governmental efforts to ban writings as obscene.

Obscenity actions first came before Hand in his 1913 decision in *United States v. Kennerley*. In *Kennerley*, Hand had bowed to higher authority in permitting the jury to determine whether the novel *Hagar Revelly* could be banned from the mails. But the aspect of *Kennerley* that preoccupied him ever after lay in his compelling criticism of the then prevailing standards of obscenity. In *Kennerley*, he had argued against the *Hicklin* rule, the English judicial approach followed by American courts at the time, that permitted a book to be condemned as obscene on the basis of an isolated passage rather than requiring consideration of the work as a whole, and that also made the most susceptible audience, not the average reader, the measure of obscenity. Hand's *Kennerley* plea for a vastly reduced governmental role in censoring literature expressed his strong belief in freedom of expression.

Hand's work on obscenity cases during his years on the Second Circuit can best be understood as a ceaseless effort, behind the scenes as well as in published opinions, to infuse his ideals about freedom of literary expression into the law. He was remarkably successful in moving the Second Circuit in that direction; *how* he succeeded offers us another illuminating example of the creative capacities of a judge duly respectful of confining authorities. In *Kennerley*, he had set forth the arguments he believed higher courts should heed in dismantling the stultifying reign of *Hicklin*. After he himself became a member of a higher court, he could more openly advocate that the restrictive *Hicklin* approach should be explicitly repudiated. But not until 1936 did Hand have an opportunity to write an opinion in an obscenity case; by that time he could justifiably write that *Hicklin* was dead (a perception that the Supreme Court would not be prepared to articulate, with an acknowledged debt to Hand, until 1957). His pre-conference memos before then show that Hand deserves the lion's share of the credit for interring the suppression-oriented *Hicklin* regime.

The first obscenity case that came before Hand after his promotion was *American Mercury, Inc. v. Kiely*, decided in 1927.[128] This was an attack on a Post Office Department order holding the April 1926 issue of *The American Mercury* unmailable on the ground that it was obscene. The appeal was an effort to set aside a temporary injunction issued by the trial judge against the postmaster of New York and the postmaster general. The sprightly, widely read magazine was published by Alfred A. Knopf and edited by H. L. Mencken, with George Jean Nathan, a prominent drama and literary critic and the *Mercury*'s cofounder, serving as contributing editor. (Mencken and Nathan had established *The American Mercury* after their association on *Smart Set*.) The Post Office's obscenity condemnation rested mainly on two articles—articles that today seem incomprehensible bases for a ban even then. One was a segment of a monthly column by George Jean Nathan himself, a segment subtitled "The New View of Sex." Nathan commented wittily on the times' changing attitude toward sex, suggesting that it was moving from "a grim, serious and ominous business" to the view that sex involved "a very considerable humor": "Sex, once wearing the tragic mask, wears now the mask of comedy. And whenever one laughs at a thing, one is no longer afraid of it." Though the postal officials did not specify their reason for outrage, it may have lain in Nathan's passing remark that sex was often "purely and simply a diversion of man, a pastime for his leisure hours and, as such, on the same plane as his other pleasures."[129]

The government's second major target was a memoir, "Hatrack," by another prominent journalist of the day, Herbert Asbury.[130] Asbury, a descendant of the first American Methodist bishop, was then on the editorial staff of the *New York Herald Tribune* and engaged in writing the first of his many books, *Up from Methodism.* "Hatrack" criticized the hypocrisy of the fundamentalist preachers and their congregations in his Missouri hometown: it presented a sketch of a pathetic young woman, "Hatrack," who on Sunday evenings worked as the town's only prostitute, having sex with townsmen in local cemeteries in exchange for a few pennies—but only after she had attended church services where preachers condemned harlotry and talked about forgiveness, yet ostracized the young woman. Hatrack, Asbury recalled, would retreat to the cemetery only after she had been given to understand in church "that there was no room for her in the Kingdom of Heaven": "From the Christians and their God she got nothing but scorn. Of all the sinners in our town Hatrack would have been easiest to convert; she was so eager for salvation." Yet she never gave up hope "that the brothers and sisters who talked so volubly about the grace and the mercy of God would offer her some of the religion that they dripped so freely over everyone else in town. But they did not, and so she went back down the street to the Post Office, swishing her skirts and offering herself to all who desired her."

On the panel that heard the *American Mercury* appeal—Manton, Hand, and Swan—Manton was a staunch defender of established morals, while Hand had an equally strong reputation, ever since *Kennerley* and *Masses,* as a defender of freedom of expression. Their pre-conference memoranda were true to those expectations: both went immediately to the obscenity issue and differed sharply on it. Manton, in a brief, dry statement, found the articles "harmful," with "a tendency to corrupt the morals of the young, and their publication should be forbidden." Hand, by contrast, continued his campaign for enlightened standards that he had begun in *Kennerley.* Nathan's essay, he insisted, "certainly" could not fall within the obscenity ban: "At worst it goes no further than to belittle the going morality in respect of sex. It contains nothing which stimulates lewd emotions, however it may indirectly give rein to them by condemning the prevailing restraints upon them." Nor did Asbury's memoir contain anything that, "at least to normal persons, would arouse lewd feelings": although it described lewd conduct, "it makes it squalid, ridiculous and pathetic"; descriptions such as this could be banned only "when they present such conduct . . . so as openly or covertly to attract, not to disgust, the reader. The utterance must promote, not depress, the evil against which the statute is directed."

But the most important part of Hand's memo lay in his discussion of the legal standards appropriate for obscenity cases. "Obscenity" was limited to the "lewd or lascivious": "the evil aimed at is the stimulation of sexually impure feelings in the minds of readers, and by sexually impure I mean no more than the sexual appetite in its directly animal aspects." The "really troublesome question" was "whether the standard to be taken is the susceptibilities of the naturally lascivious or of normal persons." This brought "Lord Cockburn's remarks" once again to the fore. Cockburn had written the dicta in the *Hicklin* case, and one of Cockburn's observations widely followed by American cases was that books could be banned because of their effect not upon "normal persons" but merely upon particularly susceptible ones. Skills in distinguishing prior cases, either because they had not truly held what had been ascribed to them or because they were not binding on the Second Circuit, were once again Hand's tools in his effort to dismantle an abhorrent position. And once again he argued against the narrow *Hicklin* approach, which would make "unlawful all literature, however inoffensive to normal persons, because the inordinately lewd can find in it a gratification of their propensities. That seems to me an impossible test which would include medical works and nearly any fiction which described love in any other than denatured language. . . . It is an impossible standard to apply and would effectively destroy letters."

Hand next turned to a new question, "whether discussion which attacks the accepted canons of morals" was barred by the obscenity law, and his response was firm and eloquent:

> On that I am clear. Morals, like religion or politics, must be open to criticism, whether or not it be conducted in good taste or without offense to the feeling of others. An utterance is not lewd because it assails the canons of continence which generally prevail. While this may, by releasing readers from the restraints which those canons impose, predispose them to the gratification of their appetites and so indirectly promote the evil aimed at, it is within the range of debate and the possible evil must be tolerated in the interest of freedom of discussion. . . . The statute has no such

petrifying purpose and would be subject to the gravest possible
constitutional doubts if it had. . . . The question in this aspect is
similar to that of seditious utterances.[131]

These comments uniquely and justifiably linked Hand's views about
obscenity with those on speech that was critical of the government's
political policies. When obscenity suppressions were in fact disguised
efforts to bar criticism of prevailing norms, it was indeed appropriate
to draw on the distinction regarding subversive speech Hand had emphasized in *Masses*: talk that would only indirectly encourage resistance
to government views was protected free speech; only when the speaker
directly incited illegal conduct could such expression be banned.

The debate between Manton and Hand in *American Mercury* never
saw the light of day and never went beyond the confines of the judges'
pre-conference memos. For his part, Swan paused to take a more careful
look at the specific facts. He noted that the Post Office's condemnation
had not been issued until April 8, 1926, and pointed to Mencken's
affidavit stating that essentially all copies of the magazine had been
mailed three days earlier, on April 5. "The question of the mailing
and the number was thus purely academic." Mencken himself no doubt
hoped that the court would rule on the obscenity question, to remove
the cloud over future issues of his magazine, but Swan thought that,
on these facts, the trial judge's issuance of a preliminary injunction had
been improvident: such injunctions could be issued only to prevent
immediate, irreparable injury; and here, since the April issue had already
been mailed, no such injury was possible. Swan accordingly hoped that
his colleagues would simply reverse the injunction on the ground that
no case had been made for such relief, without getting to the obscenity
problem (although he ended his memo by indicating that, if forced to
vote on the merits, he would side with Hand).

Swan's way was taken by the court. Manton wrote the opinion, and
the district judge's temporary injunction was set aside on the sole ground
that the papers had failed to show that the magazine would suffer
"irreparable injury during the pendency of the action."[132] The battle
between Hand's speech-protective position and Manton's restrictive one
was postponed to another day.

In a 1930 case, *United States v. Dennett*,[133] a unanimous Second
Circuit reversed an obscenity conviction concerning the mailing of Mary
W. Dennett's scientific pamphlet *Sex Side of Life*, designed to provide
accurate sex education for children. Learned Hand did not sit in that
case; his cousin Gus Hand wrote the opinion for a unanimous court,
joined by Thomas Swan and Harrie Chase. Gus Hand concluded that

obscenity law was not "designed to interfere with serious instruction regarding sex matters unless the terms in which the information is conveyed are clearly indecent"; here the pamphlet tended "to rationalize and dignify [such sexual] emotions rather than to arouse lust"; and any "incidental tendency to arouse sex impulses . . . [was] subordinate to its main effect." He did not directly challenge the restrictive *Hicklin* approach, but his generous opinion lent itself, with only a little straining, to later invocations by Learned Hand as an example of the circuit court's refusal to follow *Hicklin* in judging a book on the basis of isolated passages.

Hand did not have another opportunity to participate in an obscenity case until 1934, in the litigation over James Joyce's *Ulysses*. The Second Circuit bench in this case consisted of Manton and the two Hands; Gus rather than Learned wrote the majority opinion finding *Ulysses* nonobscene; but the pre-conference memoranda disclose that Learned's influence was the most powerful.

James Joyce's *Ulysses* had been, as the brief for the claimants accurately put it in the district court as well as the Court of Appeals, "a *cause célèbre* in literary circles for more than a decade." Litigation about it was the most publicized obscenity case in American judicial history, in part because of the deliberate strategy of the American publisher and its attorneys.[134] The book had encountered difficulty with censors ever since its first publication by Sylvia Beach's Shakespeare and Co. in Paris in 1922. Americans had brought home contraband copies of the book for years, but officially the government considered it obscene.

The lawsuit that ultimately found its way to Learned Hand's court was the result of careful planning by a publisher, Bennett Cerf, and a lawyer, Morris L. Ernst. In 1925, Cerf had acquired the Modern Library series; two years later, he helped establish Random House and became its president; though not yet thirty, this made him a major figure in publishing. Random House's Modern Library had gotten off to a good start by publishing well-established classics, but Cerf was eager to publish *Ulysses* as well. As he recalled in his reminiscences, "*Ulysses* was our first really important trade publication. . . . Here was a big commercial book—with front-page stories to help launch it— and it did a lot for Random House."[135] In March 1932, Cerf asked Ernst whether he would defend *Ulysses* in the courts if Random House could acquire American rights to it. Ernst readily agreed, even though Cerf assured him that he could not "pay you fancy prices": instead, Cerf offered an unusual contingent-fee arrangement, by which Ernst would get a royalty on *Ulysses* for the rest of his life if it were successfully published in the United States.

Ernst's agreement to handle the case was predictable. As Cerf recognized: "He loves publicity just as much as I do!"[136] In fact, Ernst and his partner, Alexander Lindey, had already spent months discussing the possibility of defending *Ulysses* against obscenity charges when Cerf made his inquiry. Ernst had already made a name for himself in obscenity law: in 1928, he had coauthored a flamboyant attack on literary censorship; beginning in 1929, he began handling some especially controversial obscenity cases, including *Dennett*. As early as August 1931, Lindey had told Ernst that he felt "very keenly that this would be the grandest obscenity case in the history of law and literature, and I am ready to do anything in the world to get it started."[137] By October 1931, Ernst was speculating about the useful publicity such a case would bring: "Possibly the controversy attending the proceedings will aid the sale."[138] No wonder, then, that Ernst was eager to handle the case when Cerf approached him in the spring of 1932.

Ernst and Cerf planned the case with extraordinary care, shepherding the legal proceedings carefully and assuring at every step that there would be maximum attention for their actions and the forthcoming book. Their first step was to engineer a seizure by American customs officials of a copy of the book shipped from France to Random House. (Investing merely the cost of a single copy of the book was far more attractive than publishing it in the United States and then awaiting an obscenity prosecution; moreover, they made sure that the seized copy contained added material about the book—reviews and the like—so that these, too, became part of the evidence in the case.) In the briefs submitted to the district court and the circuit court, Ernst and Lindey began their arguments with quotations from Hand's 1913 *Kennerley* opinion, and they quoted far more copiously from Hand than from anyone else throughout. Moreover, they maneuvered adroitly, even at the cost of postponing proceedings by several months, to get the case before district judge Woolsey, whom they justifiably thought to be the trial judge most receptive to anti-censorship arguments.

The Customs Service seized the book according to the Ernst-Cerf plans in May 1932, and by December the government had filed a proceeding to condemn it. Another year passed before, on December 6, 1933, Woolsey handed down his decision finding *Ulysses* not obscene,[139] a ruling that received enormous coverage. Cerf quickly published the book in his Modern Library series, with a brief foreword by Ernst and the full text of Woolsey's opinion. (The Woolsey opinion became one of the most widely read judicial opinions in history, for it appeared in every one of the hundreds of thousands of copies Random House sold.) "The New Deal in the law of letters is here," Ernst began.

> It would be difficult to overestimate the importance of Judge Wool-
> sey's decision. . . . It is a body blow for the censors. [Woolsey's
> opinion] raises him to the level of former Supreme Court Justice
> Oliver Wendell Holmes as a master of judicial prose.

And Ernst went on to rejoice: "The first week of December 1933 will
go down in history for two repeals, that of Prohibition and that of the
legal compulsion for squeamishness in literature. [We] may now imbibe
freely of the contents of bottles and forthright books."[140]

Woolsey and *Ulysses* were made for each other. Woolsey had come
to the federal court as a skilled admiralty lawyer, but his personal
idiosyncracies soon overshadowed his professional abilities. Sporting a
gold ring around his cravat and almost invariably waving an ivory
cigarette holder or a long-stemmed pipe, the ruddy-cheeked Woolsey
behaved and often wrote quite flamboyantly. He loved the late eighteenth
century: Samuel Johnson was his demigod (Woolsey tried to collect
every Johnson first edition available), and he fancied himself an expert
in the architecture and furnishings of Colonial America.[141] Hand's files
contain photographs that Woolsey had taken of himself wearing the
wig and robes of an English judge, photos Woolsey proudly circulated
among his fellow judges.

Judge Woolsey's reputation was built less on any command of legal
niceties than on his "literary" writing and rhetorical flourishes, and of
these there were many in his opinion in *United States v. One Book
Called "Ulysses."* Much of it was a quite persuasive depiction of the
purpose of Joyce's stream-of-consciousness style; one commentator who
thought he was praising Woolsey's ruling aptly described it as "a decision
which read like an exceptionally intelligent and enthusiastic book review."[142] Woolsey's opinion was indeed readable, quotable, and not
excessively burdened with legal analysis. He concluded that *Ulysses* was
"a sincere and honest book, and I think that the criticisms of it are
entirely disposed of by its rationale." Woolsey's personal reactions to
the book, and those of friends he had consulted about it, filled most of
the opinion; the legal standards for obscenity were barely addressed.
The near circus atmosphere generated by his ruling and the ensuing
book publication preoccupied the press for weeks. Government attorneys
recommended against an appeal, but after weeks of indecision, a newly
appointed U.S. attorney, Martin Conboy (once a lawyer for Anthony
Comstock's anti-vice crusade), decided to press on to the Second Circuit.

By the time the arguments began in the Second Circuit's courtroom,
on May 16, 1934, thirty-five thousand copies of the Random House
edition had been sold. Before a bench composed of Martin Manton and

the two Hands, Conboy condemned the book as "filthy, offensive to modesty and subversive to decency."[143] In his brief, he rested squarely on the continued vitality of the *Hicklin* test, and in his oral argument, after describing the book as dealing with "one day in the life of a Hungarian Jew in Dublin, together with his thoughts and ruminations and those of his wife," insisted on spending hours reading lengthy passages aloud, with emphasis on Joyce's concluding forty-six pages, "the stream-of-thought soliloquizing of Mrs. Molly Bloom at the end of a hard day,"[144] a soliloquy that is widely considered to be one of the finest, as well as most erotic, passages in modern literature. The newspapers had a field day describing the "three solemn, elderly gentlemen" on the bench "staring self-consciously" at the book while the U.S. attorney, "flushed and determined," voiced Molly Bloom's reverie. At one point, Learned Hand interrupted Conboy to ask, "Are you going to read the whole book?" "Well, I'll give you a generous sampling," Conboy replied. Hand persisted: "Do you believe the court should read it?" "No," Conboy replied, "I will read a generous sampling from this product of the gutter. I do not believe it will be necessary for your Honors to read the entire book." To Hand, the government's emphasis on a selected passage rather than the whole book clearly demonstrated the weakness of Conboy's case under the obscenity standards he had advocated ever since *Kennerley*.[145]

The pre-conference memos in the *Ulysses* case reveal three distinctive minds at work, with the Hands on one side and Manton clearly on the other. To Manton, it was clear that the *Hicklin* rule was the appropriate standard. He wrote: "The last pages of this book clearly support the charge against it—that is, that the tendency of the novelist [is] to excite lustful and lecherous desires." Gus Hand, on the contrary, believed that "[m]uch standard literature will be excluded if we do not hold that a book is to be judged as a whole in respect to general effect and objective purpose." Still, he was always the sober judge, never an enthusiast, and far less enamored of Joyce than Woolsey had been: "I think the greatness of the book is somewhat exaggerated but that it is powerful a careful reading seems to me to demonstrate":

> Perhaps the monologue of Mrs. Bloom in its immediate effect is erotic but on the whole it is pitiful and tragic and much of the book is so. The comedy in it is mixed up with the tragedy. I think it is less light than such passages as that where Rabelais describes the bridegroom who went to bed with a mallet. Such humor is simply coarse and not erotic at all, whereas some of "Ulysses" certainly is.

But none of this warranted finding the book obscene.

In his laconic way, Gus Hand made clear he was better acquainted with literature than Woolsey claimed to be, and more sensitive to Joyce's basic purpose: "The lampoons on religion and sacraments and priests and nuns are very rough and coarse but that is old stuff that we have no right to deal with as such. . . . The same attack of course might be, and is made, on the Protestant clergy and I have known of the fall of many of them who were prominent from accepted morals." (Long a senior warden of one of the oldest Episcopal churches in the city, Hand had reason to know.) And above all, "I cannot say the 'Ulysses' deals in smut for smut's sake or is calculated to be read generally." In his subdued way, he was by now moving closer to Learned's level of commitment to freedom of literary expression: "If we held *Ulysses* obscene as a matter of law we should be forced to the same conclusion as to Venus and Adonis, Ovid's Art of Love, certain poems of Catullus and many other classics." Still, he was not prepared to embrace Learned's permissive approach in its entirety.

Learned Hand clearly had a higher opinion of *Ulysses* than either of his colleagues: he called it "a very notable contribution to literature." More important, he tackled the precedents on which the government had relied and the underlying policy issues obscenity cases presented. He conceded at the outset that there were passages in the book "which could excite lustful feelings not only in the mind of a youthful person, but of a normal adult." If that were enough, "the book ought to be condemned." But, he added, "I think that it is not enough." A lower federal court decision had indeed endorsed judging a book on the basis of selected passages, but, he argued, another case had in effect repudiated this, and he hoped "very much" that the Second Circuit would now "expressly overrule . . . the doctrine . . . saying that nobody can have lawful access to any works any part of which may harm young people. Whatever courts may say, they would not live up to any such doctrine as that."

Characteristically, Hand addressed the most basic issues:

> Different occasions involve interests of different value and the result depends on how the law appraises the values at stake. If a man writes a book which is all libidinous, he has and should have no immunity. But there are themes whose truthful and complete expression involves what taken alone ought to have no immunity; the whole portrayal does not excite libidinous feelings. The conflicting interests are the freedom of authors to express themselves fully and as they wish as against the debauching of their readers'

> minds. . . . [I]t is clear that without taking the work as a whole
> we cannot decide; [there] is an interest in completeness of expres-
> sion even when it leads to matter sexually exciting. Personally I
> should be disposed to make relevance the test almost always.

But Hand himself doubted that his court was willing to go quite so far
in embracing his "relevance" test. And so he concluded:

> Here at any rate the offending passages are clearly necessary to the
> epic of the soul as Joyce conceived it, and the parts which might
> be the occasion for lubricity in the reader are to my thinking not
> sufficient to condemn a very notable contribution to literature.[146]

By the time the judges conferred about these memoranda, it was
clear that they could not arrive at a unanimous opinion. Gus Hand,
who like Learned was annoyed about the enormous flood of publicity
the litigation had already generated, urged: "In my opinion we should
affirm without opinion. It will give the book a minimum of adver-
tising." But Manton was determined to write a strong dissent proclaiming his moral righteousness. Thus, a majority opinion on behalf of the
Hands became essential. Yet how was that to be produced without
following in Woolsey's footsteps and providing grist for the publicity
mill?

Learned Hand certainly did not want the Second Circuit to rebuke
Woolsey personally; all he sought was to discourage judicial opinions
as performances in a publicity circus. With respect to Woolsey himself,
Hand's evaluation was measured and temperate. Reminiscing years later,
when in his late eighties, he said, "I came to like [Woolsey], to be
very fond of him," but he had only limited respect for Woolsey's judicial
work: "I never thought [it] showed much acuteness and perception.
. . . He was a bit of a show-off, . . . given to phrases." That would
have been acceptable if Woolsey's typical phrases had been apt and of
high quality. But, as *Ulysses* demonstrated, "[M]ost of them weren't
—and yet they got a great deal of quoting." Woolsey clearly thought
himself "literary," but, as Hand commented, "[T]hat's a very dangerous
thing for a judge to be. I didn't say it was a *bad* quality; I said it was
a dangerous one. . . . If [a judge is] brilliant, that's very good. [But
that requires] a complete aptness for the occasion." And Woolsey's
weakness for language was "not perfectly apt."[147]

Faced, then, with the need to produce an opinion that would clarify
the law, reject Manton's approach, but not insult Woolsey, Gus and
Learned agreed that the opinion affirming Woolsey's ruling should, if
at all possible, contain "not a single quotable line." Given this goal,

the choice of the author was inevitable: the cousins both recognized that Learned would have a hard time producing an opinion devoid of quotable language no matter how hard he tried; solid, plainspoken Gus was clearly the right choice.

As it turned out, Gus Hand's opinion in *Ulysses* was not so colorless as his opinions often were, perhaps because he was prompted to vividness by Manton's unusually long and contemptuous dissent.[148] Manton insisted that the *Hicklin* rule stood unimpaired; he argued that a court "cannot indulge any instinct it may have to foster letters" and ended with this peroration:

> The people need and deserve a moral standard; it should be a point of honor with men of letters to maintain it. Masterpieces have never been produced by men given to obscenity or lustful thoughts—men who have no Master. . . . A refusal to imitate obscenity or to load a book with it is an author's professional chastity. Good work in literature . . . requires . . . a human aim—to cheer, console, purify, or ennoble the life of people. . . . It is by good work only that men of letters can justify their right to a place in the world.[149]

Gus Hand's majority opinion was laconic by comparison. It focused on clarifying the law, essentially in the direction Learned had set forth in his pre-conference memorandum. And the legal conclusion Gus drew was very similar to that which Learned had long advocated. The obscenity statute, he insisted, should not apply to literature

> where the presentation, when viewed objectively, is sincere, and the erotic matter is not introduced to promote lust and does not furnish the dominant note of the publication. The question in each case is whether the publication taken as a whole has a libidinous effect. The book before us has such portentous length, is written with such evident truthfulness in its depiction of certain types of humanity, and is so little erotic in its result, that it does not fall within the forbidden class.[150]

Gus Hand acknowledged that *Ulysses* had "become a sort of contemporary classic," but added, "We may discount the laudation of *Ulysses* by some of its admirers and reject the view that it will permanently stand among the great works of literature." Still, he thought, borrowing Learned's formulation, it was "sincere, truthful, relevant to the subject, and executed with real art." Such a book "of artistic merit and scientific insight" could not be condemned as obscene.

Despite a conscious effort at self-control, Gus Hand not only wrote a lucid statement of ideas for which his cousin had been chief advocate, but also produced more literary and quotable prose than either of them thought appropriate for the case. Still, he could take satisfaction that his analysis was germane to the legal issues.

The law of obscenity in the Second Circuit had come a long way indeed from the shape it had been in when Learned Hand first encountered it in *Kennerley* in 1913. With *Ulysses*, the *Hicklin* approach was dead. Another two years passed before Hand had a chance to speak for his court at last and to restate the position he had shaped so tirelessly over the years. This opportunity came in 1936, in *United States v. Levine.*[151]

Levine had been convicted for mailing obscene advertisements for several books that were quite close to run-of-the-mill pornography. The books were *Secret Museum of Anthropology*, a collection of photos of "female savages"; *Crossways of Sex*, a pseudo-scientific treatise on sexual pathology; and *Black Lust*, a fictional study of sadism and masochism that Hand found "of considerable merit, but patently erotic," adding that it "would arouse libidinous feelings in almost any reader." The Second Circuit panel consisted once again of the two Hands and Manton. Predictably, Manton had no difficulty in labeling all three books as "obscene." Gus's pre-conference memorandum cited both *Crossways of Sex* and *Black Lust* as obscene. In Learned's view, only *Black Lust* could be found obscene by a jury.

Gus, as if to underline the differences between himself and Learned, made it clear that he was not willing to apply Learned's speech-protective approach to materials that were not endorsed by "respectable" people. "The works are neither classics, nor in any proper sense works of science," he emphasized in his memo; instead, they were "pornographic and designed to reach the class of readers who are after that sort of stuff."[152] He was unenthusiastic about obscenity prosecutions, but the practicalities were most persuasive to him: he doubted that obscenity laws really served their purpose; their main effect seemed to be to "greatly promote distribution" of the books sought to be banned. For Learned, by contrast, a broad-ranging freedom of literary expression— one aspect of freedom of thought and speech—was the central concern. And free expression was not limited to high literature or pure science; to him, it was precisely in the application of protective standards to more marginal writings that true protection of speech would be assured.

Fortunately, there was no need in the reported opinion in the *Levine* case to explore the obscenity of the books. Instead, Learned Hand announced that the conviction was reversed solely because the trial judge had not charged the jury adequately about the proper standards. And this in turn allowed him to make crystal clear the hard-won protections of *Ulysses*; it is undoubtedly his best as well as most authoritative writing on the subject of obscenity.

In his memorandum, Hand emphasized his perception that the district judge "was clearly wrong in his charge about the class of people whom the statute protects." The trial judge had been confused, "hopelessly at sea about the whole thing; he didn't know what he thought and first said one thing and then another." From his charge, "the jury could not conceivably know what he did mean; the charge was a mere jumble of words, . . . mere nonsense."

The focus of Hand's memo became the theme of his opinion. But assuring that his approach would be adopted by a majority of his court was no easy task. The division among the judges was unusual: Manton, even while condemning the books as obscene, reluctantly agreed that the charge was "contradictory" and unacceptable after *Ulysses*. That meant two votes for reversal of the guilty verdict. Yet Gus Hand was reluctant to make it unanimous. While agreeing that the trial judge "was mixed up as to his charge," he was unsure that this was a valid ground for reversal: he considered the obscenity of the books so clear that the jury verdict "ought to stand in spite of some inconsistencies of the charge."

Eventually, a Learned Hand majority opinion emerged, based on an awkward coalition. It noted that Learned Hand and Manton believed the mistakes in the jury charge "were serious enough to upset the conviction," though adding that Augustus Hand thought some of the material "was so plainly obscene that the errors may be disregarded." Only by having a majority agreement (by Learned Hand and Manton) that the case should go back for a new trial could Learned write an opinion (endorsed by him and Gus) couched as guidance for the second trial. This tenuous foothold was sufficient to support a magnificent restatement of where obscenity law stood at the time.

Hand's *Levine* opinion allowed him to repeat for the official reports the arguments he had made about the precedents in his memos in both *American Mercury* and *Ulysses*, and he provided his own incomparable gloss on the reasons that justified a truly speech-protective view. Most of the perceptions in his confidential memos of the past were now published for the guidance of the future. The earlier, more restrictive doctrine of the *Hicklin* era, he wrote,

> necessarily presupposed that the evil against which the statute is directed so much outweighs all interests of art, letters or science, that they must yield to the mere possibility that some prurient

person may get a sensual gratification from reading or seeing what to most people is innocent and may be delightful or enlightening. No civilized community not fanatically puritanical would tolerate such an imposition. . . . As so often happens, the problem is to find a passable compromise between opposing interests, whose relative importance, like that of all social or personal values, is incommensurable. We impose such a duty upon a jury . . . because the standard they fix is likely to be an acceptable mesne and because in such matters a mesne most nearly satisfies the moral demands of the community. There can never be constitutive principles for such judgments, or indeed more than cautions to avoid the personal aberrations of the jurors. We mentioned some of these in [*Ulysses*].

In his own summary of what he claimed had been established by *Ulysses*, a single sentence expressed not only all of the guidance found in Gus Hand's many *Ulysses* paragraphs but also his own elaborations of the principles of that case. The determinative "cautions," as Learned Hand saw them, were that

the work must be taken as a whole, its merits weighed against its defects; if it is old, its accepted place in the arts must be regarded; if new, the opinions of competent critics and published reviews or the like may be considered; what counts is its effect not upon any particular class, but upon all those whom it is likely to reach. Thus "obscenity" is a function of many variables, and the verdict of the jury is not the conclusion of a syllogism of which they are to find only the minor premises, but really a small bit of legislation ad hoc, like the standard of care.[153]

Levine was the apex of the most speech-protective position for which Learned Hand could find support on his court. True, this did not go as far as he would have wanted, but it did bury *Hicklin* once and for all, more crisply and more clearly than ever. Another twenty-one years passed before the Supreme Court, in *Roth v. United States*,[154] was ready to agree that *Hicklin* was indeed dead, that a book had to be taken as a whole rather than on the basis of selected passages, and that the response of the average reader, not of those most susceptible, was critical in determining obscenity.

In these obscenity cases, Hand demonstrated his characteristic traits. Repeatedly, he argued that allegedly binding and widely followed precedents had not in fact held what they were assumed to have decided; he perceived the underlying value conflicts at stake and steadfastly delineated the proper path out of the morass; and he managed to fashion new law even though he was genuinely respectful of the binding commands of legislative judgments and applicable decisions. And, especially, he left no doubt that he was impelled to work so assiduously over so many years to achieve a more enlightened view of the law because of his deep commitment to a liberal skeptic's basic belief—a commitment to freedom of thought and expression.

VIII

Achieving National Renown During the Nation's Complacent Years, 1919–1928

BY THE END OF WORLD WAR I, after a decade on the bench, Hand was already considered an excellent judge in New York professional circles, but he was not yet nationally known. Soon, however, his reputation would rise dramatically: by 1930 he had received serious consideration for appointment to the United States Supreme Court.

Hand's growing national stature was not the result of increasing involvement in public controversies. To the contrary: his attitude about the propriety of a judge's participation in partisan politics changed in the opposite direction. In 1912 and 1913, he had felt few compunctions about being active in the Progressive–Bull Moose campaign, even to the point of running as a candidate for the highest state court while holding a lifetime position on the federal bench. After World War I, by contrast, he became self-conscious and restrained about such activities, typically refusing public identification with causes that could be seen as "agitation" or "propaganda." By November 1922, for example, Hand had firmly insisted, "If [a judge] is to become actively interested in politics, I think he should resign."[1]

Of course, the political environments of the prewar and postwar years differed greatly. Teddy Roosevelt's pleas to invoke national powers in order to deal with America's economic and social problems had stirred a unique enthusiasm in Hand. In the 1920s, by contrast, no such persuasive and charismatic leader was in sight. Hand had vast contempt for Harding (he had hoped the Republicans would nominate Herbert Hoover) and nearly as much for Coolidge; he voted for their Democratic rivals because they seemed the lesser evils; and in a drab political atmosphere, the temptation to participate actively in politics diminished sharply.

But the more important, basic explanation for Hand's postwar abstention from "agitation" lay elsewhere. The central truth was that an older, wiser, and more reflective Learned Hand had decided that it was essential to the fairness of courts (and to the public perception of it) that judges eschew partisan engagements. Far and away the most important stimulus to his change of attitude came in a conversation with Justice Oliver Wendell Holmes. "Holmes once told me to avoid all 'heated subjects,' " Hand often recalled; "[he] once said to me that he had always avoided entrance into heated fields."[2] For Hand, Holmes was an unblemished idol on the bench, and his personal advice, rarely received, was bound to have a profound impact. Holmes's "advice was good," Hand concluded; as he explained to his old Harvard friend the journalist Norman Hapgood:

> A judge will necessarily show his point of view on subjects which show strong feeling, probably in his work, probably also by the company he keeps and the things he says. That is inevitable, but it is much more if he identifies himself with projects designed to arouse public feeling on one side or the other. . . . I do not want to take on the appearance of a partisan. . . . While I am afraid that my record in the past has not always been good in this regard, that is no reason for making it worse.[3]

Keeping clear of "heat" was far easier for Holmes than for Hand. While Holmes read widely and engaged fully in the intellectual life of his times, his was an attitude of remote, Olympian detachment: he was rarely interested in contemporary political battles or concerned about their outcome. Hand, like Holmes, was a skeptic, increasingly committed to judicial detachment in the interest of an independent judiciary, but he cared deeply about the progress and outcomes of political skirmishes, as his private correspondence amply reveals. It took far more self-restraint to decline public participation in causes that elicited strong sympathies from him. Nevertheless, beginning in the postwar years, Hand strove valiantly never to overstep the all but invisible yet important line between permissible and impermissible statements to be made by a judge. He did not always succeed.

The most important ingredient of Hand's mounting renown was clearly his work on the bench. The public had no way of knowing about the great way he decided his numerous little cases;[4] but reports did appear in the press, whether because of the notoriety of the litigants or because of a particularly well turned phrase in his opinion. Lawyers, professional journals, law professors, and judges had more substantial reasons to appreciate his towering talents, and among this professional elite, Hand was rapidly elevated into the very front rank of American judges. Even by the early 1920s, Holmes had hoped that Hand would be named to the Supreme Court, and Holmes continued to sing his praises, telling visitors that he considered Hand's judicial work "the *real thing.*"[5] Supreme Court justice Louis Brandeis and New York Court of Appeals judge Benjamin Cardozo, two other jurists at the apex of the American legal system, also chimed in. Cardozo was perceptive enough to fear that he would "stress the wrong note" to talk simply of "the qualities of mind,—the keen analysis, the close reasoning, the capacity for deft and incisive phrase—that have given to Judge Hand such distinction among the judges of our day"; he thought even "greater" was Hand's commitment to free speech in contexts such as the *Masses* case.[6]

Peer evaluations eventually affect a broader elite of journalists and scholars. Hand's excellence was acknowledged, for example, in the request that he participate in the formation of the American Law Institute in the early 1920s, in his selection to many honorary societies and advisory boards from the American Academy of Arts and Sciences to the Social Science Research Council, and in his being awarded his first honorary doctor of laws degree by Columbia University in 1930 (by the end of the decade he would receive another five honorary LL.D.s, and additional ones would follow). His mounting fame had a great deal to do as well with his speeches and writings outside the court reports. From time to time he accepted invitations to give addresses, and these, directed not merely to professional audiences, slowly captured the attention of more and more listeners and readers. Hand, an engaging conversationalist in small social settings, dreaded and avoided extemporaneous speechmaking. He was not satisfied with hastily drafting and delivering vacuous rhetoric. He labored hard over these extrajudicial addresses, and he imposed on himself very high standards, as he did on the bench. His compulsive perfectionism assured that he spoke only when he had something substantial to say and when he could say it well.

This drive meant that he declined far more invitations than he accepted. Since he was incapable of taking his speaking engagements casually, since he knew that he would spend hours drafting and revising his addresses, he refused to give speeches whenever his judicial workload was heavy. For much of the mid-1920s, while the Second Circuit judges pleaded with Congress to give them additional personnel, the huge caseload precluded frequent public addresses. After a new judgeship was established in 1929, Hand spoke more often, but then an onslaught of cases in the early 1930s once more compelled his near exclusive attention to adjudication. Yet there was enough time during less pressing periods to permit the reluctant Hand to do a memorable amount of public speaking. His inhibitions and his painstaking efforts compelled many hours of work for drafting and polishing, but the result was a glittering collection of literary gems, which often found their way into print, not only in professional journals but also in magazines and newspapers.

Preparing public speeches that have genuine content is especially difficult for a judge seeking to avoid engagement in the controversial issues of the day, but Hand managed to do this. Without being partisan, he addressed some of the most basic issues of American democracy: he preached the virtues of moderation, skepticism, tolerance, and freedom of thought in a way that elaborated some of the most basic tenets of a civilized society and that helped to inform his audiences' reactions to ongoing controversies. Heeding Holmes, he usually succeeded in avoiding the "heat," yet he managed to contribute greatly to the light.

ON MAY 21, 1920, district judge Learned Hand wrote a letter to "His Excellency Hon. Alfred E. Smith," the governor of New York:

> Nothing has given me greater satisfaction for many months than your veto of the Lusk bills. It is refreshing to learn that a public officer has the courage in the face of determined and vindictive opposition to assert his faith in free institutions. Shocking as it is that it should be necessary to show such courage, it is none the less grateful that you have been found willing to do so. All citizens who believe in popular government will not soon forget this check upon the most sinister and disintegrating influence that can beset a democracy, the attempt to establish political orthodoxy.[7]

Hand's unusual letter illustrates his difficulty in mustering the restraint needed to avoid the open identification with contentious debates that he had come to think inappropriate for a judge. Hand did not know Smith personally and had had no other correspondence with him. Moreover, his unsolicited applause was addressed to a Tammany Democrat carrying a label long distasteful to him (indeed, Smith had first been elected to the New York Assembly in 1903 after a campaign in which

Hand had engaged in street-corner speaking on Smith's East Side to battle against Tammany). Smith was already moving in a more independent, progressive direction, and when Hand praised him for his "consistent liberalism," he had in mind the orientation of Smith's proposals in support of workmen's compensation and minimum-wage and factory-inspection laws, all issues dear to Hand's Bull Moose heart. Hand could see, as many ex-Progressives did, that despite the despised Tammany label, Smith was a rare reformer in the standpat political atmosphere of the 1920s.

Hand was moved to write mainly because of the governor's "courage" in vetoing the so-called Lusk bills, a package of six "anti-sedition" bills largely directed at the Socialist party and its sympathizers. The governor's messages explaining his vetoes of these bills (each dated May 18, 1920, and sent in typescript to Hand on May 25) forcefully condemned the entire package and repeatedly invoked "fundamental" principles. Portions of the bills, he insisted, struck at "the fundamental right of people to enjoy full liberty in the domain of idea and speech"; the country did not need "a system of intellectual tyranny"; and a provision denying official recognition to political parties advocating views threatening to the government, he claimed, would deprive unpopular minorities of "their basic rights of representation."[8] Smith's vetoes understandably resonated with Learned Hand, for the principles Smith emphasized closely resembled those Hand had articulated in his *Masses* ruling.

Writing a letter to Al Smith was unusual for Hand, but he was a constant defender of freedom of expression in many forums. During the war, persecution of dissidents was perhaps to be expected, although Hand had condemned it even then, but the greater hysteria that gripped the nation in the postwar years was far more troubling. All over the country, strikes and bombings made many Americans imagine that the shadow of the Russian Revolution was lurking on domestic soil and that the "Red Menace" should be counteracted. In late November 1919, Hand remarked to Justice Holmes that

> the merry sport of Red-baiting goes on, and the pack gives tongue more and more shrilly. I really can't get up much sympathy for the victims, but I own a sense of dismay at the increase in all the symptoms of apparent panic. How far people are getting afraid to speak, who have anything really worth while to say, I don't know, but I am sure that the public generally is becoming rapidly demoralized in all its sense of proportion and toleration. For men

who are not cock-sure about everything and especially for those who are not damned cock-sure about anything, the skies have a rather sinister appearance.[9]

The skies looked no less dark five months later, when the New York Assembly approved the Lusk bills. For Hand, Governor Smith's veto was a welcome breath of fresh air, so strongly in contrast to the "sinister" outlook for freedom of thought during the preceding year.

In this period of his life, Hand was far from an obsessive newspaper reader. During the Progressive era and for a while thereafter, he had subscribed to as many as five New York dailies; by early 1921, he could confess to Zechariah Chafee, with some exaggeration, of being guilty of "never reading the papers."[10] But Hand's rich circle of acquaintances—people who delighted in being on top of everything, like Walter Lippmann and Felix Frankfurter—assured that he knew about important contemporary controversies. Though Hand may not have been aware, for example, of the strong support for the Lusk bills in the very conservative editorial pages of *The New York Times* (in one editorial, the *Times* praised the Lusk recommendations as "excellent" and "wise" and condemned the "sentimentalists or amateurs" who "raise the cry of 'free speech' and 'liberty of the press' for the purpose of sheltering persons deliberately striving to overthrow the government"),[11] he knew well the speech-chilling winds blowing through his own state and the entire nation.

New York had gained the unenviable reputation of being the most energetic state in the anti-radical crusade. For a full year before the Lusk Committee (named after its chairman, State Senator Clayton R. Lusk) recommended its package of bills, it acted as a combination fact finder, prosecutor, police, and propaganda agency in investigating "seditious activities." Its most attention-getting techniques were raids on alleged hotbeds of subversives, including the Rand School of Social Science and the Socialist party headquarters.[12] But its apogee was reached with its headline-making efforts to bar the seating of five Socialists who had been elected to the New York Assembly. The Socialist party was legally recognized, and its gubernatorial candidate had received more than 120,000 votes in the 1918 election, but two hours after the Socialist legislators took their oath in January 1920, their fellow assemblymen suspended them from serving because they had been "elected on a platform that is absolutely inimical to the best interests" of government.[13] Full-fledged expulsion proceedings followed, and on April 1, shortly before the Lusk bills were enacted, the Assembly overwhelmingly voted to expel all five.[14]* (One of the Assembly's lawyers in "prosecuting" the case was Martin Conboy; ten years later, as U.S. attorney in New York City, Conboy would read Molly Bloom's soliloquy before Learned Hand's court as part of his speech-suppressive effort to ban *Ulysses*.)

These expulsion maneuvers, engineered by the Lusk Committee, ironically resulted in calming the hysteria that had beset the state, for a significant part of New York City's legal elite, as well as most of its newspapers (including the *World* and the *Tribune*, but not the *Times*) protested the action. Charles Evans Hughes, the respected Republican back in Wall Street practice after his service on the Supreme Court and his unsuccessful candidacy for the presidency in 1916, took the lead. He wrote an outraged letter to the Speaker of the Assembly as soon as the maneuvers began in early January; he battled before the City Bar Association to assure appointment of a committee to present the anti-expulsion case in Albany; and he spoke out repeatedly in the ensuing months on behalf of "free speech, free assembly and the right of representation."[15]

Learned Hand did not follow the newspaper stories about the expulsion moves day by day, but he was well aware of the controversy. He frequently used the bar association's library on West Forty-fourth Street; he knew lawyers on Hughes's committee; and he discussed with Hughes the legal issues involved. In January, soon after the Assembly's opening moves against the Socialists, he contributed $25 to the *New York World*'s fund "to defray the expenses of counsel in defense of the Socialist assemblymen."[16]† And even if Hand had not had these prior

---

* The same procedure, resulting in another vote to expel the Socialists, was followed at the legislature's special session in September 1920. As the result of the Republican landslide in the 1920 election, Al Smith lost the governorship. In the November election, New York City's voters elected four Socialists to the state legislature—two of them among those twice expelled from the Assembly a year earlier. A new effort to expel the Socialist assemblymen was opposed by the Republican governor Nathan L. Miller; the Lusk forces pressed ahead; but the expulsion move was defeated in April 1921. (Miller opposed expulsion because he feared Republican election prospects in New York City would be permanently damaged, but he did support the Lusk Committee's legislative proposals.)

† Hand's $25 contribution presumably seemed permissible to him because it was for a legal-defense fund. Six months earlier, by contrast, he had rejected an appeal to sign a public letter of protest against the New York attorney general's court proceeding to annul the charter of the Rand School of Social Science (an effort that failed in the New York courts, and that produced the inclusion of the school as a target of the Lusk bills). On July 9, 1919, the director of the National Civil Liberties Bureau asked Hand to sign. (Hand was the only judge asked to sign; among the others asked were Herbert Croly, C. C. Burlingham, Mrs. Willard Straight—the financial angel of Croly's *The New Republic*—and Walter Lippmann.) Hand replied: "I do not approve of political agitation designed to influence the conduct of a court, however much I may disapprove of [the attorney general's] effort in itself." He acknowledged that, so far as he knew, "there is absolutely no ground" for revoking the school's charter, and he added that the

exposures to the issues, he would have become fully informed when, in late 1920, he read every page of Zechariah Chafee's *Freedom of Speech*, a book Chafee had dedicated to Hand for his courage in *Masses*. This influential book devoted more than thirty pages to the expulsion of the New York Socialists and contained by far the fullest contemporary treatment of the facts and legal arguments against the assembly's action.

On January 2, 1921, Hand sent Chafee a ten-page handwritten letter full of praise for Chafee's scholarship and civil libertarian instincts, but with critical commentary as well. The most important part of Hand's letter was devoted to his renewed defense of his "incitement" standard and his criticism of Holmes's "clear and present danger" test. But Hand also showed a special interest in the chapter dealing with legislative expulsions of duly elected members, which "interested me immensely," he said; and he left no doubt that his general sympathies lay with Chafee and Hughes. "I am of your faction," he assured Chafee, "which at least for N.Y. would admit no extra-constitutional tests."[17]

Supportive as Hand was, he had reservations about the legal arguments Hughes had made and Chafee had endorsed, arguments essentially stating that once the legislators had taken their oaths, the Assembly had no business to inquire into their qualifications. "About a year ago I had this out w. Hughes," Hand told Chafee. What if there was clear evidence that an assemblyman had taken his oath in bad faith? Could not the assembly at least consider *that* evidence? Hand agreed that the particular inquiry to which the five Socialists had been subjected was wholly indefensible, but he also saw some plausibility in the Assembly's claim that it could exclude a member if there was clear-cut evidence he had taken his oath in bad faith. Hand stated his position with characteristic wit, challenging Chafee with a humorous hypothetical problem:

> Suppose this case: Claessen [one of the Socialist assemblymen] is about to take the oath to support the Constitution etc. On the way up Capitol Hill in Albany while arm in arm with two Bishops he says that he knows that he must take the oath, but that it is all nonsense, he does it only "to bore from within." As for him the

---

effort seemed "directed simply toward the prevention of free speech." His refusal produced a second appeal, from Walter Nelles, counsel of the bureau and a civil liberties lawyer whom Hand respected. But Hand adhered to his refusal, with added force: "If one side begins to agitate the other will necessarily follow. I am unalterably opposed to any such tactics regarding matters that are in court. It is hard enough for judges to eliminate such considerations from their minds in any event, but direct propaganda seems to me to strike at the very foundations of propriety. All this is particularly applicable to the case of one who, like me, is a judge himself." (The correspondence is in box 33, file 24 of the Hand Papers: see Albert DeSilver, director of the bureau, to LH, 9 July 1919, with enclosed protest statement; LH to Albert DeSilver, 10 July 1919; LH to Walter Nelles, 14 July 1919.)

shortest way is the best and a General Soviet with an Extraordinary Commission of the modern equivalents of Fouquier-Tinville, Couthon, Saint Just and Anacharsis Kloot is what he means to get and that P.D.Q. Meanwhile he will do his best to befuddle the poor dunderheads up there and reduce their efforts to miserable and ridiculous confusion.

> Is there a question justiciable before the Committee on Privileges, or whatever it is, and before the House, when the two Bishops somewhat treacherously peach on Claessen? "No," says Carolus the justiciar, (ci-devant) [Hughes], "No, not if Claessen once takes the oath. The test is the oath." Well, much as I should like to avoid the possibility, which became an actuality, of letting in all the mischievous tittle tattle on which the Five were excluded, I find it a little troubling going along. . . . Of course I don't mean that they [the legislators] should go any further than to inquire whether Claessen *meant* to support the Constitution as C. *understood* it, but mayn't they go so far? This great man [Hughes] said no, and God forbid that a D.J. should say no [to Hughes]. But he is entitled to doubts.[18]

In short, Hand insisted on criticizing the legal elements of the Socialists' defense, even at a time when he was quite passionately committed to defending their right to serve. At about the same time, when an acquaintance asked him to join other liberals at a dinner, Hand replied:

> It is kind of you to think of me as a liberal. I sometimes am afraid that I am not a very good one, that I am a conservative among liberals and a liberal among conservatives. . . . [A]t the present time the essence of liberalism is that one should be tolerant. I sometimes think that the advocates of free speech are as intolerant about their side as the others about theirs. It is a hard thing to be tolerant.[19]

Hand was clearly a partisan of liberal values in his defenses of free speech and toleration. But unlike many of his fellow liberals, his devotion to the cause never deteriorated into self-righteous, uncritical allegiance. Off the bench as well as on, he retained the capacity truly to listen to the other side's arguments and agonizingly to reexamine his own premises.

HAND WAS WELL AWARE of the massive federal Espionage Act prosecutions, which produced about two thousand sedition convictions of antiwar dissidents: he had himself tried to protect freedom of speech in his *Masses* ruling in 1917, and soon realized that his views were not shared by most American judges. But he was less well acquainted with the other curbs on civil liberties that had occurred during the war.

For example, Hand did not follow closely the harsh treatments employers meted out to workers and their unions. During the early months of the war, strikes broke out all over the United States, and the major reason for the walkouts was often not wage demands but employer hostility to unionization: employers vented their anti-unionism with unbending determination and justified their behavior by invoking the fear of the allegedly anarchist and violent International Workers of the World.

Hand's friendship with Felix Frankfurter deepened his understanding of this mounting labor strife. Frankfurter left Harvard for Washington early in the war to serve Secretary of War Newton D. Baker as a principal civilian adviser. In September 1917, President Wilson established a mediation commission in the hope of resolving the major strikes threatening the war production effort, and Frankfurter became counsel to the commission. Its first assignment was to look into the disorders in Arizona's copper industry. Frankfurter and the commission spent nearly two months in Arizona, and Frankfurter kept Hand well informed.

The situation Frankfurter found there quickly convinced him that the nation was losing its "perspective" in "this war for democracy." As he told Hand in a long letter he wrote from the Copper Queen Hotel in Bisbee, Arizona, on November 6: "The manifestations of shoddy patriotism this trip reveals are wide and deep. You would be surprised, even you, [by] the tyrannies that are exercised in the holy name of 'loyalty.' " His deepest progressive feelings were outraged by the greedy, hypocritical bosses:

> The thing is so shallow and so pathetic, as well as brutal. These old bags, who have fought labor and unions as poison for a decade, now wrap themselves in the flag and are confirmed in their old bias . . . by a passionate patriotism. Gee—but it's awful and then they wonder at the fecundity of the I.W.W.s, the [W]obblies, as they are picturesquely called. They breed the IWWs—they and the neglect of the old fashioned trade unions [Samuel Gompers's A.F. of L.] of the needs of the immigrant, non-English speaking seasonal workers of the West.[20]

What especially stirred Frankfurter's anger was the lawless behavior in Bisbee itself. Frankfurter, on behalf of the mediation commission, prepared a report to the president on the "Bisbee Deportation" and sent Hand a carbon copy.[21] In deference to the more conservative sentiment of the commission, Frankfurter could not air his full emotions about what he considered an outrageous story of vigilantism, but his report called the "deportations" that had taken place in Bisbee during the summer "wholly illegal." What had happened was that the head of the copper-producing Phelps, Dodge & Co. had persuaded the townspeople to solve its labor problems by ejecting more than 1,000 strikers and their sympathizers from Bisbee: under the sheriff's aegis, more than 2,000 residents rounded up 1,186 men on the morning of July 12 and put them on a train that carried them to a town in New Mexico. When that town refused to accept the "deportees," the train left them at a station in the desert, "wholly without adequate supply of food and water and shelter for two days . . . abandoned by the guards who had brought them [and] left to shift for themselves." Nearly half the deportees were citizens; the rest were aliens from over twenty countries. (Not until the War Department was notified two days later were federal troops sent to escort the deportees to a nearby town, where the government maintained them for months.) Additional deportations of "large numbers of others" continued for weeks until the governor of Arizona finally put a stop to the vigilante regime late in August. Frankfurter flatly rejected the claim that the deportations were necessary to avert risks to life and property.

Frankfurter did not know that his bulky envelope would reach Hand in the depth of a serious illness: for much of November and December, Hand was having "a rather anxious time" because of another life-threatening bout with pneumonia. But when Hand at last was able to catch up with his mail, he was shocked. "Your Bisbee report was absolutely right and courageous," he responded. "No matter what comes of it, it is a good stroke of service and I have no doubt that you are correct in your general belief about the situation, although I must take your word for that."[22]

By this time, Hand had also heard of criticisms leveled at Frankfurter, despite his report's moderate tone. Among the critics was Theodore Roosevelt, who had turned into a super-patriot during the war, to the dismay of his old Progressive sympathizers. Frankfurter sent to Hand copies of his exchange of letters with Roosevelt; in these, TR charged Frankfurter with smearing the reputation of patriots and with coddling anarchists: "You are engaged in excusing men precisely like the Bolsheviki in Russia, who are murderers, . . . who are traitors to their allies, to democracy, and to civilization."[23] There was no doubt for Hand as to which side he was on. "I much admire [how] you handled the matter," he wrote Frankfurter. "I am glad that you stood up to [TR] as well as you did, and you certainly had him backed against the ropes. As usual with Teddy, he speaks before he has any adequate knowledge of the facts and when he is wrong, he is all-fired wrong."[24]

The Bisbee deportations were the result of vigilante action aided by local officials, but the Wilson administration itself added fuel to the hyper-patriotic fire. Civil libertarians who supported the war were dismayed by the tenor of Wilson administration statements, but they hoped that once peace came the administration would return to more tolerant ways. These hopes collapsed in the postwar months. "Now the starch is out of the administration," Frankfurter wrote Hand in January 1919. "Cold feet prevail in a wide area. [Wilson] has given up—*pro tem*— the U.S. to make a world . . . and his paralyzed subordinates are meek and timid. They have practically announced bankruptcy and have invited the Republicans as receivers. God help us!"[25] With America turning into "the most reactionary country in the world,"[26] Frankfurter resigned from the administration and returned to Harvard.

Worse was yet to come. Though ineffectual on most policy issues in 1919 and 1920, government leaders mustered the energy to engage in a virulent wave of anti-radical hysteria that exceeded anything the nation had seen even in the midst of the war. The postwar witch-hunt began in the early summer of 1919, initiated in part after a bomb exploded at the home of Wilson's new attorney general, A. Mitchell Palmer, who quickly became the leader of the repressive forces. He set up a General Intelligence Division in his Justice Department and placed an ambitious twenty-four-year-old, J. Edgar Hoover, in charge of it. Hoover set up elaborate files on radicals, while Palmer made plans to use the federal power to deport aliens as a central measure to deal with Communists, anarchists, and other radicals. Almost exactly a year after the Armistice, in November 1919, Justice Department personnel launched a wave of mass raids and arrests. In early January 1920, just as the Lusk Committee's moves to expel Socialist assemblymen surfaced in Albany, the "Palmer Raids" rounded up about six thousand aliens. By late spring, these "Red Raids" were blocked by the Labor Department, but the "Deportations Delirium" was marked by inhumane detention centers, charges of brutality, and numerous violations of statutory and administrative rules.

Hand did not fully appreciate how massive and widespread the phenomenon had become until he read Chafee's *Freedom of Speech*. Though on the bench he frequently complained about the harshness of particular deportations even as he felt compelled to apply the law unless he could find procedural irregularities, Chafee's lengthy recital of deportation abuses shocked him. He agreed with Chafee that the government had used its power over aliens atrociously, though he doubted that courts could legitimately strike down the laws.

> My God, but I never knew [the deportations] were like that. [But] your doubts about the constitutionality of any deportation law I think I don't share. On the whole I believe that while the justification for freedom of speech is public enlightenment, historically the "right" . . . is vested in the speaker, and our legislators can engage ad lib in obscurantism, provided they don't impinge on an individual who [is entitled to] cry out. Now [the congressional policy] is inhumane enough, and it has filled me with loathing to have to recognize it, but it is the fact that if I come here & don't get out my [naturalization] "papers" I stay on sufferance. I don't think we judges could intervene if they deported all aliens who ate with their knives. After all a court which doesn't recognize the post "as of common right" [i.e., views use of the mails as a privilege rather than a right] is not going to strain at gnats like deportations.[27]

For Hand, once again, commitment to basic liberal values coexisted with an undiminished capacity to examine skeptically his own side's legal arguments.

MUCH OF THE FUEL for the zealotry of the postwar witch-hunters stemmed from fear of the Russian Revolution. For the organizers of the administration's dragnets, pursuit of domestic radicals was justified by the belief that the Soviet Bolsheviks were trying to replicate the revolution in the United States. News from the U.S.S.R. (which the administration staunchly opposed recognizing) also strongly affected the country's foreign policy. Hand viewed nonrecognition with distress: he was convinced that, like the persecution of domestic dissidents, it could only make martyrs of Communists and feed the flames of unrest. In the summer of 1920, he explained to a British acquaintance, an admiralty lawyer, his disagreement with the policy:

> [Wilson] is taking just the attitude that the Powers did toward the French [Revolution] which plunged Europe into twenty years of destructive warfare. If the Russians are content with the kind of militant oligarchy they have got now, or if not being content they have not the public spirit to overthrow it, we do our best by our present attitude to consolidate its power and to give it the enormous

support of all national Russian sentiment. . . . [W]hile it is an intolerable government, we are all doing our best to maintain and consolidate it, and this last announcement of Wilson is only another prop.

Yet he dreaded the prospect of Harding, whom the Republicans had just nominated:

Harding seems to me impossible. His nomination represents nothing but an appeal to apathy, little Americanism and the tacit assumption that the old crowd of wire-pullers playing in with the "big interests" is on the whole most to be trusted. All of what Theodore Roosevelt stood for in public life has been wiped clean off the slate by the party which he led. That party to-day stands just where it stood in 1900, when Mark Hanna and the little crowd of magnates for whom he spoke were the . . . bosses of the whole country. . . . They have no program, no policy, no ideas.[28]

Unlike Frankfurter, however, Hand refused to sign protest statements or join public meetings. His correspondence amply reveals the ensuing tension. For example, in the midst of the war—in January 1918—the National Civil Liberties Bureau (the predecessor of the American Civil Liberties Union) had invited Hand to join about seventy other people selected because of "their well-known liberalism" to serve on a committee calling a mass meeting on "American Liberties in War Time" to protest the nationwide "denial of constitutional rights" and particularly "the insidious use made of the war and patriotism by privileged interests to intimidate labor and radical movements." He declined, citing his avoidance of "any agitation of a political character" on matters "likely constantly to come before me as a judge."[29] After the war, in December 1919, he once again privately expressed his "sympathy" with the "general attitude" of a movement to unite "the liberals of America" in an "Americanization" program saner than the flag-waving "knownothingism" of "blind distrust of the foreigner, [of] thoughtless insistence upon an undefined Americanism," reflected in the right-wing attacks on alien workers.[30] And as the 1920 presidential campaign began, he became ever more frustrated with Congress's preoccupation with the "Red Menace." Writing to a college friend who had written in *The New York Times* to advocate American economic aid to Europe's postwar reconstruction efforts, Hand doubted that Congress could be gotten to focus on the issue, even though it would be to "their own self-interest":

They worked themselves up into a frenzy of witch-hunting over the Bolsheviki and are willing to spend millions to suppress half-crazy enthusiasts. In doing that my own judgment is that they make two for every one they suppress, besides losing their heads and forgetting their most honorable traditions.[31]

The tension between Hand's privately expressed convictions and his abstention from taking public stands put him to severe tests. As a judge, he was bound by the higher court's reversal of *Masses* and the federal judiciary's rigorous enforcement of the sedition laws; but he hoped that the defendants would be granted amnesty as soon as possible after the Armistice. Accordingly, when his friend the District of Columbia judge William Hitz asked for help in persuading the administration to pardon the defendants, Hand enthusiastically agreed.[32]

More questionable, given his self-imposed restraint, was Hand's response to an appeal to contribute to an umbrella organization sending funds to various jailed dissidents. He contributed $25 to the Workers' Prison Relief Committee, which organized a mass meeting pressing for the release of political prisoners, many of them Wobblies. Accurately anticipating that the contributors would be listed, Hand requested that his donation be listed simply as coming from "L.H."; the list was indeed thus printed. What Hand may not have anticipated was that his own contribution was the second biggest of all. Many well-to-do New Yorkers contributed only two or three dollars, and Hand's own gifts were usually modest; the unusual size in this instance suggests both the depth of his feelings and a somewhat reckless inability to follow through consistently on his own determination to avoid heated issues.[33]

Hand's innate moderation, his capacity to perceive shades of gray, and his hostility to emotional demagoguery were all in evidence when, in December 1919, the conservative Boston establishment attacked his friend Felix Frankfurter for alleged radicalism. On Armistice Day, Frankfurter had, at the request of several members of Boston's elite, chaired a mass meeting at Boston's Faneuil Hall in support of American recognition of the Soviet Union. Two days later, Thomas Nelson Perkins, a former Progressive and now a conservative, in Frankfurter's eyes, member of the Harvard Corporation, telephoned Frankfurter to ask about "this Communist meeting you presided over." A letter had come to Perkins from "a man of influence and large property" who had earlier criticized a number of alleged "left-wingers" associated with Harvard Law School—Zechariah Chafee, Roscoe Pound (since 1916 the law school's dean), and the visiting English Fabian socialist Harold Laski as well as Frankfurter.[34] Frankfurter, outraged, launched an extensive, agitated correspondence with Perkins; Hand did not whole-heartedly embrace Frankfurter's position—and this brought upon him-self copies of the entire exchange as well as several Frankfurter letters of self-justification. As Hand told Frankfurter, "I can only say that my instinct—whatever its source—rather tends against agitation here & now looking to a change towards Russia, little as I personally share the common feelings [against recognition]. I suppose I was born to be in the Centre, a little to the left, but in Le Marais [the swamp]." What was needed in these reactionary, Red-baiting times, he thought, was "cement, not explosives"; he could see no point "in nailing your colors to the mast in a cyclone." Hand added, "Not a very stimulating position to occupy and without the joys of Freedom, as you say. Anatole [France] says this in M. Bergerat somewhere: 'Je comprends, c'est mon faiblesse; il y a beaucoup de face de ne pas comprendre.' [I understand, it's my weakness; there is much face-saving in not understanding.] There is a time when we should not weigh too nicely the pros & cons. Perhaps you have hit it right and that the time is full for a gesture of indepen-dence, even when there are no traceable results to be got. I honestly don't know; I guess no. It must be a little disappointing not to have one's friends more courageous."[35]

Frankfurter scrawled on this letter, "Isn't he Honesty itself." His response was to launch a new tirade: Did Hand want to leave the field entirely to the reactionaries? That was what "it gets down to—if Pound and [*The New Republic*] and I (let alone Holmes and Hand J. in the 'Masses') keep quiet." Freedom was "a subtle thing," and the attitude behind Perkins's letters was a "very corrosive force" subverting liberty.[36*]

This was not the last time Hand and Frankfurter clashed because of temperamental differences. Hand was repeatedly bombarded, in person and by letter, with Frankfurter's arguments and documents. Hand deeply respected his friend's "very great capacities and his generous enthusiasm for the right side, on which he gets nearly always," but, as he once told Lippmann, "I wish to God he wouldn't feel that every case was a signal for a moral crusade, or if he does, I wish his controversial manner would be a little more consonant with one's own self-respect." When the crusading spirit seized Frankfurter, Hand suggested, he could be

---

* Interestingly, the entire correspondence occurred in the context of Frankfurter's impending marriage to Marion Denman, which occurred in December 1919. Frankfurter had asked Holmes to marry them; Holmes told him that a Supreme Court justice had no authority to marry in New York. Frankfurter then turned to Hand to perform the ceremony in Hand's chambers; Hand at first agreed, but at the last minute, after checking the New York laws, had to tell Frankfurter that he, too, lacked authority to conduct the ceremony. Benjamin Cardozo ulti-mately did the job, in Hand's chambers, at Hand's suggestion.

more than "a bit trying," even "intolerable." Whenever Hand voiced a rare criticism of Frankfurter's other heroes on the bench—Holmes, Brandeis, or Cardozo—he was made to feel as if he were "sinning against the Holy Ghost." Hand thought it "preposterous to suppose that even the best men can never be wrong"; yet Frankfurter's vehemence revealed "almost a clansman's spirit, and it is certainly out of place in matters that justify and require any serenity or the contemplative spirit."[37]

Yet Frankfurter's sense that the postwar hysteria had made him a major target of attack at Harvard was rooted in fact, and he was not alone in perceiving this. Frankfurter reported declining morale on the Harvard Law School faculty to Hand—"some have turned turtle in their opinions and others are scared out of their [Levis]"; alumni and the university administration, including its president, A. Lawrence Lowell, were attacking Roscoe Pound and Harold Laski; and after the faculty had recommended a promising young scholar for appointment, "he was turned down as a 'Bolshevik' " by the university.[38] That news truly troubled Hand,[39] and soon there were even more reasons for concern about "the cowed atmosphere" enveloping the Harvard faculty.[40] Zechariah Chafee, with Frankfurter, had (at the invitation of the federal trial judge involved) joined the legal team attacking the Justice Department's mass deportations of aliens, and they had managed to set aside some of the deportations, persuading the judge that the government had denied the aliens' due-process rights.[41] Soon after, they joined other critics of the "Red Scare" in signing a lawyers' report sharply critical of the Justice Department's practices.[42] Predictably, these engagements provoked new charges against the Harvard "radicals."

Though Thomas Nelson Perkins apparently had no part in this, Frankfurter again complained to Hand about him: He lacked "*guts.* . . . He knows I am not 'a Red' (whatever that may be) [and] that [Attorney General] Palmer *is* a 'dangerous' man, . . . *but* he hasn't guts" to speak out. "*Per contra* he doesn't want to have [to] bother on my account—and wants me to be a quiet, well-behaved, boot-licking harmless teacher, who doesn't defend 'communists.' [He simply] sits around and listens to damnations of Holmes and Brandeis and Pound and Chafee and me—all 'dangerous' and Bolsheviks as State Street and the gang here rate them. What's the use of all of Nelson's 'red blood-edness' and 'bowels' if they don't move?"[43] Hand didn't want to engage once again in arguments about Perkins as a representative of the Boston right wing: "We shall have·to let the matter stand," he told Frankfurter, and indeed proceeded to defend Perkins—and, indirectly, himself.

Hand, like Frankfurter, had known Perkins for some years, and as he told Frankfurter, "I save my friends at possibly some expense to the chastity of my intellect." To Frankfurter's charges that Perkins lacked "moral courage," he replied sharply that Frankfurter was simply "wrong." Perkins, he thought, had in his nature "an undue diffidence of his own conclusions" that prevented him from having "very well-defined or constant convictions." And, he added,

> I have a good deal of sympathy for such a one, being much like him in that respect, and it makes me perhaps over sensitive for him when he is charged with lack of courage. . . . You may abuse such a make-up as much as you please; God knows, I should be the last to fly to its defence, but bet[ween] high-brows like you & me, il faut toujours preciser [one must always be precise].[44]

Frankfurter was not appeased. As a member of the Harvard Corporation, Perkins simply had to make decisions, "however diffident he may be as to his own conclusions." And he added, "The fact is that somehow or other this diffidence—what you claim is an intellectual humility—does not prevent him from making decisions always on the side of his own comfort and his own crowd."[45]

What Frankfurter saw as the right-wing harassment of Harvard Law School liberals reached its climax in May 1921, with Chafee as the "defendant" at the "Trial at the Harvard Club," a hearing before the Harvard Board of Overseers Committee to Visit the Harvard Law School on charges, submitted to the Board of Overseers by a conservative New York lawyer, Austen G. Fox, that Chafee's article on the *Abrams* case—the notorious prosecution of antiwar dissidents that produced the first strongly speech-protective Holmes dissent in the Supreme Court—contained numerous errors. (The errors were in fact few and minor.) Even though the committee members included Judges Benjamin Cardozo, Gus Hand, and Julian Mack, Harvard liberals feared the worst. Frankfurter viewed the proceedings as "heresy trials" and condemned "the coxcombery of Austen Fox."[46] But to the liberals' surprise, Harvard president Lowell, whom they had long considered a part of the conservative Boston establishment, turned out to be a hero in this instance. He spoke out at the hearing in strong defense of academic freedom, his arguments prevailed, and his intervention was lauded as changing the repressive atmosphere at Harvard into one of genuine freedom;* the

---

* Chafee was so grateful for Lowell's defense of academic freedom that he changed the dedication page in his revised 1941 version of his 1920 *Freedom of Speech*. The 1920 volume had been dedicated to Learned Hand for his courageousness in *Masses*. The 1941 volume, *Free Speech in the United States* (Cambridge: Harvard University Press, 1941), was dedicated instead to "Abbott Lawrence Lowell, whose wisdom and courage in the face of uneasy fears and stormy criticism made it unmistakably plain that as long as he was President no one could breathe

committee concluded unanimously that Chafee had "made no statements in his article which were consciously erroneous."[47] Even Frankfurter had to recognize that the Harvard president was not all bad: "Lowell was really very fine about it," he wrote Hand. He asked Hand to get from "Julian [Mack] and the other eminent judges . . . the gossip of the conference room" about the goings-on,[48] but Hand had no success: "As far as I can find," he told Frankfurter, "the heretics will have to be content with an acquittal by silence." Hand was more disturbed by the fact that some of his acquaintances (for example, the lawyer James Byrne, who had helped him get his district court appointment) seemed "greatly concerned" over Chafee's alleged "inaccuracies." "That attitude," Hand exploded, "makes me a little tired." Gus Hand apparently expressed similar reservations, and Learned argued with him in Chafee's defense. "I had it out with Gus lately," he reported to Frankfurter:

> The good thing about old Gus is, that however much to me he may rave and curse, you will always find him in the end on the right side and there is no doubt that he has a great deal more influence on the other side than people like you and me, who are regarded as radical. Radical—God save the mark! Think of anybody thinking me radical,—a man who always finds the new experiments too hazardous to be tried just now. That charge always amuses me.[49]

Frankfurter was so relieved by the outcome of the Chafee "trial" that, with rare optimism, he suggested to Hand, "Don't you think the wartime hysteria is letting up a wee bit? I do."[50] But the less volatile, more sober-minded Hand was not so sure: "Are the hysterica [sic] disappearing? Only because there is nothing on. They would appear again just as soon as anybody tried to start anything."[51]

HAND WAS THE MORE ACCURATE. Though by the summer of 1921 the anti-Red hysteria had waned at Harvard, as it had throughout the nation, soon something new was "on"—a threat that Harvard would impose an explicit quota to restrict the admission of Jewish students. Frankfurter and Hand both became engaged in the battle over Harvard's "Jewish problem." Frankfurter quickly identified the main villain in the story: President Lowell. Once again, Hand was skeptical at the

---

the air of Harvard and not be free." On the Chafee "trial," see Donald L. Smith, *Zechariah Chafee, Jr.: Defender of Liberty and Law* (Cambridge: Harvard University Press, 1986), 50–57. See also Harlan B. Phillips, ed., *Felix Frankfurter Reminisces* (New York: Reynal & Company, 1960), 176.

outset, but his major focus was on the underlying issue; and on that, he spoke out fearlessly.

Lowell's proposal to limit the admission of Jewish students to Harvard College became public knowledge in late May 1922, and soon it was front-page news in *The New York Times*. Lowell had long worried about the rise in Jewish student enrollment at Harvard: during the first two decades of the century, Jewish enrollment had risen from about 7 percent to over 20 percent. In Hand's class in the 1890s, there had been a scattering of Jews, primarily assimilated descendants of German Jews. The new wave of Jewish immigration from Russia and Poland that began in the late nineteenth century swelled the numbers, and these Jews' ghetto background led some faculty and alumni to fear subversion of the cherished Harvard atmosphere. "The anti-Semitic feeling among the students is increasing," Lowell claimed, "and it grows in proportion to the increase in the number of Jews." To Lowell, there was clearly "a problem—a new problem," and in his view the appropriate solution to the "racial question," "in the interest of the Jews, as well as of every one else," was to have every college "take a limited proportion of Jews."[52] He urged Harvard to lead the way with an overt quota: Harvard should impose a maximum 15 percent quota on the admission of Jewish applicants.[53]

The quota proposal stirred widespread controversy. Lowell had hoped to keep the discussion confined to Harvard circles; indeed, he had initially tried to attain a quota scheme by quiet action of the admissions committee, but that committee insisted that the question go to the full faculty. On May 23, the Arts and Sciences faculty had considered a motion—by President Lowell's brother-in-law—to instruct the admissions committee that "it [was] not desirable that the number of students in any group which is not easily assimilated into the common life of the College should exceed fifteen percent of the whole College."[54] This figure, it was clear to all, was aimed at Jews. Initially, the faculty turned quite panicky in the face of the rising Jewish enrollment statistics, and it adopted a slightly revised proposal, urging that certain categories of applicants be admitted only if the admissions committee were satisfied "that their presence as members of the College will positively contribute to the general advantage of the College." Toward that end, the committee was to "take into account the resulting proportional size of racial and national groups in the membership of Harvard College." Moreover, the faculty voted to establish a special committee "to consider principles and methods for more effectively sifting candidates for admission."[55]

The claims that the concerns prompting the quota proposal were limited to "unpolished" East European Jews were soon pierced. Instead, as a Jewish student at Harvard reported, "[W]e learned that it was *numbers* that mattered; bad or good, *too many* Jews were not liked. Rich or poor, brilliant or dull, polished or crude—*too many Jews*, the fear of a new Jerusalem at Harvard, the 'City College' fear."[56] The "City College fear" was spurred by the experience of the College of the City of New York, where Jewish enrollment had climbed to 80 percent. Other colleges in metropolitan areas with a large Jewish population trembled lest a similar flood inundate them. Harvard's response to the fear was distinctive in proposing an overt Jewish quota; other colleges had already taken their own covert measures to stem the tide. Thus, Nicholas Murray Butler's Columbia University, with Jewish enrollment approaching 40 percent just a year or two earlier, had adopted "personality" tests, "character" inquiries, and revised questionnaires to bring its percentage of Jewish students down to below 20.[57] Lowell himself saw the threat of a 40 percent Jewish Harvard just around the corner ("If their number should become 40 per cent. of the student body, the race feeling would become intense"), and he was proud that Harvard was confronting the problem candidly rather than through subterfuges ("Some colleges appear to have met the question by indirect methods, which we do not want to adopt").[58]

Lowell's proposal encountered obstacles within days of his initial success. On second thought, many Harvard faculty members concluded that they had acted in excessive haste, and they signed petitions urging Lowell to convene a special meeting to reconsider the vote. On June 2, by a nearly 3–1 margin, they rescinded most of their earlier action, leaving in effect only the appointment of a special "sifting" committee.* For the next year, while this committee (chaired by Professor Charles H. Grandgent) deliberated, there was no further official action, but the debate about restrictive quotas raged both on campus and off. Ultimately, in April 1923, the faculty endorsed the committee's central proposal: official rejection of any limitation on admissions based on race or religion.

Lowell's preoccupation with "the Jewish problem" reflected broader national trends. Clearly, consideration of restrictions on college admissions was not limited to Harvard. And the issues went beyond higher education. First, there was mounting anti-Semitism after World War I. The opinions and actions of Lowell and his supporters were not so crude as the Henry Ford–sponsored propaganda about an international Jewish conspiracy or the Ku Klux Klan's xenophobic activities, but

* Harvard's Board of Overseers diluted the proposal still further three days later: on June 5, it expanded the membership of the "sifting" committee to include faculty from the entire university, not just the college.

Harvard's polite fears about the flood of Jewish applicants drew nourishment from similar emotions. In the 1890s, Harvard's social clubs had hurt even Hand by their exclusionary practices; Jews were "outsiders" far more clearly than he had been. Second, the "Americanization" campaign that was used to whip up persecution of aliens was but one aspect of a broader concern to maintain the dominance of WASP, North European stock in the American population. Lowell himself expressed this. Not only was he the most prominent Brahmin advocate of a Harvard quota, but he simultaneously served as the national vice president of the Immigration Restriction League, actively opposing large-scale immigration by "alien races."[59]

Learned Hand could not help being informed about the Harvard quota debate, for several of his friends were intimately engaged in the battle. His judicial colleague Julian Mack, the first Jew to serve on Harvard's Board of Overseers, was the most regular source of information, and of course there was also Frankfurter. (When Mack pressed Lowell to name Frankfurter to the "sifting" committee, Lowell refused, claiming that Frankfurter was too committed to the anti-quota position to be suitable.) At first, Hand thought Frankfurter once again too ready to impute bad motives to Lowell. Frankfurter insisted to Hand that Lowell's conduct on "the Jew matter" was contemptible, for "his methods in pursuing his ends and in covering them up."[60] Hand ultimately agreed: "[I]n the present showing you seem to me justified about Lowell. This I say in the faith [in] Julian's report and he is a strictly accurate reporter, so far as I have ever found."

More important, Hand, as early as June 1922, was clear about where he stood in the controversy. He did not "like this business" of excluding Jews, but he thought the overt quota proposal at least "better than Nick Butler's way" of following covert routes at Columbia. And with open debate, he accurately perceived, the proposal was doomed: "[The College] will not dare to do it; that is the advantage of playing above board at least in result." Throughout, Hand's deepest belief held firm: "I want most of all to have a Harvard that means still all that Harvard has stood for. . . . If we are to have in this country racial divisions like those in Europe, let us close up shop now."[61]

During much of the summer of 1922, Hand was touring Europe with his family. When he returned home, he found emotions still high, and his concern was strong enough to stir him to take a step unusual for him in these years of deliberate abstention from public controversy: he labored over and finally sent a letter to Professor Charles Grandgent setting forth a rational, principled case against Harvard's adoption of any Jewish quota. In it he identified "the real difference" between "those who would limit and those who would not": "A college may gather men of a common tradition, or it may put its faith in learning. If so, it will I suppose take its chance that in learning lies the best hope, and that a company of scholars will prove better than any other company."[62]

Hand tried hard to understand the arguments of those advocating restrictions: the difficulties caused by the growing number of Jewish undergraduates, he thought, were "no doubt real in a sense that a graduate of thirty years ago would find it hard to realize." He was prepared to assume the accuracy of what he had been told: that Harvard now had many "insensitive, aggressive, and ill-conditioned [Jews] whose presence causes much hostility among the Christians" and that admission of still more Jews would indeed "drive away many students of the kind to which we have been accustomed." Yet none of this justified a quota: "Notwithstanding, I cannot agree that a limitation based upon race will in the end work out any good purpose. If the Jew does not mix well with the Christian, it is no answer to segregate him."

Of course, segregation or total exclusion of Jews was not being proposed, but Hand thought a quota was "if anything worse." For him, any plan "to prevent Jews from concentrating in too great numbers in any one college" was subject to "the same vice" as segregation or total exclusion: "They are spread involuntarily, which must mean that some are excluded," and those admitted "are only tolerated." Focusing on the ultimate purpose of universities—to serve as centers of learning rather than as social clubs—he insisted that "students can only be chosen by tests of scholarship. . . . [S]o far as there are any who will be turned away because they find themselves in too great a company of the uncouth, their prime purpose is not scholarship."

Although the letter was a private one, Hand knew it was bound to get widespread attention, and he himself sent copies to some acquaintances.[63] Its low-keyed, calm tone deliberately concealed the depth of his emotions on the Jewish quota issue. But when he sent a copy to Miss Grace Norton of Cambridge, the daughter of Charles Eliot Norton, his fine-arts professor at Harvard, he explained:

> I cannot disguise from myself the fact that whatever reasons I may give, my position is dictated in the end by my feelings. Perhaps it would have been franker to say so. At least I can be frank now and with you when I say that I do not believe it would have been possible to be led by my reason to another conclusion. . . . I cannot bring myself to believe that in Harvard College we can afford to draw lines based upon race and if it really comes to a

pass where we must endanger the existence of the college in a defence of its prejudices, . . . I think we must take the risk. But I have tried to discover "good" reasons as distinct from "real" reasons for my feelings.[64]

In his willingness to be an outspoken opponent of Jewish quotas, and in the depth of his hostility to them, Hand was an atypical member of his circle. Whether because he himself could sympathize readily with the feelings of outsiders or whether because he was accustomed to dealing with individuals on the basis of their personal qualities rather than their clan identifications, he spoke from the heart as well as the head.

In the otherwise genteel circle of Hand's predominantly non-Jewish friends and colleagues during the 1920s, slurs on Jews as a group were commonplace, but Hand himself was not guided in his personal behavior and attitudes by the prevalent stereotypes. He liked and admired Julian Mack, as he did the philosopher Morris Cohen; his friendship with Felix Frankfurter was as intimate as any in his life; and he formed a warm attachment to most of his law clerks, many of them Jews. Moreover, he pressed for the admission of psychoanalyst Carl Binger to the Century Association even though he was aware that a Jew faced an uphill battle there, and he refused to join another social club because he could not invite Jewish friends to lunch there.[65]

Hand knew that the Harvard faculty's acceptance of the committee's report in April 1923 did not mean the end of anti-Semitism at Harvard or in the society he moved in. And that Harvard's anti-Semitism was not limited to student admissions was brought home to him in the later 1920s when he got to know, admire, and like Nathan Margold, a young Jewish lawyer on the U.S. attorney's staff in New York. Margold was one of Felix Frankfurter's many protégés, and Hand supported his appointment as a lecturer at Harvard Law School during the 1927–28 academic year. But when the law school faculty recommended that he be named to a five-year nontenured faculty position, President Lowell refused to submit the proposal to the Board of Overseers and instead sought to persuade Margold to leave quietly. Frankfurter was sure that Lowell objected to Margold as one more Jewish "radical," but Roscoe Pound, weary of friction with the university administration, urged the faculty not to battle; after a bitter meeting, a majority of the faculty supported him.[66] Meanwhile, Hand learned from his friend Morris Cohen that Columbia Law School might be willing to have Margold on its faculty. Hand promptly volunteered his assistance and wrote a warm recommendation letter to Columbia Law School dean Young B. Smith.[67] Hand made clear that he knew Margold personally as well as from his court appearances, that he was "much impressed" by him, and that "his manners and personality are to me very agreeable." Hand had had few dealings with the school and did not know its new dean; he therefore had no reason to know that the appointment of a Jewish professor was as rare a phenomenon at Columbia as at Harvard, and that Smith often took the lead in blocking prospective Jewish appointments. Columbia took no action.

A few months later, in November 1928, Hand learned from the Wall Street lawyer George Welwood Murray that the Commonwealth Fund's legal research committee was thinking of sponsoring a study of workmen's compensation at Columbia and that Margold had been suggested to conduct it.[68] Hand's recommendation of Margold to Murray was even warmer and stronger than his letter to Dean Smith had been. He told Murray:

> I recommended him for trial at the Harvard Law School and I am sorry that they did not keep him there. Their reason was never, at least publicly, declared, but I do not think it concerned the character of his work. I had rather guess that they did not want to get many Jews upon the faculty.[69]

But once again, Margold did not get the job. (Margold eventually did find absorbing employment: like many of the best Jewish graduates of the best law schools of his day, he moved to Washington to become a New Deal official.)

BY 1920, Hand was incontrovertibly an internationalist. He had closely followed European developments in the prewar years and strongly supported America's entry into the war; his hostility to isolationism deepened during the postwar debates about the proper shape of the peace settlement and over American participation in the League of Nations. As his breach with his old friend Herbert Croly illustrated, he was convinced that the United States should join the League of Nations even if it meant accepting the Senate's reservations about it. To Hand, a reluctance to compromise and an insistence on perfectionist versions of world order were bound to fail, and would incur the unacceptable cost of curtailing sharply American engagements with the rest of the world.

With the Harding and Coolidge administrations, the United States seemed once again to be turning its back on foreign entanglements, a change that Hand repeatedly bemoaned. For him as for most of his friends, the international scene was usually synonymous with Europe, and he considered that his nation's historical, cultural, and economic ties with Europe compelled anti-isolationism. His opportunities to see the European situation at close range and to befriend many Europeans gave texture to his interest in international relations. As he watched the rise of dictatorial regimes in Europe, his belief in international alliances intensified.

Although Hand took frequent trips to Europe, he was not always an eager traveler. Heavy judicial labors absorbed him from early October of each year until the following July, by which time he would often be close to exhaustion. Left to his own choice, he would have preferred to spend his few weeks of respite from court work with family and friends in Cornish. He was never an enthusiastic sightseer, and he became impatient with the continual packing and unpacking required when visiting three or four European countries. The main reason the Hands crossed the Atlantic so frequently was Frances's irrepressible wanderlust. Indeed, in the winter of 1929–30 she set off for Europe on an extensive midyear tour with her friend Louis Dow. But during the summers, Learned, free to join her, accommodatingly went along, and while their three daughters were young, the Hands took many opportunities to show them foreign lands. By the 1930s, when the couple normally traveled alone, the European trips offered Learned welcome, uninterrupted time with his wife. At home, the two were often separated: when court was in session, Frances often spent many weeks in Cornish, while Learned commuted between his chambers in downtown Manhattan and the empty house on East Sixty-fifth Street. As he told her soon after they returned from an unusually long European trip in 1929, "It was the greatest joy to have those two and a half months with you, when we were not separated for a day and scarcely for an hour."[70]

When the judge did travel, Europe was clearly his preferred destination. Only twice did he head for the open spaces in the West: in 1917, to visit New Mexico, see the Rockies, and hike in Wyoming; and in 1930, when he ventured all the way to the West Coast, traveling from southern California to San Francisco and farther north. California left Hand so unimpressed that he headed home with no desire ever to return. "I shall never [again] willingly go to the Coast," was his verdict after traveling more than eight thousand miles. Frances was even more negative: she "enjoyed very little of it," Learned reported to his oldest daughter, Mary,[71] and the couple canceled their plans to continue up the West Coast as far as Jasper National Park in Alberta, Canada, deciding instead to head back east from Oregon.[72]

As Hand told Walter Lippmann, he found Los Angeles ultimately "intolerable": "Braggarts and Babbitts all."[73] Only the chance to see a movie scene shot at the MGM studio kept him in town briefly. A flow of copyright cases had required him to deal with film scripts; now there was a chance to see the industry in action. As he put it to Mary, though, "The ingenuity of the craftsmanship is so out of proportion to the fatuity of the result, as to leave me somewhat despondent about the fate of man. If after all this fabulous skill in mastering the secret of nature, men are no better able to produce beauty and value than this, what is the use of it all?"[74]

Characteristically, Hand was a discriminating tourist. Just as he had mixed feelings about travel in general, so he was ambivalent toward many of the countries he and Frances visited. For example, although he was interested in Greek culture throughout his life—even using Greek phrases (written in Greek) in his letters—he could not bring himself to visit Greece during the 1920s. His reluctance was a rebellion against what he considered to be the uncritical and often uncomprehending enthusiasm that English intellectuals had for ancient Greece. When Walter Lippmann told him of a day spent at Delphi in the company of the British classicist Gilbert Murray, Hand burst out, "Oh my God, those English and their god-damned Greeks!" For himself, he was "entirely clear" that the English "would have bored the Greeks" with "all their decencies," their "sentimental overlays," and "their myoses" [excessive smallness or contraction of the pupil of the eye, i.e., narrow vision]. "I am so sick of the Greeks and the canting solemnities that prove how we owe the Ford car to Anaximenes!" (He added that he had reservations about Gilbert Murray, giving several examples to show why "I have always distrusted [Murray's] translations."[75] Actually, Gus Hand was far better at reading Greek than Learned—he read Greek classics in the original until the end of his life—but Learned could read Greek, albeit not fluently.)

For Hand, England was a more attractive destination than Greece, and he and Frances went there often. Yet to England, too, his response was ambivalent. Intellectually, he was an Anglophile: British history and British institutions were in his blood. As Frankfurter once put it to him, "Anglophiles like you and me . . . care about England not only because of intellectual and emotional congeniality, but also because politically she is the most civilized society."[76] But the emotional commitment that made Hand a strong supporter of England during most of the international crises between the wars stemmed mainly from his love of its ideals and values rather than any affection for its countryside and people. He did not think that the terrain offered great attractions to an American tourist. "I do not find England really a foreign country," he told Lippmann; "the general look of things is so much like our own."[77] More important, he felt ill at ease, inadequate and inferior, in the presence of upper-class, well-educated Englishmen. He repeatedly noted the characteristic "British complacency" that could be penetrated only by flattery; and he was sensitive to what he considered the typical Englishman's superciliousness: "Sneering is as congenital with them as with Pooh-Bah."[78]

Only one European country evoked virtually no criticism from Hand: Italy was clearly his favorite, and he always tried to find time for Florence, Venice, or Rome, and, especially, the Tuscan countryside he loved. In September 1939, Hand called Italy "the love of my mature years, but as strong a love as though it had been youthful."[79] Italy did indeed stir an extraordinary passion in him: there and nowhere else did he spend hour upon hour enthusiastically touring museums, absorbed in the art of the Renaissance; there and nowhere else did he relish each new vista of the varied landscape.

His special affection for Italy's landscape and art was strengthened through his long acquaintance with Bernard Berenson, the expatriate connoisseur. Hand and "B.B." were friends for nearly forty years; over that time, they exchanged more than two hundred letters.[80] They first met in New York City in 1920, during the last of Berenson's visits to the United States; Lippmann probably introduced them.[81] Soon after B.B. returned to Italy, he sent the first of many invitations requesting that the Hands visit him there, either at his villa, I Tatti, near Florence, or at his summer retreat in Consuma, in the cooler mountains an hour away. Berenson watched the world from an emotional and physical distance. He had come to Boston as a ten-year-old Jewish immigrant from Lithuania in 1875; twelve years later, after a Harvard education, he left for Italy and an astonishing career as a prolific writer about Renaissance art; he became rich by authenticating paintings for wealthy collectors, especially through his long association with the powerful art dealer Joseph Duveen. By the time Hand first called on him at I Tatti, Berenson had long been ensconced there, entertaining a steady flow of socially prominent visitors who assured him that he was admired and accepted. Berenson loved to talk to the great and famous who joined the retinue of acolytes who would follow him on his walks through his gardens; Hand was one of the very few he would actually talk *with*.[82]

Berenson was at the peak of his fame when Hand came to know him. Nearly seven years older than Hand, the poised, self-assured fifty-five-year-old was a small, slim figure, always impeccably groomed and dressed. He usually wore a carefully tailored gray suit; the color matched his graying hair and his neatly clipped, pointed beard, which reminded some of that sported by England's King George V. And I Tatti itself had become a splendid, luxurious showplace. The villa and its setting were indeed integral parts of Berenson's self-image. I Tatti was known as the epitome of "Beauty and Art" and, like its owner, was a symbol of the reflective, scholarly life. The luxurious retreat, a perfect setting for the development of the finest aesthetic sensibilities, exuded classical restraint. The villa was set on the hills rising behind the village of Settignano, only a few miles from Florence. A grove of cypress and fir trees covered the hillside behind and embraced the villa on three sides. Originally a sixteenth-century Tuscan farmhouse, the villa, set on forty acres of land, had expanded over the years into a residence of forty rooms.

Berenson's egocentric, upper-class affectations and I Tatti's atmosphere seem unlikely attractions for a man such as Learned Hand. Yet Hand looked forward to being Berenson's guest, if only because the visits assured a few days of comfortable respite from Frances Hand's sight-seeing schedule. Both men had wide interests: they had similar educations at Harvard; they were lifelong readers; and they were both interested in political developments—Hand with more depth and engagement than Berenson. Occasionally, Berenson would stroll with just one companion, and this was the case with Hand. For Hand, these walks along the gravel paths of I Tatti's formal gardens were times to relish and cherish. Hand had always liked walking, and he loved beautiful landscapes—from the Adirondacks and the Swiss Alps to the verdant countryside of New Hampshire and the more imposing vistas of the Rockies. But no landscape moved him more than the Tuscan countryside. As they walked together, Berenson, with his eye for scenery and an ardent physical enthusiasm for the land, would stop to point out an especially lovely view, and his infatuation infected Hand.

Berenson also lifted from the judge's shoulders the burden unwittingly left by Professor Charles Eliot Norton at Harvard. The supercilious Norton, preaching his ethereal and arcane standards of "High Culture," had made Hand feel that he could never appreciate "Art" without endless labors and expert knowledge in art techniques and art history. Norton, Hand once told Berenson, "made me think that the enjoyment of art was possible only by a discipline which made a Yogi seem like a voluptuary. 'Art' was something to approach with awe and humility; it must never be a mere spontaneous outgoing." But Berenson managed to make Hand believe at last that he might be "good enough" to "get" some of the "wonderful artistic things." Spending time with Berenson and reading his work conveyed to Hand the "consolatory thought" that "when all is said, you give one the right to trust to his untutored feelings": "That is a boon greater than perhaps you can realize."[83]

BY THE MID-1920S, most Americans had settled into a complacent enjoyment of Coolidge prosperity. Hand thought Coolidge nearly as hopeless as Harding had been, and was sarcastic about the Democrats as well, but refused to follow Frankfurter into the La Follette Progressive camp; he was convinced that all hope lay in working through the major parties. (Hand's reluctance to support La Follette reflected the old view of eastern Progressives that La Follette was a wild man; not until several years later did Hand acknowledge that he might have dismissed the 1924 Progressives too readily.)[84] But civil liberties problems continued to fester, and liberal intellectuals worried about the recurrent majoritarian repressions of dissent. In talks and correspondence with friends like Frankfurter and Lippmann, Hand struggled to form his own opinions; and, characteristically, he often went his own way.

Two aspects of Hand's reactions distinguish him not only from the complacent majority but also from his liberal friends. First, Hand was too much a doubter to rush passionately to embrace any cause, and his typical open-mindedness often frustrated those of his acquaintances who were not averse to letting their emotions prompt wholehearted involvement in causes. Second, for Hand, the appropriate role of the courts was always a major concern. He had criticized judicial obstruction of majoritarian rule regarding economic policy for too long to look eagerly to the courts for help in pursuit of liberal ends. Ever since his classes with James Bradley Thayer in the 1890s, he had opposed the courts' reliance on the vague terms of the due-process clauses of the Fifth and Fourteenth Amendments to block legislative decision making. But the events of the 1920s put this to a severe test. Government repression of dissident views raised a question: Should liberals ask the courts to rely on the same due-process clauses to strike down speech-curtailing laws? Many liberals took heart from signs that the Supreme Court was becoming more lenient about economic reforms. The Bull Moose attack on the justices, it seemed, had put "the fear of God" into them;[85] the judicial ogre slaying hard-won economic reforms seemed a thing of the past. In 1921 correspondence, for example, Hand and Frankfurter agreed that the "damned Bill of Rights"—specifically, the due-process clauses—allowed judges to pour their pro-laissez-faire economic biases into the Constitution.[86] By December 1922, Hand found signs that the Supreme Court was once more moving to the right and thought the prospect not at all "pleasing"; and with Harding pondering new appointments to the Supreme Court, Hand regretfully acknowledged that the nominees' ideology was a legitimate consideration, given the lethal policy-making tools the justices had made of the due-process clauses.[87]

In April 1923, any belief that legislatures had been unshackled from the constitutional restraints of economic due process was rudely shattered when a Supreme Court 5–3 ruling in *Adkins v. Children's Hospital* held that a District of Columbia law prescribing minimum wages for women violated due process.[88] *Adkins* was a startlingly reactionary decision, and Hand wrote to Frankfurter about it the next day: "The whole thing we thought gained in 1912 [in the Bull Moose campaign] is now thrown overboard and we are just where we were." He had had higher hopes: "I confess I did not expect [such a result] again."[89]

Hand had followed the evolution of the *Adkins* case, for Frankfurter had argued on behalf of the minimum-wage law in the Supreme Court, and during his months-long preparation, Hand had cheered him on: "God be with you; strength to your brain."[90] Yet the Court, speaking through the newly appointed justice George Sutherland—who had been expected to be the most able and flexible of Harding's appointees— found minimum wages for women unconstitutional, though only fifteen years earlier it had shown a rare permissiveness toward regulation of women's working hours.[91] Now, though, Justice Sutherland insisted that freedom of contract was "the general rule, and restraint the exception," and suggested that any regulation of wages, for women as for men, was unconstitutional. And since the grant of women's suffrage by the Nineteenth Amendment, Sutherland added, the civil inferiority of women was near the "vanishing point." Justice Holmes, predictably, dissented forcefully from the majority's discovery of one more "naked, arbitrary exercise" of legislative power: he once again attacked that "dogma, Liberty of Contract," and he could not, he said, understand how the power to set minimum wages could be denied by a majority that had conceded the power to fix maximum hours for women. He added, "[It] will need more than the Nineteenth Amendment to convince me that there are no differences between men and women, or that legislation cannot take those differences into account." Even the normally conservative Chief Justice Taft was moved to dissent.*

The "real need," as Hand put it to Frankfurter, was "not to get angry over [*Adkins*], but to have some idea what one ought to do." It was clear to him, as always, that "the danger"—the justices' infusion of

---

* Justice Sanford joined Taft's dissent; Justice Brandeis did not participate in the case. Taft sounded remarkably Holmesian in insisting that "it is not the function of this Court to hold [laws] invalid because they are passed to carry out economic views which the Court believes to be unwise or unsound."

their personal views into the open-ended due-process clauses—"persists"; "I can't see anything we get out of the 5th and 14th Amendments in the least commensurate with that danger," he insisted. Frankfurter promptly agreed: "[The] possible gain isn't worth the cost of having five men, without any reasonable probability that they are qualified for the task, determine the course of social policy for the states and the nation. For, of course, it is silly to assume that the ordinary questions of law that you and other judges are concerned with, the mental habits, the stream of precedents, etc. that have come down through centuries, have any reasonable relevance to the kind of issues involved in determining whether a minimum wage law is included within 'the vague contours' of the due process clause."[92]

Prescribing a suitable remedy was a harder question. "It seems to me the place to hit is the Amendments themselves," Hand suggested. Initially, he rejected a proposed constitutional amendment advocated by Senator William Borah to require a 7–2 majority for any Supreme Court decision striking down a state law. "I am opposed to the 7:2 rule, if applied generally," he told Frankfurter; "I shouldn't want to have a state statute stand in the path of federal power [because] 3 judges stuck out for it," he commented.[93]

Further reflection led Hand to revise his thinking about remedies. Eliminating the due-process clauses might be the wisest approach, but it surely was not a practicable one: "I have no idea that you could possibly get through what would amount to a repeal of those amendments." Instead, he temporarily embraced the notion of requiring a 7–2 majority for Supreme Court invalidations, provided it were limited to due-process issues: "I am inclined to think that a good compromise is seven-two, on the Fifth and the Fourteenth Amendments. . . . If you look back you will see that a seven-two vote would have answered practically all the difficulties."[94] Eventually, Hand bowed to Frankfurter's criticism that this was little more than mechanical tinkering and that more basic changes were needed, that the "due process clause ought to go," that it was simply too open an invitation for judicial infusions of personal biases into the Constitution.[95] Hand accepted that view: it was the purest in terms of the principles he stood for, even though, as he had accurately warned Frankfurter, it was the position least likely to be implemented in practice.

WHILE HAND AND FRANKFURTER were exchanging and refining their views on *Adkins*, the Court decided another case that used the approach so long abhorrent to liberals to produce a liberal result, and that decision divided liberals, on the Court and off, in a way that has still never been healed. As long as the concept of substantive due process that the justices had relied on for decades was invoked in opinions favoring laissez-faire and economic reforms, liberals were united. But what if that concept were used for liberal ends? Should liberals applaud or condemn? This question was at the heart of the controversy among FDR's appointees to the Court in the late 1930s—appointees who, albeit all New Deal liberals, promptly split over how to wield judicial power on behalf of civil liberties. In the late 1930s, as the Court withdrew from second-guessing legislative policy choices in economic matters, many liberal justices adopted a "double standard," keeping hands off in the economic sphere even while intervening to protect individual rights. During the 1970s, this controversy grew more intense when the Court majority revived an explicit reliance on substantive due-process notions in order to protect open-ended "liberty" on behalf of such rights as that of access to abortions. And this debate persists.

This divisive issue first arose in 1923, when, two months after *Adkins* had struck down minimum-wage laws more vehemently than ever, the Court handed down its ruling in *Meyer v. Nebraska*.[96] The majority opinion in *Meyer* was written by Justice McReynolds, well known as the most reactionary (and bigoted) member of the Court's dominant conservatives. *Meyer* invalidated a state law on substantive due-process grounds, with Justice McReynolds relying on the economic-regulation cases from *Lochner* through *Adkins* that had read "liberty broadly," that had imported the "dogma, Liberty of Contract" into the Constitution, and that had condemned "arbitrary" interferences with "liberty" except in "emergency" circumstances. So far, the opinion sounded like one more obstructionist Court ruling against legislative reforms of economic affairs. But there was a big difference in result in the *Meyer* case, a difference large enough to prompt some liberals to reexamine their hostility to the Court.

Nebraska had enacted a law prohibiting the teaching of foreign languages in primary schools. Robert T. Meyer, a parochial school teacher, had been convicted of teaching German to a ten-year-old student. In the Supreme Court, Nebraska defended its law as a reasonable policy instituted so "that the sunshine of American ideals will permeate the life of the future citizens of this republic."[97] The statute was a legislative response to the xenophobic obsession that had swept the nation in the time of World War I; twenty-two states prohibited the teaching of foreign languages. Justice McReynolds, building on the restrictive due-process rulings of the previous two decades, insisted that "liberty" included not only freedom of contract but also the rights "to acquire useful knowledge, to marry, . . . [and to] bring up children," together with other privileges long recognized "as essential to the orderly pursuit of happiness by free men." Every one of these rights so read into the vague due-process clause was implicitly declared to be outside the reach of state regulatory power except in extraordinary circumstances. According to *Meyer*, the "right" of the German-language teacher "thus to teach and the right of parents to engage him so to instruct their children" could not be abridged without the strong justification required by the justices' due-process rulings; and thus the teacher's "liberty" had been unconstitutionally curtailed. For the first time, substantive due process had been used to reach a result liberals could cheer.

Justice Brandeis silently joined the majority, and among the Court's liberals, only Holmes dissented. (Sutherland, who had written *Adkins*, joined his dissent!) Holmes hinted that he, like all liberals, did not like the Nebraska law; but, he insisted, it was one "upon which men reasonably might differ and therefore I am unable to say that the [Constitution] prevents the experiment being tried."[98] This was the typical Holmes-and-Brandeis rationale in the many cases in which these Great Dissenters defended legislative experimentation in the economic sphere.

Meyer was a watershed: in every threat to civil liberties for the rest of the decade, the *Meyer* precedent prompted liberals to look to the courts for the protection of those personal rights they cherished, and the split in *Meyer* among the liberal justices was soon echoed throughout the civil liberties community. Hand and Frankfurter quickly embraced Holmes's position: they had battled too long against quasi-political due-process rulings to turn now to an opportunistic embracing of what they considered to be an illegitimate constitutional tool. As Frankfurter wrote Hand the day after the ruling:

> For myself, I should have voted with the minority [in *Meyer*]. Of course, I regard such know-nothing legislation as uncivilized, but for the life of me I can't see how it meets the condemnation of want of "due process" unless we frankly recognize that the Supreme Court of the United States is the revisory legislative body. If legislatures of our polyglot communities in their folly deem it desirable to exclude foreign languages from our schools and the 14th Amendment forbids, then I must say they are circumscribed far beyond what "fundamental principles of liberty and justice," by the most liberal conception of "fundamental," limit. . . . That kind of confinement of the activity of our legislatures shrinks their responsibility and the sense of responsibility of our voters much

beyond what is healthy for ultimate securities. The more I think
about this whole "due process" business, the less I think of lodging
that power in those nine gents at Washington.[99]

(Frankfurter's position in 1923 on *Meyer* was essentially his position
in the controversial 1940 and 1943 Supreme Court decisions on the
flag salute mandated in some states for schoolchildren.[100] In 1940, he
was in the majority on the Court, upholding the flag salute, but by
1943, the majority changed its mind, and he was in dissent. Most
modern commentators have criticized his position; few try to understand
it in terms of his long-held position on due process.)

A day later, Hand endorsed Frankfurter's position, and unlike many
liberals, he found the underlying issue easy: "I can see no reason why,
if a state legislature wishes to make a jackass of itself by that form of
Americanization, it should not have the responsibility for doing so rather
than the Supreme Court. But then, like you, I am ultra-latitudinarian
in such matters"—that is, he supported the broadest freedom for legislative experimentation, even when he did not like the product of the
lawmaking process.[101]

Most of the Court's increasingly restrictive interpretations of due
process after *Meyer* continued to void economic regulations. But two
years later, substantive due process produced a second ruling with a
liberal result. In June 1925, in *Pierce v. Society of Sisters*,[102] the reactionary McReynolds once again struck down an outgrowth of the rabid
Americanization movement, a law requiring children to attend public
schools and in effect banning private schools. The law, which was
challenged by a parochial school as well as a military academy,[103] had
been enacted under Oregon's direct democracy methods, through an
initiative measure adopted in 1922. The initiative drive had been heavily
backed by the Ku Klux Klan, and tinges of the campaign infected the
state's defense of the law: among the justifications relied on by Oregon
were that the voters sought not only to stem "the rising tide of religious
suspicions" and to "safeguard against future internal dissentions and
. . . foreign dangers," but also to further the "Americanizing [of] its
new immigrants and developing them into patriotic and law-abiding
citizens." Although most of Oregon's private schools were religious
ones, the state warned that similar ones might be established by "believers in certain economic doctrines entirely destructive of the fundamentals of our government. Can it be contended that there is no way
in which a State can prevent the entire education of a considerable
portion of its future citizens being controlled and conducted by bol-
shevists, syndicalists and communists?"[104] Anyone listening to the state's

counsel in the Supreme Court in 1925 could not but think that the postwar "Red Scare" still raged in Oregon.

Justice McReynolds's opinion found *Pierce* even easier than *Meyer*: there was nothing to indicate that nonpublic schools were educationally inadequate; accordingly, there were "no peculiar circumstances or present emergencies which demand extraordinary measures relative to primary education." Under the doctrine of *Meyer*, then, "[W]e think it entirely plain that the [law] unreasonably interferes with the liberty of parents and guardians to direct the upbringing and education of children under their control. [The due-process clause] excludes any general power of the State to standardize its children by forcing them to accept instruction from public teachers only."[105] This time, unlike *Meyer*, there was no dissent at all in the Supreme Court; both Brandeis and Holmes joined the McReynolds opinion.

Hand read about *Pierce* while he was visiting Albany, attending to the estate of his recently deceased sister, Lily. During a spare moment, he took up his pen in his old house at 224 State Street in order to write to Walter Lippmann. After Lippmann had left *The New Republic* to direct the editorial page of the *New York World,* Hand had drawn closer to him: Lippmann's calm, rational commentary on the passing political scene seemed increasingly attractive. They saw each other frequently in New York, and they often exchanged notes. In Albany, Hand was anticipating that he might not see Lippmann for weeks: Lippmann was in Baltimore, at the hospital bed of his wife, who was recuperating from a serious operation; Hand would soon leave for a European trip. Hand, who recognized that Lippmann's strength lay in displays of sheer intellect and that he rarely displayed genuine sympathy with people, thought that Mrs. Lippmann's illness might afford her husband a rare chance to escape the constraints on his emotions. He also suspected that Lippmann could handle personal problems with greater equanimity than he himself could: "I think of you as keeping an evener keel than I should"; in family crises, Lippmann would not be tortured by the feelings that would beset Hand—"the sense that your lid will blow off"; Lippmann, Hand thought, probably had "an enormous advantage over the ill 'integrated' " such as he. Yet he wasn't wholly sure, and so he wrote primarily to extend the warmth of his friendship to his cool young friend: "[I]t will be pleasant to know that you are in the minds of your friends. You are."

But Hand found it impossible not to address other issues when writing to so ostentatiously intellectual a person as Lippmann. By the sixth page of his eight-page letter, he turned to the just decided *Pierce* case. "I was amused that the Oregon school case came out of their Nibs without a scratch. Even old Holmesy couldn't stomach that," he wrote. But Holmes's and Brandeis's silent acquiescence was difficult to accept intellectually:

> [I]t's a little hard to see why if the State may say to Alvin Johnson [the former *New Republic* editor, now head of the New School for Social Research] "We won't let you keep your children out of school till we give the wiff the once-over and see whether she is up to our curricular standards"; why if the State may say that, it mayn't say "On the whole we decide that the education we want must be in our schools."

Yet he sympathized with the liberals who joined the ruling: "Well, it's all a matter of degree, and as the Klan was at work, I can't complain at the lack of logical integrity. Had I been there I should have been recorded [as] a 'me too,' I fancy." Still, he was bitter about the enormous judicial power that had been infused into the vague words of due process: "One might as well confess that the 'nine' are a superior legislative house and be done w. it. But let them be on guard that they assume no more than an overwhelming consensus of the vocal folks will admit." He could not resist closing with a sarcastic remark about his view of justices who enforced their political preferences under the guise of due-process rulings: "That's a fine doctrine for judicial independence."[106]

Above all, Hand feared that the justices' use of the due-process clauses to resolve heated partisan issues would subvert their authority to decide disputes about more concrete legal norms. Within days of *Pierce*, he made clear that he disagreed with those liberals who were ready to abandon their traditional antipathies toward due process so long as the laws they were attacking threatened civil liberties rather than laissez-faire. The battle was joined over an issue that had arisen in Tennessee even while the *Pierce* case was before the Supreme Court; and Hand's views emerge most clearly in his sharp rejection of Lippmann's suggestion that it was time for liberals to abandon the old progressive faith and look to the courts for help in causes they favored.

In March 1925, Tennessee adopted a law forbidding public school employees "to teach any theory that denies the Story of Divine Creation of man as taught in the Bible, and to teach instead that man has descended from a lower order of animal."[107] Tennessee's anti-evolution law—the "monkey law"—was a triumph for the enemies of Darwinian theories led by the WCFA, the World's Christian Fundamentalist Association. In 1925, the recently formed American Civil Liberties Union, at first preoccupied with the evils of Americanization programs and with Klan-supported attacks on Catholic schools, added the fundamentalist crusade to its targets. The civil libertarians persuaded a young science teacher, John T. Scopes, to stand trial in a criminal prosecution under the new law, and recruited a prominent legal team led by Clarence Darrow to defend him; the WCFA persuaded William Jennings Bryan, the Democrats' Bible-preaching three-time presidential candidate, to lead the prosecution. The ACLU's objectives in the Scopes case were twofold: first, to expose (and mock) the ignorance that had produced the law; second, to test its constitutionality by ultimately carrying the question to the Supreme Court.[108] But the ACLU succeeded only in its first aim. The enormous publicity surrounding the trial reached its high point when Darrow managed to call Bryan to the stand and ferociously examine and effectively ridicule his literal interpretation of the Bible. Hundreds of journalists had descended on Dayton, Tennessee; most of them portrayed the anti-evolution crusade as a backward, rural, southern, ignorant phenomenon; and the ACLU could justifiably proclaim a propaganda victory. (The crushed Bryan died a week after the trial.)

But the ACLU could not claim a legal victory. Scopes was convicted and fined $100. Darrow knew all along that his courtroom fireworks (dramatized decades later in the play and movie *Inherit the Wind*) would not exonerate his client; indeed, he had hoped that the jury would convict Scopes so that he could then attack the "monkey law" on appeal. But the Tennessee Supreme Court managed to foil the ACLU's efforts to reach the U.S. Supreme Court: the state court rejected all the ACLU's constitutional arguments and yet reversed Scopes's conviction on a technicality (that the fine had been imposed by the trial judge rather than by the jury). One of the ACLU lawyers charged that this was a state "subterfuge . . . to prevent the legality of the law [from] being tested." But the state court ruling ended the case: without a conviction, there was nothing to appeal to Washington.[109]

Although the "monkey law" trial was a national public-opinion victory for the ACLU, it took four more decades for a similar law to reach the U.S. Supreme Court and be struck down there,[110] and despite many historians' verdict that *Scopes* struck a death knell for anti-evolution laws, the issue was not ultimately settled even in 1968; instead, new test cases were needed to challenge the modern wave of "creationism" laws. Moreover, the legal aim of the ACLU in the 1920s has never been achieved. In *Scopes*, the ACLU wanted to ensure a constitutional right of academic freedom for public school teachers; yet any right to present subjects according to the teacher's best lights is still very much in doubt. True, the modern legal attacks on "monkey" and "creationism" laws have succeeded,[111] but the victories have rested on the ground that the laws constitute a state "establishment" of religion, a ground not available in the 1920s and only made possible after various Supreme Court decisions, starting in the late 1940s, held that the First Amendment's ban on "establishment" was applicable to state governments.

The publicity about Tennessee's anti-evolution law and the *Scopes* trial escaped neither Hand nor Lippmann. Both thought the law abhorrent. Lippmann turned out one impassioned editorial after another; Hand—like Clarence Darrow, an agnostic—was deeply disturbed by Tennessee's policy. In his Albany letter to Lippmann in Baltimore, he had remarked, apropos of medical research, "We shall in the end know a good deal about this complicated chemical combination which has so strangely appeared in a tiny satellite of a modest star. That is, we shall unless the besotted Tennesseans and their ilk do not engulf us." And Hand continued his musings:

> There's a fine passage somewhere in Gilbert Murray where he says that the Greek always lived w. the consciousness that he was on a little island likely to be overwhelmed by the seas of barbarism at any time. Finally it was. I have always felt that we were secure. The last ten years ought to give anyone some pause. Still I think it will be O.K., but it's a long fight, and the end always uncertain. [112]

Hand's speculations struck only a partially responsive chord with Lippmann, who was growing ever more sympathetic to efforts to have the Supreme Court strike down anti-evolution laws on substantive due-process grounds. He replied:

> I want your advice badly on the Tennessee case. [Constitutional-law professor Thomas Reed] Powell and Morris Cohen take the view [that] the constitutionality of the law ought not to be attacked. Such foolishness should be within the province of the legislature. . . . Now I know this is progressive dogma as we all accepted it in the days when the courts were knocking out the laws we wanted. Powell and Cohen are consistent, but I wonder whether we don't have to develop some new doctrine to protect education from majorities. My own mind has been getting steadily antidemocratic: the size of the electorate, the impossibility of educating it sufficiently, the fierce ignorance of these millions of semiliterate priest-ridden and parsonridden people have got me to the point where I want to confine the actions of majorities. At any rate we have got to fight this Tennessee business somehow. What do you think? [113]

Hand disagreed, and wrote promptly and firmly to that effect. He was no more willing to trust the Court with issues of school policy than with those of economic theory:

> I think you are wrong about Tennessee. . . . What I said about the Oregon case [*Pierce*] indicates my attitude. Left to myself I would have swallowed even that, a fortiori this. . . . Somebody must determine the curriculum. Who shall it be? The judges? Well, if so, only when the preponderance is overwhelming. It's a case in the end of protecting [the judges'] independence and nobody knows how important that is who has not served in the job. If they are to act at all in such matters, as to which I have some doubt, it must be only in the extremest cases.

For Hand, the notion of seeking the courts' aid under the due-process clauses in order to protect liberal values was ultimately negated by his belief in the democratic process—the right of the people and their representatives to decide controversial issues for themselves, rather than being ruled by the policy choices of an unelected, unresponsive, undemocratic judiciary. This was a position he would in later years often identify with E. M. Forster's *Two Cheers for Democracy*: support for popular decision making under a system whose flaws and risks one perceived but whose essentials one considered the best among the alternatives. As Hand told Lippmann:

> We are in for democracy and while I am as shaken as you [by its excesses], I ask for any available substitute. These are the conditions: a principle of continuity,—that rules out dictators,— enough power to ensure stability, that in modern times means the acquiescence of great masses of the people,—some assurance that intelligence in the conduct of government will not cost too much in selfishness and exploitation—that on the whole seems to me to forbid an oligarchy, though as to that I am open to conviction. On the whole the principle of counting heads apparently assures the first & second, at least the first. If I could get far enough away I might be more doubtful about the third, but at close range I am disposed to guess that even the modern technique of suggestion [i.e., political propaganda] will not allow such absolute exploitation as uncontrolled power. Ignorance may yet overwhelm us but I am laying my odds against it.[114]

Hand's admiration for Lippmann had been consolidated several years earlier, when Lippmann's *Public Opinion* was published, probably his most important and certainly his best-received book,[115] which went

beyond the political analysts' traditional preoccupations with institutions
and formal governmental processes and drew heavily on the new field
of social psychology. In it he suggested that biases, stereotypes, and
propaganda were undermining the traditional foundations of popular
government: the assumption that the masses had the information to
make policy decisions, the "original dogma of democracy," was outmoded in the complex, modern age. "The common interests very largely
elude public opinion entirely, and can be managed only by a specialized
class." Yet he concluded on a note of optimism: "It is necessary to live
as if good will would work," he claimed. "It is not foolish for men to
believe . . . that intelligence, courage and effort cannot ever contrive
a good life for all men."[116]

Hand read *Public Opinion* with enthusiasm: he shared Lippmann's
concern with mass psychology and competence as well as his seeming
faith that somehow democracy would survive. He recognized that
the book could not have been done without "the pioneer work" of
Graham Wallas, the Fabian sociologist who was an early mentor of
Lippmann and Hand's longtime acquaintance; but he also acknowledged
Lippmann's originality, though he perceived an increasingly conservative tone in the younger man's work. Hand, too, after all, had lost
some of his reformist zeal of the early *New Republic* and even earlier
Bull Moose days; still, he never turned as conservative as Lippmann,
and he retained greater affection for the days when life seemed simpler.
Lippmann's prescription of rule by experts struck him as too mechan-
istic, too neat, too intellectual. In theory, it made sense "to let the
experts work" lest the "barbarian invasion" of the demagogues of
the press and of politics—"the Hearsts, the Thompsons" ("Big Bill"
Thompson was then mayor and boss of Chicago)—overwhelm all. But,
Hand suggested, Lippmann's incomplete analysis did not take sufficient
account of the complexities of human drives:

> Your faith that stepping down the voltage of disputes by taking
> out the exciting phrases may serve in part, but where I stick is
> the hopeless proclivity of us all to enjoy getting discharged emo-
> tionally. The glorious reality of the welter of the good old reliable
> manly reflexes. The gruesome mortification of checking our im-
> pulses by the real environment. How in Hell are we ever to be
> rid of the delights of these?

Amid his praise and genuine admiration, then, Hand was dissatisfied
with Lippmann's simplistic reliance on "experts" and his inadequate
appreciation of the power of mass emotions:

In a foolish way I fondly hoped you may be going to point the way. . . . [But] how could anyone? The diagnosis is sound and scorching; we must pry about here & there for meliorating therapy. "Trial and error," yes that will serve, but [as] I read it last night, I said "yes trial & error," but "trial & error with record." I suppose the Banderlog have trial & error, but of what account is it to them, for they forget to-day what they did yesterday. And so it is too with Demos. Can you give him a memory? I would pay you more for that than [for] anything else. Then he could learn.[117]

Hand's questioning speculations helped Lippmann to press forward with his analysis and to seek resolution of his incongruous juxtaposition of a sophisticated, pessimistic analysis with a simplistic call for "experts" and a vaguely optimistic conclusion. Lippmann's sequel, entitled *The Phantom Public*, was not published until 1925, soon after the Scopes controversy.[118] That summer, Lippmann ended a letter to Hand with "another favor to ask":

My book "The Phantom Public" is to be published in the fall. . . . I want to dedicate the book to you, and I am embarrassed because I feel you ought to have a chance to say no, and I am afraid you won't say no whatever your feeling about it. I am quite prepared to believe you will think it crude and even unsound, because I have taken a flyer into a rather strange field of theory. Please be frank enough to say just what you would like best.[119]

Hand happily accepted the honor:

[This] has given me a satisfaction greater than anything else . . . in a long time. I don't need to read the proofs: I know you and what you have said even if I don't go along with it pari passu. [It] will so nearly accord with what I think at least after I have read it that there is no chance taken. Besides, I don't suppose that one assumes a foot to foot concurrence in such matters. Now that you have suggested it I can only say that it would be a grave disappointment to me if I didn't get what seems to me one of the greatest honors I have had.[120]

But Hand must have read the book with very mixed, often disappointed emotions. He never wrote to Lippmann about it; unlike *Public Opinion*, it elicited no superlatives from him. Lippmann abandoned the optimism with which he had ended *Public Opinion* and now pronounced that it was a "false ideal" to believe that the masses had the interest or the capacity to govern themselves. The traditional democratic premise that the voters direct the course of government was simply wrong; such a public was a "mere phantom." Even Lippmann's faith in experts had waned: the true distinction was between insiders and outsiders, with only the former having adequate data to act on. "The public must be put in its place," he insisted, "so that each of us may live free of the trampling and the roar of a bewildered herd." Hand, too, sometimes referred to the masses as "the herd"; but his fears were mixed with empathy, and his conclusion was never so bleak. Lippmann wrote as a disillusioned ex-romantic, ex-idealist, ex-Progressive: as he suggested in an especially personal passage in the book, he had "lived through the romantic age in politics" and was "no longer moved by the stale echoes of its hot cries"; he was now "sober and unimpressed," no longer a crusader. But Hand could no more accept Lippmann's broad condemnation of majoritarian experimentation than he could endorse his flirtation with judicial intervention under the due-process clauses.

NEAR THE END OF 1925, Lippmann reminded Hand that Justice Holmes would turn eighty-five on March 8, 1926, and asked Hand to write a short appreciation of him for the *World* on that occasion, "signed preferably."[121] Hand wrote the essay, was characteristically unhappy with its quality, but sent it along to Lippmann, insisting that it be anonymous, as indeed it was.

> Plainly I cannot sign it; it too clearly commits the writer to the Holmesian point of view. . . . [I]f you use it, I must ask that you keep its authorship to yourself. I tried to make it colorless enough to bear a signature, but that took out of it even such guts as it has. It's impossible to say anything extra-judicially if you are a judge.[122]

Despite Hand's self-deprecating letter, his tribute to Holmes is in fact a significant and elegant little work in which, as if continuing his argument with Lippmann about the Scopes trial, he elaborated Holmes's (and in effect his own) position on constitutional questions:

> There are two schools, rather two tendencies; one is to impose upon the Constitution the fundamental political assumptions which for the time being are dominant; it views the general clauses of the amendments as protecting the individual from the vagaries and extravagancies of faction. The other does not depart from the first in theory but in application is more cautious. That caution in the end must rest upon a counsel of scepticism or at least upon a

recognition that there is but one test for divergent popular convictions, experiment, and that almost any experiment is in the end less dangerous than its suppression. Of the second school, Justice Holmes . . . has been one of the foremost members.

Holmes's views on challenged legislation did not turn on whether he agreed or disagreed with the law; instead, Hand emphasized, they "indicate his settled belief that in such matters the judges cannot safely intervene, that the Constitution did not create a tri-cameral system, that a law which can get itself enacted is almost surely to have behind it a support which is not wholly unreasonable." He elaborated (as if speaking for himself) that Holmes's advocacy of judicial deference to legislative choices reflected the justice's concern about which branch of government should bear the "odium of disappointing large numbers of persons": "Shall the courts bear it, and can they while they keep an official irresponsibility to public opinion? To withdraw them from such controversies may in the end be the surest protection of their powers."

Hand also spoke perceptively about Holmes's personal traits; and as usual in his tributes to others, he spoke more truly of himself than of his subject. He attributed to Holmes one of his own qualities: "a sceptical disposition," concededly "hazardous equipment for a judge." Holmes's special characteristics, Hand noted, had always had their fullest recognition "among those"—Hand was clearly one of them—"to whom life is complex and universals slippery and perilous; to whom truth is a dangerous experiment and man a bungling investigator."[123]

How could a judge be skeptical and genuinely open-minded? Was this "temper of detachment" the ready product of an Olympian disengagement from the problems of mankind, or did it result from an agonized emotional struggle, a difficult act of will, a conscientious effort?

The temper of detachment and scrutiny is not beguiling; men find it more often a cool jet than a stimulus, and it is a little curious that they ever can be brought to rate it highly. Yet, in the end, it has so obvious a place in any rational world that its value is forced upon their notice and they look behind to the disposition which produces it. If they do, they find it anything but cold or neutral, for the last acquisition of civilized man is forbearance in judgment and to it is necessary one of the highest efforts of the will.[124]

When Hand described "forbearance in judgment" as a painful effort of the "will," he accurately described his own agonies during several of the civil liberties disputes of the 1920s, certainly those of the *Meyer* and *Pierce* cases and the Scopes controversy. But on several others he vacillated, and this irresolute behavior showed the uncertainty, even fearfulness, that had been part of his makeup ever since childhood; some of his greater caution was less the product of self-disciplined "forbearance" than of what he himself sometimes called a lack of courage.

This fearfulness could be seen in 1919, when he refused to join the widespread liberal outrage about the attacks on Felix Frankfurter for chairing the Boston meeting advocating recognition of the Soviet Union. But no controversy of the 1920s illustrates Hand's vacillation more poignantly than the Sacco-Vanzetti case. That case engaged Frankfurter's emotions more deeply than any other controversy of the 1920s, yet, despite his efforts to rouse Hand's interest and feelings, Hand only very slowly, and only very late, came to believe that there might indeed have been something wrong with the criminal proceedings against the Italian immigrants.

Nicola Sacco, a shoemaker, and Bartolomeo Vanzetti, a fish peddler, both anarchists, were arrested in May 1920 for the holdup and murder of a guard and a payroll clerk. They were tried in Dedham, Massachusetts, before Judge Webster Thayer, and they were readily convicted and sentenced to death. At the beginning, the Sacco-Vanzetti case was mainly an occasion for a battle between extremists: those on the left viewed it as an opportunity to spread the gospel of class warfare and to indict the corruption of American society; those on the right saw it as one more chance to vent their hatred of foreign radicals. Judge Thayer was indeed biased—he referred to the defendants privately as "those anarchistic bastards"[125]—but he was careful to keep his prejudices out of the trial record.[126] (In fact, the evidence was complex and conflicting, and the question of the defendants' guilt or innocence continues to be debated to this day.)

For five years after the convictions in 1920, Frankfurter paid virtually no attention to it. Then, in 1925, a new, middle-of-the-road defense lawyer charged that the prosecutor had misled the court and that the administration of justice had thereby been subverted, and Frankfurter became convinced that the defendants had not received a fair trial. Once roused, he worked indefatigably: in addition to coordinating strategy and publicity in the final months of the long proceedings, he buried himself in the huge trial record and produced a long article designed to appeal to the "best people," which was published in *The Atlantic Monthly*.[127] And in March 1927, soon after Frankfurter first wrote about the case, he began to besiege Hand with letters designed to stir in him a similar concern.

Hand initially shrank back from immersion in it;[128] and reluctance to become engaged remained his stance for months thereafter. What explains Hand's disinclination to take sides in this controversy? To some extent, it was his faith in the established judicial order; to some extent, it was his congenital uncertainty. But the explanation lies in other sources as well. For one thing, Hand instinctively recoiled whenever Frankfurter vented the self-righteous certitude of the passionate zealot; and for another, he often doubted that the American criminal-justice system was truly sensible when it afforded defendants seemingly endless opportunities to challenge their convictions.

As early as 1923, for example, Hand had been irritated by Frankfurter's intense, aggressive adherence to the causes he embraced, that year the cause being the forced resignation of Amherst College's president Alexander Meiklejohn, a gifted educator and philosopher. Meiklejohn's reforms at Amherst were popular with students, but he had managed to alienate most of his faculty and lose the confidence of his trustees, both because of campus schisms over educational reforms and because of his mismanagement of finances. Frankfurter was convinced that Meiklejohn's departure from Amherst constituted a violation of academic freedom. "I am rather on the warpath about [it]," he told Hand. "Hardly any American episode since the Armistice has stirred me up as much as this has." He was especially short-tempered when Hand protested that given an insufficient "information for judgment," he was "inclined most to trust" the Amherst trustees he knew (the trustee Hand knew best was the liberal Republican Dwight Morrow); trustees of private colleges, he argued, should be judged on the basis of broad institutional results, not individual personnel decisions.[129] In the face of Frankfurter's whirlwind of argumentation, Hand simply abandoned correspondence about the issue: there was no point in continuing, he told Frankfurter, "especially as you feel so strongly about it."[130] He found Frankfurter "highly wrought," as he put it to Lippmann, and commented resignedly, "Well, we are differently made."[131] (Lippmann, it turned out, had for weeks borne the stings of Frankfurter's outrage about the *World*'s equivocation regarding the Amherst matter. Lippmann had written in praise of Meiklejohn, but also condoned the action of the trustees,[132] and Frankfurter had lectured him that his business was to interpret, not to act as a mere impartial reporter. "[W]hat in Sam Hill has got into Felix to make him so suspicious, so querulous, and so argumentative?" Lippmann asked Hand.)[133]

Only rarely did Hand have the stomach to explore more deeply the differences in temperament that produced his repeated irritations with Frankfurter. One revealing exchange in the late 1920s shows just how "differently made" they were. This time the issue was a quite technical debate about the appropriate jurisdiction of the federal courts. Frankfurter, the originator of scholarly interest in this subject, repeatedly argued that the federal courts should not be in the business of deciding disputes simply because citizens of different states were battling one another; Hand did not fully agree, believing that even in the twentieth century there was still reason to afford a neutral federal judicial forum to out-of-state residents who might encounter local prejudices if they had to submit their cases to state courts. As usual, Frankfurter persisted in pressing his views at length, Hand repeatedly voiced his disagreements, and after numerous letters and conversations, Hand expressed his annoyance to Frankfurter's face—and promptly turned regretful. In an April 1929 note, Hand apologized. Oliver Wendell Holmes had once suggested, Hand said, that the ultimate "upshot" of Frankfurter's tireless activities "would be to invest affairs with more rationality," and Hand agreed.

> I suppose I am not much unlike other men when I find that generally when my friends seem to impinge upon me, it is because they are touching spots that I have comfortably glazed over, but where I am really in conflict. They awaken those conflicts and the result is disturbing. Brandeis once said to me that the chief virtue in a democracy was militancy. I will not go quite to that degree, for militancy so often breeds militancy and contention obscures judgment; yet I cannot deny the value of that virtue. It is easy to conform; years make it doubly easy. You are an influence which helps disturb me from that vice, to which I suppose I am getting more and more prone. You will have to accept at times the price from one who has always been somewhat irritable.

In a moving passage, he acknowledged his own weaknesses and combined criticism of Frankfurter's off-putting traits with an expression of the deep affection that helped assure the survival of their friendship for more than fifty years:

> I would at times wish that you did not so often espouse causes, but may not this be because I do not find the energy or the will,—perhaps the courage,—to espouse any myself? Do not think that this can obscure to me what you do and what you will continue to do. There must be those who act; it is not enough to affect an

aloofness which may be the cover for incapacity to make up one's mind. Do not believe that I shall ever fail to see these things in you; whatever at a distance I may feel, never do I meet you alone when my heart does not warm to your friendship.*[134]

But Hand's reluctance to join Frankfurter's crusade against the Sacco-Vanzetti convictions was also rooted in his views regarding the risk of unjust convictions in criminal cases. Hand had made his position clear to Frankfurter several years before the Sacco-Vanzetti controversy reached its peak. In 1923, in a district court opinion in *United States v. Garsson*, he had made harsh, law-and-order remarks critical of excessive solicitude for criminal defendants: "Our dangers do not lie in too little tenderness to the accused. Our procedure has always been haunted by the ghost of the innocent man convicted. It is an unreal dream. What we need to fear is the archaic formalism and the watery sentiment that obstructs, delays, and defeats the prosecution of crime."[135] These sentences stirred Frankfurter's interest and wrath, but Hand held firm:

> Like you, I vary somewhat in my views about the procedural protections accorded to defendants. Occasionally the show goes wrong. On the whole when it does it is because the public is in a hanging mood and I doubt in those cases the efficacy of the safeguards you mention. Perhaps I underestimate them. In ordinary times you will agree that American criminal jurisprudence has been fettered by the web of red tape which has always surrounded it. We must in some way learn to deal more directly and effectively with the commission of crime if we are to check the lawlessness which is our curse. I had rather take my chances of occasional judicial lynchings than hamstring the usual course of justice, though I admit it is a matter of degree.[136]

By March 1927, when Frankfurter sent his *The Atlantic Monthly* article to Hand, one motion for a new trial of Sacco and Vanzetti had already failed; soon, the denial of a second motion was affirmed by the highest Massachusetts court. Amid these legal maneuverings, Frank-

---

* Frankfurter's even briefer reply returned the warmth and conveyed a rare sense that he could at times recognize the prickly aspects of his own personality:

> For [a] good twenty years now, I have had a solid and steadily growing affection for you apart from mere admiration for your great talents. And it has pained me to realize that from time to time I have irritated you. . . . You brought me much peace by analyzing the source of "irritation." I suppose there is a gaudium certaminis [joy in certainty] in my nature. But, know that at all times it is truly innocent [Felix Frankfurter to LH, 28 April 1929, 104–15].

furter published his study charging that the judge and prosecutor had jointly created a hysterical atmosphere at the trial, and that the evidence against the defendants was in any event circumstantial. Soon after, Massachusetts governor Alvan Fuller refused to commute the sentence. Yet when Hand received Frankfurter's article, he seemed in no hurry to read it. He hoped to be able to get to it "when the occasion offers," he wrote. "I find myself unconsciously tending more strongly than I wish I did toward the position of my order," he confessed: he presumed that after a full trial and repeated appeals in the state courts, serious error was unlikely; he gave the benefit of the doubt to convictions validated by the formal judicial machinery. Still, he reassured his friend that "I believe that when I come to read this I shall be able to overcome any prejudice with which I may instinctively approach it."[137]

For the next few weeks, Frankfurter, with unaccustomed gentleness, persisted in trying to arouse Hand's interest. Early in April, for example, he sent Hand a letter that the Harvard historian Samuel Eliot Morison had written to the *Boston Herald*, in order "to let you know how the very best mind and spirit of New England feels about the Sacco-Vanzetti business, when not in the grip of bogies and fears about the onrush [of] Bolshevism into State Street."[138] But once again, Hand shrank from taking a stand. To reach a firm judgment, he told Frankfurter, "involves more inquiry than I have had any opportunity to make." Yet Frankfurter managed to elicit a few comments, at least suggesting that Hand was beginning to harbor some doubts about capital punishment.[139]

Ultimately, Hand did pay closer attention to the controversy, but not in exchanges with Frankfurter: there was no mention of Sacco-Vanzetti in their letters for the next two years. Instead, they reached an implicit understanding to avoid the issue entirely. When they met at a conference in New Hampshire, late in the summer of 1927, Hand reported to Lippmann,

> I did have to sit at the table when he got started, and it was to me exquisitely painful. That he knew the case in its least details was of course true, but while that made it impossible to dispute with him, his conclusions at least for me were without weight, because it was so apparent that no more light could then come into his mind, and that passion had seized all. What I needed was someone who would give me conclusions that I could accept. Plainly he was in no condition to do that.[140]

Yet with the mounting debate about the case, Hand could not help but follow the unfolding of the Sacco-Vanzetti tragedy more closely. Frankfurter's *The Atlantic Monthly* article, and its reprinting in his ensuing "little book" about the case, *The Case of Sacco and Vanzetti*, had significant consequences. Before Frankfurter wrote, most of the protests had come from those quite far left on the political spectrum. Frankfurter's withering attack troubled the Boston establishment, as it had been intended to do; and it generated widespread attention around the world. Frankfurter himself was busier than ever in consulting on strategy to save the defendants. At about the time of his final effort to rouse Hand's attention, Frankfurter concluded that further appeals to the courts on behalf of Sacco and Vanzetti were not likely to be productive. Instead, he and his fellow lawyers tried to attain executive clemency. They hoped that Massachusetts governor Fuller could be persuaded to commute the death sentences, especially if he would name a group of impartial citizens to investigate the trial. The governor did indeed agree to appoint a review board, but the group was headed by Harvard president A. Lawrence Lowell, Frankfurter's old nemesis. Frankfurter did not expect Lowell to be any more fair-minded on this issue than he had been on the "Jewish quota," but the defendants' supporters hoped the board would raise enough doubts about the trial to encourage Governor Fuller (whom Frankfurter later described as "crude, illiterate, self-confident") to commute the death sentences.

But when the Lowell report was published in early August, the liberals were stunned: the board announced that the trial had been fair and the defendants guilty. John F. Morrs, an old friend of Lowell and a member of the Harvard Corporation, commented that the review board had been "incapable of seeing that two wops could be right and the Yankee judiciary could be wrong." Frankfurter fervently agreed: Lowell "couldn't transcend his belief in his crowd."[141] After this setback, Frankfurter and his associates went on trying to avert Sacco's and Vanzetti's executions. But it was all to no avail. On August 23, Sacco and Vanzetti were electrocuted. As the final crescendo of the long campaign on their behalf, mass protest demonstrations were held throughout Europe as well as the United States; with their death, Sacco and Vanzetti elicited an anger and sympathy that have reverberated in newspapers and books, in novels, poetry, and drama, to this day.[142]

During the final weeks before the executions, Hand was at his summer home in Cornish. Surrounded by his old liberal friends, uniformly partisans of the defendants, he paid more careful attention to the proceedings; and most of his day-by-day information came from the pages of Lippmann's *World*. By the climax, he was fully absorbed at last. Slowly, he came to conclude that the trial had indeed been unfair and that class bias had infected the Lowell board. Ironically, his most probing introspection about the controversy came in the weeks *after* the execution, when he finally mustered the energy (and the time) to think more carefully about it; only then did he feel ready to make up his mind; only in retrospect did he express the "wish that I could have come to a more certain conclusion with myself" while the defendants were still alive, as he confessed to Lippmann.[143]

Even then, even when Hand finally realized that an injustice had probably been done, he was almost equally preoccupied with how Europeans were assessing the case: "The foreign press has been extremely irresponsible, in my judgment, and would not have been so if the occasion had not been so apt to vent their hatred of all things American." He was especially annoyed by "the English, who have their blissful faculty of making one feel the Scythian manners and Scythian mores with which one is branded. . . . I can get the sense of what it feels to be one of an oppressed race, with all its dangers to one's mental symmetry. I confess to a considerable Anglophobia just now."[144]

In a September 20 letter to Lippmann, Hand continued to be beset with inhibitions, doubts, and vacillations. He agreed that a "miscarriage of justice" had probably occurred; yet he continued to agonize about how the legal system should have responded. He was troubled about giving in to emotional appeals that threatened the calm façade of the law; he was troubled about caving in to European hysteria; he was troubled by the system of criminal procedure whose recurrent errors were more likely to let the guilty go free than punish the innocent; and, at bottom, he was deeply uncomfortable with his own deep-rooted uncertainties. Long after his friends had taken sides, and after the defendants had been executed, Hand was still searching for an escape from the swamp he found himself in once again.

One aspect of the case that especially disturbed him was that massive public protests had exerted unaccustomed pressure upon the normal operations of the judicial structure. And the temptation to bow to European outcries troubled him deeply: to have had the courts or the governor save the defendants "because the world outside" was outraged seemed to Hand "a very doubtful proposal." Bowing to public opinion was beyond the pale for Hand. The "only tenable attack" on the convictions, in Hand's view, had to rest on "the merits," "taking all the proceedings as a whole." And if the Sacco-Vanzetti pleas had been limited to those grounds, Hand was not at all confident that a new trial or clemency would have been appropriate. Hand once again sought shelter in his perceptions of the problems of American criminal procedure. Hand could not condone the "introduction of passion of any kind into judicial procedure." Usually, passion served to acquit the guilty; the Sacco-Vanzetti case was a rarer one in which passion did perhaps convict the innocent. But to battle the bias in any trial by resorting to mass protests was unacceptable: that represented another illegitimate "introduction of passion" into a system he wanted cleared of such distorting influences.[145]

Hand's ultimate judgment on the case was a thoughtful, responsible one from his judicial perspective; yet his retreat from the case's specifics to generalities about the error-prone qualities of American criminal justice was also an ultimate vacillation that, as Hand himself occasionally recognized, could be taken as a lack of courage. Frankfurter, reminiscing about the Sacco-Vanzetti storm in his old age, identified a central problem in the controversy: "What is it that makes so many men timid creatures?" He wondered why "those who are economically independent, those who have position, those who by speaking out [would] turn on the currents of reason and check the currents of unreason," were silent.[146] Frankfurter would no doubt have placed Hand among these "timid creatures," even though his judicial position gave him a reason not to speak out publicly.

The worldwide uproar over Sacco and Vanzetti faded quickly after their executions in August 1927. Hand was amazed that after all the turmoil "the whole thing seems now to be drifting into the realm of forgotten things," as he put it to Lippmann, and he related this dreamy indifference to the era's "mythical, unbelievable, though actual, prosperity. . . . People want to be rich and comfortable, and are quite contented so long as they are. All of us reformers, and betterers in general, had best accept that with as good grace as we can. It ought not to be such a surprise to moralists, who are never tired of telling us that we reach holiness only through our tribulations."[147]

But the nagging issues would not wholly fade for him, and reminders arose in unanticipated contexts. In November, for example, Frankfurter sent Hand a copy of the major scholarly book of his career, *The Business of the Supreme Court*.[148] During a brief winter vacation in Charleston in January 1928, Hand finally had a chance to read the tome and promptly wrote an effusively appreciative letter to the author: "What an amazing mine of information it is! How extraordinary that anyone can find the opportunity for such detailed and thorough work!" Then, near the end of his long and supportive letter, he included a remark that reopened old wounds: "Your temper in this book was so severely detached, so 'scientific,' that there is little to carry away for propaganda. I wish those who complain of Sacco & Vanzetti would be forced to see how dispassionate you can be, when you are engaged in real research, and are not trying to accomplish a specific purpose."[149]

Frankfurter was understandably stung by the implicit distinction between his professorial detachment when he undertook "real research" and his less dispassionate temper when engaged in "propaganda" to "accomplish a specific purpose." After delaying a response to Hand's note for over six weeks, he erupted:

> I know the criticisms that have been widely made. But, personally, I think that exactly the same spirit of scholarship which produced the Business was behind the S. V. [the Sacco-Vanzetti book]. I aimed at accuracy & thus far no one . . . has pointed out any omissions or commissions. If ever you know of anyone who is prepared to be specific in his criticisms I should be genuinely obliged to you to let me have such criticisms.[150]

ON A LESS WELL KNOWN ISSUE that arose within months of the executions of Sacco and Vanzetti, Hand demonstrated an even stronger opposition to abuses of governmental power than did Frankfurter. The issue was the power of the United States Senate to bar elected members from serving in Congress.

In December 1927, two investigations of recently elected members got under way in the Senate. Both senators—William S. Vare of Pennsylvania and Frank L. Smith of Illinois—were Republicans who had been elected after free-spending primary campaigns. A few years earlier, the Supreme Court had held that the Federal Corrupt Practices Act could not constitutionally apply to primary elections,[151] and now, senators who were eager to curb excessive campaign spending tried to implement their objectives through another route: they moved to "exclude" Senators Smith and Vare, to bar them from serving, relying on the constitutional power of each house of Congress to "Judge [the] Qualifications of its own Members" (Article I, Section 5). A large majority voted to bar the two men from taking their seats.*

Both Hand and Frankfurter had long been concerned about the excessive influence that money had in political elections. Both, moreover,

---

* Arguably, Hand had special reason to applaud the criticism of Senator-elect Vare of Pennsylvania, for the losing candidate in the challenged primary he won was the Senate incumbent, George Wharton Pepper. Pepper, a vice president of the American Law Institute, had become a close friend of Hand.

The allegedly excessive primary spending for which Vare lost his seat amounted to less than $800,000; ironically, Pepper, his opponent, had spent more than twice as much, nearly $2 million. Similarly, Senator Smith of Illinois was successfully excluded for spending about $460,000 in his campaign, even though the losing candidate in that election, incumbent senator William B. McKinley, spent about $50,000 more. (See Senate Document No. 71, 87th Congress, 2d Session, *Senate Election, Expulsion and Censure Cases from 1789 to 1960* [1962].)

ordinarily sided with the liberal forces that had been behind the expulsion maneuvers, forces led by the progressive Republican senator from Idaho, William Borah. Frankfurter eagerly embraced the strategy the progressives took to exclude elected members when they had gotten to Washington on a road strewn with gold, but Hand forcefully disagreed: he believed that the Senate's expulsion efforts were unconstitutional and, worse, that the Senate liberals were being heedless of their own long-term interests.* In judging the "Qualifications" of its "Members," he thought, each house of Congress was limited to the explicit constitutional "Qualifications" of age, citizenship, and residence; in his view, the Senate could exclude an elected member only when it determined that he failed to meet these constitutionally prescribed qualifications (or he had won election through outright fraud).

The disagreement between Hand and Frankfurter concerned far more than constitutional technicalities. What prompted Hand to oppose Frankfurter so sharply was neither legalistic pedantry nor sympathy for conservative, free-spending Republicans but, instead, historical memory and a prescient perspective about the future. The exclusion efforts brought to Hand's mind the efforts to exclude elected Socialist members from the New York legislature in 1920 and recalled the House of Representatives' earlier bans on Socialist congressman-elect Victor Berger. Believing strongly that the Senate was not to be trusted to wield the broad exclusion powers Frankfurter was willing to concede to it, he argued that liberals should be especially opposed, for liberal dissidents were likely to be the most frequent victims in the long run.

In 1967, not long after the deaths of both Hand and Frankfurter, the longtime liberal Democratic congressman from Harlem, Adam Clayton Powell, Jr., was excluded from taking a seat in the House because of his alleged financial improprieties. Two years later, the Supreme Court at last decided the issue that Hand and Frankfurter had debated more than forty years earlier. Chief Justice Earl Warren's 1969 opinion held that Congress could *not* exclude elected members on any-

---

* The dispute was prompted by an editorial Lippmann published in the *World*, strongly attacking the position of those who supported the power of the Senate to exclude members on grounds going beyond the "qualifications specifically laid down in the Constitution": anyone urging so broad a Senate power, Lippmann wrote, was guilty of "lawlessness and hysteria." Frankfurter promptly shot off his dissenting views and simultaneously sent a copy of his letter to Hand. He was surprised at Lippmann's "intimation that a dispassionate Court" that included "B and Gus Hand" would say that Lippmann's position was the only permissible one, and on the copy he sent Hand he scrawled, "I hope I have not invoked your name in vain." Hand's response was quick and firm: "I think Walter was in substance right" (carbon copy of Felix Frankfurter letter to Walter Lippmann, 13 December 1927, with a scrawled note by Frankfurter on Hand's copy, 104–14; LH to Felix Frankfurter, 16 December 1927, 104–14).

thing other than the constitutionally prescribed qualifications; his *Powell* ruling[152] was in effect a ringing endorsement of Hand's position.

On this issue, unlike Sacco-Vanzetti, Hand had not agonized or vacillated at all. "My views," he told Frankfurter, "are very positive and based upon what people used to call 'the philosophy' of the situation."[153] When Frankfurter replied, heatedly but not very persuasively, and tried to articulate an intelligible moderate position that would give the Senate an exclusion power going beyond the narrow confines Hand insisted on, he got nowhere. "The 'compromise' I have in mind," he explained, "is a denial of the suggestion that the alternatives are either the specifically enumerated qualifications of the Constitution or absolutism"; the Senate should be held to a "moral exercise of authority," and that meant "judgment according to standards relevant to service in the Senate." This was a vague and slippery criterion indeed—"I am aware that is a loose standard"—and Hand was unmoved.[154] "You don't convince me," he told Frankfurter flatly. It was certainly conceivable, he acknowledged, that one could have a legislature with "the power to purge itself of those of whose moral qualifications it disapproves," but for Hand "the absolute right of each constituency to select the man it wants seems of greater importance . . . In some things I would be an absolutist, though not for absolutist reasons."[155] Hand, who was always opposed to the stifling of dissidents, believed deeply, despite his skepticism, that legal principles and precedents could help safeguard dissidents in the real world. It is no accident that his speculations about risks in the exclusion context of 1927 bear a striking resemblance to his defense of his 1917 *Masses* doctrine.

HAND'S THOUGHTS on all these civil liberties issues of the 1920s were confined to his correspondence with a few intimate friends, but his renown grew with a larger audience that came to hear the off-the-court addresses he gave, several of which also attracted newspaper attention and were printed in magazines. By the early 1930s, thousands of Americans knew that Hand was one of the nation's most penetrating and gifted writers.

None of Hand's speeches dwelled at length on contemporary controversies, and only a careful listener would catch his passing, ironic remarks on the news of the day. His central concerns in his addresses were more basic, longer-range problems. Again and again, he spoke of the obstacles to the survival of the autonomous individual in an increasingly homogeneous mass society; considered how democracy might survive amid the pressures toward conformity in twentieth-century

America; tried to delineate the essentials of individual liberty, which he saw threatened; and reflected on the nature of judging, and the satisfactions, even joys, of doing one's job.

Hand labored hard over his speeches. He spoke the truth when, in declining the growing number of invitations, he protested that preparing an address meant agony and torture for him. His repeated claim that he could not lecture extemporaneously speaks more to his self-imposed high standards than to his gifts of expression, which were great.

One unfortunate consequence of Hand's elegant literary style was that many in his audience had difficulty grasping his speeches' quite substantial content. The very richness of his style, the distinctive subtlety of his analysis, made his addresses more suitable to reflective reading than to immediate comprehension. Small wonder that Hand was often frustrated by the failure of commentators to grasp his central points. This occurred with the very first of his public addresses that was widely publicized, a commencement speech at Bryn Mawr College given on June 2, 1927.[156] The Bryn Mawr invitation had been difficult to resist: Frances had of course studied there and had remained involved as an alumnae trustee; all three of his daughters attended the college, and his eldest, Mary, was graduating that year. Hand's words managed to turn a pious ceremony into an occasion to applaud the rebelliousness of youth and, more important, to assert how an individual could preserve a distinctive self in a conformist world.

Hand wrote "The Preservation of Personality" in the midst of the Roaring Twenties, when flappers and their beaux, in flashy new cars, bent on nothing but self-gratification, it seemed, were causing their elders unprecedented consternation about "the younger generation dancing down the primrose path," as he put it. But Hand embraced the youthful rebelliousness. "[Y]ou are sceptical and unsatisfied," he told the graduates. "[A]t the risk of finding neither treasure nor skeleton in any, you wish to open all the closet doors, so that nothing shall be left to hearsay." And he had no difficulty accepting this questioning spirit: "I do for myself approve that temper. Experience soon teaches the seeker, not so much that he can find the key to the universe, as the limits of his search and the paucity of his trove." Though the college generation's iconoclasm carried dangers, Hand clearly preferred these risks to unquestioning surrender to traditions:

> They may not know where they are going, but the fact that they
> are on the way is charming. I can talk with them, feel with them,
> enjoy them, and, fatuously enough, allow myself the illusion that
> I am at one with them, better than with many of my coevals who

so often seem to wear their defenses on the outside, like crabs and lobsters, long since outclassed for their timidity.

Hand's praise of "Irrepressible Youth" (which was the title of a condescending *New York Times* editorial on the speech published two days after a long news article about it)[157] attracted attention. One Pennsylvanian wrote to him that she was certain he had been misquoted: she could not believe that he had "preached a non-sacrificial doctrine" instead of providing "guidance in the quest of a GREAT happiness & life, which is in conquest of self."[158] Another woman, who signed herself simply "An Indignant Mother," insisted that Hand "should be committed to the nearest lunatic asylum *for life*": "Your selfish lesson is exactly the manners on a hog ranch at feeding time. Graduates of Bryn Mawr may now be rated as educated hogs."[159] Even sympathetic friends who applauded Hand's speech commented on the controversy he had stirred. Helen Thomas Flexner congratulated him for "goading the conventionals into emitting desperate squeals":

> How do you enjoy standing out as a protagonist of Bolshevik parents? Like Socrates I fear you are a corrupter of youth! I am extremely glad you said what you did, as you did and when you did, because I think it will make things a little easier for some young people.[160]

The stir caused by Hand's speech startled him. "What is to be thought of a man of his age and dignity who delights in the rebellious spirit of youth?" the *Times* asked. But the critics had misconstrued his point. His central concern, ignored by the press, was this:

> Our dangers . . . are not from the outrageous but from the conforming; not from those who rarely and under the lurid glare of obloquy upset our moral complaisance, or shock us with unaccustomed conduct, but from those, the mass of us, who take their virtues and their tastes, like their shirts and their furniture, from the limited patterns which the market offers.[161]

This risk of choking conformity was a consequence of the twentieth century's means of mass communication. What especially concerned Hand was the modern techniques of manipulating people's tastes and views, and this problem had preoccupied him ever since his exchanges with Lippmann in the early 1920s. Never before had there been so many people

> who felt alike, thought alike, ate alike, slept alike, hated alike— so far as they hate at all—loved alike, wore the same clothes, used

the same furniture in the same houses, went to the same games, saw the same plays, approved the same sentiments, believed in the same God. . . . Over that chorus the small voice of the individual sounds not even the thinnest obbligato; it seems senseless and preposterous to sing at all. Why not accept the accredited chant and swell the din?[162]

This astute, prophetic perception of modern mass culture framed the central questions: Should individuals simply embrace the "new discoveries in mass suggestion" and adopt "the high calling of Manipulator"? Or could they somehow survive autonomously? Machiavellian manipulations were "not confined to Russia or Italy," Hand warned. "[O]ne may find them all about even in this Land of the Free . . . Our problem, as I see it, is how to give the mannikin, assailed on all hands with what we now so like to call propaganda, the chance of survival as a person at all, not merely as a leaf driven by the wind, a symbol in a formula."

In searching for answers, Hand rejected the normal American reliance on "ambition" and "competition" as self-defeating. Nor would he endorse the escape route of the hermit. Instead, he argued, individual self-realization came ultimately from choosing one's work on the basis of one's personal preference and then performing it well. The choice of a job, he insisted, should not stem from yearnings for renown or riches, or even a desire to "serve mankind" (his repudiation of this public-service ideal shocked his audience). Rather, he urged work "because one likes it and for no other end," for doing it with "an acute sense of craftsmanship" best assured personal satisfaction and creativity.

Somewhere there lurks a craving to impress some form upon the stuff about us. . . . I must be friendly with the whole of this Me, in which I live and move and have my being, this formless thing, wayward, unaccountable, inconsequent and wanton. In its deep recesses it has the itch to leave upon an indifferent universe even the print of its hands upon the clay.

Hand confessed a "still amorous" recollection of attending a circus as a little boy, awed by the trapeze artists displaying their hair-raising skills:

They had done their bit, and done it as they had planned it. . . . They had exhibited in their conduct a pattern of their own making; they had done a job, and done it handsomely. If others knew it, so much the better; if not, for themselves it was there, the manifestation in action of a purpose, the realization of an imagined plan.

In what way was this like being a judge?

> A judge's life, like every other, has in it much of drudgery, senseless bickerings, stupid obstinacies, captious pettifogging, all disguising and obstructing the only sane purpose which can justify the whole endeavor. These take an inordinate part of his time; they harass and befog the unhappy wretch, and at times almost drive him from that bench where like any other workman he must do his work. . . . [But] when the case is all in, and the turmoil stops, and after he is left alone, things begin to take form. . . . [O]ut of the murk the pattern emerges, his pattern, the expression of what he has seen and what he has therefor made, the impress of his self upon the not-self, upon the hitherto formless material of which he was once but a part and over which he has now become the master.

> [This] obdurate and recalcitrant world is perhaps in the end no more than a complicated series of formulae which we impose upon the flux. . . . [A]nd as we consciously compose, a happy fortuity gives us the sense of our own actuality, an escape from the effort to escape, a contentment that the mere stream of consciousness cannot bring, a direction, a solace, a power and a philosophy. . . . If it be selfishness to work on the job one likes, because one likes it and for no other end, let us accept the odium. I had rather live forever in a company of Don Quixotes, than among a set of wraiths professing to be solely moved to the betterment of one another. . . . [A] community of creatures engaged primarily in serving one another, except for the joy of meddling in other people's business, appears, to me at least, so dreary and so empty, that I had as lief sing for eternity in the heavenly choirs as to have any part or parcel in their pallid enterprises. Let us then, if one insists on candour, do our jobs for ourselves; we are in no danger of disserving the State. . . . [You] will have a chance to save yourself, and that is quite enough to ask in a time when the streets are so full of motorcars, and the radios bark at every other corner.[163]

A temporary decline in Hand's judicial workload allowed him to give more speeches between 1929 and 1932. In 1929, when Congress provided relief at last for the hardworking Second Circuit judges by creating a fifth position on the court and Harrie Chase joined the Hands, Swan, and Manton, Learned Hand had a few years' respite from an unrelenting press of court work. In his speeches of the time, he was able to develop and deepen his reflections on the major theme of his Bryn Mawr remarks.

In March 1930, for example, Hand gave an address at Harvard Law School on the occasion of the presentation of Charles Hopkinson's portrait of Justice Holmes.[164] Holmes was Hand's idol, and on this favorite subject, he readily accepted the invitation to speak: "I feel rather flattered to be asked," he wrote to Frances. At first, he had his usual self-doubts: he would "try to say something worthy of him, but can I?"[165] For once, though, he managed to suppress his tendency toward hypercritical judgments of his own work: "I really think that it is pretty good," he wrote to Frances just before he traveled to Cambridge for the event on March 20.[166] And the large audience there seemed enthusiastic. As he told Frances soon after, "You know how it is; everybody says it is grand after you get through, and more or less means it. I rather think that it went well. . . . [M]aybe they really did like it."[167]

Hand's tribute to Holmes was especially memorable because of Hand's elaboration of the ingredients he had identified at Bryn Mawr as "the surest fabric of a self," the sense of craftsmanship and the resultant joy in creativity, depicting Holmes as the president of the "Society of Jobbists"—the mythical assembly of those committed above all to doing their jobs well. And what were the standards for admission to this guild of Jobbists?

> It is an honest craft, which gives good measure for its wages, and undertakes only those jobs which the members can do in proper workmanlike fashion, which of course means no more than that they must like them. [Its work] demands right quality, better than the market will pass.[168]

At least in America, Hand continued, the membership of the Society was "not large,"

> for it is not regarded with favor, or even with confidence, by those who live in chronic moral exaltation, whom the ills of this world make ever restive, who must be always fretting for some cure; who cannot while away an hour in aimless talk, or find distraction for the eye, or feel agitation in the presence of fair women.* Its members have no program of regeneration; they are averse to propaganda; they do not organize; they do not agitate; they decline to worship any Sacred Cows, American or Russian.

---

* In an earlier draft, he wrote of those who "feel a painful, yet blissful, agitation in the presence of fair women." (File 132–24 contains several revised drafts of the Holmes address.)

By doing their work well, Jobbists could achieve "a certain serenity" that "must come from being at home in this great and awful Universe, where man is so little and fate so relentless."[169]

In Hand's view, Holmes, that skeptical imposer of "the forms," had attained serenity and experienced the joy of creation. Learned Hand— less detached than Holmes, more brooding and more self-doubting— found it harder to attain this serenity and joy. For him, solace was usually the more modest consequence of commitment to craftsmanship. "The pleasure of the job, as in every other job, is in doing the work itself. If you like it, it's good; if you don't, it's hell. Personally, I like it."[170]

Soon after, Hand spoke to the Juristic Society of the University of Pennsylvania Law School, a group of "younger lawyers" interested in the "academic aspects of law." If his audience expected a pedantic exegesis of a technical subject, they must have been disappointed. In "Sources of Tolerance,"[171] Hand's central concern was once again the capacity of the independent individual to survive in an age in which the propagandistic forces of salesmanship were ever more pervasive and effective, and he offered a precise remedy. Hand began with an historical foray: He invited his audience to think back a century and a half, to compare the nation as it was then with what it had become. He contrasted the competing hopes of Hamilton and Jefferson in the Founding Era—Hamilton favoring strong national government, Jefferson suspicious of all authority; Hamilton with no faith in "the perfectability of human nature," Jefferson believing "in the basic virtue of mankind."

All of the Hands, ever since Grandfather Augustus, had adhered to the old Jeffersonian Democratic faith; yet as a young Albany lawyer, in his first act of political independence, Learned Hand had rejected this notion of minimal government as unsuitable to the twentieth century. He recognized early on that the national government's powers, rather than being scorned as a threat, should be embraced as a tool of reform. In Philadelphia, Hand urged the preservation of the Jeffersonian ideal of individual liberty and autonomy against the forces of homogeneity and uniformity. He acknowledged that in many ways Hamilton had proved the better prophet, yet the Jeffersonian ideal of liberty was worth preserving.

> It is intolerable to feel that we are each in the power of the conglomerate conscience of a mass of Babbitts, whose intelligence we do not respect, and whose standards we may detest. . . .
> Certainly there was a meaning in Jefferson's hatred of the inter-

position of collective pressure. . . . [S]hall we not feel with him
that it is monstrous to lay open the lives of each to whatever current
notions of propriety may ordain?[172]

Hand's rare endorsement of Jeffersonian aspirations brought him to
his central question: How could Jefferson's idea of liberty be preserved
in twentieth-century America? He suggested:

[Liberty] is the product, not of institutions, but of a temper, of
an attitude towards life; of that mood that looks before and after
and pines for what is not. It is idle to look to laws, or courts, or
principalities, or powers, to secure it. . . . It is secure only [in]
that sense of fair play, of give and take, of the uncertainty of
human hypotheses, of how changeable and passing are our surest
convictions.

There was no certain safeguard for liberty, Hand knew; but "[p]erhaps
if we cannot build breakwaters, we may be able to deepen the bottom."
And for him, the best hope lay in education; only education could help
people see past the passions of the day. When he prescribed education
in "history" as well as "the Liberal Arts, Fiction, Drama, Poetry,
Biography," he was not urging mere "education for education's sake"
or for "polish"; indeed, he repudiated a "general cultural background"
as a valid goal in itself, for that was "so often a cloak for . . . the prig,
the snob and the pedant." Instead, he insisted on the importance of a
liberal education on ultimately *political* grounds, as the best way to
"meet and master the high-power salesman of political patent medi-
cines." Hand recognized that most students preferred "something they
can immediately use"—"science, economics, business administration,
law in its narrower sense." But he argued forcefully against such
curricula.[173]

Hand made his theme more vivid by drawing on an illustration
especially apt for his audience of lawyers. This passage, among Hand's
best known, reflected a lifetime's preoccupations:

I venture to believe that it is as important to a judge called upon
to pass on a question of constitutional law, to have at least a bowing
acquaintance with Acton and Maitland, with Thucydides, Gibbon
and Carlyle, with Homer, Dante, Shakespeare and Milton, with
Machiavelli, Montaigne and Rabelais, with Plato, Bacon, Hume
and Kant, as with the books which have been specifically written
on the subject. For in such matters everything turns upon the
spirit in which he approaches the questions before him. The words

he must construe are empty vessels into which he can pour nearly
anything he will. Men do not gather figs of thistles, nor supply
institutions from judges whose outlook is limited by parish or
class. They must be aware that there are before them more than
verbal problems; more than final solutions cast in generalizations
of universal applicability. They must be aware of the changing
social tensions in every society which make it an organism; which
demand new schemata of adaptation; which will disrupt it, if rigidly
confined. . . . All I want to emphasize is the political aspect of
the matter, of the opportunity to preserve that spirit of liberty
without which life is insupportable.[174]

Hand brought unaccustomed public attention upon himself in 1929
by choosing to begin a speech at the American Law Institute, "Is There
a Common Will?," with several concrete examples drawn from recent
events. His aim was merely to illustrate the philosophical issues at the
heart of his address; the examples were meant to show that though the
masses might believe in free speech and fair criminal procedures in
theory, they were often ready to endorse abuses. Thus prefacing his
philosophical speculations with specific illustrations inevitably risked
precisely the reaction he claimed to dislike: public notoriety for engaging
in contested political battles. And indeed, he risked—and received—
enormous press coverage with the very opening of his May 1929 speech:
in scathing terms, he described events that had taken place in New
York City only a few months earlier. A new police commissioner had
taken office, "a gentleman of urbanity and elegant apparel" who for
years had "officially welcomed all distinguished guests to our city."
The police commissioner was Grover A. Whalen, a debonair, striking
figure appointed by New York City's equally flamboyant mayor, the
scandal-plagued James J. Walker.

Then and for decades to come, Whalen was one of New York City's
most prominent public figures: until the early 1950s, he was the city's
official greeter. He perfected the art of ticker-tape parades cheering
heroes from Charles Lindbergh to Douglas MacArthur, and his
appearance—the carefully groomed mustache, the dark suit set off by
an ever-present carnation boutonniere, the impeccable light-blue shirt,
the dark homburg hat—caught the public's imagination. In December
1928, Jimmy Walker had persuaded Whalen to leave his job as general
manager of Wanamaker's department store to take on the police com-
missionership. Whalen had tackled his duties with immediate and impressive élan: his war on speakeasies, gamblers, and assorted gangsters

provided steady front-page news for every New York newspaper; he organized "gun squads," groups of brawny policemen under orders to enforce "nightstick law"; his detectives became experts in the use of the ax and crowbar to demolish the speakeasies they raided. The public applause of Whalen's rough-and-ready tactics was what concerned Hand. The attitude of the commissioner and his supporters, he assured his Washington audience, no doubt commanded "the overwhelming assent of the good citizens of New York," though "if you ask them whether they believe that any man should be punished at the will of an official without some evidence of his guilt, they would resent the question." At one and the same time, they were fiercely proud of constitutional protections of individual rights, yet supported police tactics that were, as one Brooklyn judge put it, "un-American, illegal, unfair and un-just."[175] Hand's general observation was that the public's will was indeed "uncertain and self-contradictory."[176]

The central concern of the speech was virtually ignored by the press. Instead, "JUDGE HAND ASSAILS METHODS OF WHALEN," *The New York Times* trumpeted,[177] and other newspapers echoed this theme. "The New York papers as usual seized upon the one thing which they could make sensational," Hand wrote to a Connecticut judge who had applauded the speech, "and neglected to present what at least I was trying to do, so that a mere illustration became the only thing that got out. I suppose I ought to have anticipated this, but it irritated me."[178]

Hand was especially stung by an editorial in *The New York Telegram* that called his speech "extraordinary judicial doctrine" and charged that "some of the language Judge Hand used seems especially extreme com-ing from one who is considered to be among the soundest members of the federal bench."[179] Hand promptly assured the editorial writer that faulty reporting was to blame, "for the reporters seized upon what seemed to them most likely to interest their readers." The journalists' version was quite inaccurate, he insisted: "Broken from its context it gave quite the opposite impression from what I had intended, and what I have hoped reasonably intelligent people would gather, if they read it all."[180] But this was not quite the whole story: although the Whalen illustration was certainly not Hand's central point, neither was it inconsistent with his theme.[181]

For once, Hand had not managed to avoid the heat, as he had promised himself to do ever since the early 1920s. The notoriety of his "Common Will" speech had beneficial consequences for him, despite his pained reaction in the immediate aftermath. The misleading newspaper pub-licity prompted Hand to develop his themes more fully, as later speeches showed, and for better or worse the controversy added to Hand's growing renown.

IN BETWEEN THE SPEECHES and the court work, the book reviews and the other writing, Hand was also busy on the social front, and accepted invitations to join dinner groups where opinion leaders from law, business, and the arts met for informal discussions. Already an active member of the Century Association (he served for several years on the club's admissions committee), he now also joined monthly gatherings of something called "the Dinner Party," which met at the University Club, where he would see C. C. Burlingham and other public-spirited lawyers such as James Byrne, Charles Evans Hughes, Henry Stimson, Henry Taft, and George Wickersham, as well as some of his favorite judges, including his cousin Gus. At the even smaller dinners of the "Round Table Club," at the Knickerbocker, he could talk away the evenings with Judge Benjamin Cardozo, the architect Cass Gilbert, and Columbia's president Nicholas Murray Butler (who sponsored Hand), as well as the financier Thomas Lamont. Moreover, he became a member of the Council on Foreign Relations and the Foreign Policy Association, and he read *Foreign Affairs*, the council's magazine, avidly.

At Harvard, Hand had been excluded by the Porcellian and other elite clubs, and he had carried with him ever since the sense of being an "outsider." But in New York City's social gatherings, he was now a welcome guest at last: a lively, brilliant conversationalist with enormously wide interests, a gift for the ribald story and delightful mimicry, a relish for rubbing elbows with cultivated acquaintances. Yet deep within himself, the "outsider" feeling never wholly disappeared.

Partly because of the friendships deepened at these informal gatherings, Hand had to deal with ever more invitations to join the boards of organizations. He declined most, either because participation would have conflicted with his desire to avoid current controversies or, more often, because he was reluctant to serve as a figurehead when he had not time to participate fully. Yet he did join groups particularly close to his interests. With the Council on Foreign Relations, for example, he reduced his participation over the years, but he remained a member at least into the late 1930s.[182] With groups interested in scholarly research, he engaged more freely, as he did with the Committee on Crime of the Social Science Research Council and the Committee on Legal Research of the Commonwealth Fund.[183]

Especially revealing is Hand's readiness in 1929 to become a founding member of the National Advisory Committee of the Institute of Law at Johns Hopkins University, a short-lived effort to promote empirical social-science research in the law. Conservative legal scholars considered the institute's members avant-garde radicals, though the membership included quite a few judges (among them the two Hands and Cardozo), not to mention Franklin D. Roosevelt. Hand readily supported the institute's efforts to study the law in action rather than through abstract theorizing, though he himself was no social scientist. As he said in a supporting letter to the president of Johns Hopkins, the "presuppositions" about law had "scarcely even [been] looked at. . . . We are still largely living in adolescent dogmas, uncriticized, often emanating from purposes of which we are but dimly conscious. The Institute would at least make us aware of our assumptions; that is much."[184]

Hand's heightened eminence was symbolized by the award of the first of his many honorary LL.D. degrees in 1930. At Columbia's commencement exercises late in the afternoon of June 3, he was praised as a "righteous judge" who had "interpreted justice to modern needs."[185] Hand greeted this honor ambivalently, welcoming it publicly but privately belittling it, partly because he thought that Columbia awarded honorary degrees too promiscuously. As he told Frances when he first learned from "Nick Butler" about the university's plans, this "is rather a job lot distinction; they distribute their LL.D.'s to all sorts of scurvy critters"—even John Woolsey, the flamboyant but not very able judge in the *Ulysses* case, had gotten one—and they were "mostly Jews" (an extremely unusual slur for him, though Frances was prone to making such remarks).* What really upset him was that his first LL.D. came from a source other than his beloved alma mater, Harvard. Not only had Hand held Harvard in awe ever since his student days; he had also been an increasingly active alumnus. He had long belonged to New York City's Harvard Club; he had served on visiting committees to the Harvard Law School and been an informal adviser to a number of its law professors; in 1929, moreover, he had become a member of the Board of Overseers, elected by a narrow margin to serve for a year to fill an unexpired term; in 1930, he was easily reelected as a nominee of the alumni association to a full six-year term. Actually, his membership on the Board of Overseers probably precluded his being considered for an honorary degree, but it still rankled: "Really the only

* See Frances Hand's occasionally pejorative remarks about Jews in the LH–Frances A. Hand Personal Correspondence. See also LH to Frances A. Hand, 9 October 1929, commenting on one of his daughters: "She has changed a great deal in her attitude about Jews whom she can now see as humans. This is due very largely to the Bingers who she likes very much. She even regretted that she did not have a tincture of Jew in herself. So you see there has been a great change." (Carl Binger was a leading Freudian psychoanalyst.)

one I would give a tinker's dam for is Harvard's and that they won't give [it to] me."[186]

Harvard did not get around to awarding this honor to Hand until 1939, but other honorary degrees soon followed Columbia's—Yale in 1931, the University of Pennsylvania two years later. Yale's reasons for recognizing Hand were far more specifically and thoughtfully stated than Columbia's. Professor William Lyon Phelps, who presented Hand, seemed especially aware of his commitment to civil liberties, and the formal citation was equally forceful.*

EVEN WHILE HAND was gaining ever greater visibility with the general public, his standing reached new heights with a smaller but especially important audience. Lawyers had long been aware of Hand's distinguished judicial work, but nothing confirmed his professional renown as much as his work in the American Law Institute.

The ALI, founded in the early 1920s, is the elite incarnation of the American legal establishment, a select group of leading practitioners, scholars, and judges committed to "the improvement of the law."† Hand took part in the ALI's founding and held major positions in it for the rest of his life.

The creation of the ALI was the result of arduous work by a Committee on the Establishment of a Permanent Organization for the Improvement of the Law that began its sessions in May 1922. The committee roster, with nearly forty members, was a virtual Who's Who of leaders of the profession: Elihu Root, "dean of the American bar," was chairman; former attorney general George W. Wickersham was the vice chairman; its members included not only leading practitioners of the day such as C. C. Burlingham, James Byrne, John Davis, and Victor Morawetz, but also some of the law schools' leading lights, including

---

* The citation stated that the degree was awarded "in recognition of eminent service in making the law a living agency for human betterment, through the wise adjustments of its provisions to the confusing flux of contemporary life, and equally for your influence in aiding to restore to the bench, by the dispassionate sanity of your decisions, that needed public confidence too often in recent times denied." (See *The New York Times*, 18 June 1931.) Judge Swan probably helped with the Yale citation.

Later honorary degrees were as follows: Amherst, 1938; Dartmouth, 1938; Harvard, 1939; Princeton, 1947; New School for Social Research, 1950; New York University, 1951; Cambridge University (England), 1952; State University of New York, 1952; University of Chicago, 1952; Yeshiva University, 1953; Washington University (St. Louis), 1953; Wesleyan University, 1957.

† During its early decades, the ALI's elected membership was well below 1,000. Not until 1987 did it go above 2,000 (to 2,044); soon after, its bylaws were amended to increase the maximum from 2,000 to 2,500.

Harvard's Samuel Williston, Joseph Beale, and Roscoe Pound, as well as Columbia's Harlan Fiske Stone. And there were a few judges as well: not only Learned Hand but also Julian Mack from the federal circuit court and Benjamin Cardozo and Cuthbert Pound from the New York Court of Appeals.[187] Although Hand was still only a district judge in 1922, he was already sufficiently distinguished to be among the first invited to join the committee,[188] which, after nearly a year of meetings, published a detailed blueprint for a permanent American Law Institute and called a national meeting of "prominent American judges, lawyers and law teachers" to consider its proposals.[189] About five hundred men convened in Washington on February 23, 1923, to launch the ALI.[190] Conservative corporate lawyers predominated, but Hand's own suggestions for inclusion sought to assure geographical diversity and the presence of broad-gauged lawyers: he named attorneys such as Henry L. Stimson and Joseph P. Cotton as well as his judicial colleagues Augustus Hand and Charles Hough, and also included Morris Hillquit, an East European immigrant who became a leader of the American Socialist party. (Hillquit chose not to attend.)

During its first two decades, the ALI's substantive work consisted mainly of the preparation of a series of "Restatements of the Law" in various areas of judge-made common law, from contracts and torts to property and restitution. The Restatements sought to identify and articulate the governing principles of the common law for the guidance of judges and lawyers, "to help make certain much that is now uncertain and to simplify unnecessary complexities, but also to promote those changes which will tend better to adapt the laws to the needs of life."[191] Hand's attraction to the enterprise as originally conceived is understandable: as a judge, he knew well the uncertainties created by the mounting flood of reported decisions, and one of his special gifts was to divine the underlying principles amid the morass of particulars.

Yet from the outset, the ALI's founders circumscribed their roles severely. The original aim to "adapt the laws to the needs of life"— an objective that suggested a willingness to go beyond the logical structure of the law to the realities of the society—soon fell by the wayside; controversial subjects—including, for example, "advocacy of novel social legislation"—were out of bounds. Hand supported this limitation: repeatedly he urged that the Restatements confine themselves to articulating the law "as it is," not as it should be; repeatedly he insisted that the ALI's task was to "restate, not legislate";[192] just as he was opposed to unelected courts dictating public policy, so was he critical of a legal elite's substituting its dictates for democratic choices on contentious issues.

In preparing its Restatements, the ALI followed a rigid routine. For each common-law subject, it designated a legal scholar as "reporter," who, with a group of advisers, prepared the drafts. These were then debated by the ALI's council, and then submitted for discussion and approval at the annual general-membership meeting. At the outset, the council consisted of twenty-one members, and Learned Hand was a member from the start. Practitioners and academics predominated, but joining Hand in 1923 was his good friend Benjamin Cardozo.[193]

Work on the first five Restatements—on contracts, torts, agency, conflict of laws, and restitution—began immediately. Among the first group of reporters selected were two of Hand's law teachers at Harvard, Samuel Williston in contracts and Joseph Beale in conflicts. Year after year, some of the nation's best scholars, in collaboration with some of its best lawyers and judges, hammered out their statements of black-letter law and commentary and hypothetical examples in order to lay out the principles of contracts and torts, of agency and property. Usually it took a decade or more before each draft made its way through the ALI mill: the first five Restatements, for example, commissioned in 1923, were not completed until well into the 1930s. Nevertheless, the ALI and its minions carried on, launching additional Restatement projects on an increasing number of subjects. And by the 1950s, after it became clear that the earlier work had not stemmed the flow of conflicting precedents, the ALI commissioned new series in fields it had already "restated"—the ALI's "Restatements Second."

Given the ALI's self-imposed constraint to limit itself to "restating" the law rather than "adapting" it "to the needs of life," the work was bound to be technical and ultimately confining to so zestful a mind as Hand's. Occasionally he complained that an ALI session had been "boring," and he often bowed out of advisory-group meetings by citing competing obligations.[194] Yet he continued his affiliation over the years, and even accepted election as a vice president in 1935, thereby taking on the additional duty of presiding for part of the time at the annual meetings in Washington. What prompted a man with Hand's capacious mind to remain so engaged with the ALI?

In part, but only in part, the very concept of Restatements did attract him. Though they resembled the ambitious schemes of C. C. Langdell, the Harvard Law School dean of his student days, to construct a logical legal structure that would form an airtight system of its own with little regard for the law's social context, an enterprise that Hand had long criticized—he knew that law dealt with human beings and social forces, that it could not be analyzed with the detached mathematical precision of the botanist, that it reflected social forces, not mere logic for its own sake—his craftsman's spirit unceasingly pursued the underlying principles amid the flood of precedents, and he appreciated the Restatements' potential of guidance for judges and lawyers.

Hand himself rarely mentioned Restatements in his own opinions, not even in the years before 1938, when federal judges still had the authority to articulate common-law rules independently of state courts. In 1934, when George Wickersham asked the judges who belonged to the ALI for endorsements of its work's utility, Hand's reply did not show great enthusiasm. "I have found considerable use for the Restatements," he told Wickersham. "Just as I anticipated, they save a great deal of labor, especially on questions which are not controversial but which take a long time to look up." But he thought it too early to tell how useful they would ultimately be.[195]

During his early years in the ALI, Hand insistently argued against proposals that the group prepare model laws, particularly if they impinged on contentious issues. For example, when the ALI prepared its first "Model Code," a "Code of Criminal Procedure,"[196] Hand opposed it, both because it might interfere with the completion of the planned Restatements and because "this shoemaker should stick to his last," because lawyers should not usurp popular resolution of controversial questions.[197] Only slowly did he reconcile himself to the ALI's codification efforts, and only because the public pressed for such reforms and the ALI seemed best equipped to do the job well.[198] Then, in the 1950s, the ALI undertook preparation of a "Model Penal Code," its most ambitious project yet, in the most controversial area it had ever touched; despite his philosophical reservations, Hand found this more stimulating than any of the Restatements. Beyond the meetings and council sessions, Hand served many hours on a range of ALI advisory groups. Herbert Goodrich, a longtime official of the ALI, and by 1940 a judge on the Third Circuit Court of Appeals, once praised Hand's contributions to the theoretical debates as ranking with those of Benjamin Cardozo: "His comment upon any legal question carried such great weight that an expressed doubt by him was a source of danger to the acceptance of any proposition, no matter how plausibly urged."[199] But it is also true that the types of projects the ALI chose to tackle only rarely stirred Hand's genuine intellectual excitement.

What, then, explains Hand's decades-long loyalty to the ALI? One reason was that it appeased his hunger for associations with law teachers. Ever since his days at Harvard, Hand had a very high regard for legal scholars, viewing them with an awe that suggests a repression of his usual skepticism. Of course, the enthusiasm also went the other way: when in 1925 he addressed the annual meeting of the Association of

American Law Schools in Chicago (even though this required a trip of unaccustomed length), he was introduced as a hero, called an "idol of the bench."[200] Hand clearly relished the opportunities the ALI afforded him to chew over basic issues of law, albeit deferentially, with these admired legal scholars. As he once put it to a Yale law professor working on the Restatement of Torts, "It awakens me, and brushes my mind, to come in contact with such a scholar as you."[201]

The other reason Hand liked the ALI was purely social: he looked forward to the opportunities for dinners, drinks, and informal chats with congenial associates. When he went to the ALI annual meetings in Washington each spring, he would usually stay with his old friend Ned Burling, either at Burling's Georgetown residence or, even more happily, at his "cabin" in the nearby Virginia hills. And during the early years, he could count on Benjamin Cardozo's attendance; Hand deeply admired the saintly, often lonely, Cardozo.

Hand enjoyed the social aspects of ALI sessions even more after he became a vice president of the organization in 1935. His selection came about partly because of George Wickersham's final intervention on his behalf. In 1909, it had been Wickersham, as President Taft's attorney general, who had in effect placed Hand on the district court. The relationship between Hand and Wickersham, a Republican pillar of the New York bar, had been respectful though not close; several months before he nominated Hand for the vice presidency, Wickersham, with rare warmth, congratulated Hand on the twenty-fifth anniversary of his selection for the bench. "I am glad I had a part in putting you there," he wrote. "I wish I could be as proud of everything I did in official life as I am of that act. You have made a distinguished record."[202] Early in February 1935, Wickersham notified Hand that the ALI council had unanimously nominated him to become a vice president. The other vice president was to be George Wharton Pepper, the former Republican senator from Pennsylvania and a leading Philadelphia lawyer.

Wickersham died a year later, and Pepper succeeded him as president of the ALI; Hand replaced Pepper as first vice president. The Pepper-Hand team worked happily together over the years: the two shared a love for literary allusions and wordplay, for Gilbert and Sullivan, for jokes and fun. There is no evidence that Pepper perceived Hand's brooding traits, and he was ever ready to praise his associate's "great personal charm, keenness of perception, abundance of humor, . . . and hearty dislike of affectation and sham."[203] Beginning in 1936, the two friends worked closely "to put life into the ALI banquet," an occasion that had "degenerated into a boring affair."[204] During the months before each year's meeting, they corresponded frequently to assure interesting programs and to plot practical jokes. They would recite nonsense poems or lyrics from Gilbert and Sullivan at the banquets—though Pepper thought they shouldn't sing.[205] (Hand, whose booming voice would often burst forth from his chambers with old Calvinist hymns, sea chanteys, and G&S numbers, would probably have been willing, if asked.) And they also tried to find interesting speakers. In 1936 they produced an erudite Englishman, Sir Willmott Lewis, the London *Times* correspondent in Washington during most of the interwar years. Pepper ended Sir Willmott's introduction with some verses from "When Britain Really Ruled the Waves."

In planning for another banquet, Hand and Pepper concocted a "conspiracy" under which a young Harvard law professor, W. Barton Leach, would appear in the regalia of a British jurist. They were going to tell the dinner audience that the speaker would be the "Rt. Honourable John Popham, Chief Justice of England"—in fact, there had been no such British dignitary since the early seventeenth century. Pepper would ask Hand to escort the "Chief Justice" into the banquet room; Leach, dressed in wig and scarlet robe, would then be led by Hand to the dais; Pepper would announce that the "Right Honourable Chief Justice" preferred to render his decisions "in verse set to music"; and Hand would proceed to "read a letter from the British Museum that they had been willing to lend a rare musical instrument made in the reign of King James in order that the Chief Justice might have the wherewithal with which to accompany himself," whereupon Leach would play his accordion. The plan didn't work out quite that way because Leach wouldn't agree to the costume; but he did make music.[206]

The Hoover Years and Hand's Missed Chance for Promotion to the Supreme Court

DURING THE EARLY MONTHS OF 1930, the nation sank into its deepest economic crisis; the Great Depression compelled Hand to reexamine some cherished views. The stock market had crashed the previous October; by the end of 1930, more than a thousand banks had closed and the number of unemployed rose to 4.5 million. In 1928, Hand had cheered the election of Herbert Hoover as a welcome relief from eight years of conservative Republican rule. He had known Hoover for a long time. They were both "Centurions"—members of the Century Club—and Hand had admired "the Great Engineer," as he called him,[1] for the European relief efforts he directed during World War I. Hand had hoped the Republicans might nominate Hoover in 1920, but he had not been surprised that the Old Guard's candidate, Warren Harding, had become president, thanks to the party's Bourbons; Hand had been alienated from the party for most of the decade. In 1928, he voted enthusiastically for Hoover.[2] But as president, Hoover fell far short of the expectation that he would be an effective problem solver: he proved timid in the face of mounting catastrophe, a captive of his party's traditional faith in individualism and free enterprise, and ideologically and temperamentally reluctant to urge resort to national powers. In November 1930, Republicans suffered their first defeat in congressional elections in a decade and a half; only then did the president seek public-works legislation to cushion the impact of unemployment.

As the Depression deepened, Hand could only bemoan the mounting stagnation and melancholy. For much of the time, he was preoccupied with his work on the court: as he would repeatedly tell friends, he was absorbed in his "cross-word puzzles," "fiddling while Rome burns."[3]

Yet he had never been a disengaged observer, and he was not now. Hand's reactions to the economic crisis and the efforts to solve it reveal much about his distinctive makeup. His characteristic skepticism surfaced repeatedly, but so did his capacity to question his own assumptions. And because of the open-mindedness generated by his self-doubts, he came to empathize with the plight of the poor and perceive the need for strong measures.

When Franklin D. Roosevelt ran for reelection as governor of New York in 1930, Hand confidently voted against him. He knew FDR only as an amiable politician who, after an unspectacular few years as a New York lawyer, had become assistant secretary of the navy during World War I, vice presidential candidate on the losing Democratic ticket in 1920, and successor to Al Smith as New York governor in 1928. Hand thought him an intellectual lightweight, a charmer who sought to be all things to all men, without inner values or a capacity to devise a coherent long-range program, and he was far from alone in that view. In 1931, for example, Walter Lippmann viewed FDR as a "kind of amiable boy scout" who didn't "happen to have a very good mind."[4] And even Felix Frankfurter would remind Hand that he too valued "brains and culture" and was well aware of Roosevelt's "limitations" in those respects.[5] For Hand, it was enough that FDR had at times allied himself with the hated Tammany Hall; that meant, Hand told Frankfurter, that "his victory will be their victory, though they love him not too well." Hand had no greater love for FDR's Republican opponent, former United States attorney Charles H. Tuttle, who seemed a publicity-hungry politico marked by "shoddy aspirations"; but, as Hand put it, "rotten apple for rotten apple, I had rather bite into him."[6]

Hand had expected that Roosevelt might win by as much as a quarter-million-vote margin, but FDR's landslide victory was three times larger than that, and the Democrats scored enormous gains in the midterm congressional races as well. Hand found this Democratic sweep "a surprise"; no one in his New York circles, he told Frankfurter, "had the faintest suspicion of the feeling" of the people.[7] Yet he still had faith in Hoover's greater intellectual power.

Only slowly, only as the seriousness of the Depression grew, did Hand begin to recognize that Hoover was not up to meeting the crisis; slowly, Hoover's dour nature and poor political instincts became clear. Hoover remained a captive of his faith in individual initiative too long, and his rational nature paralyzed him in dealing with the emotional currents generated by growing unemployment, bank closures, and business failures. Frankfurter helped to educate Hand about Hoover's weaknesses. Washington politics had turned "miasmatic," he reported soon after the 1930 election; even Joseph Cotton seemed uncharacteristically subdued in the face of the prevailing "malaise"; "the man in the White House" was having "an irreclaimably miserable time."[8]

In 1931, Hand truly awakened to the crisis:

> We roll slowly along down into our industrial avenues, everybody acting dejected, sans teeth, sans hope, sans everything. Nobody has any guts left; all sit and groan like the companions of Odysseus in Polyphenus' Cave.

He was aware of the mounting complaints about "lack of leadership" and "spinelessness." "Next winter is a spectre," he added in a letter to Lippmann, and "horrid doles" lay ahead. For the first time, he showed his awareness that his own sheltered life risked breeding an unduly narrow attitude: he recognized "the possibility of entire industrial prostration," and he acknowledged that "it will hurt a good deal more than I can realize, sitting here for a pleasant week-end out of the hot city." He wondered whether it was appropriate for Harvard to be giving an honorary degree to Thomas Lamont, a J. P. Morgan partner; he might be a liberal banker—public-spirited and interested in ideas, as well as an agreeable dinner companion—yet Hand was concerned about the symbolism of it: "At times I wonder at it, but no more than I wonder at much else."[9]

During a European trip that summer, Hand paid a visit to Bernard Berenson in his luxurious cocoon at I Tatti. B.B. had shown no sign of discomfort in his villa. Hand, returning to the United States on a luxury liner, was ill at ease: he hated this kind of luxury, he told B.B., and he knew that he was returning to a nation in crisis: "Maybe the whole system is on the chutes. Apparently there is neither hope nor courage left among our captains of industry. At least I can't see that the dawn has shown the faintest glimmer on the horizon."[10]

NOTHING TESTIFIES more tellingly to Learned Hand's growing renown during these years than his first genuine prospect of promotion to the nation's highest court: early in 1930, as he turned fifty-eight, he was seriously considered for a seat on the Supreme Court when Chief Justice William Howard Taft retired because of failing health.

In selecting a new chief justice, President Hoover confronted a difficult choice: Should he name his close friend, fifty-seven-year-old associate justice Harlan Fiske Stone? Or were there stronger reasons to select Charles Evans Hughes, the sixty-eight-year-old elder statesman of the Republican party, who had resigned from the Court in 1916 in order to serve the Republican party by challenging Woodrow Wilson for the presidency? Hoover chose Hughes, but only, it has been said, after he considered promoting Stone and filling the resulting vacancy with Learned Hand.

This notion stems from a report of a conversation in late January 1930 between the president and Joseph Cotton, then acting secretary of state. The "Joe Cotton story" has been widely discussed and occasionally challenged. Cotton himself died soon after; a few years later, when the story first appeared in print, both Hoover and Hughes went out of their way to deny it; historians have debated its reliability ever since. But another look at the old evidence and an examination of new materials demonstrate that Hand was indeed very much in the running.

Joseph Cotton was an able Wall Street lawyer. Three years younger than Hand, he had entered New York City law practice in 1900 (two years before Hand left Albany), became a partner in the well-established Cravath firm while Hand was still struggling to make his way, and formed his own, very successful law firm about the time Hand became a district judge. (Today's Cahill, Gordon firm is the successor to Cotton & Franklin.) A "gifted," "attractive," remarkably "capacious-minded" and "effective" man, Cotton earned huge fees in what he called "the green goods business," advising large financial interests in corporate affairs.[11] Cotton's heart was never in the legal work that brought him his large income, though; his deepest interest lay in public affairs. Yet most of the time he refused to leave his law practice, declining offers of government positions and invitations to join the Harvard faculty.

Cotton's rare ventures into public service were, however, important ones. In 1910, he was counsel to the New York State Commission on Workmen's Compensation and wrote a report (after consulting Hand) strongly defending the constitutionality of workmen's-compensation laws (only to find his efforts foiled when the New York Court of Appeals struck down the laws in a ruling that incurred the wrath of Teddy Roosevelt, Hand, and other Progressives). During World War I, he served as legal assistant to Hoover in the Food Administration, which helped feed postwar Europe and brought Hoover to national attention. And in 1929, he became Henry L. Stimson's right-hand man in the State Department.* As under secretary of state, he became a trusted political adviser to Hoover, and Stimson was delighted to have additional

---

* When Hoover named Stimson secretary of state, Stimson in turn asked two old friends—one was Felix Frankfurter—to find a lawyer to serve as his undersecretary; Frankfurter persuaded Cotton to take the job. "I—this arch fiend of the New Deal—was really responsible for selecting the Under Secretary of State in the Hoover Administration" (Harlan B. Phillips, ed., *Felix Frankfurter Reminisces*, 228).

access to the White House through him. Indeed, he claimed that Cotton was "the only man who could do anything with the President.")[12]

During the week of January 27, 1930, Cotton was acting secretary of state while Stimson was in London at the Naval Disarmament Conference. Hoover was occupying temporary quarters in the old State, War, and Navy Building (now the Executive Office Building); Cotton's office was "just down the corridor and around the corner" from Hoover's, and the "President's door was open to him at any hour."[13] On January 30, when news of Taft's imminent departure made the rounds, Cotton, according to the story he related repeatedly, was in the president's office. He told the president that the vacancy was "a great opportunity": "Now you can promote Justice Stone to be Chief Justice. And then you can appoint Judge Learned Hand to fill Stone's place, and thus put on the Supreme Court the most distinguished federal judge on the bench today."[14]

In advancing this suggestion, Cotton had little interest in Stone as such; his motivation was his long friendship with and admiration for Hand. As Felix Frankfurter recalled, "Joe Cotton saw his great chance when Taft retired, namely, to shove Stone up, to leave a vacancy, and appoint L. Hand to the vacancy. That was his interest; he didn't give a damn about Stone, less than a damn."[15]

According to Cotton, President Hoover expressed some doubts: "I feel I must offer the Chief Justiceship to Governor Hughes. As a former Justice there can be no question of his qualifications, and I feel so greatly obliged to him for that splendid speech he made for me on the Saturday before election [in 1928] that it would be unforgivable ingratitude on my part not to offer him this position." Cotton quickly pointed out to the president that Hughes couldn't take the chief justiceship:

> His son Charles, Jr., is your Solicitor General, and in that job he handles all government litigation before the Supreme Court. That comes to about 40 percent of all the cases there. Consequently, if the father is Chief Justice, the son can't be Solicitor General. That means that Governor Hughes won't accept.

Hoover's response was that if Hughes declined, "that solves our problem. Then I can promote Stone and appoint your friend Hand. But, since the public knows Hughes and not Hand, it would be fine to announce that I had offered the post to Hughes before appointing Stone and Hand. So I really must make the offer to Hughes." Hoover promptly picked up the telephone and called Hughes in New York City. As Cotton related it, Hughes did not decline out of hand. Cotton was shocked; he thought, "The son-of-a-bitch never even thought of his son!"

Hughes came down to Washington on the overnight train, had a breakfast meeting with the president the next morning (January 31), and quickly agreed to become Chief Justice. Three days later, on February 3, Taft's formal retirement letter reached Hoover; that day, Hoover nominated Hughes to be the next Chief Justice of the United States. Stone's chances collapsed, and so did Hand's.

In the days immediately after this turn of events, Cotton told his story to a number of people, and it was widely retold. Joseph Cotton died on March 10, 1931. Several years later, after the story finally appeared in print, doubts about it were raised. Did Cotton really tell that story? Was there any basis for it—that is, did Cotton and Hoover in fact talk about the chief justiceship? And did Hoover ever consider anyone but Hughes for the position?

That Cotton did in fact tell the story seems most certain. Felix Frankfurter claimed to have heard it from Cotton within days of the conversation with the president, and subsequently retold it throughout his life. (Had he first voiced it only decades later, there would be good reason to question his recollection: Frankfurter was subject to a revisionist memory and was rarely a wholly reliable witness about events long past.) And there is written evidence that Frankfurter told essentially the same story to three of his recently graduated Harvard Law School protégés at a dinner in Providence in February 1931. One of these—Orrin G. Judd, then serving as a Frankfurter-recommended law clerk to Hand (later he was a federal judge himself)—kept a diary, in which he related that on February 5, 1931, he "heard Hand, Hughes story" from Frankfurter.[16]

More than fifty years after the putative Hoover-Cotton conversation, Joseph Cotton's only daughter, Isabel, vividly remembered her father's immediate reaction to his session with President Hoover. She had never seen her ordinarily calm and poised father so livid, outraged, and emotional as when he came home that evening. This "extraordinary behavior," in her words, was a response to Hughes's apparent disregard of his son: Cotton himself was very close to his children and especially fond of his only son; it was unthinkable to him that a father would so willingly risk his son's career; moreover, he "just couldn't stand" that the Stone-Hand idea, which he had thought so readily within reach, "went wrong" so dramatically. And his daughter remembered the same contemptuous line Frankfurter and others had recorded: "The son-of-a-bitch never even thought of his son!"[17]

But most of the attacks on the Cotton story turn on its substance, on the question of whether Cotton's account of his conversation with Hoover was truly reliable, particularly with respect to the phone call to Hughes and Cotton's understanding of Hoover's predisposition and motives. The question arose when the story of the phone call was told in a three-part "Profile" of Hughes written by Henry F. Pringle, later Taft's biographer,[18] and published in *The New Yorker* in June and July 1935. Hughes was "greatly disturbed" when he read the piece, and thought of writing to Hoover, but "let it pass" at the time.[19] Two years later, the investigative reporters Drew Pearson and Robert S. Allen published a book, *The Nine Old Men*, that received enormous attention: it was a slashing attack on the justices, published amid the controversy over FDR's Court-packing plan, and it included a garbled retelling of the Cotton story.[20]

Ex-President Hoover promptly wrote to Chief Justice Hughes about this "scurrilous book," assuring him that "your own recollections will confirm mine that I never had any telephone conversations with you at all on the subject."[21] The next day, Hughes thanked Hoover for "disposing of this story" and asked (and received) permission to show Hoover's letter to Pringle: "He may be tempted to repeat this story and I should like to see it suppressed."[22] A few days later, Hoover sent Hughes a fuller recollection of the 1930 events. Reiterating that "no telephone conversation" ever took place and adding that "one would think it improbable that Presidents use the telephone in such vital matters," Hoover insisted that Attorney General William DeWitt Mitchell was the only official with whom he had discussed the succession to Taft: "The question required no consultation with others. It was the obvious appointment." And, Hoover added, he could not have talked with Cotton about it because Cotton, as a State Department official, "had nothing to do with judicial appointments."[23]*

In 1951, Merlo Pusey's biography of Hughes was published; it fiercely defended his subject and sought to demolish the Cotton story.[24] But Alpheus Thomas Mason's 1956 biography of Justice Harlan Fiske Stone amassed evidence that Stone had indeed been a serious candidate in 1930, and concluded that "[f]or some reason" Hoover "changed his mind at a late hour."[25] In the same year, Mason's review of a new book about Hughes reiterated that "Hoover, it seems, offered the post

---

* Hoover also claimed that Hughes had not accepted the position until a few days after their meeting. Hughes corrected this, reminding Hoover that he accepted on the spot; and he reiterated that he was "glad to have your emphatic repudiation of the absurd story which it seems has gained considerable currency" (Hughes to Hoover, 8 March 1937, *Autobiographical Notes*, 294). Some years later, Hoover sent an even more forceful denial to Merlo Pusey, Hughes's biographer, stating (according to Pusey), "There was not a shred of truth in that Cotton story" (quoted in Pusey to Frankfurter, 19 November 1956, Frankfurter Papers, Library of Congress).

to . . . Hughes with the not unreasonable expectation that he would decline it."[26] Hoover promptly sent a denial to the author of that book.[27] For his own part, Justice Frankfurter soon after launched a well-reasoned series of letters to Merlo Pusey in which he insisted on the basic reliability of Cotton's story.[28] This battle continued well into the 1980s.[29]

Where does the truth lie? The evidence strongly suggests that Cotton did discuss the nominations with Hoover, that Cotton made the Stone-Hand suggestion as he said he had, and that Hoover promptly telephoned Hughes, in Cotton's presence, to ask him to Washington the next day. Cotton's outrage about Hughes's interest in the chief justiceship was entirely understandable in light of what he knew.

Hoover's ultimate choice of Hughes, however, rested on factors that Cotton did not know about. Unbeknownst to Cotton, powerful forces were pressing Hoover to name Hughes rather than Stone; and Hoover, a weak and vacillating president, bent to those pressures. Cotton was angry about and surprised by Hughes's response, but Hoover was not.

Hoover frequently used the telephone for important presidential business; indeed, he used it when he offered a seat on the Supreme Court to Benjamin Cardozo in 1932. And Merlo Pusey himself interviewed a man who had been an associate at Hughes's law firm and who was present when Hughes received Hoover's telephone call. At the time, Hughes and the associate were revising a letter providing a legal opinion for a private client, and when Hughes put down the phone, he said, "Hold up that opinion. It may not go out."[30] Hoover probably did not make a firm offer of the chief justiceship on the telephone; but it is equally probable that Hughes knew what Hoover had in mind when he agreed to take the night train to Washington. The focus of the "shrewd" Cotton's shock was on Hughes's not rejecting outright any thought of the Supreme Court.[31] Nor is there more credibility in Hoover's protestation that he could not have discussed the appointment with Cotton because the acting secretary of state "had nothing to do with judicial appointments," a protestation that rests on a wooden, formalistic notion of organizational structure that was belied by the closeness and breadth of the two men's association. Far more plausibly, Hoover would have listened willingly to advice from a highly respected lawyer and influential government figure.

But the linchpin of Hoover's denial was his insistence that Hughes was the only candidate he considered, that Hughes was "the obvious appointment." Yet Associate Justice Stone had been widely talked about as the successor to Taft, and Stone and Hoover were old friends. They had been colleagues in Coolidge's cabinet before Stone went to the Court in 1925; they remained close friends for the remainder of the Coolidge administration and in the early part of Hoover's as well. Hoover had tried to persuade Stone to become secretary of state in 1928 or early 1929, then tried to get him to become chairman of the National Commission on Law Observance and Enforcement. They were both self-made men, both from rural backgrounds; they and their wives regularly dined together at each other's homes; and Stone was well known to be a member of the president's "Medicine-Ball Cabinet"—the small group of men who gathered early each morning at the White House to engage in a favorite exercise of the day, tossing around a medicine ball, and then to chat informally over a hearty breakfast in the White House basement.[32]

No one was more aware of, and concerned about, the rumors concerning Stone than Taft himself. Throughout his chief justiceship, he had been imbued with the mission to preserve the Court as a bulwark of property rights; it was this preoccupation that had prompted him to offer his advice freely to his administration friends whenever names of such untrustworthy liberals as Learned Hand surfaced in speculations about Supreme Court appointments. The conservative justice Pierce Butler wrote to Taft in September 1929 about the mounting "publicity in reference to Stone's elevation." Taft had no doubt that there was "a good deal of truth" to this rumor, for he had long worried about the risk that Hoover, whom he considered excessively liberal, might promote Stone. What troubled Taft most was the risk that he would thus undermine the six-man conservative majority on the bench; to Taft, all the dissenters—Stone, Brandeis, and Holmes—were "hopeless," as he wrote to his brother Henry, and his great fear was that "if a number of us die, Hoover would put in some rather extreme destroyers of the Constitution."[33]

Speculations that Stone would be named Chief Justice continued right up to the moment that Hughes's nomination was announced,[34] the source being one of Hoover's press secretaries, who had "tipped off" his press-corps friends that Stone would be the selection.[35] In fact, Hoover moved up his announcement of Hughes's nomination by a day when he realized that the Stone rumors were on the wires to newspapers around the country. Among those who believed Stone was a genuine candidate was Stone himself. When the Hughes nomination was announced, Stone's secretary later recalled, it was "a keen disappointment" for him, "which he took on the chin."[36]

In view of Stone's strong chances to become Chief Justice in 1930, then, Cotton had ample reason to mention him to Hoover. And it

arned Hand at mid-career, probably in the 1930s, appearing unusually self-assured. *(Family Collection)*

For more than three decades, Dartmouth French professor Louis Dow was a permanent houseguest at the Hands' summer home in Cornish, a companion to Frances while Learned was in New York. *(Harvard University Archives)*

Charles Culp Burlingham, New York City attorney and reformer, befriended Learned Hand soon after Hand's move to New York City in 1902 and urged his judicial appointment seven years later. *(Harvard Law Art Collection)*

Learned Hand at a family gathering, probably in the 1940s, taking satisfaction in his after-dinner performance of Gilbert and Sullivan songs. *(Family Collection)*

Learned Hand at seventy-five, demonstrating the strength of sailcloth to his grandson, Jonathan Hand Churchill, during a summer visit to Northeast Harbor, Maine, in 1947. *(Family Collection)*

Learned and Frances Hand, in September 1951, preparing to embark on the *Mauretania* for Europe. *AP/Wide World Photos)*

The Judge, probably late 1940s.
(Richard Saunders)

The great triumvirate on the Second Circuit Court of Appeals, ca. 1953—three friends who had served together since 1927 and brought the court its greatest renown: (left to right) Judge Learned Hand; Chic Judge Thomas W. Swan (Hand had retired from that post in 1951); Judge Augustus N. Hand.
(Erich Hartman/Magnum)

arned Hand, far right, in the academic procession at Cambridge University, England, June 1952, en ute to receive an honorary doctor of laws degree. *(News Chronicle)*

the judges' robing room prior to the Special Session of the U. S. Court of Appeals for the Second rcuit, in commemoration of fifty years of federal judicial service by Hand on April 10, 1959. Left to ht: Chief Justice Earl Warren, Judge Hand, Justice Felix Frankfurter, and Justice John Marshall arlan. *(The New York Times)*

Learned Hand in 1957, at eighty-five.
(Philippe Halsman © Yvonne Halsman)

Learned Hand, delivering his *Bill of Rights* lectures at Harvard Law School in 1958. *(Harvard Law Art Collection)*

Learned Hand in 1959, at eighty-seven, in
a portrait by Alfred Eisenstaedt.
*(Alfred Eisenstaedt, Life Magazine, © Time
Warner Inc.)*

Another portrait by Eisenstaedt in 1959,
showing Hand in a characteristic pose,
studying the briefs and record in a case
before him.
*(Alfred Eisenstaedt, Life Magazine, © Time
Warner Inc.)*

An especially well-known portrait of Learned Hand, taken in 1952, included in the Museum of Modern Art's photographic exhibit, "The Family of Man." *(Don Weiner, courtesy Sandra Weiner)*

should also be remembered that Hoover's 1937 denial of the story coincided with Roosevelt's Court-packing plan, a scheme that made Hoover dislike his successful rival even more than he already did, and that drew heavily on a dissent Stone had written a year earlier, the most vehement attack yet on the Court's conservative majority.[37] Hughes was taking the lead on the Court in undermining support for FDR's plan (he wrote a critically important letter to Montana senator Burton Kendall Wheeler opposing it), and no anti-Rooseveltian would have wanted to undermine him. Hoover thus had good reason to give Hughes a flawed version of the 1930 events, and Hughes equally good ones to embrace it.

In the White House, Attorney General Mitchell was the chief spokesman for maintaining a conservative majority on the Court. He was close to Justice Butler, who had discussed the Stone rumors with Taft for months; it was probably Butler who helped to persuade Mitchell that Hughes was the ideal choice for Chief Justice. Mitchell, in turn, had urged Justices Butler and Willis Van Devanter to dine with Hughes in New York just two days before Hoover's telephone call, to get his reaction to a possible nomination; the justices had returned convinced that Hughes was interested. Mitchell told Hoover this, and Hoover, despite his liberal Republicanism and his friendship with Stone, bowed to the conservative pressure. It was for this reason that Hughes's response to Hoover's telephone call on January 30—the conversation that Cotton overheard—was not nearly so surprising to Hoover as it was to Cotton. And thus it was that William Howard Taft bore at least indirect responsibility for preventing Hand's promotion to the Supreme Court for the second time.[38]

LEARNED HAND'S OWN REACTIONS to the Hughes appointment confirm that he had had a genuine shot at promotion to the Supreme Court. A worried Frankfurter wrote to him, "Poor Stone must be deeply disappointed—but I suspected that the [conservative] influences against him would be too strong. . . . Altogether—I should have been much happier with Stone." And then he added a consoling word: "I'm afraid this rules out anybody else from N.Y.—both you and B.N.C. [Cardozo]."[39] Hand's reply was stoic:

Yes, I am sorry for Stone, who must have had much disappointment. But a man has only himself to thank if he allows himself to count on such things. Tis a world where the unaccountable is the most certain, and nobody over the age of consent ought to go along without that always in mind. What you say about me is comprised in the same.

Hand evaluated his own prospects as having been quite marginal, as only an outside chance:

> If anyone had been making a "book," he would have had to put me among the entries at mere odds. Personally, I should have put myself down as what the sports call "a long shot," but it is true I should have been on the "book." To have that "long shot" finally wiped off is a slight matter; in a sense it is as well that now it is closed. Anybody who is a judge and says that he would not like it is a damned liar, but then so is anyone or nearly anyone who says he wouldn't like to be President or King of England, I guess, or nearly any other "face card." So we are made, little as it is creditable to us that we are.

Hand sensed, too, that Chief Justice Taft, his old nemesis, had exercised his waning but still considerable influence: "I had heard that the old C.J. had freely expressed himself on the subject and was very set. I can't blame the President for yielding, though I don't doubt it cost him a very genuine personal pang."[40] To Frankfurter, Hand insisted that his chances to get on the Supreme Court in 1930 had always been remote. But slowly he brought himself to acknowledge the true extent of his chagrin; he voiced these private feelings only in a series of letters to his wife.

On January 31, 1930—the day after Joseph Cotton's meeting with Hoover—Frances Hand, accompanied by Louis Dow, had embarked on a three-month voyage to Europe and the Near East.[41] Learned wrote her two or three long letters each week she was away. These letters make clear that they had often discussed the possibility of a Supreme Court appointment before she left—and that her hopes had been high. Frances, indeed, had told one of her friends that Learned's promotion was "probable." Still, in his first letter to her, written while she was on the high seas and he had just heard the news about Hughes, he insisted, "You will do me the justice to say that I always warned everybody that while it was possible, the odds were all against it. . . . I must allow that for a while I felt a pang or two, but as in so many other things in life, once the die is cast we have unusual means of adapting ourselves to new situations. I had thought of this as a possibility all the time and of course knew that if [Hughes's appointment] came through, it would end any hopes I might have. . . ."[42] Four days later, he revealed his feelings more fully:

> Really, I am not so sorry about the closing of the door for me to Washington. That damned thing was in my thoughts all the time; it made a kind of coward of me. After the first, which I will agree was a little of a dasher, I began to feel as though something had been lifted from my spirits and now I feel freer.[43]

Part of Hand's adjustment was to seek rationalizations: he looked for reasons why Hughes's designation might after all be for the best, and he accurately suspected that "the whole thing was arranged and that Taft may have had much to say about it; he did not trust Stone,— thought him too ambitious"; "in Hoover's place I think I should have taken Hughes, because I doubt Stone's ability to preside over a court, a number of whom do not like or trust him." Anyway, "perhaps Charley will turn into a good 'liberal,' God knows the Court needs one very badly."[44] A few days later, this rationalization had taken firmer hold: "It was rather a hard blow for Stone, but Hoover was absolutely right. Stone was not man enough to handle the Court, made up in such large part of old fierce mastiffs who despise and hate him." He remarked on the beginning of an attack on Hughes in the Senate, from people like George William Norris of Nebraska and Robert La Follette.[45] In fact there were a large number of votes against the confirmation, on the grounds of Hughes's representation of corporate clients in his Wall Street practice and the impropriety of naming someone who had once left the Court to engage in presidential politics.

Despite Hand's best efforts to find solace, it took him nearly a month after the Hughes appointment to achieve calm acceptance. Not until March 1 did he write convincingly that he had put his disappointment behind him:

> I have really ceased to care about the Sup. Ct. Yes, it is true I still am unable to say finally to myself that it is outside the possibilities. That curious disposition of us all to wonder whether some turn of the wheel may not change it all, will persist, unlikely though it now is. But I can truly say that I have no longer any sense of disappointment, and that it is a relief not to have the damned thing so much in my mind.[46]

Hand's "curious disposition . . . to wonder" about a possible promotion found a new outlet within days. On March 8, the Court's second youngest justice—the sixty-four-year-old Edward Terry Sanford, Harding's last appointee—died, and immediate widespread speculation was that "Hoover will be likely to take a Circuit Judge." For Hand, this report simply opened new wounds: "I feel fairly sure that if Hughes had not been appointed, it might well have been me."[47] He promptly pushed for the appointment of a New Orleans lawyer friend, Monte Lemann. But he quickly found that his effort would not get anywhere: Lemann was a Democrat, and he was not a judge. (Hand thought these reasons for barring Lemann were silly.) The nomination went to a very young federal circuit judge from North Carolina, John J. Parker. Parker was promptly attacked for an alleged anti-labor decision and alleged racism; he was defeated in the Senate. Ultimately, this seat went to Owen J. Roberts, a Philadelphia lawyer.

Two years later, when Justice Holmes retired, Benjamin Cardozo of the New York Court of Appeals was the widely expected choice to succeed him, and Cardozo was indeed appointed.[48] The differing circumstances in 1932 explain the selection of Cardozo over Hand: there was a great demand for another renowned common-law judge to succeed Holmes, and Cardozo was the most respected in the nation, with a distinguished career on a highest state court very similar to Holmes's in Massachusetts prior to *his* Supreme Court service. In 1930, the Hoover administration had been eager to promote a judge from a lower federal court, but that interest had declined considerably by 1932. In the changed context of 1932, by contrast, Cardozo had wide support for the Holmes seat.[49]

EVEN WHILE HE WAS STILL BROODING about the missed Supreme Court opportunity, Hand unexpectedly found himself the probable American nominee to succeed Charles Evans Hughes as a judge on the Permanent Court of International Justice—the World Court, as it is commonly known—that sits at The Hague.[50] "[T]hings certainly have been popping about here of late," Learned wrote Frances as he apologized for filling his letters "w. so many things about appointments to public office."[51] The news about the World Court threw Hand into several weeks of agonized, indecisive turmoil: personally, he did not want to go to the Netherlands; yet the honor was undeniable, and the court might have a real chance to contribute to international order, a cause close to his heart.

The League of Nations had established the World Court in 1920 as an autonomous body in which nations could participate even though they were not members of the League. Elihu Root, Theodore Roosevelt's secretary of state, had been a leader in organizing the court, and Hughes, as secretary of state from 1921 to 1925, had pressed repeatedly for American acceptance of the protocol governing it, though the Senate never ratified. Yet despite the American refusal to submit to the court's jurisdiction, the United States usually supplied one of its judges. (Nominations were made by members of the pre–World War I International Court of Arbitration, and the formal election was by the League. American nominators in effect determined the occupant of the "American seat" on the World Court.)

The unanticipated development stunned Hand. As he told his wife: "First, was Hughes' appointment which put so new a face on my life; interiorly anyway. Then . . . this World Court business. . . ."[52] He first learned of "this World Court business" in a conversation on February 10 with Walter Lippmann, who was a good friend of Newton Baker, the onetime mayor of Cleveland who had been Wilson's secretary of war (and for whom Frankfurter had worked during World War I). Baker, as a member of the Permanent Court of Arbitration, was one of the nominators of the American judge for the World Court. (The others were Hughes; Hughes's predecessor on the World Court, John Bassett Moore; and Elihu Root.) Baker was keen on nominating Hand and so advised his colleagues on the committee; Lippmann was deputized to find out how Hand felt about it.[53] Hand did not know Baker well and was surprised by his interest; but Baker proved a very determined advocate. "[H]e's an emotional cuss," Learned wrote Frances, "and for some reason or other is determined that I shall take The Hague job, though I ought to be on the Supreme Court."[54]

This surprising development preoccupied Hand for more than a month: it surfaced in every one of his many long letters to Frances— who, on her overseas travels, was not likely to see any of them for weeks. On the day after his talk with Lippmann, Hand wrote his wife about

> a momentous decision in our lives that I have got to put before you. . . . I can't tell you what a funk this has thrown me into. Really I don't want to do it and yet that may be no more than my great dread of taking on something so far from home and of the great and final breach it makes in my life.

Hand did not want to appear ungracious to his supporters, yet he could find little attraction in the idea of spending his life at The Hague:

I have absolutely no acquaintance w. international law and my French you know the extent of, though for that matter everything is done in two languages. Of course I should have to resign here and I must be bound not to practise law or have any other activity except that, although apparently I could lecture here if I wanted to.* The term is six years† and you must be about five months at The Hague w. opportunity to get away from time to time.[55]

But the strongest negative aspect was the actual work of the World Court. Hand had observed the court in action while in Europe during the previous summer, and he had told Lippmann about his reactions to its "burdensome" work. Since the court dealt with disputes among sovereign nations, it "must treat the parties with such respect that they can talk & talk ad libitum; they may repeat themselves, reply, rejoin, retort till the cows come home, and the judges must hear it all." They might "hear" it all, but they scarcely paid attention. "One judge spent his time writing poetry,—he was a Frenchman;—another went to sleep, an old Dutchman." Hughes had told Hand in The Hague that "getting to a decision was more trying than the argument"; Hand could not "see how they could get men willing to endure the agony for such meager results."[56]

Yet there were pulls in favor of the position, and the need to make a decision left Hand in a mood of "perturbation" and vacillation. He thought he ought to feel "elated"; he kept telling himself, "What kind of person are you that you should not feel it?" He mentioned to Frances that the salary was $20,000 a year, a good deal higher than his judicial salary; and he wrote repeatedly about the need to give money to their daughters to provide for their security (he had no hesitation in urging $100,000 to each, as a minimum, to assure at least a $4,500 annual income).[57] Week after week, Hand agonized, consulting everyone he could think of. Gus Hand and Tom Swan told him that there was "no good reason to take it"; only Benjamin Cardozo disagreed.

Further brooding brought the family situation to the fore. Leaving his daughters in the States for nearly half a year, he was certain, was "a bad thing." And the uncertainties about his professional life *after* World Court service haunted him even more insistently. Yet turning down the position continued to seem out of the question. Central to Hand's anxiety was his fear that he would have to tell President Hoover face-to-face that he would not accept: Hoover would press him, he

---

* In fact, Hughes practiced law both before and after his few months at The Hague in 1929.
† Actually, nine years normally; "six" presumably because this was the unexpired portion of the Hughes term he would fill.

feared, if only to "help get the Court accepted here." He wanted to make a decision before Hoover summoned him to an interview; yet he could not bring himself to make one.[58]

In mid-March, he postponed decision once more—until June, mainly because Joseph Cotton wanted him to remain a candidate, if only to head off more unsuitable ones. Going to The Hague seemed ever less possible "for personal reasons"; yet at the same time, the World Court's "work as work" seemed ever more attractive, for Hand now believed that he could expect to play a leading role on it.[59]

Fortunately, Learned Hand never did have to resolve his ambivalence: he soon learned that the issue had been put off indefinitely, mainly because of the disagreement among the nations at the London Naval Disarmament Conference. Hand was relieved: "[I]t is quite possible that the whole thing was only a flare-up at best," he told his wife.[60]*

This series of events should have reassured Hand of his reputation and standing. Yet his uncertainties and shaky self-esteem persisted: he had difficulty believing he was as serious a possibility for the Supreme Court as in fact he was; he wasn't sure he was equipped to sit on the court at The Hague; and above all, the dark undercurrent of his indecisiveness, so noticeable in his response to the Sacco-Vanzetti controversy, was dramatically evident in his vacillation over the World Court appointment.

THE DEATHS of two very good friends within months of each other in 1931 related, in a poignant way, to the erosion of Hand's faith in Hoover as well as to his detachment from the economic crisis. In March, Joseph Cotton succumbed to a long, debilitating illness; in October, Dwight Morrow, who had seemed in the best of health, died after a sudden stroke. For Hand, the deaths of these two contemporaries— Cotton was three years younger than Hand, Morrow only a year younger—brought more than intimations of mortality.

Hand had been extraordinarily fond of both men, even though—and in part because—they were both so different from him. Cotton was a warm friend with a genuine breadth of outlook and liberal instincts; Morrow, too, was a close acquaintance, although as Hand once told Frankfurter, Morrow was "so continuously occupied that he scarcely had time for warm personal relations."[61] But Morrow, like Cotton, was broad-gauged and progressive. After a few years in a successful Wall Street practice at Simpson, Thacher early in the century, he had

---

* The World Court vacancy was not filled until months later: on September 17, Frank B. Kellogg was elected to replace Hughes.

spent an even more lucrative period as a partner in J. P. Morgan's banking house, but like Cotton he had found time for enlightened public service; and he moved permanently into the public sector when he served as ambassador to Mexico from 1927 to 1930. On returning to his northern New Jersey home, Morrow ran successfully for the Senate, and that victory catapulted him immediately into contention as a potential Republican candidate for the presidency.

What distinguished Cotton and Morrow from Hand, and what attracted him to them, was that they were men of action. Both were impatient with long-range speculations, and forceful in seeking immediate results. As Hand reported to Frankfurter after a "good time" during a weekend visit with the Morrows, "He is always a stimulating person, deft and wise, with as good a practical sense for the immediate as I know." Partly out of envy, Hand admired such men of action, yet he could also regret that they were not more deliberative. As he told Frankfurter, he did not find this practical sense for the immediate "wholly adequate": "Are human affairs so accidental, so capricious, so unaccountable, that all remote speculations are mere vanity?"[62]

With the loss of Cotton and Morrow, Hand had grave doubts about the Hoover administration's capacity to grapple with the economic crisis. Their deaths meant more than a "crushing blow";[63] their loss also prompted a chilling sense that the country might need a stronger captain to steer it through the economic crisis. By the beginning of 1932, with Cotton and Morrow gone, Hand was convinced that Hoover would not "have another term" and that "the next [president] will be a Democrat."[64]

During the long months of 1932 that preceded the November presidential election, the Depression deepened. Conservatives continued to preach self-reliance and thrift; liberals urged more vigorous governmental action; radicals foresaw the end of capitalism and the bankruptcy of democracy. Felix Frankfurter and Walter Lippmann, both convinced that the end of Republican rule was at hand, busied themselves in maneuverings directed toward the Democratic convention in late June. Hand kept aloof from the political machinations, not only because of the restraints of his office but also because he could muster little enthusiasm for either side. But with his longer-range perspective, he made clear that he cared deeply about the survival of his country and its system of government.

In March 1932, for example, Hand delivered an eloquent address to the Federal Bar Association in Washington. In "Democracy: Its Presumptions and Realities,"[65] he recognized the challenges to representative government from totalitarians of the left and the right, argued against rule by "supermen," and acknowledged the imperfections of American democracy while nonetheless giving it his two cheers as surely the most "tolerable system." For many Americans, the economy's roller-coaster ride from boom to massive unemployment and Depression was stirring anti-democratic attitudes. But Hand drew moderately optimistic conclusions from deeply pessimistic premises: for him, the democratic process, redefined to take account of the modern context, remained the best system of government, despite its flaws.

"Democracy: Its Presumption and Realities" depicted how far modern American politics fell short of the expectations of the Founding Fathers; yet in his speech Hand rejected the widespread despair that prompted so many, at the depth of the Depression, to embrace totalitarian ideologies. Hand insisted on taking his chances with imperfect individuals participating in the democratic process as best they could. Modern democracy was "not as bad as it seems," he argued, and "good or bad, we still derive from it advantages which are irreplaceable in any other system." He conceded that "counting heads is not an ideal way to govern," but pointed out that "at least it is better than breaking them."

> We do more than count; we measure political forces by the aggressiveness and coherence of conflicting classes, and this, though it may be the despair of the reformers, I should like to put in a more respectable light. It may not be an ideal, [but] I shall argue that it is a tolerable system; that it can insure continuity and give room for slow change, since it allows play to the actual, if unrecognized, organs of society.

For Hand, then, the proper response to the flaws of democracy was to develop the habits essential to the survival of the democratic system, to "learn a little; . . . to forbear, to reckon with another, accept a little where they wanted much, to live and let live, to yield where they must yield; perhaps, we may hope, not to take all they can."

As he was wont to do, Hand closed his remarks by invoking the image of his idol, Oliver Wendell Holmes (who was celebrating his ninety-first birthday on the night Hand spoke). And he ended with a peroration of extraordinary poetic eloquence:

> Beware then of the heathen gods; have no confidence in principles that come to us in the trappings of the eternal. Meet them with gentle irony, friendly scepticism and an open soul. Nor be cast

X

The New Deal

HAND TURNED SIXTY IN 1932, and he repeatedly worried that his advancing age was making him resistant to new ideas. Quite the contrary was true: his very awareness of the dangers of calcification reinforced his capacity to listen, to think, and to rethink. His acquaintances, from the fear-filled wealthy to reform-oriented intellectuals, overflowed with their contrasting certitudes, but Hand steered an independent path. He knew all too well of the need for reform to believe blindly in the capacity of the free-enterprise system to right itself, yet he was too doubting to embrace uncritically the vast and often incoherent proposals being made for large-scale changes.

Hand's changing evaluation of Franklin Delano Roosevelt illustrates his lack of dogmatism and his capacity for growth. In 1930, when Hand still hoped that President Hoover would yet prove effective, he was quite aware of FDR as an emerging rival—FDR was reelected governor of New York in that year—but found nothing to admire in him. In 1932, Hand voted once again for Hoover, although with diminished enthusiasm, for he recognized that the nation was in greater distress than ever: the number of the unemployed had reached twelve million; bank closures had climbed to new highs; and all the economic indicators—wages, dividends, industrial production, farmers' purchasing power—had dropped nearly by half since 1929. Slowly, Hand began to appreciate FDR's strengths: his personal courage, especially in living with the effects of polio; his buoyant optimism; his ability to restore self-confidence to the shaken nation. He voted for FDR in 1936, 1940, and 1944; he appreciated the need for leadership and action, even though he never abandoned his skepticism about New Deal measures.

Hand was never an uncritical enthusiast of the New Deal, in part because of his concern about the threat to individual liberty inherent in the burgeoning national establishment. For decades he had had few qualms about a broad reading of national powers, but the pervasive exercise of these powers, and the growing dominance of the presidency over Congress, were worrisome in a decade that saw the spread of totalitarianism in Europe. For many of those who voiced fears about the New Deal's threats to liberty, including the conservative Liberty League, the concern about personal freedoms was a mere façade for greed. Not so for Hand.

Hand's evolving views about the Depression and the New Deal can be seen most vividly in his extensive correspondence with three friends, Bernard Berenson, Walter Lippmann, and Felix Frankfurter, where the distinctiveness of their positions—and Hand's own—emerges clearly.

Berenson was, as always, the aesthete, the snob, and the aristocrat. To him, Western culture, for which he lived and from which he made his living, was always on the verge of being submerged by demagogues and the masses. Predictably, he had little patience with political leaders: throughout the 1930s, Berenson sneered at FDR; at bottom, he disdained democracy. He once provoked a clash with Hand by advocating the desirability of an aristocracy that would "hold down" the masses. B.B. was convinced "that we are hierarchical animals with pyramidical societies, governed from the top & not from the base"; Hand vehemently disagreed. Whatever might be said for aristocratic rulers in theory, he told Berenson, he knew of no system by which they could be safely selected. Plato's scheme, he insisted, was "desperately unconvincing"; and there had never been a period of aristocratic rule when "they did not abuse their powers before long."[1]

Lippmann shared some of Berenson's appreciation of high culture and aristocratic values, but he was far more engaged in current events. In 1931, when the *New York World* folded, he commenced a "Today and Tomorrow" column for the *New York Herald Tribune*, where his commentaries evoked widespread admiration, including Hand's, for their seemingly detached, calm, rational critiques of governmental policies. Yet Lippmann's responses to the Depression and the New Deal were far more volatile than Hand's, and indeed fluctuated wildly. He was an early enthusiast of FDR: in 1932 he called for strong executive leadership and urged the exercise of near dictatorial powers by the president during the early part of Roosevelt's first term. Yet by 1935, he had swerved sharply to the right, suddenly perceiving a threat of totalitarianism in Roosevelt's leadership, and in 1936, he urged the election of the Republican candidate. And when FDR launched his ill-fated attack on the Supreme Court in 1937, Lippmann berated FDR in a tone shriller and more hysterical than that of most critics.

Hand did not share Lippmann's enthusiasm for Roosevelt in 1932, and from the beginning perceived the risks of totalitarianism in strong executive leadership. But Hand's admiration for the president steadily rose, and in the 1936 election, he left no doubt that he preferred Roosevelt to Alf Landon. And Hand strongly disagreed with the vehemence of Lippmann's attack on FDR's Court-packing plan: he did not like FDR's tampering with the institution, but he insisted that the opposition's hysteria was unwarranted.

Felix Frankfurter continued to be Hand's most frequent correspondent of all during these years. In contrast to Berenson's distant contempt for the New Deal and Lippmann's erratic course, Frankfurter was always the emotionally committed, fully engaged supporter of FDR and the New Deal's objectives. Frankfurter had supported Alfred E. Smith against Hoover in 1928, but with Smith's defeat he quickly switched his allegiance to Roosevelt as the next great hope of the Democratic party. By 1932, Frankfurter had become a trusted adviser to FDR, a loyal, increasingly sycophantic and also an increasingly influential consultant.

Frankfurter had long been distressed about the greed that motivated so many law students' career choices; with the advent of the Roosevelt presidency, he was able to steer some of the best to Washington and a career of public service. (Opponents of the New Deal referred to the hordes of young lawyers swarming to the capital from Cambridge as "Happy Hot Dogs.") Typically, he battled with FDR's original "Brain Trust," the triumvirate of Columbia economists—Raymond Charles Moley, A. A. Berle, and Rexford Guy Tugwell—who were early suppliers of grandiose economic schemes, for he admired Roosevelt more for his leadership capacities than for the New Deal's detailed economic programs. Hand, doubtful about the efficacy of rigid, centralized economic planning, accurately viewed Frankfurter as among the most conservative of FDR's advisers.

Frankfurter was crucial in helping Hand to see the need for FDR's dominance—he was far ahead of Hand in seeing the central significance of the maldistribution of wealth that made the Depression so terrible and that required national leadership to correct—and both realized that they thought alike on many essentials. "Whatever may be our difference on specific measures," Frankfurter wrote to Hand, "you and I are a pair of old-fashioned democrats, crowded on the left by the discontented and on the right by the too comfortable."[2] This was an accurate assessment. Frankfurter was too much a disciple of Louis Brandeis's fears of big government to convert his personal admiration for FDR into support for the economic planners' most radical proposals. And Hand was too much the thoughtful skeptic to embrace either Berenson's total hostility to the New Deal or Lippmann's love-hate pattern, any more than he could join Frankfurter's unqualified enthusiasm for FDR.

Yet their agreement on basics could not obscure the very real differences between Frankfurter and Hand: throughout early 1932, their letters had erupted with them. Although Democrats as well as Republicans continued to advocate a balanced budget during the election campaign, Frankfurter and other Roosevelt advisers were moving toward support of more basic economic reforms, in the belief that only deficit spending could give adequate relief to the needy. Hand, by contrast, adhered to fiscal conservatism, perhaps still influenced by his associations with the wealthy and still a captive of the preconceptions of his own comfortable economic class. Frankfurter, however, devoted all his passion and conviction to castigating the underlying sources of the economic crisis: the smugness of status-quo defenders, their preoccupation with moneymaking, and the uneven distribution of wealth shown in the growing gap between rich and poor.

SOME OF HAND'S GROWTH in understanding occurred while he was caught in a cross fire between Frankfurter and Lippmann about who the Democratic nominee should be in 1932. Frankfurter staunchly supported FDR; Lippmann worked vigorously to assure the nomination of Newton Baker. Baker had been a Wilsonian idealist and a strong supporter of the League of Nations, but Frankfurter insisted that the Baker of 1932 was not the Baker of 1918: he had become a lawyer and lobbyist for industrial and financial interests in Cleveland; he was not the man to get the country out of the Depression. Hand thought Frankfurter's antipathy excessive, but Frankfurter, as usual, persisted. What was wrong with Baker, he claimed, was his complacent attitude toward "the basic economic questions of our day": he had a fundamental "distrust of the democratic direction" and was unwilling to challenge "those in control of financial power," those responsible for the "disparity in wealth and social power which in the long run will not be tolerated." (As a law teacher, Frankfurter had an added reason to dislike Baker, for the example he set: many Harvard students wanted to emulate Baker's successful corporate law practice; but Frankfurter's reasons for being at Harvard did not include helping others make money.) Roosevelt was surely preferable, Frankfurter insisted, at least for his "basic general direction." "I don't see any use for brains and culture if they are not energized and, in effect, make for complacency or if their weight is thrown in what seems to me the wrong directions."[3]

Hand continued to defend Baker: Roosevelt still seemed to him no more than "vaguely well meaning, without much capacity or willingness to make himself plain"; his kind of talk could "mean anything or nothing."[4] Frankfurter insisted that FDR, unlike Baker, understood the basic problem of American society. A commitment to greater egalitarianism, he argued, had become part of the "bones and marrows of people": "One does not have to be much of a radical . . . to satisfy the desire for greater fairness, for less arrogant power in the hands of those who have financial power."[5]

A few days after the election, Frankfurter called Hand's attention to Hoover's final, self-righteous and vindictive campaign speech, and only then did Hand at least concede: "I quite agree with you that Hoover's crabbed and somewhat churlish nature was a great defect."[6] And at last he began to see that some of the qualities that he had disparaged as weaknesses in Roosevelt might indeed be useful traits. As Frankfurter put it, those " 'soft' human qualities in him which grated on so many people may turn out to be one of the most important factors for a tolerably successful administration. Are we not apt to forget that perhaps the most indispensable function of a democratic statesman is the capacity to mediate among the feelings and irrationalities of his people?"[7] In reply, Hand wrote:

> About Roosevelt I try to remember always this. A man who has conquered such a terrible calamity as he, must have somewhere in him "virtues." When I reflect what [polio] would have done to me, I must stand in respect of him. But the human soul is a curious melange, and what may be heroism in one, may be no more than an unconquerable optimism in another. It is a pity that it was impolitic to emphasize this, by far the greatest claim in my opinion that he has upon our confidence.[8]

In accepting the Democratic nomination in June 1932, Roosevelt had pledged "a new deal for the American people." But the platform on which he ran was fiscally orthodox, and the nation that overwhelmingly voted for him on November 8—he won all but six states—had little idea what was in store, beyond knowing that a jaunty optimist would move into the White House. With the Twentieth Amendment [changing the date of inauguration from March to January] not yet effective, the country had to wait four months until FDR could assume office on March 4, 1933. During this long delay, the Depression continued unrelieved while Roosevelt, lacking clear plans of his own, listened to the debate among his advisers. The advocates of central planning, led by his "Brain Trust," battled with a Brandeis-inspired group—including Frankfurter—suspicious of big national government.

Once in office, FDR moved quickly, replacing the long lethargy with visible action through a program that sided with the central planners. He promptly declared a bank holiday and called a special session of Congress to convene on March 9. During this three-month session—the "First Hundred Days" of the "First New Deal"—an overwhelmingly Democratic Congress enacted a broad program of social and economic experimentation. The Agricultural Adjustment Act sought to reduce crop surpluses and provided financial aid to farmers; the Tennessee Valley Authority was created; the Securities Act promoted reliable information in securities transactions; and in the most ambitious program of all, Congress, just before adjourning in mid-June, passed the National Industrial Recovery Act. The NIRA established a National Recovery Administration (symbolized by the Blue Eagle) to stimulate business and reduce unemployment by setting up a system of industrial self-regulation, with businesses adopting fair-trade codes under government supervision and obtaining immunity from the antitrust laws in return. The NIRA contained other important provisions as well: a National Labor Board was set up to assure collective bargaining rights to labor; and a Public Works Administration was formed to reduce unemployment through construction projects.

By the summer, Hand had abandoned many of his doubts about the president and indeed found reasons to applaud his forceful actions. True, Hand continued to have ample reservations, but not out of a rich man's blind hatred toward the perceived enemy of private property. Instead, Hand's concerns stemmed from his long-held beliefs in the American constitutional structure, with its division of power between president and Congress, and in the tenets of liberalism, with its hostility to totalitarianism and its insistence on room for individual autonomy. Hand recognized the economic emergency, but he would not join Lippmann's campaign to bestow dictatorial powers on FDR. He wrote to Frankfurter:

> [M]ake no mistake, win or lose, our revered Constitution of checks and balances has gone. The American people is getting used to the idea that when the wind blows, the Captain is the boss, and that what he says, goes. If there is opposition, he goes "on the air," and bullies recalcitrants into line. . . . I confess I wince; it has too much resemblance to Russia, Italy, Japan and Germany

for my relish. I see a very small place left for the kind of [procedure]
for which I . . . am suited and to which my heart is wed.

Hand drew on the words of an English scholar whose ideas would
soon capture the imagination of many New Dealers, ideas about fiscal
policies of countercyclical government spending: higher governmental
expenditures in bad times and higher taxes in good ones in order to
even out business cycles. Hand told Frankfurter that he had been impressed by a recent essay by John Maynard Keynes in *The New Statesman*;
Keynes, he reported, "while acknowledging that there must be drastic
upsets economically if a shred of capitalism was to stay," insisted that
"if the cost was to be the suppression of all dissent and the general
atmosphere of the Big Bully, he was back to 19th Century Liberalism."
Keynes's concern was Hand's: even while Hand perceived the need for
FDR's policies in 1933, he worried about the long-term impact of the
New Deal's methods. The "feel of the thing is not pleasant to me," he
told Frankfurter:

> If you once get used to brow-beating the whole crew and the
> passenger list whenever the wind rises to a half-gale, your Beaufort
> scale will be half-gale whenever you don't have your way. I
> shouldn't mind so much if the way out was by upsetting capitalism,
> but Russia is not an encouraging alternative. And so I stand as I
> generally do, like G. Santayana, "perplexed aside from so much
> sorrow."

The White House's dominance of all public debate and the adulation
of the president without effective political opposition especially troubled
Hand: "I seem to see everywhere the spectre of Fascism, and I hate
that something fierce; it stops my breathing apparatus. If they won't
let me talk, I might as well die."[9]

HAND OFTEN CLAIMED that he was uninformed about Washington affairs. But again and again, his self-deprecating remarks were
followed by astute observations. In June 1933, for example—with
Lippmann in London for his first long meeting with Keynes—Hand
sent his friend vivid descriptions of the Washington atmosphere, writing
on the very day that Congress enacted the NIRA. The capital was

> a mad-house; junior clerks dictating, God save the mark, funda-
> mental statutes to their stenographers; their superiors being inter-
> viewed and interviewing all the live-long day, and repeating clichés

that they hear from the aforesaid j.c.'s. Nobody thinking; everybody feeling and acting.

Yet despite his sarcasm, Hand left no doubt that he recognized the need for forceful leadership: "Well, there is a time when, merely to keep from blowing up, there must be action, or the appearance of acting. This is said time; FDR has to give the semblance of an efficiency engineer, and by God, he has done it. And most excellently." Hand was also sarcastic—and somewhat apprehensive—about the flood of litigation that lay ahead as a result of the New Deal legislation: "Lord, how the puzzles have piled in. I suppose it isn't a patch on what we shall get out of the coruscations of this best galaxy of talent in this or any country, in this or any other time."[10]

Hand recognized that economic experimentation might well take unforeseeable turns, but he insisted that forceful governmental action was necessary: "[W]e had to have something of the sort . . . if for no other reason than that people would not have been willing to wait longer," he told Bernard Berenson in September 1933. And so far, Americans had "proved more toughly-knit than I should have expected—four years survived under circumstances that to most people would have been prohibitive of anything but introspective self-pity."[11]

In a significant reflection of the differences he had with Berenson, Hand rejected B.B.'s dismissive linking of FDR's program with totalitarian varieties of materialism. In a comment sharply at odds with what he had been saying about Roosevelt just a year earlier, he acknowledged that "Roosevelt, in spite of some serious blunders, carried us on and gave us a little dash of self-confidence. It was sadly needed, and the hypodermic worked." Hand especially resisted Berenson's arguments that excessive materialism was the source of the global trend toward totalitarianism. "If I didn't know where the next meal was coming from, and was likely to be thrown onto the street next week, I rather fancy that I should be relatively cool towards the dangers of materialism," he remarked sharply. "Our blessed capitalistic democracies" might be no "less materialistic than Stalin, Hitler, Mussolini & Co.," yet he insisted on distinguishing democrats from totalitarians:

> I don't care for any of the partners [in the totalitarian group], largely because they would cramp me, a divine soul, nearly 62 years old, and especially wouldn't let me express my ideas about the Good, the True and the Beautiful.

Hand ended his musings with a characteristic "I'm in some doubt; I'm always in doubt," but his judgments were strikingly perceptive.[12]

Totalitarianism's abuses of power—its rejection of impartial justice, its reliance on arbitrariness, its resort to terror—offended Hand's deepest values, and this antipathy to dictatorship well antedated the rise of Hitler. In February 1928, for example, writing at the moment when Mussolini in Italy and Stalin in the Soviet Union were consolidating their powers, he had set forth his creed for Judge Charles F. Amidon of North Dakota (one of the few federal judges who had been on Hand's side in objecting to Espionage Act prosecutions of dissenters during World War I). Liberalism, Hand told Amidon, meant "a frame of mind," not an "espousal of any definite program." The "liberal," he said, was "the man who disbelieves in the power of the human mind to see far in advance" and who therefore could not be committed to "far-reaching programs." That was why "the Bolsheviks and the Fascists hate liberalism as they hate nothing else, and with justice, for they know that the spirit of skepticism is death to their program."[13]

Hand's anti-totalitarianism was also stirred by his human sympathy for its victims. One of the first anti-Fascists he came to know was Max Ascoli, a young Italian political scientist with a letter of introduction from Berenson whom Hand met on an ocean voyage from Europe in October 1931. He perceived "substantial gifts" in this "most charming and intelligent" young man[14] and quickly sensed that Ascoli was attracted to living in the United States because he yearned for "surcease from Fascism." Hand took care of Ascoli in New York, and when the Italian headed for Harvard, he urged Frankfurter to look after this "very remarkable chap; erect, poised, moderate, with a good sense of humour, and—at a guess—a genuine scholar."[15]

Ascoli's stay in the United States proved permanent. In 1933, he became one of the first twelve anti-Fascist scholars—all the others were German, primarily Jewish refugees—to be appointed to the faculty of the new University in Exile, one of America's major havens for those fleeing Fascist regimes. The University of Exile was the creation of the New School for Social Research in New York City and its director, Alvin Johnson; within a year, the group of exiled scholars became the New School's graduate faculty.

Both Learned and Frances Hand were friends and supporters of Alvin Johnson, and Learned's interest in the New School stemmed not only from his approval of its mission but also from personal ties. The New School, organized in 1918, had grown out of discussions among *The New Republic*'s founding circle, which met regularly at Herbert Croly's home. Johnson saved the New School from ruin by emphasizing only one of its original twin missions, adult education; but by 1933, the presence of the refugee scholars allowed the school to pursue its other mission—systematic research. And the Hands were major financial supporters of the institute.[16*]

Hand's long-standing hostility to anti-Semitism made him an unusually early opponent of Hitler's crusade against the Jews. In 1933, while many of Hand's acquaintances, including Walter Lippmann, underestimated Hitler's speeches and writings and saw the Nazi phenomenon as merely a short-lived phase in German politics, Hand was quick to perceive and recoil from the dangers of Nazi anti-Semitism. In November, Franz Boas, the influential Columbia scholar who had almost single-handedly refashioned anthropology into a scientific discipline, invited Hand to participate in a meeting to devise ways to counteract Nazi racial theories with empirical data. Hand declined to do so because of his self-imposed abstention from any activity he viewed as "agitation of a political character," but his reply to Boas disclosed the depth of his disdain for the mania sweeping Germany: "I need hardly assure you that I am as much out of sympathy as you can be with the whole Nazi movement and particularly with its preposterous talk about race."[17]

A few days later, Frankfurter, then a visiting professor at Oxford, wrote to Hand about his encounters with "various German exiles" who had fled to Great Britain. "It's really ghastly, and we don't know even a tithe from the public press, of the madness and the brutality that are in the saddle in Germany."[18] Unlike many Americans, Hand readily sympathized with Frankfurter's concern, and his contempt for master-race theories reflected his special sensitivity to anti-Semitism. He was a good deal more ambivalent about other European crises, however, and he watched the growing threats of conflict with mixed feelings. Like most people in the nations that ultimately joined as the Allies in World War II, Hand dreaded war; yet he also recognized that genuine threats of force might be necessary to curb Hitler's and Mussolini's expansionist ambitions. As early as 1932, Hand opined that "the world has determined to go to hell in a hand basket," as he told Frankfurter. "If I were to lay my finger on the rotten spot, I should say it was the sense of nationality."[19]

Between the frenzied lawmaking efforts of early 1933, the First New Deal, and the more deliberate enactments of the Second New Deal in 1935, Hand's views of the Roosevelt administration continued to evolve. He was disturbed by the atmosphere of improvisation and chaos in Washington. "Perhaps," he wondered, "if we get through, we shall at

---

* Felix Frankfurter and Thomas Lamont were then members of the New School's board of trustees; C. C. Burlingham and Frankfurter were also members of its advisory committee. Hand himself had been on the advisory committee in the 1920s.

least hear less of planned economy; [or] perhaps we shall hear that the planning must be more radical and that the State must, like God, be all in all." But Hand was never convinced that apocalypse was at hand:

> Somehow I can't feel as though Americans were prepared for that kind of [statist] organization; our tradition had been from the outset too anarchic, and when the first fine frenzy is passed, I dare to hope that we may relapse into our accredited method, [and follow a more] individualistic theory.[20]

Even Frankfurter, though a committed reformer, was unhappy with just about everything the First New Deal produced—except the TVA and the Securities Act of 1933, which he helped to draft. In the event, most of the reforms of 1933 proved evanescent. The more permanent effects of the New Deal, and its most successful months, did not come until 1935, by which time Brandeis-Frankfurter ideas had become influential. Frankfurter spent more time in Washington than ever, often collaborating with bright young lawyers such as Benjamin V. Cohen and Thomas Corcoran to draft major parts of significant New Deal laws. By then, the president's major goal was no longer revival of the national economy but, rather, greater economic security for ordinary people. Steering a course between the economic centralizers to the left, headed by Rexford Tugwell, and the advocates of reasonable accommodations, led by Raymond Moley, Roosevelt increasingly pursued a left-of-center course. On the right, the Liberty League, organized by big business, fought him tooth and nail, and on the left, various extremists from Dr. Francis Townsend* to Governor Huey Long of Louisiana pressed for measures to curb economic inequalities. In response, FDR moved toward redistributive measures of his own. In April 1935, Congress adopted the Works Progress Administration, designed to put millions on the public payroll; in May, farmers were offered aid by the Rural Electrification Administration and the Resettlement Administration; and the late summer brought the most important change of all, when the Social Security Act, drafted in part by Frankfurter along Brandeisian lines, was adopted.[21]

Learned Hand watched the Supreme Court with growing concern after the change in personnel in 1930, when Hughes rather than Stone succeeded Taft as Chief Justice and when Owen Roberts of Pennsylvania filled the vacancy created by the death of Justice Sanford. The ever optimistic Frankfurter believed that the new justices would join the liberals in not interfering unduly with legislative reforms,[22] but Hand

---

* The Townsend Recovery Plan called for government payments of $200 a month to everyone over age sixty, with the proviso that the recipient had to spend the money.

was more cautious. He respected Roberts's integrity but never forgot, as he occasionally reminded Frankfurter, what Joseph Cotton had said about him: "Anyone who takes Owen Roberts for a liberal is going to be mistaken."[23] Occasionally, Roberts did join the liberals in refusing to view due process as a restraint on economic regulations,[24] but more often he joined the conservatives in blocking regulatory action.

Due-process adjudication had been Hand's constant target ever since the early years of the century, but it was not the New Dealers' only concern. With the administration invoking congressional power to an unprecedented degree, the potential obstacles to national authority imposed by the federal system loomed ever larger. The Supreme Court was confronted with a choice among contradictory lines of authority: one construed congressional power over interstate commerce broadly, in the light of economic realities; the other limited national authority rigidly to those activities "directly" related to interstate commerce and barred national regulation of most "local" activities, including manufacturing, mining, and farming.

In 1934, the Court sent its first warning signals to the New Deal: with Justice Roberts writing for the majority (in an opinion that prompted Frankfurter to call him an economic reactionary), it struck down a law regulating railway workers' pensions, even though the railroad industry had been found the most readily regulatable in pre–New Deal decisions.[25] Soon after, the Court challenged the administration directly by striking down more New Deal laws. The most sweeping ruling came in the *Schechter* case, holding the National Industrial Recovery Act unconstitutional.[26] The act itself was flawed—it was the most loosely drafted product of the Hundred Days of 1933—but the overtones of the opinions were ominous, and FDR promptly blasted the ruling as an effort by the justices to take the country back to "the horse and buggy days." This confrontation first arose in March 1935, when the case of *United States v. A.L.A. Schechter Poultry Corporation* came before the Second Circuit.[27] Schechter, a poultry wholesaler in Brooklyn who bought and slaughtered chickens for resale to local dealers, was convicted of violating the National Industrial Recovery Act. The act authorized the president (ordinarily upon application by trade associations) to promulgate "codes of fair competition for [a] trade or industry." Several hundred codes had been adopted, and the National Recovery Administration's Blue Eagle symbol soon appeared in the windows of the nation's businesses. The typical code contained provisions regarding unfair trade practices, minimum wages and prices, maximum hours, and collective bargaining. One code governed the live-poultry industry in the metropolitan New York area; the

Schechter conviction was for violating its wage-and-hour as well as trade-practice provisions.

At the outset, the NIRA had had widespread public support and worked well, but by the time *Schechter* came to Hand's court the regulatory structure was disintegrating in the face of waning enthusiasm, administrative difficulties, and court injunctions. In two earlier test cases challenging the act's constitutionality, the government had amassed elaborate data to demonstrate the economic magnitude of the industries involved (oil and lumber); but neither case produced a broad Supreme Court ruling on the constitutionality of the law.[28] *Schechter* was not the government's chosen vehicle for a test of the NIRA: although the Depression affected businesses large and small, the poultry business hardly constituted a major industry; moreover, the record in *Schechter* did not specifically demonstrate how the wages and hours paid by poultry slaughterers in Brooklyn affected interstate business sufficiently to bring it within the congressional power over commerce. Nevertheless, the case was properly in the courts, and Hand and his colleagues Martin Manton and Harrie Chase had no choice but to decide it.

Two constitutional objections were raised in *Schechter*. The first was the "delegation" issue: Did the act adequately channel the president's discretion in promulgating codes of fair competition? Or had Congress, instead of legislating policy itself, granted too much unconfined authority to the president, thereby unconstitutionally delegating Congress's legislative power to the executive branch? Hand and his colleagues had little difficulty rejecting this challenge. Hand pointed out in his pre-conference memorandum that the Court had long sustained broad delegations, as in the provision authorizing the Federal Trade Commission to delineate "unfair methods of competition."

The far more troublesome issue in *Schechter* was the scope of congressional authority to regulate interstate commerce. Hand had no doubt that trade practices were sufficiently connected with interstate business to be within the reach of national powers; it was the regulation of the hours and wages of employees in Schechter's business that was the truly difficult problem. To deal with this issue in 1935, before the Supreme Court had expressed itself on the NIRA or any other major New Deal law, was a difficult task for a judge. The precedents were chaotic: one line of cases—dealing with the railway industry and stockyards, for example—had sustained national regulation of "local" intrastate business in the interest of effective exercise of the authority over interstate commerce; another, far more restrictive line had indicated that the proper analysis did not look to economic relationships between intrastate and interstate commerce, but instead relied on logical connections, hinting that all traditionally "local" activities—manufacturing, mining, agriculture, and presumably chicken slaughtering—were beyond congressional power, since any relation these activities had with interstate commerce was only "indirect" rather than "direct." How, then, was the *Schechter* dispute to be resolved?

Hand had long held a broad view of the national commerce power. Ever since his association with Herbert Croly and his support of Teddy Roosevelt's Bull Moose program, he had believed that a nationally integrated market was the constitutional ideal; he was convinced that congressional authority was broad enough to reach any significant national economic problem. Yet in 1935 Hand also had to recognize that the Constitution had after all set up a federal system of nation *and* states, and this implied a national government with only limited, delegated powers, and presupposed that some matters were left to state control. It was ultimately Hand's felt allegiance to the constitutionally established federal structure that convinced him that some limits to national power had to be recognized, even though he believed that a federal system was too cumbersome and inefficient to regulate modern economic problems.

In his pre-conference memorandum in *Schechter*, Hand accordingly concluded that the hours and wages of employees in Schechter's business could *not* be regulated by the national government:

> I cannot see how these have a direct relation to interstate commerce unless everything else does which affects the dealings of the market men and slaughterers, as for example, the rent of their depots or warehouses or the price they pay for their antiseptics or for any tools they may use, the knives of the butchers for example. Of course all these have an effect upon the demand for fowls and that is transmitted to interstate commerce. So would an ordinance which raised the cost of maintaining the shops by requiring them to be kept outside the city or to be stinkproof. Yet nobody would say that Congress might regulate these things. The line is no doubt in the end arbitrary, but we have got to draw it, because without it Congress can take over all the government.[29]

Harrie Chase agreed with Hand; Martin Manton, in a wholly uncritical memorandum, was blithely blind to any constitutional difficulty. Manton wrote the opinion for the court, devoting himself almost entirely to explaining the unanimous rejection of the "delegation" claim; on the commerce-power issue, he stated merely that the "majority of the court" had found it unconstitutional. It was left to Hand, in a concurring opinion joined by Chase, to explain why the wage-and-hour provisions were invalid. His opening remark was not mere rhetoric: "It is always a serious thing to declare any act of Congress unconstitutional, and especially in a case where it is a part of a comprehensive plan for the rehabilitation of the nation as a whole."[30] He immediately added that the extent of the congressional commerce power went "to the very root of any federal system at all." Barely hinting at his own doubts about the utility of the American federal system, Hand added, "It might, or might not, be a good thing if Congress were supreme in all respects, and the states merely political divisions without more autonomy than it chose to accord them." But his task was to apply the constitutionally delineated scheme; abolishing it would require a constitutional amendment.

Hand's analysis eschewed the logic-chopping distinction between "direct" and "indirect" in the restrictive precedents and instead insisted on what would within a few years become the accepted view:

> In an industrial society bound together by means of transport and communication as rapid and certain as ours, it is idle to seek for any transaction, however apparently isolated, which may not have an effect elsewhere; such a society is an elastic medium which transmits all tremors throughout its territory; the only question is of their size.

Yet this realistic recognition could not mean unlimited congressional power if the federal framework was to be preserved. With characteristic, unflinching candor, Hand insisted that the distinction between matters that were congressionally regulatable and those that were not was not fixable by any bright line. Few judges of the day were ready to confess what he insisted on: "The truth really is that where the border shall be fixed is a question of degree, dependent upon the consequences in each case."

To permit congressional regulation of wages and hours in the poultry business was simply going too far: "[T]here must come a place where the services of those who within the state work [goods] up into a finished product are to be regarded as domestic activities." Hand accordingly concluded that the workers in the poultry industry were "immune" from congressional regulation. He thought this conclusion unavoidable. The Second Circuit decision came down on April 1, 1935. The Schechter company promptly sought review by the Supreme Court of its conviction under the constitutional portions of the act. This appeal confronted the government with a quandary: it had no real interest in testing the law so late in its life, and especially none in risking an unfavorable constitutional decision on a record so thin, about an application so remote from the workings of a major industry. Yet the United States chose not to oppose review: the solicitor general's office, traditionally the most principled among government law offices, concluded that seeking to block review, although well within its power, "would not [be] a seemly course for public officials."[31] The Supreme Court promptly granted review, heard argument on May 2, and decided *Schechter* on May 27, less than three weeks before the NIRA would have expired of its own force.

The Supreme Court dealt a far more devastating blow to the NIRA and the national regulatory power than Hand had. Several of the justices—Brandeis, Stone, and Cardozo—were known to be receptive to most economic-reform measures, yet all of them joined the *Schechter* decision striking down the act. Moreover, they invalidated the law not only on the commerce-power ground that Hand had relied on, but also on the ground that the act unconstitutionally delegated legislative power to the president, an objection that Hand had readily rejected. The administration reacted promptly and bitterly. What FDR saw as the "big issue" was this question: "Does this decision mean that the United States Government has no control over any national economic problem?" If all the Court's "phraseology" were accepted, it would prescribe "forty-eight different controls over national economic and social problems."[32]

The Court's language was indeed cause for great concern. Striking down the NIRA merely because of the president's excessive discretion was not ominous, even though Justice Cardozo's concurring opinion blasted the act's "unconfined and vagrant" executive authority as "delegation running riot";[33] this flaw could have been readily corrected by redrafted legislation. But the Court's approach to Congress's power over commerce threatened *all* New Deal regulation of traditionally "local" activities. There had been far less threat in Hand's opinion: he had left open the possibility that regulation of *major* industries would be sustained in future cases. But the Supreme Court took a less flexible approach, emphasizing the allegedly "necessary and well-established distinction between direct and indirect effects."[34] (This suggestion was spelled out even more clearly by the majority a year later, when it invalidated a post-NIRA effort to regulate hours and wages in the coal industry; the Court made it clear that it would not be interested in the economic dimensions and would instead focus solely on the logical connection between the local and national; and this placed any regulation of local production beyond congressional power.)[35]

.   .   .

AS AN OBSERVER from the sidelines, Hand could and did criticize New Deal programs with regularity. But as a judge, Hand knew that his doubts about the effectiveness of these reforms could not legitimately affect the exercise of his official duties. The spurt of new regulatory programs soon made itself felt in the business of the Second Circuit: the workload of Hand's court steadily increased, and many of the cases arose from the flood of New Deal laws. Many issues came before Hand in these lawsuits: challenges to the constitutionality of reform measures; questions about the extent of coverage Congress had intended under the new statutes; judicial review of the increasingly powerful and pervasive administrative agencies. None of Hand's rulings reveals any sign that his private doubts about the New Deal ever affected his judgment. Instead, his decisions usually enforced New Deal laws more sympathetically than even the post-1937 Supreme Court; unlike many of his fellow judges, he gave genuine deference to the administrative agencies even while he periodically doubted their expertise and impartiality.

The cases involving claims of unconstitutionality gave Hand the greatest difficulty. His judicial philosophy always made him reluctant to strike down legislative acts. Ever since James Bradley Thayer's classes at Harvard in the 1890s, he had believed in giving the lawmakers every benefit of the doubt; ever since his criticism of the *Lochner* due-process philosophy early in the century, he had been opposed to the invalidating of laws because of their asserted unreasonableness. Moreover, he had long believed in a strong national government and a broad interpretation of congressional powers, and he admired vigorous presidents. Yet twice during the early New Deal years, he took the very unaccustomed step of holding legislation unconstitutional.

The first of these cases, *Seelig v. Baldwin*,[36] in August 1934, was the easier one, yet Hand had qualms even about it. The law he struck down was a response to the Depression, but it was a state law, not part of FDR's New Deal program. New York sought to cure the economic chaos in its dairy industry by stabilizing milk prices. It did so by prescribing the minimum prices that New York dealers could pay milk producers. As applied to purchases made by New York dealers from New York farmers, the law had survived a due-process challenge a year earlier.[37] But in *Seelig*, the law was applied to a New York dealer's purchases of milk from Vermont dairy farmers and therefore raised questions about a state's power to regulate interstate commerce. Vermont prices were lower than New York's, and New York, seeking to protect its price-control scheme, insisted that its dealers pay its prescribed minimum price to Vermont as well as in-state producers. The clear effect (and probable purpose) of this application of the New York law was to protect local dairy farmers from out-of-state competition.

Seelig involved the implied limitations imposed on the states by the Constitution's commerce clause. Although in form simply a grant of power to Congress to regulate interstate commerce, the clause had long been interpreted as safeguarding nationwide free trade by curbing some state restrictions on interstate trade. In principle, Hand should have had no difficulty invalidating the New York law: he had long believed in judicial responsibility to safeguard interstate trade against obstructions. His view was much like that of Oliver Wendell Holmes, who had said in a famous remark years earlier, "I do not think the United States would come to an end if we lost our power to declare an Act of Congress void. I do think the Union would be imperiled if we could not make that declaration as to the laws of the several states."[38] Accordingly, Hand's opinion found that the law sought "to protect a local industry by excluding foreign competing goods, and that is exactly the kind of activity against which the commerce clauses are primarily directed"; the opinion concluded, "No matter what the local need, as a nation we are without protective economic barriers between the states, certainly until Congress sees fit to allow them."[39] The Supreme Court unanimously affirmed Hand's ruling in an opinion by Justice Cardozo—an opinion more famous but less incisive than Hand's.

In short, *Seelig* arose in a context in which Hand had the least misgivings about striking down a law.[40] Yet even in this case, he felt uncomfortable. On reading Hand's opinion, Frankfurter, with gentle sarcasm, congratulated him "on having at last found a statute that is unconstitutional, at least unconstitutional in its operation."[41] Hand promptly repudiated any implication that he was happy to exercise his power in this manner: "No, I was rather unhappy about that unconstitutional statute. I have a kind of feeling that my record ought to be clean [regarding rulings of unconstitutionality], and it comes always a little hard for me when it is not." Yet he conceded that the striking down of a law was especially justified in a situation such as *Seelig*:

> I regretted it here less than in most instances, for it does seem to me that this kind of legislation if lawful without the concurrence of Congress would quickly Balkanize these United States. The effort to build up in each state economic barriers for the protection of the local industry seems to me a direct way toward an interstate protection system, and I am satisfied that our economic advancement in the past has been largely due to the free trade area which was insured. No such effort ought to be permitted without the

concurrence of Congress, so I found a case that I could act on *con amore*. I can hardly imagine feeling so about the Fifth or Fourteenth Amendment.

"In twenty-five years this is only the second time"[42] he had struck down a law, Hand accurately told Frankfurter. The first time was eight years before, in *Frew v. Bowers*. There, Hand had written a concurring opinion joining a decision striking down a provision of the 1921 Revenue Act. To Hand, the unusual tax scheme involved in *Frew* was "too whimsical to stand," too "capricious" to be sustained. And the legal ground he invoked, quite startlingly, was the due-process clause of the Fifth Amendment. Hand had argued throughout his life against excessive invocations of due process to invalidate allegedly "unreasonable" laws; repeatedly he had suggested that a law that had the support of a majority of legislators was probably reasonable by that fact alone and was hardly likely to be so arbitrary as to justify judicial invalidation. Yet in *Frew*, he concluded that "[i]f there be any [due-process] limit whatever, I own I cannot, except in fancy, think of a case more plainly beyond it than this."[43] Yet in December 1934, Hand was telling Frankfurter that he could "hardly imagine" being moved to strike down a law as violative of due process. Evidently he had forgotten about *Frew*, the only case in his life in which he struck down a law on due-process grounds.

EARLY IN 1935, Walter Lippmann turned into an overwrought alarmist. He was concerned about the rise of totalitarianism in Europe and perceived the seeds of an American fascism in Huey Long's demagoguery; in response, he advocated sharp curtailments of free speech, insisting that First Amendment rights belonged only "to those who are willing to preserve it."[44] But Hand refused to retreat from his belief that freedom of expression was the most basic right. Then, when the Second New Deal was enacted, Lippmann turned sharply against FDR and charged Congress with "abdication."[45] By contrast, Hand turned warmer toward the president. "I find myself increasingly friendly to what actually goes on in Washington," he told Frankfurter in October 1935.[46] Soon after, he reported to Bernard Berenson, with unusual optimism, "We seem to be emerging . . . in this country, still slowly, but with some certainty."

But despite his growing respect for Roosevelt's leadership, Hand was especially concerned about two aspects of the New Deal: the steady growth in federal spending, with the expectations this generated; and the expanding size of the federal bureaucracy, with the risks to personal autonomy this engendered. "Once the people have become used to an open tap," he remarked to Berenson, "it is most dangerous politically to turn it off, and while [Roosevelt] has announced that he means to do so, he has put the people into a frame of mind . . . which may override him."[47] And to a young lawyer who had gone to work for the Agricultural Adjustment Administration and was eager to leave because "work with the New Deal, at least in my vicinity, is becoming a hazardous and not too pleasant experience,"[48] Hand replied sympathetically, "I cannot help having a feeling that the pitch gets higher, more dictatorial, more bureaucratic, all the while."[49] (The young lawyer was Telford Taylor, who had been Gus Hand's law clerk.)

Soon after, Hand erupted with a mix of sarcasm and annoyance when he was asked to fill out a long questionnaire for the TVA, which was considering hiring one of his former law clerks. In response to the question "To what extent is he motivated by professional ethics and considerations of the public good, rather than by the desire for personal profit?," he drafted this reply: "I suppose he wants to make a living. I decline to answer such a silly question." And at the question "What contribution has he made without financial gain to himself to the well-being of his community?," he exploded:

> I don't know. Do you want competent lawyers, or unctuous self-righteous busy bodies? You can get here a perfectly reliable, capable young man with a sense of obligation to his job. I can't tell you more and would not answer such an absurd inquiry if I could.[50]

Not for the last time, Hand had second thoughts about risking damage to an applicant's chances by venting his annoyance: he requested another copy of the form and sheepishly explained that the first questionnaire "had been destroyed."[51]

To his acquaintances, Hand was freer in airing his antipathy toward overzealous reformers. He once referred to a man who had sought his financial help in order to complete a book as having

> a good many of the stigmata of the uplifter—a class of saint who more and more I have come to deprecate. I would give them crowns of glory, and a separate universe of discourse in which to function, but I should not welcome their intervention in the affairs of a world so wolfish as I apprehend this human world to be. Nevertheless, he may have some substance to contribute, in spite of the fact that he appears to be a "governmental planner." In my

old age I do not wish to lose all the ardors of my youth, become
a moss-back and accept the status quo without condition.[52]

ON ELECTION DAY 1936, Hand cast the first of his three presidential votes for Franklin D. Roosevelt. The national debt had increased
by 50 percent during FDR's first term; the texture of federal regulation
had grown ever more dense; and most of Hand's acquaintances in the
financial community had followed the Liberty League into vehement
opposition to Democratic rule. Lippmann was wholly disillusioned with
Roosevelt and threw his support to the liberal Republican candidate,
Alf Landon of Kansas. Hand still doubted Roosevelt's inner strength
and the wisdom of many of his measures, but he recognized the country's
demand for reform measures and believed that the Democrats, who had
begun them, should be entrusted with their implementation. As he put
it to Lippmann at the end of September, "I think on the whole that
. . . it is safer to have the unsafer party in power than the safer. There
may be things to be done that I should hate to see the Republicans do."
And a month later, just a few days before the election, he reaffirmed:
"I shall plunk for 'the more abundant life' on Tuesday, with a rather
sick heart."[53]

In letters to acquaintances less partisan than Lippmann, Hand found
it easier to disclose his complex reasons for opting for FDR. The
respected Wall Street lawyer Grenville Clark was one of these more
congenial correspondents. Clark, ten years Hand's junior, had co-
founded a leading corporate law firm and was known for his thoughtful
interest in public affairs; best known for his advocacy of world government in the post–World War II years, he was an occasional participant in the political scene. His was not an "agile" mind, but in his
"slow," careful way he had a capacity to probe deeply.[54] In late October,
Clark included Hand among a small group of acquaintances with whom
he shared a memorandum entitled "Notes on the Election, or The
Dilemma of an Independent-Conservative Voter."[55] Clark had more
confidence in FDR personally than Hand did—he had known FDR
since childhood, and they had been contemporaries at Harvard (with
Clark a member of the Porcellian, and FDR, like Hand, excluded from
it)—but he had doubts about the president's programs.[56]

In his response, Hand set forth his own views at unusual length.
His doubts about FDR's personal capacities persisted:

He seems to me too suggestible and too emotional in nature to be
capable of anything I should care to call convictions, and, so far

as I can gather, he is nearly devoid of critical faculty— . . .
because his mind seems quite at sea in dealing with abstractions.
. . . I credit him with some real sympathy with oppression, but
it seems to me very largely that of the social worker, with whom
he shares a truly vindictive feeling towards the ruling classes. (I
am disposed to put down much of his venom towards them to the
fact that he was unsuccessful at the bar.) Indeed my chief hesitation
about him personally . . . is his willingness to fan incendiary
animosities; he has repeatedly shown himself reckless and irresponsible in ways I shall never forgive him.

Despite these continuing doubts, Hand insisted on voting for FDR, for

at the moment the Republican Party is not fit to take power. . . .
I entirely agree with you about the political necessity of a program
of "Reform," doubtful as I am about its practicability. Such a
program will be more likely to succeed in the hands of its friends.
. . . It is a good program in its objectives and it may succeed.
. . . [But the] program may go wrong. . . . If it does go wrong,
I do not want a conservative party in power. . . . At the present
time only Leftist governments ought to be in the saddle when
periods of great strain come, as [French premier Léon] Blum has
shown.[57]

In another pre-election letter, Hand gave added reasons for choosing
FDR over Landon. Hand agreed with a pro-Roosevelt article that the
Harvard philosopher Ralph Barton Perry had written for the *Harvard
Crimson*, resting his choice on the underlying policy of the New Deal's
programs: "the saving of capitalistic and democratic institutions by
correcting . . . their defects."[58] Hand said of Perry's position, "He
represents about my own notions. . . . I shall somewhat unwillingly
put in a ballot for Roosevelt, not that I love him more, but Landon
and the Republicans less."[59]

Roosevelt won reelection in 1936 by a landslide: his popular vote
was nearly twenty-eight million to Landon's fewer than seventeen million. And his Electoral College majority was the greatest in history,
with only two states going for Landon. (Postmaster General James A.
Farley quipped, "As Maine goes, so goes Vermont.") Moreover, FDR's
victory swept the Democrats into more overwhelming control of Congress than ever. Hand was not disheartened. The glum Berenson asked
him "what you prognosticate for America now that Roosevelt is in again
with a mandate to do as he likes."[60] "I voted for [FDR] and am extremely
glad I did," Hand replied, for "it is not a time for a government of the

right to be in power. Besides, he is sensitive and adolescent and he has high histrionic gifts; all very important qualities in the ruler of a democracy."[61]

But not all of Hand's concerns had evaporated. Late in 1935, for example, John L. Lewis, chief of the United Mine Workers' Union, had formed industrial unions within the A.F. of L. that threatened to be more class-conscious and militant than the traditional crafts union. Lewis's techniques, Hand feared, might prove "the first step towards what comes to Fascism—or it might be Communism." Hand had confidence in FDR's ability to tame the tiger: "Roosevelt is acting as though he was going to let [Lewis] fall by his own weight. R.'s judgment is so much better than others' that if he does not smear him, it will mean that the groundswell is running against him." To Berenson's recurrent pessimism, Hand countered, "His Nibs in the White House may have his hands full before he gets through, . . . [but] he is an adept at keeping balls in the air."[62]

Yet Hand was not so sanguine about the long-range implications of the 1936 election. Big government, he recognized, was here to stay, and this development carried risks. Still, despite all the forebodings, the fear that Roosevelt's election victory would bring in its wake a vast array of new national regulatory programs proved groundless. In his second inaugural address, on January 20, 1937, the president did indeed promise new measures to battle the conditions that left "one-third of a nation ill-housed, ill-clad, ill-nourished." But rather than pursuing the elimination of these evils, his first proposal to Congress lit a firestorm that would cripple the New Deal.

On February 5, 1937, Roosevelt proposed legislation to expand the size of the Supreme Court from nine to a maximum of fifteen members by authorizing the appointment of one additional justice for each incumbent who chose not to resign or retire upon reaching age seventy. At the time, six of the justices were over seventy. Four of these were consistent enemies of reform legislation (Justices Butler, McReynolds, Sutherland, and Van Devanter); one was only a sometime opponent (Chief Justice Hughes); and the sixth was the oldest member of the Court, the eighty-year-old Louis D. Brandeis, who had been attacked as too radical at the time of his nomination in 1916.

FDR's Court-packing plan provoked not only predictable outrage from conservatives, but also intense hostility from New Dealers and other liberals. The overwhelming Democratic majority in Congress was torn asunder, never to be wholly joined together again. The president was attacked for seeking to subvert a fundamental American institution, and he was charged with disingenuousness as well. In a February 5 message to Congress, he sought to portray the plan as merely a reform measure in the interest of greater judicial efficiency, but in a March 9 radio address, he insisted the plan was needed because "we must take action to save the Constitution from the Court and the Court from itself"; he wanted additional justices in order "to bring to the decision of social and economic problems younger men who have had personal experience and contact with modern facts and circumstances under which average men have to live and work. This plan will save our National Constitution from hardening of the judicial arteries."

For the next three months, the plan dominated the nation's political debate. On June 14, the Senate Judiciary Committee issued an "Adverse Report," castigating the proposal as "a needless, futile, and utterly dangerous abandonment of constitutional principle" and claiming that its enactment would make interpretation of the Constitution open to change "with each change of administration. It is a measure which should be so emphatically rejected that its parallel will never again be presented to the free representatives of the free people of America."[63] Soon after, Roosevelt's proposal collapsed. Paradoxically, however, the Supreme Court soon ceased to be an obstacle to his economic-reform legislation: largely because of FDR's sweeping election victory, two of the justices, Hughes and Roberts, switched sides in April and began to vote to sustain New Deal laws that would no doubt have been struck down only a year earlier. (On April 17, for example, the Court upheld the National Labor Relations Act—the Wagner Act—as within congressional power, with the majority taking a fact-oriented approach to the scope of the national commerce power, an analysis sharply different from the logic-driven obstructionism of the year before; and a few weeks earlier, in upholding a law prescribing minimum wages and maximum hours for female workers, it shrank the due-process barrier that had barred such economic regulation for so long.)[64]

Roosevelt would later suggest that he had lost the battle but won the war. This was an accurate assessment with respect to judicial obstruction of economic regulation, but it was not a persuasive evaluation of his political capacity to achieve additional major reforms. When he called Congress into special session in the fall of 1937 to enact laws aiding farmers and workers and to promote conservation, he met defeat, largely because the opponents of the Court-packing plan blocked the bills. In 1938, Roosevelt intervened in the congressional primary campaigns in order to purge the Democratic party of his new enemies. Once again, he failed; and in the November elections, the Republicans scored their first congressional gains since 1928.

Amid the intense controversy over the Court-packing plan, Hand once again trod a calm and independent path. Lippmann led the press outcries against the plan. Usually he managed to present his emotion-laden opinions with surface calm; but in this instance he became hysterical. In thirty-seven columns over the five months beginning in February—half his newspaper pieces during this period—he denounced the plan. FDR was "drunk with power," he insisted, and plotting a "bloodless coup d'etat."[65]

Hand believed the widespread hostility to the plan was far too extreme; he was convinced that the Supreme Court had acted politically, willfully wielding broad policy-making powers under the guise of enforcing constitutional norms, and hence political retaliation was predictable and understandable: "Until we can arrange our institutions more in accordance with our professions I shall not be overwhelmed by such perversions; the perversions which are inherent lead to perversions in detail," he wrote to Lippmann.[66] True, FDR's plan was an inappropriate response to a Court run amok. But the Supreme Court's recent rulings had been "perversions" of judicial power; it was these abuses that had bred the "perversions" of proposed institutional curbs.

Lippmann's biographer, Ronald Steel, has sought to justify his subject's vehement hostility to FDR's Court-packing effort as resting on his legitimate "concern over the spread of totalitarianism."[67] But Hand, who was equally sensitive to the rise of absolutism in Europe and almost as disturbed by the excessive reliance on presidential rule in the United States, did not succumb to extreme emotional oscillations, and could not shed tears over an abusive Court's becoming the target of attack. Just before the 1936 elections, when Grenville Clark criticized FDR for making political appointments to the federal courts, Hand had rejected this concern, asking Clark, "By the way, how *do* you get so het up about judges? Of all R.'s faults that which I mind least is 'debauching the federal judiciary.' "[68] In a similar vein, Hand now told Lippmann, "Insofar as you are discharging your artillery against totalitarian absolutism, tempered by plebiscite, I am with you; it is only when a bunch of judges is used to fill the voids that I protest."[69] For Hand, excessively politicized judging remained a central evil.

Hand, from his occasional meetings with Frankfurter at this time, assumed that his friend supported the president, but he did not know the details of Frankfurter's involvement in the Court-packing campaign. (In fact, Frankfurter cheered on FDR enthusiastically and opposed any compromises.)[70] During most of the embattled months of the controversy, Hand and Frankfurter did not discuss the issues at all in their letters to each other. Usually Hand responded to Frankfurter with no more than "I wish I could have an hour with you." But he added once,

"The longer I go, the more revolutionary about the whole matter of constitutional law do I become."[71] From this kind of remark, Frankfurter could infer that he had Hand's support for any campaign to bring home to the American people the full story of judicial excesses, but he soon learned that Hand did not join him in endorsing FDR's remedy. A month after the startling rulings of April, Hand spent five days in Washington at the annual meeting of the American Law Institute. There he found the controversy dominating every conversation: "All the music was 'Court, Court, Court,' " he told Frankfurter. "It's a real fight, and his Nibs may have to stoop to conquer." Hand suggested that Roosevelt at least accept a revised, compromise plan: "I should say that now the chance of getting six [new justices] was about even; but he can get two, I fancy, at the drop of a hat." Hand did not like Roosevelt's most extreme remedy, but he was as strongly opposed to the obstructionist, biased Court actions that had produced this political reaction. As he told Frankfurter, "I am against the whole business, but I can't lash myself into a hashish fury or cut myself with clam shells about it."[72]

Hand's even-tempered equilibrium with Felix Frankfurter over the Court-packing scheme had everything to do with his distress a year before when, in the coal case, and in *United States v. Butler*, in which the Agricultural Adjustment Act of 1933 was invalidated on a narrow reading of the congressional spending power,[73] the Court majority had dug in its heels against the New Deal: over the dissenting votes of Brandeis, Cardozo, and Stone, the Court had insisted that Congress could not reach "local" activities related only "indirectly" to interstate commerce, no matter how large and substantial their economic dimensions. These were willful, obstinate rulings, and Hand believed they justified FDR's virulent criticisms of the Supreme Court. "It seems to me that the Court was pretty clearly wrong in the AAA decision," he wrote a former law clerk about *Butler*.[74] After analyzing the power of Congress to impose conditions on funds it appropriated for the "general Welfare," he conceded, realistically, that upholding Congress's power to enact conditional spending programs so long as they promoted an open-ended "general Welfare" might in practice leave federalism an empty shell; but he did not consider this a tragedy. For the Old Guard majority on the Supreme Court, creating obstacles to national power remained the central obsession; Hand, by contrast, was ready to accept national control of the national economy well before the justices were ready to loosen the chains on Congress.

. . .

ON ''BLACK MONDAY,'' April 12, 1937, the reign of the Old Guard ended. In *NLRB v. Jones & Laughlin Steel Corp.*, a 5–4 majority of the Supreme Court sustained the Wagner Act, adopted in 1935 to curb strikes by assuring workers the right to unionize and engage in collective bargaining.[75] As a test case, the government chose a lawsuit involving the steel industry, and compiled a voluminous record to show the potential impact of steel strikes on interstate commerce. But the law would not have survived had the majority adhered to the rigid constraints on the commerce power announced and applied in the previous years: under the narrow notion that manufacturing, no matter how large the enterprise, was "local" and related only "indirectly" to interstate commerce, the national government could not have safeguarded unionization in factories. Yet the Wagner Act was upheld.

The government's legal team in the labor board cases included a thirty-year-old Justice Department lawyer, Charles E. Wyzanski, Jr. Wyzanski, an outstanding Harvard student, had clerked for Augustus Hand from 1931 to 1932; and when Learned Hand's new clerk had to delay his service for the judge in September 1932, Wyzanski stayed on as Learned's assistant for a portion of the fall. Learned Hand had come to know and like Wyzanski in 1931 and grew even fonder of him when he served in his own chambers. They shared many views, including those about the role of the courts and the meaning of the Constitution, and Hand followed Wyzanski's subsequent career with absorbed interest. In the early weeks of the New Deal, Wyzanski became solicitor of the Labor Department, the chief legal aide to the new secretary of labor, Frances Perkins; then, in 1935, he moved to the Justice Department, where he participated in the 1937 *Jones & Laughlin* case.* As soon as Hand learned of the government's success in the Labor Board cases, he sent his effusive congratulations to his ex-clerk:

> That was a great victory. You will be saying that you didn't do it; that God—or his stooge, F.D.R.,—did it; or what not, like that. Well, I won't insist that these present discontents may not have had their share in changing Owen's [Justice Roberts's] mind; but, my dear boy, you must not disclaim your own. If you had not done your bit as you did do it; if you had been opinionated and arrogant and overbearing, as the New Dealers are,—at least

* Wyzanski worked on the brief in *Jones & Laughlin*, but did not undertake the oral argument in that case. He also participated in writing the brief in the companion Labor Board cases. His only oral argument was in one of these, a case decided on the same day, *Associated Press v. NLRB*, 301 U.S. 103. This was a feather in Wyzanski's cap, for in the *Associated Press* case, the opposing oral advocate was John W. Davis—probably the nation's most distinguished appellate lawyer—then sixty-three years old, to Wyzanski's thirty.

so often are—you might have put the fat in the fire. No, Charles, you must take this as your own and it's a grand affair, all around. . . . I rejoice to see my prophesies about you coming true: I hadn't expected to be justified so soon.[76]

But Wyzanski's reply more accurately described the central cause of the Court's turnabout: "it was not really Mr. Wyzanski who won the Wagner cases, but Mr. Zeitgeist," he told Hand.[77] Hand recognized this phenomenon as well as Wyzanski did. He viewed the Court's change of course—welcome as it was as a matter of constitutional doctrine—as a confirmation of his deepest misgivings about the increasingly politicized nature of judicial review.

The Court's 1937 decisions in *Jones & Laughlin* and its companion cases, upholding the application of the Wagner Act to the steel industry and other large businesses, resembled the permissive approach Wyzanski had suggested in 1935.[78] As advocate in the Labor Board cases, Wyzanski had not dared to advocate anything so bold; but the Court majority, chastened by the 1936 election results, went beyond the arguments of the government's lawyers and began to shape a broad authorization for national regulation of all local activities with significant national economic effects. In 1937, the new authorization seemed limited to truly national industries. Yet the new standard proved as "amorphous" as the old: in the years since, the Supreme Court has not struck down a single national law as exceeding the ever more leniently construed scope of Congress's delegated powers.

OCCASIONAL CONSTITUTIONAL CHALLENGES to New Deal laws continued to come before Hand, but by 1937 he had little reason to brood any longer about federalistic limitations on congressional powers. None of the later cases presented real difficulties under the new, permissive Supreme Court interpretations. As he said in one of his post-1937 memoranda: "I don't know that there is anything more to say than that the law today extends the interstate commerce [power] much further than it used to go."[79] And as Hand knew—and was content to accept—a similar observation could be made about the other powers of Congress as well, from those concerned with taxing and spending to that over the mails. Yet despite the waning constitutional restraints arising from the federal system, Hand never sloughed off constitutional objections: he was far too much a craftsman to ride roughshod over important issues, and his memoranda were characteristically more meticulous and thorough than those of his colleagues.

After Hand's agonized ruling of unconstitutionality in the *Schechter* case in 1935, he had to confront only two more cases raising constitutional objections to major New Deal laws, both in 1937. In each, Hand rejected the constitutional attack; in each, he went his distinctive way. Each ruling met criticism, but Hand's independent analyses stood the test of time especially well. The first case, *United States v. Kay*,[80] was an attack on one of the New Deal's major relief efforts, the Home Owners' Loan Act of 1933, enacted to relieve the distress caused by mass foreclosures of home mortgages during the Depression. The law established a government corporation authorized to spend a limited amount of appropriated funds and the vastly larger amount of money it could borrow in order to extend financial relief to hard-pressed mortgagees. In his pre-conference memorandum, Hand labeled the constitutional arguments against the law "frivolous and absurd":

> As to appropriations there can be no doubt that the United States may tax and spend for any purpose that is "common welfare"; if it can tax, it can borrow for the same purposes; no limit is laid on the borrowing power and it must be that the money raised may be used as money raised by taxes can be used. It would be an absurd government which, having power both to tax and borrow, and tax to pay loans, could not use the money acquired in either way for the same purposes.[81]

The unanimous Second Circuit opinion, written by Martin Manton, adopted this approach.

In hindsight, this was clearly the correct analysis, but in March 1937, when the case was before the circuit court, there was some reason for doubt, not only in view of the Supreme Court's general hostility to New Deal laws but also because of the *Butler* case less than a year earlier, which had left clouds over the government's fiscal powers. Hand and his Second Circuit colleagues managed to distinguish *Butler* readily; but the Supreme Court took a far narrower route and managed to sidestep the constitutional issue.[82]

The other 1937 case that came before Hand, *Electric Bond & Share Co. v. Securities and Exchange Commission*,[83] involved a more important and complex New Deal law than *Kay* and gave Hand somewhat more difficulty. *Electric Bond & Share* was the beginning of decade-long litigation to test the constitutionality of one of the New Deal's most lasting regulatory measures, the Public Utility Holding Company Act of 1935. The act was designed to curb the excessive economic power of holding companies that had repeatedly harmed not only investors but also the customers of utility companies. The regulatory scheme was intricate; its provisions ranged from mandatory registration of the companies to simplification of their structures and, in some cases, to the "death sentence" of breaking up the financial networks.

In enacting the law's sweeping measures, Congress had relied primarily on its powers to bar the use of the mails and the facilities of interstate commerce in specified circumstances. Hand's memorandum in *Electric Bond & Share* took a very broad view of these powers:

> I cannot see any difference between forbidding the use of the mails for an immoral or dishonest purpose, and for any other purpose which people generally disapprove; Congress is limited to its powers, but it can use them for the general welfare as it understands it. . . . [Congress] could say to registered companies: "You may not use the mails or interstate commerce to sell securities that we disapprove of; or to make or perform service contracts; or to acquire securities."[84]

But the case itself involved only the constitutionality of the first step in the regulatory scheme, the registration requirement. Senior judge Manton wrote his usual verbose, turgid, rambling opinion but ultimately limited himself to sustaining only the registration provision: he insisted that none of the more drastic additional measures in the act needed to be ruled on. By contrast, Hand, who had written the most precise and lengthy pre-conference memo, composed a separate concurring opinion, only a paragraph long, that managed both to sustain the core of the act in broader terms than Manton's and yet to cast doubt on the constitutionality of some of the law's peripheral provisions.[85] Hand did not think that the registration requirement could be sustained unless there were other, valid sections dealing with the consequences triggered by registration. Some marginal aspects of these added sections, he suggested, might not be valid; but even if "all these doubtful provisions are deleted," a valid "workable system of controls would still be left"; he briefly sketched some of these to show that registration would not be an empty gesture.

In casting his analysis in these terms, Hand was aware that he would offend some of those to the right of him, those who defended the status quo and opposed the constitutionality of the entire act. Soon after the decision, he discovered that he had offended New Deal reformers as well. The conservative and liberal forces battling in the case were symbolized by the lawyers who argued the case in the Second Circuit: Wall Street's Thomas D. Thacher argued for the holding companies; New Dealer Benjamin V. Cohen argued for the government. Thacher was a longtime friend of Hand: during the 1920s, with Hand's support, he had become a federal district judge in New York; during the Hoover administration, he resigned from the bench in order to serve as solicitor general, once again helped by Hand's recommendation letters; and when he left his government post in order to return to private law practice after Roosevelt's victory in 1932, Hand repeatedly urged Frankfurter to press FDR to reappoint so able—albeit Republican—a judge. Thacher argued the *Electric Bond & Share* case with his usual sense of conviction, but admiration and friendship could play no role for Hand in deciding the case. Soon after his ruling, Hand wrote to Frankfurter, "I was sorry to have to disappoint Tom Thacher so much as I know we did in the . . . case; he feels things so strongly and sees them so clearly that it must be hard to have others turn aside from the straight path."[86]*

When he received Frankfurter's reply to these comments, Hand discovered he had managed to displease some New Dealers as well. Professor Frankfurter, in an anticipatory display of a technique that would repeatedly annoy his fellow justices on the Supreme Court in later years, proceeded to lecture Hand rather patronizingly about the flaws in his approach. Urging Hand to read one of his law-review articles "about withholding constitutional dicta," Frankfurter announced his "preference against the expression even of such doubts as to matters not before you, as you express in El B & S." In offering this stern, unsolicited advice, he tried to sound like a principled academic observer. He reminded Hand that a Harvard colleague had "once reprovingly said to [Frankfurter] 'You do take law seriously.' " And he added, to Hand: "Well—I do!"[87] But so did Hand, and he hardly needed the lecture. Indeed, Frankfurter, despite his pose, was not really writing primarily in his academic capacity. He had been prompted to write as he did— characteristically, he failed to disclose this—by a letter he had received just a few days earlier from Benjamin Cohen.

Cohen was a former student and protégé of Frankfurter; together with Thomas Corcoran (cocounsel in the *Electric Bond & Share* case), he was among the hottest of the Harvard "Happy Hot Dogs." Cohen, Corcoran, and Frankfurter had worked closely together in drafting the Public Utility Holding Company Act. Cohen's long letter to Frankfurter was devoted to explaining his opening comment: "My pleasure over the C.C.A. opinion has been considerably marred by Judge Hand's concurring remarks." Cohen was annoyed that Hand had expressed his

---

* Hand went on, poignantly, to speak of the temperamental differences between him and Thacher and to reveal once more his acute self-awareness: "I am sometimes tempted to envy those to whom this muddy world can seem so bright and clear; but of course that would be merely wishing that this particular me had never been born. I am often discouraged but not quite as much as that."

doubt that "all parts" of the law were valid. Cohen did indeed agree that something had to be said about the validity of other provisions of the act in order to sustain the registration provision; what he objected to was that Hand had pointed not only to provisions that were clearly constitutional, but also to possibly challengeable ones. To his credit, Cohen confessed that Hand's endorsement of the constitutional provisions was more helpful to the government than Manton's narrow opinion, yet this concession did not restrain him from filling two single-spaced typewritten sheets with carping complaints about Hand's temerity. Frankfurter's stern note to Hand was simply a distillation of this message, with the inspiration not revealed.[88] He ended by predicting that the Supreme Court would sustain the Second Circuit ruling in which Hand participated, and he was right: several months later, the Court affirmed, in a 6–1 decision.[89]

Several more years of litigation were needed before all the complex provisions of the Public Utility Holding Company Act could be tested and sustained, in a series of landmark decisions by the Supreme Court.[90] None of Hand's mild doubts about a few of the tangential provisions proved persuasive to the 1940s Supreme Court, solidly composed of New Deal sympathizers; and all of his speculations about the validity of most portions of the act were vindicated. Thus, the *Electric Bond & Share* case illustrates once again that Hand, despite his doubts about the efficacy of many New Deal programs, repeatedly proved ready to sustain their basic constitutional validity at an earlier time than the Nine in Washington.

THE SUPREME COURT'S RECOGNITION after 1937 of Congress's broad authority to regulate the economy by no means ended the Second Circuit's concern with the copious products of the New Deal's legislative mill. To the contrary: removal of the constitutional obstacles opened the door for the most burdensome chores the new laws imposed upon Hand and his colleagues. The flood of New Deal statutes had to be interpreted and applied to particular situations. Statutory interpretation, far more than the settlement of constitutional disputes, had always made major demands on federal judges' time; and the torrent of New Deal laws assured that statutory cases represented an ever larger portion of the Second Circuit's workload.

Delineating the meaning of congressional acts demands close, meticulous attention to the statutory words and their animating purpose. Making sense of the intricacies of the regulatory schemes and disentangling the subsections, exemptions, and cross-references without losing sight of the forest—the objectives Congress sought to achieve—is a formidable task. As Hand once described the work of a judge finding "his way through thickets of verbiage in statutes and regulations":

In my own case the words of such an act as the Income Tax, for example, merely dance before my eyes in a meaningless procession: cross-reference to cross-reference, exception upon exception— couched in abstract terms that offer no handle to seize hold of— leave in my mind only a confused sense of some vitally important, but successfully concealed, purport, which it is my duty to extract, but which is within my power, if at all, only after the most inordinate expenditure of time. I know that these monsters are the result of fabulous industry and ingenuity, plugging up this hole and casting out that net, against all possible evasion; yet at times I cannot help recalling a saying of William James about certain passages of Hegel: that they were no doubt written with a passion of rationality; but that one cannot help wondering whether to the reader they have any significance save that the words are strung together with syntactical correctness. Much of the law is now as difficult to fathom, and more and more of it is likely to be so; [yet] it will be the duty of judges to thread the path—for path there is—through these fantastic labyrinths.[91]

Hand, long a master craftsman in statutory interpretation, never displayed his skills more effectively than in his handling of cases arising under New Deal laws. Some of his decisions under the Fair Labor Standards Act (FLSA) offer especially apt illustrations of his outstanding work. The FLSA, a 1938 law establishing minimum wages and maximum hours of work for employees, was an achievement of FDR's second term. With the Supreme Court's new generosity toward the scope of congressional authority, there was little doubt that its constitutionality would be upheld.[92] Yet this left many questions about the extent to which Congress had chosen to exercise its authority. In the Wagner Act, Congress had clearly sought to go as far as the Constitution permitted, for it covered all activities "affecting" interstate commerce. But in the FLSA, Congress had not tried to go to the limits of its constitutional power. Determining how far it had in fact gone became a much litigated question, producing numerous cases before Hand as well as the Supreme Court. Two of these prompted especially notable Hand opinions—*Fleming v. Arsenal Building Corp.* in 1941[93] and *Borella v. Borden Co.* in 1944.[94] Both cases presented statutory issues that were difficult in their day; in both, the Supreme Court affirmed Hand's holding that the employees involved were covered by the act; in both, the Court relied on parts of Hand's approach; and in both, Hand's analysis was not only more persuasive than the Supreme Court's but also more generous in its delineation of the reach of the law.[95]

Under its terms, the FLSA covered not only employees themselves working "in [interstate] commerce" but also those engaged "in the production of goods for commerce." The *Arsenal* and *Borden* cases both involved the "production" provision. The act defined this provision as including anyone "employed . . . in any process or occupation necessary to the production" of goods for commerce. In both cases, the central question was whether the employees involved fell within the law even though they themselves were not physically engaged in production activities. In each case, the employees claiming the benefits of the FLSA were building maintenance workers. Could they be considered "necessary" to the production of goods? How far could courts go to protect workers not themselves engaged in the actual process of production without subverting the deliberately limited reach of the act?

In *Arsenal*, the defendant was the owner of a large New York City loft building that leased most of its space to manufacturers of women's clothes. The suit was to compel payment for overtime work by the maintenance employees. The owner insisted that it, unlike its tenants, was not producing goods for interstate commerce and claimed that maintenance workers were too far removed from the manufacturing process to be considered "necessary to the production" of goods. Hand, both in his pre-conference memo and in his opinion, went straight to the heart of the case. He noted that maintenance employees would clearly be protected if the manufacturers owned the building: "[A]lthough such people may not perhaps 'work on' the goods, [they] are certainly in an 'occupation' which is 'necessary to the production' of the goods. The cloth can't be cut and sewn in a cold filthy building; nor can it be taken up to or down from an upper floor by hand."[96] In light of this expansive coverage, Hand found no reason to exempt the workers just because the building was not owned by the clothing manufacturers. As he put it in his opinion, "[I]t would as much defeat the purpose of the act . . . to deprive such workmen of its protection when they chance to be employed by a different employer, as when they are employed by the employer of the cutters and stitchers."

Hand's skills in statutory interpretation came most clearly to the fore when he answered the defendants' claim that so stretching the reach of the law proved "too much, for Congress could not have meant to impose 'fair labor standards' upon everyone who might chance to contribute any necessary 'ingredient' . . . to the production of goods." Hand replied that it might well be true that Congress had not intended to cover the "miller who furnishes the flour to a baker who sells bread in other states" or "the cutler who sells knives to a wholesale butcher," but that was no reason to exclude the workers in this case: "[H]ere, as so often, the test [is] one of degree." And Hand added that more extreme applications need not be resolved in this case, for

> the work of the defendant's employees is in kind substantially the same as it would be if the manufacturers employed them directly. That is the substance of the matter. Since the words and the purpose of the act coalesce so far, we will not allow ourselves to be drawn into dialectical niceties which are not before us and whose answer need not compromise the step we are taking.[97]

Hand put forth this surefooted analysis even though, as he recognized, other courts of appeals, by a 4–1 margin, had resolved the issue against his position. As he ended his opinion, "Obviously the question will not be set at rest until the Supreme Court makes an authoritative ruling."[98] The Supreme Court ruling came soon after; but it did not wholly "set at rest" the central question. The majority opinion was by Hand's old friend Frankfurter, now on the Court, and Frankfurter, although he paid tribute to the circuit court's "weighty" opinion[99] and partly followed—indeed, paraphrased—Hand's analysis, took a quite different tack. Instead of Hand's broad, liberal approach to the law, Frankfurter warned against an interpretation that might upset the federal system and intrude upon the traditional power of the states. He agreed with Hand's result but took issue with his approach. It was an ironic stance: the enthusiastic architect of so much of the New Deal, now placed on the Supreme Court by FDR, embraced a far more cautious approach than the doubting Hand, who had long questioned New Deal policies.

But Judge Hand ultimately had the last word in his exchange with Justice Frankfurter. In the *Borden* case, he once again construed the FLSA broadly and in effect repudiated the rebuke Frankfurter had administered in *Arsenal* four years earlier. "[A]ny hesitation to give [the purpose of the law] its full scope," he insisted,

> must proceed from a vague compunction that to press the statute so far, is unduly to invade fields which Congress must have meant to leave to local regulation. We do not share that compunction. It is of course true that the whole statute invades fields which were formerly left to local regulation. That Congress did not mean to exercise its power to the full is not important; rather the question is whether we shall say that the borders of those fields which it

did choose to occupy, are to be found by considering its object, or whether the realization of that object shall be truncated by irrelevant considerations.[100]

This was a crisp and compelling response to Frankfurter. Hand perceived accurately that the airing of "a vague compunction" about threatened inroads on traditional state spheres contributed little to proper interpretation. Instead, the language and, above all, the purpose of the act, not tangential abstractions, had to govern. Hand's more focused approach was endorsed by the Supreme Court on review, with Frankfurter concurring only in the result of the majority opinion.[101]

The particular context of *Borden* involved one of the "dialectical niceties" Hand had found unnecessary to reach in *Arsenal*. This time, another group of maintenance workers claimed coverage under the FLSA, but in circumstances that went beyond those in *Arsenal*. The maintenance employees in *Borden* worked at the New York executive headquarters of the Borden Company, where only the administrative functions of Borden's "enormous" milk and dairy business were conducted.* Were these employees so remote from the physical processes of production as to fall outside the scope of the act? Once again, as in *Arsenal*, Hand assured "a liberal judicial application" of the FLSA.[102]

Hand's pre-conference memorandum in *Borden* was succinct: the Supreme Court's affirmance of the *Arsenal* ruling made it clear who was "necessary" to the production of goods; that affirmance "was really the long step; and might well never have been taken at all." And so, he concluded:

> The administrative offices of a large business are, I should think, as "directly" and "immediately" engaged in "production" as anyone else. . . . After all, as James Mill once said, all human beings can do is to move things about in space; that comprehends all industry. If so, how can we distinguish between the men who use their hands to move, and those who tell them where to move? I don't know; it's a gamble at best, but I bet on the plaintiffs.[103]

Of greatest interest are the more general passages of Hand's opinion in *Borden*. Probably reacting to Frankfurter's lecture on proper statutory interpretation in *Arsenal*, he spelled out his own approach with special care. His proved more focused than Frankfurter's and less distracted by unhelpful, "irrelevant considerations" about the nature of the federal system. The coverage provisions of the FLSA regarding employees engaged "in the production of goods" used "words of colloquial speech";

---

* "Enormous" was Hand's adjective. See *Borden*, 145 F.2d at 63.

these were inevitably indefinite words, and so it was "to be expected that interpretation will vary"; statutory language was "unlike the terminology of science, deliberately fabricated for its definite outlines." Legislators, "like others concerned with ordinary affairs, do not deal in rigid symbols, so far as possible stripped of suggestion." And these perceptions shaped his stance:

> We can best reach the meaning here, as always, by recourse to the underlying purpose, and, with that as a guide, by trying to project upon the specific occasion how we think persons, actuated by such a purpose, would have dealt with it, if it had been presented to them at the time. To say that that is a hazardous process is indeed a truism, but we cannot escape it, once we abandon literal interpretation—a method far more unreliable.[104]

This did not mean that the words of the law were unimportant: as Hand pointed out, in any "interpretation of language, the words used [are] far and away the most reliable source for learning the purpose of a document"; he meant only, but significantly, that a literal reading of the words was not fully adequate to the task of an empathic effort to understand the purpose of a law and its authors.

Passages such as these illustrate Hand's remarkable perceptiveness in approaching statutory interpretation. True, admonitions to respect the lawmakers' words yet not be imprisoned by them, to go beyond and to be guided by legislative purpose, are only vague generalizations. In particular cases, literalism and purposive analyses can point in conflicting directions; general advice can only suggest a mood. Yet Hand's commentaries, in numerous cases and frequent extrajudicial statements, are among the most perceptive and influential on the books. If they are understood as no more than general maxims, they can be helpful; but the real test of distinguished judging comes only in concrete circumstances.

Hand himself called the interpretation of statutes "an act of creative imagination," an "undertaking of delightful uncertainty."[105] Sometimes, Hand would insist that words not be stretched beyond their natural meaning; at other times, he would feel free to go beyond and even contrary to the words, if he found the underlying purpose clear and the statutory language at odds with that purpose.[106] The relative emphasis on each of these seemingly contradictory guides must inevitably vary from case to case. Whether a judge achieves the proper balance turns on the specific provision and facts of each case. A distinguished federal judge rightly said that Hand's record in statutory interpretation represented "a field in which he was to achieve what perhaps was his greatest mastery."[107] That this accolade was well deserved is demonstrated in hundreds of cases in which Hand skillfully applied his general principles.

Hand never stated his approach to statutory interpretation more crisply and lucidly than in a nationwide radio address he gave over the Columbia Broadcasting System early in the New Deal, on the evening of May 14, 1933. A National Advisory Council on Radio in Education, formed in 1930 and devoted to raising the quality of programs on the fledgling broadcasting medium, sponsored lecture series on various topics from economics to political science; the subject in 1933 was law, and the May 14 broadcast had two speakers, Hand and Frankfurter. A host of new laws had already been launched by the administration, and soon, the lecturers knew, the flood would inundate the courts. Frankfurter discussed constitutional litigation, emphasizing that the "Justices of the Supreme Court are in fact arbiters of social policy," with broad discretion to interpret the vague constitutional phrases. The Constitution, he was confident, was "flexible enough to meet the needs of our society." Hand recognized that his topic, the interpretation of statutes, might "seem abstract and dry," yet he insisted that "it is important, and it is well for us to try to come to some understanding about it." His two thousand words contributed magnificently to this "understanding," and his concluding paragraph illustrates his gift for speaking directly and perceptively in an unadorned style. A judge interpreting statutes was "in a contradictory position," he noted, "pulled by two opposite forces":

> On the one hand he must not enforce whatever he thinks best; he must leave that to the common will expressed by the government. On the other, he must try as best he can to put into concrete form what that will is, not by slavishly following the words, but by trying honestly to say what was the underlying purpose expressed.

He appealed to the public to understand how complex judicial work was, and not to criticize judges for such alleged flaws as lacking "common sense":

> Nobody does this exactly right; great judges do it better than the rest of us. It is necessary that someone shall do it, if we are to realize the hope that we can collectively rule ourselves. And so, while it is proper that people should find fault when their judges fail, it is only reasonable that they should recognize the difficulties. Perhaps it is also fair to ask that before the judges are blamed they shall be given the credit of having tried to do their best. Let them

be severely brought to book, when they go wrong, but by those who will take the trouble to understand.[108]

ONE FINAL TYPE OF CASE recurred in Hand's court during the New Deal years: disputes involving judicial review of the burgeoning number of administrative agencies. Administrative agencies were not invented by the New Deal: the Interstate Commerce Commission (ICC), created in 1887, and the Federal Trade Commission (FTC), established in 1914, long antedated FDR's agencies. But during the 1930s, the alphabet-soup jumble of new boards and commissions proliferated. Often, the New Deal established agencies to take a crack at determining whether a given new law applied to particular contexts; the courts entered this arena only after an agency's application of the law to a particular dispute. This was the pattern followed, for example, in the creation of the Securities and Exchange Commission (SEC) to implement the securities laws of 1933 and 1934 and the National Labor Relations Board (NLRB) to effectuate the Wagner Act of 1935.

These independent administrative agencies—the fourth, "headless" branch of government, partly shielded from direct presidential control —have prompted societal ambivalence for decades. Making expert regulators do the initial task of adjudication has been hailed as a step toward sensible, efficient government; at the same time, people have been concerned about giving excessive discretion to the agencies, about such a system breeding lawlessness and politicization.[109] Hand was not immune to this ambivalence. Privately, he repeatedly doubted the political neutrality and genuine expertise of the administrative agencies, but in his official capacity, he deferred generously to their resolutions of disputed facts and relevant policy judgments, and he intruded only when he found that the administrators had misinterpreted the applicable statutes.

Hand's ambivalence, and yet his steadfast deference to agency discretion nonetheless, is well illustrated by his pre-conference memoranda in dozens of cases in which he reviewed decisions by the NLRB. The Wagner Act had established a national policy on a particularly contentious issue: amid bitter and sometimes violent strikes, Congress clearly endorsed the workers' right to unionize, and barred employer interferences with union activities as "unfair labor practices." During its early years, the board was widely criticized as excessively pro-labor, and Hand at times agreed with this charge; yet he was known from the beginning as especially ready to enforce NLRB orders.

Under the Wagner Act, the NLRB had to seek enforcement of its orders in the appropriate court of appeals. The judges were directed to give broad deference to board findings of fact, with instructions to sustain them if they were based on "substantial evidence." Hand took this admonition very seriously, sometimes excessively so, despite his private doubts. As he put it in one of his pre-conference memos, this was the kind of issue "upon which courts are supposed not to be as competent as the Board. The Board was in part created because it was thought that through its specialized experience it had better capacity than a court to judge what would be the result of events in this field." In theory, it was as if a "judicial board of chemists" had been created to advise the judges in complex patent cases*; inevitably, deference would be due not only to their specific findings of facts but also to their general expertise. Applying this approach to labor issues, he insisted that the NLRB deserved deference not only as to what actually happened, but also about the effect of the events on labor's right to unionize: "We must assume that the Board is specially gifted in deciding such questions." Still, he recognized the practical flaws:

> In the hands of a biased Board such a power can become a fearful engine of oppression; and I am personally extremely skeptical as to their superior insight into this range of industrial facts. However, there cannot be any doubt that acquaintance with the field does make one's judgment better than that of the ordinary boob judge. . . . If Congress wants such tribunals, it is not our business to thwart the purpose.[110]

In the early years of the NLRB, Hand expressed his distrust of the experts' impartiality even more vigorously. But as the years went by, he became increasingly convinced that the rulings of the "Sacred Board" were conclusive in almost all cases:

> If we are to assume, as we must, that the Board understands both these interests [of the employer and the employee] better than we can, what is there left? I submit that we must so assume, and indeed there is some ground for supposing that the Board does understand these facts better than we.[111]

In his ready deference to "expert" NLRB evaluations, Hand occasionally went too far for the Supreme Court. Much as Justice Frankfurter had rebuked him for an excessively broad approach to the

---

* Using the chemical-experts example, he cited an essay in 15 *Harv. L.Rev.*—his own first published essay at the beginning of the century, advocating the use of independent court experts rather than relying on experts hired by the parties. See p. 60.

interpretation of the FLSA in the *Arsenal* case, he chastised Hand for his excessive deference to NLRB findings. This renewed confrontation between the judge and the justice arose in a famous case, *NLRB v. Universal Camera Corp.*, that came before the Second Circuit in December 1949,[112] after the judges had ruled on NLRB matters for more than a decade, with an unusual number of divided 2–1 decisions. The case arose, moreover, only a short time after a growing national skepticism about the NLRB had manifested itself in congressional action: in 1947, the Republican-controlled Eightieth Congress had enacted the Taft-Hartley Labor Relations Act, a revised law passed by both houses over a veto by President Truman, who had branded it as excessively anti-labor.

The judicial review provision of the original law, the 1935 Wagner Act, had made the NLRB findings of fact "conclusive" so long as they were "supported by evidence," but from the beginning the Supreme Court had interpreted this language to mean that the findings of fact had to rest on "substantial evidence."[113] Hand and other judges given to interpretations deferential to agencies had long rested their enforcements of NLRB orders on this "substantial evidence" standard. The 1947 Taft-Hartley Act changed the statutory language to read that NLRB resolutions of factual issues should be considered "conclusive" only "if supported by substantial evidence on the record considered as a whole." The question for the federal courts after that change, most authoritatively resolved in *Universal Camera*, was whether the "record considered as a whole" phrase was intended to require the courts to scrutinize board findings more carefully than they had in the past. The legislative history contained scattered charges that the NLRB had been guilty of "partisan bias," and that there had been too much "abdication" of the power of judicial review;[114] yet the legislative language did not necessarily change the courts' authority, and judges such as Hand could legitimately claim that they had always examined the "record as a whole."[115]

The *Universal Camera* case itself involved a fairly simple situation. The company had fired an employee; the issue was whether he had been discharged on the legitimate ground of insubordination (he had accused the personnel manager of drunkenness), or on the illegal ground of anti-union bias, in reprisal for his testimony in support of the union in an NLRB proceeding a few months earlier. The trial examiner (these officers are now called administrative law judges) believed the company's witnesses, found that no anti-union sentiment had motivated the firing, and therefore recommended dismissing the "unfair labor practices" complaint. The NLRB itself reached the opposite conclusion. The question for Hand and his colleagues was whether the board's order should be enforced.

In his pre-conference memo, Hand agreed with the majority of circuit courts that the Taft-Hartley Act had left the scope of the courts' authority "unchanged." The Second Circuit's decisions, like "all the sound decisions," had always believed that "the record as a whole must show 'substantial' evidence"; hence, the new law "did not change" judicial review authority.[116] As he put it in his opinion:

> It appears to us that, had it been intended to set up a new measure of review by the courts, the matter would not have been left so at large. We cannot agree that our review has been "broadened"; we hold that no more was done than to make definite what was already implied.[117]

Moreover, he refused to attribute any special significance to the NLRB's reversal of its own trial examiner: "[I]t is practically impossible for a court . . . to consider the Board's reversal as a factor in the court's own decision."[118]

In the Supreme Court, Hand's ruling was overturned and the case sent back to the Second Circuit. The Court's opinion was far clearer in demonstrating that the justices thought the case important than in clarifying what their disposition meant. In a long, laborious, and often murky opinion, Frankfurter elaborately reviewed the legislative history of the statutory change and tried to provide guidelines for reviewing courts; what he did clearly decide was that the Taft-Hartley Act *was* intended to change the courts' role. Congress had simply "expressed a mood," but this attitude had to be enforced. Congress believed that some courts had sustained NLRB findings so long as they could find any isolated fragments of evidence to support them (although Frankfurter did not accuse Hand's court of such a practice); the aim of the "record considered as a whole" language was "to impose on courts a responsibility which has not always been recognized"; the new law required courts to "assume more responsibility for the reasonableness and fairness of Labor Board decisions than some courts have shown in the past." And the Second Circuit had clearly been wrong in believing that little if any weight was to be attached to the board's rejection of its own trial examiner's contrary findings; on remand, the Second Circuit was instructed to "accord the findings of the trial examiner the relevance that they reasonably command."[119]

Frankfurter repeatedly emphasized that reviewing standards were inevitably unclear: in this area, "precise definition is impossible."[120]

This impossibility was demonstrated by the subsequent history of the case. On remand, the Second Circuit once again split, and Hand again wrote for the majority, changing his mind in view of the Supreme Court order. His opinion in the second *Universal Camera* case[121] read Frankfurter's rebuke very broadly. The Supreme Court, he found, had held that the act, "although in form it did no more than incorporate what had always been the better practice—our own included," was intended to

> prescribe an attitude in courts of appeal less complaisant towards the Board's findings than had been proper before; not only were they to look to the record as a whole, but they were to be less ready to yield their personal judgment on the facts; at least less ready than many at times had been.

As a result, since the disputed facts were not within the board's "specialized experience," Hand rejected the NLRB's argument "that we are not in as good a position as itself to decide what witnesses were more likely to be telling the truth in this labor dispute." And so he concluded that on reexamining the record and "giving weight to the examiner's findings—now in compliance with the Court's directions as we understand them," his "first disposition of the appeal" had been "wrong."[122]

The imprecision of Frankfurter's "guidance" was demonstrated when Judge Jerome N. Frank, one of Hand's colleagues, wrote a separate opinion insisting that Hand had read too much into the Supreme Court's ruling:

> Recognizing, as only a singularly stupid man would not, Judge HAND'S superior wisdom, intelligence, and learning, I seldom disagree with him, and then with serious misgivings. In this instance I have overcome my misgivings because I think that his modesty has moved him to interpret too sweepingly the Supreme Court's criticism of our earlier opinion written by him.[123]

But Hand cannot be faulted for reading the Frankfurter ruling as he did. As he had insisted before his second decision was handed down, the justices "meant us to adopt a more exacting scrutiny over the Board's findings in *all* cases. This they found implicit in the amendment, which is just what we had decided was not there."[124] Certainly, Hand did not misperceive the dominant tenor of rebuke in Frankfurter's verbose dissertation. Nevertheless, Hand probably had it right the first time: despite the Supreme Court's insistence in *Universal Camera* that more intensive review by the courts was required by the 1948 revision of the act, the decades since have suggested that "considerable deference to agency findings of fact,"[125] which Hand had always been willing to give, has in fact persisted. And NLRB cases, so plentiful and troublesome in Hand's day, are still a major segment of the federal judicial workload.[126]*

For Hand, the decisive ingredients were always a separation of personal views from the duty to enforce legal commands, a skepticism about the utility of abstract guidelines, and a judicial obligation to discern and vigorously enforce the legislature's expression of the common will. It was these tasks that he performed so superbly; it was these themes that permeate the hundreds of statutory and administrative cases that came before him.

---

* A common complaint by court of appeals judges is that too many NLRB appeals involve "merely factual issues"; one judge, when asked what appeals he would like to be rid of, said, "I'd pick the most important one of all—labor—the most colossal waste of time. The aperture of review is so narrow. To call upon us to read thousands of pages is the most colossal waste of time I know" (J. Woodford Howard, Jr., *Courts of Appeals in the Federal Judicial System,* [Princeton: Princeton University Press, 1981], 287, n. r).

XI

The Road to War
and the Break with Lippmann

BY THE MID-1930s, Europe's totalitarian, expansionist regimes posed an ever growing threat to the world's peace. In March 1935, Germany openly began to rearm, after denouncing the Treaty of Versailles; in October of that year, Mussolini's forces invaded Ethiopia; in March 1936, German troops reoccupied the Rhineland; four months later, a bitter civil war erupted in Spain. The Spanish battles quickly became a testing ground for the totalitarian combatants in World War II: Hitler and Mussolini aided the Fascist challengers to the Spanish republic; Stalin assisted the defenders.

Hand watched with anxiety, yet he remained remarkably confident for several years that skillful diplomacy could avert a wider war. Writing to Bernard Berenson in January 1937, for example, just after reading a recent book about the onset of World War I (*The Eve of 1914*, by the veteran anti-Nazi newspaper editor Theodor Wolff, first published in Switzerland in 1934, and published in the United States in 1936),[1] Hand reflected on "the inherent instability of it all" in 1914—"more instable I insist than today, even with a possibility of a dictator's last throw of the dice." Like many others in America and Europe in 1937, he was not yet ready to believe that even the Nazis would plunge the world into war, despite their ominous rhetoric and militaristic actions: "I do not believe . . . the German Loki is going to set his world afire; after all there are limits to imbecility." And without Hitler taking the lead, Hand recognized, "I should think the play could not begin." Even then, he avoided being dogmatically confident: "I know how tenuous it all is." Yet he reiterated that "the world on the whole" was "less instable" now, and he assumed that the world leaders of the 1930s had better judgment than those of 1914.[2]

Hand was more eager than most in the democratic nations to urge strong diplomatic pressures to curb expansionism. In a rare show of strength, the League of Nations in November 1935 did impose sanctions on Italy in an effort to halt its aggression upon Ethiopia. But to Hand's dismay, that effort collapsed, because of loopholes in the measures as well as divisions among the future Allies. Hand, as usual the internationalist bemoaning American isolationism, had no hope that the United States would move to strengthen the backbone of resistance to the dictators' adventures. As he remarked at the end of 1935, most Americans, faced with Germany's rearmament, Italy's imperialism, and "the amazing somersaults of the British government," were disposed "to adopt the role of disinterested observer." He saw no prospect that Congress would support the League sanctions; at most, there might be minor revisions of American neutrality laws. Predominantly, however, Americans would persist in their

> strong desire to make sure that we shall not become involved in any way with European troubles, to say nothing of European wars. . . . Except for people who are pro-League because they are anti-Fascist, the bulk of the community is in the typical American tradition, apparently supposing that nothing can touch them if they do not enter into alliances and do not sell goods [to the belligerents]. In the large cities, there are of course strong groups, strong rather in feeling than in numbers, who take sides, extending their hatred of Hitler to all forms of dictatorship which is not red.[3]

By the fall of 1937, Hand's optimistic belief that diplomatic pressure could avert war was fast fading. He was especially distressed by the weak responses to the Axis intervention in the Spanish civil war. Italian and German supplies and troops poured into Spain on Franco's rebel side, and the Fascist insurgents were soon better supplied than the republic's defenders. Early on, the British and French advanced an international agreement against intervention, only to be ignored by the Germans and Italians. In response to this defiance, they continued to vacillate; Great Britain, indeed, soon began negotiating a weak pact with Mussolini, which was eventually concluded in April 1938.

Hand was distressed by these developments, for several reasons: American voters were hardly likely to abandon their isolationism if European democracies showed no greater resolve than this, and the weak British response was especially painful to the Anglophile Hand. His disappointment was heightened by a visit to Italy in the late summer of 1937, when he found the Italians "in a most dangerous frame of mind," with an arrogance encouraged by English weakness. As he reported to Frankfurter, "[T]hey really think that Britain will not intervene and that they may not only tweak her nose but take away all of her toys. The poor fish really believe they can do their will with her; that was the worst single thing I came to believe on my trip."[4]

For a moment, the outlook seemed more encouraging at home. Hand increasingly admired Roosevelt's leadership, especially because he seemed to be doing his best, within the limits of the dominant isolationism, to lead the nation toward anti-totalitarianism. The president gave a heartening speech on foreign affairs in Chicago on October 5 in which he condemned "unjustified interference in the internal affairs of other nations" and "invasion of alien territory" and alerted Americans to the risk that "the very foundations of civilization" and "the peace of the world" were under threat.[5] This cheered Hand: "FDR made a ten strike in the Chicago speech," he wrote to Frankfurter, "just the right note at the moment. Growl but do not say when, or if, you are going to bite; that's another matter; but just now it pays for us to be nasty, to show that we are not too 'snail conscious.' "[6]

But the ray of hope offered by FDR's remarks proved short-lived. The Chicago speech proved to be merely a trial balloon, quickly deflated: isolationists promptly attacked it, and Roosevelt soon reverted to a less determined tone. Moreover, Britain's foreign policy continued to be weak. Frankfurter predicted that the British would soon turn more resolute. Hand, ordinarily as aware of complexities as anyone and certainly no more bellicose than Frankfurter, suggested that his friend was being too simplistic and ineffectual, and he urged a more forceful stand:

> [A]ll that Mussolini and Hitler will recognize is a determined attitude, back of which there is a real and immediate possibility of war. The trick will be, having armed, for Britain to make that so clear that [the totalitarians] will recede, and yet not to force them to too quick retreats. That will be where the statecraft will come in.[7]

The year produced little support for Frankfurter's faith or Hand's hope that Great Britain would take this stronger stand. Instead, the world's attention turned from Mussolini to Hitler as the greater threat to peace. The new area of contention was the Sudetenland section of Czechoslovakia, a third of Czech territory inhabited by about one third of the country's population, mainly by a linguistically German people. For several years, Sudeten Germans, enthusiastic supporters of Nazism, had demanded autonomy and at least ideological union with Germany. In the spring of 1938, at about the time of the *Anschluss*, Hitler's annexation of Austria, the Sudeten crisis came to a head, producing the greatest mobilization of troops that Europe had seen since 1918. Konrad Henlein, the leader of the Sudeten German party—not openly Nazi, but in the secret pay of Germany and clearly loyal to Hitler— publicly set forth his demands, including full liberty for Sudeten Germans to proclaim their adherence to "the ideology of Germans." The Prague government firmly rejected the demands, while both Britain and France pressed the Czech leaders to make concessions.

During the ensuing summer of negotiations between the Henlein group and the Czech government, Hitler mobilized forces and built new fortifications. Occasionally, the British hinted at war if the crisis continued, and the French called up their reserves. But more typically, the British shied away from force, and the French followed their lead —even though Czechoslovakia, as the last remaining democratic outpost in Central Europe, had reason to hope for greater British support, and even though it had a treaty with France pledging French assistance in case of armed attack. On September 12, Hitler demanded that the Sudeten Germans be granted self-determination, widespread disorders broke out on Czech streets, the government proclaimed martial law, and Sudeten leaders fled to Germany.

The threat of imminent war at last forced Prime Minister Neville Chamberlain into action, of sorts: he proposed a personal conference with Hitler. When they met at Hitler's Alpine retreat in Berchtesgaden, Hitler demanded control of the Sudetenland and implied that he would go to war if necessary to achieve this end. Chamberlain consulted with French premier Edouard Daladier and promptly urged the Czech government to accept Hitler's terms, offering in return only an international guarantee of Czechoslovakia's new borders. When this offer was rejected, Britain and France threatened that they would not come to Czechoslovakia's aid and, indeed, hinted that if war broke out the blame would rest on Czech shoulders for failing to make concessions to Hitler. In the face of this pressure, the Czech government in effect yielded on September 21, but this did not end the crisis. When Chamberlain made a second visit to Hitler, at Bad Godesberg, the German chancellor increased his demands, insisting, for example, that the contested territory be turned over immediately. Chamberlain appealed to Hitler for one more conference so that the already agreed-upon surrender of Sudeten territory could be handled peacefully; other world leaders, including President Roosevelt, supported his appeal.

Hitler agreed to meet with Chamberlain in Munich, and on September 29 Hitler emerged with an agreement that gave him almost everything he had demanded. Chamberlain promptly returned to England and proclaimed that he had achieved "peace for our time." At the base of the Anglo-French position was a deep fear of war, a passion to preserve the peace at almost any cost, and a widely held conviction that communism was a greater threat than fascism, along with a related belief that the German arguments for control of the German-speaking Sudetenland were too persuasive to justify war. But Chamberlain's critics, domestic and international, charged him with shameful appeasement—a term that would echo through political debates for decades— and claimed that Chamberlain had deserted a bastion of democracy in exchange for a piece of paper, that he could have stopped Nazi expansion had he met Hitler's threats with a strong stand of his own.

Given Hand's long advocacy of a strong anti-totalitarian policy by the Western democracies, he might have been expected to join Chamberlain's critics. But for several months after the Munich settlement, Hand did not do so. Just before the outbreak of the final Sudeten crisis, for example, he told Berenson, "I suppose you think little of Chamberlain, but I don't agree. . . . [He] is teetering on the edge of a chasm, either way, and who am I to know what is the best way across?"[8] He could not abide "the children of light, the [former] pacifists" who were now "howling for war," he told Frances. He conceded that Foreign Minister Anthony Eden might be right in urging more forceful measures, yet he also recognized the difficult responsibilities of national leaders: "[I]t's a dreadful decision and it . . . makes me sick to have yells and dogmaticisms exchanged about it. Thank God, I have not such a terrible decision to make." He could not reject Chamberlain's stance out of hand: "On the whole I am with [him,] for if the dictators can be kept out of the powder magazine long enough, there is a good chance that they will break their backs." But, torn as he was, he added, "Still, it is ominous that France is a cypher and Britain always taking a crack in the snoot."[9]

More than three months after Munich, Hand could still be irritated by categorical judgments about Chamberlain's behavior, though he was now ready to agree that a different prime minister might have been "a better poker-player than [he] and would have got more out of Der Fuhrer."[10] But not until mid-January 1939—a few weeks before Nazi troops marched into Prague, a few months before the final dismemberment of Czechoslovakia—did Hand even concede that Chamberlain might have been mistaken. Frances Hand, with Louis Dow on a visit to Europe, reported to Learned that she had spent some time with her old Bryn Mawr acquaintance Alys Russell, Bertrand Russell's former wife, who vituperatively attacked Chamberlain. Hand replied that the account of Alys Russell's outburst "made me perceptibly angry": "It's quite likely that Chamberlain was wrong, but this vilification of him is rotten mean."[11] This reluctance to criticize Chamberlain's Munich policy placed Hand out of step with the dominant anti-Fascist mood of his circle, and it showed qualities central to his makeup. Characteristically, he saw both sides of the question, and his self-tormenting doubts were especially intense over the Munich issue.

Hand's reluctance to endorse military resistance to Hitler evaporated in the face of renewed German aggression later in 1939. In March, a week after extinguishing the Czechoslovak state, Hitler demanded a path through Poland to assure access to the German-speaking state of Danzig; only British and French pledges to aid Poland in case of an invasion kept Hitler from unleashing his armies immediately. By then, Hand had gotten a better, though still incomplete, understanding of the situation in Germany. Frances Hand and Louis Dow had joined Hand's old friend George Rublee on a ten-day diplomatic mission in Berlin, and Frances's letters from Berlin, although more concerned with museums and opera than with politics,[12] distressed her husband: "So many sudden changes, volte-faces, without explanation—all the external marks of a people at the mercy of two palace cliques, of which now one, now another, is in the ascendant," as Hand put it to Bernard Berenson.

The mounting volatility in Europe made Hand a more enthusiastic supporter of FDR, and he reported to Berenson that "little as I like his mind, his measures, or his friends," he was still "our best bet" for the election in 1940.[13] But soon Hand had the opportunity to see the situation in Europe at close range. Frances, returned from one trip with Louis Dow, was eager to continue with the schedule of biennial visits to Europe with her husband. The judge, more attuned to the crisis than she, feared that "we shall get marooned" but yielded to her insistence: "FAH has decided and who am I to gainsay her?"[14] His fear of war prompted him to cancel the original plan to visit Berenson after touring in France: Italy "would be a particularly poor place to be caught in, if there were a war," he told Berenson in late June. "We don't want to be caught [in Europe] if the baboons all get to cutting throats." And by then, he conceded, "[I]t looks as though that might happen—fifty, fifty."[15]

The Hands returned to the United States on August 23—the day after the British government reiterated its pledges to Poland while appealing to Germany to negotiate, the day on which Foreign Minister Joachim von Ribbentrop was in Moscow to sign Germany's pact with

Stalin's representatives, the day before Roosevelt pleaded once more for an avoidance of war. One week later, on September 1, Germany launched its successful blitzkrieg against Poland; two days later, Britain and France declared war on Germany and the Second World War was launched. Hand wrote to Berenson from Cornish that his stay in France had given him "a sense of impending calamity which I found it impossible to shake off," and he added, "I thought I could see that things were steadily heading towards an impasse from which neither side could or would withdraw." And for the first time in his correspondence, he heatedly referred to the Nazi leaders as the "madmen of Germany." He was relieved, in a way, that now at last the Allies were taking a firm stand, but, he added, "I have tried to hold myself in from warlike exhortations. Nothing is to me more unbecoming than the bellicosity of an old man who cannot be exposed—especially if, as in my own case, he did not embrace the opportunity to join in war when his age allowed." Despite his earlier reluctance to advocate force, Hand was clearly glad that war had erupted: "I could not hope that this occasion [of the invasion of Poland] should turn out to be merely another scalp in Hitler's belt. Even after the curious conduct of Stalin & Co. it seems to me better, and in the end safer, to take a stand now."

More than ever, Hand was preoccupied with the persistence of isolationism in the United States, but he also recognized that there were "a number of people who see in the whole thing nothing more than an unseemly squabble for power. The *Chicago Tribune* takes that view; I suppose that [Senators William] Borah and [Hiram] Johnson do. Yet I scarcely think that the Republican Party will care to espouse it."[16]

Hand could take heart from the fact that Roosevelt, though still hemmed in by isolationists, greeted the outbreak of war with immediate moral support of the anti-totalitarian side. Over the next year, the president slowly edged the nation closer to the Allies: in early November, Congress repealed the arms-embargo clauses of the Neutrality Act of 1937 and authorized trade with belligerents on a cash-and-carry basis; and even though both parties' 1940 platforms opposed involvement in foreign wars, Roosevelt successfully pressed for increased defense appropriations. After massive German air raids launched the Battle of Britain in August 1940, the United States transferred fifty old destroyers to Britain in exchange for long-term leases of some British possessions; on September 14, Congress passed the first peacetime draft act; in January 1941, FDR began his third term by asking for additional aid to the anti-Axis nations; early in March, he signed the Lend-Lease Act; in June, he suspended diplomatic relations with Germany and Italy.

Hand shared Frankfurter's enthusiasm about Roosevelt's victory in the 1940 election. Both welcomed the defeat of Republican Wendell L. Willkie as above all a major blow to the isolationist elements in the Republican party. For Hand, moreover, Roosevelt was preferable to Willkie for still another reason: convinced that the United States needed to be at least the major supplier of arms for the Allied side, he viewed FDR as more likely to assure the national harmony necessary to make this effort succeed; in addition to "more far-reaching reasons," then, Roosevelt was "the better bet on production, and production is the means by which alone we can save Britain."[17]

Yet despite all these signs that American policy was moving steadily toward open support of the Allies, Hand grew increasingly impatient with the snail-like pace, and as Allied prospects turned dimmer, he found it increasingly difficult to control his emotions. His self-restraint diminished sharply by the spring of 1940, as he watched the Nazis' inexorable march across Western Europe. At first, he managed to limit expressions of his intense anti-isolationism to private conversations. In April, for example, a social acquaintance of the Hands, a self-described uncertain isolationist, acknowledged that Hand's heated feelings had "certainly jarred [his] complacency," even though he was not ready to yield to the insistence that Americans must "arouse and wake up the democracy so that it will be ready to act before it is too late."[18] By February 1941, less than a year later, writing to a state judge whom he did not know very well, Hand felt free to burst out in the midst of an otherwise routine note: "We shall not keep our liberties unless we are wiling to fight for them; there are many who do not understand this."[19] By August, less than four months before Pearl Harbor, his emotions were even more aroused. As he wrote to an English judge whom he had met only once:

> Over here we still hang fire in that curious way which I fear is the habit of democracies; a sort of "yes-and-no" attitude which distresses those of us who feel how vital it is for us not to wait, almost as much as it must you to whom the peril is more immediate, though, in my judgment, scarcely less threatening in the end. Roosevelt is doing all he can but the attitude of the Republicans is incredible.[20]

Hand's feelings were so strong that they periodically erupted to a circle wider than his acquaintances. Less than two months after World War II began, for example, the depth of his anti-Axis feelings was already so great that he decided to abandon temporarily his "invariable rule not to write letters to members of Congress about current matters, because I think it improper for a judge," and wrote to Warren R.

Austin, the internationalist Republican senator from Vermont. Although unacquainted with Austin (they later became friends), Hand was moved to congratulate him for giving a speech that made him "less ashamed to be an American."

> I do not feel able to be silent about your manly declaration yesterday in the Senate; the only one, so far as I have seen, which broke the supine and ignoble chorus of those who seem to believe that any ignominy, any concession should be patiently endured from . . . ruffians and barbarians, rather than risk war. I am proud that there was at least one voice which was raised against so craven an attitude.[21]

Hand sent a similar enthusiastic note to a public figure he hardly knew in January 1941, when Al Smith, the former New York governor and 1928 Democratic presidential nominee, ended a long breach with Roosevelt by giving a radio talk urging stepped-up "wartime production" and aid to all nations resisting the Nazis. Hand promptly wrote to him: "It is encouraging beyond words to have someone who stands as you stand, rise above all personal considerations and sink everything [into] the sense of our common peril and of our need for common action."[22]

Despite substantial private contributions that the Hands made to war-relief efforts in 1940 and 1941, Hand refused to become a committee member of the British War Relief Society, citing his practice not to have any public connection with committees engaged in what could be regarded as political, including international, affairs. Yet in declining, Hand did not try to hide his emotional support: "I trust I need not assure you where my own personal feelings lie, or that they are very strong."[23]

Once during the difficult years of 1939–41 Hand's passions did burst through the dam of his self-imposed restraint. On May 17, 1940, several hundred members of the American Law Institute gathered in Washington for their annual banquet, where Hand, as one of the two ALI vice-presidents, was asked to speak briefly. The Nazi armies, after contenting themselves for several months with facing the Maginot Line, had launched an attack on the Low Countries just a week earlier and quickly overrun the Netherlands and Belgium. Within a month, France surrendered and the British saved what troops they could by evacuating them from Dunkirk. Hand had planned simply to convey greetings to the ALI gathering and prepared no formal speech. But the gloomy news from Europe moved him to extend his extemporaneous remarks: in a few words, he conveyed a message that his audience understood as an unmistakable call of warning that the democracies were under mortal threat and that preparedness and help from America were urgently needed.

Hand's impromptu eloquence struck a responsive chord: many in his audience told him that they had seldom been so moved. For the first time in his life, Henry J. Friendly—then a young New York lawyer, decades later a successor to Hand as chief judge of the Second Circuit —wrote to Hand:

> I have been privileged to hear two—and only two—addresses from which one got the same sense of elevation of spirit and perfection of form that one feels in reading Lincoln's greatest speeches. . . . You brought us something for which we were all waiting, in a way that no one else could have done. It is only decent to thank you for it.[24]

And the legal scholar Laurence H. Eldridge, another member of the audience, told Hand that he was "filled with something of your emotion, and as you closed there were tears in my eyes." Eldridge wished that the banquet had ended right then: he could not bring himself to applaud; he just wanted to leave "silently and reverently"; "I have had the same feeling when the last bars of Parsifal have faded into silence."[25]

Hand, long without illusions that American public opinion would readily support outright war against the Axis, knew that mere exhortations would not be enough and that a more dramatic event was needed to stir the United States into firmer action. He confided to Raymond B. Stevens, an acquaintance who was chairman of the U.S. Tariff Commission, that

> if there could only be some armed collision which would bring us at last into a real state of war, I should feel that we were safer. It sounds ruthless to say this, but the times call for ruthless conduct and we shall not be safe until we are at grips with those competent bandits who seem to be carrying everything before them. If we go down, at least it will be better to have had our try; we shall certainly go down much more painfully and shamefully, if we stand aside now.[26]*

* Stevens had written a vituperative outburst against Charles Lindbergh, attacking him for his "unsound, dangerous, cowardly, and craven" isolationism and for the "cool superiority" of his personality. Stevens apparently knew Louis Dow: "Louis told me that you shared more or less my views" (Raymond B. Stevens to LH, 27 May 1941, 80–13). In his response, Hand observed that Lindbergh was doing "so much damage at the moment that it is hard for me to appraise him justly, which I want to do, because in spite of all I have a deep regard for his wife" (LH to Stevens, 29 May 1941, 80–13). Lindbergh's wife was Anne Spencer Morrow, the daughter of Hand's late friend Dwight Morrow, and Hand had known her since her childhood.

Hand was right in believing that the American people were in fact not ready to engage in war wholeheartedly unless the Axis committed some "grisly enormity," but soon, such a "horror"[27] was launched, by the Japanese rather than the Germans: on December 7, 1941, they attacked the American fleet at Pearl Harbor. Hand had no illusions that the Japanese attack was unanticipated. As he later recounted it for Bernard Berenson:

> Of course, we made the most of that "treacherous" and "foul" blow below the belt, struck in a time of "profound peace." Nonsense, my dear B.B., as you and I know. It is one thing to say that decency—supposing that to be among the conventions of any kind of war—should require a declaration; it is another to scream, when, after being fully advised that the other chap does not fight like Tybalt "by the book," he has caught us off guard. However, moral indignation, justified or not, is a strong weapon, and we were very heartily in earnest in our sense of righteous superiority —rather a specialty of ours and J. Bull's anyway, is it not?[28]

Listening to oral arguments in the Supreme Court a few days after Pearl Harbor, Justice Frankfurter turned to his favorite remedy against boring advocates: he busied himself by scribbling notes to his friends on small Supreme Court memorandum pads. On nine such sheets, he wrote Hand of his exultation about the recent turn of events:

> Well, we're in it, as you and I long felt we should be, in all good decency & honor. But we didn't quite bargain for an "incident" that should be a volcanic explosion. And yet . . . if the papers on Dec. 8 . . . could have truly headlined
> <u>Navy Licks Japs</u>
> we should have gone into a Maginot Line of complacency. Emerson is too right—"Mankind is as lazy as it dares to be."[29]

Soon after, Hand echoed Frankfurter's relief: "I vary in mood about [the progress of] the war; but then, every once in a while I ask myself to think back a year or to the summer of 1940, and then my soul rises on wings of confidence."[30]

IN THE EARLY FALL OF 1937, as American observers followed the news from Europe with growing anxiety, the friendship between Walter Lippmann and Learned Hand suddenly ended. That friendship had been long and close. Ever since 1914, even before they helped launch *The New Republic*, the two men had carried on an extensive and intimate correspondence; in May 1917, Hand was among the first whom Lippmann told of his plans to marry Faye Albertson,[31] and Hand had been delighted with this revelation of love and humanity in his usually aloof friend.[32] Their personal as well as intellectual ties had flourished during dinner parties at each other's houses, in frequent encounters at the Century Club, and in lunches near their downtown offices. What caused the break in 1937 between such old and intimate friends?

Both Lippmann and Hand were intellectuals, and both inclined toward internationalism; as war approached, they puzzled over the divisions in the Western democracies and fluctuated between hopes and fears in observing the increasing assertiveness of the totalitarian regimes. Given these shared concerns, the contrast in their reactions to European developments of the mid-1930s stands out starkly.

Two examples illustrate the differences. Hand repeatedly lamented America's isolationism and the Allies' failure to back up their occasional protests against totalitarian expansionism with any convincing threats of force. Lippmann, however, publicly supported American neutrality and noninvolvement in European affairs almost until the end of the decade. In 1935, for example, his characteristically cold, detached appraisal of American interests compelled him to conclude "that we can contribute nothing substantially to the [peace] of Europe today": "For the time being," he wrote, "our best course is to stand apart from European policies."[33] The onset of the Spanish civil war in 1936 did not alter this position: although he feared that it might start a general European war, he had no great interest in it for its own sake. Unlike Hand, he offered no criticism of the Western democracies' weak response to the use of German and Italian arms and supplies in Spain. When FDR launched his trial balloon deviating from American neutrality in his October 1937 "quarantine the aggressors" speech, Hand praised it enthusiastically; Lippmann was not yet willing to go so far. And later in 1937, while Hand was telling Frankfurter that mere diplomacy would not stop the aggressors and that the Allies had to back up their threats with force, Lippmann opposed any military alliance to combat aggression as too "desperately dangerous a remedy," and confessed, "For my own part, I honestly do not know what I think should be done."[34]

The differences between Hand and Lippmann in the 1930s appear even more clearly in their early reactions to the racial policies of Hitler's Third Reich. From the start, Hand abhorred Nazi racism and sympathized with the plight of its victims, while Lippmann, himself a Jew, responded to the Nazis' early anti-Semitism with apologetic remarks about Hitler and, throughout the 1930s, never raised a public voice against the persecutions. Both Hand and Lippmann took note of the excesses of Nazi propaganda in 1933, but Lippmann viewed the persecution of Jews and others as a subject for detached foreign-policy analysis rather than one for shocked human concern. Early in May, after the Nazis' first round of book burnings, he suggested in his column two factors that might prevent Hitler from throwing the world into war: the French army and, paradoxically, Nazi persecution of the Jews. This was the first of Lippmann's very rare mentions of pogroms; he suggested that they might, "by satisfying the lust of the Nazis who feel they must conquer somebody and the cupidity of those Nazis who want jobs," serve as "a kind of lightning rod which protects Europe."[35] Frankfurter, as old a friend of Lippmann as Hand was, promptly sent Lippmann a note of concern about "the implications of attitude and feeling behind that piece."[36]

Undeterred, Lippmann, a week later, published a more elaborate assessment of Hitler, as remarkably optimistic about the Führer as it was insensitive to the fate of the persecuted Jews.[37] This second column was prompted by Hitler's having given a speech with unusually moderate passages, which Lippmann pronounced "reassuring": "The Chancellor went further than anyone had dared to hope in offering specific guarantees that he does not wish to disturb the peace."

> [W]e have heard once more, through the fog and the din, the hysteria and the animal passions of the great revolution, the authentic voice of a genuinely civilized people. . . . To deny today that Germany can speak as a civilized power, because uncivilized things are being said and done in Germany, is in itself a deep form of intolerance. Like all intolerance it betrays a lack of moral wisdom, in this case the religious insight into the dual nature of man.

Having hit his moralistic stride, he warned against judging any man or any nation by the evil rather than good qualities. Germans and their leaders should not be judged by their "crimes" and "sins" any more than others:

> Who that has studied history and cares for the truth would judge the French people by what went on during the Terror? . . . Or the Catholic Church by the Spanish Inquisition? Or Protestantism by the Ku Klux Klan? Or the Jews by their parvenus? Who then shall judge finally the Germans by the frightfulness of wartimes and of the present revolution?[38]

The column reeked of Lippmann's typical rationalism and disinterestedness, yet his words were indeed, in the words of his biographer, "deeply offensive."[39]

One of those offended by the column was Felix Frankfurter. The Austrian-born Frankfurter was no more an observant Jew than Lippmann, who was of German Jewish descent, but he was more comfortable with his Jewishness. Frankfurter did not write to Lippmann at the time; instead, he simply stopped corresponding with him. Not until three and a half years later did he explain his sudden silence. On November 28, 1936, Frankfurter wrote to Lippmann that he had heard that the columnist believed he had been "dropped" "because we happened to differ politically." Frankfurter denied that political differences were the reason:

> When, in your column for May 19, 1933, you described Hitler as "the authentic voice of a genuinely civilized people"—I'm not unaware of the context—and likened the Reich's cold pogroms and the expulsion of some of its greatest minds and finest spirits, merely because their grandmothers or their wives happened to be Jewesses, to the fact that "Jews have their *parvenus*," then something inside of me snapped.[40*]

Hand did not learn of Frankfurter's rebuke to Lippmann for another seven years, but in April 1943, in the course of a short note to Hand, Frankfurter made passing reference to a recent Lippmann column. In an even briefer reply, Hand remarked with some surprise:

> So you keep up with Walter? I daresay I should do well to do the same, but I don't. My position reminds me of that of an old hymn I used to hear in my infancy: "Lord, it is my chief complaint, that my faith is weak and faint."[41]

Hand's comment provoked a typical response: "Since you ask about my relations with Walter, let me answer with pedestrian accuracy." Frankfurter sent Hand not only an explanatory letter but a substantial enclosure of supporting documentation, including the exchange of letters in 1936 and a typescript of the 1933 column. Frankfurter recounted his old experience with Lippmann: whenever he praised a column, Lippmann would reply with "the most incandescent words of appre-

---

* In reply, Lippmann claimed to be "astounded" by Frankfurter's letter. He said he had reread his 1933 column and concluded that Frankfurter's tearing of "phrases from their context" and ignoring of "the historical circumstances in which the article was written" was "inexcusable." He added: "It betrays a lack of personal goodwill" (quoted in Ronald Steel, *Walter Lippmann and the American Century* [Boston: Little, Brown, 1980], 332).

ciation both for my devotion and for my wisdom"; when he was occasionally "at all critical of anything he wrote," "I was put in my place and made to feel that I did not understand." "For my taste," Frankfurter added, "he became more and more worldly-wise, and there set in a imperceptible alteration in our relationship." And that "incredible article on Hitler's 'peace' policy snapped the cord and I ceased writing him."[42] But by then, Hand had "dropped" Lippmann for nearly as long as Frankfurter.

The story of Frankfurter's break with Lippmann may have provided some comfort, both in showing that Hand was not the only one who had severed relations with an old friend and in reminding him of why he had been so irritated by Lippmann's writings. But the mounting differences between Hand and Lippmann over European developments were not themselves sufficient to end a friendship. The publication of Lippmann's book *The Good Society*[43] in the fall of 1937 was a more important cause.

The Good Society attracted widespread attention and large sales, not surprising for a major effort by a writer of Lippmann's reputation. But in fact it was a very strange book that "suffered from a split personality," as Lippmann's biographer has put it.[44] Its first part was a broad attack on collectivism and central economic planning, phenomena that in Lippmann's analysis were common to all totalitarian regimes. Central planning required regimentation and thus suppression of human freedom; Hitler's Nazism, Mussolini's fascism, and Stalin's communism all suffered from these vices. And so, according to Lippmann, did FDR's New Deal.

In this first section of *The Good Society*, Lippmann urged avoidance of central governmental controls and reliance on the free market, admiringly citing such laissez-faire economists as Friedrich von Hayek and Ludwig von Mises. But in the second part, he shrank back: the self-styled liberal, with roots in socialism and Herbert Croly's New Nationalism, was reluctant to sound like an ordinary economic conservative. Instead, the book propounded a remarkably wide-ranging agenda of reforms for a liberal democracy—public works, social insurance, and elimination of wealth inequalities through taxation. The inherent contradiction in Lippmann's book left the obvious question of how his reforms could be implemented without considerable state intervention that might arguably threaten liberty. A dictatorship of the bureaucracy could be avoided, he thought, through reliance on the common law and above all on judges as the ultimate decision makers. Citing authorities from Grotius and Saint Thomas Aquinas to Lord Coke, he heaped praise upon "the law" and the "spirit of the higher law." If citizens could sue officials in the common-law courts, he claimed, they would avert the curbs on liberty that an activist government might otherwise impose.[45]

Few careful readers found this satisfactory. Critics on the left—Edmund Wilson, Lewis Mumford, and John Dewey—denounced his attack on collectivism, particularly his inclusion of the New Deal. Challengers on the right ignored Lippmann's liberal agenda and instead praised his discovery of the "higher law" as a safeguard of liberty.[46] Learned Hand, the judge Lippmann knew best, was profoundly unimpressed by the book his friend had labored over for nearly four years. Hand believed that invoking vague notions of a "higher law," a version of "natural law," promised far more harm than good. And he had special contempt for the notion that a better society could be achieved by entrusting judges with the task of giving content to these vague concepts. Hand had always insisted that the abuse of judicial discretion was a major evil.

From conversations over the years, Hand had gained some sense of Lippmann's themes before they were published. And on September 10, 1937, writing from Consuma, Bernard Berenson's summer residence, Hand, having expressed his regret that he would have to sail home without seeing Lippmann, who was to arrive a few days later, added this preliminary appraisal of the unfinished *The Good Society*: "Insofar as you are discharging your artillery against totalitarian absolutism, tempered by plebiscite, I am with you; it is only when a bunch of judges is used to fill in the voids that I protest."[47] At the end of his letter, Hand expressed hope that he and Lippmann could see each other more often when they both returned to New York. But they did not see each other again for years.* (In 1955, Hand at last conveyed to Lippmann his criticisms of *The Good Society*, the occasion being the publication of an even more popular book by Lippmann, *The Public Philosophy*.[48] He congratulated Lippmann for his "most impressive background of reading and reflection, which gives what you say initial impetus and power," and for having "leapt at once into the 'best sellers' list. You are likely to stay there for a long while." He acknowledged that the new version of Lippmann's philosophy was "a contribution 'more life enhancing,' as B.B. likes to put it, than my own forbidding

---

* Hand elaborated his objections to *The Good Society* in correspondence with several friends during the late 1930s. He told Berenson, for example, that the book seemed to him to be "a disastrously insufficient performance: how the man who had written the first half of *A Preface to Morals* [Lippmann's book published in 1929] could have written that, passed my comprehension. It seemed to me greatly padded, full of false reasoning. . . . [T]he book will stand pretty well between us" (LH to Bernard Berenson, 3 August 1938, 99–16 [photocopy from Berenson Papers, I Tatti].)

gospel." Yet he left no doubt that he continued to reject Lippmann's rosy generalities:

> As I look back on the masters who trained my youthful thoughts, they did not, or at least I did not understand them to, believe that there were any ascertainable general principles of government that could be made to serve as guides for the solution of concrete problems; we used to think that we had put the quietus on "Natural Law."

That hope had proved wrong, for there was a "strong renascence" of an "equivalent" to natural law "cropping up all around in legal philosophy, quite independently of any theological background; it is an outstanding movement of the time."* Hand clearly rejected these natural-law tendencies.

> If I have understood you, . . . you do think that there are enduring and ascertainable concepts of "civility" without which no society can reach a tolerable Good Life. Frankly, I cannot agree. I do not mean of course that we do not have the Kantian basic principle: A counts for as much as B, and no more; Prince and Pauper stand alike; we must love our neighbors as ourselves. . . . [I]n the end I adhere to the notion, well, though rather brutally, stated by Holmes, that in politics—and for that matter in ethics—we are always faced with the insoluble problem of striking a balance between incommensurables, and that for the solution there are no standards or tests, save what will prove the most nearly acceptable compromise; what will most accord with existing conventions. Maybe at long last some fixed standards or tests will emerge; theoretically it is not impossible that we may come to find some, should our physiology go deep enough. Out of it could then perhaps come an adequate ethic and aesthetic on which politics could depend. But all that is centuries away. Strangely enough, all this comes out, or so I think, when one examines our own constitutional system with the Supreme Court on top as the final negative authority. . . . Perhaps your way out is possible, but for the moment I cannot see my path in that direction.[49]

With that forceful statement the eighty-three-year-old judge ended his critique.)

---

* For example, Hand's former law clerk, by now a friend and a federal judge, Charles E. Wyzanski, Jr., had recently given a speech as mystical in nature and as natural-law-oriented in flavor as the objectionable parts of Lippmann's new book. (See LH to Walter Lippmann, 23 May 1955 [retained copy], 23 May 1955, 106–18.)

The notion that his own tone and arguments were the causes of the 1937 break of his relationship with Hand never occurred to Lippmann. To him, there was only one reason, and that had to do with what was happening in his private life. The matter involved four people, all of them friends of Hand: Lippmann; Lippmann's wife, Faye Albertson Lippmann; Helen Byrne Armstrong, who had become Lippmann's lover in the spring of 1937; and Hamilton Fish Armstrong, Helen's husband and for years Lippmann's closest friend. Hamilton Armstrong himself discovered the affair when several of Lippmann's love letters to Helen accidentally came into his hands. Faye and Walter Lippmann were divorced; so, shortly thereafter, were Hamilton and Helen Armstrong; Walter and Helen soon married and moved to Washington.[50]

Hand had known Walter and Faye Lippmann for almost a quarter century, and Helen Byrne Armstrong for even longer; she was the daughter of James Byrne, a highly regarded leader of the New York bar since the turn of the century.* Hamilton Armstrong, an engaging, warm-hearted man, was a journalist who had joined the staff of the Council on Foreign Relations and become the editor of its influential magazine, *Foreign Affairs*. Hand had belonged to the Council for decades, and he read *Foreign Affairs* avidly. The Armstrongs, like the Lippmanns, saw the Hands frequently at dinner parties.

By the beginning of 1937, the marriage between Walter and Faye Lippmann had long been distant: Faye cared little about the issues of politics and philosophy that increasingly preoccupied her husband. But together they saw a great deal of their engaging friends Hamilton and Helen Armstrong, in both the city and country; they even went to Europe together. Walter and Hamilton were especially close. They saw each other regularly at the Council on Foreign Relations, lunched frequently at the Century, and talked almost daily on the phone. Helen Armstrong, a shrewd, quick-witted woman with an inquiring mind, had interests that extended to politics, and she was a good listener to boot. At a dinner party in January 1937, Helen and Walter had a conversation about love and marriage couched in the most general, impersonal terms, but at the end of the conversation, Helen lightly touched his hand, and Walter could not forget this gesture. A few days later, he left New York for Florida for more than three months, to complete *The Good Society*, and he spent a lot of time thinking about Helen while he was away. He returned to New York in April and

---

* Byrne was one of those who supported Hand for his first judicial appointment in 1909, and Hand gave him a substantial part of the credit for assuring that he achieved his dream of reaching the bench. He was the first Catholic to be elected to Harvard's Board of Overseers.

resumed seeing Helen, although only in Hamilton Armstrong's company.

One afternoon in May, Hamilton Armstrong called Lippmann to say that he had to attend an evening meeting; would Walter take Helen to dinner? Lippmann took her to the fashionable Rainbow Room, atop Rockefeller Center. Lippmann, usually the model of a detached, disinterested analyst, uncharacteristically spoke to her about his feelings —his fatigue with writing newspaper columns, his loneliness, and, finally, his disillusionment with his wife. The marriage, he told her, lacked all passion and real affection, and he felt even lonelier with his wife than by himself. That May evening, which ended with much wine and dancing, changed their lives. Helen later recalled that she had decided in early May that she was ready to leave her husband for Walter Lippmann. But thoughts of such an upheaval were not in Lippmann's conscious mind then, or for many weeks to come.

The day after, Lippmann asked Helen to have dinner with him again on the next evening Hamilton would be away. When the opportunity arose, they went to a quiet restaurant and to a hotel thereafter. Soon, Helen rented a small apartment on East Ninety-fifth Street where they could meet nearly every afternoon.

No one seemed to have an inkling of what was going on, but years later Helen remembered an uncanny, prescient conversation with Learned Hand that expressed his extraordinary perspicacity, both off the bench and on. As Lippmann's biographer tells it:

> One evening at a dinner party, having come straight from a rendezvous with Walter at the flat, Helen was astounded when Learned Hand, who was seated next to her, turned and said "How well do you know Walter Lippmann?" Taken aback, she mumbled a noncommittal, "Why, you know we've been friends with the Lippmanns for years." "Well, my dear," Hand said, his bushy black eyebrows setting off his piercing glance, "I'm sure then you realize that despite his impassive front he is really a highly sensitive person. Don't do anything to hurt him." Her face flushing, Helen protested she was hardly in a position to hurt him. The Judge smiled and changed the subject.[51]

Meanwhile, Lippmann continued to see Hamilton Armstrong frequently. He had little difficulty maintaining a composed public demeanor and deceiving his closest friend: he was caught up in the passion of the liaison, and he was in love for the first time in twenty years. When he brooded about the situation, his energies were directed exclusively to the prospect that Helen was soon to leave for a three-month stay in Europe; so long a separation seemed unbearable to him. Helen tried to lift his gloom. She pointed out that her husband would return to New York at the end of July, while she and their thirteen-year-old daughter could stay for another month in France; perhaps they might meet in August at a hideaway in southern France? Lippmann, much cheered, looked forward to their reunion. During their separation, he wrote virtually daily letters to Helen, whose responses edged ever closer to asking him for a commitment; he seemed not to understand what she meant, and for weeks his letters to her, though far more passionate than his detached public writings, contained no explicit promises.

When Hamilton Armstrong returned to New York in early August, he and Lippmann saw each other several times; Lippmann still said nothing about Helen. Lippmann later claimed that as of early August, he had given no thought to ending his marriage with Faye or to any long-term plans regarding Helen. But while he was sailing to Europe in mid-August, the consequences of the affair came into sharp focus. Four letters he had written in mid-July to Helen care of an Austrian Alpine resort she was visiting arrived after she had left, and the hotel, instead of forwarding his letters to her elsewhere in Europe, sent them to her husband's American address. Lippmann's love letters reached Hamilton Armstrong's New York office on August 16. The secret was out.

Armstrong read only the first few lines of the first letter, promptly called Helen, and persuaded her to return to New York immediately. An hour later, Lippmann, now in France, phoned Helen and learned of Armstrong's discovery. His rendezvous with Helen was canceled; instead, they met briefly at a Paris railroad station. Lippmann was bewildered. He urged Helen to return to her husband with an open mind, not to decide about the future until she had talked with him.

On returning to New York, Helen wrote Lippmann that she could not bring herself to stay with her husband, and pressed him for an answer about their future. Finally, Lippmann resolved not only to leave Faye but to marry Helen. Helen responded by cabling him—by then, he was Bernard Berenson's houseguest at Consuma—that she was ready to go forward as fast as he wished. Lippmann still had to struggle with the problem of telling his wife; he could not bear facing her personally and enlisted her stepfather, Ralph Albertson, to do it for him, insisting to Helen that this was not really cowardly.

Lippmann returned to the United States at the beginning of October. Less than two weeks later, on October 19, Faye Lippmann filed for divorce in Florida; soon after Christmas, Helen Armstrong went to

Reno for hers. Even before the divorce became final, Lippmann, in January 1938, moved to Washington; he and Helen were married in March, a month after her marriage to Hamilton Armstrong was ended.

In November 1937, Lippmann had written Armstrong to explain why he had not told his old friend in August about what was happening, and to say that he was truly sorry about the end of their friendship. Armstrong refused to read the letter. He never allowed Lippmann's name to appear in *Foreign Affairs* again for the remaining thirty-five years of his editorship. At his death in 1973, Armstrong left to Helen the love letters that had accidentally been delivered to him in August 1937; only one of them had been opened. It was her first chance to read them since they were written thirty-six years earlier.

The affair and the divorces fueled gossip among the Armstrongs' and Lippmanns' friends for months. Adultery was not unheard-of in that circle, but an affair followed by two divorces affronted conventions. Armstrong was widely viewed as the victim: Lippmann was condemned as being sneaky toward his closest friend and cowardly with Faye. Some of Lippmann's friends quickly dropped him, and Lippmann, believing the Hands were among the deserters, was especially hurt by what he considered Learned Hand's disloyalty, attributing it to his and Frances's conventional attitude about divorce.

But Lippmann was for the most part wrong. Only one aspect of the scandal did play a role in the breach. Learned Hand was never revulsed by divorces or even extramarital affairs. What bothered Hand in this instance was how Lippmann had behaved toward Faye and toward Hamilton Armstrong. But the Hands, unlike some of Lippmann's other friends, did not "drop" Lippmann peremptorily. They talked with him soon after the divorce and extended dinner invitations, which he declined.[52] As the years went by without further contact, the breach fed upon itself: the very momentum of the drift apart made revival of the friendship progressively more difficult.

Lippmann's biographer notes that Lippmann was "particularly hurt by Hand's disloyalty" and claims that the break between the writer and the judge "was largely due to Frances Hand, a domineering woman who had no compunctions about a second man in her own life, but who was offended by a scandalous divorce." The New York City novelist and lawyer Louis Auchincloss was the source of this description of Lippmann's reaction. While there is no doubt that Lippmann voiced such views late in his life,* it is not at all clear that these were his conscious thoughts in 1937. One of his obsessions during these years

---

* In his last, failing years (he died in 1974), Lippmann frequently uttered crushing judgments about acquaintances.

was the alleged abandonment by the Hands at the time of his divorce. As his biographer reports, he said of "a man [obviously Hand] who had once been a close friend and then turned his back during the scandal of the divorce: 'The first task of that man's biographer will be to enquire why he remained for so long on such goods terms with his wife's lover.' "[53] The unconventional relationship between Louis Dow and Frances Hand was certainly a subject of comment during its day, but it is by no means clear that they were in fact lovers, even though some people, especially in Lippmann's generation, thought so.[54] It is even less clear that the relationship played as central a role in the Hand-Lippmann break as Lippmann's late-life musings would have it.

During the six weeks' climax of the Lippmann-Armstrong crisis, from mid-July through September 1937, Learned Hand knew nothing of the contretemps besetting his friends. He was on his European tour, unavailable to any of the parties, even if they had wished to confide in him. A six-day visit with Berenson at Consuma was on his schedule, and throughout his planning, he had hoped that his visit with B.B. would coincide with Walter Lippmann's. Hand's first inkling that Lippmann was in extraordinary turmoil came from Berenson, although neither man yet understood the cause. A few days after Hand left Consuma, and just after Lippmann arrived there, B.B. wrote to Hand that Lippmann was "more delightful than ever, so discursive, & informing & wise," but added a worried qualification: "[H]e seems to hang *over* the brink of a serious breakdown" (the emphasis is Berenson's). B.B.'s diagnosis was that Lippmann had exhausted himself in his feverish efforts to finish *The Good Society*: "I can't persuade [Walter] to remain here till he gets better. A demon urges him on as it does all destined to neurasthenia. Let me pray he may escape it."[55]

Hand received that note on September 21, just as he was preparing to board the S.S. *Roma* back to the United States. He replied to Berenson during the first days of the voyage, and his opinion here is a subtle, striking intuition about not only Lippmann but himself:

> I am distressed at what you say about Walter; and to be frank, I find it hard to believe that you are right. In my experience people do not break down from work, but from continued emotional strains. Of course nobody knows the strains of anybody else, and Walter may have plenty. But it seems curious, that that level, unimpassioned wisdom should not be equal to whatever demands may be made upon it. And yet I will confess that at times I too have seen symptoms of stress in him. It would be a great shock to me.[56]

Lippmann spent his few days with Berenson knowing that he would leave his wife but uncertain about the course Helen Armstrong would choose. While he awaited word of Helen's decision, he resolved, he claimed soon after, to retire from journalism if she turned him down. Indeed, he claimed that he planned to live permanently in a little cottage on the I Tatti estate.[57] For days B.B. watched him brood, then suddenly, on September 19, Helen's cable to Lippmann arrived from New York, probably just a few hours after Berenson sent his worried letter to Hand; Lippmann promptly disclosed his secret to B. B. Berenson was full of sympathy; he focused on the impossible, loveless marriage of Walter and Faye Lippmann. "The strain he was under must have been awful," Berenson wrote to Hand. "I hope he can disentangle himself, & return to see the stars. He had been in hell for many years."[58]*

By then, Hand was hearing a good deal of the story himself. Hand wrote to Berenson that after Lippmann had twice refused dinner invitations, Hand "began to hear various pretty circumstantial accounts that the *way* he went about it was bad"—accounts dealing mainly with Lippmann's deception of Armstrong. Hand quickly added, "I have never allowed myself to form a judgment, nor shall I until, if ever, and it won't ever be, I hear from [Lippmann] his own account." But he did not rest with this:

> No, that's really nobler and more judicial than I am or shall be: I shall *say* that I shan't come to any conclusion, and I shall try to leave it open, but neither I, nor any other man or woman, can quite do that. The circumstantial stories did leave their effect on me, and I do feel a little differently about him.

Then Hand brought up his views on *The Good Society*. "[W]as that because I had made up my mind subconsciously against him?"

> I think not; my recollection is that I read the book before the Armstrong motif had developed in the bassoons. . . . He may think I have joined the pack against him, which at least I haven't, whatever defection you may choose to read into the above.[59]

* A year later, Berenson added to his interpretation: "If there was harshness & roughness in the wrench, I should be inclined to lay it at [Helen's] door rather than his. She makes the impression of being far more of an actor—I mean act-or, one who produces actions, not actor in the theatre sense—than he ever could be. Indeed I wonder whether he has an inkling of what [she] is up to. I have no idea myself, but I fancy she knows just what the instrument Walter can do for her & himself. I imagine she is worldly ambitious unconsciously & as a matter of course. She seems very able & with brains to sell" (Bernard Berenson to LH, 2 September 1938, 99–16).

For more than a decade, social relations between Hand and Lippmann ceased. Friends, especially Berenson, repeatedly urged Hand to resume the friendship; and Hand repeatedly berated himself for feeling too awkward to do so; he recurrently felt pangs of loss. When, two years later, in August 1940, with the United States still a bystander in World War II and the Allies reeling under Hitler's onslaught, Lippmann turned his back on noninterventionism, Hand began to read Lippmann's columns again occasionally; he found his voice "the sanest, the sagest, and the most prophetic which is being heard in the land," as he put it to Berenson. Yet he continued to keep his distance from Lippmann personally. The treatment of Hamilton Armstrong clearly still rankled:

> And yet I have never heard [Lippmann's] side, and of course never can; and, if I did, I would never hear Armstrong's authentically; so that I should end where I began. I know all this very clearly, and say to myself that when next I am in Washington I shall break through my ridiculous shyness, which no doubt he interprets in a very different way; and shall go to see him, but, somehow or other, I have never seemed to find the time. But I shall, I shall . . . it is too preposterous to leave things as they are.[60]

Hand never mustered the will to do so. In February 1941, in a final letter to Berenson before communications with wartime Italy were cut off, he returned, more defensively, to his continued lack of contact with Lippmann.[61] Several more years passed before Hand and Lippmann resumed their friendship, but it never regained the old intimacy.

XII

The Chief Judgeship and World War II

IN FEBRUARY 1939, after fifteen years as a circuit judge, Learned Hand became the presiding officer of his court. Hand acceded to the chief judgeship not as a reward for outstanding work, but automatically: the position is given to the sitting judge with seniority of service.[1] Far more dramatic than the elevation itself were the circumstances surrounding it, for the position became open in 1939 because the incumbent chief, Martin Manton, resigned under threats of impeachment and criminal indictment.

Hand and his fellow circuit judges had never held Manton in high esteem. Manton, who had become a district judge in 1916 at the age of thirty-six, had had a few years in private practice that were very remunerative, and through his partnership with the Tammany politician W. Bourke Cockran he had become a favorite of New York Democratic party officials. These political connections, together with support from the Roman Catholic hierarchy in New York, gained him the federal judicial appointment. And Manton's political associations continued after he became a judge: the waiting room in his chambers always seemed to be filled with his political friends, and his Tammany connections set him apart from his fellow judges.

Hand had revealed his low opinion of Manton as early as 1917, when the two were rivals for promotion to the Second Circuit, and in 1923, he had openly criticized the idea of naming Manton to what was considered the "Roman Catholic seat" on the Supreme Court. Chief Justice Taft's energetic intervention blocked Manton and his many political and religious supporters, so that the appointment went instead to Pierce Butler, a Minnesota Catholic.

But nothing had prepared Hand and his friends for the charges against Manton that exploded on the front pages of New York City's newspapers in late January 1939. The storm erupted on January 27, when the *New York World-Telegram* printed the first installment of an exposé series delving into Judge Manton's business activities while serving on the federal bench. The next day, U.S. Attorney General Frank Murphy announced that the Justice Department was investigating the allegations of misconduct.[2]

On January 29, far more detailed charges surfaced. Thomas E. Dewey, then New York County district attorney—at the beginning of a crime-busting career that brought him the governorship of New York and repeated nominations as the Republican candidate for president— released a letter he had sent to Congressman Hatton W. Sumners of Texas, who chaired the House Judiciary Committee, whose tasks included considering possible impeachments. Dewey told Sumners that his office had been investigating Manton for the past year with a view toward prosecution under New York's income-tax law.* The nub of Dewey's charges was that Manton and his associates had corrupted the administration of federal justice by soliciting and accepting bribes in the form of payments and loans (to Manton himself or to companies he controlled) from litigants in cases pending before the court—essentially, that Manton had taken money to cast votes in favor of his bribe givers. In his elaborate, detailed letter, Dewey alleged six incidents, beginning in 1932, in which Manton or corporations owned or controlled by him had received more than $400,000 from parties involved in litigation before the Second Circuit.[3]

Soon after, Manton offered his resignation to President Roosevelt, to be effective in March. Unwilling to wait until then and to link his administration unnecessarily with an allegedly corrupt judge, the president accepted Manton's resignation effective on February 7.

Hand was aware that Manton was under investigation even before the *World-Telegram* story broke, but he did not expect that Manton would be forced from office. Rumors that Dewey's office was checking into Manton had been spreading through New York legal circles, and Hand mentioned these rumors in letters to his wife, who was in Europe with Louis Dow. "The cloud still hangs over Manton," Hand wrote to her on New Year's Day, "and there are various rumors, but my guess is that the longer nothing breaks, the less likely any break is.

---

* Dewey apparently sent the letter to Sumners because he recognized that the two-year statute of limitations under the state income-tax law would bar prosecution of most of the charges under that statute.

He will, I think, come through with smirches, but nothing more."[4]
A few days later, he wrote to her about a City Bar Association dinner
at which both he and Manton spoke. "Manton got off some of the most
preposterous 'crap' you can imagine." The lawyer who chaired the event,
Albert ("Bert") Milbank, "was terribly afraid [Manton] would be indicted just on the eve of the dinner; but although one hears they are
still fussing about it, I have no idea that anything will come of it."[5]

Within a week, however, Augustus Hand was urging Learned and
the other member of the great Second Circuit triumvirate, Thomas
Swan, "that *we* ought to do something about it." Learned thought there
was "nothing to do"[6]—presumably believing that the only information
the judges could offer to Dewey was that they did not think much of
Manton's craftsmanship and that he was always surrounded by political
hangers-on; this fell far short of evidence of criminal behavior.

By the time Hand succeeded to the senior circuit judgeship on February 7, gloom enveloped the court that had long been considered the
nation's outstanding federal appellate tribunal. A week earlier, a federal
grand jury had begun to hear the case against Manton, and within a
month, it began handing down a series of indictments[7] that culminated,
on April 26, in a superseding indictment under two criminal statutes,
one prohibiting conspiracies to defraud the United States and the other
barring the corrupt obstruction of justice. The indictment alleged a
series of acts done in furtherance of the conspiracies, some that were
among District Attorney Dewey's charges submitted to the House Judiciary Committee, and some new ones as well.[8] Of most obvious
concern to Hand was the indictment's pervasive theme: that Manton
had gotten money in exchange for his votes on cases before the Second
Circuit, bribes that he himself had solicited through intermediaries.

Manton's trial began on May 22. Since all the federal judges in New
York City had some acquaintance with him, none of them could properly preside. Accordingly, it was requested that Chief Justice Hughes
assign a judge from outside New York to hear the case. The Chief
Justice selected Judge W. Calvin Chesnut of Maryland. (After Manton
was convicted in the trial court, the specter of potential disqualifications
reappeared with Manton's appeal to the Second Circuit. Once again,
judges unacquainted with Manton were designated to sit on the appellate
panel: retired Supreme Court justice George Sutherland and active
justice Harlan Fiske Stone, together with a recently appointed Second
Circuit judge, Charles E. Clark.)[9]

The newspaper coverage of the case, which for months had competed
on the front pages with reports of the impending war, expanded even

further when the trial began. Day after day, detailed reports filled the papers as the scandal unfolded in the courtroom; *The New York Times* often printed the transcript of the testimony as well.[10]

Only one very short passage in the voluminous trial transcript directly involved Hand, and that is because he and his colleagues Augustus Hand, Thomas Swan, and Harrie Chase all appeared on the witness stand, not voluntarily, but subpoenaed by the defense. While the defense called a parade of luminaries to testify to Manton's good reputation for truthfulness and integrity—including two former Democratic nominees for the presidency, John W. Davis and Al Smith—Manton's judicial colleagues were not part of this array of "character witnesses." Instead, they took the stand on the last day testimony was heard (June 2), just before the cross-examination of Manton began, and each was asked only one question; none was cross-examined. All they were asked was whether, in any of the cases in which they sat with Manton, they *observed* anything that led them to believe "he was acting otherwise than according to his oath of office and the dictates of his conscience." Each answered that he had observed nothing to indicate that Manton was deciding on anything other than the merits of each case.[11] Their appearance seems to have had little effect on the jury, which did not deliberate long: on June 3, after less than three hours of discussion, Manton was convicted. On June 20, Judge Chesnut sentenced him to two years' imprisonment and a $10,000 fine. Manton spent seventeen months in the federal penitentiary in Lewisburg, Pennsylvania, before he was released on October 13, 1941. (Five years later he died in upstate New York, remembered as a judge whose twenty-three years of judicial service "ended in unprecedented disgrace.")[12]

The trial record made clear that Manton had sold his office to protect his substantial business investments from the effects of the Depression. His financial position had indeed been seriously eroded. He had come to the court as a millionaire, but he was effectively insolvent by 1931. His criminal behavior began soon after, and for most of the 1930s, as he tried to preserve his many investments in real estate and other enterprises, he relied on outright payments and loans from litigants to protect his holdings.

For Learned Hand, the most painful and embarrassing revelation was that he himself had sat in two cases in which Manton had accepted bribes. Each involved patent litigation: the first dealt with patents for parts of automobile ignitions; the second, patents for cigar lighters.

In the first, *General Motors Corp. v. Preferred Electric & Wire Corp.*,[13] the Second Circuit unanimously invalidated the General Motors patents on which suit was brought. The pre-conference memoranda show that all three judges—Manton, Hand, and Swan—agreed on the disposition from the outset, and nothing on the face of Manton's memorandum suggested that he had been paid to reach his decision.[14] True, Manton's memorandum was not as erudite as Hand's, but this was the norm; also, he had throughout his appellate career a reputation of being a "scissors and paste-pot" judge who produced many of his opinions simply by lifting useful passages, complete with precedents and legal authority, from the briefs of the prevailing side.

In *General Motors*, then, nothing in Manton's memorandum could clearly provoke suspicions of corruption. By thus limiting his corrupt votes to reasonably close cases and arguably plausible positions, Manton made much of his dishonesty difficult to detect. In the *General Motors* case, it was particularly difficult to perceive the corruption, since his memorandum and opinion closely resembled the analyses of his colleagues. Indeed, when the Second Circuit granted a rehearing in the case after Manton was convicted, the court, after a fresh review of the old record and with full knowledge of Manton's bribery, once again found the patents invalid.[15]

In the second corrupted lawsuit in which Hand sat with Manton, however, the situation was more complex. In that case, *Art Metal Works v. Abraham & Straus*, Hand disagreed with Manton from the outset.[16] The legal battles in *Art Metal* began when Art Metal's combative president, Louis Aronson, filed a lawsuit claiming that his rival, Alfred Reilly, and Reilly's company, the Evans Case Company, had infringed Aronson's patents on the popular Ronson cigar lighter and had sold the copied lighters through a Brooklyn department store, Abraham & Straus. Art Metal's suit—only the first of a series—resulted in a victory for the plaintiff's Ronson patent, with the Second Circuit holding in August 1932 that Evans had infringed that patent. Reilly, Evans's president, quickly began to search for ways to save his business. An acquaintance introduced him to William J. Fallon, Manton's bagman. Fallon assured Reilly that he was a "great friend" of Manton and that he would talk to the judge. Soon after, Fallon passed the word that Manton thought the case not completely hopeless. Reilly's strategy, encouraged by Manton, was to try to block Art Metal from enforcing the judgment it had won.

The crux of Reilly's new claim was that Art Metal and its sales personnel had misrepresented the judgment upholding the Ronson patent by claiming that it barred *all* competing lighters and had thus misused its patent victory. Accordingly, he argued, Art Metal should forfeit its right to sue for patent infringement. The trial court rejected this, and the case once again went to the Second Circuit. While this appeal was pending, Reilly again got together with Fallon, who sought $10,000 for himself and $15,000 for Manton in exchange for Manton's favorable vote. On the day of the decision, April 30, 1934, Fallon called Reilly asking for an immediate payment of $15,000 because "the Judge . . . was in bad circumstances for the money." Reilly promptly paid most of that amount, mainly in cash, and Manton's was the decisive vote in a 2–1 ruling accepting Reilly's argument that the Ronson patent was not enforceable because of Art Metal's alleged misconduct. Soon after the decision, Fallon introduced Reilly to Manton, and the two became close social friends. Moreover, Reilly put Fallon on his payroll, assuring continuing payments to Manton's bagman.

When District Attorney Dewey's charges against Manton became public in 1939, *Art Metal* was not on his list of cases, but Manton feared that the investigation might turn up the misdeeds in that case, and on February 5, just two days before he left the court, he phoned Reilly about the Evans Case Company's relationship with Fallon and suggested that it would be "very embarrassing" for Manton if it were found out that Fallon was on the payroll. "Couldn't you pull out those pages?" he asked. Reilly doubted that was possible, and later on that day called Manton to discuss the problem again. Manton, fearing that it might not be safe to talk from his home, called Reilly back from another phone a few minutes later, using an assumed name. Presumably as a result of these calls, Reilly tried to persuade his bookkeeper to burn all the records of payments to Fallon. After some resistance by the bookkeeper, most of the papers were in fact burned; the few that were not were used as prosecution evidence at Manton's trial.[17]

From the outset of the Second Circuit's consideration of the case, Hand was unpersuaded by Manton's argument that a patentee's misbehavior, particularly through its sales personnel in the field, could in effect invalidate the patent. This time—perhaps for the only time in all the cases for which he was convicted—Manton sold his vote in a case that was very difficult to justify on the basis of precedent.[18] His memorandum insisted that Art Metal was engaged in trying to eliminate its major competitor and "capture [its] business," that it was "bound by what the salesmen agents said to the defendants' customers," and that this "constituted inequitable conduct which should forbid both their right to an injunction for violation [by] infringement and also to an accounting."[19]

Hand thought that Manton's analysis was wholly misguided. The very meaning of a patent, he pointed out, was to grant a monopoly to the patent holder. He conceded that "a ruthless insistence upon the monopoly [by the patentee] will drive the other man out of business," but he insisted that the right to do this was the very essence of the patent scheme:

> It may not be Christian, but it is certainly lawful to press for monopoly . . . and it is merely mawkish to wince at the consequences. . . . I count as nothing all this chatter about "threats"; the plaintiff had received power to stop everyone from selling [the lighter it had patented], and was wholly within its legitimate rights in threatening everybody who sold them with legal proceedings. That was the very purpose of the whole suit.

True, the inventor could not lawfully "lie about what the court had decided." Whether there had been that kind of lie was really the central issue. On his own review of the facts, Hand found "no evidence of any such lie": meticulously examining every allegedly unconscionable act by Art Metal, Hand found no "impropriety" at all.[20]

When the *Art Metal* case was reheard by the Second Circuit in 1939, several months after Manton's conviction, the new panel consisted of Learned and Gus Hand and the newly promoted Robert P. Patterson. This time, the judges were unanimous in siding with Hand's earlier dissent, and Manton's 1934 opinion was overturned. Learned Hand's own memorandum in what he called "the Unclean Hands Case" was very brief. In the course of it, he wrote one especially fascinating sentence: "I thought [in 1934] that our lamented chief was doing dirty business of some kind here, and now I know it."[21] By the time he wrote this, he knew, of course, that the Ronson patent litigation had played a major role in Manton's criminal trial. Hand may well have suspected in 1934 that Manton had strained so hard to articulate such strange patent-misuse principles because of his friendships with old political allies, but there is no indication that he suspected Manton had been bribed.

For years after Manton left the bench, Hand worried that somehow he was partly responsible for Manton's corruption, though he had not known, and had no real reason to know, that any of Manton's votes were prompted by bribes. He repeatedly speculated about what he might have done to keep Manton from temptation: if only he and Gus Hand and Tom Swan had done more to bring Manton into their circle, he would muse, if only they had not watched from a distance as Manton churned out marginal work while political hangers-on filled his anteroom. These self-tortures were unrealistic, given what Manton was like, yet to the end, Hand refused to exculpate himself entirely.

This somewhat farfetched soul-searching reflected the psychological strain the Manton scandal had imposed on Hand and his court. For years, most of the Second Circuit judges had been considered not only the weightiest intellects in the federal judiciary but also models of integrity. The well-publicized reports of a bribe taker among them were bound to scar their institutional and personal self-esteem (and patent law was among the court's renowned strengths). The scar was long-lasting: when Hand stepped down from the chief judgeship in 1951, for example, a letter to Calvin Chesnut, the judge who had conducted Manton's criminal trial, left no doubt that the passage of twelve years had not eradicated the scar: "Again and again have I thought of what our position would have been if you had not undertaken that most unwelcome duty. I know that I have often repeated my gratitude, but let me say it once again. . . . We owe you an enduring debt which never can be repaid except in our hearts and minds."[22] Seven years later, Hand told Chesnut, "I have never forgotten your service many years ago when you came to try the case against Judge Manton. Maybe I have told you before of my enduring gratitude, but I never tire of remembering it."[23] He was similarly effusive in a letter to Justice Sutherland, who wrote the Second Circuit opinion affirming Manton's conviction, although he had long criticized Sutherland and other members of the Supreme Court's dominant conservative bloc; Hand thanked Sutherland profusely for his willingness to sit "and so help us out of what otherwise would have been a very difficult position."[24]

Hand's intense brooding over the Manton scandal may well have had something to do with the old and deep friction that had marked their relationship going back to the first days of Manton's chief judgeship. One of the chief's tasks was to prepare assignment schedules, designating the weeks in which the court would hear arguments and who would sit each week. Manton repeatedly irritated his colleagues by the overbearing manner in which he exercised these duties, and well before the impact of the Great Depression led him to criminal behavior, he circulated a schedule that sharply departed from past practice and especially irritated Hand. (After a flurry of angry correspondence, in which the other judges joined Hand's side, Manton modified his assignments.)[25]

Even more vivid in Hand's mind was Manton's high-handed and ill-motivated behavior in appointing receivers for insolvent companies, who were supposed to run a company so that it might continue and recover rather than be chewed up by the claims of competing creditors. Usually, the trial judge in charge of a case appointed lawyers as receivers. Hand was well acquainted with the abuses in receivership appointments from his fifteen years as a district judge; in 1909, only a month after taking his seat on the bench, he had complained about the pleas of politically well connected attorneys seeking appointments, and he knew that receivership appointments were patronage plums controlled by judges, obstacles in the way of a truly independent judiciary. He often advocated reforms in the system, but no significant change occurred during his district court days.

The problem did not come to a head until after Hand moved to the Second Circuit, and then Manton became a major figure in the battles that erupted. As insolvencies mounted with the onset of the Depression and the need for receivers grew, complaints about favoritism in the appointment practice stirred separate congressional investigations of two trial judges in the Second Circuit (Grover Moscowitz and Francis A. Winslow; Moscowitz was ultimately criticized but exonerated while Winslow resigned under fire). The publicity over what Manton himself called "the so-called bankruptcy scandal"[26] prompted the trial judges in the Southern District to take corrective action: they designated one trust company, Irving Trust, as the exclusive "standing receiver" in bankruptcy and awarded most equity receiverships to it as well. Hand supported this move, but Manton publicly criticized the Irving "monopoly" and instead strongly supported the appointment of private attorneys, chosen case by case by the supervising judge.[27]

Manton soon found a characteristically imperious way to resolve the conflict between his views and those of the district judges. Relying on a provision of the Judicial Code permitting the senior circuit judge, "if the public interest requires," to designate any circuit judge to hold a district court within his circuit, he occasionally designated *himself* as district judge, took over the receivership, and gained power to appoint a private receiver. He first tried this scheme in June 1932 in the case of the insolvency of the Fox Theatres Corporation. In response, the district judges unanimously amended their own rules of court, "to deprive, if possible, the Senior Circuit Judge, duly designated, from all power to act [in receiverships] except in such measure as the Senior District Judge might permit."[28] The angry Manton insisted that the new district court rules violated the Judicial Code to the extent that they circumscribed his powers, and he vowed to exercise his powers as he had.

Manton followed precisely the same pattern within weeks in the well-publicized insolvency of the Interborough Rapid Transit Company. The IRT, with properties worth about $500 million and with thousands of employees and trains, operated a substantial part of New York City's rapid transit system.* Fearing that the district judge who would supervise

* The Manhattan Railway Company, which held the franchise for and owned the elevated trains in Manhattan, had leased its property to the IRT. A separate receiver was appointed for Manhattan as well, in a related part of this complex set of proceedings.

the receivership would select a corporate receiver, Manton decided to prevent that outcome[29] and issued an order once again designating himself as the district judge to supervise the IRT receivership, in defiance of the district court rules.* Manton's intervention quickly led to a showdown. District judge John M. Woolsey ruled that Manton's order was illegal; he insisted that when the senior circuit judge designated himself as a district judge, he was subject to the district judges' rules of practice.[30]

Woolsey's ruling was appealed to the Second Circuit and assigned to a panel of Learned Hand, Thomas Swan, and Harrie Chase.[31] Considering only the question of Manton's power to act, they decided unanimously for him and reversed Woolsey's ruling in a unanimous opinion written by Hand. Manton had been careful to cross all the *t*'s and dot all the *i*'s in issuing the orders designating himself to sit as trial judge in the case. In form, he had the statutory authority to act. That was enough for the Second Circuit: the judges felt bound to affirm Manton's position on technical grounds. All three judges concluded that the question of whether "the public interest" truly required his self-designation was *not* open to reexamination.

Yet the Second Circuit judges clearly had private doubts that Manton's order was in fact justified by "the public interest." Swan, for example, in his pre-conference memorandum voted to reverse Woolsey "[w]ith regret (because I deprecate a circuit judge being able to select special cases to be tried before himself in the District Court").[32] Similarly, Chase stated that there "was in fact no basis" for Manton's "public interest" finding, though he could see "no way by which Judge Manton's administrative order can be judicially reviewed."[33]

The Second Circuit's ruling was promptly challenged before the United States Supreme Court. In a unanimous opinion written by Justice Van Devanter,[34] the Court laboriously set forth the law and the facts at the unusual length of twenty-three pages and firmly upheld the Second Circuit's ruling; but whereas the Second Circuit opinion never criticized Manton, the Supreme Court ended with some words of reproof and advice for him. Justice Van Devanter wrote: "[Manton] acted hastily and evidently with questionable wisdom. This action has embarrassed and is embarrassing the receivership." This "embarrassment would be relieved" if Manton withdrew from the case, and so the

---

* Manton named one Thomas Murray as one of the receivers. Murray, it turned out in the later investigation of Manton, was one of the judge's cronies and had paid more than $20,000 for worthless stock in one of Manton's corporations shortly before his appointment. The other receiver was Victor Dowling, who became a partner in Chadbourne, Stanchfield & Levy, a law firm with which Manton had had a series of questionable relations—especially those with Levy.

justices announced their "belief . . . that, on further reflection, he will recognize the propriety of [stepping down] and, by withdrawing, will open the way for another judge with appropriate authority to conduct the further proceedings."[35]

Hand presumably followed the IRT proceedings with care, not only because of the extensive newspaper coverage and because they had come before his court, but also because of his long interest in cleansing the receivership process of opportunities for patronage and cronyism. Yet none of these events could reasonably have provoked him to suspect Manton's criminality. Still, if Hand had any grounds for self-reproach, it lay in not doing more to determine whether Manton's long-known penchant for cronyism was prompting abuses of his judicial powers. His brooding about his own partial responsibility for Manton's corruption mainly reflects his almost masochistic penchant for self-doubt and self-criticism.

Ultimately, Manton's behavior did not leave as deep and permanent a scar on the reputation of the Second Circuit as Hand feared. By restoring the court's high standards of ability and integrity, Hand and his colleagues reestablished the Second Circuit's renown as the nation's leading intermediate appellate court. A few months before he died, Hand could comment that "the standards of judicial conduct are [now] a good deal better" than they had been.[36]

THE POSITION of senior circuit judge that Hand assumed in February 1939 was more than a titular honor. It required him to take on many administrative tasks, both petty and significant, and all potentially burdensome. Within the Second Circuit, Hand was responsible, for example, for scheduling the weeks in which his court would hear arguments and for designating the three-judge panels assigned for each week—tasks that Manton had performed so insensitively. He not only chose the opinion writer when he was in the majority, but also wrote most of the per curiam opinions of the court—summary opinions when the court did not think it useful to explain its reasoning at length. To assure adequate personnel to keep up with the workload, Hand frequently had to ask trial judges to serve, and he sought help as well from circuit judges in other parts of the nation, a procedure that required the permission of the Chief Justice. As chief judge, Hand also controlled some personnel decisions regarding the court's staff, such as selecting the Clerk of the Court. In addition, he had the statutory obligation to convene an annual conference of all of the judges of the circuit, trial and appellate, to consider problems in the administration of justice.

There were responsibilities outside his circuit as well: every year, the chief had to attend the Conference of Senior Circuit Judges (later renamed the U.S. Judicial Conference), which demanded participation in numerous committees as well as preparation for and attendance at meetings. The conference made recommendations on many subjects affecting the operation of the federal courts and their relation to the other branches of government.[37]

The actual dimensions of the task depend mainly on the philosophy and attitude of the incumbent. For many modern judicial administrators, administrative tasks absorb half or more of their working time.[38] Hand himself occasionally complained that his new administrative tasks were time-consuming,[39] but he probably spent less than 10 percent of his time on formal administrative duties. This remarkably small percentage reflected his personality and philosophy. He had no interest in using his position for ego gratification or displays of power; he had no desire to put any more time than necessary into the often dull job of administration; he firmly believed that his main job was to decide cases, not to manage a growing bureaucracy, and to foster harmonious collegial relations through informal measures rather than by dictating solutions by power of office. As he put it on February 3, 1939, the added duties imposed on the senior circuit judge did not seem "very formidable": "He does of course have some [administrative] work, but I believe that could be so arranged as to take very little time." Hand suspected that the burdens imposed by the chief's statutory duties were "largely imaginary. The Senior goes to the Judicial Conference once a year; he asks District Judges to sit in other Districts; he has some other duties too which at the moment I do not recall." Most important, Hand crisply articulated the consideration that would govern his own behavior for the next twelve years: "After all, a judge spends substantially all his time in judging—or at least he ought to. . . ."[40]

When Hand took over the position, he sought to improve relations between the chief and the other judges, and to purge the courthouse staff of second-rate political appointments. One of the stables to be cleaned was the Office of the Marshal for the New York federal courts—in effect, the courts' police arm. Justice Stone, who had served on the special panel that heard Manton's first appeal, and U.S. Attorney John Cahill, who had prosecuted Manton, were both eager to see "a better sort of man" appointed as marshal, and each sought to enlist Hand's aid. Hand shared their desire. As he told Justice Stone, "[T]he corridors and some of the court rooms . . . are filled with bondsmen and hangers-on, and there has at times been a breath of scandal about it. . . . [T]here have been one or two instances, indeed, where, as I recall, the deputies have been tools in jury fixing, though I am not sure." But the marshal's appointment of deputy marshals had proved to be of "a great deal of financial importance to the political party which has the appointment," and "[t]hese places have always been filled . . . by a low grade of political workers of small intelligence and at times doubtful morals."[41]

In a second letter to Stone, Hand told the Justice that Cahill thought New York City's federal courthouse was "a sort of volcano which might break out in more scandal at any time." Hand himself insisted that it was "highly important that someone be appointed who will have the courage to appoint only reliable deputies, and not to make the office a 'pay-off' for party workers." He endorsed a candidate Cahill suggested, one Julian Starr, a "life-long Democrat, though not active in the party," who was *The New York Sun*'s reporter in the federal courthouse and was "thought to know the ropes as well as anyone."[42]

After such efforts to purge the evils of the Manton era, Hand turned to more routine administrative duties, which he performed with a characteristic hostility to pomp and formality. His attitude on en banc hearings was typical. En banc hearings are hearings by the full complement of judges on the circuit, at the request of losing litigants who prefer to have their cases reexamined by all the circuit judges rather than to seek immediate review by the Supreme Court. Some circuits, acting on their inherent powers, had already begun to hold en banc hearings even before the law explicitly authorized them, but in 1941, a bill was introduced in Congress formally to grant en banc authority to the circuit courts, about which Hand stated bluntly: "I am really against this bill."

Throughout his life, Hand had nothing but scorn for the utility of en banc hearings. In 1941, there were six judges on the Second Circuit, normally hearing cases in panels of three. Hand could see no point in using the valuable time of all six judges to review any panel decisions: "[F]or myself, I should never vote to convene" an en banc hearing. He recognized that for most people, including lawyers, "numbers really are impressive," and thus en banc decisions by a number of judges greater than three would likely be viewed as more authoritative than rulings by the usual three-judge panel. Yet the "scheme of judicial hierarchy" was that all circuit courts of appeals were of "presumed equal authority." "For this reason," Hand argued, "the bill does disturb the general judicial scheme."[43]

After Congress explicitly authorized en banc review, Hand adhered to his promise that he would "never vote to convene" an en banc court, and he mocked those courts that resorted to the practice with ever increasing frequency. As he once wrote to his friend Herbert Goodrich, a judge of the Third Circuit: "I cannot but admire [Third Circuit Chief Judge] John Biggs' device of having all the judges of a Circuit sit together; it so much increases the certainty of the result. For example, here [in an opinion Goodrich had sent Hand] your vote is four to three, when it might have been only two to one."[44] And he proudly reported to the chief judge of the District of Columbia Circuit, after nearly four years as chief, that the Second Circuit had never sat en banc.[45] (Hand's hostility to en bancs has remained a tradition in the Second Circuit to this day, although they are not wholly unknown there. Chief Judge Wilfred Feinberg has written, "The tradition in the Second Circuit, a tradition that goes back to Learned Hand, is that in bancs are not encouraged. My view, and that of my predecessor, Irving R. Kaufman, is that for the most part in bancs are not a good idea: They consume an enormous amount of time and often do little to clarify the law.")[46]

Hand's insistence that judges devote themselves primarily to judging—deciding cases and giving adequate reasons for their rulings—set him firmly against the increasing bureaucratization of the federal judiciary. In 1939, for example, when the Administrative Office of the United States Courts[47] was established, a structure that spurred parallel bureaucracies within the various circuits and districts, Hand tried to shield the judges under his supervision from additional administrative preoccupations. When the chief judge of the Ninth Circuit sought Hand's advice on establishing and developing his own comprehensive organization, Hand swiftly replied that in the Second Circuit, "We have no organization, no offices, and no standing committees."[48]

Hand, who preferred personal relations among judges to formal, bureaucratic ones, was especially resistant to the Circuit Judicial Conference he was required to call annually. He once described an impending conference to a former law clerk: the conference members "will all be there, feeling pretty important. . . . We shall talk a great deal to show each other how sagacious we are; . . . we shall settle some things to present to Congress which Congress will probably not do. Then we shall go home with a sense that we are rather nice chaps, which is really the case."[49] Instead, he followed his own independent path. Though a federal statute adopted within a few months of Hand's succession to the chief judgeship mandated an annual meeting of all of the active circuit and district judges of the circuit, "for the purpose of considering the business of the courts and advising ways and means of improving the administration of justice within [each] Circuit,"[50] Hand followed the law's requirement only in form. In most circuits, the annual conferences quickly became two- or three-day affairs, often at resort retreats, where the judges could socialize, attend seminars and discussion sessions, and mingle with invited members of the bar. Throughout his years as chief judge, from 1939 to 1951, Hand would have nothing to do with the grand gatherings, common in other circuits, that often brought together five hundred to one thousand people for a mixture of camaraderie and business.[51] He scorned that kind of pomp, and instead typically sent a brief annual notice to every judge, citing the statutory provision requiring the meeting and announcing that the year's conference would take place in a room at the Foley Square Courthouse in downtown Manhattan at a specified date and hour. He expected the proceedings would take very little time, and he sometimes added a blanket excuse in advance for the absence of any judge who had more important business to transact on that day (under the law, attendance by each judge was mandatory, "unless excused by the chief judge"). While Hand did once seek the aid of a trusted district judge to help prepare a minimal agenda for the annual conference, even then he made clear that they should avoid the extravagance indulged in at many other circuits—which occurred, as he told the district judge, "perhaps because they are not so busy" as the Second Circuit.[52]

Despite—perhaps because of—his low regard for elaborate bureaucratic structures, committees, and formal meetings, Hand proved to be a superb administrator, eliciting enormous respect and affection from the judges of his circuit. He attended to all important administrative chores punctiliously, but he did not let them govern his life, or his work as a judge. Only in giving primary attention to his task of deciding cases and explaining judgments, not in basking in the formal honors of his office, did Hand take pride in his work.

FURTHERING COLLEGIAL HARMONY on the Second Circuit was a major challenge to Chief Judge Hand. Until Manton's forced resignation, the court had been unchanged for a decade: the Hands, Swan, and Chase had all been named in the 1920s, and they formed a tightly knit group. But then, in less than three years, three new judges joined the court: Robert P. Patterson replaced Manton in 1939; Charles E. Clark was named to a newly created sixth seat in the same year; and in 1941, Jerome N. Frank was appointed to occupy the seat left vacant when Patterson resigned. The composition of the appellate court then remained unchanged for Hand's final decade as chief judge.

Maintaining the court's cohesion would have been a challenge even if the new members had been as even-tempered and open-minded as Thomas Swan and Gus Hand. But of the three new appointees, only

Patterson had a background and temperament similar to those already on the court, and only he was quickly accepted by his colleagues. Clark and Frank, both products of the New Deal, had emerged in a political environment far different from the one that had shaped the senior members of the court.

Robert Patterson had been a district judge for a decade, one of the very best in Hand's eyes. From the beginning, he and Hand felt a remarkably close personal affinity, and before long, they became intimate friends. Each viewed the other as heroic, with Hand, characteristically, questioning the accuracy of Patterson's evaluation. Hand once said that Patterson

> endowed me with some of his own qualities in which I was sadly lacking. I used at times to try to undeceive him, but always without success; and it usually followed when we parted, that I had a desperate feeling that we could never come to a common footing because he so obstinately refused to listen to the truth about myself which I knew and he would not believe. Out of this there generally came the compulsive conclusion that, as he insisted that I had been made in the heroic mode, I ought to try to make good his faith. The sense of duplicity came from the fact that long experience had taught me that, however elevated I might feel at the moment, the effect would not last.[53]

Hand and Patterson shared common backgrounds. Nineteen years younger than Hand, Patterson, like Hand, was born in upstate New York and attended Harvard Law School. After more than a decade in successful corporate practice, he accepted the district court appointment from President Hoover in the spring of 1930. Although Hand then knew him only by reputation, he greeted him warmly: "Nothing has pleased me more since my cousin came to join me. . . . You will be a distinguished judge, a pride to us all." From the beginning, Hand treated him as a family member—indeed, almost as a son—admiring his strengths and delighting in his achievements, and once, while lauding Patterson for his willingness to give up a successful career to take on a lower-paying judge's job, he was moved to sentimental reflections about his own accession to the trial bench twenty-one years earlier: "I can assure [that it] will always seem to you nearer the Good Life than any other open to a lawyer. . . . You will not regret it. . . . I welcome you to your new life, with the assurance of one who has lived it for long and finds it good."[54]

Patterson, who had been wounded in battle and decorated for his service during World War I and who served for years as a high official in the War Department, had a passion for military history. Hand, always an admirer of what William James had called the "tough-minded" rather than the "tender-minded," had a special respect for such men, and this part of Patterson's background enhanced his admiration. During the 1938 Washington debates about adding a sixth judgeship to the appellate court, Hand supported Patterson so enthusiastically that, notwithstanding his view that the new judgeship was unnecessary, he pressed friends to "jog up the Attorney General about Bob Patterson for our court,"[55] and when Manton resigned, FDR selected Patterson to succeed him. Ordinarily, the president might have been inclined to select a New Dealer, but in the wake of the Manton scandal, a person with notable judicial experience and of especially unimpeachable integrity seemed the wiser choice. Very shortly, Patterson gained the affection and admiration of Hand and his colleagues. Even the ordinarily restrained and taciturn Vermonter, Harrie Chase, was saddened by Patterson's departure only a year and a half later, telling Hand, "He was a man—take him for all in all, you shall not see his like again."[56]

Patterson resigned from the court in July 1940 to become assistant secretary of war. Patterson and Hand had talked about the offer at length, and Hand, though reluctant to see him go, had nonetheless bowed to Patterson's sense of duty.[57] The Second Circuit judges tried their best to keep Patterson's judicial position open for him, since as the presidential election approached it was not at all clear that FDR would retain the White House against Wendell Willkie's challenge; after learning from Felix Frankfurter that "a horde of insects" was after the Second Circuit vacancy, Hand instigated a round of letters to Attorney General Robert H. Jackson, pressing him to postpone a replacement appointment for as long as possible.[58] The judge's efforts had some success: Jackson told Hand that the place would not be filled until it was decided "whether [Patterson is] going to be [in Washington] permanently or not"; Hand understood this to mean a delay "until after the election."[59]

Roosevelt did of course gain his third term, and Patterson, after a quick promotion to undersecretary of war, served throughout the war as head of the U.S. Army's vast procurement program. When Jerome Frank was named to Patterson's seat on the Second Circuit early in 1941, Hand was still not persuaded that it was necessary to replace him: "[T]here was no need whatever to fill Bob's place and shut him out; we need six judges about as much as a cat needs two tails," he wrote James M. Landis. "But I suppose we ought not to have expected them to hold open any place for perhaps a couple of years, no matter how little it needed to be filled."[60]

When Henry Stimson retired as secretary of war, Patterson succeeded him and led the planning of the merger of the armed services into a single new Department of Defense. Hand, immensely proud and nearly overcome with emotion,[61] swore Patterson in as secretary of war in 1945.[62] They had maintained their social ties, and their mutual admiration had only deepened throughout the war years. And when Patterson resigned from the cabinet in July 1947, Hand wrote approvingly that Patterson was "in line for the next vacancy on the Supreme Court."[63] But Patterson returned to corporate law practice, and as he did so he told Hand, "Let me say that you are my true friend and closest friend; that your support and your approval have been of great help to me all these years; that my debt to you is beyond calculation."[64] Indeed, close observers believed that Hand had been "largely responsible for [Patterson's] rise."[65]

Patterson never returned to the bench. After apparently declining an offer from President Harry Truman to return to the Second Circuit,[66] his life was cut short in January 1952, when he died in an airplane crash in Elizabeth, New Jersey. Hand was devastated by the news, which he heard just five days before his eightieth birthday. He abandoned plans to attend a dinner, explaining to his host, the publisher Alfred A. Knopf, that "I did not feel equal to facing a party. I fancy he would have thought [this] my weakness [which] perhaps it was for he was of much sterner stuff; but he was one of those closest to me and to have him snuffed out like that put more of a strain on me than I felt I could quite carry in company."[67]

As Hand put it in a condolence letter to Patterson's widow, their friendship had "ripened into one of my most precious possessions."[68] Hand and Patterson sometimes disagreed about legal issues, but there was never a hint of personal irritation or impatience. And as Patterson said of Hand in an essay for the 1952 Harvard Law School Yearbook written just before his death: "How hard it is to write a tribute when emotions for a friend and companion keep pressing their way into the stream of thought. . . . Above all else, [Hand] is the free man, far more civilized than the world he lives in. But the world is a better world because of him. All history, so Emerson says, resolves itself into the lives of a few stout and earnest persons. The life of Learned Hand is on that select list." Hand's memorial tribute to Patterson included the following: "He was guileless, indifferent—indeed too indifferent —to money, careless of the impression he made on others, fearless, generous, without envy or jealousy, merciful and even tender with the weak, and neither deferential nor assertive with the strong; and he was too apt to ascribe these qualities to others."[69]

Hand feared that FDR's other appointments to the Second Circuit would not be so perfect a fit as Patterson, that New Dealers might seriously disturb collegial harmony. He thought that many of them tended to be zealous, a cast of mind uncongenial to his pervasive skepticism. He saw no room for political enthusiasts on the bench, for he had "an unconcealed scorn for that temper . . . which transfigures a judge into a crusader for righteousness as righteousness may appear to his incandescent conscience," as he put it in memorializing Patterson.[70] He had no difficulty agreeing with the general direction of New Deal social reforms, but he worried that the reformers' devotion to social goals might shake his court's commitment to even-handed, apolitical judging. In selecting nominees for the new, sixth seat and for the vacancy caused by Patterson's resignation from the fifth in 1940, FDR followed his political inclinations and chose two unquestionably loyal as well as able and experienced New Deal supporters. To Hand and his fellow Coolidge-era appointees, the specter of discord loomed large.

Charles Clark and Jerome Frank did indeed disturb the harmony of the Second Circuit; frictions and divisions on the court increased; but the cause was usually not an ideological clash but, rather, personality conflicts, primarily *between* the two new appointees themselves. Yet amid these frequent clashes, the court's reputation survived undiminished and was even enhanced. The outstanding quality of its work reflected in part the judges' high level of ability and in part Hand's skillful, sensitive leadership in becalming the incipient feud between Frank and Clark.

Charles Clark came to the court after nearly twenty years at the Yale Law School, whose faculty he had joined in 1919, during Thomas Swan's tenure as dean. After years of teaching and writing in the areas of procedure and property law, Clark had become dean himself in 1929. He was long "noted for his liberalism," as *The New York Times* put it, and was apparently the only law school dean to testify publicly in favor of Roosevelt's controversial Court-packing proposal in 1937.[71]

After taking his seat on the Second Circuit in March 1939—the same month Patterson joined the court—Clark did indeed prove to be a recurrent source of friction: in his absorption in one area of the law, and in his prickly, combative personality, he proved to be a crusader on the court not on behalf of the New Deal social ideals, but rather for procedural reform. The rules of practice and procedure in the federal courts had been his major interest for years. He was the "architect" of the Federal Rules of Civil Procedure that were promulgated in 1938, as Justice Potter Stewart put it.[72] As a member of the Supreme Court's Advisory Committee on Civil Procedure and as its reporter, he was responsible for drafting an important reform that combined the old separate practices in law and equity in order to assure "the litigants a just, speedy, and inexpensive determination of their lawsuit, rather than a welter of moves in a judicial game of chess."[73] Clark's appointment to the nation's most important intermediate appellate court soon after the Federal Rules were promulgated gave him a strategic position to influence their interpretation: not only did he remain a member of the Advisory Committee, which prepared revisions of the rules, and serve on the relevant committees of the U.S. Judicial Conference, but he also used his voice and his vote on the court.

Unfortunately, but understandably, his Second Circuit colleagues did not share Clark's passion for the centrality of procedural rules. As Clark himself once bemoaned in a letter to Hand, "[T]he greater the judges, the less patience they will have with procedural matters."[74] It was not that Clark's colleagues were dismissive of procedural problems, but they frequently grew impatient with Clark's insistence on his own interpretation of a particular rule. Hand himself, in pre-conference memos that Clark would not see, frequently referred to him as "the GLAPP"—his abbreviation for "the Greatest Living Authority on Practice and Procedure." Within a year of Clark's appointment, Hand sent Harrie Chase, who sarcastically called Clark "the great dissenter,"[75] a copy of an opinion referring to "the new 'wules' "—Clark apparently thus pronounced his favorite word—and added:

> Dare we construe any wule sans Charles? I submit the following verses:
>
> > There once was fellow named Clark
> > Who thought it a Hell of a lark
> > To discuss about wules,
> > And then call us fools,
> > Because we were so in the dark.[76]

Clark's obsession with procedural issues was especially irritating because he was so certain that his interpretations were right. A descendant of New England Puritans, he considered the Federal Rules a matter of high principle and viewed compromises as tantamount to sin. He once praised a fellow academic for his "lack of facility in compromise; for I recall how often being conciliatory or tactful means in essence a yielding and ultimate retreat from principle, making immediately for quietude, it is true, but ultimately for forfeiture of leadership."[77] Yet Clark's comments often struck his colleagues as harsh and supercilious, a problem made worse because his discomfort in face-to-face negotiations made him rely on written, often didactic, communications. The other judges quickly grew impatient with his rigidity and tenacity, his proclivity for separate opinions, and his self-righteousness. Chase vented a widespread feeling when he burst out to Hand: "[Clark] has been *so damned* irritating."[78] Once, when Clark had "made up his mind to write another one of those opinions he sponsors alone," Chase, in thanking Hand for his "last effort to stop a tempest in a teapot," bristled at Clark's delivering to his colleagues "a little lecture we could have done without, just as we did without him for a good many years before he became the judge he is."[79] A few weeks later, the thin-skinned Clark got upset about Chase's referring to one of his proposed separate concurrences as "one of those opinions," and Chase at first resisted Hand's efforts to make him back off: "[H]ow many times should a certain so-and-so be allowed to get stubborn about nothing and get away with it?"[80]

Beginning at least as early as August 1940, a little more than a year after Clark joined the Second Circuit, he proposed that the court regularly identify in its opinions the name of the trial judge whose judgment was under review. Hand, who had no strong feelings about this issue, explained to his new colleague that while it had been "our custom in the Second" not to disclose the name of the trial judge, this practice had evolved "only out of tenderness to their supposed sensibilities." He thought that some of the trial judges "would object very decidedly" to any change in policy, but he agreed to solicit their reactions, as he promptly did.[81] The survey showed, as Hand informed Clark, that only four of the circuit's twenty-three trial judges supported such a change (and one of these had just retired); a few had no opinion; and thirteen clearly "preferred" continuing the present practice.[82] Yet, even on this relatively minor matter of form, Clark relentlessly pressed the issue[83] and repeatedly raised it at the Circuit Judicial Conferences. (In 1944, he warned Learned and Gus Hand that he planned to raise the issue once again at the forthcoming conference, even though he had been accused of "making a mountain out of a molehill.")[84] And he was an even more vigorous battler when it came to the proper interpretation of his Federal Rules. Hand recurrently found himself at the receiving end of Clark's demands for greater attention to the Federal Rules at the U.S. Judicial Conference on which Hand sat; and he was the target of several sharp Clark dissents on matters of Federal Rules interpretation. Hand assured him that he did not mind the dissents' caustic tone, and that Clark's approach might indeed be the wave of the future.[85]

In his official relations with Clark, Hand managed to retain his equanimity, and on the surface their relations were respectful and cordial, but Hand never developed affection for Clark; the most that can be said is that Hand brought Clark as much as possible into his court's collegial fold. But if Hand ever had reason to fear that a New Deal appointment would disrupt the Second Circuit, it was the selection of Jerome Frank. Yet Frank proved to be neither an irritant nor a burden, and his friendship with Hand quickly flourished into one of the court's most affectionate and intimate.

The reason lies mainly in the important similarities in their personalities. Frank was above all an individual of enormous vitality and range, an insatiable reader and irrepressible writer, a generator of a seemingly endless flow of ideas, as well as an engaging conversationalist. Hand had always loved such people, for they stimulated him to address new questions and reexamine old approaches. The core of his affinity with Frank, despite their profound philosophical differences, was a shared skepticism, a common urge to challenge received wisdoms wherever they surfaced.[86]

Frank, nearly eighteen years younger than Hand, had spent his early years at the bar (after his undergraduate and law school education at the University of Chicago) in the intricacies of corporate reorganization, at first in Chicago and then for a few years on Wall Street. Soon after Roosevelt won the 1932 election, Frank enlisted Felix Frankfurter's help to find a place in the New Deal,[87] and soon he was named general counsel of the Agricultural Adjustment Administration. There, Frank opposed the idea that the New Deal's elaborate farm-price support program should substantially benefit middlemen rather than the farmers themselves; early in 1935, Secretary of Agriculture Henry A. Wallace fired him because of his strong stand on behalf of tenant farmers and sharecroppers. Frank was then quickly named special counsel to the Reconstruction Finance Corporation, but at the end of 1935 he returned to New York to resume private practice. Frank's return to the more lucrative world of Wall Street was short-lived. In 1937, on the recommendation of William O. Douglas, then the chairman of the Securities and Exchange Commission, Frank was named a commissioner, and when Douglas left for the Supreme Court in 1939, Frank became the SEC chairman.

Although Hand had not followed the details of Frank's government career, he was well aware of the stir Frank had created in 1930 with the publication of his first book, *Law and the Modern Mind*, which catapulted him to the front lines of a new jurisprudential movement, "legal realism." Drawing heavily on a recently developed interest in psychology and psychiatry, Frank launched a vigorous attack on the notion that the law consists of a set of rational, predictable rules that govern judicial decisions. Instead, he emphasized the personality of the individual judge as the central factor in decision making and argued that legal rules curbed judicial discretion to only a very limited extent. He ridiculed the idolatry of certainty and predictability in the law, likening it, on the basis of his fascination with Freudian ideas, to the childish need for an authoritarian father.

Law and the Modern Mind thus challenged central beliefs of the American legal system—beliefs that Learned Hand in a sense personified—and implicitly attacked the very legitimacy of judicial authority. The core of Frank's iconoclastic ideas became fashionable in the 1930s, with other legal realists developing similar challenges, albeit with different emphases. Traditional law schools, like Harvard's, felt especially stung by these critiques and identified them closely with the Yale Law School, the perceived hotbed of legal realism.[88] At a meeting of the Harvard Board of Overseers Committee to Visit the Harvard Law School in the spring of 1932, the subject of what Hand called "the new movement in the law" had come up, and Hand made a disparaging comment about it. Thomas Reed Powell, a Harvard constitutional-law professor whom Hand admired, interrupted him to say that the new legal realists "were doing more thinking than anybody else in the profession." Hand promptly apologized for speaking so harshly: "What I said was really the outburst of an irritated person who I suppose had got tired of trying to digest new notions, who had put too much capital into the old to want to see them scrapped. In other words, I am afraid it is a typical old man's point of view. At any rate, I had no right to abuse without understanding, and I certainly have read too little to understand." Hand asked Powell what to read to become more familiar with the new movement: "I think it would be undesirable for me to begin on Jerome Frank, don't you? Who presents that outlook in a less extravagant way? Who is the best one to read?"[89]

Frank's statement of his thesis in 1930 had indeed been "extravagant"—his "rule-skepticism," or doubt that legal rules and precedents were very important, was expressed too broadly, and his claim that judges had virtually free rein in choosing among competing, indeterminate legal rules was overstated. Yet Hand would have found much to agree with had he read Frank's book. He was never a wholehearted admirer of C. C. Langdell's efforts to construct airtight logical structures, nor would he have doubted the role of personality and personal biases in judicial decision making.

In fact, Hand greeted Frank cordially when Frank was named to the court in 1941, and from the beginning, expected to get along well with him. As he wrote to Frankfurter at the time, "I don't doubt I shall like him."[90] (Frankfurter, in responding, was happy that Hand felt that way: "He is worth the patience necessary for an adequate understanding. You will find him a first-class craftsman and one of the sweetest of men. He does, however, have all the verbal difficulties of one who has messed around . . . with psychoanalysis as much as he has. His has been a complicated life. The core of the man is really very good and sweet.")[91] Hand knew of Frank's reputation for boundless energy: in his first letter to his new colleague, Hand wrote that Frank might "find the life a little too quiet for [his] tastes."[92] Within months, a remarkably deep affection developed between them. By the summer of 1942, for example, Hand wrote Frank, "You give me a stimulus and a companionship that I would not forgo for much."[93] And in 1955, after Hand had stepped down from the chief judgeship, he could write, "Certainly the fourteen years that we have been together have been happy ones to me; and I have got from you a constant source of suggestion and information that I have not had from any of the other associates that I have had throughout the long years I have had on the bench."[94]

Frank warmly reciprocated Hand's affection. At about the same time, he wrote to Hand, "No one else I have ever known has excited in me such admiration and affection. You are my model as a judge. More, you've influenced my attitudes in incalculable ways towards all sorts of matters, intellectual and others. For your eminence lies not alone in the singular nature of your mind, but in the manner in which you infuse your ideas with emotions, both noble and humorous. You are, par excellence, the democratic aristocrat. God bless you!"[95] In 1949, by which time Frank had abandoned his crusade against the importance of rules and precedents and instead launched a vehement critique against the inadequacies of fact-finding processes in the courts and the flaws of jury determinations, Frank dedicated his second major venture in legal philosophy, *Courts on Trial*, to Hand, saluting him as "our wisest judge."[96] Soon after Frank's appointment, a book reviewer, calling this "perhaps [President Roosevelt's] happiest appointment," likened it "to the choice of a heretic to be a bishop of the Church of Rome."[97]

But the real Jerome Frank who took his seat among his eminent senior colleagues in 1941 was not the revolutionary, eager to burn down the temple, that some of the most extreme passages in *Law and the Modern Mind* might have suggested. He was nothing like the ogre his colleagues might have expected. He appeared to be and was approachable. His face was marked by a high forehead, a full mouth, and, most notably, deep-set eyes surrounded by dark shadows and with enormous bags under them. Richard Rovere, the *New Yorker* writer who became Frank's close friend while trying to write his biography, aptly described him as resembling a "zealot" with "a burned-out and dissipated look." But, as Rovere accurately added, Frank was "an enthusiast, not a zealot."[98] The colleague Hand grew to know and like had a quick and fertile mind, and his wide reading—in psychology, philosophy, history, indeed on almost any subject in print—found its way into his lively, free-flowing conversations and his often overflowing opinions. He wore his interdisciplinary learning lightly, especially in face-to-face sessions. As Justice William O. Douglas once put it, "His mind was too eager to be pompous, too skeptical to be arrogant."[99] While often looking disheveled and spouting words with great rapidity in order to keep pace with the quickness of his mind, Frank struck those around him as a warm, humane man, endlessly fascinated by ideas and genuinely interested in communicating and debating them with others.

Like Frank, Hand loved books, though he did not read them as widely; like Frank, Hand took ideas seriously and loved to argue about them; like Frank, Hand often looked disheveled, despite his Savile Row suits. Above all, Hand sought and appreciated stimulation and challenge. He ranked his law clerks on the basis of how effectively they criticized his drafts and questioned his ideas; similarly, he valued critical minds among his colleagues, and none was more critical and iconoclastic than Frank's. Hand was clearly astounded by "the extraordinary— sometimes, for me, the amazing—extent of [Frank's] reading," and the "readiness with which it was mobilized. . . . He seemed to carry [everything] in his head."[100] He was awed by Frank's inexhaustible mental energy, remarking that he seemed always "in perpetual cerebration."[101] As he once wrote to Frank: "I look with unmixed admiration at your ability to hit on all twelve—or is it sixteen?—cylinders for twelve—or is it sixteen?—months in every year."[102] Hand not only admired the fruitful restiveness of Frank's mind but also appreciated the challenges Frank's feisty independence posed to him. Once, after acknowledging the "stimulus" Frank provided, Hand confessed that "at times it does make the old horse take some jumps that he would probably run around if he were [deciding cases] alone."[103]

Yet the mutual admiration that marked the dealings between Hand and Frank did not mean that all was tranquil in their collegial relations. Some of the disturbances arose from the differences between Jerome Frank the warm, engaging friend and Jerome Frank the writer of a flood of books, articles, and judicial opinions. In intellectual jousts, Frank would pierce pretensions and inconsistencies as he saw them, and he could hurt; while he was himself quite sensitive to perceived slights, he was uninhibited in inflicting wounds on his adversaries.

Frank's opinions were notable not only for the sharpness of their tone but for their length and discursiveness. In his first month on the court, Frank sent Hand a draft opinion far longer than the Second Circuit norm, exploring at length the history of the legal doctrine under consideration. Hand questioned its elaborateness, predicted that Frank would not be able to delve into such extensive detail when the "workload got busier," yet concurred in the opinion.[104] But even when the court's burdens increased, Frank kept producing long essay-opinions citing works of philosophy, history, and literature in elaborate footnotes that from anyone else might have been dismissed as pretentious. Harrie Chase was sarcastic about this: "I have agreed to the foot-note by Aristotle, as amplified, to which Jerry attached his opinion," he noted once to Hand. "Such authority has the tang of old and mellow liquor, which especially appeals to me and I was unable to resist it during the festive holiday season." He then appended his own footnote: "Foot-notes, foot-notes, foot-notes. Blah!"[105] James Landis, then the Harvard Law School dean, had warned Hand when Frank was appointed that he would have to be taught to be "less prolix than he is customarily,"[106] but Frank was incorrigible. Hand had once written to a state judge that "[p]ersonally, I . . . abhor footnotes. . . . But the practice has become so general that I fear I am enlisted in a lost cause. My objection to this is that it tends to make the opinion more a legal treatise, and to that I greatly object. It is not the tradition of the American or the English bench; it tends to prolixity and gets the judges professorial; after all, we are not speaking to eternity, but deciding disputes."[107] But Hand could not persuade Frank of that view. He warned Frank once that "very few people read such long opinions." He added, "[B]ut then, I was reared at an earlier age, and maybe the world is going to use judges' opinions for jurisprudential treatises. BUT! I DON'T BE-LIEVE THEY EVER WILL. I *THINK* YOU ARE PUTTING YOUR MONEY ON THE WRONG HORSE."[108]

Yet Hand quite readily accepted these differences. Unlike some other judges, he refused to get very exercised about Frank's opinion-writing style. As he once told Frank, the style of a judicial opinion is, after all, a matter of "the personal taste of the writer."[109] To Felix Frankfurter, whose own penchant was for didactic opinions decorated with extensive footnotes, Hand wrote, "[I]t is impossible to control [Frank's] exuberant mentality. . . . This is a world in which we can't do very much for another chap. . . . On the whole I think that he will slowly pull in his sails."[110] And when Frankfurter sent Hand copies of his letters to Frank criticizing his opinions, Hand persisted in avoiding the fray.[111] Frankfurter criticized Frank for his extensive essays, telling him, in one case, that he saw "no reason why you should take a simple case which Holmes would have disposed of in a page and a half and use it as a peg for an essay on mercantilism," but Frank eloquently, lengthily, and pedagogically (during most of his years on the Second Circuit, he gave a very popular Friday afternoon class at Yale Law School) made a good case for his expansive, idiosyncratic style: "[T]he best way to educate the bar is through opinions. Few lawyers read the law journals. Fewer still read books dealing with 'jurisprudence.' But most of them do read opinions."[112] And some of his separate opinions did have substantial impact: his concurring and dissenting opinions repeatedly served in effect as petitions for review to the Supreme Court, and quite often they succeeded.*

The stormy relations between Frank and Clark were all but inevitable, for Frank was strong precisely in those areas in which Clark was weak—he was a warm, delightful person, while Clark seemed uncomfortable in verbal battle, ponderous, and relatively humorless—but some of their similarities intensified their conflicts. Both were sensitive to personal affronts. Both would take their complaints about each other to Hand, who often expressed the wish that they would speak to him about their problems rather than resorting to lengthy, inflammatory letters.

The first outburst occurred about a year after Frank joined the court, and how Hand resolved it shows his characteristic touch. Frank wrote to Hand about Clark's having made an "unfair" charge that Frank buttressed his position in panel conferences by referring to the informally expressed views of other judges not sitting in the case. Hand admonished Frank in a letter, where he tried hard, almost too hard, not to sound exasperated:

> The fact is that we shall get into continuous hot water—all of us—if our casual talks are to be considered as important. I would be dreadfully sorry to have this happen; it is a great assistance to us all, I am sure of it, that we can break in and gas to each other. But it will prove fatal to any freedom if such talks are thought to be responsible opinions. I am sure you will agree with me that you don't feel that what you say represents more than a superficial, horse-shed judgment, unless you have studied the opposite arguments and had time to consider. . . . I know you agree with all

---

* The best-known example involved the first of the major obscenity cases in the Supreme Court, *Roth v. United States*, 354 U.S. 476 (1957), where Frank's concurrence—full of references to materials on sociology and psychology—pressed the Supreme Court to decide the permissibility of obscenity controls under established First Amendment doctrine. He succeeded in having the Supreme Court grant review, but was unsuccessful in persuading it of his views. (See *United States v. Roth*, 237 F.2d 796, 801 [2d Cir. 1956].)

this and the only question is how we can best preserve our freedom and yet not misunderstand each other. I can think of no way except that we should all go on as we have been, but should not quote what one says who is not of the three judges, as though it were very important—which it is not. It is all a question of the mood in which we deal with such talk; if we lose the proper mood, we shall have to readjust our mutual communication at a loss. I don't know how to go about keeping the proper mood; it is all a question of nothing too serious about it, and nobody likes to have anyone else think he is too serious about something that seems serious to him.[113]

The same day that Hand wrote this letter to Frank, he had written to Frankfurter, in their correspondence about Frank's writing style, that his younger colleague was "so sensitive and so responsive that he is likely to overreact."[114] Frank's response to Hand's letter illustrated the accuracy of Hand's observation. Evidently, Hand's admonition got under Frank's skin, for Hand had to becalm his ruffled feelings later on in the same year: "My, Jerry, but you're a sensitive cuss; no, my boy, you certainly do *not* take your work of any kind too seriously; and my words were only meant as a pleasantry—and a feeble one at that."[115]

The issue that aroused the most heated battles between Clark and Frank involved Rule 54(b), which governed the complex, technical subject of how the courts should handle "interlocutory" appeals, piecemeal appeals such as those from a pretrial order admitting or excluding evidence. The general rule about trial court judgments is clear: only a "final" judgment in a district court can be appealed to the appellate court of the circuit. Thus, interlocutory appeals are ordinarily not permitted; the aggrieved party must wait until the trial court has issued a "final" order, such as entering a judgment for one of the parties. Difficulties arise, however, when a trial involves several claims. The question that the Second Circuit repeatedly considered was whether all the claims in a particular case had to be disposed of before an appeal could be taken, or whether the final rulings applicable only to particular claims might be appealed separately. The original Rule 54(b) provided that in multiple-claim situations, a trial court could enter a separate judgment disposing of a single claim, and that such a judgment could be appealed immediately.

Clark interpreted Rule 54(b) as giving the ultimate discretion about interlocutory appeals to the trial judge, and he fought vehemently to preserve his interpretation. Frank and Hand strongly opposed him. Frank preferred to give the ultimate discretion to the circuit court judges to determine whether justice required them to hear the separate appeal, and Hand agreed. Both he and Frank opposed Clark's repeated efforts to draft and redraft rules that would specify in ever greater detail how judicial discretion should be exercised. To Frank, no procedural rule should ever be permitted to interfere with doing substantial justice in a case. Decisions "ought not to be made merely to afford satisfaction to those interested in maintaining the aesthetic proportions of procedural theory. More important than delight in such verbal symmetry . . . is the avoidance of needless unfairness to litigants."[116]

When this battle first erupted on the Second Circuit in 1943, Clark at first thought that Hand's better judgment had been overcome by Frank's personal charm and intellectual salesmanship. Hand had to inform Clark that his views on interlocutory appeals were entirely his own.[117] Three decisions in 1951 added fuel to the fire that had burned for years. In the first, Clark interpreted a revision of Rule 54(b)—a revision he had helped draft—as clearly granting the final say on appealability to the district judge. Frank insisted that these comments were not necessary to the decision and could be disregarded as mere "dictum." Then, eight days later, a different panel, in an opinion by Learned Hand, claimed to be free to disregard this earlier "dictum." The revised rule, Hand wrote, could not be read to intend "so revolutionary an inversion of what had been the uniform custom theretofore."[118]

Clark was outraged. He complained privately to Harrie Chase:

> Do you see what Learned Hand has been doing . . . ? I don't know whether to laugh or cry over what seems to be almost a pursuit of your humble servant by our distinguished colleagues who seem ready with a sledge hammer to smash my poor feeble attempts—now continued over some years on the Rules Committee and elsewhere—to work out a rule of appeal that anybody, even lawyers, can understand.

Hand's opinion, he thought, seemed "rather strange medicine for a colleague's work—without notice or any consultation."[119] A few months later, when Clark found an occasion to vent his anger with Hand in a printed opinion, it was apparent for all to see.[120]

But the dispute did not end there. In cases subsequent to the 1951 trilogy, Clark managed to get majority support for his position. Frank ultimately conceded as much, but he intensified his efforts to obtain congressional legislation granting the circuit courts broader discretion to hear appeals from otherwise nonfinal orders, and he collaborated with Hand to get the issue considered by the U.S. Judicial Conference and ultimately by Congress. A legislative compromise was adopted in 1958, a year after Frank died. Even Felix Frankfurter was drawn into the squabble over Rule 54(b), at one point suggesting to Clark that he had been rude toward Hand in his opinions. Clark, never one to let a stinging remark pass unanswered, began an extensive correspondence to "rehabilitate" himself by rebutting this "devastating" comment.[121]

Frankfurter's protective remarks on Hand's behalf were unnecessary, for Hand always assured his colleagues that tough, argumentative opinions were entirely appropriate and he did not take them as personal insults. "[A]s I think you know, I rather like to have a dissent hit hard," he once wrote to Frank.[122] But he became exasperated with the waste of energy involved in the constant bickering. "After you and Jerry get through amending your opinions, and stop shouting, for God's sake file the opinions," he once wrote to Clark.[123] And he put it even more colorfully in a memorandum on a petition for rehearing in a case where he sat with the two of them:

> I like to dance in the moonlight as well as any man, but my wind is not as good as it once was, and I cannot keep time with the antiphonal strophe and antistrophe of my youthful colleagues. "When, as, and if" between you—supposing that happy time shall ever arrive—you come to the point of exhaustion, I shall play upon the harp and timbrel and lift up my voice in praise to God. BUT, while all this agitating cerebration remains in parturition, I shall merely sit on the side lines, contemplate my navel, and repeat the syllable, OM.[124]

The Clark-Frank battles erupted with respect to other portions of the Federal Rules of Civil Procedure as well, though not with the same duration and intensity.* And in the criminal arena, too, Clark and Frank were often on opposite sides. Here, however, Hand repeatedly sided with Clark. Frank and Clark diverged sharply in their sympathy with criminal defendants and in their level of concern for what Hand once referred to as "the ghost of the innocent prisoner." Typically, Clark disliked what he perceived as "a present, strong trend toward special care and consideration [for the defendant] in criminal prose-

---

* This was particularly the case on the issue of summary judgments, as illustrated by the 1946–47 litigation in *Arnstein v. Porter*, 154 F.2d 464 (1946). Clark strongly favored enhancing the power of judges to award a summary judgment rather than submitting the case to a jury. Frank was no lover of juries, but distrusted judges even more. Moreover, he, like most liberal judges (such as Justices Hugo Black and William Douglas), feared that broad power to grant summary judgments would ultimately hurt underdogs bringing lawsuits—e.g., railroad employees and seamen—and Hand sided with Frank on this issue. (*Arnstein* was a colorful case involving Cole Porter's alleged plagiarism in some of his most famous songs.)

cutions," particularly when "the guilt of the accused [is] clear."[125] Hand himself was not strictly anti-defendant. On the question of excluding evidence seized in violation of the Fourth Amendment's guarantee against unreasonable searches and seizures, for example, he was committed to penalizing misconduct by law-enforcement officials and often sided with the defendant, but he was not one to search for procedural errors, particularly when they did not rise to constitutional dimensions. Frank, by contrast, was ahead of his time in adopting what became the approach of the Supreme Court majority in the 1960s: a strict enforcement of the protections of criminal defendants, accompanied by a great reluctance to view any trial error as "harmless."[126] His solicitude for criminal defendants' claims was the source of recurrent dispute between Frank and all the other judges.

The harmless-error doctrine—the principle under which it was maintained that not every trial that contained an error should lead to a reversal of the conviction on appeal, and that required instead that the defendant show that the trial error had actually affected the outcome—became of vastly diminishing significance on the Supreme Court during the Warren years. (One major indication of the Supreme Court's change of direction beginning in the 1970s was its revived resort to affirmances resting on the conclusion that the error at trial was harmless.) But from 1943 on, Frank was reluctant to consider any trial error as "harmless." In *United States v. Liss*, Hand, for the majority, insisted that "a remote chance of prejudice should not balance the extreme probability that the jury came to the right result."[127] Frank strongly disagreed.

In his views on the harmless-error rule, Frank stood alone on the court, and disputes over this issue generated yet another round of sharp personality clashes between him and Clark. In 1945, for example, Clark complained to Hand that "Jerry has been down lobbying with the Supreme Court law clerks against what he likes to term the dreadful 'Second Circuit rule' of harmless error." (Hand unsuccessfully tried to defuse this squabble.) And Clark repeatedly complained that Frank was using his course at Yale as a forum for venting his disagreements with his colleagues on the Second Circuit. The issue came to a head in early 1946, in *United States v. Antonelli Fireworks Co.*, decided by a panel consisting of Learned Hand, Clark, and Frank. The defendants had been convicted of conspiring to defraud the government by producing defective munitions. The major ground for the appeal was the prosecutor's summation of the case, in which he appealed to the patriotism generated by World War II. The trial judge had instructed the jury to disregard the prosecutor's remarks, because "[w]e would do our government a disservice if we allowed the hysteria of war to usurp the place of calm deliberation in deciding this case, and we would do these defendants a great injustice," but he did not declare a mistrial. Clark wrote the majority opinion affirming these convictions; joined by Hand, he found that the passing references to patriotic sentiment at the end of a long prosecutorial statement were "harmless error," that there was "no reasonable ground for attributing such emotional irresponsibility to this jury."[128]

Frank's scathing dissent insisted that the prosecutor's remarks were wrong and inevitably prejudicial. However weak the data on the impact on the defendants might be, he argued, the court should reverse the conviction in order to deter future prosecutorial misconduct. He sharply criticized the affirmance of convictions "merely because the judges of this court believe those defendants guilty. If [this court] does so, it is, I think, helping to undermine a basic tenet of the American faith. . . . Perhaps my sense of humor has indeed deserted me, and I indulge in exaggeration; but I think not."[129]

Clark, hurt and angered by Frank's tone, exchanged vehement letters with Frank for weeks. Clark never forgave Frank for this dissent, harping on it even after Frank's death more than a decade later. Hand could not avoid involvement in the extended crossfire. Frank flooded him with copies of the correspondence, including Clark's remark that Frank had made "violent, unrestrained personal attacks upon the individual members of this court."[130] Frank also sent Hand a series of letters from his former law clerks, now clerking for the Supreme Court, trying to demonstrate that his lunches with them while visiting Washington did not constitute improper lobbying, as Clark had alleged.[131] He apologized for any affront he might have caused Hand by his dissent in *Antonelli*—"you know my profound admiration for you both as a man and judge"—but he complained that Clark kept spreading rumors that the other judges, including Hand, shared his view that Frank was exceedingly difficult to get along with, and he was deeply worried about the suggestion that if Hand indeed viewed him as a "disturber of the judicial peace," Hand might be tempted to resign from the bench.

Hand, vacationing in Cornish, felt compelled to respond to this barrage of materials from Frank. In a letter of August 9, 1946, he told Frank he was sorry the issue had not been raised when they had been together just a week earlier, "for I am sure that in such matters five minutes of talk is better than reams of correspondence." Once again, Hand tried to reassure his colleague:

> I can only say, to answer categorically, that I have never found you in the least difficult to get along with, or obstinate in your

opinions, or uncooperative, or unwilling to accept suggestions. On the other hand, I get a stimulus from you, not only in our work, but in our talk.

Yet Hand conceded that he had been upset by Frank's *Antonelli* dissent:

Yes, I was annoyed by the Antonelli dissent, which seemed to me to castigate us for our deliberate perversity. I did not say so to you, because, as I have told you, I feel very strongly that, when a man is writing for himself, he should be absolutely free to say his mind without let or hindrance. Not only is that a part of his own liberty, but it is a condition upon his fellows' freedom from any shadow of responsibility for what he may say, without which they cannot wholly disown it, as they should be able to do. . . . As for Antonelli, forget it; I have long since cashed it in.[132]

AFTER THE UNITED STATES at last entered World War II in December 1941, Hand followed the ups and downs of the nation's battle with the Axis powers with deep interest and recurrent anxiety. As during World War I, he felt a "fatuous sense of futility at sitting about doing crossword puzzles," as he wrote to his former law clerk Louis Henkin, while others made sacrifices for truly important goals.[133] With the judges' workload declining in the early war years,[134] Hand felt especially relegated to a marginal position: he turned seventy in January 1942, and he did not even seek opportunities to serve in government, as he had done so eagerly during World War I.

Throughout the 1930s, Hand had advocated American aid to the countries battling the totalitarian powers, and he had criticized America's powerful isolationist forces. The Pearl Harbor attack was in one sense a blessing, he argued to Bernard Berenson: the Japanese decision to wage war against the United States, quickly followed by declarations of war from the Hitler and Mussolini regimes, "did us a good turn, for if they had not, it seems to me quite possible that we might have let Europe go hang." Even after Congress declared war, Hand at first feared that American sentiment would press the war against Japan and ignore the war in Europe: "[I]n very influential groups, especially in the Mississippi Basin, the Nazi war had always been regarded as a British business, and the old hatred of Britain flared up as it always does in a crisis."[135]

During the early months of the war, when the Japanese seemed unstoppable in Asia and the German war machine continued to gobble up large parts of Europe, Hand felt gloomy about Allied progress. By

August 1942, just a few weeks before the Nazi army entered Stalingrad in what at first appeared to be another important Germany victory, he confronted the possibility that the Axis might indeed win the war. In rhetoric unusually strong for him, he told Felix Frankfurter that he yearned for some participation "in [this] effort to redeem the world. For really, that is what it is." Frankfurter was far more optimistic, thinking that the war would soon be won, but Hand could not endorse such a rosy view. A few weeks later he wrote:

> Well, nothing but your most incorrigible optimism . . . would give you the belief that we will be out of this horror in 1943. Maybe, of course. Possibly; but not with any probability. The fight has now become a death grapple into which [the European Axis] and their yellow friends will put all they have because they will be exterminated if they lose. . . . But it is good to have you voice your confidence.[136]

To Louis Henkin, Hand offered the small consolation that even if the Nazis won, "their empire would fall apart in their hands, for it has no rational basis; it does not admit of any statement, except in terms which are so untrue as to be preposterous, and, were it not for the terror of it, ridiculous." He tried hard to find some rays of hope: "In spite of the rather discouraging Russian campaign, and the U-boat successes, I can't help feeling that things are not so bleak as the faint-hearted keep saying. After all, [the Nazis] have got to do this job within ten or twelve weeks or they will never be able to do it. That is a large order."[137] Hand fervently hoped the Russians would be able to avoid collapse and told Henkin that "if they can keep 'an army in being' until the winter, I don't quite see how Adolph [sic] & Company are going to pull off the job."[138]

Hand's hopes came true. The Germans so overstretched their supply lines during their late-summer campaign that the Soviets were able to counterattack successfully. The remnants of the German divisions cut off at Stalingrad surrendered at the beginning of February 1943; Leningrad was relieved from its seventeen-month siege; and by the summer of 1943, the Soviet forces, armed with massive shipments of military supplies from the West, undertook a major campaign. Better news from the Eastern Front, as well as the first American successes in the Pacific and against the Nazis (after the successful landing in North Africa), caused American hopes to soar. By early 1943, Hand began to see signs of overconfidence in the United States, and he became increasingly worried about American complacency. All the reports of victories— the counteroffensive in the Soviet Union, the Allied bombings of Germany, the collapse of Mussolini—gave Americans "something more than we deserve of confidence," he wrote to Henkin. "And I rather fear that there is some disposition to think that the war is 'in the bag.' "[139] By December, he no longer thought it likely that the United States would lose the war, but he despaired at the decline in national unity and the "general breakdown of the common interest as against special interests":

> What curious nonsense it is that a society will take its young men for death and mutilation at low wages during their most productive time; and yet will not put the necessary pressure on the rest of us to do our very small part. . . . Of course, the chief reason here is that we have been so untouched by the war that we don't truly realize it. As [Undersecretary of War] Patterson said to me less than a year ago, a few bombings would do wonders for us.[140]

Yet even Hand could not deny that despite these domestic divisions, the American economy had achieved "fabulous" wonders in its war-production efforts, for which he gave much of the credit to his old colleague and friend Robert Patterson. As Hand reported to Bernard Berenson in January 1945, in the letter that resumed their war-interrupted correspondence:

> [T]his country of ours baffles me. . . . A more undisciplined, ill-accorded group it would be hard to find . . . ; a melange of all races, all traditions, all environments, swept together with a history of comfort, ease, and wealth, such as has never descended on this creature since he jumped down from the trees and began to use his thumbs. And what did we do? Really, the most stupendous performance that has ever been done on the Planet—I mean of its kind, of mass production. Make no mistake about that; we have done it; somewhere, somehow, suddenly, as though inspired by some apparition, we did unite, and this inexhaustible flood of ingenious contrivances began to appear in absolutely incredible profusion. . . . Somebody with a genius for organizing had to be there to keep everybody from stumbling over everybody else; and to supply the "assembly belts," so that the things rolled out of the factories with the spark plugs already snapping. There must be in some way a future for a society which can do that.

Such optimism was rare for Hand. Yet he also believed that the United States had had a quite narrow escape from a worse fate. And the greater casualties brought by the American landings in France on

D-day, June 6, 1944, and the invasion of Northern Europe had made Americans "a sober people, and a sad one." He continued:

> I do not see any evidence that our will has been blunted; but at times I feel glad that this, the real part of our ordeal, did not come until success was to all intents certain. Had we had to bear these losses, while the result was in the balance, and with a chance to stop with some kind of compromise, I am not so sure.[141]

PART OF HAND'S PREOCCUPATION with the war's progress stemmed from his strong personal empathy with the tribulations undergone by American soldiers. He often revealed a sense of regret, even guilt, for never having served in the armed forces, and became quite emotional over the difficulties confronting the soldiers he knew personally: his former law clerks and the sons and grandsons of his friends, whose courage and sense of duty he admired. In the darkest days of the war, for example, during the Christmas season of 1942, a fellow judge, Orie Phillips of the Tenth Circuit, included in his holiday note to Hand a remark on the "threat of darkness over the earth, with three despots undertaking to decree that there shall be no light"—a message that stirred Hand. In a lengthy reply, he alluded to "what those young men are going through, and the gay and grave spirit with which they have faced their deadly peril. . . . While we can breed such men we are safe"; he added, self-consciously, "I wish I could look back now on a past which contained such heroism as these men are showing; but, alas, how many of them will live through it?"[142]

Nowhere did Hand express these emotions more strongly than in his correspondence with former law clerks serving overseas. W. Graham Claytor, Jr., for example, Hand's law clerk in 1936–37, who became a naval officer nearly a year before Pearl Harbor, served on a number of ships in the Pacific and ultimately commanded a destroyer escort; like Hand's other clerks, he sent the judge blow-by-blow accounts of his exploits.[143] Hand devoured these letters as eagerly as he had once relished the sea stories of Richard Hallet, his law clerk during his early district court years, who had abandoned the law to seek adventure. Repeatedly, he reached out to encourage, console, and sympathize with his former clerks, but even as he tried to share their feelings, he recognized that he could not really know what it was like to be at the front.

Eventually, Hand allowed his sense of frustration to alter his usual behavior. While since the end of World War I he had tried to avoid public participation in "heated issues," he now came to be quite active in various organizations. He had maintained only a pro forma affiliation with the Council on Foreign Relations during the 1920s and 1930s, for example, but he once again became a regular member in 1939.[144] From 1940 through 1944, he attended council dinners eagerly and regularly, to hear foreign guests reporting on developments—the ex-premier of Belgium, Lord Halifax, the king of Greece, the American ambassador to Italy, the prime minister of Australia, and the Soviet Union's ambassador to the United States, Maksim Litvinov.[145]

Hand also devoted time and energy to organizations assisting particular nations that were victims or foes of the Axis.[146] Hand's public concern with the fate of Greece was especially notable. Perhaps spurred by his wife's affection for Hellenic culture, Hand repeatedly lent his name and voice to public appeals on behalf of beleaguered Greece, to which, after it was invaded by Italian troops in 1940, American supporters organized to assure adequate war relief. Hand was approached in April 1941 by the American Friends of Greece to endorse these war-relief activities, and he declined in accordance with his usual practice,[147] yet this aversion to public identification with potentially heated issues evaporated as soon as the United States entered the war. Within days of Pearl Harbor, he received an appeal from the American-Hellenic Student Committee for Medical Aid to Greece to write a formal statement for a volume of letters to be presented to the exiled king of Greece at a reception in New York. Hand promptly wrote a letter "to His Majesty, George the Second, King of the Greeks," advising the king that Americans had "faith that in the end the free peoples of the earth will maintain their freedom against those enemies who seek to enslave them."[148] Soon after, moreover, he became active in both the American Friends of Greece and the Greek War Relief Association. On March 25, 1943, for example, he addressed an audience at the American Friends' Greek Independence Day, sharing the platform with Wendell L. Willkie. A year later, the American Friends asked Hand to write an article about Greece and postwar reconstruction for their magazine, *Philhellene*. Hand carefully prepared a draft praising the Greek people for their "heroism," "constancy," and "martyrdom for the right," using the occasion to reflect on the desirable shape of the postwar world. A few days later, Hand revised it to amplify and clarify his theme, and this revision was printed in *Philhellene* under the title "The Debt of the World to Greece."[149]

Hand's emotional engagement in the war against the Axis prompted him to participate in activities far more controversial than those praising the courageous Greek people: early in the war he joined organizations sympathetic to the Soviet Union's battle against fascism—both Russian War Relief and the National Council of American-Soviet Friendship. He began supporting these organizations in 1942, at a time when he, like many Americans, "look[ed] anxiously to Russia" to help defeat the Nazi war machine.[150] Hand's enthusiastic support of the Soviet Union at a time when it seemed the only obstacle to a speedy Nazi victory later proved controversial when World War II ended and the Cold War began.

As early as April 1942, Hand responded generously to Russian War Relief's appeal for contributions to buy medical supplies, food, and clothing.[151] Then, at the instigation of the Wall Street lawyer Allen Wardwell, he attended a dinner on May 7, 1942, for the former American ambassador to the Soviet Union, Joseph Davies; Russian War Relief promptly thanked him for his attendance. Hand spoke on behalf of the organization at two other major dinners, and only when he was asked to chair the speakers bureau of Russian War Relief—evidently in order to take advantage of his prestigious name—did he draw the line. "I don't want to identify myself too much with public movements," he said belatedly.[152]

Hand's involvement with the National Council of American-Soviet Friendship became an even greater source of discomfort. Hand had permitted his name to be listed as a sponsor of the council in late October 1942, even as the German armies advanced upon Stalingrad,[153] and his name remained on the letterhead into late 1946. The sponsors—there were about one hundred of them—included many people from the liberal and left side of the political spectrum, including Thomas Mann and Albert Einstein; three lines down from Hand's in the alphabetical listing appeared the name of playwright Lillian Hellman. Hand was the only judge on the list.[154] (He would resign from the council in October 1946, by which time the press was alleging that the council, which had supported former vice president Henry Wallace's attacks on postwar American policy toward the U.S.S.R., was excessively pro-Soviet. By then, Hand thought it was time to return to his prewar abstention from "heated issues.")[155]

Hand served only one very brief tour of duty in an official position directly related to the war effort: he spent the last few weeks of 1943 in Washington as chairman of the Advisory Board on Just Compensation, a body established by President Roosevelt to draft guidelines for the War Shipping Administration, which had requisitioned for wartime use virtually all privately owned ships in the American merchant marine and which would soon confront the shipowners' claims for just compensation for their seized property.[156] The board's task was to digest mountains of empirical and legal data in order to develop fair standards for valuing the ships. While, as Hand told the staff director of the board at the end of his labors, "my heart [did] not as deeply bleed for [the shipowners] as perhaps my colleagues' did,"[157] he performed his task dutifully. It was "an important job,"[158] Hand thought—the least he could do while younger men were sacrificing so much more year after wartime year. When Roosevelt thanked Hand for his contribution, Hand's acknowledgment expressed the attitude with which he had taken the job: "In times such as these, such services are so trifling, compared with all that is being done, that it scarcely seems right that they should be noticed. It was a privilege to be allowed to contribute."[159] (Hand had one more opportunity to serve in war-related matters, shortly after the war ended, when President Truman pressed him to serve as chairman of a new labor-management board to work out procedures for settling impending postwar disputes between unions and employers. After some hesitation, Hand declined.)[160]

THROUGHOUT THE WAR, Hand maintained an avid interest in domestic political developments. His internationalism led him to support Roosevelt's bid for a fourth term in 1944, as he had supported FDR's candidacy in the two preceding elections. And Hand feared not only the renewed isolationism that FDR's 1944 opponent, Thomas E. Dewey, seemed to symbolize,[161] but also the wartime tendency to encroach on freedom of expression and association—a tendency later institutionalized in the McCarthy era.

In the spring of 1943, a witch-hunt launched by the House Un-American Activities Committee prompted Hand to speak out on a heated political issue in the name of civil liberties. Ever since the late 1930s, the committee (known as "the Dies Committee" after its chairman, the Texas Democrat Martin Dies) had engaged in a crusade against "subversive" activities. In February 1943, Dies, in a long floor speech, claimed that thirty-nine government employees were "irresponsible, unrepresentative, crack-pot, radical bureaucrats" and affiliates of "Communist front organizations." Dies urged that Congress refuse to appropriate money for the salaries of these "subversives." Ultimately, the House adopted a resolution authorizing its Appropriations Committee, acting through a special subcommittee, to investigate these charges. The subcommittee, headed by Representative John H. Kerr, quickly commenced hearings, in secret executive sessions, and soon concluded that three named individuals, including one Robert Morss Lovett, had indeed engaged in "subversive activity."

Lovett, Hand's contemporary at Harvard College, had after decades as a professor of English literature at the University of Chicago joined the federal government as secretary to the governor of the Virgin Islands.[162] Hand's friend Ned Burling, an admirer of Lovett, urged acquaintances to send protest letters to Congressman Kerr while the subcommittee was holding its secret hearings. Hand, despite his special reluctance to speak out on issues that might reach the courts (as Lovett's case ultimately did), promptly complied. On April 19, 1943, he wrote Kerr, in a letter very similar in tenor to one he had sent during World War I to defend the sale of *The Masses* on New York's subway newsstands:

> I have heard that a sub-committee of which you are Chairman has been asked to discontinue the appropriation for the salary of Robert Morss Lovett as secretary to the Governor of the Virgin Islands, and I am writing in the hope that I may be able to contribute to persuading the sub-committee not to do so. I have known Lovett for over fifty years, first as a college acquaintance and later as a friend, with increasing affection and esteem. I know no one whose life has been more selflessly devoted to the cause of justice and the relief of distress; his courage and devotion have been proof against unpopularity, and risk to his position as a teacher. He has never flinched from standing openly for those things which have aroused his pity and offended his sense of fair play. It is quite true that at times I have differed from him very markedly; his opinions are by no means the same as mine; but it is altogether mistaken to suppose that he has ever fostered subversive activities or that he believes in them.
>
> I should indeed be happy to feel that I could look back upon a life so consistently, so generously and so unremittingly devoted to the welfare of my fellows; it would seem to me a shocking end to a life so spent, now to deprive him of a position in which I am absolutely persuaded he is able to do, and is doing, much to help a small group of people who on any showing are in need of understanding and assistance.[163]

But this was moderate rhetoric masking his deep outrage. Four days later he wrote to Felix Frankfurter: "Are they really going to lynch Bob Lovett? Ned says it is not exactly the Dies Committee but a peculiarly savage witch-hunter named Matthews, an ex-Communist with the holy zeal of the Holy Office. Why must there be so many bastards born in wedlock?"[164]

Neither Hand nor Lovett's other supporters could stem the anti-subversion tide in the House. The House Appropriations Committee rejected a "strong appeal" from the secretary of the interior for permission to retain Lovett in his position. Instead, it reported that it could not "escape the conviction that this official is unfit to hold a position of trust with the Government, by reason of his membership, association, and affiliation with organizations whose aims and purposes are subversive to the Government of the United States."[165] Arguments on the House floor that a bar on Lovett's salary would be unconstitutional fell on deaf ears; instead, the House passed a rider to a major appropriations bill forbidding funds to be disbursed to three specified individuals, including Lovett, unless their names were resubmitted to the Senate and confirmed. The Senate, after first voting unanimously to reject the rider, ultimately yielded to the House. When FDR signed the bill, he stated, "The Senate yielded, as I have been forced to yield, to avoid delaying our conduct of the war. But I cannot so yield without placing on record my view that this provision is not only unwise and discriminatory, but unconstitutional."[166]

The appropriations rider barred payment for any service rendered after November 15, 1943. Lovett remained in the government's employ for some time after that date but received no pay for his work. He and the two other individuals named in the rider promptly filed suit in the Court of Claims for payment for their services. Their cases did not reach the Supreme Court until 1946; in the summer of that year, Justice Hugo Black's opinion for the Court held the rider to be a bill of attainder—an unconstitutional imposition of punishment by the legislature without a judicial trial. Hand's appeal to the House represented an unusually sharp break with his usual abstinence from public statements on controversial issues. Yet the pursuit of Lovett offended one of his most deeply held beliefs. During the war, there were only limited occasions to speak out on civil liberties. A few years later, Hand was to have far more occasions to defend civil liberties against anti-subversive hysteria.

DURING AND IMMEDIATELY after the war, there was much talk in the press and in Hand's circle about the arrangements needed to assure peace. The proposals ranged from the articulation and strengthening of principles of international law to the creation of a system of world government that could effectively curb the nationalistic impulses that had produced two world wars in thirty years. Hand rejected all such proposals. He thought the efforts to draft new "principles" would merely produce meaningless exhortations, and he viewed all schemes for world government as both utopian and dangerous. Such grandiose schemes promulgated impracticable goals, he believed, and would only cast the United States into revived isolationism—much as the refusal of "principled" internationalists such as Woodrow Wilson and Herbert Croly to compromise on the Treaty of Versailles had led it into the isolationism of the 1920s and 1930s. Only old-fashioned balance-of-power arrangements among the great nations, he insisted, would assure relative tranquillity in the world; and he doubted that even these could avert all new conflicts.

Even before Pearl Harbor, for example, Hand was notably cool to an inquiry from the Carnegie Endowment for International Peace about what international-law projects might be undertaken to prepare for postwar needs: "I do not see how anything can profitably be done while the present turmoil is on. . . . I am not everlastingly pessimistic about [international law]"; at some distant time, perhaps, nations would no longer be governed only by force, but that time, Hand suggested, did not lie immediately ahead.[167] And when near the end of 1944 James Shotwell, an international-relations scholar chairing the Commission to Study the Organization of the Peace, asked Hand to support a draft of an International Declaration of Human Rights, he declined:

> [S]o far as I can see, we are in grave danger of losing everything by aspiring to too much. We must not expect to create a newer and better world in which those things which are the subject of your proposal would indeed be taken as a matter of course. We shall have to be content with something very like "Power Politics," which has now become the Devil's alias. It would ordinarily not be a mistake to aim for more than you are likely to get; but in this instance it will, I believe, play exactly into the hands of those who wish to cut us off from the rest of mankind, just as the [Henry Cabot] Lodge crowd did twenty-five years ago.[168]

During the war, Hand repeatedly encountered advocates of new worldwide institutions, such as Supreme Court justice Owen J. Roberts and Clarence Streit, president of the United World Federalists. When in 1947 he was asked to comment on a proposed World Federalist Constitution, he declined because anything he said "would have to be discouraging, and not constructive." "Frankly," he added, "I cannot help believing that efforts of the kind are so far in advance of anything practicable that they make against the only steps which can help us in our appalling situation."[169] As he had written to an American Law Institute staff member just three weeks after Pearl Harbor:

I am not very sanguine that when we get out of this, if indeed we do, we shall do very much to make a better world. I suppose that it is bad to harbor such doubts, and certainly to express them, but I question whether there is much use at the present time in trying to prepare for the peace. Its terms will depend so much on the temper with which the democratic nations end the war, if they are successful; if they are not, nothing matters anyway. I wish I felt more certain that our nation, which has always been unwilling even to reduce its tariff barriers, could be made to feel more its dependence upon others.[170]

By 1944, Hand had told his ALI colleague George Wharton Pepper, "I am as much opposed as I gather that you are to any effort to form a society of nations which will include everybody and attempt to regulate all international relations." In another letter to Pepper a few days later, he added, "For an indefinite time, I know of no way by which we can keep the world from lapsing periodically into the shambles which it is now, except by an alliance of the powers strong enough to make their will felt."[171]

Hand was consistently hostile to ambitious international statements and organizations. A few days before V-E day, for example, an old acquaintance asked him to sign an "open letter" to the American delegation to the U.N. Conference on International Organization then meeting in San Francisco to establish the United Nations. The letter urged the delegates to strengthen a proposed U.N. police force and press for a Supreme Court of the United Nations. Hand refused to sign, since his views put him "in quite another school":

> The general expressions in the Atlantic Charter, while very well as aspirations, are not in my opinion fit to be incorporated as law, doctrine or rule, and should remain as ideals. I fear that, by proclaiming a benign desire for justice and a bill of rights, we shall think that we have helped perceptibly the promotion of peace. Quite to the contrary, I am inclined to believe that our best hope lies in as durable a combination of Great Powers as is possible.[172]

Hand had only one formal occasion during the war to express his doubts about the utility of international-law principles and world-government blueprints—his "The Debt of the World to Greece" essay for *Philhellene* in 1944.

> [W]e are too ready to suppose that we can find the solution, if only we bring good will to the search. We are flooded with vague concepts, like "sovereignty," "democracy," "rights of small na-

tions," "equality before the law," put forward as though they had
some definite content. The Greeks will not be so put off; complacent generalities, however well meant, will not serve.

Merely helping the Greeks to rebuild their country would not assure
them "what they really fought for." Small nations—Belgium, the
Netherlands, Denmark, Greece—would still be at the mercy of destructive weapons in the hands of greater powers:

> We shall have to devise altogether new concepts for what we mean
> by "independence" and "liberty" and "autonomy." The problems
> which we shall have to face will demand concrete thinking; our
> answers will inevitably repel and disgust visionaries, who are never
> content with less than the City of God, who will decry all com-
> promise as treason. . . . [The Greeks] ask of us, and they ask
> rightly, not some dream of a better world, some vision of Utopia,
> but a viable arrangement within which they can live and work
> with security. [173]

Hand was similarly out of step with many in his circle in vehemently
opposing the legitimacy of the Nuremberg war-crimes trials adjudicating
the case of Nazi leaders soon after the war. Hand's opposition to the
trials did not mean that he viewed the Nazi regime with any less
antipathy than he had for years. Rather, he recalled all too well the
effect of the Versailles treaty's draconian terms after World War I, and
he did not think an orderly postwar world could be built on excessively
harsh peace terms. In 1943, he wrote, "I cannot believe that an out-
and-out vindictive peace, a 'Carthaginian peace,' will in the end make
for an enduring peace." He could understand how the Soviet Union
would be moved "to hang the savages who massacred their comrades;
but I wonder whether at the last, that will serve to make Germans
more understanding and tend to cure them of their notion that force is
all." During the war, he rejected the widely held view reflected in the
Morgenthau Plan—the imposition of permanent disarmament on Germany and the gutting of its industrial capacity. As he wrote to Louis
Henkin:

> I do not believe that the nations now together will continue to
> keep [Germany] disarmed; and the temporary disarmament at the
> end of the last war only led to a greater frenzy of armament when
> the restraint was off. You know, at times I have wondered whether
> the wisest plan would not be merely to take away all their territorial
> gains and leave the Germans with nothing more to show for their
> suffering than their efforts and their wasted cities and the lost and

maimed young men. It would be harder for them to nurse a grievance out of that than if Hitler and Goebbels and Himmler and Goering were all hanged.

Vengeance by the European victims of Nazism, such as the Russians, Czechs, and Poles, Hand thought, was "natural and easily understood," but, he added, if "we're looking to a more tolerable society, to a world where men are not continually to kill, these retributions are not a good path towards it."[174]

For Hand, the charges against the Nazi leaders at the Nuremberg trials, including the charge of waging "aggressive war," were efforts to cloak vengeance in the robes of law. Very few Americans made similar arguments at the time. Judge John J. Parker of the Fourth Circuit, one of Hand's colleagues on the 1943 Advisory Board on Just Compensation, who served as a judge at some of the Nuremberg trials, pleaded with Hand to abandon his criticism, in the hope "that the genius who has supported so many worthy undertakings may not in this instance be employed to raise doubts with respect to what I regard as an important step in the establishment of world order based on law."[175] Hand was not moved. As he repeatedly made clear, vengeance was an understandable human emotion, but calling it "law" while trying to impose retroactive standards of decency on the Nazi leaders was unacceptable. Hand confessed to a strong bias against "the whole notion of 'aggressive war' as a crime,"[176] and even as late as 1948 he said that "nothing could be further from my liking than the Nuremberg trials."[177] He described as "apt" an acquaintance's view of the trials: "Nobody would have complained if the leading Nazis had been shot when captured. The difference between vengeance and justice is that justice must apply to all."[178]

UNTIL THE FINAL YEAR of World War II, Hand, despite his thirty-five years on the federal bench, was not a widely known public figure: most Americans had never heard of the judge with the unusual name. Not until one Sunday afternoon in May 1944 did Hand utter words that would catapult him into popular fame. On May 21, 1944, Hand was one of the speakers at the annual "I Am an American Day" ceremony in New York City's Central Park, where 150,000 newly naturalized citizens were to swear their oaths of allegiance. He had been asked to make a few remarks and then lead the assemblage in the Pledge of Allegiance. Hand had always dreaded extemporaneous speaking, and in this instance as usual he spent some time writing out his talk ahead of time. His brief speech, little noticed at the time of the gathering, proved to be long remembered. More than any other statement he ever made, this address spread his reputation far beyond the legal profession and assured him nationwide fame.

The speech was heard by the largest audience ever gathered in New York City. (In addition to the 150,000 new citizens, more than a million others, no doubt attracted by the mild, sunny summer weather and by the promise of Broadway entertainment, heard the proceedings over loudspeakers scattered throughout the park.) Under "an almost cloudless blue sky," nearly one and a half million people attended the ceremony. Patriotism was at its zenith. The fortunes of the war had clearly turned in the Allies' favor, and anticipation of an impending invasion of Nazi-held Northern Europe was in the air. New York Mayor Fiorello La Guardia's welcoming remarks expressed the mood: "We are set for it. We are waiting. Nobody knows when it will come. But we have the utmost confidence in our commander. . . . Whenever it comes we will back those men and give them everything we've got."[179] A little more than two weeks later, on D-day, June 6, the invasion began.

The crowd that heard Hand's words must have been fatigued by the time he rose to speak, well after four o'clock in the afternoon. The first members of the gathering throng, many bringing picnic lunches, had begun to fill the park at ten-thirty in the morning. The program began at two-thirty, with occasional relief from the extensive speech-making supplied by the music of three bands and performances by the casts of several Broadway musicals, from *Carmen Jones* to *Oklahoma!* New York's New Deal senator, Robert F. Wagner, delivered the longest speech, outlining a program of "American ideals" that should guide the nation after victory. Remarks by a number of city officials and by clergymen of three major faiths added to the festive occasion.[180]

Of all the speeches that afternoon, Hand's was the briefest. In little more than five hundred words, he reminded the audience that all Americans were immigrants or descendants of immigrants, that all arrived on American shores in search of "liberty." He then posed his central question: "What do we mean when we say that first of all we seek liberty?" Courts, laws, and constitutions could not be the primary protectors of freedom: "[B]elieve me, these are false hopes. Liberty lies in the hearts of men and women; when it dies there, no constitution, no law, no court can save it; no constitution, no law, no court can even do much to help it."[181]

Liberty, he insisted, was not "the ruthless, the unbridled will"; it was not "freedom to do as one likes. That is the denial of liberty, and leads straight to its overthrow. A society in which men recognize no check upon their freedom soon becomes a society where freedom is the possession of only a savage few; as we have learned to our sorrow." Against that background, Hand uttered the most memorable words of his address, certainly the most widely quoted he ever spoke:

> What then is the spirit of liberty? I cannot define it; I can only tell you my own faith. The spirit of liberty is *the spirit which is not too sure that it is right* [italics mine]; the spirit of liberty is the spirit which seeks to understand the minds of other men and women; the spirit of liberty is the spirit which weighs their interests alongside its own without bias; the spirit of liberty remembers that not even a sparrow falls to earth unheeded; the spirit of liberty is the spirit of Him who, near two thousand years ago, taught mankind that lesson it has never learned, but has never quite forgotten; that there may be a kingdom where the least shall be heard and considered side by side with the greatest.

And in that spirit, "the spirit of that America for which our young men are at this moment fighting and dying," he asked his audience to rise and join him in reciting the Pledge of Allegience.[182]

Hand's brief words garnered no immediate acclaim whatever. The front-page coverage of the occasion in the next day's *New York Times* quoted at length from Senator Wagner's speech and more briefly from the other addresses, but printed not a word of what Hand had said. Yet within a few weeks, Hand's remarks about "the spirit of liberty" were the subject of enormous publicity.

There would have been no public attention to Hand's speech had the Central Park ceremonies not been broadcast by New York City's municipal radio station, WNYC. Philip Hamburger, a staff member at *The New Yorker*, tuned his radio to WNYC that afternoon, hoping to find the classical music that was the staple of the station's programming. Instead, he heard the "I Am an American Day" ceremonies. He was deeply impressed by Hand's eloquence. Discovering the next morning that "not a newspaper in town quoted [the] remarks," as he reported later, he called Hand's chambers and went to the Foley Square Courthouse to borrow Hand's typescript of his speech and to speak briefly with the judge.

Hamburger was one of the writers of the "Talk of the Town" segment that begins each issue of *The New Yorker*. For the June 10, 1944, issue, he wrote a short, chatty essay, "Notes on Freedom," in which he reported on his brief talk with Hand and quoted some excerpts from the speech.[183]* While the readership of *The New Yorker* was a good deal larger than that of the law reviews and the court reports in which Hand's prose usually appeared, it did not by itself guarantee the enormous attention Hand's remarks ultimately received. Several weeks later, *The New York Times* made amends for its initial neglect by printing the speech in full in its Sunday magazine.[184] The next day, *Life* magazine also printed the full text, calling it "a new stone in the edifice of American oratory. It is not in the great Webster tradition, but in the greater, simpler tradition of Lincoln."[185] *Reader's Digest* quickly followed suit, assuring Hand an even larger audience.[186]

The surge of publicity was not yet at an end. More than two years later, Philip Hamburger wrote a splendid biographical profile of Hand that appeared as a feature article in *Life*'s November 4, 1946, issue. Prominently featured next to the title, "The Great Judge," and facing a full-page photo of Hand was a bold-faced paragraph entitled "The Spirit of Liberty," quoting Hand's definition.[187] Hand, who had so often scorned the capacity of modern mass culture to homogenize tastes, suddenly found himself a folk hero; he received far more mail about this single brief address than about any of his opinions or other speeches. He had written his address hastily, spurred by a sense of duty that stemmed from his ongoing participation, since 1941, in Mayor La Guardia's committee to celebrate "I Am an American Day," on which Hand had served through most of the war years—in large part because his son-in-law Newbold Morris, his daughter Constance's husband, served in the La Guardia administration as president of the city council.[188] Moreover, the Conference of Senior Circuit Judges had implemented an earlier congressional resolution by passing one of its own in September 1942, urging all federal judges to emphasize the importance of naturalization proceedings, which were seen as vital to furthering wartime patriotism.[189] Thus, when Hand was asked in 1944 to administer the Pledge of Allegiance, he did not feel free to turn down the invitation. Though he did not think that he was composing a memorable speech, and was puzzled and surprised by all the acclaim,

---

* Hamburger also reported that he was astonished to hear that Hand wrote out all his decisions and speeches in longhand, "frequently after hours of intensive struggle." The judge could not bear dictating, and so he agonized over his long yellow pads with pen in hand. "For me, writing *anything* is like having a baby," he told Hamburger. Hand also told Hamburger that while he admired orators when he was growing up in Albany, he had become disenchanted because too much modern oratory was not genuine. "Too many people have other people write their speeches," he said. "Why, just the other night I was sitting on the dais with the waxworks at some banquet and a fellow rose and made some intelligent introductory remarks. Then he reached into his pocket, pulled out a paper, and said 'I paid fifty dollars for this speech, so I had better deliver it.' *I* ducked out" (*The New Yorker*, 10 June 1944, 18–19).

he occasionally confessed that he actually enjoyed it. And as public acclaim for the address mounted, he found it increasingly difficult to insist that his remarks "did not seem to . . . have great quality."[190] Writing to his friend the drama critic John Mason Brown, Hand commented on the praise: "I suppose if I say that it seemed to me so extravagant as to be silly, it would only be put down to false modesty; so consider it unsaid."[191] A year later, in response to another enthusiastic letter from Brown, Hand confessed, "[Y]ou please me absurdly, in spite of your wild Bacchanalian madness." He could no longer deny the enormous public attention that Hamburger's efforts had brought him. He referred to himself as "[a]n old gent whom a pleasant chap from *The New Yorker* put on the front page and pushed into a publicity which, in accordance with the nature of that Beast, has rolled up into a snowball. Why not all draw a deep breath and relax?"[192]

Only a few of those who complimented Hand on his remarks had actually heard them in person. Among them was the secretary of the New York City Bar Association, who told him, "I felt . . . that we were listening to an address by you that perhaps will be as memorable as that called 'The Gettysburg Address,' "[193] a comparison that reverberated in ensuing years. The president of the Virginia State Bar Association also insisted, "For simplicity and beauty, [your speech] rivals Lincoln's Gettysburg Address."[194] An old acquaintance told Hand that she had first learned of the address when her cook came home from Central Park and told her "what [Hand] said to her (to *her!*) and how much it would always mean."[195] A particularly perceptive acquaintance hoped that Hand would truly accept and take satisfaction in the applause, because of its importance in Hand's "unending quest for validation."[196]

Hand, though never without misgivings, relished this applause. As he wrote to a friend, Harry King:

> [L]ike nearly everybody else, I adore applause and so I "lapped up" this. If a man says he doesn't, he lies. Still, I felt ashamed that I liked it so much. I suppose nobody who has any sense, when he gets into bed, pulls up the bedclothes, and thinks over his past life, does not feel a shudder at the recollection of the times when he has been a coward, or a liar, or a weakling, or an ass. So I feel, when people like you say what you [do], as though it was only by a streak of luck that folks have not found me out. But I am glad they never have, and if I can continue to play you along, I shall do it.[197]

Hand was especially touched by reports of how much his speech meant to servicemen, including a navy officer who carried a copy of the speech in his uniform and read it out loud to anyone who would listen until the magazine clipping fell apart.[198] But no one saw the irony of Hand's newfound fame more clearly than Louis Henkin. Writing to Hand from his post in France, Henkin reported that he had read Hand's remarks in both *Life* and in the *Reader's Digest* and that he was very impressed—"proud of the old boss, as if I had something to do with it."

> But what struck me, enough to say it aloud to some "Looey" up here, was the fact that here you are at near 73, gaining popular acclaim for a few hundred words you dashed off some evening when the deadline began to oppress you. And for 35 years you worked your work and lived your life as Judge Learned Hand, so that someone on the Court in Washington once told me I was working for "the greatest living Judge of the English speaking world." And to our great citizens of the Republic, Learned Hand was probably a character out of a New Amsterdam folk tale, or an old English description of a local village scribe! . . . But I'm still pleased.[199]

The strongly favorable response to Hand's Central Park speech was to some extent paradoxical. Hand, for decades an agnostic, delivered an address with notable religious overtones, including an invocation of Jesus Christ.[200] The speech was unusual, moreover, in its plea for equal respect for all members of the community, with its reference to "a kingdom where the least shall be heard and considered side by side with the greatest." But Hand's dominant theme was his claim that the spirit of liberty was skeptical. After all, his remarks were delivered in the midst of war, at a time when unquestioning loyalty to the cause was considered every American's duty. Yet here was a federal judge at an important patriotic ceremony admiring the "spirit which is not too sure that it is right." Even at a time when the survival of democracies was at issue, he adhered to his commitment to the doubting spirit. Skepticism and doubt are not fashionable traits in the midst of battle, but his forceful eloquence and praise of doubt even amid clamors for certainty struck a responsive chord with a large audience.

XIII

The Last Chance
for a Supreme Court Appointment:
The 1942 Vacancy

HAND'S FINAL OPPORTUNITY to attain a seat on the United States Supreme Court came in the fall of 1942, when he was nearly seventy-one. The nation was embroiled in a war whose outcome was still uncertain: the Japanese had encountered little opposition in expanding their hold on ever larger portions of the Pacific; the Axis war machine had driven the Western Allies from the European continent and was piercing into the Soviet Union, with Nazi troops reaching Stalingrad. The Allies, anxiously seeking omens of better fortunes to come, could cherish victories only rarely: the naval battle of Midway, the Marines' fight for Guadalcanal, the landing of Eisenhower's troops in North Africa.

The pervasive domestic impact of the war effort touched even the composition of the Supreme Court that fall, when at the beginning of October, President Roosevelt persuaded James F. Byrnes to resign from the Court in order to become director of the Office of Economic Stabilization.* By then, FDR, whose frustration over his inability to name even a single justice during his first term had helped to provoke his Court-packing plan in his second term, had had ample opportunity to assure a solidly New Deal Court: starting with his appointment of Alabama senator Hugo Black in 1937, he had placed seven new justices on the highest court: Stanley Reed, Felix Frankfurter, William Douglas, Frank Murphy, James Byrnes, and Robert Jackson, in addition to

---

* Byrnes was on the Supreme Court from June 1941 to October 3, 1942. He then held the post of director of the Office of Economic Stabilization for less than a year, becoming director of the Office of War Mobilization in May 1943, a position he held until 1945. Later, he was Truman's secretary of state (1945–47), and then governor of South Carolina (1951–55).

Hugo Black.[1] (Byrnes had been appointed in 1941 to replace the last, and most reactionary, of the anti–New Deal Old Guard, Justice McReynolds.)

With the new vacancy created by Byrnes's resignation, several friends of Hand, led by Felix Frankfurter and Charles C. Burlingham, launched a massive campaign to persuade President Roosevelt to name Hand to the Court. A few years earlier, such an effort would have been out of the question: the claim that judges over seventy were inadequate to their task had been FDR's main ground for pressing his Court-packing proposal. But five years after the Court-packing battle, Hand's supporters could hope that FDR would no longer be embarrassed to nominate a septuagenarian.

Felix Frankfurter was the originator, and a chief promoter, of the plan to have Hand named to the Court. The close ties between him and the president had survived his transformation into a justice in January 1939, and although Frankfurter tried to stay away from issues that might come before the Court, he continued to offer copious advice to the White House throughout the war years. Moreover, Frankfurter and Byrnes had formed a close relationship during their year on the Court together. Byrnes had become a justice in 1941 after a very active political life, including more than two decades as a member of the House and the Senate. Frankfurter had not expected much when Byrnes joined the Court: he had anticipated that Byrnes would show "practical-mindedness" but little judicial detachment; he was surprised to discover an "uncommon sagacity" and a "real judicial temper" in the South Carolina politician.[2] (That Byrnes tended to side with him on an increasingly divided Court no doubt helped.) And he knew, before any public announcement, that Byrnes would resign from the Court in order to join the administration. From his contacts with FDR, Frankfurter was well aware of the president's months-long efforts to press Congress for an economic-stabilization act to curb inflation and wartime profiteering. So he lost no time in launching his plan to assure Hand's elevation.

On September 30, three days before Byrnes's resignation from the Court became public, Frankfurter wrote two notes to the president. In the first, he applauded FDR's selection for the directorship of Byrnes, his "most congenial pal"; in the second, he revealed his mind, already in its characteristically engaged mode, focusing on maneuvers regarding a successor to Byrnes on the Court. "Naturally," he wrote, "Jim [Byrnes] and I talked about the effect of his going [off] the Court. He and I agree, I believe, that you again have a chance to do something for Court and Country comparable to what you did when you made

Stone the Chief Justice [in 1941]. And I have good reason for believing that Stone would agree with the notion that Jim and I have on this matter."[3]

Frankfurter quickly unleashed his enormous reserves of energy to organize a campaign to persuade the president to select Hand. For the next month, he worked mainly behind the scenes, rousing potential supporters. He recruited C. C. Burlingham as his leading ally. In 1942, Burlingham was eighty-four years old, but his mental agility and his delight in pulling wires behind the scenes remained undiminished. He had demonstrated his continuing vitality in forging the Fusion coalition that brought New York City's mayoralty to Fiorello La Guardia in 1934; now he quickly helped to compile lists of influential people who might help persuade FDR.

The campaign reached its peak with a barrage of letters to the president in November. Frankfurter, who talked to Roosevelt face-to-face and on the telephone a half dozen times about Hand, wrote on November 3, a day after one of their conversations:

> Especially on the score of politics, L. Hand is the only lad who will create no headaches for you—or, if you will, break no eggs. He is *the* one choice who will arouse universal acclaim in the press. . . . *His* youth—*his* non-hardening of the social and modern veins, is established. By virtue of his work he has, as it were, been on this Court for years. This will only make it known [to] all men. . . . I never was more sure of anything—as a matter of *Politics.*

In a postscript, Frankfurter sought to reassure the president that Hand's age should not stand in the way: "Third term [of FDR's presidency], Bernie [Baruch] at 72, Leahy at his age [Fleet Admiral William D. Leahy, FDR's military chief of staff, was sixty-seven], Jimmie [Byrnes] taken off Bench—all more extraordinary than the Hand business."[4]

Three days later, Burlingham put in his oar:

> Dear Franklin:
> Let me suggest for the Supreme Court the one man who would be acclaimed by the entire Bar as Cardozo was when President Hoover appointed him. LEARNED HAND.

He conceded that Hand was past seventy, and that he was from New York, which already had two justices on the Court. "But," he insisted, "he is an ox for work, and he is far and away the best judge on any Circuit Court of Appeals, learned as his name, liberal, wise." He reminded the president of Hand's distinguished career, including his just missing the Court in 1930: "(You know the story of Hoover and Joe Cotton.)" Burlingham proceeded to spell out the reasons, and added that there was special "political and poetical justice in promoting Hand; he will fit into the Court instanter without apprenticeship, continuing the work he has done so grandly for 33 years." He concluded: "You are on top of the World and can do anything. . . . As I began, so I end. Hand would be as good and as well received as Cardozo was and would add as much weight to the Court as he did."[5]

A week later, Augustus Hand added weighty, moving words. Learned's cousin had been privy to the maneuverings from the start: a month earlier, he had told Learned he was convinced there was a serious possibility that Learned might get to the Supreme Court after all.[6] And Gus—like C.C.B., but unlike Learned—could write to the president as a lifelong Democrat. This was a rare opportunity for the usually reticent Gus to voice his affection and enormous regard for his cousin—who, he told FDR, was "more like a younger brother"; being "the only men of our generation in the clan," they were "much more together than brothers generally are." On the basis of their intimate friendship over decades—"playmates in our boyhood," "daily associates on the U.S. Court for the past twenty-five years"—Gus could justly claim that he knew Learned "more thoroughly than anyone else."

Like Frankfurter and Burlingham, Gus Hand wrote in order to overcome presumed resistance from a president who did not know Learned well. And so he testified to Learned's "inquiring mind that would put Socrates to shame" and also to, "what is more important, [his] imagination [and] human qualities that enable him to understand current movements, to view them sympathetically and to adapt his outlook to a changing world. Indeed, I have long called him 'Heraclitus' because he really feels the truth of the old philosopher's maxim: 'Nothing is, everything becomes.' "[7]

Gus's three-page letter noted the attention given to Learned's opinions, justly renowned not only for their reasoning and style but also "because they have shown a rare capacity to treat subjects before him with imagination and understanding." No judge then sitting had "a larger academic following"; his appointment "would bring the same kind of popular acclaim that came when Cardozo's name was sent to the Senate." And, concerned about FDR's possible reservations about Learned's political credentials, he added words of praise for "his liberal outlook" and emphasized that he had been "one of the very earliest prophets, indeed, long before he was on the bench," of the modern constitutional position that opposed judicial obstacles to legislative reforms such as the early New Deal had encountered. Augustus Hand concluded with a special appeal:

> His vigor and alertness have not diminished and his talents are truly of the first order. . . . Now you may say L.H. is too old, but you would not be selecting a man with any known weakness and would be obtaining one who is perfectly trained for the position by long experience, rare general culture and philosophical depth.[8]

After this initial barrage, Frankfurter and Burlingham worked feverishly to generate additional pressure on the president. One of their main targets was Chief Justice Stone. Though Frankfurter had confidently assured FDR that Stone would agree with the selection of Hand, he was actually not so sure: increasingly alienated from Stone because of the many decisions on which the two disagreed, Frankfurter told Burlingham that he thought the New Hampshire "Farmer" was "timid," too unwilling to state his convictions forthrightly. Burlingham, long an admirer of Stone, disagreed: he thought it was merely "etiquette that restrains him," not to mention his being a Republican.[9] Stone was indeed reluctant to volunteer his views, but he spoke favorably about Hand in response to an official request from the administration. The chief justice told Burlingham, "I stated very emphatically my view that the appointment . . . would greatly strengthen the Court and that I should be made very happy by it."[10] This strong support fell short of praising Hand as uniquely qualified, and Stone sounded a warning: "I suspect . . . that the age question stands in the way."[11]

The promoters of the Hand candidacy turned next to Attorney General Francis Biddle. Frankfurter's relations with Biddle were somewhat strained, but Burlingham had no inhibition about giving the attorney general his characteristically curt, forceful advice: "To appoint a man of 70 may seem inconsistent with F.D.R.'s position in '37 on aged judges; but L.H. is an exception. . . . As for consistency *vide* Emerson's Self-Reliance [as] that hobgoblin of little minds."[12] A few days later, the indefatigable Burlingham wrote the president a second letter, to assure him that support for Hand was widespread and to defuse the nagging age issue. "Man after man has spoken to me pro L.H.," he reported; that Hand was seventy should not stand in the way: "The grand Climacteric of the Romans was 63 (9 × 7). The survivors are tough. And this is especially true of judges, who usually lead regular and cloistered lives." And as Burlingham had told Biddle three days earlier, he now advised the president:

Consistency [is] "that hobgoblin of little minds." In '37 you conceded that there were exceptions. L.H. is one. His appointment would be an outstanding confirmation of your own open-mindedness. H's mental arteries are as normal and free as yours.[13]

FDR's first responses were not encouraging. To Burlingham, he wrote merely a noncommittal, amused reply: "Thank God . . . that you were never a judge! There never would have been a C.C.B. if you had ever led a regular or cloistered life."[14] A letter to Gus Hand was more ominous: with humor yet also with an unmistakably serious undercurrent, the president expressed the wish "that as a member of the family [Gus] might alter in the records the date of B.'s birth."[15] The president's reluctance was not sufficient to still C.C.B.'s voice: Burlingham wrote several more letters to FDR to press the case for Hand. Early in December, for example, he teased the president about the suggestion that Gus alter Learned's birth record: "I doubt whether Gus would say to you, as he says to me, that as a Senior Warden [of an Episcopal church] he is shocked that any Senior Warden should suggest to him that he commit a crime by changing a birth record. I am a warden too, and as one warden to another, I say no crime is needed." Hand was about to go to Washington to speak at the Supreme Court's memorial session for Louis Brandeis; if the president could only "by hook or by crook, see him" there, Burlingham assured FDR, he "wouldn't hesitate a second—you'd appoint him on his face, which is the very embodiment of a JUDGE, worthy of the best of the British bench or even of Gilbert & Sullivan."[16]

Soon after Burlingham sent this plea, Frankfurter submitted his own last appeal to FDR:

> Knowledge of what greatness has done for Court and Country—and surely Holmes, Brandeis and Cardozo were the only truly great judges here since the Civil War—makes me covet for you that you give to the history of your presidency the only man worthy to rank with Holmes, Brandeis and Cardozo. Were you to name Learned Hand, five minutes after the news flashed to the country, all considerations of age, geography, and the like would be seen to have had no relevance. If only for a few years, Hand could not but bring distinction to the Court and new lustre to the President who made it possible.[17]

This was the last of Frankfurter's many oral and written pleas. But he preserved one more notable document pertaining to the Hand nomination. He drafted a public statement for FDR, announcing Hand's designation to the Supreme Court:

> I have nominated Learned Hand, the Senior Circuit Judge of the Circuit Court of Appeals for the Second Circuit, as an Associate Justice of the Supreme Court in succession to James F. Byrnes.
>
> In time of national emergency when each must serve where he can be most useful, it is fitting that in replacing a member of the Court who has been drafted into the war effort, considerations of age and geography—which in normal days might well be controlling—should yield to the paramount considerations of national need.
>
> Judge Learned Hand enjoys a place of pre-eminence in our federal judiciary. His long experience as a judge, his deep knowledge of all phases of law, especially of federal law, makes him uniquely qualified for the Supreme Bench. His choice at this time is clearly indicated. He will bring to the Court a youthful vigor of mind and a tested understanding of the national needs within the general framework of the Constitution.[18]

According to the editor of the Roosevelt-Frankfurter correspondence, who spent many hours with the justice in his last years, Frankfurter prepared this announcement with the president's approval.[19] Frankfurter, ever optimistic—often excessively so—no doubt believed he was acting on FDR's authority, but his high hopes were soon dashed: the next day, the president replied in a note marked *"Private"*:

> The words "prayerful consideration" rarely mean what they say. In the present they do. In the same way "the exception proves the rule"—but one of the requisites for the exception is the very important element of timing.
>
> Sometimes a fellow gets stopped by his own words and his own deeds—and it is no fun for the fellow himself when that happens.[20]

By which he meant his own 1937 Court-packing plan, in which he had opposed septuagenarians. The message was clear: his reluctance to go forward with Hand's nomination pained him, but the age issue seemed insurmountable.

With receipt of this note, Frankfurter abandoned his efforts on behalf of Hand. The country would suffer from what had been, in his view, "the most foolish part of the whole Court fight," the age issue:

F.D.R. now well knows this to be so, and he should have known at the time, for the most liberal judges on the Court had been Holmes, although ninety, and Brandeis, although past eighty. But F.D.R., as he told one or two people, felt he could not get over his attitude in 1937 as to age and the use that would be made of it by his critics. I have no doubt that was an error of judgment on his part, for even though some wag might have poked a little fun at him, the acclaim that would have greeted Learned Hand's appointment would have drowned the fun-poking. In any event, to have a man of Learned Hand's stature on the Court would have been worth the price of a little fun.[21]

Burlingham was not inclined to give up so quickly. "It was right that you should succumb with quiet dignity," he wrote Frankfurter, "but I insisted on dying hard."[22] Even C.C.B.'s hopes waned when he heard "gossip" that Wiley Blount Rutledge, Jr., of Iowa was to be named, yet he refused to believe that all chance was lost: "I am strongly opposed to Old Age—more so every day in every way," said the eighty-four-year-old Burlingham; but age was more a matter of psychology than chronology, and Hand did not seem too old to him. Burlingham had never heard of Rutledge; on checking, he found that he was a former law professor and a current dean, and erupted at Frankfurter: "Well, without offense may I suggest that the Court doesn't need another Professor. You & Dean Stone & Professor W.O.D. [William O. Douglas] are enough." Eleven days later, Burlingham added, "I think it would be a public calamity to have another professor on your Court unless he was seasoned by experience."[23] On the day before Christmas, Burlingham accordingly sent his last plea to the president, and he took up the same theme about law professors: "Their weakness is that they have never had to come up against reality. They can think and say one thing this term and the contrary the next term or the next week. They are freed from responsibility for the consequences of their preachments. In a Trial Court they go to school and learn to be judges; on an Appellate Court they are a real danger."[24]

On January 11, 1943, the White House announced that Wiley Rutledge of Iowa was the president's choice.[25] Rutledge was twenty-two years younger than Hand, only forty-eight years old in 1943. Most of his career had been spent on law faculties; Roosevelt had named him to the Court of Appeals for the District of Columbia in 1939, and this experience satisfied the demands that FDR appoint someone with experience on the bench. But the age issue was a chimera: Justice Rutledge served for only six years and died in 1949, when Hand was still an active judge on the Second Circuit, as he remained until his death, twelve years after Rutledge's.

For the rest of their lives, both Frankfurter and Burlingham were convinced that Hand was not named to the Supreme Court in 1942 solely because of Roosevelt's preoccupation with the age issue and the constraints imposed by the hobgoblin of consistency. But Roosevelt repeatedly left his acquaintances uncertain, and at times misled, about his plans and motivations: among his great political skills was his ability to keep his own counsel after hearing a range of views and ultimately to go his own way; Frankfurter was certainly not the only one who believed that his desired end was about to be embraced by the president, only to see the prize withdrawn at the last moment. In fact, there were other, unstated grounds for the president not to choose Hand.

One probable reason was the very persistence of Frankfurter's campaign. Attorney General Biddle, who never became a forceful advocate for Hand, was an intimate observer of the maneuverings over the vacancy, and he claimed in later years that Frankfurter's zeal had been more of an obstacle than an aid. As Hand himself recalled in his eighties, Biddle had told him, "If Felix hadn't pushed, pushed, pushed, you'd have had a better chance—if he hadn't been so importunate." And Hand added, "[T]hat's true. That's one of Felix's faults."[26] True, Biddle's report to Hand was not made until nearly a decade after the events, for he did not come to know the "wise and witty" judge until 1951, when he and Hand were fellow shipboard passengers on a trip back from Italy. And what Biddle told Hand then was probably no more than old Washington gossip: as he wrote in his 1962 autobiography, "I heard *later* [italics mine] that [FDR] resented what he called the 'organized pressure' in Hand's behalf."[27]

This surmise is substantiated by the autobiography of Justice William O. Douglas. More than thirty years after the event, Douglas related that he frequently played poker with the president at the time of the Hand campaign. At one poker party in January 1943, FDR teased Douglas about the prevalent curiosity regarding Justice Byrnes's successor. Douglas finally asked the president who was "not going to be appointed," and Roosevelt, throwing back his head and laughing, answered, "Learned Hand is *not* going to be appointed." Douglas claims that he told FDR that he was "passing by a fine man." But the president replied, "Perhaps so. But this time Felix overplayed his hand. . . . Do you know how many people asked me today to name Learned Hand?" Answering his own question, he went on: "Twenty, and every one a messenger from Felix Frankfurter." Douglas concludes: "Pausing for another second, he thrust out his jaw and added, 'and by golly, I won't do it.' "[28]

This tale is somewhat suspect. By the time Douglas wrote, he looked back across years of service with Frankfurter on the Court marked by a mounting, increasingly intense animosity. Casting clouds on Frankfurter's reputation must have had special appeal. Moreover, the date Douglas gives is questionable: he reports that the poker-party exchange took place just a few days before Rutledge's nomination: yet by then, Frankfurter had long since abandoned his campaign, and it is highly unlikely that "twenty" messengers from Frankfurter pleaded with the president that day. More probably, Douglas recalled some Roosevelt annoyance over Frankfurter's tendency not to know when to stop pressing whatever his current cause might be—a tendency that Hand himself had observed repeatedly, on the Sacco-Vanzetti issue and others.

The more significant meaning of Hand's rejection lies in political-philosophical factors stemming from the internal dynamics of the 1942 Supreme Court. The New Deal appointees were increasingly divided; Frankfurter increasingly found himself in a minority; Hand's appointment would have given another vote to his side, just as the designation of Rutledge instead assured a strengthened opposition to it.

That there was a risk of political opposition to Hand was always clear to Frankfurter and Burlingham. Their correspondence reveals, for example, that they were eager to keep Hand's name from being mentioned prematurely, for fear of unleashing attacks by unspecified political opponents, for fear "if [Hand's name] leaks out, the wolves will be rampant," as Burlingham put it.[29] But what was the source of the potential hostility to Hand? In all likelihood, the failure to select Frankfurter's candidate in 1942 reflected not only impatience with Frankfurter's maneuvers but also disagreement with his conception of the role of the Supreme Court.

Frankfurter had come to the Court in January 1939, self-confident and renowned as an influential adviser to FDR, as an old acquaintance of most of his fellow New Deal justices, with a well-earned reputation as a leading scholar of constitutional and administrative law, an expert on the history and contemporary business of the Supreme Court. And he fully expected to be the Court's intellectual leader. At the outset, all seemed to go smoothly. Justices Black, Douglas, Reed, and Murphy all had warm relations with him and usually deferred to his views. But by 1942, Frankfurter's confidence was severely shaken; colleagues were turning into foes and he often found himself in a minority.

Frankfurter's role declined for both philosophical and personal reasons. The philosophical issue pertained to the proper function of the Supreme Court in protecting individual rights. Roosevelt had given little thought to personal-rights problems, and he was therefore surprised when his nominees split so sharply and quickly on these. His central concern had been to find justices who would end the Supreme Court's decades-long efforts to establish obstacles to legislative regulations of the economy—obstacles reflected in narrow interpretations of congressional powers and broad views of due-process restraints upon legislatures. He achieved this objective without any difficulty: beginning in 1937, the Court abandoned judicial intrusions into economic reforms; soon, rulings upholding the constitutionality of economic regulations were assured. But another kind of battle quickly erupted, concerning the Court's role in protecting civil liberties and civil rights: for example, should the Supreme Court be more active and interventionist when such rights as freedom of speech and religion rather than property interests were threatened?

This major constitutional battle had been foreshadowed as early as 1938, in a famous footnote by Justice Stone in the *Carolene Products* case.[30] In the course of rejecting a constitutional challenge to an economic regulation, Stone suggested that there might be a "narrower scope for operation of the presumption of constitutionality" when laws restricted the "political processes" or were "directed at particular religious . . . or racial minorities"—situations in which "prejudices against discrete and insular minorities" might "curtail the operation" of the political process.[31] The central issue soon became whether judicial restraint—broad deference to legislative resolutions of policy debates—should be the across-the-board position of the justices as to *all* types of laws, or whether there should be something of a double standard under which the justices would keep their hands off economic regulations and at the same time scrutinize more carefully those laws attacked as impinging on personal liberties.

All the New Deal justices agreed that the hands-off attitude was appropriate for economic laws, but they differed sharply about the proper approach to individual-rights cases. The Frankfurter wing insisted that a double standard was inappropriate: judicial deference to majority rule should govern even when the challenged law curtailed personal rights, not only when economic interests were threatened. The opposing side, led by Justices Black and Douglas, argued just as vehemently that a more activist, interventionist role for the Court was appropriate when personal rights sought protection. This battle over contending philosophies was at its peak in 1942, when the Byrnes vacancy arose. Most notably it was symbolized by cases in which schoolchildren belonging to the Jehovah's Witnesses sect challenged, on First Amendment grounds, local requirements that students salute the American flag in classroom exercises. The Jehovah's Witnesses claimed that the requirements violated their religious obligation of literal adherence to the Ten Commandments. The Court gave its first full consideration to this claim in 1940, in the *Gobitis* case,[32] where Frankfurter's draft opinion rejecting the Jehovah's Witnesses' attack was greeted with applause by most of his colleagues;[33] he spoke for eight of the nine justices in a ruling that supported the school board's right to determine "the appropriateness of various means to evoke that unifying sentiment without which there can ultimately be no liberties." "[P]ersonal freedom is best maintained," he explained, "when it is ingrained in a people's habits and not enforced against popular policy by the coercion of adjudicated law."[34] Only Justice Stone dissented: applying his *Carolene Products* suggestion, he concluded that he was "not prepared to say that the right of this small and helpless minority . . . is to be overborne by the interest of the state."[35]

Off the Court, criticisms of Frankfurter's *Gobitis* position were far more widespread. Many newspapers and most liberals condemned what they considered excessive judicial restraint, and soon, these attacks began to affect several members of the *Gobitis* majority. By the fall of 1940, Douglas had told Frankfurter that Black would no longer join the decision. Frankfurter asked, "Has Hugo been re-reading the Constitution during the summer?" And Douglas replied, "No—he has been reading the papers."[36] Within a year, by the 1941–42 Court term, the Court's "liberals"—Black, Douglas, and Murphy—were in increasing rebellion against Frankfurter's leadership. By June 1942, the three— Frankfurter came to refer to them as "the Axis"—had taken the occasion of another Jehovah's Witnesses case (not involving the flag salute) to make an extraordinary public statement that they had changed their minds about their votes in *Gobitis*: "[W]e now believe," they announced, "that [*Gobitis*] was wrongly decided."[37] This open disagreement with Frankfurter made the term a difficult one for him: the rate of his dissenting votes rose sharply, the Douglas-Black-Murphy group coalesced, and, as one scholar put it, "[T]he 1941–42 Term was definitely a turning point for the Roosevelt Court."[38]

Thus, when the Byrnes vacancy arose at the beginning of the Court's fall 1942 term, Frankfurter's leadership position was under siege and in real danger of crumbling. On the flag salute itself, for example, he knew that Stone as well as "the Axis" were against him. This may help to explain the timing and intensity of Frankfurter's effort to persuade FDR to name Hand to the Court. His friendship with and admiration for Hand were genuine and long-standing, to be sure, but the embattled justice may have been tempted to wage his campaign for Hand with special fierceness at this critical time in his own judicial career. Thus, the unidentified political opposition to Hand that both Frankfurter and Burlingham feared may well have been the partisans of the Court's liberal judicial activists.

Frankfurter was correct in anticipating that FDR's selection of Byrnes's successor would be critical. Rutledge was a solid vote to join the Black-Douglas-Murphy-Stone side; Hand, by contrast, would probably have sided with Frankfurter on the civil liberties issues dividing the New Deal Court. Although a lifelong believer in the First Amendment, he, like Frankfurter, generally refused to embrace a double standard, a more interventionist judicial stance toward "personal" rights than to "property" ones.*

When the flag-salute issue returned to the Court in 1943, Frankfurter's *Gobitis* ruling was overruled, in *Barnette*.[39] Frankfurter submitted one of his most emotional opinions, an unusually long and personal dissent. (As if to rub salt into his wounds, the majority opinion was written by Justice Jackson, usually an ally.) Frankfurter proclaimed his long liberal record of sensitivity to the rights of political minorities. "One who belongs to the most vilified and persecuted minority in history is not likely to be insensible to the freedoms guaranteed by our Constitution," he proclaimed,[40] but his personal views could not determine

* Hand made this most clear, ironically, in a tribute to Stone. In a famous passage, he claimed (erroneously) that Stone would *not* have been on the side of those who thought individual rights deserved greater judicial protection than property rights:

> Even before Justice Stone became Chief Justice it began to seem as though, when "personal rights" were in issue, something strangely akin to the discredited attitude towards the Bill of Rights of the old apostles of the institution of property, was regaining recognition. Just why property itself was not a "personal right" nobody took the time to explain . . . but the fact remained that in the name of the Bill of Rights the courts were upsetting statutes which were plainly compromises between conflicting interests, each of which had more than a plausible support in reason. . . . It needed little acquaintance with the robust and loyal character of the Chief Justice to foretell that he would not be content with what to him was an opportunistic reversion at the expense of his conviction as to the powers of a court. He could not understand how the principle which he had all along supported, could mean that, when concerned with interests other than property, the courts should have a wider latitude for enforcing their own predilections than when they were concerned with property itself ["Chief Justice Stone's Concept of the Judicial Function," in *The Spirit of Liberty*, 201, at 205–06].

The views Hand here ascribed to Stone were more truly his own. As Professor Paul Freund once put it, "Memorial addresses often provide an even truer insight into the speaker than into the subject; and it is probably safer that the views so pointedly put by Judge Hand be ascribed to himself than to the late Chief Justice" (Paul A. Freund, *The Supreme Court of the United States: Its Business, Purposes, and Performance* [New York: World Publishing Co., 1961], 34).

constitutionality: as a constitutional matter, legislative policies warranted great judicial deference, whether or not they affected the economic sphere or civil liberties.*

More than philosophical differences explain Frankfurter's waning influence. His personal style also accounted for his increasing isolation in dissent: his colleagues' dislike of the abrasive aspects of his personality made it easier for Black to build majorities that led the Court into a liberal activist direction.

For decades before becoming a justice, Frankfurter had been extraordinarily influential with a very wide circle of acquaintances. He drew effectively on a quick and shrewd mind and an enormous body of learning; and his success rested also on his persistence and his skill at flattery with men ranging from Henry L. Stimson to Louis Brandeis and Oliver Wendell Holmes to Franklin D. Roosevelt. Yet on the Supreme Court, this style was often counterproductive. None of his colleagues knew so much as he about the Court and constitutional law, but he was only one of nine justices, each with his own ego and pride, each holding a commission for life. With most acquaintances—whether older, younger, or his contemporaries—Frankfurter was engaged, warm, charming, and persuasive. Yet on the Court, among equals in rank, his flattery, cajolery, and proclivity for professorial instruction backfired. An endless flow of memoranda circulated from his chambers, supplemented by even more numerous personal calls upon his colleagues. With every new appointee, Frankfurter perceived a new ally; again and again, he was disappointed. At the Court's private conferences, his raised, high-pitched voice was the one that most frequently and readily penetrated the thick oaken doors of the justices' conference room.

DURING THE FALL OF 1942, while wheels busily turned within wheels over the Byrnes vacancy, Hand remained silent, but he was by no means uninterested and disengaged. He knew about his friends' efforts, but he was never optimistic about his chances for promotion. In his view, his best opportunity had come and gone in 1930. Still,

---

* Jackson's majority opinion flatly disagreed: "The very purpose of a Bill of Rights was to withdraw certain subjects from the vicissitudes of political controversy, to place them beyond the reach of majorities and officials and to establish them as legal principles to be applied by the courts." The "fundamental rights" guaranteed by the due-process clause "may not be submitted to vote; they depend on the outcome of no elections" (*Barnette*, 319 U.S. at 638).

After his defeat in *Barnette*, Frankfurter repeatedly defended his position on flag salutes in his correspondence. More than two decades later, he would say, "I know what the Hands thought of [*Gobitis*]. I know what Learned Hand thinks because he wrote me." (See Harry N. Hirsch, *The Enigma of Felix Frankfurter* [New York: Basic Books, 1981], 175.)

he was clearly disappointed by the outcome, in 1942 as in 1930. But Hand, better than Frankfurter or Burlingham, understood that the obstacles to promotion went well beyond his advanced age, that FDR might have philosophical reservations about him.

Soon after the rumors of Rutledge's impending selection began to circulate in December 1942, Burlingham reported to Frankfurter that the "Hand cousins" were now claiming that "F.D. wouldn't appoint B. [even] if he were ten years younger."[41] C.C.B. disagreed, and so did Frankfurter, who argued ever more vehemently that FDR's fear of embarrassment over the age issue was the *sole* reason that the campaign for Hand had failed:

> I go further. If Biddle [once law clerk to Holmes] had really caught the greatness of Holmes & Holmes' realization of the importance of great talents for the Court—if the N.H. Farmer [Harlan Fiske Stone] had cared the way Taft cared, about having the right men on the Court, FDR would not have resisted. But, both the A.G. and the C.J. assured F.D. that Rutledge was O.K. . . .[42]

Hand himself had a more perceptive, capacious sense of the situation:

> I don't believe a word of what F.F. says about what F.D.R. would have done; he wants to believe it. He doesn't like Biddle much now, and he is getting a little out with the New Hampshire Farmer. I am sorry. He has great possibilities where he is, and he is somewhat—indeed a good deal—injuring them by talking too much, and misbehaving on the bench. I wish he wouldn't; especially as the New Dealers are now fast running out on him, and he will never be quite "kosher" with the other group. I am too fond of him to want him to fall between two stools; besides, as I said, he is really the best.[43]

In fact, Stone and Biddle had assured FDR that they approved of the selection of Hand, although not to the point of opposing the Rutledge alternative.[44] Thus, Biddle told the president that among lower court judges Hand was "head and shoulders above all the others," "far more distinguished than any of the others," yet he also dutifully compiled data on "the others" and reported that Rutledge was "the most promising," "[o]utside of Hand": even though he was "long-winded," he was "lawyerlike" and "a liberal who would stand up for human rights."[45] Alas, it was not until a decade later that Biddle came to believe that "I should have urged the President to appoint [Hand] in spite of his age."[46]

Hand's own analysis appeared most clearly in a touching note of appreciation he wrote to Burlingham on January 12, thanking him for the "affection" that had prompted the efforts on his behalf:

> I never had more than the faintest notion that you and Gus and Felix could get F.D.R. to appoint me. I think that there was a deeper difficulty than age, though that was enough. Probably I should have voted as he would have liked, but not for the reasons he would have liked, if he had ever known them, which he never would. He has a sensitive nose for people, and my ways of going at things are so different from his that he may well have felt me alien; I fancy he did.[47]

In all the speculation about FDR's reasons for not naming Hand, this comment ranks among those with the greatest insight. Roosevelt was not acquainted with Hand, but he knew enough about him to recognize that he was no ideological crusader. Hand was a probing skeptic, a judge committed to independent, reasoned decision making; and these traits were indeed "alien" to the president.

Abstractly, Hand was no doubt the best-qualified individual for the Supreme Court in 1942. But the choice of a Supreme Court nominee is rarely a merit-selection process. Some would say that luck is predominant, but a seat on the Court results from factors more concrete than that. It was expecting too much of a president besieged by wartime problems to name someone who was not a personal acquaintance, who was not a dyed-in-the-wool New Dealer or even a Democrat, who was from a state already represented by two members on the Court, and who was over seventy years old. Instead, the seat went to a much younger midwesterner with well-organized supporters of his own, a long record of personal support for FDR, a predictable judicial philosophy of liberal activism, and the prospect of a long tenure on the Court. Hand wrote to Frankfurter soon after Rutledge's death:

> Poor little Wiley—so humble, so virtuous, so painstaking, so infinitely serious and industrious and so monumentally dull! The Great Reaper really has at times a sense of irony; why lay his hand on one for whom early prophetic intimation would foresee an indefinite continuation of patient, long-winded, gentle question-begging, always suffused with kindly sympathies and a vague sense of beneficence?[48]

In 1959, in a ceremony at the federal courthouse in New York City marking the fiftieth anniversary of Hand's appointment to the bench, Felix Frankfurter addressed a distinguished audience that included Chief

Justice Earl Warren and Justice John Marshall Harlan.[49] A major theme of his speech was that Learned Hand's life had been a "lucky" one, and he claimed that Hand "was lucky in not having drawn a successful ticket in that odd lottery by which men are picked for the Supreme Court of the United States."[50] Later on he reiterated that "although I spent not a little part of my life to promote that end as opportunity availed, I insist with deep conviction that he was lucky in not having won out in that strange lottery." Frankfurter suggested, here and elsewhere, that Hand's influence on the Second Circuit was greater than it would have been on the Supreme Court, for in Washington "his views would have been diluted eight-ninths." He claimed, moreover, that Hand lacked "the joy of battle" and therefore would not have enjoyed the "controversies" that were "more strident" on the Supreme Court than in the Second Circuit.[51]

But Hand himself had set the record straight nearly a decade earlier. In June 1950, he drafted, painstakingly revised, and then sent an especially moving letter to Frankfurter—a letter he requested Frankfurter not to answer or "indeed to mention . . . when we meet." "I can write such things to another if they do not provoke a reply," he explained, "but discussion of them would be excruciating." Hand's letter was, precisely, about his thwarted ambition to be on the Court:

I remembered [on seeing a recent photograph of all the justices] how during the last—shall I say five—decades the spectacle of the nine men who have had so much power has affected me with varying moods. I remember how I used to impute to them, not so much superior wisdom, and certainly never great dialectical acumen, but that sort of detachment and subjection to what vaguely we all think of "law" that has an authority beyond the court that interprets it; and this gave them a dignity and entitled them to a respect that somehow overcame my differences from them.

Part of his ruminations concerned his lowered respect for the Nine: now, there were only one or two justices, Frankfurter among them, "who any longer satisfied that demand of mine." Yet thinking about the Supreme Court had "curiously enough" become "soothing" for him:

I can say it now without the shame that I suppose I should feel —I longed as the thing beyond all else that I craved to get a place on it. Don't, for God's sake, say I have done as well; that would miss the very point. (This is a penitential confession.) It was the importance, the power, the trappings of the God damn thing that really drew me on, and I have no excuse beyond my belief that I am not by a jugful alone in being subject to such cheap and nasty aspirations. It was in my case particularly inexcusable because I was living all the while with a person [Frances Hand] who of all I have ever met—except perhaps Gus—was least inflated with this especial effort to escape insecurity.

Yes, he had indeed aspired to promotion over many years: he could not deny that he would have liked to sit on the Supreme Court, and that the failures to be named *did* hurt. Only now could he accept his disappointment:

> I remember Holmes used to say that at 90 he had bid defiance to the imperatives of Good & Evil. I shall never get there, but I do allow myself to hope that they may seem in time to be less imperious. Even a glint of Freedom is welcome.[52]

Hand was at peace at last—at least almost so—about his missed opportunities. But neither he nor the nation was "lucky" that he had missed becoming a justice of the Supreme Court of the United States.

THE EARLY 1940S brought Hand peace not only about his career hopes; he found greater peace in his marriage as well. At the beginning of 1944, Louis Dow, who had for so long complained of physical ailments, fell fatally ill. Frances hastened to be with him in Cornish. As usual, Learned was supportive. A few months earlier, Hand had told his wife that he wondered "how you found Louis, thinking of the light in his face when he saw yours."[53] During Frances's final visit to Louis, in February, Learned had planned to join her, but was held back by a nagging cold. He wrote Frances:

> I hope Lou will not be too much disappointed; I know he will feel much repaid by your staying over as you mean to do. I shall be quite all right here, as you know; . . . I feel that Louis gets so much out of your being there, that it is as nothing that you are not here. . . . The difference in our positions is so huge that I should be ashamed to have you even let me drift for an instant across your choice [about your date of return].

Yet even here he could not suppress his impatience with not knowing the details of her midwinter trip:

> When you make up your mind as to the day you mean to come [home], let me know. . . . Only, would you do this? When you decide on the day, not to put it off later? That seems silly to ask;

but it does make just a little disappointment. . . . [D]on't, pray
don't, feel any urge on my account. . . . But if you could hold
it [the date of your return] open until you know, and then not
put it off, I should feel a little less disappointed.[54]

Ten days later, Dow's life was clearly fading. Learned had a long
telephone conversation with his wife that evening, and wrote her the
next day:

I hate to think of you having to bear this all alone; . . . I woke
up early this a.m. and of course began to think about you and
how staunch you were. This end brings back to me the past years
in a curious way. Some people seem to be able to think with
satisfaction of their past; I do not. As I look back, they seem to
me so confused, so agitated, so concerned with what was less
important, and so anxious. You should, and I think you do, have
a better account to give of yourself to yourself; you have always
much better understood yourself; or, if not that, at least you have
been much better friends with yourself.[55]

On March 5, Louis Dow died, with Frances Hand at his side. Frances
telephoned Learned to report the news. The next day, Learned wrote
her:

I think of you all the while, really now more than Louis. But the
whole past thirty years keeps coming to me with a strange sense
of unreality; so many emotions that now that the end has come,
have a curious appearance of futility. How we do import into the
past unreality! As though it was not as real as the future.[56]

A few weeks later, Frances returned to New England to clear out
Dow's Hanover home. In a will that Dow had executed during the last
months of his life, he had left the Hands his collection of wines and
whiskeys as well as his automobile. Frances inventoried everything in
the house carefully, sorting through his books, papers, clothes, and
furniture, and kept silent about the whiskey legacy ("I don't want the
community here to know that I have all this liquor," she told Learned).[57]
The Hands promptly had the car reregistered in their name and used
it for years. In August, Frances supervised Dow's burial; she thought
it "better to do it quietly without anybody" and was accompanied only
by an old friend, an undertaker, and a minister.[58] Throughout this
period, her letters to her husband were remarkably cheerful and un-
troubled. Perhaps she was trying to spare Learned's feelings; perhaps it
was another manifestation of her capacity to live for the present, a trait

that Learned admired so much. Louis Dow was gone, and as she had shown after her mother's death, she was not one to mourn. Her joy in life remained as great as ever, but now was more warmly directed toward Learned.

As she cleaned out Louis's house, she wrote to Learned, "I love you *very* much. I feel just as you do, about the shortness of our lives, and the necessity of not letting the gray melancholy take possession of us. We must not waste any time. But must try to live until we die."[59] At long last, Learned received the kinds of warm endearments from Frances that he had long sought. "I was sorry to miss your sweet old voice," she told him.[60] And soon she was signing letters with "Kisses xxx," exclamations that Learned had not seen for three decades.[61]

Learned reciprocated with unrestrained, even exuberant affection. His letters to his wife now glowed with a playful, youthful love that he had not expressed since the earliest years of their marriage. Thus, he sent her a note addressed to "Beloved of My Heart; likewise Sweet Little Homebody," and ended with "I LOVE YOU. BUNNY LOVES KITTY" (adding a little drawing not of a cat but an arrow piercing a heart, with the initials "FAH" and "LH" inside). In response to her "Kisses" signatures, he would repeatedly write, "I love you, I love you, I love you." He was determined that they would spend more time with each other, and she was happy to go along. "I love you and hate to be separated from you," he wrote in June 1950, when he was seventy-eight. "It must not go on; we must manage to be together till one of us leaves for all."[62]

XIV

The Postwar Years,
the Cold War, and McCarthyism

ON JANUARY 27, 1947, Hand turned seventy-five. More than the usual round of birthday greetings poured in, but he claimed to see no reason to consider the completion of three quarters of a century extraordinary; as he remarked to Felix Frankfurter, "[I]t seems as though there ought to be some sort of 'turning-point' about it, but there ain't. Same as every other day."[1] Three days later, he told an old friend, "The awful day passed and plunged me unharmed into the abyss of my fourth quarter century." Only the calendar told him he was getting old, and he loathed to listen: "Now the question is: 'How long, oh Lord, how long?' Curiously perhaps, I don't want to shorten it a day; I am having a good time. . . ."[2] His good health and undiminished acuity gave him no reason to break his vigorous stride. Instead, he continued busy and absorbed as the presiding judge of the Second Circuit, and pursued his interest in the politics of the day.

The world was not so ready to let the seventy-fifth landmark go unnoticed. Instead, the occasion prompted an enormous new outpouring of applause. In February 1947, the *Harvard Law Review* took the unusual step of devoting its entire articles section to praise of a living alumnus, dedicating the issue to Hand, "whose wisdom and eloquence have made his seventy-fifth birthday an occasion to be celebrated by all who serve the law."[3] Eight articles by distinguished judges and lawyers analyzed and praised his contributions. In March, his law clerks and the Harvard Law School Association presented a bronze bust of the judge to the Harvard Law School. The *American Bar Association Journal* called him "the best judge in America," the historian Arthur M. Schlesinger, Jr.'s, article for *Fortune* deemed him "the wisest American judge," and *Life*'s extensive profile by Philip Hamburger described Hand as "the judicial giant whom the U.S. Supreme Court missed." The Theodore Roosevelt Memorial Association conferred upon him its Medal of Honor, citing him as "the foremost jurist of the English-speaking world."[4] Major newspapers echoed the praise. The *New York Herald Tribune*, for example, called him a "worthy successor" to Holmes and noted Hand's rare talents: "[N]ot many men possess urbanity without brittleness, erudition without ostentation, judicial detachment without chilliness."[5] And *The Washington Post* insisted that Hand,

> probably more than any other American jurist still active on the bench, typifies the spirit of sincere and open-minded inquiry into the facts and detached formulation of judgments on the basis of those facts. . . . He has won recognition as a judges' judge. His opinions command respect wherever our law extends, not because of his standing in the judicial hierarchy, but because of the clarity of thought and the cogency of reasoning that shape them.[6]

As always, Hand had difficulty accepting such lavish praise, and his acknowledgments were marked by recurrent self-doubt. When a Boston lawyer named Robert Dodge, a Harvard contemporary, congratulated him on the *Harvard Law Review* issue, Hand responded wistfully:

> As I look about it seems to me that one advantage of a judge's life—there are many—is that as one gets older, provided one has been industrious and reasonably competent, an encrustation of approval builds itself up about one. . . . I account for what these boys have got up about me largely in this way: years of somewhat obscure but laborious work, and an aloofness from the stream of conflicts.[7]

Yet the wide-ranging applause was not so easy to discount. Even Hand had to admit, as he did to Dodge, that the praise was absurdly gratifying. When one's friends "apparently do take it seriously," he wrote another old acquaintance, "it exposes [the subject] to the danger of beginning to wonder whether there may not be something in it after all."[8]

Hand's doubts were real. He denied that his self-effacing responses constituted suppressed vanity and attributed the applause largely to his longevity and his capacity to stay out of trouble. He told Frankfurter about the conflict he felt between satisfaction and uncertainty:

Of course, [the praise] is hugely gratifying . . . and it has this curious effect: I wonder whether there may not be some truth in it in spite of so many years of "autoptic evidence" to the contrary. Then recurs the more authentic version—so it seems—and I say of these judgments: "As a dream doth flatter, in sleep a king, but waking no such matter."[9]*

Though the laudatory outpourings temporarily allayed his brooding lack of self-esteem, Hand could never quite escape this "more authentic version" of himself, and he continued to doubt that his achievements warranted the acclaim.

This "more authentic" self was hypercritical, as it had been for decades. In fact, however, the accolades were largely written with great analytical care and were well grounded in the record, as well as in friendship. Hand's old sponsor, C. C. Burlingham, then eighty-eight years old, described Hand as "the most reasoning" of all human beings who was "now unquestionably first among American judges,"[10] and his former law clerk Archibald Cox praised his "wisdom" and "deep-seated tolerance."[11] And at the presentation of the bronze bust to the Harvard Law School, Judge Thomas D. Thacher of New York's highest court sensitively portrayed both Hand's "earlier frailties of indecision" and his "rejection [of] a complementary mechanism," and concluded, "His beliefs have clothed him with true humility and with a conscience which spares him never. Couple these with his learning and his craftsmanship and we have a great judge."[12]

In this instance, Hand's only objection was aimed not at the tone of the ceremony but at the shortcomings of the bust itself, a creation by New York sculptor Eleanor Platt. In fact, the bust is an adequate likeness, although the dense, protruding eyebrows in the artist's version suggest a caricature, and the image conveys little of Hand's humanity. But Hand's reaction revealed more than a trace of vanity. How could an "unsure, timorous creature" such as he, he asked the artist, impress anyone as being like this intimidating bust?[13] To another judge he wrote, "One of my intelligent friends told me that it looked like nothing so much as a paleolithic man. As for me, I would say that if I saw that old Bozo I would never want to come before him; he looks to me like a typical 'hanging judge.' "[14] To others, he complained that the bust made him look like a "grouchy old man," a "ghastly" portrayal of a "gargoyle."[15] The artist's failure to convey any warmth rankled

---

* "Autoptic" derived from "autopsy," in the sense of a critical examination of the past. The line LH quoted—"as a dream doth flatter . . ."—is from Shakespeare's Sonnet No. 87.

with him, even though the official photograph he had used for many years (probably because he had gotten a large number of copies for a very low price) made him look even more remote and detached.*

The homage from so many quarters did not significantly disrupt Hand's normal routine. At the time of the birthday hurrahs, he was preoccupied not only with judicial work but with crafting a critical response to a proposal in the *Saturday Review of Literature*: in its February 1, 1947, issue, its editor, Norman Cousins, had urged New York's representatives in Washington and Albany to adopt a "group libel" law that would ban defamatory remarks about minority groups. Noting that defamation of individuals had long been a basis for lawsuits, Cousins suggested that the libel remedy be expanded to curb those "who use our freedoms as battering rams against freedom," as Hitler and his Nazi cohorts had done in their racist and anti-Semitic crusades in Germany. Advocacy of group-libel legislation was widespread after World War II, and the *Saturday Review*'s editorial proposal was a part of this campaign to curb "hate specialists." As Cousins argued, group-libel laws could have an "antiseptic value" in deterring "hate speech": "Such stock canards as pertain to the Protocols of Zion, or the mental or constitutional inferiority of races or religious groups, can be effectively nailed and precedents slowly built up which may serve as a sort of legal sprinkler system against totalitarian arson."[16]†

Six weeks later, when the magazine ran two pages of comments by public figures about its "editorial proposal," one of the responses was from Hand, who unhesitatingly condemned it, stating that he was "quite certain that any law creating a 'group libel' would be undesirable." Reiterating once more his commitment to open debate and free expression, he wrote:

> It is quite true that the kind of defamation you have in mind has that tendency to promote disorder which has been the conventional justification for all criminal libel; yet, if one thinks through the

---

* Hand never reconciled himself to Eleanor Platt's sculpture. Six years after its presentation, when the New York City Bar Association solicited money to commission her to do another bust, Hand observed, "I much regret the choice of Miss Platt for the job. I agree that the heads she did of Einstein and Brandeis were good; but that of Stimson seems to me insipid, and she perpetrated a gargoyle of me, which now stands in the Harvard Law School, that will be a perpetual libel for all time, because the damned thing is in bronze. This lady has for some reason captivated Burlingham, who throws all the work to her that he can. He has no competence in such matters. . . . Why don't you go to somebody who really knows? We lawyers are not fit to decide, little as we appear to be able to be convinced that we are not" (LH to George A. Spiegelberg, 21 October 1953, 95–32).

† At the time, the staff of the *Saturday Review* contained several friends of Hand: Henry Seidel Canby was the chair of its editorial board; the critic John Mason Brown was an associate editor.

working of such prosecutions in practice, I should suppose that their effect would be rather to exacerbate than to assuage the feelings which lie behind the defamation of groups. . . . The passions which lie at the root of such utterances do not have their bases in evidence, and will not yield to it. . . . There is no remedy for the evil, but the slow advance of the spirit of tolerance; and I believe that the suppression of intolerance always tends to make it more bitter. This is a result most unsatisfactory to ardent natures and it may be wrong; I can only tell you what I believe.[17]

As Hand forged ahead in his "fourth quarter century," he had many more occasions to defend free speech, advocate tolerance, and oppose repression.

THE EUPHORIA that greeted the Allied victory in World War II in 1945 was short-lived. Throughout 1945, several Allied conferences with the Soviet Union regarding a peace treaty with Germany foundered;[18] so too did any agreement on the prohibition of nuclear weapons. Winston Churchill's 1946 speech in Fulton, Missouri, captured the new tone when he warned against the "expansive and proselytizing tendencies" of the Soviet Union, and asserted: "From Stettin in the Baltic to Trieste in the Adriatic, an iron curtain has descended across the Continent."[19] As the nation became preoccupied with restraining these perceived Soviet tendencies, Hand was an intent observer of international tensions and a dismayed critic of their repercussions at home.

Hand had never had any illusions about Stalin's regime. During the 1930s, when he already believed that America must go to the aid of those who opposed totalitarianism, he typically linked Stalin with Hitler and Mussolini as the enemy. True, when the Soviet Union fought valiantly against Nazi Germany, he supported the activities of the National Council of American-Soviet Friendship, but the immediate postwar developments, especially the frustrating treaty negotiations, left him in no doubt that the U.S.S.R. was a nation to be viewed warily. As he wrote to Bernard Berenson in the summer of 1946:

It may be that our good friend, Uncle Joe of Moscow, is not so formidable as he looks; better—not as formidable as he seems to be going to be. But I confess, after dickering with him for a year, the Hitler pattern has so nearly repeated itself, that I am full of trepidation. Besides, I am a shameful coward in the presence of any Authentic Faith—having none of my own to match against one—and I can discern no such Creature upon the Planet to-day, unless it be the Gospel according to St. Karl [Marx].[20]

A year later, Hand, though heartened by a new resistance to isolationism at home, was gloomier than ever about Soviet intransigence. As he told Berenson in August 1947, "Our Slavic friends in the last two or three months have lost much ground; their disclosure of their utter unwillingness to enter into any cooperation except on their own terms has alienated a good many of their former sympathizers."[21] By then, the Truman administration had indeed adopted a "hard" line toward the Soviet Union. The previous spring, while yet another conference of foreign ministers was failing to reach agreement on postwar Germany,[22] President Truman had announced his policy of containment of the Soviet Union expansion, and requested and secured economic and military aid for Greece and Turkey to strengthen them against "attempted subjugation by armed minorities or by outside pressures." In response, the Soviet Union attacked the United States as "warmongers." A year later, in June 1948, when Secretary of State George C. Marshall proposed a plan for massive economic aid to cooperating European nations, the Soviet Union and its satellites quickly denounced the scheme as hostile to the U.S.S.R. and designed to enslave Europe. The Cold War was fully under way.

Hand, like most Americans, never doubted the need for American firmness in the face of Stalinist foreign policy. But unlike most Americans, he also perceived from the start the domestic damage that American obsession with international communism was inflicting. In writing to Berenson in August 1947, for example, he said that "the frantic witch hunters are given freer rein to set up a sort of Inquisition, detecting heresy wherever non-conformity appears."[23] The way that the battle with communism bred domestic witch-hunts had haunted Hand ever since World War I. He remembered, too, the chilling effects on speech generated by the Dies Un-American Activities Committee before World War II, and his public defense of Robert Lovett after Congress had cut off his salary during the war. Hand had warned law-enforcement officers in no uncertain terms about the danger of resorting to unfounded accusations of alleged subversives. On July 16, 1941, the New York head of the FBI had called a gathering of three hundred state and local police to coordinate their efforts as the nation approached war; Hand addressed the conference (as a last-minute substitute for John Knox, the chief district judge). His central concern being to "preserve the essentials of democracy and the essence of freedom" at home in the midst of international crises, Hand told the officers that he feared that "once people feel that rumors and idle, foolish suspicions of enemies may land them in concentration camps, disunity sets in." And, he somberly warned, "[T]here is quite as much danger in overdoing fears, excitement and punishments that come from a state of peril as there is from neglecting to take necessary remedial steps."[24] As he put it in a letter to an acquaintance who congratulated him on speaking out against "the growing intolerance on the part of the public towards aliens and radicals, and the strange doings of the FBI, so reminiscent of the last war," "[O]ur most pressing need [is] unity and . . . you can lose whatever modicum we can get of it—not too much at best—as well by witch-hunting as by failing to run down traitors and spies. Like everything else in life, nothing is any good except when it is done in moderation."[25]

These concerns quickly ripened into outright hostility not only to Wisconsin senator Joseph McCarthy, the most visible and most demagogic crusader against domestic subversion from 1950 to 1954, but the whole phenomenon that attached to McCarthy's name, pervading American public life well before and for some years after. Often a partisan effort to discredit opponents of right-wing Republican policies, McCarthyism was marked by the circulation of sensational, unsupported charges and innuendos accusing a wide range of people of subversion. The increasingly hysterical charges were well under way before McCarthy himself took center stage with his claim, in a well-publicized speech in Wheeling, West Virginia, in February 1950, that he had "here in my hand a list of two hundred and five" subversives working in the State Department.[26] As early as March 1947, President Truman had issued his Executive Order 9835, establishing a loyalty program for federal employees, the standard for dismissal being the existence of "reasonable grounds . . . for belief that the person involved is disloyal to the Government of the United States"; in its application, the program and its successors produced recurrent abuses. Employees were scrutinized for any left-of-center political associations and even asked whether they read *The New Republic* or possessed books dealing with Russia. By 1948, the House Un-American Activities Committee, with Congressman J. Parnell Thomas having replaced Martin Dies as its chair, intensified its investigations into alleged Communist infiltration of labor unions, education, Hollywood, and other aspects of American life. A young California lawyer named Richard Nixon gained his seat in the House in 1946 with the help of the Communist issue and soon garnered a national reputation as an active member of the Un-American Activities Committee.

The search for subversives severely divided the American liberal community, between those who considered all domestic uses of the communism issue as improper Red-baiting and those who distrusted Stalinists and supported the search for genuine spies. Hand was not a formal member of any liberal group, but his views most closely resembled those of the latter type; he considered international communism a real danger, not a bogey, but he feared that loose charges against dissenters by political conservatives threatened American civil liberties. By 1951, when he retired from "regular active service" as a judge, Hand considered the McCarthyite campaign so dangerous that he denounced it publicly. Continuing work on the Second Circuit as a "senior judge," he made additional public condemnations of McCarthyism that were among the earliest attacks on the phenomenon by an establishment figure.

Much of Hand's heightened sensitivity to the reckless charges that became known as McCarthyism was roused by the ceaseless attacks made on Dean Acheson, the longtime State Department official who was Truman's secretary of state. Acheson was a vigorous anti-Communist in foreign affairs, the architect of the plans for international control of atomic power in 1946, of the Marshall Plan in 1947, of Truman's containment policy in 1948, and of the NATO alliance in 1950, yet he was virulently attacked for being "soft" on communism. Senator McCarthy attacked him for harboring security risks in the State Department, for lack of foresight in failing to support Chiang Kai-shek's China and causing Chiang's replacement by Mao Tse-tung. McCarthy's charges were nothing new: Senator William F. Knowland of California, Congressman Nixon, and other members of the "China Lobby" had long targeted Acheson. A State Department white paper had discussed the "corrupt, reactionary and inefficient" Chiang regime in China, concluding that "the unfortunate but inescapable fact is that the ominous result of the civil war in China was beyond the control of the government of the United States. [It] was the product of internal Chinese forces, forces which this country tried to influence but could not." To the right-wing critics, the "loss" of China was the result of American, and especially State Department, perfidy.

Acheson was a natural target, having served in the State Department for many years, as assistant secretary of state beginning in 1941, and as under secretary from August 1945 to July 1947 (with many stretches as acting secretary while the secretary was abroad).* A graduate of the Harvard Law School, a former law clerk to Justice Louis Brandeis, a

---

* Acheson was briefly out of the State Department for eighteen months in 1947–48, when he returned to his financially rewarding law practice but remained influential behind the scenes. In January 1949, Truman named him secretary of state.

friend of Felix Frankfurter by the 1930s, Acheson became an even closer friend when Frankfurter moved to Georgetown in 1939. Frankfurter's admiration for Acheson and his outrage about the unfair attacks were frequent subjects in his correspondence with Hand, and Hand readily shared both Frankfurter's admiration and outrage. He viewed Acheson's appointment to the State Department as a rare ray of light amid the lowering darkness.[27]* In mid-January 1950, he wrote, "I think the Republicans are acting with such inconceivable savagery [but] Dean will come out [of it], in spite of his unhappy Chinese inheritance. But it is all very awful."[28] A few days later, he elaborated:

> The violence of the attacks upon [Acheson] is distressing evidence of the savagery of modern life. [When] I look back on my Nineteenth Century kit of feelings and beliefs, it is not with any complacent satisfaction at the changed times I have lived into. Quite the contrary; in all that makes for human progress, if there is such a possibility, those days appear to be better than the regnant faiths to-day. [T]he ethos of those days forbad so ready a resort to violence: violence of feeling; violence of expression; violence of suppression; violence in action of every kind. . . . So that when I look at Dean and his work, my soul dares again to take wing at its own low altitude and to believe that there may be at least a fighting chance that man has a significance, different, and I dare hope, better, than a baboon, whatever "better" may mean.[29]

Two weeks after this dejected comment, Senator Joseph McCarthy catapulted into fame with his Lincoln Day speech in Wheeling, West Virginia. Hand wrote to Bernard Berenson at about the same time,

> [T]he local hysteria in this country has now reached such a peak that there are few who would dare to acknowledge any Communist inclinations, if they had them. We are in a convulsion, likely in the end, as are most such violent reactions, to do more towards fostering what we have come frantically to dread, than if we could keep better hold on ourselves. We especially dread the spread of the gospel, recognizing, as in our bowels we do, that it is a living faith, however Satanic and false.[30]

Berenson had been puzzled as to why so many of his cultivated intellectual European friends had turned into advocates of "the Soviet religion." Hand ascribed that tendency to a desire for certainty at all

---

* "But there are lights here and there at times when Der Anblick Gibt den Engeln Staerke [the prospect gives strength to the angels]. Dean did get the job; I never thought it. . . ."

costs, and his analysis once again underlined the philosophical strength
of his skepticism:

> The relief of finding something which will take the place of the
> "intolerable labor of thought"—with all its attendant sense of
> futility—makes us the prey of the most obscene and monstrous
> faiths, from which, if thinking were not itself such a perversion
> of our nature, thinking would protect us. I believe that your in-
> tellectual friends, just because of their habit of "intellectualizing,"
> are the easiest victims of Marx. They have today only two escapes
> from that world of Trial and Error in which all that we have
> hitherto relied upon, has come into just suspicion. For we have
> burrowed so deep, and are so God damned smart in our burrowings,
> that nobody who is inflexibly reasonable, can be confident of much,
> if anything. The juster he is rationally, the more unbearable be-
> comes the outlook. One escape is into the bosom of the Holy
> Mother, and it is curious that over here [many] have chosen that.
> . . . [T]he other escape is into the hairier embraces of that strangest
> of all strange deities, the enraged egoist—Karl Marx. . . . It all
> comes down, I believe, to whether we have the guts to face the
> Universe with a consciousness that it is a perpetual question-mark.
> . . . My despair, when I do despair, which is oftener than I wish,
> is grounded in the fact that it does seem as though the last achieve-
> ment of mankind was a detachment, a scepticism, an aloofness
> from conviction, which has proved the best road, and nearly the
> only road, that has led us out of the trees. . . . [A]s a consistent
> sceptic, I must be sceptical as to the supreme value of scepticism,
> and that too I shall try to be.[31]

As McCarthyite extremism grew shriller and shriller, North Korean
forces invaded South Korea, and the United States persuaded the U.N.
Security Council to urge member nations to supply armed forces to
curb this; near the end of June, Truman authorized the use of American
ground forces in Korea under the command of General Douglas
MacArthur. After some early successes, American troops encountered
strong resistance and were driven south. The U.N. forces counterat-
tacked; though their Korean "police action" was supposed to be limited,
MacArthur, exceeding his instructions, moved into North Korea, all
the way to the Yalu River, prompting Chinese "volunteers" to cross
the Yalu in force to support the North Korean response. During the
winter of 1950–51, North Korean and Chinese troops pushed the U.N.
forces into a drastic retreat. General MacArthur, convinced that an
attack on the Chinese at the Manchurian border was necessary in order

to win the war, threatened to bomb China. Within days, President Truman relieved MacArthur of his Far Eastern command. An unrepentant MacArthur returned to Washington to address a joint session of Congress and urge military action against China.

The American defeats in Korea proved enormously divisive domestically, and provided fertile soil for a sharp increase in McCarthyism, with the right wing attacking the administration for vacillation and continued "softness" on communism. Hand and Frankfurter bemoaned the mounting hysteria and sought to understand its causes. The attacks on Acheson became a central theme of their letters. Frankfurter, particularly, was distressed by the newspaper columns of Walter Lippmann, his old bête noire, who was urging that Acheson, having lost the nation's confidence, be forced out of office. Lippmann's columns, he was convinced, were "just the kind of talk that some of the weak and woolly minded GOP Senators, like Lev Saltonstall [a Massachusetts Republican], need to feel they are *vox populi*." The attacks had focused on Acheson, he thought, for "three reasons heavily exploited by the worst forces in our society": Acheson's statements in defense of Alger Hiss, recently convicted of perjury (and implicitly of stealing government documents on behalf of the Soviet Union);* his "foolishly candid disclosure" that he had removed several homosexuals from the State Department; and his refusal "to be a tail to Chiang & the 'China Lobby.' "[32] Hand was not convinced that these three factors alone accounted for "the appalling load of vindictive vituperation that has been dumped on Dean." He thought the charges that Acheson bore responsibility for America's setbacks in Asia were especially unfounded: "I am not aware that he has fumbled about Formosa, and the Korean adventure everybody agreed to—well nearly everybody. He has been enmeshed in the Asian enterprises, not because he chose them but because the Republicans kept yelling 'appeasement' whenever we show any abatement from what they wanted."[33]

In response, Frankfurter redoubled his attacks on Lippmann exercising a "mischievous influence": "There were several Senators . . . who were moved to vote in the Republican caucus for the motion against Dean because of what Walter wrote the morning of their meeting. They argued that even if so detached a liberal writer as Lippmann reports that Acheson has lost the confidence of the country that establishes his loss of public confidence."[34]

By the turn of the year, Hand came around to sharing Frankfurter's distress about Lippmann's work, attributing the columnist's attacks on

* Acheson testified at the Hiss trial as a reputation witness and announced that he stood by his old friends, stating, "I do not intend to turn my back on Alger Hiss."

Acheson to "a very deep insecurity" and "real timidity." He perceived in Lippmann "a kind of apocalyptic quality, descending from on High, . . . which is probably what puts it over on the illiterates." He was surprised to learn that senators took him so seriously: "I should have thought that he would be set down as nothing but a wordy highbrow."[35] Frankfurter continued to berate Lippmann for his "pathologically vindictive" attitude on Acheson for many a season. He had nothing but disdain for such an "educated & intelligent scribe" joining the McCarthyites in attacking the secretary of state; it only effectively reinforced and stimulated the "Enemies and Obscurantists" who, he believed, now held Acheson a prisoner.[36]

Hand probed deeper than Frankfurter to explain the reasons for the extremist attacks on the administration. The Republicans' pent-up hatred of FDR's New Deal, their search for a way of returning to power, the distaste of most Americans for the superior airs that East Coast intellectuals conveyed, and the continuing strength of isolationism had a good deal more to do with the vituperation than the three immediate factors Frankfurter had listed. As Hand told Bernard Berenson in September 1950:

> The Republicans have, in my judgment, behaved with indecency. . . . By what fantastic perversion they have been able to justify their concentrated attack upon Acheson because of mistakes made four or five years ago over China, I cannot comprehend, except for the obvious reason: they are willing to do anything to get back into power. . . . [I]t may be that the Republicans, who shriek that all Democrats are disguised Communists, will ride in [at the next election] on a hysterical tidal wave which is more passionate, more blind and more dangerous to the eventual unity of the country than anything I remember in my time, even including 1920.[37]

A month later, Hand elaborated more fully on the right wing:

> Perhaps it was wrong to go into Korea, though I still think, as I did at first, that we had no alternative. However, we have made an honest effort; we did what we engaged to do; and it has proved too much for us. I cannot believe that it is wise to persevere throwing in all we have while it will count least, and giving up any hope—at best thin enough—to protect Western Europe. Yet we seem to be bedeviled by cliches; "there must be no appeasement"; "we must not yield to aggression"; "to fail now is to abandon our principles"; "we must be true to what our honor demands," etc., etc. I fear we . . . shall embark whatever strength

we can muster in the very worst place to put it—Asia—leaving nothing for Europe which is infinitely more important to us. It is hard for me to comprehend why the articulate feelings have become so Orientally directed; but apparently it is so.

If I were to guess the real basis, it is made up, in part, of our past fighting against Japan, in part of a strange sense that we are a kind of foster parent to China—although we have always treated them as inferiors—and in part of the worship of General MacArthur. The last factor has been tied in with the Republicans' impotent fury at being excluded from power for 18 years and at the egalitarian policies of the dominating influences in the Democratic Party.[38]

Yet despite these acute and outspoken evaluations of the partisan political situation, Hand, like most Americans, still failed to speak out publicly against McCarthyism. Of course, he defended this position by his well-known argument that it was "very undesirable for a judge to take public positions on matters likely to come before him." He declined an invitation to speak on the Bill of Rights and civil liberties at the annual meeting of the National Association of Magazine Publishers, for example, even while acknowledging that his attitude might seem to some "a pusillanimous evasion."[39] And he refused a request from an old acquaintance, the Wall Street lawyer Allen Wardwell, to support lawyers attacked for defending people charged with disloyalty:

We have a number of appeals in such prosecutions and there is an even chance . . . that I may be called upon to sit in any given one. The public expression of sympathy with either the prosecution or the defence is . . . to the last degree undesirable. . . . I am disposed to believe that it is wiser while I stay on the bench to keep away from all "hot spots," as Holmes once told me.[40]

Yet, as Hand himself recognized, he was not always "quite consistent in my own practice," as he wrote to Walter White of the National Association for the Advancement of Colored People, declining to participate in a public tribute to a retiring federal judge, J. Waties Waring, a courageous anti-racist in South Carolina.[41] For example, he attended and even spoke at a meeting of New York lawyers supporting the work of the International Commission of Jurists in publicizing the abuses of Soviet totalitarianism, and he signed a resolution endorsing the commission's program of "exposing systematic injustice and denials of human rights in countries lying behind the Iron Curtain."[42] More commonly, however, he abstained from public comment on Cold War issues.

Hand's avoidance of other controversial issues was not ironclad. For example, his commitment to making birth control devices available to all women—at a time when this was a highly controversial position—was deep, and this was only in part because his daughter Frances was for a time president of the Planned Parenthood Federation of New York and his wife was a strong supporter of the cause. Hand permitted Planned Parenthood to use in its publicity materials a statement he had made at one of its luncheons: "Concerning the survival of democracy as we know it, I believe Planned Parenthood is the most important thing in the world."[43] "[T]he cause seemed to me important beyond any other save the public safety," he said on another occasion.[44] Hand's usual observance of judicial proprieties was no doubt a major reason why he avoided speaking out against McCarthyism until 1951.

The principal factor involved here was, surely, Hand's own fearful nature. It is fascinating to note how closely he identified with Caspar Milquetoast, the famous H. T. Webster creation in the *New York Herald Tribune* editorial-cartoon series entitled "The Timid Soul." When Webster died in September 1952, Hand wrote a letter to the newspaper expressing his "sense of personal loss":

> I was often on the point of writing to ask [Webster] by what mystic power of divination he came to know the intimate springs of my own self without ever meeting me; for Caspar Milquetoast appeared to me accurately and specifically personally biographic. Nor was this all; in most of his characters I came to feel a part of myself; they appeared to me day after day as pleasant, if corrective, instances from my own experience.[45]

Hand's decision finally to speak out on McCarthyism can be explained in part by his decision a few days earlier, on May 15, 1951, to retire from "regular active service" as a federal judge. His retirement note to President Truman produced an unusually eloquent response, which may well have relied on the advice of Dean Acheson. Truman wrote:

> Your profession has long since recognized the magnitude of your contribution to the law. There has never been any question about your pre-eminent place among American jurists—indeed among the nations of the world. . . . [I]n your day to day work for almost half a century, you have added purpose and hope to man's quest for justice through the process of law. As judge and philosopher, you have expressed the spirit of America and the highest in civi-

lization which man has achieved. America, and the American people, are the richer because of the vigor and fullness of your contribution to our way of life.[46]

But Hand continued to sit frequently on the Second Circuit; he continued to hear cases arising from the subversion hysteria, and the restraints of judicial propriety did not significantly loosen. Yet at one of the tributes to Hand on his partial stepping down—the meeting of the American Law Institute in Washington where the annual dinner was devoted to Hand, with Felix Frankfurter as one of the speakers—Hand rose to acknowledge the laudatory speeches and spoke, briefly and extemporaneously, publicly and bluntly, against the evils of McCarthyism. His remarks, which were taken down by a stenographer, show that Hand could be at his eloquent best speaking without a prepared script, as he preferred.

> My friends, our future is precarious. I do not know if you remember the time . . . in 1940 when we were here just on the eve of those dreadful days when it seemed not unlikely that the whole of all which made life precious might be overwhelmed. Today we stand in as much danger as we did then. . . . I like to hope we have a good chance . . . of victory, but *on one condition: that we do not go to pieces internally.*

At the heart of his remarks was a deeply felt, powerful warning:

> [M]y friends, will you not agree that any society which begins to be doubtful of itself; in which one man looks at another and says: "He may be a traitor," in which that spirit has disappeared which says: "I will not accept that, I will not believe that—I will demand proof. I will not say of my brother that he may be a traitor," but I will say, "Produce what you have. I will judge it fairly, and if he is, he shall pay the penalties; but I will not take it on rumor. I will not take it on hearsay. I will remember that what has brought us up from savagery is a loyalty to truth, and truth cannot emerge unless it is subjected to the utmost scrutiny.' "—will you not agree that a society which has lost sight of that, cannot survive?

Hand concluded: "You remember in *The Cloister* [*and*] *the Hearth*, in tight moments how Gerard's companion used to say: '*Courage, mon ami, le diable est mort.*' No, my friends, the devil isn't dead; but take heart of grace; we shall get him yet!"[47]

The Washington Post, a leading critic of McCarthyism, obtained the stenographer's transcript and printed the heart of Hand's speech as its lead editorial on May 27, 1951. His remarks also brought Hand considerable private praise.* But a year later, Hand was writing to Herman Finkelstein, who had been his first circuit court law clerk and was in 1952 general counsel to the American Society of Composers, Authors, and Publishers (ASCAP), "I am thrown into perplexity whether it would not be better for me to free myself from all judicial scruples, so that I might say something which it might not be seemly to utter while still a judge."[48] Hand did not leave the court, but instead overcame his scruples and publicly denounced McCarthyism anyway. The occasion was his return to his native Albany to accept an honorary LL.D. degree from the University of the State of New York. He had been asked to prepare the principal address to the six hundred education officials attending the eighty-sixth convocation of the Board of Regents.[49] As usual, he struggled over his speech and wrote it with care. While his major theme was the importance of a liberal arts education to intelligent democratic participation, the point of his closing passages was clear:

> Risk for risk, for myself I had rather take my chance that some traitors will escape detection than spread abroad a spirit of general suspicion and distrust, which accepts rumor and gossip in place of undismayed and unintimidated inquiry. I believe that that community is already in process of dissolution where each man begins to eye his neighbor as a possible enemy, where non-conformity with the accepted creed, political as well as religious, is a mark of disaffection; where denunciation, without specification or backing, takes the place of evidence; where orthodoxy chokes freedom of dissent; where faith in the eventual supremacy of reason has become so timid that we dare not enter our convictions in the open lists, to win or lose. Such fears as these are a solvent which can eat out the cement that binds the stones together; they may in the end subject us to a despotism as evil as any that we dread; and they can be allayed only in so far as we refuse to proceed on suspicion, and trust one another until we have tangible ground for misgiving. The mutual confidence on which all else depends can be maintained only by an open mind and a brave reliance upon free discussion. I do not say that these will suffice; who knows but we may be on the slope which leads down to aboriginal sav-

---

* E.g., W. Graham Claytor, Jr., to LH, 3 July 1951, 85–41. W. Graham Claytor, a former Hand clerk and a partner in Covington & Burling, a leading Washington law firm, commented that his colleagues agreed that "these few paragraphs are not only magnificent, but also terribly important." Claytor reported that John Lord O'Brian, Claytor's senior partner, one of the very few senior lawyers who spoke out almost as early as Hand did, in a speech at Washington and Lee University, had used those very words to describe LH's speech.

agery. But of this I am sure: if we are to escape, we must not yield a foot upon demanding a fair field and an honest race to all ideas.[50]

Hand himself knew this explosive passage was "not entirely relevant to the main theme," as he told Frankfurter, yet it seemed "relevant enough to drag in, as a kind of 'stinger' in the coda, what I fear most in the present time—McCarthy and the Cartesian Crew."[51] This carefully considered outburst was so startling that the Albany speech proved to be one of the most widely publicized and quoted of all Learned Hand's addresses. It was front-page news in the next day's *New York Times*, and a day later, the *Times* editorially praised Hand for his "courage as well as wisdom" in speaking out "in these days." The address was promptly reprinted by the *Saturday Review* as its lead article; other publications soon reprinted it as well; several newspapers around the nation published commendatory editorials; Edward R. Murrow, the most respected radio commentator of the day, devoted most of a broadcast to long excerpts; and Hand's mail contained an unprecedented number of enthusiastic approvals.[52] Herbert Bayard Swope, the former editor of the *New York World*, suggested that Hand send a copy of his speech to Senator McCarthy, but in reply, Hand emphasized that he had in mind not only Joseph McCarthy but Richard Nixon—who had recently become the Republicans' vice presidential nominee—as well. He shuddered at the risks of a Nixon vice presidency, a prospect that gave him "an attack of vertigo," even though he planned to vote for Dwight Eisenhower.[53] One of the most heartening comments came from Norman Thomas, the longtime presidential candidate of the Socialist Party of America: "You are in a position to speak with peculiar authority. I do not think your words will be forgotten." Hand was very pleased by that note: "For many years I have regarded you as a noble and useful figure in our political scene," he told Thomas, "and to learn that in spite of our wide political differences and practice, you should be able to write me as you did, is more gratifying than perhaps you can know."[54]

Despite the enormous publicity and wide acclaim that his Regents address received, Hand continued to suffer from uncertainties about such public statements. "Sometimes I ask myself whether a deep demon does not really lead me to publicity 'stunts,' while my public upper cortical centers strike noble attitudes in apology. Which is the Real Self?," he wrote to Felix Frankfurter.[55] A few months after his Regents speech, he declined an invitation to attend an ALI discussion of congressional investigations into communism.[56] Similarly, he told the Columbia University law professor John Hazard, who had asked him to participate in a discussion of national security restrictions, "Sometimes I feel that I may [not have] been reserved enough [about speaking out publicly on such questions], but that would be no excuse for failing again."[57] And just a month after the Albany speech, he declined an invitation to attend an ACLU luncheon to celebrate the Bill of Rights, explaining, "Perhaps I am carrying too far my unwillingness to join in such a public celebration, however much personally I may be in favor of it; but I still think that it is better for judges not to appear on such occasions."[58]

With the nation torn by McCarthyism, President Eisenhower incurred the criticism of many liberals and Democrats because he refused to take a firm public stand against the Wisconsin senator and limited himself to veiled remarks opposing "book burners" and "thought control." Hand, who voted for Eisenhower in the 1952 election despite his strong dislike for Nixon, found himself increasingly isolated when defending the president. "I would have treated the McCarthy matter about as he," he wrote in the fall of 1952,[59] and throughout the McCarthy years, he urged his friends: "Don't be hard on Eisenhower. . . . [H]e may indeed look feeble and indecisive; but to my mind that is an inadequate judgment."[60] Indeed, he applauded the president's skill in "temporizing" with the Republican right wing and gave him credit for helping to bring about McCarthy's ultimate downfall.[61] He also supported Eisenhower because of the president's outspoken opposition to the so-called Bricker Amendment, an isolationist proposal to amend the Constitution to weaken the nation's treaty-making power and the president's power to make executive agreements. Hand's wrath was mainly directed against the Republican party organization, particularly the right wing that Eisenhower was afraid to alienate.

Senator McCarthy's demise came more quickly than Hand had anticipated. The war with Korea, which Eisenhower promised to end during his 1952 campaign, concluded at last with an armistice in July 1953, and that took away one source of the anti-subversion hysteria. More important, through the deft efforts of counsel Joseph Welch in the Army-McCarthy hearings, from April to June 1954, the shamefulness of McCarthy's tactics and the senator's deep flaws were revealed to a national television audience. On December 2, 1954, the Senate dealt McCarthy a fatal blow by formally condemning his tactics by a 67–22 vote. Hand himself gave credit for McCarthy's downfall to the president, reporting to Bernard Berenson with relief that Eisenhower had "finally extinguished the baleful light of McCarthy; and although he has not, and cannot, convert his malevolent following, which is perilously large and formidable—especially through the support the

[Roman Catholic] Church gives it—at least the eclipse of the leader has had a discouraging effect for the moment."[62] Even then, after McCarthy's rebuke by the Senate, a poll indicated that 44 percent of the American public still regarded him favorably. And McCarthy's supporters still continued their master's method of reckless accusations. Hand, upset by the continuing witch-hunt, gave another widely reported address, even more felicitous and eloquent than his Regents speech, at the forty-eighth annual session of the American Jewish Committee, on January 29, 1955,[63] where he received the organization's first American Liberties Medallion. Hand's carefully prepared response addressed the continuing evils of McCarthyism. No one could mistake his target, especially after former New York State justice Joseph M. Proskauer presented Hand to the audience and conferred the medallion in a short address that quoted a passage from Hand's Regents address.[64]

Hand's speech took special pains to link his hostility to McCarthyism to his lifelong philosophy. In speaking about the "principles of civil liberties and human rights," as he had been assigned to do, he began by reminding his audience that "a beehive or an anthill" was not "a perfect example of a free society." Americans, he claimed, had traditionally held the "deepest hostility" to "such prototypes of totalitarianism." Why was that so? Surely not because conformity could not be assured in fact; it could, as Aldous Huxley's *Brave New World* and George Orwell's *1984* had prophesied. The world had already seen such prophecies nearly fulfilled, he noted, yet groups were now at work in America to press it toward such a conformist society, "large and powerful groups . . . who see treason in all dissidence, and would welcome an era in which all of us should think, feel, and live in consonance with duly prescribed patterns." The widespread charges of "subversion" were Hand's special target: "[A]ll debate, all dissidence," Hand told his audience, "tends to question, and in consequence to upset, existing convictions: that is precisely its purpose and its justification." And the basic assumption of the American system counseled tolerance of those who challenge our most basic beliefs. The true "principles of civil liberties and human rights," he insisted,

> lie in habits, customs—conventions, if you will—that tolerate dissent and can live without irrefragable certainties; that are ready to overhaul existing assumptions; that recognize that we never see save through a glass, darkly; and that at long last we shall succeed only so far as we continue to undertake "the intolerable labor of thought"—that most distasteful of all our activities.[65]

Hand ended by restating the modest skeptical faith he had preached for decades. He was not confident about the ultimate outcome of the battle against conformity, but, speaking as much biographically as philosophically, he reverted to the idealization of the craftsman of Oliver Wendell Holmes's "Society of Jobbists," which he had evoked many years earlier, in 1930, at the presentation of a portrait of Justice Holmes to the Harvard Law School:[66]

> By some happy fortuity, man is a projector, a designer, a builder, a craftsman; it is among his most dependable joys to impose upon the flux that passes before him some mark of himself, aware though he always must be of the odds against him. His reward is not so much in the work as in its making; not so much in the prize as in the race. We may win when we lose, if we have done what we can; for by so doing we have made real at least some part of that finished product in whose fabrication we are most concerned: ourselves. And if at the end some friendly critic shall pass by and say: "My friend, how good a job do you really think you have made of it all?" we can answer: "I know as well as you that it is not of high quality; but I did put into it whatever I had, and that was the game I started out to play."[67]

Hand's address attracted nearly as much public attention as his Regents speech of 1952: newspapers printed excerpts, and Senator Herbert Lehman of New York promptly inserted it into the *Congressional Record*.[68] And again, congratulatory mail poured in. Felix Frankfurter quoted his wife's remarks: " 'This is really terrific! (A word I do not recall having heard from her.) I only hope that there were some people there who could fully appreciate his English.' Frankfurter J. concurs."[69]

HAND'S CONCERN that his public statements might keep him from working on cases involving Cold War issues was perhaps justified, for increasingly they came before him as a judge. The espionage and perjury cases he had to decide put to a severe test his intellectual commitment to detached, impartial judging. Three cases illustrate his responses to this challenge: *United States v. Coplon*,[70] a review of a conviction for stealing and delivering "defense information" to a Soviet citizen;[71] *United States v. Dennis*,[72] an appeal of the convictions of the leaders of the American Communist party for conspiring to advocate and teach the violent overthrow of the United States government; and *United*

States v. Remington,[73] an appeal of a conviction for giving perjured testimony regarding the defendant's Communist involvements.*

The *Coplon* case was one of the most absorbing spy trials of the Cold War. The chief defendant was Judith Coplon, a young Barnard College graduate who had been employed by the Internal Security Section of the Department of Justice. Her codefendant was Valentin A. Gubitchev, a United Nations employee who had been an official of the Soviet Foreign Affairs Ministry. From the moment Coplon and Gubitchev were arrested in New York on March 4, 1949, while Coplon was passing to Gubitchev documents she had stolen from the Justice Department, the case captured the imagination and fed the fears of the American public and received extensive coverage in the press. There was no real question about the guilt of the defendants. Both drew fifteen-year sentences.† Gubitchev's sentence was suspended at the request of the State Department, on a condition he readily accepted—that he immediately return to the Soviet Union. Coplon was thus left to appeal the conviction on her own.

The appeal came before a Second Circuit panel of Learned Hand, Thomas Swan, and Jerome Frank. That the prosecution had introduced sufficient evidence of guilt was not seriously disputed. The central issue was rather the legitimacy of the government's law-enforcement methods. On this score, Coplon raised two objections: first, she charged her warrantless arrest violated the Fourth Amendment's guarantee against unreasonable searches and seizures; second, she claimed she had not been given adequate opportunity to demonstrate that the evidence against her derived from illegal wiretaps of her telephone.

The FBI had been tracking Coplon for some time before she was arrested. She had been a Justice Department employee in New York from 1943 until early 1945, when she was transferred to Washington to work in the division that had charge of the registration of foreign agents. In October 1948, she was transferred to the more sensitive

---

* The congressional investigations repeatedly produced prosecutions for contempt of Congress against those who failed to answer questions in hearings of the House Un-American Activities Committee and the Senate Internal Security Committee; but the contempt-of-Congress cases were typically brought in the federal courts for the District of Columbia rather than in New York. The New York federal courts, including the Second Circuit, did decide two other major cases of the era, the perjury conviction of Alger Hiss and the espionage convictions of Julius and Ethel Rosenberg, but Hand did not sit in either of these.

† The sentences were imposed by Judge Sylvester J. Ryan in the Southern District of New York. Before the New York trial, the defendants had also been tried in a federal court in the District of Columbia. Formally, the D.C. charge was that Coplon copied, removed, and secreted Justice Department files; the New York charge was that she attempted to deliver the information to Gubitchev in New York and conspired with him to steal the documents.

Internal Security Section. By early 1949, her section chief was told that she was under suspicion, and he transferred her back to the Registration Section. During February, Coplon went to her successor in the Internal Security Section, pressed her to see some of the reports filed there, and took some of them away, asking the woman to send Coplon any reports pertaining to foreign embassies and, particularly, to Russian agents.

The stimulus for her arrest in March came from three trips she made to New York, in January, February, and March of 1949. During each trip, FBI agents kept her under close surveillance. On the first and second trips she spent considerable time with Gubitchev, but apparently passed him no papers. She rendezvoused with Gubitchev once again on March 4. According to Hand's opinion, "[B]oth appeared to be acting with even more circumspection than before." At about 9:30 p.m., they were arrested by the FBI, without a warrant; a sealed packet in Coplon's purse contained many government documents. Although the defendants did not know it at the time, the FBI, at the personal direction of the attorney general, had been tapping the phones at Coplon's Washington home, her Washington office, and her Brooklyn home since January.

Hand's opinion pointed out that during all three New York City meetings, Coplon and Gubitchev "had wandered aimlessly about, meeting, separating, rejoining, going hither and yon, continually looking back, and in general giving every appearance of persons who thought they might be shadowed and wished to escape being trailed." He noted that all the documents in her purse, "taken with the repeated instances in which she had shown an insistent wish to get access to such records, and with her meetings in New York, made out a case which must have satisfied any fair minded jury that she was engaged in the conspiracy with which she was charged; and that, when the right moment came, she meant to pass the packet to Gubitchev." The defendants' activities, according to Hand, constituted an illegal "attempt" to commit a crime rather than an unprohibited "preparation."[74]

Hand then turned to the question of the legality of Coplon's warrantless arrest. Under the law, warrantless arrests were permissible only when the arresting officer had "reasonable grounds to believe that the person so arrested is guilty of [a] felony" *and* "where there is a likelihood of the person escaping before a warrant can be obtained for . . . arrest." The trial judge had found that the arresting FBI agent reasonably believed that Coplon was likely to escape. Hand rejected that conclusion. In his view, the defendants' behavior indicated that their March 4 meeting was not a final one: if Coplon had not been arrested, it was almost certain that "she would go back to Washington and hold her job." Even if there had been reason to fear her escaping, the FBI had no justification for arresting her without a warrant, Hand wrote: "It is apparent that even in the morning the Bureau had decided to arrest her that day; and there was not the least need of doing so without a warrant. No sudden emergency forced the hand of the agents." The law requires a warrant whenever there is time to obtain one; accordingly, Hand concluded: "We have no alternative but to hold that the arrest was invalid, and concededly that made the packet incompetent [as evidence] against her."[75]

Hand next turned to the most important question in the case: Coplon's claim that she had been a victim of illegal wiretapping. At the time, while wiretaps were illegal under Section 605 of the Communications Act of 1934, the Supreme Court had never held that a wiretap violated the Fourth Amendment. Over passionate dissents by Justices Brandeis and Holmes, the Court had ruled 5–4, in *Olmstead v. United States* in 1928,[76] that wiretaps were not searches and seizures for Fourth Amendment purposes. Thus, while as early as 1939 he had expressed the view that "possibly *Olmstead v. United States . . .* is no longer law,"[77] Hand had to decide *Coplon* mainly on statutory grounds, despite its evident constitutional overtones.*

One genuine constitutional issue did enter Hand's analysis, however. The normal rule governing wiretap data is that once the defendant establishes that conversations have been unlawfully tapped, the government must then prove that none of the evidence it used to convict was derived in any way from the wiretapping. The defendant must be given access to the data in order to counter the prosecution's claim that its evidence was not tainted. However, the trial judge had withheld some of the wiretap records from Coplon on national-security grounds. Instead, he examined all the records in private and concluded that the wiretaps had not led to any evidence introduced at the trial. In an especially carefully reasoned part of his opinion, Hand found that the trial judge's refusal to disclose all the wiretap records to Coplon required a reversal of her conviction. Withholding the records, he argued, had violated her Sixth Amendment right "to be confronted with the witnesses against [her]." Thus, though in Hand's view Coplon's guilt was "plain," he concluded that her conviction had to be reversed. He refused to dismiss the indictment against her entirely, however, since it was "pos-

---

* Not until nearly twenty years after Hand's *Coplon* decision did the Supreme Court formally overrule *Olmstead* and hold that wiretapping was indeed a search and seizure for Fourth Amendment purposes (*Katz v. United States*, 389 U.S. 347 [1967]).

sible [at] another trial that there may be more evidence of the likelihood of an escape; [and] that the prosecution may decide to divulge the contents of the 'taps.' "[78]*

Hand had no sympathy for spies and no illusion that international communism carried no threat to American security. His powerful opinion in *Coplon* thus represented not sympathy for the defendant but rather loyalty to his basic belief that government must cut square corners in prosecuting the accused. He expressed this belief fervently in one passage of his opinion:

> Back of this particular privilege [to confront one's accusers] lies a long chapter in the history of Anglo-American institutions. Few weapons in the arsenal of freedom are more useful than the power to compel a government to disclose the evidence on which it seeks to forfeit the liberty of its citizens. All governments, democracies as well as autocracies, believe that those they seek to punish are guilty; the impediment of constitutional barriers are galling to all governments when they prevent the consummation of that just purpose. But those barriers were devised and are precious because they prevent that purpose and its pursuit from passing unchallenged by the accused, and unpurged by the alembic of public scrutiny and public criticism. A society which has come to wince at such exposure of the methods by which it seeks to impose its will upon its members, has already lost the feel of freedom and is on the path towards absolutism.[79]

These were stirring words but hardly novel sentiments for Hand. Such sentiments had made him an especially strong defender of the Fourth Amendment search-and-seizure guarantee since his district court days. Hand was never as eager as his colleague Jerome Frank to overturn convictions simply because of some "harmless" error. Moreover, he was not inclined to broad interpretations of the Fifth Amendment's privilege against self-incrimination: while he was indeed harshly critical of secret questioning of the accused by the police, he saw no reason

---

* Judith Coplon was never retried in New York: in 1955, the Justice Department admitted that it did not have sufficient evidence independent of the wiretapping to warrant a retrial, and the indictments were finally dismissed, in 1967. (See Hershel Shanks, ed., *The Art and Craft of Judging: The Decisions of Judge Learned Hand* [New York: Macmillan, 1968], 283–98.)

After the existence of wiretaps became known in Coplon's New York pretrial hearing, she moved to set aside her earlier District of Columbia conviction as well. She succeeded in the D.C. Circuit Court of Appeals, after it was discovered that the D.C. taps encompassed conversations between Coplon and her attorney, both before and during her D.C. trial. This, the D.C. Court of Appeals held, deprived her of her Sixth Amendment right to "effective and substantial aid of counsel" (*Coplon v. United States*, 191 F.2d 749 [D.C.Cir. 1951]). She was never retried in the District of Columbia either.

why the Fifth Amendment privilege needed to be broadly interpreted to bar comments on an accused's refusal to answer questions in open court. But in a long series of search-and-seizure opinions, he was steadfastly on guard against government misconduct that violated the Fourth Amendment. As long ago as 1923, he had as a trial judge imposed safeguards to assure that genuine "probable cause" existed before a search warrant could issue.[80] In 1926, he wrote a landmark, widely cited opinion restricting the right to conduct searches of an accused's papers or home as an incident to a lawful arrest.[81] In this particular case, under the National Prohibition Act, Hand commented, "[W]hat seems fair enough against a squalid huckster of bad liquor may take on a very different face, if used by a government determined to suppress political opposition under the guise of sedition." And although the law governing the scope of permissible searches incident to a valid arrest continued murky for many years, Hand steadfastly defended the accused's rights.[82] For example, Hand sharply criticized the Supreme Court's decision in *Harris v. United States*[83]—a decision in which it approved, as incident to a legal arrest, a five-hour search of every room of a defendant's apartment while he remained handcuffed in his living room. Hand expressed to Frankfurter (who had dissented) his disdain for the majority ruling. He could not understand, he told Frankfurter, "how anyone can take the majority's view in whose bowels there is any fire of freedom. Worse. This is the kind of thing on which Totalitarianism lives and without which I rather guess it cannot live."[84] He expressed similar views less than a year later, in commenting to Frankfurter on the need to curb interrogations of a suspect after arrest:

> But on what happens to a man under arrest your guts and mine move—doubtful simile?—alike. I suppose it would go too far to make inadmissible everything said after arrest which was not in the presence of a judge etc. etc., though I confess that temptation is strong to me to go so far. But this goddamn questioning for hours under Klieg . . . lights outrages me. Such things are only next door to torture: to me they would be.[85]

In 1949, Hand had faced a question very similar to the one the Supreme Court had decided in *Harris* in 1947. By relying on a 1948 Supreme Court ruling,[86] he was able once again to reverse the conviction on the basis of governmental misconduct.[87] But the Supreme Court renounced its own 1948 ruling and reversed Hand's decision, eliciting a fierce Frankfurter dissent that concluded "I have yet to hear the answer to Judge Learned Hand's reasoning below."[88] Given these shared views, it is no surprise that Frankfurter, when he read the first reports of Hand's *Coplon* decision in the press, wrote to him promptly:

> I don't have to wait for text of your *Coplon* to congratulate you —[though] one ought not to praise a judge for doing what he knows is right.[89]

But while Hand had indeed done what he thought was right as a matter of law and constitutional principles, many followers of the *Coplon* trial disagreed, and he became a target of hate mail, most of which bemused rather than shocked him—he saved a sampling in his papers.[90] As he wrote Frankfurter:

> You would be amused at my Judy Coplon mail; the Jews bribed us to let her off and we are now rich because, being "rats," "curs," "traitors," etc., we cashed in "big." I will own that I am a little disturbed at the rather constant note of anti-Semitism; but the rest entertains me.[91]*

Writing in 1968, Hershel Shanks, a Washington lawyer and a perceptive commentator on Hand's decisions, captured Hand's approach especially well:

> The point is . . . simply that no facile evaluation can be made of Judge Hand's judicial product in terms of the currently fashionable liberal-conservative equation. The values he served were at once higher and more subtle: impartiality, intellectual detachment, respect for the higher authority of sometimes murky Supreme Court guides, an awareness of the limited authority in which courts must operate to justify their untouchable independence and the belief that reason must lead to the result, not vice versa.[92]

SHANKS'S ADMONITION is also apt in assessing Hand's 1950 ruling in another notorious case of the Cold War era, *Dennis v. United States*. In that decision, Hand affirmed the convictions of eleven leaders of the Communist party of the United States under the Smith Act of

---

* Frankfurter replied: "I am deeply saddened that a completely disinterested exercise of judicial duty such as you performed in the *Coplon* case should open the sluices of the sewer even against you. I can only say that if you had a glimpse of the stuff that for years has been coming through the mail to me you would be less surprised but not less saddened by the infection of anti-Semitism that Hitler and his epigni have brought to this country" (Felix Frankfurter to LH, 29 December 1950, 105–15).

1940* for forming a conspiracy to advocate or teach the duty and necessity of overthrowing the government by force and violence, and to organize the Communist party as a group so to teach and advocate.[93] In upholding the constitutionality of the Smith Act in *Dennis*, Hand restated and diluted the most speech-protective interpretations of Holmes's "clear and present danger" test. When the Supreme Court affirmed Hand's decision, Chief Justice Fred M. Vinson's plurality opinion adopted Hand's version of the "clear and present danger" standard, calling it "as succinct and inclusive as any other we might devise at this time."[94]

The Supreme Court's *Dennis* decision was viewed by many as a debacle for the First Amendment, and critics have attributed a share of the blame to Hand's opinion in the Second Circuit. But the story behind Hand's decision is more complicated than that. On a more discriminating assessment, the ruling does not truly cast doubt upon Hand's strong hostility to McCarthyism or the genuineness of his long commitment to civil liberties.

The appeal of the Communist leaders came to Hand's court after they were found guilty in the trial court of Judge Harold Medina, who presided over a rambunctious, nearly nine-months-long proceeding. The defendants were indicted in July 1948; their trial began on January 17, 1949, and it did not end until the jury's guilty verdict on October 14 of that year. The central constitutional question before Hand's court, as it would be for the Supreme Court, was the constitutionality under the First Amendment of the Smith Act. The defense relied mainly on its interpretation of the "clear and present danger" standard that Justice Holmes had announced in *Schenck v. United States* in 1919: the "question in every case is whether the words used are used in such circumstances and are of such a nature as to create a clear and present danger that they will bring about the substantive evils that Congress has the right to prevent. It is a question of proximity and degree."

As stated and applied in *Schenck*, the "clear and present danger" test was not very speech-protective. Indeed, during and immediately after World War I, Hand had argued extensively with Holmes, unsuccessfully trying to persuade the justice that the "incitement" standard Hand articulated in the *Masses* case was far more speech-protective than, and preferable to, the "clear and present danger" standard. Hand objected from the outset that speech should be punishable only if the speaker

---

* The original indictment was of twelve leaders; the defendants included William Z. Foster, the chairman of the party, but his trial was deferred because he was ill with a heart disease. The name of the case, *Dennis v. United States*, comes from the defendant Eugene Dennis, the party's general secretary.

used words that explicitly counseled violation of law—words that counseled the audience that it was their "duty" or in their "interest" to
violate law. This incitement standard, Hand thought, was a far safer
"qualitative formula," "hard, conventional, difficult to evade." Hand
also insisted from the outset that the "clear and present danger" test
was far too slippery and open-ended, for it required a judge or jury to
prophesy about the likelihood that the speech would produce danger.
That, he feared, would make courts far too vulnerable to the prevailing
winds of public opinion. But by the time of *Dennis*, Hand had come
to believe that his *Masses* approach had been a failure: it had found
"little professional support,"[95] and he had been compelled to "bid a long
farewell to my little toy ship which set out quite bravely on the shortest
voyage ever made."[96] And while Hand's *Masses* approach sank into
oblivion in the years between World War I and World War II, the
Supreme Court had adhered to and struggled to clarify its "clear and
present danger" test.

As a judge of a lower court who took seriously his obligation to
follow Supreme Court precedents, Hand devoted a substantial part of
his opinion to a painstaking and what he himself called a "weary
analysis" of the Supreme Court decisions.[97] He found no clear guidance
there, and he cannot really be faulted for sensing that the Supreme
Court rulings meandered. On the one hand, for example, *Gitlow v.
New York*,[98] still on the books, had upheld the application of a New
York law very similar to the Smith Act to a left-wing agitator, despite
dissents by Holmes and Brandeis; on the other hand, some sharp separate
opinions by these two Great Dissenters had attempted to put more teeth
into the speech-protective aspects of "clear and present danger."[99] As
Hand said of one series of cases, "[T]he situation in all was wholly
different from that in the preceding decisions," and none "attempted
to define how grave, or how imminent the danger must be, or whether
the two factors are mutually interdependent."[100] Faced, then, with an
array of rulings on "clear and present danger"—a standard he disliked
from the outset—Hand concluded that it amounted only to "a way to
describe a number of occasions, even the outskirts of which are inde-
finable, but within which, as is so often the case, the courts must find
their way as they can." And as he rephrased the standard, in words
Chief Justice Vinson would adopt for the Supreme Court, "In each
case [the courts] must ask whether the gravity of the 'evil,' discounted
by its improbability, justifies such invasion of free speech as is necessary
to avoid the danger."[101]

Hand thought that the *Dennis* defendants' teachings seemed "to kick
the beam" by going far beyond the protected area of speech as delineated

by the "clear and present danger" test. A "bitter outcast" might be permitted to "vent his venom before any crowds he can muster and in any terms that he wishes," but this case presented "something very different":

> The American Communist Party, of which the defendants are the controlling spirits, is a highly articulated, well contrived, far spread organization, numbering thousands of adherents, rigidly and ruthlessly disciplined, many of whom are infused with the passionate Utopian faith that is to redeem mankind. It has its Founder, its apostles, its sacred texts—perhaps even its martyrs. It seeks converts far and wide by an extensive system of schooling, demanding of all an inflexible doctrinal orthodoxy. The violent capture of all existing governments is one article of the creed of that faith, which abjures the possibility of success by lawful means. . . . Our democracy, like any other, must meet that faith and that creed on the merits, or it will perish; and we must not flinch at the challenge. Nevertheless, we may insist that the rules of the game be observed, and the rules confine the conflict to weapons drawn from the universe of discourse. The advocacy of violence may, or may not, fail; but in neither case can there be any "right" to use it.[102]

Among the criticisms launched against Hand's and the Supreme Court's analysis of *Dennis* is that Hand's formula put much less emphasis on the "immediacy" of the danger than earlier opinions had. Hand did not in fact deny the relevance of "the question [of] how imminent . . . that is how probable of execution" the alleged conspiracy of the Communist party was in 1948, the time of the indictment. Like the majority of the Supreme Court, however, he relied heavily on the world situation during the Cold War rather than evidence on the record, which consisted mainly of the teachings of Communist literature.

Justice William O. Douglas's strong dissent in the Supreme Court decision in *Dennis* targeted that aspect of the approach. He claimed that the case was argued as if the defendants had been teaching "the techniques of sabotage" and similar illegal behavior. But, he insisted, "[T]he fact is that no such evidence was introduced at the trial."[103] Instead, the emphasis in the trial record was on the teaching of Marxist-Leninist doctrine as reflected in books by Stalin, Marx and Engels, and Lenin. The Supreme Court had not outlawed these texts, but had instead made "freedom of speech turn not on *what is said*, but on the *intent* with which it is said," because the Smith Act had been construed to require "the element of intent—that those who teach the creed believe in it. The crime then depends not on what is taught but who the teacher is."

In Douglas's view, there had been no showing of "some immediate injury to society that is likely if speech is allowed."[104] He therefore opposed the Supreme Court majority's finding of danger on the basis of "judicial notice."

Hand, too, relied on this doctrine—on facts so readily known to judges that they do not need to be proven by trial evidence.

> [I]n most of West Europe there were important political Communist factions, always agitating to increase their power; and the defendants were acting in close concert with the movement. The *status quo*, hastily contrived in 1945, was showing strains and tensions, not originally expected. Save for the unexpected success of the airlift, Britain, France and ourselves would have been forced out of Berlin, contrary to our understanding of the convention by which we were there. We had become the object of invective upon invective; we were continuously charged with aggressive designs against other nations; our efforts to reestablish their economic stability were repeatedly set down as a scheme to enslave them; we had been singled out as the chief enemy of the faith; we were the eventually doomed, but still formidable, protagonists of that decadent system which it was to supplant. Any border fray, any diplomatic incident, any difference in construction of the *modus vivendi*—such as the Berlin blockade we have just mentioned— might prove a spark in the tinder-box, and lead to war. We do not understand how one could ask for a more probable danger, unless we must wait till the actual eve of hostilities. . . . True, we must not forget our own faith; we must be sensitive to the dangers that lurk in any choice; but choose we must, and we shall be silly dupes if we forget that again and again in the past thirty years, just such preparations in other countries have aided to supplant existing governments, when the time was ripe.[105]

This reliance on "judicial notice," by Hand and in the Supreme Court, to establish the danger of Communist activities has been widely criticized. Yet this approach was in effect invited by the traditional formulations of "clear and present danger." The emphasis on prophecy of the future, the insistence on forecasting the danger of speech at some future time, was inherent in the "clear and present danger" test, and this made that standard especially vulnerable to such wide-ranging inquiries, as Hand himself had warned as early as his debates with Holmes at the end of World War I.

Today, the affirmance of the *Dennis* convictions is widely seen as a blow to the First Amendment. Indeed, Justice Hugo Black expressed this view in his dissent in *Dennis*:

> Public opinion being what it now is, few will protest the conviction of these Communist petitioners. There is hope, however, that in calmer times, when present pressures, passions and fears subside, this or some later Court will restore the First Amendment liberties to the high preferred place where they belong in a free society.[106]

That greater protection of free speech did indeed soon come from the Supreme Court, within a few years of *Dennis*. In the course of subsequent prosecutions, a series of Supreme Court opinions by Justice John Marshall Harlan reinterpreted the Smith Act and *Dennis* itself. In cases such as *Yates v. United States*, *Scales v. United States*, and *Noto v. United States*,[107] the Court required far stronger evidence of actual unprotected speech by the specific defendants than *Dennis* had. In fact, these Harlan opinions rekindled the torch lit by Hand in his *Masses* ruling of 1917 and in his debates with Holmes. Harlan insisted on strict statutory standards of proof emphasizing the actual speech of the defendants—a variation on the "hard," "objective," words-oriented focus of Hand in *Masses*. Harlan claimed to be reinterpreting *Dennis*; in fact, Harlan's opinion represented a doctrinal evolution in a new direction, a direction back to the *Masses* "incitement" standard.[108] And in 1969, less than two decades after *Dennis*, Hand's *Masses* position was vindicated by the Supreme Court at last: in *Brandenburg v. Ohio*,[109] the Court established a new standard of speech protection, a standard in which incitement to lawless action—Hand's *Masses* standard—became a central prerequisite for justifying convictions under the First Amendment.

Clearly, Hand's performance in *Dennis* was neither a sudden surrender to McCarthyism nor an act of cowardice. Thus, he insisted repeatedly that he thought the Smith Act prosecutions of the Communist leaders a mistake. As he wrote to Bernard Berenson in Italy after the decision, "For myself, although of course it has nothing to do with my job or what was before me in [*Dennis*], I deprecated the prosecution! If one is going to take any action against Communism, it is of no use to put some of the leaders in prison for three or four years. 'The blood of martyrs is the seed of the church.' "[110] "Personally I should never have prosecuted those birds. . . . So far as all this will do anything, it will encourage the faithful and maybe help the Committee on Propaganda."[111]

The central answer to the puzzle of how Hand could write so speech-restrictive an opinion as *Dennis* lies in the fact that as a lower court judge, he was bound by and faithful to Supreme Court precedents. He had never liked Holmes's "clear and present danger" test, and he continued to feel this way at the time of *Dennis*: "As res integra, I think that Holmes—nomen clarrisima et venerabilissime—for once slipped his trolley on 'clear and present'; at most a mere side spark anyway," he wrote to Frankfurter.[112]

Hand's contemporaneous correspondence makes clear that he continued to adhere to the essence of his *Masses* test of 1917, but, since the Supreme Court and the profession had not adopted it by 1950, he was not free to apply it in *Dennis*. Had he been more free to follow his own beliefs, there was a better answer than the Supreme Court's approach, he thought. It lay in the incitement analysis he had set forth in *Masses*.

> I have never felt satisfied that there was not an adequate qualitative distinction, baffling as any rule must become in application. I tried to state it years ago in the *Masses* case but have had to abandon it.

> So far as the constitution goes, I cannot see why it should protect any speech which contains "aid[ing], abetting, counsel[ing]" etc., to *violate* any law. If that is mingled with otherwise permissible speech I would leave it to Congress to require the utterer to separate the wheat from the chaff. Holmes was wrong I think when he said that every argument is an "incitement";[113] that was too loose use of language, for incitement more properly means making yourself a party to the venture: an accessory. Maybe in the end the crux is purpose; I rather think it is; and I am as aware as you can be how unreliable a litmus test that is. Still, we do use it all the time.[114]

Hand also insisted on this preference for *Masses* as a constitutional rule in a letter a few months later to Elliot L. Richardson, who was Hand's law clerk in the 1947–48 term and clerked for Frankfurter soon after. Richardson wrote a lengthy defense of the Supreme Court's approach in *Dennis* in the *Harvard Law Review*,[115] on which Hand commented at length:

> I dissent from the whole approach to the problem of Free Speech which the Supreme Court has adopted during the last thirty-five or forty years. . . . I would make the purpose of the utterer the test of his constitutional protection. Did he seek to bring about a violation of existing law? If he did, I can see no reason why the

constitution should protect him, however remote the chance may be of his success.

My reasons may sound didactic and too generalized; but here they are. Every society which promulgates a law means that it shall be obeyed until it is changed, and any society which lays down means by which its laws can be changed makes those means exclusive. . . . If so, how in God's name can an incitement to do what will be unlawful if done, be itself lawful? How do words differ from any other way of bringing about an event? . . . Of course, I do not mean that it would be wise to punish all utterances whose purpose is to provoke unlawful conduct. Much of it is much better to ignore; too repressive a policy though in itself lawful may often discourage legitimate and even profitable discourse. But that, I submit, is not a constitutional objection, or at least it ought not to be.[116]

Thus, Hand thought his court really had no choice but to reject the defendants' challenges in *Dennis*: "[W]e had no alternative. Many is the time that I have declared valid a law I should never have voted to pass."[117] But his uncommon self-confidence about his ruling did not diminish his insistence that even those who were clearly guilty were entitled to the full protections of the law. And he had repeated occasion to act on this commitment in a controversial series of rulings intertwined with the *Dennis* appeal. The recurrent issue was whether Dennis and his codefendants were entitled to be freed on bail after they were convicted in Judge Medina's trial court, an issue that first arose on October 14, 1949, when, immediately after the trial, the defendants asked Judge Medina to free them on bail and the government opposed their request. Judge Medina, who had no doubt about the constitutionality of the convictions, refused to grant bail. The defendants promptly appealed to the Second Circuit. The argument on the issue was held on November 1, before a panel over which Hand presided.[118] From the outset, Hand was notably cool toward the prosecution's insistence that the eleven Communists remain in jail pending appeal or, if bail were granted, that it be set at $1 million "for security reasons."[119] The defendants relied on a federal rule stating that bail may be allowed pending appeal where the case involves a substantial question that should be determined by the appellate court.[120] From the prosecutor's murky responses to his questions, Hand drew the conclusion that "the prosecution concedes there is doubt on substantial questions." This simplified the case for him: "It comes down to whether bail should be allowed, and on what terms."[121] Two days later, Hand's court granted bail at a total of $260,000.[122] The Civil Rights Congress promptly posted the requisite amount in government bonds and the defendants were released on the evening of November 3.

After the Second Circuit affirmed the *Dennis* convictions in early August 1950, the defendants sought bail while they pursued an appeal to the Supreme Court. The zealous United States attorney, Irving Saypol, had initiated this proceeding by moving to revoke the bail of the defendants on the ground that they were continuing "to do the same things [of] which they had been convicted." Once again, Hand sat on the Second Circuit panel, joined by Judges Swan and Chase. These last two, somewhat moved by the impassioned arguments of the prosecutor, granted the motion to revoke bail, but postponed its effectiveness for thirty days to permit the defendants to appeal the issue to Justice Robert Jackson. Hand would not curtail the defendants' rights that way. He dissented from the majority ruling of his court, stating, "I would continue bail until either the petition for certiorari [the petition to invoke the Supreme Court's discretion to review the case] is denied or granted."[123]

Hand's independent, courageous judgment was soon vindicated by Justice Jackson. On September 25, Jackson found that the "substantial constitutional question" in the case had not "completely disappeared." He rejected the prosecution's claim that the defendants had forfeited their right to bail because of their "misbehavior after conviction":

> Imprisonment to protect society from predicted but unconsummated offenses is so unprecedented in this country and so fraught with danger of excesses and injustice that I am loath to resort to it. . . . [T]he right of every American to equal treatment before the law is wrapped up in the same constitutional bundle with those of these Communists. If in anger or disgust with these defendants we throw out the bundle, we also cast aside protection for the liberties of more worthy critics who may be in opposition to the government of some future day.[124]

Repeatedly quoting from Hand's dissenting views in the Court of Appeals, Jackson (who ultimately voted to affirm the *Dennis* convictions) accordingly continued the bail of the defendants until the Supreme Court ruled on their appeals.

Hand's bail rulings did not sit well with politicians and portions of the public. Some of the very people who hailed his decision affirming the convictions criticized his bail arguments. Republican senator John Bricker of Ohio—the author of the isolationist Bricker Amendment

and Thomas Dewey's vice-presidential candidate in the 1948 election
—issued a press release in late March 1951 urging an investigation by
the Senate Judiciary Committee of "the whole situation" of federal
judges releasing convicted Communists on bail. Bricker stated: "I do
not believe the courts of our country are sacred cows that are . . .
protected by some kind of sanctity which absolves them from investigation by Congress as to whether they are carrying out their oaths of
office."[125] Bricker had in mind not only Hand's grant of bail to the
Dennis defendants, but the Ninth Circuit's grant of bail to the West
Coast labor leader Harry Bridges, an Australian émigré who had been
convicted of swearing falsely at his naturalization hearing that he had
never been a Communist party member. Chief Judge William Denman
of the Ninth Circuit angrily retorted that Bricker's charge amounted to
"smearing," and sent a copy of his statement to Hand, addressing it
"Dear Bull Moose and Sacred Cow," and noting the impression in
Washington that "Bricker seeks to McCarthyize Roosevelt's and Truman's appointments."[126]

Hand must have been especially surprised by a letter of praise from
the very left-wing artist Rockwell Kent, who sent Hand a copy of a
letter he had written to the editor of the pro-Communist cultural magazine *Masses & Mainstream*. The magazine had repeatedly criticized
the judges in the *Dennis* litigation and called for public protests against
them; demonstrations in Foley Square in front of the federal courthouse
had become commonplace,[127] so the magazine, as well as Communist
party chairman William Z. Foster, had attributed the decision to grant
bail to the force of such public opinion. Kent rebuked such statements:

> Foster, and others, have done serious injustice to three exception-
> ally able and conscientious men who, by the righteousness of their
> decision, are makers rather than followers of public opinion. There
> is a deep strain of justice and fair play in the American people. It
> was given authoritative expression by the decision of the Circuit
> Court.[128]

The "battle of Foley Square"[129] that went on during the *Dennis* trial
had indeed directly affected Hand in some ways, even before he came
to review the convictions. During the trial, pro-defendant pickets gathered in the little park across from the courthouse every day, carrying
placards and yelling slogans; inside the courtroom, Judge Medina, the
defendants, and the defendants' lawyers were increasingly at one another's throats, with motions endlessly argued, exchanges of sarcasm
and derision, and mounting complaints of fatigue from Medina, who
was convinced he was being deliberately harassed. "It is more than any

human being can stand," he complained.[130] He repeatedly responded to the tensions by threatening the lawyers with contempt, but he refused to interrupt the trial to pursue his threats, fearing that to do so would play into the hands of the defense. Instead, he waited until after the jury verdict to cite the lawyers—including Eugene Dennis himself, who conducted his own defense—for contempt. This produced a new round of appeals; Hand did not sit in these but he did have a chance to examine Medina's behavior in reviewing the Smith Act convictions.

One of the defendants' claims was that Medina's alleged bias and misconduct had deprived the accused of a fair trial. Hand's opinion for the Second Circuit concluded that Medina had not exceeded all proper bounds, although his tongue was often sharp. As Hand summarized the trial atmosphere:

> The record discloses a judge, sorely tried for many months of turmoil, constantly provoked by useless bickering, exposed to offensive slights and insults, harried with interminable repetition, who, if at times he did not conduct himself with the imperturbability of a Rhadamanthus, showed considerably greater self-control and forbearance than it is given to most judges to possess.[131]

Hand was normally inclined to grant trial judges considerable leeway in conducting trials. Although he conceded that Medina had "at times . . . used language short of requisite judicial gravity," he refused to sustain the charge that Medina had been guilty of hectoring counsel and unduly limiting them in the presentation of the defense. Nor could Hand find any evidence that Medina had revealed a pro-prosecution bias; indeed, "if anything," his rulings had been "too favorable to the defense."[132]

After the trial and the contempt rulings, the exhausted trial judge quickly became a national hero, reportedly receiving fifty thousand congratulatory letters within a week of the trial's end;[133] Medina, who never seemed to suffer from a shriveled ego, obviously relished the acclaim. Two years later, in 1951, he was promoted to the Second Circuit to fill the seat vacated by Hand's retirement; since Hand continued to sit on the Court of Appeals, he and Medina were colleagues for the remaining decade of Hand's life.[134]

The Hand-Medina relationship is intriguing. Although Medina had come to the federal bench after a long and successful career at the New York bar and as a law teacher, Hand never thought that he had a distinguished or penetrating mind, and he was repelled by some of Medina's bombast and sentimentality; still, he found Medina quite charming personally. As Hand once said of him, he was "a most attractive companion. He is quick, alert, gay and garrulous, with a most engaging naivete."[135] (Supposedly, Augustus Hand once told Medina that he talked too much. Medina replied, "Yes, but I can't help it"; he couldn't think, he explained, unless he was talking.)[136] The short, dapper, mustached Medina was indeed an entertaining talker, full of stories, whether about his passion for sailboats or his recollections of his colorful career. Hand, a considerable conversationalist himself, was not bothered by Medina's loquacity and even enjoyed it.

Medina paid lengthy visits to Hand's chambers after they became colleagues on the circuit court, and Hand would often emerge with a wistful, even envious response to Medina's self-assurance and stability. Medina, the son of wealthy Mexican immigrants and a loyal alumnus of Princeton, was a devout Episcopalian, and he was always ready to tell the world about the strength he derived from his faith in troubled times such as the difficult months of the Communist trial. The agnostic Hand listened to these tales with bemusement and regret—regret that he himself could not ever hope to enjoy the religiously derived stability of people like Medina and his cousin Augustus.

Hand and Felix Frankfurter delighted in sending each other news clippings about Medina's cloying speeches. Three months after the *Dennis* trial ended, for example, Hand enclosed for the justice an article from *The New York Times* about a Rotary Club speech Medina had delivered.

> As a piece of searching analysis, pregnant patriotism and gorgeous rhetoric [this] ranks with the great outbursts of recent times. And incidentally it certainly gave the most uncontaminated delight to the audience who had they given expression to their feelings would have said: "By God, there speaks a real American. None of your dirty 'on the one hand' and 'on the other hand,' but true forthright Americanism. We can understand that; he's got our money."

Yet, Hand added:

> And the curious part of it is I like the cuss; I have got so low that I like everyone who's having a good time—even a safe-cracker. In spite of all [Medina] is a good fellow.[137]

A few weeks later, while the Supreme Court was considering the *Dennis* appeal, Frankfurter in turn sent Hand a clipping of the text of a speech Medina had given to the Church Club of New York, entitled "The Judge and His God." In one passage of his talk, Medina recounted his inner life at the time of the *Dennis* trial, recalling how

I suddenly found myself in the vortex of the trial of the Communists, in the midst of the play of great forces upon which, for all I know, the destiny of the human race may hang. Later it suddenly dawned upon me that some queer turn in the wheel of fate had singled me out, for the moment, to feel the impact of America's love of justice. And the result was what must be inevitable under the circumstances, that I found myself to be a small, indeed a very small and insignificant particle in the scheme of things. It has been an extraordinary experience. . . . It took me a long time to realize what [the Communists] were trying to do to me. But as I got weaker and weaker, and found the burden difficult to bear, I sought strength from the one source that never fails.

After recalling that fortunately, "I was taught to pray from so early a time that I cannot remember going to bed at night without saying my prayers," Medina concluded:

After all is said and done, it is not we who pull the strings; we are not the masters, but the servants of our Master's will; and it is well that we should know it to be so.[138]

The clipping had been sent to Frankfurter by Justice Jackson, with a scrawled note: "I think it will help you resolve any doubts about the [*Dennis*] case to know which side God is on. You will not want to undo God's handiwork."[139]* To this merriment Hand genially responded, "That speech has been old stuff around here for a long time. Personally, I prefer not to take off all my clothes in public, but it's only a question of taste and doesn't affect his capacity as a judge."[140]

For Hand, some of Medina's traits were irritating and regrettable, but usually tolerable; for Frankfurter, then and later, they produced disdain. This had an effect upon actual judicial work when Medina summarily found the lawyers for the *Dennis* defendants guilty of contempt and sentenced them to various jail terms of up to six months; the lawyers promptly appealed. Although there was no legal doubt that a trial judge had the power under the Federal Rules of Criminal Procedure to act summarily *during* a trial,[141] Medina's strategy of waiting until the end of the *Dennis* trial was questionable, notwithstanding his repeated trial warnings that he found the lawyers' behavior outrageous and contemptuous. Still, the Second Circuit affirmed the contempt convictions in a 2–1 decision. (Learned Hand did not sit; Augustus

---

* Frankfurter's and Jackson's notes were on Supreme Court memorandum paper; probably both were written while the justices were listening to arguments on the bench.

Hand wrote the main opinion, stating that the lawyers had engaged in "persistent obstructive colloquies, objections, arguments, and many groundless charges against the court.")[142]

The defendants promptly sought review by the Supreme Court. At first, the Court denied review. Frankfurter, concerned about the possible procedural unfairness to the defendants and especially outraged by the growing hostility to lawyers defending unpopular clients, supported the defendants' request for further review, and lobbied strongly (and with eventual success) with his closest colleague, Jackson, urging that the Court should speak out on "the responsibilities of both the bar and bench as part of the trial process, as well as the obligation of an independent bar in a democratic society."[143]

The case was finally argued before the Supreme Court in January 1952, and decided two months later.[144] Justice Jackson wrote the majority opinion affirming the contempt convictions. Medina had not abused his power, Jackson insisted: "These lawyers have not been condemned, as they claim, merely by the impulse of one lone and hostile judge. Their conduct has been condemned by every judge who has examined this record under a duty to review the facts," and he quoted Learned Hand's characterization of Medina's behavior in the Second Circuit's ruling in *Dennis v. United States*. Frankfurter, dissenting at extraordinary length and with extraordinary heat, lectured Medina about proper standards of judicial decorum and charged him with engaging in "dialectic, in repartee and banter, in talk so copious as inevitably to arrest the momentum of the trial," and went on to claim that Medina failed to exercise "moral authority," concluding that Medina should not have tried the contempt charges himself and in doing so had violated the "belief that punishment is a vindication of impersonal law."[145]

Frankfurter's dissent provoked Hand to a rare outburst. He told Frankfurter:

> I have read your dissent in the contempt case and I am shocked at the general low tone of Medina's constant talk; surely he failed in maintaining the very minimum of dignity required of a judge. I am not on the other hand as much impressed as you with his inability to give them a hearing which would measure their deserts. On this issue, . . . it is what they did which counts; and what he said is important only in so far as it throws light on his animus. . . . Medina does not seem to me, taking the whole of what he said including his protests of impartiality, to have so far committed himself to a conclusion . . . as to make necessary a new trial.[146]

For Frankfurter, the demands of procedural regularity and the risks of intimidating lawyers who represented politically unpopular clients, as well as his personal dislike of Medina, were determinative. For Hand, a less harsh view of Medina and an appreciation of the practical reasons for supporting a trial judge's discretion were controlling.

THE LAST OF THE MAJOR CASES of the Cold War era to come before Hand's court was that of William Walter Remington, a government economist whose perjury conviction was affirmed by the Second Circuit in 1953.[147] Learned Hand wrote a strong dissent, insisting that the conviction could not stand because governmental misconduct was responsible for the trial at which Remington had allegedly perjured himself. A careful observer characterized the *Remington* case as "a shameful example of the excesses of the McCarthy era,"[148] and that is the way Hand viewed the case. His dissenting opinion was the product of a long struggle over many weeks that pitted his long-maintained hostility to overzealous prosecution tactics and his deep disdain for McCarthyism against his belief that he could justify overturning the conviction only if supported by precedents—precedents not readily apparent in this case. In *Remington*, Hand's emotions were at war with the existing state of the law, and he agonized as a result.

William Remington was an earnest young intellectual trained in economics who had spent his entire career in government service. He entered Dartmouth College as a sixteen-year-old in 1934, stopped out after his sophomore year to work as a messenger for the Tennessee Valley Authority, returned to Dartmouth to graduate at the top of his class in 1939, and earned a master's degree in economics from Columbia University in 1940.[149] Remington left Columbia to work in Washington, first for the National Resources Planning Board in 1940, and then, after a year with the Office of Price Administration, beginning a two-year stint at the War Production Board in 1942. In 1944, he was commissioned an ensign in the U.S. Navy and was assigned to serve with the Office of War Mobilization and, later, with the Office of Naval Intelligence, where he was trained as a specialist in Russian affairs. He left the Navy in 1946, joined the staff of the president's Council of Economic Advisers and then transferred to the Department of Commerce, where he became the director of export programs to the Soviet Union's allies in the Office of International Trade.

Remington did not become a public figure until July 30, 1948, when, at a hearing of the Investigations Subcommittee of the Senate Expenditures Committee, he was accused of having passed secret data to the Soviet Union. His accuser was Elizabeth Bentley, one of the major ex-Communist witnesses who testified frequently before congressional committees and grand juries in the 1940s, and who had acknowledged that she had been a courier for a Soviet espionage ring during the war.[150] By then, Remington had already come under suspicion and was under FBI surveillance. A month before Bentley's Senate testimony, he had been suspended from his Commerce Department position pending disposition of a charge of questionable loyalty before a Civil Service Commission regional loyalty-review board. Remington consistently denied that he had spied for the Soviet Union; he did admit that he had met Bentley under her assumed name, but thought she was a researcher for left-wing journalists.[151] Soon after the Bentley testimony, the regional loyalty-review board ruled that there were "reasonable grounds to believe" that Remington had been disloyal. Remington appealed that decision to the president's Loyalty Review Board, which reversed the decision. Remington promptly returned to his government position, with reduced responsibilities.

A year later, additional testimony was given in congressional hearings about Remington's having been a Communist party member when he worked as a teenager for the Tennessee Valley Authority. The Commerce Department began a new investigation that was terminated when the secretary of commerce, though asserting that he did not intend "to reflect in any way on the loyalty of [Remington]," requested that he resign "in the interest of good administration." Meanwhile, Remington had been called before a federal grand jury of New York investigating espionage charges; that grand jury ultimately indicted him, not for espionage but for perjury during those proceedings: allegedly, he lied in denying that he had ever been a member of the Communist party.[152] Remington thereupon resigned from the Commerce Department, claiming that he was unable to fight two proceedings—the loyalty investigation and the perjury charge—at once.[153]

While Remington denied that he had ever been a Communist party member, he did acknowledge that he was a "philosophical Communist": he believed in organized labor, as well as nationalization and public ownership of industry. He drew a sharp distinction between those who believed in such ideals and those who were actual members of the party, who believed in "dictatorship of the proletariat and overthrow of the Government by force and violence."[154] In his own testimony before the Senate subcommittee and at a press conference immediately thereafter, Remington regretted ever having spoken with Bentley, admitted that he "was very gullible," praised Bentley's courage in "exposing Communism," and emphasized that he had simply been a twenty-four-year-old idealist when he worked for the War Production Board and spoke with her.[155]

After a thirty-two-day trial, Remington was found guilty of having lied to the grand jury when he denied that he had "ever been a member of the Communist Party."[156] He was sentenced to five years' imprisonment and fined $2,000. On February 8, 1951, the day of the sentencing, Remington's counsel announced that he would appeal the conviction and sought Remington's release on temporary bail of $5,000. U.S. Attorney Irving Saypol (whose term in office covered the *Dennis*, *Hiss*, and *Rosenberg* cases as well) refused to consent to the bail that would have been normal in a case such as this. When the district judge denied bail, the issue came to Hand, who heard the case sitting alone. In this first encounter with the *Remington* litigation, he asked Saypol whether he would object to temporary bail overnight until a three-judge panel could hear the matter in the morning. "I certainly do," Saypol responded. "Overnight? Nonsense," Hand shot back. He rose abruptly, left the courtroom, and immediately signed an order releasing Remington.[157] The next day, the full Court of Appeals continued the bail.[158]

Remington's appeal of his perjury conviction was argued on June 15, 1951, before a panel consisting of the circuit's three old friends— Thomas Swan, who had succeeded Learned Hand as chief judge earlier in the year, Gus Hand, and Learned Hand himself.[159]* From the outset, the judges' pre-conference memoranda make clear, Thomas Swan and Learned Hand were sure that the conviction had to be reversed and the case remanded for a new trial; the trial judge's instructions to the jury, they thought, had been inadequate.[160] Only Gus Hand leaned toward affirmance: although he had been "quite convinced that there was reversible error" at the time of the argument, he told his colleagues, "I now doubt this very much to say the least and I am inclined to think otherwise." Accordingly, he concluded, "Tentatively I vote to affirm the conviction."[161] Ultimately, however, Thomas Swan and Learned Hand persuaded Gus Hand to join in a unanimous opinion reversing the conviction. Chief Judge Swan's opinion found that the judge's instructions to the jury were indeed too "vague and indefinite": the jury had not been told which "overt acts" they could rely on to find that Remington had lied in his denial of membership in the Communist party.

---

* On Saypol's brief in the appeal was a young assistant U.S. attorney named Roy Cohn. There is evidence that Cohn played an active role in the case. By the time of Remington's second appeal, in 1953, Cohn had become counsel for Senator Joseph McCarthy's Senate subcommittee, which catapulted them both into fame and notoriety.

Among Remington's challenges to his conviction was the claim that the indictment was invalid because of misconduct in the grand jury room: the grand jury foreman, Remington charged, had "a financial interest in a book which the government's chief witness [Elizabeth Bentley] was writing and . . . exercised undue influence in the procurement of the indictment, particularly during the grand jury's examination of the defendant."[162] With respect to this charge, the Second Circuit now assured Remington access to the grand jury minutes before any second trial.*

Hand found his work on the first *Remington* appeal exhausting. Just a few months after his theoretical "retirement," he was working harder than ever. "I have been busy pretty steadily all the summer," he told Frankfurter. "Think[ing] of how [Holmes] disposed of such stuff" got him depressed, when he contrasted it with what he described as his "lumbering mind": "My head is like an old attic full of every kind of junk."[163] He looked forward to a trip with Frances to France and Italy during the early fall months.

As it turned out, Remington was not retried on the original perjury charge. The prosecution instead obtained a second perjury indictment, suspiciously like the first, from a new grand jury. The new indictment charged that Remington had lied when he took the stand in his own defense at his first perjury trial. This time, the charge did not include perjury in denying Communist party membership; however, all the charges were related to alleged Communist activities. Remington was convicted on two of these five counts: denying that he had ever delivered government information to Bentley, and denying any acquaintance with the Young Communist League while he studied at Dartmouth.

Remington's appeal of this second conviction brought his case before the same panel that had reversed his first conviction—Learned and Gus Hand and Thomas Swan. This time, Remington put all his hopes into what Gus Hand would call "a rather new and novel argument": having now been able to study the grand jury minutes, he argued that misconduct by both the prosecutor and the grand jury foreman in the first proceeding had led to the trial that gave rise to the second perjury charge. This misconduct, he contended, required that "the first indictment [be] quashed and [the first] trial be declared a nullity." Since

---

* The court also provided one additional bit of guidance for any retrial: it admonished the prosecution that "there should be no repetition of the cross examination attack upon defense witness Redmont's change of name." Redmont was Jewish; Chief Judge Swan noted that "the prosecutor continued his inquiry of this matter long after it became clear that the change of name had no relevancy to any issue at the trial, and could only serve [to] arouse possible racial prejudice on the part of the jury." This admonition flowed directly from comments in Learned Hand's pre-conference memorandum. See LH memo of 31 July 1951, 213–18.

he would never have been put on the stand at his first trial "but for the procurement of that indictment by illegal conduct of the Government," he maintained, the government should not be permitted to "gain a benefit from its illegal conduct" by prosecuting him for perjury at a trial that should never have taken place. Augustus Hand quickly made clear that he was not at all impressed by this defense argument. In a very brief pre-conference memorandum, he wrote, "I do not think that the grand jury proceedings in the first case are relevant to the charges of perjury in the case before us. It is a completely novel extension of any doctrine I know of that Remington can come before the court and commit perjury under the last indictment and be immune from prosecution. I feel sure [that] the judgment of conviction must be affirmed." Swan was less sure, but nevertheless concluded, "With some doubt and regret I vote to affirm." In his view, whatever arguments might once have been made about the first indictment, the second trial after all rested on a new one; the trial court had jurisdiction over it; "and hence perjury committed [at the trial on that indictment] was a crime." Swan found it "difficult to answer this argument [l]ogically." To overturn the second conviction was not justified by any clear Supreme Court precedent; "I am disposed to think the Supreme Court should make the extension if it is to be made."[164]

For Learned Hand, the second *Remington* appeal was intellectually and emotionally far more complex than the first. The intellectual problem was difficult enough. Supreme Court precedent did not clearly support Remington's arguments, and, as Gus Hand argued, to immunize the defendant from perjury charges in the circumstances of this case might be seen as suggesting "that perjury, although a crime, is an inevitable occurrence in judicial proceedings." Nevertheless, Learned Hand persisted in his view that Remington's conviction had to be reversed. His dissent focused on the first grand jury's interrogation of Remington's former wife, Ann, who had tried to avoid testifying because "her husband's conviction would imperil the support he gave her and her children." Mrs. Remington's refusal to incriminate her ex-husband led to immense pressure being put upon her in the grand jury room; as Hand pointed out, she had been "questioned continuously for about four hours," up to the point where she broke down and finally admitted that Remington did " 'give this money to the Communist Party.' " Once her resistance was broken, "she became generally complaisant, and gave testimony exceedingly damaging to him."[165]

Hand acknowledged that a grand jury was free to press a reluctant witness "hard and sharp," but he insisted that here "the examination went beyond what I deem permissible."

Pages on pages of lecturing repeatedly preceded a question; statements of what the prosecution already knew, and of how idle it was for the witness to hold back what she could contribute; occasional reminders that she could be punished for perjury; all was scattered throughout. Still she withstood the examiners, until, being much tried and warned, she said: "I am getting fuzzy. I haven't eaten since a long time ago and I don't think I am going to be very coherent from now on. I would like to postpone the hearings. . . . I want to consult my lawyers and see how deep I am getting in." This was denied, and the questioning kept on until she finally refused to answer, excusing herself because she was "tired," and "would like to get something to eat. . . . Is this the third degree, waiting until I get hungry, now?" Still the examiners persisted, disregarding this further protest: "I would like to get something to eat. But couldn't we continue another day?"

The coup de grace that broke Ann Remington's resistance consisted of harangues by the member of the prosecutor's staff in the grand jury room, Special Assistant to the Attorney General Thomas Donegan, and by the grand jury foreman, John Brunini, who said to her:

> Mrs. Remington, I think that we have been very kind and considerate. We haven't raised our voices and we haven't shown our teeth, have we? Maybe you don't know about our teeth. A witness before a Grand Jury hasn't the privilege of refusing to answer a question. You see, we haven't told you that, so far. You have been asked a question. You must answer it. . . . You have no privilege to refuse to answer the question. I don't want at this time to—I said "showing teeth." I don't want them to bite you.

Hand was especially troubled by the fact that "the examination was *ex parte* and without the presence and control of a judge or any other important official." Hand noted that the Fifth Amendment privilege against self-incrimination had itself arisen because of the abuses of the Star Chamber in the seventeenth century—the one-sided coercive pressure upon witnesses in secret proceedings. "Save for torture, it would be hard to find a more effective tool of tyranny than the power of unlimited and unchecked *ex parte* examination."

Yet Hand was willing to assume for the sake of argument the validity of the grand jury's indictment even considering this controversy. But there was more. The "added circumstance" was that "a very large part of Ann Remington's testimony consisted of confidential communications from her husband to her"; this tipped the scale and convinced him that the indictment had to be invalidated. Confidential communications between husband and wife during marriage are clearly privileged in any courtroom. Hand plausibly assumed that the Remingtons' subsequent divorce did not end the privilege; "indeed, any other view would be completely inconsistent with the theory of the privilege," which allows spouses to communicate freely with each other without fear that either would ever be forced to disclose such communications. Yet, as Hand emphasized, Mrs. Remington was misled about her right to remain silent. Foreman Brunini, he noted, "not only threatened her with contempt proceedings, but expressly told her that she had no privilege." True, Brunini was a layman and might not have known that his assertions were false, but the prosecutor "did not intervene to correct the mistake." Although ordinarily a grand jury had only to find reasonable ground to suppose an accused's guilt, Hand was "convinced" that other testimony normally sufficient to support an indictment did not "excuse pressure and deceit in procuring [this] indictment. . . . [O]nly by upsetting convictions so obtained can the ardor of prosecuting officials be kept within legal bounds and justice be secured; for in modern times all prosecution is in the hands of officials."

Clearly, excessive pressure on Mrs. Remington might well have supported a dismissal of the first indictment against Remington, but that finding formed only the background of the central issue, which was that Remington had *not* been retried on the first indictment but instead, at the government's request, another grand jury had issued a second indictment, and the second trial had convicted him of perjury not before the first grand jury but at his first trial.

Hand thought the irregularities before the first grand jury justified reversal of Remington's conviction at his trial on the second indictment, and in the most vulnerable part of his opinion, he spelled out two theories as to why this was so. Hand relied, first, on an analogy to the "exclusionary rule," a long-standing prohibition against evidence obtained in violation of the Fourth Amendment guarantee against unreasonable searches and seizures. More particularly, he noted the prosecution's obligation to show, if challenged, that none of its evidence was a "fruit of the poisonous tree"[166]—obtained, that is, as a consequence of an illegal search or seizure. What was the underlying premise of this rule? Hand asserted that it was applicable here:

> Now the finding of the first indictment was a necessary part of the evidence in the case at bar, because without it nothing that Remington said in the first trial would have been perjury, no matter

how false it was. I do not see any difference in principle between obtaining the first indictment by the unlawful extraction of evidence, necessary to its support, and obtaining a document by an unreasonable search.

This was not an ironclad, totally convincing analogy, but neither was it wholly implausible; it was the best anyone could do.

Second, Hand relied on another well-established principle, that which makes "entrapment" a defense in a criminal proceeding.[167] This defense, as he explained, "depends . . . upon the repugnance of decent people at allowing officials to punish a man for conduct that they have 'incited' or 'instigated,' and to which by so doing they have made themselves accessories." Hand conceded that the first indictment and prosecution did not, in the narrow sense, incite Remington "to repeat on the first trial the testimony that he had given on the grand jury proceeding," but he thought the entrapment rationale, though not strictly applicable here, "should [not] be so narrowly confined." After denying Communist party membership before the grand jury, Remington had in effect no choice but to repeat the denial in his first trial, since failing to take the stand would have been equivalent to pleading guilty. The prosecutors knew that in bringing the first indictment to trial, they had created a situation in which Remington would certainly perjure himself on the stand. "Therefore," Hand concluded, "I do not see how it can be denied that the finding of the first indictment was as direct a provocation of the perjury for which he has been convicted, as the persuasion of agents or officials of the prosecution would have been, had they 'incited' or 'instigated' him to perjure himself; so that in point of causation I insist that the situations are the same."

In the present case, Hand contended, the government's methods of obtaining the indictment were independently unlawful. "For these reasons," he concluded, "it seems to me that the case at bar is within the implied ambit of the doctrine of 'entrapment' as well as it is within that of the doctrine against using evidence unlawfully obtained."

Learned Hand's long opinion was a lone dissent; Gus Hand's majority opinion, joined by Thomas Swan, rejected Learned's argument. Indeed, rarely had he been so vigorously disagreed with, and repudiated by, his colleagues. He had tried to meet the intellectual puzzles in *Remington* as best he could; he could hope that his dissent might move the Supreme Court to review the case and perhaps overturn the conviction. Hand's efforts to stretch existing precedents were unusual for him; typically, he was an obedient lower court judge, not eager to extrapolate from the Supreme Court's principles too readily. As he had said in a case a decade earlier, "Nor is it desirable for a lower court to embrace the exhilarating opportunity of anticipating a doctrine which may be in the womb of time, but whose birth is distant; on the contrary I conceive that the measure of its duty is to divine, as best it can, what would be the event of an appeal in the case before [it]."[168] Yet in *Remington*, Hand told himself, the situation was different. He certainly hoped that the principles he was advocating were not ones "whose birth [was] distant"; he thought there was truly a reasonable chance that the Supreme Court would agree with his extension of the search-and-seizure and entrapment principles.

In some ways, the writing process that produced the *Remington* dissent was consistent with Hand's usual practice, discussing with his law clerk the approach he proposed to take, arguing back and forth about whether it was defensible, with Hand always eager for critical comments from the "puny judge" who held the clerkship that year. In this case, the back-and-forth process with his clerk continued for weeks, virtually to the exclusion of anything else. I was the clerk that year, and I remember that Hand produced thirteen complete versions of his dissenting opinion, each recast to accommodate whatever criticisms I had raised that he found telling.

After seven weeks, he handed his most recent effort to me. "Now look at this one; see if this one holds water any better." I studied the new draft for several hours and returned to his desk. Hand looked up eagerly: "Well, will it wash?" I responded that portions of the opinion now seemed reasonably airtight, but there were still weaknesses in other sections.

Hand looked at me darkly, pain and annoyance clouding his face. He heaved a deep sigh, then picked up a small paperweight on his desk and threw it in my general direction, missing me by only a narrow margin. "Damn," he shouted, "I can't go on forever like this! Thirteen drafts and it's still not satisfactory? Son, I get paid to decide cases. At some point, I have to get off the fence and turn out an opinion. Enough!"

I had never heard Hand speak in such anger. I turned pale and retreated, shaken, to my desk in the adjacent office. I flung my head down on the desk and tried to regain my composure. After a minute or so, I felt a hand gently tapping the back of my head. Judge Hand, in his stocking feet, had silently left his desk, come into my office, and hoisted himself to a sitting position on my desk. I raised my face and looked up into his bemused countenance. "Now, now," he gently consoled, "you can't take it that way! It's all part of the job! Don't take it so hard—you did your job; I have to do mine."

That evening, my wife came to pick me up at the office so that we could go together to a social engagement. She told me that she had encountered Hand on her way in and that he had chided her, "Come on, now, you've been married three or four years. Don't you ever yell at him? You must yell at him once in a while. He's not used to it. He's got to get used to people yelling at him!"

The *Remington* case upset Hand not just because of the unseemly pressure the grand jury exerted on Ann Remington but also because of other grand jury misconduct Hand did not feature in his dissent. One of the "other alleged irregularities" he referred to in passing was the collaboration between the grand jury foreman, John Brunini, and the major witness against Remington throughout the congressional and judicial hearings, Elizabeth Bentley. While cross-examining Bentley at the first trial, Remington's counsel elicited testimony from her that, during the time the grand jury was deliberating the first indictment of Remington, she had been under contract to write a book about the people she had named as Communists; she testified that Brunini had done "editorial work" on her book and gave her "moral encouragement" in writing it; another witness testified that Brunini even had a financial interest in the book's success.* As Hand's dissent pointed out, Brunini had taken a leading role in browbeating Ann Remington, and as the defense suggested, the Remington passages in the Brunini-Bentley book would probably have had to be dropped unless Remington were indicted. Nor did the alleged conflicts of interest end with Brunini's involvement. Bentley also acknowledged at the trial that Thomas Donegan, the chief prosecutor in the grand jury room, had been her lawyer before he joined the Justice Department.

Privately, Hand was deeply disturbed by this additional evidence of McCarthyite witch-hunting. He may also have been inclined to accept Remington's steadfast denials of anything more than youthful "philosophical" or "intellectual" communism because he knew and respected Remington's lawyers. Bethuel Webster, a business lawyer who was a leader of the New York bar, had represented Remington at the time of his first arraignment; William C. Chanler, another leading New York lawyer who had been the city's corporation counsel, was Remington's principal attorney in the first trial.[169] In style, they were a far cry from the rambunctious attorneys who had wrought havoc in the *Dennis* trial,

---

* The contract with the Devin-Adair Company was dated 2 June 1950. An employee of the publisher testified that there was an earlier contract, even before June, under which Brunini was to share in the proceeds of the book, and that Brunini and Bentley were treated as "one party" for purposes of the contract.

and Hand may have been especially suspectible to the advocacy of lawyers from his own circle and class.*

While the *Remington* appeal was pending before him, Hand's emotions were also stirred because of his recollection of an earlier case involving Henry Julian Wadleigh, a relative of Frances Hand. The Hands had repeatedly tried to help Wadleigh's widowed mother in finding employment. In 1943, for example, Learned Hand had unsuccessfully recommended her for a job with the United Nations Relief and Rehabilitation Administration (UNRRA); near the end of the war, he prepared a script for broadcast by the Office of War Information (where she was then employed) to commemorate a Nazi massacre. And in 1946, he recommended Wadleigh's brother for a position with the UNRRA.[170] Wadleigh attained considerable notoriety in December 1948, when Whittaker Chambers named him before the House Un-American Activities Committee as, together with Alger Hiss, Chambers's source in obtaining State Department documents for delivery to a Soviet KGB agent. At first Wadleigh denied that he had been a member of the Communist party or even a Communist sympathizer; he refused to answer any other questions, invoking his Fifth Amendment privilege against self-incrimination. However, by the time of Hiss's first perjury trial, in 1949, Wadleigh testified for the government as a surprise prosecution witness, admitting that between 1936 and 1938 he had, as a young man in his twenties, "collaborated with the Communists," delivering up to five hundred State Department papers to Chambers, who relayed them to the Soviet spy ring. After the 1939 Nazi-Soviet pact, Wadleigh testified, his attitude toward communism changed and he developed "very serious misgivings" about his activity and decided that he "was no longer willing to take the risks and face the other factors involved."[171] That Hand repeatedly mentioned Wadleigh in his critical comments about McCarthyism and its victims, both while he was preparing his *Remington* dissent and in later years, is remarkable. True, Wadleigh's mother was a close acquaintance, and Wadleigh's Communist sympathies, like Remington's, could be interpreted as mere youthful idealism. Still, Wadleigh was a confessed collaborator with a Soviet spy ring.

* An outburst by C. C. Burlingham may have helped arouse Hand to the lurking McCarthyite tone of the Remington prosecutions. At Remington's arraignment, Bethuel Webster, then Remington's attorney, reported that he had found no surety company to post bond for the defendant's $5,000 bail. All of the companies had refused because "a loyalty question was involved." This prompted an angry, sarcastic letter from Burlingham to *The New York Times* branding the companies' behavior as McCarthyite: "Bizness is bizness and must keep itself unspotted by any suspicion of sympathy with Communism!" (C. C. Burlingham letter to editor, *New York Times*, 20 June 1950.)

Hand's hostility to the McCarthyite enterprise helps to account for the extraordinary intensity of his emotions when he considered the second *Remington* appeal—emotions in tension with his creed of disinterested, unbiased judging. And in *Remington*, Hand was not only emotionally engaged but also uncommonly firm about the conclusions he reached. As he wrote in response to a letter praising his dissent: "I seldom feel much assurance in the results of my opinion; but I must confess that that case seemed to me so clear that I was a good deal distressed when no one appeared to agree with me. I could not have helped asking myself whether my powers had not begun to fail, if I was so out . . . with the expert professional opinion of my calling."[172]

Hand's deep absorption in his dissent attests to his insistence on articulating adequate legal basis for his position. His opinion was a craftsman's effort to identify the underlying principles of Supreme Court rulings, and his careful analysis suggests that he had surely not abandoned reason.

Hand's lack of success in persuading his colleagues in *Remington*, painful as that was, was not the end of his suffering about the case. The Supreme Court denied review in December 1954; as usual, the order did not indicate whether any justice had dissented. The decision was a grievous disappointment to Hand, and for the first time in his long relationship with Felix Frankfurter, Hand sent his old friend a cri de coeur:

> I felt, shall I confess it?, a sense of professional incapacity when your distinguished Group would not even hear the *Remington* Case. But it does serve as a warning, never to be forgotten, though never really learned, that what may seem to oneself [entirely clear], may seem to others plain tosh. After all, an old dog who has been in the ring for nearly forty-five years mustn't yelp at another bite.[173]

Frankfurter was no more accustomed to discussing a denial of review of a Second Circuit case with Hand than Hand was to complaining about it. Yet he quickly tried to soothe Hand's disappointment:

> You should have no disquietude about *Remington*. The fact is that three of us voted to hear the case—and the fourth didn't because [the] extreme views expressed by that essentially lawless [Hugo] Black indicated the hopelessness of agreement even among those who were outraged by the Government's behavior. As you know, I am dead against noting dissent from denial of certs [certioraris].[174]

It was probably Justice Jackson who declined to provide the fourth vote necessary to grant review, so Hand could take some solace from there being four justices as "outraged" as he "by the Government's behavior." In any event, four votes would not have been sufficient to reverse *Remington*'s conviction. "Apparently," he wrote to Frankfurter, "there was some measure of truth in what I had thought a possible explanation [for the denial of review]. Clark being out of it [Justice Tom Clark had yet been attorney general at the time the *Remington* indictment was brought, and therefore could not participate in the case], [a grant of review] would have been worse than [none], if the vote was sure to be a tie." With Clark not sitting, a 4–4 division on the Court would simply have affirmed the lower court decision from which Hand had dissented. Fierce and saddened, Hand continued, "The most discouraging part of all this [is] how pervasive is running this madhouse hysteria. Hardly a day passes that I do not get some evidence about the quite unconscious drift away from all that we have professed, and much that we have practiced, from the beginning of history."[175]

On April 15, 1953, William Remington began serving his three-year term at the federal penitentiary in Lewisburg, Pennsylvania. Nearly a year later, Remington's second wife, Jane, and his attorney appeared in a New York federal court to plead for a reduction of his sentence. Remington's counsel reminded the judge that his client had been "immature when he fell under the spell of Communism." The second Mrs. Remington was also allowed to speak, on behalf of herself and the couple's nine-month-old son. The pleas were unsuccessful.[176] Then, on Monday, November 22, 1954, eight months before he was due to be released, Remington was resting in his dormitory after working at his assigned task—he held a job reserved for model inmates, in the prison hospital during the midnight–to–8:00 a.m. shift—when three fellow prisoners entered, beat him over the head with a brick wrapped in a sock, and inflicted multiple fractures on his skull. He died two days later.[177]

The motives for the assault were never made clear. At first, the prison's acting warden and the chief of the regional FBI office both presumed that anti-Communism was the cause. "You'll get pretty much the same reactions concerning loyalty in a prison climate as in any other community."[178] But soon after, both the FBI and the prison authorities suggested that the killing stemmed either from gang rivalries or an attempted robbery.[179] Unexpected support for the robbery explanation soon materialized: On the day of Remington's funeral, November 27, 1954, one of Remington's fellow prisoners at Lewisburg, Alger Hiss, was released from the penitentiary after serving forty-four months of his five-year sentence for perjury, his trial having taken place in New York City just a few months before Remington's first conviction. Outside the prison gates, Hiss held a press conference, renewing his claims of innocence. A reporter asked about the slaying of Remington. Hiss promptly endorsed the robbery explanation for the assault, adding, "I can assure [you] that none of the inmates feel anything but revolt. Actually, they were horrified."[180] The three prisoner assailants were indicted on second-degree murder charges, to which they initially pleaded innocent; they changed their plea to guilty in May 1955, and were sentenced to terms between twenty years and life imprisonment after a hearing at which the prosecution insisted that "robbery was the motive in the killing."[181]

The image of Remington being bludgeoned to death in prison haunted Hand for the rest of his life. He would repeatedly refer to the brutal assault in conversation; often, he would wonder whether he could have done more to block Remington's imprisonment for a conviction upon an indictment that, he was convinced, had been unlawfully obtained.

HAND HAD ONE MORE BRUSH with McCarthyism. At the beginning of 1953, he agreed to serve as the head of a presidential advisory board to review disloyalty charges against John Carter Vincent. Vincent, then fifty-two, was a longtime career diplomat who had specialized in Chinese affairs, one of the "China hands" who had become a special target of right-wing Republicans. In 1950, Senator McCarthy had charged that Vincent was "number two" on his list of alleged Communists in the State Department. A year later, the former Communist Louis Budenz, once managing editor of the party's *Daily Worker*, told the Senate Internal Security Subcommittee that Vincent had been "under Communist discipline."[182]

In February 1952, however, the State Department's Loyalty and Security Board completely cleared Vincent of disloyalty charges. Yet that exoneration was reviewed by the Civil Service Commission's Loyalty Review Board, which found that Vincent had expressed "studied praise of Chinese Communists and equally studied criticism of the Chiang Kai-shek Government throughout a period when it was the declared and established policy of the Government of the United States to support Chiang Kai-shek's Government." On December 15, 1952, the State Department suspended Vincent because of the Review Board's conclusion that "there [is] reasonable doubt as to his loyalty to the Government of the United States."[183]

By this time Harry Truman was a lame-duck president: Dwight D. Eisenhower had won the election from Democrat Adlai Stevenson a month earlier. But Truman and his secretary of state, Dean Acheson, were still in office, and Vincent's fate ultimately lay with Acheson. Skeptical of the Review Board's actions, Acheson proposed to Truman that an advisory review panel be established, composed of persons "of highest judicial qualifications" and with experience in diplomatic affairs, to guide him in reaching his decision. Hand agreed to chair the panel, which also included his friend John J. McCloy, former U.S. high commissioner for Germany.[184]* Acheson's review panel promptly encountered criticism, none harsher than that offered by Walter Lippmann. Frankfurter was predictably outraged; commenting to Hand on "the suggestion of the Great Elucidator the other day that in appointing an advisory committee consisting of L. Hand, McCloy & Co., [Acheson] was abdicating his responsibility," he remarked: "I just wonder how far a jaundiced eye, vis-à-vis Dean, and a boot-licking attitude toward [John] Foster Dulles [Eisenhower's soon-to-be designated secretary of state], can warp a man's understanding."[185]

An enormous number of documents soon landed on Hand's desk, including Acheson's and Truman's memoranda.[186] Hand and his fellow review-panel members diligently plowed through the materials for more than three weeks in January 1953. As Hand told Frankfurter soon after:

> I do not think I ever have been so much "philogrobolized" by any mass of incoherent documents as those on which I put in three or four weeks' work in January. . . . I realized . . . how the pursuit of truth depends upon sharpening of the questions to be answered and limiting the material to be considered. The volumes of verbiage almost broke the back of one of the smartest boys [his law clerk] I have had for a long time.[187]†

---

* The other members were James Grafton Rogers, former assistant secretary of state under Henry Stimson; G. Howland Shaw, former assistant secretary of state under Cordell Hull; and Edwin C. Wilson, a retired Foreign Service officer and a former ambassador.

† In using the word "philogrobolized," Hand was borrowing from one of his favorite authors, Rabelais. Frankfurter promptly asked him how he came to use the term and Hand explained in a response summarizing the relevant passages in Rabelais's *Gargantua* with wit and succinctness. Hand explained that he had referred to Panurge's judgment:

> [It] had been a great law suit between the Lords Suckfist and Kissbreach; it had gone on, as I remember, for twenty years, and all the jurists of France had delved into it and groped about. . . . Finally the exhibits and testimony had grown so great in bulk that it required twenty mules to carry them. The jurists having debated and debated, and quarreled and quarreled, finally declared that they were at an end. They were completely "philogrobolized," and so they asked Panurge to give judgment. That he did expeditiously and with a torrent of judicial wisdom which has never been equalled.

Hand suggested Frankfurter study "that celebrated judgment and [consider] whether you ought not to take it as at least a model of whatever you collectively say" on the Supreme Court (LH to Felix Frankfurter, 30 March 1953, 105–18).

But Hand and his panel never got to render judgment on Vincent's loyalty. On Inauguration Day, Eisenhower named John Foster Dulles as his new secretary of state, and Hand wrote to Dulles that the Review Board had made some progress and was prepared to continue on the job, but asked "whether Mr. Dulles would think it necessary to proceed."[188] A few days later, Dulles told Hand that the data before him were "adequate to give me guidance" and therefore concluded: "I do not think it will be necessary for you and your associates to act as a special review group to consider this particular case." A month later, Dulles cleared Vincent of the loyalty and security charges but criticized him on the ground that he had failed "to meet the standard which is demanded on a Foreign Service Officer of his experience and responsibility at this critical time." Vincent was permitted to retire and retain his eligibility for a pension—a disposition promptly attacked by Senator Patrick McCarran as a "subterfuge."[189]

Hand heard about Dulles's decision through a telephone call from the secretary of state. By then, the review group had completed only about half of the necessary "damned hard work."[190] As Hand reported later, when Dulles "said [he did not need us], I answered him: 'Is there any thing that I can give you as a present?' "[191] Hand was content and even happy to be relieved of the burden: it "was a nasty job we took, and we were by no means through, so that I . . . confess that I was jolly glad when Dulles cried 'Hold, enough!' "[192]

Hand never disclosed how he was inclined to resolve Vincent's case, because "[a]ll the members agreed when the committee was dissolved that we would not give any indication whatever of any opinion that we might have reached about Mr. Vincent."[193] Corresponding with Hand, Frankfurter manifested no such inhibitions: "Is it timidity or stupidity, or stupidity begetting timidity or timidity begetting stupidity, that makes people think they can woo to reason a Hitler or a Huey Long, or the McCarthys and McCarrans?"[194] No doubt, however, Hand's contempt for witch-hunting and McCarthyism at least elicited considerable sympathy for Vincent.

Hand's antipathy toward witch-hunts lasted well beyond the termination of the Remington and Vincent controversies. For example, in a letter to an old friend, the New Orleans lawyer Monte Lemann, who had written to criticize Attorney General Herbert Brownell, Jr.'s, assertion that he would try to get the National Lawyers Guild listed as a subversive organization, Hand agreed that "this business of 'subversive lists' is utterly detestable. In the first place I do not know what a 'subversive' is, unless he is a man who disagrees with me politically and violently. If it were confined to people who could prove to be engaged in a conspiracy to overthrow the government, that would be one thing, but there is more evil packed into that one word than into anything else that is going on politically today. . . . Our only hope is that the President [Eisenhower] will have not only the courage—which I think he does have—but the power, to keep his party . . . from going over, holus bolus, to the witch hunters."[195] Hand's feelings were especially well expressed during the controversy spurred by Harvard University's invitation to the nuclear physicist J. Robert Oppenheimer to serve as its 1957 William James Lecturer on Philosophy. A number of Harvard alumni immediately protested because of Oppenheimer's alleged "fundamental defects" of character, supposedly demonstrated by the fact that he had been denied security clearance by the Atomic Energy Commission. Hand received such a protest from Arthur Brooks Harlow, a 1925 Harvard graduate, writing on the letterhead of a self-styled "Harvard 'Veritas' Committee," which had undertaken an investigation of how Harvard had come to invite Oppenheimer. Although the broadside was an impersonal form letter, Hand took the unusual step of writing a personal reply, "from an alumnus, who could not more completely disagree with your effort, or think it more to the disadvantage of the University." He noted that he had read "a considerable part of the evidence" in the security hearings before the Atomic Energy Commission, but preferred not to discuss it at length. Instead, his blistering note stated,

> I need say no more than that I am wholly satisfied that Dr. Oppenheimer is qualified morally, as he certainly is professionally, for the position for which he has been chosen. I should say no more, were it not for the statement of the purpose of your committee. This says that it is "to serve the cause of Truth," yet there immediately follows the statement: "We believe that our University . . . has been the target of Communists and subversive infiltration." I can only read this as meaning that "the cause of truth" must be kept safe from becoming a target of "subversive infiltration," and I cannot imagine a postulate more at variance with all that I value about Harvard.

He could barely contain his anger:

> We do not conduct a kindergarten; the premise derived from all our history is that we shall teach students to think for themselves, and that if we do, they will be able to detect "infiltrations," good or bad. We do not seek to teach truth; but how to think; that is

the chief difference between ourselves and all totalitarians. Anything else would be a surrender of our most precious possession and make us unfit to exist.[196]

DURING THE YEARS WHEN Hand struggled with the intellectual puzzles and emotional strains created by the Cold War and McCarthyism, his court also had to wrestle with another difficult problem. United States naturalization laws required the applicant to show that during the five years immediately preceding the filing of a petition for naturalization, he or she was "a person of good moral character, . . . well disposed to the good order and happiness of the United States."[197] Hand made two major rulings during these years on this requirement: in the first, *Repouille v. United States*[198] in 1947, he had to decide whether a man who had committed euthanasia on his thirteen-year-old blind, mute, and deformed son could be admitted to citizenship; in the second, *Schmidt v. United States*[199] in 1949, he had to determine whether an unmarried thirty-nine-year-old college teacher who, "in a moment of what may have been unnecessary frankness," told the naturalization examiner that he had "now and then" engaged in acts of sexual intercourse with single women, could nevertheless qualify as "a person of good moral character."

Applying the "good moral character" requirement presented special difficulties for a judge like Hand. His was a modest rather than activist view of judging, and he considered it beyond a judge's duty and competence to impose his own moral standards upon the community. Moreover, he was of course a skeptic, doubtful of any absolute moral standards. Yet Congress had commanded the judges to give content to the vague phrase "good moral character," and obedience to the lawmakers' will was among Hand's most basic beliefs.

Hand did his best to pour content into the statutory phrase. He first articulated the approach he followed throughout his life in a 1929 case, *United States ex rel.* [upon information from] *Iorio v. Day*,[200] which involved the meaning of the phrase "a crime involving moral turpitude" in the law governing deportation of aliens. The question was whether violation of a local Prohibition ordinance involved "moral turpitude." Hand insisted: "We do not regard every violation of a prohibition law as a crime involving moral turpitude." A criminal conviction alone did not suffice to justify deportation; Congress, with its "moral turpitude" language, had added the additional element that the crime "must itself be shamefully immoral." And in order to determine this elusive question of immorality, Hand, deciding against deportation, put forth his standard:

> There are probably many persons in the United States who [would] regard either the possession or sale of liquor [as "shamefully immoral"]; but the question is whether it is so *by common conscience*, a nebulous matter at best. While we must not, indeed, substitute our personal notions as the standard, it is impossible to decide at all without some estimate, necessarily based on conjecture, as to *what people generally feel*. We cannot say that among the commonly accepted mores the sale or possession of liquor as yet occupies so grave a place; nor can we close our eyes to the fact that large numbers of persons, otherwise reputable, do not think it so, rightly or wrongly. Congress may make [violation of Prohibition laws] a ground of deportation, but while it leaves as the test accepted moral notions, we must be loyal to that, so far as we can ascertain it [emphasis added].[201]

Hand never liked the open-ended, vague nature of the "good moral character" standard. Still, as a dutiful lower court judge, he did not feel free to refuse to take on the "absurd" task imposed by Congress. His resort to the "common conscience" formula was an effort to escape judicial subjectivism by relying on some outside source. One commentator has suggested that his escape route was in effect a plea "to Congress to get him out of the morals business"; but since Congress did not do so, his approach seemed "the best that can be done with good moral character provisions."[202]

More than two decades later, several Supreme Court justices indicated sympathy with Hand's doubts. Justice Jackson's 1951 dissent in *Jordan v. De George*, joined by Justices Black and Frankfurter, insisted that the phrase had "no sufficiently definite meaning to be a constitutional standard for deportation": Congress had "knowingly conceived it in confusion"; none of the judicial efforts "to reduce the abstract provision . . . to some concrete meaning" had been successful; not even a phrase akin to Hand's "common conscience" test—"the moral standards that prevail in contemporary society"—was sufficiently definite. "How should we ascertain the moral sentiments of masses of persons on any better basis than a guess?" Justice Jackson asked, citing Hand.[203] Yet this position, which Hand might well have supported had he sat on the Supreme Court, was voiced in a dissenting opinion. Chief Justice Vinson's majority judgment insisted that the statutory language "conveys sufficiently definite warning as to the proscribed conduct when measured by common understanding and practices."[204] And so Hand was essentially following what became the majority command of the Supreme Court in *Jordan v. De George* when he struggled over the years to give content to his "nebulous," "common conscience" standard for determining what was and what was not "moral."

Hand found every alternative to his "common conscience" approach—an approach that became the dominant view in the courts —even less attractive. One was offered in 1951 by the legal philosopher Edmond N. Cahn, who extensively criticized Hand's analysis. Cahn suggested that Hand had irresponsibly sought to evade his judicial responsibility by relying on the "common conscience"; instead, he should have filled in the vague statutory words with "his own moral principles": "[B]y subordinating his own moral principles to those of the marketplace, Judge Hand seriously distorted the function of the court as pedagogue and moral mentor in a democratic society." In Cahn's view, the judge's task was to exercise "such influence as he could to raise the morals of the marketplace to a level approaching his own." He regretted that "it is the best and finest of judges who afflict themselves with the whips of doubt": "What the community needs most is the moral leadership of such a man as Learned Hand and the full benefit of his mature and chastened wisdom."[205]

For Hand, this was no solution, for it substituted for one evanescent standard, "community conscience," the even more flawed and uncertain one of asking that judges exercise a function they were not fit to undertake. As he once told Cahn, he could not accept the notion that in difficult cases of statutory interpretation, a judge should use his private conclusion of what is "right."[206]

Hand's colleague Jerome Frank, himself a considerable legal philosopher, offered still another alternative to reliance on the "common conscience," suggesting "that the correct statutory test (the test Congress intended) is the attitude of our ethical leaders. That attitude would not be too difficult to learn."[207] Hand was profoundly unimpressed by this idea. As he wrote to Felix Frankfurter about Frank's "outré dissent" in the euthanasia case, *Repouille v. United States*, where Frank had launched his "ethical leaders" suggestion:

> I assume that he expected the district judge, sua sponte [on his own initiative], to call the Cardinal, Bishop Gilbert, an orthodox and a liberal Rabbi, [Protestant theologian] Reinhold Niebuhr, the head of the Ethical Cultural Society, and [literary critic] Edmund Wilson; have them all cross-examined: ending in a "survey." Oh,

Jesus! I don't know how we ought to deal with such cases except by the best guess we have.[208]*

In any case, the naturalization cases seemed to Hand to be difficult and borderline; each one, he was aware, changed a person's life. He maintained intellectual detachment as best he could—not "the disinterestedness of the calloused or the heartless,"[209] but the detachment of a judge committed to performing an unwelcome task. Many of these rulings, like those involving McCarthyism, were agonizing to Hand, and his decisions reflected his turmoil. They repeatedly illustrate C. C. Burlingham's comment that but for the fact that a judge must decide a case, "not a few of Hand's opinions might well end with a question mark."[210]

In every one of Hand's major naturalization cases, his first reaction was that the alien's behavior did not disqualify him on "good moral character" grounds; and in only one did he write an opinion barring citizenship. That case was *Repouille v. United States*.[211] Louis Repouille filed his naturalization petition on September 22, 1944. Not quite five years earlier, on October 12, 1939, he "had deliberately put to death his son, a boy of thirteen, by means of chloroform." Hand related the facts about Repouille's "tragic deed" with evident sympathy: the blind, mute child had "suffered from birth from a brain injury which destined him to be an idiot and a physical monstrosity malformed in all four limbs. . . . He had to be fed; the movements of his bladder and bowels were involuntary, and his entire life was spent in a small crib." Repouille had four other children to whom he had always been a responsible parent. Presumably, the killing of his deformed son "was to help him in [the] nurture" of his other children. At his criminal trial, the sympathetic jury had brought in a verdict of second-degree manslaughter with a recommendation of the "utmost clemency," and the trial judge had imposed only a brief sentence and stayed its execution.

In writing his majority opinion, Hand invoked his "common conscience" approach, insisting that the "good moral character" test called not for "those standards which we might ourselves approve, but whether 'the moral feelings now prevalent generally in this country' would 'be

---

* Frankfurter responded: "It really is fantastic to assume that the kind of confused ethical judgments you would get from Jerry's imagined panel of experts would be a dependable basis for a judicial judgment on such an issue. . . . Jerry too often is just a learned child—if, indeed, learning is the product of a voracious appetite for reading without considering the contents of books both backwards and forwards—backwards, by placing them in the movement of ideas, and forwards, by viewing new ideas with proper skepticism in determining their implications. Jerry too often reminds me of Holmes in the reverse. You remember Holmes' remark: 'I don't know facts; I merely know their significance.' Jerry knows a helluvah lot of books, but not their significance" (Felix Frankfurter to LH, 11 December 1947, 105–13).

outraged' by the conduct in question: that is, whether it conformed to 'the generally accepted moral conventions current at the time.' "[212] That, as always, was a difficult task for him. He recognized that it might be preferable to have the legislature prescribe ground rules regarding euthanasia, but the fact that there was no such law on the books did not mean "it must be immoral to do this": "Many people—probably most people—do not make it a final ethical test of conduct that it shall not violate law; few of us exact of ourselves or of others the unflinching obedience of a Socrates." Clearly, the jury had not felt "any moral repulsion at Repouille's crime." The second-degree manslaughter conviction "was flatly in the face of the facts and utterly absurd," and the jury's clemency recommendation "showed that in substance they wished to exculpate the offender." Should the benign jury serve as an adequate, reliable "measure of current morals"? At first, Hand was strongly tempted to defer to it. But he ultimately declined, noting that a similar offender in Massachusetts had recently been sentenced to life in prison for euthanasia:

> Left at large as we are, without means of verifying our conclusion, and without authority to substitute our individual beliefs, the outcome must needs be tentative; and not much is gained by discussion. We can say no more than that, quite independently of what may be the current moral feeling as to legally administered euthanasia, we feel reasonably secure in holding that only a minority of virtuous persons would deem the practise morally justifiable, while it remains in private hands, even when the provocation is as overwhelming as it was in this instance.

Hand reached this rare conclusion only after extensive discussion with his colleagues. Having at first been prepared to admit Repouille to citizenship, relying mainly on the jury's obvious compassion—"Not only does the law at times fail to keep pace with current morals; but current morals at times may make law morally inadequate"[213]—he found this impulse was not shared by his colleagues Gus Hand and Jerome Frank. Gus, while announcing that he was "sorry for this poor fellow," was not prepared to find that the "common conscience" would find Repouille's behavior to be consistent with "good moral character": "We may favor 'mercy killing' but if sanctioned by law it should have the most careful safeguards to make it accord with social safety." He noted the Massachusetts case his cousin later mentioned, pointing out that "a father living near Pittsfield was convicted last year of murder in the first degree for a mercy killing of an idiot child. . . . That disposition was pretty barbarous, yet has a bearing on the sentiment of

American communities."[214] Frank insisted that the jury verdict was "a pretty good indication of the 'commonly accepted mores' "; his pre-conference memorandum did not mention the "ethical leaders" suggestion in his published dissent.[215]

Hand presumably changed his mind because of the Massachusetts euthanasia case. Perhaps, too, he was concerned that he might be seen as endorsing euthanasia more broadly than he intended, in the face of the legislature's failure to legalize it. Moreover, rejecting Repouille's petition was not a harsh judgment in this case: as Hand knew all along, and as he made explicit in his opinion, "a new petition would not be open to the objection," because any future effort to attain citizenship would begin more than five years after the deed. This clearly made it easier for Hand to rule against Repouille, since "the pitiable event, now long past, will not prevent [him] from taking his place among us as a citizen."[216]

In every other major naturalization case, Hand, both before his conferences with his colleagues and in his final decisions, found for the petitioner on the "good moral character" question. Two years after *Repouille*, in *Schmidt v. United States*, he found that sex outside of marriage did not bar a finding of "good moral character." Once again he emphasized that determining good moral character was "at best only a guess, made without any opportunity of checking it": "[W]e must, I believe, decide that a single man does not forfeit his claim to good moral character, because he is not celibate."[217] Referring to Alfred Kinsey's recently published *Sexual Behavior in the Human Male*,[218] Hand's colleagues agreed with his proposed disposition. Judge Thomas Swan noted, "The Kinsey Report shows how the majority of unmarried males regard promiscuous sexual relations." Similarly, Judge Charles Clark commented that "[i]n the face of the Kinsey Report and common-sense ideas," he was unwilling to find that Schmidt's conduct was "repugnant to the mores of the community."[219] Frankfurter soon sent Hand a clipping from a Washington newspaper with the headline "N.Y. MORALS—'IF ANY'—HIT HERE." The paper carried a United Press story that reported an immigration official's response to *Schmidt*, a response suggesting that "what New York's federal judges accept as 'good moral character' is not good enough or moral enough for the rest of the country." The official proclaimed that despite Hand's ruling, immigration authorities would continue to apply their "normal Christian standards": "There is no use to subject the rest of the country to the moral standards, if any, in New York." Frankfurter attached a note addressed to "Dearest B" and stating, "You have already justified your stay on the bench!"[220]

Hand's compassionate view of those who had strayed from the wholly virtuous path was also central in a 1947 ruling, *United States v. Francioso*.[221] There, the alien applying for citizenship had married his niece in 1925 and lived with her and their four young children between 1938 and 1943, the relevant five years before he filed his naturalization petition. He had entered his marriage knowing that it was a forbidden, incestuous one under the law of Connecticut, the state in which he resided. Later on, a Catholic priest had "solemnized" the union with the consent of the local bishop. The question was, as Hand put it: "Would the moral feelings that are now prevalent generally in this country be outraged because Francioso continued to live with his wife and four children between 1938 and 1943?" To Hand, the answer was quite clear. It would be inhumane and intolerable to demand that the husband leave his wife and young children: "Cato himself would not have demanded that he should turn all five adrift . . . and we have for warrant the fact that the Church—least of all complaisant with sexual lapses—saw fit to sanction the continuance of this union."[222] Hand's pre-conference memorandum was even more vigorous in insisting that Francioso's conduct had been consistent with "the most rudimentary decencies," and Hand, always contemptuous of insensitive administrators, added, "Perhaps even so low a form of animal life as an examiner in the Naturalization Bureau would go so far as that." Hand was outraged by the claim that Francioso should be deemed as lacking good moral character because he had not turned to celibacy: "Once more I wish to pay my respects to the sanctimonious, hypocritical, illiterate animaleulae who infest and infect the Naturalization Bureau."[223]

Until the very end of his life, Hand adhered to his "common conscience" standard in "good moral character" cases—often over the resistance of his colleagues and always with sensitivity to the human beings affected by his rulings. In one of his early cases, in 1939, he succeeded in eliciting a unanimous opinion that possession of a "jimmy," a burglary tool, with criminal intent did not constitute a crime of "moral turpitude." His colleagues, the tough-minded Robert Patterson and the New Deal liberal Charles Clark, were both at first convinced that deportation was clearly in order, but Hand found the issue less simple. He argued that although jimmies were designed for burglary and larceny, their main function was to pry things open, and not all crimes that might be committed with one necessarily showed "moral turpitude."

> This alien was then a boy of seventeen and such boys might delight in having jimmies to pry their way into buildings or boxes or

barrels merely for curiosity or mischief. Those would be crimes, it is true, but they would not be morally shameful.[224]

And as Hand ultimately put it in his opinion for a unanimous court:

> Such crimes by no means "inherently" involve immoral conduct; boys frequently force their way into buildings out of curiosity, or a love of mischief, intending no more than to do what they know is forbidden. Such conduct is no more than a youthful prank, to which most high-spirited boys are more or less prone; it would be to the last degree pedantic to hold that it involved moral turpitude and to visit upon it the dreadful penalty of banishment, which is precisely what deportation means to one who has lived here since childhood.[225]

That final passage discloses a mainspring of Hand's zeal to permit aliens to remain in this country: for as long as he had been a judge, he had been especially critical of deportation orders against aliens who had lived in the United States for many years and whom the authorities now proposed to expel because of actions in their youth.

Hand displayed his skill and artistry in sympathetic adjudication of naturalization cases throughout his remaining years on the bench. Two of his last decisions, rendered just a few months before his death, *Posusta v. United States* and *Yin-Shing Woo v. United States*,[226] are illustrative. In each case, he overturned the trial judge's denial of naturalization, applying his "common conscience" approach with compassion and flexibility.

In the first case, Marie Posusta, the petitioner, was a Czechoslovakian woman who had been the mistress of, and lived with, a man named Posusta since 1936; they had married in 1959. Posusta had been married to another woman for most of those years; he had one child with his first wife and then two children, during the 1940s, with Marie, the eventual second Mrs. Posusta, whose naturalization petition was filed in April 1959, soon after she and Posusta finally married. The central question was whether she had been a person of "good moral character" during the five years preceding her filing, when she and Posusta lived together before he separated from and divorced his first wife. (Mr. Posusta and the petitioner had in fact taken out a marriage license in October 1954. In explaining the delay in their marriage, Mr. Posusta said that he "wanted to take charge of" the education of his son by his first wife, which he thought he "could do better than" she; if he married again, he thought, "she would not give me the child at all.")

Hand's opinion emphasized again that "the test is not the personal moral principles of the individual judge or court before whom the applicant may come; the decision is to be based upon what he or it believes to be the ethical standards current at the time."[227] Moreover, that a person had "been delinquent upon occasion in the past" did not preclude a finding of "good moral character"; "it is enough if he shows that he does not transgress the accepted canons more often than is usual":

> Obviously it is a test incapable of exact definition; the best we can do is to improvise a response that the "ordinary" man or woman would make, if the question were put whether the conduct was consistent with a "good moral character." Values are incommensurables; and the law is full of standards that admit of no quantitative measures; the most frequent instances are those that require "reasonable" appraisals between conflicting values or desires.

Applying this slippery standard to the facts, Hand concluded that Marie Posusta's conduct "was consonant with 'good moral character' ":

> So far as appears, Posusta was her only lover and she had been true to him for over twenty years. Her relations with him were not concealed; indeed when they were both in this country they lived under the same roof. People will of course differ in their degree of condemnation of such breaches of the moral code; we can say no more than that even a continued illicit relation is not inevitably an index of a bad "moral character."[228]

In *Yin-Shing Woo*, the second 1961 case, the trial judge had denied an application for naturalization because the petitioner had not proved that he was "well disposed to the good order and happiness of the United States," another phrase in the statute. The petitioner, a native of China and a translator for the State Department who had been a permanent American resident since 1948, had been arrested in New York City in September 1957 as a "scofflaw": he had failed to answer twenty-three parking tickets; he was released from jail after paying a fine of $345. The question was whether these violations of city ordinances indicated that he was not "well disposed to the good order . . . of the United States." Hand refused to adopt "a rigid interpretation of the words": "Like any other statute, this one is to be read with its purposes in mind, which are to admit as citizens only those who are in general accord with the basic principles of the community. Disregard of parking regulations, even when repeated as often as this was, is not inimical to its 'good order,' so construed."[229]

This was simply one more instance, Hand argued, of a legislature leaving "to the judge the appraisal of some of the values at stake." Any time the law adopted a "reasonableness" standard, for example, the lawmakers really granted to the courts "legislative power, although we call the issues questions of fact": "They require of the judges the compromise that they think in accord with the general purposes of the measure as the community would understand it." All a judge could really say, Hand insisted, was that he was doing his best. Overcoming the reluctance of Judge Clark, Hand managed to obtain a unanimous ruling in the *Yin-Shing Woo* case.[230]

These naturalization decisions were characteristic of Hand the judge and Hand the man. In the decade after his seventy-fifth birthday, he continued to wrestle honorably with his judicial business and the issues of the day. He never escaped his self-doubts; he never abandoned his skepticism; he never forsook the craftman's efforts to do his job well; he spoke out, publicly and vigorously, against the evils of the McCarthy era; and he confronted his assigned tasks with discipline and humanity. In these ways, Hand's wisdom illuminated a dark decade. As he had once said in another context: "No doubt the answer is not as clear as one might wish . . . but we can only follow what light we have."[231] His light was brighter than most.

Active Retirement from
"Regular Active Service"

LEARNED HAND'S RETIREMENT from "regular active service" in 1951 by no means ended his public life. Not only did he continue to participate in many cases on the Second Circuit; he became ever better known to an ever larger audience. The greatest single factor that propelled Hand to the rank of American folk hero was the publication in 1952 of *The Spirit of Liberty*, a collection of his extrajudicial papers and addresses.

For years, Hand had turned aside invitations to write his memoirs, offers to do his biography, and requests to appear on radio and television programs. He thought it "unseemly" for judges to garner publicity through anything other than their judicial opinions. And the book did not represent a change of heart, for it was initiated by his wife and oldest daughter. When a prospective publisher and editor appeared, and family support was thrown their way, Hand's reservations were overcome.

The liberal editor of the *St. Louis Post-Gazette*'s editorial pages, Irving Dilliard, was an admirer of Hand. Dilliard's persistence was mainly responsible for the compilation of the *Spirit of Liberty* essays. Dilliard had no real personal acquaintance with Hand when he came up with the idea of editing a book of Hand's essays and speeches. They had had only one chance encounter: in the library of the City Bar Association, where Hand often worked on weekends and holidays, on Thanksgiving morning in 1949. But Dilliard had written editorials praising Hand, and he mentioned these when he first wrote Hand in February 1951 requesting an inscribed photo. "I admire you in a way that I admire no other American today," he told Hand. Only a postscript, addressed

to Hand's secretary, hinted at the project Dilliard had in mind: he noted
that he had been compiling a list of Hand's writings over the years and
asked whether Hand's office kept a similar list against which he could
check his own.[1]

A few weeks later, Dilliard first broached the subject to Hand. He
proposed to "gather up some 15 to 20 of your essays . . . and addresses
before law students and at memorials and commencements for a suitable
volume." He had already spoken, he told Hand, with the publisher
Alfred A. Knopf and Knopf's wife, Blanche, and they as well as
Knopf's editorial board were "delighted with the idea."[2] The Hands
knew the Knopfs socially, and this prompted Hand to take the inquiry
more seriously than usual, though he still balked. He wrote Dilliard
that Frances Hand and the Hands' oldest daughter, by now Mary Hand
Darrell, had already planned "something of the same kind which they
hope to get published by my eightieth birthday, next January."[3] Within
weeks, Dilliard managed to elicit the family's cooperation in a single
project. Learned drafted a letter for Frances's signature promising full
cooperation and insisting that the Hands would not "ask, or indeed
take, any royalties from the sale of the book."[4]

During the rest of the year, Hand and Dilliard corresponded frequently, deciding which pieces should be included. Dilliard had long
admired Hand for his liberal opinions on such issues as freedom of
expression, but he did not so readily understand that Hand's liberalism
also included a strong belief in limits on judges' power to fashion
constitutional values. But Dilliard's puzzlement and even disagreement
with some tenets of Hand's faith did not get in the way of his doing a
first-rate job in assembling the materials. Dilliard's collection ranged
from the student Hand's Class Day oration at Harvard College in 1893
to Judge Hand's reflections on liberal education, the courts, and the
democratic process, as well as his tributes to a wide range of acquaintances and other judges. Dilliard also successfully pressed Hand to allow
use of one piece of his private correspondence, his November 1922
letter to the chair of Harvard's special "sifting" committee, opposing
the adoption of a Jewish quota by the university. Dilliard wrote brief
introductory remarks to each of the pieces, as well as a lengthy foreword
containing a biographical sketch, and Hand readily supplied biographical
data and background material for these.

Dilliard completed the manuscript by Lincoln's Birthday 1952. Hand
helped him in the reading of the galley proofs, complimenting Dilliard:
"The book will be the greatest satisfaction to me and to my children,
though I can hardly suppose that many others will care for it. But,
after all, that is the risk that Knopf thought it wise to take."[5] In May,

a few months after Hand's eightieth birthday, the book came off the press. Hand was still protesting. "I don't understand," Hand wrote, "why you should have thought it worthwhile to go the trouble you have taken to try to put my notions . . . in a permanent form."[6]

Hand's doubts about the interest his essays would have to a general audience were not mere modesty. Neither Hand nor the publisher expected great success. As Alfred Knopf put it in mid-April, just weeks before the official publication date, "[P]ublishers are always publishing books on which they lose money, and isn't it a lot better to lose on a book by Learned Hand than on, say, some unpretentious and at best second rate piece of fiction?"[7] A few months later, Knopf could tell Hand that "what started quite differently, has become a successful venture": "I am afraid that when we embarked on the publication of The Spirit of Liberty no one involved took the book quite as seriously, from a purely business point of view, as it deserved."[8] By August 15, only three months after publication, 7,300 copies had already been shipped to bookstores (the initial store order had been only 1,300), and the book was about to go into its fourth printing. With the book now an assured financial success, the publisher tried to persuade Hand to accept a royalty check.[9] Hand flatly refused, as he had done ever since the project was launched. As he explained to Dilliard, "All the stuff was written con amore and without any idea that I should get paid. I could not look myself in the face and take anything for it."[10]

By October 1954, the total print run had reached 20,000, and sales continued to hold up.[11] On the third anniversary of the publication, sales exceeded 18,000; on hearing that news, Hand exclaimed that he was "amazed and delighted."[12] When sales of *The Spirit of Liberty* passed the 20,000 mark in 1956, Knopf pressed Hand to agree to a book of selected judicial opinions, but Hand declined. The publication in 1958 of a paperback edition of *The Spirit of Liberty* assured an even wider audience. The delighted publisher tried once again to provide Hand some monetary reward. Alfred Knopf sent Hand a $1,000 check, urging him to divide it among his grandchildren if he did not want it for himself. The check reached Hand just before his eighty-eighth birthday, in January 1960. But Hand's attitude about accepting compensation remained unchanged. He told Knopf that he had been left "almost speechless" by the "staggering enclosure":

> It is rather I who should give to you, for it was you who took the chance, by no means negligible, that the book might be a "flop" and useful only as a "deduction." Now that it proved to get a certain degree of welcome, I can only credit it to your backing,

and it gives me a gratification that I shall not forget, [that is] so ample that I should feel more in your debt as I always shall anyway.[13]

And so Hand returned the check, explaining that he would not feel comfortable about spreading the money among his grandchildren, and urging that it go to Dilliard, if to anyone. For him, the satisfaction "for the chance you gave me of spreading about my desultory talks among so many people" was reward enough.[14]

The unanticipated success of *The Spirit of Liberty* was no doubt helped by the enthusiastic reviews. In *The New Yorker*, Philip Hamburger was the apt commentator, stating that readers would be "astounded" by "the depth and breadth of the man's wisdom, of his learning, of his compassion, and of his monumental struggle with himself and his era in his pursuit of truth in the deepest and darkest corners of his experience."[15] *The New Republic*'s review, like many, emphasized that Hand had found that "skepticism rather than dogmatism is the key to human freedom."[16] In the *Saturday Review of Literature*, the historian Richard Morris concluded: "Wise and urbane, scornful of pretense, shibboleths, and standpattism, [Hand] exemplifies the best in the tradition of American liberalism."[17]

In the ensuing months, professional journals added to the mounting encomiums by judges, legal scholars, political scientists, former law clerks, and practitioners.[18] Only a very few questioned any part of Hand's philosophy. The most common target of criticism was Hand's belief that the courts had no more warrant to intervene on behalf of personal rights such as speech and religion than on behalf of economic rights, as they had in the *Lochner* era. Harvard law professor Louis Jaffe, for example, thought the courts had a larger role to play in the protection of civil liberties. "There is so much truth in [Hand's] whole analysis and so much felicity in its expression that one hesitates to question it," he wrote, but question it he did.[19] The occasional sounds of dissent, however, were submerged by the overwhelming chorus of praise. Repeatedly, the reviewers referred to Hand as the greatest living American judge, the best writer among judges, and the de facto "Tenth Justice" of the Supreme Court; as Jaffe put it, the essays provided "a vivid picture of the man thinking and feeling his way through life."[20]

As the Knopf volume went through quick reprintings and new editions (and Hand continued to deliver addresses), the thirty-four papers collected in *The Spirit of Liberty* were expanded to forty-one.[21] None of the many reprints of the collection gave Hand more personal pleasure than the decision by Hamish Hamilton to publish a British edition in

1954. In writing a preface for British readers, Hand struck a characteristic stance: "It is a collection of papers written on odd occasions over a great many years without much, if any, coherence. I should hardly think that it would interest readers in Britain; but the publishers apparently think it may, and, after all, the risk is theirs."[22] In a lead review entitled "A Great American Humanist," Britain's influential *The Economist* viewed Hand's essays as an important antidote to "certain cliches used by the English in thinking about Americans," especially "the best loved cliche of all," that the United States was "a society which has passed from barbarism to decadence without any intervening phase of civilisation," a cliche that had seemed confirmed by the appeal of McCarthyism. Hand's work, by contrast, revealed "a style and a view of life as far removed from the common, trivial and the undercivilised mass mind as it is conceivable for a man to be." The reviewer concluded: "As for the cliche-mongers, they can at least reflect that the society which produced McCarthy has also formed, advanced and honoured the most eloquent exponent of liberty and tolerance living in our day."[23]

BY 1953, Hand was still carrying nearly a full workload of Second Circuit cases; he was mentally as alert as ever, and in satisfactory physical condition. Though a bad back kept him from continuing his routine of daily walks to the courthouse on Foley Square from his home on East Sixty-fifth Street, he traveled to Europe more often than ever, for sight-seeing and visits to old friends in several countries. On his summer visits to Cornish, he regretted that so many of his old friends had died, but he found new ones to maintain the intellectual verve of his circle. A special favorite was a young man, the novelist J. D. Salinger, who had bought a house near Low Court and who, though generally a recluse, developed a warm affection for Hand. During the long New Hampshire winters, Salinger and Hand exchanged letters, with Salinger's notes— from "Jerry" to "Dear Jay and Mrs. Hand"—filled with news of the weather, his family life, and, soon, his thoughts on spiritualism and Eastern religions as well.[24] Hand considered Salinger "a close friend" for whom he had "the utmost regard, not only for his intelligence, but for his personal character."[25] He knew of Salinger's penchant for privacy,[26] and respected it. Thus, when a *Newsweek* reporter sought to interview Hand about Salinger, Hand refused: "I know that Mr. Salinger does not want any publicity, and as his friend I am certainly unwilling to be a party to impose upon him what he would regard as an invasion of his privacy. Moreover, I may add that I am quite in accord with his feelings."[27] Hand's young neighbor may have found in the judge "the kind of father Salinger might wish to have had";[28] certainly Salinger's letters to Hand disclose a very special fondness.

Summering in Cornish during these years, Hand was able to express his love of song and mimicry more frequently than ever. He and Frances put on musical evenings for guests where he sang and she played the piano. Once, presenting his version of Shakespeare's *Othello*, he acted out the title role with such verismo that, in the last act, he broke his Desdemona's nose. When his growing number of grandchildren visited, he would recreate stories and nightly fables, and perform songs and pantomimes—such as his "Story of the Crooked Mouth Family"— with which he had captured the imagination of his own three girls in earlier years.[29] Many of his law clerks remember Hand bursting out in song and mimicry at unanticipated moments in order to lighten the atmosphere. One of the clerks, Daniel M. Gribbon, recalls an occasion when he had retreated to his desk disheartened after failing to persuade Hand on a legal issue. A few minutes later, Hand came in "dancing a jig and singing at the top of his voice, 'You're mad at me, you're mad at me!' "[30]

Learned was also able to spend far more time with Frances during these years. For him, these were among the happiest years of his marriage: "I think of you very often, always realizing that you are my pearl without price. How did I ever get you?"[31] When he received one of her notably warmer letters, he replied, "[M]y God, how I like to get them. They positively ooze with your dear serenity and loveliness." And he added, in a note of self-reproach rare during his final years, "It seems to me as though I really never came to realize what you were until these last years. The early ones were too full of urgencies—self, really—I never came to look at you or understand you till almost the other day." His gratitude to her for what he saw as her rescuing him from an unhappy, psychologically crippled life was a constant in their nearly sixty years of marriage. Congratulating her on her seventy-fifth birthday, he wrote, "[O]h what a fortunate day it has been for me. What should I be; where should I be if you had not come to bless this twisted introvert and guide him through the years?"[32]

Frances Hand continued to enjoy her life to the fullest. After the years of effusive birthday letters from Learned, she, after taking only slight note of his earlier birthdays and even forgetting some of them,[33] had taken time when he turned seventy-three in 1945 to compose a little poem about her "thoughts of Bunny & his love so warm."[34] True, when she visited Cornish she occasionally admitted, "I miss Lou [Louis Dow] here a good deal."[35] But she also expressed sentiments unlike any she had voiced for decades, such as "I hate to leave you alone, darling, & shall be so glad to see you again."[36] And in thanking him for a "little love letter," she affectionately endorsed his determination not to be so often separated again: "I know how you feel about the fact that there must necessarily be an end to our so-long accustomed ways of parting & meeting."[37]

Learned's expressions of love suffused his letters to Frances till the end. "I love you more all the time"; "You are very precious to me"; "I think often of you and feel always how much you are to me. . . . I love you, I love you, I love you!!"[38]—in the warmth of endearments such as these they shared their last years. And even though they spent far more time together than they had for decades, Learned craved more: "I love you, I love you, I love you!!! and I don't like these separations"; "I do *not* enjoy these separations from you; I mind them more than I used to."[39] And now when Frances went to Cornish, as she continued to do with undiminished joy for a few summer weeks each year, Learned could appreciate her life renewal there with unreserved satisfaction: "I think of you as falling easily into that state of ease in which you are not pestered by this and that but can let the hours slip away in pleasant reading. . . . Don't ever forget that the hours—better the days—that I do not spend with you, my best and dearest, are far from being 'a string of pearls to me.' " And after sending greetings of "love" from several friends, he ended with "I can 'send' you none, for you already have all my store, past, present and future."[40]

But Hand could not deny the calendar, and the "irreversible process of getting older"[41] was increasingly on his mind. For some years he had routinely written the law clerks newly designated by the Harvard Law School that they should make alternate arrangements for their clerkship year, tenure being "insecure" because of his advancing age: "I want to reserve the absolute freedom not to work next year. . . . As Holmes used to say: 'I reserve the right to die or resign.' "[42] These warnings never rang true when the clerks reported for duty. When I began my clerkship in the fall of 1953, I found the eighty-one-year-old judge remarkably vigorous, with no signs of failing health and no indication of any thoughts of resigning. Yet Hand's ruminations about old age were now far more dominant in his conversations than they had been earlier.

The immediate reason for Hand's heightened preoccupation with aging lay in his concern for his cousin Gus, down the hall on the twenty-fourth floor of the Foley Square courthouse. Neither Learned Hand nor the judges' law clerks could help noticing that Gus, only a little more than two years older than Learned, was declining. True, he was still a genial conversationalist, reminiscing about earlier years and frequently invoking his beloved Latin and Greek classics to illustrate a point. Yet he had frequent difficulties in maintaining his attention; his mind wandered and his eyelids drooped while on the bench; and in conferences as well as in his own chambers, the mental powers of the older of "the Hand Boys" were clearly not as acute as they had once been.[43]

Learned Hand had premonitions. As he wrote to a former law clerk in the fall of 1953, after the great triumvirate of the Second Circuit —Learned and Gus Hand, and Thomas Swan—had sat together hearing thirteen cases argued over four days:

> [I]t had a touch of finality about it for it is so unlikely that we shall be together again. It was like a living representation of the past: "Observe the final appearance of the Dinosaurs."[44]

And as Hand recalled a year later, the unavoidable reality was that Augustus Hand

> was steadily, but slowly, failing. When his attention was awakened, his wit seemed to be as good as before, but I do not think he was any longer capable of any long sustained effort, and it is my guess that he would not have been able to hold court again. . . . Of course I prefer to think of him as he was in his prime.[45]

Augustus's failing powers troubled Learned greatly. He would brood repeatedly about the possibility that he, too, might be failing, even though there were no signs of it in his own behavior and work. His recurrent refrain was "Will you tell me? Will anyone tell me when I'm really slowing up, when I'm in fact declining?" He dreaded the thought that he himself might unknowingly be slipping, and he repeatedly sought reassurances that he was not.

During Gus's final months, Learned sadly watched his cousin "getting very gradually more and more weak," often "rather torpid in company," though he remained physically healthy until the end. Often, he "easily lapsed into what seemed to be a revery, and what very probably was a rather empty state of blank contentment."[46]

On October 28, 1954, Augustus Hand died: he "simply went to sleep and didn't wake up."[47] Learned was consoled that "no one could have had a more perfect end if the end had to come than to go to bed and not wake up."[48] Moreover, "it was right that [Gus] should go. . . . [W]hat remained would inevitably have been a descent."[49]

The consolation that Learned Hand found in the manner of Gus's death could hardly be sufficient, though, for as he put it to a friend a few days later, "His death has ended my longest intimacy—nearly eighty years—and I cannot yet quite realize that it has happened."[50] To Felix Frankfurter he mused, "I ask myself what [Gus's death] means. We knew each other—each of us—longer than we knew anyone else; we had in one sense been as intimate as men can be—the kind of intimacy that does not express itself in words, but takes things for granted."[51] Learned and Gus had indeed been as close as brothers: Learned the agnostic, Gus the vestryman of Grace Church; Learned the more mercurial one, swinging from gloom and depression to occasional joys and satisfactions, Gus the even-tempered, placid one. Learned was vividly aware of the contrast: he had written to the editor of a religious magazine the year before, "[I]f I reach Paradise, it will have to be on [Gus's] coattails; they are ample, and perhaps I shall."[52]

Gus once said to a young man writing a doctoral dissertation on Learned's judicial work, "Why not do a study of my work? I am the balance wheel in the Hand combination."[53] He said it with a twinkle in his eye, but Learned would have agreed that this was a fair assessment. Justice Robert Jackson once related that as a young country lawyer in upstate New York, he had been taught "to quote Learned, but cite Gus." Learned was indeed better at fashioning prose that sang, but Gus had a reputation as the more solid of the two—less creative perhaps, less liberal in his politics, less daring in his public statements. Gus and Learned did not always agree, on law or on politics, but "there was such a genuine unity (*not* unanimity!) in the great Hand-Swan-Hand court."[54]

UNTIL THE VERY END of his career, Learned Hand had no occasion to deviate from his usual reluctance to interfere in judicial appointments. Thomas Swan and Gus Hand had both retired in 1953. Their successors were Carroll C. Hincks, a well-respected, conscientious district judge from Connecticut, and the Wall Street lawyer John Marshall Harlan, whom Hand admired enormously. (When after only a few months on the Second Circuit Harlan was considered for a seat on the Supreme Court, Hand, in a letter to President Eisenhower, praised Harlan effusively for his "detachment," "balance," "horizons," and "sense of public duty.")[55] Similarly, Hand was pleased when J. Edward Lumbard, a former U.S. attorney for the Southern District of New York, joined the court in 1955, replacing Harlan, and when Judge Sterry Waterman of Vermont succeeded to Judge Harrie Chase's seat.

Later, however, the appointments to the Second Circuit turned highly contentious. Hand, fearing that the court's high quality was at risk, actively pressed for the appointment of individuals he considered best qualified.

Intense rivalry for a position on the Second Circuit first erupted in the wake of the sudden, unexpected death of Jerome Frank on January 13, 1957. Shortly thereafter, Felix Frankfurter, never as reluctant as Hand to offer advice, wrote a long, forceful letter to Eisenhower's attorney general, Herbert Brownell, Jr., urging the naming of Henry J. Friendly to succeed Frank. Friendly, a partner in a Wall Street law firm, had been Frankfurter's student at Harvard, and Frankfurter had selected him as law clerk for Justice Louis Brandeis. Frankfurter sent to Hand a copy of his Brownell letter with a note: "B—What say you to this? FF"[56] Hand hesitated only briefly before endorsing Friendly, though he scarcely knew him. He told Frankfurter that he would normally oppose appointing a practicing lawyer if he thought that "an honest effort would be made, regardless of devious political pressures, to select the best of the district judges." In his view, the best way to select circuit court judges was to promote from the ranks of the lower courts, and he had been "disgusted" for years by "the base considerations that have dictated judicial . . . appointments." But now he had little faith that trial judges with "the most capacity" would be promoted: "We may get a district judge, it is true; but you may bet your boots that the eventual determinants will be other than fitness, though he will have to be fit enough not to stink. . . ." Since promotion of the best was politically unlikely, Hand was happy to support a practitioner such as Friendly.[57] Friendly's reputation at the New York bar was rightly high, and Hand knew it; as he wrote to Frankfurter, he did not expect Frank's successor to be the late judge's "match morally . . . unless it should be some gift of God be Friendly."[58]

Hand guessed that the leading candidates to succeed Frank were Whitney North Seymour, Eli Whitney Debevoise, and Irving R. Kaufman.[59] The first two were prominent New York business lawyers; Kaufman was a well-publicized district judge who had gained considerable renown by presiding at the espionage trial of Julius and Ethel Rosenberg in 1951 and sentencing them to death. Kaufman soon emerged as a major candidate for the vacancy, even while Hand's preference for Friendly became more fervent by the day; soon, indeed, he took the unusual step of following in Frankfurter's footsteps and writing to Attorney General Brownell himself.[60]

By the end of January 1957, Hand learned (from Justice Harlan) that Friendly would probably not be named to Frank's place; Hand told Frankfurter he was "very sorry, truly sorry, that Brownell did not come around to Friendly. He was worth a sacrifice of the principle of promotion."[61] Two weeks later, a *New York Times* story, headlined "Big U.S. Court Job Hotly Contested," and subtitled "Naming Appeals Judge to Succeed Frank Involves High Political Figures," revealed how deeply mired in politics the succession to Jerome Frank had become. The *Times* reported that the contest was now between Kaufman and Leonard P. Moore, the U.S. attorney for the Eastern District of New York. Former governor Thomas E. Dewey and the two Republican senators from New York, Jacob Javits and Kenneth Keating, were in Moore's corner, but, as Hand knew, Kaufman, a Democrat, had strong, bipartisan support—not only from Emanuel Celler, the Democratic chair of the House Judiciary Committee, but also from the influential New Hampshire Republican senator Styles Bridges and from Democratic senator Estes Kefauver of Tennessee.

The *Times* story included a passage that disgusted both Hand and Frankfurter: "One of the main arguments being used in favor of Judge Kaufman is that his promotion would constitute an expression of Presidential and Senatorial approval for his conduct of the Rosenberg trial. During the trial and since the execution of the two convicted spies, he has been under heavy attack from left-wing groups."[62] When Hand read this, he erupted to Frankfurter:

> Did you see today's Times and the reasons said to be put forward in Washington for moving up Kaufmann [*sic*]? "To show the President approved his decision to execute the Rosenbergs."

> Oh, oh, oh! How low people can get! I don't mean K. [Kaufman]; he didn't start that, I believe; but the Swine, the Swine, the Swine!!![63]

Soon after, the 1957 political battle ended with a victory for Leonard Moore. Hand was left with such contempt for the political process in filling vacancies that he wrote Frankfurter that he was "thoroughly sick of my government, especially quoad [with respect to] the appointments of judges. What a mistake it was to let the Senate in on any appointment anyway! Democracy! How many crimes are committed in thy name!!!"[64]

But the political tempests that swirled around Court of Appeals appointments were not yet over. Another vacancy on the Second Circuit arose in March 1958, when Judge Harold Medina retired, and this time, Friendly and Kaufman were the only contenders. Once again, *The New York Times* reported (in mid-January 1959) that an "extraordinary struggle," marked by "political infighting," had broken out,[65] and the struggle was entangled with a dispute over a judgeship bill: the

Eisenhower administration proposed creating forty-five new federal judgeships; the Democrats were threatening to block the bill in order to await the outcome of the 1960 election.* Henry Friendly, nominally a Republican but never active in political affairs, had stronger support this time than in 1957. New York's Republican leaders and Republican senator Keating endorsed him, but Republican senator Javits had not yet announced his support.

Hand watched this renewed battle with great concern. As in 1957, he was eager to see the most qualified person—in his view, Henry Friendly—on the bench. Hand had written Frankfurter in January 1958: "I fear [Medina's] successor is settled—Irving Kaufman—a thoroughly competent lawyer, but interested primarily, if not completely, in recognition of Irving Kaufman."[66] By late January 1959, Hand decided to intervene once more. This time, suspecting that Attorney General Brownell had committed the Justice Department to Kaufman, he wrote directly to President Eisenhower:

> I think there have been not more than two occasions during the long period that I have served as a judge when I have felt it permissible to write a letter in favor of anyone for a judicial appointment.[67] However, I feel so strongly that the Second Circuit would be greatly benefitted by the appointment of Mr. Henry J. Friendly that I cannot forbear writing you to express my hope that you may see fit to fill the vacancy now existing in the Circuit by selecting him. I have not the slightest doubt that as a Circuit Judge he would be an addition to our court, as great as, if not greater than, anyone else you could choose; not only because of his unblemished reputation and high scholarship, but because of his balanced wisdom and wide outlook.[68]

The president promptly replied: "Your opinion is greatly valued by me, and I assure you that I will give Mr. Friendly the most earnest consideration."[69]

The winds rapidly shifted in Friendly's favor. William P. Rogers, the new attorney general, decided to back Friendly, despite his predecessor's apparent assurance to Kaufman after the 1957 appointment. And Hand's weighty support clinched the matter: on March 10, Friendly's nomination went to the Senate. Frankfurter, who once again supported Friendly, predictably applauded Hand's endorsement and Rogers's stand. He wrote Hand elatedly:

---

* According to the *Times* story, Kaufman supporters claimed that the administration was using the judge as "an unwitting pawn by promising to promote him to the Second Circuit if the judgeship bill is passed."

It took no little guts for Rogers to stand his ground against the powerful pressure that Irving Kaufman brought to bear on him and on the White House. And I give the President a high mark for supporting Rogers, considering the fact that Brownell had made a commitment to name Kaufman before he left office. The sources of K's strength in all sorts of quarters beats me. It can't be, or is it, merely his Rosenberg sentences? I have no doubt that your letter to the President was an important factor in Ike's decision to ditch K. and name Friendly.[70]

Learned Hand, too, thought the nomination gratifying, although his public intervention on Friendly's behalf raised doubts in his own mind about the propriety of taking so active a role. He told Frankfurter:

I felt very strongly, else I should not have written the letter; indeed, I have some doubt whether I ought to have done it. Maybe, as you suggest, it was a makeweight; but it was a "trifle light as air" nevertheless. I look to Friendly to put the court on a new footing; and I join in your cheers for Rogers.

I'm really sorry for [Kaufman] for he is reported to be absolutely crushed. His support appears to have come largely from the moving picture people. I doubt that the Rosenberg sentences played a part.[71]

As Hand had feared, Friendly's confirmation was delayed. Hand grew increasingly impatient about the political machinations that seemed to be keeping an outstanding candidate from the bench. He decided to undertake one more unusual intervention in the process. In early August, with the nomination bottled up in the Senate Judiciary Committee, he wrote a very careful letter to Frankfurter. The draft of the letter contains numerous revisions—a practice unique in the fifty years of Frankfurter-Hand correspondence—and the careful revisions suggest that this letter was intended to be shown to others. (Nonetheless, Hand, as on occasion, misspelled Friendly's name as "Friendley," as he did Kaufman's as "Kaufmann.") Frankfurter did indeed use the letter in his on-the-spot Washington lobbying for Friendly: he showed it, most significantly, to Senate Majority Leader Lyndon Johnson. Within a few days, Frankfurter told Hand:

Your letter done it! Senator Lyndon Johnson just phoned me that he has "seen the gentleman," one [Senator Thomas J.] Dodd of Connecticut, and "all will be O.K." A week's notice for a hearing has to be given and that has been done, & the hearing will be next Tuesday. L.J. assured me there'll be no difficulty. Armed with

your nifty letter, I saw the great man and he started things going
at once. I got a good glimpse, incidentally, on how the wheels of
government move—or, are made to move. How jejune almost all
books on "political science" are.[72]

Friendly was indeed promptly confirmed, on September 9. A year later,
Hand, now in his eighty-eighth year, sitting with Friendly on the
Second Circuit, told Frankfurter with pride: "Friendly is realizing all
our hopes."[73]

Irving R. Kaufman, the losing candidate in two successive campaigns, remained on the district court for a while longer, and finally
achieved his ambition of moving to the Second Circuit in 1961—with
the hitherto withheld help of Learned Hand. Soon after John F. Kennedy succeeded Dwight D. Eisenhower in the White House, Congress
at last enacted a bill creating seventy-three new federal judgeships—at
that time, the largest increase in the federal judiciary in its history; this
provided three new judgeships for the Second Circuit, a 50 percent
increase in its size, and one of these judgeships went to Kaufman.

Hand's decision to support Kaufman in 1961 is understandable: he
had never charged that Kaufman personally claimed to deserve promotion because of the sentencing of the Rosenbergs; and he had sympathized with Kaufman's earlier disappointments, even though he did
not then consider him sufficiently distinguished. But in 1961, just two
months before his death, Hand was moved to write President Kennedy
urging the appointment of Kaufman "as one of the three new circuit
judges." He now described Kaufman as a man of "exceptional capacity,"
but Hand mostly emphasized his long-held principle that "the promotion
of those best qualified in the lower levels is one of the most important
considerations of efficiency."[74] (There were indeed district judges whom
Hand would have preferred in earlier years, such as the widely admired
Edward Weinfeld, but Weinfeld was now too old.) Irving Kaufman
ultimately succeeded to the chief judgeship of the Second Circuit, as
Henry Friendly had done earlier.*

EXTRAORDINARY EXCITEMENT was in the air on the Harvard
campus on the cool, moonlit evenings of February 4, 5, and 6, 1958.

---

* Repeatedly in his career, Kaufman, especially when he was a target of criticism, defended
himself in part on the basis of Hand's supporting letter in 1961, sometimes conveying the
sense that he was Hand's enthusiastic choice. But as we have seen, the record suggests otherwise:
Hand had twice actively supported Friendly over Kaufman, and when he finally endorsed
Kaufman, his tone was much less fervent than his interventions on behalf of Friendly had
been.

Harvard Law School's parking lots filled rapidly with cars carrying the audience for a series of lectures. The scheduled speaker was Learned Hand, "the most revered of living American judges," as *The New York Times* called him. The large number of students, faculty, and alumni emanated anticipation as they entered Austin Hall for the Oliver Wendell Holmes Lectures (funded by a bequest in the will of Holmes), which brought distinguished invitees to the law school from time to time.[75]

Hand was in his eighty-seventh year. His strong, barrel-chested, stocky body no longer reached a full five feet ten inches, but it was only slightly stooped. He walked slowly and had requested a tall chair that he could lean on, to alleviate discomfort from his bad back,[76] but he stood erect throughout. His shock of silver-gray hair, his bushy eyebrows, his wide mouth and strong chin, his high forehead and strong cheekbones, were as striking as ever. His rich and deep voice had the vigor of a man years younger. His eyes, often melancholy and moody in repose, gazed piercingly at the audience, and they glistened with emotion—partly from sentiment, partly from the intensity of his urge to convey a deeply felt message.

Hand had been graduated from Harvard Law School more than sixty years earlier, but part of him had never left Cambridge. Amid the competing attractions of the campus, Harvard Law School authorities were at first uncertain whether a sufficiently large audience would appear for the Holmes Lectures, even though the series was the school's most distinguished and the 1958 speaker its most eminent living alumnus. But as a last-minute precaution, the law school installed loudspeakers in two large classrooms to accommodate an overflow crowd. These arrangements proved necessary: on each of the three evenings of Hand's engagement, every seat in Austin Hall's large Court Room was taken by 7:30 p.m. for the 8:00 p.m. lecture. Outside the building, the scene reminded one observer "of the entrance to a big theater where a hit was playing."[77]

Hand was surprised that the audience remained so large throughout all three lectures. "I did expect a substantial audience the first night," he told Frankfurter, "but a diminishing return each of the other two. It was not so; apparently the stuff went down their throats with less effort than I should have thought."[78] An overflow crowd for the first night was not startling, if only because of the rare opportunity to see the man whose towering reputation was familiar to so many.

For most of the listeners, the high point of the lectures no doubt came with Hand's peroration, at the end of his final lecture on February 6, when he movingly delivered an elegant tribute to his law school teachers and a poignant avowal of his ultimate, modest faith in legal craftsmanship. "More years ago than I like now to remember," he began his final paragraph, "I sat in this building and listened to—yes, more than that, was dissected by—men all but one of whom are now dead." And what he got from his teachers was "much more" than technical rules:

> I carried away the impress of a band of devoted scholars; patient, considerate, courteous and kindly, whom nothing could daunt and nothing could bribe. The memory of those men has been with me ever since. Again and again they have helped me when the labor seemed heavy, the task seemed trivial, and the confusion seemed indecipherable. From them I learned that it is as craftsmen that we get our satisfactions and our pay. In the universe of truth they lived by the sword; they asked no quarter of absolutes and they gave none.[79]

He paused, fixed his piercing eyes on some of the students in the hall, and added, before the audience rose in applause: "Go ye and do likewise."[80] Deeply felt as these words were, they were not the heart of the lectures. Their core—and their controversy—lay in what had gone before.

The nub of Hand's message was a modestly phrased but unmistakably bold challenge to what was already well on its way to becoming the reigning philosophy of the widely admired Warren Court. Hand attacked the propriety of the Supreme Court acting as a "third legislative chamber"[81] and behaving in the manner of lawmakers by second-guessing the merits of legislative choices via constitutional adjudication. For the Warren Court, the achievement of social justice through invocation of the Bill of Rights and the Fourteenth Amendment was well on its way to being the justices' central preoccupation, especially for the Chief Justice and Justices Hugo Black, William O. Douglas, and William Brennan, Jr. Hand, by contrast, questioned the desirability of judicial activism and preached an extreme version of judicial self-restraint.

What made Hand's lectures particularly contentious was that he spoke at a time when the Warren Court was itself deeply entangled in political controversy, widely criticized in Congress and by many political leaders and editorial writers. The attack on the 1954 decision in *Brown v. Board of Education*,[82] holding racial segregation in public schools unconstitutional, was near its zenith; subversion hunters had also joined the anti-Court cries, especially because of two 1957 rulings: *Watkins v. United States* suggested constitutional barriers to congressional investigations of subversion;[83] *Yates v. United States* read the Smith Act, the major criminal weapon against Communists, narrowly.[84]

Warren Court admirers could dismiss the most vocal critics of the Court as extremists; yet here was the nation's most highly regarded judge, renowned as the most articulate advocate of liberty, apparently joining the Court's enemies. And Hand's lectures were in fact an attack both on the Warren Court's general jurisprudence and on some of its specific rulings. He insisted that courts were not justified in upsetting honestly reached legislative accommodations of clashing interests and values; and in the course of doing so, he even questioned *Brown v. Board of Education*.

Hand's focus was the exercise of judicial power in constitutional cases. His stance was modesty; his philosophy, that of a skeptical democrat and experienced judge, doubting the courts' competence to decide the problems of public policy that tend to come before them under our Constitution, worried lest judicial interventions undermine the maturing of democratic processes. He loved to invoke E. M. Forster's phrase "Two Cheers for Democracy"; he sometimes suggested that perhaps one cheer or a cheer and a half might be even more appropriate. But he never swerved from his conviction that democracy was the system clearly preferable to any alternative.[85]

His first lecture dealt with the most "well-worn" issue:[86] the legitimacy of the power of judicial review, the Supreme Court's authority to hold governmental acts unconstitutional. His conclusion—that there was no constitutional basis for the power, no ground in text or history to infer it—challenged conventional wisdom and thus raised many eyebrows. But most listeners overcame any concern about Hand's claim because of his added submission that it was "not a lawless act to import into the Constitution such a grant of power," for "without some arbiter whose decision should be final the whole system would have collapsed." For him, the necessity to avoid turmoil and anarchy, not logic, was the only defensible justification for judicial review. Moreover, the courts "were undoubtedly the best 'Department' in which to vest such a power, since by the independence of their tenure they were least likely to be influenced by diverting pressure." Yet even this concession carried overtones of restrained judicial review: Hand insisted that because their power rested only on the need to prevent the "collapse" of the constitutional system, judges should use this power only in truly necessary situations.[87]

The most provocative aspect of Hand's message did not emerge until his second lecture, "The Fifth and Fourteenth Amendments." This segment focused on the due-process clauses—the requirements that governments not take life, liberty, or property "without due process of law." At the outset merely a guarantee of procedural regularity, due process had for decades been interpreted as authorizing judicial invalidation of statutes whenever it was determined that the latter "unreasonably" interfered with life, liberty, or property. Hand's startling thesis, clearly outside the mainstream of modern legal thought, was that "due process" and similarly vague constitutional phrases were essentially unenforceable by the courts. He argued that these provisions were merely "admonitory or hortatory, not definite enough to be guides on concrete occasions." Judicial review, he insisted, should be limited to court enforcement of the boundaries of the powers of each organ of government, those pertaining to state and national power in the federal system, rather than individual rights. Ever since the closing years of the nineteenth century, the Supreme Court had in fact authorized judicial inquiries into the reasonableness of other laws, but he was convinced that such a power left "no alternative to regarding the court as a third legislative chamber," and that this was "a patent usurpation" of powers not properly belonging to courts.[88]

The opposition to the early New Deal Supreme Court had by 1937 prompted the justices to withdraw from careful review of laws, "at least when economic interests only were at stake." But before the end of the decade, the Court had embraced a new version of its old activism, promising careful scrutiny in situations where laws impaired "personal" rather than "economic" rights. Hand condemned this as an "opportunistic reversion"—as he had called it elsewhere—to judicial intervention, on behalf of personal rights, under the guise of vague notions of due process. He rejected the widely accepted view—which underlay some of the Warren Court's most criticized decisions—of a legitimate "double standard" justifying judicial activism on behalf of personal rights even while keeping hands off economic regulations:

> I can see no more persuasive reason for supposing that a legislature is a priori less qualified to choose between "personal" than between economic values; and there have been strong protests, to me unanswerable, that there is no constitutional basis for asserting a larger measure of judicial supervision over the first than over the second.[89]

In the course of this second lecture, Hand voiced one of his most provocative opinions. He asked whether the school segregation case— the Brown v. Board of Education case, decided in 1954—illustrated the abuses he had discussed. Did the Court, he asked, "mean to 'overrule' the 'legislative judgment' of states by its own reappraisal of the relative values at stake? Or did it hold that it was alone enough to invalidate the statutes that they had denied racial equality because the amendment inexorably exempts that interest [racial equality] from legislative appraisal?" He concluded that the Court had paid too much heed to the special importance of education to permit reading its decision as resting solely on an absolute prohibition of racial inequality. (He toyed with but rejected the proposition that the segregation cases "meant that racial equality was a value that must prevail against any conflicting interest." Striking down segregation on that ground, he suggested, would have rested on a clear rule that he *could* accept.) And so he was driven to the conclusion that in its focus on the single area of racial segregation in schools, *Brown* constituted impermissible second-guessing of legislative choices.[90]

This criticism was bound to attract especially wide attention in 1958. But Hand was not yet through. His third lecture, "The Guardians," proved the most controversial of all; it dealt extensively with the First Amendment—a seemingly specific command, not marred by the vague language of the due-process clauses—and summarized his hostility to the prevailing judicial attitudes. He reiterated his agreement with the First Amendment's underlying premise—"that in the end it is worse to suppress dissent than to run the risk of heresy." Yet even as to this valuable interest in freedom of expression, Hand argued that there was no justification, *"in point of constitutional interpretation"* [emphasis added], for heightened judicial protection of the First Amendment vis-à-vis other sections of the Constitution. Where the legislature had made choices between speech and legitimate competing concerns, such as preventing illegal action, extreme judicial self-restraint was warranted: as in due-process cases, a statute attacked as unconstitutional under the First Amendment must prevail "unless the court is satisfied that it was not the product of an effort impartially to balance the conflicting values."[91] This was probably the most startling assertion of all by the courageous author of the *Masses* opinion and the well-known articulator of tolerance, liberty, and the protection of dissent.

But the extensive criticism of these passages did not adequately heed what Hand went on to say about protection of free expression. He had spoken initially of simply the question of special protection for the First Amendment, but he promptly noted that he had not yet addressed what judges might appropriately do under the modern "custom to go further and correct patent deviations from a court's notions of justice." He acknowledged that the judiciary had in fact evolved into an organ available to block legislative excesses. Expressing doubts about the desirability of such "a third chamber," he rested part of his argument on the assumption that such an organ might be desirable, and turned to the issue of "whether the courts should be that chamber."[92]

As a matter of desirability and statecraft, not constitutional interpretation, Hand did find a plausible basis for the judicial "power to review the merits" of laws impairing First Amendment interests. "I agree," he acknowledged, that "those who wish to give the courts" such a power "have the better argument so far as concerns Free Speech. The most important issues here arise when a majority of the voters are hostile, often bitterly hostile, to the dissidents against whom the statute is directed; and legislatures are more likely than courts to repress what ought to be free." Having the courts available to avert "serious damage" that "cannot be undone" *was*, he conceded, "a substantial and important advantage of wide judicial review." In short, in his discussion of the *desirability* of having the courts act as a "third chamber" (rather than their constitutional warrant for doing so), Hand very clearly distinguished their function in First Amendment disputes from their function regarding "other interests covered by the 'Bill of Rights.' " Only on First Amendment issues did he explicitly agree that the defenders of judicial review "have the better argument."[93]

But with respect to Bill of Rights guarantees other than the First Amendment, Hand was not persuaded that there were practical policy advantages to judicial supervision. Most of the Bill of Rights guarantees are indeed quite specific, dealing with issues of criminal procedure such as self-incrimination and confrontation of witnesses. Hand had no objection to their enforcement to the extent that they were kept to their "historical meaning." Yet, still speaking about the expediency of (rather than the constitutional warrant for) judicial protections, he was concerned about guarantees such as those involving "unreasonableness," that had acquired vague judicial glosses. For judges to set aside legislation on the basis of the law's "arbitrar[iness]"—a term that simply shrouded the jurists' personal views that "the legislators' solution [was] too strong for the judicial stomach"—was undesirable for many reasons. It was "apt to interfere with [the] proper discharge" of the judges' vital, albeit less glamorous, duties, especially the interpretation of statutes; moreover, given the lack of standards, appellate judges inevitably disagreed about the results, and these divisions tended to undermine popular respect for the law.[94]

And so, Hand said poignantly, "Each one of us must in the end choose for himself how far he would like to leave our collective fate to the wayward vagaries of popular assemblies." His own choice was clear:

For myself it would be most irksome to be ruled by a bevy of Platonic Guardians, even if I knew how to choose them, which I assuredly do not. If they were in charge, I should miss the stimulus of living in a society where I have, at least theoretically, some part in the direction of public affairs. Of course I know how illusory would be the belief that my vote determined anything; but nevertheless when I go to the polls I have a satisfaction in the sense that we are all engaged in a common venture.[95]

Hand concluded with words Benjamin Franklin had delivered to the Constitutional Convention in 1787, a passage especially congenial to him. Franklin had said, " '[T]he older I grow, the more apt I am to doubt my own judgment, and to pay more respect to the judgment of others.' " To Hand, this represented "the combination of tolerance and imagination that to me is the epitome of all good government, when coupled with a rare courage that, as Holmes used to put it, will risk life on a conclusion that tomorrow may disprove."[96]

Those words from Hand's heart could not but be moving. Yet this was not the passage that attracted widespread public attention. It was his doubts about modern judicial review, his criticisms of the prevailing Supreme Court philosophy, and his attacks on recent decisions that soon filled the newspapers and quickly made their way into the ongoing congressional debate about the Court.

On the day after Hand's last lecture, Alistair Cooke observed in the *Manchester Guardian* that the Holmes Lectures would "flutter the gowns" of the Supreme Court justices, for Hand had challenged the activist jurisprudence that had become "chic," and Cooke also predicted that Hand's words would "set off bonfires in Dixie" and make the judge "the latest idol of the South."[97] Cooke's shrewd guesses soon proved accurate. When the book version of the Holmes Lectures came off the press—*The Bill of Rights* was published by the Harvard University Press at the end of February—opponents of the Supreme Court quickly moved to embrace it. David Lawrence, editor of *U.S. News & World Report* and a widely syndicated conservative columnist, took the lead. In his magazine and his newspaper columns, Lawrence focused on Hand's criticisms of the segregation decision and his charge that the Court had set itself up as a "third legislative chamber." He praised the judge for rendering "a great service to contemporary understanding of the true limits of the Supreme Court's powers"—limits, he urged, that Congress should strengthen "lest we fall victim to absolutism in our own institutions."[98] A few days later, he applauded Hand, "known as a liberal," for stripping away the Supreme Court's pretensions, and pleaded that

Congress not "abdicate its functions by inaction."[99] Southern editorial writers quickly jumped on the bandwagon, cheering especially Hand's criticism of *Brown*.

Lawrence's appeals for vigorous congressional action were not uttered in a vacuum, for the Warren Court was already the subject of extensive debate in Congress. In the summer of 1957, the conservative Republican senator William E. Jenner of Indiana had introduced a bill sharply curbing the Court's power by eliminating its jurisdiction to entertain appeals in specified types of cases—admissions to the bar, congressional investigating committees, the federal loyalty-security program, and state subversive controls. The bill was plainly a reaction to recent Court decisions that had restricted governmental power to deal with the alleged evils of communism and subversion. Senator McCarthy had disappeared from the scene, but his spirit lived on in the work of Senator Jenner and those of his colleagues who accorded internal security the highest priority. Neither the Jenner bill nor its successors mentioned school segregation, but southern opponents of *Brown* were obviously delighted by it. Not since the post–Civil War years had Congress, in a retaliatory action, stripped the Supreme Court of parts of its appellate jurisdiction. In February and March 1958, the Senate Judiciary Committee held extensive hearings on the Jenner bill, in which northern conservatives and southern segregationists quickly embraced the unanticipated help from Hand. Senator Roman Hruska of Nebraska was the first to call the committee's attention to Hand's remarks, presenting an editorial which praised "the distinguished Judge" for "saying that the High Court does legislate," and adding that "that conclusion is quite like the premise on which Senator Jenner [had] based his bill to curb the Court." In ensuing weeks, these references to Hand's lectures and renown became prominent themes.[100]

Soon after the hearings ended, the Senate Judiciary Committee approved the amended Jenner bill. Opponents of this amended version, now known as the Jenner-Butler bill,* were sufficiently disturbed by the supporters' efforts to wrap themselves in Learned Hand's mantle to ask the judge himself about his views on the pending bill, as the liberal Democratic senator Thomas C. Hennings, Jr., of Missouri, did on May 2. Hand promptly explained that since he was still a sitting judge, he would not disclose his position on the bill's constitutionality, but

---

* Modifications of the Jenner bill were made by Senator John Marshall Butler of Maryland. The new bill left only one curb on appellate jurisdiction of the Supreme Court, that regarding bar-admission cases. Other new provisions were substantive, strengthening investigating committees' powers, amending the Smith Act, and so forth.

he added, "I do not feel the same compunction [in] expressing my opinion that such a statute if enacted would be detrimental to the best interests of the United States." Limiting himself to comment on the proposal relating to curtailment of the Supreme Court's review power, he made it clear that he did *not* think that the Court's jurisdiction should be curbed: "It seems to me desirable that the Court should have the last word on questions of the character involved. Of course, there is always the chance of abuse of power wherever it is lodged, but at long last the least contentious organ of government generally is the Court. I do not, of course, mean that I think it is always right, but some final authority is better than unsettled conflict."[101]

Hand's position here paralleled those he had taken in every other political crisis that the Supreme Court had encountered throughout his lifetime. In 1908, he had attacked the conservative majority of the Court for reading its economic biases into the due-process clause in *Lochner v. New York*; the same hostility to perceived abuses of judicial power in the name of economic due process had led him into Progressive party politics and into being a candidate for chief judge of New York in 1913. Notwithstanding this, he had always opposed the institutional reform most favored by the Progressives—the "recall" of judicial decisions, permitting state legislatures to overturn unpalatable constitutional rulings by state courts. Hand repeated this pattern in 1937, at the time of FDR's effort to overcome obstacles to economic reform by naming additional justices to the Court: then, too, Hand sided with Court critics in condemning the Court's antediluvian rulings, yet also rejected efforts to tamper with the institution itself.

The Jenner-Butler bill was the most serious challenge to the Court's institutional role since 1912 and 1937. Once again, Hand strongly disagreed with the Supreme Court, and his lectures clearly aided the Court's enemies, yet he drew the line at tampering with the Court's powers. His aim was to influence public opinion, including judicial opinion, in the direction of greater judicial self-restraint; it was not to strike at the heart of the Court's power itself, only at its misguided exercise.

Hand's letter to Senator Hennings cut the ground out from under reactionaries' and segregationists' efforts to invoke him in support of their plans. But Senator Butler, dismayed, wrote to Hand that his letter to Hennings was inaccurately "being construed as a condemnation of the bill in toto." Hand, responding, agreed that he "did not mean to express any . . . opinion" on the merits of those portions of the bill unrelated to Supreme Court jurisdiction. Yet there was no way that

Butler and his associates could continue to rest their case on Hand's endorsement: they could no longer suggest that the judge supported the proposed curbs on Court jurisdiction.[102]

On August 20, the Jenner-Butler bill was brought to a vote, and the Senate voted 49–41 to table. The Court had escaped by the skin of its teeth; with more than 40 percent of the Senate supporting this drastic anti-Court measure, the Jenner-Butler bill was clearly the high-water mark of congressional hostility to the Warren Court. And there was no denying that the Court's critics could legitimately draw some comfort from Hand's strong opposition to judicial activism and the direction of the Warren Court. When the flood of book reviews of *The Bill of Rights* appeared, the reception of Hand's message proved almost universally negative. Most commentators—academics, lawyers, and laypersons alike—rejected his questioning of the constitutional basis for judicial review, his doubts about the judicial enforceability of the Bill of Rights, and his criticism of specific rulings such as that in *Brown*. The academics' response was especially predictable: most of them were supporters of the Warren Court; even those who had doubts tended to suppress them in the face of the more obvious evil of assisting the reactionary critics during a time of political crisis. And most of the rare praise of the judge came from the South.[103]

Among the most careful of the analyses were those by Yale law professor Alexander M. Bickel and the New York lawyer Herbert Prashker, who had once clerked for Justice Stone. Bickel[104] described Hand's thesis as "a radical doctrine of judicial restraint" and accurately pointed out that the Court had never "adhered to quite so uncompromising a position" as his. Hand's hostility to "Platonic Guardians," stated at the end of his lectures, made clear that "judicial restraint *à la* L. Hand, J. is very strong medicine indeed"—it amounted essentially to "total abstinence" in the areas he had discussed. But, to his credit, Bickel went on to say that "it will not do to dismiss Judge Hand's position simply on the ground that just now one dislikes its consequences." Nor could it be met by resort to "magnificent, self-winding certitudes about the meaning of the Bill of Rights," with their allegedly "unequivoca[l] guarantees." That approach—which was indeed the approach of many of the sharpest critics—assumed away the difficulties and paradoxes of judicial review "by drawing a veil of words over the process of judgment." This was, Bickel thought, "an atavistic regression to a mode of thinking that every so often grips the law and has always to be unlearned again," an approach that "converts the words into answers"; it aimed "to solve the problem which Judge Hand faithfully faces—and painfully, with the lucidity of pain—by gingerly walking around it with eye firmly averted." In the end, Bickel struggled to state a function that somehow managed to assign to the courts "the weighing of choices," yet "which differs from the legislative and executive functions." He found an answer that satisfied him by insisting on Supreme Court decisions "properly attuned to our people's traditions and aspirations and resting on deeply felt first principles," an approach he argued was distinguishable from "more personal or group preferences." In short, he tried to solve the conundrum by allying himself with an essentially Frankfurterian restrained approach, which he thought distinguishable from the even greater judicial abstinence advocated by Hand.

Prashker[105] began his commentary by predicting accurately that the lectures would "strike many as a Jovian thunderbolt, loosed from a place securely won on Olympus by one of the greatest American judges never to sit [on] the Supreme Court." Yet he immediately went on to note, as no other reviewer did, that Hand's position was not "a belated withdrawal from the animating libertarian principles of a lifetime. The case is precisely the opposite." He saw that *The Bill of Rights* had

> its source in the struggle of a half-century against the dominance
> of the Court on matters of economic policy, a struggle in which
> its author was deeply and personally involved . . . [But now the]
> principal battleground [had] shifted from economic issues to "Per-
> sonal Rights." . . . For Judge Hand, if the Court's role under the
> Constitution bars it from making policy judgments on matters of
> economics, its role . . . must be similarly limited where "Personal
> Rights" are in issue.

Prashker was also the only commentator who was attentive to Hand's concession that as a matter of policy about whether we should have a "third chamber," those advocating a greater Court role had "the better arguments so far as concerns Free Speech." Prashker showed unusual sensitivity to the subtleties of Hand's argument, concluding, "Still skeptical and doubting of himself no less than others, [Hand] cautions us now that judges should be sparing in their use of power, which is probably why he is the archetype of the judge to whom wider power might be safely entrusted."

Of the other critical reviews, that of Edward L. Barrett, Jr., then a law professor at the University of California at Berkeley, stands out for its fairness and thoroughness. Barrett pointed out that while most critics of Supreme Court directions were angry and intemperate, and though most criticism depended "on whose ox is being gored at the moment," Hand's discussion was "lucid and temperate." Yet Barrett thought that

Hand rested too much of his argument on questioning the constitutional legitimacy of the judicial review power, an issue that, Barrett said, had been "irrevocably decided by a century and a half of practice," and urged that Hand had posed "a false dilemma—obviously we need not choose between 'the wayward vagaries of popular assemblies' and rule 'by a bevy of Platonic Guardians.' "[106]

Hand stood, then, virtually alone. On the surface, this was a very different Hand than that of the judge in *Masses* in 1917. What explains this seeming turnabout? Had Hand turned against liberal values? Had Hand turned conservative?

AS A JUDGE and as a private citizen committed to freedom of expression, Hand clearly had not changed in the four decades since the *Masses* ruling. His record provided powerful evidence of that, with his outspoken public attacks on McCarthyism and his courageous opinions— *Coplon* in 1950, the *Remington* dissent in 1953. The key difference, I believe, is that his doubts about judicial activism had increased during his last years.

Hostility to judges' tendency to pour their personal preferences into vague constitutional phrases was Hand's most consistent, deep-seated feeling about courts, and as we have seen, the due-process clauses had long been his special target. The courts' invocation of due process as a prescription of substantive justice, not merely a requirement of procedural regularity, seemed to him the primary evil underlying judicial excesses. To him, substantive due process meant that judges had to act without adequate guidance and would inevitably second-guess legislative resolutions of value conflicts.

After the ghost of economic due process was banished during the New Deal, many liberals sought rationales to distinguish between personal and economic rights, and to justify continued judicial interventions on behalf of the former. Hand, as we have seen, could not accept this "double standard"; to Hand, enforcing personal rights more vigorously than property rights was an "opportunistic reversion."[107] This hostility to the "double standard" became a central theme in Hand's 1958 lectures. But this was no sudden emergence of conservatism. Indeed, the judge's prescription of a "hands-off" attitude by courts facing value conflicts couched as constitutional issues had earlier roots. In 1942, in a speech at the 250th anniversary of the founding of the highest court of Massachusetts, Hand had said, "[T]his much I think I do know— that a society so riven that the spirit of moderation is gone, no court *can* save; that a society where the spirit flourishes, no court *need* save;

that in a society which evades its responsibility by thrusting upon the courts the nurture of that spirit, that spirit in the end will perish."[108]

Hand was criticized for posing too starkly the choice between intense involvement by the judiciary and abdication, overlooking the possibility that even though courts could not "save" an intemperate society, they could serve as an educational force to foster the constitutional spirit. As the Harvard legal scholar Paul A. Freund put it, "The question is not whether the courts can do everything but whether they can do something."[109] In short, Hand's provocative message of 1958 did resemble, even if it exceeded, those he had articulated earlier.[110]

The 1958 lectures were rightly seen as unusually sharp criticisms of the Supreme Court and judicial review. Despite the lifelong continuities in Hand's view of judicial power, he was indeed advocating a more extreme position than he had taken earlier. Clearly, Hand was more doubtful than ever about courts as "Platonic Guardians"; his skepticism produced a prescription of self-restraint—indeed, near abdication—that went well beyond his earlier views.

The best explanation of Hand's extreme, stark position can be found in his private correspondence of the time, where the Warren Court's performance evoked comments as bitter and sarcastic as those he had directed at the product of the Nine Old Men in the 1930s. A major reason for this was that his views of the Court were being largely influenced and shaped by the perceptions of Justice Felix Frankfurter. Since Hand himself did not read most Supreme Court decisions with care by the 1950s, Frankfurter's letters were his only direct pipeline to the Court and his most important source of information about Court decisions. Frankfurter, Hand's sole intimate correspondent on the Warren Court, had grown increasingly bitter about most of his colleagues. He poured out scathing denunciations in letter after letter—and often added an "I could unto you a tale unfold" refrain.[111] Partly, he shared many of Hand's doubts about judicial excesses, but in part, his contempt rested on personal pique, on disappointment because his influence on the Court had been less than he had anticipated. Hand accepted Frankfurter's often excessive invective uncritically.

Hand was affected also by Frankfurter's reports on specific rulings, reports that were sometimes slanted to serve the ends of his own judicial agenda. The effect was especially dramatic in the evolution of the single most contentious paragraph of Hand's 1958 lectures—the paragraph criticizing *Brown v. Board of Education*, where he viewed it as an example of a Court action overruling a legislative judgment "by its own reappraisal of the relative values at stake," thus sharing the distasteful characteristics of a long sequence of due-process cases with the Court acting as a "third legislative chamber." Were it possible to read the *Brown* opinion as holding that "racial equality was a value that must prevail against any conflicting interest"—resting therefore on a principle that the Fourteenth Amendment absolutely prohibited racial discrimination—it was in Hand's eyes a manageable, judicially enforceable rule. He strongly implied that he would accept *Brown* if the Court had truly meant that the Constitution prohibited legislatures from imposing *any* racial inequalities. So viewed, the Court's invalidation of school-segregation laws would rest not on the quasi-legislative ground that a state's reasons for racial inequality were not strong enough but, instead, on a constitutional command that *no* reasons would do, that *all* statutes imposing inequality were invalid. But Hand had ultimately concluded that the somewhat opaque *Brown* opinion could not be interpreted that way, that the Court had *not* meant to propound an absolute rule against racial inequality but had instead engaged in its own reappraisal of legislative judgments.

This view of the meaning of *Brown* in 1958, it turns out, came directly from Felix Frankfurter, who repeatedly told Hand between 1956 and 1958, in letter after letter, what meaning the Supreme Court intended to convey in *Brown*. Frankfurter's reading of *Brown* differed sharply from Hand's own interpretation during those years; the correspondence shows that Hand changed his mind, and largely because of Frankfurter's incessant hammering. Frankfurter had his own reasons for reading *Brown* both more flexibly and more narrowly than Hand had initially thought proper; Hand did not succumb to Frankfurter's interpretation until the autumn before he gave the Holmes Lectures. The most controversial paragraph Hand uttered on those three February evenings in Austin Hall was thus a last-minute, in retrospect unfortunate, addition.

THE REASON the two judges wrote to each other so often about the proper meaning of *Brown* stemmed from a troubling issue that seemed likely to come before the Supreme Court quite soon: the issue was the constitutionality of southern miscegenation laws—prohibitions on racial intermarriages then on the statute books of most southern states that stood as the most emotional symbol of the racial inferiority of nonwhites. Frankfurter was worried that a Court ruling holding miscegenation laws unconstitutional would stir additional southern resistance to the implementation of the Court's command that public schools be desegregated: his twin aims were to avoid a Supreme Court ruling on the issue and, if it were forced to rule, to distinguish the miscegenation laws from the issue of school segregation, all in the interest of furthering the smoothest possible implementation of school desegregation.

In 1955 and 1956, Frankfurter twice successfully persuaded his colleagues on the Court to dismiss cases that raised the question of the constitutionality of miscegenation laws.[112] The grounds the Court gave have rightly been called "wholly without basis in the law."[113] The avoidance of a ruling on miscegenation was basically an exercise of a Court discretion that was justified neither by anything in the Constitution nor by the congressional statutes that then obligated the Court to review all cases in which a state court had rejected a federal constitutional attack on a state law.

Faced with the dreaded prospect that the miscegenation issue would soon be pressed upon the Court once more, Frankfurter turned to Hand in the fall of 1957 for "helping wisdom" on what he feared were impending cases. The intimacy of their correspondence notwithstanding, Frankfurter had never asked Hand for guidance on any specific issue he had soon to decide. He wanted Hand to tell him "with particularity what you would do in my place, were the constitutionality of the conventional miscegenation statute before you," and he asked Hand to base his answer on the premise that he accept "loyally the Court's decision on school segregation."[114]

This inquiry about the miscegenation laws and the meaning of *Brown* came at an important time in the evolution of the Holmes Lectures: as Hand told Frankfurter in his first response, he was close to finishing "those thrice accursed 'Lectures.' "[115] At this time, Hand's drafts of the lectures included no mention of *Brown*.*

Hand rejected Frankfurter's efforts to distinguish the miscegenation laws from segregation-in-education issues. There was no legitimate escape from ruling on miscegenation, he bluntly told Frankfurter, and no possible constitutional distinction between that issue and school segregation. He thought *Brown* had to be interpreted as announcing a flat, absolute ban on racial discrimination; so read, it compelled the Supreme Court to invalidate miscegenation laws as well.

He would have "gone along with the Segregation decision," he told Frankfurter, although he would have liked to know a good deal more about the history of the Fourteenth Amendment's equal-protection clause. He assumed that the Amendment was designed to assure that

---

* Hand, who did not follow the Supreme Court's docket very closely, thought that the miscegenation issue might actually be pending in the Court already. Frankfurter clarified the matter in a letter of 17 September 1957: "No, [the miscegenation issue] is not immediately here, but vividly in the offing. We twice shunted it away and I pray we may be able to do it again, without being too brazenly evasive."

the "legal rights" of "Negroes" "were to stand upon an absolute equality with Whites," so that black Americans had a constitutionally recognized interest in "being exempt from race discrimination." He went on, "I cannot see how we can possibly say that it does not deny 'equal protection' to Negroes to forbid their marriage with Whites." Whatever possible policy reasons might underlie miscegenation laws were not relevant to the issue. They *would* be relevant were the question one of due process, which permitted all the balancing arguments regarding competing interests that Hand had despised for so many decades; but the miscegenation issue was a question not of due process but of equal protection.* And to Hand, equal protection, in light of *Brown*, was "an imperative command by the nation that, so far as concerns the laws of a state, . . . race must not be considered as a determining factor, regardless of the 'values' at stake." Normally, states could impose conditions on marriage, but "there is this exception, based upon the Fourteenth Amendment, that a state shall not make race—Negro race—one of those conditions."

In short, Hand believed that under *Brown*, the Fourteenth Amendment essentially prescribed a "color-blind" principle, and he insisted that miscegenation laws would therefore have to be held unconstitutional: "That is what I cannot avoid concluding. . . ." He acknowledged that such a holding might well have "unwelcome" practical consequences for the progress of school desegregation. And he doubted the wisdom of a constitution framing absolute generalizations for all kinds of unpredictable circumstances. But as judges, he insisted, neither he nor Frankfurter could legitimately avoid heeding the absolute rule he thought propounded by *Brown*:

> [W]hen you inscribe in your fundamental charter such a prohibition, and there is no honest way to say that it [is] not intended to be enforced just as it reads, what alternative have you? . . . If I could see any honest way of escaping the conclusion that the taboo on race discrimination was an "absolute," I should seize upon it. I do not see any and the "Segregation" case has closed it, if there was one I do not see.

Hand's seven handwritten pages implicitly repudiated a central characteristic of Frankfurter's approach to judging. Frankfurter, despite his

---

* Hand elaborated: "It may be that there are good reasons [for] such a denial; Negroes may be biologically inferior, though, so far as I know, anthropologists do not say so. They may be culturally so backward that it is desirable to suspend intermarriage until they catch up. Neither of these considerations is relevant, as they would be [were] the question one of Due Process."

general avowal of a restrained position on judicial review much like Hand's, was given to expediency, discretion, and manipulation in the interests of prudence and avoiding political attacks on the Court. His stance on the miscegenation-law cases was characteristic. But as late as September 1957, Hand refused to go along with it.

Had Hand adhered to his view of *Brown*, he would have had no reason to criticize the school segregation case in the Holmes Lectures. Frankfurter would not rest, though, and he bombarded Hand with suggestions for how the miscegenation issue might be distinguished from that of school segregation. Acknowledging that Hand's reasoning and conclusion had made him "extremely uncomfortable," he then offered the argument that the Fifteenth Amendment, which explicitly bars denials of the right to vote on the basis of race, might undercut the claim that the Fourteenth Amendment should be read as an across-the-board prohibition of color lines; since "color" was not explicitly mentioned in the Fourteenth Amendment, consideration of the context of the classifications—marriage rather than education, for example— might be legitimate in equal-protection litigation. Frankfurter added, "I shall work, within the limits of judicial decency, to put off decision on miscegenation as long as I can."[116*]

Hand was not persuaded by Frankfurter's contrast between the text of the Fourteenth and Fifteenth Amendments. In another long handwritten letter, he said, "I should regard it as a very tenuous inference that the contrast indicated that the XIV had not originally been intended primarily to protect Negroes." And he concluded emphatically: "[A]s to miscegenation, I don't see how you lads can duck it."[117]

As soon as he received Hand's second letter, Frankfurter sent what proved to be a decisive response: he asserted his inside knowledge of the Court's deliberations on *Brown* to persuade Hand that the Court had *not* intended an across-the-board rule barring discriminatory racial factors in state laws. The *Brown* case, he insisted, "did not rest on the absolute that the XIVth in effect said '[every] state law differentiating between colored and non-colored is forbidden.' . . . I'm confident that as comprehensive a proposition as yours in dealing with miscegenation . . . would not have commanded unanimity. I know I would not have agreed to it—nor, I'm sure would several others." In short, he was not persuaded by Hand's view of *Brown* and claimed that he knew that

---

* Frankfurter succeeded for a while in his avoidance aims: the Court did not in fact rule on the question until a decade later, when it held miscegenation laws unconstitutional, in a unanimous ruling written by Chief Justice Warren in *Loving v. Virginia*, 388 U.S. 1 (1967). (The ruling was foreshadowed by *McLaughlin v. Florida*, 379 U.S. 184 [1964].)

the Court did not intend, in *Brown*, an absolute ban on disadvantaging racial lines. He ended his letter by posing another question, in effect inviting another response: "Or am I all cock-eyed?"[118]

Frankfurter never told Hand, and Hand was not a sufficiently careful follower of Supreme Court rulings to know, that the Supreme Court had in fact extended *Brown* very quickly and forcefully to areas well beyond the educational environment. A number of lower courts had struggled with the meaning of *Brown* in the course of efforts to determine whether segregation was constitutionally permissible in public facilities other than schools. When some of these lower courts noted the emphasis in *Brown* on education and suggested that its anti-segregation rule did not apply in less important settings, the Supreme Court did not even dignify these attempted distinctions with a full opinion; instead, in a series of summary, unexplained orders in 1955, it ruled that segregation was equally impermissible on public beaches and golf courses and in public parks and buses. Soon after, the Court extended that principle to reach restaurants and municipal airports and public courtrooms.[119] In short, the Court's own record, which Frankfurter knew far better than Hand, demonstrated much more support for Hand's original impression that *Brown* meant to establish a broad rule against racial distinctions than for Frankfurter's position that *Brown* was an education case and that the permissibility of racial discrimination in other areas had to be decided by a context-specific, case-by-case balancing analysis.

In answering Frankfurter's letter on October 10, Hand still adhered to his view that *Brown* meant "that race must not be a determinant" in any legislation. He continued to adhere to his original position: "that in the setting of 1868 the 'Equal Protection Clause' *was* an 'absolute,' much as I revolt from all of them [i.e., all 'absolutes']." And Hand added a fateful final sentence: "I suppose I *must* say something about all this in my goddam Lectures."[120]

Frankfurter, sensing incipient victory, promptly sent one more letter in support of his position that *Brown* could not be read "as an absolute" and instead rested on the fact that it involved "the field of public education" and "separate educational facilities." But he disavowed any intention of advising Hand to include this in his lectures. Yet, he added, "But for the love of Mike don't say anything that lawyers and the cynical, unscrupulous Bill [Justice William O. Douglas] can quote as the clear view of 'the greatest living judge' that the Segregation decision covers miscegenation!!"[121]

Meanwhile, other lawyers, acquaintances, and Hand's own law clerk were telling him that he had to discuss *Brown*: "You simply cannot duck that one."* And so Hand proceeded to tackle *Brown,* "very regretfully and under . . . pressure," as he later put it to Frankfurter, and, on reexamining it, reluctantly accepted Frankfurter's gloss on the ruling. Frankfurter, he told the justice after succumbing, must have been "right in saying that [the Court] had not treated the 14th Amendment as making race an 'absolute,' as I had supposed":[122] after all, Frankfurter had been part of the Court that decided *Brown* and Hand had not.

The most controversial passage in the lectures, then, represented Hand's delayed surrender to Frankfurter's self-serving interpretation of *Brown.* In effect, he paraphrased Frankfurter's repeated arguments; the justice's advocacy succeeded in ultimately pressing Hand to say that the Court had in fact "overrule[d]" the "legislative judgment" of states "by its own reappraisal of the relative values at stake."[123] So viewed, *Brown* was yet one more example of the Court's acting as a "third legislative chamber"; and this had to be condemned by Hand.

Hand was no doubt also vulnerable to Frankfurter's ceaseless advocacy because he was suffering from fatigue about the lectures. He recognized that they would be his farewell statements, and he dreaded the overwhelming responsibility they represented. He produced revised draft upon revised draft of his "goddam Lectures." He was eager to rid himself of what Frankfurter called "his albatross," yet for years could not and often wondered whether he ever would. (Hand had originally agreed to deliver the Holmes Lectures in the late 1930s, when James Landis was dean at Harvard Law School. He begged off because of the pressure of judicial work; then in 1951 he made a renewed commitment, this time to Dean Erwin Griswold.) Hand spent an enormous amount of time worrying about them, as well as drafting and redrafting them, between 1951 and 1958. Some of the earlier drafts were far less extreme than the final version. In the face of the pressures to get the job done, in the face of letters from Frankfurter saying that the justice wanted to see those lectures in order to help him in his losing battle with his brethren, and obsessed by his drive to produce logically airtight arguments, Hand articulated a more rigid, more negative view of judicial power than any he had ever voiced before, and he knew it. Just before he delivered the lectures, he wrote to Frankfurter, "[They] will go quite a bit further than you, and will be as welcome to [persons in] our calling as a skunk in the parlor." Later he wrote, "The 'Jesus Choir' of your NINE will think my work the most errant heresy, if

---

* The law clerk was Ronald Dworkin, now professor of jurisprudence at Oxford and New York Universities. Hand called him "That Law Clerk to Beat all law-clerks Roland [*sic*] Dworkin" when relating this to Frankfurter.

they ever read it. Anyway, the damned things are done and my relief is very great."[124] Ultimately, the bleakness, pessimism, and extremism of Hand's final major statement did not do full justice to the richness, subtlety, and complexity of his lifelong search for a delicate balance between the competing pressures of passionate devotion to free speech in an open society on the one side and sensitivity to the legitimate restraints on courts in a democracy on the other.

A HORDE OF GUESTS crowded into the Second Circuit's courtroom at Foley Square on the afternoon of Friday, April 10, 1959, for a very special occasion. The Court of Appeals had decided to hold an "extraordinary session"[125] to commemorate Hand's completion of fifty years of consecutive service on the federal bench. The glittering event was unique in several respects: no federal judge had ever served so long;[126] no federal court had ever held such a session to honor a judge still hearing and deciding cases; and the record of such a special session had rarely been included in the *Federal Reporter*, the official reports of decisions of all federal courts of appeals.[127]

There was a formidable audience and an impressive list of speakers, with Chief Judge Charles Clark presiding. Hand's friend and fellow civil libertarian the Washington lawyer John Lord O'Brian praised Hand for his "intellectual skepticism" and his courage in questioning public policies that threatened individual rights.[128] Harrison Tweed, a leader of the New York bar and president of the American Law Institute, thanked him for bringing "human understanding of the broadest and deepest sort" to the work of the ALI, at whose meetings Hand's "contributions . . . of philosophy and poetry [were] probabilities, and of wisdom and profanity certainties."[129] Attorney General William P. Rogers, representing the executive branch, brought Hand a letter from President Eisenhower, who saluted the judge's integrity, learning, and dedication to the nation's system of jurisprudence as "an inspiration to your colleagues in the law and in the community at large."[130] Fellow circuit judge Carroll C. Hincks expressed his and his colleagues' "affection for our beloved companion, mentor and friend."[131] Chief Justice Warren and Justices Harlan and Frankfurter represented the Supreme Court among the speakers.

Frankfurter spoke extemporaneously and eloquently, in especially moving words that, wrote one journalist, "seemed to touch both Judge Hand and the audience most deeply."[132] Hand had described his life as "uneventful, unadventurous, easy, safe and pleasant," Frankfurter noted, but all these adjectives were "inadequate and inaccurate."

"Safe—has his life been safe, secure? He, safe and secure, who has been buffeted and battered by the largest self-doubt of any human being I have ever encountered?" He suggested that "daring, romantic, antediluvian, sophisticated and lucky" were more appropriate adjectives. He concluded: "But luckier have we been that he was endowed with these gifts and has put them to the uses to which he has put them. After every one of us in this room will no longer be here, long after that, Learned Hand will still be serving society so long as law will continue to exercise its indispensable role in helping to unravel the tangled skein of the human situation."[133]

Hand's response to the tributes began in his characteristic self-deprecating mode. The speeches reminded him of the widow who listened to all the eulogies at a wake and finally looked in the coffin: "Well, after all they said, I didn't know whether it could be Mike who was there." Remarking that Chief Judge Clark had assured him that the ceremony was not for him at all but "for the circuit," Hand likened Clark's situation to that of the operator of a zoo with a chimpanzee who had been in captivity longer than any other chimpanzee on earth. After the zookeeper gathered an audience, he asked the chimpanzee, Loki, to climb a ladder. Loki managed to get up the ladder "in one way or another." Then the owner said, "Loki, make noise like chimpanzee." Hand continued: "And 'Loki' made a noise that some people might think sounded like a chimpanzee. All this helped to advertise the zoo."

Turning serious, Hand reflected that his decisions had seemed to him "for the most part trivial" and gave him "a little sense of fatuity." But there was the "excuse" and "adequate defense" that judges were after all "absolutely essential" to society; "[w]ithout them we should be even more of a cut-throat community than we are." In identifying the essential qualities for judging, he suggested once more the necessity of "complete personal detachment. . . . [A]s far as it is possible—it is never quite possible— . . . you must keep your personal choice out of the frame you select to impose upon the written words." And then, "[Y]ou must have as much imagination as is possible." For him, the work had after all been "a most engaging and pleasant occupation"— an occupation somewhat "in the nature of an art," like that of a poet or sculptor who "has some vague purposes and . . . an indefinite number of what you might call frames of preference among which he must choose." Hand concluded by reciting Shakespeare's 123d Sonnet:

> No, Time, thou shall not boast that I do change;
> Thy pyramids built up with newer might

To me are nothing novel, nothing strange;
They are but dressings of a former sight.
Our dates are brief, and therefore we admire
What thou does foist upon us that is old;
And rather make them born to our desire
Than think that we before have heard them told.
Thy registers and thee I both defy,
Not wondering at the present nor the past,
For thy record and what we see doth lie,
Made more or less by thy continual haste.
　　This I do vow, and this shall ever be;
　　I will be true, despite thy scythe and thee.[134]

Increasing physical pain and recurrent groundless fears that his mental acuity was failing marred Hand's final years. The quality of his writings—in judicial opinions, addresses, and letters—remained high until the end. The inner forces that drove Hand to remain engaged in ideas were not only the lifetime habits of an intellectual, but also a product of fear—fear of boredom and uselessness were he to abandon his regimented life on the bench.

The pain in his back did not become a major preoccupation for Hand until he was very old. Not until the summer of 1958, which he spent in Cornish, did his physical ailments begin to trouble him. For the first time, he was gripped by depressing thoughts of becoming a cripple. "I can just manage, with not infrequent pauses, to walk about a third of a mile," he told Frankfurter. "My feet get very numb and my back painful. The truth is that 86 is too long."[135] For decades, he had enjoyed conversations with his friends while walking through the New Hampshire woods; now these joys seemed ever more out of reach. The environment appeared to him increasingly "mournful": "[n]early all the old lot are dead." Moreover, the late eighties seemed "a rather solemn time to live into. The restoratives, even liquor, don't restore as much as they used; and one can't keep asking: 'What's the use?' "[136] Frankfurter offered repeated reassurances. "86 is not 'too long' when your bean works as it does," he wrote cheerfully in September 1958.[137]

Hand's physical condition continued to deteriorate when he returned to New York City to resume court work in the fall of 1958: "I am rather dispirited, partly because I am crippled so that I can't walk more than a quarter of a mile and partly because in general I am a feeble old poop, who will be 87 in three months."[138] Yet the very letters in which he told old friends about his physical difficulties testified that he was mentally as alert as ever. Still, he bemoaned the decline in the number of opinions he was able to produce.

> I have developed the art, most appropriate to my mature years, of stringing out "judicial" work for what would have seemed to me, only a few years ago, an unconscionable period. Besides this, so far as I am aware, my senility in general has not seriously affected more than my legs, though these have indeed practically gone on strike and refuse to carry me more than two or three blocks, and that too with a constant threat they mean to quit. What other defects consonant with my 87 years—or almost—have appeared higher up I of course don't know and no one will tell. Except that I do get tired very easily. Why not, for God's sake?[139]

Hand's physical deterioration continued inexorably. Within a few months, the pain and numbness in his legs had intensified so much that he had to resort to crutches. Yet somehow he found the strength to remain active, both on the court and extrajudicially. Some of his inspiration came from his judicial idol, Oliver Wendell Holmes. He repeatedly related his recollections of Holmes when the justice was about ninety; whenever Holmes would talk as if it did not seem worthwhile to go on, he would add: "When I think that way, I have an imaginary talk with the Great Panjandrum, who says to me, 'Well, Wendell, if that's how you feel, I can arrange it. How about tonight?' And then I always know that I should answer, 'Boss, could you just as well put that off a fortnight?' "[140]

A similar drive to carry on as long as possible propelled Hand. In the fall of 1960, as he felt "more and more crippled and less and less useful," he continued to affirm that, "strange to say, I still prefer not to cash it [in] while I don't have to."[141] And as he told a former law clerk soon after his eighty-ninth birthday in 1961: "Things do lose a good deal of their flavor, but still one wants to go on and see it through, and I want to do that like the rest of us."[142]

But Hand never saw in himself the kind of courage that he thought Holmes, a Civil War veteran, had. As he once told Frankfurter, "There is nothing to do about [my physical condition] but play the Stoic—a part I have always admired, but have never felt much qualified to play."[143] Instead, Hand's life force was spurred mainly by his near terror of the decrepitude of total inactivity. This theme surfaced often in his letters to close friends: "I should feel lost if I couldn't run around in my little paddock";[144] "I have spun the wheel in my squirrel's cage for so many years that I dread its standing still."[145] The "squirrel cage" Hand knew best was work on the Second Circuit. "How far my brains have failed I cannot tell, and no one will advise me," he told a former law clerk. "Never mind, they let me still make a noise like a judge, which at least occupies my time."[146]

Despite his failing physical condition by 1960, Hand thought for a while that continued judicial work might not be enough to fully occupy his time. In February 1960, President Eisenhower, at the beginning of his final year in office, appointed a Commission on National Goals to articulate the ideals that should guide the nation's "next decade and longer."[147] The president wanted a distinguished group to undertake that task, and Hand was asked to join it. The chairman, Henry M. Wriston, former president of Brown University and the Council on Foreign Relations, pressured Hand to accept the appointment, and Hand gave in. Working over the preliminary documents that were circulated to commission members,* Hand found that the work kept him "quite as busy as my strength permits" and indeed called for "a little more than I have"; but at first he thought it "better than sitting still and contemplating the past."[148]

Soon, friends began to reinforce Hand's doubts about the utility of the whole endeavor. Paul Bender, a former law clerk who had turned to teaching, wrote him, "Were I with you, I would ask you to defend yourself for participating in such mass public soul-searching. I suppose it is an honor one doesn't decline, but between you and me, isn't it all a load of you know what?"[149] In reply, Hand acknowledged, "Yes, I fancy it deserves a good deal of [the] epithet that you bestow on it. But I must do something, . . . even if it does prove no more than 'a load of you know what.' "[150] Before long, Frankfurter expressed concern over rumors that the commission would urge the Supreme Court to turn even more activist on "Civil Rights" and warned Hand about pressures toward "out-Blacking Black or out–gallery playing Douglas."[151] By then, Hand had resigned from the commission, for the stated reason that "it involved more work than in the present state of my health I care to add to the judicial work that I am still trying to do."

The quality of Hand's judicial work continued at its old level, as Frankfurter tried to reassure him. Hand was relieved: "I am glad that, since I have got to start rotting somewhere, you think it is not at the top."[152] Soon after, Frankfurter told him, "If you don't look out, your goddam fecundity will kill you yet. In the latest bunch of opinions from your [court] I find three written by 'Hand, Circuit Judge.' . . .

* Wriston was the chair; Frank Pace, former secretary of the army, vice chair. The eleven-member commission also included the chairman of M.I.T., the president of the University of California, former presidents of Harvard and the University of Virginia, as well as George Meany, president of the AFL-CIO.

I'll eat my hat if I am wrong in believing that you wouldn't have written them better twenty years ago."[153] "I am glad that you did not discover any falling off above the ears," Hand replied, for "[o]ne can never judge about that for one self, and people don't volunteer to say: 'Old boy, you are a nice fellow, but you don't quite realize how your nut has gone off.' " But he could not help noticing that "in speed I have failed greatly," consoling himself with a wry "but then the Union rules make allowances for a falling off in output."[154]

Yet the task of solving legal problems seemed no longer quite so absorbing as once it had: "I will concede that the game interests me much less than it used. . . . When all is said, this old age stuff ain't what it is cracked up to be."[155] More disturbing still was that the search for ultimate answers seemed as fruitless as ever:

> At times I get a strange hypnotic hope that after I do get through, perhaps I have seen *into* things further than I did before. However, accompanying this is a rather disconcerting doubt whether the LAW, as I used to think of it, has any genuine "principles" and is, or can be, more than an effort to forecast imaginatively what some other human beings, who have final power, would say, if they were faced with the existing, concrete occasion before me. . . . Oh, to have the inner certainties of those Great Four [Chief Justice Warren and Justices Black, Douglas, and Brennan] of your colleagues![156]

But "certainties" and confident answers never had been Hand's forte; his strength always had lain in asking the probing questions and in skepticism about any proffered Truth, including his own. As he wrote to another friend, "I wish I knew better than I do what the whole show is about; I wish, in short, that the years had brought wisdom, or at least a measure of illusion of wisdom. All I can see is that we do best when we think of ourselves as aiming [for] some construction, some embodiment, some objective impress, in and upon the world about us, that bears a resemblance to what appears to us fair and just in understanding and imaginative of others."[157]

Hand's concern about his productivity continued right to the end. On June 13, 1961, in Hand's final letter to Frankfurter, he complained, "I have fallen into near idleness; I have taken part in not more than 25 or 26 cases this year and I would take up some other job if I could find one. . . . I suppose that I should lie back and thank God that I have had almost 90 years without becoming worse crippled than I am."[158] In reply, Frankfurter once again sought to calm Hand's anxieties:

I wish I could exorcise your concern that you don't toss off 60 or 70 opinions. For me the wonder is the dog performs not merely at all, but so well. I have just read your two latest admiralty opinions. What are you griping about? The old master appears in them. If it were not so—I wouldn't lie to you. What a puritan conscience is driving you, with all your pagan admixture. Why should you be working at near 90 with a head of steam at 50 or 60 or 70 or even 80? Why should you, and why should you fret that you don't?![159]

By then, Hand's physical condition had deteriorated further. Because of his difficulty in walking, he had to use a wheelchair by the beginning of 1961: "[T]he old back grinds the spinal cord . . . when I have to stand on my legs."[160] No medical help was possible, he knew: "The wiseacres all . . . assure me that my back will not and cannot get right; it's an architectonic malady that would make chipping and hewing unthinkable in a gent who is in his 90th year."[161] Even then, he managed to preserve some humor about an ailment that had turned excruciatingly painful. The trouble, he suggested, was that "I walk on my hind legs which my back was never intended for. I tell [the doctors] that it is not my fault that I was badly brought up, that I started on four legs, and that it was my parents who insisted on my walking on two; indeed they were very pleased when I began to do so."[162]

The Hands, faced with the judge's difficulty in getting about, sold their house on East Sixty-fifth Street, in which they had lived for more than fifty years, in order to occupy a more accessible apartment a block away, on East Sixty-fourth Street.

Hand bore the pain of his final years with a courage he did not think he possessed but admired in others. In one of his last formal addresses, at a memorial service for his friend the architect William Delano, he paid a special tribute to "the way he bore his infirmities for so long." Delano had been "very infirm," which, Hand added, "is not pleasant, as I am finding out myself a little bit."

I tell you that extreme pain, what we call agony, seems to me as dreadful as anything can be; and if it were not relieved, I don't know how we should carry on. It *excludes*; it *concentrates*; it *minimizes* the whole self; it takes over the whole being—there is nothing left but that. I am talking about extreme pain; and that a man could take that, not with clenched fists and pursed lips, but take it and not make evident what it is, is beyond me and beyond anything. I just leave it to you whether you can think of any greater heroism than that.[163]

Hand, too, showed that he could take the pain and not make it evident to most acquaintances; he continued his work despite his crippling infirmities. The end came soon after he had finished his final week's work on the bench. In June 1961, he went to Cornish, where in early July he suffered a heart attack. He seemed to recover quite well, but his daughter Frances brought him back to New York City in an ambulance, and soon after, he had a second heart attack. He was taken to St. Luke's Hospital "in no pain but not clear mentally."[164] A few days later, on August 18, 1961, he "died peacefully."[165]

Felix Frankfurter immediately issued a statement from his chambers for the press: "A truly great man has left, but he has left behind an important addition to our national heritage."[166] The next morning, a front-page obituary in *The New York Times* reminded readers that Hand had been called "the greatest jurist of his time,"[167] and the *Times* of London said elegiacally, "[T]here are many who will feel that with the death of Learned Hand the golden age of the American judiciary has come to an end."[168]

Frances Hand outlived Learned Hand by two years. After his death, she would often sit by the fireplace in their apartment, opening beribboned packages of letters from Learned, rereading them, and tossing occasional bundles into the fire. She had not realized all of Carey Thomas's aspirations for Bryn Mawr students, but she had been true to herself, and she had taken her pay in a life fully lived day by day. "I don't think that I shd. *ever* be willing to be the door-mat of a man of genius—(for all my life—)," she had written to Mildred Minturn;[169] the "straining for success" was "apt to make life . . . so arid in other directions."[170] By placing the highest value on inner development and personal fulfillment rather than earthly manifestations of success, she had avoided Mildred's agonized struggles.

Perhaps it can be said that Learned Hand, who did not believe in a Hereafter, had in the accomplishments of his life and work nevertheless realized the version of Heaven that he had repeatedly portrayed anecdotally. Recounting his notions of what he hoped his first day in Heaven would be like, he would say that in the morning there would be a baseball game, with the score 4–1 in favor of the opposing team in the bottom of the ninth. Hand's team then loads the bases, and it is Hand's turn at bat; he promptly hits a home run, clearing the bases and winning the game.[171] In the afternoon, there is a football game between the evenly matched teams, tied in a scoreless match. With a minute left to play, Hand catches a punt, weaves his way down the sidelines, and scores the winning touchdown. The highlight of the day is an evening banquet, with civilization's greatest minds—Socrates, Descartes, Benjamin Franklin, and Voltaire—among the guests. The designated speaker for the evening is Voltaire. After a few words from him, the audience shouts, "Shut up, Voltaire, and sit down. WE WANT HAND!"[172]

Notes

Much of this book is drawn from Learned Hand's private correspondence, manuscripts, and court papers in the Learned Hand Papers at the Harvard Law School Library. References are from that source, unless otherwise indicated. The location of most of the manuscripts in the Hand Papers is indicated by box and file number. Thus, 107-13 refers to box 107, file 13, of the Hand Papers. Many of the Learned Hand–Frances A. Hand letters are identified herein as Personal Correspondence because box and file numbers have not yet been assigned to them.

I have used abbreviations only sparingly in these notes. The abbreviations are:

LH   Learned Hand

FAH   Frances A. Hand, Learned Hand's wife

STH   Susan Train Hand (Augustus N. Hand's wife), editor of *Letters of the Hand Family, 1796–1912* (New York: Edwin S. Gorham, 1923)

C.C.B.   Charles C. Burlingham

B.B.   Bernard Berenson (Berenson's papers, including his extensive correspondence with Learned Hand, are in The Berenson Archive, Villa I Tatti, The Harvard University Center for Italian Renaissance Studies, Florence, Italy.)

Minturn Papers   The papers of Mildred Minturn (Scott), Frances A. Hand's classmate at Bryn Mawr College, are in the possession of her daughter, Mrs. Leslie Minturn Allison, in Fordingbridge, Hampshire, England.

I have also used several interviews, primarily interviews conducted by me with Learned Hand's family members and acquaintances. I refer to interviews by others as follows:

F.I.   Family Interviews—interviews of Learned Hand by members of his family

Henkin Interview   "Reminiscences of Learned Hand" (1957), in the Columbia
                    Oral History Collection—interviews conducted by Louis
                    Henkin, former law clerk to Learned Hand and professor of
                    law at Columbia University, for the Oral History Research
                    Office at Columbia University

I
The Early Years

1. Henkin Interview, 27.
2. U.S. Bureau of the Census, *Twelfth Census of the United States, 1900: Population, Part I* (Washington, D.C.: Bureau of the Census, 1901), 430.
3. See Aunt Harriet to LH, 18 July 1935, 114–12.
4. F.I. II, 19.
5. Id., 18.
6. Ibid.
7. Gunther Interview, 162; see also F.I. II, 99.
8. F.I. II, 37.
9. Henkin Interview, 3.
10. Id., 2–3.
11. Id., 4.
12. Id., 3.
13. Id., 3–4.
14. F.I. II, 20–24.
15. Henkin Interview, 20.
16. F.I. II, 19.
17. Id., 20–24.
18. Ibid.
19. Id., 19–20.
20. See materials in 113–14.
21. Samuel Hand biographical sketch, edited by LH, in 113–14. See also 102
    New York Reports, 743–48.
22. Ibid.
23. Samuel Hand to Augustus C. Hand, 11 September 1876, 113–9.
24. F.I. II, 12.
25. Ibid.
26. F.I. II, 20.
27. Samuel Hand obituaries transcribed by LH, 113–14, pp. 51, 52.
28. F.I. II, 12.
29. Samuel Hand's manuscript of 1869 lecture, 113–10; LH transcript of lecture
    (22 June 1896), 113–11.
30. F.I. II, 12, 19–20.
31. See chapter 2, below.
32. Henkin Interview, 16–17.
33. Id., 16.
34. Id., 143–146.
35. LH to FAH, 4 October 1929, Personal Correspondence.
36. Henkin Interview, 145.
37. On Hand family data, see LH recollections in Gunther Interview, the Family

Correspondence, and two secondary sources: Susan Train Hand (Augustus N. Hand's wife), *Letters of the Hand Family, 1796–1912.* (New York: Edwin S. Gorham, 1923) [hereinafter STH]; Jeannette Edwards Rattray, *East Hampton History* (Garden City, N.Y.: Country Life Press, 1953), 350–367.

38. Henkin Interview, 5, 9.
39. Anna Hand to Samuel Hand, 15 July 1796, STH, 24.
40. Henkin Interview, 10; compare STH, 10.
41. Henkin Interview, 9.
42. F.I. II, 5, 36.
43. STH, 11 (by Richard Hand, LH's great-uncle).
44. See the daguerreotype portrait of Elizabeth Sill Hand in STH, 43.
45. F.I. II, 6; Henkin Interview, 9.
46. F.I. II, 4.
47. Augustus C. Hand to his sister Nancy, 22 August 1826, STH, 57.
48. Augustus C. Hand to his father, 20 January 1828, STH, 65.
49. Augustus C. Hand to Marcia S. Northrup, 23 November 1824, STH, 52.
50. F.I. II, 4, 7, 8, 38.
51. Augustus C. Hand to sons Samuel and Clifford (at college), 16 September 1848, STH, 187–189.
52. Augustus C. Hand to sons Samuel and Clifford (at college), 21 September 1847, STH, 183, 184.
53. Augustus C. Hand to brother Richard, September 1839, STH, 118.
54. Augustus C. Hand to Dr. and Mrs. Chipman, 28 January 1839, STH, 113, 114; see also Mrs. A. C. Hand to husband, 28 November 1839, STH, 125, 126.
55. Samuel Hand to his mother, 13 October 1847, STH, 184–185.
56. Samuel Hand biographical sketch, 113–14, 2.
57. Samuel Hand to brother Clifford, 18 June 1851, STH, 212.
58. Richard L. Hand to brother Samuel, 20 July 1858, STH, 235, 238.
59. Samuel Hand to brother Richard, 5 November 1859, STH, 248, 249 (emphasis by Samuel).
60. Samuel Hand to brother Richard, 25 February 1862, STH, 268, 270 (emphasis by Samuel).
61. See p. 13 of fifty-seven-page typescript prepared by LH and entitled by him "Speeches and Newspaper Articles Concerning Samuel Hand on the Occasion of His Death—May 21, 1886," 113–14.
62. F.I. II, 20.
63. Augustus C. Hand to his wife, 9 February 1845, STH, 161, 163 (emphasis by Augustus).
64. Clifford A. Hand to his aunts, 18 April 1878, STH, 301.
65. LH in F.I. I, 6.
66. Mrs. Mary Noyes Learned to Mrs. Augustus C. Hand, 19 July 1872, 114–16.
67. F.I. II, 28.
68. Henkin Interview, 14, 17.
69. Samuel Hand to his mother, 16 December 1880, 113–13.
70. F.I. II, 19.
71. Samuel Hand to Gus (Augustus N. Hand), 18 January 1880, 109–1.
72. LH to "Gussy," 7 March 1881, 109–1.
73. Ibid.

74. Henkin Interview, 22.
75. "Bertie" (childhood friend) to LH, 21 April 1959, 98–33.
76. Henkin Interview, 17–18.
77. Samuel Hand to Gus ("Gustle"), 18 January 1880, 109–1.
78. LH to Gus, 10 February 1884, STH, 310, 311.
79. Henkin Interview, 17, 20.
80. F.I. II, 21.
81. Id., 21–23. See also LH to Gus, 7 March 1881, 109–1.
82. LH to Gus, 10 February 1884, STH, 310, 311.
83. F.I. II, 36.
84. F.I. I, 108.
85. Samuel Hand to his mother, 16 December 1880, 113–13; Samuel Hand to Gus, 18 January 1880, 109–1.
86. Gus to his mother, 27 August 1882, STH, 309, 310.
87. LH to Gus, 10 February 1884, STH, 310, 311.
88. F.I. II, 32–34.
89. Id., 35–36.
90. LH to Gus, 23 May 1886, 109–1.
91. Id., 31 May 1886, 109–1.
92. Id., 13 June 1886, 109–1.
93. Henkin Interview, 20.
94. F.I. II, 23–26.
95. Id., 22–23.
96. LH to Albany Academy, 29 April 1902, 11–11.
97. Henkin Interview, 20, 140–141.
98. F.I. II, 24.
99. LH to Gus, 2 September 1888, 109–1.
100. F.I. I, 24–25.
101. Id., 35, 41, 56; LH to William Constable, 9 August 1940, 69–4; LH to James L. Fly, 20 March 1944, 71–11.
102. LH to Uncle Richard, 12 January 1890, 110–6.
103. Henkin Interview, 23.
104. Samuel Eliot Morison, *Three Centuries of Harvard, 1636–1936* (Cambridge: Harvard University Press, 1936), 427.
105. Henkin Interview, 23.
106. F.I. I, 36.
107. Morison, *Three Centuries of Harvard*, 422, 424.
108. F.I. I, 33–35.
109. Robert G. Dodge to LH, 18 March 1947, 70–7.
110. LH to Uncle Richard, 12 January 1890, 110–6.
111. LH to Matthew Hale, 31 July 1902, 4–27 (the younger brother of the addressee was Robert Lee Hale, later a law professor at Columbia).
112. Matthew Hale to LH, 25 August 1902, 4–27.
113. LH to Matthew Hale, 6 September 1902, 4–27.
114. F.I. I, 48.
115. Morison, *Three Centuries of Harvard*, 419.
116. F.I. I, 27–28.
117. Id., 33, 45.
118. Henkin Interview, 24.
119. F.I. I, 45–47.

120. Henkin Interview, 22–23.
121. F.I. I, 41, 42.
122. E.g., LH to Gus, 20 July 1890, 109–1.
123. F.I. I, 44, 47–48.
124. Id., 49.
125. LH to Thomas Tileston Baldwin, 15 April 1916, 14–11.
126. F.I. I, 49.
127. E.g., LH to President James Bryant Conant, 4 March 1949, 69–3.
128. LH to James Bryant Conant, 12 April 1939, 69–3.
129. Henkin Interview, 27.
130. F.I. I, 29.
131. F.I. II, 41.
132. F.I. I, 30, 31, 37, 40.
133. Morison, *Three Centuries of Harvard*, 330; see also Samuel Eliot Morison, ed., *The Development of Harvard University Since the Inauguration of President Eliot—1869–1929* (Cambridge: Harvard University Press, 1930), lix, lxii–lxiii, and Frederick Rudolph, *The American College and University—A History* (New York: Alfred A. Knopf, 1962), chapter 14.
134. F.I. II, 48.
135. F.I. I, 38.
136. F.I. II, 43–44.
137. Gunther Interview, 155. (LH added at this point: "This was, of course, very painful to my mother.")
138. F.I. II, 46.
139. Ibid.
140. F.I. I, 38.
141. F.I. II, 44.
142. Id., 44, 59.
143. See, e.g., Gay Wilson Allen, *William James: A Biography* (New York: Viking, 1967).
144. William James, *Pragmatism, A New Name for Some Old Ways of Thinking: Popular Lectures on Philosophy* (New York: Longmans, Green and Co., 1907).
145. See F.I. I, 60–61; F.I. II, 46.
146. E.g., LH–Felix Frankfurter Correspondence, box 105.
147. F.I. II, 44–45.
148. F.I. I, 39–40; F.I. II, 42–43.
149. F.I. I, 55.
150. *Harvard College Catalogue 1891–92*, 85.
151. Morison, *Three Centuries of Harvard*, 352.
152. See Kermit Vanderbilt, *Charles Eliot Norton: Apostle of Culture in a Democracy* (Cambridge: Harvard University Press, 1959); see also F.I. I, 48–58.
153. F.I. I, 50–51.
154. Id., 52.
155. LH to Gus, 30 July 1892, 109–1.
156. LH to Bernard Berenson, 24 May 1949, 99–20.
157. LH to Uncle Richard (Richard L. Hand), 4 January 1893, 110–6.
158. Ibid.
159. F.I. II, 48.
160. Ibid.
161. Henkin Interview, 25.

162. LH to Uncle Richard, 1 January 1899, 110–6.
163. F.I. II, 48–49.
164. Id., 49.
165. Henkin Interview, 24.
166. On the pedagogical premises and institutional changes at Harvard Law School, see generally, in addition to LH's letters and reminiscences, Arthur E. Sutherland, Jr., *The Law at Harvard—A History of Ideas and Men 1817–1967* (Cambridge: Harvard University Press, 1967); Charles Warren, 2 *History of the Harvard Law School and of Early Legal Conditions in America* (New York: Lewis Publishing Co., 1908); *The Centennial History of the Harvard Law School, 1817–1917* (Cambridge: Harvard Law School Association, 1918); Roscoe Pound's essay in Morison, *The Development of Harvard University Since the Inauguration of President Eliot*. See also a range of secondary sources on educational and professional developments—e.g., Burton J. Bledstein, *The Culture of Professionalism: The Middle Class and the Development of Higher Education in America* (New York: W. W. Norton, 1978); Robert S. Stevens, *Law School: Legal Education in America from the 1850s to the 1980s* (Chapel Hill: University of North Carolina Press, 1983).
167. See Dean Christopher Columbus Langdell's address at the 250th anniversary of Harvard University in 1886, in *Centennial History*, 231. See also Sutherland, *The Law at Harvard*, 175, and LH Memo for Williston, November 1948, 83–11, reprinted in *Harvard Law School Bulletin*, January 1949. (See also Langdell's preface to the first edition of his *Cases on Contracts* (1871), reprinted in Sutherland, *The Law at Harvard*, 174–175.)
168. Henkin Interview, 25–27.
169. 8 *Harv. L.Rev.* 51 (1894).
170. Albert E. Dacy to LH, [1909], 19–4.
171. Henkin Interview, 30, 32.
172. Data in letter from Prof. Austin Wakeman Scott to LH, 9 June 1947, 79–36 (information requested by LH), sending class standings of honors graduates 1880–1901 (as modified on basis of supplemental information from registrar of Harvard Law School).
173. LH to Prof. Austin Wakeman Scott, 11 June 1947, 79–36.
174. Henkin Interview, 29, 30.
175. See *Harvard Catalogue, 1893–94*.
176. LH's foreword to Samuel Williston, *Life and Law—An Autobiography* (Boston: Little, Brown, 1940), reprinted in Irving Dilliard, ed., *The Spirit of Liberty: Papers and Addresses of Learned Hand*, 3d ed., enlarged (New York: Alfred A. Knopf, 1960), 140.
177. F.I. II, 50; Henkin Interview, 27.
178. LH Memo for Williston, *Harvard Law School Bulletin*, January 1949, 7.
179. 8 *Harv. L.Rev.* 65, 66 (April 1894).
180. LH Memo for Williston, *Harvard Law School Bulletin*, January 1949, 7.
181. Ibid.
182. LH to Samuel Williston, 9 April 1940, 83–11.
183. The only faculty member LH did not study under was Eugene Wambaugh.
184. "They were a great set of men." LH in Henkin Interview, 27.
185. F.I. II, 50; Henkin Interview, 25–27.
186. LH Memo for Williston, *Harvard Law School Bulletin*, January 1949, 7–8.
187. LH to A. James Casner, 10 November 1959, 89–27.

188. Henkin Interview, 29.

189. Arthur E. Sutherland sketch of Beale, *Dictionary of American Biography, Supplement 3* (New York: Charles Scribner's Sons, 1973), 43.

190. LH Memo for Williston, *Harvard Law School Bulletin*, January 1949, 8; Henkin Interview, 28.

191. LH to A. James Casner, 10 November 1959, 89–27.

192. LH Memo for Williston, *Harvard Law School Bulletin*, January 1949, 8.

193. LH's foreword to Williston, *Life and Law*, vii–xi.

194. LH to A. James Casner, 10 November 1959, 89–27.

195. LH Memo for Williston, *Harvard Law School Bulletin*, January 1949, 8.

196. LH to A. James Casner, 10 November 1959, 89–27.

197. LH Memo for Williston, *Harvard Law School Bulletin*, January 1949, 7.

198. LH to A. James Casner, 10 November 1959, 89–27.

199. Ibid.

200. F.I. II, 51.

201. LH's foreword to Williston, *Life and Law*, vii.

202. LH Memo for Williston, *Harvard Law School Bulletin*, January 1949, 7.

203. F.I. II, 50, 1; LH to A. James Casner, 10 November 1959, 89–27.

204. *Centennial History*, 277.

205. For the best sketch of Thayer, see id., 276–283. That sketch is based on a longer one by James P. Hall in William Draper Lewis's *Great American Lawyers* (Philadelphia: John C. Winston Company, 1909). See also sketch—by Samuel Williston—in 9 *Dictionary of American Biography* (New York: Charles Scribner's Sons, 1935), 405–406.

206. LH Memo for Williston, *Harvard Law School Bulletin*, January 1949, 7.

207. LH recalled that there was about Thayer "a kind of Rhadamanthine detachment that has always remained to me a paragon of what a lawyer's attitude to law should be" (LH to A. James Casner, 10 November 1959, 89–27). But detachment can be subversive of a practical advocate's zeal. In Greek mythology, after all, Rhadamanthus was a judge, and detachment is a more clearly desirable trait in a judge or scholar than in a practitioner. And it was indeed Thayer as a probing, impartial scholar, "a great innovator" (F.I. I, 1), whom LH most admired.

208. See James B. Thayer to LH, 14 February 1898, 10–16. LH's article dealt with the courts' use of expert witnesses, as noted below.

209. Harlan B. Phillips, ed., *Felix Frankfurter Reminisces* (New York: Reynal & Co., 1960), 299–300.

210. LH Memo for Williston, *Harvard Law School Bulletin*, January 1949, 7.

211. F.I. II, 1.

212. LH Memo for Williston, *Harvard Law School Bulletin*, January 1949, 7.

213. LH to Bernard Berenson, 26 March 1958, 99–26.

214. LH to A. James Casner, 10 November 1959, 89–27.

215. LH to Arthur Dehon Hill, [1902], 5–4.

216. LH Memo for Williston, *Harvard Law School Bulletin*, January 1949, 8.

217. Learned Hand, *The Bill of Rights* (The Oliver Wendell Holmes Lectures, 1958) (Cambridge: Harvard University Press, 1958), 77.

218. Ibid.

219. LH to Augustus N. Hand, 4 June 1896, 109–1.

220. Ibid.

221. Arthur Dehon Hill to LH, 24 July 1901, 5–4.

222. LH remarks recounted in George Blow Elliott to LH, 13 May 1897, and 4 February 1899, 3–20.
223. Learned Hand, "Restitution or Unjust Enrichment," 11 *Harv. L.Rev.* 249 (1897).
224. LH to James B. Thayer, 12 April 1897, 10–16.
225. LH to Uncle Richard, 1 January 1899, 110–6.
226. Marcus T. Hun to LH, 15 July 1907, 115–24.
227. Clifford Hand (Uncle Clifford) to LH, 13 June 1897, 110–1.
228. Marcus T. Hun to LH, [July 1901], 115–13.
229. LH to Uncle Richard, 1 January 1899, 110–6.
230. Gus to LH, 27 January 1899, 109–2.
231. LH to Uncle Richard, 1 January 1899, 110–6.
232. The correspondence pertaining to this case is in 11–9 (starting with 17 November 1898).
233. See LH letters of 18 November 1898 and 18 January 1899, in 11–9.
234. See LH to Charles Ware, 17 March 1899, 11–9.
235. Charles Ware to LH, 15 March 1899, 11–9.
236. LH to Charles Ware, 17 March 1899, 11–9.
237. LH to Gus, 11 February 1901, 109–4; see also LH to Clifford Hand, 31 January 1901, 110–2.
238. LH to Gus, 11 February 1901, 109–4.
239. Gus to LH, 10 February 1901, 109–4.
240. LH to Clifford Hand, 31 January 1901, 110–2.
241. LH to General Robert Shaw Oliver, 15 July 1902, 7–20.
242. Gus to LH, 7 January [1899], 109–2.
243. LH to Lucius Ward Bannister, 17 September 1901, 1–22.
244. LH to FAH, 7 April 1906, Personal Correspondence.
245. Recollected in LH to FAH, 17 February 1920, Personal Correspondence.
246. LH to Julian T. Davies, Jr., 6 May 1899, 3–17.
247. LH to Edward H. Childs, 13 October 1900, 2–14.
248. Gus to LH, 1 March 1900, 109–3.
249. Learned Hand, "Historical and Practical Considerations Regarding Expert Testimony," 21 *Albany Medical Annals* 599 (November 1900), reprinted as Learned Hand, "Historical and Practical Considerations Regarding Expert Testimony," 15 *Harv. L.Rev.* 40 (1901).
250. Gus to LH, 2 November 1900, 109–4.
251. LH deleted the reference to the common law as "the foster mother of all absurdities." LH to Gus, 3 November 1900, 109–4.
252. Prof. Hugo Munsterberg to LH, 14 June 1902, 7–11.
253. LH to George B. Dorr, 19 June 1901, 3–18.
254. See especially LH to Gus, 6 November 1898, 109–2, the source of the quoted passages that follow.
255. LH to Gus, 3 November 1900, 109–4.
256. Ibid.
257. See clipping from (unidentified) Albany newspaper, 2 December 1898, 115–2.
258. See *Albany Evening Journal*, 1 June 1901, printing the underlying correspondence relating to the report of the committee that had been released on 31 May 1901.
259. LH to Gus, 6 November 1898, 109–2.

260. Mary Vida Clark to LH, 5 November 1902, 2–20.

261. LH's report of 3 November 1902, in 9–17 (quoted phrases from pp. 9 and 10 of report).

262. Howard Townsend to LH, [1897], 10–17.

263. James B. Ludlow to LH, 20 November 1900, 6–13.

264. The correspondent, Davis R. Vail, also urged LH to try to get his mind off depressing emotions by looking for physiological causes, explaining that "when I wake up to find myself blue and ready to worry myself sick, I try to feel that it's only my liver, or spleen or some other obscure organ that is getting me fretting. . . . It helps me and perhaps it may help you." See Davis R. Vail to LH, [1900], 10–23; see also id., 21 January 1901, 10–23.

265. Id., 14 June 1901, 10–23.

266. LH to [acquaintance in Boston], [mid-1901], 115–1; LH to Gus, 23 October 1901, 109–5; LH to Lucius Ward Bannister, 17 September 1901, 1–22.

267. Charles Lowell Barlow to LH, 18 March 1902, 99–5.

268. LH to Gus, 23 October 1901, 109–5.

269. James B. Ludlow to LH, 15 November 1901, 109–5.

270. Id., 12 December 1901, 6–13.

271. Hector M. Hitchings to LH, 24 October 1901, 5–12.

272. LH to Hector M. Hitchings, 9 November 1901, 5–12.

273. LH to Henry K. McHarg, 14 November 1901, 6–18.

274. A. Leo Everett to LH, 30 January 1902, 3–23.

275. LH to J. Archibald Murray, 9 February 1902, 7–3.

276. LH to FAH, 10 June 1923, Personal Correspondence.

277. Id., 7 April 1906, Personal Correspondence.

II

Learned Hand and Frances Fincke

1. LH to FAH, 11 June 1949 (her seventy-third birthday), Personal Correspondence.

2. See, e.g., LH's letter to Cousin Gus during his first European trip at sixteen: "You ought to see how pretty these French girls know how to make themselves; they beat anything we have got in dress. . . ." LH to Gus, 12 August 1888, 109–1.

3. Id., 20 July 1890 (at the end of LH's freshman year at Harvard), 109–1.

4. Id., 4 June 1906, 109–1.

5. The Bowditch invitations were the only ones not primarily turning on the presence of unmarried young women. Edward Bowditch, Sr., and his wife, Lucy, were close enough to the Hands to call LH "Bunny" (see Lucy R. Bowditch to LH, 12 July 1901, 2–1); LH was an occasional counselor to the Bowditches' son, Edward Bowditch, Jr., who attended Harvard College and (unsuccessfully) Law School, about a decade after LH. The young relative was Mary R. (Mysie) Bowditch. In congratulating LH on his engagement a couple of years later, Bowditch, Sr., wrote LH: "What is Mysie going to do?" See Edward Bowditch, Sr., to LH, 25 August 1902, 2–1.

6. See the Tremain material in 10–8 (Emily) and 10–18 (Mabel).

7. See, e.g., Mabel Tremain to LH, [July] 1898, 10–18.

8. During visits to the Tremain country place, LH was also subjected to some mild flirtations by two visiting girlfriends of Mabel, Katharine and Elinor

Wilson of Wilmington, Delaware. LH played croquet with them and, to his eventual regret, sent them boxes of chocolates when they returned home. Letters from them followed, including invitations to visit them in Wilmington, where "we could show you the beauties (all kinds) of Delaware." See 11–22.

9. See LH to Davis R. (Davey) Vail, 14 June 1900, 10–25: "I have learned that the particular reason for my unwillingness to go to the place in question is uncalled for. The ladies will not be there at all."

10. LH comment, quoted in Davey Vail letter to LH, 4 December 1900, 10–25. (About this time, late in 1900, Fred Townsend and Coco Oliver decided to end their engagement, which increased the risk to LH.)

11. Invitation in Mrs. Oliver to LH, 26 July 1898, 7–23; Elizabeth Shaw Oliver to LH, 28 December [1898], 7–23. (The reference was to LH's achieving a salaried partnership in the Hun firm at the end of 1898.)

12. Fred Townsend to LH, 3 July 1899, 108–1.

13. See, e.g., Bessie Oliver to LH, 4 October 1900, and [November] 1900, 7–23.

14. Bessie Oliver to LH, 24 July 1902, 7–23.

15. Charles L. Barlow to LH, 25 October 1903, 99–5. Barlow's sister was Louisa Barlow Jay ("Loulie"), who had married Pierre Jay, a New York banker, in 1897. The Barlows were related to the Minturn family, at whose summer home LH first met Frances; the Jays had a summer home in Mount Kisco, where the Hands, soon after they married, built their first summer home.

16. Ernst Berg to LH, 17 November [1902], 1–25; LH to George B. Elliott, 13 March 1897, 3–20; LH to Herman F. Gade, 1 February 1899, 4–21; George Rublee to LH, 21 September 1899 and 3 October 1902, 107–1.

17. E.g., Charles L. Barlow to LH, 17 November 1903, 99–5 (on moving to a Boston law firm, recalling his years in New York City, where "the haunts of the beautiful" were well known).

18. Id., 15 November 1898, 99–4.

19. LH to FAH, 7 March 1932, Personal Correspondence.

20. Charles L. Barlow to LH, 21 June 1899, 99–4.

21. At the southern end of the bay, a spit of land known as Point-à-Pic jutted out into the river. LH referred to the resort by that name rather than as Murray Bay. (Point-à-Pic was in fact a small hamlet; the names were often used interchangeably.)

22. Leslie Minturn Allison remembers the river as usually too cold for swimming, and bathing normally taking place in a nearby hotel pool. (She spent the early World War II years at the Minturn cottage, with her young children.) See Gunther Interview with Mrs. Allison, 1986. (For general background on Murray Bay, see also Andrew Hepburn, *Great Resorts of North America* [New York: Doubleday, 1965], and George M. Wrong, *The Canadian Manor and Its Seigneurs* [Toronto: Macmillan, 1908]. See also Gunther Interview with R. Minturn Sedgwick, 1973. Sedgwick was the last member of the Minturn family to occupy the Minturn cottage.)

23. Pleasure seekers had begun to arrive at Murray Bay around the time of the American Civil War. For the next two decades, residents of Quebec comprised the modest, rustic summer community. But in the 1890s, Americans began to dominate. They built their more opulent summer "cottages," and they tolerated Anglo-Saxon Canadians but shunned the Quebecois. See Gunther Interview with R. Minturn Sedgwick, 1973. Sedgwick recalled, for example,

that, as a young offspring of a wealthy American family, he was rebuked by his elders for associating with the son of a (Roman Catholic) Quebec cabinet minister. (Among the Americans who often summered in Murray Bay was William Howard Taft, the president who appointed LH to the district court in 1909. LH first met Taft at Murray Bay.)

24. Charles L. Barlow to LH, 22 September 1901, 99–4.

25. LH to Gus, 23 October 1901, 109–5.

26. See, e.g., Tom Lee to LH, 4 September 1902, 6–9 (referring to the period before the public announcement of the engagement).

27. Mother to LH, 22 August 1902, 113–4.

28. Gus to LH, 23 September 1902, 109–7 (reminiscing, after Frances accepted, about the agonies of courtship he had seen LH go through).

29. For the invitations, see 2–1 (Bowditch) and 7–20 (Oliver); on the split stay, see correspondence with Thomas Lee of Westport, 6–9; on LH's travel arrangements, see, e.g., 9–5.

30. On riding lessons, see 10–1. On riding clothes, see correspondence with Gibb & Co., Montreal tailor, 4–15.

31. This is FAH's recollection, related to R. Minturn Sedgwick sometime after LH's death in 1961 and before she died in 1963, as recounted to me. See Gunther Interview with Sedgwick, 1973. (There is some confirmation of Sedgwick's account in LH to FAH, 11 June 1949, Personal Correspondence, suggesting that FAH told LH in later years about her ambivalent feelings that night and morning.)

32. LH to FAH, 11 June 1949 (her seventy-third birthday), Personal Correspondence.

33. Gus to LH, 23 August 1902, 109–7.

34. LH to Frances Fincke, 13 October 1902, Personal Correspondence.

35. Id., 11 October 1902, Personal Correspondence.

36. Id., 22 October 1902, Personal Correspondence.

37. Gus to LH, 6 October 1902, 109–7.

38. See LH-FAH Personal Correspondence; see also LH to Davis R. Vail, 25 September 1902, 10–23.

39. Mother to LH, 22 August 1902, 113–4. See also id., 30 December 1902.

40. Fred Townsend to Mrs. Hand, 28 August 1902, 113–4.

41. See LH to F. Ottway Byrd, 6 September 1902, 2–6 ("From the way matters looks now, I think it not likely that I shall be married until after January.") See also Gus to LH, 17 September 1902, 109–7.

42. LH moved the hour of the ceremony from 2:30 p.m. in order to allow the newlyweds to catch a late-afternoon train and to avoid a long, inebriated gathering: "I am in every way anxious to get rid of the incipient . . . drunks as soon as possible, and for that matter those who will be in a state of somewhat mournful sobriety as well" (LH to Frances Fincke, 22 October 1902, Personal Correspondence).

43. See Gus to LH, 5 November 1902, 109–7. Among the other ushers: Gordon Knox Bell, Charles L. Barlow, Robert Pendleton Bowler, Harold Coolidge, and Davis R. (Davey) Vail. Among LH's old friends, only George Rublee, who was traveling in Europe, could not attend. See George Rublee to LH, 3 October 1902, 107–1.

44. See Frederick G. Fincke–LH correspondence, especially Fincke to LH, 24 October 1902, 113–20.

45. LH to FAH, 7 March 1932, Personal Correspondence.
46. Id., 11 June 1949, Personal Correspondence.
47. See, e.g., as early as LH to Frances Fincke, 22 October 1902, Personal Correspondence. (On Frances's knowledge of Latin, see, e.g., the comment by an old family friend from Utica congratulating the Hands on the birth of their first child in 1905: "I'll bet she is spitting Latin now!" [Edward Brandyn to LH, 7 August 1905, 2–2]).
48. In his letters, LH often commented on his halting efforts to use French. Both LH and Frances, however, were quite comfortable with German. See, e.g., LH to Frances Fincke, 22 October 1902, Personal Correspondence, addressing her as "Meine Kleine Geliebte" [My Little Beloved].
49. LH to Frances Fincke, 11 October 1902, Personal Correspondence.
50. Ibid.
51. Ibid.
52. As related in Charles L. Barlow to LH, 17 September 1902, 99–5.
53. Gordon K. Bell to LH, 15 October 1902, 99–9; Charles L. Barlow to LH, 22 September 1902, 99–4.
54. Gus to LH, 23 August 1902, 109–7. See also George Rublee to LH, 3 October 1902, 107–1: "Few men seem more capable of being happy in marriage than you and few seem to need such happiness more."
55. Fred Townsend to Mrs. Hand, 28 August 1902, 113–5.
56. LH to Frances Fincke, 10 October 1902, Personal Correspondence.
57. LH to FAH, 10 June 1923, Personal Correspondence.
58. Id., 22 June 1917, Personal Correspondence.
59. Id., 12 June 1917, Personal Correspondence.
60. Id., 17 February 1920, Personal Correspondence.
61. Id., 12 June 1929, Personal Correspondence.
62. Id., 28 December 1938, Personal Correspondence.
63. Edward Bowditch, Sr., to LH, 25 August 1902, 2–1.
64. LH to Frances Fincke, 10 October 1902, Personal Correspondence.
65. LH to FAH, 2 July 1905, and LH to Frances Fincke, 10 October 1902, Personal Correspondence.
66. Helen Ekin Starrett, *After College, What? For Girls* (New York: Thomas Y. Crowell & Co., c. 1896). Starrett noted that after college the college graduate finds herself suddenly confronted "with blank nothingness in so far as a worthy occupation of her time is concerned" and that the immediate post-college years of women graduates are thus typically "years of deep and perplexing unhappiness." "I want *something to do*," she states, is the characteristic cry of the young woman graduate (id., 5, 12, 14).
67. LH to Gus, 30 November 1901, 109–5.
68. Edward Brandyn to LH, 7 August 1905, 2–2 (in the course of congratulating LH on the birth of his first child and speculating whether the new mother-daughter relationship would be like that in the Fincke family).
69. Class of 1873. (He obtained a law degree from Columbia in 1875.)
70. LH to FAH, 19 July 1904, Personal Correspondence, after dining with an acquaintance who had been a college contemporary of Frederick Fincke.
71. Frederick Fincke to LH, 12 December 1908, 113–22.
72. Class of 1901 (three and a half years after Frances graduated from Bryn Mawr).
73. Frederick Fincke to LH, [September] 1904, 113–21.
74. LH borrowed these nicknames after he married Frances, most often calling her

"Kit." He often called himself "Cat" in his correspondence with her, frequently ending his letters with a deft little drawing of a cat. (He also occasionally called her "Puss" rather than "Kit" [e.g., LH to FAH, 4 July 1917, Personal Correspondence].)

75. Frederick Fincke to LH, 12 December 1908, 113–22.

76. Id., 15 September 1908, 113–22.

77. See, e.g., the supporting letters he sent to Bryn Mawr when she applied there. Gunther correspondence with Bryn Mawr College.

78. Barbara Miller Solomon, *In the Company of Educated Women: A History of Women and Higher Education in America* (New Haven: Yale University Press, 1985), 62.

79. Edith Finch, *Carey Thomas of Bryn Mawr* (New York: Harper, 1947), 36. The most useful sources I have relied on are this biography; Cornelia L. Meigs, *What Makes a College? A History of Bryn Mawr* (New York: Macmillan, 1956); and the superb essays and original documents in *The Making of a Feminist: Early Journals and Letters of M. Carey Thomas*, ed. Marjorie Houspian Dobkin (Kent, Ohio: Kent State University Press, 1979). On women's education of the day in general, as well as Bryn Mawr in particular, I have also found useful Roberta Frankfort, *Collegiate Women: Domesticity and Career in Turn-of-the-Century America* (New York: New York University Press, 1977), and an earlier essay by Roberta Wein (later Frankfort), "Women's Colleges and Domesticity, 1875–1918," *History of Education Quarterly* (Spring 1974), 31–47. See also Nancy Woloch, *Women and the American Experience* (New York: Alfred A. Knopf, 1984), and Nancy F. Cott, *The Grounding of Modern Feminism* (New Haven: Yale University Press, 1987). On M. Carey Thomas, see also the biographical essay by Laurence R. Veysey in 3 *Notable American Women 1607–1950*, ed. Edward T. James (Cambridge: Harvard University Press, 1971). Some of Thomas's speeches are collected in Barbara M. Cross, ed., *The Educated Woman in America* (New York: Teacher's College Press, 1965).

On the conflicts and choices facing graduates of women's colleges of the period, see also Joyce Antler, " 'After College, What?' New Graduates and the Family Claim," 32 *American Quarterly* (Fall 1980). On the themes of this section, I have also been helped by three fine, unpublished student papers, all by Stanford Law School students: Bonnie J. Sheldon, "Changing Choices: A Study of Frances Fincke Hand" (1988), Robin Cooper Feldman, "Learned and Frances Hand: A Puzzle" (1988), and Sonja Alpert, "Frances Fincke Hand" (1987).

80. Meigs, *What Makes a College?*, 72.

81. For example, Wellesley did not begin posting grades until years after. See Frankfort, *Collegiate Women*, 53.

82. *Bryn Mawr College Program*, 1895, Bryn Mawr College Archives, as quoted by Frankfort, *Collegiate Women*, 51.

83. M. Carey Thomas, "The Curriculum of the Women's Colleges—Old-Fashioned Disciplines," 10 *Journal of the Association of Collegiate Alumnae* 590 (May 1917).

84. The major examples of this kind of literature, insisting that "race suicide" would be the consequence of women's education, were Edward Clarke (a professor of medicine at Harvard), *Sex in Education; or, A Fair Chance for the Girls* (Boston: J. R. Osgood & Co., 1873), and G. Stanley Hall, *Adolescence* (New York: D. Appleton and Company, 1904), which spurred a large number of

popular articles about women's education. See, e.g., A. Lapthon Smith, "Higher Education of Women and Race Suicide," *Popular Science Monthly* (March 1905). Eliot insisted that "the prime motive of the higher education of women should be recognized as the development in women of the capacities and powers which will fit them make family and social life more intelligent, more enjoyable, happier, and more productive. . . ." See Carroll Smith-Rosenberg, *Disorderly Conduct: Visions of Gender in Victorian America* (New York: Alfred A. Knopf, 1985), 259. Thomas responded that women's education was a "dark spot" in Eliot's otherwise luminous intelligence. See Cross, *The Educated Woman in America*, 142.

85. See Wein, "Women's Colleges and Domesticity," 34; Frankfort, *Collegiate Women*, 26. Similarly, Thomas attacked Edward Clarke's volume as "that gloomy little specter" (M. Carey Thomas, "Present Tendencies in Women's College and University Education," 25 *Educational Review* 64–85 [1908]).

86. Mildred Minturn Diary, 61–62 (entry made at Mount Kisco, 25 November 1902), Minturn Papers, England.

87. See Frankfort, *Collegiate Women*, 52, 54–56.

88. Id., 56.

89. See id., 54–64, especially the data on Wellesley graduates during the same years. Thus, for the entire 1889–1908 period, 57 percent of Wellesley graduates married, and even during Frances's years, 1894–98, when only 36 percent of Bryn Mawr graduates married, 54 percent of Wellesley graduates did.

90. Id., 57. After 1910, far more college-educated women married and had children. "Defiantly different lifestyles promoted by a college education were, by 1910, only sporadically noticeable as college women clung to domesticity under the guise of sanatory science and domestic hygiene" (see Sheldon, "Changing Choices" 19). Moreover, fewer women pursued graduate studies or had careers after 1910, so that the statistical differences between Bryn Mawr graduates and those of other women's colleges such as Wellesley virtually disappeared. Frankfort, *Collegiate Women*, 72–78.

91. See Liz Schneider, " 'Our Failures Only Marry': Bryn Mawr and the Failure of Feminism," in Vivian Gornick and Barbara K. Moran, eds., *Women in Sexist Society: Studies in Power and Powerlessness* (New York: Basic Books, 1971) 419, 426.

92. Frankfort, *Collegiate Women*, 54–55.

93. In later years, Thomas softened her anti-marriage stance. By 1901, she recognized that some women graduates would marry but that an intellectual education was nevertheless important to them "because men and women are to live and work together as comrades and dear friends and married friends and lovers, and because their effectiveness and happiness and the welfare of the generation to come after them will be vastly increased [by getting] the same intellectual training and the same scholarly and moral ideals" (M. Carey Thomas, "Should the Higher Education of Women Differ From that of Men?" 21 *Educational Review* 1, 10 [1901], reprinted in Cross, *The Educated Woman in America* 36).

94. See Frankfort, *Collegiate Women*, 74. Thus, she no longer uttered statements such as "Of all things, taking care of children seems most utterly unintellectual" (Nancy Woloch, *Women and the American Experience* [New York: Alfred A. Knopf, 1984], 279).

95. From a letter by Thomas's father, James Carey Thomas, at his daughter's

request, to President Gilman of Johns Hopkins, trying to elicit an invitation to Russell from there as well. Quoted in James Thomas Flexner, *An American Saga: The Story of Helen Thomas and Simon Flexner* (Boston: Little, Brown, 1984), 299. (Helen Thomas—Mrs. Flexner—was Carey Thomas's sister.)

96. Alys was the first of Russell's four wives; this marriage, like most of Russell's, ended in divorce. As his fourth wife, Russell married, at the age of eighty in 1952, Edith Finch, a lecturer in English at Bryn Mawr, a former companion of Lucy Donnelly (also long on the Bryn Mawr faculty), and a biographer of M. Carey Thomas. (Edith Finch and Lucy Donnelly were both good friends of the Hands, as was Helen Thomas Flexner, who, before her marriage, was Donnelly's closest companion. See Flexner, *An American Saga*, 299, 307, 410).

97. Alys Russell to her family, 25 October 1886, Minturn Papers, England.

98. Finch, *Carey Thomas of Bryn Mawr*, 194.

99. Alys Russell to her family, 25 October 1886 (as well as a subsequent letter by her, [fall] 1896), Minturn Papers, England. (Alys also wrote that another young woman [quite possibly Frances Fincke] repeated to her "every word we had said to Miss Minturn.")

100. See generally the Mildred Minturn correspondence of the 1890s, Minturn Papers, England. (Mildred Minturn was Frances's housemate at Bryn Mawr and her closest friend.) Mildred repeatedly visited the Russells in England after graduation, and in later years Bertrand Russell, who always had an eye for attractive young women, carried on a flirtation with her. See, e.g., Bertrand Russell to Mildred Minturn Scott, 12 April 1914, in response to a letter in which she referred to their long walks eighteen years earlier and described herself as then "ardent and lanky"; Russell replied that the "lanky was inappropriate, . . . if you had had less beauty I should not have been always thinking" of you.

101. Frances Fincke to Mildred Minturn (after visiting the Russells, writing from Nice), 12 February 1899, Minturn Papers, England.

102. Id., 9 June [1898], Minturn Papers, England.

103. Mildred's father, Robert Bowne Minturn, Jr., had bought the famous clipper ship *Flying Cloud*, which set several speed records. He died in 1889; her mother, born in 1839, lived until 1926. See Jean Stein, *Edie: An American Biography* (New York: Alfred A. Knopf, 1982) (edited with George Plimpton), 21, 430. *Edie* is the story of Edith Minturn Sedgwick, a grandniece of Mildred Minturn, born in 1943, who died a suicide in 1971. Edie Sedgwick was an Andy Warhol groupie who appeared in several of his movies; she was a victim of the drug culture in that circle.

104. See Mildred Minturn–J. G. Croswell (English teacher and sometime headmaster at the Brearley School) correspondence, Minturn Papers, England.

105. Susanna Shaw Minturn ("Mama") to Mildred Minturn, 20 March 1897, Minturn Papers, England.

106. See Frances G. Gosling, *Before Freud—Neurasthenia and the American Medical Community 1870–1910* (Urbana: University of Illinois Press, 1987), and Tom Lutz, *American Nervousness, 1903: An Anecdotal History* (Ithaca, N.Y.: Cornell University Press, 1991).

107. Mildred Minturn Diary, 30 (speaking of fall 1899 and early 1900), Minturn Papers, England.

108. Id., 30–33 (1900 and 1901 entries). The Mrs. Stetson to whom Mildred referred was Charlotte Perkins Gilman (Stetson was her first husband, Gilman

her second). The book (also mentioned by Frances Fincke in her letters) was *Women and Economics* (Boston: Small, Maynard & Co., 1899), a major feminist manifesto of the day. It was essentially an argument for female economic independence; it insisted that the female had become wholly dependent upon the male for food and shelter, so that women's capacities for autonomy, careers, and economic independence had atrophied. Gilman argued that women would achieve economic independence by planning their own lives. It bears noting that Charlotte Perkins Gilman was also a neurasthenic, and was also, like a number of pathbreaking independent women of the era (such as Jane Addams), required to submit to the prescribed therapy of extensive rest and limited intellectual activity. See Lutz, *American Nervousness*, and Ann J. Lane, *To Herland and Beyond: The Life and Work of Charlotte Perkins Gilman* (New York: Pantheon, 1990).

Mildred's periodic bouts with neurasthenia and her seeming nervous breakdowns continued after Frances and LH were married. Mildred spent most of the early 1900s in Europe, especially Paris. There she was treated for several years by a Dr. Gorodizche and subsequently by a Dr. Janet, "a specialist in women's nervous disorders." Both attributed her illness in part to her failure to assume a normal young woman's life and her overdeveloped intellect.

109. As a result of the leave, she did not get her degree until the end of the fall semester of 1897, even though her classmates had graduated at the end of the preceding spring.

110. Frances Fincke to Mildred Minturn, 9 June [1898], Minturn Papers, England.

111. Id., [March 1899], Minturn Papers, England.

112. Id., from Nice, 12 February 1899, Minturn Papers, England.

113. Id., [March 1899], Minturn Papers, England.

114. Id., "Friday" [1899], Minturn Papers, England.

115. Id., 9 June [1898], Minturn Papers, England. See also her letter from Europe, and her comments about Bernard Berenson, who was then working with Mrs. Costelloe (Alys Russell's sister, and, later, Mrs. Berenson), id., 12 February 1899, Minturn Papers, England.

116. See ibid., and id., 21 December 1904, Minturn Papers, England.

117. See Barbara Harris, *Beyond Her Sphere: Women and the Professions in American History* (Westport, Conn.: Greenwood, 1978), 104.

118. See the many letters from Frances to Mildred, 1897–1908, in the Minturn Papers, England. There are fewer preserved letters from Mildred to Frances, although the Minturn Papers contain two (2 August 1906 and 4 September 1906); most of Mildred's references to Frances are in her diary of nearly 120 pages, from 1898 to 1906.

119. See Sheldon, "Changing Choices," 14.

120. Mildred Minturn Diary, 61–62 (23 November 1902), Minturn Papers, England.

121. See, e.g., id., 64–70 (17 January 1903).

122. For other examples, see Sheldon, "Changing Choices," 15 et seq.

123. For the use of these phrases, see Mildred Minturn Diary, 69–70 (17 January 1903), Minturn Papers, England.

124. See Lillian Faderman, *Surpassing the Love of Men: Romantic Friendship and Love Between Women from the Renaissance to the Present* (New York: Morrow, 1981), 191. The term came from Henry James's *The Bostonians* (New York:

Macmillan, 1886) and refers to "one of those friendships between women which are so common in New England," as James wrote in his *Notebook*.

125. Mildred Minturn Diary, 59–60 (entry made at Mount Kisco, 13 November 1902, shortly before Frances's marriage), Minturn Papers, England.

126. Mildred, for example, had undertaken a "labor investigation" in the winter of 1901–02, studying the education of working girls by visiting clubs and interviewing about 120 girls. She had also read and summarized the Webbs' book on Fabian socialism and had "tackled the reports of the [New York State Labor] Commissioner at length." She shared some of the results of her studies with Frances during a visit to Utica, where she "discussed economics & the labor law." See Mildred Minturn Diary, 50–53 (1902), Minturn Papers, England.

127. Id., 55–56 (23 November 1902), Minturn Papers, England.

128. Frances Fincke to Mildred Minturn, on returning to Utica, Thursday noon [spring 1902] [written at the time Mildred's mother was ill, which, according to her diary, 54, was in the spring of 1902], Minturn Papers, England.

129. Mildred Minturn Diary, 55 (23 November 1902), Minturn Papers, England.

130. "The blow didn't fall till we were together again in August." Id., 56 (23 November 1902), Minturn Papers, England.

131. Id., 57–60 (23 November 1902), Minturn Papers, England. Mildred went on that she was thankful that "it all happened when we were together, so that I went thro' every stage with her & she took me in in the most wonderful way. It was not all bitterness, bec. I was truly happy to see her so radiant aft. her long year—some days I was hardly even sad."

132. Id., 67 (17 January 1903), Minturn Papers, England.

133. Id., 72–73 (6 September 1905), Minturn Papers, England.

134. FAH to Mildred Minturn, 13 August 1905, Minturn Papers, England.

135. LH to FAH, 10 October 1902, Personal Correspondence.

136. LH to Francis W. Lee, 25 May 1903, 6–7.

137. See correspondence about house searches in 8–6.

138. See correspondence with Dr. Deas Murphy in 7–2.

139. See, e.g., letters of FAH to LH in 111–14.

140. See LH to Francis W. Lee, 25 May 1903, 6–7, for complaints; see LH to real estate broker J. Metcalfe Thomas, 30 November 1903, 10–5; see also negotiations reflected in correspondence in 10–5.

141. LH to Fred Townsend, 16 November 1903, 108–2; see also LH to Lewis Parker, 6 November 1903, 8–1.

142. This amount included $2000 for improvements (e.g., parquet floors). See correspondence with architect William Delano, 3–11. (The Hands remained in the house until the late 1950s; not long before LH died, they moved into an apartment, because of his ailing back. [In the late 1970s, former president Richard M. Nixon bought the house for about $750,000; he sold it soon after for more than $1 million.])

III
From Wall Street Lawyer to Federal District Judge

1. Fred Townsend to LH, 17 November 1902, 108–1.

2. Zabriskie did most of the legal work; the other partners were supposedly in charge of attracting business. J. Archibald Murray, who recruited LH, was

genial enough but supervised only a few cases of his own. Middleton S. Burrill, the third partner, seldom set foot in the office.

3. Mother to LH, 28 July 1903, 113–5.
4. FAH to LH, 6 July 1903, 111–11.
5. Frederick Fincke to LH, 22 April 1903, 113–20.
6. Id., 10 January 1904, 113–21.
7. LH to Frederick Fincke, 29 July 1903, 113–20. Fincke resented this criticism. See his reply, 30 July 1903, 113–20.
8. Mother to LH, 28 July 1903, 113–5.
9. Frederick Fincke to LH, 22 April 1903, 113–20.
10. See id., [July] 1903, 113–20 [erroneously marked "Fall 1903"]. (This letter indicates with unusual clarity that FAH was keeping her father informed about LH's thinking even when LH was not directly communicating with Fincke.)
11. Ibid.
12. See id., 30 July 1903, 113–20.
13. See the summary of LH's complaints about the firm in id., 8 January 1904, replying to LH's letter of 7 January 1904, 113–21.
14. Frederick Fincke to LH, 10 January 1904, 113–21.
15. Id., 8 January 1905, replying to and quoting from LH's anxious, depressed report of 7 January 1905, both in 113–21.
16. Frederick Fincke to LH, 8 January 1905, 113–21.
17. Ibid.
18. John L. Wilkie to LH, [1905], 11–15.
19. The latter controversy involved litigation between the Genets (George C. and Augusta G. Genet) and the Delaware & Hudson Canal Company. LH had to educate himself to become something of a mining expert. The lawsuits had been under way for years when he entered the case. He dropped some of the pending cases and settled the rest for nearly $200,000, with Mrs. Genet, by then a widow, paying the law firm a $20,000 fee. See correspondence with Mrs. Genet, 1904–08, 4–10 to 4–13; see also correspondence with W. P. Butler, February 1909, 2–6.
20. Fred Townsend to LH, 26 December 1905, 108–4.
21. See Gus to LH, 15 July 1905, 109–8.
22. See FAH to LH, 6 March 1908, 111–11.
23. See, e.g., LH's comment on Gould in LH to FAH, 7 April 1906, Personal Correspondence.
24. FAH to LH, 6 March 1908, 111–11.
25. Frederick Fincke to LH, 21 July 1908, 113–22.
26. Mother to LH, [2] April 1909, 113–6.
27. From LH's extemporaneous remarks to a dinner of the New York Legal Aid Society, 1951, recorded by a stenographer, and filed with Allen Wardwell–LH correspondence, 82–39.
28. See C.C.B.'s remark to LH in a letter of 11 November 1933, 100–29: "The truth is, I like messing about in public or quasi-public business." See also Gunther Interview with Charles C. Burlingham, 1957, and LH–C.C.B. correspondence, 100–24 to 101–6 (1904–59).
29. Charles C. Burlingham to LH, Easter 1905, 100–24.
30. The Social Register Co. to LH, 11 January 1907, 9–27.
31. Plunkitt's often wise and corrosive wit was preserved by a New York journalist: William L. Riordan, *Plunkitt of Tammany Hall: A Series of Very Plain Talks*

*on Very Practical Politics, Delivered by Ex-Senator George Washington Plunkitt,
the Tammany Philosopher, From His Rostrum—The New York County Courthouse
Bootblack Stand* (New York: Dutton, 1963).

32. Id., 17.
33. Richard L. Hand (Uncle Richard) to LH, 31 October 1903, 110–10.
34. LH to Alice Lee, 20 October 1903, 6–5.
35. LH to Marcus Hun, 21 October 1903, 115–19.
36. Id., 27 October 1903, 115–19.
37. Fred Townsend to LH, 25 October 1903, 10–14.
38. LH to Richard L. Hand, 4 November 1903, 10–10.
39. Gus to LH, 16 September 1900, 109–3.
40. See Norman Hapgood to LH, 18 September 1900, 5–8.
41. Gus to LH, 16 September 1900, 109–3.
42. LH to Gus, 19 September 1900, 109–3.
43. Former judge John Teller (of Auburn) to LH, 14 July 1904, 10–4.
44. Arthur Dehon Hill to LH, 22 August 1904, 5–4.
45. See Richard L. Hand to LH, 18 November 1904, 110–11.
46. LH to *New York Times*, 16 September 1904, 10–17.
47. Cecile R. Swartz to LH, 28 February 1902, 10–3.
48. LH also had friendly relations with another Jewish classmate, Jesse Isidor
    Straus, whose father, a German Jewish immigrant of the mid-nineteenth cen-
    tury, was an early owner of the Macy's and Abraham & Straus department
    stores. Jesse Straus became president of Macy's (and ambassador to France in
    F. D. Roosevelt's administration). But not even Straus made it into the inner
    circles of Harvard's clubdom; and Howard Gans, from a far more modest
    background, was doomed to remain even further from the core.
49. See Howard Gans to LH, 11 December 1902, 4–21.
50. Fred Townsend to LH, 19 November 1903, 108–2.
51. Howard Gans to LH, 9 November 1903, 4–21.
52. See id., 21 November 1903, 4–21.
53. Fred Townsend to LH, 17 November 1903, 108–2.
54. Id., 19 November 1903, 108–2.
55. Howard Gans to LH, 21 November 1903, 4–21.
56. LH to Fred Townsend, 8 November 1903, 108–2.
57. Ibid.
58. LH to Howard Gans, 17 November 1903, described in LH to Fred Townsend,
    [November] 1903, 108–2.
59. The trustees LH appealed to included Robert Olcott, assistant cashier of the
    Mechanics and Farmers Bank of Albany (see Robert Olcott to LH, 21 November
    1903, 7–23), Charles L. Pruyn, Embossing Company of Albany (see Charles
    L. Pruyn to LH, 21 November 1903, 8–18), and Luther H. Tucker, Jr.,
    publisher of *The Country Gentleman* (see Luther H. Tucker, Jr., to LH, 23
    November 1903, 10–19).
60. Luther H. Tucker, Jr., to LH, 23 November 1903, 10–19.
61. Fred Townsend to LH, 7 November 1903; id., 19 November 1903, 108–2.
62. Howard Gans to LH, 24 November 1903, 4–21.
63. Id., 14 December 1903, 4–21.
64. Id., 11 December 1902, 4–21.
65. Id., 24 November 1903, replying to LH to Howard Gans, 21 November 1903,
    both in 4–21.

66. It was not the last time the Hands would go to the Lower East Side. A few years later, LH and FAH became engaged in raising funds and serving on governing boards of tenement houses, joining Jane Addams's movement to provide educational and recreational facilities for the children of immigrants and others in the underprivileged neighborhoods. (LH and Howard Gans were also in touch during the 1905 municipal campaign. Gans asked LH for a contribution to District Attorney William Travers Jerome's successful reelection campaign, and LH sent an unusually large amount, $100—in part, perhaps, as one more token of respect for Gans, who was treasurer of Jerome's campaign. They drifted apart thereafter, perhaps because Gans's main business was in the highest state court and LH had turned his back on most Albany matters.)

67. 21 *Harv. L.Rev.* 495 (1908).

68. 198 U.S. 45 (1905).

69. U.S. Constitution, Amendment XIV, § 1. The Fourteenth Amendment's due-process clause applies only to states, but identical language in the Fifth Amendment imposes the same prohibition on the national government. Thus, the restrictive *Lochner* ruling bound the hands of Congress as well as of state legislatures.

70. *Slaughter House Cases*, 83 U.S. 36, 78 (1873).

71. Thayer set forth these ideas in a *Harvard Law Review* article published in the very year Hand entered law school, an article that became a classic. Thayer, "The Origin and Scope of the American Doctrine of Constitutional Law," 7 *Harv. L.Rev.* 129 (1893). (LH's class notes in Thayer's course, preserved in the Hand Papers, reveal how much emphasis Thayer gave to the proper role of courts in a democratic society—and how carefully LH recorded his lectures.)

72. *Allgeyer v. Louisiana*, 165 U.S. 578, 589 (1897).

73. 198 U.S. 45, 58–61 (1905).

74. Id., 75–76.

75. One invalidated a federal law against "yellow dog" contracts—employment contracts barring employees from joining trade unions—on interstate railroads. The other, upholding a paternalistic law limiting the hours of work for women (on the ground that "women's physical structure" made them so unequal as to justify state intervention), reiterated *Lochner*'s message that the Court would not tolerate "unreasonable" state interventions in the operations of the free market. *Adair v. United States*, 208 U.S. 161 (1908); *Muller v. Oregon*, 208 U.S. 412 (1908).

76. 21 *Harv. L.Rev.* 495, 507.

77. LH called it the "laisser faire" theory (rather than the more conventional "laissez-faire").

78. 21 *Harv. L.Rev.* 495, 507–08.

79. Id., 500.

80. Id., 505–06.

81. Veeder, one of LH's acquaintances, was appointed in 1910 to the district court for the Eastern District of New York.

82. Charles C. Burlingham to Attorney General George W. Wickersham, 12 August 1910, 100–24.

83. This is based mainly on Frederick Fincke to LH, 9 March 1907, 113–21, the first letter in Fincke's spring barrage. (LH's letters to Fincke are not preserved, but his thinking is well reflected in his father-in-law's responses.)

84. Ibid.

85. Frederick Fincke ("Dad") to FAH ("Dear Kitten"), 10 March 1907, 113–22 (mislabeled 15 March).
86. Augustus N. Hand (Gus) to Frederick Fincke, 12 March 1907 (copy in 113–22). Even if LH did not explicitly ask Gus to write, LH clearly knew about the letter from the start, for Gus gave him a copy. (Gus's letter was written on the Tuesday after the Saturday on which Fincke first wrote LH. From the body of Gus's appeal, it is quite clear that he knew about not only Fincke's 9 March letter to LH but also Fincke's 10 March letter to Frances.)
87. See Frederick Fincke to LH, 12 March 1907, 113–22.
88. Augustus N. Hand to Frederick Fincke, 12 March 1907, 113–22.
89. Frederick Fincke to LH, 12 March 1907, 113–22.
90. Id., 9 March 1907, 113–22.
91. Id., 12 March 1907, 113–22; Frederick Fincke to Augustus N. Hand, 15 March 1907, 113–22.
92. Frederick Fincke to LH, 9 March 1907, 113–21.
93. Id., 2 May 1907, 113–22.
94. The quoted comments about Semple and Ordway are from Augustus N. Hand to Frederick Fincke, 12 March 1907, 113–22. (I have had to reconstruct the story of the competition for the position from the correspondence because the official files cannot be located. The Justice Department files in the National Archives usually contain the various letters of recommendation for federal judgeships, and I have indeed gotten the files on Ordway and Semple from that source. However, several years of searches for LH's files [aided by Justice Department officials] proved unsuccessful. The LH files did exist, but they were removed by attorneys general who were preparing various tributes to LH in the 1940s and 1950s. The last one, apparently, was Attorney General William P. Rogers. The files have not turned up either in the attorney general's office or in the National Archives and evidently were mislaid.)
95. Ibid.
96. See 43 *Congressional Record*, pt. 3, 2483–84.
97. Democratic representative William Sulzer of New York, id., 2484.
98. 22 February 1909. (The Senate, as in earlier years, relied largely on extensive studies and debates in the House.)
99. Act of 2 March 1909, 35 Stat. 685.
100. See receipt for dues—$4—paid by LH to 29th Assembly District Republican Club, 21 May 1907, 2–27.
101. See LH's correspondence with John Boyle, Jr., chairman of the Speakers Bureau, 2 October 1908 et seq., 2–1.
102. See George E. Mowry's sketch of Wickersham in 11 *Dictionary of American Biography, Supplement* 2 (New York: Charles Scribner's Sons, 1958), 713, 714, and his *Theodore Roosevelt and the Progressive Movement* (Madison: University of Wisconsin Press, 1946), 184.
103. Frederick Fincke to LH, 21 March 1909, 113–23 (in response to LH to Frederick Fincke, 16 March 1909, paraphrased in Fincke's letter).
104. See Frederick Fincke to LH, 2 April 1909, 113–23.
105. "If the President could have foreseen that in less than three years Hand would be supporting Theodore Roosevelt as the Bull Moose candidate for the Presidency, and a year later would be running for Chief Judge of the [New York] Court of Appeals . . ., he would not have considered Hand for a moment" (C. C. Burlingham, "Judge Learned Hand," 60 *Harv. L.Rev.* 330 [1947]).

(See also Gunther Interview of Charles C. Burlingham, 1957, and the Second Circuit's Commemorative Proceedings on Hand's half century on the bench [264 F.2d], including remarks about Burlingham's influence by Chief Judge Charles E. Clark and Attorney General William P. Rogers. The same emphasis on C.C.B.'s influence appears in Whitney North Seymour's "Tribute to the 'Old Chief' of the Bench," *New York Times Magazine*, 5 April 1957, 17 [reprinted as an appendix to the 1959 Second Circuit Proceedings at the beginning of 264 F.2d].)

106. Felix Frankfurter, "Judge Learned Hand," 60 *Harv. L.Rev.* 325, 326 (1947).
107. E.g., Charles J. Buchanan to LH, 6 April 1909, 2–4.
108. Fred Townsend to LH, 2 April 1909, 108–7.
109. Frederick Fincke to LH, 2 April 1909, 113–23.
110. LH to James Byrne, 5 April 1909, 2–6. (Byrne, a Roman Catholic leader of the bar, was the father of Helen Byrne, Walter Lippmann's second wife.)
111. Fred Townsend to LH, 8 August 1908, 108–7.
112. Id., [April] 1909, 108–7.
113. George E. Mowry's sketch of Wickersham, 11 *Dictionary of American Biography, Supplement 2*, 713, 715.
114. The account that follows is largely based on an enterprising journalist's reconstruction, in the *Brooklyn Eagle* of 5 May 1909 and preserved by LH in his files, 2–4. The story is datelined "Washington, May 5." Quotations not otherwise cited are from this article.
115. The other New York senator, also a Republican, was the recently elected Elihu Root, Sr., not a likely opponent of George Wickersham's apolitical nomination: Root, a distinguished, high-minded New York lawyer who was a close acquaintance and political associate of Wickersham, had been President Roosevelt's secretary of state from 1905 to 1909. (His son, Elihu Root, Jr., was a reform-minded New York City lawyer, a close friend and law school classmate of Felix Frankfurter.)
116. For example, Taft had called a special session of Congress to consider tariff reform as soon as he was sworn in, and the ensuing debates created the first fissure between conservative and liberal Republicans in the new administration. Wickersham's unilateral behavior on LH's nomination struck Depew as one more irritant. See Mowry, *Theodore Roosevelt and the Progressive Movement*, chapter 2 ("Taft, Tariff, Trouble").
117. See the transcript of LH's oath-taking ceremony, 30 April 1909, 42–20.
118. Lydia Coit Learned Hand (LH's mother) to LH, 2 April 1909; see also her letter of [3] April 1909, 113–6.
119. Id., 30 April 1911, 113–7.
120. Id., [January] 1911, 113–7.
121. Id., 29 January 1911, 113–7.
122. Id., 2 April 1909, 113–6.
123. File 113–6 contains more than a dozen typewritten letters LH sent to his mother between 13 May and 17 June 1909. She did not preserve his handwritten notes, his usual way of writing. (His uncomfortable sense of duty toward his mother is suggested by the fact that he maintained the correspondence even when he did not have time to write a letter by hand, by resorting to a method he rarely used—dictating to his secretary.) All of his mother's notes to him were handwritten; he retained almost all of them.
124. Mother to LH, 25 February 1911, 113–7.

125. LH to Mother, 13 May 1909, 113–6.
126. Id., 14 May 1909, 113–6.
127. Id., 18 May 1909, 113–6. This concern about talking persisted. See LH to Charles C. Burlingham, 5 June 1909, 100–24: "I wonder how I am doing. I am certain of one thing, and that is, I have an irrepressible tendency to talk too much. The only thing to be said in my favor is that I have followed your advice and talk in a very loud voice, which I think can always be heard."
128. Felix Frankfurter to Charles C. Burlingham, [January 1933], Burlingham Papers, Harvard Law School.
129. LH to Mother, 21 May 1909, 113–6.
130. Id., 28 May 1909, 113–6.
131. Id., 19 May 1909, 113–6.
132. Id., 28 May 1909, 113–6.
133. Id., 3 June 1909, 113–6.
134. Id., 4 June 1909, 113–6.
135. Receiverships involved application of traditional state equity principles. By contrast, when the federal bankruptcy statute was invoked, court-appointed referees in bankruptcy supervised the initial handling of claims against the bankrupt, and these referees were regular employees of the court.
136. LH to Charles C. Burlingham, 5 June 1909, 100–24.
137. LH to Mother, 8 June 1909, 113–6.
138. Id., 11 June 1909, 113–6.
139. Id., 17 June 1909, 113–6.
140. Id., 4 June 1909, 113–6.
141. See the often routine but frequently revealing correspondence with the Justice Department (filed under "U.S. Attorney General") throughout his district court years, 42–1 through 42–10. On ribbons, see, e.g., U.S. Department of Justice to LH, 25 January 1912, 42–2; on books, note that the judges' chambers did not even have the *Federal Reporter*, the reports of the federal court decisions, and that LH repeatedly had to plead for authorization to buy technical manuals, especially seafaring guides for his maritime cases.
142. See, e.g., two pamphlets published in 1985 by the Second Circuit Historical Committee and the Federal Bar Council, *The Federal Courthouse at Foley Square* and *The Successive Locations of the United States District and Circuit Courts in the Borough of Manhattan*.
143. LH to U.S. Department of Justice, 5 February 1924, 42–10 (LH writing, as often, on behalf of his colleagues as well as himself). See also LH correspondence with Winfred T. Denison in 18–22, when Denison, a friend of Felix Frankfurter, was chair of the Association of the Bar's Committee on the Court House.
144. 1919 *Report of the Association of the Bar's Committee on the Court House* (see Denison correspondence, 18–22).
145. See *Successive Locations*, 14. See also correspondence in 23–21.
146. Not until 1936, long after LH had been promoted to the Second Circuit, did the federal courts move into their new, spacious quarters in architect Cass Gilbert's high-rise building on Foley Square. (Gilbert, who had designed the Woolworth Building, also planned the U.S. Supreme Court Building. He died in 1934; his son Cass Gilbert, Jr., supervised the completion of both the Foley Square and Supreme Court buildings.)
147. E.g., circuit judges Lacombe and Noyes before the end of World War I, and circuit judge Mayer in 1924.

148. See LH's repeated pleas for an increase in his stenographer's salary from $1,000 to $1,200, achieved only after years of effort. (See, generally, correspondence in files 42–3 to 42–5, and note the granting of his request in U.S. Department of Justice to LH, 12 March 1917, 42–5.)

149. E.g., LH to William Henkel, Jr., 25 November 1914, 25–3.

150. The only judge who had used law clerks before then was the Supreme Court Justice Horace Gray, Professor John Chipman Gray's brother.

151. LH to John Chipman Gray, 2 April 1909, 21–27.

152. See John Chipman Gray to LH, 14 April 1909, 21–27.

153. LH to John Chipman Gray, 2 April 1909, 21–27.

154. John Chipman Gray to LH, 27 April 1910, 21–27.

155. See Arthur L. Robinson to LH, 14 April 1911, 37–9.

156. On authorizations to hire the early law clerk–stenographers, see Justice Department files, 42–1 and 42–2. For correspondence concerning early clerks, see especially 21–1, 21–27, 22–24, and 37–9, on Collett, Hallet, and Robinson.

 In 1930, a law clerkship for every federal judge became a federally funded position at last. LH's law clerks of this later vintage were typically officers of the *Harvard Law Review* who frequently moved on to Supreme Court clerkships after their year with LH. With them, LH usually formed very close bonds. He asked them to criticize his drafts mercilessly as his written opinions evolved, relishing and attending to their critical comments with extraordinary open-mindedness and forming a near collegial relationship with what he called his "puny" judges—a takeoff on "puisne" judges ("inferior" judges). But even with the second generation of his law clerks, LH was notoriously unwilling to delegate any part of his opinion-writing task: not one of the succession of over thirty law clerks who served LH on the appellate court ever wrote a single line of any of his opinions, or indeed submitted a single research memo; LH, unlike most other judges, used his clerks entirely as critical sounding boards as he worked out his position and developed his written opinions in face-to-face encounters with them.

157. Collett and Robinson died young—Collett in 1913, of a heart attack (see George B. Guthrie, Portland, Oregon, to LH, 30 April 1913, 22–16), Robinson in an accident while running to catch a moving train in 1923 (see John W. Frost to LH, 10 March 1923, 21–1); see also LH's reply to Frost, 13 March 1923, 21–1: "I feel genuinely grieved that such a good fellow would have been lost in so needless a way."

158. See LH to Richard (Dick) Hallet, 12 August 1957 and 29 May 1957, 89–12. [LH's earlier correspondence with Hallet and his father is in 22–24 (Richard) and 22–23 (Richard's father, Andrews Hallet).]

159. R. Hallet to LH, 19 December 1911, 22–24; see also id., 11 August 1911, 22–24, and LH to R. Hallet, 29 May 1957, 89–12.

160. LH to Andrews Hallet (regional sales manager for a Boston cement company), 27 March 1912, 22–23. (See also LH to R. Hallet, 11 May 1912, 22–24, about LH's enjoyment of Dick's letters: "I read them to my wife, we both greatly enjoyed them and envied you the adventures which you have known.")

161. LH to Andrews Hallet, 19 April 1912, 22–23, in response to Andrews Hallet to LH, 22 April 1912, 22–23.

162. LH to R. Hallet, 11 May 1912, 22–24.

163. See R. Hallet to LH, 11 August 1911 and 6 September 1912, 22–24. Hallet

recalled that the editor of the London *Times* rejected his story "but gave me a drink of whiskey"; the *Post*, by contrast, accepted it but "withheld the whiskey." See R. Hallet obituary [from unidentified newspaper] in 89–12. See also Hallet entry in 4 *Who Was Who in America* (Chicago: Marquis—Who's Who, 1968), 396.

164. R. Hallet to LH, 15 May 1957, 89–12.

165. LH helped Hallet repeatedly, lending him money and encouraging him to join the crew of additional ships. In 1917, LH drew on his friend George Rublee's connection with the War Shipping Board to get Hallet a job as third mate on a hastily built ship while America prepared for World War I. See R. Hallet–LH correspondence in 1917, 22–24, and R. Hallet to LH, 15 May 1957, 89–12.

166. R. Hallet to LH, 15 May 1957, 89–12.

167. LH to R. Hallet, 29 May 1957, 89–12.

168. Hough became a circuit judge in 1916; LH frequently sat with him before he himself moved in 1924 to the Second Circuit, where they became colleagues. Hough died in 1927. See Hough-LH correspondence, 24–6 to 24–11, and 54–34 to 54–35. Hough, a maritime-law expert, had a scholarly bent as well. See his booklet, *The United States District Court for the Southern District of New York—Its Growth, and the Men Who Have Done Its Work*, written in 1923 and published posthumously by the Maritime Law Association of the United States in 1934.

   (The authorized personnel for the Southern District bench remained at four until 1922. The changes after 1909: Julius M. Mayer succeeded the deceased Adams in 1912; Gus Hand replaced the retired Holt in 1914; Martin T. Manton came on when Hough became a circuit judge in 1916; and John C. Knox was named in 1918, when Manton moved up to the circuit court. In late 1922, Congress authorized two more seats, and Francis A. Winslow and Henry W. Goddard were sworn in at the beginning of 1923.)

169. Although the circuit court had original (trial) jurisdiction, not only appellate power, it sat solely as an appeals court for most of LH's years as a trial judge.

170. By the time Mayer himself resigned from the court to enter private practice in 1924, LH and Mayer had reasonably close relations. Indeed, Mayer supported LH as his successor, much as LH had supported Mayer in 1921, once he recognized that he himself had no chance for the vacancy.

171. The Second Circuit did not gain true distinction until Yale Law School dean Thomas W. Swan (in 1926) and Augustus N. Hand (in 1927) joined LH on it.

172. For the statistical data, see Hough, *The United States District Court*, 34: 1,346 bankruptcy cases; the remainder was comprised of 380 admiralty, 400 criminal, and 950 law and equity cases. (Figures are rounded.)

173. Ibid. The 1920 figures: 1,503 bankruptcy cases; 7,620 for the rest, including 1,904 admiralty cases (up from 380), 2,620 law and equity (up from 950), and 2,740 criminal (up from only 400).

174. Henry J. Friendly, "Learned Hand: An Expression from the Second Circuit," 29 *Brooklyn L.Rev.* 6, 13 (1962).

175. Published in 3 *Lectures on Legal Topics* (New York: Macmillan, 1926), 87, containing the lectures delivered in 1921–22. The series of *Lectures* ultimately ran to ten volumes. (Among the other lecturers in volume 3 are Benjamin N. Cardozo, Charles M. Hough, and Augustus N. Hand.)

176. E.g., Judge Julius M. Mayer's remarks on bankruptcy, in 1 *Lectures on Legal Topics* 283.
177. E.g., Judge Augustus N. Hand's remarks on constitutional law, in 3 *Lectures on Legal Topics* 343.
178. Id., 104.
179. Id., 105.
180. Ibid. (This passage has been widely quoted, typically without citing a source other than Jerome N. Frank's use of the sentence as the opening words of one of his classics in legal realism, *Courts on Trial* [Princeton: Princeton University Press, 1949].)
181. This and the following quotations from id., 90–91, 93–96, 98–99.
182. Id., 102–03. LH also commented on the unsatisfactory rules regarding expert testimony. He urged that judges use "disinterested" experts, rather than witnesses hired by each side; the latter left "difficult questions quite beyond [the jury's] possible comprehension" to "the conflicting opinions of partisans." This is a problem LH had written about while still an Albany lawyer, in his first law-journal publication. He confessed that the subject was his hobbyhorse ("He is really only a pony, not a full-grown hobbyhorse, but I love him very much; I mean the expert witness"). LH said in 1921, much as he had at the beginning of the century: "My thesis is that help should come to [the fact finders] from an assistant who can inform them and not from one who inevitably . . . must take on the attitude of a partisan, for partisan they surely become" (id., 103–04). (This kind of reform is still being proposed—and has not yet been achieved.)
183. Id., 104, 106.
184. 209 Fed. 119 (S.D.N.Y. 1913).
185. Hershel Shanks, ed., *The Art and Craft of Judging: The Decisions of Judge Learned Hand* (New York: Macmillan, 1968), 30.
186. LH's dissenting opinion in *Spector Motor Service, Inc., v. Walsh,* 139 F.2d 809, 823 (2d Cir. 1943), *vacated,* 323 U.S. 101 (1944).
187. The novel was written by Daniel Carson Goodman, a New York physician. The defendant, Mitchell Kennerley, published the book in 1913. For a modern biography of Kennerley, see Matthew J. Bruccoli, *The Fortunes of Mitchell Kennerley, Bookman* (San Diego: Harcourt Brace Jovanovich, 1986). Kennerley's trial in LH's court is discussed at pp. 68–74.
188. 1868 L.R. 3 Q.B. 360 (1868).
189. The jury acquitted Kennerley (Bruccoli, *Mitchell Kennerley,* 73).
190. 209 Fed. 120–21.
191. See *United States v. One Book Called "Ulysses,"* 73 F.2d 705 (2d Cir. 1934) (discussed below, pp. 333–40.).
192. *Butler v. Michigan,* 352 U.S. 380 (1957).
193. See *Roth v. United States,* 354 U.S. 476 (1957).
194. *Kennerley,* 209 Fed. 120–21.
195. E.g., *Roth,* above, and *Miller v. California,* 413 U.S. 15 (1973).
196. *United States v. Levine,* 83 F.2d 156, 157 (2d Cir. 1936) (discussed below, p. 340–2).
197. 244 Fed. 535 (S.D.N.Y. 1917), *reversed,* 246 Fed.2d 24 (2d Cir. 1917).
198. Act of 15 June 1917, ch. 30, 40 Stat. 217.
199. 246 Fed.2d 24 (2d Cir. 1917).
200. For my fuller analysis of the *Masses* case, its context, and its consequences, see

Gerald Gunther, "Learned Hand and the Origins of Modern First Amendment Doctrine: Some Fragments of History," 27 *Stan. L.Rev.* 719 (1975). (An appendix to that article prints the text of all letters relating to free-speech issues between LH and Justice Oliver Wendell Holmes, Jr., and between LH and Professor Zechariah Chafee, Jr., during the World War I era.)

201. For background on the magazine, see Leslie Fishbein, *Rebels in Bohemia—The Radicals of "The Masses," 1911–1917* (Chapel Hill: University of North Carolina Press, 1982), and Rebecca Zurier, *Art for "The Masses"—A Radical Magazine and Its Graphics, 1911–1917* (Philadelphia: Temple University Press, 1988).

202. *The Masses*, January 1913, 2, quoted in Fishbein, *Rebels in Bohemia*, 18.

203. Max Eastman, *Enjoyment of Living* (New York: Harper, 1948), 481–82.

204. Max Eastman to LH, 26 June 1916, 20–1.

205. LH to Max Eastman, 27 June 1916, 20–1.

206. LH to FAH, 16 July 1917, Personal Correspondence.

207. Hand printed the articles and the poem as addenda to his opinion, 244 Fed. 535, 543–45. For a description of the challenged cartoons, see 244 Fed. 535, 536–37.

208. Act of 15 June 1917, ch. 30, 40 Stat. 217, 219.

209. Act of 14 July 1798, ch. 74, 1 Stat. 596.

210. *New York Times Co. v. Sullivan*, 376 U.S. 254, 276 (1964).

211. See Walter Nelles, ed., *Espionage Act Cases* (New York: National Civil Liberties Bureau, 1918), passim.

212. LH to Zechariah Chafee, Jr., 3 December 1919, Chafee Papers, Harvard Law School, 4–20; id., 2 January 1921, 4–20.

213. Id., 8 January 1920, 4–20.

214. 244 Fed. 540.

215. Ibid.

216. LH to Zechariah Chafee, Jr., 2 January 1921, Chafee Papers, Harvard Law School, 4–20.

217. 244 Fed. 540.

218. Id., 542.

219. Id., 541–42.

220. LH to Zechariah Chafee, Jr., 2 January 1921, Chafee Papers, Harvard Law School, 4–20.

221. Van Vechten Veeder, "Charles Merrill Hough," 5 *Dictionary of American Biography* (New York: Charles Scribner's Sons, rev. ed. 1958), part 1, 249.

222. *Masses Publishing Co. v. Patten*, 246 Fed. 102, 106 (2d Cir. 1917).

223. Id., 24, 38.

224. LH to Charles C. Burlingham, 6 October 1917, 100–26.

225. LH to Walter Lippmann, 3 October 1917, Lippmann Papers, Yale University.

226. LH to Charles C. Burlingham, 6 October 1917, 100–26.

227. LH to Oliver Wendell Holmes, Jr., 22 June 1918, Holmes Papers, Harvard Law School, 43–30.

228. E.g., id., 3 March 1933, 43–30; id., 8 March 1921, 43–30.

229. Id., 22 June 1918, 43–30.

230. *Abrams v. United States*, 250 U.S. 616, 630 (1919) (dissenting opinion).

231. Oliver Wendell Holmes, Jr., to LH, 24 June 1918, 103–24; *Jacobson v. Massachusetts*, 197 U.S. 11 (1905).

232. For analyses of the differences between Holmes's "clear and present danger"

standard and LH's incitement test, see, in addition to Gerald Gunther, "Learned Hand and the Origins of Modern First Amendment Doctrine," and Gerald Gunther, *Constitutional Law*, 12th ed. (Westbury, N.Y.: Foundation Press, 1991), 1008–25, Yosal Rogat, "The Judge as Spectator," 31 *U.Chi. L.Rev.* 213 (1964); James M. O'Fallon and Yosal Rogat, "Mr. Justice Holmes: A Dissenting Opinion," 36 *Stan. L.Rev.* 1349 (1984); Fred D. Ragan, "Justice Oliver Wendell Holmes, Jr., Zechariah Chafee, Jr., and the Clear and Present Danger Test for Free Speech: The First Year, 1919," 58 *J. Am. Hist.* 24 (1971); Harry Kalven, "Professor Ernst Freund and Debs v. United States," 40 *U.Chi. L.Rev.* 235 (1973); Douglas H. Ginsburg, afterword to "Ernst Freund and the First Amendment Tradition," 40 *U.Chi. L.Rev.* 243; David M. Rabban, "The Emergence of Modern First Amendment Doctrine," 50 *U.Chi. L.Rev.* 1205 (1983); Liva Baker, *The Justice from Beacon Hill: The Life and Times of Oliver Wendell Holmes* (New York: HarperCollins, 1991), chapters 24 and 25; and G. Edward White, "Justice Holmes and the Modernization of Free Speech Jurisprudence: The Human Dimension," 80 *Calif. L.Rev.* 391 (1992).

233. 249 U.S. 47 (1919).

234. 249 U.S. 204 (1919); 249 U.S. 211 (1919).

235. Oliver Wendell Holmes, Jr., to LH, 25 February 1919, 103–24.

236. Id., 3 April 1919, 103–24.

237. LH to Professor Ernst Freund, 7 May 1919, 21–1.

238. 249 U.S. 47, 52 (1919).

239. Kalven, "Professor Ernst Freund and Debs v. United States," 40 *U.Chi. L.Rev.* 235, 237–38.

240. Zechariah Chafee, Jr., *Free Speech in the United States* (Cambridge: Harvard University Press, 1941), 86.

241. LH to Oliver Wendell Holmes, Jr., [late March, 1919], Holmes Papers, Harvard Law School, 43–30.

242. Oliver Wendell Holmes, Jr., to LH, 3 April 1919, 103–24.

243. 250 U.S. 616, 624 (1919) (dissenting opinion).

244. See Richard Polenberg, *Fighting Faiths: The Abrams Case, the Supreme Court, and Free Speech* (New York: Viking, 1987).

245. 250 U.S. 616, 628–30.

246. LH to Oliver Wendell Holmes, Jr., 25 November 1919, Holmes Papers, Harvard Law School, 43–30.

247. Oliver Wendell Holmes, Jr., to LH, 26 November 1919, 103–24.

248. Zechariah Chafee, Jr., to LH, 25 October 1920, 15–26.

249. See id., 28 March 1921, 15–26.

250. Zechariah Chafee, Jr., *Freedom of Speech* (Cambridge: Harvard University Press, 1920), iii.

251. LH to Zechariah Chafee, Jr., 2 January 1921 (LH draft), 15–26.

252. Id., 2 December 1919, Chafee Papers, Harvard Law School, 4–20.

253. Id., 8 January 1920, 4–20.

254. Id., 2 January 1921 (LH draft), 15–26.

255. Ibid.

256. LH to Walter Nelles, 20 April 1923, 33–6.

257. Chafee, *Free Speech in the United States*, v. President Lowell had protected Chafee against alumni attacks on some of his libertarian writings in 1919, especially his criticisms of the *Abrams* prosecutions. See Arthur E. Sutherland, Jr.,

The Law at Harvard (Cambridge: Belknap Press of Harvard University Press, 1967), 250–59.
258. 341 U.S. 495 (1951).

IV
The Marriage and Its Tensions

1. LH to William C. LeGendre, 27 September 1905, 2–10. (LeGendre was the seller; transactions completed in 1906.)
2. See Gunther Interview with Frances Arnold, Cornish, New Hampshire, 1973.
3. Gunther Interview with Frances Holter Vicario, New York City, 1982.
4. LH to FAH, 26 February 1938; see also id., 6 March 1944, Personal Correspondence.
5. See Arthur Dehon Hill to LH, 24 May 1905, 5–4; Benjamin L. Knower to LH, 25 April 1905, 6–3; Alice Lee to LH, 23 November 1905, 6–5; Edward M. McKinney to LH, [summer 1905], 6–24.
6. John L. Wilkie to LH, 7 May 1905, 11–15.
7. LH to FAH, 6 March 1944, Personal Correspondence.
8. Dr. Henry Hun to LH, 3 April 1904; see also id., 16 June 1904 (both in 115–1).
9. LH to FAH, 2 July 1905, Personal Correspondence (recounting the advice of Boston lawyer Harold J. Coolidge).
10. Dr. Henry Hun to LH, 5 November 1905, 115–1.
11. Id., 25 September 1906, 115–1.
12. Id., 2 October 1906, 115–1.
13. Id., 15 April 1907 (congratulatory note), 115–2.
14. Id., 31 December 1907, 115–2.
15. Ibid. See also id., 29 January 1908, 115–2.
16. Id., 27 January 1910, 115–2.
17. See LH to FAH, 7 April 1906, 23 May 1906, 6 June 1911, 13 June 1911, Personal Correspondence.
18. E.g., id., 23 May 1906, Personal Correspondence.
19. E.g., id., 1 December 1905, 9 March 1906, Personal Correspondence.
20. Dr. Henry Hun to LH, 27 January 1910, 115–2; see also id., 31 December 1907, 115–2.
21. LH to FAH, 9 March 1906, Personal Correspondence.
22. Id., 7 April 1906, Personal Correspondence.
23. Id., 10 June 1923, Personal Correspondence.
24. E.g., FAH to Mildred Minturn, 21 December [1904]; 7 March [1904]; 30 March 1904, Minturn Papers, England.
25. Id., 7 March [1904], Minturn Papers, England.
26. Id., 31 July [1903], Minturn Papers, England.
27. Id., 7 January 1906, Minturn Papers, England.
28. Id., Christmas [1905], Minturn Papers, England.
29. Id., "Sunday," 6 October [1904], Minturn Papers, England.
30. Id., 7 March [1904]; see also id., Christmas [1905], Minturn Papers, England.
31. Id., 15 March [1904], Minturn Papers, England.
32. Ibid.
33. See, e.g., LH to FAH, 25 June 1918, Personal Correspondence.
34. Mildred Minturn Diary, 73–74, Minturn Papers, England.

35. FAH to Mildred Minturn, 15 March [1904]; 30 March 1904; 31 May 1904; 6 October [1904]; 20 March [1905]; 13 August [1905], Minturn Papers, England.
36. Id., 15 March [1904]; 13 August [1905]; 20 March [1906]; [1903], Minturn Papers, England.
37. Id., 29 August [1905], Minturn Papers, England.
38. Mildred Minturn Diary, 82, Minturn Papers, England.
39. See, e.g., FAH to Mildred Minturn, [February or March 1906], Minturn Papers, England.
40. Id., 7 April 1906; see also id., 12 August [1906], and id., [February or March, 1906], Minturn Papers, England.
41. In fact, Scott was only two years younger than Mildred (Mildred Minturn Diary, 83, Minturn Papers, England).
42. See id., 80–120. I do not have Mildred's letters to FAH about this, but Frances's responses make it clear that she was kept informed about Mildred's fluctuating emotions.
43. FAH to Mildred Minturn, 12 August [1906], id., 2 September [1906], Minturn Papers, England. (FAH repeatedly wrote "W. Scot" instead of "A. Scott"—the same spelling she used for the British novelist Sir Walter Scott.)
44. Mildred Minturn to FAH (from The Hermitage, Effingham), Friday, [2 or 3] August 1906, Minturn Papers, England (letter apparently returned by Frances to Mildred).
45. Mildred Minturn to FAH, 4 September 1906, Minturn Papers, England (letter apparently returned by Frances to Mildred).
46. FAH had written Mildred Minturn, 12 August [1906]: "I must tell you here dear O.S. that I am pretty sure I am going to have another soft one. I am about 10 days overdue which is pretty certain for me. Of course I am delighted for it means that Mary will have a companion two years younger." Mary had been weaned only a few months earlier. See FAH to Mildred Minturn, 21 January [1906], Minturn Papers, England. (The Hands' second daughter, Frances, was born in 1907.)
47. Id., 18 September [1906], Minturn Papers, England.
48. Mildred Minturn Diary, 119, Minturn Papers, England.
49. FAH to Mildred Minturn, 25 September [1906], Minturn Papers, England.
50. Id., 15 June 1908, Minturn Papers, England.
51. Id., "Sunday evening," [February or March 1906], see also id., Christmas [1905], Minturn Papers, England.
52. Id., 30 March 1904, Minturn Papers, England.
53. See id., 12 August [1906]; 21 January [1905]; [February or March 1906], Minturn Papers, England.
54. LH to FAH, 27 June 1919, Personal Correspondence.
55. On Louis Dow, see, in addition to his letters and my interviews, Prescott Orde Skinner, "Louis Henry Dow: A Tribute to the Late Tuck Professor of French," *Dartmouth Alumni Magazine* (April 1944), 19.
56. The first letter is Louis Dow to LH, 12 October 1909, 100–29. (That Dow letter closed with "I never said goodbye to Madame, but I like her immensely." Throughout the occasionally difficult years that ensued, LH and Dow sustained a frequent correspondence, in the files beginning with 102–29.)
57. Mrs. Dow was initially hospitalized in Brookline, Massachusetts. See, e.g., Louis Dow to LH, 28 October 1913, 102–29, reporting the latest news about

his wife, Rebecca, as being "rather discouraging." He referred to her "apathy and rebelliousness" and reported that she was "weaker and harder to manage." (Dow rarely mentioned her in later years, did not seem especially perturbed about her, and did not visit her often—in part because, at least at the outset, the doctors urged him to stay away.)

58. Louis Dow to LH, 18 October 1913, 102–29. (Among their other common traits, Dow and FAH apparently shared a degree of anti-Semitism. In that letter, for example, Dow spoke of George Rublee's spending some time with Louis D. Brandeis, "which is no relaxation, for the atmosphere is surcharged with seriousness unrelieved by humor, and there is a sickening sense of Jewdom about the Brandeis household.")

59. Dow had one child of his own to take care of at his home.

60. Louis Dow to LH, 16 November 1914, 102–31.

61. See, e.g., the first letter during their marriage in the Personal Correspondence, FAH to LH, [January] 1908: "I shall be perfectly *overjoyed* to get back. . . . I shall be very thrilled to have your dear arms around me to-morrow. . . . All my love dear." See also another letter of [January] 1908, FAH to LH, "I always feel a thrill of love when I get your letters. . . ."

62. Id., [January] 1908, Personal Correspondence.

63. LH to FAH, 13 June 1911, Personal Correspondence.

64. E.g., FAH to LH, [1919] and [June] 1920, Personal Correspondence.

65. LH to FAH, 12 June 1918, Personal Correspondence.

66. Id., 16 June 1918, Personal Correspondence.

67. See, in addition to Louis Dow–LH correspondence in box 102, Louis Dow to Mary Hand, 16 July [1920]: "Daddy is right and you can trust him." Mary Hand Darrell–Louis Dow Personal Correspondence.

68. Thus Louis Dow told LH repeatedly on the 1930 trip to Europe and the Near East that "[w]e think and talk of you constantly." See, e.g., Louis Dow to LH, 2 February 1930, and id., 21 February 1930, both in 103–5. The Louis Dow–FAH trip in the winter of 1929–30 came at an especially difficult time for LH, because he spent some anxious weeks wondering about his prospects for an appointment to the Supreme Court. After these hopes were dashed, Dow, with characteristic sensitivity, wrote LH, "It seems as if all the eventful things in your otherwise quiet life were destined to be crowded into the one month that Frances was away from you" (Louis Dow to LH, 23 March 1930, 103–5).

69. See, e.g., id., 2 March 1935, 103–7: "It's very good of you to urge [Frances] to extend her visit with me. . . . Her life-giving presence has done more than anything else to pull me out of this hole"; see also id., 6 May 1935, 103–7: "I can never thank you enough . . . for [Frances's] coming up to be with me these last few days."

70. FAH to LH, June 1919; id., 5 June 1919, Personal Correspondence.

71. Id., 11 June 1924, Personal Correspondence.

72. Id., 18 June 1919, Personal Correspondence. (Her letters several times mentioned her joy in taking off her clothes to walk or swim.)

73. Id., 12 June 1924, Personal Correspondence.

74. E.g., id., 24 July 1924, Personal Correspondence.

75. Id., 15 July 1920, Personal Correspondence.

76. LH to FAH, 20 July 1918, Personal Correspondence.

77. Id., 16 July 1918, Personal Correspondence.

78. FAH to LH, 6 June 1919, Personal Correspondence.
79. Id., 7 October 1919, Personal Correspondence.
80. Id., [1918], Personal Correspondence.
81. E.g., id., 12 January 1918, Personal Correspondence: "We read aloud & Lou reads to me, and it is really just as nice as it can be."
82. See Gunther Interview with Frances Arnold, Cornish, 1973.
83. Thus, Walter Lippmann, nearly eighteen years younger than LH, was convinced until his death that Louis Dow and FAH were lovers. This is related in Ronald Steel's biography of Lippmann; the source was Lippmann's last lawyer, Louis Auchincloss. (See, e.g., Lippmann's comment about LH, at the time Lippmann was failing and near death: "The first task of that man's biographer will be to enquire why he remained for so long on such good terms with his wife's lover." Lippmann never forgave the Hands for allegedly turning their backs upon him during the scandal attending Lippmann's divorce during the 1930s. See Ronald Steel, *Walter Lippmann and the American Century* [Boston: Little, Brown, 1980], 597.) Moreover, Judge Charles Wyzanski insisted to me that they were lovers (see Gunther Interview with Charles E. Wyzanski, Jr., Cambridge, 1973). It is striking, however, that this was the view of people in the generation *after* the Hands, a view not shared by the Hands' contemporaries. Thus, Archibald Cox's mother, who lived for many years across the Connecticut River from Cornish, was quite firm in denying that there could have been a physical relationship (see Gunther Interview with Mrs. Archibald Cox, Sr., Windsor, Vermont, 1973). She, like Frances Arnold, emphasized the morality and even prudery of FAH, though she was also convinced (and Frances Arnold so suggested) that Louis Dow may well have been in love with FAH. Mrs. Cox felt that FAH was such a cold human being that she could not have been emotionally involved with anyone.
84. LH to FAH, 25 June 1918, Personal Correspondence.
85. Id., 13 June 1919, Personal Correspondence.
86. Id., 18 July 1918, Personal Correspondence.
87. Id., 2 September 1919, Personal Correspondence.
88. Id., 10 June 1923. In that letter, LH also told FAH that without her he would have long been "melancholic, a failure, as they say, . . . single and hopelessly hypochondriac." He also wrote, "At times I feel that we have not as much in common as we might have, I mean our tastes. You would have had more company and society from another sort of man. Whether I should have had from another sort of woman I doubt; I was more or less destined to be driven about by internal compulsions which spoil me for a steady companion. But . . . we have learned so well now to accommodate ourselves to each other. . . ."

V

The Peak of Political Enthusiasm: Herbert Croly, Theodore Roosevelt, and the Progressive Years

1. LH to Herbert Croly, 5 November 1909, 102–17.
2. Harlan B. Phillips, ed., *Felix Frankfurter Reminisces* (New York: Reynal & Co., 1960), 88.
3. Charles Forcey, *The Crossroads of Liberalism: Croly, Weyl, Lippmann, and the*

Progressive Era 1900–1925 (New York: Oxford University Press, 1961), 11–17.

4. LH to Herbert Croly, 5 November 1909, 102–17.
5. Id., 6 February 1911, 102–18.
6. Id., 3 December 1909, 102–17.
7. Herbert Croly, *The Promise of American Life* (1909), ed. Arthur M. Schlesinger, Jr. (Cambridge: Harvard University Press, 1965), 135–37.
8. Id., 133–34.
9. LH to Herbert Croly, 5 November 1909, 102–17.
10. Id., 3 December 1909, 102–17.
11. Herbert Croly to LH, [early December 1909], 102–17.
12. LH to Herbert Croly, 6 February 1911, 102–18.
13. LH to Dean Byron S. Hurlbut, 29 March 1910, 24–16.
14. Dean Byron S. Hurlbut to LH, 28 May 1910, 24–16 (including the text of a letter to the dean from George Haskins). See also, on the negotiation with Harvard, LH to Herbert Croly, 8 April 1910, 102–17; LH to Dean Byron S. Hurlbut, 31 May 1910, 24–16; and Herbert Croly to LH, [June] 1910, 102–17.
15. See David W. Levy, *Herbert Croly of "The New Republic": The Life and Thought of an American Progressive* (Princeton: Princeton University Press, 1985), 132–35.
16. Felix Frankfurter, "Croly and Opinion," *New Republic* (memorial issue on Croly's death), 16 July 1930, 247, 249. See also Phillips, *Felix Frankfurter Reminisces*, 88.
17. Walter Lippmann, "Notes for a Biography," *New Republic*, 16 July 1930, 250.
18. Croly, *Promise of American Life*, 167–75. (The two sections were entitled, revealingly, "Theodore Roosevelt as a Reformer" and "The Reformation of Theodore Roosevelt"—the first fairly descriptive; the second, an idealized gloss.)
19. Id., 167, 175.
20. Id., 168–73.
21. Id., 175.
22. Id., 454.
23. LH to William B. Wheelock, 19 January 1910, 37–21.
24. William B. Wheelock to LH, 20 January 1910, 37–21.
25. LH to Theodore Roosevelt, 8 April 1910, 37–21.
26. Theodore Roosevelt to LH, 22 April and 30 April 1910, 37–21.
27. Herbert Croly to LH, 6 May 1910, 102–17. (See also LH's reply, 7 May 1910, and Herbert Croly to LH, 11 May 1910, 102–17.)
28. Theodore Roosevelt to Herbert Croly, transcribed in Herbert Croly to LH, 1 August 1910, 102–18.
29. Levy, *Herbert Croly*, 137.
30. Herbert Croly to LH, 1 August 1910, 102–18.
31. Levy, *Herbert Croly*, 138–39.
32. "The New Nationalism" in 19 *The Works of Theodore Roosevelt* (memorial edition), ed. Herman Hagedorn (New York: Charles Scribner's Sons, 1925) [hereinafter *Works*], 10–30.
33. George Mowry, *Theodore Roosevelt and the Progressive Movement* (Madison: University of Wisconsin Press, 1946), 144.
34. Croly, *Promise of American Life*, 169.

35. 19 *Works*, 18, 24, 27, 30.
36. Henry Cabot Lodge to Theodore Roosevelt, 5 September 1910, Roosevelt Papers, Library of Congress (microfilm), reel 93, 5 September 1910, quoted in Mowry, *Theodore Roosevelt*, 144.
37. Levy, *Herbert Croly*, 141, citing 84 *American Magazine* 23 (November 1912).
38. Theodore Roosevelt, "Nationalism and Popular Rule," *Outlook* 98 (21 January 1911), reprinted in 19 *Works*, 86.
39. E.g., Mowry, *Theodore Roosevelt*, 146.
40. Levy, *Herbert Croly*, 139–40.
41. LH to Herbert Croly, 6 February 1911, 102–18.
42. See, generally, Mowry, *Theodore Roosevelt*, 134–56.
43. LH to Herbert Croly, 6 February 1911, 102–18.
44. Henry L. Stimson to LH, 7 October 1910, 39–18.
45. LH to Herbert Croly, 29 October 1910, 102–18; Herbert Croly to LH, 4 November 1910, 102–18.
46. LH to Herbert Croly, 29 October 1910, 102–18.
47. Ibid.
48. Id., 7 November 1910, 102–18.
49. Id., 22 July 1910, 102–18.
50. See LH's recounting of his exchange with Oswald Garrison Villard (LH's college classmate and at the time the owner of the *New York Evening Post*), in LH to Herbert Croly, 6 February 1911, 102–18.
51. Ibid.
52. Ibid.
53. Ibid.
54. Herbert Croly to LH, 24 February 1911, 102–18. (For a summary of the politics of the tariff battle, see Mowry, *Theodore Roosevelt*, 158–68.)
55. See Mowry, *Theodore Roosevelt*, 172–74. (Norman Hapgood was the only one in LH's circle who joined: he switched to Wilson during the 1912 campaign.)
56. Id., 188. (See, generally, id., 183–95.)
57. *Outlook* 99 (18 November 1911), 654–55.
58. LH's commentary appears (with Roosevelt's commentary) in Theodore Roosevelt, "The Tobacco Trust and the Court," *Outlook* 99 (25 November 1911), 711.
59. LH to Theodore Roosevelt, 15 November 1911, Roosevelt Papers, Library of Congress (microfilm), reel 117.
60. Theodore Roosevelt, "The Trusts, the People, and the Square Deal," *Outlook* 99 (18 November 1911), 652.
61. See *Outlook* 99 (25 November, 1911), 711.
62. "The Trusts, The Press, and Mr. Roosevelt" (unsigned editorial), *Outlook* 99 (25 November 1911), 702–3.
63. LH to Theodore Roosevelt, 8 May 1911, Roosevelt Papers, Library of Congress (microfilm), reel 106.
64. 201 N.Y. 271; 94 N.E. 431 (1911).
65. LH's friend Joseph P. Cotton, the progressive Wall Street lawyer, had been counsel to the Wainwright Commission and unsuccessfully defended the law in the New York courts. In preparing the commission's report, Cotton had understandably included a section defending the law's constitutionality, relying on frequent discussions with LH. Cotton's only doubt had been "whether the courts had been educated" sufficiently to understand that the law was valid in

principle; neither LH nor Cotton had any "genuine doubt" about its constitutionality. LH to Van Vechten Veeder, 11 December 1913, 44–6.

66. See 201 N.Y. 284–87; 94 N.E. 436–37.
67. 219 U.S. 104, 110, 111 (1911).
68. Herbert Croly to LH, 5 March 1911, 102–18.
69. LH to Van Vechten Veeder, 11 December 1913, 44–6.
70. LH to Theodore Roosevelt, 8 May 1911, Roosevelt Papers, Library of Congress (microfilm), reel 106.
71. Theodore Roosevelt, "Workmen's Compensation," *Outlook* 98 (13 May 1911), 49.
72. Id., 53.
73. See Mowry, *Theodore Roosevelt*, 171, citing *New York Times*, 16 August 1911. See also the useful Ph.D. dissertation, J. Patrick White, "Progressivism and the Judiciary: A Study of the Movement for Judicial Reform, 1901–1917" (University of Michigan, 1971). (White mistakenly claims, however, that TR never suggested the recall of judges.)
74. Roosevelt, "Workmen's Compensation," *Outlook* 99, 53.
75. Theodore Roosevelt letters to Cecil Arthur Spring Rice and to Arthur Hamilton Lee, 22 August 1911, 7 *The Letters of Theodore Roosevelt*, ed. Elting E. Morison (Cambridge: Harvard University Press, 1954), 332–35, 337–39. See White, "Progressivism and the Judiciary," 360–61.
76. Roosevelt's speech of 20 October was not published in *The Outlook* until late December (*Outlook* 99 [23 December 1911]). The full text (including the passages on the courts, omitted in *The Outlook*) is in 18 *Works*, 244, 270, 274.
77. Brooks Adams to Theodore Roosevelt, 29 February 1912, Roosevelt Papers, Library of Congress (microfilm), reel 131; see White, "Progressivism and the Judiciary," 364.
78. LH to Theodore Roosevelt, 20 November 1911, Roosevelt Papers, Library of Congress (microfilm), reel 117.
79. Theodore Roosevelt to LH, 22 November 1911, original in 37–21; retained copy in Roosevelt Papers, Library of Congress (microfilm), reel 370.
80. LH to Herbert Croly, 24 November 1911, 102–19. See also Croly's reply, [late November 1911], 102–19.
81. Theodore Roosevelt to LH, 28 November 1911, original in Hand Papers, 37–21; retained copy in Roosevelt Papers, Library of Congress (microfilm), reel 370.
82. *Mutual Loan Co. v. Martell*, 222 U.S. 225 (1911).
83. LH to Theodore Roosevelt, 15 December 1911, Roosevelt Papers, Library of Congress (microfilm), reel 120.
84. Theodore Roosevelt to LH, 19 December 1911, original in Hand Papers, 37–21; retained copy in Roosevelt Papers, Library of Congress (microfilm), reel 371.
85. *Outlook* 100 (6 January 1912), 40–48.
86. Id., 48.
87. LH to Herbert Croly, 24 January 1912, 102–19.
88. LH to Whitridge, 21 February 1912, 37–21.
89. Theodore Roosevelt's letter to a group of Republican governors, 24 February 1912, 19 *Works* (item 16), 198–99.
90. Theodore Roosevelt's Columbus, Ohio, speech, "A Charter for Democracy," 21 February 1912, 19 *Works* (item 15), 163, 178–97.

91. Mowry, *Theodore Roosevelt*, 218.
92. See George Rublee to Theodore Roosevelt, 1 March 1912, Roosevelt Papers, Library of Congress (microfilm), reel 131.
93. LH to Theodore Roosevelt, 27 February 1912, Roosevelt Papers, Library of Congress (microfilm), reel 131.
94. See Herbert Croly to Theodore Roosevelt, 28 February 1912, Roosevelt Papers, Library of Congress (microfilm), reel 131.
95. Felix Frankfurter to LH, [February 1911], 104–1. (Frankfurter was then still in the U.S. attorney's office.)
96. LH to Felix Frankfurter, 26 February 1911, Frankfurter Papers (copy in Hand Papers, 104–1).
97. Felix Frankfurter to LH, 2 March 1911, 104–1. (Soon after, LH had Felix Frankfurter as a dinner guest, to meet Herbert Croly. See Frankfurter's thank-you note to LH, 11 April 1911, 104–1.)
98. LH to Felix Frankfurter, 9 March 1912, retained copy in Hand Papers, 104–1.
99. Ibid.
100. Felix Frankfurter to LH, 12 March 1912, 104–1.
101. LH to Theodore Roosevelt, 15 March 1912, retained copy in Hand Papers, 37–21 (original in Roosevelt Papers, Library of Congress [microfilm], reel 134). The speech LH wrote and enclosed for Roosevelt is only in the Hand Papers, 37–21, in draft form [marked "Sent to TR March 15, 1912"]; it is not in the Roosevelt Papers in the Library of Congress.
102. Theodore Roosevelt to LH, 18 March 1912, 37–21 (addressed to "Dear Hand").
103. The Carnegie Hall speech is reprinted in 19 *Works* (item 17), 200–205. On the setting of the speech, see "Roosevelt Hits at Taft Again," *New York Times*, 21 March 1912, 1.
104. LH to Felix Frankfurter, 4 April 1912, retained copy in Hand Papers, 104–1 (with a slightly revised original in Frankfurter Papers, photocopy in 104–1).
105. LH to Felix Frankfurter, 11 April 1912, 104–1 (retained copy).
106. Felix Frankfurter to LH, 12 March 1912, 104–1.
107. Mowry, *Theodore Roosevelt*, 231–35.
108. LH to Norman Hapgood ("My dear Norman"), 23 May 1912, Roosevelt Papers, Library of Congress (microfilm), reel 142 (forwarded by Hapgood to Roosevelt).
109. LH to George Rublee, 23 May 1912, 107–2.
110. George Rublee to Theodore Roosevelt, 1 May 1912, Roosevelt Papers, Library of Congress (microfilm), reel 138.
111. See LH to George Rublee, 14 June 1912, 107–2 (addressed to "Roosevelt Headquarters").
112. Ibid. See also LH to Theodore Roosevelt, 13 June 1912, 37–2; LH to Herbert Croly, 14 June 1912, 102–19.
113. Mowry, *Theodore Roosevelt*, 252.
114. LH to Herbert Croly, 14 June 1912, 102–19.
115. Norman Hapgood to LH, 24 June 1912, 23–5.
116. However, calls for workmen's-compensation laws and unionization, included in the draft documents, were eliminated at the convention.
117. From the 1912 Progressive party platform, in Theodore Roosevelt, *Progressive*

Principles, ed. Elmer H. Youngman (New York: Progressive National Service, 1913), 316. (The platform runs to sixteen pages of small print.)

118. Herbert Croly to LH, 13 July 1912, 102–20.

119. Ibid.

120. Felix Frankfurter to LH, 26 August 1912, 104–1.

121. LH to Philip Littell, 15 July 1912, 106–19.

122. LH to Felix Frankfurter, 25 July 1912, 104–1 (photocopy from Frankfurter Papers, Library of Congress).

123. LH to Theodore Roosevelt, 11 August 1912, 37–21.

124. On the sociology of Progressivism, see, e.g., Christopher Lasch, *The New Radicalism in America (1889–1963): The Intellectual as a Social Type* (New York: Alfred A. Knopf, 1966), ix–xi, 168–69; and Richard Hofstadter, *The Age of Reform: From Bryan to FDR* (New York: Alfred A. Knopf, 1955), 148–63.

125. LH to Felix Frankfurter, 12 September 1912, 104–1 (photocopy from Frankfurter Papers, Library of Congress).

126. E.g., E. Hooker to LH, 11 October 1912, 35–15, thanking LH for a $200 contribution to the party. (LH enrolled in the party as a "Founder." See "Founder's Certificate," 35–15.)

127. Walter E. Weyl to LH, 25 September 1912, 35–15. (Two years later, Weyl joined Croly in founding *The New Republic*.)

128. LH to Walter E. Weyl, 2 October 1912, 35–15.

129. See Mowry, *Theodore Roosevelt*, 277–78. The speech is in "Roosevelt Stills Garden Tumult," *New York Times*, 31 October 1912, 1, 2.

130. LH to Mrs. Douglas Robinson (handwritten draft, carefully revised), 1 November 1912, 37–10.

131. "Battles Just Begun, Says Col. Roosevelt," *New York Times*, 12 November 1912, 1. See John Allen Gable, *The Bull Moose Years: Theodore Roosevelt and the Progressive Party* (Port Washington, N.Y.: Kennikat Press, 1978), 150 (quoting TR's statement reported in *New York Times*, 12 November 1912).

132. See Gable, *The Bull Moose Years*, 164 (noting annual pledges of $50 each from Hand as well as his Cornish friend the novelist Winston Churchill).

133. William L. Ransom to LH, 9 January 1913, 36–5 (referring to LH's unpreserved letter to Ransom, 17 December 1912).

134. LH to William L. Ransom, 3 February 1913, 36–5.

135. Id., 13 January 1913, 36–5.

136. T. Douglas Robinson to LH, 23 September 1913, 37–11.

137. LH to T. Douglas Robinson, 25 September 1913, 37–11 (LH's much revised draft response).

138. "Hand for Chief Judge Named by Progressives," *New York Times*, 10 September 1913, 6.

139. LH to T. Douglas Robinson, 25 September 1913, 37–11.

140. *New York Tribune*, 28 September 1913, 3.

141. LH to T. Douglas Robinson, 30 September 1913, 37–11.

142. T. Douglas Robinson to LH, 1 October 1913, 37–11.

143. E.g., LH to E. B. Styles (Saugerties, N.Y.), [October 1913], 41–1.

144. See LH to Herbert Mitgang, 18 May 1960, 93–2. In later years, LH also commented to Seabury's biographer that "perhaps [Seabury] was right." Herbert Mitgang, *The Man Who Rode the Tiger—The Life and Times of Samuel Seabury* (New York: J. B. Lippincott, 1963), 106–07.

145. E.g., "The Court of Appeals Judges," *New York Times*, 7 October 1913, 12; see also *New York Times*, 10 October 1913, 20.

146. Clipping from *New York Sun* [n.d.], in 41–5.

147. This was the adjective used by the November 1913 *Progressive Bulletin*; see Gable, *The Bull Moose Years*, 179.

148. By contrast, only four Progressives had been elected to the assembly in the 1912 election.

149. LH to Felix Frankfurter, 11 November 1913, 104–2.

150. Felix Frankfurter to LH, 3 October 1913, 104–2.

151. LH to Gilbert E. Roe, 7 November 1913, 37–13. (Four years later, Roe was the successful advocate in LH's court in the *Masses* case.)

152. LH to Charles Forcey, 6 July 1957, 88–9.

153. See William Joseph Cibes, "Extra-Judicial Activities of Justices of the United States Supreme Court" (Ph.D. dissertation, Princeton University, 1975), 1,449, concluding that more than half of the justices engaged in significant nonjudicial activities. See also Bruce Allen Murphy, *The Brandeis/Frankfurter Connection—Secret Political Activities of Two Supreme Court Justices* (New York: Oxford University Press, 1982), 345–63.

154. See, e.g., American Bar Association, *Model Code of Judicial Conduct* (1990), 34.

155. LH to Robert M. La Follette and George Huddleston, 24 November 1922, 28–25 (LH declining invitation to Washington conference of People's Legislative Service, an organization of progressives in Congress; predecessor to the [new] Progressive party's La Follette campaign for the presidency in 1924). Before the quoted passage, LH wrote, "I think it is undesirable for a judge to take an active part on political movements or agitation. . . . Of course, everybody knows that a judge, like anyone else, must in fact have his trends or convictions, and that cannot be helped. But active affiliation with political movements gives a good deal more excuse for imputing to him feelings, however disinterested, which would be likely to disturb his impartial judgment." However, after the passage quoted in text, LH added, "I trust you will not take this as indicating a lack of interest on my part in what may be done [at the conference]. It is quite clear at the present time that unless the country can find intelligent leadership somewhere, public feeling may run to deplorable extremes."

156. "Heated subjects" was LH's paraphrase of Holmes's advice. Holmes's term was "burning themes." See Oliver Wendell Holmes, Jr., to LH, 27 June 1923, 103–24: "I generally have felt that it was a mistake for judges to meddle with burning themes. . . ." (in response to LH's request for advice, LH to Oliver Wendell Holmes, Jr., 24 January 1923, 103–24 [copy from Holmes Papers, Harvard Law School]).

157. LH to Capt. Manard E. Pont, 18 November 1957, 94–12.

158. Herbert Croly to LH, [13 October 1913], 102–21.

159. LH to Herbert Croly, 14 October 1913, 102–21.

160. Ibid.

161. Felix Frankfurter to LH, 6 November 1913, 104–2.

162. LH to L. E. Opdycke, 18 April 1914, 34–15.

163. LH to George Rublee, 25 June 1914, 107–2.

164. See, e.g., FAH's friendship with Theodore Roosevelt, developed during an ocean voyage to Europe in 1914 (see LH to George Rublee, 25 June 1914, 107–2) and resulting in invitations for weekend visits by the Hands to Oyster

Bay (see Theodore Roosevelt to LH, 17 November 1914, 37–21, and LH to Theodore Roosevelt, 20 November 1914, Roosevelt Papers, Library of Congress [microfilm], reel 194).

165. LH to Theodore Roosevelt, 9 July 1914, Roosevelt Papers, Library of Congress (microfilm), reel 187.

166. Theodore Roosevelt to LH, 24 July 1914, retained copy in Roosevelt Papers, Library of Congress (microfilm), reel 384 (not in Hand Papers).

167. LH to Theodore Roosevelt, 13 June 1916, Roosevelt Papers, Library of Congress (microfilm), reel 211.

168. Theodore Roosevelt to LH, 16 June 1916, 37–21.

169. LH to Walter Lippmann, 10 June 1914, H–1, Lippmann Papers, Yale University.

170. LH became a stockholder in the *Boston Journal* in early 1914, pledged $1,000 (a remarkably large sum for him), made contributions through 1915, and did not turn in his stock until the fall of 1917. See LH correspondence with Charles E. Ware, 1914–17, in 44–25.

171. LH to Felix Frankfurter, 31 July 1914, 104–13.

172. See Herbert Croly to LH, three undated letters [before 1 August 1913], 102–21; see also Herbert Croly to LH, 22 October 1926, accompanying Croly's payment of final installment of the loan from LH.

173. Alvin S. Johnson, *Pioneer's Progress: An Autobiography* (New York: Viking, 1952), 233. See also Levy, *Herbert Croly*, 188–89.

174. See Levy, *Herbert Croly*, 206–7, and Forcey, *Crossroads of Liberalism*, 173–77.

175. Forcey, *Crossroads of Liberalism*, 184.

176. Phillips, *Felix Frankfurter Reminisces*, 91. (On the founding circle, see Forcey, *Crossroads of Liberalism*, 178–83, and Levy, *Herbert Croly*, 209–14.)

177. Theodore Roosevelt to Rómulo Sebastian Naon, 6 January 1915, in 8 *The Letters of Theodore Roosevelt*, 872.

178. Herbert Croly to LH, 5 January 1914, 102–22.

179. See Ronald Steel, *Walter Lippmann and the American Century* (Boston: Little, Brown, 1980), 55; see also Levy, *Herbert Croly*, 196.

180. When Lippmann told LH in the spring of 1917 about his engagement to marry, LH could not help remarking on the striking novelty of his young intellectual friend's rare display of human emotion. He confessed he had suspected Lippmann might be in love when he had seen him walking on Fifth Avenue months earlier arm in arm with a woman: "I said, *Tiens, Tiens*, so Walter, he is like the rest of us after all" (LH to Walter Lippmann, 3 May 1917, Lippmann Papers, Yale University, L–3).

181. See Forcey Interview with LH, 5 April 1956, 88–9.

182. Phillips, *Felix Frankfurter Reminisces*, 91.

183. Id., 92.

184. See Herbert Croly to LH, 8 January 1914, 102–22.

185. Levy, *Herbert Croly*, 213. Croly, unlike LH, bitterly opposed Frankfurter's decision to go to Harvard Law School rather than to *The New Republic* at the end of his first Washington service. "Poor old H.C.," LH told Frankfurter, "is deeply cast down by your coerced defection. To be deprived of him 'who more than any one else, understands his point of view and shares his conviction,' was hard indeed. . . . I was incontinently, unsympathetically joyous . . . , unconcealedly glad" (LH to Frankfurter, 9 October 1914, 104–3). See also

Phillips, *Felix Frankfurter Reminisces*, 92 ("Croly was very anxious, terribly anxious, to have me join him"); Herbert Croly to LH, 29 June 1914, 102–22.

186. E.g., Herbert Croly to LH, [March] 1914, 104–22.

187. Id., 29 June 1914, 102–22.

188. Id., 7 August 1914, 102–22. See also id., 10 August 1914 and 17 August 1914, both in 102–22.

189. LH to Herbert Croly, 24 October 1914, 102–22. See also LH to Lord Ratcliffe, 24 October 1914, 38–5. LH had acted as intermediary in soliciting a manuscript for *The New Republic*: "Don't hesitate to send anything [to me], as *I see those men* [of *The New Republic*] *constantly*" (emphasis added).

190. Herbert Croly to LH, 14 August 1914, 102–22.

191. LH to Felix Frankfurter, 31 July 1914, 104–3.

192. Ibid.

193. *New Republic*, 12 December 1914, 5; see Levy, *Herbert Croly*, 239.

194. Herbert Croly to Theodore Roosevelt, 11 January 1915, Roosevelt Papers, Library of Congress (microfilm), reel 197.

195. Theodore Roosevelt to Herbert Croly, 15 January 1915, Roosevelt Papers, Library of Congress (microfilm), reel 357.

196. Johnson, *Pioneer's Progress*, 245 (paraphrasing TR); see TR to Willard Straight, [1915], 8 *The Letters of Theodore Roosevelt*, 4019–21. See also Levy, *Herbert Croly*, 239–41, and Forcey, *Crossroads of Liberalism*, 192–94.

197. [Learned Hand], "An Unseen Reversal," *New Republic*, 9 January 1915, 7–8 (published anonymously).

198. Ibid.

199. LH to Felix Frankfurter, 9 October 1914, 104–3.

200. 236 U.S. 1, 13, 17 (1915).

201. "Normal" is in brackets because the majority did not use that adjective until later in its opinion, when it stated that the legislature cannot legitimately say that it is for the public good to require "the removal of those inequalities that are but the normal and inevitable result of their exercise" (id., 17–18).

Justice Holmes's one-paragraph dissent, similar in force and brevity to his earlier *Lochner* dissent that LH had praised in the *Harvard Law Review* in 1908, insisted:

> In present conditions a workman not unnaturally may believe that only by belonging to a union can he secure a contract that shall be fair to him. If that belief, whether right or wrong, may be held by a reasonable man, it seems to me that it may be enforced by law in order to establish the equality of position between the parties in which liberty of contract begins. Whether in the long run it is wise for the workingmen to enact legislation of this sort is not my concern, but I am strongly of opinion that there is nothing in the Constitution of the United States to prevent it [id., 26–27 (Holmes, J., dissenting)].

202. [Learned Hand], "Normal Inequalities of Fortune," *New Republic*, 6 February 1915, 5–7 (published anonymously).

203. [Learned Hand], "The Bill of Rights Again," *New Republic*, 17 April 1915, 272–73 (published anonymously). In another *New Republic* essay, early in November, LH returned to his attack on reform-obstructing constitutional rigidities in a comment on an article written for the magazine by Graham

Wallas, the British Fabian socialist whose works LH had read for years and with whom he had recently become acquainted. Wallas, addressing Americans interested in preparing for possible involvement in World War I, urged his audience to change the Constitution so that it would become less difficult to amend. LH thought that many would no doubt be startled by that advice, yet he found the need for greater constitutional flexibility "obvious." In his editorial comment "Government According to Law," *New Republic*, 6 November 1915, 4–6 (published anonymously), LH suggested that the pressures of war would place intolerable strains on the inflexible Constitution. If such crises could not be handled legally, he warned, "[T]he impulse of self-preservation will force the nation to adopt illegal remedies."

204. Learned Hand, "The Hope of the Minimum Wage," *New Republic*, 20 November 1915, 66–68.

205. "Felix is very anxious to have us publish [it]," Croly wrote to LH. Herbert Croly to LH, 3 November 1915, 102–23. See also Herbert Croly to LH, 11 November 1915, 102–23.

206. Hand, "The Hope of the Minimum Wage," *New Republic*, 20 November 1915, 66–67.

207. Occasionally, LH would draft a new essay, but most did not reach print. For example, he submitted an essay entitled "Taxes on Loans," on the financing of American preparations for the war, but Croly thought it too complex and technical and suggested he try something in a lighter vein (Herbert Croly to LH, 8 June 1917, 102–24).

208. [Learned Hand], "The Legal Right to Starve," *New Republic*, 2 May 1923, 254–55 (published anonymously).

209. 261 U.S. 525 (1923).

210. In commenting on *Adkins*, LH was more pithy and vitriolic than ever. He began with a graphic description of the fate of the woman involved in the case, Willie A. Lyons, a twenty-one-year-old elevator operator in a Washington hotel. The Washington, D.C., Minimum Wage Board had decided that her pay of $35 a month and two meals a day was below an appropriate minimum wage, but the Supreme Court found this an impermissible interference with her "liberty of contract" ("The Legal Right to Starve," *New Republic*, 2 May 1923, 254–55).

211. Borah's proposal was to require a supermajority—a two-thirds vote in *all* constitutional cases. LH was not prepared to accept this supermajority requirement fully: with respect to the limits that the federal system imposed on national and state laws, he thought it "undesirable" to permit a mere one third of the justices to uphold challenged laws. But the due-process clauses were "different": "There, . . . the questions are in their nature essentially legislative, as no candid person can doubt who reads more than a little of the opinions." If in principle the courts in due-process cases should uphold laws "while there is any fair doubt, it would seem to be a reasonable corollary that a fair doubt arises when nine presumably competent men decide as nearly equally as their numbers admit" (id., 255).

212. Id., 255.

213. In January 1917, Wilson, in a major speech to Congress (S. Doc. No. 685, *Cong. Record* 54 [22 January 1917], 1741–43), advocated "peace without victory"—a phrase Lippmann had used earlier in a *New Republic* editorial in a quite different context (Lippmann had used the phrase in the course of rejecting

as humiliating a German peace proposal). Wilson's echoing of Lippmann's language lent added credence to the notion that there were intimate ties between *The New Republic* and the administration.

214. See Harvard president Charles W. Eliot to LH, 14 March 1917, and LH's reply, 15 March 1917, 20–3.

215. LH to FAH, 22 June 1917, Personal Correspondence.

216. Id., 25 June 1917, Personal Correspondence. The passage continues: "Everyone feeling that next week he might be leading the Paladins to a glorious death in defence of the Cross and not knowing his lance from a barber pole!"

217. Id., 4 July 1914, Personal Correspondence.

218. Id., 22 June 1917, Personal Correspondence.

219. Ibid.

220. Id., 25 June 1917, Personal Correspondence.

221. Id., 26 June 1917, Personal Correspondence.

222. FAH to LH, "Tuesday," [late June, 1917], 111–13; id., "Saturday," [late June, 1917], 111–13.

223. LH to FAH, 28 June 1917, Personal Correspondence.

224. FAH to LH, "Sunday," [late June, 1917], 111–13.

225. See Walter Lippmann's diary entry in early October 1917, as cited in Steel, *Walter Lippmann*, 129.

226. LH to FAH, 1 June 1918, Personal Correspondence.

227. See FAH to LH, "Wednesday," [June 1918], Personal Correspondence: "[I]t made me feel mad with them for stirring us up so! . . . We'll try and remember these past experiences another time, won't we. Of course the more I think of it the more fitted I think the Judge's job is to you, but I think it would have been interesting to have you [have] a try at the other, but at no risk to your own job."

228. Most of LH's correspondence was with David Hunter Miller of the State Department, the designee of the secretary of state on these issues (see 31–8). The rest of the story is documented in correspondence scattered in several files: 27–18, 37–8, 37–18, 41–19, 42–16, 42–23, 43–16, and 46–24.

229. The group consisted of LH, circuit judge Charles M. Hough, and three New York patent, trademark, and copyright attorneys: Archibald Cox, Thomas E. Ewing, and Lawrence Langner. The hardest-working member other than LH was Langner, a young naturalized Englishman with expertise in the international law of intellectual property. See LH to Odin Roberts, 5 October 1918, 37–18, and, generally, file 27–18. (While working on the study, Langner had enough energy left to work on his favorite avocation, the theater; soon after the group's report was ready, he told LH that he had succeeded in organizing the Theatre Guild—and invited the Hands to attend the Guild's first production.)

230. The most time-consuming task was the collection of the patent and trademark laws of the warring nations. This report was promptly stamped "secret" by a Washington bureaucrat. LH successfully battled the advocates of government secrecy in order to make the collection available to the bar. The Government Printing Office ultimately published the "Basic Patent and Trademark Laws" volume in 1919 (over five hundred copies). See 41–19.

231. The text of the basic report, submitted to the State Department on November 22, 1918, is in 42–23.

232. LH to David Hunter Miller, 22 October 1918, 31–8.

233. Id., 13 January 1919, 31–8.

234. See LH to F. D. MacKinnon, 11 August 1920, 29–11.
235. LH to Walter Lippmann, 3 October 1917, Lippmann Papers, Yale University, L–5.
236. See George Rublee to LH, 2 May 1917, 107–3.
237. LH to FAH, 11 June 1917, Personal Correspondence.
238. Id., [12 June 1917], Personal Correspondence.
239. George Rublee to LH, 22 June 1917, 107–3.
240. LH to FAH, 25 June 1917 and 28 June 1917, Personal Correspondence.
241. Id., 1 July 1917, Personal Correspondence.
242. George Rublee to LH, 29 June 1917 and 1 July 1917, 107–3.
243. LH to FAH, 16 July 1917, Personal Correspondence.
244. See chapter 3, 151–61, above.
245. See LH to Walter Lippmann, 3 October 1917, Lippmann Papers, Yale University, L–5: "I must be out of it; perhaps the *Masses* was enough."
246. See FAH to LH, 16 September 1917, Personal Correspondence.
247. From a draft note sent by Felix Frankfurter to LH, 9 March 1917 (when Judge Coxe's resignation, which created the vacancy, seemed imminent). A more polished version was probably sent to Attorney General Gregory in April. Frankfurter also drafted "a memorandum of a list of cases which will indicate the range and quality of [LH's] work." The draft note and a photocopy of the list are in 104–7.
248. George Rublee to LH, 15 October 1917, 107–3.
249. See ibid. Rublee respected Hitz as knowing more "about the inside of Washington than anyone [he was] in touch with" (ibid.). See also id., 27 November 1917, 107–3.
250. Id., 15 October 1917, 107–3.
251. FAH to LH, "Saturday," [12 January 1918], Personal Correspondence. FAH urged LH not to put all his hopes into the revived possibility, "for I don't want you to be disappointed"; "yet," she told LH, "I wish *so* you could get it."
252. LH to Felix Frankfurter, 9 January 1918, 104–7. A few days later, LH still thought Manton was "out of it," for he seemed to be "exhibiting some signs of uneasiness" (id., 13 January 1918, 104–7).
253. FAH to LH, "Wed. p.m.," [March 1918], Personal Correspondence.
254. LH to Felix Frankfurter, 9 January 1918, 104–7. The full passage contains a phrase that seems obscure but is revealing: "I am an outsider and utlegatus, a man out of frankpledge." His memory was good for old feudal law and for Blackstone's *Commentaries.* "Frankpledge" was the system by which every member of a tithing was answerable for the performance or nonperformance of any other member. What LH meant was that he was not a team player, certainly not in politics. "Utlegatus"—"outlaw"—is even more obscure. LH meant he was in effect an outlaw (in terms of patronage rewards).
255. *New Republic,* 30 November 1918, 134–37. See also the related *New Republic* editorial, id., 116–18.
256. Id., 116.
257. H. Doc. No. 765, *Cong. Record* 54 (8 January 1918), 680–81.
258. LH to Felix Frankfurter, 9 January 1918, 104–7.
259. See Felix Frankfurter to LH, 21 January 1919, 104–7.
260. LH to George Rublee [January 1919], 107–4.
261. Id., 30 January 1919, 107–4.
262. Id., 3 March 1919, 107–4.

263. Lippmann's fourteen-page piece was of such an unusual length that *The New Republic* published it as a special supplement (Walter Lippmann, "The Political Scene," part 2 [Special Supplement] to *The New Republic*, 22 March 1919). The quoted passage is at p. 14.
264. LH to Walter Lippmann, 29 March 1919, cited in Steel, *Walter Lippmann*, 157. See also Lippmann to LH, 1 April 1919, 106–15.
265. LH to Felix Frankfurter, 8 November 1919, 104–8.
266. LH had had hints from Croly that the magazine was moving in this direction. See, e.g., Herbert Croly to LH, 30 October 1918, 102–24.
267. "Europe Proposes," *New Republic*, 17 May 1919, 67–71.
268. "Peace at Any Price," *New Republic*, 24 May 1919, 100–2.
269. LH to Felix Frankfurter, 6 June 1920, 104–9.
270. Felix Frankfurter to LH, 28 June 1920, 104–8.
271. LH to Felix Frankfurter, 3 December 1919, 104–8.
272. LH to FAH, 15 June 1919, Personal Correspondence.
273. Herbert Croly to LH, [1922], 102–25. See also LH to Felix Frankfurter, 8 November 1919, 104–8.
274. LH to Felix Frankfurter, 3 December 1919, 104–8.
275. See Herbert Hoover to President Woodrow Wilson, 19 November 1919 (carbon copy, forwarded by Frankfurter to LH, 104–8).
276. LH to Felix Frankfurter, 3 December 1919, 104–8.
277. This and following quotations are from LH's long letter to a British acquaintance, F. D. MacKinnon, 11 August 1920, 29–11.

VI
Promotion to the Second Circuit

1. See chapter 5, above, 257–61.
2. LH to William Fordyce, 15 December 1924, 20–25.
3. See circuit judge Charles M. Hough's Memorial of Julius M. Mayer, reprinted from *Yearbook of the Association of the Bar of the City of New York, 1926*, in file 30–24.
4. LH to Julius M. Mayer, 5 July 1921, 30–24.
5. See id., 10 May 1921, 30–24.
6. Julius M. Mayer to LH, 23 September 1921, 30–24. See also id., 26 September 1921, 30–24.
7. See, e.g., Prof. Manley O. Hudson of Harvard Law School to LH, 13 December 1924, 24–13.
8. Felix Frankfurter to LH, 26 July 1921, 104–10.
9. Id., 3 December [1924], 104–11.
10. LH to Felix Frankfurter, 5 December 1924, 104–11.
11. See Walter F. Murphy, "In His Own Image: Mr. Chief Justice Taft and Supreme Court Appointments," *1961 The Supreme Court Review* (Chicago: University of Chicago Press, 1961), 159, 165–66.
12. William Howard Taft, "Mr. Wilson and the Campaign," 10 *Yale Review* N.S., 19, 20 (October 1920) (quoted in Daniel J. Danelski, *A Supreme Court Justice Is Appointed* [New York: Random House, 1964], 29).
13. See Harold Laski to Oliver Wendell Holmes, 6 October 1923; Holmes to Laski, 19 October 1923; and Laski to Holmes, Jr., 30 October 1923, 1 *Holmes-*

Laski Letters, ed. Mark DeWolfe Howe (Cambridge: Harvard University Press, 1953), 548, 555, 557.

14. Harold Laski to Oliver Wendell Holmes, Jr., 6 September 1922, id., 446. (See also Laski's follow-up letter, 13 September 1922: "Dean Acheson tells me that neither Cardozo nor Learned Hand has a chance and I expect to see you endowed with a Republican McReynolds" [id., 450].)

    (In later letters, whenever Holmes sounded fatigued, Laski urged him to stay on until LH or Benjamin Cardozo could be named. See, e.g., Laski to Holmes, 7 June 1925: "[Y]ou must stay there until your President is sensible enough to see that Learned Hand or Cardozo is your only possible successor" [id., 748]. See also Laski to Holmes, 5 March 1927: "I doubt whether the kind of approach you make would be made by any one else except Learned Hand and Cardozo and I gather that their elevation is not within the realm of the possible. Hence my entreaties!" (2 *Holmes-Laski Letters*, ed. Mark DeWolfe Howe [Cambridge: Harvard University Press, 1953] 926).

15. See the discussion of this appointment in Danelski, *A Supreme Justice Is Appointed*, passim.

16. LH to Felix Frankfurter, [December] 1922, 104–10.

17. Felix Frankfurter to LH, 24 October [1922], 104–10.

18. William Howard Taft to Warren G. Harding, 4 December 1922, Taft Papers, Library of Congress (quoted in Danelski, *A Supreme Court Justice Is Appointed*, 42).

19. LH to Felix Frankfurter, 27 July 1921, 104–10, and Felix Frankfurter to LH, 26 July 1921, 104–10 (predicting " 'mashed potato' opinions" from Taft). See also Felix Frankfurter to LH, 26 July 1921, 104–10.

20. LH to Felix Frankfurter, 31 August 1921, 104–10.

21. LH to Henry W. Taft, 8 October 1923, 41–3.

22. William Howard Taft to LH, 3 December 1924, 41–4.

23. Harlan Fiske Stone to LH, 11 December 1924, 39–20.

24. William Howard Taft to Harlan Fiske Stone, 1 August 1924, and Stone's reply, 4 August 1924, from the Taft Papers, Library of Congress, quoted in Walter F. Murphy, "In His Own Image: Mr. Chief Justice Taft and Supreme Court Appointments," *1961 The Supreme Court Review* (Chicago: University of Chicago Press, 1961), 179, n. 85.

25. Mayer hesitated only briefly before backing LH. He moved as soon as he learned from district judge John R. Hazel in Buffalo, a fellow Republican for whom Mayer had a "sentimental and strong regard," that Hazel preferred staying on the trial court (Julius M. Mayer to LH, 26 August 1924, 30–24). See also Hazel-LH exchange, 16 December 1924 and 18 December 1924, 23–17, with LH telling Hazel that he could have gotten the appointment if he had wanted it.

26. Julius M. Mayer to LH, 29 July 1924, 30–24.

27. Id., 26 August 1924, 30–24.

28. See Abram Elkus to LH, 30 July 1924 (enclosing his letter to the attorney general of the same date), 19–17, and Thomas Ewing to LH, 30 July 1924, 19–17, enclosing a letter from Charles D. Hilles of the Republican National Committee, 26 July 1924. Ewing was among the several supporters who had approached Hilles.

29. Julius M. Mayer to LH, 26 August 1924, 30–24. At the same time, Mayer

had written his political associates that he thought it "unnecessary to delay in [Hand's] case" (ibid.).

30. See LH's exchange with New York senator James W. Wadsworth, 44–13 (including Wadsworth's telegram to LH, 20 December 1924). See Wadsworth's letter to LH, 3 January 1925, and LH's reply, 7 January 1925.

31. The documents are in 42–9. See, e.g., LH to Attorney General Harlan Fiske Stone, 29 December 1924, 42–9.

32. Gilbert H. Montague (patent lawyer) to LH, 16 January 1925, 32–13. For other congratulatory letters, see, e.g., the collection in 47–14 and 47–15.

33. *New York World*, 3 December 1924, repeatedly enclosed in congratulatory letters. See, e.g., New York Court of Appeals judge Cuthbert W. Pound to LH, [December 1924], 35–27.

34. *New York World*, 3 December 1924, 7 (in a brief news story following a longer dispatch from Washington reporting Hand's nomination).

35. Walter Nelles to LH, 3 December 1924, 33–6.

36. LH to Felix Frankfurter, 27 July 1921, 104–10.

37. J. F. Curtis to LH, 4 December 1924, 18–10.

VII

The Second Circuit Court of Appeals in the 1920s and 1930s:
Hand as First Among Equals

1. See Laura Kalman, *Legal Realism at Yale, 1927–1960* (Chapel Hill: University of North Carolina Press, 1986) 99.

2. Charles Merrill Hough to LH, 31 March 1927, 54–35.

3. LH to Ethel P. Hough (Hough's widow), on the tenth anniversary of Charles M. Hough's death, 22 April 1937, 54–35.

4. Ethel P. Hough to LH, 25 April 1937, 54–35 (emphasis added).

5. *Gitlow v. New York*, 268 U.S. 652 (1925).

6. The Hough-LH exchange is in file 54–34: Charles Merrill Hough to LH, 8 July 1926, and LH's response, 9 July 1926.

7. See Charles Merrill Hough to LH, 27 July 1926, and LH to Charles Merrill Hough, 9 July 1926, both in 54–34.

8. At the time, the Harvard approach was considered to be the truly "progressive" one, though C. C. Langdell's case method was already coming to be seen as having an excessively arid preoccupation with logically tight legal concepts. Harvard appointed Roscoe Pound as dean in 1916, the year Thomas Swan went to Yale. Pound, a Nebraskan trained as a botanist, originated "sociological jurisprudence," the philosophy that the analysis of law required a broader focus than Langdell's mechanical jurisprudence and had to concern itself as well with the social policy and empirical contexts with which both legislation and judicial decision making were intertwined. Sociological jurisprudence was a congenial approach for lawyers—including LH and Felix Frankfurter—who were sympathetic to Bull Moose Progressivism; predictably, then, both LH and Frankfurter were enthusiastic supporters of Pound for the Harvard deanship. In later years, Pound and the Harvard Law School were far more often associated with more conservative tendencies; but in 1910–30, the Harvard model was truly the more progressive one. See Kalman, *Legal Realism at Yale*; Wilfrid E. Rumble, "Sociological Jurisprudence," in 4 *Encyclopedia of the American Con-*

stitution, ed. Leonard W. Levy, Kenneth L. Karst, and Dennis J. Mahoney (New York: Macmillan, 1986), 1705; and Wilfrid E. Rumble, "Pound, Roscoe," in 3 *Encyclopedia of the American Constitution*, ed. Leonard W. Levy, Kenneth L. Karst, and Dennis J. Mahoney (New York: Macmillan, 1986), 1431.

9. See, e.g., LH's letter to Attorney General John G. Sargent [1927], 61–27.

10. Edward Burling to LH, 28 January 1959, 100–21 (a mistake by a temporary, foreign-born secretary).

11. On Mack see generally, Harry Barnard, *The Forging of an American Jew: The Life and Times of Judge Julian W. Mack* (New York: Herzl Press, 1974).

12. LH to William Howard Taft, 27 January 1929, Taft Papers, Library of Congress.

13. Harrie Chase to LH, 25 January 1929, replying to LH to Harrie Chase, 22 January 1929, both in 50–15.

14. The pre-conference memoranda fill 39 of the more than 230 boxes in the Hand Papers—boxes 178–217.

15. For the contrast between the practice in LH's day and the modern practice, see Chief Judge Wilfred Feinberg's 1986 Hofstra lecture, "Unique Customs and Practices of the Second Circuit," 14 *Hofstra L.Rev.* 297 (1986). Some of the differences (which have made the practice somewhat less useful on the modern court, although Feinberg and most of the other modern judges continue to praise it): memos today are much shorter; most are often written on the day of argument or the next day, after a good deal less thought and research than in earlier years; the memos are more commonly responsive to those of colleagues. Feinberg contrasts the last feature with the "tradition," which persisted through Harold Medina's years (especially the 1960s), of not reading other judges' memos until one's own was done, except for "a peek once in a while." See also Harold Medina, "Some Reflections on the Judicial Function at the Appellate Level," 1961 *Wash. U.L.Q.* 148 (1961), and "The Decisional Process," 20 *New York County Lawyers Association Bar Bulletin* 94 (1962). Medina, originally a skeptic about the practice, came to think it was "a wonderful system." Henry J. Friendly was, predictably, a "staunch supporter."

16. See chapter 3, above.

17. This description of the working relationship between LH and his law clerks is based on my own recollection of my clerkship with him (1953–54), my interviews of him in the late 1950s, and my interviews of a large number of his law clerks.

18. E.g., *In re United States Wood Preserving Co.* (1924 Term) 179–11.

19. Henry J. Friendly, "Learned Hand: An Expression from the Second Circuit," 29 *Brooklyn L.Rev.* 6, 13.

20. *Franklin Knitting Mills v. Groper Mills*, 181–13 (18 October 1926).

21. *Inecto v. Helvering*, 193–6 (31 May 1934).

22. *U.S. v. S.S. Manuel Arnus*, 195–17 (23 February 1935).

23. E.g., *U.S. v. Zambelli*, involving a technical defect in the service of a summons, 191–2 (16 June 1932).

24. *Branhill v. Montgomery Ward*, 189–14 (11 June 1932).

25. *Neuberger v. U.S.*, 180–10 (7 May 1926).

26. *In re Vincenzo Della Femina*, 179–23 (13 May 1926).

27. *U.S. v. Nash*, 190–25 (28 December 1931).

28. *Comm'r v. Rail Joint Co.*, 191–10 (18 October 1932).

29. *U.S. v. President Wilson*, 190–13 (20 December 1932).
30. *Transportes [etc.] v. Almeida*, 179–9 (1924 Term).
31. E.g., *Canadian Government Merchant Marine v. U.S.*, 178–4 (1924 Term).
32. *Gillespie et al. v. U.S.*, 180–1 (1925 Term).
33. E.g., *La Fontaine v. U.S.*, 180–6 (24 March 1926); *Sharron v. U.S.*, 180–17 (23 March 1926); *U.S. Steel v. Noble*, 180–22 (23 November 1925).
34. *Charles H. Cahan v. Empire Trust Co.*, 179–19 (18 December 1925).
35. *Gillespie et al. v. U.S.* (on rehearing), 180–1 (1925 Term).
36. See the correspondence about *In re Lansley* in 57–21 (October 1926).
37. *Equitable Trust Co. v. Connecticut Brass & Mfg. Co.*, 179–22 (9 February 1926).
38. *Gerli v. Cunard*, 188–08 (24 February 1931).
39. *Allied Metal Stamping Co. v. Standard Electric Co.*, 189–12 (12 January 1932).
40. *Rayahel v. McCampbell*, 190–14 (28 December 1931).
41. *Deitel v. Reich-Ash Co.*, 191–13 (27 March 1933).
42. *Gitlow v. Kiely*, 188–8 (23 April 1931).
43. *In re Syracuse Stutz Co., Inc.*, 190–19 (18 January 1932); *U.S. v. Bouchard*, 191–8 (24 March 1933).
44. *United States v. Drexel*, 190–23 (13 February 1932).
45. *Brownstein v. U.S.*, 178–4 (1924 Term).
46. *Mills v. U.S.*, 180–8 (8 June 1926).
47. *Eagle & Star [etc.] Co. v. Schliff*, 183–9 (28 February 1928).
48. *Commercial Casualty Ins. Co. v. Allied Dairy Production Corporation*, 185–3 (22 October 1928).
49. *Nieblo v. Preston*, 187–7 (13 February 1930).
50. *Lane v. Selby*, 188–14 (14 November 1930).
51. *Searfoss v. Lehigh Valley R.R. Co.*, 195–13 (11 March 1935); *U.S. v. McNaugh*, 187–14 (26 June 1930); *U.S. v. The Schooner "Marion Phillis,"* 187–15 (14 November 1929); *King v. Aetna*, 190–4 (23 October 1931).
52. *Pacyna v. Nassau Electric R.R.*, 185–24 (16 May 1929).
53. *Marine Lighterage Co. v. Netherland American*, 187–4 (15 January 1930).
54. *Pine v. Columbia Nat'l Ins. Co.*, 192–5 (10 June 1933).
55. *Spooner v. N.Y. Central No. 17*, 187–12 (26 May 1930).
56. *Heiskell, Trustee v. Furniss, Withey & Co.*, 178–14 (1924 Term).
57. *Cutler Hammer Co. v. Beaver Machine Co.*, 178–6 (1924 Term).
58. *U.S. ex rel. Mittler v. Curran*, 179–10 (22 May 1925).
59. *U.S. ex rel. Sapunachis v. Day*, 184–8 (22 October 1927).
60. *Chin Wah et al. v. U.S.*, 179–20 (3 June 1926).
61. *U.S. ex rel. Mittler v. Curran*, 179–10 (22 May 1925).
62. *U.S. ex rel. Restivo v. Day*, 187–17 (15 April 1930).
63. *U.S. v. Frommel*, 189–6 (28 April 1931).
64. E.g., LH's comments in *Mills*, 180–8 (8 June 1926): "[T]his insistence on piling up penalties . . . more and more fills me with rage"; *Gambino and Lima v. U.S.*, 181–14 (13 January 1927), protesting "against doubling, nay quadrupling, the sentence" under "a guise" and calling this a "hateful and oppressive exercise of power . . . nothing less than an outrage"; and *Spirou v. U.S.*, 184–9 (27 February 1928): "[T]he idea of expanding all this into 15 counts seems to me a damned outrage. . . . I am not going to keep still though I shall be decorous about it."
65. E.g., *U.S. v. Lonardo*, 194–1 (17 November 1933).

66. For examples from his early decades on the federal bench, see *U.S. v. Casino*, 286 Fed. 976 (S.D.N.Y. 1923), and *U.S. v. Kirschenblatt*, 16 F.2d 202 (2d Cir. 1926).
67. *U.S. v. 1013 Crates*, 189–8 (11 April 1931).
68. *U.S. v. American Surety Co.*, 193–25 (23 February 1934).
69. LH conducted extensive correspondence with members of congressional committees and with the Patent Law Association. (A specialized court was given jurisdiction over appeals from the Patent Office in patent and trademark cases as early as 1929, but a great deal of patent litigation continues to come before the regular federal courts even today. There have never been any specialized American courts for maritime cases.)
70. *Newtown Creek Towing Co. v. N.Y. Central R.R.*, 180–10 (2 June 1926).
71. *Newton Creek Towing Co. v. New York Central Railroad Co.*, 12 F.2d 1017 (2d Cir. 1926). (LH did not note a dissent; but dissents were uncommon, particularly in summary affirmances.)
72. The case is in 180–6, under the title *Norddeutscher Lloyd v. La Lorraine*, with an LH memo of 16 April 1926. It is reported under the caption *La Lorraine. The Prinz Friedrich Wilhelm* at 12 F.2d 436 (2d Cir. 1926) (per curiam opinion, apparently by Hough). On his skills in routine cases, see also the examples in five consecutive LH memos at the beginning of 193–12, all from late 1933 and early 1934: *New York v. Tug Moran* (23 April 1934); *New York and New Jersey Steamboat Co v. Ferryboat Philadelphia* (20 November 1933); *New York Trap Rock Corp. v. Tug "Edwin H. Mead"* (20 November 1933); *Nielson v. Steamtug P.R.R. No. 26* (20 March 1934); and *O'Brien Bros. v. New York* (13 December 1933).
73. *Soeller v. The Herkimer (and The Dixie)* (18 March 1932), decided as *The Harry. The Dixie. Soeller v. New York Canal & Great Lakes Corp.*, 57 F.2d 184 (4 April 1932; unanimous opinion by Manton).
74. See *Jacobus v. Tug "Alice Moran,"* 193–7 (9 October 1933).
75. *Lehigh v. La France*, 180–6 (13 April 1926).
76. *Schomburg v. The "Industry,"* 186–5 (17 October 1928).
77. *Huasteca Co. v. 27,000 Bags of Coffee*, 190–2 (22 June 1932).
78. *Parke-Davis & Co. v. H. K. Mulford & Co.*, 196 Fed. 496 (2d Cir. 1912), affirming LH's decision in 189 Fed. 95 (S.D.N.Y. 1911).
79. *Wachs v. Balsam*, 187–18 (10 January 1930).
80. *Winget Kickernick Co. v. Kenilworth Mfg. Co.*, 180–22 (4 February 1926). In this bloomer case, LH found that there had indeed been infringement, even though the defendant had made a few technical changes from the patented scheme: the infringer had engaged in "a clear effort to steal the meat and leave the shell. . . . [I]t gives lip service to the invention but leaves it so that anyone may ignore it with impunity." Mack's brief memo simply supported "all that L.H. says on this subject": "Patents, even simple ones like this, are not in my particular line," he confessed.
81. *Gibbs v. Triumph*, 183–13 (11 April 1928).
82. *Elyria Iron & Steel Co. v. Mohegan Tube Co.*, memos in 178–9, decision reported in 7 F.2d 827 (2d Cir. 1925); LH dissent id., 831.
83. *Kaumagraph Co. v. Superior Trademark Mfg. Co.*, 193–8 (31 May 1934).
84. See, e.g., LH's memoranda in 1926 in two cases each captioned *Armstrong v. De Forest*, 179–15 (12 January 1926; 7 June 1926).

85. E.g., *Technidyne v. McPhilbin*, 193–23 (1933 Term—a memo that LH, uncharacteristically, did not date; his colleagues never dated theirs.)
86. *B.G. Corp. v. Walter Kidde & Co.*, 79 F.2d 20, 22 (2d Cir. 1935).
87. *Dewey & Almy Chemical Co. v. Mimex Co.*, 124 F.2d 986, 990 (2d Cir. 1942); *Kirsch Mfg. Co. v. Gould Mersereau Co.*, 6 F.2d 793, 794 (2d Cir. 1925).
88. *Sachs v. Hartford Electric Co.*, 47 F.2d 743, 748 (2d Cir. 1931).
89. *Hookless Fastener v. G. E. Prentice Mfg. Co.*, 193–5 (18 January 1934).
90. *Dupont v. Sayford*, 188–6 (10 February 1931). Decision reported at 47 F.2d 1083.
91. *Dupont v. Sayford*, 188–6 (memo by Mack).
92. For further explorations of LH's contributions to this area, see especially Stephen H. Philbin, "Judge Learned Hand and the Law of Patents and Copyrights," 60 *Harv. L.Rev.* 394 (1947). See also Paul H. Blaustein, *Learned Hand on Patent Law* (White Plains, N.Y.: Pineridge Publishing House, 1983). I have kept the discussion of patent law to the single issue of what is an invention. I have not gone into such related areas as LH's recurrent emphases on (a) how long there had been unsuccessful search in the trade for something like the invention, and (b) the effect of the alleged patent on the conduct of the trade. Nor have I developed his subtle discussions of the relevance of the fact that the invention seemed obvious once it was patented.
93. U.S. Constitution, Article I, § 8. This clause authorizes not only federal copyright laws but patent laws as well. Although the general purposes of protecting "Writings" and "Discoveries" are similar, there are important differences between patents and copyrights, as noted below.
94. For guidance in this discussion of LH's work in copyright law, I am especially indebted to my former student Douglas G. Baird (now professor of law at University of Chicago School of Law) for his remarkable unpublished student paper, "Learned Hand and the Manichean Heresy: An Overview of His Copyright Opinions" (Stanford Law School, 1979), and to my colleague Paul Goldstein. See, e.g., Paul Goldstein, "The Competitive Mandate: From *Sears* to *Lear*," 59 *Calif. L.Rev.* 873 (1971).
95. See Benjamin Kaplan, *An Unhurried View of Copyright* (New York: Columbia University Press, 1967), 89–92.
96. 175 Fed. 875 (S.D.N.Y. 1910).
97. *Bleistein v. Donaldson Lithographing Co.*, 188 U.S. 239 (1903).
98. See the well-known statement by LH's later colleague Jerome Frank in *Alfred Bell & Co. v. Catalda Fine Arts, Inc.*, 191 F.2d 99, 102 (2d Cir. 1951), that originality amounts to "little more than a prohibition of actual copying. No matter how poor the author's addition, it is enough if it be his own."
99. John Ewen to LH, 16 July 1924, 20–6. LH and the court reporter called him "John Ewing," erroneously. See LH to John "Ewing," 17 July 1924, 20–6. The confusion probably arose because a patent lawyer named Thomas Ewing was well known to LH and the court staff; he was LH's rival for the Second Circuit appointment in 1918 that went to Martin Manton.
100. *Haas v. Leo Feist*, 234 Fed. 105 (S.D.N.Y. 1916).
101. *Stodart v. Mutual Film Corp.*, 249 Fed. 507 (S.D.N.Y. 1917).
102. *Arnstein v. Edward B. Marks Music Corp.*, 82 F.2d 275 (2d Cir. 1936).
103. "Immature tastes" in *Rosen v. Loew's*, 162 F.2d 785 (2d Cir. 1947); "cheap and vulgar" in *Fitch v. Young*, 230 Fed. 743 (S.D.N.Y. 1916); "paranoiac"

in LH's pre-conference memo in *Arnstein v. Edward B. Marks Music Corp.*, 195–22 (20 October 1936).

104. See LH to Arthur Dehon Hill, 11 October 1916, 23–27.

105. See Baird, "Learned Hand and the Manichean Heresy." Baird read all of LH's copyright opinions, and his compilation includes not only LH's overview but copies of all of the pertinent correspondence and memoranda in the files as well as copies of all the opinions. See also Hershel Shanks, ed., *The Art and Craft of Judging: The Decisions of Judge Learned Hand* (New York: Macmillan, 1968), part 8, "The Protection of Literary Property," 114–43.

106. 276 Fed. 717 (S.D.N.Y. 1921).

107. Shanks, *The Art and Craft of Judging*, 122.

108. Baird, "Learned Hand and the Manichean Heresy," 56.

109. Many years later, LH did change his mind on the reach of the statute, concluding instead that the Copyright Act's language did not mean to go as far as the Constitution permitted. See *Capitol Records v. Mercury Records Corp.*, 221 F.2d 657 (2d Cir. 1955). But the narrow reading in that case does not undercut the strength of his argument in *Reiss*.

110. The only objection to using such English cases, he said, was if the Constitution "embalms inflexibly the habits of 1789." He rejected any restriction of the Constitution to such narrow notions of original intent:

> [The Constitution's] grants of power to Congress comprise, not only what was then known, but what the ingenuity of men should devise thereafter. Of course, the new subject-matter must have some relation to the grant; but we interpret it by the general practices of civilized peoples in similar fields, for it is not a strait-jacket, but a charter for a living people [*Reiss v. National Quotation Bureau*, 276 Fed. 717, 719 (S.D.N.Y. 1921)].

111. *Fred Fisher, Inc. v. Dillingham*, 298 Fed. 145 (S.D.N.Y. 1924).

112. There was no proof at all that the plaintiff had in fact copied his accompaniment from any earlier work; as LH put it, "[F]or the purposes of this case it must be deemed to be original, if by original one means that it was the spontaneous, unsuggested result of the author's imagination" (298 Fed. 145, 148).

113. *Sheldon v. Metro-Goldwyn Pictures Corp.*, 81 F.2d 49, 53 (2d Cir. 1936), more fully discussed below.

114. After the ruling in Jerome Kern's case was published, Silvio Hein's lawyer wrote LH to ask whether he remembered his decision fourteen years earlier in *Hein v. Harris*, suggesting, quite accurately, that the new ruling sounded very different. LH replied in a most uncharacteristic way: he suggested that the error in *Hein* lay in the Second Circuit decision that had affirmed his own district court ruling in 1910. The circuit court, LH said, was "clean off in saying that for copyright infringement it was necessary that the defendant should borrow from the plaintiff. They mixed up the rule between patents and copyrights and have since that time repudiated it, so that the law is on a sound basis now" (LH to "John Ewing" [John Ewen], 17 July 1924, 20–6). Moreover, LH persisted in this view twelve years later (see LH memo in *Arnstein v. Edward B. Marks Music Corp.*, 195–22 [20 October 1936]). In this pre-conference memo, LH condemned the Second Circuit ruling in *Hein* as "just as wrong as a decision can possibly be in copyright . . . an abysmally ignorant decision. . . . Conceive of saying that a copyright owner could enjoin others from saying what he said though they did not copy." Yet the Second Circuit mistake in

Hein was in fact an affirmance of LH's own decision, a Second Circuit echo of the very mistake LH had made. It was uncharacteristic of LH to try to shift the blame from himself to the appellate judges; he was typically ready to confess his own mistakes. The most plausible explanation is that he genuinely, although mistakenly, thought the Second Circuit had addressed these issues, but that he himself, on the trial court, had not. Inadvertence, not evasiveness or blame shifting, best explains LH's disavowal of his mistake.

Not until 1936, in his opinion in the *Arnstein* case, did LH officially take back the error in *Hein*, writing, "Although we once held otherwise in *Hein v. Harris*, independent production of a copyrighted musical work is not infringement; nothing short of plagiarism will serve. . . . [*Hein*] is contrary to the very foundation of copyright law, and was plainly an inadvertence which we now take this occasion to correct" (82 F.2d 275 [2d Cir. 1936]). (Yet even here, his reference is to "we" and "our," suggesting the voice of a circuit judge speaking of past decisions of the circuit judges; even then, he apparently did not focus on the fact that the circuit judges had simply, although more clearly, echoed LH's own misperceptions in his district court ruling in *Hein*.)

115. *Myers v. Mail & Express Co.*, 36 Copyright Dec. 478, 480 (S.D.N.Y. 1919) (not published in the official reports).

116. 45 F.2d 119 (2d Cir. 1930).

117. Gus Hand, who sat with his cousin on the case, commented in his memo that it was "in fact a dreadful play," but had become "a howling prolonged success because it embodied [the] popular idea about getting the Irish and Jews together," an idea that had "become during the last ten years the basis of propaganda in New York, so much a part of the program of [New York governor and 1928 presidential candidate] Al Smith or his followers that many people have asserted that Smith's father was a Jew" (Augustus N. Hand pre-conference memo in *Nichols v. Universal Pictures*, 188–18 [1930 Term]).

118. 81 F.2d 49 (2d Cir. 1936), *cert. denied*, 298 U.S. 669 (1936).

119. LH memo in *Nichols*, 188–18 (22 October 1930).

120. 45 F.2d 119, 121–22.

121. *Sheldon v. Metro-Goldwyn Pictures Corp.*, 7 F.Supp. 837 (S.D.N.Y 1934). (LH's opinion in the case came down a year and a half later, in January 1936, for a unanimous bench consisting of Thomas Swan, Harrie Chase, and LH. This is a rare case in which the pre-conference memos were not preserved— perhaps because the case produced a later opinion, in the Second Circuit and the Supreme Court, on the question of damages.)

122. George Wharton Pepper, "The Literary Style of Learned Hand," 60 *Harv. L.Rev.* 333, 340–41 (1947).

123. Kaplan, *An Unhurried View of Copyright*, 49.

124. Shanks, *The Art and Craft of Judging*, 133.

125. This and following quotations from LH's opinion in *Sheldon v. Metro-Goldwyn Pictures Corp.*, 81 F.2d 49 (2d Cir. 1936).

126. See Baird, "Learned Hand and the Manichean Heresy," 44, 47.

127. LH explained: "Speech is only a small part of a dramatist's means of expression; he draws on all the arts and compounds his play from words and gestures and scenery and costume and from the very looks of the actors themselves. Again and again a play may lapse into pantomime at its most poignant and significant moments; a nod, a movement of the hand, a pause, may tell the audience more than the words could tell. To be sure, not all of this is always copyrighted.

. . . [But] the play is the sequence of the confluents of all these means, bound together in an inseparable unity. . . . [That] it appears to us is exactly what the defendants have done here; the dramatic significance of the scenes we have recited is the same, almost to the letter" (*Sheldon*, 81 F.2d 49, 55–56).

128. 19 F.2d 295 (2d Cir. 1927); LH pre-conference memo in 181–3 (12 April 1927).

129. From George Jean Nathan's "Clinical Notes" column, *American Mercury* 7, no. 28 (April 1926), 492–93.

130. Id., 479–83. As an afterthought, the Post Office offered a third ground for banning the magazine: a quarter-page advertisement (on p. xxxiii) by a bookshop offering four books, with "Brantome: Lives of Fair and Gallant Ladies" the allegedly obscene one. (The Post Office apparently had no difficulty with Burton's unabridged translation of *Arabian Nights*, which the bookshop also offered.)

131. LH pre-conference memo in *American Mercury*, 181–3 (12 April 1927).

132. 19 F.2d 295, 297 (2d Cir. 1927).

133. 39 F.2d 564 (2d Cir. 1930).

134. For background on the *Ulysses* case, I have relied not only on the opinions and the pre-conference memos in 194–2, but also on a volume collecting documents and commentary about the case, published on the fiftieth anniversary of the district court's decision: *The United States of America v. One Book Entitled Ulysses by James Joyce: Documents and Commentary—A Fifty-Year Retrospective*, with an introduction by Richard Ellmann, ed. Michael Moscato and Leslie Le Blanc (Frederick, Md.: University Publications of America, 1984) [hereinafter *Documents and Commentary*]. This nearly five-hundred-page grab bag of court documents, correspondence, and commentary is very useful, even though poorly organized and chaotically put together (for example, the title page spells Ellmann's name incorrectly, with one n). I have also relied on an essay by Kenneth R. Stevens, " 'Ulysses' on Trial," in *Joyce at Texas: Essays on the James Joyce Materials at the Humanities Research Center*, ed. Dave Oliphant and Thomas Zigal (Austin: Humanities Research Center of the University of Texas, 1983), 91–105.

135. From Bennett Cerf, *At Random: The Reminiscences of Bennett Cerf* (New York: Random House, 1977), excerpted in *Documents and Commentary*, 54–59.

136. Id., 54.

137. Alexander Lindey memo to Morris L. Ernst, 6 August 1931, Document 1 in *Documents and Commentary*, 77.

138. Morris L. Ernst to B. W. Huebsch, 21 October 1931, Document 5 in *Documents and Commentary*, 98.

139. *United States v. One Book Called "Ulysses,"* 5 F.Supp. 182 (S.D.N.Y. 1933).

140. From Morris L. Ernst's foreword, *Documents and Commentary*, 335.

141. See the long profile of John M. Woolsey in *New York World-Telegram*, 13 December 1933, Document 222 in *Documents and Commentary*, 341.

142. From Lewis Gannett's "Books and Things," a column in the *New York Herald-Tribune*, Document 211 in *Documents and Commentary*, 330.

143. As quoted in New York *Daily News*, 17 May 1934, Document 265 in *Documents and Commentary*, 445.

144. *New York Herald Tribune*, 17 May 1934, Document 266 in *Documents and Commentary*, 446.

145. For a rich sample of the New York press reports on the argument, see *Documents and Commentary*, Documents 263–269.
146. From the pre-conference memos in *Ulysses*, 194–2 (LH's memo was dated 6 July 1934).
147. Gunther Interviews of LH, 1957–59; see especially "side 2" of 3 January 1959 Interview (pages 171–72 of the transcript).
148. *United States v. One Book Entitled Ulysses*, 72 F.2d 705 (2d Cir. 1934).
149. Id., 711.
150. Id., 707.
151. 83 F.2d 156 (2d Cir. 1936).
152. From the pre-conference memos in *Levine*, 197–1 (LH's memo was dated 20 February 1936).
153. 83 F.2d 156, 157.
154. 354 U.S. 476 (1957).

VIII
Achieving National Renown During the Nation's Complacent Years, 1919–1928

1. LH to Robert M. La Follette and George Huddleston, 24 November 1922, 28–25.
2. The first phrase is from LH to Norman Hapgood, 12 November 1926, 54–3; the second is from LH to Frank Taussig, his old Harvard economics professor who was then editor of the *Quarterly Journal of Economics* (with LH declining to do a book review of Frankfurter's book on labor injunctions), 27 February 1930, 62–6.
3. LH to Norman Hapgood, 12 November 1926, 54–3. LH characteristically made it clear that he strongly sympathized with his correspondent's position: "It makes no difference that I should be on the right side in this"; "[I]t is unnecessary for me to tell you at least how much I am in sympathy with your object." (Hapgood had asked LH to join or endorse the National Security League.)
4. Henry J. Friendly, "Learned Hand: An Expression from the Second Circuit," 29 *Brooklyn L.Rev.* 6, 13 (1962).
5. E.g., Arthur Dehon Hill to LH (reporting on a visit to Holmes), 27 February 1925, 54–27 (emphasis added).
6. Benjamin N. Cardozo to Peter B. Olney, 7 February 1925, 59–18, expressing great disappointment about not being able to attend the small dinner given by LH's friends at the time of his Second Circuit appointment in early 1925 (letter evidently sent to LH by Olney).
7. LH to Alfred E. Smith, 21 May 1920, 39–4. LH added his "warm regard and admiration" not only for the vetoes, "but for your consistent liberalism in the discharge of your high office." Smith promptly replied with a note of thanks, enclosing his veto messages (Alfred E. Smith to LH, 25 May 1920, 39–4).
8. See the veto messages in 39–4. Despite the governor's vetoes, this was not the end of the Lusk proposals. Smith was defeated in his reelection bid in 1920 and some of the Lusk bills were readopted in 1921—and the Republican governor who succeeded Smith signed the laws. But Smith recaptured the governorship in the next election and the Lusk laws were repealed by the

legislature in 1923. See Zechariah Chafee, Jr., *Free Speech in the United States* (Cambridge: Harvard University Press, 1941), chapter 8, 306–17.

9. LH to Oliver Wendell Holmes, Jr., 25 November 1919, Holmes Papers, Harvard Law School, 43–30, printed in Gerald Gunther, "Learned Hand and the Origins of Modern First Amendment Doctrine," 27 *Stan. L.Rev.* 719, 761 (1975).

10. LH to Zechariah Chafee, Jr., 2 January 1921, 15–26 (LH draft).

11. Editorial, *New York Times*, 19 March 1920, 10. See also a second editorial, *New York Times*, 22 April 1920, 12.

12. See, e.g., Paul L. Murphy, *The Meaning of Freedom of Speech—First Amendment Freedoms from Wilson to FDR* (Westport, Conn.: Glenwood, 1972), 66–67; Lawrence H. Chamberlain, *Loyalty and Legislative Action: A Survey of Activity by the New York State Legislature, 1919–1949* (Ithaca, N.Y.: Cornell University Press, 1951), 17–24.

13. See Zechariah Chafee, Jr., *Freedom of Speech* (New York: Harcourt, Brace and Howe, 1920), 334.

14. The expulsion story is discussed at length, both factually and with a demolition of the arguments for disqualifying elected legislators in a case like this, in Chafee, *Freedom of Speech*, 332–64.

15. See, e.g., "Hughes Says League Has a Bad Heart," *New York Times*, 19 September 1920. Hughes's efforts are traced in Merlo J. Pusey, *Charles Evans Hughes* (New York: Macmillan, 1951), vol. 1, 391–94. (Hughes's stand had a national impact: even Zechariah Chafee, Jr., the leading publicist of civil liberties, gave him credit for turning the tide. See Chafee, *Freedom of Speech*, 338–39.)

16. LH to *New York World*, 21 January 1920, 33–28.

17. LH to Zechariah Chafee, Jr., 2 January 1921, 15–26 (LH draft).

18. Ibid.

19. LH to Frank W. Hallowell, 12 January 1920, 24–21. LH pleaded a prior engagement and did not attend the dinner.

20. Felix Frankfurter to LH, 6 November 1917, 104–7.

21. The report (filling five typewritten pages) is in 104–7. Frankfurter scribbled on it, for LH, in pencil: " 'Law and Order' or 'For God, for Country, and for Home.' " See also Michael E. Parrish, *Felix Frankfurter and His Times: The Reform Years* (New York: Free Press, 1982), 81–101. (The report Frankfurter sent to LH was published by the Government Printing Office in 1918: *Report on the Bisbee Deportation Made by the President's Mediation Commission to the President of the United States* [Washington, D.C.: U.S. Government Printing Office, 1918].)

22. LH to Felix Frankfurter, 23 January 1918 (retained carbon copy), 104–7. See also id., 9 January 1918, Frankfurter Papers, Library of Congress, copy in 104–7.

23. Quoted in Parrish, *Felix Frankfurter and His Times*, 99. That LH got copies of the correspondence from Felix Frankfurter is shown by LH's letter to Frankfurter, 23 January 1918, 104–7. (Only one of Theodore Roosevelt's letters— by no means the most violent one—was retained by LH: Theodore Roosevelt to Felix Frankfurter, 18 January 1918, 104–7.)

24. LH to Felix Frankfurter, 23 January 1918, 104–7.

25. Felix Frankfurter to LH, 21 January 1919, 104–7.

26. Felix Frankfurter to Walter Lippmann, 13 January 1919, Frankfurter Papers,

Library of Congress, quoted in Parrish, *Felix Frankfurter and His Times*, 117.

27. LH to Zechariah Chafee, Jr., 2 January 1921, 15–26.

28. LH to F. D. MacKinnon, 11 August 1920, 29–11.

29. L. Hollingsworth Wood, chairman of the Directing Committee of the National Civil Liberties Bureau, to LH, 3 January 1918, 46–19; LH to Wood, 4 January 1918, 46–19.

30. LH to M. E. Ravage of the Peoples of American Society, in response to Ravage to LH, 8 December 1919, 38–6.

31. LH to Eliot Wadsworth, 22 May 1920, 46–26 (Wadsworth was then vice chairman of the American Red Cross; he became assistant secretary of the treasury in 1921, in the Harding administration).

32. See William Hitz to LH, 18 January 1919, asking LH to meet with him on his next trip to Washington "as I am anxious to talk with you touching the possibility of getting pardons for the numerous ladies and gentlemen under conviction for entertaining opinions." LH's response, 22 January 1919, stated that he would come down if Hitz thought it would be worthwhile: "I am very much in favor of the suggestion." (Both are in 25–6.)

33. See Elizabeth Stuyvesant to LH (with enclosures), 13 May 1923, 41–1. See also LH's sympathy with pressures for amnesty while urging delay until after the presidential election, in LH to Jessie Hardy MacKaye, 6 May 1920, 32–2.

34. See the summary of the Perkins-Frankfurter conversation in Felix Frankfurter to LH, 9 December 1919, 104–8.

35. LH to Felix Frankfurter, 3 December 1919, Frankfurter Papers, Library of Congress, photocopy in Hand Papers, 104–8.

36. Felix Frankfurter to LH, 4 December 1919, 104–8.

37. LH to Walter Lippmann, 7 June 1929, Lippmann Papers, Yale University, H–24.

38. Felix Frankfurter to LH, 9 December 1919, 104–8. (The person denied appointment was Gerard Henderson.)

39. LH to Felix Frankfurter, 17 December 1919, 104–8.

40. Felix Frankfurter to LH, 4 December 1919, 104–8.

41. The case (discussed at some length in Donald L. Smith, *Zechariah Chafee, Jr.: Defender of Liberty and Law* [Cambridge: Harvard University Press, 1986], 46–48) was *Colyer v. Skeffington*; the judge was George W. Anderson.

42. *Report Upon the Illegal Practices at the United States Department of Justice*, published May 1920. See also Smith, *Zechariah Chafee, Jr.*, 48, and Parrish, *Felix Frankfurter and His Times*, 126.

43. Felix Frankfurter to LH, 20 May 1920, 104–9. Frankfurter added that "the Nelson Perkins that I saw in Washington in the House of Truth in 1918 is certainly a freer Nelson Perkins than he who is back in Boston in 1919–20."

44. LH to Felix Frankfurter, 6 June 1920, Frankfurter Papers, Library of Congress, photocopy in Hand Papers, 104–9.

45. Felix Frankfurter to LH, 28 June 1920, 104–9.

46. Id., 20 June 1921, 104–9.

47. The vote was narrower (only 6–5) in rejecting Fox's complaint that the errors should have been corrected in the law review; but Chafee did make some brief, minor corrections. The original Chafee article was at 33 *Harv. L.Rev.* 747 (1920); the corrections at 35 *Harv. L.Rev.* 9 (1921).

48. Felix Frankfurter to LH, 26 July 1921, 104–10.

49. LH to Felix Frankfurter, 27 July 1921, 104–10.

50. Felix Frankfurter to LH, 26 July 1921, 104–10.

51. LH to Felix Frankfurter, 27 July 1921, 104–10.

52. See "Lowell Tells Jews Limit at Colleges Might Help Them," *New York Times*, 17 June 1922, 1.

53. See, e.g., A. Lawrence Lowell to Julian Mack, 29 March 1922, Harvard University Archives.

54. This was the proposal of Professor James Hardy Ropes, Lowell's brother-in-law and "intimate friend" (Marcia Graham Synnott, *The Half-Opened Door: Discrimination and Admissions at Harvard, Yale, and Princeton, 1900–1971* [Westport, Conn.: Greenwood Press, 1979], 64). See also Synnott's "Anti-Semitism and American Universities: Did Quotas Follow the Jews?" in David A. Gerber, ed., *Anti-Semitism in American History* (Urbana and Chicago: University of Illinois, 1986), 233–71. For additional background on the Harvard controversy, see Nitza Rosovsky, *The Jewish Experience at Harvard and Radcliffe* (Cambridge: Harvard University Press, 1986), 8–26; Robert D. Shapiro, "The 'Jewish Problem' at Harvard, 1922–1923" (unpublished seminar paper, Harvard University, May 1975); and Dan A. Oren, *Joining the Club—A History of Jews and Yale* (New Haven: Yale University Press, 1985).

55. See Synnott, *The Half-Opened Door*, passim.

56. Harry Starr (then president of the Harvard Menorah Society), "The Affair at Harvard: What the Students Did," *Menorah Journal* 8 (October 1922), 263–76, reprinted in Rosovsky, *The Jewish Experience at Harvard*, 77.

57. See, e.g., Julian Mack to A. Lawrence Lowell, 30 March 1922, Harvard University Archives (recalling that Lowell had told Mack that Columbia, through its "psychological test" subterfuge, had "cut the percentage of Jews from 40 to 16").

58. A. Lawrence Lowell to A. A. Benesch, in *New York Times*, 17 June 1922, 1, 3.

59. Synnott, *The Half-Opened Door*, 34–35.

60. Felix Frankfurter to LH, 4 June 1922, 104–10.

61. LH to Felix Frankfurter, 6 June 1922, Frankfurter Papers, Library of Congress, photocopy in Hand Papers, 104–10.

62. This and the following quotations from LH to Charles H. Grandgent, 14 November 1922, 21–26, reprinted in Irving Dilliard, ed., *The Spirit of Liberty: Papers and Addresses of Learned Hand*, 3d ed., enlarged (New York: Alfred A. Knopf, 1960), 20–23.

63. LH sent copies to Felix Frankfurter, Julian Mack, Grace Norton, and the lawyer Joseph M. Proskauer, for example. See, e.g., his transmittal letter to Proskauer, 28 December 1922, 35–16.

64. LH to Grace Norton, 15 November 1922, 33–19.

65. See LH to Century Association, 10 January 1938, 50–12; LH to Carl Binger, 1 May 1939, 67–10. Recall also LH's assistance to Howard Gans in seeking admission to Albany's Fort Orange Club, chapter 3 above.

66. See Parrish, *Felix Frankfurter and His Times*, 157–58.

67. LH to Young B. Smith, 8 February 1928, 57–24.

68. George Welwood Murray to LH, 12 November 1928, 57–24. (Murray was a partner of Harrison Tweed, LH's Porcellian friend and later president of the City Bar Association of New York. Murray was interested in legal research and later endowed a legal-history professorship at Columbia University.)

69. LH to George Welwood Murray, 12 November 1928, 57–24.
70. LH to FAH, 1 October 1929, Personal Correspondence.
71. See, e.g., LH to daughter Mary, 8 August 1930 and 7 September 1930, Personal Correspondence.
72. See LH to Walter Lippmann, 21 September 1930 (on return from West Coast trip), Lippmann Papers, Yale University, L–54.
73. Ibid. After several days of sight-seeing in Los Angeles, LH called it "a hellish modern city, built recently and w. the customary disorder and ugliness." See LH to daughter Mary, 7 September 1930, Personal Correspondence.
74. Id., 7 September 1930, Personal Correspondence.
75. LH to Walter Lippmann, 31 May 1931 (a nine-page letter, nearly half devoted to Greek culture), Lippmann Papers, Yale University, L–60.
76. Felix Frankfurter to LH, 18 October 1937, 105–5.
77. LH to Walter Lippmann, 6 September 1933, Lippmann Papers, Yale University, L–69.
78. LH to Felix Frankfurter, 23 July 1933, 105–2.
79. LH to Bernard Berenson, 6 September 1939, Berenson Papers, I Tatti, 99–17.
80. The correspondence is in 99–12 to 99–26 of the Hand Papers. It includes Bernard Berenson's letters to LH (some of them printed, but only in truncated form, in Bernard Berenson's published correspondence) and LH's letters to Bernard Berenson (copies from The Berenson Archive, Villa I Tatti, The Harvard University Center for Italian Renaissance Studies, Florence, Italy). The printed inventory of the I Tatti holdings indicates fifty-eight LH letters there; in fact, there are somewhat more than that—the Hand group constitutes one of the largest in the collection.
81. See Ernest Samuels, *Bernard Berenson: The Making of a Legend*, vol. 2 (Cambridge: Harvard University Press, 1987), 284.
82. Note the comment by Sir Kenneth Clark, who had served an apprenticeship with Berenson at I Tatti: "The only person to argue with [Berenson] with impunity was the great American judge, Learned Hand." Clark added, "Mr. Berenson admired him more than any man alive. Judge Learned Hand did not admire Mr. Berenson" (Sir Kenneth Clark, *Another Part of the Wood* [New York: Harper and Row, 1974], 140).
83. LH to Bernard Berenson, 24 May 1949, 99–20 (photocopy from Berenson Papers, I Tatti).
84. See LH to Mrs. Gilbert Roe, 17 December 1930, 60–25.
85. [Felix Frankfurter], "The Red Terror of Judicial Reform," *New Republic*, 1 April 1924 (published anonymously) (photocopy in LH–Felix Frankfurter correspondence, 104–11).
86. See LH to Felix Frankfurter, 31 August 1921, and Felix Frankfurter to LH, 7 September 1921, both in 104–10.
87. LH to Felix Frankfurter, [early December] 1922 and 13 December 1922, 104–10.
88. 261 U.S. 525 (1923).
89. LH to Felix Frankfurter, [10] April 1923, 104–10 [misdated 11 April by LH, but actually 10 April; Frankfurter replied to this note on 11 April; *Adkins* was decided on 9 April 1923].
90. See id., 7 February 1923, 104–10. The case was argued 14 March 1922.
91. See *Muller v. Oregon*, 208 U.S. 412 (1908).

92. LH to Felix Frankfurter, [10] April 1923; Felix Frankfurter to LH, 11 April 1923; both in 104–10.
93. LH to Felix Frankfurter, [10] April 1923, 104–10.
94. Id., 30 April 1923, 104–10.
95. [Felix Frankfurter], "The Red Terror of Judicial Reform," *New Republic*, 1 April 1924, sent by Frankfurter to LH, in 104–11, written during the debate about the Court during the 1924 election campaign, with Robert La Follette as the third-party candidate.
96. 262 U.S. 390 (1923).
97. From Nebraska's argument in *Meyer v. Nebraska*, 262 U.S. 390, 394 (1923).
98. 262 U.S. 404, 412 (with the companion case to *Meyer, Bartels v. Iowa*).
99. Felix Frankfurter to LH, 5 June 1923, 104–10.
100. See *Minersville School Dist. v. Gobitis*, 310 U.S. 586 (1940); *Board of Education v. Barnette*, 319 U.S. 624 (1943).
101. LH to Felix Frankfurter, 6 June 1923, 104–11.
102. 268 U.S. 510 (1925).
103. *Pierce v. Society of Sisters* was decided together with a companion case, *Pierce v. Hill Military Academy*, in a single opinion.
104. From Oregon's argument in *Pierce*, 268 U.S. 510, 525–26 (1925).
105. 268 U.S. 510, 534–35 (1925). .
106. LH to Walter Lippmann, 7 June 1925, Lippmann Papers, Yale University, L–22 (photocopy in Hand Papers, 106–16).
107. See Edward J. Larson, *Trial and Error: The American Controversy Over Creation and Evolution* (New York: Oxford University Press, 1985), 55. The Larson book is an excellent study of anti-evolution efforts.
108. See id., 60, 72.
109. See id., 71.
110. See *Epperson v. Arkansas*, 393 U.S. 97 (1968), striking down, on "establishment of religion" grounds, an Arkansas version of the Tennessee "anti-evolution" law, enacted soon after the Scopes trial.
111. See, e.g., *Edwards v. Aguillard*, 482 U.S. 578 (1987), striking down Louisiana's "creationism" law on "establishment" grounds.
112. LH to Walter Lippmann, 7 June 1925, Lippmann Papers, Yale University, L–22 (photocopy in Hand Papers).
113. Walter Lippmann to LH, [8 or 9] June, 1925, (mis)dated "January 1925," but clearly a response to LH's letter of 7 June 1925, 106–16.
114. LH to Walter Lippmann, 10 June 1925, Lippmann Papers, Yale University, L–23 (photocopy in Hand Papers).
115. Walter Lippmann, *Public Opinion* (New York: Harcourt, Brace and Company, 1922). See Ronald Steel, *Walter Lippmann and the American Century* (Boston: Little, Brown, 1980), 180–85.
116. Lippmann, *Public Opinion*, 310, 418.
117. LH to Walter Lippmann, 12 May 1922, Lippmann Papers, Yale University, L–9 (photocopy in Hand Papers).
118. Walter Lippmann, *The Phantom Public* (New York: Harcourt, Brace and Company, 1925).
119. Walter Lippmann to LH, [8 or 9] June 1925, 106–16.
120. LH to Walter Lippmann, 10 June 1925, Lippmann Papers, Yale University, L–23 (photocopy in Hand Papers).

121. Walter Lippmann to LH, 16 December 1925, 106–16, L–25. See also reminder, Walter Lippmann to LH, 23 February 1926, 106–16, L–27.

122. LH to Walter Lippmann, 3 March 1926, Lippmann Papers, Yale University, L–18 (photocopy in Hand Papers). Not until five years later did LH permit his name to be identified with his essay, "Mr. Justice Holmes at Eighty-Five." For Holmes's ninetieth birthday, in 1931, Felix Frankfurter put together a volume reprinting tributes by a group of distinguished commentators. By then, LH had published another, signed piece on Holmes, and he now permitted Frankfurter to reveal his (LH's) authorship of the *World* tribute of March 8, 1926. *Mr. Justice Holmes*, edited by Felix Frankfurter (New York: Coward-McCann, 1931), contained both LH's *World* tribute and his talk accepting the Holmes portrait, originally printed in 43 *Harv. L.Rev.* 857 (1930). Frankfurter had spotted LH's distinctive style as soon as he read the judge's anonymous tribute. See Frankfurter letters and memos to LH in early March 1926, especially his comment on 10 March 1926, 104–12.

123. Frankfurter, *Mr. Justice Holmes*, 120–25.

124. Id., 123.

125. See Parrish, *Felix Frankfurter and His Times*, 179.

126. Frankfurter conceded this. See Harlan B. Phillips, ed. *Felix Frankfurter Reminisces* (New York: Reynal & Co., 1960), 203; Parrish, *Felix Frankfurter and His Times*, 185.

127. Felix Frankfurter, "Case of Sacco and Vanzetti," *Atlantic Monthly* 139 (March 1927), 409–32. This was soon published in book form (adding the footnotes omitted in the magazine) as Felix Frankfurter, *The Case of Sacco and Vanzetti: A Critical Analysis for Lawyers and Laymen* (Boston: Little, Brown, 1927). In addition to the LH–Felix Frankfurter and LH–Walter Lippmann correspondence, I have relied on William Young and David E. Kaiser, *Postmortem: New Evidence in the Case of Sacco and Vanzetti* (Amherst: University of Massachusetts Press, 1985), which reviews the continuing debate in the literature; Parrish, *Felix Frankfurter and His Times*; Phillips, *Felix Frankfurter Reminisces*, 202–17; and Steel, *Walter Lippmann*.

128. See LH to Felix Frankfurter, 10 March 1927, 104–14.

129. See Felix Frankfurter to LH, 24 August 1923, and LH to Felix Frankfurter, 11 August 1923, both in 104–11.

130. LH to Felix Frankfurter, 11 October 1923, 104–11.

131. LH to Walter Lippmann, 5 September 1923, Lippmann Papers, Yale University, L–16 (photocopy in Hand Papers).

132. Walter Lippmann, "The Fall of President Meiklejohn," editorial in *New York World*, 24 June 1923, reprinted in Gilbert Harrison, ed., *Public Persons* (New York: Liveright, 1976), 67–73.

133. Walter Lippmann to LH, 18 September 1923, H–13, 106–16.

134. LH to Felix Frankfurter, 25 April 1929, 104–15.

135. *United States v. Garsson*, 291 Fed. 646, 649 (S.D.N.Y. 1923).

136. LH to Felix Frankfurter, 26 November 1923, 104–11 (photocopy from Frankfurter Papers, Library of Congress).

137. Id., 10 March 1927, 104–14 (photocopy from Frankfurter Papers, Library of Congress).

138. Felix Frankfurter to LH, 8 April 1927, 104–14. Apparently, Lippmann also sent Morison's article to LH. See LH's acknowledgment to Walter Lippmann, 13 April 1927, Lippmann Papers, Yale University, L–32 (copy in 106–16).

139. See LH to Felix Frankfurter, 9 April 1927, 104–14.

140. LH to Walter Lippmann, 7 September 1927, Lippmann Papers, Yale University, L–33.

141. Phillips, *Felix Frankfurter Reminisces*, 202, 203.

142. For a survey of the literary impacts, see, e.g., G. Louis Joughin and Edmund M. Morgan, *The Legacy of Sacco and Vanzetti* (New York: Harcourt, Brace and Company, 1948).

143. LH to Walter Lippmann, 20 September 1927, Lippmann Papers, Yale University, L–34.

144. Id., 7 September 1927, Lippmann Papers, Yale University, L–33.

145. Id., 20 September 1927, Lippmann Papers, Yale University, L–34.

146. Phillips, *Felix Frankfurter Reminisces*, 205.

147. LH to Walter Lippmann, 20 September 1927, Lippmann Papers, Yale University, L–34.

148. See LH to Felix Frankfurter, 14 November 1927, 104–14, acknowledging receipt of Felix Frankfurter and James M. Landis, *The Business of the Supreme Court: A Study in the Federal Judicial System* (New York: Macmillan, 1928).

149. Id., 28 January 1928, 104–15 (photocopy from Frankfurter Papers, Library of Congress).

150. Felix Frankfurter to LH, 14 March 1928, 104–15.

151. *Newberry v. United States*, 256 U.S. 232 (1921).

152. *Powell v. McCormack*, 395 U.S. 486 (1969).

153. LH to Felix Frankfurter, 16 December 1927, 104–14.

154. Felix Frankfurter to LH, 20 December 1927, 104–14.

155. LH to Felix Frankfurter, 12 January 1928, 104–15 (photocopy from Frankfurter Papers, Library of Congress).

156. Printed as "The Preservation of Personality" in *Bryn Mawr Alumnae Bulletin* 7, no. 7 (October 1927), 7–14, reprinted in Dilliard, *The Spirit of Liberty*, 30–46. LH's typed drafts, some corrected, are in 132–19. LH's papers indicate that he himself provided the title (which was unusual) when arranging for a reprinting of it in a private pamphlet, in response to the many requests. This is one of LH's longest speeches—seventeen pages in print—a length not exceeded by any other, and equaled only by his "Sources of Tolerance" speech at the University of Pennsylvania Law School in 1930.

157. Editorial, *New York Times*, 5 June 1927, 10.

158. Jennie Griffith to LH, [undated], 132–19. (LH kept a typewritten copy of this outraged note with his manuscript file of the Bryn Mawr speech.)

159. Manuscript letter in 65–28.

160. Helen Thomas Flexner to LH, 11 June 1927, 52–35. (Flexner, a younger sister of Bryn Mawr's president M. Carey Thomas, was a longtime friend of LH and FAH; she was married to Simon Flexner, the first president of the Rockefeller Institute.)

161. Dilliard, *The Spirit of Liberty*, 34.

162. Id., 35.

163. Id., 36, 37, 41–45.

164. Learned Hand, "Mr. Justice Holmes," 43 *Harv. L.Rev.* 857 (1930), reprinted in Dilliard, *The Spirit of Liberty*, 57, and in Frankfurter, *Mr. Justice Holmes*, 126.

   For LH's earlier writings on Holmes, see his book review (of Holmes's *Collected Legal Papers*) in *Political Science Quarterly* 36 (September 1921),

528–30 (manuscript in 132–10), and his anonymous birthday tribute in the *New York World*, reprinted in Frankfurter's *Mr. Justice Holmes*.

165. LH to FAH, 13 March 1930, Personal Correspondence (while she was on an overseas trip).

166. Id., 18 March 1930, Personal Correspondence.

167. Id., 23 March 1930, Personal Correspondence.

168. Dilliard, *The Spirit of Liberty*, 62–63.

169. Id., 63. Here, LH, as he did in a number of places, used the motto of Rabelais's Abbey of Thélème: "*Fais ce qe voudra*" ("Do as Thou Wilt"), from Rabelais's *Gargantua and Pantagruel* (Book I, chapter LVIII).

170. LH to A. A. Ballantine, 10 June 1930, 48–19.

171. The title was apparently given to it by the *University of Pennsylvania Law Review*, which published it in its vol. 79, pp. 1–14 (November 1930). It is reprinted in Dilliard, *The Spirit of Liberty*, 66–83. The manuscript, in 132–26, contains a few introductory sentences omitted in the publication. There are no manuscript corrections in the typescripts in the files; a note in the file indicates that the original was sent to a Philadelphia judge on 18 June (the lecture was delivered on 16 June 1930) and shows that the topic (perhaps title) was originally "Hamilton & Jefferson."

172. Dilliard, *The Spirit of Liberty*, 72.

173. Id., 76, 78, 79–81.

174. Id., 81–82.

175. Kings County judge Martin's comment on impaneling a grand jury: "Judge Scores Whalen for Criminal Hunts," *New York Times*, 2 April 1929, 3.

176. Dilliard, *The Spirit of Liberty*, 49. See also Whalen's obituary, *New York Times*, 21 April 1962, 1, and *Mr. New York—The Autobiography of Grover A. Whalen* (New York: G. P. Putnam's Sons, 1955).

177. *New York Times*, 12 May 1929, 23.

178. LH to Elbert B. Hamlin, 15 May 1929, 55–7. See also Adrian B. Hertzog to LH, 13 May 1929, congratulating him after reading the report in the *New York World*. LH responded on 15 May 1929 that the paper had "failed to state what I was trying to say," "[b]ut I am used to that, and perhaps it is just as well, as I daresay it amounted to little in any event." The exchange is in 55–11.

179. Editorial, *New York Telegram*, 13 May 1929, 8.

180. LH to Dan Williams (chief editorial writer of *The New York Telegram*), 21 May 1929, 65–5. (LH enclosed his only copy of the speech for Williams.)

181. After reading the full speech supplied by LH, Dan Williams did print fuller excerpts. See Dan Williams to LH, 27 May 1929, 65–5.

182. See Council on Foreign Relations files, 51–20 and 51–21.

183. On the SSRC, see 52–16 and 51–16 (1926 to at least 1933); on the Commonwealth Fund, see 56–34 and especially 51–9 (at least during 1930–37). (With the SSRC, LH was a member of the Committee on Crime as early as 1926; see 52–16.)

184. LH to Joseph F. Ames, president of Johns Hopkins University, 15 January 1930, 55–26. See also the earlier letter from Ames, 10 December 1929, 55–26, with a list of the (then incomplete) advisory committee.

185. From the speech by Professor A. H. Thorndike, University Orator, presenting the candidates for honorary degrees, "Dr. Butler Assails the 'Insulated Life,' " *New York Times*, 4 June 1930, 18. The citation that accompanied the degree

praised "that energy and that wisdom which Cowper celebrates when he writes: 'Knowledge dwells in heads replete with thoughts of other men, Wisdom in minds attentive to their own.' "

186. LH to FAH, 6 March 1930, Personal Correspondence.

187. See *Report of the Committee on the Establishment of a Permanent Organization for Improvement of the Law Proposing the Establishment of an American Law Institute*, prepared for submission to a meeting of "representative judges, lawyers and law teachers" on 23 February 1923. See also 116–1 (the first of the files on the ALI).

188. See William Draper Lewis (dean at University of Pennsylvania Law School, secretary of the committee, and, later, first director of the ALI) to LH, 19 May 1922, 116–1. (An even smaller organizing group had held its first meeting on 10 May 1922; a few days later, LH was in the first group invited to join the committee.)

189. See Herbert Goodrich and Paul Wolkin, *The Story of the American Law Institute 1923–1961* (St. Paul: American Law Institute Publishers, 1961), an expanded version of an article in 1951 *Wash. U.L.Q.* 283 (1951).

190. See *The American Law Institute: An Account of the Proceedings of the Organization of the Institute in Washington, D.C., on February 23, 1923*, 7, 89, 122–139.

191. *Report of the Committee*, 14.

192. E.g., Judge Harold Stevens of the D.C. Circuit to LH, 11 May 1937, and LH reply of 14 May 1937, both in 61–19.

193. See the letterhead of William Draper Lewis to LH, 6 June 1923, 116–2, listing the members of the council and showing Elihu Root as honorary president, George W. Wickersham as president, and Benjamin Cardozo as a vice president.

194. On boredom, see, e.g., LH's letter to FAH, [1930], Personal Correspondence; see also, e.g., LH to Robert S. Woodworth, 19 December 1931, 61–16, saying that he could spare "scarcely any time" for the work of the Council of the ALI; and note correspondence with Warren Seavey of Harvard Law School in 1929–30, 61–7, about LH's inability to attend to the details of the Agency Restatement.

195. LH to George W. Wickersham, 14 November 1934, 64–27.

196. Adopted in 1930. See Goodrich and Wolkin, *The Story of the American Law Institute*, 21. In the late 1930s, the ALI began work on its second model law, a Code of Evidence. It was completed in 1942.

197. LH to George R. Nutter (Boston lawyer), 16 October 1925, 116–6.

198. See LH to George Wickersham, 29 January 1935, 64–27, commenting on the report of the Advisory Committee on Criminal Justice, an early proposal for the study of a Model Penal Code.

199. Herbert F. Goodrich, "Judge Learned Hand and the Work of the American Law Institute," 60 *Harv. L.Rev.* 345, 346 (1947).

200. Professor Ralph W. Aigler (secretary-treasurer of the AALS) to LH, 6 January 1926, 47–19. (For LH's speech at the meeting, see "Have the Bench and Bar Anything to Contribute to the Teaching of Law?" 5 *American Law School Review* 621 [March 1926].)

201. LH to Fowler Harper, 13 June 1933, 55–7.

202. George W. Wickersham to LH, 6 May 1934; see also LH to George W. Wickersham, 9 May 1934, both in 64–27.

203. From George W. Pepper's essay in the *Harvard Law Review*'s tribute to LH

on his seventy-fifth birthday, "The Literary Style of Learned Hand," 60 *Harv. L.Rev.* 333, 334 (1947).

204. See, e.g., George W. Pepper to circuit judge Charles T. McDermott, 20 January 1937, 59–23.

205. George W. Pepper to LH, 29 April 1936, 59–23. (All the LH-Pepper correspondence is in 59–23 and 59–24.)

206. See, e.g., George W. Pepper to W. Barton Leach, 3 May 1938, and George W. Pepper to LH, 6 May 1938, both in 59–24. See also Pepper's recollections of this banquet in his autobiography, *Philadelphia Lawyer* (Philadelphia and New York: J. B. Lippincott, 1944), 379–80.

IX
The Hoover Years and Hand's Missed Chance for Promotion to the Supreme Court

1. See LH to FAH, 9 February 1930, Private Correspondence.

2. See LH–Herbert Hoover correspondence, especially LH's enthusiastic letter to Herbert Hoover on his nomination in June 1928, 54–32. (The files also contain other letters of praise to Hoover, and a poem sent by Hoover to LH, about the Century Club.)

3. LH recurrently used such phrases throughout the early 1930s—e.g., to Walter Lippmann, 13 June 1933 and 12 April 1935, Lippmann Papers, Yale University (photocopy in Hand Papers, L–68, L–71); and to Bernard Berenson, 11 November 1933, Berenson Papers, I Tatti (photocopy in Hand Papers, 99–13). To Berenson, for example, he claimed to find "a curious satisfaction in my little cross-word puzzles": they might not "give one extended horizons," but "in a world which appears to be pretty generally quaking they do offer a quiet niche" where one could "at least console oneself that one is not much less useless than many who are doing what to gross appearance seems more brave and striking stuff." Similarly, he wrote Lippmann that he was preoccupied with the cases before him, "my cross-word puzzles": "Surely they are all I am up to in such stormy times. But it is indeed a little like fiddling while Rome burns."

4. See Ronald Steel, *Walter Lippmann and the American Century* (Boston: Little, Brown, 1980), 291, citing Walter Lippmann to Newton D. Baker, 24 November 1931.

5. Felix Frankfurter to LH, 30 January 1932, 104–22.

6. LH to Felix Frankfurter, 3 November 1930 (the day before the election) and 9 November 1930 (after the election), both in 104–19 (photocopies from Frankfurter Papers, Library of Congress).

7. Id., 9 November 1930, 104–19 (photocopy from Frankfurter Papers, Library of Congress).

8. Felix Frankfurter to LH, [25] November 1930, 104–19.

9. LH to Walter Lippmann, 31 May 1931, Lippmann Papers, Yale University (photocopy in Hand Papers, L–60).

10. LH to Bernard Berenson, 4 October 1931 (photocopy from Berenson Papers, I Tatti), 99–12.

11. Harlan B. Phillips, ed., *Felix Frankfurter Reminisces* (New York: Reynal &

Co., 1960), 218. (LH's correspondence also uses the "green goods business" phrase and attributes it to Cotton.)

12. As quoted by Felix Frankfurter in Gunther Interview of Frankfurter, 15 September 1960, part 2, p. 14; also in Phillips, *Felix Frankfurter Reminisces*, 228. (In a letter to Merlo J. Pusey, 14 December 1956, Frankfurter Papers, Library of Congress, Frankfurter claimed that Stimson added, "Probably no man in the Administration had as much influence with Hoover as did Joe.")

13. *Time*, 3 February 1930, 11. See also id., 20 January 1930, 12.

14. The quotations are from the version Frederick Bernays Wiener heard from Felix Frankfurter about a year later, in 1931, as related in Wiener, "Justice Hughes' Appointment—The Cotton Story Re-Examined," *Yearbook 1981, Supreme Court Historical Society*, 78–79. Frankfurter related essentially the same story on 15 September 1960 (see Gunther Interview of Frankfurter, part 2, pp. 13–16); it is exactly the same story that Cotton told his daughter (and, at the time, his hostess in Washington) on the day of the conversation. She affirmed this in Gunther Interview of Mrs. Robert Morse, 31 March 1982.

15. Gunther Interview of Felix Frankfurter, 15 September 1960, part two, p. 14. (Frankfurter added, "Cotton was, as some of us were for years, promoting— trying to get [LH] on the Supreme Court.")

16. See Wiener, "Justice Hughes' Appointment," *Yearbook 1981*, 78–91. Wiener had given a speech on Roger Williams that evening; Orrin Judd and Henry Hart (1930 Harvard Law School classmates of Wiener) and their law professor Felix Frankfurter attended; the four men dined together afterward. Id. 78–79.

17. Gunther Interview of Mrs. Robert Morse, 31 March 1982.

18. Henry F. Pringle, "Profiles," "Chief Justice—III", *New Yorker*, 13 July 1935, 19.

19. See Charles Evans Hughes to Herbert Hoover, 20 February 1937, in David J. Danelski and Joseph S. Tulchin, eds., *The Autobiographical Notes of Charles Evans Hughes* (Cambridge: Harvard University Press, 1973), 293.

20. See Drew Pearson and Robert S. Allen, *The Nine Old Men* (New York: Doubleday, Doran & Co., 1936), 74–75. Among the Pearson-Allen errors: they have Hoover initiating the elevation of Stone, with Cotton then chiming in to say that LH in Stone's place would be a fine idea; they quote Hoover as saying that he wanted to offer Hughes the appointment "but make sure that he will turn it down," when Cotton never put it that baldly; and they have Hughes accepting on the spot, on the phone, relating something that Cotton could not possibly have heard and clearly did not say. Moreover, they have Cotton exploding, "Well I'll be damned! Can you beat that? The old codger never even thought of his son" (every other version has Cotton calling Hughes a "son-of-a-bitch").

21. Herbert Hoover to Charles Evans Hughes, 19 February 1937, *Autobiographical Notes*, 292.

22. Charles Evans Hughes to Herbert Hoover, 20 February 1937, *Autobiographical Notes*, 292, 293.

23. Id., 25 February 1937, *Autobiographical Notes*, 292–94.

24. Merlo J. Pusey, *Charles Evans Hughes* (New York: Macmillan, 1951) (published in two volumes; see especially volume 2, 650–53).

25. Alpheus Thomas Mason, *Harlan Fiske Stone: Pillar of the Law* (New York: Viking, 1956), chapter 17, especially pp. 277, 283.

26. Alpheus Thomas Mason's review of Dexter Perkins, *Charles Evans Hughes and*

American Democratic Statesmanship (Boston: Little, Brown, 1956), in *Saturday Review* 39, no. 30 (28 July 1956), 14.

27. See Herbert Hoover to Dexter Perkins [ca. August 1956], cited in James M. Buchanan, "A Note on the 'Joe Cotton Story,' " *Yearbook 1981, Supreme Court Historical Society*, 92.

28. See the letters in container 147 of the Frankfurter Papers, Library of Congress (in the Charles Evans Hughes file). The letters are: Felix Frankfurter to Merlo J. Pusey, 14 November 1956; Pusey (then still associate editor of *The Washington Post*) to Frankfurter, 19 November 1956; Frankfurter to Pusey, 23 November 1956; Frankfurter to Pusey, 27 November 1956; Pusey to Frankfurter, 5 December 1956; Frankfurter to Pusey, 10 December 1956; Pusey to Frankfurter, 11 December 1956; Frankfurter to Pusey, 14 December 1956.

29. See Wiener, "Justice Hughes' Appointment," and Buchanan, "A Note on the 'Joe Cotton Story.' " Buchanan mentions the Pusey-Frankfurter correspondence noted above; see also Merlo J. Pusey, "The Nomination of Charles Evans Hughes as Chief Justice," *Yearbook 1982, Supreme Court Historical Society*, 95.

30. See Pusey, *Charles Evans Hughes*, 651, reiterated in Pusey, "The Nomination of Charles Evans Hughes," *Yearbook 1982*, 96.

31. Felix Frankfurter to Merlo J. Pusey, 10 December 1956: "[T]he shrewd Cotton derived from this telephone call the conclusion that Hughes would . . . accept the Chief Justiceship" (Frankfurter Papers, Library of Congress, container 147).

32. See Mason, *Harlan Fiske Stone*, 270–74. Thus Mason reports: "Close friends of the Justice were certain that Hoover would appoint him Chief Justice if the opportunity arose" (id., 274).

33. This is all conveniently summarized in Mason, *Harlan Fiske Stone*, at 274 et seq. The quotations are from Pierce Butler to William Howard Taft, 10 September 1929; William Howard Taft to Pierce Butler, 14 September 1929; William Howard Taft to his brother Horace, 1 December 1929, and 6 December 1929; all are cited in Mason, *Harlan Fiske Stone*, 274–76.

34. See, e.g., "President Names Hughes Chief Justice . . . ," *New York Times*, 4 February 1930, 1.

35. Mason, *Harlan Fiske Stone*, 277.

36. Id., 277–79. See also Felix Frankfurter to Harlan Fiske Stone, 21 February 1930, cited in Mason, *Harlan Fiske Stone*, 282.

37. See Stone's vitriolic dissent in *United States v. Butler*, 297 U.S. 1, 78–88 (1936). (Hughes thought Stone's dissent "unduly theatrical.")

38. On Taft's maneuvering in the episode, I have relied mainly on Mason, *Harlan Fiske Stone*, as well as Mason's later book, *William Howard Taft: Chief Justice* (New York: Simon & Schuster, 1964). The latter covers similar ground, with added information. In the latter book, p. 297, Mason concludes that "there is some evidence to support the belief that Stone was President Hoover's first choice." Mason also prints a memorandum from Stone's friend John Bassett Moore, 20 February 1930, concluding that "the appointment of Hughes was the result of direct prearrangement between the President and persons outside his cabinet, [and] was prompted by political considerations" (Mason, *William Howard Taft*, footnote at 297–98). See also Martin L. Fausold, *The Presidency of Herbert C. Hoover* (Lawrence: University Press of Kansas, 1985), 86 et seq.

39. Felix Frankfurter to LH, 4 February [1930], 104–17.

40. LH to Felix Frankfurter, 6 February 1930, 104–17 (photocopy from Frankfurter Papers, Library of Congress).

41. See id., 1 February 1930, 104–17 (photocopy from Frankfurter Papers). For part of the trip, Louis Dow and FAH were accompanied by Loulie Jay and by the Hands' second daughter, Frances, whom they picked up in Naples.
42. LH to FAH, 5 February 1930, Personal Correspondence. (LH thought that his wife would have been reluctant to leave New York for Washington: "Well, my dear, at least you are free from the fear of the electric chair now and can end your cunning little days w. your old man at 142 E. 65 St" [id.].)
43. Id., 9 February 1930, Personal Correspondence.
44. Id., 5 February 1930, Personal Correspondence.
45. Id., 9 February 1930, Personal Correspondence.
46. Id., 1 March 1930, Personal Correspondence.
47. Id., 13 March 1930, Personal Correspondence.
48. There was some, but not much, press speculation about LH as a possible choice for this vacancy as well. See " 'Liberal' Is Urged in Holmes's Post," *New York Times*, 14 January 1932, 15.
49. See Andrew L. Kaufman, "Cardozo's Appointment to the Supreme Court," 1 *Cardozo L.Rev.* 23 (1979), and Ira H. Carmen, "The President, Politics and the Power of Appointment; Hoover's Nomination of Mr. Justice Cardozo," 55 *Va. L.Rev.* 616 (1969).
50. See Merlo J. Pusey's chapters "The World Court" and "International Judge" in vol. 1 of his *Charles Evans Hughes*, 594–603, 640–647. See also A. P. Fachiri, *The Permanent Court of International Justice* (Oxford: Clarendon Press, 1922; 2d ed., London: Clarendon Press, 1932; reprint: Aalen: Scientia Verlag, 1980).
51. LH to FAH, 22 and 23 February 1930, Personal Correspondence.
52. Id., 13 March 1930, Personal Correspondence.
53. Id., 12 February 1930, Personal Correspondence, and Walter Lippmann to LH, 11 February 1930, Lippmann Papers, Yale University (photocopy in Hand Papers, H–26A).
54. LH to FAH, 26 February 1930, Personal Correspondence.
55. Id., 12 February 1930, Personal Correspondence.
56. LH to Walter Lippmann, 16 September 1929, Lippmann Papers, Yale University (photocopy in Hand Papers, L–47).
57. See LH to FAH, 14 February 1930, Personal Correspondence.
58. Id., 22 and 23 February 1930, Personal Correspondence.
59. See id., 13 March 1930, Personal Correspondence.
60. Id., 23 March 1930, Personal Correspondence.
61. LH to Felix Frankfurter, 20 October 1931, 104–20.
62. Id., 1 July 1931, 104–20 (photocopy from Frankfurter Papers, Library of Congress). With respect to both Cotton and Morrow, LH had developed, as he said of Morrow, strong "confidence in the purity of his character, as well as in his extraordinary sagacity and resourcefulness" (id., 20 October 1931, 104–21).
63. Id., 14 October 1931, 104–21 (photocopy from Frankfurter Papers, Library of Congress).
64. See Felix Frankfurter to LH, 28 January and 25 January 1932, 104–21 (both letters paraphrase what LH had told Frankfurter in recent meetings).
65. *Federal Bar Association Journal* 1, no. 2 (March 1932), 40–45, reprinted in

Irving Dilliard, ed., *The Spirit of Liberty: Papers and Addresses of Learned Hand*, 3d ed., enlarged (New York: Alfred A. Knopf, 1960), 90–102.
66. Dilliard, *The Spirit of Liberty*, 99, 92, 100–02.

X
The New Deal

1. Bernard Berenson to LH, 25 August 1950, 99–20; LH to Bernard Berenson, 20 September 1950, 99–20 (photocopy from Berenson Papers, I Tatti).
2. Felix Frankfurter to LH, 31 March 1932, 104–22.
3. Id., 30 January 1932, 104–22.
4. LH to Felix Frankfurter, 3 February 1932, 104–22 (photocopy from Frankfurter Papers, Library of Congress).
5. Felix Frankfurter to LH, 12 February 1932, 104–22.
6. LH to Felix Frankfurter, 10 November 1932, replying to Frankfurter to LH, 9 November 1932, 105–1.
7. Felix Frankfurter to LH, 9 November 1932, 105–1.
8. LH to Felix Frankfurter, 10 November 1932, 105–1 (photocopy from Frankfurter Papers, Library of Congress).
9. Id., 23 July 1933, 105–2 (photocopy from Frankfurter Papers, Library of Congress).
10. LH to Walter Lippmann, 13 June 1933, 106–18, L–68 (photocopy from Lippmann Papers, Yale University).
11. LH to Bernard Berenson, 21 September 1933, 99–12, written from I Tatti, where the Hands had visited for a few days, finding only Mrs. Berenson there and B.B. away (photocopy from Berenson Papers, I Tatti).
12. Id., 11 November 1933, 99–13 (photocopy from Berenson Papers, I Tatti).
13. LH to Judge Charles Fremont Amidon, 24 February 1928, 48–15. On Amidon, see, generally, Paul L. Murphy, *World War I and the Origin of Civil Liberties in the United States* (New York: W. W. Norton, 1979), 203 et seq., and Kenneth Smemo, *Against the Tide: The Life and Times of Federal Judge Charles F. Amidon, North Dakota Progressive* (New York: Garland, 1986).
14. LH to Bernard Berenson, 4 October 1931, 99–12 (photocopy from Berenson Papers, I Tatti).
15. LH to Felix Frankfurter, 14 October 1931, 104–21 (photocopy from Frankfurter Papers, Library of Congress).
16. See, generally, the LH–Max Ascoli correspondence, in 48–4, and the LH–Alvin Johnson correspondence, in 55–28 and 55–29. (The latter includes letterheads listing the members of the University of Exile in the 1930s. See, e.g., Alvin Johnson to LH, 9 March 1938, 55–29.) On general background of the New School, see Peter M. Rutkoff and William B. Scott, *New School: A History of the New School for Social Research* (New York: Free Press, 1986).
17. LH to Franz Boas, 4 November 1933, 50–1.
18. Felix Frankfurter to LH, 29 November 1933, 105–2.
19. LH to Felix Frankfurter, 16 March 1932, 104–22 (photocopy from Frankfurter Papers, Library of Congress).
20. LH to Walter Lippmann, 6 September 1933, 106–18, L–69 (photocopy from Lippmann Papers, Yale University).
21. In addition, the Public Utility Holding Company Act to curb major units of

economic power went on the books, and the Wealth Tax Act assured the most progressive revenue measure yet.

22. E.g., Felix Frankfurter to LH, 31 May 1930, 104–18.

23. LH to Felix Frankfurter, 27 May 1931, 104–20 (photocopy from Frankfurter Papers, Library of Congress).

24. In 1934, for example, he wrote a seemingly pathbreaking decision strongly endorsing a broad state police power in upholding New York's regulation of milk prices in the face of a due-process challenge (*Nebbia v. New York*, 291 U.S. 502 [1934]).

25. *Railroad Retirement Board v. Alton Railroad Co.*, 295 U.S. 330 (1935).

26. *Schechter Poultry Corp. v. United States*, 295 U.S. 495 (1935).

27. 76 F.2d 617 (decided 1 April 1935).

28. The first case, *Panama Refining Co. v. Ryan* (the so-called Hot Oil Case), 293 U.S. 388 (1935), struck down a discrete provision of the act dealing only with the petroleum industry, finding an improper delegation of legislative power to the president. In the other case, *United States v. Belcher*, 294 U.S. 736 (1935), involving the lumber industry, the government had moved to dismiss the case in the Supreme Court because, although a voluminous record had been gathered, the posture of the case did not seem suitable for adjudication. (*Belcher* was dismissed on 1 April 1935, the very day of the Second Circuit's decision in *Schechter*.) On the government's litigation strategy, see Robert L. Stern, "The Commerce Clause and the National Economy, 1933–1946," 59 *Harv. L.Rev.* 645 (1946), especially pp. 653–64. (Stern was a longtime Justice Department attorney, mainly in the solicitor general's office.)

29. LH's pre-conference memo in *Schechter v. United States*, 195–17.

30. LH's opinion in *Schechter* is in 76 F.2d 624–25.

31. See Stern, "The Commerce Clause," 59 *Harv. L.Rev.* 645, 660.

32. See FDR's post-*Schechter* press conference, printed in 4 *The Public Papers and Addresses of Franklin D. Roosevelt* (New York: Random House, 1938), 212, 218–19.

33. 295 U.S. 495, 551, 553 (1935).

34. Id., 546.

35. See *Carter v. Carter Coal Co.*, 298 U.S. 238 (1936), striking down the Bituminous Coal Conservation Act (the Guffey Coal Act) of 1935, designed to revive the NIRA scheme for the coal industry.

36. 7 F. Supp. 776 (1934). The Supreme Court, in a unanimous opinion by Cardozo, affirmed the heart of LH's ruling in what has become a landmark case—*Baldwin v. Seelig*, 294 U.S. 511 (1935). (*Seelig* was not a circuit court ruling; instead, it was an opinion by a three-judge district court that was then required for cases involving constitutional challenges to state laws.)

37. *Nebbia v. New York*, 291 U.S. 502 (1934)—the case that briefly gave rise to hopes that the Court was ready to retreat from its harsh impositions of due-process restraints on legislatures.

38. Oliver Wendell Holmes, *Collected Legal Papers* (New York: Peter Smith, 1952), 295–96.

39. 7 F. Supp. 776, 780.

40. State interferences with interstate commerce came before LH only rarely. (For another instance, see *Spector Motor Service, Inc. v. Walsh*, 139 F.2d 809 [1944], *reversed*, 323 U.S. 101 [1944] [state privilege tax on interstate commerce]. There, LH dissented, and his view was sustained by the Supreme

Court. See Charles E. Wyzanski, Jr., "Judge Learned Hand's Contributions to Public Law," 60 *Harv. L.Rev.* 348, 368 [1947].)

41. Felix Frankfurter to LH, 3 December 1934, 105–2.
42. LH to Felix Frankfurter, 5 December 1934, 105–2 (photocopy from Frankfurter Papers, Library of Congress).
43. 12 F.2d 625 (2d Cir., 1926); see id., 630.
44. Quoted in Ronald Steel, *Walter Lippmann and the American Century* (Boston: Little, Brown, 1980), 314.
45. Steel, *Walter Lippmann*, 316.
46. LH to Felix Frankfurter, 16 October 1935, 105–3 (photocopy from Frankfurter Papers, Library of Congress).
47. LH to Bernard Berenson, 22 December 1935, 99–14 (photocopy from Berenson Papers, I Tatti).
48. Telford Taylor to LH, 15 February 1935, 62–8.
49. LH to Telford Taylor, 16 February 1935, 62–8.
50. LH's draft answers, 26 April 1935, to TVA questionnaire sent on 24 April, about Alexander B. Hawes (law clerk, 1931–32), in 55–10.
51. LH to C. L. Ritchey, director of employment, TVA, 27 May 1935, 60–25.
52. LH to Alvin Johnson, 10 June 1933, 55–29.
53. LH to Walter Lippmann, 29 September 1936 and 31 October 1936, 106–18, L–80, and L–81 (photocopies from Lippmann Papers, Yale University).
54. See Gerald T. Dunne, *Grenville Clark: Public Citizen* (New York: Farrar, Straus and Giroux, 1986), 20, 28. The "agile" description is Frankfurter's in Harlan B. Phillips, ed., *Felix Frankfurter Reminisces* (New York: Reynal & Co., 1960), 27; "slow" is Emory Buckner's—see Martin Mayer, *Emory Buckner* (New York: Harper and Row, 1968), 105. Both are quoted by Dunne.
55. See Grenville Clark to LH, 23 October 1936, 50–22.
56. In addition to Clark's initial twenty-page memorandum, see his concluding section, another four pages of musings, 30 October 1936, 50–22.
57. LH to Grenville Clark, 31 October 1936, 50–22.
58. Ralph Barton Perry, "Why I Am for Roosevelt," *Harvard Crimson*, 27 October 1936, sent to LH by Harry Clark of the Harvard Alumni Association on that date, in 50–23.
59. LH to Harry Clark, 29 October 1936, 50–23.
60. Bernard Berenson to LH, 23 December 1936, 99–14 (reprinted in part in *The Selected Letters of Bernard Berenson* [Boston: Houghton Mifflin, 1963], 136–37).
61. LH to Bernard Berenson, 25 January 1937, 99–14 (photocopy from Berenson papers, I Tatti).
62. Ibid.
63. The major documents are excerpted in Gerald Gunther, *Constitutional Law*, 12th ed. (Westbury, N.Y.: Foundation Press, 1991), 122–24. On the background of the plan, see William E. Leuchtenberg's essays, "The Origins of Franklin D. Roosevelt's Court-Packing Plan," in *1966 Supreme Court Review*, 347–99, and "Franklin D. Roosevelt's Supreme Court 'Packing' Plan," in Harold E. Hollingsworth and William F. Holmes, eds., *Essays on the New Deal* (Austin: University of Texas Press, 1969), 69–115. See also the contemporaneous book, Joseph Alsop and Turner Catledge, *The 168 Days* (Garden City, N.Y.: Doubleday, 1938). On debates within the administration, see especially Harold Ickes, *The Secret Diary of Harold L. Ickes* (New York: Simon

and Schuster, 1953–54); Max Freedman, ed., *Roosevelt and Frankfurter: Their Correspondence, 1928–1945* (Boston: Little, Brown, 1967), 369–417; and Joseph P. Lash's essay in his *From the Diaries of Felix Frankfurter* (New York: W. W. Norton, 1975), 55–62. On Lippmann and the plan, see Steel, *Walter Lippmann*, 319 et seq.; on Frankfurter and the plan, see Michael Parrish, *Felix Frankfurter and His Times: The Reform Years* (New York: Free Press, 1982), 252–72.

64. See *NLRB v. Jones & Laughlin Steel Corp.*, 301 U.S. 1 (1937); *West Coast Hotel Co. v. Parrish*, 300 U.S. 379 (1937).

65. See Steel, *Walter Lippmann*, 319.

66. LH to Walter Lippmann, 10 September 1937, L–84, 106–18 (photocopy from Lippmann Papers, Yale University).

67. Steel, *Walter Lippmann*, 322.

68. LH to Grenville Clark, 31 October 1936, 50–22. (During the Court-packing furor, Clark became one of the former FDR supporters who publicly turned against the president.)

69. LH to Walter Lippmann, 10 September 1937, L–84, 106–18 (photocopy from Lippmann Papers, Yale University).

70. See, e.g., Felix Frankfurter to Franklin D. Roosevelt, 7 February 1937, printed in Freedman, *Roosevelt and Frankfurter*, 380–81.

71. LH to Felix Frankfurter, 26 February 1937, 105–4 (photocopy from Frankfurter Papers, Library of Congress).

72. LH to Felix Frankfurter, 11 May 1937, 105–5 (photocopy from Frankfurter Papers, Library of Congress).

73. *United States v. Butler*, 297 U.S. 1 (1936).

74. LH to Charles E. Wyzanski, Jr., 9 January 1936, 108–15 (photocopy from Wyzanski Papers, Harvard Law School).

75. 301 U.S. 1 (1937).

76. LH to Charles E. Wyzanski, Jr., 13 April 1937, 108–15 (photocopy from Wyzanski Papers, Harvard Law School).

77. Charles E. Wyzanski, Jr., to LH, 14 April 1937, 108–15.

78. Id., 5 November 1935, 108–15.

79. LH memo in *NLRB v. Van Deusen*, 14 October 1943, 206–18. Case decided at 138 F.2d 893 (1943), with LH writing a concurring opinion.

80. 89 F.2d 19 (1937), vacated by the Supreme Court on different grounds in *Kay v. United States*, 303 U.S. 1 (1938).

81. Pre-conference memo in *United States v. Kay*, 15 March 1937, 198–12.

82. A few weeks after the Second Circuit ruling in *Kay*, a divided Supreme Court did read Congress's fiscal powers broadly in the Social Security cases, *Steward Machine Co. v. Davis* and *Helvering v. Davis* (the former at 301 U.S. 548 [1937], the latter at 301 U.S. 619 [1937]).

83. 92 F.2d 580 (1937).

84. LH's long memo in the *Electric Bond & Share* case, 11 October 1937, 198–25.

85. 92 F.2d 593 (L. Hand, J., concurring).

86. LH to Felix Frankfurter, 23 November 1937, 105–5 (photocopy from Frankfurter Papers, Library of Congress).

87. Felix Frankfurter to LH, 27 November 1937, 105–5.

88. The Cohen letter to Frankfurter was dated 9 November 1937. A note on it, in Frankfurter's handwriting, specified that it was to be filed with his LH

correspondence, as it was (photocopy from Frankfurter Papers, Library of Congress, in 105–5).

89. *Electric Bond & Share Co. v. SEC*, 303 U.S. 419 (1938).
90. See especially *North American Co. v. SEC*, 327 U.S. 686 (1946), upholding the provision requiring each holding company to limit its operations to a single integrated public utility system, and *American Power & Light Co. v. SEC*, 329 U.S. 90 (1946), involving the "death sentence" provision and sustaining an SEC order compelling the dissolution of the company because its corporate structure was "unduly . . . complicated" and "unfairly and inequitably distributed voting power among the security holders" (id. at 96). Justice Murphy wrote the unanimous decision in each of these.
91. From LH's tribute to Thomas Swan, 57 *Yale L.J.* 167, 169 (1947), reprinted in Irving Dilliard, ed., *The Spirit of Liberty: Papers and Addresses of Learned Hand*, 3d ed., enlarged (New York: Alfred A. Knopf, 1960), 213.
92. It was indeed upheld; the basic decision is *United States v. Darby*, 312 U.S. 100 (1941).
93. 125 F.2d 278 (1941).
94. 145 F.2d 63 (1944).
95. For the Supreme Court affirmance of LH's rulings in the *Arsenal* case, see *Kirschbaum Co. v. Walling*, 316 U.S. 517 (1942) (an 8–1 decision). (*Kirschbaum* was a companion case to *Arsenal*; the Supreme Court decided both cases in the same opinion.) The affirmance of *Borden* came in *Borden Co. v. Borella*, 325 U.S. 679 (1945) (a 7–2 decision).
96. LH's pre-conference memo in *Arsenal*, 12 November 1941, 203–23.
97. 125 F.2d 279, 280.
98. Id., 281.
99. 316 U.S. 524.
100. 145 F.2d 65.
101. 325 U.S. 685.
102. Hershel Shanks, ed., *The Art and Craft of Judging: The Decisions of Judge Learned Hand* (New York: Macmillan, 1968), 165.
103. LH's pre-conference memo, 17 June 1944, 206–3.
104. 145 F.2d 64–65.
105. LH at the fiftieth-anniversary celebration of his judicial service in 1959, 264 F.2d 28 (*Proceedings in Commemoration of Fifty Years of Federal Judicial Service*).
106. See the illustrative quotations in Shanks, *The Art and Craft of Judging*, 159.
107. Henry J. Friendly, "Learned Hand: An Expression From the Second Circuit," 29 *Brooklyn L.Rev.* 6, 12 (1962).
108. See pp. 1, 4, 5–6 of pamphlet "How Far Is a Judge Free in Rendering a Decision?" in *Law Series I, Lecture No. 14* (Chicago: University of Chicago Press, 1933) (reprinted in Dilliard, *The Spirit of Liberty*, 103–10, where the date of the lecture is misprinted as 1935 rather than 1933). The draft and reading versions of the lecture, as well as a reprint, are in 133–3. (The Frankfurter lecture is printed in the same pamphlet, see pp. 9, 10.)
109. See, generally, e.g., pp. viii–ix of the preface to Richard J. Pierce, Jr., Sidney A. Shapiro, and Paul R. Verkuil, *Administrative Law and Process* (Mineola, N.Y.: Foundation Press, 1985).
110. LH's pre-conference memo in *NLRB v. Standard Oil Co.*, 11 October 1943, 206–18. The decision in the case is at 138 F.2d 885 (1943). The opinion elaborates his views, noting, for example, that the issue before the board and

court here (whether the effect of an old, disestablished "company union" had dissipated, or whether the employer influence still had an overbearing impact on the employees' will) was an issue on which "a board, or tribunal chosen from those who have had long acquaintance with labor relations, may acquire a competence beyond that of any court" (138 F.2d 887).

111. LH memo in *Republic Aviation Corp. v. NLRB*, 1 March 1944, 206–20, reported at 142 F.2d 193 (1944) (decided in an LH opinion, with Swan dissenting; affirmed by the Supreme Court at 324 U.S. 793 [1945]). The issue was a board defense of union electioneering in a plant during the lunch hour. The board, LH said in his memo, knew best "how important that kind of organization[al] propaganda is, and how much interference it is likely to occasion with the business." Similarly on the second issue, about solicitors wearing union stewards' badges: this also was "a matter preeminently for the Board, if we are to allow it its well and unfavorably known competence with which Hillbilly Hugo [Justice Hugo Black] and his pals have invested it."

112. *NLRB v. Universal Camera Corp.*, 179 F.2d 749 (1950). LH wrote the majority opinion; Swan dissented. The pre-conference memos are in 212–13; LH's memo is dated 14 December 1949.

113. *Consolidated Edison Co. v. NLRB*, 305 U.S. 197, 229 (1938). (On the evolution of the changing interpretations of the "substantial evidence" rule, see Frankfurter's opinion in *Universal Camera Corp. v. NLRB*, 340 U.S. 474 [1951], and Walter Gellhorn, Clark Byse, Peter L. Strauss, Todd Rakoff, and Roy A. Schotland, *Administrative Law*, 8th ed. [Mineola, N.Y.: Foundation Press, 1987], 355 et seq.)

114. See *Universal Camera Corp.*, 340 U.S. 478–79, 485–86.

115. The new language is in Section 10(e) of the Taft-Hartley Act; it echoed the language adopted for administrative agency review generally in the Administrative Procedure Act of 1946.

116. LH's pre-conference memo, 14 December 1949, 212–13.

117. *Universal Camera Corp.*, 179 F.2d 752.

118. Id., 753.

119. 340 U.S. 474, 487, 489, 490, 497 (1951). (Justices Black and Douglas concurred in only part of the Frankfurter opinion.)

120. Id., 489.

121. *NLRB v. Universal Camera Corp.*, 190 F.2d 429 (1951).

122. Id., 430, 431.

123. Id., 431 (Frank, J., concurring).

124. LH to Jerome N. Frank, 2 July 1951, 213–10.

125. See Pierce et al., *Administrative Law and Process*, 358.

126. In recent years, for example, one third of all administrative appeals have been NLRB cases. See Gellhorn et al., *Administrative Law*, 366, n. 1.

XI
The Road to War and the Break with Lippmann

1. Theodor Wolff, *The Eve of 1914* (New York: Alfred A. Knopf, 1936), first published under the title *Der Krieg des Pontius Pilatus* (Zurich: Verlag Oprecht & Helbling, 1934).

2. LH to Bernard Berenson, 25 January 1937, 99–14 (photocopy from Berenson Papers, I Tatti).

3. Id., 22 December 1935, 99–14 (photocopy from Berenson Papers, I Tatti).
4. LH to Felix Frankfurter, 7 October 1937, 105–5 (photocopy from Frankfurter Papers, Library of Congress).
5. "The President's Speech," *New York Times*, 6 October 1937, 1, 16.
6. LH to Felix Frankfurter, 7 October 1937, 105–5 (photocopy from Frankfurter Papers, Library of Congress).
7. Id., 19 October 1937, 105–5 (photocopy from Frankfurter Papers, Library of Congress).
8. LH to Bernard Berenson, 3 August 1938, 99–16 (photocopy from Berenson Papers, I Tatti).
9. LH to FAH, 22 February 1938, Personal Correspondence.
10. Id., 1 January 1939, Personal Correspondence.
11. Id., 24 January 1939, Personal Correspondence.
12. See FAH (from Berlin) to LH, 28 January 1939, Personal Correspondence.
13. LH to Bernard Berenson, 5 March 1939, 99–16 (photocopy from Berenson Papers, I Tatti).
14. LH to Felix Frankfurter, 27 July 1939, 105–6 (photocopy from Frankfurter Papers, Library of Congress).
15. LH to Bernard Berenson, 28 June 1939, 99–17 (photocopy from Berenson Papers, I Tatti).
16. Id., 6 September 1939, 99–17 (photocopy from Berenson Papers, I Tatti).
17. LH to the Rev. William Adams Brown, Union Theological Seminary, 22 October 1940, 67–27.
18. Laird Bell (a Chicago lawyer; president of the Harvard Alumni Association in 1946–47) to LH, 5 April 1940, 67–4.
19. LH to Irving Lehman (chief judge, New York Court of Appeals; brother of Herbert Lehman), 11 February 1941, 75–14.
20. LH to Sir Wilfred Greene, 16 August 1941, 72–15.
21. LH to Senator Warren R. Austin, 20 October 1939, 66–29.
22. LH to Alfred E. Smith, 11 January 1941, 80–31.
23. See LH to Sir Clutha Mackenzie, 15 May 1941, 67–24, in response to a request that he become a member of the St. Dunstan's Committee of the British War Relief Society. (This committee focused on helping blinded servicemen. LH's and FAH's contributions were unusually large—fifty pounds sterling in January 1940, $500 in July 1940, $200 in April 1941.)
24. Henry J. Friendly to LH, 21 April 1940, 71–26.
25. Laurence H. Eldridge to LH, 18 May 1940, 70–17. (For other noteworthy reactions to LH's speech, see William Draper Lewis to LH, 1 June 1940, 75–19, and John Lord O'Brian to LH, 30 May 1940, 78–1.)
26. LH to Raymond B. Stevens, 29 May 1941, 80–13.
27. LH to Bernard Berenson, 6 September 1939, 99–17 (photocopy from Berenson papers, I Tatti).
28. Id., 18 February 1945, 99–18 (retained copy).
29. Felix Frankfurter to LH, 10 January 1942, 105–9 (emphasis in original).
30. LH to Felix Frankfurter, 21 January 1942, 105–9 (photocopy from Frankfurter Papers, Library of Congress).
31. Walter Lippmann to LH, 2 May 1917, 106–15.
32. LH to Walter Lippmann, 3 May 1917, L–3, Lippmann Papers, Yale University.
33. "Today and Tomorrow," 2 February 1935, quoted in Ronald Steel, *Walter*

Lippmann and the American Century (Boston: Little, Brown, 1980), 334. See, generally, id., chapter 26, pp. 327–41, and chapter 29, pp. 367–78.

34. Id., 340–41.

35. "Today and Tomorrow," 12 May 1933, quoted in Steel, *Walter Lippmann*, 330.

36. Felix Frankfurter to Walter Lippmann, 13 May 1933, quoted in Steel, *Walter Lippmann*, 330.

37. "Today and Tomorrow," 19 May 1933 ("Hitler's Speech," typed copy sent by Felix Frankfurter to LH, 27 April 1943, together with correspondence between Walter Lippmann and Frankfurter in November 1936), 105–10.

38. From the typescript of the column—an accurate copy—sent by Felix Frankfurter to LH, 27 April 1943, 105–10.

39. Steel, *Walter Lippmann*, 331.

40. Copy of Felix Frankfurter to Walter Lippmann, 28 November 1936 (sent by Frankfurter to Hand in 1943), 105–10.

41. LH to Felix Frankfurter, 26 April 1943, in response to Felix Frankfurter to LH, 24 April 1943, both in 105–10.

42. Felix Frankfurter to LH, 27 April 1943, 105–10.

43. Walter Lippmann, *The Good Society* (Boston: Little, Brown, 1937).

44. Steel, *Walter Lippmann*, 322.

45. See Lippmann, *The Good Society*, passim. For the quoted phrases, see id., 338.

46. Steel, *Walter Lippmann*, 325.

47. LH to Walter Lippmann, 10 September 1937, 106–5, L–84 (photocopy from Lippmann Papers, Yale University).

48. Walter Lippmann, *Essays in the Public Philosophy* (Boston: Little, Brown, 1955).

49. LH to Walter Lippmann, 7 March 1955, H–47, 106–18 (retained copy in Hand Papers; Lippmann himself retained no correspondence from LH after the September 1937 letter quoted above).

50. See generally Steel, *Walter Lippmann*, 345–65, a masterful account of Walter Lippmann's divorce and remarriage that I have found very helpful in disentangling the strands relevant to LH's role and reactions.

51. Id., 347. In fact, it is very unlikely that LH was aware of the affair at the time (though Helen Armstrong's perception of his question is quite plausible, in view of her clandestine relationship with Lippmann).

52. See LH to Bernard Berenson, 3 August 1938, 99–16 (photocopy from Berenson Papers, I Tatti). LH wrote that the Hands had "twice tried to get Lippmann to dine": "He evaded both times. So we concluded he didn't want to come."

53. Steel, *Walter Lippmann*, 361, 597.

54. See chapter 4 above.

55. Bernard Berenson to LH, 19 September 1937, 99–15.

56. LH to Bernard Berenson, 22 September 1937, 99–16 (photocopy from Berenson Papers, I Tatti).

57. Steel, *Walter Lippmann*, 365.

58. Bernard Berenson to LH, 6 October 1937, 99–16.

59. LH to Bernard Berenson, 3 August 1938, 99–16 (photocopy from Berenson Papers, I Tatti).

60. Id., 27 August 1940, 99–17 (photocopy from Berenson Papers, I Tatti).

61. Id., 22 February 1941, 99–17 (photocopy from Berenson Papers, I Tatti).

XII
The Chief Judgeship and World War II

1. Seniority had been the basis for the designation of the presiding judge of the circuit court ever since 1891, when the circuit courts of appeals were created (26 Stat. 827 [1891]). The position of senior circuit judge (as it was known in 1939) was renamed "Chief Judge" when the laws governing the federal courts were codified in the Judicial Code of 1948, in Title 28 of the United States Code (see § 45, 62 Stat. 871 [1948]). As a result of an amendment to § 45 in 1958, a judge can be chief judge only until he or she turns seventy years old (72 Stat. 497 [1958]). [The redesignation of the position as that of "chief judge" took place "in recognition of the great increase in administrative duties of such judges," according to the Revisers' Note to the section in 1948.])

2. "Manton's Conduct Under U.S. Scrutiny; He Defers Defense," *New York Times,* 29 January 1939, 1.

3. The Dewey charges are detailed in a three-column front-page story headlined "Dewey Says Judge Manton Got $400,000 from Litigants; Sends Charges to Congress," *New York Times,* 30 January 1939. The story appeared adjacent to (and got far more attention than) the latest conjecture about what Adolf Hitler's position would be in a forthcoming speech to the Reichstag.

4. LH to FAH, 1 January 1939, Personal Correspondence.

5. Id., 6 January 1939, Personal Correspondence.

6. Id., 13 January 1939, Personal Correspondence.

7. See "Manton Indicted as a Conspirator in Case He Heard," *New York Times,* 3 March 1939, 1.

8. On the superseding indictment, see "Manton Case Told in New Indictment," *New York Times,* 27 April 1939, 32. For the earlier indictments after the first one on 2 March, see "Manton Indicted for Second Time," *New York Times,* 18 March 1939, 7, and "Manton Indicted for Fourth Time," *New York Times,* 11 April 1939, 10. On the formal charges and the statutes relied on, see the Second Circuit's decision in *United States v. Manton,* 107 F.2d 834, 837–38 (1939), cert. denied, *Manton v. United States,* 309 U.S. 664 (1940).

9. Justice Sutherland wrote the unanimous opinion affirming Manton's conviction, 107 F.2d 834. (Manton sought review by the Supreme Court, but the Court declined to hear the case.)

10. See, e.g., "Manton, on Trial, Accused of Getting Bribe from Thomas," *New York Times,* 23 May 1939, 1 (about the first day of the trial, including the news that William J. Fallon, Manton's bagman, changed his plea to guilty at the opening of the trial); id., 25 May 1939, 1; id., 2 June 1939, 1; id., 3 June 1939, 1 (including two full pages of Manton testimony); "Judge Manton Is Convicted by Jury of Selling Justice," id., 4 June 1939, 1.

11. See id., 3 June 1939, 1, 9, and the trial transcript excerpts in Transcript of Record, *U.S. v. Martin T. Manton and George Spector,* vol. 1, preserved in vol. 94 of *Records and Briefs, U.S. Supreme Court.* In addition, note the comments in Milton S. Gould, *The Witness Who Spoke with God: And Other Tales from the Courthouse* (New York: Viking, 1979), especially pp. 198 (footnote) and 227.

12. "Ex-Judge Manton of U.S. Bench Here," *New York Times,* 18 November 1946, 23 (Manton's obituary).

13. 79 F.2d 621 (2d Cir. 1935).

14. The 1935 memoranda in the *General Motors* case are in file 196–7. LH's memo there, on the invalidity of the patents, is dated 9 October 1935, accompanied by an undated Martin Manton memo and a 16 October 1935 memo by Thomas Swan. There are also two supplemental memos by LH, both dated 16 October 1935.

15. The reheard case was decided in *General Motors Corp. v. Preferred Electric & Wiring Corp.*, 109 F.2d 615 (2d Cir. 1940). The bench on rehearing was composed of LH, Augustus Hand, and Harrie Chase.

16. 70 F.2d 641 (2d Cir. 1934).

17. See the detailed recital of Manton's activities in this case in *United States v. Manton*, 107 F.2d. 834, 840–41 (2d Cir. 1939).

18. The relevant *Art Metal* memos are in file 192–17. Manton's memo (undated) concluded, "I think bad faith was fully proved." LH's memo, also undated, was unusually long (four pages). There is a Chase memo as well. (The second set of memos, on the rehearing during the 1939 term, are in file 201–6. LH's memo then, on what he called "The Unclean Hands Case," is dated 24 October 1939. On the rehearing, LH sat with Augustus Hand and Robert Patterson.)

19. From Manton pre-conference memo in 192–17. Manton's memo was notably thin in citing precedents for his ruling. One of the few cases he was able to rely on was "a very good opinion by Judge Thomas." Thomas was a federal judge on whose behalf Manton had taken money from Fallon in the criminal proceedings against one Lotsch, a lawyer and bank director involved in Manton's corruption in other cases. LH's memo argued: "It so happens that except for an unreported case of Thomas, J., which I haven't seen, no court has ever taken away a patent decree for this kind of thing" (192–17).

20. LH memo, 192–17. LH adhered to this position in his published dissent in the case, *Art Metal Works v. Abraham & Straus*, 70 F.2d 641, 645–47 (1934).

21. LH memo of 24 October 1939, 201–6.

22. LH to W. Calvin Chesnut, 22 May 1951, 69–27.

23. Id., 23 April 1958, 86–34 (acknowledging Chesnut's congratulations on LH's Holmes Lectures).

24. LH to Justice George Sutherland, 18 October 1939, 80–22.

25. See, e.g., LH to Chief Justice William Howard Taft [6 September 1927], and Taft to LH, 7 September 1927, both in 62–5.

26. The phrase is in Manton's opinion in *American Brake Shoe & Foundry Co. v. Interborough Transit Co.*, 1 F.Supp. 820 (S.D.N.Y. 1932).

27. See Manton's angry opinion in *American Brake Shoe*, 1 F.Supp. 827.

28. See *American Brake Shoe*, 1 F.Supp. 825.

29. See *Johnson v. Manhattan Ry. Co.*, 289 U.S. 479, 484 (1933).

30. *Johnson v. Manhattan Ry. Co.*, 1 F.Supp. 809 (S.D.N.Y., 13 October 1932). Manton's vehement response to Woolsey came in *American Brake Shoe*, 1 F.Supp. 822–25, decided five days later (18 October 1932).

31. *Johnson v. Manhattan Ry. Co.*, 61 F.2d 934 (2d Cir. 1932). The pre-conference memos are in 191–23.

32. Swan pre-conference memo, 20 November 1932, 191–23.

33. Chase pre-conference memo, undated, 191–23.

34. *Johnson v. Manhattan Ry. Co.*, 289 U.S. 479 (1933) (Justice Butler concurred only in the result).

35. 289 U.S. 479, 505 (1933).

36. See William Peters, "American Morality," *Redbook*, February 1961, 95 (quot-

ing an interview with LH in October 1960). See also the correspondence between LH and the magazine in 95–7.

37. For a good survey of the history and tasks described here, see Wilfred Feinberg's "The Office of Chief Judge of a Federal Court of Appeals," 53 *Fordham L.Rev.* 369, 373–83 (1984). (Feinberg was chief judge of the Second Circuit at the time.) See also Marvin Schick, *Learned Hand's Court* (Baltimore: Johns Hopkins Press, 1970), 305–27.

38. See, e.g., Feinberg, "The Office of Chief Judge," 53 *Fordham L.Rev.*, 384.

39. See, e.g., a rare LH complaint in a letter to Harrie Chase, 25 January 1940, 68–19, that Judicial Conference work was interfering with his work on cases: "I found a lot of so-called 'administrative' stuff that took my time."

40. LH to Oscar R. Ewing, 3 February 1939, 59–29. This letter is LH's response to a 2 February 1939 inquiry from Ewing, a New York lawyer who was working on a New York County Lawyer's Association Committee Report on pending legislation about the status of aging senior circuit judges. LH was skeptical about the need for new legislation akin to mandatory retirement (then proposed at age seventy-five). (In 1948, the law was changed to make retirement from the presiding position at seventy necessary for the chief judge, though this did not require retiring from the bench.)

41. LH to Harlan Fiske Stone, 16 November 1939, in response to Stone to LH, 15 November 1939, both in 80–17.

42. LH to Harlan Fiske Stone, 27 December 1939, 80–17.

43. LH to D. Roger Englar, 25 October 1941, 70–22, in response to Englar's inquiry of 24 October 1941 about the bill, on behalf of the Committee on Federal Courts of the New York County Lawyers Association.

44. LH to Herbert Goodrich, 18 November 1954, 88–35.

45. LH to D. Lawrence Groner, 24 October 1942, 72–8.

46. Feinberg, "The Office of Chief Judge," 53 *Fordham L.Rev.*, 376–77.

47. 53 Stat. 1223 (1939), codified as amended at 28 U.S.C. § 601 (1990). The Administrative Office was established by the same law that created the Judicial Conference of the United States and the Circuit Judicial Conferences. The law mandated continuous study of problems pertaining to the federal courts and prompted elaborate committee structures and bulky reports.

48. LH to William Denman, 15 June 1946, 70–1. The only exception was a "committee of district judges whose duty it is to report to the Conference [of the Second Circuit] on matters which the Conference is to report back to the Conference of Senior Circuit Judges."

49. LH to Louis Henkin, 21 September 1944, 73–7.

50. 53 Stat. 1223 (1939), codified as amended at 28 U.S.C. § 333 (1990).

51. Five hundred is the number given by Feinberg in "The Office of Chief Judge," 53 *Fordham L.Rev.*, 382. One thousand is based on my experience at Fourth Circuit Conferences in the 1980s.

52. LH to Judge Mortimer W. Byers, 8 March 1946, 67–36.

53. From LH's memorial tribute to Patterson, 11 March 1952, at the Association of the Bar of the City of New York, reprinted in Irving Dilliard, ed., *The Spirit of Liberty: Papers and Addresses of Learned Hand*, 3d ed., enlarged (New York: Alfred A. Knopf, 1960), 263, 270–71.

54. LH to Robert Patterson, 25 April 1930, 59–22.

55. LH to Harold M. Stevens (an ALI acquaintance and District of Columbia circuit judge), 20 May 1938, 61–19.

56. Harrie Chase to LH, 25 July 1940 (the day Patterson was nominated for his Washington post), 68–21.

57. See LH to John M. Woolsey, 26 July 1940, 83–13.

58. See LH to Harrie Chase, 1 August 1940, 68–21, urging Chase to write Jackson, and Chase's confirmation that he did, 4 August 1940, 68–21 (though Chase doubted that they could block a new appointment, because "the pressure of deserving New Dealers will be too great to overcome").

59. See LH to Robert Patterson, 5 August 1940, 78–8; LH to Charles E. Clark, 5 August 1940, 101–17.

60. LH to James Landis, 31 March 1941, 75–5. See also LH to Frankfurter, 18 March 1941, 105–8: "It was a damned outrage to fill Bob's place; there was not the least need of it; we haven't enough work for even five men."

61. See LH's memorial tribute to Patterson, in Dilliard, *The Spirit of Liberty*, 263, 272, recalling his emotions in swearing in Patterson both as circuit judge and as secretary of war: "Each time I feared that I might not get through without some unreasonable show of emotion. As I looked into the steady blue eyes and at the small, lithe frame, as I saw the uplifted hand and called to mind with what dedication he was accepting the post, there came over me with more force than I was certain I should manage to conceal, what was the measure of the man, and how he stood out among those whom I had known."

62. See Robert Patterson to LH, 6 October 1945, 78–9.

63. See LH's nominating letter to the Century Association for Patterson, 13 September 1947, 78–10.

64. Robert Patterson to LH, 30 July 1947, 78–9.

65. See Herbert Bayard Swope to LH, 19 November 1957, 96–1.

66. See Dilliard's claim in *The Spirit of Liberty*, 263, 264.

67. LH to Alfred A. Knopf, 24 January 1952, 91–21.

68. LH to Margaret Patterson, [February] 1952, 94–3.

69. Dilliard, *The Spirit of Liberty*, 263, 270.

70. Id., 265.

71. *New York Times*, 6 January 1939, 1.

72. See Stewart's memorial tribute to Clark at the beginning of 328 F.2d.

73. From the adulatory introduction by Charles A. Wright and Harry M. Reasoner to *Procedure—The Handmaid of Justice: Essays of Judge Charles E. Clark*, ed. Wright and Reasoner (St. Paul: West Publishing Company, 1965), 5.

74. Charles E. Clark to LH, 4 August 1947, cited in Schick, *Learned Hand's Court*, 246.

75. Harrie Chase to LH, 25 March 1940, 68–20.

76. LH to Harrie Chase, 24 April 1940, 68–20.

77. Charles E. Clark, "Walter Wheeler Cook," 38 *Illinois L.Rev.* 341, 342 (1944), quoted in the Wright-Reasoner introduction to *Procedure—The Handmaid of Justice*, 5.

78. Harrie Chase to LH, 22 January 1943, 68–24.

79. The quoted passages are from two letters from Harrie Chase to LH, both dated 21 January 1943, 68–24.

80. Harrie Chase to LH, 8 April 1943, 68–24.

81. LH to Charles E. Clark, 18 September 1940, Clark Papers, Yale University.

82. Id., 2 July 1941, Clark Papers, Yale University.

83. E.g., Charles E. Clark to LH, 22 May 1943, 101–23, and LH response of 24 May 1943, 101–24.

84. Charles E. Clark to LH and Gus Hand, 21 March 1944, 101–26.
85. E.g., LH to Charles E. Clark, 3 January 1941, 101–18.
86. See mainly the Jerome Frank–LH correspondence (both in the Hand Papers and at Yale University), the LH–Felix Frankfurter correspondence, miscellaneous articles by and about Frank (especially Frank's "Some Reflections on Judge Learned Hand," an article based on two speeches given to Yale law students in November 1955, published posthumously, with an introduction by Philip Kurland, in 24 *U.Chi. L.Rev.* 666 [1957]), Frank's major books, the recollections of Frank's law clerks and acquaintances, the relevant portions of Schick, *Learned Hand's Court* (e.g., pp. 244–45), and the study of Frank by Robert Jerome Glennon, *The Iconoclast as Reformer—Jerome Frank's Impact on American Law* (Ithaca, N.Y.: Cornell University Press, 1985).
87. See Richard Rovere's memorial of Frank (quoting the Frank to Frankfurter letter of 30 November 1932), in "Jerome N. Frank: 1889–1957," in the transcript of the proceedings at a special memorial meeting of the New York County Lawyers' Association and the Association of the Bar of the City of New York, held on 23 May 1957.
88. See generally Laura Kalman, *Legal Realism at Yale* (Chapel Hill: University of North Carolina Press, 1986).
89. LH to Thomas Reed Powell, 9 May 1932, 59–33.
90. LH to Felix Frankfurter, 18 March 1941, 105–8.
91. Felix Frankfurter to LH, 25 March 1941, 105–8.
92. LH to Jerome Frank, 12 March 1941, Frank Papers, Yale University. LH suggested that, if necessary, Frank could find an outlet for his enormous energies by sitting in the district court as well.
93. Id., [1942], Frank Papers, Yale University.
94. Id., 6 February 1955, Frank Papers, Yale University.
95. Jerome Frank to LH, 3 February 1955, 88–12.
96. See dedication page of Jerome N. Frank, *Courts on Trial* (Princeton: Princeton University Press, 1950). See also Jerome Frank to LH, [5 July 1949], 71–20 (asking LH's permission to dedicate the book to him). In responding (LH to Frank, 12 July 1949, Frank Papers, Yale University), LH said that he would "indeed be flattered" by the dedication but pleaded: "Please be moderate about it."
97. William Seagle, review of Jerome Frank, *If Men Were Angels*, in 29 *Va. L.Rev.* 664 (1943).
98. See Richard Rovere's comments in "Jerome N. Frank," 23.
99. See id., 13.
100. See LH's 14 January 1957 announcement in court that Frank had died, printed in *Yale Law Report* 3, no. 1, 9.
101. See the bar association's memorial pamphlet on Frank, n. 87 above, 3.
102. LH to Jerome Frank, 20 August 1947, Frank Papers, Yale University.
103. Id., 9 August 1946, Frank Papers, Yale University.
104. Id., 5 June 1941, 71–15.
105. Harrie Chase to LH, 29 December 1948, 68–28.
106. James Landis to LH, 28 March 1941, 75–5.
107. LH to Robert G. Simmons, chief justice of the Nebraska Supreme Court, 25 May 1940, 79–45.
108. LH to Jerome Frank, 3 May [no year given], Frank Papers, Yale University.
109. Id., 5 June 1941, 71–15.

110. LH to Felix Frankfurter, 20 July 1942, 105–9.

111. See Jerome Frank to Felix Frankfurter, 13 November 1942, Frankfurter's response, 14 November 1942, and Frank to Frankfurter, 18 November 1942 (copies in 105–9).

112. See Felix Frankfurter to Jerome Frank, 14 November 1942 (copy in 105–9), and Frank to Frankfurter, 13 November 1942 (copy in 105–9).

113. LH response, 20 July 1942, to Jerome Frank of 17 July 1942, 71–16 (copy of LH's letter from Frank Papers, Yale University).

114. LH to Felix Frankfurter, 20 July 1942, 105–9.

115. LH to Jerome Frank, 10 September 1942, Frank Papers, Yale University.

116. Jerome Frank's dissent from a Charles E. Clark opinion in *Clark v. Taylor*, 163 F.2d 940, 951 (2d Cir. 1947).

117. The 1943 flare-up centered on *Zalkind v. Scheinman*, 139 F.2d 895 (2d Cir. 1943); see the letters of Charles E. Clark to LH, 17 and 23 November 1943, and the discussion of these in Schick, *Learned Hand's Court*, 232.

118. The first case (including Clark's majority opinion and Frank's dissent) was *Pabellon v. Grace Line, Inc.*, 191 F.2d 169 (2d Cir. 1951). LH's ruling (for a bench consisting of him, Thomas Swan, and Gus Hand) was in *Flegenheimer v. General Mills, Inc.*, 191 F.2d 237, 241 (2d Cir. 1951).

119. The first quote is from Charles E. Clark to Harrie Chase, 9 August 1951; the second, from Charles E. Clark to Thomas Swan, 21 August 1951 (both quoted in Schick, *Learned Hand's Court*, 236).

120. *Lopinsky v. Hertz Drive-Ur-Self System*, 194 F.2d 422 (2d Cir. 1951); Clark's opinion included a footnote: "Nor is the blow softened by describing opprobriously a colleague's hard work as only 'dictum.' "

121. Charles E. Clark to Felix Frankfurter, 29 September 1954, with a response by Felix Frankfurter, 1 October 1954, discussed in Schick, *Learned Hand's Court*, 240.

122. LH to Jerome Frank, 10 August 1945, 71–17.

123. LH to Charles E. Clark, 26 November 1943, as quoted in Schick, *Learned Hand's Court*, 241.

124. LH's memorandum on a petition for rehearing in *Cover v. Schwartz*, 6 January 1943, 204–22.

125. *United States v. DiRe*, 159 F.2d 818, 821–22 (2d Cir. 1947), affirmed, 332 U.S. 581 (1948).

126. Frank's last book, coauthored with his daughter, emphasized the risk of convicting the innocent. Jerome Frank and Barbara Frank, *Not Guilty* (Garden City, N.Y.: Doubleday, 1957).

127. 137 F.2d 995, 991 (2d Cir. 1973).

128. 155 F.2d 631, 638, 641, 664 (2d Cir. 1946).

129. Id., 663.

130. See Jerome Frank to Charles E. Clark, 15 May 1946, and Charles E. Clark to Jerome Frank of the same date, both in 71–18.

131. LH's copies of this group of the law clerks' May 1946 letters is in 71–18. They are summarized in a letter by Jerome Frank to Charles E. Clark on 15 May 1946, also in 71–18. The file also contains Frank's defense of sending copies of his dissent to Justices Douglas, Black, and Frankfurter, pointing out that each was an old friend (id., 16 May 1946, 71–18).

132. LH to Jerome Frank, 9 August 1946, Frank Papers, Yale University, replying to Frank to LH, 4 August 1946, 71–18.

133. LH to Louis Henkin, 7 August 1942, 73–5 (a twelve-page letter from Cornish). Henkin responded on 9 October 1942, 73–5. (The especially rich World War II correspondence between Hand and Henkin, his law clerk in 1940–41, is in 73–5 through 73–7. Henkin was drafted in June 1941, did not want to become an officer, ultimately rose to sergeant, and served in North Africa and Italy.)

134. LH to Louis Henkin, 7 August 1942, 73–5.

135. LH to Bernard Berenson, 18 February 1945, 99–18, a very long letter reviewing the wartime years during which exchanges between the two had been disrupted.

136. See LH to Felix Frankfurter, 7 September 1942, 105–9.

137. LH to Louis Henkin, 7 August 1942, 73–5.

138. Id., 7 September 1942, 73–5.

139. Id., 14 August 1943, 73–6.

140. Id., 27 December 1943.

141. LH to Bernard Berenson, 18 February 1945, 99–18.

142. See Orie Phillips to LH, 21 December 1942, and LH's response, 23 December 1942, both in 78–19.

143. See W. Graham Claytor letters in 68–32 and 68–33. See also Louis Henkin letters in 73–5 to 73–7.

144. See exchange (in response to Walter Mallory to LH, 10 October 1939) between an aide of Hamilton Fish Armstrong and LH in October 1939, with LH agreeing, 30 October 1939, 69–14, to restore his full membership so that he would feel freer to attend more often.

145. See files 69–14 and 69–15, with dates of dinners.

146. Although my discussion is limited to LH's work for Greek and Soviet victims, note also his message on the Ardeatine Caves Massacre in Italy, translated into Italian and broadcast to Italy in March 1945 by the Office of War Information—a rare, one-shot LH venture into wartime propaganda. The massacre was a Nazi atrocity against Italians: Italian partisans had planted a bomb that killed thirty-three Germans in Rome; Nazis in Berlin then ordered the deportation to forced-labor camps of every able-bodied Roman, but the local Nazi commander, Field Marshal Albert Kesselring, ordered the execution of ten Romans for every German killed. Three hundred thirty-five males—not all Romans and including Jews and assorted criminal suspects as well—were rounded up, herded into the Ardeatine Caves, and shot to death (the bodies were then covered with lime, and the tunnel entrance was sealed with a blast of dynamite). There was widespread shock and anger about this slaughter of innocents. (At his war-crimes trial after the war, Field Marshal Kesselring claimed that he had acted humanely, in order to scale down Berlin's demand to deport every Roman male to forced-labor camps; he was sentenced to death, but was freed in 1952.) LH's message was transmitted on the first anniversary of the massacre. He wrote the message at the request of Julia Wadleigh, then employed at the Office of War Information; she was a distant relative of FAH and the mother of Julian Wadleigh, a target of subversion charges in the McCarthy years.

147. LH to American Friends of Greece, 18 April 1941, 66–11.

148. LH to George II, 11 December 1941, 66–33.

149. The final version is printed as no. 25 in Dilliard, *The Spirit of Liberty*, 186, reprinted from *Philhellene* 3, May–June 1944, 5–6. See file 66–11, making it clear that nos. 24 and 25 in *The Spirit of Liberty* are really the first and second

versions of the "editorial," requested by the magazine 11 February 1944, first version produced by LH 20 March 1944, final version 29 March 1944.

150. LH to Louis Henkin, 1 August 1941, 73–5. The files of correspondence with these organizations are 77–9 (National Council of American-Soviet Friendship) and 79–18 (Russian War Relief).

151. See LH's sending $200 on 23 April 1942, in response to the organization's appeal of 31 March 1942, in 79–18.

152. See, in addition to LH's correspondence with Allen Wardwell of Davis, Polk, 82–39, Edward Carter (president of Russian War Relief) to LH, 9 May 1942, Carter to LH, 28 May 1942, and LH's responses, 1 June 1942, all in 79–18.

153. LH to National Council of American-Soviet Friendship, 29 October 1942, 77–9.

154. See the photostat of the council's stationery in 83–35 and a 17 December 1945 letter to a newspaper by the Rev. William Howard Melish, vice chairman of the council, blaming the Western Allies for the mounting tensions between the U.S.S.R. and the West.

155. See LH to the Rev. William Howard Melish, 14 November 1946, 77–9.

156. See "Board Set Up to Advise on Ship Payments to Be Made to Owners for Use During War," *New York Times*, 16 October 1943, 6, describing FDR's announcement of 15 October setting up the board. The standards stated by the board, the White House announced, would greatly facilitate the determination of the specific amounts to be paid for individual vessels. In announcing the selection of three sitting federal appellate judges for the board, the White House took care to point out that their service would "not disqualify them from their judicial tasks," because any litigation arising from the shipowners' claims would ordinarily come before the Court of Claims rather than a circuit court of appeals. (In the ensuing years, millions of dollars were awarded to shipowners under the standards developed by LH's board.)

157. LH to John Parkes Davis, 24 May 1944, 69–35.

158. LH to Judge Irving Untermeyer, 15 October 1945, 82–24.

159. LH to President Franklin D. Roosevelt, 1 January 1944, responding to FDR's letter of 29 December 1943, 79–11.

160. LH to President Harry S Truman, 18 October 1945, 81–10. See also LH to Felix Frankfurter, 19 October 1945, 105–11, and 20 November 1945, 105–12.

161. LH had a strong visceral dislike for Dewey. As he once told Frankfurter, "I wonder whether some personal prejudice must not be lurking in me, that I should so thoroughly detest that little man" (LH to Felix Frankfurter, 7 April 1944, 105–11). LH was even more caustic about Dewey in his correspondence with Louis Henkin. Dewey's campaigning seemed "peculiarly ineffective. . . . [A]pparently [he] has nothing to say, as I suspected." Dewey's demand that General Douglas MacArthur be given a larger job, LH thought, was "[a]n exception, and a very dishonorable one." Dewey's demand appeared to be merely an appeal to isolationists of the *Chicago Tribune* variety: "It was a dirty thrust which [Dewey] knew very well could have no result except to arouse hate among those absurd people who have exalted that quite unpleasant person, MacArthur, beyond his deserts, a good general though indeed he has shown himself to be" (LH to Louis Henkin, 21 September 1944, 73–7).

162. Lovett was on the University of Chicago faculty from 1893 to 1936 and had

assumed his Virgin Islands post in 1939. He had also served on the editorial board of *The New Republic* from 1922 to 1930—during the period when LH had severed most of his connections with the magazine because of his disagreement with Herbert Croly's inveterate hostility to the Senate's reservations regarding American participation in the League of Nations.

163. LH to John H. Kerr, 19 April 1943, 75–36.

164. LH to Felix Frankfurter, 23 April 1943, 105–10.

165. H. Rep. No. 448, 78th Cong., 1st Sess., p. 6, quoted in *United States v. Lovett*, 328 U.S. 303, 312 (1946).

166. See H. Doc. No. 264, 78th Cong., 1st Sess., quoted in *Lovett*, 328 U.S., 313.

167. LH to Philip Jessup (chairman, Carnegie Endowment for International Peace), [8 August 1940)], responding to Jessup to LH of 1 August 1940, 69–25.

168. LH to James T. Shotwell (chairman, Commission to Study the Organization of the Peace), 2 January 1945 (responding to Shotwell to LH of 27 December 1944), 69–30.

169. LH to Robert Redfield (the University of Chicago anthropologist), 29 December 1947, 69–30.

170. LH to John R. Ellingston, 27 December 1941, 70–18. (Ellingston had sent LH his paper urging immediate planning for the postwar years, "The Sublimest Hour in History and What Shall America Do?")

171. LH to George W. Pepper, 25 January and 28 January 1944, both in 78–12.

172. LH to William H. Waddham, 8 May 1945, responding to Waddham's plea of 5 May 1945, both in 83–14. See also LH's opposition to a project to frame an international bill of rights, in an exchange with F. Lyman Windolph, 8 July 1943, 83–20.

173. Dilliard, *The Spirit of Liberty*, 187–88.

174. LH to Louis Henkin, 27 December 1943, 73–7.

175. John J. Parker to LH, 24 March 1947, 78–5.

176. See LH to Columbia Law Review, 25 July 1946, 68–37, declining to review Sheldon Glueck's *The Nuremberg Trial and Aggressive War*.

177. LH to the publisher Lynn Carrick, 24 February 1948, 69–25.

178. LH to the international economist Imre De Vegh, 16 October 1946, 70–4. De Vegh had sent LH a draft of a proposed letter to the editor of *The New York Times* (see De Vegh to LH, 15 October 1946, 70–4). On the Nuremberg trials, see also LH's comment to Felix Frankfurter, 10 April 1946, 105–12: "The whole business would be a farce, were it not so ominous." Despite LH's strong feelings, he refused to take a public stand on the issue. See LH to Lawrence Spivak, then editor of *The American Mercury*, 12 December 1945, 66–15, in which LH refused an invitation to write an article about the Nuremberg trials, citing Holmes's advice about judges' comments on heated issues.

179. "American-Day Fete in Park Attracts Record City Crowd," *New York Times*, 22 May 1944, 1. Police Commissioner Lewis J. Valentine estimated the crowd to number 1.4 million.

180. The city officials included, in addition to Mayor La Guardia, Grover A. Whalen, the official New York City host who was then chair of the Civil Defense Volunteer Office. The clergymen were Bishop William T. Manning, Rabbi Stephen S. Wise, and Msgr. Francis W. Walsh (representing then Archbishop Francis J. Spellman).

181. Dilliard, *The Spirit of Liberty*, 189, 189–90.

182. Id., 190 (emphasis added).
183. *New Yorker*, 10 June 1944, 18–19.
184. "The Faith We Fight For," *New York Times Magazine*, 2 July 1944, 26.
185. "What Is the Spirit of Liberty?" *Life*, 3 July 1944.
186. "What Is the Spirit of Liberty?" *Reader's Digest*, September 1944, 57–58.
187. "The Great Judge," *Life*, 4 November 1946, 116–17.
188. See La Guardia correspondence in 75–2. In 1945, LH was the honorary vice chairman of the mayor's committee and delivered another brief, less memorable address, "A Pledge of Allegiance," at the "I Am an American Day" ceremonies on 20 May 1945. See Dilliard, *The Spirit of Liberty*, 192.
189. See LH's correspondence in 74–4 with Carl B. Hyatt of the Immigration and Naturalization Service, discussing the September 1942 resolution.
190. LH to Felix Frankfurter, 9 June 1944, replying to Frankfurter to LH of 3 June 1944, both in 105–11.
191. LH to John Mason Brown, 11 November 1946, 67–26.
192. Id., 17 October 1947, 67–26.
193. Charles H. Strong to LH, [June] 1944, 81–2.
194. John L. Walker to LH, 25 October 1947, 82–34.
195. Elizabeth Symington to LH, 5 November 1946, 81–5 (emphasis in original).
196. New York lawyer Lewis B. Wehle to LH, 26 April 1949, 82–43.
197. LH to Harry O. King, 12 December 1946, in response to King to LH of 11 December 1946, 74–26.
198. See Ralph Hayes to LH, 25 May 1951, 73–37, telling the story of the former Navy officer who had become president of the Coca-Cola Bottling Company in Chattanooga, Tennessee. LH replied 28 May 1951 that he was truly "moved," and there was nothing more rewarding than encouraging "those devoted men who stood us in such good stead during the perilous years that are past" (73–37). LH also took special delight that word of his address reached Bernard Berenson, who had recently emerged from wartime isolation in Italy. See letter from John Walker (director of the National Gallery of Art) to LH, 27 September 1945, 82–38: "I told [Berenson] that you had delivered one of the most moving speeches I had ever read on the subject of being an American."
199. Louis Henkin to LH, 17 November 1944, 73–7.
200. In LH's definition of "the spirit of liberty," he had included a passage stating that "the spirit of liberty is the spirit of Him who, near two thousand years ago, taught mankind that lesson it has never learned, but has never quite forgotten. . . ." (Dilliard, *The Spirit of Liberty*, 189, 190).

XIII
The Last Chance for a Supreme Court Appointment

1. FDR had also promoted a Coolidge appointee, Justice Harlan Fiske Stone, to the chief justiceship in 1941, after Chief Justice Hughes's retirement.
2. "Frankfurter Memorandum on Judge Learned Hand," in Max Freedman, ed., *Roosevelt and Frankfurter: Their Correspondence, 1928–1945* (Boston: Little, Brown, 1967), 674.
3. See Felix Frankfurter to FDR ("Dear Frank"), two notes dated 30 September 1942, Freedman, *Roosevelt and Frankfurter*, 670–71 and 671–72.
4. Id., 3 November 1942, Freedman, *Roosevelt and Frankfurter*, 672 (emphasis in original).

5. Charles C. Burlingham to FDR, 6 November 1942, Frankfurter Papers, Library of Congress (microfilm), reel 20.

6. Augustus N. Hand to LH, 8 October 1942, 109–16 (typed copy of handwritten original). Gus heard about the plans from either Burlingham or Frankfurter. See also Charles C. Burlingham to Felix Frankfurter, 12 November 1942, Frankfurter Papers, Library of Congress (microfilm), reel 20, reporting that the labor lawyer Leonard Boudin had dropped in on Gus the day before, "hot to do something for B"; C.C.B. thought Boudin "powerful with the CIO," but didn't think their public approval would be helpful.

7. This and subsequent quotations from Augustus N. Hand to FDR, 13 November 1942, Frankfurter Papers, Library of Congress (microfilm), reel 39.

8. Ibid. Gus Hand added: "I may add that he has a sensitiveness that would never permit him to lag superfluous on the stage after the work became too much for him" (ibid).

9. See Charles C. Burlingham to Felix Frankfurter, 8 November 1942, Frankfurter Papers, Library of Congress (microfilm), reel 20 (repeating Frankfurter's words to Burlingham in an unpreserved handwritten note).

10. Harlan Fiske Stone to Charles C. Burlingham, 14 November 1942, Frankfurter Papers, Library of Congress (microfilm), reel 20.

11. Ibid. On Stone's qualified support, see also Alpheus Thomas Mason, *Harlan Fiske Stone: Pillar of the Law* (New York: Viking, 1956), 592; Francis Biddle, *In Brief Authority* (Garden City: Doubleday, 1962), 193–94; and Michael Kahn, "The Politics of the Appointment Process: An Analysis of Why Learned Hand Was Never Appointed to the Supreme Court," 25 *Stan. L.Rev.* 251, 281 (1973).

12. Charles C. Burlingham to Francis Biddle, 15 November 1942, Frankfurter Papers, Library of Congress (microfilm), reel 20. (Burlingham to Frankfurter, 16 November 1942, Frankfurter Papers, Library of Congress [microfilm], reel 20, shows that this was Burlingham's letter to Biddle.)

13. Charles C. Burlingham to FDR, 18 November 1942, Frankfurter Papers, Library of Congress (microfilm), reel 20.

14. FDR to Charles C. Burlingham, [20 November 1942], quoted in Burlingham to Frankfurter, 23 November 1942, Frankfurter Papers, Library of Congress (microfilm), reel 20.

15. Charles C. Burlingham to Felix Frankfurter, 23 November 1942, Frankfurter Papers, Library of Congress (microfilm), reel 20 (paraphrasing FDR's letter).

16. Charles C. Burlingham to FDR, 8 December 1942; see also Burlingham to FDR, 23 November 1942, both in Frankfurter Papers, Library of Congress (microfilm), reel 20.

17. Felix Frankfurter to FDR, 3 December 1942, Freedman, *Roosevelt and Frankfurter*, 673.

18. Undated Frankfurter memorandum, Freedman, *Roosevelt and Frankfurter*, 673.

19. Id., 19.

20. Franklin D. Roosevelt, "Memorandum for F.F.," 4 December 1942, Freedman, *Roosevelt and Frankfurter*, 673–74.

21. "Frankfurter Memorandum on Judge Learned Hand," undated, Freedman, *Roosevelt and Frankfurter*, 674–75.

22. Charles C. Burlingham to Felix Frankfurter, 31 December 1942, Frankfurter Papers, Library of Congress (microfilm), reel 20.

23. Id., 11 December 1942, and id., 24 December 1942, both in Frankfurter Papers, Library of Congress (microfilm), reel 20.

24. Charles C. Burlingham to FDR, 24 December 1942, Frankfurter Papers, Library of Congress (microfilm), reel 20.

25. Rutledge was confirmed readily, on February 8, 1943, and took his seat on February 15, 1943. See 318 U.S. iii.

26. Henkin Interview, 148–49.

27. Francis Biddle, *In Brief Authority*, 94, 194 (emphasis added).

28. William O. Douglas, *Go East, Young Man: The Early Years: The Autobiography of William O. Douglas* (New York: Random House, 1974), 331–32.

29. Charles C. Burlingham to Felix Frankfurter, 20 November 1942, Frankfurter Papers, Library of Congress (microfilm), reel 20. See also Burlingham to Frankfurter, 2 December 1942, Frankfurter Papers, Library of Congress (microfilm), reel 20.

30. *United States v. Carolene Products Co.*, 304 U.S. 144, 152 n. 4 (1938).

31. Id., 152–53.

32. *Minersville School Dist. v. Gobitis*, 310 U.S. 586 (1940).

33. See, generally, chapter 5, "1939–1943: The Unexpected Challenge," in Harry N. Hirsch, *The Enigma of Felix Frankfurter* (New York: Basic Books, 1981), 147–52.

34. 310 U.S., 597, 599.

35. Id., 606.

36. This exchange is from Frankfurter's scrapbook, as quoted in Hirsch, *The Enigma of Felix Frankfurter*, 152.

37. *Jones v. Opelika*, 316 U.S. 584, 623–24 (1942) (Black, J., dissenting).

38. C. Herman Pritchett, *The Roosevelt Court: A Study in Judicial Politics and Values* (New York: Macmillan, 1948), 40.

39. *Board of Education v. Barnette*, 319 U.S. 624, 646–47 (1943).

40. Id., 646–47 (Frankfurter, J., dissenting).

41. Charles C. Burlingham to Felix Frankfurter, 31 December 1942, Frankfurter Papers, Library of Congress (microfilm), reel 20.

42. Felix Frankfurter to Charles C. Burlingham, 11 January 1943, Frankfurter Papers, Library of Congress (microfilm), reel 20.

43. LH to Charles C. Burlingham, 15 January 1943, Burlingham Papers, Harvard Law School.

44. See Mason, *Harlan Fiske Stone*, 592–93, and Kahn, ". . . Why Learned Hand Was Never Appointed," 25 *Stan. L.Rev.* 251, 281.

45. Biddle, *In Brief Authority*, 193–94.

46. Ibid.

47. LH to Charles C. Burlingham, 12 January 1943, Burlingham Papers, Harvard Law School.

48. LH to Felix Frankfurter, 14 October 1949, 105–15 (photocopy from Frankfurter Papers, Library of Congress).

49. See "In Commemoration of Fifty Years of Federal Judicial Service by the Honorable Learned Hand: Proceedings of a Special Session of the United States Court of Appeals for the Second Circuit . . . ," 10 April 1959, printed as a special insert at the beginning of 264 F.2d.

50. Id., 21–22.

51. Id., 22.

52. LH to Felix Frankfurter, 8 June 1950, 105–15 (photocopy from Frankfurter Papers, Library of Congress).
53. LH to FAH, 18 November 1943, Personal Correspondence.
54. Id., 18 February 1944, Personal Correspondence.
55. Id., 29 February 1944, Personal Correspondence.
56. Id., 6 March 1944, Personal Correspondence.
57. FAH to LH, 13 June [1944], Personal Correspondence.
58. Id., 2 August [1944], Personal Correspondence.
59. Id., 14 June 1944, Personal Correspondence.
60. Id., 13 June 1944, Personal Correspondence.
61. E.g., id., [1945] and 1 October 1945, Personal Correspondence.
62. LH to FAH, 10 June 1950, Personal Correspondence.

XIV
The Postwar Years, the Cold War, and McCarthyism

1. LH to Felix Frankfurter, 27 January 1947, 105–13.
2. LH to Helen Woodbine, 30 January 1947, 83–21.
3. 60 *Harv. L.Rev.* 325 (1947).
4. "Learned Hand: Senior Circuit Judge—Second Circuit—Sketch of Judge Hand's Career," *American Bar Association Journal* 33 (September 1947), 869, 870. The unsigned article was written by Judge Herbert Goodrich of the Third Circuit, who knew LH well not only from his judicial activities but also because of Goodrich's role as executive director of the ALI. See LH–Herbert Goodrich correspondence, 71–39 to 71–41. See also Arthur M. Schlesinger, Jr., "The Supreme Court: 1947," *Fortune*, January 1947, 73, 201; Philip Hamburger, "The Great Judge," *Life*, 4 November 1946, 117; and, on the Roosevelt Medal, John Mason Brown to LH, 13 October 1947, 67–26.
5. Editorial, "In a Fine Tradition," *New York Herald Tribune*, 27 January 1947, 18.
6. Editorial, "Judges' Judge," *Washington Post*, 28 January 1947, 8 (in 76–41 file).
7. LH to Robert Dodge, 24 March 1947, responding to Dodge's letter of 18 March 1947, 70–7.
8. LH to William Draper Lewis, longtime director of the ALI, 27 March 1947, 75–19.
9. LH to Felix Frankfurter, 19 March 1947, 105–13.
10. Charles C. Burlingham, "Judge Learned Hand," 60 *Harv. L.Rev.* 330, 332 (1947).
11. Archibald Cox, "Judge Learned Hand and the Interpretation of Statutes," 60 *Harv. L.Rev.* 370, 392 (1947).
12. See Thomas Reed Powell to LH, 2 April 1947, 78–27, and "Judge Learned Hand: Honored by Harvard Law School," *American Bar Association Journal* 33 (May 1947), 476 (which, like *The New York Times* of 30 March 1947, contains a photograph of the bust).
13. LH to Eleanor Platt, 9 January 1947, 78–21.
14. LH to D. Lawrence Groner, 15 April 1947, in response to Groner to LH of 3 April 1947, 72–9.
15. See LH to Livingston Hall, 13 November 1957, 89–9; LH to Felix Frank-

furter, 25 November 1947, 105–13, and LH to another sculptor, Francis Minturn Sedgwick, 30 October 1953, 95–21.

16. Editorial, "Group Libel," *Saturday Review of Literature*, 1 February 1947, 20.

17. LH letter in *Saturday Review of Literature*, 15 March 1947, 23.

18. Germany was first discussed at Yalta in February 1945, then again at the Potsdam Conference in July 1945, and once more in September, soon after victory over Japan, at the London meeting of the Council of Foreign Ministers. The failure to agree there on a peace treaty with Germany was the first serious breach between the Soviet Union and its World War II allies.

19. Churchill's speech at Westminster College, Fulton, Missouri, 5 March 1946.

20. LH to Bernard Berenson, 7 August 1946, 99–19.

21. Id., 2 August 1947, 99–19.

22. At the Moscow Conference, attended by U.S. secretary of state George C. Marshall and British foreign minister Ernest Bevin, 10 March to 24 April 1947.

23. LH to Bernard Berenson, 2 August 1947, 99–19.

24. As reported in "Warns FBI, Police on Causing 'Fear,' " *New York Times*, 17 July 1941, 20.

25. LH to Alice Hamilton, 26 July 1941, responding to Hamilton to LH, 22 July 1941, 73–34.

26. The actual number kept changing in later versions. Most often, McCarthy used 57 rather than 205 as the number. See Richard M. Fried, *Nightmare in Red —The McCarthy Era in Perspective* (New York: Oxford University Press, 1990), 123.

27. See LH to Felix Frankfurter, 27 January 1947, 105–13.

28. Id., 15 January 1950, 105–15.

29. Id., 20 January 1950, 105–15.

30. LH to Bernard Berenson, 8 January 1950, 99–20.

31. Ibid.

32. Felix Frankfurter to LH, 15 December 1950, 105–15.

33. LH to Felix Frankfurter, 19 December 1950, 105–15.

34. Felix Frankfurter to LH, 29 December 1950, 105–15.

35. LH to Felix Frankfurter, 31 December 1950, 105–15.

36. Felix Frankfurter to LH, 24 April 1951, 105–16.

37. LH to Bernard Berenson, 20 September 1950, 99–20.

38. Id., 10 December 1950, 99–20.

39. See LH to William S. Chenery, *Collier's Magazine*, 16 January 1948, 69–27.

40. LH to Allen Wardwell, 31 January 1951, in response to Wardwell to LH, 30 January 1951, 82–39.

41. LH to Walter White, 11 February 1952, 93–26.

42. The meeting was at the City Bar Association on 4 May 1953. See LH correspondence with Dudley Bonsal of the bar association, especially Bonsal letter of 5 May 1953, 84–19. See also related correspondence in 84–19 and 84–26. Also, LH attended a luncheon for exiles from Eastern Europe held by the National Committee for a Free Europe early in 1951. See LH telegram to Joseph C. Grew, 2 February 1951, 77–34.

43. See LH's approving response to a letter requesting permission, 15 April 1954, 94–10.

44. LH to Miss Best, an official of Planned Parenthood, 3 July 1955, 94–10.

45. LH to the editor of *New York Herald Tribune*, 25 September 1952, which was published on 27 September 1952. See also LH correspondence with H. T. Webster's widow in 98–19.

46. Harry S Truman to LH, 23 May 1951, quoted together with LH's retirement letter, in Irving Dilliard, ed., *The Spirit of Liberty: Papers and Addresses of Learned Hand*, 3d ed., enlarged (New York: Alfred A. Knopf, 1960), xxv–xxvii.

47. Learned Hand, "The One Condition," no. 32 in Dilliard, *The Spirit of Liberty*, 223–24 (emphasis added).

48. LH to Herman Finkelstein, 16 August 1952, 88–4.

49. "Judge Hand Says U.S. Democracy Is Menaced by Suspicion and Fear," *New York Times*, 25 October 1952, 1.

50. Learned Hand, "A Plea for the Open Mind and Free Discussion," no. 36 in Dilliard, *The Spirit of Liberty*, 274, 284.

51. LH to Felix Frankfurter, 30 October 1952, 105–17.

52. Editorial, "Wise Words from Judge Hand," *New York Times*, 26 October 1952; "The Future of Wisdom in America," *Saturday Review of Literature*, 22 November 1952, 9–10, 55–56. On additional reprintings, see, e.g., LH to American Association of University Professors, 26 January 1953, 84–7, approving reprinting in *AAUP Bulletin*; also reprinted in *The Progressive* magazine, December 1952—see William L. Strauss to LH, 8 April 1953, 96–14. See also commendatory editorials in *Washington Post, St. Louis Post-Dispatch*, and *Toledo Blade*; for Murrow's use of the speech in his Monday evening news broadcast, 27 October 1952, see Myron T. Gomberg to LH, 11 December 1952, 89–4.

53. LH to Herbert Bayard Swope, 28 October 1952, in reply to Swope to LH, 27 October 1952, 96–1.

54. LH to Norman Thomas, 1 December 1952, in response to Thomas to LH, 26 November 1952, 96–18.

55. LH to Felix Frankfurter, 30 October 1952, 105–17.

56. LH to Herbert Goodrich, 6 April 1953, 88–34.

57. LH to John Hazard, 7 December 1953, 86–1.

58. LH to Whitney North Seymour, a leader of the New York bar, 21 November 1952, 95–23.

59. LH to Irving Dilliard, 31 October 1952, 87–14.

60. LH to Bernard Berenson, 24 January 1954, 99–22.

61. See id., 26 December 1954, 99–23.

62. Ibid.

63. LH's address, "A Fanfare for Prometheus," no. 39 in Dilliard, *The Spirit of Liberty*, 291–98, reprinted from the American Jewish Committee's report of its annual meeting, *"Proclaim Liberty"* . . . *Report of the 48th Annual Meeting of the American Jewish Committee* (New York: American Jewish Committee, 1955). The committee also reprinted Hand's address in a separate pamphlet in March 1955. (The title of the address derives from LH's use, at his conclusion, of the last words of Percy Shelley's *Prometheus Unbound*.)

64. See *"Proclaim Liberty,"* 25.

65. Dilliard, *The Spirit of Liberty*, 291–96.

66. See Learned Hand, "Mr. Justice Holmes," in id., 57.

67. Id., 297–98.

68. See "A Plea for the Freedom of Dissent," *New York Times Magazine*, 6 February

1955; "A Fanfare for Prometheus," *New York Herald Tribune*, 3 February 1955; *Vital Speeches*, 1 March 1955; and letter to LH from Senator Lehman's executive assistant, 10 February 1955, 87–1.

69. Felix Frankfurter to LH, 31 January 1955, 105–20.
70. 185 F.2d 629 (2d Cir. 1950).
71. The defendants in *Coplon* were also convicted of conspiring to remove and copy government documents in order to turn them over to a Soviet citizen.
72. 183 F.2d 201 (2d Cir. 1950).
73. 208 F.2d 567 (2d Cir. 1953).
74. 185 F.2d, 632.
75. 185 F.2d, 634–36.
76. *Olmstead v. United States*, 277 U.S. 438 (1928).
77. *United States v. Nardone*, 106 F.2d 41, 44 (2d Cir. 1939).
78. 185 F.2d, 640.
79. 185 F.2d 629, 638.
80. *United States v. Casino*, 286 Fed. 976 (S.D.N.Y. 1923).
81. *United States v. Kirschenblatt*, 16 F.2d 202 (2d Cir. 1926).
82. See, e.g., *United States v. Rabinowitz*, 176 F.2d 732 (2d Cir. 1949).
83. 331 U.S. 145 (1947).
84. LH to Felix Frankfurter, 10 May 1947, 105–13 (soon after the *Harris* decision).
85. Id., 16 January 1948, 105–14.
86. *Trupiano v. United States*, 334 U.S. 699 (1948).
87. *United States v. Rabinowitz*, 176 F.2d 732 (2d Cir. 1949).
88. 339 U.S. 56, 71 (1950). (In later years, the Supreme Court itself expressed doubt that its *Rabinowitz* ruling would be followed on its own facts if the question were again presented to the justices. See *Abel v. United States*, 362 U.S. 217, 235 [1960].)
89. Felix Frankfurter to LH, 8 December 1950, 105–15.
90. See 69–8, containing eleven postcards and six letters criticizing LH's ruling.
91. LH to Felix Frankfurter, 19 December 1950, 105–15.
92. Hershel Shanks, ed., *The Art and Craft of Judging: The Decisions of Judge Learned Hand* (New York: Macmillan, 1968), 298.
93. This is a paraphrase of Hand's summary in *Dennis*, 183 F.2d, 206–7 (2d Cir. 1950).
94. *Dennis v. United States*, 341 U.S. 494, 510 (1951).
95. LH to Oliver Wendell Holmes, Jr., 25 November 1919, Holmes Papers, Harvard Law School, 43–30, reprinted in appendix to Gerald Gunther, "Learned Hand and the Origins of Modern First Amendment Doctrine: Some Fragments of History," 27 *Stan. L.Rev.* 719, 760 (1975).
96. LH to Oliver Wendell Holmes, Jr., [late March] 1919, Holmes Papers, Harvard Law School, 43–30, reprinted in Gunther, "Learned Hand and the Origins of Modern First Amendment Doctrine," 27 *Stan. L.Rev.* 719, 759 (1975).
97. 183 F.2d 201, 207–12.
98. 268 U.S. 652 (1925).
99. E.g., Holmes, joined by Brandeis, in *Gitlow*; Holmes, joined by Brandeis, in *Abrams v. United States*, 250 U.S. 616 (1919); and Brandeis's concurrence in *Whitney v. California*, 274 U.S. 357 (1927), joined by Holmes.
100. 183 F.2d, 209.

101. Id., F.2d, 212.
102. Id., F.2d, 212–13.
103. 341 U.S. 494, 581.
104. Id., 583, 585 (emphasis added).
105. 183 F.2d, 213.
106. 341 U.S., 581.
107. The citations are *Yates*, 354 U.S. 298 (1957); *Scales*, 367 U.S. 203 (1961); *Noto*, 367 U.S. 290 (1961).
108. See Gunther, "Learned Hand and the Origins of Modern First Amendment Doctrine," 27 *Stan. L.Rev.* 719, 753.
109. 395 U.S. 444 (1969).
110. LH to Bernard Berenson, 11 June 1951, 99–21.
111. LH to Felix Frankfurter, 8 June 1951, 105–16.
112. Ibid.
113. LH was referring to Holmes's statement in his dissent in *Gitlow v. New York*, 268 U.S. 652, 673 (1925): "Every idea is an incitement."
114. LH to Felix Frankfurter, 8 June 1951, 105–16.
115. Elliot Richardson, "Freedom of Expression and the Function of the Courts," 65 *Harv. L.Rev.* 1 (1951).
116. LH to Elliot Richardson, 29 February 1952, 105–17 (photocopy from Frankfurter Papers, Library of Congress). (I believe that Frankfurter got this typewritten copy from Richardson and put it with his LH correspondence; there is no mention of it in Frankfurter's correspondence with LH. Richardson replied in a letter of 8 March 1952, also in this file.)
117. LH to Irving Dilliard, 3 April 1952, 87–14.
118. See "Million Bail Asked for Red Leaders," *New York Times*, 2 November 1949, 5.
119. Ibid. (The government asked for $100,000 each for seven of the defendants, $75,000 each for the remaining four.)
120. See "Out on Bail," *New York Times*, 6 November 1949 (News of the Week in Review).
121. See "Million Bail Asked for Red Leaders," *New York Times*, 2 November 1949, 5.
122. "Communists Freed in Bail of $260,000 to Press Appeal," *New York Times*, 4 November 1949, 1.
123. "U.S. Court Revokes 11 Reds' Bail, Giving 30 Days for Appeal," *New York Times*, 29 August 1950, 1.
124. *Williamson v. United States*, 184 F.2d 280, 282, 284 (1950). The case is called *Williamson v. United States* (rather than *Dennis v. United States*) after the labor secretary of the Communist party, because Eugene Dennis was then serving a jail sentence for contempt of Congress and thus was not eligible to be released as part of the Smith Act appeal. (On 7 March 1951, the Second Circuit ruled that Dennis, too, would be released on his original bail of $30,000 if the Supreme Court did not decide the Smith Act case by the time Dennis completed serving his contempt-of-Congress sentence. Dennis was in fact released on bail on 12 March 1951. See "Red Leader Dennis, Freed from U.S. Jail, Eager to Wage a 'Real Crusade for Peace,' " *New York Times*, 13 March 1951, 14.)
125. "Bricker Asks Probe of Judges Who Have Freed Communists," *Washington Post* printing of United Press story, 30 March 1951, in 70–1 (with LH's

correspondence with Judge William Denman, chief judge of the Ninth Circuit).

126. Judge William Denman to Senator John Bricker, 2 April 1951; Denman to LH, undated, but probably of the same date; both are in 70–1.

127. The demonstrators often used a slogan that became more famous some years later, during the civil rights movement: "We Shall Not Be Moved." See "Communists Freed in Bail," *New York Times*, 4 November 1949, 1.

128. Rockwell Kent to editor, *Masses & Mainstream*, 2 December 1949, enclosed with Kent to LH of same date, 74–38.

129. The phrase is the title of chapter 4, Michal R. Belknap, *Cold War Political Justice: The Smith Act, the Communist Party, and American Civil Liberties* (Westport: Greenwood Press, 1977).

130. Belknap, *Cold War Political Justice*, 101.

131. *United States v. Dennis*, 183 F.2d 201, 226.

132. 183 F.2d, 225, 226.

133. Belknap, *Cold War Political Justice*, 113.

134. When Medina was promoted, he was busy in another long trial (in the *Investment Bankers* case), so he did not in fact begin to sit actively on the Second Circuit until 1953.

135. LH's supporting letter to the Century Association, 27 January 1951, endorsing Medina's candidacy to the club, 76–19.

136. Stanley I. Kutler, *The American Inquisition: Justice and Injustice in the Cold War* (New York: Hill and Wang, 1982), 266, note 5, quoting Charles C. Burlingham to Felix Frankfurter, 17 January 1951, Frankfurter Papers, Library of Congress.

137. LH note and clipping to Felix Frankfurter, 12 January 1951, 105–16.

138. Newspaper clipping, unidentified source, enclosed with Felix Frankfurter to LH, [8?] April 1951, 105–16.

139. Justice Jackson's note is also in 105–16.

140. LH to Felix Frankfurter, 9 April 1951, 105–16.

141. Fed. R. Crim. P. 42(a).

142. *United States v. Sacher*, 182 F.2d 416 (1951); see the Supreme Court opinion in this case, *Sacher v. United States*, 343 U.S. 1, 3 (1952).

143. See Kutler, *The American Inquisition*, 161.

144. Argument 9 January 1952; decision 10 March 1952; *Sacher v. United States*, 343 U.S. 1 (1952).

145. Jackson's dissent is at 343 U.S. 1, 13. Frankfurter's dissent is at 343 U.S. 1, 23–89 (with a forty-seven-page appendix beginning at p. 42). Justices Black and Douglas also dissented.

146. LH to Felix Frankfurter, 6 April 1952, 105–17.

147. *United States v. Remington*, 208 F.2d 567 (2d Cir. 1953).

148. Shanks, *The Art and Craft of Judging*, 299.

149. In reconstructing the Remington story, I have relied on the following in addition to my own recollection: the generally accurate introduction to the *Remington* case in Shanks, *The Art and Craft of Judging*, 299–303; the *New York Times* reports on the first and second trials and their aftermath; the judges' pre-conference memoranda in the Second Circuit, especially on the appeal of the first conviction in file 213–18; and the pre-conference memoranda in the second *Remington* appeal in 214–24, with memoranda by Thomas Swan and Gus Hand, but none by LH. Remington's career is particularly well sketched in "Remington Denied Link to Red Spies," *New York Times*, 25 November 1954, 19.

150. The subcommittee was chaired by Senator Homer Ferguson (R.-Mich.).
151. Remington's attorneys later insisted that he had spoken with Elizabeth Bentley only because he was trying to be "an important guy" and a "big shot" ("Remington Tells of Bentley Data," *New York Times*, 21 January 1953), 11.
152. The grand jury hearings leading to Remington's first indictment took place in May 1950: see, e.g., "Red Quiz Again Hears Remington," *New York Times*, 24 May 1950, 26. He was indicted on 8 June 1950: see "Grand Jury Here Indicts Remington on Perjury Charge," *New York Times*, 9 June 1950, 1. Remington was thirty-two years old at the time. *The New York Times* described him as a 6'2" tall, redheaded, handsome young man, and, later, as looking increasingly haggard.
153. See "Remington Quits U.S. Post to Give Full Time to Defense," *New York Times*, 10 June 1950, 1.
154. "Remington Denies Red Membership," *New York Times*, 20 January 1953, 4.
155. "Remington Denies Party Tie," *New York Times*, 31 July 1948, 1.
156. On Remington's denials of party membership at his trial, see the summary in "Remington Gets 5 Years, Fined $2,000; Appeal Set," in *New York Times*, 9 February 1951, 1. See also "Remington: Guilty," *New York Times*, 11 February 1951 (News of the Week in Review), reporting that Remington's trial had "often" been called the "little Hiss case." The conviction laid the Truman administration open to new charges that its loyalty program was inadequate ("Anti-Subversive Forces Get Added Ammunition," *New York Times*, 11 February 1951 [News of the Week in Review]).
157. "Remington Gets 5 Years," *New York Times*, 9 February 1951, 1.
158. "Remington Continues at Liberty as Court Weighs Long-Term Bail," *New York Times*, 10 February 1951, 6.
159. See "Reversal Argued in Remington Case," *New York Times*, 16 June 1951, 6. This first *Remington* case was decided on 22 August 1951. *United States v. Remington*, 191 F.2d 246 (2d Cir. 1951).
160. See Thomas Swan memo of 25 July 1951 and LH memo of 31 July 1951, both in 213–18.
161. Gus Hand memo, 5 July 1951, 213–18.
162. 191 F.2d, 252. During oral argument before the Second Circuit, LH's questions indicated that he was already concerned about this issue. The prosecution argued that one biased grand juror would not invalidate an indictment. LH retorted, "If that's the law there will be one vote to change it"; any other view "would take away all protection from the accused" ("Reversal Argued in Remington Case," *New York Times*, 16 June 1951, 6).
163. LH to Felix Frankfurter (from Windsor, Vermont), 26 August 1951, 105–17.
164. Augustus Hand's memo in second *Remington* appeal was dated 28 October 1953 and is in 214–24; Thomas Swan's memo of 24 October 1953 is also in 214–24.
165. See LH's dissent in 208 F.2d, 571–75, for this and all following quotations.
166. The central Supreme Court case establishing this principle and relied on by LH was *Silverthorne Lumber Co. v. United States*, 251 U.S. 385 (1920).
167. The leading case relied on by LH was *Sorrels v. United States*, 287 U.S. 435 (1932).
168. *Spector Motor Service, Inc., v. Walsh*, 139 F.2d 809, 823 (2d Cir. 1944).
169. "Ex-Wife Identifies Remington as Red," *New York Times*, 27 December 1950,

1. Chanler defended Remington as merely "a college youth who embraced the philosophy of 'fellow travelers' as he 'sowed his mental wild oats.' " Chanler's opening statement described Remington as a young man who "might have talked like many other Americans who embraced the 'common front' " but added that the question was not whether Remington talked like a Communist at the age of sixteen or seventeen, "but was he a card-carrying member?" Chanler's cross-examination of Ann Remington tried to show that the "causes she and Remington supported in 1937 and 1938 were similar to those embraced by most liberals of the day." See also "Mrs. Remington Says Ex-Husband and She Were Not 'Orthodox Reds,' " *New York Times*, 29 December 1950, 1, and "Prosecution's Witness," *New York Times*, 31 December 1950 (News of the Week in Review).

170. See Julia Wadleigh file, 82–36, and Richard R. Wadleigh file, 82–37.

171. "Wadleigh Admits Giving Documents to Soviet Spy Ring," *New York Times*, 17 June 1949, 1, and Wadleigh's twelve-part memoir series, "Why I Spied for the Communists," *New York Post*, 10 July through 24 July 1949.

172. LH to Edward R. Lewis, Winnetka, Illinois, 15 June 1954, replying to Lewis to LH, 17 April 1954, both in 92–4.

173. LH to Felix Frankfurter, 25 February 1954, 105–20. (The Supreme Court's denial of review is reported at 347 U.S. 913 [1954]. The date of the order was 8 February 1954.)

174. Felix Frankfurter to LH, 3 March 1954, 105–20.

175. LH to Felix Frankfurter, 8 March 1954, 105–20.

176. "Court Rejects Plea of Remington's Wife," *New York Times*, 5 March 1954, 7. A few months later, Remington became eligible for parole and appeared before the parole board; once again, he obtained no relief. "Remington Plea Denied," *New York Times*, 26 June 1954, 6.

177. "Remington Dies in Prison; 2 Inmates Named as Killers," *New York Times*, 25 November 1954, 1; "Two in Lewisburg," *New York Times*, 28 November 1954 (News of the Week in Review).

178. "Remington Hurt in Prison Assault," *New York Times*, 24 November 1954, 9.

179. "Remington Death Laid to Robbery," *New York Times*, 27 November 1954, 5; see also, e.g., "Remington Dies in Prison; 2 Inmates Named as Killers," *New York Times*, 25 November 1954, 1.

180. "Hiss, Free, Seeks His 'Vindication,' " *New York Times*, 28 November 1954, 37.

181. "Slayers Plead Guilty," *New York Times*, 7 May 1955, 14; "3 Slayers Sentenced," *New York Times*, 27 May 1955, 45.

182. For background, see E. J. Kahn, Jr., *The China Hands: American Foreign Service Officers and What Befell Them* (New York: Viking, 1975).

183. See the *New York Times* front-page stories of 4 January 1953, "Truman Orders New Board to Review Vincent's Loyalty," and 1 February 1953, "Dulles Will Rule in Vincent Inquiry."

184. On the Vincent inquiry, see also Elliot Richardson to LH, 10 February 1953, 94–24, and LH to Claude M. Fuess, 6 April 1953, 88–29.

185. Felix Frankfurter to LH, 16 March 1953, 105–18.

186. The memos are printed in "Texts of Memorandums by Acheson and Truman on Vincent Case," *New York Times*, 4 January 1953, 49.

187. LH to Felix Frankfurter, 20 March 1953, 105–18.

188. LH to John Foster Dulles, 20 January 1953, reported together with Dulles's response in "Dulles Will Rule in Vincent Inquiry," *New York Times*, 1 February 1953, 1.
189. "Vincent Is Cleared and Then Retired," and "Text of Dulles Statement Retiring Vincent," both in *New York Times*, 5 March 1953, 8.
190. LH to Herman Hagedorn, 27 February 1953, 96–17.
191. Ibid.
192. LH to Lloyd Garrison, 6 February 1953, 88–30.
193. LH to Harold Martin, *Saturday Evening Post*, in response to 27 February 1953 inquiry from a reporter, 2 March 1953, 92–33. See also LH to Felix Frankfurter, 20 March 1953, 105–18, saying that "I wish I felt freer to talk to you about the Vincent episode, but we promised each other, and I think rightly, that we would say nothing about it outside."
194. Felix Frankfurter to LH, 25 March 1953, 105–18.
195. LH to Monte Lemann, 15 December 1953, 91–37.
196. LH to Harvard "Veritas" Committee, 28 March 1957, 90–38.
197. 8 U.S.C. § 1427(a).
198. 165 F.2d 152 (2d Cir. 1947).
199. 177 F.2d 450 (2d Cir. 1949).
200. 34 F.2d 920 (2d Cir. 1929).
201. 34 F.2d, 921. The case arose before a panel consisting of Martin Manton, LH, and Thomas Swan. All three pre-conference memoranda agreed on this disposition of the case, but only LH's memorandum addressed the "moral turpitude" question at any length. The "moral turpitude" language, he said, was "a direct appeal to the moral sense of the community, and although many people would [think so], it does not seem to me to have fallen into the class of acts which themselves are thought to involve moral disgrace" (LH memo of 11 June 1929 in *U.S. ex rel. Iorio v. Day*, 185–13).
202. Martin Shapiro, "Morals and the Courts: The Reluctant Crusaders," 45 *Minn. L.Rev.* 897, 917 (1961).
203. Justice Jackson's dissent in *Jordan v. De George*, 341 U.S. 223, 232 (1951); quotations from pp. 232, 233, 235, 237–38.
204. 341 U.S., 231–32.
205. Edmond Cahn first criticized LH in "Authority and Responsibility," 51 *Colum. L.Rev.* 838 (1951). He elaborated those criticisms in *The Moral Decision: Right and Wrong in the Light of American Law* (Bloomington: Indiana University Press, 1955). The quoted passages are from "Authority and Responsibility," 51 *Colum. L.Rev.* 844, 851.
206. LH to Edmond N. Cahn, 12 May 1952, 85–25.
207. Frank, J., dissenting, in *Repouille v. United States*, 165 F.2d 152, 154 (2d Cir. 1947).
208. LH to Felix Frankfurter, 9 December 1947, 105–13.
209. Shanks, *The Art and Craft of Judging*, 44.
210. Burlingham, "Judge Learned Hand," 60 *Harv. L.Rev.* 330 (1947).
211. 165 F.2d 152 (2d Cir. 1947).
212. This and the following quotations are from id., 152–53.
213. LH memorandum in *Repouille*, 20 November 1947, 210–18.
214. Augustus N. Hand memo in *Repouille*, 19 November 1947, 210–18.
215. Jerome Frank memorandum in *Repouille*, 21 November 1947, 210–18.
216. 165 F.2d, 153–54. Despite LH's ultimate ruling, an officer of the Euthanasia

Society of America thanked him for his "understanding of the whole euthanasia problem" (Mrs. Robertson Jones, vice president of the society, to LH, 8 December 1947, 70–27). LH replied that he was "much pleased" by her comment (LH to Mrs. Jones, 11 December 1947, 70–27).

217. LH memo in *Schmidt v. United States*, 12 October 1949, 212–17.

218. Alfred C. Kinsey, Wardell B. Pomeroy, and Clyde E. Martin, *Sexual Behavior in the Human Male* (Philadelphia: W. B. Saunders, 1948).

219. LH's *Schmidt* ruling spurred a comment in the *Marquette Law Review*, a publication by a Roman Catholic university, which Judge Frank called to his attention, urging LH to read it "[j]ust for fun" (Frank to LH, 6 November 1956, 88–14). The comment, by Earl A. Charlton in "Jurisprudence—Naturalization—Moral Standard," 33 *Marq. L.Rev.* 202 (1950), sharply criticized LH for "refusing to recognize immutable objective morality": "Fornication is just one of many transgressions long recognized as undesirable. . . . When the courts refuse to condemn such conduct as being evil, they are in effect . . . condoning a . . . moral wrong" (id., 204).

220. Felix Frankfurter to LH, 27 October 1949, 105–15.

221. 164 F.2d 163 (2d Cir. 1947).

222. 164 F.2d, 163–64. (Swan and Chase joined the opinion.)

223. LH memorandum in *U.S. v. Francioso*, 17 October 1947, 210–16.

224. LH pre-conference memorandum in *U.S. ex rel. Guarino v. Uhl, Director of Immigration*, 19 October 1939, 202–12.

225. *United States ex rel. Guarino v. Uhl, Director of Immigration*, 107 F.2d 399, 400 (2d Cir. 1939).

226. *Posusta*, 285 F.2d 533 (2d Cir. 1961); *Yin-Shing Woo*, 288 F.2d 434 (2d Cir. 1961). *Posusta* was decided 6 January 1961; *Yin-Shing Woo* on 27 March 1961; LH died in August of that year.

227. 285 F.2d, 534–35.

228. Id., 535.

229. 288 F.2d, 435.

230. See LH memorandum in *Yin-Shing Woo v. United States*, 20 February 1961, and compare Clark's, 21 February 1961, both in 217–20.

231. *Flegenheimer v. General Mills, Inc.*, 191 F.2d 237, 241 (2d Cir. 1951).

XV
Active Retirement from "Regular Active Service"

1. Irving Dilliard to LH, 10 February 1951, 87–12.

2. Id., 25 March 1951, 87–12.

3. LH to Irving Dilliard, 2 April 1951, 87–12.

4. LH and FAH to Herbert Weinstock of Alfred A. Knopf, Inc., 17 May 1951, 87–12.

5. LH to Irving Dilliard, 21 February 1952, 87–14.

6. Id., 3 April 1952, 87–14.

7. Alfred A. Knopf to LH, 16 April 1952, 91–21.

8. Id., 8 September 1952, 91–21.

9. The report of 7,300 copies shipped is in Herbert Weinstock to LH, 20 August 1952, 91–24. The offer of a 15 percent royalty, deducting only a few dollars paid to Irving Dilliard, is in Alfred A. Knopf to LH, 8 September 1952, 91–24.

10. LH to Irving Dilliard, 4 November 1952, 87–14.
11. Alfred A. Knopf to LH, 4 October 1954, 91–22.
12. Id., 9 May 1955; LH response, 12 May 1955; both are in 91–23.
13. LH to Alfred A. Knopf, 27 January 1960 (LH's eighty-eighth birthday), 91–24.
14. Ibid. (After LH sent back the $1,000 check, Knopf sent $500 to Dilliard [see Alfred A. Knopf to LH, 29 January 1960, 91–24] and sent LH a case of "quite remarkable wine"—which LH accepted [Alfred A. Knopf to LH, 22 March 1960, 91–24].)
15. Philip Hamburger, "Learned Hand" (review), *New Yorker*, 10 May 1952, 120.
16. Eugene Gressman, "With Vision and Grace" (review), *New Republic*, 2 June 1952, 19.
17. Richard B. Morris, "Wise Wit from a Legal Lifetime" (review), *Saturday Review of Literature* 35, no. 18 (3 May 1952), 16. See also Felix Frankfurter review in *New York Herald Tribune Book Review*, 18 May 1952.
18. E.g., Judge Stanley H. Fuld, New York Court of Appeals, in 27 *N.Y.U. L.Rev.* 734 (1952), Judge George T. Washington, U.S. Court of Appeals for the District of Columbia Circuit, in 38 *Va. L.Rev.* 835 (1952), Harvard law professor Louis L. Jaffe in 66 *Harv. L.Rev.* 939 (1953), Chicago law professor Karl N. Llewellyn in 20 *U.Chi. L.Rev.* 611 (1953), Columbia law professor Adolf A. Berle, Jr., in 52 *Colum. L.Rev.* 811 (1952), Robert S. Lancaster in 6 *Vand. L.Rev.* 154 (1952), Max Goldman in 47 *Nw. L.Rev.* 744 (1952), and George Wharton Pepper in 62 *Yale L.J.* 135 (1952).
19. Jaffe, in 66 *Harv. L.Rev.* 939, 941.
20. Id., 939.
21. See preface to Irving Dilliard, ed., *The Spirit of Liberty: Papers and Addresses of Learned Hand*, 3d ed., enlarged (New York: Alfred A. Knopf, 1960), published a year before Hand's death. The first paperback edition appeared in 1958, from Vintage Books. Another paperback edition (a reprint of the third edition) was published by Phoenix Books of the University of Chicago Press in 1977. The enormous attention attracted by Hand's 1952 attack on McCarthyism in his Regents speech in Albany—a speech added to *The Spirit of Liberty* in its second edition in 1953—no doubt helped the continuing sales of the book.
22. Dilliard reprinted Hand's foreword to the British edition in the third edition of *The Spirit of Liberty*, at 289.
23. "A Great American Humanist" (review), *Economist*, 22 January 1955, 267–68.
24. The LH–Jerome D. Salinger correspondence is in 95–13.
25. LH to Frederick A. Colwell, State Department cultural affairs officer, 28 September 1960, replying to Colwell's inquiry of 20 September 1960, 95–13.
26. See LH to Frederick A. Colwell, 11 October 1960, 95–13: "[Salinger] likes to be alone and live alone."
27. LH to Mel Elfin, 3 December 1959, 95–13.
28. Ian Hamilton, *In Search of J. D. Salinger* (New York: Random House, 1988), 155.
29. For these recollections, I am indebted to LH's grandson, Jonathan Hand Churchill, and his granddaughter, Constance Jordan.

30. Marcia Nelson, ed., *The Remarkable Hands: An Affectionate Portrait* (New York: Foundation of the Federal Bar Council, 1983), 54.

31. LH to FAH, 11 June 1951, Personal Correspondence.

32. Id., 12 June 1951, Personal Correspondence.

33. E.g., "I feel so badly that I did not remember your birthday" (FAH to LH, [February 1928], Personal Correspondence).

34. The full text of her poem:

> When I have fears that time
>   may go so fast
> Ere ever I have chance to
>   put in tuneful phrase
> My thoughts of Bunny &
>   his love so warm
> Which flood my memory
>   and shine in these dark
>   days.
>
> Then do I quickly on my
>   tablet write
> And say, thus lamely but
>   with utter truth,
> That Bunny is of all men
>   I have know[n]
> A changing, faithful constant
>   lovely [k]night.

FAH to LH, 27 January 1945, Personal Correspondence.

35. Id., 10 May [1946], Personal Correspondence.

36. Id., "Friday" [1946], Personal Correspondence.

37. Id., "Saturday" [1946], Personal Correspondence.

38. See LH to FAH, 7 September 1953, 3 June 1955, 17 June 1955, Personal Correspondence.

39. Id., 20 June 1957 and 21 June 1957, Personal Correspondence.

40. Id., 16 June 1957, Personal Correspondence.

41. LH to Bernard Berenson, 26 December 1954, 99–23 (copy from Berenson Papers, I Tatti).

42. LH to Harvard Law School vice dean Livingston Hall, 26 November 1958, 89–11.

43. "The Hand Boys" was a phrase used by Gus Hand to refer to himself and his cousin, as recalled by Joseph Hamlen, editor of the *Harvard Bulletin*, in a letter of 26 January 1955 to Gus Hand's widow, describing in detail a dinner in honor of the Hands at the Somerset Club in Boston in the fall of 1951. See 89–14.

44. LH to Max Goldman, 28 October 1953, 88–32.

45. LH to Monte Lemann, 11 November 1954, 91–38.

46. LH to Felix Frankfurter, 4 November 1954, 105–20; LH to Bernard Berenson, 26 December 1954, 99–23.

47. LH to Monte Lemann, 11 November 1954, 91–38.

48. LH to circuit judge John J. Parker, 11 November 1954, 94–2.

49. LH to Felix Frankfurter, 4 November 1954, 105–20.

50. LH to Judge John Knight, 3 November 1954, 91–28.
51. LH to Felix Frankfurter, 4 November 1954, 105–20.
52. LH to W. B. Spofford (editor of *The Witness* magazine), 6 April 1953, 98–24.
53. Recalled in Robert S. Lancaster to LH, 20 July 1955, 91–32.
54. See W. Graham Claytor (former law clerk) to LH, 15 November 1954, 85–41.
55. LH to President Dwight D. Eisenhower, 22 October 1954, 87–33. (Harlan went to the Supreme Court, replacing Robert H. Jackson, and enjoyed a distinguished tenure there.)
56. Felix Frankfurter to Herbert Brownell, Jr., 14 January 1957, 105–22.
57. LH to Felix Frankfurter, 15 January 1957, 105–22.
58. Id., 16 January 1957, 105–22.
59. LH's list is in LH to Felix Frankfurter, 15 January 1957, 105–22.
60. There is no extant copy of this LH letter that I know of. My basis for asserting its existence is Henry J. Friendly to LH, 6 January 1957, 88–19, thanking LH for the support he expressed in his letter to Frankfurter "and for the letter that you have written Brownell."
61. LH to Felix Frankfurter, 3 February 1957, 105–22.
62. See *New York Times*, 18 February 1957, 16.
63. LH to Felix Frankfurter, 18 February 1957, 105–22.
64. Id., 25 March 1957, 105–22.
65. "City Lawyer Gets Backing as Judge," *New York Times*, 16 January 1959, 25.
66. LH to Felix Frankfurter, 19 January 1958, 105–23.
67. I believe that the earlier occasions were his letter to Brownell on behalf of Friendly in 1957 and his letter to Eisenhower supporting John Marshall Harlan for appointment to the Supreme Court in 1954. See LH to President Dwight D. Eisenhower, 22 October 1954, 87–33.
68. LH to President Dwight D. Eisenhower, 22 January 1959, 87–33. Two weeks after LH's letter, the *Times* reported that LH had written to Eisenhower in support of Friendly and quoted LH as saying that he had "volunteered his recommendation because he was interested in 'getting the very best man we can' " (*New York Times*, 17 February 1959, 24).
69. President Dwight D. Eisenhower to LH, 29 January 1959, 87–33.
70. Felix Frankfurter to LH, 12 March 1959, 105–24.
71. LH to Felix Frankfurter, 21 March 1959, 105–24. Soon after, Frankfurter told LH that the president repeatedly "referred to Friendly as 'the man that Judge Hand wants appointed' " (id., 24 March 1959, 105–24).
72. Felix Frankfurter to LH, 19 August 1959, 105–25.
73. LH to Felix Frankfurter, 26 March 1960, 105–25.
74. LH to President John F. Kennedy, 25 May 1961, printed in "Judge Hand Gives Kaufman Backing," *New York Times*, 18 June 1961, 41. The appearance of the letter in the newspaper illustrates the influential hand of Kaufman at *The New York Times*.
75. See *Harvard Law School Bulletin* 9, no. 5, April 1958, 3.
76. LH to Assistant Dean William Bruce, 20 January 1958, 88–42.
77. *Harvard Law School Bulletin* 9, no. 5, April 1958, 3.
78. LH to Felix Frankfurter, 10 February 1958, 105–23.
79. Learned Hand, *The Bill of Rights* (Cambridge: Harvard University Press, 1958),

77. (*The Bill of Rights* was the published version of Hand's Holmes Lectures, brought out within a few days of their delivery.)

80. These words are now displayed on a bronze plaque in the Harvard Law School Library. (Nearby for several years was Eleanor Platt's bust of Hand [which had been placed there shortly before the lectures].)

81. Hand, *The Bill of Rights*, 42.

82. 347 U.S. 483 (1954).

83. 354 U.S. 178 (1957).

84. 354 U.S. 298 (1957).

85. See especially the Felix Frankfurter–LH correspondence (e.g., LH to Felix Frankfurter, 19 January 1958), 105–23.

86. "Well-worn" is in the very first phrase of his first lecture, "When a Court Should Intervene" (Hand, *The Bill of Rights*, 1).

87. Hand, *The Bill of Rights*, 29. LH elaborated, saying that since the judicial review power was "not a logical deduction from the structure of the Constitution but only a practical condition upon its successful operation, it need not be exercised whenever a court sees, or thinks it sees, an invasion of the Constitution. It is always a preliminary question how importunately the occasion demands an answer" (id., 25). (Compare the critical comments in Herbert Wechsler, "Toward Neutral Principles of Constitutional Law," *Principles, Politics, and Fundamental Law* [Cambridge: Harvard University Press, 1961], 3–15, and Gerald Gunther, "The Subtle Vices of the 'Passive Virtues': A Comment on Principle and Expediency in Judicial Review," 64 *Colum. L.Rev.* 1 [1964], challenging the view that a court has discretion to avoid adjudication on the merits in a case clearly within its jurisdiction.)

88. Hand, *The Bill of Rights* 31, 34, 42.

89. Id., 45, 51.

90. Id., 54.

91. Id., 56, 57, 61.

92. Id., 67–69.

93. Id., 69.

94. Id., 70–71.

95. Id., 73–74.

96. Id., 75.

97. Alistair Cooke, "Judge Hand Criticises Supreme Court," *Manchester Guardian*, 8 February 1958, 5.

98. "Famous Judge Rebukes Supreme Court," *U.S. News & World Report*, 7 March 1958, 108, reprinted repeatedly in the *Congressional Record*, apparently for the first time at the behest of Senator Herman Talmadge on 3 March 1958 (see *Congressional Record*, 85th Cong., 2d Sess., 3198).

99. See *Washington Evening Star*, 10 March 1958, for Lawrence's column entitled "A Third Legislative Chamber," placed in the *Congressional Record*, pt. 20, by Senator J. William Fulbright, on 12 March 1958 (*Congressional Record*, 85th Cong., 2d Sess., A 2305).

100. The committee had held a very brief hearing on the Jenner bill on 7 August 1957; the hearings reconvened 19 to 21 February, 25 to 28 February, and 4 and 5 March 1958. The hearings are printed in "Limitation of Appellate Jurisdiction of the United States Supreme Court," *Hearings Before the Subcommittee on the Judiciary to Investigate the Administration of the Internal Security Act and Other Internal Security Laws of the Committee on the Judiciary, United*

States Senate, 85th Cong., 2d Sess. on S.2646 [the Jenner bill], pt. 2 (1958). The editorial is from the 18 February 1958 edition of the *Omaha World-Herald*, placed in the hearing record by Senator Roman Hruska on 19 February 1958 (see *Hearings*, 76–77). Typically, LH's name was invoked by supporters of the Jenner bill. Occasionally, though, his lectures were mentioned by opponents (e.g., Ernest Angell, chairman, board of directors, ACLU, *Hearings*, 219, noting that LH did after all support the justifiability of judicial review). See also letter of Attorney General William P. Rogers to Senator James Eastland, chairman of the Senate Judiciary Committee, 4 March 1958, in *Hearings*, 573–74.

101. See *Congressional Record*, 20 August 1958, 85th Cong., 2d Sess., 18,673, printing LH's letter of 5 May 1958 to Senator Thomas Hennings (copy in 90–9); see also Dilliard, *The Spirit of Liberty*, 300–301.

102. See *Congressional Record*, 85th Cong., 2d Sess., 18,673, printing Senator John Butler's letter of 19 May 1958 to LH, and LH's reply. See, generally, id., 18,646–77, 20 August 1958, 18,646–77.

103. E.g., the South Carolina lawyer Robert McC. Figg, Jr., in 10 *So.Car. L.Q.* 728 (1958).

104. Alexander M. Bickel, "Judicial Restraint & the Bill of Rights," *New Republic*, 12 May 1958, 16.

105. Herbert Prashker, in 13 *The Record of the Association of the Bar of the City of New York* 382 (1985).

106. Edward L. Barrett, Jr., in 46 *Calif. L.Rev.* 859, 861 (1958).

107. See Learned Hand, "Chief Justice Stone's Concept of the Judicial Function," 46 *Colum. L.Rev.* 696, 698 (1946), reprinted in Dilliard, *The Spirit of Liberty*, 202, 206.

108. Learned Hand, "The Contribution of an Independent Judiciary Civilization," reprinted in Dilliard, *The Spirit of Liberty*, 155, 164.

109. Paul A. Freund, *The Supreme Court of the United States* (Cleveland: World Publishing Co., 1961), 89.

110. For an excellent, carefully documented study of the continuities in LH's thinking about judicial review, see Robert G. Pugh, Jr., "A Lifetime Preoccupation: Learned Hand and Judicial Review" (unpublished paper, Stanford Law School, 1979, based on extensive research in the Hand Papers).

111. See, e.g., Felix Frankfurter to LH, 13 February 1958, 105–23.

112. See *Naim v. Naim*, a Virginia ruling upholding the laws, which the Court vacated and remanded for clarification of the record (350 U.S. 891 [1955] [per curiam]); on remand, the Virginia court stuck to its guns, and this time the Supreme Court once again dismissed the appeal, for want of a "properly presented federal question" (350 U.S. 985 [1956] [per curiam]).

113. Herbert Wechsler, "Toward Neutral Principles of Constitutional Law," in *Principles, Politics and Fundamental Law* 3, 47 (1961). (I have similarly criticized the Court's prudential devices to duck cases that it has an obligation to decide [including the 1950s miscegenation cases]. See, e.g., Gerald Gunther, "The Subtle Vices of the 'Passive Virtues'—A Comment on Principle and Expediency in Judicial Review," 64 *Colum. L.Rev.* 1, 12, 23–24 [1964] [criticizing Alexander Bickel's defense of such "passive virtues"—the avoidance devices of the Court—in his *The Least Dangerous Branch—The Supreme Court at the Bar of Politics* [Indianapolis: Bobbs-Merrill, 1962].)

114. Felix Frankfurter to LH, 8 September 1957, 105–23.

115. This and following quotations from LH to Felix Frankfurter, 13 September 1957, 105–23.
116. Felix Frankfurter to LH, 17 September 1957, 105–23.
117. LH to Felix Frankfurter, 25 September 1957, 105–23.
118. Felix Frankfurter to LH, 27 September 1957, 105–23.
119. See, e.g., *Mayor of Baltimore v. Dawson*, 350 U.S. 877 (1955), and *Holmes v. Atlanta*, 350 U.S. 879 (1955). See generally Gerald Gunther, *Constitutional Law*, 12th ed. (Westbury, N.Y.: Foundation Press, 1991), 652.
120. LH to Felix Frankfurter, 10 October 1957, 105–23.
121. Felix Frankfurter to LH, 12 October 1957, 105–23.
122. LH to Felix Frankfurter, 22 February 1958, 105–23.
123. Hand, *The Bill of Rights*, 54.
124. LH to Felix Frankfurter, 19 January 1958 and 10 February 1958, both in 105–23.
125. See 264 F.2d, 6.
126. LH broke the record previously held by a nineteenth-century judge, William Cranch of the District of Columbia Circuit Court (1805–55). See Anthony Lewis's story "Judge Hand, on Bench 50 Years, Hailed," on the front page of *The New York Times* the next day, 11 April 1959. See also the *Times* editorial, "Judge Hand's Golden Years," 10 April 1959, 28.
127. The proceedings were printed in a special pamphlet, "In Commemoration of Fifty Years of Federal Judicial Service by the Honorable Learned Hand," and this pamphlet was bound into every volume of 264 F.2d, with the spine of the volume carrying the legend "Proceedings in Honor of Learned Hand." (The special pamphlet also included a reprinting of Whitney North Seymour's tribute to LH that had appeared in *The New York Times Magazine* on the Sunday preceding the ceremony, "Tribute to the 'Old Chief' of the Bench," *New York Times*, 5 April 1959.)
128. 264 F.2d, 9.
129. Id., 12. (LH's contributions to the ALI's discussions, and his demonstrations that his mind was ever ready to reexamine prior views, continued to the end of his life. At the ALI's annual meeting in 1955, for example, he argued successfully—after earlier voting to retain a criminal ban on homosexual sodomy in the ALI's Model Penal Code—that such behavior should be decriminalized. He explained: "Criminal law which is not enforced is much worse than if it was not on the books at all. . . . I think [sodomy] is a matter of morals, a matter very largely of taste, and it is not a matter that people should be put in prison about." The ALI's membership, by a narrow margin, heeded his advice. See *Time*, 30 May 1955, 13.)
130. President Dwight D. Eisenhower to LH, 8 April 1959, id., 16–17.
131. 264 F.2d, 25.
132. Lewis, "Judge Hand, on Bench 50 Years," *New York Times*, 11 April 1959, 1. (Soon after the session, LH told Frankfurter: "Everybody I've seen agrees that you 'stole the show'; it was a masterpiece, regardless of the obvious exaggerations of your estimate" [LH to Felix Frankfurter, 25 April 1959, 105–25].)
133. 264 F.2d, 20–22.
134. Id., 26–29.
135. LH to Felix Frankfurter, 10 July 1958, 105–24.
136. Id., 22 July 1960, 105–26.

137. Felix Frankfurter to LH, [September] 1958, replying to LH to Felix Frankfurter, 10 July 1958 (where LH notes that his country walks had shrunk to a third of a mile), 105–24.

138. LH to Felix Frankfurter, 1 November 1958, 105–24.

139. Id., 4 January 1959, 105–24.

140. From LH's recollection of Holmes stories for Mark DeWolfe Howe, Holmes's first biographer, 29 April 1959, 90–31. I and others remember LH telling the story repeatedly in his late eighties.

141. LH to Felix Frankfurter, 4 November 1960, 105–26.

142. LH to Max Goldman, 30 January 1961, 88–32.

143. LH to Felix Frankfurter, 26 March 1960, 105–25.

144. Id., 6 April 1960, 105–25.

145. LH to John W. Davis, 1 June 1951, 87–3.

146. LH to Max Goldman, 14 February 1959, 88–32.

147. *New York Times*, 2 February 1960, 44.

148. LH to Donald G. Hatt (of Albany Academy), 10 February 1960, 84–2.

149. Paul Bender to LH, 1 June 1960, 84–38.

150. LH to Paul Bender, 6 June 1960, 84–38.

151. Felix Frankfurter to LH, 30 July 1960, 105–26. After the commission's report appeared at the end of November, Frankfurter expressed "relief that your name was not signed, by reason of a timely resignation. . . . It would have added meretricious weight by exploiting your authority" (Felix Frankfurter to LH, 23 January 1961, 105–26). (For the final National Goals Commission Report, see "U.S. Report Maps High Goals in 60's; Tax Rises Hinted," *New York Times*, 28 November 1960, 1 [text of report on pp. 22–23]. There were no specific references to the courts in the final report, but its very general aspirations elicited a number of dissenting statements from its members.)

152. LH to Felix Frankfurter, 1 February 1960, 105–25.

153. Felix Frankfurter to LH, 22 March 1960, 105–25.

154. LH to Felix Frankfurter, 26 March 1960, 105–25.

155. Id., 6 April 1960, 105–25.

156. Id., 26 March 1960, 105–25.

157. LH to Herman Finkelstein, 27 January 1957, 88–5.

158. LH to Felix Frankfurter, 13 June 1961, 105–26.

159. Felix Frankfurter to LH, 15 June 1961, 105–26.

160. LH to Herbert Goodrich, 15 February 1961, 88–36. See also LH to Arthur Corron, 18 January 1961, 86–13: "[M]y back gets worse and worse, so that I can hardly walk at all, even with the aid of crutches."

161. LH to Felix Frankfurter, 13 February 1961, 105–26.

162. LH to Judge Richard Hartshorne, 6 April 1961, 90–37.

163. The memorial service for Delano was on 1 February 1960; LH's memorial address is in 87–8.

164. Mary Hand Darrell to Felix Frankfurter, 9 August 1961, 105–26 (the best source on LH's final illness).

165. Telegram, FAH to Felix Frankfurter, 18 August 1961, 105–26, sent at 5:21 p.m.: "B died peacefully this morning, no funeral service or flowers."

166. Felix Frankfurter statement, 18 August 1961, 105–26.

167. "Judge Learned Hand Dies; On U.S. Bench 52 Years," *New York Times*, 19 August 1961, 1.

168. "A Great American Judge" (obituary), *Times* (London), 19 August 1961, 10.

169. Frances Fincke to Mildred Minturn, "Sunday" [March 1899], Minturn Papers, England.

170. FAH to Mildred Minturn, 30 September 1904, Minturn Papers, England.

171. That LH included a winning home run in his story contrasts with remarks he made at the ALI banquet in 1959 honoring his fifty years on the bench. Attorney General William P. Rogers, introducing LH, told how his son had answered successive telephone calls from the president and the vice president. Rogers had told his son, "You can't appreciate it now, but some day you will be very proud," to which the boy replied, "Daddy, have you ever met Mickey Mantle?" When LH rose to address the gathering, he turned to Rogers and remarked, "with evident, sincere regret: 'I don't know what Mickey Mantle is or does. Is it a man?' " ("Random Notes in Washington: Judge Hand Fans on Baseball," *New York Times*, 25 May 1959, 21).

172. This version of a much told story is based on a letter from Reginald Heber Smith (Boston attorney) to LH, 28 February 1961. Smith had heard the story told at a bar dinner commemorating LH's fiftieth anniversary on the bench. LH replied that he "vaguely remembered" it as Smith related it (LH to Reginald Heber Smith, 1 March 1961, 95–28).

Index

A Note About the Author

Gerald Gunther served as law clerk to Judge Learned Hand in the 1950s, and later to Chief Justice Earl Warren at the Supreme Court, and then entered private legal practice in New York. Born in Usingen im Taunus, Germany, in 1927, he was educated at Brooklyn College, Columbia University, and Harvard Law School, served on the faculties of those institutions as well, and since 1962 has been Professor of Constitutional Law at Stanford University Law School, where he is now the William Nelson Cromwell Professor of Law. A fellow of many professional associations, Gunther is the author of *Constitutional Law, Individual Rights in Constitutional Law,* and *John Marshall's Defense of McCulloch v. Maryland,* and is a contributor to numerous legal periodicals.